Books by C. L. Sulzberger

THE LAST OF THE GIANTS *1970*

A LONG ROW OF CANDLES *1969*

(American Heritage) HISTORY OF WORLD WAR II *1966*

UNFINISHED REVOLUTION:
AMERICA AND THE THIRD WORLD *1965*

THE TEST: DE GAULLE AND ALGERIA *1962*

MY BROTHER DEATH *1961*

WHAT'S WRONG WITH U.S. FOREIGN POLICY *1959*

THE BIG THAW *1956*

SIT-DOWN WITH JOHN L. LEWIS *1938*

The Last of the Giants

The Last of the
GIANTS

C. L. SULZBERGER

The Macmillan Company

The Macmillan Company
866 Third Avenue, New York, N.Y. 10022
Collier-Macmillan Canada Ltd., Toronto, Ontario

Library of Congress Catalog Card Number: 78-119840

FIRST PRINTING

Printed in the United States of America

For Jonathan

My First Grandson

"One radiant smile disperses all the gloom
of heavy years that bend us to the tomb."

"L'art d'être grand-père"
VICTOR HUGO

Acknowledgments

I wish to express my deepest thanks to Julia Whitehurst and Susan Sevray for helping to prepare and edit this manuscript and to Marina, my wife, for reading still another effort with a shrewd and critical eye.

I acknowledge permission from *The New York Times* to print here certain of the raw material on which my columns for that newspaper have been based, as well as excerpts from my Kremlin talks with Khrushchev.

CLS

Contents

List of Illustrations

(following page 558)

Autographed portrait of Charles de Gaulle.
With Janos Kadar, Communist boss of Hungary.
Visit to Cracow with Polish government officials, 1956.
With Abd-el-Krim, chief of the Riffian rebellion against Spain and Morocco
    in the 1920's.
With the chief of a Pathan village in the no man's land between Afghanistan
    and Pakistan.
With King Hassan of Morocco.
With Chiang Kai-shek.
Party with President Sukarno of Indonesia, 1959.
Autographed portrait of Dwight D. Eisenhower.
A letter from President Eisenhower.
Marina with Greta Garbo and Stavros Niarchos during a summer holiday
    in Greece.
A bet with Franz-Josef Strauss, Germany's then defense minister.
Visiting Israel's founding father, David Ben Gurion, at his kibbutz in the
    Negev.
With President Nasser of the United Arab Republic.
Helping Mrs. John F. Kennedy ashore in Italy, 1962.
My regular golfing companions with Ben Hogan.
Talking with Chairman Khrushchev in the Kremlin, 1961.
With Khrushchev in the Kremlin, September, 1961.
Letter from de Gaulle, 1963.
Autographed portrait of John F. Kennedy.
With King Hussein in Jordan, 1963.
Bet with Stash Radziwill, December 9, 1963.

List of Illustrations

Preface

There will be a third volume to this series although I have not yet decided when. Discretion imposes increasing reticence as recollection leaps into the present. And now, with the early autumn Meltemi blowing southward over Greece, churning up the Aegean foam, the rotting grapes, the faded roses, and jasmine into a turmoil of nostalgia, I take leave.

The central figure of this book is Charles de Gaulle, a type only France seems capable of producing and, in his own words, a man of consequence. In some respects, like Napoleon before him, de Gaulle reflected that inborn French penchant for disaster, able both to surmount and to produce it, leaving a crumbling edifice behind and yet bequeathing more than legend. Each gave his countryman passing grandeur—much appreciated in vain France. Both solitary men of destiny (Napoleon conferred friendship on only one man, his aide de camp, Duroc; de Gaulle, in truth, on none), they recognized fate when it arrived and seized it by the forelock.

Now we approach an age when even de Gaulle would be hard put to recognize giants. We become the creatures of science and laboratory technicians, the latest priesthood of the newest class: spawned by artificial insemination and reared on cybernetics. This is an unfamiliar world for one like myself, of the middle class, mildly, what once we used to call an intellectual (démodé word); the oligarch of brains with its manufactured peons takes over.

And what have I learned from all this, as time rushes at my back? Little, I suppose, except that singular men can still achieve singular things in any epoch and also that only the very young and the very old are truly independent, because neither fears life nor is afraid of death. At this stage, aged fifty-seven, well-worn by years and travel, I crave peace and tranquility.

Spetsais, Greece
October 1, 1969

The Last of the Giants

MANY CHARACTERS

IN SEARCH

OF A PLOT

T HE FIRST VOLUME OF THESE RECOLLECTIONS, *A Long Row of Candles*, indulged at times in the vanity of personal experience, for then I was a young man embraced by happenings soon to be swept aside by stodgier middle age. Now, amid incipient decrepitude, I peer from my fur-lined rut to edit this second volume, conscious that journalism, while not so old a profession as whoring nor so unrespectable as smuggling, is nevertheless a passport to amusement.

It has enabled me to dine with hobos and kings; to know a press of generals, a gaggle of politicians, and a wallet of Rothschilds; to consult Popes and witch doctors; to fly with pilgrims from Mecca and demolitions experts to Israel. I have watched Pathan tribesmen in the Kohat pass fashion me a revolver from stolen rails and truck tires and I have lunched with the Cao Dai general staff where the pièce de résistance, served au bleu, erect, and staring with contumelious blue eyes, was a walking fish. In Tashkent, I have devoured fat-tailed mutton with the Grand Mufti of Central Asia and I have also sat beside a desert sheikh in Syria as he groped within a monstrous pilaff, discovered the object of his search, and plopped a sheep's eye in my mouth while I stared at the rice grains hanging from his armpit.

If you will bear with me in these pages you may find moments of some interest: Translating Pericles' funeral oration into German for dehiscent Poles aboard a train to Cracow; flying eight times around the South Pole with the U.S. Commander-in-Chief of the Pacific; watching Tito and Khrushchev totter through a Belgrade palace like drunken bears and also watching French police march on the National Assembly screaming death to

I

the government and the Jews. I have worked on all seven continents and admired mountains such as Everest, McKinley, Kenya, Popocatapetl, Kilimanjaro; the Alps, the Hindu Kush, the Tienshan and Altai ranges that separate Russia from China; and Mount Elburz where Prometheus was bound and pecked by eagles sent by jealous gods. I have visited the Congo, Indus, Nile, Niger, Mekong, Oxus, Amazon, and Volga rivers, seen the spindrift of the Red, Yellow, Black, and Bering seas, traveled by foot, horse, rowboat, caique, resplendent ocean liners, and antiquated trains: the Orient Express, Taurus Express, Golden Arrow, the Red Train to Leningrad, the Blue Train from Capetown. I have heard the mournful shawm, the squeaking of horsehair, and the whining of catgut make sad people gay and gay ones sad; and also the sound of fish leaping, bird wings whirring, and the gurgle of my own grandchildren. I have tasted champagne, Ethiopian mulse, the Bull's Blood of Eger, cognac laid down for Napoleon, fried termites, rattlesnake, bear meat, Uganda kob—and fear and sorrow.

During these times, there have been occasional excursions beyond the compass of the ordinary: A brief encounter with EOKA, the secret army in Cyprus to whose commander, subsequently, the Greek foreign minister wished to send me bearing suggested terms of peace with Britain; a short visit to the Algerian guerrillas fighting France; immersion in one enormous, round bathtub with South Korea's high command. I interpreted at a tête-à-tête luncheon between Georges Pompidou and the American ambassador to France—so confidential that the latter wished to keep the matter from his staff; and I took to President Kennedy a far more secret message from Chairman Khrushchev. At White House request I prepared for Kennedy a report suggesting how he might deal with de Gaulle at their Paris meeting. But these are exceptional intrusions into the life pattern of a columnist grown thicker around the middle and less audacious than a reporter, depending for intellectual sustenance on the ideas of others rather than the drumbeat of events and nonevents.

A newspaperman, pursuing his role of chronicler and commentator, becomes perforce a sort of scavenger, nattering at the heels of the distinguished or the great, observing—closely, if he can—those who lead us on the merry chase to nothingness. There are some who, in this epoch of befuddled, latter-day Marxism, prefer to see history in terms of unpredictable if sometimes charted forces, imponderable "things" which, as Emerson gloomily perceived, "ride mankind." My own belief places more stock in human qualities, human judgment, human decision, and the capacity of man himself to exceed his expectations and avoid the terrible rictus of disaster. Perhaps a quarter of a century earlier this might have seemed a pleasant but naively romantic approach; however, in our extraordinary era, when men, by their own initiative and in response to their own dreams, have exploded from the atomic age to the space age in a few brief years, maybe we can be reassured that mankind, when it so wishes, still rides.

These pages will serve to show, I think, that there were vestigial giants alive during the period described. This diary—as in the case of *A Long Row of Candles*—was originally written with no view to publication and as a kind of detailed notebook. I have been puzzled, on rereading and editing, to find how many people talked so freely to me, dominated by some conversational afflatus, and I can only conclude that this was because I wisely heeded my first city editor's advice: ·Keep your ears open and your mouth shut. There is much to be said for looking expectantly at a man and waiting for him to speak.

I find this, like its predecessor, a sporadic and incomplete account. Thus, I cannot for the life of me imagine why I did not note two conversations with de Gaulle in which he offered me (for *The New York Times*) U.S. syndication rights to his magnificent *Mémoires* and in which I had to go back and tell him with embarrassment that my paper wasn't interested. The only reason I imagine I omitted this was (as when Eisenhower, some years earlier, had invited me to buy the neighboring farm in Gettysburg) that nothing of journalistic note was said.

When discussing serious subjects with many people who appear in these pages I took full notes in their presence—even when it was understood I would not quote them. During every talk with de Gaulle which I have recorded (there were perhaps a half-dozen others), I listed my questions first on a sheet of paper, then laid them, with a notebook and a pencil, on his desk across from him, drew up a chair, and fired away: Whether we were in his party headquarters on the rue de Solférino, his early Paris residence, the Hotel de Lapérouse, or the Elysée Palace. De Gaulle often would assure me that he received me *en ami* and caution that what he said was not for publication; but I learned with time that he expected me to paraphrase his thoughts and cite particularly juicy phrases.

Many matters once held too confidential for publication are no longer in that category. Time cools passions and diminishes embarrassment. Thus I now see no reason why I cannot disclose in detail de Gaulle's warning that he would consider returning by *coup d'état*, an intimation which has always led me to believe the world does not yet know the full story of his comeback in the wake of an army revolt. Likewise it is permissible now to show how young President Kennedy wrote to General Gavin, his envoy in Paris, and told him he was the best American ambassador since Benjamin Franklin—at the very moment he pulled the rug from under him.

If you will bear with me in these pages you will hear Pandit Nehru say: "Both communism and fascism have the same evil features: violence, cruelty, and oppression," and Field Marshal Kaiser Shumshere Jang Bahadur Rana of Nepal, giving a long explanation of the best use of the Gurkha's *kukri* knife: "To cut off a human head it is better to use the forehand but a good backhand can do it; there is also a neat upward disembowelling stroke." Iskander Mirza, first dictator of Pakistan and a devout Muslim (despite his penchant for whisky), could not refrain from regretting: "The Arabs are worthless. If God and 120,000 prophets couldn't make something of Arabia, certainly they can't." George Kennan confesses: "It took Foster Dulles to make a Democrat of me"; Ernest Hemingway says: "The world would be a sad place if we didn't have crazy poets in it"; Field Marshal Montgomery complains: "Diplomats don't seem to understand that the game being played is poker; they play it as if it were chess."

This is a mixed farrago. Jean Cocteau observes: "The great tragedy of France is that its politicians are unsuccessful writers and its writers are unsuccessful politicians." Speidel, who prepared for his NATO command by serving as Rommel's chief of staff, foresees: "The Germans and the Americans are going to have to defend Europe." And Harold Macmillan, in a relaxed moment of whisky and whimsy, concludes: "Man is a reasonable size and perhaps that is why he has succeeded so well; he is neither a dinosaur nor a bee."

Konrad Adenauer, the crafty, righteous, wooden Chancellor, who resurrected Germany from the Nazi cloaca, thought: "In general, wealth makes people blind; thank God that has not been the case with America." And General MacArthur, always jealous of his younger, more successful rival, predicts: "If Eisenhower is re-elected President it will be the greatest disaster in American history. I know just what will happen. He will go off to the golf courses and the trout streams of the country and then he will just disappear." Jugoslavia's former ruler, Prince Paul, remembers of his grim colloquy with the Führer: "It disturbed Hitler to think of a 'pretty' English boy lying dead on the battlefield beside a 'beautiful' young German," and Hitler told him: "Some of my speeches are like those of Martin Luther and will live at least as long."

Dag Hammarskjöld, the curiously vain Swede who thought he knew God, insisted: "I cannot be succeeded by a card-bearing member of a church." Bitter, brilliant Dean Acheson described Foster Dulles and Britain's Foreign Secretary, Selwyn Lloyd, as "a pair of slick lawyers who are trying to outsmart each other." John F. Kennedy said of Johnson that he was one of a few leaders who "actually prevented our military intervention in Vietnam" in 1954. Don Juan, pretender to the Spanish throne, sneered from his exile near Lisbon: "Portugal is a republic where if you mention the word republic you are clapped into jail. Spain is a monarchy where if you mention the word monarchy you are clapped into jail." And Morocco's King Muhammed V remarked: "It is harder to fight my people than the French."

I discovered that the South Pole is marked by a circle of fuel barrels about fifty yards in diameter, set amidst an enormous, flat, empty plain of snowy waste, pockmarked and rippled by wind. In Christchurch, New Zealand, of all places, I was informed that on his campaigns MacArthur required eight pillows on his bed; these were laid out not only under his head but also under his knees and elbows.

General "Lightning Joe" Collins, a speedy, self-confident soldier, assured me: "I know damned well that I could have moved right on to Berlin and nothing could have stopped me." Georges Pompidou, subsequently President of France, confided: "There was a serious plot to oust de Gaulle, backed by American money." And, some two years before it happened, Allen Dulles, head of the CIA, confidently proclaimed: "The Russians are too smart to put bases in Cuba."

Just before his narrow election victory John Kennedy admitted: "Nixon was a damned fool to agree to debate with me on an equal-time TV basis." And, not long after that election, which made him Vice President, Lyndon Johnson spoke of his favorite dog: "Beagle always sleeps under my bed. But when I'm sick or unhappy or feeling sorry for myself, or when I cry, he comes up on the bed and comforts me."

Averell Harriman, early in Kennedy's administration, told me: "I started as a private with Roosevelt and worked to the top. And then I had to start as a private all over again with Truman and worked to the top. That is what I intend to do again." And do you know what MacArthur said to President Kennedy? "All the chickens are coming home to roost and you are living in the coop."

The Shah of Iran thought: "Democracy of the western type, when applied in underdeveloped countries, becomes only a weapon for subversion." The carcinomatous Eichmann swore: "An anti-Semite I never was . . . I tried as best I could to live according to Kant's categorical imperative." The one who supervised his capture, trial, and execution, Ben Gurion, believed: "The Arabs are out to destroy Israel . . . and we are not insane; we won't commit suicide. . . . The prophets taught that you should love your neighbor as yourself . . . but no more. They did not speak about turning the other cheek." Six years before the 1967 conflict, Ben Gurion's doughty captain, Moshe Dayan, foresaw that Israel might be forced to start a war "if there were any massive build-up in the United Arab Republic clearly directed toward Israel." Royal interludes: Queen Frederika of Greece thought Adlai Stevenson "an egghead and pinkish"; Princess Beatrix of Holland considered "all Dutch Calvinists and Puritans, even the Catholics." And, after a Jugoslav visit, Greek King Paul chuckled: "Tito certainly likes the good life."

Khrushchev boasted to me in the Kremlin: "The United States is still in the stage of jumping while the Soviet Union has learned to fly." He went on to insist (September 5, 1961): "Castro is not a member of the Communist party." He said: "Our national emblem is already on the moon, but we don't want to place a coffin beside it." He added, before asking me to take to the American President a message so secret that he enjoined me not to tell the U.S. ambassador, "Kennedy is too young. He lacks the authority and prestige." Kennedy told me (after I had delivered the communication): "Now I have been able to judge this man. Now I know that there is no further need for talking."

De Gaulle wrote Kennedy that if France demonstrated it could "tear off an arm" from Russia with its nuclear deterrent, this could be a restraining influence on Moscow. And Sekou Touré, President of Guinea, shocked prim Washington by taking his mistress to the White House. The chiliastic Jean Monnet, often called Mister Europe, said: "The only western country that can provide an example to underdeveloped lands is Israel."

Couve de Murville: "One of the first things de Gaulle asks a statesman he has never met before is how he sleeps. De Gaulle feels this is very indicative of a man's inner repose and capability as a leader." Eamon de Valera, modern Ireland's father: "I would rather drive a team that I have to hold in than to have a team I have to whip on." And Macmillan: "I feel in my knees that great movements are irresistible. [In Europe] there is a confederating spirit, a spirit of the ages, the dynasts, that takes control."

Harriman, who knew him well, remembered: "Roosevelt had his Dutch jaw stuck out on China." Jackie Kennedy, on an Italian holiday from the White House: "Bobby is immensely ambitious and will never feel that he has succeeded in life until he has been elected to something." De Gaulle, incidentally, told her to beware of Mrs. Khrushchev who was *"plus maline que lui."* And, one year before the President's assassination, that brilliant gentleman-scholar, Sir Isaiah Berlin, wondered if deep in Kennedy's mind, "he may not have a presentiment that he may not live a long time." As for Kennedy's own thoughts: "Nixon is a nice fellow in private and a very able man . . . but he seems to have a split personality."

When Acheson, on an urgent mission from Kennedy, brought de Gaulle reconnaissance photos of Soviet missiles in Cuba, the General said: "It is not necessary to show me the pictures because obviously a great government like yours would not risk war for nothing." Macmillan inscribed a photograph to the young American President: "Ask not what your country can do for you but what we can do together for all mankind." Kennedy himself said after the Cuban confrontation: "The human race remains in peril. . . . In this job there is nothing like experience." And, an extraneous footnote: "Just a short time ago Nasser was in the ash can. Now look what he is up to."

Some of the ensuing cast of characters is not well known even to current history but plays its intimate role. Ambassador Burin des Roziers: "I translated at two conversations—one between Nehru and de Gaulle and one between Nehru and Malraux. The Nehru-de Gaulle colloquy was very banal. As for that with Malraux, it simply didn't make any sense. Don't forget, it's impossible to translate Malraux into French, much less into English. I must say Nehru looked very puzzled." Or NATO Secretary-General Stikker: "De Gaulle's strategy is to defend France in Germany, to the last German." Gaston Palewski, the General's friend from the 1930s: "The only sport de Gaulle was interested in in those days was flirting."

Montgomery's simplified aphorisms: "You could not have a people more different than the British and the Americans. I have commanded both. I know. You should not try to mix them up in the same box of tricks. . . . Khrushchev is a clever fellow; he understands me. . . . Without Stalin, I think the Russians would have quit the war. . . . De Gaulle chucked out the useless politicians. Now he has a proper set-up in France. . . . Damned fool, Ike."

Couve de Murville (April 4, 1963): "It is impossible to produce any military solution in South Vietnam. . . . Nobody is going to win the war there." Chip Bohlen remembers how Stalin gave Roosevelt a lemon tree (any significance?), and Harriman recalls that Roosevelt fired Ambassador Bullitt for leaking to de Gaulle on the North African invasion. U Thant acknowledges: "No Secretary-General worthy of the name can ever afford to be morally neutral." And Khrushchev, another breed, would "no more permit disarmament inspectors in the Soviet Union than men were allowed in harems."

"In 1956 at the time of Suez," King Paul of Greece recalled, "the President sent a signal to the Sixth Fleet saying: 'Are you prepared to meet the enemy?' The reply sent to Washington was: 'Which enemy?' " The Swedish general commanding UN forces in the Yemen ordered two hundred coffins as "essential for his mission." King Hussein of Jordan believed: "It is a weakness when a nation feels it must put all its hopes on the life span or the ability of one leader." His wife, Princess Muna, thought the hardest thing to get used to was seeing Hussein, when he got dressed, strap on a shoulder holster. "Hussein is convinced he will not die a natural death and that when he is killed it will be by a man in uniform standing behind him."

And so it goes, a long, long chronicle whose only plot is history itself and whose characters are entwined within it: Outstanding and occasionally formidable men, each leaving footprints in the sand; Kennedy, Khrushchev, Adenauer; Hemingway, Malraux, Eliot, Cocteau; dictators, despots, democrats; conquerors and cowards. I have portrayed them in their own words.

The last of the giants encountered by me were those two glorious and decidedly old-fashioned figures, Churchill and de Gaulle, one whose flame had almost failed, while the other's was about to blaze. Churchill had already slipped from the active scene and de Gaulle was in self-chosen political exile when this account begins. Yet, before its end, the General rose like a genie from his dark forest refuge and came to dominate Europe in a way yet to be achieved by any other postwar statesman. During the nine years covered (1954–1963), these two were the remaining monoliths, aging and impeccably courteous men who, in themselves, typified the best of their respective heritages.

Churchill already had fulfilled his role. I spent a day with him in 1956, at his country home in Kent when, illumined by conversation, cognac, cigars, and fond memories, he glowed for a while like incandescent light. After tottering about his farmlands showing off treasures from golden orfes and fat cattle to a garden pavilion adorned with paintings of his ancestor Marlborough's victories, the filament flickered and went out. He shivered, required an overcoat on a hot summer's day, barely managed to fumble the way to his doorsill, and stood, pointing his cane at the corpse of a baby bird lying on the driveway, tears trickling down his compassionate, old face as he regarded the injustice of inevitable death.

He was a magnificent man of bitter wit, deep emotion, and the utmost resolution; a man who could pity, lead, and understand his fellows, who said of his unfortunate successor, Eden: "Poor Anthony, he used every known cliché from 'the situation is fraught with consequences' to 'gentlemen will please adjust their dress upon leaving.'" In Marrakesh, a Moroccan haven where Churchill retreated more and more as age closed in, he once complained to me over brandy and cigars, "Why would any one want to leave this planet? That would be foolish."

De Gaulle embodied the French soul and French prejudices quite as much as those of England were imbued in Churchill. The master of a precise, well-disciplined literary style, de Gaulle once commented: "Churchill has never written a properly composed book. There are just interesting observations and lots of documents" (which is exactly what the Pléiade poets might have said of Shakespeare).

Despite his subsequent political actions, de Gaulle was a man of savage prejudices which statesmanship forced him to ignore. Before his return to power, he once said to me: "Who are the Arabs? A people who since the days of Muhammed have never constituted a state successfully. . . . After Muhammed there has been nothing but anarchy." As early as May 31, 1956, he predicted: "If there is no war, NATO is doomed to disappear" (an event that has not yet happened although he himself gravely wounded that alliance). Six months later he was saying: "Things have taken control. Events are leading men. . . . Small men cannot handle great events. Great circumstances bring forth great men." He insisted "Russia doesn't need communism any more," and, finally, "War is a law of the human species."

On January 20, 1962, de Gaulle said: "To be a great man, one must realize something. One must achieve something definite." He showed himself, in his own words, both a "giant" and "a man of quality." Certainly, during his tenure of power, he managed to "realize something" even if one might argue that he did not "achieve something definite." But he was no less a man for trying, for restoring to his people a sense of grandeur outweighing history's logic and for providing them with the means for a brief strut back to the central stage. For this reason de Gaulle, the very last of the giants, is, if anyone, the hero of this invious, plotless book and the subject of more detailed scrutiny in ensuing chapters.

AS OTHERS SAW HIM

T HE TWO MOST RECURRENT THEMES IN MY CONVERSATIONS WITH
    de Gaulle have been France and the role of great men in inter-
    national affairs. De Gaulle himself was to prove, during the decade
of his return (1958–1968), that the age of giants had not entirely ended.

He was, I have discovered on rereading these diaries for 1954–1963, the
principal figure mentioned. As little as I know him, I am probably better
acquainted with de Gaulle and have known him over a longer consecutive
period than any other American. In this book I have not repeated comments by other writers nor cited the General's own public speeches or
works. This chapter derives from original material.

De Gaulle is the opposite of what Guy Mollet once said of his Socialist
predecessor: "Léon Blum, who knew where he was going but did not know
how to get there." The General always knew how to get there, but not
always where he was going. His motto might well have been that of Des-
cartes: "Larvatus prodeo: Masked, I advance." What follows may help
unmask him.

De Gaulle was far more sensitive than he permitted the world to think.
He was impeccably polite about answering correspondence, and almost
always replied in his own handwriting. I even have a note from him commenting on a book I wrote on death—a note of particular interest, as he
himself observed, since he wrote it shortly after an attempt to assassinate
him. Everyone knows what a deep, tender feeling he cherished for his
daughter Anne, who never grew up as other children do. It is less known
that he adored his Alsatian dog and allowed him to sleep on the presidential
bed despite his wife's complaints.

Of all my friends, Gaston Palewski, President of the Conseil d'Etat, knew
him longest. He first met de Gaulle in 1934, when the latter was a major
seeking to interest the Cabinet in armored divisions. Palewski, then working
for Paul Reynaud (later Premier), said de Gaulle was a relatively relaxed
and affable figure, "rather fond of women." I asked if de Gaulle was
actually able to carry on badinage and flirtation in the approved French
fashion. Palewski replied: "The badinage was in the nature of a cavalry

charge and de Gaulle seemed more intent on proving himself than in enjoying the process."

René Brouillet, de Gaulle's chef de cabinet, once assured me the General was "a very timid man and very sensitive." Brouillet considered his intellectual formation "much more Fifth Century B.C. Greek than Latin—although the envelope is Roman." Elisabeth de Miribel, de Gaulle's wartime secretary, observed that he had two different personalities—one the arch-conservative, Jansenist, minor aristocrat, family man and the other a thinker and philosopher. Madame de Gaulle saw to it that the first aspect was never forgotten. The General's great fault, Elisabeth thought, was that he never discovered the secret of translating his thoughts into the qualities requisite for action (a perceptive observation for, as de Gaulle himself told me, Bergson's philosophy alone allowed the two qualities to blend). Elisabeth said the General remained somewhat of a mystery even to those closest to him.

Pierre Mendès-France, former Prime Minister, confided an extraordinary thing. He said that once, during the war, de Gaulle observed to him: "One of my brothers, Xavier, is crazy. The other of my brothers, Pierre, is thoroughly normal. I am in between." Mendès pointed out that the General came from a distinguished family of country gentlefolk with a strange strain in its blood. De Gaulle's daughter, Anne, was completely subnormal although another daughter grew up to be a remarkable and intelligent woman.

Pompidou wrote me to deny a published report that de Gaulle had even once called him "Georges." I asked Etienne Burin des Roziers, who had for some years been the General's top aide, what he called him. He replied: "He doesn't call me anything." "But doesn't he say 'Burin' or 'Etienne' or 'Monsieur?' " "No, nothing at all." I asked if de Gaulle ever suggested at the end of a difficult day: "Wait a minute, relax and sit down," and then discussed subjects removed from the political world. Rarely, said Burin, and then only affairs of state.

Burin, who believed the secret of de Gaulle's friendship with Malraux was a common romantic patriotism, a shared belief about France, considered him unabashedly vain. He never wore glasses if he could help it, relying on a kind of haptic contact with the world. Vanity helped inspire his impressive trick of memorizing phrases in foreign languages to be used in speeches while traveling abroad—and his feat of committing to memory both television addresses and press-conference summations, so he need not appear in spectacles before his public.

Georges Galichon, at one time chef de cabinet at the Elysée, said the General's only relaxation was television, which he often watched with his grandchildren. He also enjoyed walking through the forest girding his home at Colombey-les-Deux-Eglises. Brouillet explained his isolation accordingly:

"Before the war he was quite interested in art and liked to visit museums but, quite apart from his position as French President, he is a prisoner of his stature and simply could not wander about looking at paintings because he would immediately be recognized." He said de Gaulle liked to read, even in the Elysée, and regularly skipped through newspapers and magazines in French and English. Brouillet claimed de Gaulle was fluent if imperfect in English and once knew German quite well, having learned it as a young officer and polished it while a prisoner during World War I.

The General's health was astonishing for an old man. He didn't overwork in the Elysée, never starting before 10:00 A.M. and never quitting later than 8:00 P.M. (according to Brouillet). He had a successful prostate operation and, of course, his eyes bothered him until his cataracts were cut out. Before then, his refusal to wear glasses caused frequent embarrassments and Pompidou said he would sometimes ask, on tours, if anyone was lining the route—when it was jammed with people. Once he put his hand through a glass door. General Pierre Billotte, de Gaulle's wartime chief of staff and later a member of his Cabinet, told me that after 1958 de Gaulle reluctantly agreed to see his doctor once a week. It took much persuasion to induce him to do this because he previously considered it immoral for any man to see a physician unless he was at the point of death.

By no means all Frenchmen acquainted with the General admired him. Jean Monnet told me: "I have known de Gaulle for years and I don't like him. He has an odd technique. He always creates problems in order to solve them." Billotte, irked by his enormous vanity, said that when the General, as a political exile, was invited to attend a memorial service for the King of England, he refused to go when he learned his position in church would be behind that of President Vincent Auriol. Malraux, always an activist, complained in 1954, after the Gaullist political organization collapsed: "He marched a large force to the Rubicon and then, instead of crossing, told them to take out their fishing rods." Raymond Laporte, a French diplomat, gave a reception for the General in New York and chatted with him during a quiet moment. Laporte remarked that perhaps never before had New York turned out so overwhelmingly for a foreign visitor. De Gaulle regarded him stonily and said: "And for whom else but General de Gaulle would such a reception be arranged?"

Pompidou thought one reason for de Gaulle's American success was snob appeal. He recalled that when the first volume of de Gaulle's *Mémoires* appeared the General was virtually a forgotten man living in Colombey. After a few people in the society world read this and said: "He is a writer; he is a Saint-Simon," it became chic to read de Gaulle as the modern Saint-Simon. Maurice Thorez, France's Communist boss, was in de Gaulle's Cabinet during his first administration. He described to me the General's abrupt departure in 1946. "He summoned all his ministers one day to the Matignon [office of French Prime Ministers] and said: 'Sirs, I am going.' There was no explanation. That was all." Jean Soutou, a French ambassador, recalls that de Gaulle warned Mendès-France at the time of the Algerian crisis: "We are too many parties already in France, but soon there will be another, the party of the refugees from North Africa."

Jean Laloy, the astute diplomat who interpreted between de Gaulle and Stalin in 1944, said the talks were not as successful as the General later claimed in his memoirs. "After all," he argued, "de Gaulle sent an agent to the Polish Lublin government when neither England nor the United States did." De Gaulle demanded Russian support for French control of the German left bank of the Rhine. Laloy was horrified. He agreed with Stalin's argument that it would permanently poison Franco-German relationships. Laloy pointed out to the General: "This would leave France backed by Russia and opposed by Britain and the United States." "Never mind," said de Gaulle, "Stalin won't agree."

Antoine Pinay, a former Prime Minister who served in de Gaulle's Cabinet after 1958, once started off a critique by telling me the General was very *rusé*. When de Gaulle was edging him out of the Finance Ministry and had already decided to give the job to Wilfrid Baumgartner, Pinay mentioned this and the General protested: "Baumgartner? There is absolutely no thought of Baumgartner to succeed you as Minister of Finance." Fifteen minutes later Pinay learned that not only was Baumgartner going to be appointed, but also de Gaulle had been consulting with Baumgartner on the subject for eight days. "I regret to say," Pinay told me bitterly, "but the President is a liar. He likes politics and ruse."

Even those who opposed de Gaulle appreciated his enormous pride. Simonne Servais told me de Gaulle had worked and reworked the third volume of his *Mémoires*, scribbling in corrections until it was a terrible mess. Then he insisted on copying over the entire manuscript himself because he thought the first version sloppy and wanted to leave "an original manuscript for history." Pierre Courtade, member of the French Communist party's Central Committee and a bitter anti-Gaullist, said after one of the General's speeches: "Nobody has spoken like that in France since Louis XIV."

Although a phenomenally successful propagandist who introduced an effective style to television politics, de Gaulle had little use for the press. I once asked Olivier Guichard, his ex-aide, why. He replied: "I really don't know. After all, he once was a journalist himself." In the 1930s de Gaulle wrote military articles for *L'Echo de Paris* although he didn't sign his name. The General, while he disliked its tedium, was a compulsive writer. Guichard always predicted that loneliness would drive him to write another volume of memoirs after his retirement—a forecast that came true despite de Gaulle's repeated insistence to the contrary.

Billotte was much taken by de Gaulle's sharp sense of humor and savage gift of mimicry. In London, during the war, de Gaulle, Billotte, and Hervé Alphand, later a distinguished diplomat, used to put on an act in which the General mimicked Pétain, Alphand played Laval, and Billotte was General

Weygand, each improvising comments on current developments. "De Gaulle was very good," says Billotte.

Once during that same period a British Member of Parliament called on the General to complain that a young English officer, one of Billotte's liaison aides, was sleeping with the MP's wife. De Gaulle instructed Billotte to fire the man. Billotte protested: "Why? He is a nice fellow and he does his job. The Englishman should have found his own solution. He could have shot my aide or he could have shot his wife or shot himself. It is ridiculous for him to complain to the chief of a government because his wife is unfaithful." The General replied: "That is not the point, my dear Billotte. If you and I were in the situation of that young aide, we would not have been stupid enough to be caught in bed. Obviously the man is a fool. Fire him." Billotte did.

Guichard said the General's family frequently discussed the wisdom of his standing for re-election. Madame de Gaulle even opposed his return to politics after he stepped down in 1946, as a comparatively young man. She was vigorously against his re-election, fearing either that he would overstrain himself or, indeed, that he might be murdered by army malcontents. However, according to Guichard, her family, the Vendroux, and that of his son-in-law, Boissieu, encouraged him to stay on. Madame de Boissieu, the General's daughter, had considerable influence on him.

Billotte complained that the only people with whom the General seemed to feel at ease were foreign chiefs of state like Eisenhower, Adenauer, or even Khrushchev. He did not accept any Frenchman as his peer. The General rarely invited anyone for a quiet dinner except members of the family. Billotte considered Madame de Gaulle "a loyal cipher without interest."

Nevertheless, word got around Paris that she played a subtly influential role. Jean-Jacques Servan-Schreiber, who didn't know the General, but, through the tentacles of his magazine, *L'Express*, was well clued in on gossip, told me Madame de Gaulle was always strictly enjoined against ever mentioning politics. Nevertheless, he described her as "a cunning lady and a violent Catholic" who cultivated her own friends in the Elysée entourage, above all Count de Bonneval, the General's principal military aide.

Pompidou told me the General had great admiration for Roosevelt although he preferred Churchill as a man, and that he had carefully studied Roosevelt's political techniques. There is no doubt that de Gaulle always paid more heed to foreign statesmen than to French politicians. Therefore, it is of interest to note what distinguished foreigners thought of him.

In 1959, Eisenhower, then approaching the end of a second presidential term marked by growing difficulties with France, told me that nevertheless he understood and sympathized with de Gaulle. He said Roosevelt had mistreated him during the war and hadn't understood his pride and his determination "to represent the noble things in France." This had given de

Gaulle "a complex towards us" and made him hard to deal with. Notwith-standing, he liked and respected the General. Three years later another President, Kennedy, made it quite clear that he had almost an obsession on de Gaulle. During one three-and-a-half hour conversation he kept returning to the subject. Although he admitted to having "lots of trouble with him," he conceded that the General was "a very great man."

Prime Minister Harold Macmillan confided in 1962, after an unfruitful meeting: "I told de Gaulle that I am sixty-eight and he is seventy-two and in our childhood we would never have thought of a Common Market. We would have thought of ourselves only as an Englishman and a Frenchman. But the world has changed." (Events, alas, were to prove it had changed less than Macmillan thought.) The Prime Minister continued: "De Gaulle is a very proud Frenchman. But he is in a sense an old-fashioned nationalist. In some ways he is rather advanced. And there you have a duality: Half narrow and half broad, and thus there are two ways of looking at things. The whole thing should be to get out of our private ivory towers." (Macmillan delayed too long before abandoning Britain's traditional disdain for Europe and by the time he did so de Gaulle had enhanced his own majestic disdain for Britain.)

Konrad Adenauer staked his policy on harmony with France. In 1957, a year before de Gaulle's return, the German Chancellor mused: "I definitely consider Churchill to be a great man. He saved his country when it was in a very difficult situation. But take de Gaulle, for example: He saved his country, but afterwards he was a complete failure as head of government." Yet, three years later, Adenauer thought de Gaulle's twelve-year exile in Colombey "had done him immense good and now he is the ablest statesman in the West."

In 1963 (before France's Israeli arms embargo), Nasser told me:

> I started to admire de Gaulle during the second World War. I remember his pictures. I remember the pictures showing him when he returned to Paris and marched in a parade to the Arch of Triumph. I admired him during the war as an officer who insisted on carrying on the fight despite all odds. De Gaulle was courageous also on Algeria where he faced the situation bluntly. Now he tries to be independent by all means. It is a question of dignity. I think he is a man of principle. It is different to deal with him than to deal with politicians, even if there are difficulties. It is a great advantage to deal with a man of principle.

Nasser's arch-enemy, Ben Gurion, shared this admiration, even after Israel's relations with France soured, while Levi Eshkol, Israeli Prime Minister, insisted: "There is no danger of de Gaulle trying to barter us away to the Arabs. We feel a special sympathy exists for us among the French people themselves and there has been no change in France's arms supply to us."

Dean Rusk, who wore Gaullism around his neck like a private albatross while he was Secretary of State, thought as early as 1963, that the General was drawing to a bitter, isolated end. He told me:

This will probably turn out to be the final chapter of a very great man. Personally, I deeply sympathize with any patriotic Frenchman who saw the experiences suffered by his country during all these years and who lived through these experiences himself. And I can understand de Gaulle's deep desire to restore all the prestige of France. He fought against the dry rot in his country not only during World War II, but before it.

Averell Harriman gave de Gaulle full marks for his handling of Stalin when he visited Moscow in 1944. He said the General "blandly refused all of Stalin's threats and blandishments when Stalin tried to get him to recognize the Lublin Polish government in exchange for an anti-German treaty." Stalin complained to Harriman that de Gaulle was a "very tough man to deal with." General Norstad, the NATO commander, in many respects admired de Gaulle, but in 1959, he told me he did not think he was "great." Norstad thought, "His historical perception extends from the sixteenth to the nineteenth century."

Robert Murphy, Roosevelt's diplomatic agent in wartime North Africa and later Undersecretary of State, didn't like de Gaulle, but he enjoyed reminiscing about him. He had been placed in charge of the haughty Frenchman when he was flown from London to Casablanca in 1942 to join Roosevelt and Churchill. Murphy took de Gaulle to his billet, a building surrounded by barbed wire and protected by U.S. sentries. The General turned to Murphy and said: "I would never accept living under such conditions on French soil if I did not know that this house belonged to a Danish national." Murphy told de Gaulle he should come to North Africa and stay there for three months during which time he could gain full control and eliminate his rival, General Giraud, because the latter had no political ambitions. De Gaulle remarked: "Political ambitions come quickly. Look at me."

Every diplomat serving in Paris during the Gaullist era had his own reminiscences. Cecil Lyon, U.S. chargé d'affaires in 1962, heard that when de Gaulle was advised Chip Bohlen would be coming as the next U.S. envoy, he said: "Well, if it has to be an American, he is the most suitable man." Douglas Dillon, President Eisenhower's ambassador to the Fourth Republic, said de Gaulle blamed U.S. interference for keeping him from a return to power in 1947–1948. The General claimed Washington preferred to have a weak government in France and therefore threw its weight against him. But de Gaulle told Dillon that, from an American viewpoint, he couldn't blame Washington.

There is no doubt that de Gaulle made an immense impression on visitors and also exerted an ineffable sway on mass audiences, abroad as well as at home. By the power of persistent self-discipline and a self-imposed loneliness that must have been hard for him to bear at times, he built up an air of inner mystery which had an electrical effect on others. Without question the greatest thing about the man was his personality, a combination of implacable resolution and radiant flashes; but it was rare that this held anyone indefinitely in thrall. De Gaulle himself is reported to have said: "Every Frenchman has been, is, or will be a Gaullist." Yet the mood rarely endured and, even while he maintained his majorities, their components constantly shifted. He was enormously admired and at times enormously hated. His ablation changed France as much as his intrusion, and even those who detested him did not dispute his personal grandeur—perhaps in the sense of Rilke, who wrote: *"La gloire est la somme des malentendus qui se forment autour d'un nom."*

THE KENNEDY

MEMORANDUM

I N APRIL, 1961, I WAS VISITED BY ARTHUR SCHLESINGER, JR., AND
Tom Finletter, U.S. ambassador to NATO, who asked me on behalf of
President Kennedy if I would prepare a memorandum outlining
analyses and suggestions that might be of aid in Kennedy's forthcoming
conversations with de Gaulle. The President was scheduled to make an
official visit to Paris at the end of May and I acceded.

In order to continue my analysis of the main figure in this book with
some coherence, I am extracting from its normal position in my diaries the
text of the memorandum, then classified as secret. I publish it here with
only slight deletions to save space. As is recounted later, Kennedy received
me in his apartment at the Quai d'Orsay after saying farewell to de Gaulle
and had the kindness to praise this paper as useful to him. Since nothing of
permanent value emerged from their talks, it is hard to accept this as more
than a friendly compliment. The text follows:

SECRET

Memorandum on General de Gaulle

I am impressed by de Gaulle as a powerful personality and as a major
and fascinating historical figure. But he is largely black and white by
coloration. Many of his conceptions are, I believe, either false, outdated,
or premature; at least not applicable to May 31, 1961.

Nevertheless, I have sought to show the man as I *feel* him to be and as
a human reality we have to deal with—whether his ideas are convenient
or inconvenient, sensible or totally without reason. The man is *the* fact of
French politics today. And although we may well have to postulate a
post-de Gaulle policy, while we deal with current France it means dealing
with de Gaulle.

If in any way during these talks de Gaulle imagines he is being driven into a corner or even indirectly threatened, he will become politely but adamantly obdurate. The weaker he feels vis-à-vis his interlocutor, the more difficult he will become.

Judging from the historical record rather than from private talks, I would say THIS is the cardinal rule.

Three basic aspects of de Gaulle's character must be kept in mind throughout conversations but above all at the very beginning. These are de Gaulle's curiously individual personality, his fundamental attitude towards the U.S., and his broad view toward the world and France's role in it.

De Gaulle deliberately modeled himself on past figures, most of them French, although in a curious way he is influenced by his classical education. In the latter respect, he is more Greek than Roman, and places an immensely high value on the individual qualities and capacities of superior human beings to influence their era. Technically speaking, his method of approach strongly reflects his early acquaintance with the philosophy of Henri Bergson and the mixture between pure logic and intuition. This aspect of intuition is most important to remember in any effort to influence the course of his thinking.

He is, of course, very much the old-fashioned gentleman with impeccable manners, deliberate courtesy, and an almost sensual desire to speak and hear well-phrased sentences. The question of interpretation therefore becomes particularly important.

I do not know whether at such a high-level meeting General de Gaulle might call on his Foreign Minister, Couve de Murville, to do any, much, or all of his interpreting; but I would doubt it. If he relies on Prince Andronikov, we are at a disadvantage unless we provide our own interpreter, equipped not only with superior abilities, but with a personality respected by de Gaulle. Andronikov is mechanically an adequate translator, but his colleagues say he doesn't understand the issues involved.

I would, therefore, strongly recommend that Mr. Bohlen [later Ambassador to Paris] serve as the President's interpreter, not only because of his great technical capacity, but also because of his profound familiarity with all the issues to be surveyed and his ability to give quick, sound counsel. Finally, Mr. Bohlen is one of the few Americans in whom General de Gaulle has expressed a personal interest. . . .

Beneath his superior air and frequently disdainful manner, General de Gaulle is a rather shy and timid man. He is not noted for the slightest levity or any sense of humor, although he does indeed have elements of the latter. Whether it will emerge depends, I suppose, on the rapport established during these talks.

He has been known in the past to show to intimates a rather remarkable gift for mimicry. He can display a cruelly sarcastic tongue. In terms of humor, as in terms of gallantry, one of his old friends described de Gaulle's approach as "the heavy cavalry technique."

Before getting into further "psychoanalysis," I would like to say that I think de Gaulle is favorably inclined towards youth. In this regard both the President and Mrs. Kennedy have a certain human advantage that may strike a chord of sympathy. He likes young people. I would suspect that, in moments of relaxation between the major conversations, he might enjoy a bit of quiet gaiety and laughter, a rare atmosphere in his self-chosen, austere surroundings.

In our approach, we must never forget his innermost anti-American feelings. De Gaulle tends to confuse himself with France. I once asked him what France thought of the U.S.

He said:

There is no hate for the United States in France. France remains friendly to the United States. But the French people don't like the American people. The United States is our friend and will remain so; but the American people are not regarded sympathetically.

Nevertheless, the United States will remain our friend. From time to time, in moments of great danger, only the United States and France will remain and people will tend to forget the Americans and French, who do not get on so well. Of course, during intervening periods, the fact that our interests are not really the same will continue to appear more obvious.

De Gaulle and many people around him rely upon the U.S. as a protective umbrella which will prevent war and beneath which they can proceed with their own plans to recapture some of France's lost position. But they don't enjoy having to rely upon this implied protection. They resent this dependence which is never mentioned.

The General doesn't really like us and he suspects our motives, even when they are above suspicion. He is exceedingly sensitive in this respect. But he is inclined to mask his suspicions and reactions. It is highly unlikely that he will disclose them in any frank way as English-speaking statesmen often do. On the contrary, they will always be obscured by a mask of courtesy. De Gaulle is an astute poker player—but with the European "stripped deck." We must remember this and not deceive ourselves.

De Gaulle's feelings on America stem from two causes. There is an undoubted resentment at the fact that the United States is now the great power of the West—in Europe as well as elsewhere—while France has fallen to a tertiary role. In this connection he even exaggerates the very close relationship between Washington and London. He feels there is a kind of invisible Anglo-American conspiracy designed to keep France from recovering the prestige it held, above all, on the Continent, during and after World War I.

The second basic cause is that series of "incidents" between himself and Americans and between France and the U.S. dating back to World War II. De Gaulle has a long memory. He will never forget the policy of Franklin D. Roosevelt, first of all vis-à-vis Vichy and Marshal Pétain, culminating with Admiral Darlan; and secondly vis-à-vis himself and the ultimate effort to build up General Giraud.

De Gaulle feels strongly about Roosevelt. He also feels strongly about Truman. He thinks American policy worked deliberately to develop a "third force" which would prevent his return to power when he first tried this through his Rally of the French People (RPF).

He has for long looked with skepticism at American diplomatic activities. Although he was not yet in power when Mr. [Robert] Murphy joined Mr. [later Sir Harold] Beeley in the "good-offices" mission after the Sakiet incident, his suspicions are intense. He is always prepared to lend an ear to anyone who tells him that American oil companies wish to grab control of the Sahara or that the U.S. wishes to fill a power vacuum in North Africa after France leaves.

Therefore we must exercise particular care both in our actions and in our statements concerning sensitive areas. De Gaulle was enraged when minor members of Cabot Lodge's UN mission attended an Algerian FLN party. He was more than enraged when Ambassador Walmsley in Tunis was instructed to confer with two FLN leaders. In fact, I am told that for a while he seriously thought of cancelling or deferring the visit of President Kennedy.

I think when the subject of North Africa arises naturally in conversations (and I emphasize the word "naturally" because I am not sure it should be introduced by our side), we must tread softly. While speaking with complete honesty, we should do so in the most delicate possible way.

Apropos of this, I would think it advisable for some distinguished and knowledgeable official to talk at length with M. Pompidou, at least ten days or two weeks prior to the opening of the de Gaulle-Kennedy conversations. Pompidou is no longer so close to de Gaulle as he used to be. Yet he is still listened to with respect and does see the General with some frequency. He is entrusted with confidential tasks.

Pompidou is well inclined to the United States and it might be well for someone to express our views and perturbations to him sufficiently in advance so that perhaps these may be echoed back to the General prior to May 31.

It is my thought that, when the serious exchanges begin, we should follow the formula, "first things last." In other words, I think a more favorable atmosphere could be created were the President to seize the earliest possible opportunity to steer the conversations to subjects where there *is* inherent agreement between Washington and Paris.

There *are* areas of agreement and political discussion should focus on these initially. Of those, the most important, perhaps, is Germany. Despite the Common Market and the close, if variable, relationships between de Gaulle and Adenauer, the General is still imbued with deep mistrust for Germany. And despite his distaste for clichés, he uses them when discussing this subject.

He is still likely to say, "Germans are Germans" and to talk of the danger of "Krupps" when viewing the situation. He thinks there is no difficulty as long as Chancellor Adenauer is alive. But even General de Gaulle, who has only lately become at all preoccupied with death as it may affect himself, recognizes that Adenauer will not long be in power.

Unless West Germany is firmly tied to the West (*encadré* is the word he uses), he foresees a nervous period after Adenauer. He thinks Moscow will make a new offer to Bonn and that the post-Adenauer government (Erhard or Strauss) will be pushed by "Krupps" to accept some kind of unification deal, perhaps based on confederation, which would prize West Germany from the occidental camp.

Although de Gaulle has little knowledge of and less interest in economics, he sees this problem in economic as well as political terms. He believes the Ruhr barons see in the Soviet bloc the only easily available source of cheap food and raw materials which will allow them to fabricate goods at an inexpensive cost; and also an attractive market for those goods particularly desired by Russia and China and particularly suited to German industrial capacities.

It seems to me that the United States, whether or not it shares these fears, has the same ultimate policy goal as de Gaulle with respect to West Germany. Once this similarity of essential views can be established, it will be easier to proceed to the discussion of other subjects, first those immediately related and second those only indirectly related.

Within that framework, for example, one might analyze the Common Market and ideas of English association with it; and then OECD. (A-propos of this, I believe de Gaulle feels that "sentiment" in London is moving increasingly towards British membership in the Common Market, but that "policy" in London is not.)

Only in this connection, and after this initial exploration, if de Gaulle allows Mr. Kennedy to more or less set the pattern of the talks, could NATO conveniently be brought up. And, when it is, I think it would be wise to stress the *political* over the *military* aspect of the alliance.

It could do no harm to point out that one of NATO's fundamental political purposes is to ensure not only that Germany (and therefore France) has an adequate defense, but that Germany will be linked closely with France and the Allies, and thereby will be unable to launch any adventures of its own so long as the North Atlantic Treaty endures.

I fear at this time that there is scant hope for achieving any great advance on the project for integration of French forces in NATO. Yet we may usefully stress the need to continue encouraging Germany's political and economic integration into the alliance.

It is blatantly apparent that de Gaulle has little use for our conceptions of either NATO or the UN. The only change I have detected in his NATO attitude during the past ten years or so is that while once he had absolutely *no* use for the alliance and would have been prepared to pull out completely, he is now prepared to tolerate it—but with minimal support.

As for the UN, his attitude has gone from worse to worst. He considers this a foolish "augmented Babel." He professes not even to be concerned with whether or not China is brought in because he feels this would merely add another hostile voice to insult the West. But he plans no unilateral action on Peking.

In this connection I think it might be psychologically appropriate for the President to ask de Gaulle a favor. That favor would be to mute France's public opposition to our efforts to strengthen the free world's cause in the UN.

(I specifically use the word "favor." De Gaulle is very human. I suspect he might feel flattered if asked to "give" something to a power which his brain, if not his heart, acknowledges as greater. In an Orwellian sense this might make him feel "more equal." Things might be easier if this feeling can be encouraged in the General's mind.)

Furthermore, while I dislike any thought of "buttering up" de Gaulle, it would be sensible to point out how pleased we are that the heritage of French culture (which, alas, may not last too long) in former French colonies in Africa has helped bring many of these to the support of western causes in the UN Assembly.

At this point, under ideal circumstances, it could be apt for the two Presidents to exchange ideas on "decolonialization." De Gaulle is particularly sensitive on this subject. He is in the astonishingly paradoxical position of having fought since June, 1940, to restore the entire French empire—largely against Mr. Roosevelt's concepts—and, since his return to power three years ago, has sought to yield this empire piece by piece, without wholly dislocating France.

Algeria is the last important area affected and the one on which, like every Frenchman, he is most sensitive. But even here his policy has been remarkably consistent over the last three years, despite apparently contradictory tactical public shifts.

Can the two Presidents usefully and tactfully discuss the problems of decolonization and how the West may insure that the fledgling Afro-Asian states, whether Algeria or Laos, can be kept free of communism? At this point it might be suitable for President Kennedy to "ask the General's advice" concerning not only Cuba but all of South and Central America.

We are no more bound to follow his advice than he is bound to follow ours. Nevertheless this represents his conception of consultation, what has been falsely called his proposal for a "*directoire.*"

De Gaulle wants France to be accepted by Washington on a basis of complete parity with England. I think that, concerning the so-called "*directoire,*" he is far more interested in establishing Big Three consultative machinery for what he calls a "western policy" in regions *outside* the North Atlantic Treaty area, not *inside* it.

As for nuclear arrangements: This vitally important subject will, I venture to say, have to be raised by President Kennedy. If it is not, I doubt if it will ever be raised by President de Gaulle. Therefore, I think we should be very careful to choose what appears to be the most propitious psychological moment before the subject is brought up. And no matter how generous an offer we might suggest to the General (even after explaining the difficulty of U.S. congressional approval), we should be prepared for de Gaulle's statement that, in fact, he doesn't want any atomic assistance from us.

He has told me twice that he doesn't require access to our nuclear secrets and that, if he were at the helm in Washington, he himself would not offer such assistance to France. It is most desirable that we have answers to this possible approach and that we have them ready in advance.

De Gaulle has blazing areas of ignorance. For example, he really knows nothing about economic matters, although he is very proud that the French fiscal situation has improved and that the Common Market has accelerated the growth of French production. This ignorance must be remembered should the General, now more than ever concerned with his own constitutional and political problems, solicit from Mr. Kennedy some of our President's ideas

We should not forget that de Gaulle is essentially a liberal (in the old-fashioned sense) and (in the French sense) more left than right, despite his autocratic methods. He is, indeed, a benevolent despot; but he regards himself as the benevolent custodian of democracy in France. Also, while he has contempt for the Communists as "foreign" agents, he dislikes the extreme right more than the non-Communist left.

Even before the recent insurrection he was thinking of the problem of arranging a post-de Gaulle governmental system for France which clearly would require still another constitution. De Gaulle imagines this should be based on what he calls the "presidential" system along lines he imagines *à l'américaine*. The fact of the matter is that he has very little real understanding of the American formula.

I suspect he might be truly interested to hear some of Mr. Kennedy's ideas on this. De Gaulle recognizes that one basic problem in France is the virtual impossibility (according to himself) of evolving a two-party system. He considers that today there is really only one "party" in France; and that is the Communist party. He does not see much likelihood of being able to organize two broad, non-Communist parties on *any* basis. Yet he still thinks paradoxically that an "American presidential" method can be established here.

De Gaulle has another feeling these days; and he applies it to the United States as well as France. He told me:

Whatever his intentions, President Kennedy will find himself increasingly pushed towards strong government and the U.S. economy will find itself increasingly pushed towards *dirigisme*. This is a necessity of our times.

The United States will simply have to abandon its shibboleth of free enterprise and accept ever greater controls for its economy. There is no escape from this. The problems and pressures of our era are simply too great to permit the luxury of laissez-faire. We are now finding this out and we will all have to react to the enormous events of our time.

This kind of formula represents the type of idea I imagine General de Gaulle might very well like to discuss informally with President Kennedy. Here again, such exchanges might help to establish that feeling of "equality" and close rapport which de Gaulle craves, but is so awkward in achieving. This conviction of the need for a "strong government" is, of course, in line with de Gaulle's oversimplified view of history and his feeling that "small men cannot handle great events."

We are not yet in a position to discern whether, in the following connection, de Gaulle is "the man of the day-before-yesterday" or the "man of the day-after-tomorrow." He has a feeling of *oneness* with the white people of the West. That is one reason he resents what he considers the lack of relationship with Washington and deplores the absence of what he calls a "western" policy.

He has a dim prevision of vicious racial cleavage between the white race and other races—somewhat along the lines entertained by William Randolph Hearst in the 1920s. For some time he tended to think of the Soviet Union solely in terms of "eternal Russia" rather than in terms of a dynamic Communist power. He somehow felt that the white peoples dominating Russia would eventually accommodate themselves to the West; he regarded their ideology as a passing thing, because of the menace on their southern and eastern borders from a vast bloc of non-white nations headed by China and eventually aided by Japan.

This view was possibly dampened by Khrushchev's visit to Paris in 1960, and by his harsh behavior at the Summit Conference. But I suspect that deep down, de Gaulle (who does not yield ideas easily) still cherishes this vague vision of the future.

To sum up, I would venture the opinion that in psychological relationships between the U.S. and France, four rules should be recalled by our Chief Executive in terms of maximum desire for a successful conclusion to these talks.

1. We, as the stronger power (and therefore per se at a disadvantage in conversations with this haughty man), must display a patient and willing interestedness to listen.

2. At no point during the conversations should we *press* de Gaulle. Rather it is wiser to seek to induce him into *mutual* discussion. He is most difficult when he feels weak and at a disadvantage.

3. We must never forget, no matter how friendly the atmosphere, that he *sus*pects the U.S. more than he *res*pects us—much as he knows he depends upon us. He feels that for geographical reasons as well as the logic of current history we depend almost equally on him.

4. In concluding, I urge that when serious conversations are started, if possible these should be begun on points where the policies of France and the United States are evidently in basic accord.

DE GAULLE

ON DE GAULLE:

COUP-MAKING

I AM A JOURNALIST, NOT A HISTORIAN, AND THEREFORE SUBJECT TO
the intuition adduced by de Gaulle's favorite philosopher, Henri
Bergson. Perhaps because of this I suspect that when this period's
history is written we will find the General seized power in 1958 by helping
to manipulate events and did not return to France's helm by accident, a
generous savior. He was out to destroy the funest Fourth Republic, to
impose his massive personality and warp France to his indomitable will.

De Gaulle adored France, but he held Frenchmen in contempt. He disliked their constitutions, their political parties, the frequent intrusion of
their army into politics. A talented plotter, he was willing to take over by
illegal means and, indeed, spoke quite frankly of his use of the *coup d'état*
when circumstances became auspicious. I am convinced that someday we
shall learn in detail how de Gaulle subtly encouraged the officers' conspiracy on whose back he rode to the Elysée. If this was not a Gaullist
coup it was a perfect simulacrum.

The General saw French history as a zigzag progression. In November,
1954, he told me: "The big trouble with France is that in one hundred and
fifty years it has had thirteen constitutions and has been invaded six times.
This only covers the lifetime of two old men." He never had a clear view of
a maturing, steadfast body politic and, indeed, acknowledged as viable only
the Communist party which alternately he cajoled or used as a threat to
galvanize the chaotic center and right.

Nevertheless, in this as everything, de Gaulle is not easily categorized. He
was in many respects more of the left than the right, despite his haughty,
monarchistic methods, and when he faltered and withdrew from the scene

he was planning the most profound social reform France had known since its revolution. Likewise, although by instinct authoritarian and contemptuous, he was no tyrant. As long ago as 1949, when he had already started working for his comeback, the General told me: "My enemies say I wish to be a dictator. I had all the power in my hand, once. Was I a dictator?"

The Fourth Republic was formed in 1946, shortly after the General retired into political exile. De Gaulle began immediately to plot its sepulture and contemplate a return. However, for long it was evident he thought of comeback in terms of conventional means. He overestimated his popular support, underestimated the effectiveness of U.S. opposition, and proved too pessimistic in forecasts of imminent war or chaos. Nevertheless, the possibility of extra-legal action was always just below the surface of his mind.

In May, 1947, when I asked if he would accept the Prime Ministry were President Auriol to offer it, the General answered: "I cannot forecast such things. That is a question of tactics. If events force such a choice, the Constitution will have to be amended." I remarked that this would take time but he replied: "Some events such as those of 1940 show that a Constitution can be changed quickly—even in one afternoon." That was the first direct hint I had that he would not exclude some form of pressure tactics.

By 1949, he was pronouncedly bitter. He told me (Oct. 26):

The entire French problem is that the regime considers itself only as an apparatus against General de Gaulle and works exclusively against General de Gaulle. [I was always fascinated by this usage of the third person and his tendency to talk about himself as if analyzing some remote historical figure.] The French ambassador in Washington is the ambassador of that regime and tries to misrepresent my views in the United States. The entire regime is constructed against me. Its papers, its radio, its news agencies, and its ambassadors work only against me. When one understands that, one understands the entire problem. Without comprehending that, one comprehends nothing.

The French people are very tired and very fed up with the regime. But they are absorbed in their own difficulties and will wait a bit more. Already the people of France realize that their Constitution is not good and is at the root of all present difficulties. It is now really impossible to re-establish any serious government. Naturally, I think we should have a new election as soon as possible, but it won't take place now. The reason is that here—unlike any other country—dissolution of the Assembly depends upon the deputies themselves.

Unfortunately, there is no way of forcing the deputies to dissolve. The Constitution permits the deputies to remain in office right up to the moment of catastrophe, because the Constitution was devised by the parties now in control. If catastrophe comes, the deputies will vanish. But they sit waiting for a catastrophe just as in 1940; and that is what I fear.

In an ordinary parliamentary regime, as in England [except in the United States where the governmental powers are divided] the dissolution comes from the government itself. The English king can dissolve parliament and ask for elections. In France, unfortunately, this depends upon the deputies.

Early in 1951, he told me that so long as he was in a position to carry out his ideas, "the question of title is not important. I will be chief of the government. Of course I would accept the title of President of the Council [Prime Minister]."

It was clear from the moment the General abruptly yielded power in 1946, and retired to Colombey-les-Deux-Eglises that he had no use for any political parties as the basis for France's future, and that he would seek a new formula on which to build. At first he attempted this through what he called a "rally," the Rassemblement du Peuple Français (RPF). This, however, failed in its come-back attempts. That failure helped drive the General along the road he chose in 1958, a road which, as he had long foreseen, was studded with violence.

Early in 1947, he told me:

At present there are five parties in France: the Communists, Socialists, Radicals, Moderates, and MRP [Popular Republicans]. The Communists are not a French party; therefore it is impossible to imagine making a French policy by relying on the Communist party. There remain four political groups, but these four are continually fighting each other. No one of these parties has the support of an important part of the French public. These parties cannot be relied upon because they cannot agree on policy.

The aim of the RPF is to group the French people in such a way as to permit a system whereby policies can be decided and responsibilities assumed in the interests of France, independent of any single political party aspirations. The Communist party cannot take part in the RPF for just this reason. Of course the Communists will fight us and of course we will fight them. They don't play a French game. But set this question aside.

He even went so far, at the time, as to say that when he regained power it would be "indispensable" to dissolve the Communist party. He added with sardonic humor, "We don't want to shoot them all." Apart from the Communists, he said: "We are willing to receive men from all parties. The RPF addresses itself to all men able to promote a French policy who will come to us as men and not as political representatives." He counted on his empathy with the masses and on backing from the non-Communist left, adding:

We do not have the support of the right. The French right is very bourgeois and mistrustful. Many of them were for Pétain and therefore mistrust General de Gaulle.

[Nevertheless] an enormous number of French people tend towards us psychologically but have not yet come over to the RPF actively. If events prove that we are right, they will. On the other hand, if within a year it is seen that the present system can keep afloat, then they will not have to join the RPF. This type of reasoning, this spirit and psychology, is that which most of the French displayed towards the Free French Movement in 1940 and 1941. They were sentimentally favorable, but they figured that if the Germans won, General de Gaulle would be wrong. If the Germans lost, General de Gaulle would be right and they would then shout "vive de Gaulle."

Everything depends upon events. If events keep the present system going we will not come to power and the movement [RPF] will no longer interest me. But I fear and believe that the present system cannot survive future events. If that is the case I think that the principal crisis will come early next winter [1947–1948]. At that time the present system of parties will be paralyzed. At such a moment France will have only a choice between the Communists and the RPF. I do not believe it will choose the Communists.

The strategy was to help other forces weaken and infibulate the Fourth Republic. Although that winter proved to be tense and marked by mass strikes and hardship, de Gaulle was evidently wrong. The United States intervened quietly to support Third Force elements (between the extremes of communism and Gaullism) which upheld the regime—a policy never quite forgiven by the General who quite accurately discerned its hostility toward his own movement. "I regret to say that you succeeded all too well," he once told me. Nevertheless, he did not immediately abandon the RPF.

In 1949, he still thought the Rally would get 40 percent of the vote in a national election and that six months afterwards it would have 55 percent of the vote because of the political and financial deterioration he foresaw. Even in 1951, he was talking of an electoral victory in which his movement would gain at least 170 seats in the National Assembly, forcing the regime to recognize that no government could be organized "except with me or with the Communists—one or the other; that is a fact."

Reliance on his own renown and fulgurous personality failed as a political tactic, and by 1954, he had abandoned the Rally as a lost cause and was turning to other conceivable solutions for the country that he felt required his leadership. He told me (January 21):

The real remedy in France is a great France, *une grandeur Française*. Now there is despair here. Those Frenchmen who are despairing go to the Communist party. That is why you need a great French policy to eliminate communism. This is not easy. But on this we have not received much support from our allies [meaning the United States].

During the war I made war. I finished by success. Now France is divided again. In 1947, when the Communist party was dangerous, I made the RPF to stop them. Now that they are not so dangerous, the French are again dispersed—the RPF also. Now all I want to do is to prevent stupidities like the European Defense Community [EDC—the European army]. I cannot achieve positive progress all alone but I can block absurdities.

By Autumn, 1955, de Gaulle was telling me he feared it was almost too late to halt the decay in France because the Fourth Republic would never reform itself. He added: "No regime ever does reform itself. It is not possible for a government to be formed under this regime. It is not a question of men; it is a question of the political regime itself." The following year he was even more gloomy, if repetitive, saying:

Regimes never reform themselves. They simply fall. They collapse. France has had 13 regimes in the last 193 years. [Note how the statistics change.] None of these ever reformed themselves. The monarchy did not know how to reform itself. It fell to the revolution. Then the revolution and the *Directoire* did not reform themselves. They were succeeded by Bonaparte. Then Bonaparte did not know how to reform himself and he was wiped out by Waterloo. When the Restoration monarch came, he fell because he did not know how to reform things. The same was true afterwards with Louis Philippe. Napoleon III, who could not change things, fell at Sedan. The Third Republic also fell at Sedan [in 1940]. Then came Pétain; and then the more recent period.

By this time—nine years after his abdication—it was clear that de Gaulle was seriously contemplating some form of "dramatic" return. On October 14, 1955, I asked how he thought he might manage this. He answered: "I would never come back except with real power. That would require a dramatic situation. While things remain as they are it is impossible. This regime can only offer the Presidency of the Republic—which means nothing —or the Prime Ministry—which means nothing. It is impossible to do anything in either of these positions. These are not for General de Gaulle." He had concluded that even the top position in France—which he had previously indicated he would be willing to accept—no longer suited his purposes.

He continued: "Present events are not dramatic enough; they do not press hard enough. This regime must first vanish—as the regime vanished in 1940." The General then spread his long arms and hands and said he was desolated, desperate, but what could he do? He said he had twice tried to save France, during the war and again by organizing the RPF; but now "I know of no third way." He did not mean by this that France would "disappear"; its national vitality remained very great. But it was too disparate and had been terribly weakened by past events. National opinion had become nonexistent and France was becoming detached on everything. Indifference was growing as a national characteristic. This seemed to him to be unbelievable but it was true. He had personally tried to shake off this national indifference; the Communists had tried; but nobody could budge the French from this mood. Nevertheless, "in France nothing is ever definitive—not even impotence."

During the subsequent year de Gaulle appeared embittered but irresolute. In May, 1956, he sneered at Poujade, the petty bourgeois, right-wing tax-protester who organized a briefly influential movement, saying: "That is not serious. There are many discontented people; but they do not represent a power. You cannot make a France with a Poujade." He added: "The other parties are no more serious than the Poujadists. You cannot make a France with them either." Six months later, after the double blow of unsuccessful intervention in Suez and defeat of the Hungarian uprising, the General realistically asserted:

> The [French] Communists have lost a few voices—but not much faith. [*Des voix mais pas beaucoup de foi.*] Many people have the habit of voting for them. The workers seem to consider that the Communists are the party which defends the workers—even if they don't think that communism will renew society. Other parties have little to offer the workers. They offer the workers no hope.

Nevertheless, he admitted, the Socialists (who had furnished the Prime Minister of the Suez debacle, Guy Mollet) would not be destroyed. He explained this by saying: "French parties depend upon a clientele, not a doctrine. The Socialists will retain their clientele. Their patronage system continues to work. The little man who hopes to advance in the government or in the party will continue to vote Socialist no matter what he thinks."

Already in May, 1956, de Gaulle had assured me: "It is impossible to reform the Constitution now. The politicians won't do it. I cannot imagine *any* circumstances under which I could come back into active political life. This regime will not reform itself. One needs a drama first." I asked what he meant by the word "drama" and he said: "Not necessarily a war. Revolution or some form of tumult might be the answer. It is not always necessary to have a war. Charles X and the Restoration disappeared without war. Then there was a revolution. The 1848 Republic disappeared without a war. But we *do* need a drama."

By December 12 of that year, he made plain that he was increasingly pondering the possibilities and circumstances of extra-legal violence as a means to personal power and national reform. He said:

> It is true that the more complicated affairs get and the more apparent the danger seems, the more people will come to recognize that the French regime lacks force, willpower, or popularity. Naturally the French people will then be inspired to look elsewhere. But so far any such development is purely speculative, not political. How it develops in the future depends upon events. We need responsible men in power. Small men cannot answer to the responsibilities of the world. Small men cannot handle great events.

Once again I asked if the President (now René Coty) could summon him to assume power. He replied in the absolute negative, adding: "If there is a war and a bomb falls on the Palais Bourbon [home of the National Assembly] it would be impossible for the President under this Constitution to make a government, any sort of government. The government must be invested by the Assembly. The Constitution says so." I inquired whether the French army could be considered a potential political force. He replied (interestingly for a general, a career officer):

The army in France has no political force. It is, of course, always for order and *la patrie*. It is also always against weak governments. But that does not suffice for the army to wish to be the state. No revolution in French history was ever made by the army. The eighteenth-century revolution was made by the bourgeoisie. The people made Bonaparte. Not even Pétain was made by the army—that was Parliament. And de Gaulle was not made by the army.

I asked how he thought a revolution could succeed in France if both the political forces represented by the Assembly and the military forces represented by the army were excluded. He said (December 12, 1956): "Revolutions in France must be made by the people. When the people *desire* a change, such a change is brought about quickly. This has been true each time there was a revolution in our history." I inquired how one could know in advance that the popular mood was ready to demand change—for example a return of de Gaulle? He answered:

"That will not be difficult to see. You will even see it in the newspapers, bad as they are. When the people wish change you will see this reflected in the newspapers because the newspapers are always ready to sell themselves to the new authorities." He considered that there had not yet been any more than faint intimations of this, but he knew enormous shifts in public attitude could develop very quickly. Thus, he told me, he had recently read a collection of newspapers from the year 1815, when Napoleon came back from Elba and marched northward from the Mediterranean to Paris (a fascinating insight into de Gaulle's thought patterns some eighteen months before he regained power after an army coup). The General recalled that at first, papers were saying in their headlines: "Order restored on the Mediterranean coast." Then, when Napoleon reached Lyons, headlines read: "Tyrant arrives at Lyons." Finally, according to de Gaulle, when Napoleon got to the capital, the same newspapers printed in their headlines: "His Majesty the Emperor in Paris."

To conclude this colloquy, I asked the General if he thought it necessary to have a period of chaos in France before he could come back. He replied "Yes" and added: "We must have some chaos first. This regime was made against me. Therefore it cannot call upon de Gaulle to save itself. De Gaulle is not prepared to save this regime." Did he think, I inquired, that chaos would be accompanied by bloodshed? He replied: "Blood? There is always a little blood. There is blood being shed in Hungary today. *Hélas. Que faire?*"

By 1957, I was convinced the Algerian war pointed toward catastrophe for France and that de Gaulle, given his previous analyses, was obviously preparing to use this terrible event as a means of re-establishing his own authority and re-creating France in his personal image. But on July 19, he said he didn't foresee a "catastrophe" in Algeria. And also that it was obvious the existing parliamentary parties would never summon him back. Very well, I asked flatly, how about a *coup d'état*?

"Why not? I have already staged two *coups d'état* in my life. In June, 1940, I staged a *coup d'état* when I established our movement in London. In September, 1944, I staged a *coup d'état* in Paris. When I came back to Paris I established the government. I was the government. The only thing is that one should not stage a *coup d'état* unless public opinion demands it. Public opinion must be entirely behind you—like Napoleon with the eighteenth Brumaire." I asked him how, in this complicated age, public opinion could express itself in such a way as to satisfy him the moment had come for a coup. He said he wasn't sure. Many things could happen.

For example, the army could decide no longer to obey the government or its officers. Or there could be a general strike provoked by exterior events —like Algeria. He didn't know exactly how, but there had to be some such expression before any coup could be considered. He did not think that another man could stage a *coup d'état* for him.

This is the final crystallization of his views on the subject—some ten months before an actual coup destroyed the Fourth Republic. It is to be noted that: The very first of the necessary preconditions he outlined occurred in May, 1958—the army decided not to obey the government; and, although, for the record, the coup was made by leading French officers in Algeria, many top Gaullist agents were there, helping and inspiring them, and *de Gaulle himself did not think there was any man who could stage a coup for him.*

It appears to me to have been but a short step from the analytical conclusions reached by the General in July, 1957, to the complex and exceedingly well-masked (*Larvatus prodeo*!) military operation of May, 1958. It was clear when I talked with de Gaulle on February 20, 1958 (less than three months before the Fourth Republic collapsed), that some kind of action was pending as the government appeared increasingly weak and incompetent. Air force officers, without orders from Paris, bombed Algerian rebel installations across the Tunisian border in Sakiet; counterintelligence authorities, without governmental permission, kidnapped the Algerian rebel leader, Ben Bella, from an airplane, and hijacked a Jugoslav ship, *Slovenija,* bearing arms to the guerrillas. De Gaulle commented:

"The situation is worse now than it was a few months ago. But it is not yet dramatically bad. The French people eat well. They are contented. They do not suffer. That is the trouble. Because in the meantime, if this regime continues, France will lose all North Africa." (It should be noted that the officers who led the antigovernment coup in Algiers thought that by bringing de Gaulle to power they could hang on to Algeria. Yet de Gaulle, once in power, was the man who yielded that territory. Again: *Larvatus prodeo.*)

The General said:

> Alas, only a disaster can change things. The French people must *personally* suffer before there can be a change. They don't know what misery is. They must experience disaster and personal suffering the way they did during the German occupation and the war. Perhaps a serious economic depression could accomplish this. This regime could not stand up against a big depression. A big depression would bring anger and suffering among the population which would throw out this regime.

De Gaulle thought the Algerian mess might—but by no means necessarily would—aggravate the situation sufficiently to bring about a change. He doubted if enough people would suffer to cause a revolution or *coup d'état*. The army was restive, but as things stood it would not rise up. And the General reminded me:

> The army in France has never been a political force. The army has never made a *coup d'état* in France. Sometimes a military man has made a *coup d'état* but not the army. Even Bonaparte, when he made his coup, made it himself because the country wanted a *coup d'état*. It was not the army that made it. I made two *coups d'état* myself. That was because the French people wanted them. The army did not make them. It only followed after I had succeeded.
>
> Before a *coup d'état* one situation that could provoke it would be a military anarchy. But that does not exist today. Nevertheless, the army has no confidence in the government. The Sakiet affair, the Ben Bella affair, the *Slovenija* affair—all these were made by special services and not by the government. They were made by the proconsuls. Afterward the government learned about them and accepted them; because there is no government in France. There are only the people who inhabit the palaces of the government.

February 20, 1958—less than three months before the coup that restored de Gaulle—was the last time I saw him as a political exile. The situation was already so ripe the General could almost taste it. The army was restive and his necessary precondition for forced change, military anarchy, was already starting as proconsuls took over the reins from Paris. And if the army as such was not a political force capable of engineering a coup, it was evidently becoming the instrument with which "a military man" could do so. The Fourth Republic—which de Gaulle regarded almost as an occupying regime, unjustly tenanting "the palaces of the government"—had almost fallen through its own inertia.

Only one man was capable of capitalizing on such a situation, the experienced coup-maker who proudly admitted to having already staged two and who had learned from his keen study of the technique that the leader of such an enterprise must strike at the moment when public opinion would tolerate and support him. In a sense de Gaulle again practiced a perfected version of that French institution, the coup-plus-plebiscite which two Napoleons had brilliantly managed.

I suspect that when all the memoirs have been written and when scholars have studied the evidence, we will at last learn that the events of May, 1958, were no unguided military plot lacking political leadership. My own suspicion is that a most audacious and resolute Frenchman carefully seeded the storm and then directed it by masterly suggestion. He used the army's frustrations, the anti-Communist visions of nationalist iconodules, and the fears of a nation ground between the millstones of a quern to achieve his own goals. These goals, as it turned out, were contrary to those of the praetorian guard that brought him back. He employed the right against the left to regain power and then employed the left against the right to hold it.

DE GAULLE
ON DE GAULLE:
PROGRAM

LOOKING BACK ON MY NOTES OF TALKS WITH DE GAULLE SINCE 1946, I find an astonishing consistency in themes. Certainly the landmark of his internal vista was always the creation of a powerful executive. He acknowledged that France could not be expected to develop a two-party system as in Britain or America, but he wanted "equilibrium among the legislative, executive, and judiciary powers." He envisioned that "The fundamental differences between the new French Constitution and that of the United States would be that the government would be responsible to Parliament; the President would be able to choose his Cabinet and dissolve Parliament. In America the President is not responsible to Congress and cannot dissolve it."

Within this framework, he foresaw economic and social reform to modernize France. Although his vision was clear, his knowledge and approach were sometimes obscured by contradictions. One might say, looking back at the record, this was the greatest weakness of his administration and in the end abetted its downfall.

Early in 1947, he told me that in France:

It is necessary to restore full productive capacity and in order to do so we must provide for full free enterprise. Simultaneously we must find a solution for the problems relating to the working of capital and labor. For France, it is necessary to organize a system of associations in which labor and capital could participate directly as interested parties. This implies also that labor unions should have no political background. They must be professional and not political organizations.

No political party in France should be permitted to interfere in their affairs. And exactly the same should apply to capitalist organizations. We must organize a completely free system to increase the productive capacity of France and prevent political interference among the workers. The associations should include all those who participate in any industry—whether worker, technician, or executive. They would all be associated together and not separated into individual organizations. They would all hold stock in their industry.

De Gaulle thought one political requirement to achieve this was the curbing of French communism. In May, 1951, he told me he intended to outlaw or limit the Communists if he regained power, saying:

They are already illegal in many ways. They are acting in the trade unions, but this is against the law because the law specifies that trade unions must only be professional and not political. It is easy to prove they are political. Up to now, the law permits the expulsion of the Communists from unions. The legislative position vis-à-vis the Communists must be further defined. You cannot have a state within a state. We cannot prevent people from being for the Soviet Union but we can prevent them from favoring the Soviet Union against France.

De Gaulle wanted to isolate unions from Russian influence and to isolate capitalists from American influence. During his political exile he intended, if he came back, to seek a new law permitting the creation of labor-capital associations. He pointed out that existent statutes permitted *Sociétés Anonymes.* He wished to encourage the responsibility of the workers as well as that of capital. He wanted to let the law "allow" rather than force the creation of associations. French missions studying American industry had been struck by the "moral" interest in production on the part of U.S. workers and, he concluded: "We must establish new contractual relationships between the worker and the owner and develop their joint interest in output."

He never did get around to this project of social-economic reform, for several reasons: he never decided just what should be done; it was difficult to unite his disparate following on this issue; he was too preoccupied with the Algerian war and exerting control over his restless army; and he was, more than anything, fascinated by the game of international diplomacy.

Already in 1961 he confided that France's new Constitution "doesn't work badly. It assures our political stability and I don't see any reason to change it [in order to provide for a Vice President.]" But he admitted there might have to be alterations. "After me, I think it would be wise to create a formal presidential system like yours which would include a Vice President. But that is not for now."

A few months later he explained: "You, of course, have a two-party system, but I do not think this is possible in France. We have a quantity of parties and this suits our nature. In fact, each party has many factions and divisions within it." In January, 1963, he amplified this:

There could never be a two-party system. Why? At the very best it would be a three-party system because the Communists are always there with 20 percent of the vote. This is a fact and you cannot elude facts. But there will always be internal differences among the people on different matters. Some people will always believe themselves to be left and right on different issues. All I can say is that the political party, as such, in France is ended for a long time as a real factor. This is also a fact. The Communists are the only organization and they are not really just a party, they are an enterprise, an army.

The parties, the other parties, have no use at this time. They represent a vacuum; they have no leaders, no programs, no doctrines. Of course, they will receive a certain number of votes in any election because it is the habit that their adherents should vote for them. But it is only a habit. No one believes in the old parties any longer.

I venture to say that this is true in America also. In America the people elect their President as a President. They don't really believe in the parties. For example, they believed in General Eisenhower, not because he was a Republican but because he was Eisenhower. He could just as easily have been elected President as a Democrat. But it was only because he was Eisenhower and the people had faith in him. Today the people believe in President Kennedy; but they believe in him because he is Kennedy and not because he is a Democrat.

There is no possibility that there could be only two or three parties in France. On the contrary, there could be seven or eight or ten. There are no other possibilities.

De Gaulle had already resolved in January, 1962, that direct election of the French President was desirable. He explained to me:

You are familiar with our system [selection of the President through balloting by national and provincial officials], and you can see that it is unsatisfactory. There must be truly universal suffrage instead of merely voting for electors. Of course, I don't care. It does not affect me. This is a question for my successor. I am here. But for my successor it is necessary to give him greater authority over the different parties and tendencies of France. For this a more universal method of suffrage is necessary—*après moi.*

However, he thought the new system of a strong President was working effectively. He explained:

I favor our present Constitution in its philosophical structure. We must have a chief of state who orients fundamental policy and is responsible for the basic line on basic things—like Algeria or Europe or defense. The President must give the broad lines of policy, but he should not mix in daily events. He should not be responsible for daily leadership requirements as under your system. He requires a Prime Minister as a chief of administration. The President, the Prime Minister, and the Cabinet must often work together. And the President must be popular. The country must think of the President as a chief of state who is responsible in big moments, in critical moments. But this is not a real "presidential re-gime." The President does not and should not make administrative deci-sions. I believe this is imperative.

On January 31, 1963, he told me he did not oppose the idea of a French President serving two terms, adding:

If the people want to re-elect a President, why shouldn't they be able to? The Constitution permits this and you may recall that two presidents of the Third Republic were re-elected to second terms [Jules Grévy and Albert Lebrun]. As it happened, neither of the two was able to finish his term but this was because of events that supervened [death and France's 1940 defeat]. It wasn't for any other reason. It would be perfectly normal for the people to re-elect a President if they thought it useful.

After putting through the constitutional reform providing for direct popu-lar election of the President, de Gaulle, in 1963, said he intended no further amendments although: "Look at your own history and your own Constitu-tion. You have had a great many amendments to your Constitution and, I suppose, in the future it may be necessary from time to time for France also to amend its Constitution." (A tone different to the warning from his exile that a Constitution could be scrapped overnight.) But he saw no chance of altering the fundamental nature of the regime. Thus he sniffed at rumors that he planned to restore the Royalist pretender, the Comte de Paris, to his throne. He said:

I don't think there is any tendency towards a restored monarchy in France at present. But the French people have the desire to decide for themselves who shall be their principal responsible chief. This is just the way the people of America elect their President and the people of Eng-land elect their Prime Minister. In such a way the people of France choose their President. Someday the Germans will have to adopt a simi-lar system of directly choosing their principal executive.

There is no other way in which you can provide for the necessary continuity of government, and that is an absolute requisite. But, as for the monarchy, that is an illusory idea. I don't wish to say that one day it could not happen in France; that it could not happen, for example, that a member of the former royal family should be chosen as President. One should not exclude possibilities of this sort for the indefinite future. Now I cannot imagine any restoration of the monarchy. The idea seems to me most illusory. The most important thing is that the country itself should choose its leader, and this system, I am happy to say, has been estab-lished and will continue.

Some months later he put period to the thought: "The proof of the value of our Constitution is that it works and that it is good for France, even if it is not good for the opposition."

Whether the General's Constitution will long outlive his personal administration is an open question. As he pointed out before his return, France had 13 constitutions within 150 years. A country so dominated by Cartesian logic is more likely to scrap a document than modify it—as is the English or American wont. His contribution to the theory of government was less notable than his contribution to the art of governing; and in this respect his adroit, ruthless diplomacy was more interesting to him and more fascinating to those who can now look back and observe its application.

EUROPE

De Gaulle had certain essential views on external affairs before he returned to the Elysée and these he tried to follow, even though he was often forced by events to shift tactics and pursue a zigzag course. Europe—the concept of an organization among the western states—is a case in point, demonstrating both the General's early vision and the frequent changes in his methods.

On May 30, 1947, during his first year in political exile, he told me:

As far as foreign affairs go I am convinced that it is necessary to re-create a Europe. If this is not done the world will be divided into a rivalry between Russia and the United States. That would lead to war—a horrid war. To re-create Europe the first condition is that France should be on her feet. France is a western power and Europe is a symbol of western civilization. Europe, to be restored, must be built upon occidental civilization. Such a Europe would be an element of strength and equilibrium.

The name "United States of Europe" is not a good one. It implies a federalized Europe. We cannot do that in the same way as the United States has federalized its separate states. But it should be possible to build a Europe on the basis of treaties between the European nations and to establish a method under which they would systematically be meeting at conferences to study common economic, political, and social problems. They would also have to study common imperial problems as many European countries have possessions abroad. It has always been impossible to organize such a Europe before. Always in the past one nation has sought to dominate the others. France in the seventeenth and eighteenth centuries attempted to do this. Then England. Then, during the last fifty years, Germany. But, for the first time, such conditions no longer exist. No European nation has the ambition or the capacity to dominate.

Nevertheless, from the start de Gaulle opposed any form of integration under a supranational body which would submerge the national identity of France. The first attempt to embody such an idea came in the European army (European Defense Community, or EDC) scheme under which it was originally intended to rearm West Germany. This scheme failed, thanks in part to the General's opposition from the wings. On May 11, 1951, he scoffed at the idea and told me only national armies made sense, although it was possible to form international expeditionary corps from them. The European army, however, was "a joke of the politicians."

He insisted a "true European Federation" must be preceded by an arrangement between France and Germany, adding: "Above all I am for a direct arrangement with Germany which would be political, economic, and strategic. My intention has always been [this was early 1951] for a direct entente between the French and the German people. The necessary initiatives are ready. On that basis a European federation can be formed." But even then he was highly skeptical about Britain. He expected London to oppose the idea and do all it could to prevent it in order to maintain a "disequilibrium in the balance of power on the European continent."

By November 10, 1954, after EDC had been killed, de Gaulle, unusually pessimistic, saw absolutely no future for Europe, for the world, or for France. He thought war was inevitable after a period of coexistence and modus vivendi. He added: "No country is very dynamic now. France remains crippled. The Germans are working hard to recover from their wartime defeat, but it is a mistake to exaggerate their dynamism." And, he continued: "Eisenhower's government has demonstrated that the Americans are no longer so dynamic and the same is true of Malenkov and the Russians."

He assured me, on May 31, 1956, that

Europe is confused and sad. It will stay like that for some time. And what will come of this? I don't know; but surely something. I must repeat, it will not be gay for the next few years. There is no West now. It is finished. There are westerners but no West. The United States is against the West everywhere. If you could replace the West, all right. But you can't. You Americans are part of the West, not the West itself. And meantime Europe will vegetate. The Germans won't do much. They have already remade their life. But they have remade neither their power nor their ambitions. And Britain is no longer very vital. This is also unfortunately the case for France.

On July 19, 1957, I asked him whether, if he were back in power, France would remain in the new "European" institutions, EURATOM and the Common Market. He observed that neither organization "existed" yet and therefore they weren't important; it was one thing to create such a body and another thing to make it work. At the time I noted, "It was perfectly apparent to me that he doesn't think either organization is going to become a reality. It was also apparent that if he comes to power he was going to do his best to destroy them."

Notwithstanding, when he finally did regain control, de Gaulle accepted the Common Market and attempted to bend it to French national advantage by excluding England from membership and insisting on ascendancy for France. On January 31, 1959, he told me he would accept no compromise between the Market and Britain's Free Trade Area, as London was advocating, and added:

The Common Market exists—not that it has had many consequences so far. But the Free Trade Area does not exist. Obviously there should be an economic accord between the two ideas; but Britain exaggerated greatly. It said that all Europe would be split on January 1, when the first phase of the Common Market began. But it did not split. There was no revolution in commercial exchanges. Then Britain wanted to support the Common Market; but this we refused to do.

This negative attitude toward Britain developed into one of the cardinal features of the General's European policy. On February 14, 1961, after a weekend of talks with Prime Minister Harold Macmillan, I asked if he thought London's policy toward the Common Market had changed and if the British now wanted to join. He raised his eyebrows skeptically and said:

British policy—no; British sentiment—perhaps.
Britain is certainly less sure of the United States now than in the past and it is not sure of the health of its own economy. Therefore, some people in England seem to think that perhaps they should eventually make a deal with the Common Market. But this is only sentiment; it is not policy. As far as we are concerned, we shall continue to make the Common Market, to make Europe. This helps us to increase our own industry and Europe's industry. It stimulates us to abandon outmoded methods and to modernize our economy. This is all to the good and I must admit that exchanges between Britain and Europe have grown a bit during the last months. Perhaps if the Common Market continues to grow Britain will be forced to change its policy; but that moment has not yet come.

On January 20, 1962, following another set of talks between de Gaulle and Macmillan, I asked the General if he thought Britain would enter the Market. He answered:

England is very divided on this question. It is difficult for her. There would be big repercussions in the British economy if they came in. Industrial production in Britain is very expensive and it would find all sorts of difficulties if Britain becomes a member of the Common Market. The same is true of agricultural production. And it is even more difficult for Britain to face taking such a step in view of Commonwealth relations. But the Common Market can never agree to Commonwealth participation. The British would like to come in because they see the consequences to themselves in Britain if they don't come in. But there are enormous practical problems. I do not see them entering except after very prolonged negotiations. This will take a long, long time.

How long I did not know then; only subsequently did the General proclaim his definitive veto of British entry.

That same day early in 1962, he proceeded to spell out the details of his vision for a Europe that clearly would be led by France. He wanted a form of loose confederation, explaining:

> As you know, this is a French proposal but we have to be realistic about this and do it by degrees. First there will be a political commission for cooperation among the six [France, West Germany, Italy, Belgium, Luxembourg, Netherlands], and only then a confederation. The big question is ideology; this is why I object to a supranational ideal. Such ideological concepts block the way. Instead of trying to create union by cooperation and then by confederation among the nations, these people [supporters of supranational control] make a fiction of a supranational Europe as one entity, one state. The problem really isn't there.
>
> These steps must be taken by states and not by commissions with their fictional ideas. It is states, not commissions, that make decisions. You have seen how in the Common Market it was necessary to bring in agriculture. But the final decision on this had to be taken by the state of Germany, not by a commission. Always, in the end, states find themselves before a national political decision. States make the decisions, not supranational commissions with their fictions. States are the reality; the rest is fiction. Some so-called experts create these fictions. But naturally *I* am against fiction, as you know.

De Gaulle was very vague about how this Little Europe would defend itself, apart from reliance of its members (including France) on NATO. He thought it "very possible" that a confederated Europe might someday build its own nuclear force but "of course, it cannot happen right away. In the meantime we [the French] are beginning to create our own atomic force. And we are in Europe so, after all, that is the beginning of a European force." Nevertheless, a year later the General told me he saw little chance of a European atomic force wholly free of U.S. participation, adding: "It could have been done right away if the British had not signed the Nassau agreement [abandoning Britain's V-bomber missile and committing it to U.S. Polaris submarines] but they preferred to choose the American formula. So that is the way things are. Someday, of course, it may be different." Nobody yet knows whether de Gaulle would, in fact, have agreed to British membership in "Europe" if it had pooled its nuclear strength. Macmillan's record of his talk with de Gaulle differs from the General's on this point.

De Gaulle was certainly confusing if not confused on the subject of Europe. He blocked its integration and blocked British admission, thus keeping it weak; yet he saw the dangers of this weakness. He told me on January 31, 1963:

> Right now it is very convenient for the U.S. There is a France and a Germany and an Italy and a Great Britain. And the U.S. plays each one against the other. But if there were a real Europe, that would be different. There would have to be a real Europe with its own economy, its

own policy, and its own defense. Once there is such a Europe, it should have an organized accord with the U.S. But what, after all, is "interdependence" [between Europe and North America, as President Kennedy wished]? I don't know what is meant by this. There must be rapport between Europe and America. That is interdependence I suppose.

But certainly in terms of defense, if there is a Soviet threat, Europe could not defend itself alone. Nor, really, could the U.S. The U.S. could defend itself with missiles but not in a moral sense and vis-à-vis the free world.

I asked him if—despite arguments between Paris and Washington—the United States could rely on full French support were there another crisis like the October, 1962, Cuba confrontation when France stood firmly by America. Without hesitation he said: "If there is a threat of world war France will be with the United States. *Evidemment. Evidemment.* That does not change."

At this point I asked the General to explain what seemed to me a contradiction in his thinking. In June, 1940, de Gaulle had endorsed the proposal of Jean Monnet and Lord Vansittart to unite France and Britain. This being so, I asked: "If you considered Britain a European country then, why isn't it European today?" He said: "Ah, but of course, Britain *can* be in Europe. It was European then. But it doesn't want to be European today. It was obliged by the circumstance of war to be European at that moment. Now it must come back to things in a European way."

By the end of 1963, the General, having shelved the project of British admission, was dominating the Common Market to suit French national interests. He took special pains to enforce upon it policies beneficial to outmoded methods of the French farmers whose political support he needed. Thus, he told me (December 12):

> Without an accord on agriculture there can be no Common Market. It is an economic community and if agriculture is not a part of its arrangement there simply won't be a Common Market. Agriculture is an essential piece of the whole. You cannot say that France would be dissolving the Common Market. If there is no agricultural agreement the Common Market will be dissolving itself.

He warned by implication that he would have his way or he would break the Market: "Either there will be an agreement on agriculture or its very lack will prove that the Common Market doesn't exist and has never been created."

GERMANY

The General was always consistent in his desire to improve relations between France and West Germany, but in such a way that France would remain ascendant. This was implied by his preference for continued partition of Germany; by his adamant refusal to tolerate nuclear arms for Bonn;

and his desire to insure a special influence for Paris both inside the Common Market and by a bilateral Franco-German treaty. Finally, one reason for his desire to exclude Britain from Europe was to avoid any chance that the British and Germans might get together at French expense.

Back in 1949, de Gaulle told me:

I am for an independent Germany. The Bonn system is not good but it exists. I am for an arrangement between France and West Germany on the basis of equality. This has nothing to do with the East German state. I have always had this idea, even before the Russians created the new East German satellite. A French-German accord could balance the effect of the Russians' East German state. This would stabilize the situation. I was against the Washington and London agreements on Germany and the Bonn system because they hinder a direct agreement between Germany and France. The creation of the Bonn system in West Germany was supported by the British primarily to prevent the strengthening of France.

Quite soon after World War II, the General accepted the idea of German rearmament. Already in 1951, he told me West Germany should be rearmed on condition that it should never be allowed to have an army stronger than any other army in Europe—above all that of France. (This limitation was met subsequently by building the French atomic *force de dissuasion,* called by almost everyone save de Gaulle the *force de frappe.*)

Three years later (January 21, 1954) he thought the question of Germany's defense could only be approached once the European army scheme was dead—an event that occurred later that year. He said:

The first question is to finish with EDC. [It was an] *entreprise manquée,* an error, stupidity. It was invented by some French politicians who aren't France. When it was submitted, France said no. Finish with the system. That is the first thing. It is absurd from a national, an international and a military point of view.

But we must incorporate Germany into the West. I have always said that. How? By a very wide European agreement—Britain, France, Germany, Scandinavia, all of free Europe in an alliance, a confederation, in which each would safeguard its own individuality. You cannot suppress nationalities. Within such an organization you can have common arms. See the way Britain has just accepted the NATO rifle. You can have a progressive rearmament of Germany. But it is an absurdity, a dream, a fantasy to think that you can suppress France and French nationality.

It is noteworthy that de Gaulle's "European" vision was then broader than it became later; at the time including England.

He continued:

The United States has walked along with this idiocy [the European army scheme]. Now you must extricate yourselves. If you put your money on a bad horse, you are lunatics if you keep throwing it away on the same horse. I guarantee that EDC will not go through. I will do everything against it. I will work with the Communists to block it. I will make a revolution against it. I would rather go with the Russians to stop it. It won't go through. It won't go through. I repeat, I will make a revolution to prevent it.

Nevertheless, while violently against the kind of integrated organization that would contain and control German rearmament, de Gaulle was afraid of where it would lead a national West Germany. He said regretfully that he had wished to make German policy while France still held all the trumps in its hand—the Saar, a piece of occupied German territory, a share in the Ruhr's coal production. But the lack of French authority, "because of the unsatisfactory Constitution," prevented this. "Not even Napoleon I or Richelieu could have made a policy under the existing French Constitution," he added sourly.

Ultimately it was the United States that got credit from Germany for rearmament, not France. The General had wanted "to introduce Germany to the western world" on France's own terms. But he was convinced that "as soon as Germany is rearmed she will negotiate directly with Russia and Russia will then pursue the policy vis-à-vis Germany" he had hoped France could pursue. Russia, he thought, would "give Germany the Oder-Neisse lands and buy Germany over to her side." The fear of such a Soviet bribe was why de Gaulle always favored good relations with Poland (which now possessed the Oder-Neisse lands and early went on record endorsing Germany's de facto frontier in the east).

Although de Gaulle negotiated the special Franco-German treaty and always went out of his way to honor Chancellor Adenauer, in private he made no secret of his typically French distrust of his neighbors. On February 14, 1961, he told me:

Germans are Germans. One reason that we must try to make a united Europe is to enclose [*encadrer*] Germany. As long as Adenauer is in control there, there will be no deal between the Germans and the Russians. But later—I don't know. I am not so sure. There are important factors pushing the Germans toward Russia and the Russians toward Germany. The Germans manufacture great quantities of industrial equipment. Look at the Ruhr; look at Krupps. And Russia never has enough industrial equipment. Krupps is very alerted to this.

Reciprocally, the Germans need cheap agricultural products to feed their workers. These products must be cheap so the Germans can keep their prices down on the manufactures they want to sell. Krupps continues to push the idea of this as the basis for a German-Russian deal. This will not take place with Adenauer. He won't treat with the Russians. But after Adenauer things may change. Russia may work out a deal on Berlin and a federation of East Germany and West Germany as the basis for such a realignment. It is not impossible to envision this after Adenauer. That is why we must have a strong Common Market Europe.

The following year (January 20, 1962) he said: "Khrushchev seeks to neutralize Germany and if he neutralizes Germany that will mean the neutralization of Europe. And if Europe is neutralized the United States is lost. For you in the U.S. cannot continue alone, alone without Europe and without the third world of the neutralists. And if you lose Europe, you will completely lose the third world of the neutralists." His remedy, at that time (more than three years after Washington and London had rejected his proposal for a three-power *directoire* to coordinate world affairs) was tripartite cooperation. In that event, he asked: "What could Germany do except follow? Anyway, Germany has no world interest, no world obligations, no political undertakings, for example, in Africa, in Asia. Those areas do not in the end really interest Germany."

On January 31, 1963, de Gaulle made plain the essence of his German policy. When I asked if France would object should a future German government decide to purchase or make nuclear weapons he looked rather startled. He said: "But the Germans are committed not to do this. It is entirely out of the question. I shall stand by these commitments and there is no reason to think the Germans will violate them. The question does not arise." I asked him if Bonn's signature of the treaty with Paris implied acceptance of the de facto Polish border for Germany which France endorsed. He said: "This is not an actual question for the Germans." I asked if France was truly working for a unified Germany and he said: "This is not a question now. Our treaty supports Germany in terms of the status quo." I asked if he would be prepared to see a demilitarized Germany in exchange for reunification. He said: "If Germany were neutralized, France would be quickly neutralized also. We are for a Germany allied to the West and militarily effective. Our view has not changed." What he did not add—nor was it necessary—was that this Germany should be western (not reunified), nonnuclear, and controlled or overshadowed by its allies.

Finally, on December 12, 1963, in our last conversation recorded in this volume, I asked if he wasn't in fact disappointed by the way the German alliance was working out. He answered:

Our alliance should not be exaggerated, as it often is by the press. This was primarily an arrangement to end a historic quarrel. And this has been done. It also had the intention of establishing closer contacts in all fields between France and Germany, particularly in matters of economics and security. The press and many people read into the alliance much more than was the actual fact, but Adenauer and I never exaggerated it. The contacts between our countries continue and will continue. I cannot tell how the future will work out.

What de Gaulle did not say but what has always been obviously at the heart of his European policy is that West Germany and West Europe, led by France, were designed in the General's mind to strengthen a position of

influence and independence vis-à-vis both superpowers, the Soviet Union and the United States. The General's view of a proper French relationship toward these two behemoths was puzzling. He always insisted that, in a crisis, America was an ally to which France would be loyal. But he calculated that its might was so enormous, in peacetime as well as in terms of war potential, that to maintain any world balance it was desirable to prop up Russia. Moreover, his diplomacy fancied the play, by an adept France, of the massive superpowers against each other.

RUSSIA

In an examination of de Gaulle's Soviet policy one discovers more shifting and tergiversation than on any other cardinal issue. On May 11, 1951, he assured me the Franco-Soviet pact which he signed with Stalin "is not important" although it hadn't been denounced. He added: "The pact I made with the U.S.S.R. was a wartime pact to prevent Germany from again becoming a nuisance. When the fate of Germany is regulated to ensure this, then no longer would any reason exist for a pact against Germany." Three years later he was developing hints of his balance-of-superpowers theory. He said: "France must not lose its independence to anyone. I prevented the Communists from grabbing power in France in 1944 and also in 1947 when I started the RPF. We cannot lose our sovereignty to the United States and we cannot lose our sovereignty to Russia." (In this respect, he steadfastly believed the French Communist party was a Kremlin tool, and he used it to frighten French conservatives. Yet, at the same time, he attracted support of some French Marxists by seeming to please the Kremlin.) He also said: "There is no chance of any serious policy being based upon the Soviet pact. We must have the United States alliance. We also want Germany with the western world—but without the simultaneous disappearance of France; everything but that."

On November 10, 1954, when post-Stalinist power contests were shaking the Kremlin, de Gaulle remarked that Russia is "just exactly as it was under the Czars, still a dictatorship tempered by assassination." Nevertheless, nine months earlier he had warned me:

> I don't think any real entente is possible between the West and the East as things now are. But I think for a certain time each can coexist with the other and trade with the other. . . . After Truman said no to MacArthur's proposal to attack China, war was excluded. The English want business with Russia. The French want an arrangement in Indochina. The United States wants export markets. These are the imponderables that make for a modus vivendi. This is not an entente; it is armed peace.

Within this framework, one could detect new tolerance toward Russia in the evolution of Gaullist thinking, even though he continued to register moral disapproval of Soviet methods. In 1956, he told me:

Even in the interior of Russia there are peoples enslaved by Russia. The question for the West, as for the United States, and you now make policy for the West, is whether to accept this situation or not. Is this [Moscow's post-Stalin policy—prior to the Polish and Hungarian troubles later in 1956] a "New Look" for the Poles, the Czechs, the Baltic peoples, etc.? Russia hasn't given them back their freedom. The West should fight the "New Look" there and show that it has not yet given freedom to those enslaved. The West should either attack or make peace; there is no other way.

You are making peace now by accepting the occupation of Eastern Europe and at the same time combating the Russian influence in the Middle East. You cannot make war and peace together. Russia has chosen to make peace for the present. But you must either make peace or war. It is a question of either war or peace. Psychological war doesn't mean anything. And if there is no war, you must make peace. [Here he added a grim warning.] NATO is an organization created to make war. If there is no war, it is doomed to disappear.

Oddly enough, by December 12 of the same year, when Soviet force had imposed sullen controls again on the restless Poles and Hungarians, the General detected for the first time signs of a favorable evolution in Russia. He said:

The fact is that the dictatorship of communism is a thing that is ending. It doesn't correspond anymore to today's requirements. It was possible in Russia after the Czars because Russia had been beaten and had to organize its economy at all costs. The price was, of course, immensely high. Millions of people lost their lives. But that is not important in Russia where they have such an enormous population. They succeeded in organizing their economy and finally, in the last war, in beating Germany.

But now they don't need communism anymore. Even Khrushchev knows this. To complete the defeat of Germany, the Russians had to control all of Eastern Europe. But now this is done. Germany is no longer an important menace. There is no need for communism in Poland anymore and all the Poles know this, even Gomulka [at that time a nationalist-minded Polish Communist who had been brought to power from the jail where Stalinism sent him]. Even Nagy [the Hungarian rebel leader, also a nationalist Communist, who was hanged by Khrushchev] knew there was no longer any need for the Russians or for communism in Hungary.

Seven months later he returned to this theme. He said that in Russia:

Communism is finished. They have lost faith in themselves. They still, of course, call themselves Communists, but it is no longer the same thing. The bureaucracy in the administration is made up of Communists; but they have no faith in their movement. They saw that they could not conquer Poland. They saw that they could not conquer Hungary—mor-

ally, I mean. Therefore they realize that they have lost their dynamism. They can no longer dream of conquering Germany, of conquering France, of conquering Italy. They cannot even hold what they have.

By February 20, 1958, only weeks before the General regained power, he had fitted this analysis into his quintessential theory of the nation-state. He told me:

The countries of the West must be for themselves, each should be for itself. France must be for the French. Nations cannot be suppressed as individualities. One reason for the success of Soviet pressure now is that the Russians have changed a lot internally. They are no longer the Bolsheviks of other times. They keep communism in an economic sense. But in an intellectual or perhaps a spiritual sense they are no longer Communists. There is an internal trend within Russia that is going toward liberty, above all liberty of the spirit. Russia used to be an ignorant country; but now it is educated, even if it is not impartially educated. And the educated people—above all the elite—are working toward liberty. This fact alone is incompatible with the old-fashioned Bolshevism. The Russians are pushing toward liberty, pushing toward the sun. They crave contact with the West. This is no longer the Russia of twenty years ago, or even of ten years ago.

They have kept the economic and social system of communism. This won't change. But in terms of the spirit they are seeking and obtaining more and more freedom. Their politicians—and we should never forget that they *are* politicians—represent this trend. This is the current of the moment. Another element which we must never forget is that the Russian people have a terrible fear of war. The Russian masses are desperately afraid of war. There won't be a war, despite the fact that Russia now has all these new [nuclear-missile] weapons. Nobody thinks anymore that Russia can conquer the world, that Russia can even conquer Europe. They have not even been able to conquer the satellites. They are there as occupying forces; but each of these countries remains Polish, Hungarian, or Rumanian despite the Russians. The Russians themselves know that they can occupy countries, not conquer them. Therefore there is less fear of Russia now. The only fear of war nowadays is the abstract fear of nuclear weapons, not of Russia.

Apropos of this, the General was tolerant of the Rapacki Plan, launched by the Polish foreign minister with the aim of reducing tensions in Europe's center, but heavily discounted by the West. De Gaulle, who did not really think the idea was "a big thing," concluded:

The Poles are obviously in accord with Russia over it. For them, of course, it is in good faith—they want to neutralize a zone in Europe. The West should not reject such projects immediately. It is not a monstrous thing for the Poles to propose that a part of Europe should be denuclearized. It is not a monstrous thing for the Poles to wish to be specially treated and not to be lumped together with the Russians in all our considerations. We should examine their project.

After he entered the Elysée, Moscow began a wary flirtation with de Gaulle, a flirtation that resulted in Khrushchev's visit to France in 1960, and the General's subsequent visit to Russia.

On February 20, 1960, I asked if he saw any reason whatsoever for reviving the Franco-Soviet treaty of 1944 which had been denounced by Moscow since I last raised the subject. He said: "There is no more reason for such a treaty. In 1944, the Germans were still in the war and we didn't know what our future alignment would be. But we are not menaced by Germany now; nor is Khrushchev, despite what he says." He continued by discussing the project for Khrushchev's state visit to France, arranged for that spring, and the subsequent four-power Summit meeting in Paris (which was to be torpedoed by the Russians after the famous U–2 incident).

I don't expect any important positive results. Perhaps I deceive myself, but I doubt it. The only thing that could possibly happen would be an acceptance on both sides of the status quo. That could facilitate a détente. There would be an implied agreement by both sides not to attack each other and, in the same sense, to keep a certain armaments balance. But I doubt if any solution can be reached. Clearly Khrushchev is applying more pressure in Berlin now. That is his game. He tries to get what he wants. But there is no sense in giving him what he wants.

Indeed, although the General was all for using Russia in his game vis-à-vis the United States, he harbored no illusions about the verity of pledged friendship and coexistence. He said: "The Russians cannot be of good faith —nor can we. Russia can think that it is in its own interest not to continue the Cold War and to pursue a temporary détente. Perhaps at the moment it is in their interest; but they won't give up on major long-range aspirations." As for Khrushchev's imminent visit to France, he sniffed:

Propaganda. Khrushchev makes propaganda. Perhaps also he hopes this might aid him in his present relaxation policy [*politique de détente*] and perhaps it is now in Khrushchev's interest in many respects to start détente. He might need this in terms of his internal position in the Soviet Union as well as in terms of his relationships with the satellite countries of Poland and Hungary. Perhaps he sees it as desirable to pursue such a détente for the moment. And a tour of this sort—his visit to France—helps propaganda. Of course, I will talk to Khrushchev. We will chat. But I don't expect anything. There is *no* question that we can solve with the Russians. There is a need for all of us to act together to solve any question—not just France.

I noted at the time: "This certainly stresses his intention to remain allied to the West even if he doesn't join in the NATO philosophy of integration." On January 20, 1962, I asked: "*Mon Général,* once you told me you thought Russia, regardless of its present ideology, was essentially a white, European and western nation. Do you think that someday we can look to a true accord with Moscow and, perhaps, even an agreement between NATO and the Warsaw Pact?" He answered: "There can never be an alliance of that sort. NATO was created against Russia and the Warsaw Pact was created against NATO."

Nevertheless, he thought:

There *can* someday be a real cooperation between Russia and the West. And, indeed, there *must* be; otherwise there *must* be war. You cannot have a cold war for an indefinite period. I suppose that someday, in the vague future, we can imagine a concord among the white people against the colored. This would not be on the basis of whiteness but on the basis of civilization. I suppose that if China continues to progress it might lead to this and China might have an increasing influence on countries like India. Perhaps one reason for Khrushchev's policy is because of China and because of this evident possibility, which he already realizes. . . .

Certainly there are difficulties inside the Communist world. This is no secret. Khrushchev himself advertises it. He has his difficulties inside Russia and also it is evident that he has his difficulties with China and Albania. It is the same thing as yesterday with Czechoslovakia. [He meant Jugoslavia.] There are big difficulties in the Soviet world but these result from what are essentially national differences. The differences between Russia and China do not stem from conditions of ideology. They merely indicate the rivalry between two big neighbors.

Also, certainly there is a progressive change in the life and the state of mind inside the Communist world. There are more and more intellectuals, more students and professors, and as a result they develop a more critical spirit. And, furthermore, the *people* want more liberty and a greater well-being. And today there is no war. There is no more war in the name of which the people can be repressed as in the days of Stalin. Khrushchev realizes these truths. He weds himself to the popular desire for more freedom and well-being because, after all, Khrushchev is a politician.

On January 31, 1963, I remarked that many rumors were circulating in Paris to the effect that de Gaulle wished to make a private deal with Russia. He commented that this was "absurd." The Communist "menace" remained, and France remained attached to its ideals and obligations. That December, in the last conversation recorded here, I asked if he had any plan to visit Russia in 1964 to repay Khrushchev's Paris trip. He answered with a categorical "No" and added that when Khrushchev had been in Paris for the 1960 Summit meeting, which failed, it had been hoped to "arrange many things and improve the situation. But you well remember what happened and nothing came of this Summit. So I am not planning any Russian journey now; but this is not to say that I will never go there." (In fact, of

course, he was to visit the Soviet Union, Poland, and Rumania before
leaving the Elysée, but these events and the subsequent dénouement of the
General's Russian policy will be recounted in a later volume.)

AMERICA

I thought it wise to recall here in some detail the development of de
Gaulle's European and Soviet diplomacy before turning to his relationship
with the United States, with which these were so intimately linked. Had the
General not felt that France's old ally was so strong and so dynamic that it
simply could not help but impinge on French interests, there is no doubt his
attitudes toward Europe, Britain, and Russia would have been different. But
to him the primordial fact of World War II and its aftermath was the
emergence of such massive American power that he felt it necessary to curb
it by any available means, although this did not, to his own mind, imply
hostility to the U.S. And, in a sense, de Gaulle reckoned that the failure of
America to use its military strength decisively when the chance was presented, more or less dictated his balance-of-superpowers approach.

He told me on November 10, 1954,

> The United States made a great mistake by not pursuing a policy of
> war. When you took your stand in Korea the free world was with you
> and was ready to be led into war. But you cannot expect other nations to
> adopt a real self-sacrificing military attitude if you do not pursue a policy
> of war. You had your opportunity when you had a definite atomic lead.
> You should have followed MacArthur's policy. But now it is too late.
> Neither America nor Russia is ready to pursue a policy of war and
> therefore a modus vivendi for a long time is inevitable.

By 1956, a note of bitterness was creeping into his remarks about the
United States. On May 31, he said:

> From the western side I think the U.S. will remain uncertain. You
> won't attack. You will make a coexistence—but without satisfaction.
> That is not a policy, it is just a series of ideas. [Marshal] Zhukov will
> go to Washington. [Secretary] Dulles will go to Moscow. You will be
> paralyzed by your elections. But you will have no consequential policy.
> And meantime Europe will vegetate.
>
> There is no West now. It is finished. There are westerners, but no
> West. The United States is against the West everywhere. It is for the
> Orient against the West—I refer to China, the Arabs, etc. [an odd
> observation]. If you could replace the West, all right. But you can't. You
> Americans are part of the West, not the West itself.

Promptly, once he returned to power, divergences became plain. On
January 31, 1959, he told me U.S. missile ramps could not be established
for NATO on French soil until other matters were settled. I asked if he
thought Washington should grant more aid to Paris on atomic weapons. He
replied, lifting his shoulders, stretching out his long arms, and raising his

eyebrows: "That is up to you. Certainly France thinks there could be more such help. Of course, we do not know how this could be arranged with your Congress; but if there were better cooperation from you on this, it would save us much time and money." He then informed me France would explode its first nuclear device "soon" although there had been "some delay."

The French decision to manufacture atomic weapons had been taken by the Fourth Republic, after the Suez debacle. De Gaulle capitalized on it, accelerated the program, and made maximum use of it in his diplomacy. On February 20, 1960, after France had staged its first test, he told me:

> There is only one subject on which it is possible to make a practicable disarmament arrangement today, and that is in the field of missiles. . . . If an agreement on missile inspection can be worked out, atomic arms will become less important. One can do something in this field, but I don't know if anybody wants to do anything. . . . All this talk about stopping tests is unimportant. Stopping atomic tests wouldn't stop atomic arms. The United States and the Soviet Union already have enormous supplies of weapons and they will continue to make arms if they stop testing. A cessation of testing will only hurt France which has not yet got its weapons.

At this time de Gaulle still vaguely hoped some kind of a deal could be worked out with Washington along the lines of Big Three cooperation (U.S., Britain, France) which he had suggested to Eisenhower and Macmillan soon after regaining authority. But, discussing his plan, he said (February 20, 1960):

> I never used the word *directoire* [in his letters to the President and Prime Minister]. That is an invention of the press. But the fact remains that there are only three real powers in the West; three powers that have world-wide support. They also have a certain force of atomic power. As far as France is concerned, we do not have an atomic military force today, but we will have. Those three powers are charged with the defense and security of the West. If one wants to organize the defense of the West, one must work through those three powers. After all, it is those three powers who will be present at the Summit [that May] with Khrushchev. Diplomatically they represent the West; and the same is true in strategy. We in France do not yet have atomic arms but we are making them.

Then the General hinted very plainly that if his views on this were not heeded he would reply by reducing France's support of NATO—precisely as happened. I had asked if he thought Big Three accord might be facilitated by the fact that France had at last crossed the nuclear threshold. He said: "I hope so. This is indispensable." However, he continued:

> If our wish in this matter is not granted we will no longer support the organization of the Atlantic Treaty. [Note the precision of the phrase: He would be against the *organization,* not the Treaty itself; he would

take the o out of NATO, the North Atlantic Treaty Organization.] We have taken back control of our fleet and certain other things. Also, we will take back our liberty in other respects if this is not granted. We will take back our complete liberty. We will, of course, remain allied; but we will only be an ally and fully independent. [This is precisely what de Gaulle's policy became six years later.]

I then asked if the General wanted American nuclear arms to reduce France's economic burden and thereby to speed up its defense preparations. He answered:

The United States will not give us aid. France is not the United States and the United States is not France. We are not the same country and we will each keep our secrets. The United States will not modify the Mc-Mahon law. I have not asked for any such modification and I will not ask for it. This is perfectly natural and I understand the American point of view. We will make our own atomic arms. That is that. It costs heavily and it will take much time, but you can be sure that we will work out this program, and basically it is better that way.

On February 14, 1961, shortly after President Kennedy had been inaugurated, I asked de Gaulle if he intended to ask for revision of the McMahon Act in France's favor, now that there was a new U.S. administration. He said: "We doubt the value of making any approach. I don't intend to make an approach. The last administration never proposed any such revision. And, frankly I wouldn't do it if I were in your place. As for France—we will continue to make our own nuclear weapons."

De Gaulle didn't seem impressed by the possibilities of better relations offered by a Kennedy Presidency. White House propagandists had put about the report that he was a personal friend of General Gavin, Kennedy's first ambassador to Paris, and I inquired if this was true. "Absolutely not," he said. "I suppose it is possible that I could have met him at some time or another and perhaps shaken his hand. But if this is the case he made absolutely no impression because I surely don't remember him." I expressed the polite hope that at least Gavin might become a friend by the time he left. *"On verra,"* said de Gaulle, without particular interest. He asked why Gavin had been chosen for the post. I said I heard it was originally offered to Chip Bohlen (he later succeeded Gavin), who would have been excellent. De Gaulle agreed. I added that Bohlen seemingly thought it better to remain in Washington because of his great experience in Soviet affairs. De Gaulle agreed that this had been wise.

I inquired whether, with a new U.S. President, de Gaulle intended to revive his suggestion for a Big Three strategy committee. He answered:

I won't renew the proposal. It met with no result. If the U.S. is interested now, it remains for you to do something about it. If the U.S. really wants to act in this world it will have to come to such an arrangement. You cannot act through such organizations as UN and NATO, which have no real meaning. We need a western policy. But American policy is not western. You are with Nkrumah and Nasser just as much as you are with General de Gaulle [a statement that rings strangely now, years after de Gaulle himself began to court the neutrals].

By January 31, 1963, there were sufficient indications of anti-Americanism in French official conversation, the Paris press, and especially on the state television, for me to raise the matter with de Gaulle. I observed that a wave of anti-Americanism seemed to be infecting the mass media.

Tiens. You think that? I think just the opposite. Do you read the *Figaro*? I think the French press is very pro-American. I think the French press is very pro-American because it thinks de Gaulle is anti-American and this is the best way to be against de Gaulle. I am surprised at your observation.

Nevertheless, I pressed on. Recalling a previous conversation, I asked if he thought the French people psychologically disliked the American people. To my surprise the answer differed considerably this time. He said:

No, how can you think that? Surely you cannot have that impression when you go about France. I think the French people like the American people and I am surprised that you should think there is anti-Americanism. I don't think such a thing exists. But you must remember that the French people, like most other nations, are xenophobic in this sense. They want to do things themselves. And they regret it very much when they cannot do things themselves. They don't like to resign themselves to letting others do things for them. That is all.

I asked if he thought France (meaning de Gaulle) retained a prejudice against the U.S. and Britain as a result of wartime disagreements. He said:

It is very evident that during the war both the United States and Britain tried to control France and the affairs of France according to their own desires. And it is true that I opposed the United States and Britain in such efforts. I opposed them for the very reason I have just cited and I can assure you I did well. Just look at the facts. Supposing you had come back to France with General Giraud as a servant and a puppet. Giraud was a brave man but he never counted for anything and the French people knew this. He would have been quickly replaced. He would simply have been refused by the French people. And if he had been *your* man, seemingly responsible for French destinies, *you* would have been detested when he was removed.

To straighten out a matter that was becoming controversial and hurting the already diminished Franco-American friendship, I asked whether his original letter of 1958 to Eisenhower, suggesting the so-called *directoire,* had ever been answered, formally or informally. He again told me *directoire* was a word he had never used and added with a sour smile: "No, there has never been an answer. Not ever." This, I was subsequently to find out, was simply not true, yet it was believed not only by de Gaulle, but also by Couve de Murville and Ambassadors Gavin and, initially, Bohlen. I can only assume the text of Eisenhower's reply to de Gaulle was mislaid both in the French archives and the U.S. Embassy. Bohlen eventually dug this text out, and, with the authorization of Secretary of State Rusk, showed it to me.

I remarked to de Gaulle that the NATO commander, General Norstad, seemed rather sympathetic to his approach, a Big Three supervision of western strategy. He interrupted before I could finish, saying: "Norstad's idea is for a committee in charge of a multilateral force which would comprise not only the U.S., Britain, and France, but also Germany and possibly some other countries like Belgium. That idea would not work. You cannot have an executive committee to decide on the West's use of such a force." Here it was evident de Gaulle was confusing elements of the Kennedy administration's nonsensical MLF (Multilateral Nuclear Force) with Norstad's own ideas. Norstad never liked the MLF and his opposition to it contributed to his downfall when Kennedy retired him.

The General continued:

My original idea was different. I had suggested to Macmillan and Eisenhower that the three of us should organize a permanent cooperation on all world subjects. Thus, for example, we would have coordinated our policy on the Congo in advance and then would have cooperated together to solve the question. There have been several occasions when such a system could have worked. We did manage, for example, to agree on a joint approach to the crisis in Laos, but not in the Congo.

Did the 1958 offer still stand, I inquired? He thought for a moment and looked skeptical. Then he said: "I ask myself if at present, things being what they are today, it would be workable. I do not think so."

Later that year (December 12) I raised this crucial subject again, mentioning that Norstad had recently spoken publicly of a nuclear "directorate" of the four leading allies: the United States, Britain, France, and West Germany. I wondered if de Gaulle favored such an approach and, on this basis, whether his own original idea might not be worth reviving. He answered:

Every day this becomes more difficult. And anyway, why should there be *four* members of such a directorate? The Germans do not have any nuclear weapons; furthermore it is better that they should not have any. Why give them nuclear weapons? And why should they be allowed to participate in such a directorate?

Certainly it would be very hard now to form such a directorate. The United States now has an American strategy, not a European strategy. Therefore it isn't practical to conceive of a directorate. Naturally, it is necessary that the allied governments should exchange political and strategic ideas and they must remain allies. They must reciprocally explain their own situations and conceptions. But the United States has chosen to take back its own freedom of action. And France has also chosen to take back its own freedom of action.

Therefore it seems to me it would be very hard to create a directorate now. Of course, if a war came there would be a directorate—as always. This is the way wars have been fought by allies in the past. But I don't see how there can be a directorate before a war. We must have contacts and explain ideas and exchange information. But this is all we can do because it is apparent we have different strategies.

Returning to the vital issue of nuclear cooperation, I asked if de Gaulle would be willing to sign the nuclear test-ban treaty if, in exchange, the U.S. gave specific information and blueprints on thermonuclear weapons to France. He said:

I doubt it, frankly. To begin with, the United States cannot offer us such information and will not do so. If I were in the position of the United States I would not do so either. And if the Americans were to offer us such information they would obviously do it under conditions that would restrain the use of these devices. We could not accept this. It is unreal, a mirage, to imagine that America might make such a move. I never believed the United States would offer to help our nuclear military development and I never asked for such aid. And now it is very late. I cannot see what we would gain. We now have the certitude of being able to construct by ourselves our own nuclear and thermonuclear arsenal and we really would not save very much money if such aid were offered, even unconditionally.

This seemed to dispose of the problem. The General had just been in the United States for President Kennedy's funeral. Johnson was in the White House. I asked if de Gaulle expected to visit the United States in 1964 (as had been planned with Kennedy).

No, I will not go. I don't envision any such trip. I had been involved in negotiations arranging to see President Kennedy in February or March but, alas, he is now dead. The exact date had not been fixed, but it would have been announced in January. I owed President Kennedy a visit because he had been kind enough to make an official visit here. But I did not plan a state visit. I had already done that under President Eisenhower. I merely planned a working visit. President Kennedy, after all, had come to see me and I was happy to repay the courtesy; but now the poor President is dead. The situation is therefore different. I think that President Johnson should come here, and I would be very happy if he were to come either on an official visit or simply on a working visit. Should he come to Europe I would receive him very gladly, but personally I do not envisage another American trip. I haven't invited him yet. After all [at the time of Kennedy's funeral], he was submerged with problems and visitors when I saw him in Washington and I did not wish to bother him. But it is possible that I shall let him know in the future that it would give me much pleasure were he to come to Paris. However, this is not urgent and nothing need be done about it now. [The two presidents never met again.]

ALLIANCES AND STRATEGY

From the moment France became allied to the United States again in 1949, under the North Atlantic Treaty, de Gaulle showed he would be a restless, highly independent-minded partner should he regain control of France. For years he held that the probability, indeed inevitability, of war was obvious and much of his diplomatic thinking was based on this gloomy assumption. But his views on French strategy and alliances differed strikingly from the opinions of Washington. And these differences were interwoven into the entire skein of relationships developed by the General with both West and East.

On October 26, 1949, the year NATO was born, de Gaulle admitted to me that the alliance was a good thing in principle, but he thought the aid foreseen under the U.S. military-assistance program was insufficient. He added: "I told my supporters that France must first count upon itself, independent of foreign aid. All of Europe faces insufficient aid from America and we must always live as if war were just around the corner." He thought the Atlantic pact gave insufficient responsibility to the French and this was "an enormous psychological error. It takes away the initiative to build our national defense. This is a result of our present political situation. Because there is no French policy, no foreign government naturally has confidence in France. Therefore the chief fault for present errors does not lie with the United States. Americans cannot have confidence in France under the present structure."

On May 11, 1951, de Gaulle acknowledged that it was in French interest to support the NATO concept and also that Eisenhower was the logical Commander-in-Chief. Nevertheless, he stressed that various allies had special interests: Britain and France particularly in the Mediterranean. Britain also was concerned with northern Europe and France with the center. De Gaulle said:

We can accept a British command in the eastern Mediterranean. We recognize that the Americans have general interests in the Mediterranean and we can accept an American commander for the whole Mediterranean—on condition that France's special rights in the western Mediterranean are recognized. But the British seek an eastern Mediterranean command and also a preponderant influence in the western Mediterranean. This, France cannot accept.

The British are playing a role against France in the Mediterranean. Britain is particularly concerned with such eastern areas as the Suez

Canal, Iraq, Jordan, and the Sudan, but to retain their influence there the British would be ready to encourage the Arabs to rise up against the French in Morocco, Tunisia, and Algeria. If the British obtain control of the entire Mediterranean command, they would work against France for the sake of British interests in the same way as, during World War II, they expelled France from the Levant with the concurrence of Stalin and Roosevelt.

This was still the old-fashioned, imperialist de Gaulle, seeking to hold together "overseas France," a policy he soon and almost wholly abandoned.

The General said in 1951 that France must be revived militarily and "therefore we must have true responsibility in the Mediterranean. If France has a greater responsibility toward NATO in Europe and in North Africa it will have more interest in working for the coalition." In this respect he thought more French divisions than were scheduled should be contributed to Europe's defense—"not only divisions, but also a greater contribution in sea and air power." France could "easily" undertake to produce twenty active plus twenty reserve divisions for Europe, thus providing an overall strength of forty divisions within eight days of the outbreak of a war. But more materiel must be received from the U.S., and military service must be increased to twenty-four months. Furthermore, France should make NATO bases available on its territory—once its own "status in NATO has been regulated and revised to assure the security of France." De Gaulle also favored admission of Greece and Turkey into NATO (not done until 1952) and the alliance's extension in the Mediterranean to include Jugoslavia and Spain. He added: "Spain cannot be excluded from western strategy—to do that would be an absurdity—even if one does not like the political regime."

Thus, in 1951, the General still thought in outmoded imperial terms and saw in NATO a means of shoring up the French empire. He also endorsed the alliance, although wishing certain modifications, and called for a larger French contribution. This view was to change radically, and soon. Even in 1955 (October 14), he thought "collective institutions" like the UN and NATO were losing vigor. He said: "The United Nations already means nothing here. Nations will come and go, enter and depart from it. But it is finished. Soon the same situation will develop in NATO."

By May 31, 1956, he was saying: "The future of NATO depends entirely on Russia. If Russia threatens, NATO exists. If Russia does not threaten, NATO will die. Of course some organizations and some of the bureaucracy and personnel will be continued; but there will be no alliance. And not much of it remains today." Seven months later this skepticism was vastly heightened. He said:

I don't believe in NATO. What real worth has it shown?
The atomic bomb has big value. There is also real value to the friendship between the United States, Britain, and France. These are the things

that kept Russia back in Europe. But NATO? Pooh! What value has that? Where are NATO's divisions? The reason the French don't mobilize is NATO. What reason is there to mobilize forty divisions if General Norstad is in charge of France's defense? You can't take away from people their own responsibilities for themselves. Yet this is what NATO has done and this is why it is failing.

The General was wrapped in gloom. He saw no governments and no statesmen seeming to know what they wanted. Their policies were to react to events not to plan for them. He added:

This is not a policy. Nowhere—in Paris, in Washington, in London, or in Moscow—do the leaders know what they wish and prepare for it. Things have taken control, events are leading men. This was just as true in the Middle East [that autumn's disastrous Suez expedition] as it was in Hungary [the simultaneous uprising] and vice versa. No one is conducting events. There are series of incidents which erupt, and the governments react to these incidents.

As a military man he was astonished by the ineptness of the Anglo-French Suez operation. It should have been planned on a lightning basis to accomplish its goals in two days. Instead of that there was a ridiculous, long-range, tedious, drawn-out plan for something equivalent to the Normandy landing in terms of time and logistics. Likewise, when the revolution in Hungary developed, Moscow and Washington were surprised. Neither of them knew what to do about it. All this pessimism led to a grim conclusion which, it was plain, transcended existing alliance requirements in his mind. He said:

In the future there is bound to be a world war. This is the future of the world. When or how it will come I don't know. It will come whether there is a revolt in East Germany, which drags in the West Germans, or whether there is no such revolt. There will be a danger to the world if Prussia revolts against Communist and Soviet domination; or equally if Prussia does not revolt. War is a law of the human species. What Bossuet called "providence" is responsible. War is the law of the species. The moment for this war will come when the people of the world wish to destroy themselves, or to risk that by changing things. But the pretext for such a war, or the men who will start it, cannot be foreseen. After all, the assassination of an Austrian Archduke was surely not an adequate pretext for the First World War with all its casualties.

While this excessive pessimism, in the wake of Suez, apparently faded, the General's early hopes for NATO never revived. On July 19, 1957, he told me:

I would not wish to withdraw from NATO but I would want NATO seriously modified. As it is, the alliance is completely unsatisfactory. America has taken everything. America has all the commands. America has all the responsibility. And America provides all the force. This is not sensible for an alliance. Look at Russia. Russia's satellites have proven valueless. I would insist upon a repartition of the responsibility and the authority of the alliance. The alliance must be something spiritual as well as physical. And it cannot be spiritually viable unless there is some sort of shake-up.

He wanted a new division of responsibility among the U.S., Britain, France, Germany and "perhaps some to Italy; the rest don't matter."

The nearer his comeback approached the more dismal his view of NATO became. On February 20, 1958, he agreed that France was heading for disaster and said:

I don't know how to stop it. If I were in power—without this type of regime—something could be done. But the only thing that can be done is to give this country back its independence. How could that be achieved? It could be achieved by ending NATO.

I would not enter into a dispute with the United States and Britain. But I would quit NATO if I were running France. NATO is against our independence and our interest. Our membership in NATO is said to be for the protection of France against a Russian attack. But I don't believe that the Russians will attack at this time. Of course, one cannot say that this will be the case forever, but there is no fear now of a Russian attack.

The development of Soviet missiles, as demonstrated when Sputnik was launched in 1957, reinforced his argument. He said:

Also, the Russians now have long-range weapons. If one of their explosives were to fall on France the United States would not fight for us. It would not go to war immediately. It would only fight immediately if a bomb fell upon the United States. If a bomb fell on France the United States would merely protest in the United Nations and make all kinds of diplomatic moves.

Thus France is not defended by NATO. And, on the contrary, NATO prevents France from serving her own interests. NATO prevents France from acting in Algeria. Under one pretext or another NATO will deprive us of Bizerte in Tunisia; and we can never forget that Bizerte is a primordial French interest.

France must take back its independence. But this regime is incapable of leading. The consequence of this is both that we will lose Africa and stay in NATO, which is meaningless to us. NATO prevents France from believing that she is responsible for her own defenses. The French people think that it is the Americans who are now responsible for the defense of our country. This is very bad. If a war came, the French would not fight. They expect the United States to fight.

NATO is no longer an alliance. It is a subordination. This is very bad. Alliance, yes; that is all right; but subordination, no. After France has regained her own independence perhaps she will be linked with the western countries in formal alliances. France can be connected with other countries which are under the same threat. But we cannot accept a superior, like the United States, to be responsible for us.

Suspecting that the ultimate logic of this position might lead in the direction of neutralism, I asked in 1958 what he thought the latter's chances were of taking over in France. He replied:

There is a difference between independence and neutralism or neutrality. If a country is neutral it means that it gives up control of its own self and its own future interests by pledging in advance not to fight. Switzerland is neutral. Therefore the Swiss cannot really run their own destiny. They are pledged in advance that they can never fight under any circumstances. France might indeed stay out of a war, remain neutral in a particular war. But it cannot renounce the idea of war. Neutralism is contrary to the idea of independence.

On January 31, 1959, I had a long talk with the General—now President —on his concept of alliances, starting off with the subject of the famous so-called *directoire* proposal to Washington and London. He said:

I told the United States and British governments that we must consider our relationships in terms of world security. NATO only covers the North Atlantic area. Together we must organize something for the whole world. This must be done by our three countries, as the three leaders of the free world which have global interests. These three leaders must organize world security both in a political and in a strategic sense. In this respect NATO is a secondary question. It comes below and after the global problems.

NATO should be reformed entirely, to include Africa and the Orient as zones of action, as well as the Red Sea. That doesn't mean the countries in those regions should become members of NATO, but those areas must be considered in our strategic interest. Furthermore, NATO must be reorganized so as to stress cooperation rather than integration. The commands of NATO must be redivided. As things are, in case of a war, the French fleet in the Mediterranean area does not belong to France. It is intolerable. And U.S. policy in North Africa, politically speaking, is not our policy. That was demonstrated in the United Nations. There must be a world security organization among the three leading Western powers and at the same time NATO must be reorganized.

I asked him if, when talking about North Africa, he thought countries like Morocco and Tunisia, as well as Spain, should be admitted to NATO. He said with a sniff that it was totally unimportant about Morocco and Tunisia. "That doesn't matter," he commented with contempt, "as long as the area is covered. But as for Spain, yes; Spain should be in NATO."

If the United States refused to go along with his ideas, I inquired, did he contemplate an alternative foreign policy? He answered: "There will be no change from NATO. We regard NATO as necessary [somewhat of a reversion from previous views] and France will not leave the alliance. But we will cease practicing our membership in the same way as we practice it at the moment. There are other ways." (I noted at the time: "This is a curious and elliptical observation. But, on the whole, it is less discouraging than when he used to tell me that NATO was useless and France would get out and establish its own series of defense pacts.")

But then he added a threatening phrase: "Only if there is no comprehension of our viewpoint, if there is no other way than war [meaning an intra-allied political dispute, not an armed conflict] will we join in the battle. We will take back our liberties. But I don't foresee this. All logic points towards an accord."

Still, a year later (February 20, 1960) de Gaulle was arguing that NATO's entire future depended upon satisfactory arrangement of Big Three global strategy. He said:

> Everything depends on this question. There are, after all, three basic powers in the West; the other powers are secondary. Strategy must be decided by the three. Already this is practically being done in the diplomatic sense. Look at the Summit. We don't exclude the other allies but they are less important and this fact must be acknowledged.

The previous month President de Gaulle had received General Norstad, the NATO commander, for the first time, in what alliance leaders regarded as auspicious circumstances. President Eisenhower had specially flown to Paris for the occasion his own interpreter, Colonel [later General] Vernon Walters, to translate. I asked de Gaulle if the conversation had been useful. He replied (and I noted then: "I think Norstad would burn with rage if he had heard this.") :

> The French government accepts the fact that certain French officers who have special charges should be dealing with certain NATO officers. The French admiral in the Mediterranean accepts to talk with Norstad's commanders. The French general in charge of air defense does likewise. But the government of France doesn't negotiate with General Norstad. When I received General Norstad it was not a negotiation; only a visit. I am happy to see General Norstad from time to time—but only as a visitor.

De Gaulle's view of allied relationships was old-fashioned. Thus, he had nothing against extensive conventional pacts, but he refused to adjust to the integrated requirements of missile defense which required instant communication and response. On February 14, 1961, he was advocating that:

> Certainly the Mediterranean powers should be coordinated. Their defenses should be coordinated. We have excellent relations with Italy and Greece and now with Spain. Maybe we will be able to develop a tighter union. This is very possible. There is much reality in the idea—and I

would include economic and cultural links. This is not an immediate problem, but it is a logical one for the future.

Nevertheless, he had little to offer in the way of similar cooperation on NATO's crucial problem, atomic arms and atomic strategy. While opposing each new formula suggested, he offered none of his own. Thus, when I asked him if he saw any value in Norstad's idea of giving NATO its own nuclear stockpile, he answered:

What is the meaning of that? It is just a question of giving a nuclear stockpile to General Norstad. That is of no interest to France. Norstad has his nuclear weapons already. In no way does this directly affect France. There is no change implied by this idea. In reality the United States would continue as before to control these nuclear weapons.

In a political sense de Gaulle was right. It was becoming increasingly clear that the General envisioned the use of his own small atomic stockpile as a diplomatic weapon against allies in peacetime and not as a military weapon against enemies in wartime. In the latter case he obviously relied upon the preponderant U.S. nuclear umbrella. But, prior to the last extremity, he could hold France's advantage over a nonnuclear West Germany and could insist on France's presence at any major international meeting because it was, after all, an atomic power in its own right.

This became plain during our conversation, when I asked if Bonn might get access to French nuclear weapons were it to invest in costly new French atomic plants. He said: "Germany is not investing in our nuclear plants. We see no reason to change. France is building atomic plants with its own money."

The General had by this time expanded and broadened his theory of another great war. He said: "If war does not come within ten years, it is possible that the white, civilized people may group together, but they will not group themselves *against* the other people of the earth. It will only be vis-à-vis them, in relationship to them, the civilized peoples banding together with respect to the less civilized." This was a vague basis on which to build an enduring alliance structure. But he blamed U.S. and British failure to accept his Big Three strategic planning formula for the lacuna, adding:

Unless there is an organized system there is clearly no engagement for a common policy. Look at the situation. The West must have a common policy in the world. But there is no common policy in the Congo or in Berlin or in the Far East. Yet a common policy is a primordial necessity. It is a primordial necessity that there would be a western-world policy confronting a Soviet world policy. The whole world looks for a *real western* global policy. Because there is no such policy the whole world suffers. We need a permanent cooperation of the three main western powers. That is indispensable. And these powers are the United States, Britain, and France. The others are less important. They would follow us; they would have to follow us.

By this time President Kennedy had offered (at Ottawa) a plan to develop a NATO force of Polaris submarines. I asked if France would participate. He said:

That goes back to the original idea of giving General Norstad command over Polaris submarines. There is nothing wrong with that plan. What do we care if the U.S. forces in Europe are under the control of an American in Europe or in Washington? That changes nothing. NATO doesn't exist. It is part of a U.S. chain of command. If it wants to have its submarines commanded by an American general in Europe, naturally I do not refuse. [He shrugged.]

I then inquired whether *any* of the forces France was bringing back from Algeria, where the war had ended, would be assigned to NATO command. Sternly he replied: "No, not NATO. We leave in NATO what is already assigned to NATO. [Prior to de Gaulle's return, France had promised to send back to the alliance troops taken away for Algeria.] We have even reinforced what is there in NATO, and there will still be some slight reinforcement. But what comes from Algeria will not be assigned to NATO. That will be our own strategic reserve."

With the new situation being created by Algerian independence, de Gaulle was losing interest in his own earlier thought of a Mediterranean pact. He told me:

There can be no such alliance. In truth, the Mediterranean countries are either western—like France or Spain or Italy or Greece—or they are not truly western. These latter countries are neutralist. I refer to countries like Egypt or Lebanon or Cyprus or Libya or Morocco or Tunisia. And I refer to Algeria, which tomorrow will be neutralist. A Mediterranean alliance is an idea and a hope, but it is not a reality. In any case, it is not a reality of the moment.

By 1963, the General had given up the last vestige of hope that he might obtain some kind of Big Three partnership recognition from Washington. On January 31, he told me that the Nassau meeting (late 1962) between Macmillan and Kennedy, when Britain made its nuclear defense dependent upon American Polaris submarines, had terminated this vision. He said:

I must say that after the Nassau meeting ended, Kennedy informed me about it and proposed that France, like Britain, should buy Polarises and put them in a multilateral force. But Kennedy didn't propose anything else. It is that simple. There was no objective to continuing negotiations. We have no submarines or warheads here. We had nothing to talk about.

There wasn't any other event that supervened. We merely understood the situation as it was and made our decision. There were no other events. This is merely a result of our own analysis of facts. But of course we remain ready to cooperate technically and strategically. I am always interested when the press talks about our *force de frappe* just the way the press talks about my plan for a *Europe des patries*. These phrases have been invented by journalists. I talk about a "nuclear force" and about "European cooperation." But the other phrases are always used.

By the end of the year (December 12—the last conversation reported in this volume), de Gaulle was evidently becoming even more skeptical about the value of NATO to France, showing great discontent with the administration of the late President Kennedy for abandoning previous U.S. strategy of immediate nuclear riposte to any attack in favor of the so-called "flexible" or "graduated" response. He said:

> The strategy formulated by the alliance in 1956, and accepted by everyone, was based on the assumption that if there should be an attack in Europe nuclear weapons would be used by the alliance right away. But this is no longer American strategy. The U.S.A. has changed its strategy and no longer wishes to make such a commitment for the immediate use of nuclear weapons. The fact that the United States has changed its strategy is no reason for the alliance to change its strategy. Without a complete agreement on strategy that pledges immediate use of nuclear weapons in case of aggression, there can be no guarantee for Europe.

I asked if he did not think it possible to conceive of a period of pause? For example, if two Soviet divisions were to invade Germany, could they not be contained and pushed back by conventional means? De Gaulle replied:

> No one can foresee just what kind of a war might take place, in advance of such a war. But it is perfectly clear that no serious Soviet attack can be met by the conventional forces we have. And anyway, it is much better to prevent such an attack by accepting the concept of a deterrent. It must be understood as the basis of strategy that all arms without exception would be used to repel any attack. If there should be an exception this would weaken the whole concept of deterrents.

I asked if, now that France's *force de dissuasion* (*force de frappe*) was coming into being, he was prepared to work out with Washington and London common NATO targeting agreements in the event of war. He said:

> We don't yet have our *force de dissuasion*. It does not yet exist. But when we have it—and this is not yet the case—we are perfectly prepared to discuss with Washington, and to a much less important degree with London, working out arrangements on the use and targets of such forces. Of course, this is primarily a matter to be discussed with Washington because it is not the least bit important with London. We are prepared to discuss what each should do with his nuclear weapons in case of war.
>
> But this does not mean that we are, or necessarily would be, in accord on strategy. The United States wants to use its nuclear weapons later, in case of war. We want to use our nuclear weapons soon, virtually immediately. So you can see that the concept of military strategy differs. But this is the nature of things.

I remarked that it seemed very difficult to me, furthermore, to contemplate any agreement between ourselves and France on the issue of nuclear forces since we preferred to strike back only at an enemy's military installations whereas France, as I understood it, would strike at an enemy's cities. "Yes," he said, "It is very hard to compromise, I admit. We certainly would attack cities."

Apart from this glaring gap on strategy, I asked if he had any ideas on how NATO's actual structure should be reformed. He said:

The states in NATO are allies and they all understand that they must make war in common if war comes. We believe in this. But NATO should have a common strategy and I don't see any such common strategy coming. We French are not happy with U.S. strategy. Therefore, I think it is better to leave things as they are without deceiving ourselves about reality as it exists. I can't see how any fundamental reform can be achieved. In theory it would be better to destroy the alliance and reconstruct it, instead of trying to reform it.

I asked whether he contemplated further reducing France's contribution to the alliance if NATO's strategy continued to differ from his own. With astonishing self-satisfaction he replied:

France has already withdrawn most of its forces from NATO. A large part of the army, a large part of the air force, and all of the French fleet are out. And now our new strategic air command will be out. All we have left under NATO is a small army in Germany and a few aircraft units. But I don't see any need to change this. For the moment I see no reason for withdrawing what is left.

He said France was no longer contemplating a military alliance with Spain, but "naturally, should there be a war, Spain intends to fight with us. France knows this and Spain knows this." And he also said that France would participate in the Geneva disarmament talks it was then boycotting,

If there are real measures discussed for real disarmament. Naturally we are in favor of nuclear disarmament. We don't wish to keep atomic weapons if the United States and Russia are ready to give them up. If they wish to negotiate a suppression of such arms, we are ready to join in talks. But the present Geneva talks are meaningless. They can lead to nothing. They have no purpose except to amuse diplomats and please the journalists. They have no reality. They only represent lost time and I see no reason to waste time.

ARABS, ALGERIA, AFRICA

Of all areas outside the hexagon of metropolitan France, that which has been most involved with the destiny of de Gaulle and the repercussions of his leadership is North Africa and the Arab world. The malady that struck down France and made the General's return inevitable was the Algerian cancer. The military putsch that destroyed the Fourth Republic originated in Algiers. The most savage debate on the intentions of Gaullism and the most confused interpretation of his delphic utterances come on the subject of Algeria. And years later, when he set out to repair France's image in the Arab world, blockaded arms sales to Israel, and referred to the Jews as a "domineering" people, the General precipitated perhaps the greatest storm of his far from tranquil career.

I have always believed that de Gaulle's single intention from the moment he took power in 1958, was to obtain for France the most favorable solution possible in Algeria. In other words, he was neither deceitful nor had any parti pris. He was simply realistic in accepting the facts and agreeing to independence. He recognized history's anticolonial tide, but this had nothing to do with whether he enjoyed floating on it or not. Therefore, with courage, skill, and mastery of ruse, he restored firm discipline over an unruly army, squashed secret terrorist movements aiming at his downfall, and, at a moment when their actual military insurrection had been defeated in the field, gave the Algerians freedom—and made the French like it.

Likewise, although he deliberately courted the Arabs after settling the North African mess and although he certainly disfavored Israel and seemed to adopt a hostile line toward Jews in general, I do not for a moment think he was by nature or personality either "pro-Arab" or "anti-Jewish." To be sure, some of his methods and aspirations derived from that brilliant if warped right-winger, the pseudo-fascist, antisemitic Charles Maurras; but his own spirit was of more noble material. As the following pages will show, he was certainly no "Arab lover" and as history has shown he was never hostile to the Jews. Léon Blum, Pierre Mendès-France, and other French Jewish leaders always spoke respectfully of him, even when they disagreed politically.

De Gaulle was a realist who tried to fit France's fortunes into the pattern of history he foresaw on the horizon; he discarded personal prejudice and sentimental inclination in favor of truth as he assayed it. Since the French empire had been built up largely in the Arab realm and the French cultural legacy remained firmly rooted there, he regarded the Arabs as pawns in the power game of an evolving France and he felt an "Arab policy" was of great importance in French relationships with other nations.

The first records in my notes of any discussion with the General on the Arabs came January 21, 1954, and involved Spain and Morocco. The Fourth Republic had ousted the Moroccan Sultan and replaced him with a puppet whom Madrid did not recognize. De Gaulle, who admitted that he too preferred the exiled Sultan, nevertheless commented: "The Spaniards quite clearly are now trying to found an 'Arab policy.' They sent their foreign minister, Martin-Artajo, to flatter the Arab League. I fear the Spaniards will keep playing this card—pro-Arab and anti-French, but I am confident it will not go too far."

In 1955, on October 14, I had my first lengthy talk with him on Algeria. He said:

Algeria was never a state. Individual Arabs and Berbers have been living in a sort of anarchic condition there for many, many centuries. They were never organized. In 1830, when the French went into Algeria, it was being run by Turkish garrisons. In the hinterland there was tribal anarchy. By contrast with Algeria, there has been a Tunisian Kingdom and a Moroccan Empire.

He pointed out that the Algerians had never been able to form a dominant political party like the Destour in Tunisia and were always divided into factional movements. He likened Algeria to a heap of dust (*une poussière*), yet he clearly saw the emotional bond between Algerians and other Arabs. On May 31, 1956, he admitted:

We can't have peace very quickly between the Arab world and the West. In Algeria, Tunisia, Morocco, and the Middle East, the Arabs are working all together. There would have been a possibility for France to find a solution with the Arabs, but it is not possible in the present situation. The Arab question is a world question, not just a French question. This question has its repercussions all over. Everybody is having difficulty with the Arabs.

Yet in no sense did this imply—as his enemies were later to adduce—that de Gaulle was an Arabophil. Indeed, he explained his personal view to me quite candidly and I have no reason to think he ever altered it. He elaborated:

Who are the Arabs? The Arabs are a people who, since the days of Muhammed, have never constituted a state successfully. Muhammed made a state because of Islam. After him there has been nothing but anarchy. Have you ever seen a dam built by the Arabs? Nowhere. It doesn't exist. It has never been seen anywhere. It has been like that for centuries. The Arabs say that they invented algebra and built huge mosques. But this was entirely the job of Christian slaves they captured [a strange distortion of fact]. It was not the Arabs themselves. We French tried to do much with them. And the Russians before us tried. But they can't do anything alone.

At the time, I noted: "I don't quite know what de Gaulle meant by 'the Russians before us'; I suppose he may be referring to Islamic Central Asia; that is a mere conjecture."

In 1957, when Arab leaders were beginning to suggest that the Algerians should deal with the exiled de Gaulle, the General cynically observed that they were just politicians and found it convenient to "deal with de Gaulle as long as de Gaulle is not in power." He thought they would be less apt to talk that way if he were running the government. He then made a rather conventional defense of the customary thesis on Algeria. He trotted out a lot of the old arguments, but rather better than most Frenchmen. He said: "There are certain basic facts. These include the discontent and desire for independence of the Algerian people. They include the injustices the Algerians have suffered from French administrations in the past. But they also include the fact that there is a large number of Frenchmen living in Algeria and the country could not survive without them. Algeria has never been independent. There has never been a state of Algeria as there was a state of Morocco and a state of Tunisia. Both in Morocco and Tunisia, the French had somebody to deal with. Even if Tunisia isn't much of a state, it is something. There is nothing that one can imagine as a state in Algeria. There are chaotic, disorganized bands of Fellagha (guerrillas). But there is no coordinated group. Furthermore, the Fellagha don't recognize the problems of independence. They have no administrative experience and no knowledge of the economic difficulties of a state. They don't seem to realize that Algeria simply couldn't stand on its feet—above all without the aid of the Europeans who are there."

De Gaulle didn't think there would be a "catastrophe" in Algeria. He thought that, "A year from now the situation would be somewhat like it is now—only worse." He thought the stalemate would persist and would get more serious and more tragic all the time. The French army would remain there and keep the Fellagha from gaining control. But at the same time there would be more and more bombings and murders.

On February 20, 1958, a short time before he returned to power, he no longer believed Habib Bourguiba's claim that it might be easier to deal with a de Gaulle government was a "*blague politique.*" He reasoned that the Tunisian chief of state felt that a France, sure of herself, could be treated with, that "It is much easier to deal with a decisive France than an indecisive France." But he had not yet gone to the end of the road, and he thought the "only reality" would be to have a "commonwealth of independent states." He favored "reciprocal engagements: economic, military, and in foreign affairs between France and the members of the commonwealth." It should resemble the "British sysem" he added.

On February 20, 1960, when, as President, he was fully preoccupied with settling the Algerian war, he told me:

> First we must have self-determination to see what the people of Algeria want. I accept that there can be a choice between one and another solutions. But Ferhat Abbas [then the rebel leader] obviously doesn't want self-determination. He wants only *his* solution—independence. And he continues the *égorgements* [throat-cuttings] he calls war so long as his solution is not accepted. This is a dictatorial and totalitarian approach. I don't want a dictatorship of any sort in Algeria.

De Gaulle then developed the three possible bases for settlement:
Secession. "If independence came, France would do no more in Algeria. But there are Frenchmen and many Muslims in Algeria who don't want to

be separated from France. They have the right to be in Algeria exactly the way the people of Ferhat Abbas have a right to be there. And they will stay. These people must regroup. Naturally, this is particularly important where they are most numerous—in the regions of Algiers and Oran." I noted: "It is perfectly apparent that what de Gaulle is saying here by implication is that Algeria will be partitioned if it votes for secession and that the Algiers and Oran areas will be kept under French control."

Francisation. I wrote: "What de Gaulle clearly means by this is what the 'ultras' have called 'integration.' Under such a solution there would be no question of separate communities in Algeria. All Algerians, regardless of origin, would be citizens like any citizen of the Metropolitan area."

Association. The General described this as "An Algeria that was not France, but that was linked with France for certain things." He said: "If this solution is chosen, Algeria must organize itself along such lines. It is a question for the people of Algeria. Algeria would not deliver the French Algerians into the hands of the Muslims. There would be an Algerian federation. Each community would have its own rights and guarantees in the French, Kabyle [Berber], Arab, and Mozabite [a small sect] communities." He added that this could be analogous to the Swiss constitutional system, binding different linguistic communities, or the Lebanon, linking different religious communities."

He then summarized the prospects:

It is, of course, conceivable under the Ferhat Abbas scheme that Algeria might become a total dictatorship which would eliminate this thought of communes or any special communities. And it could become French, and it could become a federal state. This is a very complicated problem. Suppose you in the United States had a population of forty million redskins. This fact would have to be recognized. You could not force them to become Christian and to change their status. You must think of things in this way.

By 1961 (February 14), after another year of war and simmering discontent, de Gaulle was still hopeful there could be an "association" between Algeria and France, but he noted that this depended on the Algerians. He argued,

It is necessary for Algeria to link its diplomatic destiny with France; but it is not necessary for France. France does not need Algeria, but Algeria needs France. Without association with France, there will be anarchy in Algeria.

Algeria needs the economic, cultural, and administrative aid of Frenchmen. It needs cadres of Frenchmen for the structure of its state. Furthermore, Algeria needs France in terms of its national defense. Indeed, it would be in France's interest that the two countries' defense should be combined. Nevertheless, if the Algerians decide by the processes of self-determination to break with France, they will break with France. That will be their loss—not ours.

Even then I observed in my notes: "I was very much struck by one thing throughout our conversation. De Gaulle continually spoke of Algeria in terms of a fully independent republic which could decide freely on its own whether it had any links with France or not. In other words, he has gone whole hog."

He continued:

We are not asking for anything, for any guarantees [for the French minority]. That is up to the Algerians. Obviously, the Europeans are very useful to Algeria. It is the Europeans with their abilities, their techniques, and their capital who can make Algeria work. Without them there would be economic misery. It is clearly in the interest of Algeria that the Europeans should remain. But it is up to the Algerians to make the decision. *They* must make the decision and *they* must offer the guarantees and the conditions which persuade the Europeans to stay on.

France has completely abandoned colonialism in all and every form. That includes Algeria. Colonialism is finished. It is now a question of interests. It is in Algeria's interest to receive help, not in France's interest. We will see what the Algerians want themselves. But we are resolved to follow whatever course the Algerians decide on. It is up to them. We *want* them to decide freely—in complete freedom. We don't want anybody to have any doubts about this.

I asked if de Gaulle preferred a separate Algeria or one linked to Tunisia and Morocco in a Maghreb (North African) state. He answered:

This is not important to us. It is only a dream. The three of them will never get together. Each will remain alone and try to follow its own individual destiny. You have already seen a similar development among the Middle Eastern Arabs. The Egyptians, the Jordanians, and the Iraqis all talk about a glorious united Arab state. But they never get together.

Of course, in the Middle East they formed the Arab League and it is possible that the North African states might try to create something like it. But it would be wholly impractical—just as impractical as the Arab League. See what the Arab League has done. For six years the Arab League has been saying that each and all of them *must* help the Algerians in their revolt. Do you know how many non-Algerian Arabs are fighting there today? Less than fifty! There are less than fifty Arab volunteers from Iraq, Egypt, and Morocco, from all over, who are actually fighting. This is the result of a six-year-old Arab League decision.

Oddly enough, considering that he had just offered the Algerians full independence if they wished, the General insisted that France had won the war itself, the military campaign. He told me:

You may not realize it, but the war in Algeria is now over. You can go anywhere. There is no fighting. There are a few murders—perhaps six a day, four Muslims and two Europeans. But that is not a war. The only war now is a war in the press—not in Algeria. But that doesn't mean that serious political questions do not remain to be settled.

By January 20, 1962, when Paris was filled with rumors of an imminent settlement in Algeria, I asked the General once again if he envisioned the possibility of a unified North Africa, a Maghreb. He waxed sarcastic, exposing his gift for mimicry by gestures and facial expressions as he imitated the Arabs about whom he was talking.

He said:

When one speaks of the Arabs one can never know what one is talking about. One can never be sure of what one says. They are always boiling. They are always unpredictable. Such is the nature of the Arab. They are nomads. They are anarchic; not anarchists, anarchic. They are engulfed in their own inherent rivalries. Nasser tried to create a union of the Middle Eastern Arabs. He couldn't. Nor will he ever be able to succeed. And who can do this for the western Arabs? No one, I venture to say. But the question is unimportant.

I inquired whether he expected trouble with the OAS, the Secret Army Organization led by General Salan in its effort to keep Algeria French and even seize France, should he make peace with the Algerian rebels. He sniffed:

The OAS does not make agreements. It is France that makes decisions. It is France that is seeking to make a peace in Algeria. France is finding a solution together with the rebellious Algerians, the FLN. The OAS does not matter. We accept the principle of an independent Algeria, but of course this can only be decided by a free vote in Algeria. Yet we know how this will result. [Later on de Gaulle said he was sure Algeria would have a neutralist government.]

We accept the idea that the French will cooperate in a free Algeria—which is necessary for the sake of a free Algeria. We will help economically and with schools and in other ways. We accept the idea of cooperation in an Algerian Sahara and there are no big differences on military bases. We will be able to remain in Mers-el-Kebir [naval base] and in a Sahara *participation* for a long time to come. And for some time, during the provisional period, we will remain in Algeria.

There are no longer any big differences. There are no serious difficulties on our side, but they, the Algerians, have difficulties. They are a poor people. They are not united. Each one of their leaders has his personal ambitions and his clan. Each one of them wants to be President. Now that they are on the verge of responsibilities instead of conspiratorial activities, they are overwhelmed by the prospect. Until now they have been agitators. But now they wish to be a government and, in truth, they are not very capable of this and they know it—and it irks them.

I hope soon they will prove able to recognize this new situation and to accept their responsibilities. I deeply hope so but I cannot know. If not, if nothing happens, we will have to act. We will then have to regroup the French in separate zones. This is not partition; it is regroupment. Partition means two Algerias; regroupment would first mean the establishment of separate zones administratively. And when that happens many of the French in Algeria will leave. There would be one main zone running from the region of Oran to the region of Algiers. But there would be secondary zones, for example, in the region near Bône. But this would be provisional. It would not be a commitment to partition; it would be temporary.

After all, already there are important zones in Algeria where there are no troops. There are mayors, prefects, and gendarmes, but there are no soldiers. Fighting has ended. There are only occasional assassinations, but there is no combat. And I can assure you the war will not start again.

As for the OAS [and here he spread his hands], the OAS is tedious [*assommant*]. The OAS is manufactured of passion and disorder. But it is not a political reality. It is not a political reality in France. And one must deal with reality. In Algeria the OAS is a sentimental reality. It is based on deep emotions. But it does not count in France. In France the OAS is made up of a few individuals who make plastic-bomb incidents. If we were to have a vote in France tomorrow there would not be twenty thousand votes for the OAS.

He said the OAS had no important influence left in the French army which had met its last test in April, 1961. At that time the army's commanders in Algeria had tried to revolt but, he said, apart from a few very special units like some of the Foreign Legion, the army did not "follow the insurrectionists." I inquired if violent trouble came to Algeria, whether he would ask the army to act by all necessary means to preserve order. Somewhat sternly he replied: "The army will make order; I shall command it and the army will follow." When I inquired whether the French government would release Ben Bella he said: "The moment there is an agreement for a cease-fire I will release Ben Bella and all the other prisoners right away, right away." And, thanks to the General's firm leadership and truly generous approach, peace came. By December 12, 1963, he was able to assure me: "Our relations are not bad with them. There is no hostility on either side."

The General's personal views on Black Africa were far from egalitarian although even there, in the vast Francophone belt of states that emerged like flimsy strawmen from the French West African colonies, he acknowledged the current tide of decolonization. He eventually established an odd system whereby shadow independence was both protected and controlled by France's airborne *Force d'intervention*. On May 31, 1956, I asked him how he foresaw the future of French Equatorial Africa. He didn't seem to understand the question very well, but I didn't get a chance to elucidate. He launched off again, talking about Arabs and Negroes together and explaining in a rather arrogant, kindergarten way that there really was a difference between Equatorial and North Africa. He said:

Those are Blacks, not Arabs. They are black. Before the whites came they were savages. I don't think the Black Continent can civilize itself all alone. There *is* a western civilization. There has also been a Chinese civilization. One cannot replace the West in Africa. It is indispensable for civilization. The world cannot exist without civilization. Barbarism, anarchy, and misery can indeed take over. But otherwise the West must exert an influence if there is to be a civilization.

When, on February 14, 1961, I inquired whether he thought settlement of the Algerian fracas would improve relations between France and its former Black African colonies he remarked with mild indignation: "Why should it? Our relations are already excellent except with people like Sekou Touré [the Guinea President who was then leaning far to the left]. There are no differences."

But he savagely opposed UN intervention in the former Belgian Congo (a French-speaking area), saying:

The first thing to do is to end this ridiculous UN intervention. France was against it from the start. We didn't exercise our veto power, but we voted against the project. UN doesn't exist. UN is Touré, Nasser, and Morocco. UN is an augmented Babel. Its intervention merely increased the trouble inherent in the Congo.

Last summer, when the Congolese crisis began to assume its very grave proportions, I proposed to Eisenhower and Macmillan that we should establish an entente among the three of us [again the old Big Three concept] to insist to both parties that they should live up to their treaty [acknowledging Congolese independence]. We would then have been in a position to cut off any intervention from the East. We could have reorganized the former Belgian Congo the way France organized the French Congo [Brazzaville], the Chad Territory, the Ivory Coast, and other former colonies. But Eisenhower was against the idea. He wanted to leave everything to the UN.

The General's observations over the years on the cruelly complex African question, so torturous for France, are of especial interest because they show so plainly the way he controlled his emotional prejudices and subjected them to the dictates of his brain. It was always obvious, whether he was discussing the Arabs or the Africans, that he tended to look down upon them personally with all the prejudices of his class—the conservative, Catholic, imperialist, and traditional Frenchman who, all too often, worshipped at the altar of the Bourbon pretenders and Maurras. But reason and reality ruled his highly disciplined policy for Africa and for decolonization just as they had ruled his behavior in 1940, when he broke with the entire military hierarchy of France, headed by Marshal Pétain, his own patron and namesake of his son, because he saw what was right for the France of his time and pursued that all-embracing vision. He didn't like the English or the Americans a generation earlier and he didn't like the Arabs or the Africans; but he did discern history's tide and swung his countrymen with it.

ASIA—ABOVE ALL, VIETNAM

The degree of American involvement in Vietnam was relatively subdued during the period covered in this volume and the General's observations on Southeast Asia are far less pungent than they were to become. Nevertheless, the main thrust of his analysis was already evident prior to France's own withdrawal from the area and long before the United States had unwittingly begun to assume the burden of its defense.

On January 21, 1954—a few weeks before the start of the fatal Dien Bien Phu campaign—I asked him what solution he could see to the war then being waged against Ho Chi Minh's Viet Minh (progenitor of the Viet Cong).

Solution? I can't see anything but evacuation of Indochina or a continuation of the present situation. [How odd this rings in American ears more than half a generation later.] For a military solution a new method and a new effort would be required. But France does not want to make that effort.

We have no really direct interest in Indochina. That is a reality. What is taking place there now is merely a prestige war. Not even the prestige of France is involved anymore. Indochina is of international interest more and more and of French interest less and less. There are only two real authorities in Indochina—France and Ho Chi Minh. There is nothing else. There are no other "authorities." The dynasties of Bao Dai [in Vietnam], Cambodia, and Laos are nothing now. They are only an appearance.

Ho is a reality. He represents independence, nationalism, communism, Asia. France is a reality. She represents the Occident. Now there is no more French authority in the country. Everything has been given up. Therefore, inevitably, the French must get out. They will get out when they have had enough. We will regret it greatly—but we must go. In 1863, Napoleon III went to Mexico. He supported Maximilian. But all the United States was against him. He had to get out. It is the same thing in Indochina.

Later the same year (November 10), after the Geneva Conference had partitioned Vietnam into two states, the General assured me that Ho was "frightened of China." He said the Hanoi chieftain wanted to build relations with France

in order to play her off against Mao Tse-tung. Ho Chi Minh would now like to come into the French Union [the shaky commonwealth which existed then] where he could speak up as a sort of Nehru on behalf of North Africa; but it is entirely out of the question to admit a Communist state to the French Union. All of Indochina is gone now and it is folly to think otherwise. There were only two *real* forces in Indochina—Communist nationalism and the French army. The French army is now being pulled out so *all* of Indochina is lost.

As for China itself, the incalculable mass Napoleon once referred to as "a sleeping giant," de Gaulle had a cautious and hesitant approach to its evident reawakening. On February 14, 1961, I said I had heard that Macmillan had recently discussed with him the desirability of admitting Communist China to UN and the recognition by other western countries of Peking. He said:

China in UN? It is all the same to us. We don't believe in UN. UN is anarchy, nothing but anarchy. It won't change if China comes in. If China comes in it won't bother us. It will just add one more orator to insult the West.

As for diplomatic relations between France and China—we are not so opposed to the thought. [In fact, he established the link in 1964.] After all, we have diplomatic relations with Russia. But we will do nothing ourselves to separate France from the rest of the West on this question. We are simply not against it. And, I repeat, as for UN—what is the difference if we bring still one more devil into it?

He had made no move on Peking by December 12, 1963, when next I raised the subject; still he confided:

We have considered this for a long time. I cannot tell you just now what we will do. But one day we will certainly have relations. I just don't know when. You must remember that the British already have such relations; and you acknowledge the existence of China and have a certain kind of relationship through the conversations you have with them in Warsaw [through the U.S. and Chinese embassies in Poland]. They represent a kind of acknowledgment, a form of diplomatic contact. It is possible, I say it is probable, that we will have diplomatic relations with China. But it is not a question of present immediacy.

This geographical focus of our conversation encouraged me to ask his views on Southeast Asia, a subject that shortly became a principal irritant to Franco-American amity. I inquired whether the area's best future lay in a neutral federation guaranteed by both power blocs, that of NATO and that of the Soviet coalition. He said this was indeed his view and added:

I have thought for a long time about this and I have told this to the Americans. I told it to President Kennedy. I have pointed out that in the present situation of Asia and Southeast Asia armed intervention—and indeed, any form of intervention—simply cannot help. We French have experimented with such intervention and now you are doing so. But it doesn't work. That is a zone where the only possibility is to establish neutrality as between East and West. Of course, any such arrangement must be guaranteed by the Communist countries as well as by the West to have any validity. But were it to be arranged, a sort of peace could be established that would end the perpetual battle—such as we now see in Laos and Vietnam—and it would provide for a détente. Then the area could begin to develop and prosper in peace. In the end that is what will come about. That is the reality. If you look at Africa you will see that it is in fact neutral. And if the neutrality of Africa were to change, or to swing either toward the East or the West, such a development could produce only war.

De Gaulle led France's dream of grandeur and a restored empire during World War II, although even then he saw the best that could be hoped for in an imperial sense was a French-led commonwealth. During the twelve years he brooded in self-imposed exile at Colombey-les-Deux-Eglises, he modernized this concept, learning from the brutal experiences of Indochina and North Africa.

Always his greatest talent in the realm of statesmanship would be the art of discerning the inevitable and exploiting it. In this way he guided and abetted his own political comeback and had a basic program to insure the effectiveness of his powers once he had regained them. He saw, even before so-called liberal and socialist Frenchmen, what the current against colonialism meant in terms of a French Algeria and West Africa, and he never permitted his undisguised personal biases to interfere with his judgment of reality.

He used the legacy of a European Common Market and an incipient nuclear arms program, bequeathed to him by the Fourth Republic, to develop his aims of increasing French prestige and the actuality of French leadership in the disorganized world lying between Russia and America. He played Germany against both superpowers and against itself and prevented a frustrated Britain from joining with a humiliated Germany inside the European political barony he carved out for France. Once he had ascertained that Washington would never grant Paris equal rights as a western capital—or even the second-class parity accorded London—he struck out on an independent line, protected by NATO and at the same time somewhat hostile to it, using the U.S.S.R. against the U.S. and vice versa, combining the talents of jiujitsu expert and tightrope walker in a fulgurous diplomatic display. He employed his tiny atomic force both to assert France's superiority over other Continental lands and to claim representation in any great power consultations, an arm more effective against allies than menacing to enemies; he also used it to give new pride and sense of purpose to a French army that had been defeated in successive wars since June, 1940.

The performance was remarkable and dazzling. And if it was foredoomed to failure because of the very limitations of France's geographical, demographic, and economic position, what, after all, endures? When de Gaulle sat down in the Elysée to play his hand in the international poker game, he had few cards and fewer chips. Yet for a long time he dominated the game.

THE MAN BEHIND

THE MASK

D E GAULLE WAS REGARDED IN STRIKINGLY DIFFERENT WAYS BY
those who supported him, opposed him, or were disappointed by
him. The extreme right called him pro-Communist and the extreme left called him a dictator; and I have tried to show how he played
these extremes off against each other. He was seen as ruthless by those he
smashed, guileful by those he deceived and disloyal by those who expected
a reward for their fidelity.

I can only describe the General in terms of my own experience. I was
certainly not even remotely an intimate, but he did show patience and
understanding to me for a quarter-century and some of his staff went out of
their way to tell me he had confided a feeling of friendship. If so, I am both
pleased and proud; for he was a great man and a singular one.

De Gaulle had an obviously justified reputation for using harsh, earthy
barracks language on occasion, but I never once heard this myself. With me
he always spoke exquisite, occasionally rather literary phrases. Although he
learned quite workable English during the war and kept reading that language, I never heard him use a word of it, not even Yes or No.

He also wrote magnificently. It is my feeling that his has been the best
French prose style since World War II, rivaled only by that of the late
Albert Camus and transcending that of his minister and friend, André
Malraux. It may be noted that the General always wrote his own speeches,
unusual in this age of ghosts. He is the only statesman with whom I
have talked who could easily and quite accurately quote Sophocles or
Goethe or Charles Péguy during the course of a routine chat.

Although he deliberately cultivated remoteness, solitude, and a disdainful
aspect, he at times showed compassion. He was always impeccably courteous and patient. Whenever I talked with this polite old man, he rose from
his desk and came forward to greet me with extended hand and similarly, at

the end, escorted me to the door with an affable farewell phrase. He always seemed to have time, or to make time, even in the midst of crises.

I have glanced through my notes of different meetings over the years and here recall some of my impressions of him.

(October, 1949): De Gaulle still talks of himself in conversation in the third person which certainly gives one an uncomfortable feeling of an autocrat. Whether he is by instinct a diffident dictator or an autocratic democrat is something impossible to judge.

(May, 1951): He was extremely gentle and courteous and forthright during our talk. He gave the impression of being less arrogant than during previous conversations we have had. He seemed older and tired. His face was gray and lined. He was wearing a double-breasted black suit, a white shirt and a black necktie. His headquarters at 5, rue de Solférino were bustling with activity. Dozens of RPF workers were wrapping up brochures and sending out letters. It certainly does not give the impression of being a wealthy organization. The furniture is rather ramshackle and the General's office is quite astonishingly simple and bare.

(January, 1954): The headquarters are, if anything, shabbier than ever before. Some of the lights don't work. The furniture is rickety. The General's office itself is spartan with a desk and a few not particularly comfortable chairs. De Gaulle has aged a great deal during the last year or two. He looks far more distinguished in civilian clothes than uniform, unlike most military men. He was, for him, about as informal as I suppose he ever gets. He offered cigarettes and told me to go ahead and take notes if I wanted to, even though he stressed that this was off the record, because (he said): "It is you and I have confidence in you."

(October, 1955): I was interested to look around the antechamber of his dilapidated and shabby office building. It is a gloomy little room with Chinese silk drawings on the walls, a model airplane strung up in one corner, a cross of Lorraine, a picture of de Gaulle with a pine branch across the top of the frame, an Arab sword in a leather scabbard, and a plaque of the Foreign Legion's golden book. Strange and rather sordid. When I went in to see the General he was as usual extremely friendly in his diffident way. He had on very thick, smoke-tinted glasses. His eyes, I know, have been bothering him a great deal. He looked considerably older again and drawn. But there was something more gentle in his face. His office is simply furnished. The desk is very neat with one or two papers carefully placed upon it. On the wall are two maps, one of France and one of de Gaulle's own native district. There were a few logs burning in the fireplace. The room is bare and has no carpet.

(May, 1956): De Gaulle impressed me more than ever by his arrogance, his obstinacy, his conceit, and his bitterness. Nevertheless, he surely does retain a certain quality. I don't know what it is, apart from the fact that he has a strange magnetic appeal and writes the best French of any living Frenchman.

(December, 1956): This afternoon I went over to General de Gaulle's headquarters and had a long talk with the General who is in town for a day or so. As usual, the office looked pretty seedy. But the faithful

Commandant Bonneval [Count—eventually General—de Bonneval, his loyal aide for years] was there, looking pale and harassed. He told me the General's eyes were now much better.

(July, 1957): I don't know if there is any significance to this but I must say the place [5, rue de Solférino] looked a bit less dilapidated today than it has for the last few years. They have a few colored photographs of the Riviera hanging along the staircase, which has actually been cleaned and waxed. De Gaulle has a couple of comfortable armchairs in his office. Bonneval as usual was extremely friendly and talkative. He said: "I want to warn you that the General is going to seem very negative to you and to pretend that he is not particularly interested in current affairs. But that is just a front." When I went in to see de Gaulle he was most amiable. He has mellowed quite a bit. He greeted me almost affectionately and asked me how my eyes were. I told him fine. He asked me what I had done to improve them. I told him I had changed my glasses. "Is that all," he chuckled quite merrily—for him. "Well, that wasn't much trouble. That wasn't very serious was it?"

(February, 1958): He is almost sixty-eight years old now and he is beginning to show it; but he is not exactly aged and decrepit. Behind a mild and withering exterior he is still the vigorous prophet of doom. . . . On leaving I remarked to de Gaulle that he seemed particularly pessimistic today. He said: *"Je ne vois pas les choses très gaies."*

(January, 1959): Good talk with de Gaulle, the first since he became President of the Republic. I saw him in the Elysée Palace, France's White House. He looked a bit pale and tired but much, much better than he appears in recent photographs. He was wearing a double-breasted gray flannel suit, a little rumpled, and his usual spectacles, and had a slight air of end-of-the-day fatigue. He came halfway to the door to greet me and then motioned me to a chair across from him before he sat down himself behind his desk. His office was warm and comfortable, with a red carpet, gilt-legged chair, a desk with gilt-metal work at the corners, high ceiling, high windows with long brocade curtains, and a view through the gardens toward the Champs-Elysées. The desk was more cluttered with papers than it used to be in the barren rue de Solférino. (Incidentally, Brouillet—his chef de cabinet—told me de Gaulle had never lived in the Elysée before he became President of the Fifth Republic. When Paris was liberated in 1944 he scrupulously avoided moving into the Elysée or the Matignon—where Prime Ministers reside—since he only headed a provisional government and did not wish to imply any kind of de facto take-over.)

I started off the conversation, as de Gaulle sat opposite me with somewhat the expression of an elongated owl, peering over his spectacles, by stating that both Brouillet and Bonneval had explained to me that de Gaulle wished to see me as an old friend but did not wish me to quote him on anything. "Yes," he replied, "I wanted to see you as a friend; but this is off the record." At the end, he rose and came to the door with me and, as he shook my hand and wished me well, he leaned over a bit and said in a somber voice, *"Rappelez-vous, je n'ai rien dit."*

(February, 1960): I found [de Gaulle] in excellent health and extremely talkative. He reminded me again that this was a conversation "*à titre privé*." I told him Brouillet had told me this but said I would like to ask him questions and take notes as I had done in the past. With a shadow of a smile, de Gaulle said: "I expected you to ask questions."

(February, 1961): He [de Gaulle] was in very good form and talked freely about everything. I sat across from him at his desk and exhausted my entire list of questions before he showed any interest in getting rid of me. As usual, I wrote down the answers and he was perfectly agreeable. When I had tucked my questions [as always typed on a separate sheet of paper] and notebook in my pocket, he spread out his long arms and said: "Well, how are you and how do you see things?" I said that I was pretty well personally but pretty unhappy about the world. He advised me not to be so sad because if people and nations had resolution they could face difficulties whatever they were.

(January, 1962): I have a strange feeling that conceivably this might be the last time I ever see him. [He was then under constant threat of assassination by the OAS.] And apart from my journalistic relations with him and my intellectual fascination for this strange character who does not belong to our era, I have genuine affection for him. Today he was not only particularly friendly but he was warm, extremely thoughtful, reminiscent, optimistic, fatalistic, and, above all, relaxed. In the past it has been my experience to find that although I prepared a large number of questions to ask him, at the end he always seemed to have time to spare and he would throw out his arms and say: *"Tiens. Qu'est-ce que vous pensez de la situation?"* Therefore I decided today not to risk running short on questions. I had thirty-eight to ask. He answered them all, patiently and amiably.

(January, 1963): He said he had noticed *The New York Times* had been hostile to him. I said I just wrote my own articles and my own opinions. "I know that," he said. "And I want to tell you once again how much I appreciate your book [*The Test: de Gaulle and Algeria*]." I then hauled out a massive list of questions, spread them out in front of me on his desk, and took out my notebook. He went through the usual old rigamarole and said: "Of course, this is not an interview." I said: "I understand but I would like to make use of this as usual and take notes." "*Allons-y,*" he said. He looked at me rather shrewdly and I was amused to see the reflection of his strangely small head looming in the mirror behind him, sort of seeing him from two angles at once.

(December, 1963): De Gaulle seemed active, healthy, and not at all tired. Physically he gave me the impression of being in better shape than last time. But just a tinge of his former courtly *politesse* and patient friendliness seemed lacking and he was clearly not in a very philosophic mood. There was just a faint something missing. I wondered if it might not be that his bitterness at the U.S. and his irritation with the press are taking somewhat of a hold on him.

I have tried in this summary to indicate the ambience of our conversations. He was always infinitely courteous, never wholly informal, usually exceptionally friendly. He seemed ready to discuss anything and it was very rare that he either dodged or refused to answer a question for reasons of discretion. I am not aware that he ever told me a lie. Practically every time we talked I took notes in front of him. As a consequence there could be no misunderstanding on this score and I retained a full and accurate record of his views. I discovered early that his conception of "off the record" was a bit flexible, and that he not only expected me to echo his views but was pleased when, from time to time, if rarely, I quoted one or another of his more striking phrases. During his last few years in the Elysée his audiences with me were mentioned in the official bulletin.

For me perhaps the most fascinating portion of this series of conversations dealt with the General's views on personalities, his own tastes, literature, philosophy, fate, and his own private plans. He never showed reticence when discussing such things and, indeed, I have been told by those who knew de Gaulle quite well that he enjoyed these discussions because few—if any—people ever raised such subjects. The interludes could conceivably have helped him escape from the terrible loneliness this sternly disciplined man had early imposed upon himself in order to accomplish his role.

During his political exile he devoted much time to reading, writing, and abstract thought. Thus, on November 10, 1954, I noted:

He told me he spends most of his time in Colombey-les-Deux-Eglises and comes to Paris once a fortnight at most. He is now writing the second volume of his memoirs. This will be ready by the end of next year. Then there will be a third volume which will deal with delicate and explosive French matters; but, says he: "I am going to write it anyway."

The General says writing comes very hard to him. He tries to do a regular stint of several hours a day. He writes in long hand in ink, and never dictates. I remarked to him that Churchill always dictated. He scoffed at this and said: "It shows. He has never written a properly composed book. There are just interesting observations and lots of documents."

(October 14, 1955): He says it takes him a long time to "compose" his books and the work is very difficult. He has reference material sent down to him at Colombey. He writes very slowly.

(December 12, 1956): De Gaulle told me that he was still working very hard on his book. It takes him two years to finish a volume. He works from three to four hours a day almost every day. He has a great deal of reading of documents to do and the job of condensation is immense.

(July 19, 1957): I must say he works very slowly. Of course he writes it all laboriously in his own handwriting. On the table in front of him were a series of pages which had been scribbled on in ink; many words were crossed out and changed.

De Gaulle never intended to continue his literary career after retiring from the Presidency. When I asked him (January 31, 1963) if he planned to write a fourth volume of his memoirs (which ultimately he did) he answered:

No definitely not. Not at all. You must remember that the other three volumes were *mémoires de guerre*. For the period since then, the period after that which I covered in those three volumes, history can speak for itself in facts and documents even if not through the press, which has been most distorted. But there were no such facts and documents really available for the period of the war and therefore I could not leave that tale untold. But I can assure you I will not write a fourth volume.

Another time (January 20, 1962) he assured me: "Retire, yes. Write another volume? No. Writing about the war, that was one thing. Now, that is another. Retire? Yes. But not another volume. Colombey? Yes. But not writing."

His cultural tastes were highly conventional; what you would expect of any well-educated Frenchman of his generation. Once when we were discussing music, I noted (January 20, 1962): "I was rather struck when putting the names in correlation by an apparent fondness for composers who reacted to the Napoleonic Wars." This is what he said:

I am very fond of music and in the evening I often listen to it, both on records and on the radio. Certainly I like Beethoven more than Mozart —although I can say I am surely fond of Schumann and Schubert. Also there are moments—I say moments—when I like Wagner. I must admit to a liking for nineteenth-century French music like Debussy and Delibes. Unfortunately I am not a musician. I am not a qualified judge. I love and I seek music. I crave music. But I am not creatively competent. My tastes are difficult to define.

I asked him if he had ever learned a musical instrument. He said he had studied piano while living at home until the age of sixteen but that he had made no headway. He had not continued afterward.

When I inquired whether any single person had particularly influenced his life, his character or his personality he replied:

I suppose it is something like music. No single individual. Many men took part. First of all, there was my father. He was a professor and he was very cultivated, very human. He contributed. He contributed much. Then, of course, looking through the past, there were many others. There were the Greeks, certainly, the classical Greeks. And then I suppose there were the Romans. There were the French classics. Above all, there were the tragedians—Corneille and Racine. And also, of course, Bossuet. There were all the French classicists who had grandeur. *Ça, c'est toujours mon gout.* [He became enthralled by the idea, I noted.] Foreigners [as if to include the Greeks and Romans among Frenchmen]? Yes, there is Goethe and Shakespeare. Shakespeare! What grandeur. What power.

I continued this interesting colloquy by observing I had heard that Henri Bergson, the philosopher, was a good friend of de Gaulle's father and that the General had known him as a young man. He commented:

No, he was not a friend, but he was great. Yes, indeed, Bergson also. And before him August Comte. Much of the world; yes, much of the world. But you must know that in history I always admired *les gens efficaces*. Like our history. Clovis. Charlemagne. Jeanne d'Arc. Charles VII. Henri IV. The real statesmen, the people who accomplished something. Napoleon—*bien sûr*. And among the living, the people who were alive when I was alive, surely Poincaré and Clemenceau.

My notes run on: "At this point I couldn't stop him. He was dreaming away in a thoughtful and rather moving fashion, looking out of the window at the bare trees in the Elysée garden on a humid, warm winter day, when the entire world was talking about the agony of France and the imminent possibility of disaster [because of the OAS insurrection]." He continued:

And in America your great Presidents. Surely your great Presidents. Jefferson. Above all Jefferson. And then there was Washington, a very great man. I have big admiration for him. And my contemporaries? Theodore Roosevelt. He was a brave man who never hesitated. And I admit to an admiration for Franklin Roosevelt despite the differences I had with him. He had the grand manner.

And the English? Among the English, Churchill is surely a great man. And the Germans? Bismarck was a real statesman. He did great harm to France but one cannot forget the fact that he was a real statesman, that he accomplished something.

Hitler? Hitler, no. Hitler, no! Because of his crimes. Not because of his nationalism. Because of his crimes I reject him.

On another occasion I again brought up the subject of Bergson whose theory of intuition so evidently influenced the General. He told me (January 31, 1963):

Bergson was not a friend of my father's, but my father admired him very much. You probably know that my father was a professor of philosophy. And he did know Bergson. I even saw Bergson myself in my youth and I deeply admired him. In fact, I was much influenced by Bergson, particularly because he made me understand the philosophy of action.

Bergson explains the role of intelligence and analysis. He saw how necessary it is to analyze questions in search of the truth. But intellect alone cannot act. The intelligent man does not automatically become the man of action. Instinct is also important. Instinct plus impulse; but impulse is also not sufficient as a basis for action. The two, intellect and impulse, must go together.

Bergson showed me that action comes from the combination, the combined application of intellect and instinct, working together. All my life I have been aware of this essentially important explanation. Pure intellect cannot by itself produce action and impulse can produce folly if it alone serves as a guide, whether in politics or in military affairs.

The two must be linked and this is Bergson's theory of intuition. The great men have both intellect and impulse. The brain serves as a brake upon pure emotional impulse. The brain surmounts impulse; but there also must be impulse and the capability for action in order not to be paralyzed by the brake of the brain. I remember this from Bergson who has led me here in my entire life.

But surely you will agree with me that philosophy has never changed anyone. Men are still what they are. Philosophy helps them to express themselves better and to understand each other better, but no man has even been *created* a philosopher.

Throughout his long life de Gaulle was preoccupied with the impact of individual personalities upon history and he took careful pains to shape his own personality so that it could have maximum effect when its moment came. His view of contemporaries was always fascinating and he expressed frank opinions to me on many world leaders. Thus:

(January 21, 1954): I like Eisenhower. But he is not a giant. Giants can do nothing now. Churchill is the only survivor. Roosevelt is dead. Stalin died—too late. This is the epoch of Malenkov, Fanfani, and Queuille [a wonderfully mellifluous trio of nonentities].

On July 19, 1957, I asked him what he thought of Khrushchev. He said:

I have never [at that time] met him, but it is apparent he is only a politician. He is not a big man, like Stalin. He is a little man who makes speeches. His speeches are rather good, but so are the speeches of many politicians.

I then asked him if Stalin had really impressed him as being a big man when he met him during the war.

Yes, undoubtedly. He was certainly a big man. Of course he tried to be affable and almost charming. But even that was merely an exterior. And sometimes he didn't even show that. He was a grand figure, a tyrant, a real czar. He controlled everything. He had absolute authority and absolute confidence. He did everything himself. Yes, there is no doubt that he was a great man.

I asked him if he had met any other men of similar stature or if he thought any other similarly "great men" had existed during his time. He said yes; he said Churchill was a great man "during the war years. Not before the war and not after the war; but during the war he was a great man, despite certain deficiencies."

He then went back to his old theory that there are no longer any giants. And he saw none on the horizon. He said that now we had an era of Eisenhower, Macmillan, and Khrushchev. I reminded him of his phrase, used three years before, that "The age of giants is over; this is the epoch of Malenkov, Fanfani, and Queuille." I remarked to de Gaulle that I thought his original phrase had been somewhat more euphonious. He seemed to miss the point. At any rate he wasn't at all amused.

Incidentally—and I almost forgot this—de Gaulle said one thing of interest this time during our discussion of the absence of "giants" from the present political scene. He said this fact indicated a real détente in the world situation because it is only in times of crisis that nations throw up "giants." They don't come in normal times. Thus, for example, his statement that he did not consider either the prewar or the postwar Churchill a "giant." I wonder if he refers at least subconsciously to himself in this analysis, and therefore does not seem to give himself much chance of returning to power.

That was but ten months before he staged his come-back. After that event I returned to the subject of giants.

On January 31, 1959, I reminded him that after Stalin's death he had explained that the world situation was then against the return of dominating figures. I remarked that now that he was back in power, I wondered if the world situation had changed and whether he foresaw a new age of giants. He said:

I don't know. I suppose that depends upon the world situation. When that situation is grave the giants come nearer to a return.

Also, you must remember, people grow in stature. One speaks of giants when it is all over. Sophocles said that one must wait until the evening to see how splendid the day was; that one cannot judge life until death.

On January 20, 1962, after he had met Khrushchev, I again asked him if—as a man who had had the privilege of knowing the great men of our time—he thought Khrushchev was a big man. What did he think of Khrushchev? He said:

I don't know. You cannot judge a man except in the light of achievement. When Khrushchev has achieved something I shall tell you. I can only give you the answer then. No man can finally be judged except in the light of achievement.

Stalin was a great man. He did something. He was a brutal man, but he created a modern state. Churchill was a great man. He forged a victory. And Franklin Roosevelt was a great man; although, as you know so well, I had many differences with him. He led the United States into war and through the war on to victory. He was a man of quality.

To be a great man, one must realize something. One must achieve something definite. If Khrushchev can achieve peace, he will be a great man. Or if he seeks war and can win a war he will be a great man. But if he does neither, he will not be a great man.

As for John F. Kennedy (December 12, 1963—quoted *in extenso* at the end of this book), the General observed with sad acuity, after returning from his funeral and in the midst of the emotional torrents of a world hysterical with grief: "History will probably say that he was a man of great ability who lacked the time to prove himself."

HOW TO START

A COLUMN

NEW YORK, *September 27, 1954*

LONG TALK WITH CABOT LODGE TODAY—THE FIRST TOUR D'HORIZON I've had since he was named ambassador to the United Nations a couple of years ago.

Lodge complains that the United States cannot be put in the position of having everybody expect us to be "an international Miss Fix-it." It is impossible to get an absolutely pat formula on colonialism. The issue of Cyprus is quite different from that of Western New Guinea, where a backward people's future is affected and where it must be considered whether they can be best advanced by Dutch or Indonesian rule. He intrudes the argument: "How about colonial peoples subject to the Soviet Union such as the Kazakhs and the Uzbeks?"

He describes our present policy on colonialism as: "We favor national independence for all peoples providing they are not engulfed by communism." However, he adds that since January, 1953, when he joined the executive branch of the American government, there has been no overall policy on colonialism. Each issue has been faced as it arose.

The Republican administration takes the view that the UN is far less a vehicle designed to go to heaven than merely a method preventing you from going to hell. The Truman administration, having inherited San Francisco, regarded the UN strictly as what it was intended to be—an idealistic and ideal organization. We take it as what it really is. . . . We recognize world opinion is an enormous force, and so we are using the Assembly as a forum and a propaganda sounding-board. We are using the United Nations for what it is. We are not condemning it completely because the Security Council has been hamstrung by vetoes. Thus, for example, I always reply to a Communist speech on the same day it is made in order to grab the headlines away in the world press.

I asked what U.S. policy was on coexistence. He replied that he disliked the word, which was too negative. It certainly wasn't true that you must have either coexistence or war, as Attlee says. Lodge claims we are in competition with the Soviet system and coexistence implies acceptance of a peaceful state. He thinks we must be much more active and in constant opposition to communism, economically, politically, and in propaganda, fighting it out with the Soviet system by all these methods.

We are certainly not at peace in a sense that we can demobilize, but it is probable that we will never again be in such a blissful state. Lodge thinks it is impossible for the United States to define its own idea of "coexistence," and to lay down terms under which this could be applied. The Russians are always taking over countries by subversion and we must continually try to press forward countersubversion. He concluded that we are now neither at peace nor at war in the old-fashioned sense.

I asked Lodge if he thought the UN was now to be doomed as a complete failure. He replied that it had been oversold by its founders. It is impossible to have an "automatic war-preventor peace-producer." Lodge thought the United Nations was "doing damned well if it works as an automatic burglar alarm." He went on to draw the following comparisons. When the Wright brothers had flown their first airplane, it only rose a few inches and flew a few seconds. But the airplane wasn't condemned and torn apart as a result. Instead it was improved until it could fly better. This is what must be done with the UN.

NEW YORK, *September 28, 1954*

LUNCH today with Admiral Strauss, head of the Atomic Energy Commission. He claims Oppenheimer and his lawyers hired special public-relations counsel to use the press in the famous Oppenheimer case. Strauss said he received the President's top-secret letter that was distributed to the heads of the AEC, Defense Department, National Security Council, and a few other top agencies, removing Oppenheimer from the list of those to whom classified documents were accessible, the very morning of the day he left with Eisenhower for Bermuda.

Turning to the other subjects, Strauss said he suspected the British were making convenient use of the theory that there was no point in England participating in any alliance since it could be wiped out by a single bomb; therefore British policy should be one of neutrality. He thought Churchill, through his deafness, might have misunderstood when it had been explained that radioactive ash from the hydrogen bomb had fallen two hundred miles away. As a matter of fact, this ash wasn't terribly dangerous, and anyway it was part of a cigar-shaped pattern, with the extreme end two hundred miles distant, blown there by the wind. Churchill managed to reinterpret this by taking a compass, putting its point in the heart of the British Isles, and then swinging it in a two-hundred-mile arc in all directions, indicating Britain could be destroyed. This wasn't actually the case, Strauss thought. However, he wondered if it would not be a good idea to withdraw many of our bases from abroad so as not to provoke fears of attack among reluctant allies.

Strauss thinks that when many small as well as large nations have atomic weapons, a completely new attitude toward security policies will be required. No nation, no matter how powerful, would then be able to launch an unprovoked, surprise attack on any other single nation because in order to obtain world supremacy and win a war, the aggressor nation would have to destroy everybody else. In other words, the day may soon come when the atom bomb is as much of an "equalizer" as the revolver was between big and little men when it first came into play along the U.S. western frontier.

NEW YORK, *October 1, 1954*

DINED last night with Gastone Guidotti, Italian observer at the UN with rank of ambassador. He surprised me by saying Clare Luce was the best ambassador the United States had ever had in Rome. "She is the first member of your politburo you have sent us. She can call the White House to get things done."

NEW YORK, *October 5, 1954*

THIS morning I had a satisfactory talk with Dag Hammarskjöld, Secretary-General of the United Nations. He was extremely friendly, self-assured, and perfectly willing to talk; in fact, he is a bit too long-winded and takes a long time to get to the point.

Hammarskjöld said that when he became Secretary-General he considered he had completely dropped his national passport as a Swede. A country of origin does not exist either for himself or for other international UN servants. But one cannot change one's heritage or personality. The political training he received naturally had a special flavor and derived from a background with a certain tradition which, despite Sweden's so-called neutrality, was extremely western—"more western than that of certain other nations in the West," he added.

Hammarskjöld thinks his two primary obligations are to analyze all problems in a detached manner, and to interpret the Charter in the best way to help humanity. The Secretary-General has a very special position. Every nation, in principle, consults with him. No countries have a "minister for human affairs," but in a sense they all share an interest in one—namely, the Secretary-General of the UN. It is a duty to advise nations in terms of human interest.

Regarding the loyalties of his staff, he repeated that he considered himself completely denationalized aside from blood and traditions and that this was his view concerning the position of his staff. For example, if an American or a Russian working in the UN could not free himself from a bias in terms of his own nation's interests, they became less useful. If they sought to influence UN actions along lines of partiality, he was forced to ban such efforts. Nevertheless, he expected every man in private to retain his sentiments of patriotism.

He did not think present American "loyalty" concepts necessarily conflicted with these views. A man who is patently disloyal to his country lacks integrity, and therefore is of no use to an international body. If a man is regarded as an enemy by his own country because of his own *intellectual* views—either in the United States or the Soviet Union, for example—it does not necessarily constitute the type of disloyalty to his country to which he was referring. He could imagine a man in the United States having intellectual sympathy with Communist philosophy and still not being disloyal to his country; thereby retaining his integrity as a UN servant. There are two entirely different concepts of loyalty; but a basic lack of loyalty to one's own country would be a serious disqualification. Political dissenters of any sort cannot be permitted to let their beliefs influence their national attitudes in the UN.

There is no right of asylum in the UN, either in the sense that church buildings could grant asylum during the Middle Ages, or in the sense of international extraterritoriality. After all, who could negotiate such questions of asylum or of extradition for the United Nations, which lacks the machinery for such. He asked: "Could the Secretary-General negotiate such an agreement with the United States when, after all, he is partly employed by the United States?" The UN office was international territory but without sovereignty. If a crime occurs there, the police cannot come in until they are invited in—but this is immediately done.

I asked if he didn't think the UN was seriously handicapped because its members ignored the body's decisions whenever they ran counter to individual national interests of their own. Hammarskjöld said the mere existence of the United Nations exerted a pressure in the right direction. After all, he said, it is harder to behave badly in the public marketplace than in the privacy of your own home, and public discussion focused world attention on national attitudes.

This afternoon I ran into Selim Sarper at the UN. He is now permanent Turkish representative here, all hot and bothered about Cyprus. It has already wrecked the Greco-Turkish alliance and the Balkan entente. The British, of course, will not give up Cyprus, but even if they intended to do so the Turks wouldn't permit them. Two divisions of Turkish troops could be moved into Cyprus "by rowboat" across the straits within a few hours if necessary. Sarper is generally moderate so this kind of talk indicated how bad things now are. He believes Moscow is deliberately encouraging Communist activity in Cyprus in order to promote trouble among the Allies.

Talk with Selwyn Lloyd, minister of state and head of the British delegation to the UN. Lloyd is a Tory lawyer and very smooth. I have a feeling he is a bit too self-confident and thinks his bland double-talk is accepted at face value. He is certainly clever, but imagines himself more clever than is actually the case.

Lloyd developed the idea that the United States had a natural priority in leadership in Korea, Formosa, and perhaps Japan. Likewise, Britain had a priority among the Colombo powers—above all, Ceylon, India, and Burma. This concept of sharing spheres of influence in terms of diplomatic leadership is very traditional for London.

I inquired whether Lloyd thought there had been a basic change from the Democratic "containment" policy to a Republican "liberation" policy. He said this was mainly a matter of party politics. When the British Conservatives were in opposition, they shouted "scuttle" whenever the Labour government gave anything away. But when the Tories came back to power, they had to "work" the India settlement. The same thing applied over here in terms of "liberation" and the argument over that word. What a party says in opposition is no clue to what it is going to do when it's in government— with all the facts at its disposal.

Lloyd said that in the realm of trade and tariffs "there *is* a difference in policy." He reflected: "It would be hard to imagine a Republican Marshall Plan." He believed that the President and the Secretary of State favored good credits and free trade, but it was difficult for them to implement this.

Lloyd strongly denied that Britain ever engaged in vote-trading in the UN. He said: "We never bargain that way." He observed that it would be too dangerous if one was caught. He added: "Votes cannot be bought because there are too many votes. Britain simply doesn't have enough to give. If everybody started asking for a price before they voted with Britain, the bank would go bust. It would encourage blackmail."

WASHINGTON, *October 8, 1954*

THIS afternoon I had a very interesting talk with Foster Dulles. I must say, he shows physical signs of strain. He looks his full age (sixty-six); the twitch he always has in his left eye is more pronounced; he has lost a bit of weight, but his jowl seems to hang. He has the appearance of a tired man and a slightly unnatural flush.

I told him that I was going to begin writing a column and wanted to launch it with an article quoting him. He was very reluctant, but I reminded him that he owed me a debt for the article I held back at his request in May, 1952, saying he would be Eisenhower's Secretary of State. He then started off somewhat hesitantly, but he soon relaxed and, as it were, dove in.

I asked if he thought it possible to arrange terms for coexistence between the United States and Russia. He replied:

I take a somewhat philosophical approach to this question, just as the Soviet leaders do. With their materialistic approach to problems, coexistence means to them merely physical coexistence in the sense that everybody would be alive together in the world at the same time and following a particular pattern. Their idea of coexistence is to have a completely ordered universe, patterned completely according to a harmony set in terms of total conformity. Everybody and every nation would move in a fixed orbit the way planets do. I can understand what they mean from a purely materialistic point of view.

But we believe in a spiritual view of the world. We believe in a world that is governed by more than material things. People are entitled to their individual beliefs in their own minds and to their individual spiritual faiths and loyalties. The differences of their opinions not only represent the theory of freedom, but they are a source of richness in themselves. This is the exact reverse of the conformity desired by the Russians. Such conformity breeds sterility, whereas individual differences in thought breed freedom.

The Russians do not and cannot admit that type of coexistence which is basically contrary to their own fanatical beliefs. When we are talking about coexistence, we are talking about something entirely different from the Russians. I can give you an example of this. When I spoke to Molotov at Berlin earlier this year, I asked him why he wasn't prepared to give the Germans their independence the way we granted independence to Japan. Molotov said he didn't trust them and that they could not be relied upon. Freedom would be dangerous for them because the Germans have already shown in the past how they abuse it. The Russians mistrust freedom. There is a basic philosophical difference between their conception and our conception of coexistence.

This doesn't mean that you do not and cannot settle matters. It is, of course, necessary for nations to adjust themselves and make compromises on international problems. We can coexist with the Russians under our own system as long as we don't abandon basic principles in the sense that we can live together at the same time. That kind of coexistence is possible, but always on a limited and provisional basis. We must recognize that our two systems are inherently incompatible. In this, Lenin was quite right. Lenin said that the capitalist world and the Communist world could not exist indefinitely side by side; that one or the other must win. This, of course, does not mean that war is inevitable, nor does it exclude provisional settlements.

However, Molotov seems to think of coexistence in terms of wanting to order the world along lines of enforced conformity and according to certain agreed, fixed principles. I could never agree to coexistence based

upon a deal, for example, permitting the Poles and the Czechs to stay
under Russia in exchange for benefits to the United States. I do agree
that we should not go to war to free the Czechs and the Poles. War
produces more evils than the evils you are trying to eradicate. But I don't
believe in a form of coexistence surrendering the basic rights of other
human beings in order to procure advantages for ourselves.

Nor do I believe that the Russians would live up to any such agreement for coexistence any more than they lived up to the Litvinov agreement not to support communism in America. Likewise we could never
agree, for example, not to let Christians send missions abroad. There are
some things that people believe in too strongly for governments to stop.
This is, of course, true not only of our Christians, but also of Communists. Even if the Russians formally abandoned communism abroad, the
Communists themselves are fanatical believers.

I asked Dulles if he thought the foreign policy of this Republican administration differed from its Democratic predecessor, and, if so, how. He replied by referring to George Kennan's last book which deals with this point.
He said Kennan argues that morality has no place in the conduct of foreign
affairs.

He argues in terms of expediency for the sake of the individual nation.
I don't share this view at all. As a matter of fact, this was one of the
reasons I wasn't anxious to have Kennan stay on in the service. Kennan
was Acheson's principal advisor. Under his thesis you would be justified,
for example, in making any deal affecting the Poles or the Czechs if you
could gain in exchange for the interests of the United States. This is not
in accordance with American foreign policy. It is not in accordance with
the principles of the Declaration of Independence which states that *all*
men have certain inalienable rights.

Everybody howls because we have not yet liberated the Poles, Czechs,
and other enslaved peoples. But it takes years to do these things. One
thing we have refrained from doing is anything that would condone or
put the mark of approval on enslavement. One of our great troubles
undoubtedly is a reluctance to undertake anything if it doesn't show
results by the next election. It takes years to accomplish policy objectives. I think this realization and this approach show a vast difference
between our policy and that which we inherited.

As far as the actual transaction of business goes, this administration
has shown greater patience, competence, and resourcefulness in getting
problems solved. I would like to point out that we have settled many of
the problems we inherited such as Iran, Egypt [1970—how odd that
rings!], and Trieste. Our objectives are often the same as those of the
Democratic administration. But I think our planning is better.

A great many people have argued in the past that the two great wars
came partly because the United States did not state clearly in advance the
principles for which it would fight. It claimed that Germany would not
have moved in either case had she known that the United States was

prepared to take action. The great weakness in the past was in our not stating clearly where we would stand. Perhaps it could be said the Korean war would have been prevented had we done so.

But if you want to wait until the last minute to decide what would be expedient, you cannot state principles in advance. President Wilson at first was much influenced by Bryan's extreme pacifism when Bryan was Secretary of State, although later his belief in his principles triumphed. We are trying to make it reasonably clear that there are certain issues on which we would fight rather than give in. We hope that this expressed attitude can keep the peace. The other system did not work; maybe this one will. In the past the United States has been criticized for not making clear in advance its basic position. Now that we are doing so some people charge us with being warmongers.

The conversation rambled off considerably at this point, but several times Dulles observed that he considered Soviet communism the most powerful fanatic movement and the most menacing since the spread of Islam in the seventh century.

WASHINGTON, *October 14, 1954*

THIS morning I had an excellent discussion with Dean Acheson at his law office. I wanted a precise comparison of his views with Foster Dulles's. Acheson was in his best form, relaxed, talkative, thoughtful, and considerate.

We started off with an analysis of coexistence. On this Acheson said:

Coexistence is not different from "peace" as a word. But the problem is different. The phrase is "peaceful coexistence." This is a flabby and unrevealing phrase. Really, one might call it "competitive coexistence." The world has seen something develop that is not explained solely by the development of the Soviet Union—which has upset the balance of power. More than that is involved. It is more than a question of differing ideologies. Now we are faced with a direct challenge to all the values of civilization. These values are moral, spiritual, and ethical. They have been the underlying element of society and civilization for hundreds of years. Now they are called nonsense by this new system. That challenge is perhaps more important than the challenge of the Soviet state.

The truth of the most fundamental beliefs of the free world is now denied—not merely in propaganda—but in fact. They deny the goodness of truth. They regard everything as an instrument. They want only to produce results. There are no basic values—like the individual human spirit—important to them. They see as fundamental their immediate objectives. And they twist the human spirit by the will of the state.

Such a challenge has two sides—the vigor and strength of both the challenger and the defender. Is our civilization strong enough and vigorous enough to resist? No. Our civilization must reinvigorate itself.

Behind the new barbarism is a combination of a powerful state and its allies plus a powerful doctrine. In the light of this, we must examine coexistence. It is a little bit more than working out an adjustment between two competing systems. Coexistence has various sides—political, military, and moral. This is a matter of moral strength. We must build up economic and military cohesion. But we must translate our moral beliefs into practical expression. McCarthyism and totalitarianism challenge here and undermine our moral worth. These challenges occur both within the country and within the individual. McCarthyism denies the truth of ourselves and of our country. It undermines us in the world's concept. Other people are losing faith in us.

The security system of the United States is sowing fear and mistrust. The same undermining, unless this trend is checked, will affect our universities, our churches, our labor unions, and our families. In twenty years it could bring a complete change in the intellectual, spiritual, and moral values of the American people. Is what we call Athens now the same that was Athens in Pericles' age? Only the name is the same. And that same comparison may someday be made for us unless we awaken to our moral responsibilities.

This part of the problem of coexistence is merely a portion of it. What is coexisting? We must maintain western civilization while in the same world there exists a new barbarism that cannot be confined to the distant reaches as in the days of the Romans. We must have a rebirth in ourselves and in our ideals. There are two other possibilities in theory. One is to eradicate the challenge—and impress our own image on the world. That means, of course, preventive war. We cannot do this. We are not strong enough. We would destroy ourselves and everyone in the process and we would end up by accepting the imprint of the enemy. The world would arise from the ruins a totalitarian world. The other possibility is to withdraw. We might argue that our allies are weak and so forth. But we cannot withdraw into ourselves. We are trying to defend a civilization and that very civilization would be lost if we gave it up. By the process of elimination we must accept coexistence. We must live through it without destroying ourselves and others.

It *can* be done. But it is very difficult. And this is a competitive affair, competitive coexistence. It is like two cabbages in a field that exist if they are not planted too close together.

When Islam rose and the Roman Empire fell, Europe went back to a more primitive order. There was no state, no administration or law such as there had been under Rome. The Mediterranean, heart of the Roman Empire, came under Islam. For almost one thousand years Europe was slowly bringing itself back to the conception of civilized life as under the Roman Empire.

It is perhaps not thoroughly valid to compare the coexistence between the Christian and Islamic worlds during that period. There is more nourishment in comparing the period of the seventeenth and eighteenth centuries in Europe between the religious wars and the French revolution. The religious wars were held in an atmosphere like that sought by the advocates of preventive war today. They had a total objective: To destroy states and to destroy all believers in another faith. Everyone sank back in the ruins when these wars were over—like they might do after an atomic war. Following that chaos there was a general return to limited objectives —no longer total objectives such as all or nothing. But the French revolution again changed that. The idea of the Directory was again total: To push to the ultimate, to take over all of Europe.

We and the Russians must recognize that we *do* have a capacity to destroy each other. We also must recognize that China is a pretty ominous thing. The Russians must be aware that if they get into a dogfight with us, their Chinese neighbors might inherit the earth.

There is no particular formula for coexistence. But to keep our balance we must continue to build strength internally. As a balance of strength is established the Russians will recognize the fact and adjust themselves to it.

The Russians are not quite realists. The difficulty is they believe their own doctrine enough to color whatever they see and thus warp or tint realities. Thus they often deduce wrong conclusions; but the Russians seem to be adjusting themselves more realistically today.

I wondered what Acheson considered the basic differences between the foreign policy of the Republican administration and the previous Democratic administration. He said:

There is no difference in essential philosophy. They are not different in what they would like to do—reducing taxes, expenditures, and the military establishment. They say the same words—but the music is different. They can't achieve the same objective. The idea, of Eisenhower, Dulles, and others, that you could appease the extreme isolationist wing of the Republican party was false and impossible. You do just enough to please them and hurt the overall program at the same time.

The net result is to please Senator Knowland in Asia and frighten the allies in Europe. But Knowland is not really pleased. Likewise, Senator McCarthy may seemingly be pacified by burning books—but McCarthy remains just as hostile as ever, and our respect in the world has been undermined. This is bad judgment—not just a different philosophy of a different administration. The essential objectives have remained the same under both parties. But in foreign policy the means are more important than the ends. The means in foreign policy are always limited and become ends. If wishes were horses, beggars would ride.

We then turned to an analysis of Eisenhower's technique as President. Acheson said: "The President is a man and not a committee and he must determine the quality of a foreign policy. But Ike by nature is a composer of difficulties, not a vigorous decider. He regards himself as a sort of board chairman. But the President must use all his powers to get things done—to escape from logrolling tactics."

Acheson objected to the slogans now being employed. He said the concept of containment associated with his foreign policy was "to do our best to prevent the extension of the Soviet system." He said the slogan of liberation was dangerous because we are issuing a check we cannot cash. "An example of this was the riots in East Berlin. They took place, but nothing happened; that is to say, we were unable to do anything. The people involved felt as if they had been sold down the river. Liberation therefore is a phrase without meaning—except a dangerous meaning. The policy of the Republicans is really not different—only the words."

I asked what Acheson considered to be American policy on diplomatic recognition of foreign states—with particular reference to the impasse over China these days. He replied:

> We have a clear policy, but we always shy off at the wrong moment. And whenever we pretend to have a different policy it is costly. It was silly not to recognize the Soviet Union for twenty years. Likewise, it was silly not to recognize Peron. We get stuck every time.
>
> In China we must be realistic. There were three points always deemed necessary to meet prior to the act of recognition—which is not actually an act of real importance. We must certainly straighten out and protect our interest in Formosa. Otherwise we will be in an awkward position. We would be at a disadvantage if we recognize Communist China and agree to have her in the United Nations and if we are at the same time in a position of defending a rebellion against the constituted authority of China—by Formosa. We are going to have to recognize China someday. Our three points of basic discord have been Korea, Indochina, and Formosa. Korea and Indochina, for better or worse, are no longer points at issue. The sole remaining point is now Formosa.
>
> Pan-American conferences have shown the trend on this issue of recognition. The rules were quite clear there. There were three tests for an authentic government: Does the government seeking recognition in fact exercise effective control in the country? Is there some degree of acquiescence by the people of the country for the control of that government. (If the people are prepared to fight against that government rather than to accept it, the answer of course is no.) The third point is: Does the government prepare to recognize and carry out the international responsibilities of the particular nation? These tests were supposed to exclude whether you like or dislike a government. This has always been the doctrine of the United States—except when we have departed from it.

WASHINGTON, *October 15, 1954*

THIS morning I went over to State to see Scott McLeod, the much-debated young man in charge of the department's security program. I found McLeod youthful, heavyset, with ruddy face and glasses. He has hair clipped short and an agreeable manner. He is definitely bright and knows how to make himself charming. During our conversation we were interrupted several times by telephone calls. I used the intermissions to wander around his office and look at his gallery of signed photographs. Among them I saw signed pictures from McCarthy, Dirksen, Bridges, and Jenner. I also saw one from Eisenhower, the only picture inscribed by Ike I have ever seen that did not say "from his friend."

McLeod, whom I tackled on the subject of morale, said it was difficult to pin down as a factor. He admitted that he was sure "we have done things that can be regarded as inept" in the effort to tighten up security. He said: "In any change of command there is uncertainty about the future and this is damaging to individual morale." When the Republicans took over from the Democrats, the employees of the government felt just as uncertain about the change in management as the employees of Montgomery Ward feel now that it is being taken over by new management. For twenty years the government and its employees have had one kind of leadership, and it was replaced by a new type which had ridden into office on "a cleanup crusade." Naturally this very factor disturbed thousands of people and there was a period of uneasiness, alarm, and low morale all over when McLeod moved into the State Department.

In this atmosphere a security check was started under the President's security order. Everybody knows his own personal history and people with good personal and private records had no reason to be nervous. Nevertheless, the whole question of security of federal employees was a relatively new factor in our history—at least at times when the country wasn't at war. We had never had a Cold War situation before. The idea of the disloyal employee had never been thought of.

During the Cold War we have developed awareness of this problem. In April, 1947, President Truman issued his first loyalty order. This provided for a loose screening system. Some people were discharged as disloyal or bad risks. The order was amended in 1949 and 1951. Each time the mesh of the screen was made finer. Each time employees had to be passed through this new screen. Of course, this whole business of rescreening created a morale problem. However, McLeod observed: "In the security trade it is hard for us to feel sorry for any person who by his own actions feels guilty and therefore has a bad morale because of his record. Why should we be concerned? What can we do about it?" McLeod said homosexuals were not considered security risks until 1949–1951. When the government decided to fire them, morale again deteriorated.

McLeod said that when he worked for the FBI, he investigated applicants for FBI jobs, and when doing so, he used to think: "Would I like him to be behind a tree with me in a gun fight? You get pretty high standards if you think along such lines, and that's the way I like to think in these investigations."

This afternoon I went over to the Pentagon for a talk with Admiral Radford, chairman of the Joint Chiefs of Staff. He was extremely courteous and friendly in his cold and emotionless way, but he scares the hell out of me. He's the American equivalent of the Soviet mechanical man. Later at lunch, Eugene Meyer and Phil Graham of the *Washington Post* told me they thought he was brilliant—"although he doesn't read." Personally, I think that's a non sequitur. I think one of the most dangerous things at Radford's disposal is the collection of quotations of Soviet leaders which circulates around Washington and which provides an easy answer on any subject to those who have never taken the trouble even to read a kindergarten study of Marxism.

I asked what Radford thought were the chances of working out a system of peaceful coexistence. He replied that based on the public writings of the Soviet leaders they will coexist only until they are ready to strike us. Their objective remains conquest of the world, and they have never deviated from this. This does not necessarily mean armed conflict—provided that we are willing to give in. But if we don't give in, it does. He said the leading Communists such as Lenin and Stalin have predicted the inevitability of armed conflict and the pattern of their armed forces today indicates they still believe this. Unless there is a change in this pattern, we cannot assume anything else about the intentions of Soviet leaders.

I recalled the Soviet leaders were all keen students of Clausewitz, starting with Lenin. Bearing this in mind, did he think that the Russians were perhaps expanding the Clausewitz theory and carrying out a cold war as policy implemented by other means. He replied that the Russians are able to conduct offensives during a period of so-called peace that are just as disastrous as military offensives. He referred particularly to economic and propaganda offensives. Even Clausewitz was a kindergarten student compared with Soviet leaders. Radford said:

> We have tried to coordinate counteroffensives in this field—but without much success. What is needed to do this is close cooperation. The Russians direct the Soviet bloc with one man at the controls. Our counteroffensives are directed and controlled by a number of nations. It is physically impossible for a group to act with the same efficiency and unanimity as one man.

Radford considered that we were now in a state of war—only without shooting. A military solution will come "only when the Russians are convinced that their other offensives have failed." In other words, if you follow Radford's thinking to its logical conclusion, the moment we begin to win the Cold War the Russians will start a hot war.

I asked how it was possible to decide when a war should be kept limited, as in Korea, or when it should be made unlimited and, in other words, total. (I particularly asked this question because he is the man who, by interfering at Dien Bien Phu, wanted to turn the Indochina conflict into an all-out war with China). He replied: "Our tendency is to limit wars. But we must be careful not to limit them as in Korea to such an extent that we cannot win them. At any time a little war starts we must recognize that the Russians have already calculated the risk that it may explode into a big war."

WASHINGTON, *October 19, 1954*

I SPENT two and a half hours in the White House seeing the Eisenhowers. It started off when I visited Mamie with Marina. We went up to the second floor—the private apartments—and she took us on a big sightseeing trip. Mamie was sitting in her study writing letters with the television set on beside her and three hillbillies blaring away. She was wearing a pink negligee and looked exceptionally young and fit. She embraced us and chatted away merrily. She said their holiday in Denver had been a real vacation; she had just stayed at home and had seen no one. She showed us through the rooms one by one. I noticed they still share a double bed. There were a couple of paperback "westerns" on the night table at the President's side. Mamie had been reading a Steinbeck collection and a book on Father Divine.

She showed us a model of their Gettysburg farm. Mamie and Ike have agreed that she will be complete boss on decorating the inside of the house and he can do whatever he wants to the outside. She also took us into the oval trophy room where we saw the President's foreign decorations. These included the Ethiopian Order of the Queen of Sheba; a Greek decoration supposedly containing a sliver of the true cross; a ruby ring from Mexico contained in a brass jewel box brought over by Cortez; and signed portraits from Haile Selassie and his empress inscribed to "President Aisenhower."

As we were standing in Abe Lincoln's bedroom an envoy came up from downstairs to tell me the President was waiting. So I rushed down to Bob Schulz (now a full colonel). He took me to the inner office and in a moment I was with the President.

Ike's study didn't seem changed from when I saw it last November, but Eisenhower is showing visible signs of strain. He looks markedly older and his face and neck show new lines and signs of worry. Worse than that, I found the strain seemed to be affecting his personality. Although he couldn't have been friendlier, his mind seemed to wander and his conversation strayed curiously. Twice he got up to mix some kind of powder with ice water, stir it, and drink it—obviously for his digestive system.

He was wearing a brown suit and tie. He strode up and down restlessly, but when I suggested after forty minutes that I should go, he went right on talking and kept me there another quarter of an hour. He was very distracted by something; kept referring to this being a "bitch of a day"; referred to "all those damned son-of-a-bitch politicians" (meaning his Republican colleagues now running for election). When I told Ike I had a new job and would be writing a column, he looked rather blank, expressed the mildest of interest, and remarked, "Well, that should be interesting; a new type of work, I suppose." The only thing he talked spiritedly about was golf.

Eventually I got him talking on foreign policy. He said he was proud of the record in Iran, where "we virtually carried the ball alone"; Egypt, where we were "most responsible for a settlement"; Trieste and Guatemala, where we "accomplished a victory without losing friends." On the whole he had gotten through his objectives. His party had now come to realize that he meant what he said and was a man of his word—which is why he fought with them often.

The "damned politicians" didn't remember that the victory in 1952 had been won by a combination of three factors—resentment at the Democratic administration; the Republican platform; and "a certain amount of popularity of Dick Nixon and myself." Now, the first point didn't apply "because nobody resents an administration that's out of office." And all of a sudden the politicians were running to him for help in the election. He didn't seem happy about giving it to them. He cursed the fact that Saturday he has to go to Pennsylvania "so every god-damned Republican congressman there can come and be photographed with me." He said many congressmen had relaxed and boasted of their victory in 1952. He warned them victory wasn't achieved; it was only the start. They had to carry out their promises. But they had relaxed. Now they were hollering for help. When they came in 1952, they were horrified to find there was no more patronage available. "The Democrats had been in for twenty years, and they put everybody into the civil service so the Republicans couldn't get them out again."

Ike thought a President ought to have a Congress controlled by his own party in order to achieve his foreign-policy goals. As chief executive he had to use his power as head of the dominant party. To gain his objectives through congressional approval, he had to be in a position to influence and cajole logrolling congressmen. He had such influence and authority within his own party, but not within the opposition. The Democrats were, of course, patriotic and would support the national interest on any major issues such as national defense. But he thought they would try to hamstring him on anything not of top importance and this included foreign policy. And he couldn't control them. He remembered when he was chief of staff in 1946, he was discussing something with Truman who said, "I'd be glad to put the request to Congress, but there's no point because as soon as they see my name on it they'll vote it down."

Wilson, Hoover, and Truman had all been crippled at times by the lack of congressional support. (I recall that Truman did get through the Truman Doctrine and Marshall Plan plus the Korean war.) Hoover had warned Ike when the latter said he intended to have a middle-of-the-road, moderate government that he would inevitably be unpopular because the extremists of both left and right would oppose him. Yet he intended to pursue this course. The country needed calm and cleaning up. Just like the Tories in Britain hadn't tried to return to everything of pre-Labour days, he didn't want to make over what the Democrats had left—entirely. But he wanted a moral cleanup and was getting it slowly. He was proud that his policy on McCarthy had proven right. McCarthy's name is mentioned now much more rarely; his influence is slipping. He had always been determined not to attack McCarthy personally and thus build him up as the single symbol of opposition to the President; he didn't want to give him that importance. And he was surer than ever now he had been proven right.

I noticed that Eisenhower used the words "leftist" and "Socialist" rather loosely, like so many Republicans. He was very irked by the whole power issue and claimed it was unfair to give federal aid to the people of Tennessee any more than to the people of some other state. He was referring in this case to TVA and the big Dixon-Yates squawk. He claimed he was a firm believer in states' rights, and pointing behind me said: "Anybody who reads the Federalist papers as I have will see that the people who wrote our Constitution thought this over for a long time and very carefully before they came to any decisions on it. And they wanted to protect the rights of the states that had voluntarily banded together."

He said the Russians were talking softly now because they had been frightened by the successes of our policy. He beefed about all his visitors—the President of Liberia, the President of Pakistan, etc. He said this job was "hell." He couldn't do it properly and see "all these people." And he felt a deep responsibility that he ought to be doing his job better.

The President had been terribly distressed by the cut in the foreign-information program. That should be getting half a billion dollars instead of $76,000,000. He had to go to Connecticut and then New York to talk at a Jewish tercentenary. "I don't know what the hell to talk about at a thing like that, so I suppose I'll just talk about peace." He had to receive the Forrestal award. "Now what the hell is the Forrestal award; they haven't even told me yet what it is."

I was rather amused at one point when the President was talking about some of his difficulties and the slowness of procedures. He said: "Supposing I wanted to appoint you, a good Republican, to some job or other. Why, it might take months before I could get it through." This is the first time I have ever been described by anybody, even by implication, as a good Republican.

On the whole I found the President uneasy, irascible, crotchety, and not quite sure of himself. I felt sorry for him.

Ike talked rather bitterly about the Democratic leadership in Congress right now. He expressed the opinion that Senator Lyndon Johnson and Representative Sam Rayburn were of no use and were representing selfish party motives. In this connection he talked about former Vice President Garner and said that he was "a terrible old man" of the same "selfish politician" variety.

Marina stayed on with Mamie after I had gone down to see the President, and I asked her to tell me about her conversation. She said:

After you left, Mrs. Ike took me around some more rooms and then as I offered to leave her in peace, she said, "Oh, do have a cigarette." We had three. We talked about the difficulties of entertaining people who sometimes spoke no English. Also about their finances which are going to the dogs, as their huge salary is taxed 90 percent. She said it costs them about $25,000 for Ike to be President. She is obliged to buy dozens of evening dresses and hundreds of hats. She says that it is quite tiresome being a First Lady, as she never gets a chance to go for a walk by herself or browse around in little shops. She said one day in Denver she walked into a five-and-ten in an act of revolt and had a lovely time. She was just about to buy a brassiere when she remembered the secret policeman behind her and was too embarrassed to have her measurements taken, so had to give up the whole idea. She told me that all the food and flowers and upkeep, which is upstairs, for the two of them and any unofficial friends they entertain, is paid for by them. Also any repairs to the top of the house—this I am not quite sure I did not misunderstand. She said that nothing had been done to the White House until she came because Mrs. Truman was "too busy doing nothing" and Mrs. Roosevelt was "too busy running around the country." She repeated that Ike hated being President but had "only done it because he felt it was his duty."

WASHINGTON, *October 27, 1954*

TODAY my first column was published. I chose this as the moment to dive into my new domain because it is my forty-second birthday, which I hope will prove an omen of good luck. I decided to start with a piece that is plainly an interview with President Eisenhower (although disguised in order not to embarrass him) and which will be followed up by two columns based on Dulles.

GERMANY REARMS

THIS MORNING I SAW HERVÉ ALPHAND, LEADING FRENCH QUAI d'Orsay expert on German rearmament. He considers the British pledge to maintain troops in Europe subject to the approval of the Western European Union is actually a hoax and a wonderful stroke of propaganda. The text of the treaty proposed between Britain and EDC (the suggested European army) plus the public commitment Eden then made in the British House was actually stronger and provided for a greater commitment. At that time, April, 1954, they promised to maintain permanently a fair share of their troops on the Continent. They promised to integrate one of their four divisions plus tactical aviation with EDC. They pledged complete cooperation on logistics, staff methods, etc. Alphand says he fought hard to prevent the resurgence of a German national army and German general staff. I recall that a long time ago he also admitted to me that he thought EDC would mean final accomplishment of Richelieu's policy—keeping Germany partitioned—because the Russians would never permit East Germany to go over to EDC. Hervé says the Germans will now have twelve divisions ready for M-Day as compared with five France is to make available. Furthermore, the Germans will be allowed to make twelve new divisions each year, demobilize the earlier ones, and thus build up a huge army while not exceeding the twelve-division limit—just like the old one-hundred-thousand-man Reichswehr.

This afternoon I had a chat with Douglas Dillon. I must say he is a very wise young man. Although he is a Republican ambassador, he said he considered the American elections very satisfactory—despite the Democratic victory in both Houses. He thought this had put the kibosh on McCarthy.

Douglas is extremely impressed with Mendès-France. He says Mendès has developed a technique of playing the people over Parliament and the rank and file of different parties over the heads of party leaders. For the moment he has even gained the support of rampant Gaullist deputies.

PARIS, *November 5, 1954*

LARRY Norstad says it is undoubtedly true the generals feel happier about having a German national army rather than EDC. It will be far less complicated integrating into NATO and they expect to get German contingents more quickly and more efficiently. However, quite apart from political implications, Norstad thinks EDC might have provided better economic and psychological support for European defense ten years hence. The real trouble with EDC was that it was too much to ask Europe to swallow at this time.

He admits the British are no further committed to continental defense by the September agreements than they were previously, because of legal loopholes, etc. Nevertheless, Eden's commitment is a very serious thing to both the British and the Europeans and has had far-reaching psychological consequences. British prestige is at an all-time postwar high.

PARIS, *November 8, 1954*

THIS morning I had a chat with General Speidel, Rommel's former chief of staff and chief German rearming negotiator. As usual it was fascinating. For the first half-hour we also had with us Freiherr von der Heydte, a colonel in one of the best parachute units during the war, who won the highest grade of the Iron Cross and served in Speidel's headquarters.

Von der Heydte told me one of the difficulties in rearming Germany was going to be psychological. The United States has two basic objectives in its occupation—de-Nazification and demilitarization. We failed in the former, but have succeeded beyond all belief in the latter. Recently, von der Heydte asked among his two thousand students how many of them would be prepared to become officers in the new German army. Not a single one was willing.

Speidel said the moral and psychological change was serious, but would not prevent the forming of a new army. He thought this revolutionizing of German opinion was due to several factors. Not only had the defeat in the war and the postwar demilitarization program crushed the old military spirit, but Germany was now going through an era of such prosperity that all young people want is to go out and make money while they can. Finally the supernational elements of Germany are only in favor of immediate German reunification and are therefore opposed to the present plan of West Germany joining NATO.

Speidel admitted to me that plans drawn up for German contingents in EDC had been prepared "with a view to any eventuality"—in other words, no changes in plan were necessary in order to develop the new national army.

The commander-in-chief will be General Ludwig Crüwell. The chief of staff and by far the most important man will be General Adolf Heusinger. Heusinger will be the key. The post of commander-in-chief will be the most unpopular post in Europe. Everybody who fears German militarism and the Germans themselves will be gunning for him. Therefore, Crüwell, who hasn't got much of a future anyway, is being sacrificed.

PARIS, *November 9, 1954*

YESTERDAY afternoon I went to see Al Gruenther out at SHAPE and after a talk of about an hour and a half I went over to his house at Marnes-la-Coquette where we sat around and had a few drinks.

Gruenther says flatly that we have such an enormous edge over the Soviet bloc that there is absolutely no danger of their attacking us now, nor is there any indication of war.

By the time the Germans have rearmed, we will be in a position to prevent any Soviet overrunning of Europe. At present, although we are confident we would win a war, the Russians could certainly, during the initial phase, overrun most of the Continent.

Gruenther said the real object of German rearmament is to restore political confidence to the West. Actually, war has become so dangerous now that it is doubtful if there will ever be one. But the Cold War seeks to wear us down by fear. A restoration of political confidence will help us in Cold War terms.

I told Gruenther about my conversation with von der Heydte. I pointed out that we are in the paradoxical position of having created Nazis who won't fight—rather than de-Nazified soldiers. He admitted there was a good deal of truth in this. Likewise, we are having a very difficult time getting Germany's national defense started, despite the long military tradition of Germany.

PARIS, *November 10, 1954*

INTERESTING talk with General de Gaulle. He looks old, gray, and is more cynical and pessimistic than ever. He told me he stays almost all the time in Colombey-les-Deux-Eglises and comes to Paris once a fortnight at most. He spends his time now entirely on writing the second volume of his *Mémoires.**

De Gaulle says the real trouble with France today is that Frenchmen were used to glory and prestige. They are disinterested in what happens to their country or government now because they have the habit of thinking in terms of French grandeur; and there is no French grandeur.†

* See de Gaulle's further comments, pp. 8, 83.
† See de Gaulle's further comments, p. 25.

He now sees absolutely no future for Europe, the world, or for France. He says war is inevitable although a period of coexistence and modus vivendi will continue for a considerable time. This is demonstrated in the improved relations between England and China, by Malenkov's soft talk, by the new attitude toward Jugoslavia, and by Ho Chi Minh's efforts to develop good relations with France.*

The General clearly does not have very much use for Mendès-France. He talked rather freely about his famous secret interview with the Prime Minister. He said that Mendès-France himself admitted his pessimism and his eventual incapacity to govern France. De Gaulle said the political parties will bring Mendès down when they are ready to do so. There are 37 men in the Assembly right now who wish to be Prime Minister and 126 men who want Cabinet posts, and when they are prepared, they will assassinate Mendès's government. They have only let Mendès remain in office in order to unload some of the burdens France carried which they themselves had been afraid to shed. "Likewise, he has been permitted to let Germany rearm because there is no way of preventing it. But the minute Mendès tries any real social reforms or fundamental changes, they will cut his throat. It is impossible for Mendès to improve the situation under the present Constitution. And it is impossible to change the present Constitution unless there is a dramatic event to wake people up."

I remarked that there were rumors that Mendès would like to oust President Coty and replace him with de Gaulle—at the same time giving de Gaulle executive powers. De Gaulle said this was impossible ("Why should Coty be removed? He was only elected this year and he's a nice fellow.") Anyway, de Gaulle said Mendès could not extend the powers of the Presidency under the present Constitution.

De Gaulle said Mendès had made no such request to him. Anyway he said he was completely out of politics now. In the 1951 elections he had hoped to get at least 200 deputies which would have made him strong enough to force through a constitutional reform. He said he only got 122 and his movement was thwarted. While he remained the titular head of the RPF, he was entirely removed from politics and had absolutely no interest in what the "Social Republican" or Gaullist group in Parliament did. He contended that when members of the Social Republican group like Dio Catroux joined the Mendès-France government, they demonstrated at best an ambivalent attitude because the RPF had actually been founded to overturn this system of governments.

I asked if he had tried to prevent Soustelle from joining the Mendès-France Cabinet. He said no, that he hadn't made any efforts to exert any influence on Soustelle. But he implied that he doubted that the latter would enter the Cabinet.

To sum up, it is perfectly clear that de Gaulle views the relationship of

* See de Gaulle's further comments, pp. 40, 45, 76.

Mendès-France to the other governments of the Fourth Republic just the way Moscow analyzes the Democrats and Republicans in the United States; that is, he considers them precisely the same thing.

PARIS, *November 12, 1954*

MOST pleasant and interesting lunch with David Bruce who is leaving soon to resume private life as a result of the failure of EDC. David, bless him, really laid it on. We had a private room at Calvet's with a magnificent meal based upon rognons and a 1947 Chateau Talbot.

His job has been to serve as American observer on EDC and representative to the Coal and Steel Community. He requested the State Department to terminate that mission. Bruce's departure coincides with the waning of the "European Idea." Monnet, Alphand, and Schuman are out of office. De Gasperi is dead. Adenauer is in a cleft stick.

It is highly unlikely that the mechanism now devised for German rearmament will really allow international control of German militarism. SACEUR has greater control of troop movements than under the EDC, but the Western European Union is not a supranational institution. Britain could of course make it so, but won't. The net result of the whole business is that France is permanently relegated to the position of being a second-rate power vis-à-vis Germany.

The present situation presents two alternatives for U.S. policy. We could take a less active part in European affairs and let Britain exercise its influence in the power scales, but does Britain wish to do this? Britain tends to think in terms of a bloc comprising the United States, Britain, and Canada, rather than in terms of Britain as a part of Europe. The other alternative for the U.S. is to remain permanently committed in Europe now that a superstate is impossible here.

Eisenhower, as NATO commander, became convinced in the field of economics that European integration was necessary. He saw clearly that the big object was to incorporate Germany into the West—not just to rearm Germany. At first he opposed EDC, but he was converted by Bruce and Jean Monnet. The EDC scheme started after Acheson proposed German rearmament in 1950, and Monnet reacted with a plan for a European army.

Bruce admits his own mission was a failure. In an immediate sense United States policy succeeded since a more practical way of dealing with the Germans was devised and the power of NATO increased. But American policy was to back a "European" idea and this did not succeed.

The big question now is how to control the interference of the German General Staff in politics—the nemesis of power. EDC would have done away with a German General Staff. The German industrialists are not yet eager for war contracts because they are grabbing markets around the world and benefiting from low taxes.

It is paradoxical that EDC should have been easiest to ratify in France—where it failed. France was offered a fifty-year guarantee to control Germany. This, says Bruce, was France's one last chance to recover her great power position.

PARIS, *November 17, 1954*

LAST night we attended a small dinner party where the Windsors were present. It has been some time since I last saw him. He ingratiated himself to me all over again by announcing that he thought Joe McCarthy was a wonderful fellow. He added, "Of course I don't approve of *all* the methods he applies, but, after all, he has taken the lead in showing you people what is wrong with communism and we cannot let the Communists get away with it."

Windsor confided to me that his job as governor of the Bahamas during the war had been "very difficult." He explained that there were some training bases for troops there and the economy of the island depended upon American visitors. Americans would not stay in hotels in which Negro troops were admitted as guests. Therefore, although British law did not provide for segregation, it had to be arranged on the quiet that no Negroes were allowed in these hotels.

PARIS, *November 18, 1954*

I HAD an extremely interesting and stimulating conversation this morning with Bidault at his home in St. Cloud. It is a simple, little, suburban house, furnished without luxury and looking just exactly like what you would expect of a professor's home: Bookshelves completely filled and extending to the ceiling; other books piled all over the place; papers scattered about; and a broken photograph frame on his desk mended on the back with a strip from a cigar box. Bidault was in excellent form: extremely intelligent, sarcastic, vital, and biting. He seemed in good health. He was not smoking and obviously was not suffering from a hangover.

He is furious at the English. Of course, although he did not say this, the reason is that they helped Mendès-France get through his rearmament program for Germany and they did not give Bidault enough assistance on EDC. Bidault says the English have no logic to their policy, unlike the French. They only see "as far as the end of their nose, and in a fog they cannot see even that far." Bidault said the British had brought a "British peace" to Indochina at the Geneva Conference and this had ruined Southeast Asia. They had brought a "British solution" to Europe torpedoing EDC and ruining Europe. They were now in the process of arranging a "British formula" in Africa which would ruin Africa. What he meant by this was that the terrorist bands operating in Tunisia and Algeria had been smuggled across from Libya, which is independent but still under British control.

Bidault said the British aspiration was to have a series of "Jordans" all across North Africa. He recalled with savage acerbity the policy of Sir Edward Spears in Beirut and Damascus. Bidault said there was something strangely chemical about it, but any Frenchman who had ever served in Asia or Africa came home an Anglophobe and any Englishman who had served in those regions came home a Francophobe. He agreed that it was imperatively necessary for the United States, Britain, and France to consult and coordinate their policies in the "gray zone" of the Middle East and Asia, but he demonstrated how difficult this will be by immediately saying that of course France would consult with no one concerning Morocco, Algeria, and Tunisia. The only solution for those areas, he says, is force. He is afraid Mendès-France will not apply it.

He said the Russians are successfully employing nationalism and Islam to foment trouble. For a time the Russians supported Israel against the Arab states because they saw vitality and force in Israel and no cohesion in the Muslim world. But then they shifted to support the Arab countries because they saw they were ripe to fall. The revolution in Egypt is by no means over, but the Egyptians, unaware of this, are calling for holy wars and meddling in the affairs of other countries.

The situation in Indochina is rotten. Bidault is convinced this is due to the treason of at least two members of the present French government. A formula had already been arranged to sell out Indochina before the Geneva Conference convened last spring. Even then, he said that only four days would have sufficed to make the rotten deal that Mendès-France accepted. Bidault said Bao Dai was a corrupt, contemptible coward. He added: "It was not I who installed him, but Ramadier, the Socialist."

Bidault said the present Prime Minister of Vietnam, Ngo Dinh Diem, was an obstinate idiot who could not get along with anybody, adding: "I say that even though he is a good Catholic." Referring to the press conference General Collins held yesterday in Saigon, Bidault said he wanted to put through a rule that any general who made any statement in public should be given forty days fortress imprisonment.

Bidault said Mendès-France deliberately sabotaged EDC. At Brussels the experts had agreed upon a compromise solution, but Mendès personally changed this with his own handwriting and then said that unless his amendments were accepted he would not take it. Bidault clearly detests Mendès and says that if he lasts six more months he will have accomplished the ruination of France. He has lost Europe and the potentiality of French leadership. He has lost Southeast Asia. He is in the process of losing Africa.

Bidault says de Gaulle is now a complete zero in the country. There is no such thing as a Gaullist. De Gaulle could not run as a candidate for office successfully in a single French election district. "Today de Gaulle is a writer, that's all," Bidault concluded.

PARIS, *November 19, 1954*

DRINKS this evening with British Ambassador Sir Gladwyn Jebb at his residence. He thinks Mendès-France is a remarkably intelligent man doing a good job, who will get his throat cut anyway. The leaders in that operation are going to be Pinay and Maurice Schumann. Jebb was horrified when I told him Dulles had described Mendès-France as a "superman" in Washington today. "My God, that will finish him in France," was his observation.

PARIS, *November 20, 1954*

LAST night we dined with the Ismays; Pug was in a great mood of reminiscence. Poor fellow, he confided to Marina that he has been working for the British government since 1905 (as an army officer), and when he retires next year—after fifty years of service—he won't have a bean. He said that, next to his wife and children, the thing he loves best in the world is his farm in England. However, although he had some money of his own, he has always held positions which cost him more than his salary plus expense allowance. As a result, he is going to sell his farm.

Despite that, he was in an exceptionally cheerful mood and told some remarkably amusing stories. Only four times during the European war was Ismay called up at night at his home in London. The first time was when Norway was invaded. The second time was when the Low Countries were overrun. The third time was after Pearl Harbor. The fourth was when the armistice was signed in Rheims.

On that occasion, Ismay was sound asleep when the phone rang and a voice came on, saying: "This is Bedell [Smith] calling from Rheims. Ike wants to speak to you." Eisenhower then got on the phone and said: "Hello Pug, I just wanted to tell you that it's all over; they've signed on the dotted line." Ismay said he replied, "I don't know what to say. I don't know what to do, whether to cry or to have a drink." Ike replied: "I'm going to do both." Ismay heard Ike pouring a drink by the telephone.

After Ismay hung up, it suddenly occurred to him that Ike wanted him to pass the message on to Prime Minister Churchill. He picked up the phone to call 10 Downing Street and found it dead. By one of those curious accidents, the phone remained connected to Rheims and he could not disentangle it. So he put on his dressing gown and stumbled out in the middle of the night to the corner local pub to use the pay telephone. He had only two-pence with him. He called up his own office in the War

Office and said: "This is Ismay speaking. You simply must believe me. I've only got two-pence and I always push the wrong button in these damned telephones. Connect me urgently with the PM's office." He was finally put through to Downing Street, where a tired functionary's voice assured him that everybody was asleep and the news was known.

Lady Ismay recalled the first time she met Churchill. They were invited to a dinner party at Ditchley. It was the night after the horrible raid on Coventry and everybody expected a repeat performance. She had delivered Pug at Ditchley for a series of meetings and then had to go home herself to change. She put on her only evening dress of red chiffon and started off in the pouring rain for the country. Halfway along, the car broke down. Finally, she flagged a passing motorcycle and got a ride in the sidecar to a nearby town where she rented a dilapidated old car and drove out to Ditchley. She arrived a few minutes early. She was just trying to tidy herself up, shake the rain out of her hair, and powder her nose when the door opened and Churchill came in scowling. He looked at her bluntly and asked: "What kind of a night is it?" She replied: "It's pouring rain." He strode to the wall switch, turned out the lights because of the blackout, and then stuck his head out of the window. A moment later he pulled it in, his face glistening with raindrops and remarked: "It looks quite all right to me." Then he stumped out of the room.

Both Ismays roared with laughter when they recalled Churchill's first experience with his "scrambler." The scrambler was a device on the telephone which completely jumbled up the conversation of important men so that nobody tapping the lines would understand anything, and yet most secret things could be discussed. As soon as Churchill got his scrambler, he called up the War Office and got on the telephone a young clerk who did not know what a scrambler was, who had no idea who was talking, and who was utterly bewildered at the weird noises he heard in his receiver. At his end of the phone Churchill was saying: "I have beshide me a mosht shecret device." All the clerk heard was mumble, bumble, rumble. The Prime Minister was furious.

Another time, when Eden visited Turkey on highly secret negotiations seeking Turkey's aid in the war, it was agreed that a private code would be established so that Eden and Churchill could discuss the visit by long-distance telephone. The code was based upon an ironmonger's shop. But Churchill forgot all about it. After his visit, Eden called the Prime Minister in great excitement and said: "I ordered two frying pans, but I could not get those three boilers with them. Something can be done about the kettles." Churchill kept grumbling back to him: "What on earth are you talking about?"

Ismay recalled that after the Moscow conference of 1944 was over, he and everybody else were most hopeful that they were going to get a lot of caviar and vodka to take back to austerity London. At the airport, as they were about to board their plane, a bunch of huge parcels wrapped in khaki cloth was delivered. A Russian kept muttering that the bundles contained caviar and vodka. Everybody was delighted. They loaded the huge parcels into Churchill's and Eden's planes. When they got to London, after much difficulty, they cleared them through customs as gifts for the Prime Minister and his party. With representatives from the Foreign Office, the War Office, and the Prime Minister's office present, the loot was shared out. Churchill got six kilos of caviar, Eden got about five, Ismay three, etc. Everybody in the party got some caviar and vodka. Then they all went home and divided up their own caviar, putting it in little jugs and bottles and giving it to their friends and relatives. Soon afterward, an inquiry came from the Soviet Embassy saying: "We simply cannot understand what happened to the caviar and vodka consigned by our government to the Soviet mission here in order to celebrate the October revolution." Everybody was horror-struck, but there was nothing to do about it. The caviar had been eaten or given away and the vodka drunk. Ismay immediately ordered the War Office to purchase a dozen cases of whisky. Eden was informed of this and he was supposed to give them to the Soviet Embassy as a replacement. But Eden, who was himself a culprit, did not have the nerve to face the ambassador when he was summoned to the Foreign Office. Instead, this duty was given a junior diplomat. The Soviet Embassy accepted the twelve cases of whisky in obvious bewilderment.

PARIS, *November 22, 1954*

ANOTHER pleasant chat with Ismay. I asked him what he considered was wrong with NATO, pointing out that too much is written about what's right with it and that it is never going to be improved unless we look at it more skeptically. He thought NATO's greatest weakness was that "we don't have much to show for Article 2. If we don't proceed with Article 2, NATO remains a purely military alliance, which it isn't. We should pray for the day when we won't have to spend all our money on arms and can improve the condition of peoples."*

Militarily, he thought NATO had been successful within the limitations imposed upon it, "beyond the wildest dreams of its founders." Politically, its fundamental weakness was that you cannot run foreign policy and strategy in watertight compartments bounded by geographical areas. For example, any event in the Persian Gulf is outside the NATO area. All countries that

---

* Article 2 reads: "The Parties will contribute toward the further development of peaceful and friendly international relations by strengthening their free institutions, by bringing about a better understanding of the principles upon which these institutions are founded, and by promoting conditions of stability and well-being. They will seek to eliminate conflict in their international economic policies and will encourage economic collaboration between any or all of them."

would resist Soviet aggression are not in NATO, such as Jugoslavia and Spain. NATO was established to safeguard the "heart" of the western world. Now it must be extended. Pug hoped that there would be a Middle East pact and a Far East pact linked up to NATO. Then someone at the top could get a global view.

PARIS, *November 23, 1954*

LAST night we dined at Pamela Churchill's. She told me old Winston is a pronounced agnostic. Once, she asked him whether he believed in an after-life. He said no, he thought there was only some kind of velvety cool blackness. He then added: "Of course I may be wrong. I might well be reborn as a Chinese coolie. In such a case, I should lodge a protest."

LONDON, *December 1, 1954*

EXTREMELY enjoyable lunch today with Randolph Churchill. He was in good form, mostly about his father. Sir Winston is extremely fond of playing cards. But he plays very badly, according to Randolph. He played bridge for years, finally gave up and went in for six-pack Bezique. Later, during the 1920s, he was a roaring Mah-Jong player. He has since successively taken up gin rummy and Oklahoma. Now, in his old age, he has gone back to Bezique. It is the easiest thing on earth to win money from him.

Randolph says Churchill had an exchange of letters with Eden early this year in which he advised Eden that he planned to retire as Prime Minister in the fall. However, since then he had changed his mind. This embarrasses Eden no end, but there is nothing he can do about it.

Randolph boasts: "Winston will probably bury Eden, and then he will deliver himself of a magnificent oration in which he will talk of the sad and premature death of this promising young man."

Randolph told me he is moving to the country shortly to write almost entirely biographies. He wants to go into politics, but only after his father has died. He complains rather mournfully: "I could do nothing while he is alive."

He said that when Foster Dulles used his "agonizing reappraisal" phrase in December, 1953, Churchill at the time remarked: "That young man understands the use of the English language." ("Young" Mr. Dulles was 66.)

LONDON, *December 3, 1954*

LAST night dined at the Radziwills. Randolph was there—at his worst. He got completely tanked and then proceeded to insult everybody successively. Poor fellow! He is his own worst enemy. He was also inconceivably gluttonous and as happy as a little boy as each successive dish arrived and he ploughed in, stuffing his ever-increasing belly. At the end he was tottering. Finally his best friend made the cruelest remark I have ever heard: He said: "Randolph, it is perfectly plain why your father despises and hates you; he despises and hates drunkards."

(P.S. Next day Randolph sent flowers to all the Ladies with a note: "I should never be allowed out in private.")

This morning I called on Harold Macmillan, minister for defense, publisher and head of the famous family property of Macmillan & Company. He will almost certainly be foreign secretary when Eden becomes Prime Minister.

We were chatting quietly around eleven o'clock when a shrill bell began to ring. A secretary popped his head into the room and said excitedly: "It's a division." Macmillan leapt out of his chair as if he had been stuck with a pin and shouted: "Come along with me—this should be fun." I ran downstairs after him and we piled into his large car which the chauffeur drove speedily to the House of Commons. Then I had to run upstairs as he rushed in to cast his vote. The Labour party had pulled a surprise test on the government, but they did not get away with it. Before, during, and after this brief exercise, we had rather a good talk. This is what I recall of it:

The mere existence of new weapons imposes a brand-new kind of problem. The weapons are so awful to use that a kind of paralysis has set in. In the old days a country like Peru could never lay claim to two hundred miles of sea and grab shipping within it. A British gunboat would have intervened immediately. After all, refusing to tolerate this type of behavior by Spain was a basic British policy that led to the founding of the New World, but right now gunboats are out of fashion.

Despite the particularly dreadful implications to a little island like Britain of the hydrogen bomb, there has been no change in policy which remains founded on the awareness that Britain must keep strong. The offense has a large advantage over the defense. Therefore, Britain's greatest protection is the knowledge by an enemy of British striking power. This has a great deterrent value in preventing wars.

The theory now is that if a war were to come there would be a brief and terrible period during which the two sides would exchange atomic bombardment. After that would come the "broken-back" phase. Millions of Russians would be swarming around Europe like the Goths, but without any lines of communication back to their own country. These would have to be driven out by more traditional methods.

Macmillan thought it would be very useful if some Middle East defense organization could be established. This might eventually be easier now that the Suez argument with Egypt has ended. His predecessor, Lord Alexander, had never cared about remaining in Suez, because he argued the canal has to be defended far to the north in Turkey, not down around the canal zone itself.

Macmillan (unlike Eden, but like Montgomery) favors a direct link between NATO, SEATO, a Middle East defense organization, and a Pacific pact. He argues that a tidy arrangement of this sort would make it much easier to draw a line dividing the free world from the Communist world and that then we could arrange terms of coexistence on a kind of spheres of influence basis.

After I finished with Macmillan, I went to the Foreign Office for an extremely agreeable talk with Eden. He looks better than any time I have seen him since his operation a couple of years ago. He seems to have gained a bit of weight and appears cheerful and energetic. Tony Rumbold sat in with us and at the end Lord Salisbury came along.

Eden thought it would be nice to have a Middle East treaty organization, but this was entirely out of the question right now. We were really not getting anywhere in terms of settling the Palestine argument and there had been a new shooting incident yesterday. Nevertheless, patient, quiet diplomacy, similar to that used in the Trieste settlement, was the only way to approach things in the Middle East. He said Cyprus remains extremely important to Britain. Cyprus is essentially a British matter and the UN has no business discussing it.

He was furious with Peru about its contention that there is a two-hundred-mile limit in which whale fishing is banned. According to international law, the three-mile limit is the only one generally recognized. In the Baltic Sea, Russia has established a twelve-mile limit, and we go along with this. But a two-hundred-mile limit is ridiculous and outrageous. The United States is helping Britain out by having Panama raise the matter at the next Pan-American conference. Of course, Britain is particularly interested in the matter because right now it affects Lloyds, who have insured the Onassis ships seized by Peru. Eden said it was a bit embarrassing to have to work so hard to protect Onassis who is "a rather unsavory character."

I asked if he saw any evidence of *real* change in the Soviet Union as a result of the post-Stalin "new look." He said there was no evidence of any changes concerning the two things we are most interested in—Germany and Austria. That was the area we kept looking at, hoping to see signs of change; but so far none. However, no doubt there has been a change as far as Jugoslavia goes. The Russians have now climbed down entirely and it is a tremendous victory for Tito. The Russians have indeed admitted that he is a good Communist and turned the blame for the row on Stalin.

Eden does not think the new Soviet (Warsaw) Security Pact amounts to anything. It does not change the situation in the least. They are just a bunch of satellites, he added, and: "I don't remember any opposition leader in the whole pack of them, do you?"

PARIS, *December 6, 1954*

BILL Gibson of our Paris Embassy told me today there is a little purge in
the State Department to get rid of all the old Indochina boys because the
Department is so embarrassed about its persistently wrong policy. The
Department still adamantly insists that the only way to save the southern
part of Indochina is to support the Diem government. This is lunacy.
Everyone is against him. But apparently the CIA has for the moment bought
Diem the support of the sects, including the Cao Daiists.

Bao Dai actually wants to go back now, but *we* for the first time (not the
French) are begging him to stay in France. That ain't hard. Gibson went
down recently to give him such a message and the Emperor hardly listened
—he was so excited about a new Jaguar he had bought. We don't want him
to go back and interfere with the chaotic Diem government.

The French are saying if we don't play ball soon they'll pull out entirely.
We say their army isn't really needed; that if crisis comes SEATO can
intervene. This is a lot of crap since SEATO is not much more than a figment
of Dulles's imagination. However, the French can't pull out very easily
because they would first have to evacuate between 250,000 and 500,000
French citizens and pro-French Indochinese to prevent them from being
massacred. General Ely is quite aware of this.

The odds in favor of the Communists gaining *all* of Indochina no matter
what we do, Gibson says, are at least ten to one. And the process will
probably succeed before elections are ever called in 1956, as provided for
by last summer's Geneva settlement.

U.S. policy hopes vaguely to establish a strong enough government in the
South (with its larger population) to influence the North favorably prior to
the 1956 elections. But Diem, the instrument chosen to carry out this
policy, is a failure. We are disillusioned but reluctant to admit it. So we
have prolonged this dead-end policy to a point beyond repair. Meanwhile,
the French have sourly agreed to go along with us for the present in order
to avoid a major split with the United States. But they would prefer to make
a working arrangement with Ho Chi Minh, saving Tonkin (the North) from
China.

PARIS, *December 10, 1954*

LAST night we went to a party at the Dillons. Ismay said he was convinced
Montgomery, in his recent speech in the United States, had cribbed from
my column on the difficulty the allies were having in constructing a world-
wide organization and "groping for the light." Ismay pointed out that Montgomery's speech came a day or two after the column was published and
added: "Monty never has any ideas of his own."

Norstad told me he had a long talk with Ike and Mamie when he was home a few days ago. Eisenhower confided to him that despite all the propaganda in favor of Mendès-France he (Ike) did not trust him.

DÜSSELDORF, *December 12, 1954*

LUNCHED today with a group of Ruhr magnates in the home of Dr. Ernst Schneider, president of the Düsseldorf Chamber of Industry and Commerce and board chairman of large bridge building, construction, and chemical concerns. Schneider's apartment is fantastic. Looks like a tenement on the outside, but contains among its clutter, ornaments and bibelots, two magnificent Holbeins, and the finest collection of porcelain I have ever seen, including four eighteenth-century Meissen figurines so valuable that Schneider cannot afford to insure them.

These men, who will be the ones to finance and construct the weapons for Germany's rearmament, said the following: They are glad to have atomic, biological, and chemical weapons banned from manufacture here because this would only arouse the suspicion of Germany's neighbors. But they insist German troops should receive such equipment from the allies.

There is no sentiment for soldiery. Many young men are saying half-jokingly, half-seriously that they will run away to France or Spain rather than be mobilized. It will be even harder to get officers than soldiers because, as Rösler observed: "Officers learned in the last war they can be hanged if they lose."

They are worried about possible serious trouble in Germany when people realize that Adenauer's policy of a NATO link isn't leading toward unification. Any deal by the U.S. with Russia, even for an Asian settlement, would be a disaster because the Germans would immediately conclude that their permanent partition had inferentially been agreed upon.

There are great industrial problems in rearming. The industrialists have not been given a clue as to what they will be expected to make or in what quantity. They can't plan on this basis. They will need much capital and labor. The only large, important capital source will be the United States.

They will need much labor as industry expands and at the same time young men are drafted. What they want is unskilled foreigners who would replace unskilled Germans—the latter being trained for skilled jobs. Of course, economically, this boils down to a program of "we'll make arms if you finance the program and provide serf labor."

BONN, *December 13, 1954*

TODAY I had a long talk with Adenauer. As usual, he looked remarkably healthy for a man of his age, but a little bit of the pep seems to be running out.

There is no alternative to joining the West and rearming, Adenauer said. He did not think there was a danger of militarism. During the recent local election campaign he addressed many meetings himself and the audiences showed a reasonable attitude "with no trace of militarism." But he added:

> They are convinced we cannot avoid becoming soldiers again. We must consider the situation as it is today. We are supposed to get twelve divisions. This is a ridiculously small force compared to the United States or Soviet Russia. It is absolutely unimaginable that Germany could again become a military state and lead a militaristic future. When Germany was a strong military power we had our own factories to support our armies. Such is no longer the case. The past will not be repeated—*Das ist alles vorbei.*

Did Adenauer think there had been any material change in the Soviet attitude? He saw no change whatsoever and said: "There will not be a change so long as the unity of the free West is not completely reestablished. Until then, there is no reason for Moscow to change." (What he means is until Germany is part of NATO.)

Adenauer said it was wrong to think Germany's war potential would be increased if East Germany is added to West Germany. On the contrary, he contended, the West would have to rebuild and colonize the East. Miles of railroad track, factories, and equipment have been shipped from East Germany to the Soviet Union. Roads and houses have collapsed and the population has fled to a considerable degree. It would take a long time to rectify this. (This argument is rather specious.)

I told Adenauer that everybody in England knew Eden would succeed Churchill when the leader retires. "Who is your Eden?" I asked. He smiled and replied: "Churchill is an old man."

BONN, *December 14, 1954*

I HAD a very interesting talk today with Lt. General Adolf Heusinger. He will certainly be the most important man in the new German army.

Heusinger started off by saying old-fashioned divisions are no longer practicable in an atomic age. Units must be smaller and very mobile. They must have a high rate of firepower, but not too many supply installations. The latter are too vulnerable to atomic attack. Germany is planning small, fast units of about twelve thousand men—smaller than those originally planned for EDC. These German divisions will be divided into three combat teams similar to American regimental combat teams. Each will have its own artillery and transport and be capable of independent action.

Heusinger said 25 percent of the German army will be professional and will enlist for a minimum period of four years with regular renewals on a volunteer basis. German rearmament will start with the organizing of cadres from volunteers. A considerable time afterward, the conscription of the twenty-year-old class will commence.

It is necessary, both by law and by education, to insure that the army will be kept out of politics. Heusinger advocates regulations forbidding soldiers from taking part in political assemblies when in uniform. However, soldiers must have *all* civilian rights, including that of voting; but they cannot vote when in barracks. No political propaganda shall be allowed in barracks, but every soldier will be allowed his own political opinion. Nevertheless, military discipline must never be endangered.

Officers will be trained carefully in the political situation and political problems. If an officer wants to go into politics he must first leave the army, although it has not yet been decided if he must permanently resign his commission.

Today it is said that the officers of the old Reichswehr were too unpolitical. When Hitler came to power, he demanded that the officers corps become political. The problem of officers' politics is a problem for every officer and government. The officer must be well-informed on internal and external politics or otherwise he cannot fulfill his obligation to answer soldiers' questions. Officers should never engage in political activity in the wrong sense. An officer can never represent one party; that is to say, he can belong to a party but as an officer he should not make propaganda for it.

BONN, *December 15, 1954*

LONG talk with Vice Admiral Helmuth Heye, an extremely loquacious individual, nice but vain. He seems to think strategically in terms of 1939, and he speaks fluent English with an accent like one of the Katzenjammer Kids. He said pompously: "Of course my accent is not American because I studied at Oxford for six months." He has a rough sea dog's face with one slightly cocked eye.

It is evident Heye would like to have a big job when Germany rearms. But he does not know if he is going to get anything. He seems to be the highest ranking admiral still loose. He commanded naval forces during the invasion of Crete and was later the German equivalent of Mountbatten, being in charge of naval secret weapons and commandos.

Heye thought the role of the new, small German navy must be to close the Allied defense ring in the Baltic and North Sea area. Denmark cannot do this job alone. Britain and the United States have enough big ships for Allied defense purposes. The need now is for more small ships such as the German navy will have and lots of air squadrons to protect the Baltic bases on both the northern and southern shores. Germany must have plenty of E-boats and small submarines.

Incidentally, Heye has recently returned from a visit to the United States where he said he was treated with great friendship and courtesy by Admiral Radford and other members of "our international trade union of the navy."

ESSEN, *December 15, 1954*

TODAY I had a talk with General Ludwig Crüwell, commandant of the Afrika Korps until he was shot down by the British on December 30, 1942. He was taken prisoner and sent off to a camp in Mississippi where he spent the rest of the war, hating the climate.

He is sixty-two, a well set-up bald man with spectacles. We drank Italian Vermouth and nibbled pretzel sticks during our conversation. At the end, he asked me if I would mind if he gave me and "dedicated" for me a copy of the book *Schicksal Afrika* put out by the Afrika Korps veterans society of which he is president. I said of course not; he wrote an amiable inscription.

Crüwell will almost certainly be either Commander-in-Chief of the next German army or at any rate troop commander if the titular boss is the chief of staff. He has a highly romantic idea of the North African war and says "on both sides this was a chivalrous, knightly war among brothers." I asked him what was the best novel on the campaign in the desert and he replied: "Desmond Young's biography of Rommel." I don't think Crüwell realized he was being funny.

He said the new German army had a fundamental psychological problem of improving relations between officers and men by making relations more democratic. There is also the problem of improving relations between the army and the state. Von Seeckt had the former problem when he created the one-hundred-thousand-man army for the Weimar Republic; but he did not have to worry about the latter.

He wants to see a democratic soldiery, an army of citizens. He wants to do away with "kommiss" or excessive heel-clicking discipline. In this connection, Crüwell remarked that he discovered when he was captured that the British army discipline during the last war was like that of the Prussian army in 1870.

PARIS, *December 18, 1954*

SAW Dulles for a brief chat. He looked tired and more twitchy than ever. I have a feeling this constant traveling is quite a strain.

Concerning Indochina, Dulles insisted there was complete cooperation between the United States and France on political matters and no effort on either side to impose views. When Mendès-France was in Washington last month, he hinted the French would be glad to accept a primary U.S. responsibility in the Far East. Dulles refused this because he thought the French were at least equally responsible in Indochina.

There had been extraordinarily close cooperation in Vietnam between General Ely and General Collins. The French have not asked us to withdraw our support from the present Diem government. We and the French have both recognized that Diem is "not 100 percent perfect" but there is no movement to replace him.

There is a program for the progressive reduction of French forces, but this must be done in stages and over a period of time in order not to leave a power vacuum. No total withdrawal of French forces is contemplated unless it is requested by the Vietnam government.

We hope Vietnam forces will be increased in efficiency although their number will be drastically cut. The main problems for the military in Vietnam are of internal security and aggression from the outside and must be handled by the deterrent power of SEATO.

PARIS, *December 22, 1954*

THIS afternoon I called on General Guillaume, French chief of staff, in his office in the Cour d'Honneur at the Invalides. I must say these are pathetic offices. I only hope they do not represent the present status of France's army.

Guillaume, who was wearing civilian clothes, seems somewhat subdued compared to when I saw him last in Morocco. He asked me not to quote him because generals now had the reputation of talking too much. He explained his theory that France has three military vases—Indochina, Africa, and Europe. When the level of water in one is increased, it reduces the level in the others, or vice versa. Thus, water dipped out of the Indochina vase will fill those in Africa and Europe.

Guillaume also thought Soviet strategy now was to outflank the West through Asia and Africa. There would be no direct Soviet assault in Europe while we had our eyes fixed on Moscow. Instead, the Communists were trying to undermine our position in the East and in Africa. If we lose North Africa we cannot hold Europe because North Africa is Europe's southern flank.

I asked if France were planning to make atomic weapons. Guillaume said so far the French were working only on abstract nuclear science and atomic piles, but the possibility of producing plutonium exists. The question of atomic arms has not yet been decided, but it is under discussion.

PARIS, *December 25, 1954*

THIS Christmas morning I went over to see Prime Minister Pierre Mendès-France at his apartment on the fourth floor of 23, rue du Conseiller Collignon, near the Muette. Poor Mendès had taken a bad beating last night when the Assembly voted him down on German rearmament. But he is now making this a question of confidence and hopes to squeak through when the matter is posed again Monday.

Mendès has a quiet middle-class neighborhood. Outside, a couple of gendarmes were the only sign that anybody special lived there. His apartment is very bourgeois and not attractive. In his study I noticed a porcelain tobacco jar with his name on it, a four-volume set of Dante, and three volumes of Stendhal's novels as well as a silver taste-vin serving as an ashtray. That is the only use such an object would have with Mendès because he hardly ever drinks—even wine.

Mendès was friendly, quiet, and grave. He is not having a very merry Christmas, poor fellow. He and his wife had a *réveillon* last night in the form of a quiet *tête-à-tête* dinner with water. It was the first time they had been alone together for months. They never drink wine when they are alone "of course," he said. He added: "But I am not against a drink and sometimes I lift a glass of champagne with friends." Today he was planning to work all day, but said if he were lucky and had the time he wanted to go to a movie with his wife. He is calm, sad-looking, and polite, with the appearance of a reflective rabbi which belies his reputation as a fighter.

I told Mendès some of his advisors say it would be a good idea if he were ousted from office after the German rearmament agreements are ratified in order to better prepare his popular position while in opposition and thereby to come back stronger in general elections. Mendès said he knew they felt this way, but he did not agree. He did not want to be ousted and added: "I want to continue my fight in the government and I don't want to be thrown out even if it would enable me to make propaganda. I prefer to continue my job in office—that is to say, my job of pushing through my program."

I asked if he thought it would be good to form a new party of the non-Marxist left in the event he should be ousted despite his wishes. He answered: "I don't think it would be good to have a new party or a new rally [referring to de Gaulle's RFP]. In all the existing parties there are good men as well as bad sectors. The fight must go on inside each party in order to rejuvenate them."

He agreed that France's political life would be better if it had fewer parties "but I don't see how we can get that result because it is contrary to our tradition." He then added: "As for myself, I prefer to work within the Radical party rather than in any new one."

PARIS, *December 31, 1954*

LAST night we dined at the Norstads' and had a long gossip. I recalled that Larry was the only American general I knew during the war who was as interested in winning the peace as he was in winning the war, and therefore favored military operations in eastern Europe to save that area from the Russians. He said that after the conference between the British and the

Americans on this subject, the British got him into bad trouble. They also wanted the same approach but Marshall was dead against it. Marshall was strictly a military man and did not think in these terms. Therefore, the Americans were furious with Slessor who suggested Norstad should go back to Washington to explain the argument for an eastern European campaign to Marshall. Larry, of course, was then a junior one-star general. "I was almost court-martialed," he recalls ruefully.

VIENNA, *January 5, 1955*

AFTER seeing Chancellor Julius Raab (a waste of time), I was taken through the complex corridors and staircases of the Ballhausplatz (from the antechamber in which Dollfuss bled to death) to the office of Leopold Figl, former Chancellor and now foreign minister. Figl is a highly sympathetic, agreeable, intelligent little man who has the reputation for being somewhat overly fond of Austria's sweet-tasting wines with their deadly after-effects. He looks like a dressed-up fox with spectacles. His face is ruddy. His eyes are red-brown and twinkle behind their glasses. His moustache is flaming red. His hair is rubicund. His expression is humorous.

Figl thought Moscow's initial goal, vis-à-vis Austria, is to try and neutralize the country in order to prevent it from becoming a member of any western European bloc or grouping, even economic. He stressed that the Russians were thinking not only of the military and strategic aspects, but also of the economic; that they don't want Austria's economic cooperation with the West. Moscow hopes eventually to gain economic control of Austria and then bring it slowly into its political orbit; much as it is patiently trying to do with Finland.

Austria insists on full sovereignty when the state treaty is finally signed and this means the state shall have the authority to decide independently if it wishes to be neutral; it cannot accept that this should be imposed in advance by other powers.

Moscow fears the effect in the satellites if a free Austria appears on their borders. The net result is a new problem for Austria, which faces further delays on its treaty.

There is no chance of the Soviets trying to partition Austria. This is a single, compact country with one government, unlike Germany. It is impossible to split it in two. The Austrian Constitution, government, and Parliament are all in Vienna under Four Power agreements to which Moscow is a party. It is impossible for the Russians to blockade Vienna like Berlin.

Lunched with Tommy (Llewellyn) Thompson, our ambassador and high commissioner. He spent most of the last year away from his post—in London, representing the United States in the secret Trieste negotiations.

Tommy said creation of a Soviet NATO for eastern Europe (the Warsaw

Pact) should give the Russians a chance to get out of Austria because they will then have an excuse to put their troops in all satellite countries under a "unified" command. They would no longer need the excuse of keeping soldiers in Rumania and Hungary to protect lines of communications to their zone in Austria.

The Russians are unhappy about their occupation of Austria. Their troops are contaminated by a happy populace. But the Russians want to maintain their position here for bargaining purposes in the diplomatic market.

PARIS, *January 13, 1955*

LAST night I had a most interesting talk with Harold Stassen, now head of the Foreign Operations Administration and here for the current meeting of OEEC. We sat in his rather unattractive suite and had a drink. While I sipped a scotch and soda, to my astonishment he ordered and drank a daiquiri—a strange after-dinner libation.

I started off by asking Stassen if he would talk on the following subjects: Wherever Russia advances into Europe—in other words moves toward the west—she brings a lower standard of living. Therefore the odds are on our side. However, wherever Russia pushes to the south or east—in other words into Asia—she tends to bring with her a higher standard of living. Therefore, the odds are on her side.

Basically he agreed with this observation, which he considered very wise. He went on to say that the question at the heart of the matter was the availability of capital. He continued:

Availability of capital is almost a complete key to the standard of living of any people. Capital is not just gold. It is available resources—available for immediate translation into living standards. In this respect Europe is of course above the Soviet Union. And when I say Europe I include eastern Europe. On the other hand, all of Asia is below the Soviet Union in this respect.

The basic economic method of the Communist system is to utilize manpower and spend it to create capital. Thus, the Communists spend men for railways, roads, mines, transportation, equipment, etc., just the way they spent men at Dien Bien Phu. Therefore, a large population becomes a capital asset because of the entire disregard for human life applied under the Communist system. They are able to translate unskilled manpower into capital in a way that no civilized nations are able to do—at any rate, no civilization based upon the Judeo-Christian philosophy.

In doing this the Communists cannot create capital as rapidly as an advanced free society can with its incentives and other means of encouraging. But it can create capital more rapidly than a backward society for the first time endeavoring to use the rules of freedom.

Stassen continued:

In Asia people from the non-Communist countries see as a consequence of the Russian system, which spends men, the creation of the new
capital assets such as railways, and they do not worry about the value of
life that has been spent in order to accomplish these things. They do not
tend by tradition in Asia to regard the value of life as highly as we do.
The question is: How can we reply to this situation?
The contest for Asia which is now on can be won by the free world
through supplying a capital element and at the same time the necessary
skills to use it. We must bring in from the outside a factor to counterbal-
ance what the Communists are able to accomplish with sheer manpower.

Stassen said: "We now feel the Communists cannot take Indochina except by force." The main problem is: "Are you going to maintain an army
so big that you need a dictatorial system in order to maintain it, or are you
going to build an army only large enough to defend the internal security of
the country and at the same time permit the improvement of living standards by not being too big a burden on the country's economy?"
We had decided an army was needed that would only be large enough to
maintain security and to serve as a sort of a glass windshield on the frontier.
By this he meant that any invader would have to visibly break it in order to
try and take over the country. That symbol would then permit reaction from
abroad. The rest of the money saved by cutting the army would be used for
long-term economic development in Indochina.
Nobody could be sure that we are going to be able to hold Vietnam but,
on the other hand, we cannot give up while there is even one chance in fifty.
He told a story about a certain man who had once been condemned to
death by the emperor. The man told the emperor that he begged only one
last favor. When asked what that was he said: "Before I die I would like to
be able to teach the emperor's favorite black horse to speak."
This intrigued the emperor who asked how long he thought it would take
to do this. The condemned man said probably he could accomplish it within
a year. When he was returned to prison his cellmates asked how he had
been able to save himself from execution. He explained. They asked then:
"But do you really think you can teach the horse to speak?" The man
replied: "Anything can happen within a year. I might die a pleasant, peaceful death. The emperor might die. And, who knows, I might even be able to
teach the horse to speak." Stassen said that after all, we were playing for
time in a similar way in Indochina.

PARIS, *January 24, 1955*

THIS afternoon I had a long talk with Gruenther out at SHAPE. Al thought:

We should be in the guerrilla and subversion field more than we are.
But this is a national problem rather than a SHAPE problem. We must

take first steps first. Guerrilla-type action must take a second place because it would occur in national territories. In other words, if any army began to occupy part of a country, guerrilla action in that occupied country would be the responsibility of the nation itself. It is very difficult to coordinate guerrilla planning and subversion planning during peacetime. This requires a high degree of centralized authority—as in Russia.

[Militarily speaking] we are in a new era. A surplus of manpower is subject to a greater destruction in the war of the future than a small amount of manpower. Even right now, this matter is beginning to be difficult. We have a big ultimate advantage over the manpower of the Soviet bloc.

DULLES ON

A-BOMBS IN ASIA

BEIRUT, *January 29, 1955*

I AM JUST WINDING UP A TWO-DAY STAY HERE DEVOTED LARGELY TO looking into the Arab refugee situation which is handled by UNRWA, of which Harry Labouisse is boss. I dined with Harry and Eve (formerly Curie) tonight and last night and had two long talks with Harry before and after inspecting pitiful camps. He told me he intends from now on to leave the administration of UNRWA almost entirely to his English deputy, and to spend his own time seeking a basic solution for the problem. At present, he feels the U.S. and Britain should get tough with both sides, telling Israel it must take back some of the refugees and settle them between the de facto frontier and the original partition line and compensate the rest, largely from German restitution funds; then the Arabs must be told this is the best that can be done for them, they must recognize Israel and permanently resettle the remainder of the refugees.

Harry says the Federal security program is utter nonsense. It took six weeks for the U.S. to clear Harry for his job. He has on his staff a former Federal security officer; it took eight weeks to clear him. Most American applicants take from six to nine months to be cleared and as a result get fed up and take other more remunerative jobs. As a result Harry has to depend heavily on British or other nationals; he can get them quickly and they don't have to be cleared by the U.S. He says it would be far easier and simpler for him to hire any Russian instead of an American. And there isn't the slightest security aspect to UNRWA.

KARACHI, *January 31, 1955*

FLEW in yesterday afternoon from Beirut and went straight to the Metropole Hotel which is unchanged except that most of the midgets whom Mr.

Soso, the Italian manager, had collected seem to have departed. Two years ago there were still about a dozen. Now there are only two or three tiny little men with white suits and white turbans bound by green bands. To see them march off carrying a suitcase on their heads makes it appear as if the baggage has sprouted legs.

In the early evening I went to see Ghulam Muhammad, who is governor general. The poor old man is a pitiful wreck. He had another stroke (at least his second) a couple of years ago and it left one leg paralyzed and finished the job of wrecking his ability to speak. He is also rumored to have tuberculosis. He is a fine looking fellow with long intelligent face and pendulant lower lip, brilliant eyes, and a good brain, still unimpaired. But I sat beside him on a sofa for forty minutes and although he spoke continually I couldn't understand more than a few phrases; the rest was utterly incomprehensible. He clearly has little time to live and his long, fine hands are already the waxen consistency of death.

As on earlier occasions, he said,

> [American capitalism is] selfish and narrow. It hasn't enough energy or broadness of concept. America hasn't met its global responsibilities properly yet. You take five years to think about a problem and then three years to act. This process costs too much. Look at China or at Vietnam. In threatened countries you have two choices: Either you must defend them against Russia or you must build up their economies. You are always too late. You are going to lose many things. You are going to link us up in the mess too. You must end your policy of half measures. One curse of capitalism is that it always wants to be efficient in terms of dollars. By the time experts have computed an efficient cost, things have already gone too far.

This morning I visited the minister of finance, Choudhri Mohamad Ali. Mohamad Ali recognizes the defects in democracy here but says: "Democracy is an ideal to be aspired after and worked for. It can never be perfectly achieved. My good friend Iskander Mirza sometimes talks of 'controlled democracy' and people think he means something like the Kemalist movement in Turkey. But I ask him: 'And who is to control the man who controls democracy?' "

Mohamad Ali said the word "Pakistan" had been invented by a group of Muslim students at Cambridge University in the 1930s after Iqbar, the greatest Muslim poet of British India, had written of a state of the Muslims in the west of India. Actually it means "land of the pure," but the name was originally an anagram: *P* for Punjab; *A* for Afghans (referring to the Pathans); *K* for Kashmir; *S* for Sind; and *Stan* for Baluchistan.

KARACHI, *February 5, 1955*

THIS morning I saw my old friend Iskander Mirza, who is now a major-general (lieutenant-colonel when I first knew him) and minister of interior. He is the "strong man" of the government and probably is going to make a play for dictator one of these days. He is chunky (about five feet ten) and a bit fat but with a determined face and character.

Mirza said the country had been "ruined" by complete adult suffrage for all men and women. "You can't have suffrage on that scale with 86 percent of the population illiterate. The big problem here is to spread literacy and education and this takes precedence over democracy. Eventually there should be a version of the American system but with even more power for the President."

Mirza said the Afghans were being damned fools with the Russians; one Afghan minister is a known Communist. He claims the Indians are "still" financing the Pakhtoonistan movement, although they claimed during the Delhi talks with Pakistan last week that they don't want the northwest frontier or the Khyber pass to change hands. "The Durand line is a sound geographical and strategic border," Mirza says.

Then I had lunch with a group of young Pakistani businessmen and intellectuals in Wajid Ali's concrete "bubble-house" on Victoria Street. The young men there—all of whom stuck to fruit juice and avoided alcohol—were a nice and impressive lot.

They all agreed you could have no "controlled democracy" and that dictatorship would lead to bloodshed—although it might be attempted. They said if you start on the premise that the country isn't ready for democracy it will never be considered so—as those men in power cement their power.

They also said the United States is not nearly so popular as we fancy. It is not a question of our Palestine policy but of our China policy. The people here think we are trying to squash a legitimate Asiatic government which may yet provide a pattern for all Asia to follow.

This evening I dined with Chester Bowles (former ambassador to India, former Democratic governor of Connecticut) and his wife. Steb (Mrs. Bowles), a tall angular woman, was dressed in a violet sari. She looked like a Daughter of the American Revolution at a masquerade. I was amused when Chet, who himself asked for the moon on behalf of Nehru, observed critically: "I have no use for American envoys abroad who try and represent the country they are accredited to instead of the U.S.A. and who take on its flavor instead of remaining American."

Bowles is bright and charming but much too overconfident. He keeps citing statistics—like any good advertising man—as the answer to everything. He says Russia is saving 8 percent of its gross product annually as against 4 percent for us (a CIA figure). We could "save" India easily if we just promised her $500,000,000 a year which, he claims, is necessary to her development, and which is "nothing out of our annual budget of $60,000,000,000." How about Pakistan, I asked.

On the way home, as I was walking toward the hotel, a voice came out of the shadows followed by an evil, leering face: "Anywhere you want, Sir," it said. "Any go, Sir. Girl, maybe? Maybe boy? Maybe please change money? Maybe drink, Sir?"

NEW DELHI, *February 8, 1955*

DONALD Kennedy, U.S. chargé d'affaires and a man who seems to have a lot of practical horse sense, analyzes anti-American feeling here as deriving from:

1. *Racism*—the American white-domination attitude.

2. *Imperialism*—the white man was the imperialist in Asia. We supported the French in Indochina and Chiang as a dummy against Mao. We are the all-powerful representative of the white West.

3. *Brutal honesty*—Americans are far too forthright, frank, and open when the Indian would prefer subtle indirection.

4. *Bossiness*—the Indians tend to resent our aid because they feel we try too much to tell them what to do.

5. *Sense of humor*—their sense of humor is more restrained and subtle.

6. *Nehru*—Nehru is an intellectual snob who dislikes most Americans as "uncouth." Our ways irritate him: private investment, advertising, pushiness. And those around him, like Krishna Menon, share this view and feed it. When Nehru came to the United States on an official visit in 1949, he felt there was much too much ostentation. At a dinner given for him by a group of bankers the host boasted that so many billion dollars were represented by the people around the table. Nehru shuddered. At a White House dinner he sat on Truman's right, Vinson on Truman's left. Most of the meal was taken up in a debate between Truman and Vinson on the relative merits of Maryland and Missouri bourbon whisky.

NEW DELHI, *February 9, 1955*

THIS morning I had a good chat with C. D. Deshmukh, minister of finance, and reputedly one of the most pro-American Indians in authority. I was amused to note sparrows twittering about the room and flying in and out of the open window, perching on the heavy brocade curtains behind his desk.

He said the impression of growing American unpopularity in India was really based on what journalists wrote and younger members of the Congress party said. Journalists here tended to be left-wing and critical. Regretfully, Deshmukh conceded, there was a "touch of a sneer" on both sides— American toward Indian and vice versa. And in any ideological dispute, people in Asia would prefer to risk communism on the theory that it would be national communism as against any dependence on the West.

Deshmukh said:

We don't misunderstand your motives, but you *are* helping colonialism
—just as you say we are helping communism by our actions. You feel we
are walking into the spider's parlor. We feel you are wrong in the assumption that military power is needed to negotiate with communism
from strength. Even you now realize that massive retaliation is too dangerous. But we remember that you considered atomic intervention at
Dien Bien Phu even if this was canceled. We fear that another time it
may come about and that the same thing will happen to us, as the result
of a distant explosion, as happened to the Japanese fishermen. Too many
people live in this part of the world.

Many of us resent America's desire for public expression of "gratitude" for aid. You should believe in your remedy—not in what people
say they think of it. We have reason to suspect we are more disliked in
the United States than you are here. After all, we have never made fun of
your leaders, whereas Nehru is referred to in slighting terms in many
American publications.

NEW DELHI, *February 10, 1955*

THIS morning I called on Sir Alexander Clutterbuck, British High Commissioner, who looks just like his marvelous name: tall, moustachioed, pale
blue popeyes, slightly vapid expression. Yet he is clearly no dope. He says:

"Nehru made a great mistake in Tibet and now seems to realize it. The
first tenet of Indian policy had always been to preserve Tibetan autonomy.
Now it's gone. Nehru lamely says he couldn't go to war on the issue. But he
is doing his best to be careful on Nepal where the Chinese are edging in. By
destroying medieval rule in Nepal, India replaced it with chaos."

CALCUTTA, *February 16, 1955*

DISCUSSION with Bob Reams, American consul general, with whom I am
staying, and some of the CIA and State Department people here in Calcutta,
concerning the situation in Tibet and the border states on the Tibetan
frontier.

The ruling families of Bhutan and Sikkim are unsure about supporting
India nowadays. China's influence is growing. The Chinese are building
roads in Tibet. Tibet is very remote. Until the Chinese came, the only
communications were across caravan routes. A railway is being built
through Jyekundo from China to Urumchi, in Sinkiang. Eventually a spur
from this railway can come down to Chando. There are now airfields at
Chando and Jyekundo.

The Dalai Lama went to Peking last summer (1954). He still retains the
personal loyalty of Tibetans, both secular and religious. The Chinese have
not been able to reduce his prestige. So far the Chinese have been content to

leave the Lamaist government. They have even rebuilt destroyed monasteries and subsidized others. The Panchen Lama of Shigatse is also in Peking. He is strictly religious. He has no secular authority. The Chinese thus have *both* leading Tibetan figures.

Imperceptibly and slowly the Chinese have undermined the position of the Dalai Lama. Since he has been in Peking he has made many statements on how good for Tibet the Chinese administration is. China wants to organize a triumvirate committee to run Tibet, including a Chinese general, the Dalai Lama, and the Panchen Lama.

No Chinese government has ever accepted the MacMahon line as a boundary. If China gets Nepal it will have crossed the Himalayan mountains. Great Britain considered Nepal, Bhutan, and Sikkim as the buffer states which constituted a strategic frontier for India. The British considered the northern boundaries of those states as essential to the defense of India. Nehru has organized Nepal as India's own "colony." China is nevertheless trying to take it over by subversion. And the situation there has gotten more chaotic since the Ranas were expelled as hereditary Prime Ministers. If the Chinese gain control of Nepal and Bhutan all of fermenting Bengal will undoubtedly fall to them. If Nepal goes Communist, India has probably had it.

BANGKOK, *February 21, 1955*

THIS evening, Jack Peurifoy, our ambassador, dropped in to see me at the hotel where I've been laid up with gout. He says this is the "most pro-American and most corrupt government" he's ever seen.

Peurifoy says it is imperative that the SEATO Conference come up with something positive that can have favorable propaganda repercussions. The Pentagon boys, who have already arrived, are dead against any supreme command setup for SEATO or commitment of any United States forces; they want to rely on our air and sea power in the west Pacific.

The U.S. is making good use of Thailand to support tottering Laos, Cambodia, and Burma. He thinks Burma is beginning to lean our way. China has organized subversionist movements north of Thailand (the Pathet Thais headed by Pridi) and in northern Laos where they control two provinces.

BANGKOK, *February 22, 1955*

BANGKOK is a lovely quaint town with red water lilies in the canals, bougainvillea trees, banana groves, flowers everywhere, ducks swimming about beside the streets, orange-robed Buddhist monks, and gabled, slope-roofed pagodas.

Called on Raymond Offroy, French ambassador and friend. Offroy is pessimistic about SEATO. The Laotian Premier, who is here, told Offroy: "You must *convince* us that we will be protected."

There is too much rivalry and regionalism in SEATO. The French are interested only in Indochina; the British in Malaya; the Americans in Thailand. The headquarters cannot be put in Singapore as the British want; that would indicate a peripheral strategy and would be like establishing NATO at Lisbon.

BANGKOK, *February 23, 1955*

THE SEATO Conference opened today in the Throne Hall of Ananta Samakom Palace, a curious and gaudy bit of oriental baroque with lots of gilt, marble, curlicues, and twittering sparrows flying around inside. Outside, gangs of schoolchildren marched up and down waving paper flags and bearing slogans such as "SEATO for Democrat" and "Democrat Asia."

Dulles arrived during the afternoon. Despite a bath, shave, and fresh white suit he has aged greatly and is haggard and always twitchy. He told me last night:

I have been working a long time to bring about a cohesive security arrangement for this part of the world. We talked about this while fighting was still going on in Indochina. But the President didn't have the necessary authority from Congress to intervene then and there was no assurance that we would have had any allies if we had acted. We hope to do away with such impediments through this treaty. This area is demonstrably important to the United States and the treaty assures our interest in it and assures that we have allies here.

To us there are three strong points: South Korea with its strong army of 500,000; Formosa with its army of 300,000; and the SEATO powers. This creates a situation so that if there is aggression in this area there could be retaliatory action in other areas. China would face a war on three fronts. China wouldn't like this. When the Chinese fought in Korea they didn't activate the fronts in Formosa or Indochina.

There will not be any permanent committal of United States ground forces in this area. We don't expect to duplicate the NATO setup. We rely primarily on sea and air power and retaliatory action at places and by means of our own choosing.

The French have a substantial military force in South Vietnam, which is part of the treaty area. That is France's principal role. Also, they have special relations with the three Indochinese states. Geneva bars the importation into Indochina of new military aid. The United States can't increase the number of its military advisers. If they were to leave, under one interpretation of the armistice, they could not be replaced. That places a strong dependence on France. If the French were to pull out of Vietnam there would be chaos. They are indispensable for the present.

The striking power Communist China faces now makes open aggression unlikely. The greatest danger faced is subversion. The situation now is like a hand with fingers—but no direct interlocking arrangements except U.S. participation in several agreements.

Eventually it will be desirable to integrate Japan into the defense of Southeast Asia. There is some thinking of a closer link among Japan, Korea, and Formosa. That would probably be more logical as a next step. But within the next few years, not months.

BANGKOK, *February 25, 1955*

THE SEATO Conference ended today—not with a bang but a whimper. Everybody is glad to get out of this miserably hot, overcrowded, inefficient town.

Dulles said:

> The conference was a complete success. Everything we hoped for came out of it and nothing that we feared. I am glad to say that the presentation I made on the first day swept away the last vestiges of efforts to have specific forces allocated to this theater.
>
> It was agreed that security against subversion from without was a recognized problem that could best be dealt with on a bilateral basis and not by a central agency or pool. The reason for this was fear of leaks. That kind of business must be done on a very restricted basis. I remember Magsaysay once told me in Manila that he avoided leaks on his campaign against the Huks by never telling anyone what was on his mind.
>
> It should be borne in mind that we are operating on a basis where more and more we treat atomic weapons as conventional. There is a slow but steady turnover in our navy, changing ships and shifting over to the use of atomic weapons for tactical purposes. It doesn't make sense to use one hundred shots or bombs to do exactly the same job as one atomic weapon and it is much more expensive. Throughout history there has been a steady development of more powerful explosives.
>
> I would like to point out that "international communism" is mentioned in the communiqué. It had been left out of the draft produced by the working committee, but we insisted on its inclusion. Now we have made the words respectable here.

I was appalled by his remarks. The Conference did nothing and he boasts of scotching its economic or antisubversion collaboration efforts. He brags about getting the words "international communism" mentioned once in the communiqué. He is getting caught up in the political semantics of a holy war.

Note: Today was his sixty-seventh birthday.

SINGAPORE, *March 1, 1955*

INTERESTING conversation with Malcolm MacDonald, British Commissioner General for Southeast Asia, at his residence, Mallaig, a lovely place with magnificent gardens and grounds just outside Singapore.

MacDonald started off by saying it was most important that we hang on to Laos. The Pathet Lao is doing a lot of infiltration there. But if the government counts the votes we should be able to block the Communists in the August elections; I hope to hell they do the counting. If Laos goes, MacDonald admits, the overseas Chinese of Malaya and Singapore "would sit more firmly than ever on the fence. Siamese [Thai] opinion would be rocked. Northeast Siam [Thailand] would be outflanked. The Viet Minh would be able to penetrate Siam at will."

He admits, Chinese propaganda is having a big success here. It stresses Peking's diplomatic triumphs and the feeling of China's irresistability; not ideology. Chiang Kai-shek has virtually no remaining influence. The propaganda Peking puts out (largely by newspapers, magazines, and word of mouth; not radio) stresses China, China, China, as MacDonald puts it.

MacDonald says Britain hopes eventually to work out a federation among independent Malaya, Singapore, and the three British colonies in north Borneo. London's policy is now working toward this in a series of steps. It is hoped the area would become a single self-governing unit with the Commonwealth. Against this, some Indonesians are thinking of a great Malaysia, including the above area. If that dream ever came true, Singapore, with its commercial and industrial position and population, would be an immense asset.

Australia and New Zealand want Britain to get on with self-government in Malaya and Singapore to avoid the development of a passionate anticolonialist movement in these parts. But they don't want Britain to get out too quickly and leave the area naked. He adds: "They want the best of both worlds; but they can't have it that way."

Yesterday afternoon I took a brief tour around the island. The Singapore River, hot and stinking, is lined with junks mostly loading rubber. In the Chinatown area the narrow streets are jammed; stores sell gaily painted lanterns and palm-leaf fans. Laundry is strung out like banners on poles extending from housefronts. Outside, on the edge of the jungle, thatched Malay huts stand on stilts under the palms; little old women in pyjamas, their pigtails done up in buns, hurry along under the sun, shielding themselves with paper parasols.

Spent most of the morning talking with Hugh Cumming, our ambassador in Indonesia, and Lambton Berry, U.S. consul general here. Berry said the British were irked when we established ANZUS and excluded them, and ANZAM was set up as a salve to Churchill's pride in 1952. It was established secretly and included Australia, New Zealand, and Malaya (Britain).

The Australians don't think this is enough. Australia feels it was bitten twice in the last war because of inadequate preparations—in Greece and in Malaya. One out of seven Australian families suffered a loss. Australia won't stand for another commitment without a proven fighting chance to avoid disaster; it wants to feel able to make a stand. Britain must be able to assure Australia of sufficient strength; otherwise it will turn to the United States.

The British, Australians, and New Zealanders are irritated because we will not tell them anything specific concerning our commitments militarily in this area in the event the balloon goes up. The United States regarded Geneva as a diplomatic defeat and we don't want to commit ourselves precisely in any more real estate that may be lost.

The British staff chiefs feel they can only hold Malaya at the narrow waist of the Kra Isthmus in Thailand, north of Malaya, with the forces that would be available. They would be prepared to make a stand further north if forces were pledged, but they won't be.

Militarily, the Malayan civil war is at a stalemate and has remained there approximately since the departure of General Templer. Now it is more of a political than a military problem. Without a completely disproportionate and uneconomical military commitment in the area, Britain simply cannot totally clean out the jungle.

India wants to protect Southeast Asia and Singapore for strategic reasons. Nehru, after visiting China, indicated publicly he opposed the idea of the Chinese trying to move into Laos or Cambodia. Recently the Indonesian police confiscated Communist textbooks whose maps showed China as including all of mainland Southeast Asia (including Burma) plus Sumatra, Borneo, and the Celebes (not Java).

SAIGON, *March 2, 1955*

LUNCHED today with Lucien Bodard, *France-Soir* correspondent: a big, awkward fellow with thick, dark-rimmed glasses. He has three cats who wander all over his apartment, above all on the table and through the food.

There are growing indications Diem won't agree to elections. Diem can claim he's not a party to the Geneva agreement. Also that freedom doesn't prevail in the North. But if there is no election in 1956, says Bodard, there will be either open war or a real coordinated subversion effort. It depends how far China, which controls Ho, will let him go.

The Viet Minh is now busily organizing the villages of South Vietnam. Their agents take pictures of Ho Chi Minh and Bao Dai around and ask the peasants "Which will you vote for?" Naturally they say Ho—because Bao Dai is detested by everyone. "Don't forget that," warn the agents.

The Cao Dai and Hoa-Hao sects are split into segments. They have men in the government in order to assure income, and they have factions opposing the government to prevent it from becoming too strong.

Bai Vian (or Le Van Vian) is head of the Binh Xuyen gang. This is not a sect but simply an organization of tough racketeers. He was named chief of police for all Vietnam by Bao Dai. Previously Bao Dai had rented him the concession for Le Grand Monde, the famous and incredibly rich gambling concession at Cholon, outside Saigon. Bai Vian gave up the Grand Monde concession when the lease expired because it was getting too unpopular. He is no longer officially chief of the police, but he continues to run the police department under the Diem government. His Binh Xuyen gangsters make very efficient cops. Even his allies, the Cao Dai and Hoa-Hao sects had been jealous of his "take" from the Grand Monde. The Grand Monde has been suppressed. But he has organized all the Saigon brothels into one huge barracks system. This reorganization was financed out of U.S. aid money.

The Binh Xuyen started before the war as a half-patriotic anti-French, half-gangster organization. Bai Vian was jailed by the French but liberated by the Japanese when they took over. He then joined the Viet Minh and conducted a successful pillaging raid against arms shops. In 1945, at a victory march-past, his troops paraded proudly under the banner: "Pirates of Binh Xuyen." The French helped to develop the sects after the war because they didn't want the central government to get too strong. They preferred to use the feudal sects to weaken it.

SAIGON, *March 3, 1955*

THIS afternoon I saw General Ely at his office. He remains High Commissioner—or rather resident general—for all three Indochinese states, but he spends most of his time in Vietnam because Collins is accredited only to Vietnam. Ely still looks withered, pale, old, bloodless. The tropical climate and his uniform bring this out more than ever. And his bad right arm accentuates it.

I asked him what are the ultimate aims of France in Indochina. He said Paris was seeking to bring about an organization similar to the British Commonwealth. But there would be differences. France has no crown to serve as a symbol of loyalty. There would probably be serious mistakes if one sought to copy the British form exactly. But Ely wants the principle of absolute equality established within the French Union.

I asked Ely if France would seek to obtain defense agreements with the three states here before pulling out entirely—as Britain intends in Malaya and Singapore. He replied that the problem is to strengthen the local military forces. The defense of these countries cannot be assured by accords alone. Then, however, Ely admitted, France would seek to negotiate agreements for bases and defense privileges. France's expeditionary corps here must be largely evacuated.

In case this country remains partitioned, the South can continue to live alone; its economy is self-supporting. The North will suffer more. It is already under Chinese pressure and Viet Minh brutality is growing. The refugees are no longer mainly Catholic; they are Buddhist and from all classes: peasant, worker, intellectual. The refugee influx since the cease-fire is an immensely important factor. These people abandoned everything for freedom. There are now about 700,000 and there will be a million. They cannot be permitted to lose again the liberty they have made such sacrifices for—even if no solution for Vietnam is visible today.

Ely said:

We are obliged to say firmly that there will be elections and we are obliged to prepare openly for them. If we could be sure of *free* elections in the North we would win easily; the exodus of refugees is indicative of public opinion there. But there has never been a *free* election yet in the Communist world. So it is unlikely there will really be a nation-wide election. But we cannot admit this openly. If the Viet Minh realizes there will be no elections they will step up their subversion and infiltration program in the South now. This must be avoided. The oriental sense of time is not urgent. As long as the Viet Minh think there will be an election which they expect to win, they are not bothering too much about subversion preparations.

The above, I must say, sounds like hopeless naiveté to me. Ho Chi Minh has proven time and again he's not dumb.

Ely said a National Assembly had been created here two weeks ago. It was approved by Premier Diem and the absent chief of state, Bao Dai. It is largely appointed. But elections will be held this year for a constituent assembly. This will prepare the Constitution. Then, presumably, the dead weight of Bao Dai can be shed. But Ely, like everyone else, says France has to keep Bao Dai going as the legal cloak for the Diem government. I cannot understand this mystique—as if it were part of the line of ordained priests in the Catholic hierarchy. It is something like the Czech system whereby they had to subvert a bishop before he could "legally" ordain phony priests.

Randolph Kidder, United States chargé d'affaires, says it is reported the Binh Xuyen paid 41,000,000 piasters for control of the police; quite a concession!

Diem came to power halfway through the Geneva Conference. The battle was already lost. He had lived a sequestered life abroad for seventeen years. He was forced to pick a government immediately; therefore he selected some bad eggs. Furthermore, his administration had absolutely no French aid to get it started—no French experts or technicians. The situation was chaotic. When Diem came in he didn't even control the army or the police.

Things began to get better about four months ago when Diem gained control of the army and U.S. support was thrown solidly behind him. There has been marked recovery from the low point; but there is a discouragingly long way to go.

Diem's self-confidence has grown. He is honest and uncompromisingly nationalist. But he is uselessly stubborn and has no political savoir faire. He is a devout Catholic and somewhat mystic. A great idealist, he nevertheless basically distrusts most people. If Bao Dai goes, there will be no constitutional means of changing the government. There must first be a Constitution and a National Assembly. The day Bao Dai leaves, Diem becomes a dictator. That would bring his enemies together.

The French had been playing with the idea of bringing in Prince Buu Hoi, a politically naive scientist, but not a Communist. This was more of Mendès-France's "coexistence planning"—like the Sainteny mission to Hanoi.

If Diem falls there would be a setback of at least six months in the processes of land reform, army reorganization, refugee care, etc. Whoever came in would have to start again from scratch. Whether Diem is the best man or not, the point of no return has probably been reached. We have to support him now because there is no alternative.

PHNOMPENH, CAMBODIA, *March 6, 1955*

I AM just winding up a brief visit to Cambodia. King Norodom Sihanouk abdicated suddenly Wednesday. Ambassador Rob McClintock was in Manila at a U.S. diplomatic conference and had to fly back in a hurry. So I got aboard his private plane at Saigon and came along. These are the views of McClintock, an amusing, energetic fellow.

King Norodom Sihanouk, the thirty-three-year-old monarch who has just abdicated, has little use for politicians whom he considers troublemakers. In the elections scheduled for June, he would have had only his own hand-picked candidates. This is admittedly unconstitutional. But he argues that the people want it that way.

The Geneva agreements specified that the Democratic partisans could vote in free elections. It is the obligation of the International Control Commission (India, Poland, and Canada) to adhere to the Geneva agreements. The King decreed that nobody could vote who had not resided in the same place for the last three years. Partisans from the Democratic party had been in the woods during that time. Therefore they would automatically have been excluded.

When Dulles was here, he told both the French and the Cambodians that the United States must be given the chief responsibility for training the new Cambodian army or it would be difficult to persuade the United States Congress to approve military aid for Cambodia. The Cambodians want the French out of the country.

Phnompenh is a clean, typical, French colonial town. The Cambodians speak of it as the "inhabited park." There is an extraordinary complex of

Royal Palace and pagodas with two white elephants, chained in stables at a corner of the enclosure, bowing politely when fed with bamboo shoots. Outside the palace gate is a company of helmeted troops, with rifles, standing at ease while yellow-clad Buddhist priests stroll by and little carts are drawn by tiny horses trotting unconcernedly along.

Yesterday afternoon I took a boat trip along the river with McClintock. The vast bulk of the population lives, in squalid, unpainted rickety shacks erected on stilts, by fishing and drying fish. Curious boats like gondolas use little trawling nets. The banks of the river stink of drying fish. They hunt tigers here on elephants wearing a lamp like a miner's lantern affixed to their hats so they can shoot them at night by the reflection of their eyes.

The King has been on the throne twelve years. He was elected King from among several candidates by a crown council, thanks largely to the dominating personality of his ambitious mother. He is the grandson of a previous ruler. His mother rigged things so that he could gain the throne. During his early years he was a French puppet. He spent some time learning to be an officer at Saumur and is a good horseman as a result. But as he grew older he became more independent.

In 1953, the King took a round-the-world trip. When in France he was rebuffed by the French who gave him the brush-off. Enraged, he flew to the United States and denounced the French as oppressors.

When France finally resolved to parley, the Cambodians were clever enough to negotiate a series of conventions to assume control of the different facets of government without worrying about the country's juridical status in the French Union. By the end of 1953, Cambodia had its *real* independence. A national referendum was held asking whether the King had done well. He was approved by a majority that even a Communist plebiscite might envy.

After his famous popular referendum, the King had been led to believe that the people of Cambodia didn't even want elections and didn't want a popular assembly. Crowds of peaceful peasants had been showing up at the palace during recent weeks bearing banners proclaiming their faith in the King's personal rule. The King thought these demonstrations were genuine. On Tuesday, to his horrified amazement, he found out they had been rigged by his parents and were not at all bona fide protests against the idea of elections. This broke his heart and precipitated the abdication. And he didn't even tell his father, whom he named as his successor, or his doting mother of his plan—until after it was announced. Then he moved into his father's villa and his father took over the palace.

The King is a young man with a martyr's complex. He thinks of himself as a royal Robin Hood. He wants to go to the country and come back to his throne as a popular hero. In the interim, while his father rules, there will be no basic change in policy.

Cambodia is a sort of oriental Graustark. The political experience of the people is not far beyond that of the Bronze Age. There is very little means of spreading information. The country claims 40 percent literacy, but this is an exaggeration. The priesthood is archconservative. One of the King's hobbies is to make home movies in which he acts himself and in which he makes his cabinet and household participate. He likes to dress up as Tarzan and have himself filmed swinging from limb to limb.

SAIGON, *March 7, 1955*

THIS afternoon I had a long chat with British Ambassador Stevenson. He says the effect of American aid to Diem has been to freeze the political situation. No political forces are being developed. The sects always operate by having a dissident general in the bush and the official bosses in the government. They gained their military power when the French armed them and gave them areas to control during the anti-Communist war. They levy their own taxes and are good propaganda for the Communists.

Bao Dai is an intelligent, venal, evil man with an immensely bad reputation among such neutral nations as India and Burma. Last November, Donald Heath, still U.S. ambassador then, told Stevenson that if Bao Dai came back as a constitutional monarch with his family and settled in Saigon he would have the country behind him within six months; but Heath reckoned he wouldn't come back. (I think this statement proves once again that Heath is thick.)

The government is paralyzed by Diem's insistence on doing everything himself. Recently the British offered to train six Vietnamese police officials in anti-Communist techniques at a school in Malaya. But Diem, after long delays, vetoed all candidates. He is honest but his entourage is not.

It is all-important that the Viet Minh should not be allowed to capture the slogan of "Unification" and paint Diem as one who advocates partition of Vietnam. Thus we should certainly proceed on the basis that national elections for all Vietnam are to be held in 1956—even if they aren't.

Except for secret Communists, there are no political parties in South Vietnam. Throughout the eight-year war the French permitted no real political activity by nationalists. But there are armed sects. The Viet Minh strategy is to infiltrate the South's population and crumble it from within.

The appallingly low standards of living in these parts is indicated by the status of children. Last night, while sitting at the Continental Café, a beggar boy of about seven came dragging himself up to my table like a crab, both legs twisted and crippled. Later I saw him quite happily chasing after some other kids, moving like a fast little crab, hurtling forward on his hands, his hind portion slapping dead on the pavement as he progressed. Nearby, a mother was selling peanuts and using her tiny son, about three, as an assistant. He was dressed only in a ragged pyjama top, much too small for

him. Later, on the way home, I saw another child (it was now about
10 P.M.) winding a large snake merrily around his neck to help his peddler
father gather a crowd.

This evening Ed Stansbury, an old friend who now runs USIS, came down
to see me. He said one of Diem's chief weaknesses is that he trusts no one.
Therefore he himself insists on signing all entry and exit visas. He has to do
this at night, his only spare time, and everything is hopelessly delayed and
fouled up. He wants to prevent the departure of people against whom corruption charges might later be filed. And he wants to prevent his opponents
from entering. The result is that just about nobody can get any sort of visa
these days.

TAY NINH, *March 9, 1955*

I SPENT an extraordinary day at Tay Ninh, headquarters and holy city of
the Cao Dai sect, a curious melange of religion, free masonry, secret society,
and private army. The Cao Dai religion was founded thirty years ago and is
a blend of Buddhism, Taoism, and Confucianism with an organization and
hierarchy like Catholicism. Cao Dai runs what is virtually a feudal state
near the Cambodian border. Its agents have check points and frequently
levy tribute from trucks going through their territory. They have their own
flag, arms depots, military insignia, and ordnance factories where they
make Sten guns, automatic pistols, and rifles out of retempered steel. Their
organization includes male and female priests and priestesses, bishops, car-
dinals, and a "Superior." There used to be a pope. However, after his death,
no new pope was elected, so the Superior acts instead.

Cao Dai means "supreme being." The cathedral is extraordinarily hideous and ornate. When I approached, dozens of white-clad priests and priestesses were standing outside, the women wearing strange white hoods on
their heads. On either side of the cathedral are carved portals and gaily
painted pillars with designs, including twisting serpents and flowers. Overhead are representations of demons bearing axes and crude world maps, as
well as the slogans in French and Vietnamese: "God and Humanity" and
"Love and Justice." The three principal saints of the Cao Dai faith are a
character named Nguyen Binh Khiem, Victor Hugo, and Sun Yat-sen, the
Chinese revolutionary. The symbol of Cao Dai, equivalent to Christianity's
cross, is a human eye.

Inside the cathedral, windows are latticed with eyes and lotus flowers.
The aisle is dominated by two long rows of pink and blue pillars carved
with painted dragons. The Superior has a special cushioned throne mounted
on huge plaster cobras. On an altar, at the far end of the cathedral, incense
burns in honor of Cao Dai, Buddha, Christ, Confucius, and Lao-tse. Beside
the incense burner is the holy red tocsin of the religion, beaten on special
occasions.

After visiting the cathedral, I was taken outside through lines of priests and priestesses where I found still more prelates assembled to escort me to the Superior's residence. We formed a little parade. First there were white robed priests with tambourines and cymbals. Then there was a portable altar on which were tied fruit, flowers, and burning incense. This was borne by four priests. Two others held tall red umbrellas above it. Then I came with a cardinal. Then a batch of priests who had put on white conical hats to keep off the broiling sun. Making a hell of a racket, we marched toward the Superior's house. This was guarded by two squads of soldiers in white uniforms with berets. They were well-armed with automatic Sten guns.

The Superior, Pham Cong Tac, a smiling intelligent-looking man who appears to be about sixty, came down the stairs to greet me and then escorted me to a group of armchairs in the foyer where we sat and chatted. His French is quite good and, unlike most Vietnamese the accent is actually comprehensible. The Superior, like the other priests, was dressed in white from toes up.

Although Cao Daiists have the reputation of great purity and supposedly don't drink, we were served good champagne as soon as we seated ourselves. This was filled with lumps of dirty ice and accompanied by stale lady fingers covered with flies. The Superior chatted away merrily, contradicting himself all the time. At the start he said: "The situation in Vietnam is so difficult that we must all unite. All the nationalists must get together behind the government." He explained that the agreement of Cao Dai, Hoa-Hao, and Binh Xuyen was not aimed against the government. (Actually their aim is to bring down Premier Diem.) He talked happily about the need for a free press and free speech. He praised Diem as a real nationalist, but complained that the country lacked two essentials: a Constitution and a National Assembly. Bao Dai should come back and set these up in "a constitutional monarchy like England's."

He said there were more than two million Cao Daiists. They have three ministers in the Diem government. Their private army numbers more than twenty thousand. The Superior wound up his confusing talk by saying this government was illegal because Bao Dai had had no right to select Diem as Premier. He added: "I am pro-American but your General Collins is making a great mistake in backing Diem. Diem is unpopular and only the Catholics have any use for him."

I then drove off some miles to the Cao Dai military headquarters where, after China tea, I lunched with the operational general and his staff, several colonels, two majors, and a captain. The captain, obviously European, turned out to be Walter Schumann, aged thirty-three, late of the German Wehrmacht and the French Foreign Legion. After fighting throughout the Russian campaign of World War II, he fled from his native city of Leipzig to Berlin, then joined the Legion as a private (he had been an Oberleut-

nant). He eventually married a Vietnamese, has several children, became a
converted Cao Daiist, now bears the name Nguyen Thanh Duo, and is an
instructor in infantry tactics at their military school. He seemed quite merry,
although half toothless, and eats away with the best of them with chopsticks.

Before lunch, we discussed the other sect, Hoa-Hao (which has the
reputation of even more military fanaticism than Cao Dai—plus the charming habit of occasionally devouring raw the livers of defeated enemies) and
the Binh Xuyen gang. Hoa-Hao has about 1,500,000 adherents and controls a big piece of the South. Binh Xuyen has no mass support but runs
Saigon through the police, brothels, etc. Hoa-Hao, the Cao Daiists claimed,
now has squeezed its own men into 40 percent of the police force—which I
doubt is true.

The Chinese style (they called it Vietnamese) lunch we had, eaten with
dirty red chopsticks, consisted of rice, some gristly, bloody nuggets of meat,
strange soup, fish, red wine, beer, coffee, and green bananas. The fish was
that unattractive sort they catch in rice paddies which is said to be capable
of walking across the road during the dry season. It was served au bleu,
naked, standing on a platter and staring at me with its blind eyes. It tasted
like mud.

The general, who spoke excellent French, complained that Diem was
trying to force unification of the private armies too fast. He said soldiers of
the regular Vietnamese army were selling their arms to the sects. The
country is in a state of anarchy and Diem does not control the non-Catholic
communities. Things have gotten so bad in the South that once more, as
during the war, cars had to travel in convoys—in order to avoid piracy.

SAIGON, *March, 11, 1955*

SPENT a couple of hours talking with General Joe Collins, our chief representative, over drinks at his house. Collins is a likeable, smooth-talking man
with a gift for clarity; but his is not a first-class brain and I think he
oversimplifies things here. He stressed his friendship with Ely, who has just
returned to Paris to discuss the Indochina budget. Collins feels there has
been a definite change in French policy. They used to keep talking about
replacing Diem with other candidates, but that has halted. And the French
very recently ceased paying the armies of the sects. These will now wither
away, Collins thinks. He says the North is having a difficult time under the
Communists and the failure of the rice crop makes famine probable.

In the afternoon I had a long talk with Diem at the President's Palace. It
was, in fact, much longer than I wanted. Diem became heavily boring. He is
exceptionally youthful looking for his fifty-five years: short, with stubby
small hands and placid brown face. His office contains few decorations aside
from a colorful map and an ancient Khmer head.

Diem has an odd way of talking. He speaks excellent French. But as he gets warmed up on a subject both his voice and his gaze seem to drift far away; he takes on an almost drugged expression (although his only vice seems to be cigarettes and he is so puritanical that his enemies say he doesn't even know what a woman looks like).

He claims there has been no change in French policy. The provisional Assembly will meet before May 1. It will approve a budget and prepare the machinery for an elected constitutional assembly. The budget will be unable to support a large army. But at the end of this spring, classes will be called up for training in compulsory military service. The sects' armies receive no more pay, except for the three thousand Cao Daiists integrated into the national army. Diem admits that the biggest problem is to get back control of the police from Binh Xuyen; there is no plan on this yet.

He repeated many times that individual rights and property must be respected. His government was advancing. It has received the powers of administration from France and the backing of the United States. Land reform has already started and previously uncultivated land is being tilled by refugees. Financing this reform is difficult however. Diem talked rather vaguely of establishing a *"crédit populaire."*

He made no secret of his skepticism about elections in 1956, and said it was impossible to know what was taking place behind the Iron Curtain in the North. He claimed that the Vietnamese there were even more disgusted with the hypocrisy of Viet Minh than with the tyranny of communism; that they resented more the continual lies along the path to communization than a frank and brutal dictatorship.

I came away rather puzzled. Diem seems to border on the fanatic, and doesn't appear to be very bright.

MANILA, *March 12, 1955*

BEFORE flying here today I spent an hour at Saigon airport talking with Graham Greene whom I had seen on and off in Saigon. He has been waiting around a month trying to get to Viet Minh territory in the North but they have kept him cooling his heels waiting for a visa; no answer—the usual Communist response. He is flying up to Haiphong today to see if he can prod some response out through the International Control Commission there. Apparently he hopes to finish a novel on Indochina. Although he is a dilapidated looking character, he is certainly adventurous enough and was describing a walking trip across Liberia he took with a cousin years ago; his long stay on government wartime business in Lagos and Freetown (which he liked); and a three-day sortie with British antiguerrilla forces in Malaya a few years ago which tired him so cruelly that he wanted to commit suicide to avoid the embarrassment of having to be carried out of the jungle.

MANILA, *March 14, 1955*

THIS morning I talked with Admiral Spruance, American ambassador here, a mild-looking man with the voice and manner more of a college professor than of an old sea dog. He is clearly most intelligent, wise, thoughtful, and open-minded.

Spruance admitted that Magsaysay had disappointed him and other observers. He is honest and has good ideas, but he is intellectually lazy, never reads, and has no political aptitude. He just doesn't follow through. For example, he called a special session to enact needed land reforms. Then he permitted the Congress to bottle up the bills he wanted. He could have avoided this had he been more energetic. He has great popular appeal with the people though.

Magsaysay should have one or two really efficient Philippine advisers on political matters. This is a big lack. An American adviser would be suspect and therefore useless. One of the big problems is the unequal distribution of land and the big estates of absentee landlords. There are still many heritages from feudal Spain. This land must be better shared because the Republic's 20,000,000 population increases by 400,000 annually.

The Filipinos back our Formosa policy and realize the island must be kept out of Communist hands or the whole U.S. defense system will be penetrated. But Spruance thinks our attitude on Quemoy and Matsu is foolish. These are military positions of weakness and should not be defended. Furthermore, the Communists can take them whenever they want if they are prepared to sacrifice the men. And they can profitably trade losses with Chiang at a rate of ten to one. Chiang would be stronger if he pulled out his troops now; he probably wouldn't be able to extricate them once the Communists attacked. He could never return to mainland China from the islands through Fukien which doesn't lead anywhere. He would much more logically return through Canton or just south of the Yangtze.

MANILA, *March 15, 1955*

LUNCHED with President Ramon Magsaysay at Malacañan Palace. It is an old Spanish residence which the Spanish government took over as the summer palace for its governors in the early nineteenth century; then it served the American governors and now the Filipino presidents. White, surrounded by large deciduous trees with creepers, a small private menagerie, and deer strolling about, it has much charm. The main room is hung with portraits of American governors and Filipino dignitaries and fitted out with immense Bohemian crystal chandeliers. Lunch was at 12:30—showing the American influence—hot soup, fish, crayfish, steak, spinach, rice, salad, mangoes, ice cream, bread and butter, and water and coffee—plenty for a broiling day.

Magsaysay is large for a Filipino—about five feet ten, strong with heavy shoulders. He has a broad face with a big jaw. His manner is affable. He is very fidgety, however, and throughout lunch his fingers were writhing about. He seemed moderately pessimistic. He complained about the amount of work he has to do—every night at least three hours of going through the complaints system he has established and answering letters and telegrams. He obviously knows little about foreign affairs and doesn't have much interest in them. For the most part he is still working to stamp out communism. Its military apparatus has been squashed but land reform and corruption remain to be rooted out. There is still corruption in the Army as well as in civil life. The only way to kill it is by ruthlessly exposing and punishing those involved. He found this out when fighting the Huks. He said he freely used bribery to beat the Huks: so much per dead Huk. He bribed informers with automobiles. He used to distribute doped Coca-Cola to be given to Huks by peasants who would then murder their visitors to collect head money.

TAIPEI, *March 16, 1955*

I FLEW here yesterday and found myself immediately plunged into the powerful atmosphere of intellectual incest that is inescapable and within minutes has you thinking like Senator Knowland. In the afternoon I visited my old friend Karl Rankin, American ambassador here four years. He had asked me to stay with him but I told him I preferred not to risk tarnishing his reputation by what I might write.

Rankin makes an excellent argument on the need to hold Matsu and Quemoy, the famous offshore islands. The Chinese Communists are very weak on logistics. While Chiang Kai-shek's Formosa has jet airfields and pipelines to pump fuel to them, the Communists have no effective air bases yet in the south from which to attack Formosa and no railways near the coast and only a few poor roads over which to transport fuel when those bases are built. The only supply route now is by sea—which Chiang, with our aid, controls. The two offshore islands help interfere with the build-up for an eventual Formosa invasion by assisting in the control of the Straits.

Quemoy and Matsu don't lead anywhere in terms of an eventual invasion —either by Chiang into China or by China into Formosa. But the Communists must gain control of the Formosa Straits before they launch any adventures into Southeast Asia, in order to protect their flank and ease their logistical problem.

Rankin feels it is pointless to give up the islands in exchange for a Communist promise to coexist or respect a cease-fire because the Communists have always broken their promises when it so suited them and are now doing so in Korea, where they are building up forces in open violation of the armistice. There is no point, says Rankin, in throwing another babe from the fleeing sled to the wolves; soon we will run out of babes and the wolves will scramble into the sleigh.

Someday there will probably be a showdown. We must convince China and Asia that we are not merely a paper tiger. It might be best to have this showdown over the offshore islands where an attack could be squashed in a strictly localized battle that would not risk world war as would an attack on Formosa itself. The Nationalists could handle a small or medium-sized attack. Anything really big would probably involve more than the two islands and that would bring us in anyway.

My own observations: For five years, Chiang's soldiers have been told they are going back to the mainland. Now they are beginning to realize they won't. And the Communists are offering bribes to pilots to desert with their planes. Eight million Formosans of the ten million people of Nationalist China have no interest in the mainland. The army is getting old. It will gradually be replaced by levies of Formosans commanded by Chinese generals.

Now the Communists are not tied up in Korea and can occupy themselves elsewhere. In 1951, when they were in Korea, Chiang's forces raided all over the place because Peking could concentrate its efforts only at one place. However, now the Communists may be strong enough to man the Southeast coast as well as Korea; and at the same time they have Ho Chi Minh's effective army in Vietnam. They are also improving their logistical position. Already through-connections have been established by rail from Hanoi to Peking. Vietnam is being increasingly integrated into the Chinese imperial system.

There are three answers to the present impasse:

1. Radford's idea of total preventive war;

2. To clear out of Asia entirely and hope for the best, giving up Indochina and praying for a "neutralist" Japan;

3. To continue a delaying action, as now, hoping that someday Communist China may make a mistake or be thrown against Russia.

China wants to be the key country in Asia. It wants to extend its economic orbit. Peking wants to be the keystone of a new system: some countries would be Communist, some neutralist—but Peking would dominate. Peking views us as the sole power in the way.

The question of recognizing Peking was not really a United States decision anyway. After Mao Tse-tung visited Moscow in 1949, he deliberately made it plain that he would never recognize us because he needed the U.S. as a propaganda whipping boy and the motivating excuse for unpopular measures. China said it had to industrialize *against* the imperialist U.S. It said life was hard *because* of the United States's threat.

Chiang has many weak points. He has no program at all. He is a good, shrewd politician who can hold the people. He has limited cultural attainments. But he has nothing to offer people—only the negation of communism.

When pressed, Chiang says he would retain the Communist land-reform program if he goes back to China. His program is anomalous: (1) to apply Sun Yat-sen's vague theories (which, for a platform, is about as precise as being a Darwinist); (2) Confucianism and belief in the old Chinese virtues, such as obedience of children to their parents—and this doesn't "send" Chinese youth today; (3) Christianity in its ethic, but only in terms of its relationship to Confucianism.

Last night I dined at the Rankins who live about a half-hour out of town in a former Japanese spa (sulphur baths). Their house is made of two joined Japanese houses and is near the Generalissimo's summer residence. Karl recounted the behavior of visiting Congressmen. One complained to the Chinese about where he was seated at a formal lunch for his group, saying: "I should think you guys would know which party is supporting you." Another, when introduced to Chiang Kai-shek, noticed some long hairs creeping out of the Generalissimo's high collar from a mole (the Chinese always leave the hairs to grow from moles). So he reached out and gave the hairs a yank; was surprised when they didn't come loose; later explained: "I just saw those loose hairs and thought I'd help the old man by pulling them away—just the sort of thing I'd like someone to do for me." Chiang apparently remains impassive throughout these performances, but he secretly regards westerners as very stupid. He spends much time meditating and reading Chinese classics. He rises at six each morning to pray (Methodist species).

This afternoon I visited General Chiang Ching Kuo, elder son of Chiang Kai-shek. Chiang Ching Kuo lives in a rather modest Japanese style house (although he has a handsome Cadillac), and the room we sat in, built for diminutive people (low door frames) contained hardly any ornaments aside from a gold athletic trophy and a large portrait of his father. He resembles the old man but is far less distinguished looking. In his forties, the son has a bland inexpressive face with a sullen mouth. He lived for years in Russia (when he didn't get on with his father), was a Communist, and has a Russian wife. He broke with Stalin and came back to China; acted as his father's agent in Manchuria when the end of World War II came. He is now assistant secretary general of their equivalent of a National Security Council. Actually he is in charge of morale, political commissars in the army, some aspects of the secret police, and security, etc.

TAIPEI, *March 19, 1955*

TODAY I flew down to Kaohsiung in order to spend the day with Chiang Kai-shek. He has a simple house outside Kaohsiung on a beach at Sitzewan.

Sitzewan means Beautiful Bay in Chinese. He has been there several days
because he has had a cold and is resting up. It is a flight of about an hour
and a quarter from Taipei to Kaohsiung. I went down in a special plane
used for government VIPs, accompanied by Samson Shen, Chiang's official
interpreter.

Chiang Kai-shek's house is a large unattractive establishment. The sitting
room where we sat before and after lunch was square, particularly ugly,
filled with hideous, comfortable chairs and sofas covered with artificial
leather.

A few moments after my arrival the Generalissimo and Madame Chiang
came in. He is a good deal shorter and smaller than I expected, no taller
than five foot six, slender: a trim-looking man who is certainly extremely fit.
He was wearing what the Chinese call a Sun Yat-sen uniform, a military-
looking khaki garment with high collar similar to the sort of uniform Russian Communist leaders often wear. It bore no insignia. Madame Chiang
was wearing a long cylindrical black Chinese dress. Although she may have
been beautiful once, now she has a rather evil and tough face. She has a
lovely voice with a slightly southern accent, but it is quite apparent that she
is a hard, ruthless woman.

Nevertheless, the two of them seemed to be very much in love. Since he
had a cold, she frequently made him put on a black velvet skull cap to keep
his shaven head warm. This cap slipped off a couple of times but she made
him put it on again. Apparently she does not speak Mandarin Chinese but
only the Shanghai dialect. Therefore she would converse with him in Shanghai, although he was talking to my interpreter in Mandarin. She speaks
absolutely perfect English but did not do any interpreting, except once or
twice to add comments of her own or explain the Generalissimo's views.

Chiang Kai-shek is a handsome, distinguished-looking man with gray
moustache, smiling countenance, and a pleasant soft voice. He has an odd
habit at times of protruding his jaw a bit and also his lower lip—giving him
a strange sort of oriental Hapsburg appearance. This may be because of his
false teeth.

Our conversation took place in three sections over a period of about
three hours. At first we sat around before lunch and I asked a series of
questions. Then, during lunch, at which we were joined by his military and
civilian aides, thus making a table of six, the conversation was general.
Then again after lunch, we repaired to the sitting room and continued.
Incidentally, the luncheon was relatively simple Chinese food, but finished
up with apple pie as, I suppose, a concession on the part of Madame Chiang
to her American guest. I noticed that the Generalissimo polished it off with
enthusiasm. Before lunch, both the Generalissimo and Madame bowed their
heads for about half a minute in silent grace.

My overall impression was that Chiang is far nicer than I had expected
and rather wiser and more reflective. However, I was not impressed by his

ideas and he did not strike me as being exceptionally intelligent: more wise than bright.

I started off by asking if he thought the dominance of Russia by Khrushchev had in any way altered the relations between Moscow and Peking. He replied that certainly Khrushchev's role would strengthen ties between Moscow and Peking.

I then said to the Generalissimo that it was frequently reported there had been a division between China and Russia of spheres of influence in Asia— that Russia was supposed to have been awarded Korea and Japan as its sphere of influence while allocating Southeast Asia to China. I asked what he thought of this report. Chiang was not sure there had been such a "distribution of assignments," but there was one single overall plan governing the activities of both countries. Moreover, there was no doubt that Russia was the country emphasizing activities in Korea and Japan.

Chiang did not believe rumors that Russia had agreed to transfer Outer Mongolia gradually into China's sphere of influence because he did not think Moscow could ever afford to give it up. It required control of Mongolia as well as of Sinkiang and Manchuria for strategic reasons. He added rather smugly, "Through my years of experience in dealing with the Communists, I have learned that one must judge them only by deeds, not words. The entire Chinese mainland is actually in the Soviet sphere of influence right now and the Chinese Communists are merely Moscow's puppets."

I asked whether he had any recommendations on how the overseas Chinese should be organized in order to help the free world's cause. He said,

> The first and most important thing is for the United States to cooperate openly with us on this. The overseas Chinese are influenced by the attitude toward them of the countries in which they reside. Often they suffer from restrictions as a result. The overseas Chinese look to us as the only government of China, but they are not allowed to express this feeling. The United States must press for their freedom of expression to support our cause. There is no doubt that most of the overseas Chinese are strongly anti-Communist and are our supporters. The United States must insist with the colonial countries that these overseas Chinese be allowed to cooperate with us.

What Chiang says here is a lot of poppycock. My investigations in Southeast Asia showed that his prestige was extremely low with the overseas Chinese. A great many of them are indeed anti-Communist, but they do not look to him as the savior. That is one of the difficulties of the situation and I don't see how the United States can help.

I asked Chiang if this were the lowest point in his long personal career of fighting to establish a unified government over China. He replied that the nadir of his fortunes came in 1926, just before he took off from Canton with less than five hundred followers bearing arms. "Now we are in a much better position—especially concerning the psychology of our people," he said.

I asked if the United States had ever formally guaranteed to defend the offshore islands of Matsu and Quemoy. He suggested I should rephrase my question and eliminate the word "formally." He then answered his own rephrased question by saying, in a series of oblique sentences, that he had only agreed to evacuate the Tachen Islands because he understood the United States would defend Matsu and Quemoy. (This, of course, all adds up to nothing. I don't believe any specific guarantee of any sort was ever given and that is why Chiang is being so cagey.)

When our conversation got onto the subject of the offshore islands, Chiang talked with such vigor that I told him I would like to quote him verbatim on this particular point although the rest of our conversation was on a background basis. He agreed with pleasure, and said:

> It would not be fair to try and force us to give up the offshore islands without a fight. That would be contrary to all international justice and to the obligations of our allies. The United States should not accede to British ideas on this. Whether the United States joins in the defense of these islands or not, she should not try and compel free China, an ally, to give them up. Under no circumstances will our forces withdraw from them. We shall not yield to any pressure. We are determined to fight to the last man. It is a mistake to think that because we evacuated the Tachons we will evacuate Matsu and Quemoy. We will certainly fight for them. And this may turn into the decisive battle for China.

All I can deduce from these statements is that we are trying to persuade him to get off the islands but don't seem to have made up our mind yet to get really tough with him. Obviously he wants World War III to start over the islands. However, since they are militarily indefensible—above all with his weak fleet and air force—it would be a pretty senseless place to begin a major campaign.

Throughout our conversation Chiang always referred to the British with the utmost of asperity and bitterness.

After lunch, when we returned to the mausoleum-like sitting room, I told Chiang I had heard he believed World War III would start in 1956. Why? He replied:

> That is correct. I think that next year Russia will be ready for war for the following reasons: You will remember that as soon as the Russians had completed the Trans-Siberian Railway they started their disastrous war with Japan fifty years ago. Russian strategy depends upon railways. According to Communist planning, new railways linking China and Russia across Mongolia and Sinkiang will be ready. As soon as these roads are finished the Russians will figure that the moment has arrived for war. And at the same time, economic and agricultural conditions are such that if Russia and China don't start a war in 1956 they will risk collapse.

I asked if it was not fair to describe Chiang's long-range policy as one of seeking to remain in being and to gather strength until the arrival of an inevitable World War III. He answered:

This is a common idea of our plan. It is a part of it. But we don't have to wait for a general conflict. There will be other opportunities. For example, if an uprising develops on the mainland we won't have to wait for a war. And once the Communist problem on the Chinese mainland has been liquidated we can actually avoid World War III.

This I feel sounds like whistling in the dark. But Chiang emphasized again, "The only way to prevent communism from winning the war without a new all-out war is to eliminate Chinese communism first." He then concluded that the only way he admittedly saw of returning to the mainland was either after a popular uprising or a general war.

I asked Chiang how he was spending his spare time down here at Sitzewan. He said he went for long walks with his wife and was reading Hegel and Wang Yang Ming. He was studying the gloomy German in order to improve his understanding of the basis of communism. He had finished Hegel's books on dialectics and was now reading his work on spiritual phenomena. Wang was a great Ming scholar of the sixteenth century who believed that true knowledge must be coupled with action.

TOKYO, *March 22, 1955*

THIS afternoon I visited Ichiro Hatoyama, the Prime Minister, at his home. The Prime Minister, who is seventy-two and partially paralyzed by a stroke, received me in his study; a strange, crowded room filled with books, snapshots, and odd little souvenirs and trinkets accumulated over the years. Among the objects on his desk I noticed a bronze rabbit and a statuette of a naked woman of the sort one finds at Atlantic City auctions.

Hatoyama, who sat in a swivel armchair, was wearing a gray cardigan, gray trousers, and felt bedroom slippers. He has nondescript features, thin, short gray hair, a scrubby gray moustache, and wears glasses.

I started off by asking if Hatoyama would not raise Japan's budgetary contribution for national security. At present only 2½ percent of the gross national product is assigned to defense. This represents 13 percent of the annual budget and covers Japan's own defense forces and its contribution to the maintenance of the U.S. security force. We are trying to prod Japan to increase this to 4 or 5 percent of the GNP.

Hatoyama indicated he has no thought of playing ball on this. He argued that the Socialists had demonstrated in last month's elections a gain in strength which must be checked. To do this the government had to settle the housing problem and for this: "We must reduce our share of the defense costs." In other words, things are going in precisely the wrong direction insofar as we are concerned.

Hatoyama said Japan was still in a state of war with Russia and, since it had no relations with Communist China, a "similar state of war with Peking." His policy was to normalize the situation so that "We can carry on trade and thus decrease international tension."

It is perfectly evident he is skillfully playing off communism against the United States. He says we must allow Japan to pay less for defense in order to prevent the growth of communism in Japan. At the same time, he says he has to trade with the Communist powers in order to reduce the threat of war.

Tokyo, *March 23, 1955*

THIS morning I visited Mamoru Shigemitsu, the foreign minister. Shigemitsu, who signed the armistice for Japan in 1945, is a gray-haired, distinguished-looking man with a remarkable similarity to the stage conception of what a Japanese diplomat should look like. He was wearing a frock coat, gray, striped trousers, and a bat-wing collar because today he is lunching at the Imperial Palace. He has a thoughtful, handsome face, and one artificial leg (bombed off in China), using crutches to walk.

Shigemitsu said the so-called "Two Chinas" formula was "a very realistic way of thinking" on the Formosa question. He thought the status of Formosa was certainly different from that of continental China. "Legally speaking, the disposition of Formosa has not yet been settled internationally," he said. "We gave up our rights to Formosa permanently at San Francisco, however."

When I asked about the offshore islands—Quemoy and Matsu—he replied without hesitation: "They belong to the continent of course and therefore to Communist China."

However, he admitted their loss might damage Chiang Kai-shek's prestige and weaken Chiang's ability to defend Formosa. Therefore, he thought they should be disposed of as part of a bargain establishing a cease-fire.

What would be the position of the United States bases here in case war started over the offshore islands? He replied:

Japan would have no choice. We are more than allied to the United States. We stand on the same common security arrangement. But we certainly hope that the means for peaceful settlement can be found. We are against the idea of making war in this part of the world. Communist China should not use force to realize its policy. It should negotiate any difficulties by peaceful means. There should be no recurrence to violence in the world for the settlement of disputes. We hope Communist China will abstain from violence. At least for the time being the "Two Chinas" formula is the only sensible solution, with Formosa giving up the offshore islands in exchange.

Shigemitsu said Japan and India certainly had to cooperate in order to develop a free Asia. He hoped ties with India could be strengthened. The idea of a free Asian arc led by Japan and India was quite sound.

This afternoon I saw Ambassador John Allison. Forthright, brisk, and practical, he was Dulles's right-hand man in our peace negotiations with Tokyo.

He said that at the Baguio Conference of our Far Eastern envoys both Admiral Spruance, ambassador in Manila, and General Collins, special ambassador in Saigon, told their colleagues the offshore islands were very bad military positions without strategic value. Therefore, Allison, when he came back here, had examined the situation from a Japanese point of view and reported back to Washington that if we get into a war as a result of the dispute on these islands we would get no support from the Japanese. Furthermore, if such a war developed into an atomic conflict we would meet with active hostility here.

The Japanese, according to Allison, don't regard China and Soviet Russia in the same light. China to them remains an oriental country and more Chinese than Communist. Japan's attitude on this is perhaps similar to what ours was five or six years ago. They say: "We don't have to fear the Communist Chinese. The Chinese never invaded us; we always invaded them."

OSAKA, JAPAN, *March 26, 1955*

SPENT the day talking over Chinese commercial prospects with Japanese businessmen in Osaka, the inland seaport which used to be the main center for the China trade.

The business community claims trade with China is necessary. It fears Chinese competition in the textile field because Japan left many spindles there. China may become a rival in the Southeast Asian market. Japan now depends too much on U.S. aid and cannot afford to disregard six hundred million Chinese because, despite communism and economic isolation, some market certainly exists there. Red China knows this and is going to exploit the situation as best possible to weaken Japan's ties with the United States. If Japan starts to trade with China it may help to draw it away from the Soviet orbit a bit. It's ridiculous to have Japan buying coal from West Virginia instead of Manchuria. China has always been a big factor in the development of the Japanese nation. It is rich in natural resources and has a huge population, even though its people are ignorant and accustomed to hard life. U.S. policy is wrong to throw it back on its own autarky.

KYOTO, JAPAN, *March 27, 1955*

CAME here last night from Osaka and stayed in a Japanese hotel called the Dai Monji. This hotel has had only one other American visitor during its fifty years' existence. It is a tiny place off a narrow, bustling street of shops. The service—despite the absence of bells and telephones—was magnificent. I had two little rooms with sliding panels so that they could open up into one. They had a private garden of about four yards by one yard, but it included miniature willow and cherry trees. The floors were covered with rice straw mats (*tatami*). The only heat was from an hibachi with charcoal burning inside in a mass of ashes. My bed was a pallet with comfortable quilts and clean sheets. I slept like a log. Both in the evening and in the morning I had a hot bath, far hotter than I imagined I could stand. Diminutive women kept bringing in tidbits like salted cherries and green tea, whose surface was covered with floating bits of puffed rice.

Kyoto is the ancient imperial capital, a city of festivals, sweets, temples, and dolls. During the Gion Festival in the geisha quarter huge gaily painted carts are drawn from one shrine to another while musicians play from the tops of the carts and throw rice cakes to the crowd.

After a delightful series of visits to shrines and temples I dined with Sei Wada, deputy editor-in-chief of *Asahi,* and the Kyoto bureau manager, at the Ichiriki geisha house which was built in the late seventeenth century, and is the place where Oishi, leader of the 47 Ronin, used to get plastered with his favorite geisha while plotting his conspiracy. We had a long and complicated discussion with the geisha girls about what the American occupation had done to Japan. The geishas are unabashedly slaves and if they run away they are brought back by the police; except they don't run away. Mariko, a seventeen-year-old, was the most attractive, a "maiko" or apprentice. It will be two years before she is a full geisha; and she has already been working two years. She is a lovely little girl with hair worn in a high black eighteenth-century pompadour filled with combs and cherry blossoms, a blue and pink kimono, and an immense extra-long obi belt.

None of the geishas had the least bit of interest in the changing world. All but Mariko said they voted, but it was clear they didn't know what this meant and, if they had no current boy friend to instruct them, they cast blank ballots. They encouraged us to play drinking games called the "thunder game," the "drinking God game," and another one in which you burn paper stretched taut across the top of a glass and the coin balanced on top falls in.

Wada thought the occupation had brought democracy and its way of thinking to Japan. It had freed the country's women, and taught them to express their opinions. We had also brought in a new constitution replacing the old authoritarian German way. The girls said there were visible American influences in the form of soft drinks, jazz, G.I. uniforms for Japanese defense forces, and quiz programs on the radio.

IN A KOREAN

BATHTUB

SEOUL, KOREA, *March 29, 1955*

ARRIVED IN SEOUL AS AMBASSADOR ELLIS BRIGGS'S GUEST, JUST IN time for a cocktail party for army Secretary Stevens and Generals Taylor and Lemnitzer. There I saw Van Fleet for the first time in civilian clothes. And, to my absolute astonishment, feeling no pain. This is a mystery because Van Fleet is a teetotaler.

Briggs says Syngman Rhee believes he can make Korea not only *an* but *the* Asian nation. He is pushing the idea of alliance with Formosa and the Philippines. He is the first Korean President, but it is a half-country and this burns him deeply. For him it is not enough to be the liberator. He wants to free *all* Korea—time is getting short. Therefore, he wants to start a war and the sooner the better. Rhee wants World War III. He wants it right away and wishes it had started a year ago. He admits frankly he would have started war himself if he hadn't been rationed on gasoline. Rhee has continually won from us economically. He insists we give him privileges and he violates one after another agreement. Right now the American government is *totally* financing Korean rearmament and yet, at the same time, they are finding money to invest in television and CinemaScope projects which hardly seem essential.

Usury is incredible. Interest rates range up to 15 to 20 percent a month. This, of course, boosts prices enormously. Inflation is so bad that many lenders insist on high interest rates; otherwise, money repaid will have no value. The pay of Cabinet ministers is only 40 dollars a month. Therefore, many participate in corruption, as do many army officers. The gasoline black market is enormous. An American military check found that there were some truck owners who had never bought a single gallon of gas on the legal market.

One of our biggest problems is that you can't keep a big enough army here to fight off the North, if again attacked, and at the same time, not powerful enough to attack the North alone. North Korea is steadily violating the armistice terms. Hundreds of boxcars have been checked coming in. This would seem to indicate that North Korea must be the largest manufacturer of freight cars in the world—highly improbable.

The United States will be stronger militarily if we can keep the Koreans out in front and meantime have our mobile air and sea power behind them. This is what keeps the Chinese from renewing the war. We put 700,000,000 dollars into South Korea this year; this produces a fighting force of about 700,000 men in uniform. At 1,000 dollars a man, including all the slippage in graft, etc., this is a damn sight cheaper than our own soldiery (a curiously mercenary outlook).

CHIN-HAE, KOREA, *March 30, 1955*

FLEW here this morning on a rough trip in a tiny air force plane to see Syngman Rhee at his summer hideaway. Chin-hae is the South Korean naval base, but Rhee built himself a place here which is, I suspect, as much a spot to get away from bombs as it is a resort. It used to be a big Japanese naval base and it was from here that the Japanese fleet steamed out in 1905 to destroy the Russian navy in the battle of Tsushima. There is a lovely bay with a rocky coast, half like the Mediterranean and half like traditional Japanese prints.

Rhee's house is small and extremely simple. Outside are plum trees in blossom and forsythia bushes. Rhee spends a good deal of his time gardening and is also an enthusiastic angler—still-fishing with bait, hook, and line. Today it was raining and the old man had to stay inside. He was expecting Secretary Stevens and Generals Taylor and Lemnitzer. In fact, I was supposed to join their party here and ride on to Japan this afternoon. As a result, Rhee had along his foreign minister, his minister of defense, and his army chief of staff. But during my conversation with him Rhee got word that the weather was so bad Stevens' plane couldn't land so he invited his ministers and generals in to join us in our talk.

Rhee is a little old man with a face like a squeezed orange, covered with wrinkles. He has snow-white hair and smiles constantly. He was wearing a rumpled blue suit with a cardigan over his vest. I started the conversation by asking whether he agreed with the idea Dulles had voiced at Bangkok of a three-pronged Asian strategy that would be launched against China in the event of any Chinese aggression elsewhere in Asia. Rhee said he thought this was fine.

He said:

The Communists are trying to conquer the world whether you Americans still believe this or not. We are on the frontier in Asia. We don't

believe we can coexist with communism. The United States sent an army
here to defend us. Therefore, this all-for-one-and-one-for-all spirit prevails in our war against communism. We want to help to defend other
areas. As a matter of fact, we offered to send twenty thousand soldiers to
Vietnam just before the Geneva Conference. General Hull thanked me
for this offer, but someone in Washington turned it down.

Did he think we should start a preventive war against the Communists
and if so, where and over what issue? He said the war was already on.

The Communists are advancing all the time. They improve their position daily. How long will you let them keep on? My proposition is, as I
told General Eisenhower, that the sooner we cripple Communist aggression the easier for the whole world. Preventive war is the only solution.
Eisenhower and Dulles can try all they can, but there is no other solution. The American people should now realize that negotiations and
conferences with the Communists lead only to disaster. Look at Panmun-
jom. You are saving the world for peace by surrendering the world. The
only hope for peace is by war first. You have to protect yourself forcibly
against gangsters trying to break into your house.

I must say that it is astonishing how belligerent this amiable looking little
old man (eighty now) seems to be. He said:

We would have driven to the Chinese border on the Yalu River in
1953, if you had permitted us. But you control all logistics. Our gasoline
and ammunition are locked up; we have only two days ration. Have you
ever heard of such a thing? What kind of a world is this?
The sooner we stop these gangsters the better. You people are too
afraid of world war. If war is the worst thing you can imagine, then you
should surrender everything, give up Washington. Give up your stocks of
atom bombs. The only alternative is to stop the Communists and the
sooner the better. Fewer lives will be sacrificed.

At this point Rhee was getting very excited. His voice rose to a scream
and he started waving his hands around. His wife, a plump little Austrian
woman around sixty, tried to calm him down. She kept saying that he had
come to Chin-hae to rest, and that he shouldn't get so excited. She passed
out nice home-made Viennese cake and coffee to all of us except the
minister of defense. She remembered that he has a bad heart and gave him
tea.

But this interlude was brief. I had just had time to look around the room,
scrutinize its ugly, comfortable furniture, the silken tablecloth on the table
between Rhee and myself, the Chinese painting on the wall, when the old
President started off again on favorite subject No. 2—Japan.

He said: "Japan is rapidly turning toward communism. I don't know
what Dulles thinks, believing he can make a faithful ally of Japan by
building it up. Why, the Japanese claim that 85 percent of all Korean

property is still theirs. I asked Dulles to make clear our situation to the Japanese, but he doesn't seem to have done much."

At this point the telephone rang and an aide came in. Rhee rushed out. It was Stevens trying to apologize in person for not showing up. We all looked at each other as we heard Rhee's anguished screams into the phone. It apparently was functioning as most Asian telephones do. After some minutes of obvious lack of communication he came back with his hair all rumpled saying: "I hate telephones. I would like to tear them all out and use the wire to strangle the man who invented them."

He then started talking about the exchange rate between the hwan and the dollar. He is bull-headedly insisting that it be kept at 180 hwan to the dollar although the black market rate is around 600. He claims that when ECA started in 1948, the rate was 15 hwan to the dollar. When war came two years later it brought inflation. He said the United States insisted on raising the legal rate despite his argument that this would inflate commodity prices. We forced him to accept, but prices were doubled immediately. By 1953, the black market rate had gone to 23,000 hwan to the dollar.

He continued:

If you really want to rehabilitate Korea's economy you must start by stabilizing the hwan currency. Otherwise, all endeavors are foolish. We have learned. You talk for eight years about economic theory, but we have come almost to the breaking point. By ruining the Korean economy you build up Japan. Is that the idea? What is the idea?

Here the defense minister, the foreign minister, and the chief of staff rose, bowed politely, and left. They weren't going to get Stevens and they'd had enough of me. But Rhee continued without taking notice. He said that there was a lack of agreement now on the exchange rate because we wouldn't go along on military conversion. He said the American army was trying to keep the black market rate up.

Rhee claims there are 23,000,000 people in South Korea now and less than 7,000,000 left in the North. But North Korea has an army of 430,000 North Koreans plus 600,000 Chinese. He complained bitterly that we weren't building up his air force and were more interested in building a Japanese air force. He had wanted to oust from South Korea as spies the Communist members of the neutral nations commission, but Dulles had prevented him. This made him remark, "All our allies are teetering too much."

I asked if he thought it would be possible to build any kind of free Asia without the active participation of India and Japan. He snorted: "In an anti-Communist bloc you can't include wavering nations. Nobody believes Japan and India are anti-Communist."

He then launched a new attack on Japan. He said that if the Japanese had wanted peace with Korea they could have had it long ago, but "they don't want a settlement until Japan has a strong military force again." He admired the Philippines for asking for a billion dollars in reparations from Japan and said, "They were only occupied for four years. We were occupied forty. I am going to increase our claims."

He ranted on about war and Japan. Obviously Korea has been so battered about and he is so old that war doesn't mean the same to him as it does to other people. His wife boasted to me with pride and affection that a large bit of Chinese calligraphy on the wall behind Rhee was a poem that he had composed and painted himself for her last birthday. He translated this for me accordingly: "A woman has three duties. A woman must be contented and she must be pleased with simple living and she must be happy doing her duty." As poetry that doesn't strike me as being very good but the sentiments seem remarkably well phrased for a Teutonic wife.

PUSAN, KOREA, *March 30, 1955*

WHEN I left Rhee the defense minister, Admiral Sohn Won Il, invited me to join him, the foreign minister, Young Tai Pyun, and the chief of staff, General Chung Il Kwon in the ride over to Pusan on a Korean navy PT boat. This suited me fine. The weather was so lousy that I had no particular desire to fly back the way we had come down, in our little three-seater monoplane by the Braille system, bouncing through the passes following the railway tracks in the mist and clouds. Therefore, we had a glass of good Korean beer and were driven down to a pier and piped aboard an old U.S. PT boat, taking off in a tremendous gale at 36 knots. As we plunged from roller to roller, I stayed on the bridge trying to see Tsushima; but it was far away.

When we got to Pusan a navy car met us and we were taken 15 miles to a dilapidated hotel with a natural steam bath. We squatted down on the floor. Odd characters, both male and female, kept coming into the room and jabbering away in Korean. I was in one round tub with all the top brass— the most high-level bath I shall ever have. Some visitors were in police uniform and did much bowing and scraping.

Finally around 6:30 we were taken to another room where a magnificent banquet was set out on a low, long table. Three Ki Saing (Korean geisha girls) were already squatted on cushions by the table to serve and amuse us. The poor things looked like the original prototype peasant women and didn't have any of the charm of their Japanese equivalents. They were wearing little short silk bodices and long high-waisted skirts and their hair was done in pigtails bound close to the head. The food, served with chopsticks, resembled what I imagine the Mongols ate: strongly spiced meat balls, dried spiced beef, hot soups, rice, tea, beer, and sake.

I was very interested in the haphazard origins of these Korean big-shots. The foreign minister, who is sixty-two, taught English in a Japanese secondary school in Korea for many years. He first met Rhee in 1909, when he was still a youngster. He knew that Rhee had lived in the United States so he went to see him at the YMCA in Seoul to improve his English pronunciation. Incidentally, his English is only fair at best. The foreign minister is an amiable-looking little man with kind eyes and a bristling moustache. He resembles the figures one sees on eighteenth- and nineteenth-century Korean screens and he ought to be wearing one of the old costumes topped by a flat black hat. After the war he became a college professor of English and used to help Rhee with translations. He was rewarded by being named foreign minister.

The admiral, prior to the war, was a sailor in the Japanese merchant marine. The general was a captain in the Japanese cavalry. He attended the Japanese cavalry school and later was an instructor. He is rather Japanese in appearance and has a somewhat aggressive manner. He is the oldest of Korea's three four-star generals, although only thirty-nine. At one time during the war he was second in command of a corps with a large number of American troops under him.

They said MacArthur had made two tremendous mistakes: He had split up his command so that when the Communists punched a hole in the middle between them there was chaos; and he refused to believe the Chinese would intervene and therefore had no prepared alternative position to fall back on. Ridgway, they seemed to think, was definitely the best and most combative of our generals. They felt that Van Fleet was not only a good fighting man but had a wonderful inspirational gift with his troops.

They all echoed Rhee's fears concerning Japan. They could see the logic, from an American point of view, of suggesting to the Koreans that they buy military equipment in Japan, but this left them dependent upon the Japanese and someday would subject them to Japanese pressure. They desperately want to establish industry in South Korea—both a heavy industry and a munitions industry. But they know it is a long, long road.

They are pathetically nice and simple people, forthright and friendly. But they are not really very impressive from an intellectual point of view. Although I am told their soldiers are extremely courageous, the country is so beaten up and impoverished that it's hard to imagine how a satisfactory economy and industry can be developed. It must depend on us indefinitely for subsistence. During their occupation the Japanese deliberately crushed the intelligentsia and made the Koreans into second-class citizens, with the result that there was really no human material available with which to build an adequate state.

HONOLULU, *April 4, 1955*

LONG talk at his Pearl Harbor headquarters with Admiral Felix Stump, United States Commander-in-Chief for the western Pacific and also Chief of

U.S. Naval Forces in the whole Pacific area. He said we were at a permanent disadvantage vis-à-vis the Communists because they know not only that they can start a war at any time but that they can also stop it any time, as they did in Korea. Because of public opinion and our political organization we do not have the initiative in any respect. A new order has just been issued by Defense Secretary Wilson cautioning officers of all services against talking to the press.

We started a discussion of the offshore islands. Stump observed that we would never have started "Overlord" (the invasion of Normandy) had the Germans held the islands in the mouths of the English river estuaries. The inland communication system of Fukien province was rotten, but the Chinese could coolie-back supplies and use junks to mount the short-range invasion of Matsu and/or Quemoy. He personally thought it would improve their chances of invading Formosa if they held the offshore islands first.

Stump reflected that this was the first time in history when the enemy (communism) had told us for thirty-five years what he was going to do next. Right from the start they announced their goal of world conquest and have never deviated.

WASHINGTON, *April 14, 1955*

THIS morning I saw Couve de Murville, now French ambassador. He said France requested postponement of the scheduled talks with the United States on Vietnam because there is no point discussing election procedure and aid terms until there is a really established government. There is no government in South Vietnam now. As a matter of fact, there never was, outside Saigon. Diem is an illusion. The United States supports him so vigorously that our prestige is bound to suffer when he goes down. Actually Diem never controlled anything beyond Saigon. The rest of the countryside is divided among the sects and the Communists.

Lunched with David Bruce at his lovely Georgetown house. David had just caught the grippe, but he stayed up for me and we had a couple of martinis each and an excellent lunch. He was rather bitter about Dulles and the State Department. His present status is that of "consultant"; this means that he is still cleared to talk with anybody who has access to secret information. But he quit the Department January 20. He has seen Dulles only once since his return from Paris. He also saw Eisenhower once at the President's request. Ike said that he heard Dulles had offered him a government job, but that Bruce turned it down: Was this correct? Bruce said yes. Then the President said: "Okay, let's not mention the subject any more."

Ike went on to say he had been reading Bruce's book on the first fifteen Presidents and he wanted to know who David thought were good Presidents. David said he cited Washington, John Adams, and John Quincy

Adams as effective Presidents and stressed that they sought to represent the electors. He went on to tell Eisenhower that Lincoln had been a complete flop until he entered the White House; he had been an ambitious trimmer and was also very lazy. However, Lincoln learned well. David thinks one of Eisenhower's greatest troubles is his own laziness.

He said Jean Monnet believes he understands the Chinese although David sometimes wonders whether he knows them any better than he knows the French—which is to say not much.

David asked me whether I thought he should take a job in the State Department or merely try to be a consultant available when he, rather than the State Department, wished. I told him I thought he should accept a position with the Department on a permanent basis because it was necessary to have his influence there.

I went from Bruce's house to the Capitol where I saw Senator Knowland in his office. He is a powerful man with an earnest, tough face. He speaks slowly in moderate tones and was extremely courteous and forthright. He admitted that he disagreed with the view expressed in my columns but showed no hostility. He tried to draw me out on my opinions, but I told him I was more interested in learning his.

We started off on Vietnam. I asked what Knowland thought we should do. He replied:

> If there is any defensible line in the situation I think that line should be defended. But I would want the advice of the Joint Chiefs of Staff on this to see if there is such a defensible line that should and could be defended. If South Vietnam goes, it will demonstrate that the President is correct in his "falling dominoes" theory. Laos and Cambodia would fall. And then Malaya and probably Burma. And Thailand would be in a very vulnerable position.

He regards Quemoy as the cork in the bottle of Amoy harbor. He also says that Matsu "at least hampers Foochow." But he continued:

> More important is their morale value. To give up these islands without a fight would so undermine the morale of the Chinese Nationalists, the Filipinos, the Thais, etc., that it would have a very detrimental effect.
> I believe Quemoy has as much importance to a free China as West Berlin has to Germany. West Berlin is certainly not defensible. It is a land-island in a sea of Soviet territory. Our garrisons and families there are hostages to the Soviet Union. But the Communists know if they try to take West Berlin they will immediately be engaged in a war with the western powers.

NEW YORK, *April 18, 1955*

TALKED with Senator William Fulbright at lunch. Fulbright is deeply disturbed by the lack of bipartisanship in foreign policy. He resents the fact that after McCarthy was censured, the State Department kept on placating McCarthy and Bridges.

I must say that when I was in Washington last week I found growing distress with Dulles's insistence on having nothing but second-rate people among his State Department cronies. The only thing he wants from them is loyalty—not brains.

Dean Acheson is delighted with an incident that occurred recently. Acheson visited his favorite barber not long ago and asked him what he thought of the world situation and our foreign policy. The barber replied: "Well, suh, until Mr. Dulles won this heah initiative everything seemed to be going all right. Now I ain't so sure."

PARIS, *April 26, 1955*

GOOD chat with Douglas Dillon who is back on the job as ambassador after a serious illness. He said it is difficult to know just who is foreign minister today. Pinay is hardly ever in the Quai d'Orsay. Officially, Pinay has "bought" the "European" policy and thoroughly approves of German rearmament in Western European Union. But he spends almost all his time in his department taking care of internal politics.

Prime Minister Faure actually runs foreign policy. It is Faure who summons Dillon to the Quai to discuss negotiations. While Pinay is a "European" and Faure pretends to be—in order to keep the support of the MRP —the Premier is really a neutralist and happy to see the trend which may yet result in a neutral Germany. Faure, being a politician, is essentially interested in votes and remembers how popular the movement against rearming Germany is in France.

Faure has chosen as principal advisor on foreign affairs Armand Bérard, a high-ranking diplomat who deeply mistrusts the Germans. Bérard outranks almost everybody at the Quai d'Orsay. Therefore, he conducts diplomatic business for Faure, circumventing the usual machinery. The result is that often Pinay does not know what is going on.

PARIS, *April 29, 1955*

THIS morning I saw Foreign Minister Pinay. I asked what he thought of a possible neutral reunified Germany which Russia now seems to be sponsoring. Pinay thought this would be very dangerous for France. The German Socialists think of a neutral Germany as an armed Germany comparable to Sweden. But a Germany of 70,000,000 people would be far too big a power to play the role of Sweden and would be dangerous to France. Furthermore, all NATO defense plans would be reversed if Germany no longer played a part in them.

I asked what policy he thought should now be followed in Vietnam—not what policy should have been followed but what we could do considering the present situation. Pinay complained that the United States and France had decided to follow a single common policy, but they never bothered to define what that policy should be. Right now there were two generals in Vietnam—Ely and Collins—and each did what he wanted.

PARIS, *April 30, 1955*

THIS morning I had a good talk on Vietnam with Armand Bérard, virtually foreign minister these days. Bérard said Diem is defended only by his ten battalions from Tonkin. It is much the same as the defense of Louis XVI by his Swiss guards. The ten loyal battalions from the North are a particularly tough group. Diem himself is from the North, a Mandarin from Hue. He is not popular in the South. It is much the same as a man from Lille heading the local government of Marseille—only more so. Furthermore, Diem is the apostle of Catholicism. Yet he heads a part of Vietnam which is primarily Buddhist.

He continued:

Our main preoccupation is that the United States and France should work hand in hand. We have made very serious sacrifices in order to go along. We abandoned our Tonkin coal mines in order to accept conditions laid down by the United States. We ourselves knew these were impossible for the Communists and thus we had to abandon the mines. The Americans have continually misunderstood the mission of Sainteny, who is a businessman and a capitalist. The United States has false ideas of the ambiguous attitude of France in North and South Vietnam.

Bérard thought the attitude of the American Congress, based only upon moral principles, was a hindrance. Merely because Diem goes to Mass and is a nationalist is not enough to make a policy, Bérard warned:

If your policy results in a collapse, we will have to take the necessary measures to save our own interests. We have no choice. If we had no responsibility toward the French population there, it would be all right for France to be expelled from Indochina. But we cannot accept to be expelled. There is an enormous Eurasian population as well as the French population and hundreds of thousands of refugees. Remember that in the United States there would be a third of public opinion—the Catholics—requesting massive intervention if the refugees are threatened. Your Catholic lobby prevented changing the Diem government. Imagine its strength if we say that 800,000 Catholic refugees face extinction by the Communists.

France is not in a position to increase its military commitments in Indochina if a disaster comes. The United States will have to intervene in such a case. "If chaos arrives and your public opinion demands action, you Americans will be forced to act."

ROCQUENCOURT, *May 5, 1955*

THIS afternoon I went out to see Al Gruenther, a world-famous bridge-player: Is bridge of any value in training military men? The Russians emphasize chess and encourage all their officers to play it on the grounds that it improves their mental equipment for strategic purposes. The Germans, as a matter of fact, developed from chess their famous Kriegspiel.

Gruenther said he really did not think bridge had any such value—nor for that matter had chess. Chess was useful, perhaps, in an elementary sense of strategy, but it was not very important. And as far as bridge went, it did help men to make decisions quickly and gave them some idea of the elements of chance.

I asked him if he had ever known a man who was a really good officer and a really bad bridge player. He thought a while and said no. But, on the other hand, many a brilliant officer, for example Bedell Smith, could conceivably take up bridge now and play it very badly. I asked if he thought Eisenhower's bridge game was indicative in any way of his military characteristics. He said definitely not; Eisenhower's particular genius was for inspiring different allies to work together in cooperation. In no sense could this be related to bridge.

Gruenther suggested I should write a piece someday on the following subject: The Russians derived great advantages from a very simple system. They are continually rude and then when they let up slightly everybody gives them great credit. They returned Austrian prisoners of war they had never even admitted holding, and everybody said how generous they were. This is a system of complete blackmail. For example, right now the Austrians think there are still other prisoners in Russia and don't dare speak up very strongly for fear of hurting their chances of getting those prisoners out. The Germans think the Russians still have thousands of prisoners and therefore Russia strikes terror in the German heart. We let the Russians get away with this and steal the show.

On departing I gave Al a bottle of Japanese whisky and told him he could make better old-fashioneds.

PARIS, *May 6, 1955*

LUNCH with Speidel. The psychological atmosphere in Germany has improved a lot and he does not think there will be much difficulty recruiting an army. Also, despite the Russian effort to neutralize Germany, the Bundestag is sufficiently in the hands of Adenauer so that enabling legislation will be put through.

One major problem is the question of war criminals. Speidel says it is a shame that Field Marshal Liszt should still be locked up in Landsberg prison. There are over fifty officers incarcerated there. The German people feel strongly about this. Also they feel strongly about Raeder and Doenitz who are in Allied hands in Potsdam. Speidel is afraid that if we keep delaying on this problem the Russians, as part of their campaign to win over the Germans, will announce that as far as they are concerned Raeder and Doenitz should be free.

Speidel thinks Indochina is lost completely and the Asiatic situation stinks. The Russians must be getting worried about the Chinese now and certainly the Chinese are no satellites. One reason Khrushchev is trying to force hundreds and thousands of people to settle in the eastern parts of the Soviet Union is to build up a protection against Chinese expansion in that area.

PARIS, *May 7, 1955*

THIS morning I visited Edgar Faure, present Premier, in the Matignon. I noticed that Faure has shifted from the usual office of Prime Ministers to the second floor, with a fine view of the lawn and garden at the back. He is a small, short, almost bald man with glasses.

Our conversation was only about foreign policy because today the big show starts. Dulles arrives as well as Eden and Adenauer. There will be a series of conferences starting with the Western European Union and NATO and including Big Three talks and Franco-American talks about the situation in Asia.

Faure said: "We cannot recommence the eternal discussions of German unification. We must take the situation as it is and look at the prevailing detente as it exists. It is now more a question of security and reduction of arms. I think we should approach the problem from that angle." Faure is not particularly anxious to encourage German unity.

I asked if he thought it possible to save Vietnam now. He did *not* think so; it was too late. It was even too late for Bao Dai to return to Saigon. Even fifteen days or a week ago he might have done that, but now the situation had gone too fast.

Did Faure desire any change in U.S. policy in North Africa? He replied that France desired Allied support—American and British—above all on the question of Libya. France must keep control of the Fezzan for security reasons.

PARIS, *May 8, 1955*

YESTERDAY evening Dulles told me (*chez* Dillon):

At long last we are seeing the beginning of a unity of Europe which will transcend any differences jeopardizing Europe. For from fifty to seventy-five years people have tried to draw Europe together so as not to have the nations of Europe fighting against each other. The integration of Western Germany into Western European Union and NATO is a great and irreversible step in the right direction.

The unification of Germany is an attainable goal. It is more attainable now since the ratification of the Paris accords. As you take steps to unify yourself—I refer to the western world—you gain results which would otherwise seem unattainable. I remember last September the Soviets hurling threats. They practically threatened war if the Paris agreements were ratified. Many people were frightened by that. At that time I recalled that when the Marshall Plan, the support of Greece and Turkey, and the Japanese peace treaty were all accomplished, each event was accompanied by dire threats from the Russians. But after each was finished the situation became more malleable.

Now we see the first real prospect for an Austrian peace treaty. We had to wait for it eight years. It seemed we could not expect the Russians to pull their troops out of Austria. Now it looks as if this will happen. The impossible became possible because of what we did. Honestly, I believe the unification of Germany is now more possible. I believe this view is shared by Chancellor Adenauer.

At present the American position on Vietnam was the same as it had been in the past—supporting Diem. Dulles said:

We are disposed to support any government there which is competent, honest, nationalistic, and anti-Communist.

Diem, in our opinion, has been doing a good job building an anti-Communist state there. If someone came along with a good new idea we would not be opposed. But we don't pick and choose the government of Vietnam. We see no particular reason to throw Diem out. But we don't have a closed mind. We are not supporting an individual as such. We are supporting a cause. If someone else comes along, we don't consider any individual indispensable. Our support is not for one single individual.

PARIS, *May 9, 1955*

LAST night the Bohlens (ambassador to Moscow) came for dinner. Chip doesn't think the Russians are ready to make much of a deal. The Austrian agreement is the direct result of West Germany's adherence to NATO and ratification of the Paris accords. The Russians wished to hurry and prevent the integration of western Austria into NATO, thus producing a line from the Adriatic up to the Baltic. He doesn't think Moscow is getting ready to make any kind of major arrangement on Germany. Following the establishment this week of a "Soviet NATO" in Warsaw, the Russians will try and freeze the situation in Europe for a long time to come based upon continued division of Germany.

The big change has been a reemphasis of heavy industry, but this is a question of emphasis and not a changed policy. Prior to the emergence of

Khrushchev and Bulganin as bosses, a period had developed where light industry actually was expanding more rapidly than heavy industry. The Russians want to reemphasize heavy industry because an expanding economy can only be founded on this.

Chat with Bill Gibson, the main American Vietnam negotiator with the French government here. The principal issue now is the future power of the Revolutionary Committee which has been created in Saigon. The Revolutionary Committee has the facade of being spontaneous, but actually it is organized and ready to spring into action. It is led by six people, two of whom are fairly well-known figureheads. It seems to resemble the apparatus that prepared the way for Ho Chi Minh's takeover in Hanoi in 1946.

The Revolutionary Committee has prepared a meeting of what they call the "Etats Généraux," at which Bao Dai is to be deposed. They obviously fancy themselves in the role of Robespierre and the "Etats Généraux" of the French revolution. If the Communists succeed in taking over, using Diem as their Kerensky, the United States will be in the odd position of having used its own influence to bring in a proven collaborator of the Communists and having aided a Communist *coup d'état*. Last week Bao Dai warned the Americans that Diem's entourage had been in touch with the Viet Minh.

Gibson is fed up with the reputation that Diem has for incorruptible honesty. He says the Diem family is profiteering heavily. Large restaurants have been bought by their interests in Paris. Bribery and corruption and the sale of jobs are rampant. American aid is being used by the Diem family.

PARIS, *May 11, 1955*

LUNCH with Walter Robertson, Assistant Secretary of State in charge of Far Eastern affairs. Robertson said he knew Mao Tse-tung quite well and spent a weekend with him once. Mao is a devout, sincere, fanatical Communist who wants to give his fellowmen the things that poor people now lack. He is utterly ruthless in seeking this goal. Robertson considers Chou En-lai one of the most charming men he ever met; one must know him well to realize what a tough fellow he is. He has killed people with his own hands and then emerged calmly smoking a cigarette. When General Marshall went to China after World War II to try and promote a coalition government, Robertson warned him against Chou and his charm. But nevertheless, Marshall fell into the trap.

Robertson points out that we never controlled Manchuria, its evacuation by the Japanese, or its turnover to the Russians. In fact, within one week of the Soviet signature of the treaty between Moscow and Chiang, the Russians were busily violating all terms of the treaty. Incidentally, Robertson contends we "blackmailed" Chiang into signing that treaty in order to live up to Yalta and Potsdam. The Russians offered Chiang the chance to join the

Soviet orbit and depend on the U.S.S.R., above all economically. Chiang turned this down. As a result the Russians took over and handed control of the country to the Communists. It was never a revolution. The Russians merely grabbed Manchuria with all its resources of raw materials and industrial equipment and the armaments taken from the Japanese; then they reequipped the Communist Chinese army.

Each great power in turn has tried to bribe Chiang, according to Robertson: the Japanese, the Russians, and the United States. In each case Chiang refused the offer. Robertson says Chiang never violated any agreement we made with him. But we have violated our agreements with him many times and Robertson wonders why he stays with us. (The answer to that is easy: There is no other place to go.)

Robertson says the Chinese Communists are continually trying to bribe Chiang over to their side and are offering him "princely treatment." He claims such offers are not being made in public but are communicated by secret means.

The Chinese Communists never claimed Formosa prior to the move there by Chiang Kai-shek in 1949, Robertson insists. The only thing they are interested in is preventing Formosa from being a military threat to them. Prior to 1949, they were proposing the independence of Formosa. But now they realize that Formosa and Chiang's army there pose a threat to their middle if they intend to start a war either to the north (in Korea) or the south (in Southeast Asia).

I asked if he had heard any reports about difficulties between Russia and China or shooting on the border. He said he had heard none. Furthermore, he added, even if there were difficulties on a local basis, they would be unimportant. The interests of the two countries lie together. Robertson claims that already in 1940, Mao Tse-tung was writing that he wanted to support world communism under *Soviet* leadership.

The situation has changed greatly since 1940; I wonder if Mao would be as interested in Soviet leadership now as then.

Robertson said he recently told Dulles there is no hope whatsoever of Mao Tse-tung becoming a "Titoist." He told Dulles that Mao is as loyal to his own principles as Dulles is loyal to the principles taught him by his father, a Presbyterian preacher.

Robertson compared Bao Dai, of Vietnam, to Al Capone, and he claimed we could not have such a man represent us. The French want us to keep him because they think they can control and influence him. The French have definitely been playing a dirty game in South Vietnam.

PARIS, *May 13, 1955*

THIS morning I went over to have a chat with Mendès-France in his apartment. Among the leather-bound sets of books in his bookshelves were the works of Proust, Dante, Baudelaire, Stefan Zweig, Maeterlinck, and Shakespeare's tragedies in French. There were several baskets of fading flowers, all including muguet, which had obviously been sent to Madame Mendès-France on May 1. The fact that they were still there showed the frugality of the family.

Mendès talked very frankly. He said the rank and file of the Radical Socialist party had been pleased by the recent revolt in which he has kept control, although the party bosses were displeased by his success. He added: "The bosses have no means. What can they do? We now have the administration of the party and contact with the masses. Of course, the bosses can cry, can make a scandal, and issue communiqués."

Mendès said the opposition to him in the party was now trying to attract Edgar Faure to its side. Mendès admitted Faure has great influence and prestige as head of the government, something which is especially attractive in the Radical party; but, he added,

> He cannot and does not want to make an opposition to the majority of his own party. We have the party in hand. They can do nothing. We will lead the party in contact with the people. I hope to make the party more liberal. When I was defeated [that is to say when his government was defeated] lots of people wanted me to start a new party. But under our electoral law, the power rests *in* the party. This is not a pleasant situation. I would have preferred another way. But look what happened to de Gaulle. He had a great amount of support. But he had no party apparatus. And what happened? It is much more efficient to have in your hands one of the most important parties. This will give us a chance to influence the next elections.

Mendès said his idea was now to make a "truly *liberal* party of the Radical Socialists—a liberal party such as it was at the beginning." The present Radical Socialist party began in 1905, he said, when the original small Radical party and the Radical Socialist party merged. They came together as *Parti Républicain Radical et Radical Socialiste.*

The coalition of Socialists, MRP, Right, and Center parties is now finished and will not come into existence again. Therefore there is a danger of a popular front—the Communists, Socialists, and Left Radicals. As a result, he thinks it is necessary to build a new political alliance which will include the Socialists but would not be rightist. It would be an alliance that excluded the Communists. He thinks this can be done easily if the Radicals take the lead and the initiative.

CHURCHILL'S LAST FIGHT

LONDON, *May 19, 1955*

TONIGHT I HAD A FASCINATING AND VERY MOVING EXPERIENCE. I followed old Churchill around on what will almost surely be his last campaign. I was struck by the similarity between the issues he raised this evening and those he spoke about in his first by-election campaign in 1899, at Oldham.

This afternoon I went over to Randolph's and thumbed through *My Early Years* by his father. I found references to his speeches in 1899, on "Tory democracy" and "Never were there so many people in England and never before have they had so much to eat." He said almost exactly the same thing this evening. I had bet Randolph in advance that he would.

I dined at Pam Berry's. Aidan Crawley, an old friend whom I have not seen in years and who used to be a minister in the Labour government, was there together with his wife (Virginia Cowles) and Anne (Mrs. Ian) Fleming.

We took off first to East Walthamstow and later went on to Chigwell, where the old man spoke in a girls' school. I must say he was quite extraordinary. He made two speeches of about forty minutes each, and got all souped up while doing so. Like a good artist, he gave his audience full value. He peered over his archaic half-moon spectacles; he sat alternately grumpy and pleased with himself, determined, smiling, and sentimental. He played with his heavy Edwardian gold watch and chain. He shook his head in denial when introduced as "the greatest Englishman of all time."

He spoke in a lispy, heavy, resonant voice. He gazed with some pride at his round belly. He read his speeches partly from notes on a stand, but then took off on his own in enthusiastic spurts worthy of a man half his age. He uttered nothing but clichés, but he spoke them better than any man alive.

His main effort both in East Walthamstow and Chigwell (where he gave his second talk) was to swing independent Liberal voters to the Conservative candidates. He said: "There is no chance of making liberalism a party issue at this election. It is generally accepted. These famous doctrines have

175

been removed from party controversy." He made "an earnest, respectful, friendly appeal" to Liberals not to help the Socialists, and added, "I can speak for Tory democracy."

At East Walthamstow (where he never once referred to Eden) there was a picture of the new Prime Minister with mottos: "Working for Peace" and "It's Full Employment." Churchill gave his delighted audience the business. He said: "The state is the servant and not the master of the people." He said: "We have a higher standard of living than ever before. We are eating more." Then, *sotto voce,* regarding his tummy, he added: "And that is very important." Later on he said: "I have a point on which to challenge Mr. Attlee." Aside, he confided to his audience: "Mr. Attlee, you know, is the leader of the Labour party." Obviously he was enjoying himself and he worked up a good deal of enthusiasm.

Churchill went on far longer than expected with remarks such as "My policy has always been peace through strength," and "The united action of the English-speaking peoples." He referred to Mr. Bevan (emphasizing the *van*): "We must be very careful about that and not mix him up with my friend Ernie Bevin." He talked about the "chaotic and muddle-headed jibberings and jabberings of the Labour party." He made passing reference to "the decent, good-hearted people of Russia." He boastfully reminded his attendant audience that "this is no time for panic; the British are not good at panic."

We drove on to Chigwell, where there was a P. G. Wodehouse character named Biggs-Davison running as the Tory candidate. The meeting was in a girls' school. All over were signs reading "Vote for Biggs-Davison," and a large Union Jack. Just before Winston came in the audience was asking questions of the candidates: Somebody inquired, "How do you feel about education?" Biggs-Davison, a beefy, pleasant, dull individual, replied: "I am for it. Like National Service, everybody has to go through it." When Churchill came in, the emotional audience sang: "For he's a jolly good fellow," and then gave him three hip-hip-hurrays.

We sat with our backs to the platform and our faces to the audience. As Churchill spoke he told the good people of Chigwell: "We live together in a neighborly way," and "This is not the same fierce conflict I have seen in other elections." He told them, "It is a great honor to be in the House of Commons" (the only thing he is now running for).

It was embarrassing that at this moment Randolph fell asleep with his head on the table while dozens of photographers had a field day photographing him as his father spoke. The noise of the cameras woke him up and he bumbled along a long line of chairs in order to get out of the hall. This did not disturb the old man, who talked on happily: "Life is not bound by rules. It is bound by luck more than by rules," and "I have very little interest except your welfare and my personal honor."

Afterward, I had a brief chat with Winston. He sat down in a little room of the school and lit one of his enormous black cigars. He looked old and tired when he got off the platform. I cannot blame him. Altogether, he had made two speeches totaling about one hour and twenty minutes which is pretty good for a man of eighty. Looking at young Biggs-Davison, Churchill nudged me and said: "From the cradle to the summit—I just thought of that. On my feet I thought of that."

CARDIFF, ENGLAND, *May 22, 1955*

LAST night I drove to Tredegar, where Aneurin Bevan was born, to watch him campaign among his constituents in South Wales. Although it was late May and sunny, it was cold, with the wind blowing hard across the bare combs and down the winding valleys. Gray sheep grazed on the naked hillsides, but the valleys were marred by hideous slag piles, mining tipples, and scattered heaps of pit props—scars of the industrial age upon ancient Wales.

Bevan drove into town ahead of time. He stayed at his sister's home, a plain house, bigger than the others but certainly not very fancy, with a sitting room that is small, square, unadorned, and filled with overstuffed leather furniture. There he took some tea, then a hot bath, prior to his speech, which is being given on the Waunpound (an old horse fair ground on a hill pass), which is the area's traditional meeting place. The town band, followed by a few dozen marching men bearing trade-union signs, tootled by his house on its way up the hill.

At Waunpound, wild ponies with thick manes were grazing on the cold heath, while dressed-up little children played on the slope in front of the sound truck from which he was to speak. I talked to an exceptionally intelligent and quiet young steel worker who is an active Labour party organizer. He said life was pretty good and there had been full employment since 1945. But he resented the fact that any local man who let his sheep graze on the common among the wild horses had to pay an annual fee to Duke of Beaufort or Lord Tredegar.

Bevan and some local officials had to stand around until the small contingent from nearby Beaufort and Ebbe Vale arrived. Bevan was hatless; the sun shone on his shock of white hair. He is a heavy-set man with jutting jaw and a face like a slab of beef. Finally he and some Labour officials climbed on the flat truck and he was introduced by an old man with a fine Welsh voice who kept boasting about his father: "My Dad did all he could for the community and the class into which he was born." He warned that "Our real enemies are the upper ruling class," and rolling his r's, boasted that Bevan was "notorious" and not "respectable."

Bevan himself spoke in a musical voice with plenty of oratorical tricks, which the crowd enjoyed. He said Waunpound had held a special significance as a meeting place during the "dark days." The wind beat tears into his eyes as he hammered away at the Tories. He said they were not giving the workers their rightful pensions: "They must think we are mugs, eh?" He said he did not want to disturb the scars of his dispute with the Labour party. He said: "Tory property owners will want their share of the swag" if they win the elections. At the end of his speech he called for the singing of "The Red Flag" and "Three Good Cheers"—"Fill your lungs with good Waunpound air. We are not so many as we have been, but we can make a good racket."

LONDON, *May 23, 1955*

LUNCH today with Vlatko Velebit, now Jugoslav ambassador here. He says the forthcoming Russian visit to Belgrade is a fantastic development but one should not forget that the German Emperor Henry IV did homage to the Pope at Canossa, only to besiege Rome later with fire and sword.

He does not know quite what the Russians are after. They would like to neutralize Jugoslavia. But Jugoslavia insists on remaining armed and has never employed the word "neutralism." However, Velebit said that, because of American equipment, the cost of a modern army in Jugoslavia was too much for the economy to bear.

BELGRADE, *May 26, 1955*

JUST before the Soviet visit, several of Belgrade's public clocks were taken down for repairs. Remembering the Red army's greed for wristwatches, word went around: "Ah, we're getting ready for the Russians again."

All wartime street, factory, and town names have been changed back—except those named for Tito. Thus Djilasova is no more. Rankovićevo is again Kraljevo. Kardelj, speaking on this, said seven factories had been named for him and he regretted to admit that four of them were bankrupt.

BELGRADE, *May 27, 1955*

LAST night I dined with Prica, number-two man in the foreign office. He says the Russians are stupid, Byzantine, and hidebound. They always view other nations in terms of their own reactions and are deceived by bad reports from their diplomats and NVD.

Khrushchev was an ass to make his speech at the airport yesterday afternoon, stressing ideology and parties, lauding Tito and blaming Beria for all Cominform mistakes. The Jugoslavs realize that if the Russians can blame all on Beria today, they can again shift another time. Jugoslav leaders now simply speak a different language from the Russians. They have no use for pan-Slavism or monolithic ideologies. Prica, commenting on Tito's birthday party Wednesday—when runners came in from all over the country—said Khrushchev should have arrived in short pants bearing a torch.

Russia is scared of China and can't afford to pay China's needs. It fears the day when the U.S. and China get together. It fears an independent and "Titoist" policy in China. Therefore, it is moving population eastward into Asia.

BELGRADE, *May 29, 1955*

LAST night Tito gave a reception for Khrushchev at Beli Dvor, the White Palace of the Karageorgevićes. It was a rainy evening and the blossoms of the pink chestnut trees lining the long entrance driveway were beaten onto the road. Cars stacked up in a traffic jam such as Belgrade never sees, while guards checked the invitations of their occupants.

Beli Dvor is a simple palace, square, not very large, and furnished in imitation French and Italian furniture with undistinguished carpets and quite a few paintings (the least good left over from Prince Paul's tenancy, including one bad Canaletto and some sentimental French masters).

The assembled diplomats, political leaders, generals and admirals of Jugoslavia massed in a couple of small reception rooms and then the stars of the occasion arrived, walked in, and stood at attention while an unnecessarily loud band boomed out the Jugoslav and Soviet anthems. In front came Khrushchev and Mrs. Broz. Khrushchev, in an astonishingly badly cut Soviet sacksuit that looked as if it hadn't even been pressed, stood like a little gypsy dancing bear, staring dully ahead with his jaw hanging slack and his belly falling down beneath the four buttons of his jacket. A single decoration dangled incongruously from his lapel. Tito's wife, Jovanka, in a white evening gown, towered over him, a handsome, large woman with gleaming black eyes and short black hair, regular features, and white teeth. Behind them stood Bulganin, in gray uniform, with somewhat bleary, kind blue eyes, smiling behind his beard and looking for all the world like the bandmaster in a small German spa. Then came Tito, sunburned, stocky, in a dandy's uniform, with a faint smile upon his face, and Shepilov, a huge, sardonic-looking Russian with a sour sneer; then Gromyko, Mikoyan, and a pack of bodyguards.

After the anthems, the smiling party pushed through to an inner room, once a library for Prince Paul, where they dined in privacy. The other guests ate a buffet from heavily laden tables in two salons. Waiters tried desperately to pass glasses of *šljivovića*, white-lady cocktails, vermouth, beer, and white and red wine.

The Jugoslavs looked infinitely more impressive than their visitors and one would have thought that the great military power was represented by the handsome Marshal and his tall, well-groomed commanders, rather than the stubby little dictator and his guardians. Vladimir Popović, a former partisan general, former student at Moscow's Frunze military academy, former ambassador to Moscow and Washington, and newly named envoy to Peking, a towering, handsome man, remarked with ill-concealed arrogance: "I suppose this is the first time Khrushchev has ever been about among the people." Certainly, he observed, it was the first time he had ever been submitted to the badgering of photographers as was permitted here and the first time that he had ridden through the streets in an open car.

The evening was long and rather dreary because we all had to stand, save a few lucky females who found chairs, and one by one the ambassadors and Jugoslav dignitaries were taken into the bosses's dining room to chat with the lions of the occasion. Riddleberger, our envoy, discussed corn problems with Khrushchev who said he was trying to place the emphasis on silage. He was highly satisfied with his badinage, in which he assured Khrushchev he had not been converted to communism and Khrushchev admitted he was not yet a Republican. Guidotti talked with Bulganin who informed him that Russia was releasing some Italian war prisoners. "Good," said Gastone, "the Italian people will be overjoyed; they have been waiting a long time."

These interviews took hours while the other guests stood around shifting from flat foot to flat foot and occasionally shoving through the mob to the corner bar. In one unnoticed corner were two little tables of bearded, stove-pipe hatted orthodox priests and bearded, be-fezzed Muslim hodjas.

Prica told me the Russians have lowered their sights; that they were not now asking for a complete Jugoslav reconciliation but merely for good relationships at a "higher temperature" (as Khrushchev phrases it), but "not too high; about the temperature of a human body."

I was amused to note the very pleased Spanish Republican minister. The Jugoslavs are great people for lost causes: until 1941 they had a Czarist Russian chargé d'affaires; now the Spaniard, a former Berlitz teacher.

Finally, after midnight, the performance ended. The burly, gruff Soviet plainclothesman outside the door of the sanctum moved away and the massive Soviet lieutenant-general and immense Jugoslav general chatting there opened it up. Khrushchev was boiled and tottered out, clearly a victim of the power of *šljivovića.* Bulganin looked foggy and Tito himself was peering through a mist. They pushed through a cleared alley in the crowd, stood blinking while the band played anthems and photographers flashed bulbs, and then went out on the rainy porch where they bade good-bye. (Khrushchev, balancing uneasily, kissed Jovanka's hand; Tito gave her a husbandly buss.) Then the Russians piled into their cars for the station and Brioni. Khrushchev had to be loaded into his car physically.

There is certainly a curious contrast between this country's communism as it has now evolved and that of Russia. I couldn't help thinking of all the men in the satellite empire murdered as "Titoists"; by inference, it is admitted this was all a great mistake.

Sava Kosanović, head of the Jugoslav Independent Republican party, member of the executive council and former Ambassador to Washington, told me more about last night's party. He was one of of those invited to the inner sanctum with the Russians. At one point Bulganin raised his glass and said: "I drink to a neutral country." Tito, thinking he meant Jugoslavia interjected: "Jugoslavia is never neutral." Bulganin explained he meant Switzerland.

Khrushchev, Sava thinks, is merely an ignorant cunning peasant who knows nothing of the outside world. He made a foolish mistake in trying to place these talks on a party level. The Russians mean only one thing by communism—their own domination.

Tito kept stressing Jugoslav independence. When he introduced Sava he said: "This is Mr. Kosanović, head of the Independent Republican party, which has always stood for a united and independent Jugoslavia for more than fifty years—since the days of the Hapsburg empire."

They exchanged jokes. Kosanović told one on Tito: Eisenhower threatens that if Tito won't obey he will drop three atomic bombs on Jugoslavia. Tito replies: "So what. You will destroy a few factories. But I—I will send you three of our economists and destroy your country."

BELGRADE, *May 30, 1955*

THIS morning I spoke with Vlado Dedijer. He has moved to another, smaller apartment. Poor fellow, he is down on his uppers. His back is troubling him. He walks haltingly with a stoop.

He has no source of income. But he had saved some money to erect a monument to Olga, his first wife. Fortunately, he says, it hadn't yet been started and he is living on the funds. He eats mainly beans and bread and now that he is so hard up, he sees how the poor must be suffering from steadily rising prices. For a year the party tried to force his wife to divorce him. She refused and they ousted her.

It was odd sitting in this old partisan's study looking at his bookshelves —lined with books on Tito. He said almost all his friends had deserted him. He still admires Tito and says he is the "first real Jugoslav"; that he will never rejoin the Russian fold. "But after Tito, what?" He shrugged his shoulders. Vlado says: "Until 1948 Stalin was my God. Now I have no more gods. Nor will I have any."

He says he stuck by Djilas not so much because he agreed with his ideas —"Djilas went much too far"—but because he was a friend and "I am a Serb and I have been taught to stand by my friends."

Vlado said there could never be a compromise between "Europe and its Christian civilization and Soviet Russia. Jugoslavia is with Europe." He kept asking: "Why is Russia so weak now? What is going on there? Is it only economic weakness?" Inevitably, at least Czechoslovakia and Hungary must return "to Europe" from the satellite fold because "they are European."

No one, neither in Russia nor Jugoslavia, has found the answer to human incentives in terms of production. The peasants in Russia were even more strongly against collectivization than before. That was Russia's problem. And in Jugoslavia, although only 20 percent of the arable land was collectivized, peasant holdings had been cut to about eight hectares. Insufficient wheat could be grown on this; that was Jugoslavia's grain problem.

Tito and Kardelj had been against collectivization even in 1946 and 1947. But they bowed to extremists. There were two factions in the party. But Tito would surely not make any moves looking as if they were more "Communist" after these Russian talks.

Altogether, it was a striking contrast to the old Vlado I have known: calm, unrevolutionary, and non-Communist. He was most philosophical.

I do not hate anyone. I have contempt for my friends who have deserted me. But I see that everything is not black and white. There are many grays in the picture. But Milovan [Djilas] is a Montenegrin. Now he hates everyone with violence. For him, all is black or white. I always told him he went too far.

I lunched today with Vlada Popović, new Jugoslav ambassador to China. He leaves for Peking right after the Soviet talks.

Jugoslavia will not change its policy as a result of the Soviet talks. They aren't going well. The atmosphere Saturday night was *not* as friendly as it seemed. The Russians got quite drunk; the Jugoslavs didn't.

The Russians are worried about China and fear it will become friendly with the U.S.

PARIS, *June 13, 1955*

DOUGLAS Dillon said we had not informed the French adequately in advance of the Turkey-Pakistan-Iraq alliance which we promoted. Our feeling was that France was too weak to be important in that part of the world. The British wanted to keep the matter secret because they thought the French might intervene. As a result, an irritated Paris encouraged the Syrians not to join the pact. This caused Iraq to attack Syria and to claim the government there is crypto-Communist. We are taking the British side.

Dillon said practically all the State Department is anti-French. Bob Murphy is so hostile that he tried to prevent the French from getting any off-shore procurement contracts.

We have continually protested to the French against the use of U.S. equipment in Algeria. They wanted to move helicopters from Indochina to North Africa for use against the rebels in the Aures. We refused to permit this and we refused to rent helicopters to France for the operation.

Dillon says North Africa is vital to France, which cannot pretend to be a big power without it. This is not a distant argument like Indochina. It gnaws right at French vitals.

PARIS, *June 16, 1955*

THIS morning I visited Gaston Palewski, minister for atomic affairs. For the next two and a half years, France will concentrate on peaceful uses of nuclear energy. When enough plutonium is available, a decision must be taken as to whether some of it should be put to use in a weapons program.

The program now—officially dedicated to peaceful development—is exactly the same as it would be if France were going ahead with weapons because, first of all, it is a question of manufacturing enough plutonium. France must go ahead and make nuclear military plans. The question of when a program will be officially adopted for weapons production will arise in two or two and a half years.

The United States cannot, under its own legislation, provide its allies with atomic weapons. But the day will come when other countries will have atomic weapons. Then the issue will arise as to whether Germany can get any. Under the Western European Union agreement, the amount of stocks of atomic weapons on the Continent must be decided by Western European Union's own council.

In theory it might be possible to control the manufacture of atomic weapons, but there is no way of controlling destruction of weapons already made, of checking up to find out whether Russia or the United States has destroyed its atomic bombs, in case of agreement. Palewski himself thought it impossible to expect because they would be fools to do so. The only solution was to create an international control organization to which bombs would be handed over by those possessing them, rather than destroyed. They would be concentrated in the hands of this control organization. Then, if an aggression occurred, the control organization would have sufficient strength to destroy the aggressor immediately. This would be a tremendous deterrent.

Palewski was a member of French delegations in disarmament conferences prior to World War II, at which the Tardieu and Paul-Boncourt plans were proposed; these suggested an international army under a control commission, in order to prevent aggression. It is an old French doctrine.

PARIS, *June 21, 1955*

LAST night, dined at the Gruenthers. Rebecca West was there. She is incredibly vain; simply could not understand the inadequate preparation of American and British soldiers for "brain washing" after she had published *The Meaning of Treason.* It was folly that the American and British armies had not used this book as a guide in indoctrination courses.

ROME, *July 4, 1955*

TODAY I visited Giovanni Gronchi, newly elected second President of the Italian Republic. Gronchi, who was chosen by a curious combination of piqued right-wing Christian Democratic votes plus the Communists and Nenni Socialists, is a much debated character. His enemies accuse him of being a "Kerensky." I suspect our embassy, which has an extraordinary hold over American correspondents here, is touting this line for all it's worth because Gronchi's election was known to have been opposed by Mrs. Luce.

Gronchi described his foreign policy accordingly:

I am a convinced European. Europe should assume a big political position through its integration. In such a way Europe can be a third element in world politics, politically, economically, and financially. It can contribute successfully to European and world equilibrium. We must work for this within the cadre of our existing obligations. Clearly the original goal of the inventors of your Marshall Plan was in this direction. It presupposed a "Europe," not just a series of bilateral pacts for aid to each individual country. It wanted a Europe using its resources in common to employ United States aid. And the countries of Europe have not progressed far enough in this direction. The Marshall Plan is still split up into bilateral accords.

He said:

We have only three political movements in Italy with a future: the Catholic social movement expressed in the Christian Democratic party, the Communists, and socialism. It is my hope that we can separate the Left Socialists from the Communists. This has been achieved in other European countries—why not here? What is needed as a first step is agreement of the Christian Democrats on a government with a program leading to such social and economic reform that it must inevitably provoke a *crise de conscience* among the Socialists. United action between the "Social Catholics" and the Socialists is the only solid basis of democracy.

GENEVA, *July 23, 1955*

DURING the ten days of the Big Four Geneva Conference, Yuri Zhukov told me that more important than anything here was Bulganin's last report to the Central Committee of the Communist party. Bulganin said Russia was no longer the be-all and end-all of civilization; that not everything had been invented in Russia; that Russia needs a technological revolution; that Russia had to learn from the West and above all from the United States.

Chip Bohlen says the most impressive moment of the talks came when Eisenhower assured the Russians he would never be party to an aggressive war and apparently impressed them so much that Bulganin openly said he believed the President. The Russians are used to dealing in small details and in bickering arguments and were impressed by the sheer simplicity and "grandeur" of Ike's statement.

PARIS, *July 26, 1955*

LUNCH with Averell Harriman. I asked why his personal friendship with Eisenhower had ended. He simply couldn't understand why; during the campaign he had said some sharp things, but he had always pointed out in his speeches that if anybody failed to take into account the noble things Eisenhower had done for the United States "he would have a fight on his hands."

He first began to talk politics to Eisenhower in 1944, when Ike's headquarters were just east of Rheims. He last discussed politics with him in October, 1951. At first, Averell used to tell Eisenhower he thought it was his obligation to be the Democratic candidate for President. However, by October, 1951 (when Harriman was over here as one of the three "wise men") he understood that Ike really "thought" Republican. Eisenhower had been telling him the one thing that would really make him run for President would be the fear that otherwise Taft would be the Republican candidate. Therefore, Averell told him at that time it was his duty and obligation to run as Republican candidate for President—but that he should know that if he did so, he (Harriman) would oppose him as best he could.

. Averell has no use for Dulles but Eisenhower will keep him around as long as he is there. He thinks Ike definitely does not want to run for President again, but is not strong enough to turn down the pressure to run in 1956.

PARIS, *July 27, 1955*

LUNCH with Pierre Courtade, French Communist. In Geneva—as at every international conference—Courtade came up and said: "Well, Sulz, are you and I going to coexist?" As usual, I said: "Why don't you call me up and we'll lunch back in Paris." This time he did.

He says there has been a big change in Russia. It is now possible to talk openly on political matters. Stalin had obviously been a little bit gaga in his last few years and was easily deceived by people like Beria. This is a novel approach!

PARIS, *July 29, 1955*

DINED and bridged at the Gruenthers, at a party for Averell Harriman. I am glad to recall that I won every single rubber and that Al was the heaviest contributor.

Gruenther is convinced nobody really wants the unification of Germany right now and he himself would be quite happy if it were not unified. The Russians do not want unification under any conditions.

Al is disturbed by a "rider" on a recent congressional bill which makes it possible for foreign countries to purchase American crops and pay for them in foreign currencies. The "rider" insists that at least 50 percent of such purchases should be exported from the United States on American ships. As a result Norway, which has an annual deficit of 400,000 tons of wheat, purchased 80,000 tons from Russia, which has little to export. The Norwegians explained to Gruenther it was impossible for them to accept this "rider" since it would commit them to importing at least half the wheat on American boats. Norway has a large merchant fleet which it must employ.

Harriman is optimistic about Democratic chances of winning New York State in 1956. Dewey is now completely out of the picture and has not been able to bequeath his organization to anyone else.

Gruenther teased Harriman about his present tour. He pointed out that as governor of New York he was going to Israel, Italy, and Ireland. He asked him what on earth he was doing in Paris and London. Averell replied they were places where he wanted to enjoy himself.

Lunch with General Speidel, now roving ambassador for the German army: German representative on the planning group in Washington, German representative for planning discussions with SHAPE, and also with the Central European Command at Fontainebleau.

Speidel thinks the Russians will offer Adenauer reunification and rearmament as well as long-term, large-scale commercial contracts in Russia and China in exchange for German neutralization. Adenauer will of course reject this, but it is difficult for him politically. However, the Russians don't really want to reunify Germany at all—they are just playing a game. Their real objective is to have a European security system with a divided Germany —half participating in each half of the system. The French also prefer this.

PARIS, *July 30, 1955*

DINED at the Chambers, again in honor of the Harrimans. Present were René Pleven and Robert Marjolin, who used to work with Averell in OEEC days.

Pleven said the Eisenhower proposal for opening up the United States and Russia to mutual inspection of military installations was first made in 1946, by General Billotte. Harriman said the Faure plan to use funds saved from arms reductions for development of underdeveloped areas was first made by Senator MacMahon.

Averell acknowledged great respect for General de Gaulle during the latter's trip to Moscow in December, 1944. Stalin put pressure on to gain concessions in exchange for a Franco-Soviet pact. He would not agree to such a pact unless de Gaulle recognized the Lublin Polish government. De Gaulle refused.

At their final meeting, a dinner was given for de Gaulle and Stalin claimed everything had been arranged to sign a treaty according to de Gaulle's views. But when the document was brought forth to be signed, de Gaulle saw, to his horror, that it was exactly what he had refused to sign—namely, it called upon him to recognize the Lublin Poles. He was furious and started to leave. When Stalin saw this, he clapped his hands and said to Molotov: "Bring me the other treaty." Immediately, a totally different draft was produced, with no conditions concerning the Poles; de Gaulle signed it.

GENEVA, *August 6, 1955*

YESTERDAY I lunched with Winston Burdett whom I haven't seen in years. He recently testified to a Senate committee that he had been a Soviet informer from 1938 to 1942. I knew him well in Turkey (1941–1942). Winston was very nervous; arms and hands trembled. He is deeply scarred by the ordeal which he overdramatizes.

He testified that Lea, his first wife, was murdered by the Russians because she knew too much about how they were training Jugoslav partisans in North Iran during the spring of 1942. I pointed out that no Jugoslav partisan had ever been trained in Iran and, by the spring of 1942, Tito had a pretty good grip on Jugoslavia.

Dag Hammarskjöld says of the nuclear conference here that this is the most delicate and hush-hush field in history. We will restore an atmosphere of openness between scientists. We will break down neuroses. We will discover there has been *no* reason for secrecy. We are swinging from night to day.

Nils Bohr points out that the great atomic discoveries were made during a period of war and therefore a wrong emphasis was given; had they been made during the 1920s instead of the late 1930s and 1940s, the emphasis would have been different. This conference may restore the balance. We hope to reduce the destructive aspects of atomic energy to their proper proportions—an aberration, not a major aspect.

NASSER: "FEAR

DOMINATES THE AREA"

CAIRO, *August 9, 1955*

TODAY I SAW HANK BYROADE, NOW AMBASSADOR HERE. HE SAYS U.S. interest in possible loss of the Middle East was aroused when Iran almost went down the drain during the Mossadegh crisis. This woke us up to the fact that the area is our business and we cannot leave it to Britain and France. As a result, we joined in abortive efforts to establish a Middle East command.

After the inauguration in January, 1953, Dulles came here. When he returned to Washington he said we must do something about strengthening the Middle East, but the first necessity was to stop talking about it. Our rudimentary policy was then that if any Middle East state wanted assistance we should try to help. We decided to encourage an agreement between Egypt and Britain on the Suez base because we realized that until this was settled Egypt would never fight on the side of the West in case of war. Unfortunately, the Anglo-Egyptian settlement on Suez came too late.

While the quarrel between Britain and Egypt was continuing, Pakistan asked us to support her proposed alliance with Turkey. We agreed. But as the "northern tier" concept developed, this still left Iraq and Iran out in the cold. Iraq then asked us for military aid. We had already been giving such aid in varying amounts to Turkey, Iran, and Pakistan. We decided to make an arrangement with Iraq but the government consequently caught political hell from Zionist elements.

We figured both Iraq and Iran would adhere to the Pakistan-Turkey alliance if we did not talk about it too much. In January, 1955, Iraq decided to join the "northern tier" by allying itself with Turkey. We had not expected this so soon and were surprised and pleased. We find the "northern tier" useful as a moral plate glass window protection against Soviet aggression.

Nasser's advisors began to convince him that this "northern tier" arrangement had nothing to do with Middle East defense, but was purely political. Then, when Nuri el-Said asked other Arab states to join the alliance, Egypt's pride was hurt. Cairo felt this was a challenge to Egypt's leadership in the Arab world.

Nasser began to suspect the entire scheme was a move to attract Syria toward Iraq, federating the two countries under a Hashemite government and then establishing the old dream of a greater Syria. Furthermore, Nasser felt he was on the verge of being flanked by hostile elements everywhere— an inimical Arabia; Israel; a Sudan where the situation is deteriorating; and a weak Libya more or less controlled by the United States through its bases there.

He became convinced we were trying to force him to his knees in order to bring him to make peace with Israel. He began to look around for support. Saudi Arabia hates and fears the Hashemites who were ousted from the Hejaz by the Saudis. Therefore Nasser sought a new combination of Egyptian brains and Saudi Arabian wealth. He wanted to develop a "defense" pact among Egypt, Saudi Arabia, and Syria. A glance at the map shows this actually could have nothing to do with defense, but its real purpose was to prevent Iraq from taking over Syria.

This pact has not yet been signed. Syria decided to try and trade on the prevailing situation and to get economic aid from both Egypt and Saudi Arabia without committing itself.

It is impossible for us to strengthen a purely Arab coalition because of the situation vis-à-vis Israel. And things have gotten worse, not better. The situation along Egypt's Gaza frontier deteriorated this year and many Egyptians actually suspected the U.S.A. urged Israeli aggressiveness in order to put pressure on Egypt.

Now another problem is developing. We have a bumper cotton crop and seem to be getting ready to subsidize cotton exports. Egypt is the second largest cotton producer in the world and 85 percent of its exports are cotton. Many Egyptians figure that the idea of subsidized American cotton exports, which reduces world prices, is still another form of applying pressure against Egypt. Because of all these factors our popularity is shrinking and the position of the Soviet bloc has improved vastly. Now Nasser has agreed to visit Moscow next spring and Red China is buying a large amount of Egyptian cotton.

It is naturally in Moscow's interest to break the "northern tier" alliance. Furthermore, the Soviet bloc *needs* cotton. People in Egypt are beginning to wonder: Is Russia after all perhaps a better friend than the West? If Moscow ever offers arms to the Arab states it could become their greatest friend overnight.

Colonel Nasser is only thirty-seven years old. Until he went to Bandung he had never been out of Egypt. Yet he is a surprising man. He can talk for hours on end about economics. He is a very hard worker, rigidly honest, a puritan, and above reproach. He is often dejected at what he considers a lack of national support. He sees the immensity of Egypt's problem—poverty, lack of education, the difficulty of land reform. By nature he is suspicious because his is a background of conspiracy.

Nasser's big interest in Marshal Tito was how Tito was able to get help from the West without being dominated by the West. The Egyptian army is convinced we are denying Egypt the right even to purchase weapons in the United States. And since the army supports Nasser he does not dare speak too nicely about us for fear of losing its support. He knows we resent this. And yet deep in his mind he sometimes wonders whether we are trying to upset him.

The High Aswan Dam which has been planned would help Egypt's population and agricultural crisis and tide the country over for another fifteen years. But the problem of financing has not been solved. Here again Egypt suspects we are influencing the World Bank to hold back on loans in order to apply pressure.

CAIRO, *August 10, 1955*

THIS morning I talked for an hour and forty-five minutes with Nasser. I saw him in his office at the HQ of the Revolution Command Council, a simple room, unostentatiously furnished with a desk and some stuffed leather furniture. The windows look out over the Nile. The only concession to comfort was an electric fan. We drank Turkish coffee and a green lime drink and smoked his Craven-A and Filtra cigarettes. Nasser is a handsome, tall, powerfully built, and vigorous man, who resembles the massive statues of Rameses II. He speaks English fluently but not perfectly. He was in mufti —a gray suit.

All in all, before recounting what he told me, I would like to sum up my impressions. He gives one the feeling of being energetic, brave, modest, and disinterested in wealth. However, he is clearly lacking in serious education or worldly experience and this must be a handicap to him. Furthermore, he tends to look beneath and behind even the most simple proposition for invidious meanings. Undoubtedly this is part of his heritage of conspiracy and of deep resentment against colonialism and imperialism. He is surely naive and could easily be fooled. For example, he confided to me that he had once thought all Communists were "thieves" and he was therefore surprised to find how nice a man Chou En-lai was. There is no doubt of his basic sincerity. The question is: When you have a man leading a revolution in midstream, is this enough?

I started out by asking: "What is the ideology of your revolution?" He replied:

I have read much about socialism, communism, democracy, and fascism. Our revolution will not be labeled by any of those names. We seek to meet the needs and requirements of our own people and we are not trying to copy anybody else's ideology. We have many diseases and shortcomings in our country and we wish to overcome all of them. We began our revolution with principles, not a program. We find that sometimes we have to change our methods.

We are a country of twenty-three million. Eighteen million are farmers and they have been deprived of their personal liberty for five thousand years. They have always been under the domination of landlords. If they disagreed with the landlords they would lose their livelihood. They prefer to sacrifice liberty in order to earn a living and support their family.

We must liberate the individuals of Egypt. Only then will the country be totally free. To do this we must limit land ownership and liquidate the domination of the landlords. We must replace the present system with cooperatives to help the small farmers and to aid them in the distribution of their crops. Only in these ways can we make the farmers feel free.

I know how these people feel. My family are farmers. I can now tell as I visit areas affected by our revolution that the farmer feels his own master. Before the revolution the people always felt that the government was their enemy. I know. I used to feel this myself. The government used to take from the many and give only to the few corrupt, wealthy people. Now the people must be made to feel that the government is not taking from them but is working for them. They must feel that the government represents them and their needs. It is hard to convince people of this change. It is hard to reassure them that the government is not working to collect money for a few. But the people are now able to grasp these ideas.

All our western desert is ready for cultivation. The only thing it needs is water. Something will have to be done. We have a big problem of increasing population as a result of scientific advances. According to statistics, we are now in a position to double ourselves over forty years. New hygiene and medical measures are reducing infant mortality. What will happen when we are forty million people limited to five million acres of the Nile Valley and Delta?

I asked how Nasser planned to turn political power back to the people. He replied:

We face the problem of opportunists seeking to work against the nation's interest. I declared we will have no political parties. We have our own organization, the Liberation Rally. Therefore, I liquidated the old parties. We have organized syndicates of intellectuals, white collar workers, professors, and ordinary workers. It is difficult to organize the farmers. But they have started with cooperatives. From these syndicates and cooperatives the people can participate in government. But so far we have not decided on a detailed program.

I found Nasser very vague on this. As a matter of fact, he admitted as much and said he was always puzzled by ideological questions and questions of future developments. I asked if Egypt were not heading toward a system of the corporate state with representatives from the various unions, cooperatives, and other organizations each playing a role. He said he did not know; he had not thought that far ahead. But obviously the words "corporate state" did not connect in his mind with Mussolini.

I asked what the philosophy of his foreign policy was and whether it could be described as neutralism. He replied: "Neutralism only applies during a war. If you mean neutrality in a cold war, it is difficult to define. Only if there is a war does the question of neutrality arise." Nasser pointed out that the Suez agreement with Britain would be activated if there were any aggression against Turkey or the Arab world and therefore Egypt would not be in a neutral position in such a case.

I asked why Egypt was so strongly against the "northern tier" alliance. He replied:

> We are only interested in the Arab countries. We have nothing against Turkey, Iran, or Pakistan. But you must remember we have a complex on the subject of alliances with big powers. We fear that an alliance is just another form of domination. For instance, our 1936 treaty with England said that Egypt would be a completely independent country. But what happened? You know and everybody knows what happened.
>
> We must *feel* free. Our public opinion simply did not believe that the British troops would evacuate Suez. I almost lost my life as a result of that agreement. The man who tried to murder me said: "He sold the country to the British." We feel that alliance is another form of domination. We Arab countries have a population of about sixty million and we can have a big army and organize our own defense. We feel we should defend our own area and our own people—not the United States and Britain. If we feel over us any kind of protectorate, our mood would change instantly. Remember we face two threats of aggression—one from outside and the other by subversive elements within. The people of this area are losing faith in their governments. They feel that some of their leaders are agents from abroad. [Nasser did not say so but I believe he meant Nuri el-Said.] This encourages extremism and nationalism.
>
> During our revolution I saw the effect of extremist leadership on pure nationalists. Most people are innocent nationalists. But those who lead them can, with their support, run the country. If these innocent nationalists feel that their government is working for others, they will follow the extremists and this is precisely what the Communists and the Muslim Brothers tried to bring about. My battle in Egypt was to defeat these elements.

I changed the subject by asking him how the Palestine war could be ended. He replied:

> This is a question of time. First we must reach solutions on the problems of refugees and of frontiers. The Arab people refuse to live under the threat of fear. You know the effect of fear. I do not want to see my children as refugees. With my own eyes I saw refugees in Palestine. I do not want to see Egyptian refugees packing their belongings to go off to

nowhere. And, to our sympathy for the refugees, you must add nationalism.

Once I thought there could be peace. I said to my troops and officers in Palestine that we must do our best to have peace in this area. They disagreed and said Israel would not agree to peace. I replied that I had guarantees from England and the United States. But after the bloody Gaza incident, when I saw the same officers, I felt responsible for the deaths of those thirty-two men. There had been no Egyptian troops at Gaza except for administrative units. They lived in their billets without defenses—no barbed wire or trenches. They were killed in cold blood. What could I say? I said I was wrong and responsible for the lives of those people. I said if you see any Jew kill him. You are responsible for yourself and for your land and we can no longer rely on guarantees.

Fear dominates the area. What do you think I feel when I hear that the Herut party in Israel wants expansion from the Nile to the Euphrates? This was said in Herut speeches in the recent election campaign. And they said that the Arabs must be pacified by force. And after that the Herut party gained eight seats. Now they have seventeen. And at the next election they may have seventy—all of them for expansion. We live in fear and as long as there is fear there cannot be peace.

What did he want in the way of relationships with the United States? He replied that in 1946, America had been very popular in this part of the world as a result of wartime declarations.

But, by 1948, all this popularity had gone. Still, after the Israeli war, people began to hope again for America. Again they started to think the United States was working for liberation and had no colonial objectives. At the beginning of our revolution we informed the American embassy, the only embassy we informed. At that time I had only two main hopes: The agreement with Britain to evacuate her troops; and a policy of friendship with the United States. I was able to attain the first but not the second.

What is the meaning of friendship? For the army it is equipment. For the people it is help against domination and help to improve their standard of living. The army is a basic factor in Egyptian life. The Communists have made many efforts to penetrate the army. They say I am working for the United States and the United States refuses to help us. I have felt this propaganda in the army. Friendship, for the army, means equipment. Our revolution was stimulated in the army by a lack of equipment. If our officers feel we still have no equipment they will lose faith in the government.

Two years ago, your Under Secretary of Defense Foster came here and said he would help us. He asked us to send a mission. I sent my assistant. I told our officers that American equipment would be coming. They were skeptical. They said the only cargo you will receive from America is your assistant. And that is the only cargo we received.

I tell your people you spend millions of dollars on propaganda; please divert some of it to the material side. People receive all these free pamphlets but they do not read them. I know. I receive them and I do not read them. We are asked if we intend to use our equipment against Israel. I reply that I am not interested in waging war; I want to build my country; I want to raise our standard of living.

Two years ago when Naguib was still head of the regime he sent a letter to President Eisenhower pledging that any equipment we received would be used only for the defense of the country. We sent that letter because you asked for a commitment that no equipment should be used against Israel. But we have received nothing. There are still negotiations. But public opinion in the army has been poisoned.

I try to make army opinion friendly to the United States because I always fear Communist penetration in the army. I wanted to send fifty staff officers to visit the U.S.A. to counter Communist propaganda and I only succeeded after many difficulties had been raised by you.

The Turkish-Iraqi pact created bad feeling between the Arab countries and the United States. The Arab countries do not want to be divided. Everyone felt that the United States was trying to divide the Arab countries in order to dominate them. The pact put an end to the improving atmosphere in this area.

At this point I simply had to go because I was already ten minutes late for a luncheon with the British ambassador. As I said farewell, Nasser shook my hand firmly and said: "I want to see my people have some of the opportunities that I had as a child. I want them to enjoy some of the pleasures of life."

Lunched with Sir Humphrey [later Lord] Trevelyan, British ambassador. Just arrived, he has not yet presented his credentials. He talked at length and most interestingly about China, which he only left at the end of May. He thinks there is no chance for at least a decade of splitting China and Russia, no matter what policy we follow. However, our present policy has been idiotic.

It is folly for the United States to base a policy on Chiang Kai-shek. No one in China thinks of Chiang now as an alternative to the Communists. Peking intends to bring about its own solution by subversion in Formosa, and one day we will wake up to find we have been betrayed. Everything is going the way the Communists want. They have no intention of allowing us to intervene in Formosan negotiations but will drag things on until Chiang dies, or is overthrown, or makes his own arrangements. Humphrey distrusts Chiang's son who was brought up in Moscow and has a Soviet wife. He does not think there is any chance now of making a deal to offer China's Security Council seat to India. It is too late to play that game.

ANKARA, *August 18, 1955*

THIS afternoon I saw Fatin Rustu Zorlu, foreign minister (later hanged). He maintained that from the sixteenth century until 1878, when the

British took over Cyprus, it had always been Turkish. The island had a Turkish majority in 1878. Turkish Cypriots now in Turkey are very agitated, and it is difficult for the government to calm them down. Furthermore, the island has immense strategic importance to Turkey. Greece is incapable of supporting it economically. The Cyprus question has inspired a mood of Greek imperialism and a return to the idea of Megali or Greater Greece. Turkey will insist at the London conference on maintaining the status quo. British "presence" in Cyprus prevents trouble between Turkey and Greece.

Zorlu argued that 20 percent of the Greek population is Communist and that Turkey simply could not risk turning over Cyprus to Greece because someday Greece might have a Communist government and this country does not wish to be surrounded by Communists. Greece was once within "two fingers" of communism and was saved only by foreign intervention. What, he asked, would be the political future when Marshal Papagos dies?

This evening I had a long talk with Prime Minister Adnan Menderes (also later hanged). He spoke fluent English, but he called in Ambassador Nuri Birgi to help when occasionally he got stuck for a word. Menderes was friendly, calm, restrained, and unusually modest.

He said Turkey had not received its fair share of American aid. The total on a per-capita basis amounted to only $19 for each Turk, whereas Greece had received $228 per capita. Even Ireland and Sweden, who are neutral, had received more proportionate aid. (This is claptrap.)

I asked what Turkey would do if it did not get the aid. He said: "Rest assured we will not collapse." But, the American government was being misinformed about economic conditions here. The Turkish investment program was just beginning to produce goods for the pipeline that would not come out at the other end for a while. By 1958, the economy would be sound. Turkey requires an effective industry to support a modern army.

He said the Turkish press was free but the opposition was trying to use it to incite public opinion and provoke incidents. "We can't tolerate this," he said and asked if we would permit such things in the United States. Indeed we would; I told him the only restriction was in terms of libel.

ISTANBUL, *August 20, 1955*

THIS morning I saw the Greek Patriarch, Athenagoras, in his musty patriarchate in the Phanar quarter. His secretary confided that the old man, who is said to have been suffering from a tapeworm, is bothered by the damp climate.

Athenagoras looks precisely like a Byzantine mosaic of God the Father: about six foot three—and even taller with his rimless stovepipe hat and flowing black gown. Despite his seventy years he is erect and active. His white beard is at least eighteen inches long and curled in ropes like Michelangelo's "Moses." He has a white skin, well-carved aquiline nose, and piercing, hypnotic black eyes.

During his life he has held five passports: Turkish, Greek, Jugoslav, Bulgarian, and American. He hopes he will live long enough to return to the United States just once before he dies so he can "kiss the soil."

He is deeply disturbed about the Cyprus question and claims the Greek government, the Archbishop of Athens, and the Archbishop of Cyprus (Makarios) have been idiotic. It is far more important, he says, for Greece to retain the friendship of Turkey and Britain. Athens, in its hysteria, is forgetting the 100,000 Greeks in Turkey. He regrets he has no clerical authority to restrain the Archbishops of Athens and Cyprus. The Orthodox Church is a federation and both Archbishops are autocephalous and autonomous. His only influence is in matters of dogma.

Our talk was punctuated by a serving of mastika jam with a spoon and water. When I left, in addition to his blessing and kisses on both cheeks, he gave me a bottle of ouzo, one of red wine, and one of Samian white wine.

ATHENS, *September 17, 1955*

THIS morning I visited Stephanopoulos, the foreign minister. He was sitting at his desk with a batch of letters and cables before him, all urging the government to quit NATO and adopt a policy of neutrality because Greece's allies had let her down. Stephanopoulos says Athens doesn't intend to abandon NATO but he fears if there is no solution to the Cyprus question at the next UN meeting the resentment here will be such that when the next elections are held in 1956, the left will sweep in.

ATHENS, *September 18, 1955*

YESTERDAY afternoon, I went out to Tatoi and saw King Paul at his summer palace. He had just returned the previous day from his official visit to Jugoslavia.

The King looked drawn and pale. He is diffident and shy; therefore harder to talk with than should be the case for an easygoing, chatty man. He was wearing a white, summer admiral's uniform with short sleeves. The atmosphere was immensely informal. There were no guards at the gates or at the palace door and when I left there wasn't even a servant: I just picked up my hat, opened the door, and departed. One Princess was playing with her dog outside and the young Crown Prince (later King Constantine) was scooting around the property on his Vespa motorcycle.

Tito had stressed to King Paul that he would never go back to the Soviet bloc; once was enough. He didn't intend to associate with any bloc in the future that did not include *both* the U.S.A. and the U.S.S.R. By this he meant he would not support any security organization in Europe that sought to eliminate or ostracize the U.S.A. Tito wants to attract the satellites away from their outmoded concepts of Stalinism. He told the King he detested Stalin and "always had."

Paul obviously fell victim to Tito's charm. He thinks he is a fine fellow —not a hidebound doctrinaire, but a sincere and reliable realist. He was also impressed by Madame Broz, but he said snobbishly: "If you saw her in peasant costume she would probably be quite striking."

Paul said he could see no Cyprus solution in sight. The U.S.A. must help get the subject inscribed on the Assembly agenda—even if it were then buried and forgotten. It was necessary to remind Greece that America is her friend. Bilateral negotiations between Greece and Britain must be resumed under the guise of Cypriot self-government—not self-determination. Thus the Turks could be kept out of the act. The British made the great error of feeding Turkish passions on this subject and encouraging their interest.

I asked Paul if he knew who Dighenis was (Dighenis is the *nom de guerre* of the underground resistance—EOKA—leader in Cyprus). He claimed to have no idea; and he noted that Dighenis is an ancient Greek name. (Dighenis is Colonel Grivas, a right-wing Greek regular officer.)

Stephanopoulos had again repeated Paul's 1948 offer (then made through me) of British bases in Cyprus and elsewhere in Greece in exchange for enosis. But the British are determined to hang on to Cyprus as a matter of prestige.

The King said there is no doubt Marshal Papagos, the Prime Minister, will die very soon. He added:

> I don't know what kind of a game my ministers are trying to play with me. It's a farce. There are all these reports that the doctors find him recovering. Yet the last time I saw him—late in August—he was lying in bed, could be fed only through the nose, lay there with his mouth half-open, and had great difficulty in talking. Now they are feeding him through the veins. I am afraid he is going to leave us very soon.

This will produce a difficult political situation. The King would have to appoint a new government to prepare for elections before November 1956, when they are now scheduled.

At present he feels the only man he could ask to form a government if Papagos dies is Caramanlis, the minister of works, an honest and popular man.

ATHENS, *September 20, 1955*

TALKED this morning to Constantine Caramanlis, minister of communications and public works and supposedly the bright young man of the present government, whom the King wants to make Premier if Papagos dies. I asked him if he should be called on to form a government, what his foreign policy would be. He stared at me in amazement. "If I talked about a policy for myself," he said, "I would look ridiculous. And I would rather die than look ridiculous."

Caramanlis said from $150,000,000 to $200,000,000 in gold is still hoarded in the country because the people lack confidence in the currency. There is a paucity of capital. Lenders demand 40 to 45 percent interest. As a result, there are no new investments, no new factories and it is even difficult to keep existing plants in repair. Right now about 25,000 young men have had to find jobs in Belgium and Holland. There are about 200,000 to 300,000 out of work. Full employment is required, but money is short. If there were confidence in currency and capital came out of hiding, new investments would provide new jobs.

NICOSIA, CYPRUS, *September 28, 1955*

HERE in Famagusta, a lovely medieval town with Gothic ruins and a Venetian castle called "Othello's Tower" (after the Moor who governed here), George Seferiadis, Greek ambassador in the Middle East, (who writes poetry as "Seferis") introduced me to a medieval wine called Commandaria which used to be manufactured at the Commanderie (headquarters) of the Knights of St. John. It is made of heavy, sweet grapes and matured in enormous casks that are only opened for refilling purposes every twenty-five years.

Earlier I saw Archbishop Makarios III in his office in Nicosia. Once a theology student in Boston, he is head of the church and also ethnarch (national leader) of the Greek Cypriots. The ethnarch system was introduced by the Turks when they conquered the island in the sixteenth century. The Ottoman Empire wanted a responsible leader for the head of each minority community. The leading ecclesiastic has always been the Greek ethnarch here. The Cyprus church ranks high in Greek Orthodoxy and has three special privileges granted by the Byzantine emperor Zeno. The Archbishop is allowed to sign his name in red ink. He wears a purple mantle. And, on ceremonial occasions, he carries an imperial scepter instead of the usual staff.

Makarios has an El Greco face, long and ivory colored, with long, prominent nose, long narrow eyes, black beard slightly streaked with gray, the whole ensemble rendered more Gothic by the tall, orthodox stovepipe hat. He wore a black robe and around his neck was a heavy gold chain, on the end of which dangled a bejewelled religious medallion. He sat at his carved walnut desk on a throne-like walnut chair given him by a Cypriot artisan two years ago. On its back was carved the Byzantine imperial device of the double-headed eagle.

He speaks very quietly in a meticulous, precise voice and does not seem in the least a fire-eater, although he is supposed to be quite an orator. He said:

The peaceful and legal way is closed to us at present by the UN decision not to discuss Cyprus's claim to self-determination. I don't know how the situation will develop. It is the view of some people, including perhaps the United States government, that owing to international tension, the Cyprus question should be put aside for a while. This is unwise. The problem should be faced and solved now.

The people of Cyprus are against the establishment of a base here to help other people preserve their freedom while their own is suppressed. It is unjust that Cyprus should be refused her freedom in the name of freedom. Turkish arguments against us were instigated by the British. The will of the minority should not rule over the desires of the majority. Turkish minority rights should be guaranteed and safeguarded under self-determination.

Makarios admitted he often preached political sermons. The church was very nationalistic. It had a great history. That's why it was called *Greek* Orthodox, not just Orthodox. Interference of the church in politics is a Greek phenomenon. The church had led all unfree Greek territories to liberty. Cyprus was the last. The archbishop was elected both as a national and religious leader. Makarios described his technique as something similar to Gandhi's—"under very different circumstances." His passive and EOKA's active resistance policies "led to the same end." He personally was for passive measures, but EOKA was activist and underground. A large section of the Cypriot population favored EOKA. "When the island is free the church will quit politics and I will lose my job as ethnarch," he added.

NICOSIA, CYPRUS, *September 29, 1955*

LAST night, a rather interesting experience. After a series of carefully arranged and discreet contacts, I had established contact with the EOKA (National Organization of Cypriot Fighters) underground. I was called up by an unknown voice, after two days of secret exchanges, and told to be in front of Electra House at 8:00 P.M. A car with the license number J— would drive up at precisely that hour. I was to get right in beside the driver and go off.

I followed these instructions. At 8:00 P.M. on the dot, two cars came up out of the night. J— did not stop but seemed to be wandering around looking for security agents. Behind it was another car. I hopped in and off we went. There were two other people besides the driver. I did not get a good look at their faces because every time I turned around they hid them behind briefcases.

Some miles out we turned off the main highway and down a narrow road and finally came to our destination. A chunky EOKA character was standing at the gate. He greeted me amiably and conducted me into a funny little room decorated with pictures of archbishops and icons.

After a few minutes, another door opened and I was summoned into a dark room. I stumbled to a chair and sat down. When my eyes got accustomed to the darkness I could make out a couple of figures. One of them was clearly very nervous. From a crack of light under the door I noticed that he was wearing dark glasses, although we were sitting in the pitch black. He was taking no chances on my being able to recognize him again. He did most of the talking in rather good English but with a stilted imitation Oxford accent.

He kept stressing that I was the first journalist ever allowed to learn any of the secrets of EOKA. At first he did not want me to write down anything at all. I promised I would dateline anything I wrote "somewhere in Cyprus" in order not to give the British security any untoward clues. After a while —and the conversation lasted several hours—I began to take notes in the dark.

The men I talked with said they were members of the central committee of EOKA. Whether they included Dighenis (Grivas), I do not know. They told me:

> We are at war with Britain, but we have nothing against the British as a nation. After all, we are very pleased with the attitude of the Labour party on Cyprus. Therefore we have not killed any English people. Our program has been to frighten the British, but not to kill them. We kill only Cypriot traitors. But soon, we fear, we will have to kill the British too.

I asked how many "Cypriot traitors" had been executed so far. They said four men had been assassinated for collaboration. There had been other efforts to execute people, but these had failed. EOKA has agents in key positions in the Cyprus government and municipalities. It claims to number all types of Cypriots, including farmers, workers, doctors, and merchants.

The military organization of EOKA is still obviously small stuff. I asked how many armed men they could muster within forty-eight hours and they said considerably less than a battalion. The only thing that comforts them is that VOLKAN, the Turkish equivalent, is even weaker.

The central committee is called Kendriki Epitropi. Under it is a series of groups and subgroups, each of which is called an *Omas* or team. Dighenis is called the *Archigos* or leader. Each Omas is headed by an *Omadarchas*, or group leader. All the leaders use *noms de guerre*. Many do not know the real names of their colleagues. The system is supposed to be that nobody knows anybody else out of his own Omas, except for the group leader. Therefore, if one Omas is discovered, its members cannot betray other groups.

The EOKA leaders claim they will never compromise with communism. They mistrust the Communists and won't let any known Communist into their organization for fear of penetration. But there is an implicit truce between EOKA and the Communists and they avoid attacks upon each other.

I was driven home in the same complicated two-car method, but the other characters who had come along with me remained behind; there was only one driver for each car. Naturally I saw their faces: a tough-looking pair. I was finally dropped off in the early morning some distance from my Nicosia hotel.

Dropped around this afternoon to see Courtney, our consul. There was a general strike. Embarrassed troops of Her Majesty's Royal Inniskilling Fusiliers were standing behind barbed-wire positions firing occasional tear-gas shells at Cypriot kids on bicycles. The Cyprus police, a dull and inefficient lot, were wearing steel hats and carrying shields to brave occasional showers of stones and Coca-Cola bottles. While sitting in Courtney's house having highballs with him and his wife, we heard the explosion of tear-gas shells and pretty soon the room filled up with fumes.

Courtney says Britain fears its Middle Eastern prestige would be lost if Cyprus were given up. The island is a good nerve center. The Ministry of Defense insists it be kept at all costs. British Middle Eastern headquarters will be established at Episkopi. A new air base is being built at Akrotiri near Limassol.

JERUSALEM, *October 4, 1955*

GOOD talk with Moshe Sharett, Prime Minister and Foreign Minister. Sharett likes the idea of the U.S. taking commitments in stabilizing the area. He thought Dulles's approach on refugees was constructive because it stressed resettlement. But it would be very difficult to get any Arab agreement on frontiers. Israel won't cede any territory, but is prepared for minor boundary adjustments.

The Dulles approach may have been outmoded by the Soviet decision to sell arms to the Arab countries. This was "a grave turn in the evolution of the Middle East. For the first time, the Soviet factor has been injected." Now the Soviet bloc has become an active element in the Middle East and it will probably transcend the Egyptian arrangement. This is bound to start an arms race—just the thing Dulles had tried to prevent.

Israel must increase its arms purchases as a result of the Soviet move. She will now request larger sales of American weapons on a longer-term basis and for lower prices and will also probably try and buy more Mystères from the French.

The question of a big-power guarantee is also now much more urgent. Israel wants a status-quo guarantee. But this must supplement new arms purchase, and not be a substitute. Israel is still vitally interested in a security treaty with the U.S. and has only recently raised the matter again with us. Israel would like other powers to adhere to the treaty, but the United States is all-important.

JERUSALEM, *October 5, 1955*

LUNCH today at the Prime Minister's home, in honor of ex-Governor Dewey. Dewey irritated me by shooting off on Turkey (his law firm is retained as legal counsel by the Turks). He said Ambassador Warren was stupidly exaggerating the extent of damage in the recent Istanbul and Izmir riots.

It was ridiculous to think of Cyprus as Greek. It was hundreds of miles from Greece and right off the Turkish coast. The Turks required it for strategic protection. Also, they had to protect their minority on the island. If the British evacuated it the Turks would have to move in. They could not risk leaving it in the hands of the unreliable Greeks.

I kept quiet. Afterward Sharett took me in a corner and said with a twinkle in his eye: "You know, Mr. Dewey has told me some rather interesting things about Turkey." Sharett has known Turkey since 1910, speaks the language well, and went to officers' school there during World War I.

This evening I had a stimulating talk with David Ben Gurion, former Prime Minister and again Prime Minister-elect, and still Defense Minister. He is a grand old man, sixty-nine years old, beginning to show signs of age. His hair has been sparse and white for years, but he has gained too much weight and looks a bit tired. However, he still talks in a most youthful way.

Ben Gurion, upon hearing that I had been in Greece recently, complained that he could no longer get any decent classic texts from Athens, which had ceased printing them. He was absolutely horrified when I told him I had seen *Oedipus Tyrannos* in modern Greek. He said it was a crime to translate it into demotic. He went on for some time discussing Sophocles. A local company had put on *Oedipus*, but the Israeli people simply could not comprehend the idea of Greek tragedy; the idea of fate unjustly controlling man's destiny and man having no influence thereon.

It was only with some difficulty that I brought Ben Gurion back to modern times. He turned to the recent Soviet promise to sell arms (through Czechoslovakia) to Egypt. For the time being, Ben Gurion said: "The deal is only being carried out through Czechoslovakia, but Russia may eventually appear openly as a munitions salesman."

He said at first he considered Nasser a decent fellow, but now realized "He is a crafty, deceitful, Arab type." He added that Nasser has three aspirations: to be head of the Arab world; head of the Muslim world; and head of the continent of Africa. "Meanwhile," he sneered, "he has lost the

Sudan." Ben Gurion suspects the British are trying to push Nasser's interests northward toward Israel in order to keep his mind off the Sudan.

Ben Gurion said Nasser knew perfectly well Israel would never attack Egypt and therefore he was lying when he used the excuse of an Israeli threat to purchase arms from Russia. He agreed that Nasser wants to satisfy the army for the sake of its political support, but he added that once the army had arms it would wish to use them.

I inquired what Israel would do if it were discovered that the Egyptian arms purchases are as extensive as he suspects. He replied: "If it turns out to be true that they are receiving between eighty and one hundred MIGs, as it is reported, we will have to smash them." I said that this would mean war, a preventive war. Ben Gurion said, "No." He thought ten Israeli planes could stage a sufficiently accurate raid to end the whole matter and it could be done without war. He explained Russia's arms sales as an effort by Moscow to obtain a footing in the Middle East. This had been Russia's aim for three hundred years.

I then asked if Ben Gurion would mind sticking his neck out and telling how he envisaged Israel's future ten years hence. He said agriculture in the South (Negev) has to be built up. Furthermore, atomic energy had to be developed. Israel was in a position to build its own piles and reactors and within five years this would be done. It was necessary to find sources of cheap power. And it was necessary to get new manpower. Jews would be brought in from North Africa. Also, he hoped to get elite elements of pioneering youth from South Africa, South America, and the United States.

Ben Gurion said there could be no peace with the Arabs until Egypt was prepared to sign with Israel. No other country would make the move until after Cairo had done so.

He thought Israel was a big enough state to be geographically viable, adding:

> Our problem is men, not land. Hitler killed the six million Jews who should have built this country. They had the need for this country, the desire to come here, and the ability to build it. The present immigration has the need and the desire, but it does not have the ability. We have to put in a great spiritual, economic, and intellectual effort to bring the new immigration up to our own level. It takes time to make them the same as we.

Ben Gurion believed Israel could contain four million people but didn't see where that manpower potential was available. The only present large source of immigration was North Africa. In the future, he thought, if East-West relations continued to improve, Russia might permit an extensive emigration of Jews. Then there might be a time when Jews from the Anglo-Saxon countries would come. The last time he had seen Einstein in America he asked him how he could obtain young scientists to help out in Israel.

Einstein replied that many young American Jewish scientists would be ready to go to Israel because they felt they were not trusted; they were certainly not trusted in England. In England, Jews are barred from several professions, including the foreign service, the intelligence service, the navy, and atomic-energy work.

Ben Gurion thought that if Israel becomes economically stable, it will attract more young people from the United States. I asked if he were not opposed to the idea of dual nationality—I meant that many Israelis from Britain and the United States keep passports from these countries as well as Israeli passports. From his point of view, he was against the idea of any citizenship. The only important thing was the physical presence here of individuals. He did not care how many passports a man had.

If a man lives here and educates his children here and takes part in this new life, what is a passport? My boy married a Christian girl in England. She is from the Isle of Man and she is terribly proud of the fact that her little birthplace has the oldest parliament in the world. Now she lives here. She has two children. Although they know English, they insist on speaking only Hebrew to their mother. You see what I mean by the unimportance of passports?

ISFIYA, ISRAEL, *October 8, 1955*

TODAY I visited a Druze village called Isfiya on the crest of Mount Carmel. A young Druze named Kamal Mansour came along as interpreter. Although a Druze, Mansour works on a Hebrew newspaper and hopes to get a job in the Israeli foreign service.

The Druzes are of Arab stock. Their religion was founded in the eleventh century in Egypt, when Cairo was ruled by the Fatimite dynasty. Originally it was an Islamic faith but it split off as a Protestant sect. The early Druzes had a secret underground. It is still a secret religion, but a great many of the mysteries have leaked out. One must be born a Druze; one cannot join later.

There are 17,000 Druzes in Israel and only a few hundred thousand in the world: 110,000 in Syria; 90,000 in the Lebanon; 10,000 in Jordan; and 50,000 in the United States. The word "Druze" is derived from Darazi, who founded the sect. But "Druze" actually means "bug" in Arabic. The center of the Druze religion is Al Bayadeh in the Lebanon where there is a religious seminary.

PARIS, *October 13, 1955*

LUNCH today with Jean-Marie Soutou, head of the eastern European division of the Quai d'Orsay and one of the closest collaborators of Mendès-France, also an extremely brilliant young man. He spent five and a quarter years in Belgrade and seems to know Communist ideology well. He explained to me that he was "equally opposed" to capitalism and communism. He talks with sneers about "fellow-travelers."

He said when Mendès-France had his famous conversation with de Gaulle, the General announced that North Africa was now lost for France. Mendès-France asked if he meant to include Algeria also. De Gaulle said yes. De Gaulle then added: "We are too many parties already in France, but soon there will be another party—the party of the refugees from North Africa."

Soutou thinks the principal result of the summit conference at Geneva last summer was that the Russians succeeded in stabilizing the European situation. Now they are able to move elsewhere more freely—into the Middle East. Moscow seeks to make a political trade with France. It hints support of the French point of view in North Africa if the French support the Russian point of view on Germany. The Russians are always primarily interested in Germany. They even tried indirectly to make a similar deal on Indochina. Several months ago they hinted to Paris that if the French were prepared to support the Russians in all-German free elections, the Russians would support the French on the question of Indochinese elections.

DE GAULLE: "THIS

REGIME MUST VANISH"

PARIS, October 14, 1955

THIS MORNING I WENT TO SEE GENERAL DE GAULLE AT HIS OFFICE on 5, rue de Solférino.* De Gaulle—and this is hardly surprising— was exceptionally pessimistic about the future. First, we talked a bit about his book. He is now working hard on the second volume, but said it would not be ready for publication until the spring.†

From this, we went into the political situation. He hoped it might be possible to save some connection with North Africa by working out a new structure for Tunisia and Morocco. This would, of course, have to be on a somewhat different basis from the British Commonwealth. French colonizing methods were different. The French mixed with the natives, unlike the British. All Tunisians speak French as their native language. (This is not true.) It would be possible to work out a connection on the basis of their common interests among France, Tunisia, and Morocco. And after all, they are right next door to each other. It is not the same thing as the distance between Johannesburg and London. But the situation is different with Algeria. Algeria was never a state.‡ De Gaulle likened Algeria to a heap of dust—*"une poussière."*

From North Africa, de Gaulle branched on to France itself. He said he had twice tried to save France. The first time was during the war. The second time was by organizing the RPF. Now he says: "I know of no third way."

However, he added, this did not mean that France would disappear. National vitality was still very great. But it was too dispersed. France had been terribly weakened by past events.

* See de Gaulle's further comments, p. 80.
† See de Gaulle's further comments, p. 83.
‡ See de Gaulle's further comments, p. 69.

The consequences of the present French crisis would eventually be seen in a great change in French psychology, especially vis-à-vis foreigners. The French would inevitably become very xenophobic because of their misfortunes. It was hard to see where this would lead in twenty years, but xenophobia was already mounting. As a result of this, a violent French nationalism would ultimately set in.*

"The United Nations already means nothing here," he said. "Nations will come and go, enter and depart from it. But it is finished. Soon the same situation will develop in NATO." This tendency was of course being encouraged by the Russians with their new smiling methods.†

I asked de Gaulle on what terms or in what condition he thought he could return. He said: "I would never come back, except with real power. That would require a dramatic situation.‡ De Gaulle then spread his hands and said he was desolate, desperate, but what could he do?§

France was still paying off past debts. Ever since the war of 1870, France had been greatly weakened. This was not observable at first. And during World War I, France gave the impression of having regained its vigor and power. But this was not true. The consequences were only now really appearing. North Africa was one consequence of this impotence. But, de Gaulle continued, in France nothing is ever definitive—not even impotence.

Looking toward the future, de Gaulle said that when France had completed paying these "debts to the past," present events would contribute to a new French nationalism. He was sure this would be a disagreeable form of nationalism for the world, including the United States, but it was inevitable.

In the past, France had always sought to participate in international cooperation. That phase was now over. During the period of *"redressement"* (rectification) there would be an increasing attitude of noncooperation. The first signs of this move and of the new nationalism were already visible. When *"un pauvre,"* like Pinay, dares to walk out of the United Nations, it is already a sign of what is coming, de Gaulle observed.

PARIS, *October 19, 1955*

LAST night Soutou came to dinner. He said that during the Geneva Conference Bulganin emphasized to the other three powers that what Russia was after was the reestablishment of Europe on a pre-1939 basis. What Bulganin meant was a Europe with the United States back on the other side of the Atlantic. Unfortunately, nobody protested. Someone should have jumped right in and said that the Europe of pre-1939 was dominated by Nazi Germany and Fascist Italy and lead to World War II.

* See de Gaulle's further comments, p. 59.
† See de Gaulle's further comments, p. 29.
‡ See de Gaulle's further comments, p. 29.
§ See de Gaulle's further comments, p. 29.

On October 17 (two days ago), Joxe, the French ambassador in the Soviet Union, saw Saburov, now one of the leading members of the government. Saburov said Russia was having trouble with its Muhammedan minority in Turkestan. He indicated that therefore Russia could understand France's position with its Muhammedans in North Africa and sympathized. The implied gambit was that if Paris would support Russia on Germany, Moscow would support France in North Africa.

At the summit, Bulganin said Russia did not like the idea of Western Germany rearming within NATO. But he hastened to add that Russia did not expect the West to permit Germany to quit NATO. It is clear the Russians really are quite happy to have West Germany in NATO because this insures the continuation of a divided Germany. The Russians are no longer afraid of Bonn's rearmament and prefer to have Germany split. If we were to suddenly say that we are prepared to let West Germany quit NATO in order to have a neutral, reunited Germany, the Russians would be in a difficult position.

It is essential for the western powers to get together and recognize Communist China now. No Tito rebellion against Moscow would have been possible without the presence of the western embassies in Belgrade at the time. We simply must be in Peking, both in order to observe and in order to help in case of an eventual split between China and Russia.

PARIS, *October 22, 1955*

LUNCH with David Bruce. He is still technically an "advisor" in the State Department. If the Democrats win the 1956 elections he would be very anxious to become the first U.S. ambassador to Communist China. Under present conditions it is impossible to recognize Peking. First the Chinese must make conciliatory gestures and behave themselves. However, recognition is ultimately inevitable.

David said Secretary Dulles had only two personal appointments as ambassadors when the Republicans came in in 1953. One was Dillon here in Paris and the other was Allison in Tokyo. (I must say they were both good choices.) He does not think much of Dulles as Secretary of State. He is too arrogant and too unwilling to listen to advice—in fact, he never asks for advice. His is a very personal policy and an awkward one.

We had a long discussion about Eisenhower, trying to analyze the reasons for his success. David agrees that he has really become a President of *all* the people—not just the Republicans. He is undoubtedly lazy, David says, but he has immense ability on the essential things.

PARIS, *October 25, 1955*

LAST night Henry Byroade, ambassador to Egypt, came over for three hours of drinks and talk. Pretty gloomy. He is convinced we are on the verge of war in the Middle East and, furthermore, thinks there is going to be a terrible wave of anti-Semitism in the United States because people will say we lost the Middle East because we catered to Jewish political opinion.

Since June 3, he knew about the Soviet arms deal with Egypt. He tried desperately to get U.S. arms for Nasser, but we just diddled. It was only a question of $15,000,000 worth, but, "because of Jewish opinion" back home, it never came through. Now the French are getting ready to sell quite a lot of arms to Egypt and so are the British. We have been left out on a limb.

Czechoslovakian weapons have started arriving. Eight boat-loads have already reached Egypt. The Egyptians wanted to fly Soviet IL-28 light bombers in from the Balkans, but Greece refused permission for refueling stops on the way. But MIGs have already been unloaded from ships. Fourteen Soviet bloc technicians have reached Cairo and forty are expected very quickly. Egyptian specialists have gone behind the Iron Curtain for training.

Hank thinks the only thing to do is lay down the law. We must tell Israel not only to take back some refugees but to give up Elath, on the Gulf of Aqaba, and part of the Negev. I told him I was positive this would be unacceptable to the Israelis. Byroade replied: "If they don't do it, there is bound to be war."

Byroade thinks we should squeeze off all aid to Israel—either American government aid or from American Jewry—until it accepts the proposals he makes, namely to abandon Elath, part of the Negev, and take in refugees. He said Nasser was prepared to make peace on these terms. This I doubt very seriously.

Today I saw René Coty, President of the French Republic, in the Elysée Palace. He said he had done a very audacious thing at Dunkirk October 15, when he made a speech stating that the French Constitution needs reforming. After all, he was the guardian of the Constitution; yet he was demanding that it be changed. The last President who had ever ventured to do a similar thing was Millerand, in 1924, and he had to resign as a result.

Nevertheless, it was absolutely essential that there should be a change. He does not favor the Gaullist type of Constitution with more powers for the President. What he wants is a stronger Prime Minister with the ability to dissolve the Assembly and call elections when necessary, so that the government will no longer be subject to the Deputies' whims. The Presidency of the Republic has adequate powers now to operate behind the scene. He compares his position to that of a constitutional monarch in England or one of the Scandinavian countries. France could never accept the American form of government where the President has strong executive powers. This is what de Gaulle wants.

Coty explained the French would never accept this because they fear a strong executive. To the Frenchman, the state is the enemy. The French remember Napoleon III and how he established a dictatorship. They also remember Marshal MacMahon who in 1877, almost established a dictatorship. They want no more of this.

Therefore, France must find its own solution. Unfortunately, France is a very old country and traditions tend to confuse the situation here. For example, in the west around Brittany there is a distinct old-fashioned right-wing feeling which has never accepted the results of the revolution of 1789. On the other hand, among the supporters of communism—not the Communists themselves, but those who vote with them—one finds people who continue the tradition of the revolution. In other words, France still contains the basic currents of the absolute monarchy that preceded the revolution and of the revolutionary violence of the late eighteenth century.

France still is scarred by the religious issue and the religious wars. And furthermore, France is divided in many other ways. In the south (the Midi) there is one type of person; in the north there is an entirely different type. Likewise, France is divided between workers and peasants, industry and farms. All these separate trends and traditions have to be taken account of in the French governmental system. Therefore France requires a certain flexibility. Since the days of Julius Caesar, the French have always demonstrated instability. Caesar referred to the unstable Gauls. No man remains popular for four years in France and that is another argument against having a presidential system like America's.

This evening saw Dulles. The poor fellow looks haggard. He has a scab on his lip and has aged years in the last few months. His whole performance, I am afraid, was rather a Byzantine dance of death. He talked about things which simply aren't going to happen and he pretended to be optimistic on issues about which it is impossible to be hopeful—above all, Germany.

He spoke of the vitality of NATO and the North Atlantic Council; that useful new ideas had emerged. (Afterward, I had dinner with Exintaris, permanent Greek ambassador at NATO who had attended the Allied Ministers' Council. He described it as an appalling, boring display; no new idea was put forth and the whole thing was completely unrealistic.)

Dulles said the Geneva conference would start Thursday. West Germany would be represented although it probably would not participate. In bringing up the subject of Germany, it might be possible, instead of a general European security treaty, to have a limited guarantee for Russia against the potential threat of a united Germany if it joins NATO. There are certain inducements that might be given to Russia to permit the unification of Germany under free elections. There are additional inducements if Russia agrees that a united Germany should join NATO and Western European Union. (This is, of course, utter nonsense and I cannot understand why Dulles should bother to say such things.)

Dulles "doubts" if the Geneva conference of foreign ministers can consummate the full details of the unification of Germany under the Eden plan and at the same time give any appropriate security guarantee. This would require much detailed work. But if agreement in principle can be reached, experts could be appointed to work out the details. These would include military experts to handle the security aspects. Listening to Dulles talk like this is terrifying; there isn't any chance whatsoever of the Big Four foreign ministers agreeing at Geneva on any broad basis for Germany's unification.

The Middle East is not on the agenda, but "perhaps" it will be brought up, he said. (It will damn well be brought up and it will be brought up by Dulles himself, even if he does not like to do so.) I would be more pleased if Dulles were merely a liar and did not believe what he says than if he really believes it.

GENEVA, *October 30, 1955*

LUNCHED today with Chip Bohlen. He finds it interesting at this foreign ministers' conference to see Molotov seeking to adapt himself to the "Geneva spirit." In the past, Molotov always had recourse to recrimination and invective to obscure his recalcitrance. Now he must adopt the polite formulas of diplomacy.

Chip said that when Adenauer went to Moscow the Russians complained to him that West German territory was being used for propaganda purposes by the United States government. They showed him a propaganda balloon sent off by the Crusade for Free Europe. Adenauer professed to be shocked by the pamphlet material attached. When Blankenhorn informed the three western ambassadors, Chip said this was not a matter that could be raised with the U.S. government since Free Europe was a private, not a governmental activity.

Chip thinks Dulles is going to see Tito largely to throw a scare into the Russians. It is my opinion that the Russians aren't interested in any security plan at Geneva. They said at the summit conference that only small powers need security guarantees; the great powers can fend for themselves. Furthermore, the Russians have denounced enough of their own pacts—and had Hitler denounce others—to take a dim view of such agreements.

This afternoon I spent an hour and a half with my old friend Abdul Rahman Azzam, former head of the Arab league. Azzam came here two months ago as special representative of King Saud in the dispute before a Geneva court over the Buraimi oasis. Arabian American Oil Company (Aramco) and Saudi Arabia claim it, but the British took it over by force on behalf of a Trucial Oman sheikh. There is probably a lot of oil underneath the oasis.

Azzam said in 1939, just before the war started, he suggested to Weizmann in the Cairo British embassy that Zionism should establish a

"Vatican" for world Jewry on an allotted piece of territory in Palestine. Weizmann turned this down. Azzam says there is no room in Israel for all the world's Jews. Already they have conquered an occupied land instead of moving into an empty territory.

He kept referring to the crusades, saying it took decades and eleven crusades before the Arabs expelled the Christians. Now the emotions of the crusades have been revived. A generation must pass before they are calmed down and true negotiations can be held, fitting Israel into the Middle East. But clearly he wants to shrink Israel. Azzam urges that Russia be kept out of the diplomatic bargaining; that the arms deal with Egypt be regarded as a passing thing; that the Big Three reaffirm their 1950 guarantee and put teeth in it; but that Israel be made aware that it cannot enter into a full arms race nor hope for military equality with the Arabs.

Russia, he says, has no real stake in the Middle East. Moscow has no control over the North African rebels. It has only unloaded a few arms to Egypt. That is nothing compared with the reality of western interests. We shouldn't let the Russians in as guarantors. It would destroy our own prestige and build up Moscow's. Azzam says we should stick to this even if the Russians unload more arms to other Arab states.

Dulles said this evening: "I hammered Molotov pretty hard yesterday. He finally said he had some other proposals to make. These would be more in harmony with the summit directive. We suggested he should not hold things back; that we had already put our cards on the table."

Since Tuesday (All Saints Day) is a holiday here, Dulles said: "I thought I'd put it to use by going to Madrid where I have had a long-standing invitation from General Franco. I shall leave in the morning, have lunch there, and return in the evening."

When will he realize that perpetual motion is no substitute for diplomacy? He is obviously going to Madrid to offset his visit next week to Tito; to fix himself up with Congress. Yet, by pairing off Tito and Franco again, he merely infuriates both.

Dulles said he had a couple of talks on the Middle East today—an hour with Molotov, then an hour and a half with Sharett. The mere fact of these discussions "emphasizes the importance we attach to the Near Eastern situation. But it is not our policy to engage in an arms race in the area. We would consider the Israeli request sympathetically, but not with the idea that arms are necessary merely to meet the Egyptian arms."

Dulles's legal mind is fascinated by Molotov's delaying tactics on the agenda—while missing the creeping explosion in the Middle East.

GENEVA, *October 31, 1955*

INTERESTING lunch with Eliahu Elath, Israeli ambassador to London. He said that two weeks ago a high Polish official had told the Israeli envoy

Israel should not continue to risk isolating herself by playing with the West, since Nasser had already told the Russians he intends to denounce the Suez Canal agreement which would permit Britain's return under conditions of war; therefore, Israel would have nothing but hostile neighbors while her friends were distant and powerless.

There are some Englishmen, Elath admits, who would like to oust Nasser and replace him with a group headed by Naguib. But the time when this was feasible ended when the Suez base was evacuated. And Eden is committed to Nasser just the way he is committed in Cyprus. He passed the Suez deal, under pressure from Washington, over strong opposition in his own party. If Nasser falls, Eden may fall too. After all, Eden as foreign secretary, advised the Israeli ambassador in a letter October 7, 1954, on the Suez deal: "The Anglo-Egyptian agreement will result in a general lessening of tension in the Middle East. By increasing confidence between the Arab States and the West, it should facilitate a solution to major problems in that area."

Macmillan, a weak man, has inherited Eden's policy even though his own son-in-law, Julian Amery, was one of the leaders of the Tory revolt against the Suez agreement. Eden is tied to Nasser the way Dulles, thinking of the Jewish vote in 1956, is tied to Israel. (But Dulles is also tied to Saudi Arabia for Aramco, and Eden, on Buraimi, is against Saud.)

The Geneva "spirit" helps the Russians in the Middle East. No one wants world war; therefore they can gamble as they dared not in Azerbaijan during the "containment" days. Russia probably wants to arrange a deal similar to the Indochina precedent: let the situation first rot; let the West lose prestige and morale; then suggest a Big Four settlement conference. In thinking of the current crisis one should never forget the Middle Eastern aspirations disclosed by Molotov to Ribbentrop. An eye on the Turkish straits has always dominated Russian policy.

Israel told Britain it doesn't intend to be a new Czechoslovakia to be carved up as at Munich in 1938. The Israeli press is now full of the word "Munich." Israel pointed out to the British that in 1938 and 1939, Czechoslovakia could lose its independence and survive; but Israel would be totally annihilated in a similar case. Therefore, Israel warns, it is prepared to fight like devils because its very physical existence is at stake. (Elath told me Israel was prepared if necessary to use chemical and biological weapons.)

U.S. policy sought for a while to keep Egypt out of the Middle East by urging her into Africa. Britain, mindful of Libya and the Sudan, pushed in the reverse direction.

GENEVA, *November 12, 1955*

THIS evening I had a long talk, more interesting than usual, with Dulles in his suite at the Hotel du Rhône. He seemed cheerful and energetic and walked restlessly up and down as he talked, occasionally stopping for a

handful of nuts from the table on which drinks were laid out. Only at the
end did he settle into a chair and relax.

First, I asked Dulles whether he thought Molotov's unexpectedly stubborn attitude at this foreign ministers' conference might reflect some change
in the Soviet internal political situation. He replied:

> That is possible. The "Geneva spirit" has certainly been in some ways
> inconvenient for the free world by melting the glue that has been holding
> us together. But perhaps there are even more serious consequences
> within the Soviet orbit. It encouraged there a desire for more independ-
> ence and more tolerance. And the whole Tito affair put ideas in the
> heads of the people in the satellites which are still being ruled by Stalinist
> governments.
>
> The opportunity seized by the Soviets to move into the Middle East
> strained the Geneva spirit. If you add all this together it is possible that
> the people in the Soviet Union indoctrinated in the old Stalinist line may
> have swung the balance. Tito pointed out to me that there are many
> people emerging at the top in Russia now who were brought up on
> Stalinism and still believe in it. The outcome is not clear. I have the
> feeling that while I always believed they would do nothing at the moment
> to jeopardize the German Democratic Republic, the way they have han-
> dled themselves here indicates a desire for more tension.
>
> Molotov could have spared himself the charge of repudiating free
> elections. But he didn't seem to want to. Perhaps the Russians think they
> need more tension now. I suspect they have been even more unhappy
> under the Geneva spirit than we have been.

I then asked how he thought we could keep West Germany "solid" now,
with Adenauer's health failing and the Socialists talking about sitting down
on some matters with the East Germans. He replied:

> The future of West Germany, as I see it, is to revive the European idea
> and give the West Germans a sense of being more fully part of Europe, a
> sense of mission and an outlet for their energies that could be developed
> in a United States of Europe.
>
> On the last day of the summit conference here I scribbled a note in
> pencil and sent it on to Adenauer, saying that it was apparent to me that
> the big problem of unification was not security, but it was simply that the
> Russians couldn't pull the rug out from under the German Democratic
> Republic.

I asked how long he thought we could go on with a divided Germany
splitting Europe; could the entire western coalition adjust themselves to the
idea and keep the West Germans from making their own deals. After all,
Adenauer is aging fast. Dulles replied:

> We are going to have to live with it for quite a while. We don't see a
> chance of a united Germany until the entire Soviet relationship with its
> satellite empire changes. . . . Eventually this will change—in a year, or

ten years, or more. Either a different type of government will evolve in the satellites, or the people in those countries will become so indoctrinated that they willingly accept their regimes. When either of these situations develops the German Democratic Republic won't be as symbolic of the satellite position as is now the case. Only then will Russia be able to afford to unite Germany.

I asked Dulles if we had been able to make any headway with the British on Cyprus. He said:

The British have been incredibly stupid on Cyprus. On the whole they have been smart in seeing the need for change and meeting it halfway in other areas. But in Cyprus they have been bad. And if they had only offered a year ago what they are prepared to offer now, they might have gotten away with it. Not now.

I then asked how on earth he hoped to settle the Middle Eastern crisis while keeping Russia out. He said:

We probably have enough pressures—economic and financial—to prevent either side from deliberately engaging in a major war. The great danger comes from these constant episodes and reprisals where you can't really fix the blame. If you could get both sides to pull their troops back and get a demilitarized strip like Korea it would be useful. This is being considered. It would be impractical to send U.S. troops there, as Stevenson suggested. The Joint Chiefs of Staff are violently opposed.

Dulles then admitted there were Anglo-American differences in the area. He said:

The British were pretty rough with the Buraimi thing. When I was in the Middle East in 1953, I remember talking with old Ibn Saud, who was still alive then. He produced a letter Truman had sent him at the time our oil concessions and bases were granted, in which Truman said we would stand up with Ibn Saud against aggression. Of course Truman was thinking about Soviet aggression. But Ibn Saud talked about the British in Buraimi. He said: "Here it is. Help us throw them out."

I often think that the United States is the only country in the world able to work in a disinterested way in these situations. We are not trying to aggrandize or serve the national interests of the United States. We are only trying to do the right thing. I am not boasting that we are more moral than anybody else. But we have all the riches and territory we need and we are not ambitious. The British and the rest are always trying to get something for themselves and want us to take care of the consequences. The British feel they can grab a few acres of sand where they suspect there may be oil and are willing to jeopardize our oil and our bases and to let us sweat it out. Of course, the British are in a desperate economic plight and they are always seeking foreign exchange.

I asked Dulles if it were not important for us to counteract the Iron Curtain trade offensive in India. He replied:

Our disadvantage is that what we do there has to be on a commercial basis. The Russians can undercut our private businesses. Of course it might be possible to act on a governmental basis and get away from this problem.

But I'm not too worried about it. The Russians are simply not in shape to carry on a major foreign-aid program. The burden of helping China lies heavy. Moscow is in no position to do anything more than make one-shot political efforts in the economic aid field—no major programs. During the next twenty years Russia must use up most of its economic efforts at home.

Ironically, the greatest danger would come if the arms burden were removed. The Soviet Union is trying to catch up with us in the most expensive form of arms—on the basis of an economy that is a third of ours. And they are also going in for heavy capital developments. This leaves very little left over.

I then asked Dulles if the State Department, when it thought about "liberating" enslaved peoples, had ever given any thought to the "liberation" of the Central Asian Muslims of the U.S.S.R. He said:

We don't know enough about that area to have a program. There are simply not enough trained people to help us make a policy there. You might do better to talk with Allen [Dulles, head of CIA] about this. The whole personnel of our country—not just in the State Department—is lacking in knowledge about certain parts of the world. Take Africa for example. The Foreign Service has not been built to produce people of that sort. We are trying to broaden it out under the Wriston plan for lateral entry and thus bring in new elements.

GENEVA, *November 13, 1955*

LAST night at dinner, Chip Bohlen observed that Molotov had been deliberately brutal in refusing even to consider free elections in Germany this time (unlike Berlin) because he wanted to impress the Germans with the illogical, heedless, sheer power of Russia. The Russians know the Germans as well as anyone. This might drive the West Germans to seek a solution directly with Moscow. At the same time, it bolsters the confidence of the German Democratic Republic regime and ends any hopes of change in the popular opposition in East Germany.

Chip said the Soviet army, as such, didn't have any real political influence in Russia. But Marshal Zhukov as an individual had undoubtedly played a role in forging "committee-rule" decisions. Zhukov was surely the man who had explained to the government that the atom bomb was not a "class-conscious" weapon, and could destroy communism as easily as capitalism. Previously, Soviet propaganda had boasted that war would only smash capitalism, leaving the Communist bloc unharmed.

PARIS, *November 17, 1955*

THIS morning I had a long talk with Jean Monnet on the chances of European Federation. He says:

The U.S. government should say nothing now. European action must be taken by Europeans themselves. Many think EDC was defeated because it was looked upon as an end in itself—not as a European problem, but as a world diplomatic problem. Europe must be made by itself, not as an instrument in a fight. This should not be represented as an answer to East-West quarrels.

There is no way of solving the problems of Europe if the countries affected do not unite. Economic, atomic, and other problems can only be solved in that way. The individual countries are too small and too poor. We believe the Russians won't make war. But the weakness of the West is its division. This is the weakness of Germany, of France, and of other countries. We cannot raise the standard of living in these countries as it has been done in the United States without uniting. A United States of Europe is the answer.

The idea of the European movement started in 1950, with the Schuman plan. Although EDC was defeated, European federation is not dead. There can be no solution unless the countries of Europe unite and establish some sort of federation.

We make the error of keeping our eyes always fixed upon the Russians. We won't be able to rebuild Europe except for its own sake. This should not be done through fear of Russia. A federation of Europe is necessary for peace and for Europe's own improvement. But it is not a trick to be fitted into a particular diplomatic situation.

It is not easy to change the policies of countries in order to fit them into a federation. This takes time. After all, the United States of America itself was not made in a day. Everything must be done step by step. The Coal and Steel Authority was successful. It works. Its authority is accepted. The next step tried was EDC, but this failed. Nevertheless, this does not kill the idea. The necessity of rebuilding Europe remains.

What we need is a common market and an atomic community on a European basis. We must move gradually and convince people that there *is* a policy to merge into one community and that this policy continues regardless of diplomatic developments.

The whole performance must be looked upon as an action to develop a common market and federation. We will at the same time be helping peace and coexistence by strengthening Europe. So long as Europe is divided, the big forces of the world will want to control one part or the other. Europe cannot improve beyond a certain point without this unity. Our standard of living is only a third of America's. You are improving at a speed we cannot match.

It is necessary to go beyond national sovereignty in order to secure the cooperation of others. The Swiss have done this for a long time. Each canton remains sovereign, but delegates certain powers for general solution by joining together in a federation. The last war proved that Europe destroys itself when national states seek domination.

PARIS, *November 21, 1955*

CHIP Bohlen has been staying with us for the last few days. He says there has been a persistent tendency in British policy to think of Russia in traditional nineteenth-century terms rather than in terms of the Communist revolution. Thus their policy is often based upon false suppositions. However, the British are very much afraid of trying to make any bilateral deal with Moscow. They realized once and for all at Geneva that the Russians are only interested in the United States. We could always trump Britain's ace if Britain started to deal bilaterally.

One of our mistakes in World War II foreign policy was the failure to realize that after the war England would be weak and France would be a small power. We tended always to think that there would be three great powers in the world—Russia, the United States, and England. But actually there are only two. We should have seen in advance that England had denuded itself of its energy and treasure in order to win the war.

The Geneva foreign ministers' conference was really exactly what the "summit" meeting in July foresaw. We did not expect the Russians to agree with us on German reunification under any terms. Nor did we expect the Russians to "buy" our security plan. The Russians are just as relentless in their pursuit of the new policy of affability as they were relentless in hostility during the Cold War. The results of the Geneva conference will not change the Russians' tactics.

Chip took notes at the Yalta Conference and many of these notes were incorporated in the Yalta papers which we published this year. One of the things crossed out was a joking remark by Roosevelt. Roosevelt was not anti-Semitic. Nevertheless, when he was talking to Stalin once about Zionism and his desire to support the movement to create a Jewish state in Palestine, Stalin asked him why. Roosevelt observed: "Well, then we can get rid of many of our troublesome Jews." Even Stalin realized that Roosevelt was joking. Fortunately this remark was not published.

At the recent Geneva foreign ministers' meeting, during one of the official dinner parties, Chip was talking to Marshal Sokolovsky. He asked Sokolovsky why Russia was so opposed to our plan for the unification of Germany and then a security arrangement afterward, which would neutralize a zone between Germany and eastern Europe. Sokolovsky replied: "Who are you kidding? You want us to give up East Germany and then neutralize part of Poland. You want us to pull back three hundred miles while you don't pull back at all."

Adenauer took a terrible beating when he went to Russia. He announced in advance that he would not agree to diplomatic relations with Moscow except on certain specific conditions. None of these were fulfilled. Nevertheless, the pressure was such that Adenauer finally agreed to establish diplomatic relations in exchange for the return of German prisoners of war. Yet the Russians only agreed to send back about ten thousand—and would not even put that in writing. Now they are holding back half of this number until the Germans accept Zorin as the first Soviet envoy in Bonn. The only thing the Russians wanted from Adenauer was diplomatic relations with Bonn. They got that and they gave up nothing.

PARIS, *November 23, 1955*

LAST night we went to a dinner party at the Norstads. Larry says Nasser has been extremely clever about his handling of the Russian arms deals. He asked the United States to supply B-26 bomber planes. This was turned down. Then he turned to the Russians and got his arms deal through. He now is actually flying some IL-28 twin-jet light bombers and is rapidly assembling MIG fighters. Nasser was asked why on earth he had requested B-26s from us when he knew they were outmoded. Nasser replied that he knew they were not classified, there were plenty of them, and they were of no use to the United States. Therefore, he reasoned, if he were not going to get these he wouldn't get anything out of us. In such a case he would turn to Russia.

GUM FOR THE PEOPLE,

BOOM FOR BERIA

Moscow, *November 28, 1955*

W E HAVE BEEN HERE SINCE SATURDAY EVENING, STAYING AT the Bohlens. The city has changed considerably: vast new skyscrapers of overornate architecture; batches of neon lights on the main streets; a traffic problem—minor compared to Paris or New York but nevertheless Moscow's first. The standard of living has risen.

The system works, in its own haphazard way. People now accept it and do not dream of an alternative. The people are stirring and coming to life after Stalin. There is a Coolidge "back to normalcy" trend. The attitude of the police has changed; there are no more midnight knocks; the people are often not afraid to tell the police to go jump in the river; they insist upon legality and their rights.

There is a curious fast set of youngsters who study up on American jazz in the Lenin library, bootleg records, wear suits replete with zippers wherever possible, and speak to each other in phrases of Latin or English. This gang is called the *stilyagi*—"stylists" or "style-hunters." There is, among young Russians, a tremendous enthusiasm for jazz. Recently a concert of Gershwin music was given. There is an immense vogue for the translated writings of Dreiser.

(British Ambassador Sir William) Hayter has a young secretary who, after picking up a Russian girl, has been introduced into Moscow's youthful high society. They are continually intermarrying and divorcing among themselves. One of them, son of a rather bad musician named Dunachaievsky, inherited two apartments, three dachas, four automobiles including a German Horch, and a huge bank account. The smart thing among these youngsters is to go abroad; they try and get jobs in even the lowest capacity on state visits, or do things such as driving foreign cars.

Chip thinks gradually the party administration will ease up on Communist parties abroad and relax the monolithic control system; also that for a long time to come they won't worry about ideology in such countries as India and Egypt; just try and line them up on their side.

Yesterday we went to the Jugoslav embassy for a reception on their national holiday. All the brass in Moscow was there: Molotov, Mikoyan, Saburov, Suslov, a new party secretary named Aristov, Marshals Budenny, Sokolovsky, and Zorin. Budenny, who looked fine, is on the water-wagon (the first time I ever saw that). I chatted with Marshal Sokolovsky, who recalled our meeting at Vyazma in 1941, just as the battle for Moscow was beginning, and drank a polite toast. Sokolovsky, a grave man with no small talk, is quite impressive. The big shots (Molotov, Mikoyan, and Jugoslav Ambassador Vidić) all made flattering speeches about the U.S.S.R. and Jugoslavia. The Chinese Communist ambassador muscled into the act with smiles and handshakes.

The Burmese ambassador explained to Chip Bohlen that the West must be patient; the Russians were like lizards in Burma who had to be cajoled and coaxed out of their holes because they were so shy. "What do you do with them when you get them out of their holes?" he was asked. "Kill them," muttered the embarrassed Burmese.

Moscow, *November 29, 1955*

CHIP says a new GUM (pronounced "goom") general store was opened the day they announced Beria had been shot. One of his staff wanted to send a cable to the Department saying: "GUM for the people, boom for Beria."

During Yalta, Chip sat next to Beria at one dinner. They discussed postwar governments and problems. Beria insisted: "The people are nothing but sheep; they must be told what to do."

Jean Laloy, the French chargé d'affaires, came for lunch today. Laloy and Chip agreed it was impossible to figure just where Russia was heading, internally, and whether an autocracy could work without an autocrat; the Russians themselves don't know. Malenkov, they agree, is brilliant and by no means at the end of his career. In a sense he represents the Russian national versus world revolution idea—more goods for the people even if it means less industrialization. There is obviously a possible conflict between the "conservative" theorists of Stalinism and the new practical managerial class of Malenkov. Khrushchev is more of the former.

Marshal Zhukov told Laloy recently: "We will never give up any areas we have conquered"—meaning in Europe and including East Germany. It seems clear they are content to leave the status quo in Europe, trying such deals as they can and have done in Jugoslavia and Austria, hoping to win West Germany in time; but in Asia they are moving fast. The entire Middle

East diplomatic corps (save Israel) is starry-eyed in favor of Moscow now. Soviet Jews are worried sick about their future.

One of the dangers to the U.S.S.R. is the desire for a Bandung "spirit" among the non-Slav minorities. It may yet be embarrassing. It is obvious there is discontent in the Caucasus. More of Beria's henchmen in Georgia were shot and a group of demonstrators and rioters at an Armenian football game were given long prison sentences.

There is a conflict among those who desire to raise living standards, those who wish to give major aid abroad, those who want to continue the heavy industrialization program. The army, which has little political influence, remains a heavy financial burden.

MOSCOW, *November 30, 1955*

LAST night we dined at the British embassy. John Morgan, the young secretary with connections in the youthful smart set, was there. He said his group has great esteem for Molotov. They seem to have a split view on Stalin. They realize things are much better now, but they still regard Stalin's period as a "golden age."

The group dresses well, preferring foreign clothes. These are brought back by friends from official overseas trips, or, more often, each has a commission shop where clothes, jewelry, and other articles are pawned. The shop boss will send a discreet message when he thinks something of interest to the client shows up. Then they meet at a selected rendezvous and the deal is consummated. The shop boss will make a profit of about 300 percent. Vishinsky's daughter, who adores foreign clothes, paid 3,000 rubles just to be introduced to a dressmaker capable of cutting modern-style dresses.

The group lives well. One has an apartment which, although small, has magnificent silverware ("The finest I've ever seen; heavy solid silver; better than in a duke's house.") and china, including Sèvres porcelain. The group seems to have so much money they can't spend it all. They keep it in savings deposits at a 3 percent interest rate. There is considerable snobbism and most are children of important officials or artists. The only apparent exception is the son of a country doctor. The group has no connection with the *stilyagi*, who are far below them in class. There are only one or two restaurants and nightclubs they consider chic. They drink (but not too heavily), have a roaring sex life, don't play cards, and never talk politics.

Chip and Hayter agreed that Malenkov is by far the most able and intelligent of the Presidium, a real intellectual force. Hayter says he not only uses some Latin phrases but has a considerable knowledge of Turkish. Chip says there is a rumor he is half-Tatar, half-German, that Malenkov is not a real Russian name, and that he was born Klein. (I have often heard he was half Bashkir.)

At lunch today (at Walmsley's) a French correspondent said that at a diplomatic reception he heard Khrushchev apologize for almost snubbing the Indian ambassador's wife: "Forgive me. I almost didn't see you. There are so many blacks around here." She replied: "When you come to my country you'll find we are the same color as you."

MOSCOW, *December 1, 1955*

CHIP says one hears from India that both Nehru and the intelligentsia are deeply offended by the Khrushchev performance there; that he is laying it on crudely and seemingly trying to make it appear almost as if India is a member of the Soviet bloc. The mayor of Madras, who reminded Khrushchev in a speech that industrialization is not the answer to all of man's dreams, let it be known he said this just after talking with Nehru by telephone. When his guests left, he said to friends: "I am glad to see their backs."

Khrushchev, Chip observes, behaves like a politician campaigning for votes where votes don't count. He is quite a baby kisser.

MOSCOW, *December 3, 1955*

TODAY at lunch I sat next to Madame Bozykin, wife of the acting chief of the American section of the foreign office here, and an opera singer. She said her seventeen-year-old son adores jazz—above all American records. Tickets for the forthcoming *Porgy and Bess* will be very hard to get (Hayter says speculators are selling *Hamlet* tickets for 500 rubles—$125). Many people go to such foreign performances because it is the chic thing to do.

This afternoon we visited the tomb of Lenin and Stalin in the Red Square. Stalin looks as if he were asleep; the brutality of his face shows. Lenin also looks pretty tough. But his "condition" appears to be deteriorating. The back of his head seems to be missing and something has started to drip out of one of his eyes. Long silent queues wait in the cold to pay their respects. They march at a special slow pace, led by officers in fur hats and boots. Silent soldiers with bayonetted automatic rifles do sentry duty both outside the tomb and in the funeral chamber. Crows fly overhead in the dusk.

MOSCOW, *December 6, 1955*

THIS morning I had a most affable taxi driver with whom I chatted in my pidgin. He explained he came from Kaluga but had settled here after that city was destroyed by the Germans. He admires American cars immensely —much better than Russian cars. But he said "our" airplanes are good.

He said now at last "we" and the Americans are friends. "Khrushchev and Bulganin are good men and they're Russian. Stalin and Beria were awful. They were Georgians and you know they're Muhammedans. Stalin was just a Muhammedan dictator—another Romanov. But now life is better."

Yesterday we went out to the embassy dacha in the country. It was the coldest day of 1955—twenty-five below zero (Centigrade). But sunny and beautiful, even if your nose and ears fell off. Hayter and Bohlen agreed there that the system of simultaneously delivering Three Power notes was ludicrous. It would be far better to deal separately with Bulganin and Company and then fill each other in, first carefully specifying Allied areas of interest that would be allotted to each ambassador for negotiation.

I had a talk with General Avidar, the Israeli ambassador, who has been seconded by the Israeli army to serve temporarily as envoy. He was born in Russia and speaks Russian fluently. He is an exceptionally pleasant, serious man with a missing right arm. His last military job was acting chief of staff.

Avidar says Russia is using the "Geneva spirit" to weaken western defenses and preparations by influencing both government and public opinion. Russia is trying to ease the arms race in order to devote more means to internal development and also to economic aid abroad—with obvious political ends. Priority goes first to China and countries already in the Communist bloc. China remains a big drain.

Russia, he feels, is working hard in the Middle East—above all in Egypt. Shepilov was in Cairo last summer—and he's important. But officials remain unchanged in their polite attitude to Avidar.

Everything is different here—even anti-Semitism. The government is not interested in official anti-Semitism. Nevertheless, Jews don't "feel" as free as other citizens. They speak less freely than others. They are not treated as a "nationality." They have no right to use their language or to have schools, schoolbooks, newspapers, or other organizations. There are no Hebrew books printed; no Bible. The rabbis still use the prerevolutionary prayer books, including prayers to the Czar. There are no Hebrew type fonts in the country. A new prayer book is soon to be printed, but an electrolytic process will merely reproduce from the old book—omitting the pages with prayers to the Romanovs.

There is a law in this country against religious propaganda. It is applied to stop the teaching of Hebrew for prayers. Many Jews feel more safe not speaking Yiddish. There is more Yiddish in the Ukraine and White Russia; but generally among the old people. Many of them prefer to speak bad Russian to each other in the streets. There is still anti-Semitism among the people—mostly in the Ukraine and White Russia, which had been occupied by the Nazis. There are between 2,500,000 and 3,000,000 Jews here. There were more before Hitler's exterminations, despite the later influx from Poland and other newly acquired areas. Stalin's 1930 principles of nationality did not acknowledge the Jews as a nation. A small emigration is permitted to Israel for parents whose children ask for them.

Soviet joke:
After Stalin's death they don't know where to bury him. They want his corpse honored but don't want it in the Red Square. They offer it abroad. Nobody wants it. Finally the Israeli government agrees to take it and offers a wonderful burial in Jerusalem. Just as the arrangements are about to be concluded, Malenkov says: "No. We can't do that. I remember there was a fellow buried there two thousand years ago. And three days later he came back."

Yesterday morning before going to the country I saw Vidić, the Jugoslav ambassador, a bright young (mid-thirties) ex-partisan who had just graduated from Belgrade University in philosophy when he took to the woods. He said that the last plenary session showed that the state's leaders have convinced themselves that if they supported and practiced the Malenkov line they would soon find themselves further behind the West than they now are. This brought about Malenkov's downfall. In an atomic, industrialized age it is necessary to push heavy industrial development. They can't lag in the race. And under the Malenkov line they would have lagged. They would have lost the race in "competitive coexistence."

The Russians now realize that the U.S. has extended its influence in the world by its immense economic aid abroad. They would hail the day when they can spread their influence in the same way. It is no accident that Bulganin and Khrushchev are stressing the aid they can give abroad. It was no joke when Khrushchev said in India: "We shall see who has more engineers, the United States or Russia."

Moscow realizes that if war is excluded, we are entering an era in which only by economic strength and a sound economy can socialism win. The Russians have concluded nuclear war is out; that nuclear energy is classless; that every nation is compelled to alter its social structure for the peaceful atom; that nuclear weapons would affect everyone in the same horrible way.

I asked Vidić whether, if his theories of separate Socialist development now being recognized were correct, it was not possible that, revising the Marxist axiom, socialism might contain within itself the inherent contradictions that would destroy it. Lenin said this of capitalism. Vidić said it was a good question; he didn't know the answer.

Later, I spent an hour and a half with Konstantin Gubin, editor-in-chief of the government organ, *Izvestia*, in his office. He is fifty-seven (had "made the mistake of being born too soon"), a big, bald man with blond thatches, blue eyes, glasses, and a strong face. He was once a teacher and has edited *Izvestia* for eight years.

The press here has always been considered as a means of popularizing ideas among the masses. At the start of the Soviet system Lenin said that without comprehension of theory there could not be a Communist movement. And this could not be spread without propagandizing it. The press's function is to propagandize the philosophical ideas of the country. Ideas gain material force when they are spread among the masses. Gubin:

> My idea is that the press must always play a public and philosophical role. Our press doesn't spread naked ideas of Marxism; that would be Talmudistic. We would bore everyone. Lenin said one of the functions of the press should be to show the example of experience. He always said the press should talk less and show the workers and peasants more by example how to build a new life.

He went on to note that there were only 859 Russian papers before the revolution; now there are more than 8,000. Not only the big towns, but also all the district centers and special enterprises have their own newspapers. *Pravda* and *Izvestia* each fly their mats to twelve cities where they are exactly reprinted. *Pravda* is the organ of the Central Committee of the Communist party. *Izvestia* is the organ of the government. All other papers represent both party and government organizations. *Pravda* was started in St. Petersburg on May 5, 1912; *Izvestia* in Petrograd, March 13, 1917. It was first the organ of the Petrograd Soviet of workers and peasants.

Gubin says there is no rivalry between *Pravda* and *Izvestia*—"but competition." One or the other might try to get an important interview. They each try to get the best writers. *Izvestia* was ahead of *Pravda* in popularizing the use of atomic energy for peace. He and a collegium of his main department chiefs—twelve in number—decide on what's to be printed and how displayed. I asked if he ever called Bulganin or Molotov to get the government line on a point. He said if he called Molotov, the latter would say: "Go to hell. You're the editor. You should know what to write."

There is a wave of advertising, fathered by Mikoyan who was much impressed by advertisements in the U.S. Now there are neon signs saying: "Taxis are the most convenient form of transportation." Or "Drink tomato juice." Or "Drink refreshing lemonade." Or "Insure your home."

MOSCOW, *December 12, 1955*

LOUIS Joxe, French ambassador, came for dinner last night. He is leaving to become ambassador in Bonn. A nice man, intelligent and, unusual for a Frenchman, modest.

Joxe said that when Leopold Bravo, recent Argentine ambassador, saw Stalin shortly before the latter's death, he expressed polite pleasure at the honor of being received. Like some old Mongol Khan, Stalin replied: "In this country even the shepherds are well treated."

Joxe also said that Stalin, on being informed Königsberg was now called Kaliningrad (after the old president of the U.S.S.R.), expressed astonishment at the incongruity: "Kalinin—and a king!"

I spent an hour and a quarter this evening with Mikhail Alexeivitch Yasnov, chairman of the Moscow City Soviet (equivalent of mayor) since 1950. He is forty-nine, born in Moscow, by profession a builder. He was educated to be an engineer. Yasnov has been a member of the Communist party Central Committee since 1952.

Yasnov is big, tough-looking, extremely well dressed. His appearance is that of an Irish-American successful businessman or politician who fought his way up from the ranks and was once a construction gang boss.

In the anteroom of his office, completely carpeted and warm, was a large painting of Stalin and Voroshilov in uniform together on the Kremlin wall and a television set. There is another portrait of Stalin in his office; and another television set. We sat at a small table and talked through an excellent interpreter.

Yasnov says Moscow's population when the war began in 1941, was 4,300,000. It is now between 4,600,000 and 4,700,000. Moscow has no main marketing center like New York, London's Covent Garden, or Paris's Les Halles. Large warehouses and storehouses keep supplies and distribute them as needed on a retail basis. When food is brought into the city by truck it is delivered directly to shops or restaurants. The great bulk is brought by rail and taken directly to storage.

The housing problem is serious. Each Muscovite has nine square meters of living space—nine feet by nine feet isn't much when kitchens are included in the total.

The population is being deliberately held down. Many Russians would like to move here from other towns. This is discouraged. A person must find work in order to live in Moscow. And he said, "We have forbidden new industrial construction so as not to create more jobs. There is no need for us to create a giant city. It would be difficult to run."

Moscow, *December 13, 1955*

Last night the Greek ambassador came for dinner. He said that one day in 1948, 45,000 Greeks living in Russia with Greek passports (mostly around the Black Sea) were rounded up and sent off to Kazakhstan. Greece made mild inquiries about them but isn't pressing too hard because it doesn't know what it would do with 45,000 more refugees.

This morning I talked for two hours with Vassily Fedorovitch Popov, President of the state bank (Gosbank), in his office. The building is a yellow, old-fashioned structure, rather attractive, which used to house the

Czarist state bank. In the wing where Popov's office is located is still a huge full-length portrait of Stalin. In his own office are pictures of Lenin, Stalin, Bulganin, Molotov, and Khrushchev.

Popov, fifty-two, is a professional and graduated from the Leningrad Financial Academy. His first job was as deputy minister of finance to the Tatar Republic at Kazan.

Popov said Gosbank embraces the whole banking system of the Soviet Union as far as short-term credits are concerned. He defined short-term credits as anything up to one year in duration. Long-term credits vary between five years and ten years and are handled by the agricultural bank, the industrial bank, municipal banks, and trade banks, under the Ministry of Finance. But the Gosbank reports directly to the Council of Ministers.

It has an authorized capital of 4 billion rubles and reserves of 4 billion. The short-term credits it has granted exceed 220 billion rubles. The balance of public funds (individual deposits) deposited with the state and savings banks are about 50 billion rubles.

Loans floated by the Soviet Union are raised by subscription from the population. Payments are made in installments, over a period of ten months. Such bond issues are usually for twenty years and are placed through the savings banks. The only term of credit of the Gosbank is for one year. The government decides interest rates through the Ministry of Finance which makes the basic recommendations. The rate on current savings accounts is 2 percent. On accounts deposited for six months or more the rate is 3 percent.

I asked what becomes of the money deposited in savings accounts and how it was invested. He said these funds were used in the budget to finance state projects. The savings banks themselves don't make any money. They get back from the state, on the money they have advanced from savings accounts, only enough to refund to their own balances the percentage interest rates paid out plus sufficient to cover overhead expenses such as salaries.

Interest rates on loans to foreign countries are fixed in agreement with foreign governments. He added: "All interest rates are very low. On internal credits they are usually only 1 or 2 percent. Therefore interest rates for foreign loans are not terribly low relative to our own rates and we don't lose money on foreign loans. Nevertheless, when the Soviet Union grants credits abroad we are not working for profits."

The U.S.S.R. does not borrow money abroad. Many years ago credits were extended to the U.S.S.R. by Britain and Sweden and these have not yet been paid off because they are long-term loans. A foreigner living in the Soviet Union can purchase bonds, but they cannot be bought abroad because "all our loans are internal." The Soviet Union needs no foreign financial assistance.

The rate for income taxes does not change with budget requirements. By far the greatest part of state revenues come from profits on state economic enterprises, not taxes. The role played by taxes and public loans is very small as far as overall revenues are concerned. As national income through the "social sector" increases, taxes are being reduced. In 1953, agricultural taxes were cut in half.

Popov said the Soviet budget was unbalanced only during the first two years of the war, in 1941 and 1942. From 1943 on, it was in balance and still is. Most capitalist countries run on a deficit budget, but a balanced budget is an important factor in a planned economy. The highest income tax rate is 8½ percent.

Retail prices include production cost, plus state profits, plus turnover expenses. All prices are planned to take into consideration these three factors. The law of supply and demand is not allowed to have an influence upon retail prices.

I asked what was the function of gold in the Soviet financial system. He replied: "Gold is not the basic backing of our money. Our money is valued in terms both of gold and of goods in circulation. Gold is a state reserve used to back our money and it is also sold abroad." The Gosbank has large gold reserves, but Popov would not tell me how much. He said: "I see no need to publish them. In capitalist countries gold reserves figures are published to demonstrate the security of the money. But our money is backed by the value of goods produced so there is no need to publish gold-reserve figures."

Popov admitted that "If you measure prices here in terms of consumer goods they are very high when compared with American prices. But to judge correctly you can't base our price system only on retail prices. You must take into consideration the fact that education here is free, medical service is free, vacations are paid, rents are very low and there are various other social security benefits."

Moscow, *December 17, 1955*

TODAY I went to see Mulin (as he says, "Mulin like Mulin Rouge") of Intourist to straighten out our tickets for the Central Asian trip and to meet Madame Komarkova, our guide and interpreter (who has never been in that part of the U.S.S.R.)

He told me a Russian joke. In the Caucasus, people are famous for their longevity. Hearing about a 125-year-old man in one village, a tourist went to interview him. He asked how he managed to live so long. The old man answered: "I never smoke. I never drink. I don't eat meat. I have been very sparing with women." At that moment there was an awful noise of stumbling, singing, retching. "What's that?" inquired the tourist. "Oh," said the old man. "That's my older brother. He's drunk all the time."

Tashkent, *December 18, 1955*

ARRIVED here after a tedious air journey. It is astonishing how haphazard things are. After many hours wait our plane finally took off at 9:30 A.M.

The pilots wore boots and leather or cloth jackets and fur hats like any other Russian men. The hostess had on an ordinary black coat with a mournful brown shawl draped over her patient face. All twenty-one seats were full. We flew at about 10,000 feet to Uralsk (just four hours). The starboard engine sounded like a broken coffee grinder all the way but it got us there. We descended at Uralsk for an hour and then flew on to Aktyubinsk. There we waited forty minutes, drank tea, and took off in more wind and snow for Djusali. By then, flying eastward, it was dark again. We spent an hour in Djusali wondering if we'd get further because of a terrific storm whipping snow drifts along like a horizontal white curtain. We took off in the night for a two-and-a-half-hour flight to Tashkent where we had to turn back. The pilot informed us there was fog over Tashkent. Back at Djusali, we staggered out into the cold, starry night. We were taken to quite comfortable billets and, to our embarrassment, Marina and I got a room to ourselves, pleasantly warm, with nine beds, white sheets and pillow cases; the other passengers were squeezed in one small room. We were just dozing off (about 3:00 A.M. local time) when a rap came on the door to advise us the plane was going off. So we dressed, staggered back aboard, and slumped into our seats. "It seems to me the pilot of this plane isn't serious," said Shura Komarkova, our guide. We finally got to Tashkent at 6:00 A.M., pooped. It was terrifying to think how the crew must have felt: They had been up over twenty-four hours.

The Tashkent hotel is large and quite comfortable, even though there is no hot running water and the community toilet on each floor is Turkish style and used by a highly inaccurate population.

We had a huge "brunch" in the dining room at noon and then set out to see the Mufti of Central Asia, with whom I had a 2:00 P.M. appointment. Tashkent was taken (from the Emir of Kokand) by the Russians in 1865. A "new" or Russian town was then built beside the old Turki town. Apart from some large and ugly administrative buildings, the airport, and parks with silvered statues of Lenin and Stalin or nude athletes (covered with singlets), the Soviets seem to have built little. There is one large Soviet textile plant to use up the local cash crop, cotton.

The city is situated attractively. Today sunshine gleamed on the Tien-Shan mountain range in the background. The range is a barrier leading toward China (Sinkiang), India (Kashmir), and Afghanistan. Plane trees and poplars grow here and there. There are many shabby but rather attractive one-story houses painted in pastel blues and greens.

The crowd is mixed—Europeans and Asians: occasional turbans wound about colored skullcaps; Uzbek hats, slanted Asiatic eyes, many a purely Chinese or Mongol cast of feature. We waited for the Mufti outside a dilapidated blue and white little mosque where rows of Uzbeks were kneeling in prayer and a quavering, fanatical voice every now and then shrieked out from the interior: *"Allah Akbar, Ya Ho, Ya Hak!"* Arabic prayers are broadcast on the city-wide plug-in speaker circuit from 2:00 to 2:30 P.M. But I noticed during part of the service the radio almost drowned out the Imam with livestock quotations and popular songs.

The Uzbeks, wearing skullcaps or dark hats heavily rimmed with fur (like Jewish orthodox hats from eastern Europe) kneeled in rows, almost all of them wearing kidskin black boots, a last memory of their famous horseman days. But now they put rubbers on over them to walk around. They are short, lightly but strongly built, wiry, and stocky, with fierce Asiatic faces and they look a tiny bit like Gurkhas. They bowed and genuflected, placed their brows on the ground, prayed, and finally rose as the Imam directed. A few wandered aimlessly about the courtyard or washed from a tin ewer and basin.

Finally we were greeted by a youthful-looking priest (who turned out to be the acting Mufti), and we drove off to the Mufti's house, hooting our way through the throng at the open market, edging aside graceful little Uzbeks, Chinese-looking children, and an occasional rare Kirghiz woman still hidden behind a thick, horsehair veil.

In the home of the Mufti (now ninety-five years old and bed-ridden), we were taken to the main room and sat down around a table every square inch of which was crammed with food: round flat loaves of bread; dishes of somewhat withered-looking, sweet grapes (kept over from the autumn), apples, pomegranates; plates filled with yellow clustered crystals of sugar candy; dishes of raisins and nuts. There was hardly room for a fly to settle amid the spread.

Our host, the acting Mufti (and I approximate the spelling of these names as translated from Arabic to Uzbek to Russian to English) Al-Hafiz Ghazi Zia-ud-Din Babahanoff (a Hadji), the son of the old Mufti who serves as substitute, was a pleasant, Turkish-looking man wearing a tan robe and white turban. Across from him sat Ghazi Pazil Hodja, Chinese-looking, with wispy white beard and white turban. Both were Uzbeks as well as a capped (Uzbek skullcap) Russian-speaking civilian at the end of the table, youthful, friendly, and, I expect, the local agent of the party.

Babahanoff said there are about 30,000,000 Muslims in the U.S.S.R.; that there were about 30,000,000 before the revolution. (I doubt very much if there are even 15,000,000 practicing today.)

The name of the old Mufti (his father) is Ishan Babahan Ibn Abdul Mejid Khan, born in Tashkent in 1861, when it still belonged to the independent Khan of Kokand. Every year about fifteen to twenty (pilgrims) go from the U.S.S.R. to Mecca. They apply to the Council of Religions in Tashkent or Moscow, and the council helps those it approves to get passports, visas, and foreign currency. Babahanoff said the number of pilgrims is so small "because it is very expensive and we are very far from Mecca."

He says that in 1917, Tashkent had 300 mosques and a population of 600,000; now, with a population of 1,000,000, there are only 18 mosques. But, he adds with proud naiveté, "They are very crowded now and they weren't very crowded in the old days."

The Uzbeks of the U.S.S.R. and the Uzbeks south of the Oxus in Afghanistan are not free to visit each other.

At this point, our host signaled we were to break bread, which we did in the traditional style. Bowls of unsweetened tea were brought in by a fierce-looking Tadjik servant, also wearing a turban, who squatted beside a stove between courses. There were huge bowls of soup containing great greasy gobs of fat-tailed sheep. Then came heaping plates of pilaff (locally "ploff") with nuggets of fat-tailed sheep resting on mounds of rice in which raisins and pepper were mixed. Finally fruit, nuts, sweets, and always more and more tea.

After our lengthy lunch and conversation, Babahanoff took us into the old Mufti's bed chamber. Ibn Abdul Mejid Khan was sitting up in a chair, dressed in a black, flowered robe and flat, honey-colored turban. He has a wispy beard straggling down from his toothless jaw, a brown face, dull old brown eyes, and a fierce hawk nose. He is small and shrunken but clearly once had a heavy chest and body frame. He muttered a few words of blessing, but he wasn't too aware of what he was saying or to whom: merely traditional Muslim courtesies. The old man looks like something out of Omar Khayyám; he has seen a few changes in his day.

It is clear that Russia's penetration continues patiently southward—just as in the days of the Czars. To me, Afghanistan, with its Uzbek population and its screwy Pushtunistan (Pakhtoonistan) policy, cut off from sea commerce by the Pakistan blockade and thereby forced to trade with Russia, is just as isolated and nearly as ready to fall as were the states of Kokand and Bokhara.

BOKHARA, *December 19, 1955*

WE flew here this morning from Tashkent in a Soviet model DC-3. Bokhara airfield is almost nonexistent. We passed a dreary-looking lake set in the desert called, I think, Kizil Kum, and flew on to a muddy field where we taxied to a stop and walked a quarter of a mile through a rickety gate bearing the letters Bokhara, to a car which the manager of the Hotel Uzbekistan (the only one in town) had kindly brought to meet us. There is no Intourist office. We were supposed to have a regular guide, but, this being Monday, when museums are shut, he had disappeared.

We drove into town and deposited our stuff in the Uzbekistan, a tiny, rickety building, with no running water and two little foul-smelling out-houses.

Many of these people look like Confucius or Chiang Kai-shek; others like Eskimos. Some of the more dashing Uzbek youths go in for a particularly strange haircut: All the head is shaven, except for a circular patch, starting above the brow and about as wide as a saucer, which is left an inch long; looks horrible. It doesn't seem to be a traditional thing as the older men have shaven pates. Must be a form of Uzbek *stilyagi*.

Bokhara seems little like a famous ancient city. Yet it was the capital of an independent emirate until the Bolshevik revolution, when the Emir fled to Kabul in 1920, and reportedly went into the rug business. Its population (largely Uzbek) was noted for savage and fanatical Muhammedanism and its emirs were renowned for their cruelty. A usual form of punishment was to take bound prisoners to the top of the twelfth-century minaret, Minar Kalan, and toss them out (a fall of about 250 feet). The market for slaves was notorious. The bazaar was once famous for products from China (on the old caravan silk route), India, and the loot Turkmenian robbers stole. The prisons were particularly disagreeable. In the old jail, one cell was sunk into the ground and called the vermin pit. It was filled with sheep lice said to have been habituated to a special diet of meat so they could happily nibble away at prisoners. Here the Emir cast two English officers, Colonel Stoddart and Captain Conolly, and kept them there for months before slicing their heads off.

This is the shabbiest Asian town I have seen in some time; completely run down, everything crumbling into dust, the only clean-looking people are the few battalions of Russian infantry from the garrison who march through every now and then, swinging their arms and singing beautifully: European recruits, striding through their Asian colonial subjects like British regiments in Kipling's India.

We started our tour by going to the old minaret, Minar Kalan, a dun-colored brick tower constructed in 1127, and still quite sturdy despite the earthquakes common to this area. It was built by a certain Arslan Muhammad Khan and the Russians have put up a tablet to note this. On this grim height, from which so many captives had been hurled, we felt we could see almost into China and as we gazed over the endless view the eternally playing Soviet radio shifted from crop forecasts to a Bach concerto.

Then we went to a large but shabby combination mosque and medresseh across the way. This is the famous Mir Arab, once one of the most important centers of Islamic learning. It is, like most religious buildings, closed for repair. I noticed across from the Mir Arab the Communist party's Agitpunkt (agitation point) #7; it was a good deal busier than the medresseh. Mir Arab is the largest medresseh in Bokhara, it was explained by Kasim Zadeh, the Tadjik vice director of the school. He did not add—what I found out later to be true—that it is the only one functioning.

We visited the Ark, the old palace-fort of the Emir, now nothing but a huge heap, roofed in dust. From the top we viewed the fallen-down wall of the city, the tumbling gray-brown mud rooftops of the town itself, and the broken domes and minarets against the skyline; a truly miserable sight.

Finally we went back to the Bokhara restaurant and watched drunks falling into their beer while a pathetic three-piece band (one woman) of violin, drum, and accordion made loud music, some of which was faintly recognizable (one piece being a weird version of "J'Attendrai").

Outside was an old mosque, now used as a poolroom where there were three spirited games and walls of pictures of Bolshevik leaders and exhortatory posters such as: "If you get drunk you won't be able to fulfill your norm."

After a hectic wait, our taxi driver (a poor Ukrainian who had been sent here during the war to recover from wounds, had lost his family, and had nowhere to go) came for us and we headed off about seven miles along a bumpy road to the railway station of Kagan. We had discovered there would be no airplane to Samarkand tomorrow and therefore had to take the train. In the station waiting room, a squad of soldiers sat with machine pistols strapped to their backs. The walls were covered with recruiting posters boasting what the army had managed to do to Hitler, Mussolini, Mannerheim, Antonescu, Horthy, and the Kwangtung army.

Marina and I shared a train "soft" compartment with a Russian lady and gent. The gent was very tidy and friendly. They had the two lowers, we the uppers. The air up there is hotter but gives the illusion of being cleaner. It takes seven hours from Bokhara to Samarkand (a fifty-minute flight in an old plane). We were given spotless boiled sheets and pillow cases and made ourselves comfortable.

SAMARKAND, *December 21, 1955*

ARRIVED here yesterday at about 5:00 A.M. and were greeted by a friendly woman from the Hotel Registan who guided us through the rainy dark to the hotel, past huddled fellow passengers bent under their baggage. Slept a couple of hours, descended for breakfast, and then started our appointed rounds.

Samarkand is painted in pleasant blue, green, and gray pastel shades and filled with plane trees and poplars. The Russians captured it in 1868 from the Emir of Bokhara and it seems still like a nineteenth-century Czarist garrison town. Many of the mosques are closed. I noticed one across from the Registan serving as a cinema.

The open-air bazaars are pathetic: few goods, shabby, sad-looking people. As usual, radio loudspeakers are ubiquitous and silvered busts of Stalin all too common. Nevertheless, there is real charm to this city with its blue-tiled mosque domes standing out against the nearby foothills of the Tien Shan range. There is a fine blue dome over Timur's (Tamerlane's) tomb which we visited.

At last we connected with a guide, Professor Konstantin Mikhailovitch Mikhailov of the local university: middle-aged, white-haired, bespectacled, grouchy, but extremely learned.

Mikhailov said there are now only seventeen mosques functioning in Samarkand. (I didn't see evidence even of these; saw not one man praying nor heard a single call to prayer in two whole days.) There are *no* medressehs. Mikhailov admits that before the revolution there were "more than twenty-five medressehs and more than one hundred mosques."

We went to the ruined mosque of Bibi Hanum, favorite wife of Timur and daughter of the Emperor of China. In 1399, Timur returned from India with much loot, including slaves, elephants, jewels, and gold. He decided to build the finest mosque in the world and ordered his architects to erect it in five years. As a result they couldn't build it as they wanted and time and earthquakes have laid it in almost total ruins.

Timur specified that he wanted the main portal to be fifty meters high. His architect warned him it would soon collapse. But Timur insisted. Bibi Hanum, then alive, used to watch the construction. Timur went off to the wars again and the architect decided to build the portal only forty-three meters high. When Timur returned he ordered it rebuilt. It was.

The architect asked but one favor of Bibi Hanum, a kiss. This was so sweet and burning that it left a mark like a red rose. When Timur returned from a campaign and saw this he knew what had happened and had the architect killed. He went to his death smiling and was turned into a dove who sang to Bibi Hanum every morning.

The portal was paneled in marble. Its doors were immense and of an alloy of silver, iron, copper, and other metals. Four hundred marble columns (of which there are still some ruined sections) supported the immense dome. It was bigger than St. Sofia in Constantinople, so huge that the old writers used to compare the cupola with the Milky Way. But even during the lifetime of Timur it began to fall apart.

We then went to the Registan, one of the most renowned public places in the world. Registan means "place of sand." It was a famous Asian traders' mart, open on one side; the other three facing huge medressehs. In 1417, Ulug Beg decided to build a medresseh, not only as a religious school, but also as a site to teach such secular subjects as chemistry, mathematics, and astronomy. In 1429, it was completed; now it is sinking into the soft earth. The tops of the minarets are falling off. Two hundred years later (seventeenth century), Yalan Gutash built a similar medresseh right opposite it on the east edge of the square. This is called Shir Dar for the Persian lions once visible on its tiled front.

Clearly this whole area was intimately linked with Persia throughout the centuries. The poet Firdousi is referred to as "our own." The religion here was once Zoroastrian. The Museum of History contains little stone caskets where bones were placed after birds ate the Parsee corpses. Firdousi was a Tadjik from near Bokhara who lived in Isfahan when it belonged to the Bokharan emirate.

I must say Russia is gradually extinguishing Islam as successfully as China converted Mongolia to Buddhism and turned it into a pastoral grazing land instead of a military power.

This morning we went to the bazaar on a cold snowy day unusual for Samarkand. It includes stalls with government produced and owned goods and fixed prices and a mob haggling in the mud bartering for chickens, ducks, eggs, green tobacco, melons, gourd tobacco cases, Uzbek caps, cloth, kidskin boots, saddles, and bicycle chains. A hideous brown silk rug with the profiles of Lenin and Stalin cost $1,000, in what used to be an incomparable artistic center.

TASHKENT, *December 22, 1955*

SHORTLY after we boarded the train for Tashkent a short, fat, enormously wide woman with broad, brown, smiling Asian features, wearing a garish print dress came into our compartment and introduced herself as vice president of the Tadjik Soviet Republic. She bore a melon, long and yellow, done up in a reed net, as credentials of goodwill: Comrade Saida Khalikova of Stalinabad, born in 1909, a Tadjik deputy in the Supreme Soviet's Council of Nationalities, now on her way to Moscow for the Supreme Soviet meeting.

She sat down in our compartment, joined us in a cigarette, and gushed away in bad Russian with fierce gestures of clenched fists, shaking her powerful arms. She was born in Stalinabad when it was still called Dushambi, a village on the territory of the quasi-independent state of the Emir of Bokhara. When she was a girl, women were the slaves of their husbands and had to wear the veil. "Look at me," she boasted. "I was brought up as a slave behind a veil. Now I can wear anything I like and go where I please and I'm vice chairman of our republic. Before the revolution women couldn't even leave their houses, now I have a grown son and he is married to a Russian girl. When I was a child, the Emir ordered all girls to start marrying at nine."

She kept smiling, exposing two squat gold teeth and screwing up her expression remarkably like an eskimo. She claimed the Emir of Bokhara had forty wives in his harem but in addition, every night, he possessed a new virgin aged between nine and thirteen. The veil was abolished only in 1927.

This morning we visited the Tashkent museum. The most interesting thing was a wax reconstruction of Timur's head, based on his exhumed skull. Decked out in helmet, pointed beard, and drooping moustache, he looked rather like a muscular Chiang Kai-shek.

Moscow, *December 24, 1955*

WE returned yesterday. Last night Chip said older Muscovites refer to Khrushchev and Bulganin as Bim and Bom, after two famous clowns in earlier Bolshevik days who were allowed a lot of leeway for the sake of humor.

Leningrad, *December 27, 1955*

CAME up for the opening of *Porgy and Bess*, the first American stage production in Russia since the revolution. The arrival of the cast created quite a stir—the sight of flashy Negroes in this white city. Some of them sang in the streets after they arrived. A huge man ("Crown") patted some Russian admirers, saying: "Why bless your little pointed heads." One of the actors wears a nutria coat and hat and has special holes in his gloves so his rings can show through. The opening was, I thought, lousy: A poor company hampered by a bad theater. Yet it seemed to go down very well—except the prudish Russians were shocked by the sex.

Leningrad is a truly beautiful city—as lovely as any I know. But it lacks life, even if it is far superior to Moscow, more European and more civilized. Martin Malia, a young Harvard professor who has been collecting books for American libraries, finds the people here much more frank and forthgiving. Many of the older ones talk critically of the system.

Moscow, *December 29, 1955*

TODAY I went to the Supreme Soviet and heard Bulganin and Khrushchev speak. Bulganin was relatively moderate, but Khrushchev, at his vituperative worst, attacked almost everyone in the western world. Even the Jugoslav ambassador was disturbed by his zeal. It certainly sounds as if the Cold War is on full blast. Why is Khrushchev so overconfident?

Moscow, *January 2, 1956*

YURI Zhukov tells me that Shepilov, *Pravda*'s editor, is ill in a sanatorium. I wonder if his malady has anything to do with *Pravda*'s famous November 7 blooper when it published: "There is no inherent conflict between socialism and *communism*" (meaning capitalism).

Moscow, *January 4, 1956*

I HAD a good talk with Molotov in his office on the seventh floor of the foreign-ministry skyscraper. The office is a long paneled room furnished with ugly, heavy chairs and desk, and a long, green-baize conference table. The desk was covered with tidy piles of papers and documents; also marble inkwells and a lamp with a marble base as well as a small wooden clock. In one corner of the room was a standard grandfather clock. On the walls were pictures of Lenin and Stalin.

Molotov greeted me courteously but without any effusion. He motioned Troyanovsky (the interpreter) and myself over to the conference table and offered me a papirossy cigarette, lighting mine and one for himself. He took off his glasses and from then on fiddled with the matchbox.

I told Molotov that, as he undoubtedly had heard, Dulles thought that in all the years he has personally been connected with diplomacy the ablest statesman he had ever witnessed in action was Mr. Molotov. Who did Molotov consider the ablest western statesman he had dealt with? He smiled and said:

I should not dwell upon the subject. The statement about me is an obvious exaggeration. As for western statesmen, that is a difficult question. There are many experienced diplomats in the West. In the United States, Cordell Hull was certainly an experienced diplomat. I had occasion to meet Mr. Hull here in Moscow in 1943, and, during the previous year, in Washington in 1942. Also, there is no doubt that Mr. Eden in Great Britain is a very experienced diplomat. [Notice: He left Dulles out.]

I then asked whether Molotov considered open or secret negotiations more useful nowadays. By open negotiations I meant the type of international conference that we had seen at Geneva where most of what occurred was duly reported through the press. Molotov replied:

I should think that in our time it would be impossible to do without both. There is no doubt that closed negotiations of a prepared character are essential. On the other hand, wide circles of the public are now drawn so much into international affairs that it is quite impossible not to explain to them the steps that are taken. The public must receive answers to the questions it raises. Therefore, it is my view that under present conditions it is impossible to do without these semi-closed negotiations where decisions are widely publicized.

I recalled that the Council of Foreign Ministers, set up in 1945, had never been formally disbanded. Should it be reconstituted? He said:

The Council was of course formally set up as a special body and that decision to create it has never been revoked. But, in fact, it no longer exists as a body. It was never utilized except for the peace-treaty negotiations. But, we are still prepared to act according to the Potsdam decisions which created the Council of Foreign Ministers. I should think it would be useful if that body were reconstituted.

I recalled that Bulganin had mentioned a desire for another Big Four summit meeting and asked whether he thought it would be useful to have preliminary discussions of this possibility. He answered: "Such preliminary negotiations could only be discussed when the reaction to Prime Minister Bulganin's statement is known. So far there have been no reports of any reaction by other governments."

I asked what he meant by "reaction." He said: "What I have in mind is different sorts of reaction: official, semi-official, or public reactions. It is important for a matter of this kind to know both official statements and also the reaction of public opinion. This is true for the United States, Britain, and France and also for other countries."

At this point it became clear that Molotov does understand at least a little bit of English. For, Troyanovsky had failed to translate the part about "other countries." Molotov interrupted in Russian and insisted that this also be translated.

I said, in Soviet proposals for the amalgamation of the NATO allies and the Warsaw Pact members I had noticed no mention of similar proposals for economic cooperation on that particular, if somewhat artificial, basis. I asked if he also had in mind some form of amalgamation between the OEEC and CEMA (Soviet Marshall Plan). He said: "Of course that could well be discussed. But the question that has decisive importance is that involving the NATO pact and the Warsaw Treaty. First we should arrive at a political decision. *Then* questions of an economic character could be brought up."

I said I had been struck by a difference in emphasis between the Soviet-Indian communiqué and Bulganin's year-end speech; the communiqué stressed that war was now excluded as a possibility; but the year-end statement indicated it was indeed a possibility; was this not contradictory? Molotov replied:

I see no contradiction between the communiqué statements and the later statement by Bulganin. In the communiqué, issued at New Delhi, mention was made of the tremendous danger of any new world war with modern weapons. Such a danger cannot be denied. But aggressive forces exist that might nevertheless launch a new war no matter how horrible that could be. Therefore, it is necessary to secure peaceful coexistence between systems that differ from each other.

Those observations led me to ask a question which is puzzling many Americans: How is it possible to build a true basis for coexistence between two systems when one of them (communism) openly proclaims its determination to triumph ultimately over the other? Molotov replied:

Well, after all, that was first said over one hundred years ago by Marx and Engels in the *Communist Manifesto* published in 1847. Communism thinks it is scientifically true that history is moving ahead from one social system to another, to a more perfect social system. We think communism is a better system, a more progressive system, and that it will historically triumph. This is our conviction. We merely consider it a well-founded conviction. It reflects historic processes.

According to the doctrine of communism, one of two systems must be victorious and must prove it is more progressive and in accordance with modern requirements. We believe communism is that system which can bring to peoples of the world more favorable material and spiritual conditions of life. This does not mean that no important changes are taking place within the capitalist system. These changes *are* taking place. Our men of science should carefully follow how the capitalist states are developing. Changes are also taking place within the Socialist countries engaged in building communism. Those changes too should be studied.

The essential part in this historical process, as we see it, is that communism is called upon to take the place of capitalism eventually as a more progressive system. Nevertheless, we recognize that not everyone shares our views.

You see, basically the two systems are contradictory. Capitalism is founded upon a system of exploitation of one people by another people, one class by another class, and one person by another person. Communism rejects the theory of such exploitation of one man by another man. In that sense the two systems are incompatible. But the change-over depends upon historic conditions. We should like the change-over to communism to be as painless as possible. There do now exist states with different ideological systems. They should live at peace and should cooperate for their own good and the peace of peoples.

Getting down to specific matters, I then inquired how he proposed that the question of Palestine should be settled. He answered: "I think that problem should certainly be settled in the interests both of Israel and the Arab countries. Israel should adopt a more friendly attitude toward its neighbors."

I thought this a rather vague reply; did he for example think the present frontiers between Israel and the Arab states should be frozen and peace established on that basis. He answered: "What is essential is agreement on controversial questions existing in that area. I believe such agreement possible. But it requires the settlement of concrete questions."

This was the old, familiar Molotov. I asked if he thought Russia, as a member of the United Nations and as a friend of both parties (Israelis and Arabs), should join with the western powers in influencing a Middle Eastern settlement. He replied:

The trouble is that the other great powers act without consulting Soviet views. A case in point is the Baghdad Pact which introduced great disturbance into this area. The Pact was directed against the Soviet Union. Steps have been taken to draw other countries into that Pact. You realize we cannot be in sympathy with such steps against the Soviet Union. This leads to a deterioration of relations in that region and also between the great powers.

I said that while his views were indeed very well known to the American people there were a couple of very minor questions I would like to ask because his personality was by no means as familiar. Was he related in any way to the famous composer Scriabin, his own original family name? No, there was "no relationship." I had read that his hobbies were reputed to be playing the violin, chess, and even bridge. He used to play the violin as a youngster "before going into political activities." He played chess "rarely." And, he added, "I don't play bridge so I cannot tell you anything about it."

I was just about to leave when Molotov said: "Now I would like to ask you a question—only one question. Will you answer it?" I said of course. The question was: "Has this visit of yours to the Soviet Union been worthwhile?" I said it had and I had noted many changes. What changes? I said of course physical changes were obvious; for example, the building we were sitting in (the new Foreign Office) had not existed when I was last here in 1947. But, the changes that struck me most were psychological; for example, although I have been in the Soviet Union four times, I never previously had the chance of sitting down in Molotov's office and talking with him. Molotov said: "Oh, that is not much of a change. You could see people before." I said it hadn't worked out that way. He beamed, bowed, and I departed. Walking home to Spaso House I got frostbite in both ears.

KIEV, *January 8, 1956*

WE arrived here at noon. Visited the Lavra monastery which used to be an enormous feudal church holding. One of its churches was blown up by the Germans during the war. A good deal of the property has been built on by the city. One building has been turned into an antireligious museum. However, the catacombs remain open to worshippers. In addition to curious sightseers, a few old Orthodox believers still wander through, staring at the awkward glass-covered coffins of medieval saints whose miraculous bodies did not deteriorate after death. Their faces are covered, but their gnarled, withered hands protrude from embroidered robes. I saw a peasant woman wetly kissing the glass cover above an old bishop from Suzdal. It is spooky wandering through the narrow, underground passages, lit only by wax tapers which one carries oneself, having the mysterious saints explained by bearded priests who look as if they had stepped from Dostoevski's pages.

KIEV, *January 9, 1956*

SPENT most of the day at a collective farm near Dimidiv, an hour's drive from Kiev across the flat white countryside toward Minsk. There are thick pine forests in this region thrusting between snow-covered fields. Horse-drawn sleighs loaded with hay slid beside girls on skis, uninhibited by their high felt Valinki boots. Most of the cottages had thatched roofs and whitewashed walls. Almost all windows were decorated with carved and often painted shutters.

In the office of the Lenin collective farm we sat with farmers discussing their problems. The walls were covered with slogans. The vice chairman, Stepan Antonovich Oborsky, did most of the talking. The plans for output are made locally. The management presents its project to the farmers and then they vote on it. Plans are, of course, tailored to suit state requirements which outline production goals. Formerly, the state decided not only how much each farm should produce but *how* and *what* as well. Since last year, the farm is its own master.

About 260 hectares are under private cultivation. Each collective farmer's family has its own plot and can raise what it wants there: crops or poultry, dairy products. It can do what it wants with the profit, spend it or put it in the bank.

PARIS, *January 18, 1956*

BREAKFAST with John Cooper, ambassador to India. He thinks it essential to help India out in order to prevent Russia's muscling in any more. India doesn't want "aid"; only help on a loan basis so it can limit its dealings with Moscow to trade and loans also.

Nehru admitted recently that he regarded Afghanistan's willingness to accept $100,000,000 from Russia as an indication it was now entirely under Soviet domination. Since the Russians' visit to India, the Indians, curiously enough, have been much more accessible to Cooper.

Despite their caution, the Indians were undoubtedly impressed by the Russians. They liked Russian support on Kashmir and Goa. They admired the ability of the Russians to come to quick, immediate, massive decisions. Above all, the Indian white-collar class seems to have been impressed.

John thinks the Russians are playing a long-range game in India, aimed at the time—some years hence—when Nehru will be dead. They want to slowly expand the beachhead of their influence and are in no hurry. The Indian Communist party is actually at the moment weaker than before the Russian visit, but it will regain strength.

Nevertheless, there remains more interest in the United States than in any other foreign country. But we mustn't expect expressions of gratitude for our aid and we should stop talking about the need to help India in order to stop it from going Communist. This infuriates the Indians.

PARIS, *January 21, 1956*

COLVILLE, for many years Churchill's private secretary, had the following observation to make about Winthrop Aldrich's activities at the Court of St. James: "You fellows don't have an ambassador in London, you have a British agent."

PARIS, *January 24, 1956*

LUNCH with Bebler, Jugoslav ambassador and exceptionally intelligent. Khrushchev, the Jugoslavs think, is clearly the dominant figure of the Russian team. Bulganin merely played the role of a benevolent uncle at the time of the Belgrade visit. When Khrushchev drank too much, Bulganin was the man who stopped him and got him out of trouble. The Jugoslavs were impressed with Khrushchev: a bold, original man who was willing to admit he had made mistakes and would change his mind.

The Russians, as a gesture of placating Jugoslavia, accepted in its entirety the Jugoslav thesis that socialism could develop along different lines in different countries. But Bebler wonders if the Russians understand what this really means. They certainly have not understood its implications in terms of eastern Europe.

Bebler says there is more development of freedom in Poland than in any other satellite country. He is disappointed with Czechoslovakia which lags far behind, although it has such a western tradition. The Czechs have no guts and have always accepted the tutelage of others. The Poles boasted recently that although the Russians insisted that Gomulka should be hanged as a Titoist they refused to hang him. Bebler sneers at this. They did, after all, arrest and purge him.

PARIS, *January 29, 1956*

LUNCHEON yesterday with the Jebbs. Gladwyn says Macmillan summoned him to Geneva during the foreign ministers' conference. Macmillan was planning a big dinner in honor of Molotov and asked Jebb to bring along the famous silver plate from the British embassy here. He did so. A very special table was laid on for Molotov. At the end of the dinner, Jebb, carried away by the beauty of the Duke of Wellington's candelabra, turned to Molotov and said, "Don't you think they are magnificent?" Molotov replied: "We in Russia find candlelight no longer in the mode. We prefer electricity."

GENEVA, *February 1, 1956*

THIS morning I called on David Morse, director general of the International Labor Organization. He wanted to show me a security report he prepared after visiting Turkey, the Lebanon, Syria, Jordan, and Israel. He is very pessimistic. He feels our policy has been shortsighted and unsuccessful and the Russians are moving in everywhere. They are subverting the labor movement, they are raising the refugees against the West. And the Arab states obstinately insist on preserving the refugees as a problem

—not giving them any permanent hopes of settlement or work. Wherever we move in and increase the standard of living it only favors the growth of communism.

PARIS, *February 6, 1956*

THIS morning called on the Polish ambassador, Stanislaw Gajewski. He is a young man, good-looking, with excellent manners, lots of confidence, and appears highly intelligent. He is obviously a Communist, but one feels—by contrast with the Russians—he is a European. He is therefore less dogmatic, more interested in exchanging ideas.

He strongly recommended that I see a play in Warsaw called *Emergency Service*. This concerns a doctor who fought in the underground Bor army and was arrested when the Communists came in, was liberated three years later, and had a hard time finding work because everybody suspected him. He ends up in a little village where he is the only surgeon. One of the Communist bosses comes down on a trip accompanied by the chief of the secret police. He falls ill with an emergency appendicitis. An operation is necessary, but the chief of police refuses to let the suspect surgeon operate. This is the plot. The audience loves it. Gajewski boasts: "A year ago no one would have dared produce such a play."

PARIS, *February 9, 1956*

LUNCH with Raymond Laporte, now director of the Cabinet of Maurice Faure, secretary of state for foreign affairs. Raymond knew Gajewski and detested him when he was in Warsaw from 1945 to 1950. Gajewski ran French affairs in the Foreign Office. When his wife died Raymond asked Gajewski to arrange for him not to be followed by the secret police at her funeral. Gajewski denied this "ever" happened. Not only was Laporte followed at the funeral, but the police insisted on opening the coffin.

PARIS, *February 14, 1956*

LAST night we went out to the Gruenthers', dined and played bridge *à quatre*. Al said the Russians are continuing to move into the Middle East. Now they are diplomatically established in Libya. They tried to get a tall building near Wheelus field, outside Tripoli, as their embassy. They wanted to overlook Wheelus and take pictures. Fortunately, we were able to block them.

He was disturbed by the efficiency of Communist, above all Chinese, propaganda. When he was home last week General Bill Donovan introduced him to a man who had been making a study of this. The Chinese have been sending to India shiploads of propaganda material printed in English. They have some first-class books for students learning English in school. These are actually Communist propaganda booklets but well printed and amusing. Indian schoolteachers, who need reading material for their children, are delighted to receive these booklets free. As children learn English, they are thus also propagandized.

BROTH WITH

HOMEMADE HOOKS

WARSAW, *February 22, 1956*

I CAME FROM BERLIN BY A RATHER DILAPIDATED TRAIN. THE CUSTOMS were polite at the border, but they made me get out of bed so they could search beneath the mattress.

I was greeted by a Pole employed by the American embassy who horrified me by paying a porter 40 zlotys ($10) for carrying two small bags. When I reached the hotel a pleasant and exceedingly pretty young woman from Orbis, the travel agency, named Danuta, placed herself at my disposal as guide-interpreter. I called at our embassy to see Joseph Jacobs, our ambassador, then went to the Foreign Office to see Poleszczuk, head of the press section, who promised to arrange my appointments. He suggested I do my traveling first and then come back to Warsaw; most of the big shots are at the Moscow Communist Congress. Therefore, I shall go to Gdansk (Danzig), Wroclaw (Breslau), and Cracow the day after tomorrow.

Danuta guided a group of Russians recently. They were very nice but pathetic. The girls locked themselves in their rooms to smoke; they were afraid of being caught. They envied Danuta's pants at Zakopane, the ski resort. They envied the lipstick, powder, and styles of the Polish girls. And the Russian boys complained: "Why aren't our girls attractive?"

WARSAW, *February 23, 1956*

DINED late with a group of Polish journalists gathered together in the Press club by its secretary, Wladyslaw Grzedzielski. They showed a moving propaganda film on Warsaw's destruction and reconstruction. Hitler ordered the city razed in October, 1944, and for two months the Nazis worked at the job with flame throwers and dynamite squads, knocking about 80 percent of it down. The only thing not mentioned was that the Red army was parked across the Vistula watching. The reconstruction has been most impressive and to a large degree the city has been faithfully rebuilt according to old plans and architecture.

Dinner was cordial and intelligent, although we all disagreed when we got to politics. The Poles said their Communist party was in better shape than others because much of the intelligentsia stayed in the country and there was no taint of collaborationism (as in Hungary) or mass emigration of intellectuals (as in postrevolutionary Russia). Grzedzielski is of poor noble stock, the rest from the bourgeoisie except for a young reporter who boasted: "I am the most humble, a worker." One was born a Jew; one a Calvinist; the rest Catholics. None were religious now. The most militant atheists were the Catholics.

They said they were much more internationally minded than other Communists because Poland had experienced a long era of internationalism and exile during 150 years of occupation after the partitions. "We prize our liberty," they said, "because Poles fought for so many other liberation movements in Italy, France, America, and elsewhere." They insisted that theirs must inevitably be a different form of communism from the Russian.

Visited Jerzy Albrecht, president of the Warsaw city council (equivalent of mayor) and member of the Central Committee of the Communist (Peoples') party. He was in the resistance and arrested by the Gestapo in 1942.

Albrecht said Warsaw's population today is 1,000,000. In 1939, it was 1,300,000. When liberated in January, 1945, there were 150,000 people in Praga (on the right bank of the Vistula where the Russians were during the insurrection) and less than 20,000 in Warsaw itself, scattered about in the ruins. Only a handful had actually lived through the holocaust of planned Nazi demolition.

On August 1, 1944, the Warsaw uprising began and lasted until mid-October. The left bank was liberated by the Russians January 17, 1945. Between October and January, the Nazis obeyed Hitler's order to destroy the city. About 300,000 people were evacuated to concentration camps and villages and, with dynamite, gasoline, and flame throwers, a methodical destruction began.

On the very day of liberation (January 17), when the government came from Lublin to Praga, a decision was made to restore the city, to keep it as a capital, and to rebuild it much along the old lines. Within two months of liberation every rubble heap that had once been a historic or artistic monument was carefully labeled with warnings against disturbing the site so that details could be dug out of the debris.

Called on acting Foreign Minister Marian Naskowski, a plump man with a sad, pale face. He fled to Russia when Poland was occupied in 1939, and later became an officer in Berling's First Polish Army (under the Soviets). After returning to Poland, he was made chief of the Polish military mission in France, then ambassador in Moscow.

I asked whether Jugoslavia would be invited back to the Cominform. He replied: "The Cominform is a purely party matter and not for the ministry of foreign affairs to discuss."

He said about the Oder-Neisse border:

Our attitude is clear. We consider the Oder-Neisse frontier has been definitely regulated although only a peace treaty can formally confirm this fact. Frankly we don't think the question can have any influence on the future settling of the question of German unification, which we favor—under certain conditions. All Poles, regardless of politics (even the emigrés in the West) favor the Oder-Neisse border. Polish history is filled with German Drang Nach Osten. We have had enough of it.

The West doesn't understand our policy well enough. It is not imposed by Russia. There is nothing in this thesis. If on the principal questions our policy is identical with that of Moscow this is for the simple reason of common interests. Our road to socialism is in many ways different from that of Russia or of China. For example, there are different percentages of collectivization. But our general direction is the same—the socialization of production.

There is freedom for all faiths and also for those who are not religious. Before the war, thanks to the Vatican Concordat, the latter were actually persecuted. Relations with the Catholic hierarchy are developing favorably. Cardinal Wyszynski is sequestrated only because he sought to foment an antigovernment policy. But he has been forgotten already in Poland. Life goes on.

I chatted with my taxi driver on the way home. (He learned German in a labor camp.) He said life was terrible; no freedom, little food, everything too expensive. He pointed to queues of women in front of bakery shops; "They haven't any other time to buy bread. And there isn't enough bread for them."

On the English language menu at lunch I noticed a beauty: "Broth with homemade hooks [noodles]."

GDYNIA, POLAND, *February 24, 1956*

LAST night I came up by train (with Danuta) to Sopot, a seaside town which was part of the old free city of Danzig (Gdansk). Breakfast together with Blumski, "cultural editor" of the Communist party paper.

A touching little American flag had been placed on the table. The waiter had been selected for his few words of English. We ate large slabs of excellent Polish ham and drank tea, looking out over the frozen Baltic, a solid block of ice for miles. Only a few narrow channels are broken in to Gdansk and Gdynia by icebreakers.

We then toured old Gdansk where World War II started. In August, 1939, the cruiser *Schleswig-Holstein* paid a "courtesy" visit and began firing salvos at the nearby Polish naval base of Westerplatte—even before the Nazi armies struck. The last resistance in the neighborhood, on the peninsula of Hel, endured until September 29.

We lunched (enormously) in a restaurant with a group of local editors plus Znajewski. Toasts were drunk to "friendship of Polish and American journalists."

The conversation was affable but obscured by slogans, i.e.:

The only real Germans seem to live in West Germany where Adenauer is almost a new Hitler because he covets Silesia. It was terrible for the West to rearm West Germany. But the East Germans are democratic and therefore not dangerous. It is OK to give them guns.

It was a crime for Bor-Komorowski to call the Warsaw uprising, which was a criminal attempt to seize power before the Russians could arrive. As a result 200,000 people were needlessly slaughtered; no word about the Russians just sitting by on the Vistula to watch the slaughter.

Russia—a benevolent power. No talk of the 1939 partition of Poland or of the Katyn massacre. Now admitted that Stalin was a dictator, anything wrong in the past blamed on him and Beria.

After we were well filled with hooch, Znajewski, a big shot in the Gdansk Communist party, suddenly dropped all pretense about good East Germans and bad West Germans. "Maybe the American comrade is right," he shouted at the puzzled journalists. "Maybe all Germans are the same. For my part I hate them all, ours as well as his."

WROCLAW, POLAND, *February 25, 1956*

TOURED Wroclaw (Breslau) extensively and was astounded at how "slavicized" it has become. The Germans are gone and Poles from all over—but especially the eastern areas ceded to Russia—have been moved in. I talked with people born in Vilna, Warsaw, Torun (Copernicus's home town), Lublin, and many from Lwow; but no one from prewar Breslau.

I was told by the delegation of journalists who took me in charge that Wroclaw now has 375,000 inhabitants, of whom only 1,500 are Germans. From the tenth to the fourteenth centuries this, they say, was a Polish town. From the fourteenth to the twentieth centuries it was German. (There is deep faith that the Germans will never come back; but the Poles, after all, waited six hundred years.)

In the cathedral I was guided about by Father Jan Kowalski who speaks excellent French. This discouraged my German-speaking entourage who, bored, fell behind. Kowalski was born in Fribourg, Switzerland, the son of an old-regime diplomat. At the end, saying farewell, he asked: "Do you ever go to Madrid?" Puzzled, I said, "Yes." "Next time would you say hello to my sister?" "Who is she?" "Lady Mallet, wife of the British ambassador."

He says Wroclaw is now "*très croyant*"; despite great cold the churches are always filled. The population is mostly from east Poland (now Russian) and is "very near God." I remarked it was odd that Wroclaw was more religious than before the war. "I think the reasons are evident," replied Kowalski.

CRACOW, POLAND, *February 26, 1956*

ARRIVED here after an all-night third-class train ride. On the train, Danuta and I had a few drinks with a man from Zakopane who had spent two years in Dachau during the war. He asked me my impression of Poland now. I told him—frankly. He disagreed; said everything was rosy. When Danuta went out to get some coffee for us, he leaned forward and whispered in German: "You're right. Don't believe what I said. I don't dare talk. But I agree with you. So do 99 percent of the people."

That night the Zakopane man invited us to share a bottle of vodka with him and his compartment mate. When it had disappeared, I produced my sole bottle of whisky and down it went. By then we were talking freely. I showed him a book on ancient Athens and read them a bad German translation of Pericles's funeral oration with its stirring encomium of democracy. "Ah," they said, swaying backward and forward in the lurching train, "that is a proper form of government." Even Danuta, carefully vetted in advance as a loyal party representative, was most impressed.

Cracow is lovely and, thank goodness, was not destroyed. Hating Warsaw, the Germans made Cracow capital of the Governorate General and put Gauleiter Frank in the Wawel castle. At war's end they had the city all mined, but the Russians came in from the West and captured it before the demolitions began. It is a fine town, with handsome houses with stone Renaissance and baroque portals over the doorways, magnificent Gothic churches and one of the oldest universities in Europe.

On the highest Gothic spire is a golden crown. In the window a trumpeter sounds his horn every hour on the hour. This symbolizes the medieval trumpeter who acted as watchman and warned of any approaching enemy. In 1241, the Tatars under Batu Khan captured Cracow and the trumpeter was shot in the throat, in mid-song, by a Tatar archer. Since the fourteenth century he has sounded his horn every day except during the German occupation. Two days after the Germans left in 1945, he resumed.

WARSAW, *February 27, 1956*

I CAME back by train from Cracow, discovering that the lock on my brief-case had been markedly picked. There were no taxis, but a driver with a ministry of foreign trade car offered a little black-market deal—20 zlotys to the Hotel Bristol. Danuta says this is common spare-time work.

This morning, I saw Hugon Hanke, former Prime Minister of the emigré government in London who quit last September and came back. He has what would be termed a luxury apartment (four rooms plus kitchen).

Hanke accuses the London Polish government of training agents "to destroy in Poland what the Polish workmen and peasants had built dur-ing years of onerous work." (Presumably, he himself once took part in such preparations.) When war came Hanke was too old to be drafted and fled to Rumania, Jugoslavia, and finally Greece. In France he joined the First Polish Division, was taken prisoner and put in a POW camp from which he escaped in 1942.

In England, he joined the Polish Mountain Brigade. He was demo-bilized as a sergeant in the spring of 1944, when the emigré government summoned him to work with the underground in Poland on liaison. After the war, he decided to stay in London because he heard Poland was a "dictatorship." In August, 1955, he was selected as emigré Prime Min-ister. He kept the job a month. He said:

> I had been thinking for two years already of returning to Poland. I had many letters from my family and from friends telling me things were all right. In early August, 1955, the Warsaw government ap-pealed to emigrés to return and offered an amnesty. I convened a special meeting of my Cabinet to discuss this. I argued that we emigrés had nothing to offer Poles abroad; that most of them were not involved in politics at all and could not get work in England. I finally resolved to return. My family was all here when I arrived. I had not seen them in sixteen years. That was the trouble.

WARSAW, *February 28, 1956*

ROMUALD Poleszczuk, acting chief of the Foreign Office press section, requested me to come around. When I went downstairs to order a taxi through Orbis, I noticed I was being openly followed. A fellow in a felt hat standing beside a nice new Mercedes got in beside the driver when I took off. They came along behind to the Foreign Office.

Poleszczuk shook hands, offered me a Polish cigarette, then said the Polish government was very disturbed and disappointed with the first column I had written (published Saturday, February 24). The government found it offensive. As a result he had been instructed to tell me no more appointments were being made for me. I replied that I was astonished. I found it extraordinary that they censured a correspondent for being objective when that was what they said they wished. I proposed to do no favors for Poland: I would write as objectively about this country as I wrote about any other, including my own.

He said there had been many American journalists here before and this was the first time the Polish government had ever found it necessary to take such steps. I remarked that, at any rate, it was a first time for each of us.

PRAGUE, *March 1, 1956*

CAME here by train from Warsaw. Next door to my compartment was a Slovak learning how to play the ocarina; all night, all day!

On leaving Poland I have some final notes:

The bureaucracy is incredible: People have to stand in queues to wait for permits to get the most ordinary things like arranging coal purchases.

They hate all Germans, call the East German army "Dove's Hussars" (after Picasso's peace bird).

The currency is utterly phony, with each country making its own exchange arrangements; all to peg the zloty to the ruble.

Everything is done the hard way. It is considered an ideological triumph when the simplest thing is constructed.

People are so proud now to realize that Stalin was a dictator; why did it take them so long? Will they now blame him for dividing Poland with Hitler? For the Katyn massacre?

Danuta came down to see me off. To my surprise she got on the train and rode to the suburban stop outside Warsaw from which a tram goes back to town. She confessed she agreed with many of the views I had expressed; and that she was surprised to find herself agreeing. She urged me to be careful; she had heard of my trouble. When we got to the little suburb station she gave me a great big hug and kiss, then fled into the night.

PRAGUE, *March 2, 1956*

THIS afternoon I called on U. Alexis Johnson, American ambassador. Johnson is sure the last satellite to discard the vestiges of Stalinism will be cautious Czechoslovakia. When Malenkov's new industrial program started, the Czechs moved gingerly and only halfway. So they had very little readjusting to do afterward. Again, when there was a new approach in relations with the West they were careful.

Lunched with Vejvoda, the Jugoslav ambassador, a charming man with a most attractive wife. He is a good-looking Croat (as is she) and they were both well dressed, well educated, spoke several languages. They might be central European diplomats from Hapsburg days. Actually, Vejvoda, who is a cultivated man with a taste for modern art (which, he says, scares the "socialist-realist" Czechs), was a prewar Communist who studied in Prague and was a member of its party. He says: "We were all Socialists then: the Communists, the social-democrats, and the Beneš national socialists. This country was rich, well industrialized, with a real tradition of democracy. We all thought and boasted that we would make it such an example of socialism that we could really demonstrate the value of our ideology to America and Europe." But, he concludes, everyone was deceived.

PRAGUE, *March 3, 1956*

THIS afternoon I spent two hours sightseeing with a Czech woman guide who in no time was savagely denouncing the regime. Said it was a joy to have a westerner to talk with as she no longer dared even to give her views among her friends for fear of some stool pigeon.

Drove around the old town hall and square. There's a monument to the first Slovak partisans who (my guide told me) were allowed to be slaughtered in 1944 when the Russians held back aid. The Americans were so near Prague and she heard the partisans' appeal for help on the radio. But we had agreed with the Russians not to come to Prague and it took them eight days to get here with relief.

We passed the huge, grim Stalin monument above the Vltava planted about with trees from Georgian saplings. The ice pack has broken on the Vltava; how much of a thaw will there be politically? My guide complained: "We need schools so badly. But instead they spent millions of crowns on this statue." Masaryk supposedly said here: "I went to Moscow a free man and came back Stalin's servant." My guide says people aren't allowed to see the room from which Masaryk jumped. She sadly recalled Jan Hus's words: "*Pravda vitezi*—Let the truth prevail."

We passed the presidential garden gates, now with green panels obscuring the view through a wrought-iron grill. She remarked: "Under Beneš anyone could look in. I think the present leaders are afraid. Maybe before the war there were some poor and some who ate richly and drank champagne. I think now that only a different group has food and champagne."

This evening I dined alone with the Johnsons in the enormous residence. He believes our propaganda is just silly. BBC has its Bruce Lockhart who is deeply respected here. We have no one. Our balloons and leaflets are bad. The Czechs used to hope for a neutral status like Austria's. Now they see that the very best they can pray for is a Titoist status—independent communism. It is arguable whether these people can really afford to be non-Stalinist according to the new Russian line. The population is hostile to communism and prowestern. Can the grip really be relaxed? When the East German revolt boomeranged, hopes and western prestige fell. Until then many wondered, "What is the West going to do?" Now they realize the question is, "What are we going to do for ourselves?" But this nation of Schweiks knows it can't do anything.

The United States has always encouraged the masses to overthrow the regime. We have done nothing to give the impression that we will make our peace with it. But we *must* do business with the regime. This schizophrenic attitude puzzles the Czechs. Our present policy merely forces the satellites to stay in the Soviet fold. The only alternative is war; but war is out.

PRAGUE, *March 4, 1956*

I DROVE extensively through the Sudetenland, visiting Plzen, Cheb, and Karlovy Vary. It was windy, stormy, wet but interesting. One would hardly realize now that American troops had liberated this part of Czechoslovakia. Memories of their effort are being extinguished and everywhere are new monuments to Soviet soldiery and emphasis on the U.S.S.R. Also, the living standards of this traditionally prosperous part of Bohemia have visibly sunk, even if goods offered in shops at Karlovy Vary are better, more varied, and cheaper than in Russia.

Wandered through the rain to a dreary little Plzen hotel for a beer in the backroom bar where a few individuals were starting off their Sunday with large steins; some were already drunk. The beer—in this home of the famous Pilsener—was miserably bad. Apparently the only good beer is for export. Not only are living standards low, but the old Czech virtues of cleanliness and tidiness seem to have vanished. Everything is drab, sordid, and filthy.

Outside Cheb, near the German border, there is still a gray obelisk commemorating those of the U.S. First Infantry Division who were killed here. Their names, chipped into the sides of the stone, are now almost illegible because the white paint marking them has been allowed to fade away. Three unusually large road signs marking directions have been placed in front of the monument to make it invisible.

Karlovy Vary, once the world-famous spa of Carlsbad, is now the favorite haunt of the Moscow jet set—and shows it. The renowned old Pupp's hotel (called Moskva) is closed to the public. I went in and found it drab, denuded of furniture, dilapidated.

The clientele of Carlsbad has changed. Last year, one of the few German-speaking waiters said, Molotov was here several days. Also

Marshal Chu Teh. There are villas for dignitaries. Russian men in fur hats and women dressed in pathetic thirty-year-old styles solemnly drink medicated waters at the public springs, lurching and belching in formation behind their group leaders.

PRAGUE, *March 5, 1956*

WENT to the Satirical Theater to see a play called *Caesar*, first produced as a satire on fascism in 1932, and revived this winter with some mild new jokes against the present system added. It has had enormous success. The author, producer, and main actor is a huge, bearded Czech named Jan Werich who looks like the perfect Falstaff.

In the play there are a few gentle cracks which are nevertheless considered so daring in this stultified atmosphere that only Werich could get away with them. For example, one character, reincarnated after many lives, complains: "I never managed to be born to rich parents." The other replies: "You're lucky—now." Another remarks: "An impressionist painter paints what he sees. An expressionist paints what he feels. A socialist-realist paints what he reads."

After the show I went with Werich for supper at the Budapest restaurant on Vaclavski Namesti. Later he led the way to a tiny wine joint in the old part of Prague and we sat up for hours talking. Here is what he said:

There is no tradition of satire in the U.S.A. because there is no need for it. Americans don't require veiled references but can say anything on stage or screen. Central Europe is accustomed to the need for satire—oblique references that everyone can understand even if they daren't say them.

"They" is the key word here (as elsewhere in the orbit). Everyone has his "they." "They" refers to the all-powerful inner circle, the direction. But it is an invisible "they." Nobody really knows who "they" is. "They" is bureaucracy. "They" is the system. But "they" is also something else—it is the excuse for refusing to take responsibility, for inaction ("they" wouldn't like it, etc.). Once, Werich was talking with one of the highest Politburo leaders here and he made reference to "they" wouldn't like it. "My God," said Werich, "you don't mean to tell me that even you have a 'they.' " President Zapotocky came to see *Caesar*. He told Werich afterward: "The play is okay. We have decided to have satire. Since we have to have satire, I approve *Caesar*."

Werich says regretfully:

The truth is that the Czechs are not a fighting people. We have never really fought since the Hussite wars of the fifteenth century. The Hapsburgs took over complete power in 1621, after the battle of White Mountain. From then on Czech mothers brought their children up in a passive tradition. They were taught: "Don't speak up what's on your mind. There is no need for people to know what you think." The result has been Schweikism. This is a method. But it is no good as a national philosophy.

The Good Soldier Schweik by Jaroslav Hasek depicted the stupid, bumbling, but shrewd peasant mentality, always going along but passively resisting.

Werich says:

Communism is a philosophy and a game. But you people must remember that the Russians and the Chinese are prepared not to eat for thirty years if necessary until their production exceeds that of the West. You should recognize this startling fact and not just rave against communism. You talk so much about your industrial ability. But personally, I don't care whether I'm killed by a highly polished H-bomb made in America or a crudely tooled Soviet model.

He thinks our propaganda stinks.

You are wasting your money on Radio Free Europe. It misses things; or it is late; or it is wrong. It is very difficult to hear because of jamming. Once you get it, you'd like to know something. But all you get is some bumbling fool who often sounds drunk or as if he had never read his text before. The things your propaganda speaks about are silly. The broadcasts give fifteen minutes of statistics and percentages. Whom do they think they're talking to—professors of mathematics?

Any improvement in the current Czechoslovakian situation must come from the East, not from the West. You can't help us. What is, is. We have no Tito and we are isolated from the sea. The Czechs fight well only when they are in foreign armies—like the RAF. There are no good young people left. Hitler closed down the schools. He sent the youth to work in Germany. He destroyed the morale and ethic of our people. The result was that some became Communists, some became Schweiks.

PRAGUE, *March 6, 1956*

THIS morning the phone rang and a querulous woman's voice asked whether I could see her for a few minutes. I couldn't understand who it was. Discovered it was Mrs. Werich. Of course, said I. She arrived later on, very nervous, to say: "My husband told me about your conversation last night. Please don't quote him. He has been dreaming for so long of visiting Vienna—maybe even Paris. I wouldn't want anything to go wrong."

This afternoon I saw Foreign Minister Vaclav David in Jan Masaryk's old office in the Czernin Palace. What a contrast to the lively, congenial Masaryk: a dour-looking man with slow reactions, sullen face, lacking in intelligence.

He said Prague wanted to live "in mutual friendship and cooperation with all countries." He criticized U.S. import restrictions and said we refused Czechoslovakia most-favored-nation privileges.

He wants us to give up balloons, leaflets, and VOA and RFE hostile broadcasts which "infringe international customs." He added: "We undertake nothing of the sort against America." He wanted United States "leaders" to cease "hostile" speeches. "Our people are governed by a system that suits them and they want to live in peace."

PRAGUE, *March 7, 1956*

TODAY was T. G. Masaryk's birthday. One would never know it. No mention in the press of the republic's founder and first leader. *The New York Times* secretary, a pathetic Jewish woman, with the tattoo of Auschwitz concentration camp on her arm, recalled the occasion and says they have removed almost every trace of Masaryk. His name has been obliterated from streets, schools, and hospitals. She also sadly recalled that today is the anniversary of the date her mother was put in a gas oven at Auschwitz. She herself, although surviving, was sterilized by the kindly Nazis. She says there is still anti-Semitism in Czechoslovakia, on the grounds that the Jews are tied to the West, since so many of them took refuge there after Hitler's entry in 1939.

We went to the Gottwald mausoleum on a hill above the city: a huge, solid, stone building with an enormous statue of Zyzka on horseback and two flags fluttering in front—one Czechoslovakian, the other Soviet. Gottwald is pickled in the Russian-style necropolis. He looks a bit unreal, thinner than in life, belly pulled in, chest puffed out and covered with medals. His wife's ashes are in a pot beside him. Two gloomy sentries at the door. This pickling "takes" better further east. In a vast hall outside are about sixty large tombs all waiting for customers—with only three, so far, occupied by tenants.

In the afternoon I went to see Antonin Zapotocky, President of the republic, co-founder of the Czechoslovakian Communist party, member of the Politburo, and first secretary-general of the party.

Until 1940, he worked in the Communist party and Red trade-union organization. When the Nazis took over he was caught trying to escape to the Soviet Union and was put in Sachsenhausen concentration camp.

Zapotocky retains a certain personal popularity among the anti-Communists who regard him as the least bad of the lot because he doesn't always tell the people they are already living in heaven and because he occasionally admits mistakes. For a man of almost seventy-two he is amazingly youthful looking with no gray hair. I saw him in his offices in the Hradčany, one floor above Beneš's old official suite. He spoke

Czech through an interpreter. Zapotocky has a long nose, elephantine ears (with mastoid scars), kindly, little blue eyes, a pinkish complexion, and one steel tooth. All in all he looks like a successful worker—which he is. The walls of his office were lined with books and he told me that since the age of sixty ("in my old age") he himself has turned author. He writes novels (four to date).

I observed that in all the reports of the Twentieth Congress meeting in Moscow the Cominform had not once been even mentioned; was this a sign that it was now considered dead? He replied: "It is not usual at Communist party congresses to discuss the Cominform. But there has been *no* change in its status. Still, it is another question if in view of the resolutions approved by the Twentieth Congress and as a consequence of congresses to be held by various Communist parties the Cominform may not be changed in the future."

(Rather delphic.)

I then asked what changes were to be expected in the application of Czechoslovakian communism or in the party's ideology as a result of the Congress. He said:

> I believe one cannot speak of changes in ideology but of adaptations resulting from the changed world situation. Lenin's teaching was that wars were inevitable under the capitalist system and this has been confirmed as a theory and remains valid. But now capitalism is not the only sovereign system in the world. A number of countries follow a Socialist system and they have sufficient strength to prevent the inevitability of wars.

I observed to Zapotocky that Beneš had sought to make of Czechoslovakia a bridge between East and West; what did he, Zapotocky, think of the idea of following such a policy? He replied: "Czechoslovakia is certainly willing to develop friendly relations with all countries regardless of their regimes. But if by the term 'bridge' you mean a policy of fence sitting, we certainly do not wish to do this. We wish to build socialism here and we must base ourselves upon Socialist countries. The capitalist countries clearly wouldn't want to help us any more than we would seek to build up capitalism in countries elsewhere."

I inquired exactly what was Stalin's present status, after he had been raked over the coals last month in Moscow; what was his standing in the Communist hierarchy? He replied:

> Stalin deserves great merit for his fight against Trotskyism after Lenin's death. Trotsky advocated the idea of exporting socialism at the point of a bayonet. Stalin also deserves praise for his industrialization of the Soviet Union. What has been objected to is when a situation develops where one person alone makes decisions; then mistakes are more easy to make. Collective leadership reduces the chances of such mistakes.

Of course, it cannot be denied that in the course of time, rule by a single individual develops unhealthy tendencies. This has been criticized and remedied. But this process neither denies the merit nor reduces the role of Stalin. Stalin will always remain a great personage both in the Communist movement and in the history of the liberation of Czechoslovakia.

At this point Zapotocky developed a truly extraordinary lie with every external indication of sincerity. Today, Masaryk's birthday (which he seemed unaware of), he said:

In this connection in Czechoslovakia you may see a number of memorials to T. G. Masaryk. *None* have been taken down. Or, if such was done by zealots, corrective measures have been taken and they have been criticized. It is clear that Masaryk will remain a historical figure in Czechoslovakia even though our political ideas are different. Of course, you can't put Masaryk on the same level as Stalin. [How true!]

BUDAPEST, *March 11, 1956*

TODAY (Sunday) I went to see Matyas Rakosi, secretary-general of the Hungarian Workers' party and Communist boss. He received me in his office in party headquarters in Pest, not far from Parliament. There was one armed soldier at the door and a party guard dressed in black overcoat and black golfer's-type visored cap who took me and my companion, a Foreign Office press interpreter, up in the elevator to the top floor of the boss's office. Everywhere pictures of Stalin—despite his "demotion."

Rakosi is astonishingly short (barely over five feet) and very broad with a huge, powerful chest. He is built like a small ox and must be exceedingly strong. He told me that in his youth he was a "sportsman" and still likes to row and swim. But, unlike some of "my other comrades" he doesn't care for fishing: "It's too slow." He invited me to come to Lake Balaton with him next summer. He had had a briefing on me; knew I lived in Paris; thought I still ran *The New York Times*'s foreign service; knew I was here in 1953. He said frankly he didn't like the articles I wrote but hoped I would find Hungary more agreeable this time.

We spoke in English which he knows fluently. He told me he also speaks (in addition to Hungarian) Russian, German, French, and Italian. Once or twice he interjected Latin quotations; obviously a well-educated man. As a youth he prepared for the Hungarian consular service which is why he became a language specialist.

He spent nineteen years in prison, but his health didn't suffer because "my parents were very healthy." When in prison he kept himself fit by using his table as a weight for setting-up exercises. He read such books as the prison censor permitted and as were smuggled in by friends. "But for long periods I didn't have a single book."

He continued: "For seven years I was in solitary confinement, often in a dark, unlighted cell. That was no high school—a Hungarian prison in fascist days."

I asked how he kept his sanity; did he, for example, do mathematical problems, memorize and recite poetry, or what? He replied:

I have always been an optimist by nature, and I was comforted by the rightness of the cause for which I fought. This helped me. And I tried everything. I remembered the Soviet Union which I had visited. I tried to work out means of improving our illegal activities. The results were all right. The director of the prison was very dissatisfied when I emerged from his cellars without a change.

When he had poured glasses of sweet wine and suggested a mild toast to the friendship of the Hungarian and American peoples (he quaffed his Tokay in one gulp, like vodka) he observed: "Our Hungarian stock is mixed. We come of Finno-Ugrian blood but it is intermixed with German, Slav, and Greek. Our Socialist system now allows the development of our peoples's hidden capacities and their talents are flourishing."

I asked what was the principal significance of the recent Twentieth Congress in Moscow and what effect its decisions would have upon Hungary? He replied:

A stronger state is in no need of a strong hand administratively. And there is no doubt that every country within the Socialist camp feels stronger. We feel more secure. But there is no question of any changes in agriculture or economic practice. We remain strongly for collectivization. Bigger farms are a practical necessity. Even in the United States every year the size of the average farm grows; but your smaller farmers are disappearing, wiped out; they become poor whites.

How about the police? If a stronger state doesn't require a strong administrative hand, would the police fade away? His answer: (and in every case he always referred back to the Moscow masters)—"The question of the police was not raised at the Twentieth Congress. But, theoretically, as long as capitalism is strong, we need a strong state. And part of a strong state is a strong and loyal police. There will be no change in this."

I asked about the Cominform. He looked at me shrewdly:

Why do you inquire about the Cominform? The Cominform was not on the agenda of the Twentieth Congress and that was why it wasn't mentioned. But last winter Khrushchev spoke of it in clear terms. [Khrushchev said in December there would be no change in the Cominform; it was an "internal" affair]. I don't see that the Congress changed this in any way. But, of course, we are not rigid. We always change our methods and our steps as times change. When the members of the Cominform see a need for change, then they will change.

What, I asked, was the historical position and reputation of Stalin as a result of the Twentieth Congress? He replied (dutifully): "We hold exactly the same opinion as Khrushchev and Mikoyan. Everybody makes mistakes. Lenin said that even the most clever men, even geniuses, can make mistakes—especially when they get old. This was the case with Stalin."

But what, I asked, was Stalin's role in Marxist historical terms? Rakosi said:

To measure a man's historical value you must be able to look backward over a certain distance in time. For example, in the case of your American presidents, some of your historians thought Coolidge was a wise, strong, silent man; wise simply because he didn't speak. But he is no longer considered so smart by your historians. [This is an odd comparison—Stalin and Coolidge.] There is no doubt that Stalin had very great historical merits even though he committed blunders also. We Communists measure historical figures both in terms of their merits and their demerits.

I then turned to Tito and Titoism. Did Rakosi think the quarrel with him had all been a big mistake. He said:

We were misled on Titoism. This was one of the works of Beria and his group. He sought to create a situation that would weaken the bonds of Socialists and the quarrel with Tito was part of it. Khrushchev spoke of this in Belgrade last year. Now we are trying to forget this disagreeable episode and to improve our relations with Jugoslavia. I am sure our new efforts will succeed. After all, Lenin thought there was no doubt that every nation is moving toward socialism—excuse me, but I even include the United States. But every country takes its own special steps. Tito was absolutely right.

I asked: "Now that the rupture with Tito has been healed, do you intend to invite him back into the Cominform?" He replied: "It is not *healed* but *healing*. Still, when it is healed I would be glad to ask him into the Cominform. This would be a strengthening move. Still, I doubt if there has been any such proposal; but, if Jugoslavia came *fully* back to the Socialist camp it would be a good thing."

I told Rakosi I had heard he once boasted of his "Salami tactics" in making revolution, slicing the opposition off piece by piece; what were these tactics? He answered:

It was our enemies who called them "Salami tactics." They meant we were advancing every day, step by step, by taking a piece from our enemies each day. But this is the job of any good political party—

including the Communists. Many other parties have come to success that way. I won't patent the process.

What was the future of the Catholic church here?

In my opinion if the Catholics had a better preview of history to come they wouldn't be so bellicose as they had been in 1948 and 1949. They thought—and not without influence and encouragement from the United States—that we were living in a transitory situation. Now they realize they made a mistake. Without acknowledging this, they are accommodating themselves to the situation. The Catholic church is well known for its ability to make separate peaces and separate arrangements under different conditions.

I asked if there were any connection between the East German uprising in 1953, and Beria's demise. He said: "I don't know about this. But I can assure you that Beria had his dirty hands in everything."

I then inquired: in view of the fact that Rakosi now admitted Tito was on a proper Socialist course and the whole row had been "Beria's fault"; and in view of the fact that Rajk had been tried, at least in part for Titoism, was the Rajk trial an error and a miscarriage of justice? He answered:

That was a mixed grill. Beria and his agents always worked to mix up truth and untruth. This made it difficult to see things clearly. But, [and this is most significant] we wouldn't have such a process today. That is a phase that has been ended. The Peoples' Democracies and the Socialist camp are strong. We have no such trials now despite the millions of dollars the United States spends on saboteurs and spies to all countries.

Rakosi said he was born with the name of Rakosi; it is not a *nom de révolution* like Lenin, Stalin, or Molotov. He was exchanged to the Russians in 1940 for battle flags of the Hungarian revolution of 1848–1849. He added: "It is an irony of history that these same flags were taken again—but by the *Soviet* army—on Austrian territory and for a second time they were delivered to us. Every time we have a national parade these flags are at the head of our columns. And I always find it a highly agreeable sensation to see them there."

BUDAPEST, *March 12, 1956*

LUNCHED with Joszef Szall, head of the information section of the Foreign Office. He told me Rakosi's name at birth was Roth and that he changed it while a university student; it was a "Jewish name." This contrasts interestingly with what Rakosi told me yesterday. Rakosi is married to a Russian who speaks Hungarian and is a ceramic artist. They have no children.

BUCHAREST, *March 14, 1956*

Bob Thayer, U.S. minister, has invited groups to meet me at dinner and cocktails. Invitations are sent to the protocol section of the Foreign Office: Please deliver so many officials for such and such an occasion.

This evening went to the Athenée Palace bar and found one of the prewar bartenders. He complained that nobody leaves tips anymore and that he earns from 350 to 400 lei a month at most. People tell him: "You get a salary. Why should I leave a tip?" He complains that there is no caviar—all exported—except "Manchurian red caviar."

The hotel certainly has a different cast of characters from the past: plenty of bell-bottom trousered Russians, capped east Europeans; Indians, Chinese. Few cars outside—ZIS's, ZIM's, TATRAS. From "Paris of the East" this seems to be becoming "Moscow of the West."

BUCHAREST, *March 17, 1956*

Excellent morning. I started out in search of the Cominform. For some strange reason a great aura of mystery is erected around it. Bogdan, at the Foreign Ministry, told me he didn't know where the headquarters were. When I asked for an appointment with Mitin, its Soviet boss, he said: "I cannot help you. It is an international organization. It is not for our Foreign Office." American and other diplomats didn't know where headquarters were. The Jugoslav says: "After all, you must remember we made a great secret of it when it was in Belgrade. Naturally they won't tell *us* where it is."

I bought the Rumanian language edition of *For a Lasting Peace, For A People's Democracy* and looked up the address of the editorial office—56 Strada Valeriu Braniște. Then I took a legation car there. It turned out to be on a slushy street in an unimpressive quarter. There was a gate. I went in. Just inside was a sentry box with a plainclothes guard, wearing boots, a long ragged peasant coat, and a fur hat. Dozens of children, dressed very Muscovite, were playing in the snow and jabbering in Russian. Two Russian women were on their way out to market, carrying Soviet newspapers and magazines with their shopping bags. I presented my card to the guard, asked him if he spoke Russian. He demanded my *propusk* (pass). I told him I had none, that I was an American newspaperman and that I wished to see Tovarisch Mitin. He seemed surprised but picked up the phone and inquired. More surprise. He kept explaining there was an American. Finally word came over the wire to go to No. 24 Strada Turturelelor, around the corner. I found another gate to the same enclosure, again opened the door and entered. Again a sentry box and plainclothes sentry. Again the same performance: card, telephone, etc.

Talked with various Russian-speaking characters in caps or fur hats. There was a car-park with a few Pobiedas. The enclosure occupies an entire city block. It is surrounded by a wall about six feet high and includes a playground, a netted wire fence, and several arc lights. There are several shabby-looking apartment houses of five or six stories, yellow and slightly dilapidated. Obviously it is not where they print the journal but administrative headquarters and where the Secretariat lives. In one corner was a steel door with a speakeasy peep window painted over with tan paint except for a scraped-out slit through which various people peered at me.

Again I presented my card and demanded in Russian to see Tovarisch Mitin. A fellow in a black golf cap took the card while another, in leather hat and boots, offered a cigarette and started to chat in Russian. Said he didn't work there; just a messenger. I asked if the enclosure across the street was main Cominform headquarters. "Da," said he. Said American cigarettes were "beautiful."

After a while two men emerged and explained they had telephoned and had been instructed to tell me I should apply to see Tovarisch Mitin through the Foreign Office. "Rumanian Foreign Office?" I asked. "Yes," said they. Full circle.

Later, on the phone, I explained all this to the assistant of Mr. Bogdan and again demanded a rendezvous with Mr. Mitin. "Who told you apply to the Foreign Office?" asked Bogdan's aide. "The Cominform headquarters," said I. "But do you know where it is?" "Yes. If you're interested it's at 24 Turturelelor or 56 Valeriu Braniste." "You mean to say you were there?" "Yes," said I.

Went on to King Carol's former palace which is now the National Art Gallery. Regarded with interest a hideous, huge statue of Stalin (in bronze) in the stairwell by Demu Dumitru. (Boy, this will be hard to move out.) Then to the international collection on the top floor, including some magnificent Grecos, Cranachs, Tintorettos. I was standing before my favorite Greco when two young Rumanians struck up a conversation. One turned out to be thirty-three, married, a skilled worker—he showed me the callouses on his hands—who hopes someday to be a writer! The other, a student about twenty-three, hopes to be a poet. They said there aren't many painters now. "A man must paint what he feels—not Socialist realism."

The would-be writer said:

This is an experimental government. And when one experiments one makes mistakes. But this regime is not just imposed. It is something that represents the majority of the people. Look at me. I am a skilled worker. I receive only 800 leis a month. That is not much, because things are expensive. How long does an American worker have to work before he gets a new suit? It takes us two months labor to get

enough to buy one. But I have a bad liver. Last autumn the state
sent me to a sanitorium for a month and cured me. It was almost free.
We know things are cheaper and more plentiful in America. It is a
pleasure to discuss this. It is rare we can ever talk with a foreigner.
We know your country has many freedoms too although there is race
prejudice. You know about freedom because you obtained it when
all of Europe was still authoritarian. But we are working for ours.

We can understand much of what goes on. We can distinguish
truth from propaganda. But you should not be misled by slogans
either. We are for this regime, even with its faults. You can't make an
omelette without breaking eggs. Things will improve. Before the war
the worker had no chance. We don't want that back again. And nobody
—not a single person—wants war for *anything*. Ideology is misleading. We know that in America and also in Russia people want the
same thing: freedom, happiness, shelter, food, something to stimulate
their minds. We don't want to vegetate. As time goes on these things
will evolve.

BUCHAREST, *March 19, 1956*

THE Argentine minister, thinking he is being clever, employs three private
"tails" to follow him and see if he is being watched. My bet: The government pays his tails more than he does for a report.

Yesterday I drove with the Thayers to Sinaia. Stopped in an eighteenth-
century village church to look at the frescoes; a baby was being christened
by a bearded Orthodox priest. As usual, the people in the porch representation of hell seemed to be having a far better time than those on the
other side in heaven; one character was skipping rope with a snake.

Last night went to an exceptionally interesting play called *Citadella
Sfarimata* ("Crushed Citadel"). The "citadel" is the home of a bourgeois
named Grigore Dragomirescu. Starts during the war (1943) and ends in
full revolution (1948). The house changes from a prosperous family
entity to a shambles boarding house: suicides, madness, prison, and
despair.

SOFIA, *March 22, 1956*

SOFIA has grown and improved in the fifteen years since I was last here: a
fine airport; many new buildings, including a horrid party headquarters
skyscraper in Stalinist style and a pillared mausoleum where G. Dimitrov
lies stuffed under glass in a heated room. Outside in the garden is Vasil
Kolarov's tomb. The streets are appallingly empty of traffic; not even
fiacres. I note pairs of policemen with tommy guns strapped to their backs.

Maria Popilieva has been out of work for six years. Her crime: working for *The New York Times*. She spent three years in a concentration

camp under the Nazis and has suffered all over again from the present outfit.

Her brother has become a Communist party member and is practicing law. But Maria will have none of it and for eighteen months has refused to speak to him—despite the fact that they live in the same two rooms with their mother. Maria has no work; they refuse to give her permission to get a job. She earns about 150 levas a month embroidering and is almost starving. "But I'm tough," she says. Goes around in a worn old dress, frayed coat, and shawl about her head; but chin held high.

Three days before she got my cable (but after the security police knew I had a visa) they began to contact her. First a woman agent became very friendly. Last night an official from the Interior Ministry called on Mrs. T., mother of a friend now abroad, and very amiably told her the latter had been forgiven everything and would she please write inviting him back home.

I dined last night with Maria at the former Diplomats' club restaurant. Everyone stared at us, I being the only American in Bulgaria (we have no relations). Apparently the U.S. is still very popular. The taxi Maria took to the airport refused to charge her for one hour's wait when he heard it was for an American.

SOFIA, *March 23, 1956*

LAST night I dined with Maria in a small joint where I used to go for tripe soup after a night out. No more tripe soup now. Three youngsters sat down at our table. They talked timidly but frankly after cautioning me: "Whatever we say is secret." One, the nephew of an Orthodox bishop, asked, "Is it true that there is bad prejudice against Negroes in America?" I said there was but it was getting better. But, said he: "I saw an American ship once and the sailors, black and white, were sitting happily at the same table playing cards."

SOFIA, *March 24, 1956*

THERE is a story of two tram drivers stopping to admire an American car. "Is that a Russian car?" asks one. Says the other: "I know what kind of car it is. But who are you? Can I trust you?"

Russians doing jobs here are paid ten times the equivalent of Bulgarians. They are forbidden to have relations with Bulgarians. They have a restaurant above the diplomatic restaurant to which no Bulgarians are admitted.

A hen was found hanged before the city hall in Plovdiv bearing a placard: "I committed suicide when I found it was impossible to fill my norm."

SOFIA, *March 25, 1956*

BULGARIANS always asked for "Grandfather Ivan from Moscow." Now they've got him. They are interested in the Khrushchev new look. But, says Maria: "We have a proverb—the wolf can shed his skin but not his habits." Should be the bear.

Attended a dinner in my honor at the journalists' club at which the host was Vladimir Topencharov, editor-in-chief of *Otechestven Front* ("Fatherland Front"), brother-in-law of the late Traicho Kostov, and himself once in prison as a Titoist. He is pleasant but spineless. They have broken him. I asked him about Georgi Andreitchin and he solemnly assured me he wasn't in jail but alive and well. (He's dead.) They asked me what I thought of Bulgaria. I said I hadn't seen it since the day, fifteen years ago, when their "German allies" had come in. There were some good things, some bad. Good—medicine, schools, child care. Bad—no freedom and being a satellite.

EN ROUTE TO BELGRADE, *March 26, 1956*

THE Bulgarians have stretched their own Iron Curtain, a barbed-wire fence (as the Jugoslavs sneeringly point out). They search the train for anyone who might escape their heaven—under cushions, behind curtains, under seats—while booted soldiers look under and atop the cars.

BELGRADE, *March 27, 1956*

THIS morning I saw Srdja Prica who is now one of the three vice ministers at the Foreign Ministry. He says: "Stalinism was convenient to the West because it served as a unifying force. But the West should encourage those forces playing in Russia against the return of a dictatorship and isolation of the Soviet Union."

The application of communism in Russia has been a great failure, although the theory was correct. I said that in all Communist countries I had found three prevailing weaknesses: a top-heavy and inefficient bureaucracy; an agricultural crisis; a housing crisis in the cities. These factors were perhaps less evident in Jugoslavia because they had not developed as far and corrective measures had been taken sooner; but even here they existed. Prica did not like these references to Jugoslavia but happily agreed that they were the marks of Soviet inefficiency where, as he said, "After thirty-eight years of revolution they still have queues one hundred meters long waiting to buy the few goods in the shops." This government is convinced that by far the greatest trend toward freedom in the satellites is in Poland. The least is in Albania. It is pretty bad in Bulgaria and Hungary.

BELGRADE, *March 28, 1956*

LUNCH with Gastone Guidotti, Italian ambassador and a close friend. He said Jugoslav policy toward the West right now was based upon the old Pascal formula—speak the truth softly, speak falsehood loudly.

Tito is in the position vis-à-vis Russia of a man who has been pushing very hard against someone holding the door against him. The other fellow suddenly releases his pressure and he (Tito) falls in.

A country, to be independent, must have its ideological, political, and economic defense. Now Jugoslavia's ideological defenses have crumbled. At any rate they are no more a barrier against the East. Likewise, Jugoslavia's political defenses have been weakened by the fall of Stalinism. No one can now be excommunicated in the Marxist church for differing on doctrine and Moscow will no longer *force* its dogma. There is no more Cold War to stimulate defense efforts of free countries, including Jugoslavia. Economically, the Jugoslavs know they almost died by strangulation in 1948. Therefore, they are being very cautious about not aligning themselves again too closely with the Soviet orbit's economy.

The present generation of Serbs is a better generation than that before the war. Before the war the government and the ruling class were imitation Europeans. These people aren't imitation. They are real.

BELGRADE, *March 29, 1956*

DINNER with Sir Frank Roberts, British ambassador. Frank assured me the Jugoslavs are privately very concerned about the possibility that a military dictatorship may take over in Russia.

He considers the Jugoslav Communists as "Anglicans of the Communist world." They maintain that theirs is the true religious line. Nevertheless, as with the Church of England, they adjust their doctrine to suit their own needs. And, he adds, Rome never apologized to Canterbury the way Moscow did to Belgrade.

LONG talk with Dobrivoje Vidić, under secretary of foreign affairs and former ambassador in Moscow. I asked where he thought Russia was heading. He said:

There is pressure for higher living standards which can be achieved only through a long period of peace. Conditions are still bad. People wait in queues and housing remains serious. The new Five Year Plan is very ambitious and its goals can only be realized through peace.

Socialism is not an abstract word. It has a concrete meaning. It should mean a much better life than now exists in the U.S.S.R. And I am convinced that the Soviet leaders are *now* really seeking this better life. Naturally all this has important world implications.

To this must be added the ideological change taking place in Moscow. For twenty-five years there has been a process tending away from true socialism. Now they are reconsidering their position on ideological questions and this makes for renaissance. The new line makes for a practical policy of coexistence. We can *now* be confident that an ideological basis for peaceful coexistence has at last been firmly established in the Soviet Union.

I recalled to Vidić that at previous times in Russian history—both Czarist and revolutionary—there have been tendencies towards liberalization, but these had inevitably been followed by an authoritarian reaction. Did he think the present regime would be able to continue along more liberal lines? He replied: "I am sure that Khrushchev and Bulganin will be able to continue their programs. But, of course, it is very difficult to obliterate Stalinism; it is much easier just to erase the name of the man than to remove traces of the method."

Talk with Veljko Vlahović, chairman of the Foreign Relations Committee of the Socialist Alliance, the main Jugoslav ideologue. I saw him in his office at the Skupština: a six-foot-five-inch Montenegrin with a shock of black hair and dark, slightly Negroid features. He is very lame and walks with a cane as a result of a wound while fighting with the Republican army in the Spanish Civil War.

I asked him to outline for me the differences between Jugoslav Communist and Soviet Communist ideology and practice. He said:

We have tried to base the authority of the state upon individual citizens. We have workers' councils, factory councils, and much discussion at the lowest level. We try to have ideas worked upward from the bottom. Thus, for example, there are many candidates in our elections. The selection comes at the bottom. Any citizen can be a candidate. There is discussion of the choice before he is nominated, although once he is nominated he is generally elected.

All this is done by secret ballot. In Russia a candidate is chosen from the top. Here in Jugoslavia sometimes the candidate of the Communist party is actually not selected by his constituents.

Russia is highly centralized. We are based on local workers' councils. A factory council cannot only change the directors of the factory, but it can also alter the actual program of that factory.

Our conception is that you cannot socialize agriculture by force. We have many cooperatives similar to the Soviet *kholkhoz*, but we also have other forms of cooperatives. We have allowed our peasants to leave cooperatives if they desire. And the small private landowner can remain a private landowner.

Vlahović says 17 percent of Jugoslavia's arable land is socialized now, whereas in 1950, about 25 percent was socialized. In other words, the trend is away from collectivization. In Russia, 100 percent of the land is socialized and the peasant has no choice.

Vlahović said:

Jugoslavia believes the world's economy is moving toward one single economy; not two systems divided into socialism and capitalism. That is artificial. All progress of new techniques is working gradually toward a single economy. The world has become one indivisible entity. There are of course different roads, degrees, and manifestations of progress. But the Russians insist that there are two different systems.

We Jugoslavs have discarded classic deviations between revolutionary and evolutionary socialism. History has erased such a distinction. Life now pushes toward the evolutionary progress. Atomic and electronic developments are favoring this. They are bound to alter all economic structures. I think that even in the United States there is a tendency toward socialism. A big change began with your New Deal and your economy retains many of its features. For example, state intervention in the economy is much larger. Classic capitalism has almost disappeared.

Vlahović claimed there was still a big difference between Jugoslavia and Russia in the field of human relations. He said:

We seek to respect the individual as an individual. There can be no socialism without such respect. We regard Marx and Lenin as thinkers, but the Russians have tended in a Byzantine way to view them as gods. We had a period of dogmatism, but we are liberating ourselves from this. We do not believe that we are now living in the times of Marx. We adjust to the facts and traditions of history.

BELGRADE, *March 30, 1956*

THIS afternoon I had a talk with Ambassador Jimmy Riddleberger. We spoke of the Dulles-Tito talks and the Brioni press statement issued on November 6, 1955. According to Riddleberger:

Tito made no wild asseverations. He argued that changes now occurring in the Soviet Union would inevitably bring about changes in the satellites. There was a logic linking present changes in the Soviet Union with future changes in the satellites. And Tito knows about these things. He is a good Communist, has much experience, and has always been ahead on such occurrences. Tito argued that it was impossible to sit still in the satellites and to act as if nothing had happened inside the Soviet Union.

At lunch today S. told me something about her own experiences. In 1948, she was arrested one December evening, charged with being "a spy for the Anglo-Americans," and kept in solitary confinement for three months. She has not been rearrested since, but she has applied four times for a passport in order to travel abroad and was always refused. Today, to her delight and astonishment she was summoned to the Interior Ministry and told she could have a passport.

During the battle for Belgrade she and her family (her father was still a prisoner of war in Germany) looked out of the window every day as the battle progressed. They were most impressed by the way the German soldiers would get behind their tanks and shave and wash every morning although they knew they were about to die.

For some time they had sixty partisans billeted upon them. They were horrified by their barbarity and uncleanliness. One partisan girl, a Serb, was very friendly. She adored telling how she killed a young Serbian Cetnik with her own hands. She would describe this youth, aged about nineteen; sometimes she took almost half an hour to describe his beautiful blond hair and how he looked almost like a girl; how he got on his knees before her and said: "Sister, please don't kill me." She said: "I told him: 'Of course I will kill you.'" Then she would tell in detail how she tied his hands behind his back with wire and cut his throat very slightly so it took forty-five minutes before he was dead.

S. says she simply cannot understand the savagery displayed by all Jugoslav people—the Serbs, the Croats, and the Macedonians; the partisans, the Cetniks, and the Ustaši; the Orthodox, the Catholics, and the Muslims. Four of her best friends were captured by partisans and cut slowly into very small pieces; another friend of hers saw the bodies.

She admits that Tito's strong hand keeps the lid on all the repressed hatred that still exists below the surface. She and many other Serbs were highly disgruntled that the regime released Archbishop Stepinac (now more or less under house arrest in a Croatian village). "He should have been hanged," she says. "He encouraged the slaughter of Serbs."

Bob Hooker told me Tito has developed the foible of pouring a bit of claret in his champagne. He learned this unconscious snobbism from King Paul of Greece.

BELGRADE, *March 31, 1956*

LAST night I dropped around to see Milan, bartender in the Majestic whom I have known for eighteen years. Over a *šljivovića* he said: "Our government promised us better things. That's all gone. The people have been living for ten years by selling their possessions in order to bring up their children. Now there are no more possessions. Our future is finished."

I asked if things were better now. "Better?" he mused. "Maybe. Four years ago there were spies everywhere and I would not have dared to talk like this, even with nobody but you at the bar. But even today I only talk with old friends."

Dinner this evening with Vlado Dedijer and his wife, Veronica. Vera is learning English and has been invited to England to visit Jenny Lee, Aneurin Bevan's wife, although she does not yet have a passport.

Vlado still believes he gets all his mail without interference. To test censorship he writes letters to himself under various phony names and they always arrive.

He first met Tito in 1938, when Tito came to stay with him in Zemun. At that time Tito's nickname was already "Stari"—the old man. Vlado did not actually join the Communist party until 1939, but he became a secret courier in 1936.

Vlado has five children. He and his family live on 38,000 dinars a month. They order three hundred grams of meat three times a week. They have to cut out almost every luxury. He can no longer afford to go to his favorite soccer games but he and Vera still go to concerts and he insists on the one extravagance of sitting in the same seats they used to occupy three years ago before their disgrace. "When one dies one must die as an aristocrat," he says.

The only real communism in the world, he believes, is the Kibbutzim in Israel and if war comes in the Middle East he intends to volunteer for the Israeli army. Vera nods negatively at this point.

Vlado doesn't want to join any other ideology. He says: "I am just out of one Catholic church and I do not want to join another. I want to be a free lance." He claims that for thirty years Khrushchev licked Stalin's boots and adds: "That explains what is going on here."

He says:

My life is an open book. I do not try to hide my feelings. I look on things objectively. I do not want to make more trouble for my country or my family. I am not an inhuman father. I do not agree with Djilas either. Nevertheless, I owe it to my friends abroad to tell them how I feel about things. I do not hate anyone. I am the historian of this revolution and I want to be objective. Events in the Soviet Union prove that I am right.

I never learned Marx from textbooks. I learned from practice, from our revolution. Everything you take only from dogma is bad. It must be balanced against the good learned from practice. That is Titoism. This philosophy saved me. I claim that ethics cannot be destroyed. Every society has its ethics and they are constant in European society. That is now proved in Russia.

The peasants of Jugoslavia are terribly dissatisfied. For example, dogs are taxed 600 dinars each. So they are killing their dogs. Maybe collectivization is good in the Vojvodina where the land is rich, but even there people are dissatisfied. Everything is taxed—fruit trees, vineyards. The peasants complain that it is no longer worthwhile raising sheep. They do not even bother to bring to the market the cheese not needed by their individual families.

Moša Pijade recently stopped off in Zurich on his way to Paris with his bodyguard. The bodyguard admired the rich shops of Zurich. Pijade told him: "Wait awhile. They will be communized. Then they will be empty."

Marx is good in analyzing the first stage of socialism and capitalism, but he was unable to go further. There is no pure system of either capitalism or socialism, only elements of both; the new and the old order mixed up together. In 1953, Kardelj told him there was more socialism in the United States than in the Soviet Union.

Vlado says:

I am not like Djilas who, as a Montenegrin, says that everything is black. I am a good European. I am objective toward everything, including myself. In my own case Tito violated the constitution of the party.

Djilas is like a volcano. He is rich in ideas but weak in practice. Djilas once said to me: "If I had a chance I would say to the masses I am going to be a demagogue." This proves to me that Djilas is no politician. I am the happiest man in the world about events in Russia. I do not want to take any political action. My face has been saved by what is going on in Moscow. I cannot hate anyone. Perhaps this is the result of my early Christian education. I fought, starved, and died with these people. I cannot be proclaimed a spy. I cannot recant.

This has been an excellent experience for me. I was lazy and arrogant. I did not even know the price of bread. When I went to ride in a bus for the first time after my disgrace I entered by the wrong door. I found my bureaucratic life was quite different from that of the ordinary man. This has been a marvelous and true lesson. I was a stupid lug. That is life. The last time I had ever studied socialism was in high school. Then the revolution came along. Now, for the first time, I have plenty of time to learn. It is a very good experience. Furthermore, it is wonderful for my children. They were little bureaucrats. Branko used to go to the door and shout "Where is the car?" Now they know the value of money. Now they take part in our family council discussing accounts. I am the finance minister. I cannot go to football games anymore. I am much more criticized as a finance minister than poor Rab Butler ever was in England.

When all this started my children had no clothes, no shirts. I have had to put them on a different spending level. No more big luxuries. I cannot even buy books. But I still go to concerts. I like Schumann, Schubert, and Mendelssohn. The German romantics in music were a reaction to the political sterility of Napoleon.

Vlado says he is the only Central Committee member who got into trouble and refused to recant. "If you have to eat dirt once in your life you will have to say it is good forever."

BELGRADE, *April 1, 1956*

VLADO told me a joke now circulating. A priest in Croatia remonstrated with a peasant who was no longer showing up at church. He called on him and noticed four pictures clustered in an ikon corner. "Why?" asked the priest, noticing that they were Stalin, Eisenhower, Lollobrigida, and Tito. "They are my ikons." "And do you pray to them?" "Of course. To the first I say: 'My father who art in heaven.' To the second I say: 'Give us each day our daily bread.' To the third I say: 'Lead us not into temptation.' And to the fourth I say: 'Forgive us our trespasses as we forgive those who trespass against us.' "

PARIS, *April 11, 1956*

PAMELA Churchill has just been down visiting her ex-father-in-law on the Riviera. He has been staying with a publisher named Reeves and Reeves's friend Mrs. Russell. This setup has horrified all the snobs on the Riviera who would like to be able to show off the old man themselves.

Churchill has been happy for the first time since he left Downing Street. The Reeves have treated him with simple affection and as a member of the family. Mrs. Russell chatters away about clothes and flowers to his delight. In the evenings they sit around and listen to music. Churchill asked Pam: "My dear girl, did you ever hear of Mozart?" He loves to puff on his cigar after dinner and order Mrs. Russell to put on the record that goes "da-de da-da" and she recognizes the tune he wants.

PARIS, *April 14, 1956*

BILL Deakin came for drinks on his way back to Oxford from southern France. While on the Riviera he lunched with Churchill. The old man varies between great alertness and a soporific state. At lunch, where some French were present, the discussion veered to Nehru. Suddenly the old man's eyes lit up and he said: "*Il est sans peur; il est sans haine.*" A profound observation!

PARIS, *April 21, 1956*

LAST night at dinner Pug Ismay said NATO is going through another period of reorganization. He was extremely disappointed at the way Al

Gruenther's resignation was announced. It had had very bad repercussions throughout NATO, which is not too strong now. One of the German reactions was that Gruenther had disagreed with the present NATO defense plan and quit. This isn't true, but it doesn't help to have the story get around.

Al had assured Ismay his resignation was caused neither by political ambitions nor health. He told Ismay he was a bit scared when he was ill recently and realized that if he died he would leave Grace stone broke. He wants to earn some money while he still has some earning ability.

Ismay said he, himself, drew a pension of only 300 pounds a year as a result of the many years' service he did in the army, several of them as a four-star general. And his pension is larger than average because of his service in India, a hardship post. "That's precisely half of what I pay my butler every year."

Melas, new Greek ambassador to NATO, was ambassador in Cairo before coming here. Upon paying his farewell call on his Soviet colleague he mentioned Greece's population problem and the need to seek areas for emigration. The Russian said: "What kind of a population problem do you think that is? In China there are fifteen million more people born each year than die. That is a population problem." Melas concludes that Russia is very concerned about the continual growth of a huge Chinese state on its borders. He wondered if it was not possible that in ten years or so Russia might be seeking alliance with the West against China.

PARIS, *April 24, 1956*

LUNCHED today with Ales Bebler, the Jugoslav ambassador. Bebler thought Khrushchev had promised Tito to dissolve the Cominform during his Belgrade visit in the spring of 1955, when they had their long intimate talk riding to Brioni.

I told Bebler I suspected the Russians were trying to revive the scheme to federate Bulgaria and Jugoslavia in order to win Tito back. He denied this and said that Jugoslavia wouldn't play.

Stalin originally opposed the scheme but in 1947 suddenly changed his mind. He invited Dimitrov and Tito to Moscow to discuss it. Already relations between Moscow and Belgrade were cooling and the Russians had withdrawn their technical missions from Jugoslavia. Therefore Tito decided not to go and argued he was not a mere puppet to be summoned at Stalin's will. Instead he sent Kardelj, Bakarić, and Djilas. Stalin was irked. Nevertheless he told the Jugoslavs and Bulgarians he was now in favor of federation. His previous line had been that such federation could only take place with Bulgaria being an equal partner to all six of the Jugoslav republics as a lump. He knew the Jugoslavs wouldn't accept, so this was tantamount to a veto. But now he told

Kardelj he not only approved federation on any terms—which meant Bulgaria would be a seventh Jugoslav republic—but that he could go ahead and "announce it tomorrow." He demanded an immediate reply from Kardelj. Kardelj said this was too important and he first had to go back to Belgrade and report.

Meanwhile, Bakarić in a casual conversation discovered that the Bulgarians (presumably at Soviet suggestion) had brought with them a proposed list of members for the first cabinet of the new federated state. They were willing to grant the Prime Ministry and defense to the Jugoslavs, but they held out for their own candidates for internal security and economic affairs. The Jugoslavs interpreted this as a trick to put the police under a Bulgarian agent of the NKVD, and, eventually, to gobble up the country for Stalin. They refused. Shortly afterward the split between Moscow and Belgrade developed.

ROCQUENCOURT, *May 3, 1956*

THIS afternoon I went out to see Al Gruenther. I had heard that he had been asked, as a senior Catholic officer, for his opinion prior to the bombing of the abbey of Monte Cassino in 1944, when he was chief of staff to Mark Clark's Fifth Army. Was it true that he had concurred? He said it had never been put up to him this way. As a matter of fact, at the time he did not think the abbey should have been bombed. But he was thinking of it purely from a military point of view. The question was whether the Allies had all the evidence concerning the use of the abbey by the Germans. But he is not, and was not, at all critical of those who made the decision. The fellow doing the attacking, Freyberg, the New Zealander who then commanded a corps, felt he had to eliminate the troops he thought he had identified in and around the abbey. He came in with a very good case and the decision was finally agreed upon.

I then told Al there was another thing I'd been meaning to ask him. In the spring of 1952, he sent me a confidential advance copy of Eisenhower's report for his first year as NATO commander. He asked me to go through this carefully and bring it out later that afternoon when I was going to play bridge and dine with Eisenhower and Gruenther. He wanted me to mark it up and make any changes I thought advisable. One basic change I made was to strike out the word "communism" wherever I found it and change that to terms such as "Soviet imperialism" or "Russian danger," when referring to the menace that NATO was preparing to protect against. When I came out that evening, I argued that it was not correct to use the word "communism"; that we were not fighting an ideology but a system that was taking over countries for imperial purposes. We had a friendly working relationship with Tito, yet he was a Communist. Gruenther and Eisenhower both agreed. Yet, when the report was made public two months later, it had been changed back and "communism" appeared in every place where I had stricken it out. I asked Gruenther why. He replied that he had agreed with my analysis and, "I have stuck a good deal to such phrases as 'Soviet imperialism' in the speeches I have been making." He forgot what actually caused the change at the time.

I then asked what was the real significance of the decision to move back United States supply bases from Europe to America as had been announced a few days ago. This had a bad repercussion because it came just after it was announced that Norstad, an air general, was taking over the command from Gruenther, a ground general. Many people had the feeling that perhaps this was the beginning of a serious change in American strategy; that we were gradually going to pull back to the United States and rely upon a fortress-America type of defense. Gruenther denied this vigorously: "We are trying to lighten the supply load wherever possible. It is not true that this is merely a preparation to make it easier to disengage our troops from Europe."

I then turned to NATO itself. The zeal that had existed at the time of the Lisbon meeting in 1952, when there was talk of building up to ninety-six NATO divisions, had now ebbed. What was there that we could do to keep this spirit alive and to keep NATO a viable force as the threat subsided? Gruenther replied:

> If you continue to have a letdown in the atmosphere, you cannot build up an adequate defensive force. Our philosophy is that this is a challenge. We must find different methods to explain the problem. The danger is not gone yet, even if the fear complex has subsided. But indifference is fatal and that is what we are trying to fight. And just to say that the United States has a deterrent ability won't keep this alliance together. It won't keep a cold-war front going.
>
> We are trying to work out a forward strategy—right up to the Iron Curtain. Politically, this is all-important. You cannot defend Germany from behind. You have to defend it from right there. Certainly the Germans are not going to let us stay in their country if we decide to base our defenses on a Rhine River line. A Rhine strategy, of course, means the abandonment of Germany.
>
> We used to have the concept of using troops supported by weapons. Now it is a case of weapons being supported by troops. Tactical atomic weapons make the difference. I am not talking about hydrogen weapons which are so destructive that they do not affect tactical purposes. But these atomic tactical weapons must be supported by ground forces. Twelve divisions is a major factor in the necessary minimum required. The Germans say that twelve German divisions doesn't mean anything as compared with the 175 divisions the Russians have; it simply doesn't match that. The difference, of course, is in the use of tactical atomic weapons. Germans have said to me they have a hope of abolishing the use of atomic weapons. I say you can't solve this problem merely by eliminating one type of weapon.

We cannot match the Russians in conventional weapons and conventional power. The only thing to do is to make war impossible, not to abolish one category of weapons. Also, I often point out that we may conceivably reduce our living standards by trying to keep a defensive force in being, but we will reduce these living standards much more by trying to match the Russians in conventional weapons than by keeping a force going that relies upon tactical atomic weapons. Such a force is a much smaller necessary force.

Gruenther said that an old Greek alliance (I believe he was referring to Athens's Delian league) was the only precedent he could discover for this kind of organization. I observed that that had been highly unsuccessful in the end, with everyone resenting the way Athens was beating its allies for more contributions and money.

I asked if it was not obviously true that the earth satellites we plan to launch in 1957 or 1958 would really achieve the purposes of Eisenhower's "open-sky" inspection plan to prevent surprise attack. In other words, they would be able to transmit photographs down from their aerial inspection as they wheel round and round the earth.

He said of course; but the question was:

Can you send a satellite over a country without the permission of that country? These satellites have photographic value. They will be very important in a big way. But, for example, can you send them over Russia even if they are three hundred miles up in the air unless you have Russia's permission? This is a difficult point and will have to be straightened out at the beginning.

PARIS, *May 4, 1956*

THIS morning Reuven Shiloah, former head of Israeli intelligence, stopped in to see me on his way from Washington to Jerusalem. He said Bulganin and Khrushchev told the British they would be prepared to prevent further shipments of arms by the Soviet bloc to the Middle East if the western powers also ceased. What they meant was that the Baghdad Pact should be abandoned.

Shiloah doubts if the United States will ever help Egypt build the High Aswan Dam despite the World Bank agreement. We have told Nasser we will help as soon as he makes an accord with the Sudan on power and water sharing, but there is no sign of that.

Three weeks ago Dulles told Abba Eban, Israeli ambassador in Washington, the United States had decided Nasser was no longer qualified to receive "preferential treatment" from us. Shiloah concludes we are prepared to write off Nasser, but there is still a lot of opposition to this in the State Department as well as air force and navy circles particularly interested in oil.

Shiloah says American policy is to encourage other countries, particularly Canada and France, to sell arms to Israel. But Ottawa and Paris, although friendly to Israel, don't want to stick their necks out. They would like the United States to participate. The U.S. argument is that in the interest of the West we must retain a free hand and provoke neither the Arabs nor the Russians.

PARIS, *May 6, 1956*

THIS afternoon saw Dulles. He admitted there was a tendency among some NATO members to estimate the Russian danger as having decreased more than the United States thinks it is safe to assume.

Dulles thought the French had dealt with the North African situation in a statesmanlike way. They showed a sound point of view in giving independence to Tunisia and Morocco. They are trying to use force to reestablish order in Algeria, not to impose their will but in order to make it possible to arrange a permanent settlement.

The Tripartite Declaration of 1950 on Palestine was always subject to our prior obligations to the UN. The primary responsibility of maintaining peace in that area is under the Security Council. If UN processes break down we would see what we could do. As a result, it was less likely that there would have to be action in the Middle East outside of the UN.

Dulles recalled: "I have said for a long time that the Soviet Union is overextended." What he means is that they have a highly expensive thermonuclear program which they are using in trying to catch up and get ahead of us. At the same time, they are trying to enlarge their capital plant and industrial investment. They have a bad agricultural situation. They need more people for their factories and farms. They have a heavy aid bill to China and other countries. They would like to improve their own standard of living.

The West has been weakened by its own internal squabbles. Its manpower, morale, and economy have all been weakened. The fact that three NATO members are at odds over Cyprus shows the possibility of European powers falling apart among themselves.

If you really want to create unity in the Atlantic community you need a great deal more than intermittent meetings of ministers. Shall we turn the present NATO council into something else or create a new body? Is there a real desire for such a unity?

This would presumably, but not necessarily, be a body within NATO. It would have to sit all the time. Its representatives would have to be almost as high in rank and authority as foreign ministers. The NATO permanent council has never discussed such things as North Africa, the Middle East, or Cyprus. If you exclude problems like that from discussion you are heading for trouble.

BLACK-MARKETING

KHRUSHCHEV

PARIS, *May 7, 1956*

L UNCH TODAY WITH STANISLAW GAJEWSKI, POLISH AMBASSADOR. The famous Khrushchev de-Stalinization speech has been issued as a text and widely printed, distributed to all top Communist officials. It has been labeled "for party use only." Gajewski has a copy in his safe but regrets he cannot let me have it.

However, eighty thousand copies were printed in Polish in Warsaw, distributed to party leaders, and read before local conclaves. It is about fifty pages long and takes two hours to read. "Because this was done in Poland," he says, "a lot of black market copies were run off." The eighty thousand original copies were all numbered and therefore could not find their way into the black market without risk to the man who resold them. But, being Poles, the printers ran off several thousand extra unnumbered copies for the black market. The original price per copy was 500 zlotys (125 dollars). But so many copies found their way to the black market that the price has fallen to 300 zlotys.

Khrushchev said Stalin prepared his military strategy from a school-room globe of the world; that Stalin contended Zhukov founded his strategy by sniffing a handful of earth, deciding whether or not to start an offensive from the smell. Gajewski added: "We know this is obviously not true. Why does Khrushchev say these things?"

Khrushchev reported that something like 80 percent of the Bolshevik Central Committee in 1934 was shot by Stalin. Several of the old Bolsheviks wrote letters to Beria and Stalin an hour or two before their deaths, expressing confidence that if Stalin only knew about these injustices he would save them. These letters were found among Stalin's papers. He had ignored them. Stalin told Khrushchev he had but to move his little finger and he could destroy Tito. Khrushchev added that he was unable to move his little finger.

Gajewski told me he had heard of my troubles in Warsaw and was embarrassed and shocked. "They couldn't expect you to write Marxist propaganda," he said. "I thought your columns were, on the whole, positive."

He had nothing but sneers for Czechoslovakia. The Polish press was being barred from Czechoslovakia because the Czechs say it is so outspoken it is "counterrevolutionary." The Czechs haven't got "the guts to fight anyone." He was in Prague in May, 1945, and can testify to the fact that it was General Vlasov's renegade Russian army that liberated Prague. There was one house on Prague's main square, the Vaclavski Namešti, damaged by fire and the Czechs didn't repair it for years but treasured it as a souvenir of their wartime strife.

PARIS, *May 10, 1956*

LUNCH today with Walter Lippmann. He thinks NATO must inevitably shrink to the size of its original conception—the real Atlantic community of France, Benelux, Britain, Canada, and the United States. One by one the other countries will lapse back to their Scandinavian or Mediterranean obligations. He believes Germany will eventually be neutralized and that we are still maintaining decisions of September, 1950, when, during the Korean war, there was a crash agreement to rearm West Germany.

It is always useful to think back to the original impulses from which policies develop—in this case, the Atlantic community. Recently he saw Livy Merchand who, says Walter, admitted that if the West Germans want to negotiate themselves out of NATO into a neutralization settlement with Russia we would have no objection, although we cannot say so. It was shocking that we had supplied Italy with an American regimental combat team from Austria as a plate-glass window to insure that Italy would defend itself.

Walter was struck by the new thinking in England on how to defend Europe during the atomic age. Macmillan wants to abolish fighter command because he says it is impossible to build planes fast enough to intercept modern attack weapons. (Macmillan was the man who abolished antiaircraft artillery while he was minister of defense.) Macmillan also wants to abolish naval mine-sweeping detachments on the assumption that in a modern war nobody will drop mines—they will use hydrogen bombs instead.

Walter believes the only excuse for our present policy of not selling arms directly to Israel but encouraging France and Canada to do so is that Russia does not openly sell arms to the Arabs but does it through Czechoslovakia. In other words, France and Canada are our Czechoslovakia.

LAST night the Norstads and the Schuylers came to dinner. Larry says the British have always been far ahead of us in modernizing their defense planning. The whole concept of massive retaliation was evolved in a paper drawn up by several British officers, including Marshal of the Royal Air Force Sir John Slessor.

THIS morning I spent an hour and a half with Pug Ismay. He looks fine although age is gradually catching up; he will be seventy next year. Politically he was pretty gloomy. NATO simply must prepare to face the consequences of its own policy. It remains an alliance. But the Cold War has been shifted to an economic and political front by the Russians and NATO has yet to adjust and cannot stay static. It must move into the nonmilitary fields. But economic affairs are already being handled by other organizations, such as the OEEC and the Coal and Steel Community.

Ismay remains convinced that Russia has changed its tactics but not its strategy. He points out that Khrushchev still says quite openly that he wants world domination for communism. He refuses any disarmament inspection scheme. Nothing exists to prevent the Russians from suddenly switching back to Stalinist tactics. There are no democratic controls in the form of a free press or a parliament.

Ismay admits that it is hard to keep up enthusiasm when you are on the defensive. But NATO *must only* remain on the defensive. There is no offensive plan in Gruenther's files. We absolutely must have an "open-skies" and "open-minds" policy. We must exchange ideas and capture the minds of men.

Ismay says one of the military tasks of the Allies is to build up their forces in relationship to somebody else's forces, in this case Russia's. Between 1925 and 1930, Britain had no visible enemies. Consequently, the Royal Air Force took the French as theoretical opponent, the navy took Japan, and the army built its plan on the assumption of fighting a war against Russia in the Middle East. The result was chaos.

THIS morning long talk with Larry Norstad.

I reminded Larry that during the war, when I used to argue things out with him, he was the only American general I ever encountered who thought we should invade eastern Europe. He alone believed that the purpose of winning a war was to win the peace. He said:

I caught hell on that. I even caught hell from the boss, Ike. I remember that the Russians were pushing into east Europe. We were planning to make the Normandy landing. I felt that if we moved across the Ljubljana Gap into the Vienna-Budapest Plain we would have a hold on part of the Balkans. I wanted to include Austria and Hungary particularly.

I thought that was more important militarily than a landing in southern France. I had to justify this as militarily sound and prove that it would lead to a military success. At one time—and here I believe I was unsound and wrong—I thought of moving into the Balkans even at the expense of the Normandy invasion, but never to the exclusion of it. I thought also that this would put us in a better position vis-à-vis the Russians. I thought we could push up from the Budapest-Vienna Plain to the Baltic Sea across East Germany and western Poland.

But the United States was strongly opposed in principle to this. Our chiefs of staff were against it. I expressed the view personally to General Hap Arnold and also to Harry Hopkins. I argued with Hopkins on this for four hours in 1943 in the war room at La Marsa in Tunisia. Hopkins seemed impressed and said he would take it up with Roosevelt. Of course, I was wrong to do this because I wasn't going through the proper channels. I pushed this idea in late 1943. But when the decisions were basically made I lost real interest. I revived interest in 1944, prior to Anvil (the southern France invasion). But after that was decided upon I agreed and did nothing more.

Larry admitted that no alliance had ever ended in success. They all ultimately ended in failure. But some of them served their purpose for a very considerable time and very successfully. That is all that could be hoped of NATO. Nothing is permanent.

Larry thought the United States would gain much more than Russia would from earth satellites. The Russians already know where most of our installations are. We have much more to learn by photographing them. He added:

New weapons and means of delivery will make the problem of defense somewhat easier. But to carry out our objective of defending Europe—and this we must do—it will always require some conventional forces on the ground. The numbers have already been greatly reduced from what would have been the case without these new weapons. We now talk of about one-third the ground strength that was fixed in the Lisbon goals (ninety-six divisions) for the same purpose.

If you leave a substantial part of the Iron Curtain line undefended this will tend to create a vacuum. That might invite the Russians to occupy this vacuum by cooking up a fake problem as an excuse for a "temporary" occupation. The Russians could assure us they meant to get out later and make it difficult for us to decide whether or not to go to war. We cannot leave any such vacuum. That would increase the dangers of a war. Every part of our line must be defended. We must face the Russians with the problem of killing someone in order to take territory.

I asked what would happen to NATO if Germany decided to use its membership in the alliance as a negotiable asset in making a deal with Russia and agreed with Moscow to quit NATO in exchange for unification. Larry replied:

> If Bonn negotiates out of the alliance for a neutral Germany, a substantial part of the basis of NATO would be pulled out. NATO would not necessarily be destroyed. But its foundation would be vastly shifted. It would depend largely upon the reaction of other countries to such a step by Germany. NATO politically and militarily is directed towards including West Germany—the area right up to the Iron Curtain. If you remove that area then it would be time for a policy and strategy reappraisal.

PARIS, *May 21, 1956*

I PLAYED golf today with the Dillons and then lunched with them at the Talleyrand's. Douglas was in a very talkative mood. He was horrified at what Dulles said fifteen days ago about the lack of knowledge of our NATO embassy concerning American policy. Dulles simply doesn't know what he is talking about. He doesn't know what is going on in the State Department because cables just don't reach him.

Just before Doug was named ambassador to France, Dulles told him that Acheson had two great faults: He didn't know how to present foreign policy from the State Department to the American people; and he didn't know how to run the State Department. Dillon says Dulles was right to a considerable degree on the first point; but he is entirely wrong on the second. Our foreign service is in worse shape now than it ever was under Acheson. Nobody reads telegrams unless they are drastically violent and few people have the guts to stand up and fight for what is necessary. Dillon says he does and Clare Luce occasionally does, but the rest of our envoys take everything lying down.

He is distressed by the way everything is being frozen back home until after the election. Dillon has been negotiating with the Poles and Hungarians about reestablishing diplomatic relations with Sofia. He was specifically ordered by cable to advise them that we could make no further moves until after the elections. He thinks this is ridiculous and embarrassing. What kind of a Bulgarian vote is there in America?

Likewise, we refused to allow any changes in the China trade situation or to revise the list of embargoed goods until after the elections, despite Eisenhower's personal promise to ease the embargo for our allies.

The result is that Britain and France and other countries are going ahead on their own, ignoring the restrictions and some of our Congressmen are raising hell with the allies, making a bad situation worse.

Douglas took me out in the Talleyrand garden and told me the embassy had just received a very hot telegram of complaint about me. It was addressed to all our eastern European missions, with copies to Paris and Radio Free Europe in Munich. (This should destroy the last illusion that Radio Free Europe is a purely private business.) The telegram quoted at length from my column attacking American propaganda's lack of success. It asked our envoys to explain in detail to the State Depart ment how I got such a woeful impression just on the eve of the budget debate for USIA. It said this column would hurt chances of a large appropriation. Dillon said he hoped our envoys would have the guts to use this as an excuse to come back and tell the Department that our propaganda does stink and why.

PARIS, *May 30, 1956*

LAST night, dinner and a long talk with Dillon. Doug says all the answers to the State Department's sharp cable on United States propaganda and my column have been repeated back to Paris—except from Thayer in Bucharest and Riddleberger in Belgrade. He wonders if the latter were so sharp that Washington was embarrassed to send repeats?

The other cables were weasel-worded; they all said they hadn't the foggiest idea how I got such an impression of propaganda; certainly not from them. They defended the Voice of America but criticized Radio Free Europe. Warsaw admitted the movies they got stank—but blamed the army, not USIA.

Dillon also told me some thirty European Jews in Oujda (Morocco) were kidnapped by terrorists. They had the word Juif tattooed across the belly plus a star of David, and were told their guts would be cut out if they didn't pay a large ransom. They did. The French are helpless and anarchy is spreading. But Paris is minimizing this in order not to divert attention from the Algerian mess.

PARIS, *May 31, 1956*

THIS afternoon, I spent an hour with General de Gaulle at his headquarters at 5, rue de Solférino. I asked how he thought the Algerian question could be settled, given the existing circumstances, not what might have been done earlier. He explained that first of all he was in no position to say how it could be settled because he had nothing to do with the government. Nevertheless, I asked what his own personal views were. He said: "We can't have peace very quickly between the Arab world and the West. . . . Everybody is having difficulty with the Arabs."*

De Gaulle said that the Russians were working very hard with the Arabs now and winning.†

I asked de Gaulle how he thought we should face up to the "new look" policy of Moscow today. He said: "France has no policy at the moment. For America—the situation created by the Russians when they took over Eastern Europe was different."‡

I asked what he thought of Poujade and Poujadism. He said: "That is not serious. There are many discontented people. But they do not represent a power. You cannot make a France with a Poujade." Then he continued: "But the other parties are no more serious than the Poujadists. You cannot make a France with them either."

I asked him about Mendès-France. I recalled to him that the newspapers had been speculating about a new relationship between him and Mendès, a respect for Mendès on the part of de Gaulle. He sneered:

> The newspapers always lie. Mendès-France has quality and value. He *had* influence in a part of the country, but it is gone now. He is no longer in the position he once was in. Maybe he will find an influence again. Maybe he will get it back. I do not know.

I remarked that I found him particularly pessimistic today. He said: "The present is pessimistic. I live in the present, not in the future. Who knows what the future will bring. If someone drops an atom bomb, that will change all."

I asked how he foresaw the future. He said:

> For the next two or three years there will be coexistence. But it will not be sincere. There will be exchanges of visits, of ballets, of football teams, and sporting groups. During that time the Russians will continue to develop economically and to progress. And they will progress further in the Arab world. But I think they will have psychological difficulties and also political difficulties with the slave peoples—Poland, Czechoslovakia, Rumania, Hungary, and the Baltic peoples. Maybe even in the Ukraine and Caucasus.§
>
> The Germans won't do much. They have already remade their life. But they have remade neither their power nor their ambitions. And Britain is no longer very vital. This is also unfortunately the case for France.
>
> Europe is confused and sad. It will stay like that for some time. And what will come of this? I don't know. But surely something. I must repeat, it will not be gay for the next few years.

* See de Gaulle's further comments, pp. 69, 74–75.
† See de Gaulle's further comments, pp. 40, 59.
‡ See de Gaulle's further comments, pp. 30, 48.
§ See de Gaulle's further comments, p. 52.

De Gaulle impressed me more than ever by his arrogance, his obstinacy, his conceit, and his bitterness. Nevertheless, he surely does retain a certain quality. I don't know what it is apart from the fact that he has a strange magnetic appeal and he writes the best French of any living Frenchman. It is a sad experience to talk with him these days, but nevertheless it remains an experience.

PARIS, *June 2, 1956*

LUNCHED today at the Polish embassy; just Gajewski, his wife, Marina, and myself. A fantastic lunch, preceded by a brief tour of the embassy which is surely one of the loveliest in Paris. Then a session with caviar, smoked salmon, plus excellent Polish vodka, port, and so on. Then, for the four of us, the following menu: fresh brook trout baked in almonds; roast duck with baked cherries; asparagus mousseline; platter of first-class cheeses; strawberry ice-cream dessert of complex mixtures of ices and whipped cream plus cookies; wild strawberries and cherries; plus a good Riesling; a 1934 Chateau Haut Brion; Dom Pérignon champagne served from a magnum. Then coffee and liqueurs in the garden. Some spread for four; and Communists at that.

What was the purpose? As far as I can figure out it was to say no on the proposed Polish trip Gajewski had urged on me. He said today it would be difficult to see Gomulka (an appointment I had insisted on). Next, said he, it would be impossible before July. (He knew in advance and I repeated today that it had to be before July as I had another trip all arranged.) He said: "I know why you want to see Marshal Rokossovski; you want to ask him if he's a Russian. I can assure you he's a Pole."

He talked at length about the ferment in Poland. "We're through with lies," he said. He said Gomulka was no Titoist. Gomulka had taken his stand in 1946 and 1947 before the Cominform. Gomulka wanted free sectors in both agriculture and industry: state, cooperative, and private; and he opposed collectivization. Also, he was anti-Soviet. Gajewski says Gomulka is now out but still having a big argument with the party on "ideological questions."

Gajewski, incidentally, said Beria was arrested and executed at "five minutes to midnight; he had all his plans laid to round up and kill the members of the Politburo; their personal guards were all Beria men." Gajewski also insisted the only remaining case of the "cult of personality" was in the instance of Tito. I asked how about Mao Tse-tung? "That's different," he said.

PARIS, *June 5, 1956*

A STATE Department analysis concludes Tito is very anxious to keep NATO strong. He is trying to maintain a world in which there is a balance of power so that a small country can maneuver. Nevertheless, he insists publicly that there has been a basic change in Russia. He thinks there will never again be a reversion to Stalinist-type of dictatorship. He says the present change has been brought about by public pressure within Russia. However there is still a Stalinist minority in Russia—many, many people who were brought up in a Stalinist frame of mind and who are still a visible political force. If we don't extend our hand and meet Khrushchev halfway, this Stalinist minority may become more powerful.

This spring, Stalin's *Short Course History of the Communist Party of the Soviet Union* disappeared from Soviet bookstores. Stalin's biography also cannot be found. Both books apparently have been recalled from officers' training schools and are no longer considered valid for candidate officers in the Soviet armed forces. Likewise, school curricula have been revised. The teaching of the history of World War II has been suspended until new texts are issued.

On April 24, when Khrushchev saw Stassen in London, he told him that Eisenhower's "open-skies" plan had only been proposed because the United States "wanted to know everything." Khrushchev thought this a kind of "mania of greatness." He warned Stassen that the United States should cease treating Russia as a rich man treats a pauper. Several times Khrushchev asked Stassen what would be the reaction if the Soviet Union reduced its armed forces by approximately a million men and correspondingly reduced the armaments of the U.S.S.R.

The Russians have now disclosed that Voznesensky, Kuznetsov, and their colleagues were executed in 1949 by Stalin on the charge of trying to set up a separate party organization for the Russian Soviet Federal Socialist Republic with its headquarters at Leningrad instead of Moscow. In other words, they were charged with separatism.

The Chinese Communist Politburo formally accused Stalin in a report of failing to prepare the Soviet Union for World War II in a military sense and also for following an erroneous course vis-à-vis Tito. The latter charge seems particularly important because Tito has always been trying to drum up a Titoist movement in China.

PARIS, *June 9, 1956*

LAST night I attended a really extraordinary dinner party at Pamela Churchill's. Present were: Pam, who is nice, beautiful, and kind; Louise de Vilmorin, whose books are a servant girl's dream of high society, and who talks like a character from them; Prince Guido Colonna, pleasant, intelligent but innocent; Bill Patten, a combination of a Henry James diplomat and a Vilmorin diplomat and not quite sure which he wants to be; and our house guest, Vera Dedijer, a Communist, who was able to talk with Colonna easily because she learned Italian in a Fascist jail.

Louise posed decoratively by the fireplace and made a long speech about how she wanted to enjoy her death. Guido earnestly assured Louise the greatest living French writers were Louise de Vilmorin and Francoise Sagan. I bit my lip to keep from adding: "How about Minou Drouet?" Poor Vera. I'm afraid all her doubts about communism were shattered last night.

PARIS, *June 14, 1956*

LUNCH with General Navarre, who was responsible for the idiotic plans that produced Dien Bien Phu and the final disaster of Indochina. Navarre, a highly unimpressive little man, tended to blame everything on the press. He complained that once there was a very important meeting between the French and the Vietnamese, including Bao Dai. Only eight people were present. A half-hour after it broke up the two leading French correspondents in Saigon had long but completely false and inflammatory dispatches on the wire. I told him that while I do not approve of phony dispatches, I thought it shocking that the government didn't have the courage to apply efficient military censorship when there was a war on. He answered that you had to have a strong government to take such measures; unfortunately France didn't have one.

PARIS, *June 18, 1956*

YEHUDI Menuhin and his wife, Diana, came for lunch. A nice, thoughtful fellow, he has been on an extensive concert tour, including Vienna, Israel, Greece, Jugoslavia, and Hungary. He feels he can be very useful as a "propaganda ambassador." He figures that our impact should be and can be greater in the satellites whereas it won't make much difference in Russia itself. He was invited to go to Russia this year but insisted on getting his usual concert fees—payable in dollars—about $2,500 a concert. He argued that Oistrakh got similar fees when he went to the United States. He was not anxious to give an impression to the Russians that he is so eager to go there that he is ready to reduce his regular fees.

PARIS, *June 23, 1956*

LAST night Kit Steel told me an amusing story about Churchill. At a Washington dinner during Churchill's visit, President Truman made a speech. He said he was confident the decision to use the atom bomb against Japan was sound. This saved many lives by reducing potential casualties and when he got before the bar of heaven he was certain his views would be sustained. One genial officer present inquired: "What makes you think you will reach the bar of heaven?" Churchill here interjected: "Surely the Almighty must observe the principles of English common law and consider a man innocent until proven guilty."

I READ a summary which French Ambassador Dejean sent in a telegram to the Quai d'Orsay of a conversation French Socialist visitors had with Khrushchev, Mikoyan, Shepilov, and Suslov. Khrushchev admitted that agriculture was the big problem. He was seeking to stimulate production by encouraging private initiative and the development of private family plots attached to the *kolkhozes*. (This is in exact contradiction to what Khrushchev is saying publicly. Publicly, Khrushchev is trying to squash the private plots.)

Khrushchev said he had had no responsibility for the *agrogorod* scheme—the famous agricultural towns which he had publicly advocated in the early 1950s. He complained to the Socialists that this scheme had been wrongly attributed to him. (This is an absolute lie although it confirms Khrushchev's attempts to pin it on Malenkov.) Khrushchev even went so far as to confide that the *agrogorod* plan was a "phony" idea.

Shepilov was possibly the most interesting of the Russian leaders. He explained why only one party could exist in the U.S.S.R. He claimed that there was an absence of "antagonistic classes" in the Soviet Union. Then he added: "If one wished to organize a party different from ours, one would not find anyone to join it. The right of an individual to express a different opinion from that of the government is necessary in a bourgeois state because the people and the government there are opposing forces." But, he hastened to add, such is not the case in the U.S.S.R., where the government is a government "of the people."

Shepilov continued that it would be impossible to have a situation in the U.S.S.R. where an opinion is held that is *not* that of the government. He said: "It is not permitted for each Soviet citizen to be a Communist. Each citizen can have any opinion provided he does not express it and does not combat the governmental authority."

Khrushchev condoned this strange view, adding, that it would be useless to form an opposition in the U.S.S.R. He asked: "Do you wish that we should form a second party now? My children would say to me: 'Papa, have you lost your mind?'"

He continued: "There are no more classes in the U.S.S.R. Our society is monolithic. To create an opposition would be to put a flea beneath the shirt. One does not need that to fight bureaucracy. It is sufficient to stimulate self-criticism within the Communist party."

At this point, Mikoyan joined in. He said that as a youth he had wanted to be a priest but had not succeeded. The Communist party was atheistic but respected the religious sentiments of the population.

Khrushchev interrupted. He said: "Some Communists don't believe in God at party meetings, but they do believe in God at home."

The Soviet leaders insisted there was no anti-Semitism in the U.S.S.R. They described anti-Semitism as a capitalist survival. Mikoyan said that there were various kinds of nationalism still left in fragments. For example, there is still some nationalism "in Armenia, my own country." It was impossible in thirty years to extirpate all the remnants of capitalism.

The leadership explained that Jews do not have their own cultural institutions in the U.S.S.R. because they have been assimilated into the rest of the population. They contended, for example, that there were insufficient pupils for a Jewish school. The young Jews wished to study in Russian. Shepilov said the Jewish theatre had been closed because it fell under disrepair and it cost the state too much to fix it up. Mikoyan added that the famous "doctors' plot" had nothing to do with anti-Semitism; it was just another of Beria's nefarious schemes.

PARIS, *July 2, 1956*

THIS afternoon Czapski and Giedroc of the Polish emigré publication *Kultura* came to see me. They had a good deal of information on Khrushchev's visit to Warsaw last spring for the funeral of Bierut. Khrushchev showed himself to be an open anti-Semite. He was heard to remark that a second-rate Kowalski (a typically Polish name) is more useful than a first-rate Rosenblum (a typically Jewish name).

Khrushchev told the Polish leaders that Stalin had ordered him to prepare concentration camps for all Jews in the Soviet Union. He admitted he had set about this task. However, when Voroshilov heard about this he turned in his party card. Shortly after that, Stalin suffered his attack and died.

Czapski made the interesting observation that the Poznan uprising last week was the first *workers'* revolt in Poland since 1905. The Warsaw Communist regime blames the factory managers, the West Germans, and American propaganda. But it really was a workers' protest.

LONDON, *July 5, 1956*

EXCELLENT talk this morning with Hugh Gaitskell who now (succeeding Attlee) heads the Labour party. Gaitskell is fifty, an old-school-tie type, an exceedingly fluent talker (often compared with Adlai Stevenson), and quite impressive.

He said:

I don't think much of the idea of developing NATO into an economic organization. After all, OEEC and other bodies cover that. The more sterilized from politics such aid can be, the better. If aid were given through NATO it would make recipient countries more suspicious than ever.

The trouble with NATO is that member governments fail to act in concert with sufficient regularity or cooperation. Look at the extraordinary failure to give a concerted reaction to the Soviet announcements of cuts in military manpower. There were three separate reactions in the United States: one from Eisenhower, one from Dulles, and one from Stassen. And there was a fourth simultaneously over here from Eden. The alliance should have made up its mind to say nothing until agreement had first been reached.

The NATO allies don't seem able to get together quickly. After all, of fifteen NATO nations, only four or five count. There must be some kind of steering committee by which the leading powers can get together. It is ludicrous that the West can't pull together because it can't choose its own leading powers.

It has been obvious for a year that the change in the technical situation because of nuclear weapons has been bound to change our defensive policy. There is a tremendous need for reappraisal of our strategic and diplomatic policy. We have never had such a reappraisal. Why hasn't it happened? No one gives any instructions. There should have been an intensive effort on these lines long ago. But there are insufficient contacts. Part of the fault lies in the personalities involved. Dulles is well intentioned, but he doesn't see the need to push things through. And I must admit we had much more impressive Americans in Europe from 1949–1952 than is now the case. Take Harriman for example.

I then asked him how he saw the future of the Commonwealth. He replied:

Our Commonwealth ties are important. For example, I don't think this country within the foreseeable future is likely to become a part of a federal Europe. We have strong ties and we are militarily bound up with Europe. But we have two other sets of ties—with the Commonwealth and with the United States. And don't forget there is a fear here that if the United States is ever satisfied that it has a United States of Europe, it will clear out.

The Commonwealth is a queer organization. It is not a military alliance. Yet, if a member should be attacked we would find it hard not to assist her. Although this is a one-way, not a two-way feeling in certain instances. Nevertheless, my guess is that if a war came India would cease to be neutral.

Despite its vagueness, the Commonwealth is a bond that is perhaps stronger than Europe. Don't forget the serious problem of language differences in Europe. And the various political systems are often quite different from ours. This should not be underestimated.

I asked him what he thought of Khrushchev. He said:

Khrushchev is not a mediocrity. But he doesn't behave like a strong man. He talks too much but without the magnetism, for example, of a Hitler. He talks off the cuff and too rashly. He is not an intellectual; Malenkov is. Khrushchev has a chip on his shoulder. Most people who met them disliked Khrushchev and liked Malenkov. I didn't feel that Khrushchev was another Stalin. They're watching him well. I didn't feel that Malenkov was frightened. Khrushchev doesn't seem like the big, powerful chief to succeed Stalin.

This afternoon I had a good talk on the terrace of the House of Commons, overlooking the Thames, with Aneurin Bevan. He was exceptionally courteous and spoke well. His ideas seemed a curious compendium of sense and nonsense—expressed with deep conviction.

He is furious with Tito and claims Tito "betrayed" Djilas. Tito gave Djilas approval to go ahead and write the articles published in *Borba* for which Djilas was later disgraced. "My wife and I heard Tito give his OK with our own ears," says Bevan. "Tito double-crossed Djilas." Bevan says Kardelj and Djilas were always personal enemies and this represented a triumph of Kardelj, "a methodical, cool, level-headed German [he was born in Slovenia] over Djilas, a poetic, moody, courageous Montenegrin poet."

Bevan thinks Titoism and Tito will now become increasingly unimportant in and to the world as a result of Tito's Moscow visit. He says:

As long as Tito was being courted actively by both sides he did well. He will continue to try and retain an equilibrium and to get help from both sides, but now his bargaining power is lessening.

What is happening is too bad. Jugoslavia was the one country in the Communist world that promised to be the most progressive and unconventional. But Jugoslavia is now petrified. The argument between Djilas and the old guard is the argument as to whether the system should evolve and adapt itself further. And now this has been settled—against Djilas. The system has been decided upon—a system of economic decentralization and political centralization. That cannot work. As a result, Titoism has become a dated phrase. It is rot to talk of the satellites adopting Titoism. The only thing left in Titoism for them to adopt is an increasing independence from the Soviet bloc.

I asked what Bevan thought of Khrushchev. He described him as:

A forceful extrovert, but I don't know if he has the capacity for deep reflection. He is the product of a very grim period. I doubt if he can estimate the distant results of his present policy. I think that Malenkov is a much abler, deeper, more brilliant man. He seems the man of the future.

The moves by Khrushchev to develop friendship with Jugoslavia have extinguished all significance of Titoism in the Communist world. Tito would have been much more influential had Russia remained hostile. Now, unless Tito can produce big changes in his own country he will have nothing further to contribute to the Communist theory or practice.

I recalled to Bevan that in 1951, he was advocating an immediate big-power negotiation with Russia, starting out with a program to share world raw materials, including petroleum, and also including control of international waterways. How did he feel about this now? He replied:

It is even more urgent now. There should be an agreement by everyone to reduce the armaments program. A percentage of the budget, saved by this cut, should be paid into an international pool through the United Nations for the economic aid of underdeveloped countries. They don't want to receive economic aid dished out only to buttress military alliances. That system has produced resentment in much of the world. Even the White House admits today that neutrality is not a mortal offense. And now the Soviet Union is doing the same kind of thing; it uses its increased material power in the same way as the United States—except the Russians are asking for neutrality and not alliance. To use economic aid as a weapon, even in the Cold War, is a mistake. The Baghdad Pact is a perfect instance of this. Moscow retaliates by selling arms to Egypt.

I have never believed that the NATO type organization is a very effective answer to fears of Soviet aggressiveness. We have been talking for five years of the need for twelve West German divisions which we don't yet have. The West hasn't gotten stronger. On the contrary, the only change has favored the Soviets; they got the hydrogen bomb. Thus, the only shift in military balance is in favor of Russia.

We have a perfect right to have NATO in order to balance the Soviet mass. But it cannot claim success in the prevention of war because the Russians never intended a military offensive. The Russians were afraid. And because they were afraid they were rigid. The slackening of their aggressive attitude is not due to western strength. The Russians, on the contrary, have become stronger. Therefore they feel more self-confident.

I asked Bevan to reply to a hypothetical question: Were he named Prime Minister tomorrow, would he seek to withdraw Britain from NATO; or what? He answered:

I would seek to bring about a mutual security pact in Europe, including both Russia and the United States. Likewise, in Asia, I would want a similar pact including India, China, Japan, and the United States. So long as nations are excluded from such pacts, schisms are perpetuated. Pacts should be inclusive, not exclusive.

What would he, as Prime Minister, do—taking the Middle Eastern situation as it *is* today? He said:

First we must accept the fact that we cannot obtain oil by armies. It can be obtained only by commerce. Commercially, the position of the Arab world and the West is complementary. They have to sell their oil. And oil won't flow up the mountains. It flows down to the Mediterranean. Thus, the prosperity of the Middle East depends upon the West. We cannot defend our oil requirements by force. We saw this in Abadan. We will see it again.

Once this is seen and acted upon, much of the bitterness in the Middle East will recede. But this should be accompanied by a firm statement—in which the Soviet Union joins—that Israel is here to stay and that the Arabs must learn to live with it.

LONDON, *July 6, 1956*

INTERESTING and lengthy lunch with Randolph Churchill and Julian Amery. I was surprised by two things: the extreme degree of their contempt for Eden (who was referred to only as "the Jerk"); and the passion of Julian's dislike for America.

The only reason Makarios was expelled from Cyprus, they said, was as a "show of force" after the Jordanians fired Glubb Pasha. An odd show of force! That weekend, Julian, Randolph, and Rab Butler were together. Butler and the Cabinet weren't especially concerned about Glubb and weren't planning much reaction. Randolph, according to Julian, got so furious that he almost hit Butler who finally agreed to ask for an immediate Cabinet meeting—which bounced Makarios.

Randolph says if Macmillan and Butler got together they could dump Eden. But they won't—party loyalty. He says Eden, Macmillan, Butler, and Salisbury forced old Winston Churchill to resign and give Eden a chance. Churchill is still resentful. But he had picked Eden as his successor back in 1940 and stuck by him.

Randolph says his father is grumpy, lonely, and can't relax. He is used to power and misses it. He misses his morning dispatch boxes. Macmillan, as foreign minister, used to send him some cables. Even then Churchill didn't enjoy reading them when he couldn't act on them. Now Lloyd doesn't even send him any. Churchill resents depending on the newspapers. He is getting deafer and refuses to wear his hearing aid. When Barney Baruch visited him, Baruch gave him a new and better hearing aid which Churchill wore while Baruch was there; he tore it off afterward.

It's untrue his father has become fond of music. "We're all totally tone-deaf." Says the old man occasionally plays some loud Gilbert and Sullivan records. He potters about and paints a bit, works at his book. But he sulks a good deal of the time. Can't follow many conversations because of his deafness. Lady Churchill, on the contrary, is happy as a lark. Randolph says she spent her whole life looking after the old man, being financially careful in line with her Scottish antecedents. Now she is carefree and spends money without a thought.

Julian is savagely bitter about Cyprus. He blames America for pushing England out of Persia, the Sudan, and Egypt; and now trying to push her out of Cyprus. He claims we double-crossed the French in Indochina and he said *The Quiet American* is an accurate tract as well as a good book. He thinks Washington is far more hostile to Britain than Moscow and fears eventually, after we've stripped Britain, we are going to make a bilateral deal with the Russians over Britain's head.

If Britain is kicked out of Cyprus, he wants Britain to pull out of NATO and he, Amery, will retire from politics.

Randolph, curiously, seems quite calm and sensible compared to Julian. He complains that because Britain submitted a Cyprus scheme to Turkey which the Turks turned down, "Nobody runs the Foreign Office here any more. It isn't the Jerk. It isn't Lloyd. It's that shit Menderes."

Julian speaks admiringly of the Turks. "They're like us," he says, "slow to become indignant but hard to stop when they are." Amery is perfectly ready to see Greece quit NATO and become neutral rather than yield an inch on Cyprus. "If they do that," he said, "it would show they weren't worth having anyway." He has considerable importance as leader of the "Young Turk" Tory rebels in Parliament and as Macmillan's son-in-law.

LONDON, *July 7, 1956*

ADAM Watson came for a drink. He is now running the African section of the Foreign Office. He said there seems to be a sort of informal pimping arrangement between Nasser and the Russians. Nasser is allowed to lock up the Communists in Egypt and beat the hell out of them as long as he encourages other Arab leaders to go to Moscow and to do as the Kremlin desires.

Adam fears Nasser is going to get a large loan when he goes to Moscow this summer. And it won't have any strings attached to it like our own. He can use it for his High Dam or to buy weapons.

LONDON, *July 8, 1956*

SPENT the weekend in the country with Randolph Churchill. He has bought a house at East Bergholt on the border of Suffolk and Essex in the Constable country. He is working hard at becoming a country gentleman, studying up on flowers and trees, thinking seriously of growing peonies on a commercial basis. He is also working on a life of Lord Derby: perfect training for the book he regards as his life work—a biography of his father. He won't start until the old man has died. But he wants to prepare himself in the technique. Since he writes well and actually can work hard, and furthermore, since he knows how to organize himself in terms of help and secretaries, I think he'll be able to do the job splendidly.

Randolph told me his father bought Chartwell when Randolph was eleven years old. One day his father drove him and one of his sisters to the country and took them around the property. At that time the house was in very bad condition and the grounds were decrepit and overgrown. But, having been brought up in the city, they loved romping around. On the way back that afternoon the old man said to the children: "Well, how would you feel if I bought that place?" They both chimed in they would love it. He then confided to them he had actually purchased it the day before but had not yet informed their mother.

Randolph said Winston made some profits out of his book, *The World Crisis*, which helped him to buy Chartwell. As a matter of fact, at one time he was thinking of calling the estate "The World Crisis" instead of Chartwell.

LONDON, *July 9, 1956*

LONG talk with Foreign Secretary Selwyn Lloyd. He is a pretty routine sort of a fellow.

The first thing I asked was his impression of Khrushchev and Bulganin. He replied:

Bulganin could be the Prime Minister of any country. He struck me as a rather typical politician. I could see him as the Prime Minister of France, Italy, or a Scandinavian country perhaps. He is neither better nor worse than the average of those. Khrushchev I could see as a militant trade-union leader. Or, perhaps, a tough party boss. But Malenkov has more personal charm. He certainly seems more intelligent. In a hierarchical sense, certainly Malenkov is not less qualified to be a leader.

Was there any difference now between the American and the British approach on Russia and how to handle the "new look?" He said:

We must be very careful in conducting ourselves at this phase so as not to cause a new freeze-up and strengthen the eastern bloc as a separate entity. If you condemn every approach they make and say there is no change, there is a danger of congealing things again. We should encourage these new tendencies toward liberalism.

Perhaps this election you are about to have in the United States is holding back the American viewpoint. Certainly it is hard to conduct foreign policy during an election. But there is undoubtedly a difference in emphasis. You are more negative.

Of course I can understand the political reasons for this. The United States gets its defense money by being tough. We get our defense budgets passed by leaning over backward to show that we are being reasonable. We each have a different approach to our Parliaments.

I asked what was going on between Egypt and Russia. He said:

Nasser is pretty deep in with the Russians. But he believes he can avoid coming under their control. I wonder if that will be possible. Certainly the Russians now regard Egypt as within their sphere of influence. It is rather ironic that Nasser, who has been striving so hard to get out of spheres of influence, should now be falling into a new one.

We convinced Bulganin and Khrushchev of the potential dangers of the Middle East. We pointed out to them that any war in the Middle East could not be limited. We tried to convince them that the Middle East is a highly inflammable area. We think, therefore, that the Russians want to avoid war and will damp things down. They have been careful not to come out too definitely against Israel. Of course they will go on trying to help the Arabs—if it can be done at small cost to themselves.

CHURCHILL ON

"OUR ARISTOCRATIC

HERITAGE"

LONDON, *July 10, 1956*

TODAY I HAD A FASCINATING, WONDERFUL, AND MOVING EXPERIence. I spent five hours with old Winston Churchill down in the country at his home, Chartwell, in Kent. I had lunch alone with him, Lady Churchill, and a young man from the Foreign Office named Anthony Montague Browne. Montague Browne has been loaned to him to keep him in touch with foreign affairs. He shows him cables and keeps him generally advised so he will understand the reasons for government decisions; this is under the guise of Churchill being a Privy Councillor. (It is partly for humanitarian, generous purposes of keeping him in touch; and partly so he won't bring the government down by some speech objecting to a policy he doesn't understand.)

After lunch Lady Churchill slipped off and for three hours, I was either alone with the old man or young Montague Browne was with us as we sat and smoked and talked, as Churchill read from one of his books, or as we wandered around the estate while he admired his cattle, his gardens, and fed his huge, fat goldfish. (He is most proud of a little pond of twenty-five-year-old golden carp.) The greatest impression made on me was of his infinite courtesy and gentleness. He was generous in his references to every figure we discussed—save Hitler. He insisted on rising and tottering off to escort his wife downstairs. He lifted his wine glass in a little private toast to Lady Churchill across the table. And, as we were wandering back to the house after our little stroll, he saw a tiny dead bird. He pointed at it with his stick, very sadly, tears in his eyes, muttering.

Chartwell is a large, rambling brick house situated on the edge of a fine valley in Kent. Churchill, staring out through the mists of this overcast day, kept murmuring about what a pity it was I couldn't see the wonderful view—"the whole weald of Kent." I said that today with the mist it looked as if the sea were only a mile away. "Thank God not that," said Churchill. "Our island is small enough as it is." Above the house was flying Churchill's private flag as Warden of the Cinque Ports. When I arrived (greeted by the young diplomat) I noticed rows of paintings in the hall. Churchill pointed one out later (some Pierrots) which had been painted by Royal Marine prisoners of war during World War I and given to him. On the table in the hallway were small bronze statues of some of his racehorses. I went into the living room, Lady Churchill joined us, and we chatted over sherry (she took tomato juice).

Then the old man came in. He was dressed in his "siren suit"—sort of a battle dress cut of dark blue flannel with a narrow gray pinstripe. It has a zipper down the front. He wore black shoes with zippers and a silk, nineteenth-century French artist's shirt with long (about eight inches) pointed collar tabs sticking out over his siren suit like a dressed-up schoolboy. He looked like a comfortable old teddy bear, above all after lunch when he'd been puffing away at his cigar and ashes had trickled down his front.

He was very torpid at first: couldn't follow the conversation; wasn't using his hearing aid; didn't seem to understand anything. His wife would repeat things and almost translate them to him, but he sat slumped in an armchair, uninterested, confused, gazing sullenly out of his rheumy, bloodshot eyes while Lady Churchill tried to carry on a gay conversation, only dealing him in when he seemed to resent being left out in the cold. Clearly he was hungry and only interested in lunch.

We then went to lunch, the old man (despite his temper and his hunger) politely seeing me through the door first. He mounted the one flight to the dining room in his tiny, exceedingly slow elevator which Lord Beaverbrook gave him. We walked up the fine oaken stairway with rough wood steps. The hall outside the dining room is lined with Churchill's paintings, mostly Mediterranean scenes and some quite good.

We ate shirred eggs, then tournedos and potatoes with a green vegetable, then some sort of a flan; a white Rhine wine, then port (with a Stilton cheese), and then brandy with our coffee. He took three glasses of wine, two of port, two of brandy (in huge, balloon goblets which really give one an overpowering bouquet), and two cups of coffee. Finally the cigars (his immense black ones) were passed. He seemed astonished when I refused. By the time he was into his cigar, with the wines and brandy and coffee circulating about his system, he began to revive. But until then the conversational going was hard. He seemed half-asleep, staring a bit greedily, looking like a great, pink, hungry baby, far more interested in the food (and such things as where was the mustard) than the conversation.

The rest of us chatted about Chiang Kai-shek, Russia, Tito, the Middle East, and only occasionally he would butt in with a question; the answer would be explained to him, repeated, then he would subside back into his chair. Lady Churchill clearly has a nice catty view of Mme. Chiang Kai-shek (which I strongly endorse). She asked me if Madame was still so beautiful. I replied that the evil was now more visible in her face than the beauty. This delighted her. She said she couldn't abide her. Mrs. Roosevelt had told her that when Madame was staying in New York once, she and Mrs. FDR had returned to Mme. Chiang's hotel rooms and found the two FBI agents outside the door fast asleep. Next day Madame asked Mrs. FDR what had become of the agents. Mrs. Roosevelt said she assumed they'd been reprimanded. Madame said: "In China it would have been this" (drawing her hand across her throat). "Rather rude to her hostess, don't you think?" inquired Lady Churchill. Lady Churchill said her husband hadn't met Mme. Chiang until the Cairo conference. Once before, when he was in Washington seeing FDR, the President said to him: "I want you to meet Mme. Chiang; she's a beautiful woman." So FDR called her up to invite her for lunch the next day with Churchill. Mme. Chiang refused unless Churchill first called upon her. Lady Churchill also observed that although she dressed Chinese fashion she had her gowns and jewels designed in the West by the best firms. (Every now and then Sir Winston would mumble into the conversation: "Formosa? What's that? Where's that? Ah, yes. I see" . . . with a lisp.)

Lady Churchill asked me if I thought Eisenhower would run again and I said certainly yes. She asked if I was pleased. I said that I admired Eisenhower and was a friend of his, but I was very worried about his health and the possibility that Nixon might have to succeed him.

After Lady Churchill departed, we sat down in the sitting room again, he plonked himself into an armchair, ashes over the front of his siren suit, and suddenly, slowly came alive; not just the shreds of a great character and the impeccable courtesy of his personality, but the old flame and wisdom began to emerge.

He put on his tortoise-shell spectacles, called for the sixth volume of his memoirs, read several pages to me with commentary, made sage and often profound observations on the world abroad and English politics, puffing contentedly and pondering for more than an hour. (I shall list some of his observations afterward.) Then he suggested we go for a stroll. He crammed a battered old gray homburg on his head (I noticed his light tan sombrero on the hatshelf), refused a coat (later he gladly accepted one brought to him), grabbed one of his many walking sticks from a stand, and off we set. He tottered out in energetic but unsteady fashion and I feared for him. A man appeared who seemed to be either a guard or male nurse. But nobody offered the old man aid and off we went, down pretty steep slopes, up again, down uneven rock steps (he explained he had the rock brought from Wales and put in to set off the fish ponds), across steppingstones through a pond, through a field of high grass, up other slopes, through the rose garden, into the Marlborough pavillion ("I built this; my nephew Jack Churchill painted the charming frieze of the Battle of Blenheim and the Duke, the Duchess, Prince Eugene, and Queen Anne, in the four corners"), through a box hedge to the croquet ground, up some more steps (here he tired, sat down on a brick wall, and we rested), and then back into the house where we sat in the hall and talked about his American ancestors and racehorses.

He is astonishingly pink. His hands are quite delicate and not terribly large or strong; nor are they as aged in appearance as one would expect. His eyes are bloodshot but kind. His vision is good; a bit far-sighted but he can read anything (with glasses). During our stroll, he spotted in the distance and pointed out to me his black swans on a pond and a calf born last week. He is proud of his black and white cattle: "They don't need anything. They look after themselves. We don't have to bring them in, even during the winter. They don't need any help in calving—only a bull." He is devoted to his two ponds of fish; assured me they weren't goldfish but golden carp (*Orfes*). (I think all goldfish are carp.) He tapped on the edge of the pools when we arrived and his nurse or detective reached down for cans of food sitting there and the old man flung great gobs of it to the fish who ate merrily while he watched them in proud silence.

Back at the house, while we were sitting there alone in the hall, his daughter Mary (young and pretty, who lives nearby) came popping in the door, gave him a buss on the head (now almost bald, with thin strands of snow white hair), popped off again after agreeing to come for dinner with someone helping him on his book. He has finished Volume II of the *History of the English-Speaking Peoples* (it comes out in November) and is determined to do Volumes III and IV. He doesn't have much new work on them (mainly editing and cutting), but he is including an entire new section on the Renaissance in Volume II. Churchill told me that he was both surprised and delighted by the enormous sales of his book in the United States. The first volume has been a best-seller for weeks.

He wanted me to sign his visitor's book. Then, before I could even find out where it was, he forgot, rambled off on something else. You could see age and fatigue gripping him again. He got up to say farewell to me; gravely stood at the door, shook my hand, said "au revoir, au revoir" several times, waved to me, and was still standing at the open door when the car drove out of sight.

By far the most interesting part of the day and that which endured

longest was when Churchill entered into a discussion of the present-day
state of the world and what it might have been had his advice been heeded.
He asked Montague Browne to bring him Volume VI of *The Second World
War* and then he read to me from Chapter XXXVI (pp. 522–527) commenting as he went along, looking up over his spectacles ruefully. In the
end he maintained sadly that had his advice been followed, both peace and
western civilization would now be less menaced. He read to me at great
length and in a strong voice. His basic thesis was that we went to Potsdam with a bad hand of cards; that the meeting should have been held
earlier while we were at our full military strength in Europe; and that
we should not have agreed to reduce that strength without adequate and
compensating concessions from the Russians. From page 522:

> The main reason why I had been anxious to hasten the date of the
> meeting was of course the impending retirement of the American army
> from the line which it had gained in the fighting to the zone pre-
> scribed in the occupation agreement. The story of the agreement about
> the zones and the arguments for and against changing them are re-
> corded in an earlier chapter [Ch. XXX]. I feared that any day a de-
> cision might be taken in Washington to yield up this enormous area—
> 400 miles long and 120 at its greatest depth. It contained many mil-
> lions of Germans and Czechs. Its abandonment would place a
> broader gulf of territory between us and Poland, and practically end
> our power to influence her fate. [Regarding me sadly, he remarked:
> "We went to war over Poland, you know."]
>
> June 4, I cabled to the President these words, which few would
> now dispute:
>
> "Prime Minister to President Truman   4 June 45
>
> "I am sure you understand the reason why I am anxious for an
> earlier date, say the 3rd or 4th [of July]. I view with profound mis-
> givings the retreat of the American Army to our line of occupation
> in the central sector, thus bringing Soviet power into the heart of
> Western Europe and the descent of an iron curtain between us and
> everything to the eastward." [Here Churchill said: "That was the first
> time the phrase 'Iron Curtain' was ever used."]
>
> On June 12 the President replied to my message of June 4. [Here
> Churchill observed: "I am not yet at liberty to make public the text
> of Mr. Truman's message. That is his paper, you know."]

Churchill admires Truman a lot. But Truman knew nothing when he
first came in—although he learned fast. It was a tragedy that he had the
initial ignorant period. It was then we lost eastern Europe. Ike never
understood or made any recommendations. We should have taken Berlin
and Prague (where the United States had two armored divisions stranded
for days just three days' march away).

Following are some other topics Churchill discussed.

America should be temperate and wise about taking time to solve its

Negro problem. "After all, you can't take twenty million of them into your belly just like that. Nonsense to say the black is the same as the white." He called for a copy of this morning's *Daily Sketch* with a picture of a Negro Salvation Army singer followed by a white Salvation Army lass. "Is that what they are going to have in Heaven?" he asked. "Is that what I am going to find there? If so, it is no place for me. I don't intend to go to a place like that."

There is, said he, no serious anti-American feeling here. People like young Amery are "bloody fools." Our destiny is together. "I'm half-American, you know. You people pushed us out of Egypt. It was a mistake. But I harbor no resentment."

Undoubtedly in a decade or two China and Russia will be at odds. But he doesn't think China will be a tremendous power ever: It's never shown the capacity to develop so.

It is a profound mistake to back the Arabs against Israel. Turkey, Iraq, and Israel should be backstopped. Nasser is nothing. He is working with the Russians.

Woodrow Wilson was largely responsible for the crazy development of self-determination which is parcelling up the world. What about the Russian empire and colonies, the satellites and Baltic states? But the Baltic states are finished; they have been under Russia too long; too many hundreds of thousands of Balts have been deported or slain.

Churchill accepted getting out of Egypt (as a result of our pressure). But he never agreed on Sudanese independence; thinks it a bad thing. "Why should they have the same vote in the United Nations as us?"

He thought Nehru was not up to much good. India chose to go its own way. "Nehru has never done anything good for us." He is sure Nehru would never help England in another war; and might even be induced to join the Communist bloc against the West, through Russian and Chinese pressure.

The Commonwealth will get worse, not better. No point taking in all these Blacks like the Gold Coast. They will go their own way. And in another generation the Indians will be even more Indian.

He thinks Stalin was a great man; above all compared to Khrushchev and Bulganin.

Stalin never broke his word to me. We agreed on the Balkans. I said he could have Rumania and Bulgaria; he said we could have Greece (of course, only in our sphere, you know). He signed a slip of paper. And he never broke his word. We saved Greece that way. When we went in in 1944 Stalin didn't interfere. You Americans didn't help, you know.

How about the Civil War, I asked? Didn't Stalin double-cross him? No, that was local Communists.

He thought Khrushchev and Bulganin agreeable. He sat next to

Khrushchev at dinner one night and he was very pleasant. But not a great man; not like Stalin. Khrushchev and Bulganin had done their cause "measureless harm" by denigrating Stalin. They would never recover. It was an immense mistake. They could not maintain communism with liberty. And it would be much harder for them to return to dictatorship because they had proven it wrong. (Bulganin told Churchill he had urged Khrushchev to make his anti-Stalin speech.) The Russians were now faced with the necessity of becoming really European, having a European policy. Inevitably that would lead to the satellites slipping gradually away.

He thought the Poznan revolt in Poland significant. But he didn't think anything of the 1953 East German revolt. (Of course, he was in power then and could do nothing; I suppose that's why he downgrades it.)

He thinks Tito is a big man; tough, intelligent, able.

The French were up against a great crisis. They were now showing more vigor and courage. But the challenge of Algeria would be their supreme test. As for himself, he thought the French should go ahead and reconquer Morocco and Tunisia.

He thought Dulles was "quite right, quite right" to declare Goa a Portuguese province and stand against Nehru.

He spoke at length about the virtues of "our aristocratic" heritage in English leadership. He was proud of Parliament as "the oldest and most important" organ of representative government in the world—"and the most powerful." He thought it shocking that MPs are not paid more. Then and there he decided he would speak Thursday (in three days) favoring an increase to 1,500 pounds a year in MPs' salary. "The House must face these facts courageously. There is nothing to be ashamed of. What does an American Senator receive? Ah, you see." (Then he decided ruefully he would not make the speech after all; didn't want to embarrass Eden.)

Spain? "I was with Franco, you know, when he started his revolt; not physically with him, but supported him. But when he accepted German and Italian help, that was different. Step by step I changed my policy. But Franco has given Spain two decades of stability."

He thinks the basis for policy now should be firm agreement among the U.S.A., Britain, and West Germany. If the French want to come in, all right. Also the Lowlands, or Scandinavia, or Italy, anyone else. But that is the heart of it.

Adenauer "Is a fine man. But the Germans are turning against him. He's the best they'll ever get." Maybe the Germans will turn sour again; who knows?

He asked me about Selwyn Lloyd's view on Cyprus. I told him. "Nonsense," said he, "that's no policy." But he wouldn't elaborate.

He is very proud of his few racehorses. "My grandfather, you know, founded Jerome Park in America." One horse won a good race; now has a bad fetlock; but he hopes to run him next month in a pretty rich German race.

He recalls his family association with *The New York Times*. "When the Irish [I suppose he means the Tweed ring] threatened my grandfather, he set up guns in the office and told them to come ahead; they didn't dare."

In summation, the thing that struck me most perhaps was the thought of talking all day with this kindly old man who had seen the last Dervish charge against Kitchener in Omdurman and had fought with the Spaniards against the Cuban insurrectionaries.

My final impression was an extraordinary experience of seeing him come fully alive and then, tired out by the effort, by the walk, our long reading from his work, the conversation, the entire physical and mental effort, to see all that dynamism fade away. It was like watching a very strong light bulb during an electrical crisis: First a faint reddening of the filament, then a flickering, then a glow, and then a brilliant blaze of light. Finally, after being blinded by the sustained glare, again flickering, subsiding, just a red filament; then nothing.

LONDON, *July 11, 1956*

PLEASANT talk with Lord Attlee in the House of Lords. The house was very agitated, winding up a two-day debate on whether or not hanging should continue in England. Attlee said that he had mixed feelings on the subject.

Our conversation was devoted to other things. He started off by saying he thought there was a considerable revolt behind the Iron Curtain against the economic crisis which has existed there since 1917. There was a desire for a fuller life in the Soviet Union and this is now being seen within the Communist leadership itself. It was significant that they had had to make friends with Tito, who had been anathema. There is trouble in the satellites. Above all, this is true with the Poles who, as usual, jumped the gun.

He thought the present situation developing in Russia and the satellites makes for greater hopes of avoiding another war. Now there is a big new bourgeoisie developing in Russia. These people have quite a lot to lose by any change in the system. They aren't going to jeopardize things or their situation in an atomic age.

I asked what his own feeling was concerning Khrushchev and Bulganin. He replied:

We thought Malenkov was a bigger man. Khrushchev is noisy and speaks a lot. Bulganin is more cautious. One thing that strikes me is that the Communists have always thought of the Kremlin as a Vatican. What the Pope said went. But Pope Stalin is gone. Today, in their own right, Mao Tse-tung and Tito are bigger figures in the Communist world than anybody in Russia.

I asked if he himself—and he had talked with Stalin many times at Potsdam—thought that Stalin was a great man. He replied, somewhat to my surprise (Attlee is small and mousey), "Stalin was not a big man. I saw him often and he did not impress me. Of course, he had control of his show, but he was not a man of any great foresight. He was a successful dictator but not a world statesman."

However, Attlee added hastily: "Khrushchev and Bulganin were on a much lower scale than Stalin. Stalin had the talents of an oriental despot. He had what is necessary to make a man dominate. But he had no grandeur of personality."

I asked Attlee what he thought about the current impression of anti-Americanism one received in England. He said:

Our general view is that Americans are a bit brash in their international relations. There is a certain lack of understanding for the feelings of people with a rather long tradition in both Europe and Asia like ourselves. There is in America perhaps a tendency to think too much in material terms and to give the impression that because you have great economic power you would exercise it no matter what other people's feelings were. Some of us are a little apprehensive that perhaps the United States, having kept out of the international field for so many years, may try and throw its weight about too much now that it has come in. We get a bit impatient with John Foster Dulles, you know.

NEW YORK, *July 27, 1956*

LUNCH with Averell Harriman. He is in the city for a few hours and up to the ears in the political campaign. When I was taken up to his sitting room, he was seated at the telephone in shirt sleeves, having a long talk with Jonathan Bingham. They were discussing whether to put out some press statement. Averell put his hand over the telephone and asked me if I thought there would be much space in the Sunday paper. I told him I thought it would still be filled with the *Andrea Doria* sinking, so they are going to move the statement up for Monday.

I was amused, looking around the room, to notice that Averell still has a bust of Eisenhower on a table (despite his very cold relations with Ike), as well as busts of Benjamin Franklin and Franklin Roosevelt. We had a couple of drinks before lunch, Averell taking two stiff gin-and-ginger ales—something he never used to do.

While we were sipping our drinks I told him I had a message for him from Virginia Chambers—namely, that she had heard that Roy Cohn (of

the famous Cohn & Schine circus) was working for Averell; that if this
was true he would lose her vote. Averell was indignant. He said:

Of course Roy Cohn is going to vote for me, but he is not working
for me. His father is a reputable judge. Roy knows that I am not soft
on communism the way Stevenson is—but he is not working for me.
If Virginia thinks that the only people who are going to vote for me
are in the Social Register she's crazy.

We went upstairs to Averell's air-conditioned bedroom, where we had
lunch. And an excellent lunch it was: jellied soup, broiled lobster, and
strawberries. I was interested by the pictures on the wall: two Derains,
an excellent Toulouse-Lautrec, a good Picasso, a Winston Churchill still
life of a couple of bottles with the initials wsc, and a not-bad "early
Eisenhower" landscape. A rather remarkable little collection.

Our conversation ranged over a good many subjects and was interrupted from time to time by secretaries bringing messages. Averell expressed the following opinions:

Eden is a second-rater who tends to blow his top, but backs down if
you stand up to him. In 1942, Harriman was in London and was furious
with British statements put out by the Foreign Office to the effect that
Britain wanted to back de Gaulle completely but that Roosevelt would
not allow this. Harriman, who was not then a diplomatic ambassador
but was dealing with lend-lease, complained personally to Eden. Eden got
very angry and said Averell had no right to complain. Averell gave him
the name of the Foreign Office spokesman who had made the accusation
and demanded that Eden summon him immediately to his office and
Averell would make the statement to his face. Eden backed down. Averell
contends this is typical.

Several times he said Stevenson is "soft on communism." By this he
didn't mean he is in any sense pro-Communist, but that he is naive and
suffered from illusions. Furthermore, he said he had made an immoral
deal to obtain Southern votes at the convention. As a result, if he were
nominated, he would lose the party many Negro votes in the North. He
added: "Adlai simply cannot defeat Eisenhower. His only program is
Me Too. We can lick Eisenhower but we have to go out and fight."

He said he has now received definite information that if Stevenson
were nominated and elected, Chester Bowles will be his Secretary of State.
He added: "I like and admire Chet, but I have no desire to see us become
a satellite of Nehru."

Averell told me something interesting about his views in 1945. He
said that at Potsdam he was opposed to the western Allies accepting occupation sectors in Berlin. Instead, he wanted to extend our occupation
zone up to the Elbe River and establish a capital of West Germany at
Magdeburg. He admits he was probably wrong on that. But he didn't

think we could hold out on Berlin because of the limited avenues of approach. I told him about the view Churchill had given me this month on advancing to Prague and Berlin and holding the Potsdam Conference earlier. Averell didn't think we would have gained much. He added: "We would have had more acreage in Germany, but we couldn't have saved Poland. And the result would have been to make Austria a Soviet satellite, because all we held there was the scenery."

Harriman kept insisting that "we must attack Eisenhower. That's the only way to beat him. It is not just a question of foreign-policy mistakes. He has betrayed the farmers, and I found out how they felt when I went to the Middle West."

Averell told me that in 1945, when George Kennan was his minister in Moscow, Kennan advocated working out a spheres-of-influence deal with the Russians, awarding them eastern Europe. Averell said he had opposed this at the time, and still felt we had to fight the Russians on their own ground. "I want to negotiate with them," he added, "but I want to negotiate from a position of vigor."

He said he found life in Albany pretty easy and agreeable because Dewey was such an awful guy that anybody trying to be halfway human was popular succeeding him.

PRINCETON, NEW JERSEY, *August 1, 1956*

I SPENT the day with George Kennan, who is now out here at the Institute for Advanced Study. I lunched at his house and afterward we sat around in the garden analyzing the world.

He is disturbed at the tendency of minorities in the United States to be treated by politicians as if they voted in organized blocs—Poles, Ukrainians, Irish, Catholics, Jews. He was very hurt at the way Stevenson handled a letter from Representative Machrowicz (Democrat) of Michigan. Machrowicz wrote Stevenson on May 10, complaining that Kennan was opposed to any policy of liberating satellites (including Poland) and asking if it was true that Kennan was one of Stevenson's foreign-policy experts. Stevenson replied to the Congressman on May 26, saying: "So far as Mr. Kennan is concerned, I can only say that he is in no way connected with my staff, and never has been. . . . I feel no reluctance whatsoever in saying, beyond this, that although I hold Mr. Kennan and his views in great respect, I differ strongly with some of the positions he has taken." Kennan says that not only did Stevenson never consult him before replying to the Congressman, but he has not yet even been given a copy of Stevenson's letter, although he is the chairman of his New Jersey state organization.

He talked about Averell Harriman's extraordinary passion for secrecy and his refusal to take any subordinate into his confidence. When Harriman was ambassador to Moscow and Kennan was minister during the spring of 1945, Harriman wouldn't even confide to Kennan that a conference was about to take place at Yalta. When Harry Hopkins came to Moscow that year he asked to see Kennan, which was of course arranged although it rather irritated Harriman.

Hopkins asked Kennan for his views on a Polish settlement with Stalin. Kennan said he did not think any acceptable settlement was possible and therefore it was better not to link the name of the United States with any deal on Poland. Hopkins told Kennan he respected his opinion but he could not accept it because, for the sake of Roosevelt, he had to obtain some settlement. This certainly contradicts Harriman's recollections about Kennan's views in Moscow, as expressed to me last Friday.

Kennan said he was struck, in working on his book on Soviet-American relationships, by the views expressed by Robert Lansing, Wilson's Secretary of State, concerning the Bolshevik revolution. Lansing, who was an uncle of John Foster Dulles, advocated a policy of letting the dust settle before any stand was decided upon. This is precisely what the Democrats were criticized for on China more recently by the Republicans. Kennan, incidentally, considers Lansing to have been a very able Secretary of State, although obviously a profoundly dull man.

I asked Kennan if he thought it was possible for a man to be a good American Secretary of State both at home and abroad. He replied:

It's hard to be good both abroad and vis-à-vis our Congress, but possible to be successful abroad and vis-à-vis the American people. Certain political forces playing on Congress make it less able to understand good statesmanship than the people at large. Dulles has not played to United States opinion in general but to an influential part of that opinion—the right-wing Republicans—centering around Senator Knowland. Dulles could have been a good Secretary abroad and at home if he had stated the case frankly and reasonably at home, but he preferred only to convince Knowland.

The actual policies of the Eisenhower administration are very little different from those of the Democrats before. But the words have been different. There is a general insensitivity to foreign feelings in this government.

And diplomats in Washington have no sense of intimacy or contact with the administration. There are few people in Washington with whom diplomats can discuss the totality of world problems. Part of the 1953 purging operation was to remove people tinged with the charge of being intellectuals. Certainly, it was not really necessary to get rid of the entire Policy and Planning staff that served under me just when they wanted to get rid of me. Paul Nitze, for example, had always been a Republican.

I then asked what Kennan thought should be the relative roles of the President and the Secretary of State in the formulation of foreign policy. He replied:

> The two positions are in tandem. Both encompass the same responsibilities in the field of foreign affairs. But the Secretary is only an assistant to the President in foreign affairs. The President's is the basic responsibility. At some time in the future of this country, the President will have to concentrate in one person all subordinate responsibilities in the entire field of foreign affairs. This can be done either by setting up a Deputy President or Prime Minister in charge of all aspects—military, foreign trade, propaganda, diplomacy, etc.— or to make the Secretary of State what he was probably supposed to be under the Constitution. That envisioned him as the senior Cabinet member, with a predominant position in all foreign policy.
>
> The system we have today is a system of self-paralysis. There is an extreme dissipation of the means to make and execute policy. This is deeply wrong. In fact, the bane of the performance of our government lies in the committee system. We tend to tell these committees that anything they agree upon will be OK. The alternative to this, instead of allotting responsibility to committees, would be to pick one official and make him ultimately responsible for decision. He could arrive at this decision anyway he wants, consulting with committees or individuals, while his individual responsibility would be rigidly fixed, and he would stand or fall by his decision.
>
> The main frustration in foreign policy in Washington is the feeling of never being able to manipulate through the labyrinth of conflicting responsibilities and committees. We don't act enough because of this paralyzing system, and time and again reality passes us by.
>
> It might require a constitutional change to amend the system. But it could be possible to make a man like Adams into a sort of Prime Minister, or to make the Secretary of State a man of full dignity. He was supposed to keep the Great Seal of the United States, and that is why he was called Secretary of State and not Secretary for Foreign Affairs.

I asked if he did not think it would be a good thing to establish a kind of RAND set-up for the State Department, so that policy problems in the foreign field—particularly those of a long-range nature—could be studied by private individuals who could prepare careful analyses on a confidential basis for governmental use. Kennan thought this could be done. But he preferred that the government should deal with these things. He said:

> The government has the people. For example, there are plenty of men in Washington fully qualified to analyze Soviet affairs. But there is such a dispersal of staffs that people can't get together. They are stifled by restrictions. The government is muscle-bound with

good people, but they don't get together on an informal basis because of the fetish of security.

Kennan went on; there were useful private study centers. For example, Massachusetts Institute of Technology has a good center for international studies. The government reads what this produces with careful
attention. And both Princeton and Chicago have international study centers. Certainly, Kennan thought, some work could be farmed out to them.
But he added: "The security people have so intimidated those working
for the government that maybe, after all, it would be better to farm
things out to uninhibited private citizens."

He recalled that Bob Tucker, who was kicked out of our embassy in
Moscow because he married a Soviet woman, was an expert analyst and
is now working for RAND. He went on: "The government's extreme in-
flexibility and unimaginativeness on security procedures perhaps makes
private institutions a better set-up to conduct certain types of inquiry.
After all, the government voluntarily cut itself off from such a profoundly brilliant man as Oppenheimer."

At this point, Kennan interrupted the general stream to tell me that
Oppenheimer came to see him after he was bounced. Kennan told him he
should not worry, but it might be advisable for him to go abroad to work
in some university in England or France where everyone would be delighted to have him. Oppenheimer admitted this might be one way of
doing things, but said he preferred to stay here, confiding with tears in his
eyes: "I love this country."

I told George I was interested in his observations that racial prejudice
as expressed in the United States hurt our prestige abroad. But how did
he propose to eliminate such prejudice? He answered:

There is no answer but courage and political self-sacrifice on the
part of our leaders. They should say to Americans that we cannot hope
to aspire to any position of moral leadership for this country unless we
can succeed in giving a happy place in our own life to the colored
people here. Look at the people around the earth. Compared to
most denizens of this world, the American colored people are gentle
and good-humored. They are intensely human. They have a good
sense of humor and a warm sensibility. Their innate courtesy towards each other is greater than the courtesy of the whites.

There shouldn't be any problem of absorption. Fortunately for this
country they are not difficult people like the sullen Peruvian Indians. Think of what things would be like if our Negroes had organized something like the Stern Gang in Palestine. Save for a few intellectuals, the Russians never succeeded in taking them over. But
they are deeply unhappy. They don't feel admitted to equal citizenship. They have been asked to make the ultimate contribution by
joining the armed forces, but they are not totally in our society.

Of course, I feel it would be ill-advised to rush things and frighten the South. But we must impress our people with the fact that the bulk of the world is colored differently from ourselves. We can't pretend to be a model with valid standards if we insist upon conceptions of races and white superiority. I don't know if it is still true, but when I was in the State Department we used to have to maintain a special agency in Miami to keep Latin American diplomats from getting hotel rooms there and to urge them to get aboard the next plane to Washington.

I asked whether, when George headed the State Department Policy and Planning staff, any of the papers prepared foresaw the possibility of present developments such as the crises in the Middle East, North Africa, and Asia. He replied:

When I headed the staff, we produced a series of papers which I believe first interpreted a series of views on world affairs by this government. Before that, individual people had produced views and papers, but there were never combined studies. I hope the government will be asked to release these, or some of them, because, after all, almost a decade has gone by and there is no reason for classification.

Since I left, I understand the staff has been put to a different use. They have become operational pinch hitters and troubleshooters. I had a study made, covering two or three years of our staff opinions, in order to find their relationship to what was actually later done in policy. I discovered that usually these opinions were first received with shocked surprise. Then, however, they were carried out as policy, with an average delay of two years. For example, at first we found the Department still studiously avoiding any relationship with Franco. Spain couldn't even, for example, be accepted as a member of such international agencies as IATA. We recommended that this situation should be put back on an even keel; that we should cease denying Franco a place in world affairs. We wanted to return our relationships to a basis of cool normalcy. At first there was a violent outcry in the Department. But, within three or four years, the pendulum had swung much too far back in the other direction.

We have to learn, vis-à-vis Franco and Tito, that there is such a thing as correct, detached, noncommital diplomatic intercourse, in which we take no positions concerning the morality of the governments concerned. I now appreciate some of the older values of our early neutralist (not isolationist) days in American foreign policy. In those days, recognition did not imply any judgment (even to ourselves) concerning the moral qualities of the regime recognized.

I told Kennan that I was writing a series of pieces on the end of the "age of giants," and that it was my impression that in the United States Eisenhower symbolized this trend, even though in terms of the immense sentimental affection he held in American hearts he might be considered a giant himself. I said I felt that his very method of reorganizing the

White House staff and the National Security Council tended to normalize things in a direction away from great individual authority.

George said he agreed with this, and added:

There are few people in conspicuous positions of government now who combine forces of intellect and character. One must combine both. Truman was very much a man of the people. People like myself actually were more different from him than from Eisenhower and Dulles. But Truman had more good-natured acceptance of intellectuals. An intellectual could work under the Democrats. This quality has been sacrificed to the Mammon of internal security, to the concept of the colorless man.

At this point, Kennan remarked with a sour grin:

It took Foster Dulles to make a Democrat out of me. I never thought of being expelled by the State Department. I never thought I would be dropped by our government after being expelled from Moscow. Surely, this must give the Russians the feeling that they managed to eliminate me as a force in our government.

The deepest problem of United States foreign policy is introversion as against extraversion. We try to have it both ways. In reality we are introverts. This government faces inwardly and does things that look good to us in the mirror. Eisenhower, of course, is sensitive by nature, and polite. But Dulles is pretty brutal and unfeeling. For example, he did exactly the same thing with both Jack Vincent and myself when he fired us. After courteously telling us the bad news he then asked us to stay, inquired of our views on China and Russia respectively, listened with patience, and expressed great interest. It was more or less as if you told your wife you had decided to divorce her and then asked her to stay on to wash the dishes.

Of course, this hit me very hard. I had been led to believe that I had a good record. I was the youngest minister-counsellor of my time and also a very young ambassador. It is hard to make a good new life at the age of fifty, much harder than you think. It is difficult to get over the feeling, after almost thirty years of public service, that the government no longer wants me. My Policy and Planning staff never comprised more than eight or nine people. Yet, four of them, after being eased out, produced books that were particularly well received. They were people of intellectual distinction.

Kennan respects and likes Allen Dulles and said that within one hour after Foster had fired him, Allen offered him any job he wanted in the CIA. Allen fought hard to keep McCarthyism out of the CIA and maintained a high morale and an intact organization.

I asked what George would do, taking things as they are today, if he were responsible for planning United States policy on the Suez Canal and Nile River issues. He said it was, of course, difficult for him to answer this because he no longer had access to State papers. But then he went on:

For years I have felt strongly—and five years ago I wrote Loy Henderson on this—that we were making a great mistake playing up to these Middle Eastern tin-pot dictators. Today, the chickens are coming home to roost. These men are not our friends. Concessions made to them in return for nothing earn nothing for us. I would like us to stick right by France and Britain on this Suez quarrel. We must stand up to Nasser in the strongest possible way. After all, we were very influential in getting the British out of Suez.

Sooner or later, the United States government must recognize that what our oil companies do in the Middle East is so much the concern of our national interest that it must be controlled by us. The financing and the profits of these companies can remain a private matter, but the government must supervise their interests. We can't pass out such huge sums without considering it a part of our foreign policy. The royalties paid to the Arab sheikhs are not too little; they are far too high. The theory of giving 50 percent to the owner of a natural resource when someone else develops it totally—and this 50 percent is net, not gross—is absolutely cockeyed. Look how we corrupt these sheikhs. It's as if I went up to the Negro section of Princeton here and started passing out thousand-dollar bills. The place would go mad!

Finally, in his analysis of the Middle East, Kennan said:

We have been ill-advised not to let Israel buy arms. I think it gives us too great a responsibility for the future. I would not be prepared to say to the Israelis that they should not defend themselves but should rely on Papa. We can not mortgage the future actions of the United States. Everyone knows that in these matters the United Nations is largely the United States. If UN decides to act because of an attack on Israel, we are the ones who will have to put up the money and the forces.

George thought we should back France and Britain in their concept of an international authority to control the Suez Canal. He feels "We should never have let ourselves in for these great intimacies with the Egyptians," referring to the friendship between Nasser and Byroade. But, he concluded, with reference to the current crisis, "Thank God this happened now and not after we had already sunk a large investment in the High Aswan Dam."

On the subject of our pacts, Kennan thought NATO "has its own rationale and industrial basis." But he thought we should press neither the Baghdad Pact or SEATO, and should let them gradually die. He added: "The likelihood of all-out military invasions in those areas is slight. All we should do is make it clear that in such a case, a world war might be likely; but we should not define things so rigidly that big issues are made in advance. For example, during one hundred years, Russia has been in and out of northern Persia, but the Persians have always managed to wangle their way out."

I then asked his views on Formosa and Okinawa. He commented:

You can never get clarity on the problem of Formosa until we eliminate the inordinate domestic influence here of the Chiang regime.
We should not insist on military facilities in Formosa, provided that we
can insist that no other power should obtain such facilities there.

We should explore gradual ways of achieving that goal. Why
couldn't you induce the United Nations to take over the responsibility for demilitarizing Formosa? All facilities of potential military
value, such as airports, should be watched by UN supervisors. I would
be content to have the UN promise the United States that if we leave,
no other country will be permitted to establish military facilities there—
above all, Communist China or Russia.

Then would be the time to have a real consultation of local opinion
concerning Formosa's future. Of course all this might take years to
work out. You can't toss out a perfect plan on this. Nevertheless,
unfortunately, if you consider these things today and it becomes known,
Chiang and his friends would begin to howl. But we must recover
our independence of action, the independence of U.S. policy. Frankly,
I would like to give Okinawa back to Japan—and also Formosa.

We must also consider the position of Japan in all of this. No one
is going to attack Japan. They need a strong internal police force and
a good little army—enough to make it clear that there would be a
major bloodletting if they were invaded. We should try and get
guarantees that no one would be able to use Japan militarily. Then
we should get our troops out. Otherwise, we would be bound to see
trouble develop there, such as there now is in Germany.

The Japanese have learned a lot. And they can be relied upon to
surely defend their own interests. Those countries don't need the
benefit of our advice on such things. Austria has shown us how it can
protect its own interests. These people are not suicidally minded.
They know the Communists and what they are doing. The Japanese
have been handling their current talks with Moscow very well; they have
always negotiated cleverly with Moscow.

I asked George if he thought there was any indication that United
States policy was trying to work out a long-range basis to divide China
from Russia. He said:

I see no evidence of any imaginative long-range thinking by this
government. Things have become so static that within the coming six
months, I am willing to wager that no thought or initiative on the
world situation will come from us. The United States has become a
topographical feature on the world horizon. That is, of course, not
meaningless. You respect a high mountain and you have to calculate
on how to get around it, but you don't need to reason with it. We
are no longer actors on the stage.

Diplomats in Washington know our government and can estimate
what it is likely to do, but they cannot discuss things with it. Look

what happened to Adenauer. We started this new-look military philosophy after Adenauer had risked his entire political future on mili-
tarizing West Germany.

There is no one authority with whom diplomats can talk. Dulles
doesn't care about problems as long as he is getting on with Congress.
The President has become practically inaccessible. He is either away
or busy catching up on things that accumulated while he was away.
Again, look at Adenauer. He came over just to see the President at
the age eighty, and during this awful summer heat, but he couldn't
see him because Eisenhower was ill.

There is no way for effective interchange by diplomats with the U.S.
government. Power has become too diffuse. For any reasonable view
of the situation you have to talk with fifty people, not one. And
then when you *do* talk to fifty, they talk on the basis of their own individual interests politically. Other countries have to reckon with
what our behavior is likely to be and then adjust themselves to it. They
can't get to any normal authoritative source.

And finally, the status of our ambassadors has been lowered by
Dulles because of his frequent travels. His presence supersedes them.
The direct diplomacy of the Secretary of State and the President causes
the regular channels to dry up.

Kennan talked with considerable vigor on what he calls "the increasing
provincialism of the United States," which he considers, rather ruefully,
to be "the most mysterious of all countries." He believes this provincialism was caused by the drying up of the immigrant stream. When he was a
boy in Milwaukee, there was an indigenous culture there that had, for
example, separate German and English stages. Now, in Milwaukee, they
have fine industry, excellent country clubs, and comfortable homes—with
the same copies of *Time, Life*, and *U.S. News & World Report* on every
table. There is hardly a book in sight. He said:

My father was a modest lawyer and yet he had a good library of
French literature which he had had bound himself, and which was
available for me to read. He was a cultured man. A lot of the cultural influence in Wisconsin came from the immigrant Germans and
Poles. This immigration had already begun to dry up, but between
the wars, in a sense, we were saved by Hitler because the cream of the
German intelligentsia joined the immigrant stream.

The country's cultural product as a whole is not less, but there has
developed a polarization of the cultural and anticultural. The egg-
heads gravitate to centers like Princeton where they are not laughed
at as queer if they are writing a book. Certain intellectual communities
in the United States are absolutely first-rate. Cambridge [Massa-
chusetts] compares with any place in the world in intellectual
strength. Princeton also does in its philosophical sophistication of approach. The people here are very mature. But there is a consequent
impoverishment of the interior, something like that in France, where

Paris has become the completely dominant and magnetic attraction. Our poor old maligned East Coast has, I am glad to say, retained a vigorous cultural atmosphere—unlike most of the rest of the country.

WASHINGTON, *August 5, 1956*

WHEN I was in eastern Europe earlier this year, I applied in seven separate capitals for a Chinese Communist visa—Moscow, Warsaw, Prague, Budapest, Sofia, and Belgrade. Today, to my astonishment, I received a cable from Peking instructing me to pick up my visa—which had been authorized—either in Hongkong or Moscow. I have decided to go via Hongkong, after the San Francisco Republican convention.

Legally, I am forbidden to go by the State Department, but I think this is a pretty good test case. After all, we had no relations with Bulgaria when I went there and correspondents were also ordered to stay out of Hungary. But I visited both, advising the Department I would do so ahead of time, and I wasn't even slapped on the wrist. I intend to take this up with the Department, at least unofficially.

IKE SAYS KHRUSHCHEV

IS LIKE "A DRUNKEN

RAILWAY HAND"

WASHINGTON, *August 6, 1956*

T HIS MORNING I WENT TO THE WHITE HOUSE FOR A TALK WITH President Eisenhower. Ike looked thin and pale but quite healthy, considering what the poor fellow has been through. He started right off talking about the Middle East and the Suez crisis. A few days ago it looked as if things were going to blow up "but I put my foot down and stopped the drift." He sent Dulles over to London and tried to persuade the British and French that things must, if at all possible, be settled at the conference table.

But he realizes that the British and French people want action. He understands their viewpoints. The French think they can bail out their North African situation by getting tough and the British are worried about oil and the entire Mediterranean.

Ike is furious at Nasser. He says we were willing to play ball with him on the assumption he was trying to help his position. We were fully behind the project for the High Aswan Dam and were going to really assist him in financing this. But we had to call a halt when he started flirting with the Russians.

Eisenhower did not see how Nasser could possibly figure on getting $100,000,000 a year out of the Suez Canal to contribute to the building of his High Dam project. Even if he raised Canal tolls—which he will probably do—the total income (gross) of the company last year was less than $100,000,000.

To date, we have no positive information that the Russians put him up to the Suez nationalization, but they are clearly trying to "fish in troubled waters." It's too bad we don't have the old Turkish (Ottoman) empire. They still had plenty to give up, if necessary, under pressure. But none of the little successor states do. Take Syria, for example. What have they got to give up? (A curious view.) Why, a Turkish Empire could have been the third great power today!

A situation has come about in the world where the weaker powers find it possible to blackmail the stronger through their very weakness. Wilson's theories of self-determination have let loose a movement whose end cannot be seen. Last year Eisenhower prepared a speech in which he said the United States was behind self-determination for any people that wanted independence and was capable of economically supporting it. His advisors jumped on this phrase and made him strike it out. They said everyone would hop on his back if he put in that economic qualification.

But it was necessary. Take the Central American countries for example. Panama has a population of only 900,000. Its annual income is only $50,000,000. Most of this comes from the Canal. It couldn't support itself otherwise. Yet it manages to keep ambassadors all around the world. How? The President can't figure it out. There isn't, he says, a single Central American country capable of living economically or politically entirely by itself and without aid. (He has just recently returned from the Pan-American Conference.)

Swiveling from side to side in his desk chair, Ike (as he so often does) kept thinking aloud. He said it was of course possible that the Arab countries would cut off oil supplies and the pipelines, which they could easily do. Then the only thing that would happen would be of benefit to the Russians. England probably has a six-week oil reserve on hand; the Continent about four weeks. We could shift everything, open up our supplies, mobilize all available tankers, put ourselves on gasoline rationing, and help the situation along. Meanwhile, the Arab states would collapse without the money. But who would benefit by this?

The Russians can't possibly take Middle East oil for a long time to come. Even if they have the steel and the money, it would be difficult and time-consuming to build a pipeline; and they are very short on tankers.

Yet, if war comes, it would be hard to limit. Ike is convinced the Russians fear war dreadfully and, in the end, would do anything to prevent it. But it is hard to calculate their estimate of the situation. Some kind of order must be established, but it is difficult to see what it can be; or will be.

I told the President about the cable I had received yesterday from the Chinese Communist government granting me a visa. He seemed puzzled. He made no comment. I told him I was going to ask the State Department whether I could or should go. Again no comment. But, he added, he was sure things were not going too well between Russia and China and he wished we could do something about exploiting this. However, there was the difficulty about the climate of American public opinion.

Eisenhower has little respect for the Russian leader. He thinks Khrushchev is about the equivalent of "a drunken railway hand." Bulganin "looks like someone who does what he is told."

He turned then to Europe and NATO. He said it was too bad Europe was in such a bad way. NATO to him is still all-important. It's too bad Al Gruenther is leaving. When Eisenhower decided to run for President, he was positive he would never stand for a second term. Al wanted to quit government service back in 1952. However, Ike extracted a promise from him that he would stay on four years—until the end of 1956. He can't ask for any more. Al has no money. He has nine grandchildren and he has to educate them.

Ike thought the greatest public servants he had ever met were Al Gruenther, George Humphrey, Bob Anderson, and his younger brother, Milton. Eisenhower said Milton "unfortunately bears my name, but has been a devoted public servant for years." Al was the smartest man he ever knew. It was too bad that some public institution like the Ford Foundation couldn't arrange to finance people who otherwise couldn't afford to stay on in government service; to reassure their family positions. But, he supposed, that would place the individual in an embarrassing spot.

Then the President said something extraordinary, considering that next week the Democratic convention sits, then the following week the Republicans. He said: "I couldn't imagine a finer thing than to see the Republican convention nominate Al Gruenther for the presidency. After all, he is smart, diplomatic, and a devoted public servant. He is about nine years younger than I am and in excellent health; there couldn't be a better President."

At this point the President turned to his own health. He said the doctors had warned him after his operation that he wouldn't feel right for six months; that it would be a miracle if he felt even approximately well after four months. He supposed they were right. He couldn't forget his age. He didn't feel right yet.

Ike said it was a great burden to have all these problems. He couldn't shake free of them. He was reading papers all weekend on Suez and Russia.

He told me he had tried some golf for the first time since his operation, on Saturday. He said the doctors had told him that in addition to resting after lunch he should walk a mile daily.

I remarked that when we used to play he always would say: "Lord, give me strength to hit it easy." He smiled wanly and acknowledged that he certainly had. He scored one par, two bogies, and a seven in four holes at Burning Tree. "I got into a trap on that last one," he said, "and just whaled away."

Clearly, he is worried about his strength and is testing himself. He is not as sure as I would like to see him.

We roamed about all kinds of things. He talked longingly of the farm in Gettysburg. He told me his mother-in-law had gone off to Denver today. He asked me if I was going to San Francisco. He inquired after my family. He remarked of Larry Norstad: "He's a fine fellow but he's going to have to show a lot more stuff than he ever showed before if he gets up to Al's stature."

He told me he had had very bad luck at bridge recently. "I keep drawing the damnedest cards," said he. "Thank God, Al is coming over here this week [the 10th]. At least with him I can minimize my losses. He knows where every card in the deck is."

By this time (I knew that he had an official appointment already delayed a half-hour) I thought I'd better be going. I had made some maneuvers in that direction twice before, but when I half rose this time, he also got up and walked to the door with me. Ike wished me luck on my summer holiday fishing. He flashed a smile, shook hands, and off I went. He seemed sad, a bit lacking in self-assurance, when he was tired. His suit had clearly been made for a bigger man. But, at the same time, he seemed far fitter than I had expected and looked better than his pictures.

I dropped in on General Snyder for a pleasant chat. He said Ike was fine now, but that he couldn't stop worrying about things and that the little things kept getting under his skin. This was too bad, but comprehensible. He wasn't sure of his health either, despite what the doctors told him. Snyder thought he was really much better as a result of the operation and wouldn't be suffering from digestive troubles anymore.

Then he took me upstairs to see Mamie. She was having some dresses fitted. She came into the upstairs sitting room in a dressing gown, sat down, smoked and chatted. She said (Snyder sat by and nodded) that it was nice for Ike to be underweight instead of always worrying. Now, thanks to the operation, he could eat the spicy Mexican food he liked. Snyder nodded. He added: "He's regained five pounds from his minimum. These things go slowly."

I told her I had lunched with Averell Harriman and he still had Ike's bust in his sitting room and one of his paintings ("Oh, the one of Sun Valley," said she) in his bedroom. She said it was too bad politics did such strange things to people, but he had said some unforgiveable things. She added: "Averell was always coming to Ike for advice. And Marie and I were good friends."

I lunched with Bob Murphy, Deputy Under Secretary of State. Our main conversation was about the Chinese visa issue. Quite unofficially and as a friend, Bob said that in my position he would be sorely tempted to go. But, he added, the government had in no way changed its attitude banning such trips by Americans. He talked with Dulles about it this morning. They were against anyone going. If it were January (in other words, after the elections), their attitude could be less tough, but this is a hot political question.

Bob promised: "If you get locked up, at any rate, I'll send a few newspapers to you—if you go." I told him I favored going. This was a competitive business. How would I feel if a rival columnist went? Bob allowed that maybe in my position, were he abroad, he'd already be on the way. But there would be no official change in attitude.

I pointed out I'd been to Bulgaria without a validated passport; others had been to North Vietnam. That was so, he acknowledged, but this was far more dramatic. And *The New York Times* and my name made it even more so. Yet as a friend he understood my intention. Bob thinks we should do more about splitting China from Russia. But it's hard to get anything done during the present political climate.

He thinks Ike always wanted to run for President (I disagreed), and really wants to run for a second term; isn't being pushed into it. He recalls Patton saying the day he lost his command: "Ike wants to be President so much you can taste it."

WASHINGTON, *August 7, 1956*

DINED and talked until the early hours with Frank Wisner and Gates Lloyd. They are in the same trade (CIA). Frank said Allen Dulles was extremely upset by my column criticizing American propaganda. Frank simply cannot understand why our ambassadors and ministers behind the Iron Curtain don't speak right out on this subject to the State Department. Wisner told me McCarthyism is, unfortunately, by no means dead in the government, and I should not forget this. M, who was suspended from the State Department on a phony, trumped-up charge, was finally forced back by pressure. But now—two years later—he has been exiled to a consular position at the fever-hole of Paramaraibo, the nearest post we have to Devil's Island.

Frank told me that he was astonished to discover, when he went to Rumania during the war, that practically all the agents furnished by Zaslani (later Reuven Shiloah), Israeli intelligence boss, to the British from Rumanian Jews in Palestine, were working for Zaslani's network all the time—and not for the British, who didn't know.

NEW YORK, *August 9, 1956*

LUNCHED with Jock Whitney. He is going tomorrow to Seoul to represent Eisenhower as his special ambassador during the inauguration ceremonies for Syngman Rhee.

Jock and Betsey stayed overnight at the White House last week. Eisenhower asked if he would agree to be ambassador to Great Britain beginning next year—presuming the Republicans remain in office. Jock told him he could only consider the post if it were understood in advance that he was going to London with a specific mission in mind—namely, that of strengthening the Anglo-American alliance. He didn't think the post of ambassador was really terribly significant; just another guy at the end of a cable. During the Suez Conference in London, Eisenhower said he never noticed the name of Winthrop Aldrich at any of the meetings with the British governmental leaders. The President observed that if a man were a really good ambassador, he would be at such meetings.

When Jock got back to New York, he wrote a long letter to the President in which he very half-heartedly and tentatively dealt himself in on the job; that is to say, he did not deal himself out. When Eisenhower offered it to him last week, he himself pointed out that this was tentative and depended upon what the world situation was in January.

Jock said that, contrary to rumor, Betsey is extremely anxious for him to accept the job and thinks he will regret it all his life if he turns it down. Jock argued that maybe it would be more useful if he stayed home, doing relatively anonymous things for the Republican party like helping Javits to be elected to the Senate or accepting membership in a committee reporting on the necessity of foreign aid.

I expressed the opinion very strongly that this was nonsense; that if he were really prepared to work hard as ambassador he could exercise a considerable influence upon the history of this country and the western allies. After all, there are many other people who could do these anonymous committee jobs here in America. But, I added, there were relatively few people qualified for the ambassadorship in London because a man had to be wealthy and well connected, with many friends on both sides of the Atlantic. He had these qualifications, along with common sense, and he was willing to work hard. With a wry grin he said: "There always has to be a fellow like you around to spoil a guy's life."

I urged him to call the President's personal secretary, have her catch the letter and return it. He telephoned. When I left I felt completely convinced that he is going to be our next ambassador in London, and I am glad of it.

NEW YORK, *August 11, 1956*

LAST night, I had dinner with Randolph Churchill, who has come over to cover the conventions for the *London Evening Standard*. He is allowed ten pounds a day spending money by the British Treasury, but he is a big dealer and has made swift arrangements to live more splendidly.

Randolph was just down in Washington. He wanted to see Dulles but got the runaround. Bob Murphy did receive him but took the rather unusual precaution of having Burke Wilkinson of the press division along throughout the interview.

Randolph also saw Nixon. He had an early morning appointment, but Nixon was delayed because he was seeing the President. So, very kindly, he had his chauffeur drive Randolph to the airport and rode along to talk with him. Randolph was undoubtedly flattered. It was the first time he had ever met Nixon and thinks he's a very fine fellow. "Quite grown up." He was so impressed that he says: "I'm the only man in the world who supports a Stevenson-Nixon ticket."

CHICAGO, *August 12, 1956*

THIS afternoon, I had a talk with former President Truman in his suite at the Blackstone Hotel, specially papered with the seals of the various states and territories. He looked well, brisk, spry, full of confidence. Yesterday, he threw support to Harriman and opened up the Democratic convention.

He regretted that Dean Acheson wasn't here (hadn't been invited). Acheson was "the greatest Secretary of State we ever had." I told him I was going to see Bowles tomorrow morning (often mentioned as a Stevenson Secretary of State). He said: "Bowles will probably tell you he knows everything about everything."

We started talking about NATO. He said Gruenther had given him a briefing in Paris and expressed great disappointment in the lack of support he was getting in present defense planning. But when I asked Truman if he thought we should replan our defense to permit a guarantee of a fixed force for a fixed period of time in Europe, he said: "No comment," clamping his mouth shut like a vise. On Spain, he said he would only like to see it in NATO "when it gets a free government. But I don't like Franco and he knows it." On Germany, he said it was "only common sense" to keep enough American troops there for an adequate time until West Germany is rearmed.

I asked if he favored a "liberation" policy for the satellites. "Do you want a world war?" he countered. "There's no other alternative. Anything else is hooey and for political purposes." How about trying to encourage some form of national communism or Titoism there as a first step, I inquired. "You can't do that," he said. "How are you going to get behind the Iron Curtain and operate? You'd get your neck sliced off. That's hooey too. You find out how you can do this; and then it could be done. But it can't."

I asked Truman how he felt about the State Department ban on visas for correspondents in China. "No comment," he said. "Are you ready to be brainwashed? Do you think you could stand up to a brainwashing?"

I mentioned the Middle East crisis (which he dodged) and his proposal at Potsdam for internationalizing strategic waterways. He was still very much in favor of this and had put it up before the Democratic platform committee only Friday. He wanted all such waterways, including Panama, placed under the UN. I asked if direct supervision should be by committees of riparian states. He said this was merely a matter of detail. But, he added, he wanted to be "damned sure that the Black Sea straits are under the UN too."

I dropped in at Harriman's headquarters, the exact same suites at the Blackstone that Ike had four years ago. Averell and Marie came back from church a few minutes after I arrived and invited me in with great cordiality. A moment later, DeSapio joined us: a sinister-looking character with weird Hollywood-type glasses, strangely shaped and with thick lenses.

Averell has to go on the air this afternoon on Suez and is going to lambaste the administration's mishandling of the whole issue from Israel and the High Dam on. He promised to let me view the final balloting on his television—the same one I sat at with Ike in 1952, when Stassen threw his votes to him and he was nominated.

CHICAGO, *August 13, 1956*

SPENT the morning with Chet Bowles, who is rumored to be Stevenson's choice as nominee for Secretary of State if Stevenson is (a) nominated and (b) elected. According to Bowles, nine Democrats started meeting informally around the end of June to draw up recommendations to the platform committee for a foreign-policy plank. Senators Fulbright, Green, and Mansfield; Representatives Carnahan and Williams; Dean Acheson, Bowles, Paul Nitze, and Ben Cohen (former counsellor of the State Department). They prepared a series of memorandum suggestions.

According to Bowles, Stevenson agrees with him that the present is a turning point in history. The future is uncertain, but past methods and assumptions must be abandoned. Still, there are hopeful aspects concerning the real meaning of the Russian changes, and the forthcoming campaign should stress this hope.

It would be a mistake if the United States attempted to repose full powers in a "diplomatic" elite. Foreign policy must be rooted in principles understood by the masses. The British have tried an "elite" system. But it is founded on certain basic and widely understood policy concepts that even the cockney will appreciate—such as not allowing one power to dominate Europe, or keeping Suez open.

In 1955, shortly before the Bandung Conference, Bowles saw Nehru and asked him why he didn't adopt a more helpful attitude vis-à-vis Israel. Nehru said he couldn't because he had a population of forty million Muslims in India and had to get on well with the Arab League. Bowles said this was precisely the kind of logic Dulles used and Nehru should cease lecturing on moral principles. Nehru was furious.

I had lunch with Paul Nitze and David Bruce in the apartment of Paul's sister, overlooking the lake. Paul argues that *the* central issue of our foreign policy now is really not the posture of the U.S.A. vis-à-vis the U.S.S.R., but vis-à-vis the nonaligned countries which are now going over to the U.S.S.R., such as the Middle East.

Already, we are in a position of risking our European allies' friendship if we don't do something about China, and the Republicans know (even if they won't admit it) that, if they win, they must alter our relations with China right after the elections. Now Suez has been added to this. Nitze feels that our policy still addresses itself to the problem of thermonuclear war against the U.S.S.R.—massive atomic retaliation.

Nitze is very worried about Suez. Now that we've forced a conference we've taken the steam out of Anglo-French determination; they won't use military force; Nasser will establish his position together with promises he'll later violate; and the Russians are in an admirable diplomatic posture.

I spent the evening with Adlai Stevenson in his Blackstone suite with just a few of his friends and family. Chet Bowles was among those present. We watched the second session of the convention on TV. Adlai was both amused and amusing about Governor Clement's keynote speech, a real old-fashioned rabble-rouser. At one point, Clement spoke of the unity of the party. "Let us pray," observed Stevenson. When Clement said: "It's better to serve in the house of the Lord than to sit in the seat of the mighty," Adlai said: "I'm not too sure of that." He laughed a good deal and seemed in fine spirits. He kept popping off to be photographed sitting alone at a TV set in his shirtsleeves (he wore a jacket with us) in an anteroom; or to see various big wheels who kept slipping in and out.

Bowles told Stevenson that it looked as if the platform committee were going to slip into the foreign-affairs plank a pledge to never recognize Red China. Adlai said: "Oh my God."

CHICAGO, *August 15, 1956*

LONG talk with Governor George Bell Timmerman of South Carolina, one of the most reactionary segregationists and Southern "favorite sons":

tall, heavyset, young, and handsome except for a nose that looks as if it
had once been broken. He speaks in a calm, deliberate voice with a
marked Dixie accent.

Timmerman argued that integrating the armed forces hurt U.S. prestige in Europe because of crimes committed by Negroes, above all in
Germany and France.

> And as that builds up, the Communists are aided and abetted. It
> pushes Europe away from our leadership. The commission of racial
> crimes by integrated troops overseas is engendering bitter hatred
> toward the United States. It is creating a demand for these troops to
> be sent home. We in the South know from generations of experience
> that segregation is best for both the Negro and the white.
> For this party to approve the desegregation decision would be to
> ask us to support what we know is wrong and would serve only to
> further strain our relations with other nations and to lower further
> American prestige.

Timmerman argues that the peoples of Asia and Africa have no interest in "whether we have a fair system of segregation as now, or unworkable integration. And it is no concern of theirs." He went on: "China isn't
interested in the Negro [pronounced nigra]—or the white man. The same
is true of India. It is ridiculous to think these people are worrying about
what Americans think or do."

He claimed desegregation would destroy individual freedom in the
South by denying to people the right to choose the associations of their
children. This is worthy of Hitler or Stalin, not a democracy. "The leaders of other countries will not be inclined to trust a government that is
not fair to its own people."

Timmerman thought foreign diplomats (to the UN or the U.S.A.) from
"colored" nations should stay in the best available segregated hotels when
traveling through the South. He had visited South Africa, and said the
race problem there was different from our South "because they have
their jungle natives as well as their jiggaboos, an amalgamated race, part
white and part nigra." He implied that where South Africa went wrong
was in occasionally imitating Northern integration too much, not sticking
by the customs of our good old South. Appalling rot!

CHICAGO, *August 17, 1956*

THE convention is almost over now. Stevenson was nominated by a landslide last night on the first ballot. It was an extraordinary spectacle, and
television's big-brother role, even in party caucuses, is astonishing.

If a naive foreigner were to read what our politicians and parties say
about each other they would be appalled. Kerr of Oklahoma spoke of
Ike's "government by deception." He said: "Millions of farmers know
they could not survive another four years of Eisenhower."

It is strange to view democracy as represented by a bunch of middle-aged Oklahoma businessmen in painted feather bonnets, shimmying around the floor. Or the balloons, banners, and comic hats from all over; Georgians waving stars-and-bars flags. (Imagine Latvian nationalists or Bokharans waving their former banners at a Soviet convention.)

The preamble to the Democratic platform denounced the present government as "political amateurs dominated by representatives of special privilege . . . big businessmen of small mind."

The whole process amazes. The Stevenson people, controlling the party machinery and the convention, issued only a handful of tickets to the New York delegation so a Harriman hatchet man arranged the forgery of five hundred floor tickets which were distributed to stalwarts. Apparently the Chandler forces did the same for Kentucky.

While the nominating speeches were being made, and it was already apparent that Harriman was licked, I went around to his suite at the Blackstone. The same television set on which Ike saw himself nominated was there. But yesterday there were only three gloomy Harriman henchmen, no booze, no high spirits; abject silence.

SAN FRANCISCO, *August 20, 1956*

JOCK Whitney dropped around this afternoon. He told me more about that letter he had written Eisenhower. Jock called Ann Whitman in the White House, as I had suggested and asked her to hold up the letter for Ike and send it back. In other words, Jock now thinks he'd like to go abroad. He has even started toying with the idea of Paris instead of London. I encouraged this but I doubt if he'll take it; prefers the English; thinks England is a more important country where more can be done. I suggested he write Ike offering to go either to Paris or London and let Ike choose. He seemed to like the idea. He hears Herter will be made Under Secretary of State, instead of Hoover, with the idea of eventually replacing Dulles.

SAN FRANCISCO, *August 21, 1956*

CHAT with Eric Johnston. He is very worried about Suez. He lunched recently with Dean Acheson and the French ambassador. The Frenchman wanted to move in. Acheson said that had he been Secretary of State he would have advocated moving in within forty-eight hours. Johnston fears we are going to try and bribe Nasser again—with ultimately unfortunate consequences; that Nasser can't stop. He is like the hero in an old Greek tragedy, a captive of forces greater than himself.

Then I talked with Sherman Adams, Ike's "chief of staff." Adams says Ike listened to much of the Democratic convention on TV and was decidedly irked, above all by Clement's keynote speech. As a result, he is all steamed up "and in a better frame of mind for a campaign than he was in 1952."

SAN FRANCISCO, *August 23, 1956*

CALLED up Uncle Arthur to say good-bye. "Where are you going?" he asked. "China," I told him. "My God, you can't do that." "Why not? I have a visa, and quite unofficially I warned Bob Murphy I would do so."

Then the whole sad story came out. It seems that in a moment of mental aberration Uncle A promised Dulles he wouldn't let anyone from *The Times* go to China before Dulles gives his okay. "I know I was a damned fool," says A. "But I gave my word and there's nothing we can do about it. And just think, if it were broken by someone with my own name!"

I agreed he was a damn fool and we were stuck with it. Told him I'd turn around and go back East (American style). He might have some fancy excess-baggage fees to pay—unless I took a train to cool off. He chuckled, regretfully.

EN ROUTE, SAN FRANCISCO TO NEW YORK, *August 26, 1956*

LUNCHED with Lorraine and John Sherman Cooper. He was a Kentucky delegate to the GOP convention. He left India in April to come home for consultations and a throat operation. The President requested him to resign his embassy and run for the Senate from Kentucky, where Cooper has been an exceptionally good vote getter. Cooper would have preferred to stay in India where there is a most important job to be done, but he was dissuaded.

He worked out a communiqué draft in Washington and called up Gettysburg to get it OK'd, saying he was resigning and running at Ike's request. He read it to Jim Haggerty who asked him to hold the phone, then came back with approval. John resigned. A few days later Ike had a press conference. He was asked if he would "request" Dewey to run for the Senate from New York the way he had requested Cooper. He said no—and added he had *not* made any such request to Cooper. This not only hurt Cooper's own (and American) prestige in India, but it also made him out to be a liar. Now his opponent in Kentucky is already hitting him on that. John is fed up. To boot, he was misrepresented in San Francisco by the press as opposing the GOP civil-rights plank as "too strong." Actually, he thinks it is much too weak.

Tidbits: The wife of the Nepalese ambassador in New Delhi, entering the outside world for the first time, asked the Italian ambassador the first time she met him last year: "What has become of that great leader, Mussolini?"

When the King of Saudi Arabia visited New Delhi this year, Cooper asked the Saudi Arabian ambassador what the King was looking for: "Certainly not financial aid; money is the one thing we don't need."

WASHINGTON, *October 13, 1956*

LUNCH with Mates, the new Jugoslav ambassador, an exceedingly cultivated man, a Croat from Zagreb. Mates calls the Russians "two-dimensional" people. They simply do not think in three dimensions or understand those who do. The Russians were shocked to find that the common people were right in the instance of the Poznan riots. They couldn't imagine that the common people could be more right than any government. Dealing with the Russians is like trying to play music through an ultrasonic dog whistle. The United States must always remember that Jugoslavia naturally has certain complexes because it lives right next to a giant. It has its bristles out like a porcupine.

WASHINGTON, *October 17, 1956*

DINED with Dean Acheson and his wife, and David and Vangie Bruce. Acheson talked a great deal, saying France is finished as a power and it is not worth paying any attention to French views.

He has no use for Eisenhower and, despite his prestige as former Secretary of State, he would not make any effort to see the President to give him advice on the present situation. Yet, Acheson says, the world is going to rack and ruin and the United States is rapidly losing its position. He knew Ike well as a Lieutenant Colonel. Yet, on November 18, 1952, after Eisenhower had won the election, Acheson met with a group of leaders of the incoming administration and was hurt when Eisenhower addressed him as Mr. Secretary instead of Dean. Knowing Eisenhower, I'm sure he was merely trying to be respectful to a Secretary of State.

He maintains that Britain and France should have invaded Egypt within two weeks instead of dawdling on the Suez Canal issue. Acheson admitted that Henry Byroade, while he was Acheson's own Assistant Secretary of State in 1952, was working on a vague outline of what finally became the Baghdad Pact. This was only an examination of the advisability of furthering the "northern-tier" idea. Thus he confirms that the idea was not strictly a Republican invention as so many Democrats contend.

Long talk with Foster Dulles. He greeted me in a most friendly way despite the fact that I have been rather needling him in recent columns. "Why come here?" he asked with a grin. "I thought nobody in this office knew anything about foreign affairs." This morning I had written that the anger of France and Britain over the Suez situation did not yet seem to have percolated through to the State Department. He said he was used to being a whipping boy. He inquired after my gout and I inquired after his. Then we sat down and chatted.

I asked what he had to say about U.S. policy in eastern Europe. He replied:

On the whole there is a growing desire for nationalistic forms of government in that area. Above all, this is true in East Germany, Poland, Czechoslovakia, and Hungary. The example and influence of Tito is very useful. He has prospered under this. His example tends to make the mouths of the satellites water with envy. We have sharp differences with Tito on domestic policy. But his attraction on the satellites is useful. There is a parallelism there in our interest. We are not giving him aid to please him or vice versa. But it helps both our purposes. It would be a setback to the aspirations of the satellites if he had to fall back on Moscow.

I asked what Dulles knew about the Tito-Khrushchev talks. He admitted that he knew little. But he added: "We are satisfied. Tito's theory on separate roads to socialism is being opposed by Russia. That is to say, the Russians are trying to slow down the trend."

On the Middle East, he said:

It is almost impossible to foresee a satisfactory solution. The decision to carve Israel out had a great deal of merit but it raised an equal number of problems. I don't think they are insoluble. I have studied many of these jointly with the British. But we need a period of relative quiet during which the emotions must be calm. The Jews and the Arabs got along for a long time in many areas. The problem is not inherently insoluble.

The borders, incidents, refugees, and such make the tension. The weakness of Jordan is a disturbing factor. The elimination of British influence from the Arab Legion removed an element of stability. There is a fear that Jordan may disintegrate. Other nations want to be in on the kill. This creates new tensions.

If you could get a year or so without emotion it might be possible to get people to think in terms of their own welfare. The Eric Johnston water plan, for example, is a very worthy project. The United States would be willing to put up a lot of money to help resettle the Arabs.

But we must first get emotions to die down. Then Israel can become an important supplement to the rest of the Middle East. It is better equipped for industrial activity than the other countries. A solution theoretically can be seen. But it cannot be brought about during the present instability. And, of course, the Suez crisis has made everything worse.

There is a great tendency on the part of the French and the British to assume that because they are allied with us in NATO we will support them everywhere. However, I can show you the report of the Senate Foreign Relations Committee in 1949, before NATO was ratified, in which we pointed out that we were not allying ourselves in colonial areas with the NATO powers, but only in a specific NATO area.

Only if you have a complete federal union can you have one policy everywhere. For example, if Europe united, they could do this there. But apart from that—and of course no such union exists—we must stick only to specific commitments in specific areas.

Dulles thought the Russians were exerting "considerable influence" in Egypt. He said, however, Egypt seemed to be operating independently.

The Egyptians agreed to go on negotiating in the UN. The Russians had been trying to horn in. But the agreement is to continue negotiations with the Russians left out. Certainly that cannot please Moscow. We don't feel yet that Nasser is a pawn or a satellite. He has, however, a degree of dependence on Moscow which frankly we don't like.

I asked if it was time for us to do something drastic about the Baghdad Pact—either join it or allow it to die. He replied: "It would neither be useful for us to join it nor to disintegrate it at the present time. I organized the idea of the 'northern tier' countries, but I never envisioned its purpose as playing its present role in Arab politics. Iraq is using it to get backing against Egypt in a competition for hegemony in the Arab world. Iraq has ambitions to the south which preoccupy Iraq more than the northern danger."

Personally, I can't see how the State Department failed to foresee this in the beginning. The rivalry between Baghdad and Cairo is of long standing and it was perfectly clear that Iraq was going to use the pact against Egypt just as it was clear that Pakistan would use it against India instead of Russia.

As a practical matter we cannot join the Baghdad Pact unless we also make a comparable arrangement to support Israel. And this would require Senate consent. I am not sure that the Baghdad Pact members want us to join at the price of another pact with Israel.

The Baghdad Pact is useful. It shouldn't be allowed to dry up. We are closely identified with many of its principles. We are members of its economic committee. We are trying to gear in our own economic and military assistance in the area to work with the Baghdad Pact. It is better to keep it as it is.

I then asked Dulles what he thought about the present status of NATO and what could be done to help it. He replied:

There is much that we are prepared to do to shore up NATO. But not as much will be done by the others as we would like to see done or as we are willing to do ourselves. We cannot automatically commit ourselves to support policy of our allies out of the NATO area. But we would like to see the NATO Council become an important body of Cabinet rank, bringing the governments closer together. I can't be going over to Paris all the time. Lodge over at the UN is treated as if he had Cabinet rank. He goes to the National Security Council meetings in Washington. We would like to see a fellow like that hold the NATO job. When he came back to America he would attend Cabinet and National Security Council meetings. But some of our allies are not as keen on this as we are. This makes me a little discouraged. We have to develop in NATO some kind of a political equivalent to the Standing Group. The present mechanisms are not sufficient.

After seeing Dulles, I dropped in to see Bill Tyler, one of the principal deputies for European affairs who has been taking an active part in the Suez discussions.

Tyler told me that Soviet intelligence advised the Egyptians of the weakness of Britain and France when they were making military threats against Egypt. Therefore, the Egyptians knew in advance this was a total bluff. When Dulles was in London he pointed out to the British that they simply were not strong enough to undertake a military operation.

He reminded them that in 1953, they had eighty thousand troops in the Suez Canal zone. In addition to that, they had eight thousand men in an immediately disposable active reserve in Cyprus. But at that time the Imperial General Staff concluded a study in which they said that in order to take action against the Egyptians, who were then conducting a minor guerrilla war with the British, the British would have to occupy Alexandria and Cairo, as well as all the area around the Canal. This would have required more troops. And the British Government decided the entire operation was too expensive. This had an important influence upon the decision to evacuate the zone in 1954.

NEW YORK, *October 22, 1956*

LAST night, dinner with Averell and Marie Harriman at their New York house. When Marina and I arrived, Averell asked what I knew about Poland. Averell had run into General Lucius Clay. They were talking about what we could do to help the new Warsaw government. Averell immediately called Clay and put me on the phone. Clay wanted to know who was ambassador there and whether he was any good; whether there were any people in the embassy who were any good. I told him. "Just as I thought," said Clay. "We seem to have a talent for never having a good man in the right place at the right time."

He asked what I recommended. I thought it might be all right if the State Department advised Gomulka or some other Polish leader as soon as possible that we would be prepared to help economically, but we did not want to intrude. We should avoid embarrassing the new government and any such message from the United States should be kept strictly secret. He agreed. He would get in touch with the President right away.

Later Adlai Stevenson called. Adlai wanted to know what the Democrats should to do to capitalize on the Polish situation. Averell, at my suggestion, told Stevenson he should make no statements except of the most vague and general sort. After all, he did not want to embarrass the U.S. government, nor in any way exacerbate the situation in Poland. However, Averell got the impression that Adlai wanted to make some specific statement claiming credit for the Democrats and attacking the Republicans. Averell, who is very good in these crises, argued with Stevenson but had a feeling his words were not being heeded.

I asked Averell whether he would agree to be Secretary of State if Stevenson won the election. He was confident Stevenson would not ask him but would prefer either Bowles or Finletter. Between those two, Bowles was vigorous and had some ideas even "though he would like to make the United States a satellite of India." However, Averell did indicate that if asked he would accept.

Averell was bitter about our foreign policy. He thinks our world position is sagging; Eisenhower simply refuses to make decisions and anyway, he doesn't know what is going on because nobody tells him. Dulles is a disaster as Secretary of State.

Harriman, by the way, thought my idea of naming the defeated presidential nominee as our next ambassador to NATO was excellent. He is deeply worried about what is happening to NATO. The terms of reference and powers of the American ambassador have been drastically cut. Averell thinks it important that we should have a man of real stature in order to avoid just dealing with foreign governments on a bilateral basis. There must be one fellow dealing with the whole field.

Averell liked my book (*The Big Thaw*) a great deal and agreed with it totally. But, he kept asking, why on earth doesn't Harper's publish it sooner? I told him I was asking the same thing. He said: "Well you tell Cass Canfield for me that I beat you up on the subject and I think it is shocking that the book isn't out right now."

Harriman doesn't think Stevenson stands any chance of winning the election. He has made a bad campaign and has not developed the proper issues. For example, he never worked really hard on the subject of Nixon and Eisenhower's health. Averell thinks Eisenhower is likely to win by almost as big a majority as in 1952.

NEW YORK, *October 24, 1956*

LAST night we went to a party given by Marietta Tree for Adlai Stevenson and a group of Democratic leaders. James Finnegan, chairman of the Democratic National Committee, was present. He made it plain he was fed up with Stevenson's campaigning methods. He said he had missed all the important chances and had devoted too much time to things that the American people were not interested in—like foreign policy and the H-bomb. Finnegan thought the only real issue was Eisenhower's health and Nixon and that Stevenson had messed it up. I asked him who would be in control of the Democratic party—its recognized leader—after the elections if Stevenson loses. He replied: "The state of Texas." He meant Senator Lyndon Johnson and Sam Rayburn.

NEW YORK, *October 25, 1956*

AT dinner I saw Lew Douglas who told a rather interesting story about Clemenceau. When Clemenceau visited the front in 1918, a German artillery barrage was laid down and a *poilu* was mortally wounded very near him. Just before he died the boy gave him a little bouquet of wild flowers he had in his shirt. Clemenceau promised to keep these with him until he died. From then on, Clemenceau cherished these withered flowers under a glass bell in his office. His will contained a clause requesting that the bouquet be lowered into the grave with him.

Mrs. Eisenhower's secretary called up this afternoon. The President and Mamie came for a Republican rally at Madison Square Garden this evening. Mrs. Ike wanted to get hold of Marina and have a chat with her because they missed each other in Washington. The President came in for a moment and kissed her on the cheek. He asked about me and Marina said I was up to my ears working on Hungary and Poland. "Poor fellows, poor fellows," he said. "I think about them all the time. I wish there were some way of helping them."

PITTSBURGH, *October 26, 1956*

THIS evening I dined with my old friend Jim Fulton, a Republican Congressman for years and one of the most important members of the Foreign Affairs Committee. Jim argued: Why should we send money to England so that Queen Elizabeth can have a big yacht? Why should we send money to France to finance the Paris park system? Why should we send money to Italy in order to build a big new railway station in Rome? He regards Britain and our other allies merely as bases for American power, not as countries where humans reside.

PARIS, KENTUCKY, *October 27, 1956*

THIS is the seat of Bourbon County, a dreary little town despite its famous name and an especially miserable place to spend my forty-fourth birthday. Marina gave me two silver mugs in which to drink Mint Juleps. Alas, it was a Sunday and no bourbon available. The manager of our grimy hotel guided us to a Greek restaurant where I could pour a scotch under the table into a cup and thus celebrate. I prefer the other Paris; even bourbon is easier to get.

LOUISVILLE, KENTUCKY, *October 29, 1956*

LONG talk with John Cooper, who is running for the Senate again. Cooper said the attitude of most people was that Eisenhower "got us out of war" in Korea, hardly a penetrating attitude. Outside of that, John says, there is not much discussion of foreign policy, despite events in eastern Europe. Cooper argues in his speeches: "At a time when these countries are showing signs of breaking away from Russia, it is harmful for us to give the impression that we are reducing our strength by abolishing the draft and limiting the H-bomb."

John is optimistic despite the fact that the registered vote in Kentucky is 55 percent Democratic as compared with 45 percent Republican. "What distinguishes them?" I asked. Cooper said, "It depends which side your grandpappy shot for."

COLUMBIA, SOUTH CAROLINA, *November 2, 1956*

I CAME in here last night to order to see James F. Byrnes. I wanted to ask two things: Whether it is inherent in the office that a Secretary of State should be unpopular; and how one could reconcile the Southern racial situation with American overseas propaganda and diplomatic interests.

This morning, the colored porter with our breakfast tray commented on the situation overseas—namely the Middle East and Hungary: "There will always be wars as long as the little people are pushed around. Down here they kill little people like myself just for the color of their skin."

After this tragic remark I walked down the street and ran into Byrnes, looking very fit and dapper, a block from his office. As we ambled along, about one out of every five people either said hello or exchanged brief conversations. He is obviously the grand old man and elder statesman of South Carolina: once Wartime Mobilization Director, Secretary of State, Governor of South Carolina, Senator, Justice of the Supreme Court.

I told him that Judge Learned Hand had assured me often that it was simply impossible to be a really good Secretary of State and above all, to be a popular one. How did Byrnes, as former holder of that office, feel? He replied:

Any effort of the Secretary of State to please a local situation is bound to be disastrous. This makes for unpopularity in his office. I don't recall any effort to fix foreign policy to meet the political needs of a community, with the exception of the case of Israel back in 1945. Both parties were then trying to please groups interested in raising the number of immigrants to Palestine. Ernie Bevin told me representatives of the Arabs and Jews were at that time in London. Bevin assured me he had learned their conversations had been very amicable. Attlee and his Cabinet hoped real progress was being made toward satisfactory settlement in Palestine—satisfactory to both sides. The main issue at that time was the number of immigrants allowed in.

But Truman cabled Attlee, telling him the U.S. position: between 200,000 and 300,000 Jews should be immediately permitted to enter Palestine. He wanted me to reiterate this to Bevin. It was nice of Truman to tell me this and he added: "I hope I haven't thrown a monkey wrench into your machine."

I asked the President if he had already sent this request to the British. He replied in the affirmative. Truman further told me that Yom Kippur was starting and he had heard that Tom Dewey was going to make a speech in the following week advocating the same thing. He wanted to make his speech before Dewey.

I remember Bevin telling me he knew I had nothing to do with this. But he added: "You can't run foreign policy to meet the needs of your New York elections. There are too many of them." He was referring to the fact there were mayoralty and gubernatorial elections as well as presidential ones. In this particular case I believe it was the election when O'Dwyer was elected mayor.

This sort of thing cannot be done. You must keep in mind the interests of the people as a whole rather than the interests of any particular group of the people. Our Polish friends have always been enthusiastic for Polish interests. There are lots of Poles in Michigan and they managed to make life miserable for poor old Arthur Vandenberg. In New Jersey there are lots of Ukrainians and they have been very outspoken. As these various groups press their interests, the Congressmen and Senators often try to pass the buck to the Secretary of State and the President rather than offend groups of constituents and thereby lose votes. A man can introduce a resolution favorable to such pressure groups of constituents just to gain popularity.

The Secretary of State must be a whipping boy. He must be strong enough to resist demands from various groups having at heart some particular or local grievance. But the pressures should continue. That is the way our democracy works. There is no way of preventing this nor should there be. But some person in office must be strong enough to say no. That is the Secretary of State.

The Secretary has a terrible task because he has the economic division under him as well as the diplomatic division. This includes control of reciprocal trade agreements and touches the entire national economy.

For example, in the South the textile people have been severely hurt by Japanese imports to the United States. They have justifiably complained. And they were angry when our government said the Japanese could not sell their textiles to China. Yet we gave the Japanese many new mills which could compete with us. It was folly that we prevented the Japanese from selling to Communist China.

I asked if Byrnes felt it might be a good idea to have a permanent, career Under Secretary of State who was a civil servant and belonged to neither party. He replied in the negative, saying: "Because the Secretary must travel so much, the Under Secretary has to act in his absence. And he must attend Cabinet meetings. It probably would not be a good idea to have a career man in this job. It would not be practical."

I asked Byrnes how he could relate our position and prestige abroad in terms of Jeffersonian democracy with the idea of segregation at home. He replied:

There is no answer to this save the facts. The difficulty is that the Northern press so distorts the facts concerning the people from the Potomac down to the Gulf. And the information of the Northern press is what goes abroad—not the point of view of the South.

Criticisms of the role of the Negro in the United States are not justified. The Negroes in South Carolina have more automobiles than all the people of the Soviet Union together. Sunday, I drove by a little Negro country church that wouldn't hold more than two hundred people. Yet there were seventy-one cars outside—all owned by Negroes. That meant about $150,000 worth of transportation outside that little church. The Negro tobacco farmers are making money. Their land is worth from $700 to $1000 an acre. You see television antennae on almost all their houses.

The Negroes have money. They are in the banks, the stores, business. They are lawyers. There is, of course, still a shortage of Negro doctors. I am helping two Negroes myself to study to become physicians. But this economic well-being is not reported. The Negroes are making wonderful progress. Negro schools are often better than white schools because they are newer. We should prevent a picture from going abroad that is limited to the Northern viewpoint.

The Southerner wants to do his share in national affairs. The South has been in all our wars. The President must depend upon Southern support in Congress no matter what differences may be on domestic questions. The strongest internationalists are in the South. Opposition to the administration in the last two wars was in the hyphenated vote of the North.

We should stress in our propaganda abroad such things as the fact that South Carolina Negroes own more automobiles than all the Russians. The voice of America must acknowledge the view of the Southern states. We have done our share for the United States. But we are not willing to give up our way of life just to please the Soviets in a propaganda war. The 1954 Supreme Court decision to give up segregation was unconstitutional. That decision has certainly not improved our reputation among the Arab states or India but it has divided the country; and a divided country is more dangerous for the United States than a point gained in the Cold War.

If I were running the Voice of America I would point out that there is no such race feeling in the South as among the three Arab nations which decline to permit Jews to enter their country. There is no petty prejudice against religion here in the South. The South voted for a Catholic, John Kennedy, for Democratic nominee for vice president. For ten years I have been going to the mountains of New Hampshire because I have hay fever. I found out that no Jew is allowed to stay in the hotel I go to. The manager told me that other people would leave the hotel if Jews were permitted. In the University Club of New York, the son of my friend Barney Baruch was blackballed. That couldn't happen in South Carolina. The Speaker of our House for the last ten years has been a Jew and there are only two Jews in the Legislature. He was elected without opposition. No one ever heard of a Jew being kept out of a hotel in South Carolina. Our social leaders include Jews. They are among our outstanding citizens. And yet the people in New England who criticize us on the subject of racial integration fail to appreciate our lack of prejudices on one of their own blind spots.

We have a deep-seated racial problem which we cannot understand; but it exists and it is. As Disraeli said, it is a key to history. The Negroes here exercise every privilege and have progressed as nowhere else in their history. But it is unfair to make children the guinea pigs of a social problem. White children are held back by this as has been proven in Washington, D.C. This problem should have started off in the hotels where there should have been integration first if such was to be the move. There you would be dealing with adult men and women.

NEW YORK, *November 7, 1956*

LAST night, election-day evening, we dined at the Harrimans. Practically everybody there was a Democrat. The evening was pretty sad. Averell was controlled and unemotional. I don't think he felt any deep unhappiness about Stevenson getting trimmed. In his heart of hearts I am sure he doesn't think too much of Adlai. During the current crisis Averell has publicly stated that Eisenhower is President of all the American people, not just Republicans, and it is everybody's duty to be behind him as "our President." Harriman grows as the years go on.

NEW YORK, *November 9, 1956*

DINED at the home of Arthur Lall. Indian delegate to UN Krishna Menon was there. There is something pathetic about him. He is not nearly as bright as he fancies himself. But the combination of his rather shabby shoes, badly cut dinner jacket, and curious conceit was touching. He seemed very tired and fell asleep—or pretended to be—several times resting his head on the silver topped cane he carries. But I noticed that when he was presumably asleep and completely relaxed his feet kept twitching.

He didn't make much sense but was less offensive than I feared; I suppose that is the advantage of having such a terrible reputation go before you.

ALBANY, NEW YORK, *November 16, 1956*

WE came up here for Averell Harriman's sixty-fifth birthday. At dinner last night were Admiral Kirk and his wife, George Backer and his wife, Madeleine Sherwood (Bob Sherwood's widow), Jack and June Bingham (he is Averell's personal secretary), and Charlie Poletti and wife (for a brief period governor of New York). Kirk acted as toastmaster and everybody made a little toast to which Averell responded courteously and movingly.

After dinner we sat around until 2 A.M. chatting. Averell told me once again he thought Stalin was the most powerful and visibly self-confident man he had ever met. He thought Stalin had a genuine liking for both Roosevelt and Churchill. Roosevelt was seriously coming around to a strong attitude against the Russians at the time of his death. Averell was very worried about Truman when Roosevelt died. He went home from Moscow (where he was ambassador) on his own initiative right after Roosevelt's death in order to see Truman. He was pleased to see how tough Truman was and what a quick grasp he got of the world situation. When Molotov came over Truman dressed him down "as nobody had ever dared to do before."

NEW YORK, *November 20, 1956*

S. W. R. D. BANDARANAIKE, Prime Minister of Ceylon, came to lunch: an unimpressive little man, badly dressed in European style clothes, with glasses and strange tufts of hair coming out of each ear. He is naive, didactic, and overconfident.

He claims there was a split in the Kremlin between the Khrushchev group and the Stalinist group (headed by Molotov) on Hungary. Marshal Zhukov stepped in and said that under no circumstances could Russia afford to lose control of Hungary. At this point the Russians decided to move.

Bandaranaike thinks there can never be peace in the Middle East until Israel is obliterated from the map. This is an odd view for a peace-loving Asian. He argues that Israel is a false idea and despite the fact that there are 1,800,000 Jews settled there, they cannot remain forever. He asks: "Why do the Jews want this desert? After all, they run the world anyway."

NEW YORK, *November 23, 1956*

LONG talk with Habib Bourguiba, Prime Minister of newly independent Tunisia: short, rather good-looking with gray hair, strong face and light gray-blue eyes.

Bourguiba assured me Tunisia was on the side of the West in the world conflict and could not remain neutral in a crisis. He thought it probable that some day Tunisia would join NATO. Tunisian public opinion was horrified at the invasion of Egypt but equally horrified at the Soviet repression in Hungary. He feared some Arab leaders might miscalculate and act too strongly on the assumption they would be backed to the hilt by the Russians.

U.S. prestige in Tunisia has risen immensely as a result of our stand on Suez. Bourguiba had just seen Eisenhower and was much impressed. He thought him a courageous, honest man who understood the situation of the world. He had managed to disassociate the United States from the smear of colonialism.

NEW YORK, *November 26, 1956*

WE spent the weekend with Jock and Betsey Whitney at Greentree, their enormous estate at Manhasset, Long Island. Jock told me he has now been asked by the President to be ambassador to Great Britain, and he has accepted. This happened Friday afternoon. The President wants him to come right down to Washington and start doing his homework.

Jock had just looked over the letter he originally sent the President, turning down the prospects of a foreign embassy—which I got him to recall before Eisenhower saw it. He is particularly happy because he says now: "It was even a bad letter. I'm certainly glad he never saw it."

Jock told me Eisenhower confided to him he intends to drop the old guard in the Republican party—the extra-conservative Senators, etc. He simply doesn't need them anymore and he is going to do his best to stress "the new Republicanism." Herter is going to get a job in the White House for a while before eventually moving over to the State Department, where he will replace Herbert Hoover, Jr.

THE BIGGEST

DUFFER OF ALL

NEW YORK, *November 27, 1956*

L AST NIGHT MARINA AND I TOOK YURI ZHUKOV OUT TO DINNER. HE
was extremely interesting and not optimistic. He is not here for
Pravda but as a special advisor to Shepilov, Soviet foreign minister. He confided: "I know him as well as you know Chip Bohlen."

Yuri was brutally frank on Hungary. He said Hungary must stay with
the Russian bloc. If the West tried to interfere it would be considered
a casus belli by Moscow. I told him we were deeply disturbed about
Nagy's kidnapping. He made no apologies. He merely said: "Nagy was
a prowestern man. We cannot allow Hungary to go to the West." I argued
that Nagy was just a national Communist and Titoist. He claimed Nagy
was a double-dealer doing everything to work Hungary westward; that
this could not be tolerated. He added that Kadar, the present Hungarian
Prime Minister, was an anti-Stalinist and a real Titoist; that he had
suffered under the Rakosi regime. I deduced that there is not going to
be any effort to pretend that Nagy is free or that the U.S.S.R. was not
involved in his disappearance.

Zhukov admitted the Cold War was on again and thought this would
continue for some time. Then there would be a gradual return to the
"Geneva spirit." It was absolutely essential that both sides retain their
sangfroid. He warned: "You Americans should not overestimate Russia's
patience." This was a rather menacing remark.

Shepilov had absolutely nothing to do with the Middle East arms deals,
despite his highly touted visit to Cairo last year. He had originally been
invited to come to Cairo as editor of *Pravda*, but before the visit ma-
terialized he had been named foreign minister. This was accidental.

Yuri was regretful about the present state of relations between United

States and Russia. Both sides continually made mistakes and insulted each other and then reinsulted each other. Things were getting worse. If the U.S. interest in Hungary today was just Cold War propaganda, that is all right. He added ominously: "But if you want to take Hungary out of the Soviet camp, there will be war."

The Russians were worried by the aftermath of General Twining's visit. Right after Twining left Russia, American planes were sent at very high altitudes over Poland and the western Soviet Union. The Russians interpreted this as an American effort to show Russia that Twining was convinced the new Soviet aircraft he had been shown in Russia were just prototypes and were not actually in production. Zhukov added: "We thought this a very rude reply."

He said the United States was making a very great mistake by driving Russia back into a "hard policy"—which I presume is a euphemism for Stalinism. He said: "You seem to want us there—back in a Cold War position. Much has been lost as a result of your attitude."

Today, I received the following letter:

THE WHITE HOUSE
Washington

November 20, 1956

Dear Cy:

Because *The Big Thaw* deals with a subject that occupies nearly all my waking hours these days—and because you wrote it—I know I shall read it with the greatest possible interest. Thank you for sending it to me, and for your personal inscription.

Incidentally, these days I am the biggest "duffer" of all—since I have had practically no time to play in these last three months.
With warm regard,

As ever,
[s]   D. E.

PARIS, *December 6, 1956*

LUNCH at the home of Brigitte Gros (sister of Jean-Jacques Servan-Schreiber), with Jenny Lee (Mrs. Aneurin) Bevan. She is Highland Scottish, speaks with quite an accent. She is clearly bright, knows how to be amiable, and is also quite evidently power-hungry. She tried to make it as clear as possible that her husband is not anti-American. They both knew that America was at heart a liberal country, despite the McCarthy episodes of the last few years.

She said Bevan didn't harbor any resentment against Gaitskell. Gaitskell was the obvious leader of the right wing of the Labour party and the most effective of them. Likewise, Nye is the most obvious, effective leader of the left. They must work together. She resents people like Wilson and Dick Crossman who deserted Bevan for the Gaitskell group. It was perfectly understood in the party that Gaitskell would be the next Prime Minister and that Bevan would be foreign secretary.

PARIS, *December 11, 1956*

DOUG Dillon is not going to run for governor of New Jersey but is working hard to get to the Senate. He is delighted that Herter is replacing Hoover. Hoover was far too anxious to ignore France and England in favor of the Arab world. He thinks Cabot Lodge has already gummed up any chance he had of aspiring to the post of ambassador here. Dillon said Lodge loves to vote with the Arab-Asian bloc and the Russians for the sake of large impressive UN majorities. Mollet will soon announce further concessions in Algeria. This will enable the United States to either abstain or vote with France in the Assembly. With a grim smile Dillon acknowledged this would infuriate Lodge.

It will be much easier to restore relations between France and the U.S.A. than between Britain and the U.S.A. Dillon is sure a meeting between Mollet and Eisenhower can be arranged early next year. The French government did a good job in keeping down the flames of passion last month. But the British government, on the contrary, seemed to encourage them. There is not the same feeling of personal betrayal vis-à-vis Mollet and Pineau that Dulles and Eisenhower harbor for Eden and Lloyd.

PARIS, *December 12, 1956*

THIS afternoon, I went over to de Gaulle's headquarters and had a long talk. The General began one of his usual gloomy tours d'horizon by stating that nowhere in the world does any government or any statesman seem to know what he wants. He found this astonishing, commenting as an observer rather than as a participator in events. The only policy of any government was to react to events, not to plan for events.*

The General said that as a military man he was astonished by the ineptness of the Suez operation. He found it very confusing. It should have been planned to accomplish its objectives within two days on a lightning basis. Instead of that, there was a ridiculous long-range, tedious, drawn-out plan for something the equivalent—in terms of logistics and the length of time—of the Normandy landing.

De Gaulle said neither the eastern powers (meaning Russia) nor the West have any policies in Europe. Here too, they are simply reacting to

* See de Gaulle's further comments, pp. 60, 80–81.

events as they occur. When the revolution in Hungary developed, Washington and Moscow were surprised. Neither knew what to do about it.*

In the future, there is bound to be a world war. This is the future of the world. When or how it will come I don't know. It will come whether there is a revolt in East Germany which drags in the West Germans; or whether there is no such revolt. There will be a danger to the world brought about because Prussia revolts against Communist and Soviet domination; or, equally because Prussia does not revolt. War is a law of the human species. What Bossuet called "providence" is responsible. War is the law of the species. The moment for this war will come when the people of the world wish to destroy themselves, or to risk that by changing things. But, the pretext for such a war or the men who will start it cannot be foreseen. After all, the assassination of an Austrian archduke was surely not an adequate pretext for World War I, with all its casualties.

I asked whether he thought Mendès-France was now so fed up with things that he was ready to throw in his lot with de Gaulle. The General replied: "I know this man. I know his work. But nevertheless he is a man of the system. He knows the regime is against him. I told him that the regime won't change itself, won't reform itself." But de Gaulle did not indicate that Mendès in any way had gone so far as to be with him.†
I asked if he thought anti-American feeling was growing. He replied:

There is no hate for the United States in France. France remains friendly to the United States. But the French people don't like the American people. The United States is our friend and will remain so; but the American people are not regarded sympathetically. Nevertheless, the United States will remain our friend. From time to time, when moments of great danger arise, then only the United States and France will remain and people will tend to forget the Americans and French who do not get on so well. Of course, during intervening periods, the fact that our interests are not really the same will continue to appear more obviously.

In concluding, de Gaulle told me that he was still working very hard on his book. It takes him two years to finish a volume. The first two volumes are of course out; volume two having appeared in June. It will take him eighteen more months to finish volume three. He works from three to four hours a day almost every day. He has a great deal of rereading of documents to do and the job of condensation is immense.

PARIS, *December 13, 1956*

LUNCH with General Hans Speidel, here for the NATO meeting. He is now head of the Joint Services Command in Germany, which, he explained,

---

* See de Gaulle's further comments, pp. 30–31, 48, 59–60.
† See de Gaulle's further comments, p. 30.

is an equivalent position to that held by Admiral Radford, our chairman of the Joint Chiefs of Staff. Heusinger is in a position between him and the German Cabinet. For political reasons—obviously because of Heusinger's record during World War II—Heusinger can hold no command. Therefore Speidel is chief commanding officer in Germany today.

It has been agreed that in April he will be named commander-in-chief of all NATO ground troops on the central front, stretching from Switzerland to Denmark. The commander-in-chief of all central forces —ground, air, and naval—will remain Valluy, a Frenchman.

Today there are 68,000 Germans under arms. By July 1, 1957, the Germans have promised to commit to NATO more than five divisions. Speidel is satisfied with the pace of rearmament.

I asked if Germany had requested to be represented on the Standing Group in Washington. He said no. The situation was being handled differently. NATO would probably appoint a chairman of the military committee (which represents the fifteen chiefs of staff). This chairman, a sort of permanent figure of secretary-general—a military equivalent to Ismay on the political side—would serve as liaison between the military committee and the Standing Group. The first such permanent boss of the military committee would be Heusinger. In other words, Germany would get into the top level without actually becoming a member of the Standing Group.

Speidel is worried about what may happen in eastern Germany. The West German government is doing its best to calm down the East Germans and prevent them from a revolution similar to the Hungarian revolution. But they're not sure they'll be able to succeed with their advice.

NATO's great weakness remains the fact that Norstad doesn't have any authority to reply *immediately* to any Soviet action in Europe. He must first consult the governments. This is too late. He must be given authority to take immediate counteraction in case of trouble.

The Anglo-French venture into Suez was a complete military disaster. They should have been ready for a blitz—to finish the job in forty-eight hours. The French wanted this; they wanted to go in very heavily and capture Port Said, Ismailia, and Port Suez with airborne units. They did not wish to stop the Israelis ten miles from the canal. However the British overruled them on all points. The result was catastrophic.

PARIS, *December 14, 1956*

LUNCH with Evangelos Averoff, Greek foreign minister. Also present were, George Seferiades (Seferis, the poet) and Charlie Yost, now minister at our embassy here.

They're very concerned about the rise in popularity throughout Greece of Colonel Grivas, leader of EOKA, the Cypriot underground. Grivas is a career Greek army officer, a colonel during the Albanian war against the Italians. After that he organized the X organization, an extreme right-wing officers' group which fought the Communists during the occupation. Grivas was born in Cyprus but was educated at the Greek Officer's Academy. He is now on the island heading the underground and since the deportation of Archbishop Makarios and the entire Ethnarchy, he is the only spokesman for the island's Greek population. He has become a legendary figure in Greece itself and Averoff fears he might very well be elected Prime Minister some day on the basis of his patriotic record in Cyprus. This would be very dangerous because of Grivas's right-wing tendencies.

Averoff said the Cyprus situation is getting worse. A new issue has been posed which is highly embarrassing to everyone concerned. This is the question of Cyprus's demilitarization. Since the Suez expedition there has been a growing demand in the Arab world that whatever the future of Cyprus may be, it should be demilitarized. This will be highly inconvenient to Greece as well as to Turkey and England.

This afternoon I had a talk with Franz-Josef Strauss, federal defense minister for the West German Republic, a burly, powerful-looking young man. He recalled—which is true—that he had had a strongly anti-Nazi record. Our conversation roved over many subjects.

This afternoon there is going to be discussion of the NATO communiqué. As now drafted, it talks only of steps to be taken to counter any "serious" aggression. The Germans insist the qualification "serious" be eliminated. "After all, aggression is aggression. Any aggression is serious."

Strauss is very disturbed by the moral situation in which the world finds itself. Are we to remain helpless to save decent people in the Soviet bloc merely because of the fear of total war? If this is to be the case, doesn't it prove that Hitler was really right? If Hitler had had atomic weapons in 1939, he would have been allowed to get away with everything and murder anyone he wished. Not even England would have dared to go to war against him if it meant global destruction. If the present logic is followed to its conclusion, it means only that the Soviets can do things equally horrible merely because they are stronger and the weapons in existence are more dangerous. Were the war criminals of Nuremberg hanged because of their crimes or because they were not powerful enough to commit them? This is a grave moral problem. Was it a question of the Nazis' power or their wickedness?

The West must be careful not to condemn by lack of support the anti-Communists now within the Soviet orbit. These people in many cases do not wish to collaborate with the West, but they want to throw out their

Communist governments. The moral position of many of them is similar to that of the anti-Nazi officers during World War II. They did not want to collaborate with the enemy in order to get rid of Hitler. In a sense, a similar psychology exists among many anti-Communist elements in countries such as Poland. We must be careful, furthermore, to avoid having such anti-Communist elements accused of being "spies" for the West by the present regimes in eastern Europe.

The Russians have now brought seven thousand tanks into East Germany. They are in a position to squash anything and presumably the East German people are aware of this. Even if the present troubles in Poland expand into an uprising, Strauss does not think the movement will spread into East Germany.

But if it should spread, it would be difficult to prevent the West German people from trying to help their brothers across the frontier. It would be virtually politically impossible for Bonn to stop this. The only way of acting, Strauss feels, would be to permit "armed infiltration" to go from West Germany into East Germany. That is to say, volunteers and weapons would be smuggled across the border. At the same time the western powers, above all the United States, would have to issue public warnings to the Russians. I asked Strauss what kind of warnings could be issued. He was not very clear about this. But he stressed the necessity of *immediate* warning. One of the tragedies of the Hungarian situation was that for three or four days, when everyone knew Soviet tanks were rolling into Hungary, no public cautioning statements were made in the UN or elsewhere. Nothing was done until the shooting actually started.

I asked what Strauss thought about reports from Washington that the United States was again considering a new disarmament approach to Russia—based upon the idea of gradual evacuation from the heart of Europe of both NATO and Soviet troops. Strauss said that there was no chance of any such agreement for three or four years at least. First of all, intercontinental ballistic missiles and strategic aircraft would have to be developed so they could strike just as well from Africa as from Europe. Secondly, the West German rearmament program must be completed so that there would be German divisions on the scene as American troops pulled out. Only when that had been brought about would it be satisfactory to consider the evacuation of Germany—and of the entire continent—by American ground troops. And even this could not be accomplished unless we got a quid pro quo in return. The Russians would have to pull their troops totally out of eastern Europe and back of the Soviet borders. In other words, the Warsaw Pact would have to be dissolved. And furthermore we must make it clear to the Russians and to the entire world that the Warsaw Pact does not give Moscow the right to armed intervention in any eastern European country now a member of that pact.

PARIS, *December 15, 1956*

YESTERDAY evening Dulles invited me in for a drink chez Dillon. Of NATO—in the wake of Suez—he said:

I can't say that all our differences are forgotten, but the past begins to recede as one begins to work on the future.

I agree with Lloyd and Pineau that there is a need to clear the Suez Canal as rapidly as possible. But there are limitations growing out of the fact that the salvage craft there are in the British and French navies —this presents political difficulties. Britain and France have agreed to take certain steps to make it easier to use their craft.

On the subject of eastern Europe, Dulles said:

It is the policy of this administration to encourage in every way the hopes and peaceful efforts of these peoples to regain their national independence and conditions of freedom, free religion, and economy. We have never encouraged the use of violence because the Soviets had such massive power to quell a revolution and we could not intervene without causing World War III. And in such a war the peoples of eastern Europe would be the first to be exterminated. We do not wish to disparage the courage of the people who did use violence. There are people, of course, who want to fight and die for freedom. I admire and respect them, but we do not wish to encourage such an attitude.

Dulles said the main problem facing us now was this: if all our eggs are in a nuclear basket, the Russians can do things and get away with them because it simply would not be worth dropping the atom bomb in order to stop them. We have to be prepared to reply in degree according to the offense. He said: "I always wanted us to have the *capacity* for nuclear retaliatory power—but not to depend totally upon it." (I think he is revising his policy a bit here.)

When I was saying good-bye, Dulles said: "What are they doing to me? First I lost Livy Merchant to Ottawa. Now I'm losing Doug Mac-Arthur to Tokyo. It's like losing my left arm and my right arm. How do they expect me to get things done without them?"

Later I had lunch with Bill Tyler, head of the Western European Division of the State Department. As far as Washington knows, it was originally planned Israel should attack Egypt on November 7—the day after our elections. This date was moved up as a consequence of the Hungarian uprising when it was figured that Russia would be occupied in eastern Europe and UN attention could be focused there. The French and the British, who were obviously in collusion with Israel, had drawn up a list for a dummy government of Egypt. Tyler doesn't remember who was on the list. I asked if it was to be headed by Naguib. He said no; but he did not remember the name of the proposed chief. Nasser clearly got wind of this and rounded up and shot forty-five Egyptian officers, including the chief of the air force.

Tyler admits that Dulles had absolutely no policy on the Middle East prior to the Anglo-French invasion of Suez. The trouble with Dulles is that although he is a brilliant acrobat and totally flexible in the way he operates, he simply doesn't take advice from anybody else and doesn't read telegrams from his ambassadors.

PARIS, *January 3, 1957*

UNCLE Arthur today sent me a copy of a letter Al Gruenther wrote him dated December 23 in Washington (office of the Joint Chiefs of Staff). Gruenther says: "It will interest you to know that an important resident of this city read the chapter on Tito from *The Big Thaw*." Of course Al referred to Eisenhower. Ike not only read my views but was apparently influenced by them in his new policy toward eastern Europe.

PARIS, *January 9, 1957*

LAST night Marina and I dined alone with the Norstads, at Marnes-la-Coquette. They have moved into the old Eisenhower-Ridgway-Gruenther house. Larry is going to be fifty in three months. His hair is grayed; he is taut, tense, and tired. He confided that he had a heart attack last year, a coronary occlusion such as Eisenhower had. Since this, he has subjected himself to every kind of fitness check—climbing mountains, etc.—to see if he could stand the strain. He is satisfied he can. This is top secret.

Larry told me a rather interesting story. When Ike was still over here, Perle Mesta invited the Eisenhowers and Norstads for a weekend in Luxembourg. Instead of keeping it quiet she gave a big dance and got in a jazz band. Larry was bored silly when he ran into Ike who had had a couple of extra drinks and said to him: "You know I have made more than $800,000 out of that book of mine. Under the capital-gains tax I had to send 25 percent to the government. I called up the Secretary of the Treasury and told him I wanted to give him the check personally because the sum was so large. Imagine Dwight D. Eisenhower signing a check to the United States Government for almost a quarter of a million dollars." Eisenhower added: "Imagine being able to give that much money all by yourself to your government. What a wonderful system we have."

Larry says the British and French never gave him any advance information about the Suez campaign. However, U.S. intelligence had good clues once the British and French started building up in Cyprus. When the show started all intelligence dried up.

He has no use for the Arabs and thinks it is ridiculous to try to base policy on them. They are chaotic, emotional people and the countries most of them live in are mere geographical fictions. They have no military strength nor political solidity. The Israeli campaign showed as much. He says the French were far better prepared militarily than the British in the Suez affair and on the whole planned pretty well.

Norstad expressed little admiration for Admiral Radford. He said that curiously enough in all his arguments, when he was chief of staff for the army, Ridgway was right—but for the wrong reasons. He opposed intervention in Indochina and in the Chinese offshore islands. But he opposed these interventions because they would have been air-naval jobs—not army. If he had seen a way of getting three or four more army divisions out of it, he would have been for the projects.

Lunch with Marcel Boussac, the textile king, sponsor of Dior and racing magnate, at the home of Lord Granard. He strongly criticized American policy: We were merely trying to oust Britain and France from their imperial possessions in order to take over ourselves. The outcome of the Eisenhower Middle Eastern policy will either be chaos and war in the Middle East or chaos and peace—while we sacrifice our alliance with Britain and France. If there's no unemployment in France there will merely be an anti-American government. If there is unemployment France will go Communist.

PARIS, *January 10, 1957*

INTERESTING talk with Norstad. I asked if he felt NATO would fall apart should the United States vote against France in the UN on Algeria. He replied:

No—but it would give us the greatest setback we have ever had. It would hurt us more than any blow could possibly do during the near future. France is totally irrational on Algeria. The French are now close to the point, however, in terms of reforms they are offering, where we could say that although their solution is not satisfactory it is, we hope, the means to an end. Under such logic, we could vote with the French in UN. If we just get too moral and either abstain or vote against France, we stand the risk of losing our shirts—NATO itself.

I asked him what effect on NATO the Suez crisis had had, how short we were running in oil. He said while we are short of reserve petroleum, the military situation is not dangerous.

Obviously the United States had to make available to all NATO countries reasonable quantities of up-to-date arms (meaning dual-purpose weapons that can use atomic warheads). He added: "You can't hold this alliance together and maintain its high morale having first-class and second-class soldiers—Americans with first-class weapons and the others on a secondary basis. For both military and psychological reasons, therefore, we must give new weapons to those countries which need them militarily. We must arrange so that nuclear warheads can be supplied on an emergency basis when the proper American authority so decides."

Norstad admitted NATO was de facto involved in the Eisenhower Middle East program. The U.S. couldn't station troops in Middle Eastern countries just to stand and wait. If an emergency developed suddenly, we would have to pull out forces from the Sixth Fleet and possibly also from Europe to send to the Middle East. But there is a precedent for this—just the way the French pulled out forces for Algeria and the British pulled out forces for the Suez invasion.

I asked if "French North Africa" were still considered part of his responsibility, as supreme commander. He claimed it never was. I made him check the 1952 terms of reference approved by the military committee and the NATO council and he found I was right: just muddy drafting.

Norstad talked at length about the necessity of maintaining ground forces to defend NATO. He said he could become the most popular NATO commander in history if he said that henceforth NATO could be defended only by air and navy. But that isn't true. NATO's primary mission is to deter war, and to deter war you have to have conventional ground forces in place. This has great political and psychological value.

PARIS, *January 15, 1957*

LUNCH with Raymond LaPorte and Lt. Col. Louis Mangin. Mangin, in the permanent French intelligence service, is a former regular who is now a reserve lieutenant colonel officially attached to the Ministry of Overseas Affairs. He handled all liaison work with Israel prior to the Suez invasion. He is the son of the famous General Mangin of World War I and Morocco fame.

LaPorte said he had been present when Charles Malik, Lebanese foreign minister, made a long report to the French on his way to the UN meeting. Malik had a seven-hour meeting with Nasser who told him frankly that Egypt would *never* permit Israeli ships to go to Elath through the Gulf of Aqaba. In other words, Egypt definitely intended to shut off Israeli access to the Red Sea as soon as the Israelis evacuated their positions along the Gulf. Furthermore, Nasser said he would never permit British and French ships to go through the Suez Canal until Israel had evacuated the Gaza strip. Malik was asked what he considered the greatest danger to Lebanon at present. Malik: "First Syria, second Egypt, and third, Israel."

Mangin said the Israeli air force was very efficient. It had been quietly brought up-to-date in terms of quantity as well as quality before the war started. France was a realistic power and recognized that its interests were the same as Israel's in the Middle East. Therefore, France had helped Israel. After all, before World War I, there was no written alliance between France and Russia. However, France and Russia fought together and their general staffs had made common plans in advance even though an alliance was lacking.

The British and the French had constantly warned the United States that their interests in the Middle East were vital and they might have to act forcefully to protect them. It was incorrect to say Washington had not been alerted in advance. The fact that the French and the British did not tip off Washington on their precise last-minute plans had nothing to do with it. Britain and France were ready to move against Egypt from Cyprus between September 12 and 15. They refrained because of warnings from Washington. This was the background to the final intervention in the autumn. Israel had made it clear to France that she felt constrained to move on her own. Therefore, France consulted England and decided to act at the same time, after the Israeli attack at the end of October. The original September plan had nothing to do with Israel, according to Mangin.

Mangin said the only sensible plan is as follows: Iraq should absorb Syria and most of Jordan. Saudi Arabia should take southern Jordan. The former Palestinian part of Jordan (the area west of the River Jordan) should go to Iraq but should be demilitarized under a United Nations guarantee. The Gaza strip should be placed under UN protection until an eventual solution came through. Israel should be guaranteed access to the Aqaba Gulf and Red Sea. Either the UN should have a force in control of the entrance to the Gulf, or there should be some kind of supervision to prevent Egypt from cutting it off again.

There were very important Egyptian fortifications in the Gaza strip. These only had offensive value. They had been built by German engineers. It was essential for the Israelis to prevent reestablishment of this type of fortification. Otherwise the Egyptians would again menace them. The Israelis were destroying everything of military value in the Sinai peninsula as they evacuated. It would take the Egyptians a long time before they were able to reestablish their position.

Quiet supper with the Dillons, in front of their fireplace. Doug has just gotten confirmation that he will be named Deputy Under Secretary of State in charge of economic affairs. He wanted this job and was afraid he wouldn't get it because he got into trouble with Dulles after the Suez crisis and because of his statement giving Russia credit for getting the British and French out of Egypt.

Dillon saw de Gaulle yesterday. The General blamed U.S. interference for keeping him from a return to power in 1947 and 1958. He said the U.S. preferred to have a weak government in France and this was the reason for its activity. De Gaulle told Dillon that from an American point of view he did not blame Washington.

PARIS, *January 17, 1957*

WE invited the Dillons for a farewell lunch at a little bistro. Ernest Hemingway was there and joined us for champagne and coffee. Hemingway was charming. He thanked me for all the assistance I tried to give to D, his former bodyguard, later jailed as a collaborator. He agreed there was nothing to do for the poor fellow; he had thought about it a great deal and was trying to imagine writing about him; but in the end, when he boiled it down, there was nothing to write. The tragedy was the fellow did have a police record. If D had been in the British army he would have gotten the DSO—probably the Victoria Cross. Unfortunately, here, he got nothing but a kick in the pants.

Hemingway is about my height, very hefty, with a three-quarter-inch white beard. His face is rather flushed and he clearly has a slight skin disease. He speaks a bit like an alcoholic—his words come out slightly blurred and with a certain hesitation. But he has a boyish, frank, simple way about him.

I asked about his days in Paris when he was an intimate friend of Ezra Pound and whether it was true he used to box with him. He said he tried to teach Ezra how to box, but it wasn't much good. He couldn't move very well. He has immense admiration for Pound although his political ideas are simply terrible. Hemingway and T. S. Eliot had just sent a letter to the U.S. Attorney General requesting that Pound be released from St. Elizabeth's Hospital. After all he is "just a crazy—the kind of crazy you find in towns all over the United States. When he lived up in Nantucket he was regarded as the local crazy."

Hemingway said any poet is crazy. He pointed to his head as he said that. The world would be a sad place if we didn't have crazy poets in it. He thought Ezra Pound should be sent back to Italy to spend the rest of his days there writing more beautiful poetry. And if Pound started to talk to people about the necessity of "killing all the Jews," he was "prepared to tell Ezra in advance that I will go to Italy and spank him personally." After all, nobody paid any attention to Pound except as a poet.

I told Hemingway about my exchange of notes with Pound last summer and how he said he would talk with me only if I agreed to have *The*

New York Times publish the complete works of Blackstone. Hemingway laughed: this was typical. It had nothing to do with Pound's present condition. He had always been that way.

I asked if it were true that Gertrude Stein had told him to quit newspaper work or otherwise he would forget how to write. He said she told him this, and she had been right.

I asked him if Buck Lanham was the model for the hero in *Across the River and into the Trees*. He said it was largely Buck and also a fellow named X. "You probably don't know X. He was before your time. But I fought with him long ago. He was in the Foreign Legion and later on he organized an English outfit." He said X was somewhat eccentric and was always ordering people shot. He would tell Hemingway: "Take so-and-so out and shoot him." Hemingway would take so-and-so out, but would not shoot him. Later in the evening, X would ask Hemingway: "Did you carry out my orders?" Hemingway would say yes. Still later in the evening (after a certain amount of alcohol) X would say: "I wish I hadn't shot so-and-so." Hemingway would say: "I'll bring him around in the morning, Sir." Hemingway remarked: "This was an interesting experience for a kid."

I asked how his book was coming—*The Great Project*, a novel about World War II. He said it was almost finished; it would only take about two or three more years. He had been working on it eight years. He gets up at six o'clock every morning and forces himself to write. He added: "You can't write if you don't practice discipline."

Hemingway didn't drink much, but as soon as he had a few glasses of wine his speech became even more pronouncedly slurred. If he didn't have such a magnificent constitution, I think he would have died long ago from too much alcohol. I only hope he lives long enough to finish his book.

At one point—after he'd had a bit of champagne—he said: "You know, Cy, you're a nice guy. I know from your writing that you're a nice guy. You can always tell what kind of a guy a fellow is from his writing." I beamed with pleasure because, for my money, Hemingway is one of the two or three really great men alive.

Hemingway made one curious observation: "The liver is the center of fear. The nose is the sign of courage." He supported this meaningless statement by saying that every great bull fighter had a long nose. (I know few Spaniards with small, short noses.)

Hemingway had gone to the Cluny Museum that morning and thought it the finest thing in Paris. He told the curator he was lucky to be able to look at its contents every day; that he should ban tourists. But then, oddly enough, Hemingway said he hated tapestries. It was a phony form of art. He burbled on—"The Prado is the finest museum in the world. Tourists should be banned from there, too."

Hemingway said in the old days they used to make writers consuls. He turned to Dillon when he said this. He said it was a fine idea to make consuls out of writers because at the time that this was customary there was nothing for a consul to do.

Returning to the subject of poets, he said that, like Pound, all poets were crazy. "Look at Baudelaire, look at Rimbaud. They were just as crazy as Ezra."

PARIS, *January 18, 1957*

THIS morning I went to see the Spanish ambassador, the Count of Casa Rojas, a most affable, rotund gentleman. I knew him in Turkey during the war.

We talked about the secret negotiations going on between the Russians and the Spaniards in Paris. In the autumn of 1954, Vinogradov, whom he had known in a rather frigid way in Turkey, suddenly came up to him in most friendly fashion at the regular presidential shoot for diplomats at Rambouillet. He was interested that Vinogradov should be so cordial after all these years. Knowing that Soviet ambassadors don't act without instructions, he inquired and found out that Vinogradov had been told to be friendly.

Last summer, the Spaniards started negotiations with Moscow for the return of remaining prisoners from the Blue Divisions in Russia as well as the children of Spanish Republican refugees. He had several conversations with Vinogradov. Last autumn, the eventual establishment of some kind of normal diplomatic relations seemed closer. Russia never recognized either the Franco government or the Spanish Republican government in exile. Had they recognized the government-in-exile, they would have been faced with a legal claim by the Republicans for the return of the gold given them for safekeeping in 1937. Three Russian Red Cross representatives are on their way to Spain now with a boatload of returning Spaniards.

After the death of Negrin, former Republican Premier, Negrin's family gave the Franco government the official copy of Moscow's receipt for the Spanish gold. This was signed by the People's Commissar for Finance and the head of the Gosbank and the gold was specifically listed as received.

Therefore, on January 3 of this year, Casa Rojas called on Vinogradov and laid a formal claim, sending Vinogradov a photostatic copy of the official receipt. Casa Rojas hinted that if the Russians did not return the gold, Spain would be bringing the matter to the attention of the Hague International Court.

I went out to SHAPE for a long talk with Field Marshal Montgomery. He looked very sprightly and fit, although he is getting close to seventy. He didn't seem overburdened with work and talked merrily on and on.

He is browned off by the fact that he was never consulted in advance about the British invasion in Egypt. He made it plain that as Britain's senior field marshal, he should have been asked. It was evident he would have liked to have commanded the expedition himself. Just how he could have been consulted I don't know, because in a sense he is an international soldier, deputy commander in the alliance.

Monty said Russia had carefully reckoned the cost of aggression in the West and decided that, because of the existence of NATO, it was impossible. Therefore, Russia wanted to outflank Europe, going through the Middle East by purely Cold War means.

Moscow has no intention of direct attack. It is just trying to exploit the chaotic situation in the Middle East. The principal trouble there is the Israeli-Arab problem. That is the guts of the whole thing. And of course Arab nationalism is very heady wine. Also there are rivalries among the Arab states.

Russia's aims are to work on all of these points and to stir up trouble. Moscow persuaded Nasser to seize the Suez Canal in order to strangle European industry. The western alliance just looked on. It didn't do anything. That's no good.

The NATO powers must work out a good strategy and then implement it if their interests are threatened. This should have been done in the Middle East, but it wasn't. The NATO powers must keep stability in the Middle East. We must have peace there. It is a very turbulent area. The United States didn't seem to understand this. The British and French acted alone. It's a great pity. It stirred up trouble in the alliance. Russia has achieved a great success.

Nasser seized Suez. And at the same time, Russia has managed to disturb the good relations that existed between the United States, Britain, and France. Thus the Russians have achieved their objective.

I think Britain was quite right to go into Egypt. But they did it in the wrong way and at the wrong time. I have no doubt that the United States would go into Panama if the Panamanians seized the Canal. Don't you think so?

With the situation as it now is in the Middle East, the UN or the interested powers should guarantee the Middle Eastern frontiers. You don't need great atomic forces on hand to do this. All you need is light forces to implement the guarantee—enough paratroopers and amphibious units. In a military sense, the needs of that area are as different from those of western Europe as a village cricket match is from a test match. In western Europe we could only have a test match. But the Middle East is village cricket.

The Israelis hit Egypt for six. It only took them three days. We should have let them finish the job themselves. The only people who can fight in that area are the Israelis. The rest are no good. They have no unity. They are jealous of each other.

That kind of village cricket situation is different from the requirements of planning for a test match. In the next test-match war, the function of armies will be to hold, not to take the offensive. They must hold while we seize control of the skies and the seas.

But in village cricket you need less. You just need plenty of paratroopers and amphibious forces and a good airlift. You only need small forces.

It is impossible to take military action against indirect aggression. You can't stop an alliance between Syria and Russia. The best way to anticipate that sort of thing is for you people to support the Baghdad Pact. It is a very good pact. I'd like to see the United States join it. The Baghdad Pact was originally invented as a hot-war thing—when we feared Russian aggression from the north. We should turn it into a cold-war thing now. The U.S. supports it economically. But I'd like to see the U.S. join it completely.

I'm going to visit Ike in May, and I'm going to tell him this. I'm going to tell him that UN should guarantee the territorial integrity of the Middle Eastern countries. We should support any country attacked there. The UN should look after that. This would make the Arabs give up all thought of stamping on Israel.

The second thing I'm going to tell Ike is that the United States should join the Baghdad Pact. Then nothing else can happen out there. It seems to me so simple. The U.S. already sits in on the Baghdad Pact, but it's not a member.

If you do that—guarantee frontiers and join the Baghdad Pact—everything will be easy. If the Arabs attack Israel, they will be seen off by the UN. You must have a UN guarantee first.

I asked Monty if he thought there was any possible way that NATO could militarily—officially or otherwise—help rebelling organizations in the satellite countries. Specifically I spoke of Poland. I wondered if NATO could help the Poles if there is trouble there after the elections. He replied: "There is nothing you can do unless you want to start the third world war. It is all or nothing. We can do nothing. If we interfere, that means World War III. If we want World War III, OK, that's the easiest way to bring it on."

He added, however, that insurrections against Russia were useful from our point of view. He said: "It's all a very good thing. If Russia attacks the West, all those nations would rise up and bite her in the tail."

Monty dismissed as a lot of bluff the Soviet threat to use rockets with nuclear warheads against England and France if they didn't get out of Egypt. He added: "Russia never had the slightest intention of rocketing England. Russia is physically capable of doing this, but we could do the same thing back. Physically, they would be destroyed in the end. The Russians haven't the slightest intention of doing anything that would bring on a war."

It was a pity the West depended so much upon the Suez Canal. We should make preparations to have alternative routes for oil so we won't be blackmailed in the future. But it would take four or five years. The construction of a pipeline from northern Iraq through Turkey to the Mediterranean was one way. Another way was to build huge supertankers to go around the Cape. He wondered if maybe as atomic energy is developed, this would reduce western dependence upon oil.

Monty then returned to the Middle East. He said:

The nigger in the woodpile there is Russia. They're not going to attack the West. Therefore, they want to outflank Europe through the Middle East. It would be a terrible thing if communism comes to Africa. And the Russians have had a startling measure of success there.

Britain mucked up Suez. Nasser is now more firmly in power than he was before. I wish I had commanded that expedition. The politicians mucked it up. Also the military. I remember, wasn't it Clemenceau who said "War is far too important to leave in the hands of generals"? Well, I can tell you, I wouldn't leave it in the hands of the politicians. They had all the cards in their hands, but they mucked it up.

Diplomats don't seem to understand that the game being played is poker. They play it as if it were chess. There are three players in the game and all of them have got some good cards. Israel had a good deal of Egyptian territory. Nasser had the Suez Canal. And Britain had a good buildup of military strength in the eastern Mediterranean.

When the United Nations told us to stop the expedition, we should have played it like poker. We should have said: "OK, I'll see you." Just like poker. The game could have gone on. And if we had been frightened about going on, we should have let Israel go it alone. The Israelis would have had the Canal in no time.

You Americans think that everything is solved by dollars. It isn't. Dollars would ruin some of these nations. It won't achieve their stability. The only thing is to guarantee their frontiers. UN must do this.

He was convinced that the Russians would not send volunteers to fight in the Middle East. That was only propaganda.

They never had any intention of doing it. The Russians will take no steps leading to war. Russian manpower couldn't sustain a war. They have a low birth rate now as a result of the fall in birth rate during the World War II years. The Russians are totally unfit for a big war right now. This will be true for the next ten or fifteen years. I mean it will be true so long as we keep up our own strength.

The only reason there has been no war since 1948 is because of the strength we have built up as a deterrent against war. I mean NATO.

Rule one of war is, Don't march on Moscow. That is rule one of war. Lots of people have tried it. But nobody has succeeded. Napoleon got there but he had to get out. Hitler didn't even get there. You can destroy Moscow without invading it. You can destroy it with atomic rockets. The function of an army is to hold. The offensive is for the air.

Rule two of war is don't march on China. China is like a sponge. You can squeeze it and everything is forced out of it. Any army that gets into China will be squeezed and forced out. Just like a sponge. You have to stand back and pound China with rockets. There is no point in getting into it. I always told this to Ridgway, but he didn't agree.

ATHENS, *January 25, 1957*

I WENT out to Tatoi today to see King Paul at his country home. He has given up the living quarters of the palace in Athens for financial reasons. Tatoi is very close (about thirty minutes) and lovely (although the house is by no means as attractive as less Germanic taste might make it). It was a fine spring-like day with a bright warm sun.

I started off by telling him I planned to write a piece or two on one of the oldest professions, namely kingship. How did it adjust to the times; how was he preparing his son for it during the atomic age; what did he consider a good king should be or know?

He said as far as he was concerned, informality was desirable. "Of course I keep a small nucleus of officialness for state affairs. Naturally on national feast days, which I have now limited, I must put on my glory rags. But I try and maintain a really informal atmosphere otherwise and live as other people do."

Paul said he himself had not expected to be king and had not been specifically educated for the job. "As a result, I lived much like everybody else and I traveled a lot abroad. Perhaps that helped. For today we live much like the rest; I drive my own car; in the summertime I wear shirtsleeves. I lead a pretty ordinary life."

I asked how he was preparing Prince Constantine (who will be seventeen in June) for the trade of monarch. He replied:

My poor boy. He's up to there [raising his hand to his throat] in work. As you know, he goes to a school like the Hahn school in Germany and Gordonstoun in Scotland. And simultaneously he is doing his military training. That is a difficult problem. Each service academy would like to have him. So I have attached him to the three cadet schools: army, navy, and air force. He wears all three uniforms at different times. And he trains over the weekends in the essentials of each service. This summer he will go on a naval cadet cruise. Then he will spend a fortnight on army cadet maneuvers. And he will do something with the air force. Last year he did a fortnight of commando training.

When he has finished school, I want to send him around the world with a few friends—you know, slow trips by cargo boats; that sort of thing. I want him to take several months and go to odd places like Indonesia. Then perhaps he will go to an American university. But I think he should also spend some time at a German university and perhaps at Oxford or Cambridge.

Was he trying to give Constantine any special education for this complicated age? He replied: "We are trying to instill in him an interest in atomic science. After all, that is the thing of the future. And my wife is very interested in the subject."

I inquired what he thought were the primary functions of a modern king. He said:

A king should influence his people and his government in the right direction. In very few countries does the king have an active role in the affairs of state. For example, I have the right to dissolve Parliament, to choose prime ministers, to grant pardons, and to give decorations. That's about all. Of course, I'm considered the head of the armed forces. But I can't act there without my government and my staffs.

Immediate contact with the people is what is essential. My wife and I travel about the country constantly and we try and figure out ways of helping the particular traits of this people. I have done something which should have a great effect owing to the peculiarities of this country. I've started a committee to give dowries to the poorest girls. There is now a special wicket in each bank market for the dowry fund so that it can be accumulated and distributed. Some of these girls can thus set aside enough to buy a small house when they get married.

The most important thing for a king is to know the feeling of his people. And he must remember also that there is something in the theory of kingship that makes people look up to a king—if he is a decent person—not like Carol [of Rumania] of course. People tend to place their best hopes and feelings on the person of a king and, if he doesn't live up to this, they feel let down. My grandfather [King George I] had an excellent motto: "My strength is the love of my people." I think that is the best motto in kingship, don't you?

I asked if he didn't feel there were personal sacrifices in the position; lack of freedom to cut up; to make as many friends as he wished. He replied (with rather corny pomposity): "I lost my liberty so as to be able to insure the liberty of others. Of course it was a bit of a wrench for me. I had been used to living like others. But one gets used to it."

Paul thought there was more room for initiative for a king in a poor country like Greece than in a richer and better educated country as in

Scandinavia. "There," he said, "they have a higher level. Therefore there is less room for the initiative of a king. Here one has to build up everything constantly. There is plenty of room for behind-the-scenes maneuvers and endeavors even if there are strict limits on the king's actual authority."

He was amused at the fact that Queen Elizabeth had recently been challenged by the opposition for selecting Macmillan as Prime Minister before he had even been formally chosen head of the Tory party. "Just exactly like me and Caramanlis," he chuckled. "That's what they said when I asked Caramanlis to form a government in 1955. Now think of that question being raised in England too. England is a country of vast tradition, they do everything by tradition. But I suppose the Queen is technically less rigidly bound than I am because I don't believe their constitution is written like ours, is it?"

Paul told me he had always disliked Eden and hoped for better under Macmillan. He had only met Macmillan once and regretted to say it had been disagreeable; he hadn't liked Macmillan at all. It was during the war when Paul had been left in Cairo as regent of the emigré government by George II who had gone to London. Paul wanted to return to Greece as the liberation was taking place and asked Air Marshal Sir Keith Park for a private plane to fly to Italy to discuss this with his own Prime Minister (already there) and General Jumbo Wilson. Park, with great embarrassment, told him he had been instructed not to give any planes to the Greek royal family without prior permission from London. Paul wrote an indignant letter to Wilson. Eventually he got a plane. He flew to Caserta (Jumbo's headquarters) and had lunch with Wilson and several others, including Macmillan, then minister of state in the Mediterranean.

Paul told Wilson and the others he wanted to go back or that his brother, King George, should, in order to take a hand in the liberation. Macmillan looked up at him and remarked blankly: "Sir, if you were a Communist agent you could do nothing more calculated to harm your country." Paul didn't exactly like this reference. He found out the reason they delayed his flight to Italy was that they had been negotiating with the Communist guerrilla generals at the time.

Paul is quite pro-Tito now (an interesting contrast with his views a few years ago). He has full confidence in Tito's honesty, friendship, true neutrality as between blocs, and alliance. He thinks Jugoslavia would move if Bulgaria attacked Greece—"Although of course you never know; the Jugoslavs didn't act in 1940. But that was a different team."

I asked if he thought the emotional situation could ever quiet down sufficiently to restore an alliance among Greece, Britain, and Turkey; if Cyprus were settled. He thought yes. "After all," he said, "who could have imagined a German general [Speidel] commanding Allied troops?"

The British were being particularly obtuse about Cyprus. When Lord Halifax was here last Easter (1956), Ambassador Peake brought him to the palace. Paul told Halifax: "This is something to be settled by statesmen, not politicians. You should run up a Greek flag over the island and right away I would be prepared to give Britain base rights at the three finest naval bases in the eastern Mediterranean—Agostoli in Cephalonia, Milos, and Suda Bay in Crete. Why the harbor at Milos can hold all the navies of the world together." But Halifax paid no attention. "He just sat there, looking glum, holding his head in his hands. And he never passed my proposition on.

"Why don't they have sense instead of trying to treat us like a bunch of white niggers?"

Incidentally, while we were talking about Cyprus, Paul said: "Papagos made a terrible mistake in letting Grivas ['Dighenis,' the EOKA leader] go to Cyprus. I told him so at the time. I had told him before not to let Grivas go. Grivas is an extreme right-wing man. They say he was OK as a colonel, but he is very intemperate and a bad politician." (This is the first confirmation I have that Papagos—or any Greek official—knew in advance of Grivas's connection with EOKA.)

ATHENS, *January 26, 1957*

AN hour's chat this morning with Caramanlis, Prime Minister since October, 1955. We sat in his large office (containing a long green table for Cabinet meetings), with the door open onto a balcony looking out over little orange trees. He was wearing a tweed suit and, instead of smoking, played constantly with a string of amber beads.

Caramanlis started off by stating that Greece had never been in such good shape. Its security and economy were more stable; the only trouble was Cyprus. The Greeks were very fine people: brave, intelligent, hard working, but extremely excitable, above all when it came to a question of *philotimo* or national pride. And now they were truly worked up— almost at war with Britain and Turkey.

He was a man "of the West" and would always remain so, even if he were the last in Greece. He had won the 1956 elections handily, but all sixteen opposition parties (some in Parliament, some not) were gunning for him on Cyprus. He was standing for moderation. He would not allow riots against the British, and he tries to keep the lid on parliamentary discussions. He was seeking a reasonable solution, recognizing that while justice was on Greece's side, political expediency must also be considered. But his opponents were screaming for Greece to leave NATO, quit UN, become neutralist. He was confident his government could ride out the storm. But if the UN debate goes sour—above all if the U.S.A. doesn't make an adequate stand for Greece—things could change swiftly. The Greeks are very volatile.

The British had made every mistake in the book. They knew, for example, that the partition scheme could not work. They were opening the door to the Arabs who were beginning to clamor that Cyprus should be independent and demilitarized (which the people don't want). The Arabs want to include Cyprus in the Middle East.

ATHENS, *January 28, 1957*

DINED last night at Ambassador Allen's. George told an amusing story. While he was ambassador in Jugoslavia he was called home for consultations and was in Washington at the time of Ike's inauguration. He had heard informally from Bedell Smith that he was to be named ambassador to India. One day he got word the President wanted to see him. He went to the White House and was taken upstairs to Ike's private sitting room. Ike looked puzzled. "But you're not the George Allen I was expecting," he said. George explained he was the ambassador in Jugoslavia. Ike picked up a phone and called Dulles. George could hear the gist. Dulles was explaining that it was indeed the ambassador in Jugoslavia who was to go to India. But Ike seemed bewildered and had a long conversation with George about the Jugoslavs, never mentioning the new assignment. George went back to Belgrade and was only recalled later for the Indian job. Ike had imagined the new man for India would be George Allen, the fat friend of Presidents and Washington, D.C., commissioner.

KARACHI, *February 1, 1957*

LAST night, Burt Marshall had us over for dinner. Marshall, who used to be on the State Department Policy and Planning staff, has been here more than two years. Officially, he is an advisor to the government and has helped on such things as drawing up the Constitution. He is a brilliant man with slow, drawling speech.

There has, says Burt, been great political improvement in Pakistan. President Mirza is beginning to like the way politics works now that he has Suhrawardy as Prime Minister. He is not talking any more of "controlled democracy" (a simile for benevolent dictatorship). Suhrawardy believes in the democratic processes. Mirza and Suhrawardy have become political allies. Both feel the importance of ties with the West. Suhrawardy has courage. For the first time, in a sense, the country really has a Prime Minister—a man with instinct for the job. Probably Mirza is the best chief of state they have had. Now there is a proper constitutional relationship.

The Constitution is a curious document. It was adopted in 1956, and describes Pakistan as an "Islamic republic." It contains "Directing Principles" (not enforcible by law) of an Islamic nature such as promoting Muslim unity. This is like favoring motherhood. But the rights of the minorities are justiciable.

This evening, I had an hour and a half talk with Hussein Shaheed Suhrawardy, present Prime Minister, in his residence next door to where I'm staying in the Prime Minister's guest house. Suhrawardy is a strange individual, about five foot seven in height, approximately equal circumference, brown face, long, hooked, broad nose, and a habit of closing his eyes and leaning back when he talks. He speaks with a deliberate drawl, a pseudo-Oxford accent, and a careful selection of ponderous phrases.

Tea arrived, plus three plates of cookies. He filled his cup with sugar and a little milk and then ate, I should reckon, at least two-dozen sweet cookies, dipping them in the sweetened milk while he talked. In the middle a barber arrived and Suhrawardy stripped off his coat and vest, sat back in his chair, and was shaved. Eyes shut, double chins being scraped, he talked endlessly. Apart from my occasional questions, the only interruption in his monologue was a series of oddly gurgling belches. He said:

> The Suez crisis placed new problems before us. There were, of course, considerable emotional stresses. A Muslim country, a small country, appeared to be asserting its rights of sovereignty and independence and was being impeded in that assertion. It seemed to have been invaded without any apparent reason by Israel, which we consider is a foreign element implanted amongst the Arab countries. I felt from the beginning that this assertion of sovereignty by Egypt over the Suez Canal to the extent of abrogating previous agreements was not a strictly correct attitude. Nevertheless, we did support Egypt at first.
>
> But Pakistan, above all, wants no stoppage of shipping. We need a steady stream of grain and the program of arrivals from America was based on the functioning of Suez. Therefore, there is grave discontent.
>
> The people are aware of the political connection between Nehru and Nasser and their initial sympathy for Nasser has therefore veered around. Nasser went out of his way to call on Indian troops and to object to ours. This caused a very bad popular reaction.

Suhrawardy said Soviet repression in Hungary had had "a tremendous impact here. It is the Hungarian episode that brought home to people here what might happen to them if they came under Russian influence and then made an attempt later to get out of it. After Hungary they understood that once a country came under Soviet influence it was tantamount to enslavement."

He said this threatened soon to take place in Afghanistan, which he regards as by far the greatest danger point in the Middle East. The Afghans were determined to press the Pushtunistan issue and were carrying on propaganda:

> Tampering with our Pathans, creating trouble, paying and entertaining agitators—and all with Russian money being sent in to finance it. This opens the road to subversion and one day they will intensify their Pathan raids on us in order to bring our army into operations. Two bases in the Middle East are being developed by Russia—Syria and Afghanistan. Syria divides Turkey and Iraq, or comes behind them, and Afghanistan pushes into Iran and Pakistan.
>
> There is only one real force in alliances and this is the question whether a country wants to be free or on the side of Soviet Russia. The rest is a small matter.

KARACHI, *February 3, 1957*

THIS afternoon, I went over to see my old friend Iskander Mirza who is now President of Pakistan, and, although his constitutional powers are limited, remains the recognized strong man. We strolled around his garden while he talked with remarkable freedom.

He also thinks Afghanistan is down the drain. Prince Daud, the Afghan Prime Minister, is unduly influenced by the Russians. Mirza told Daud during his visit to Kabul: "You people are a novelty. Communism is usually introduced from the bottom. You are introducing it from the top." The Russians are all over the place. They are building two broad military highways south from the Oxus border to Pakistan. The King's uncle has gotten Mohammed Zahir interested in women—and as a result he has lost any faint interest in political affairs. Mirza mused: "Why is it that royal families vary so? His father was an able man. He is a useless weakling."

He still favors "controlled democracy" and fears real democracy with universal suffrage would wreck Pakistan—"which I won't permit." The Constitution was a farce and no one believed in it. The Islamic clauses were unnecessary window-dressing. I mentioned Christian persecutions. He said: "Are they after them again? I'll stop it."

Mirza is deliberately encouraging all groups wanting to speak their national languages—Bengali, Urdu, Pushtu, Sindi. "That way they make themselves more dependent on English to communicate with each other. Why should we give up English—a good, modern language. The Turks told me they envied us having an international language."

He hates Nasser and mistrusts him.

Why didn't the British plan a decent operation? If they'd had the sense to go on forty-eight hours more, Israel would have done the job for them. Then they could have pretended to save Egypt when they intervened. The British made a mess of it. The Israelis fought magnificently. They are a good, modern army. They are brave and have a cause. [Odd from a Muslim statesman!]

When King Saud was here he started to tell me about Nasser's victory. I told him he was mad; that he didn't know the facts; that he just listened to Egyptian sources. What kind of an army wins a victory, I asked him, by losing to half its number? Thirty-eight Egyptian MIGs took refuge on your Saudi Arabian airfields. Is that the way to fight?

Twenty thousand Israelis smashed forty thousand Egyptians. They could have taken Ismailia and Suez if the British hadn't messed things up. That would have cooked Nasser. I asked Saud—Who do you think is trying to upset your dynasty? Is it England or France? No. It's Nasser. Yet you employ Egyptian officers to train your army. That made him think.

The Arabs are worthless. If God and 120,000 prophets couldn't make something of Arabia, certainly they can't. Kuwatly, the Syrian President, is a mess. He told me he had come out here to make me friendlier with Nasser.

I said to him—Why don't you get friendlier with the Turks and Iraq? That shut him up. What an ass. Pay no attention to the Arabs. They're a mess. It's a pity they have the Canal—and the petroleum.

Sat around with Chet Bowles, now touring this area. He is nice and interesting but seems to have a totally one-track mind—India.

He said India did not take the Pakistan-U.S. military agreement seriously in 1954. But in 1956, the pipeline of materiel deliveries began to hit Karachi. At the same time, pressure developed from Moscow offering to supply arms to India at token prices. Lord Mountbatten talked Nehru out of such a deal. But Zhukov is now examining Indian installations. He is stressing what bad equipment the Indians have.

In 1951, the U.S.A. loaned India $190,000,000 to purchase wheat. The first repayment is due in June—*in dollars*. Furthermore, during the war we loaned the British in India 180,000,000 ounces of silver worth $120,000,000. Payment on this falls this year. Thus India must start repaying both the silver and wheat loans in 1957. Bowles thinks Congress should postpone payment or accept rupees.

India has been sending people to China who are by tradition pro-democracy, but who are intrigued by China's large village development program. He says 95 percent of rural China is now embraced by these village cooperatives. India wants to borrow and adjust that system which manages to mobilize landless labor even if it doesn't produce more food. What India talks about is adopting the Chinese system "democratically" —an anomaly since the Indians are not able even to put through a moderate land reform.

Bowles suggests the U.S. should sponsor a great-power arms embargo on the Middle East and South Asia; that "great-power disengagement is needed in Asia as in Europe." He asks: "How would the U.S. feel if Mexico were being armed by Russia? You can't gain stability by establishing a weak and provocative alliance on the border of a great power."

LAHORE, PAKISTAN, *February 5, 1957*

WE are staying in the governor's house, former residence of the British governor-general of the Punjab. The dining room is an enormous former tomb from Moghul days. The house, built around the tomb, is palatial, filled with handsomely moustachioed servants in turbans and scarlet jackets. The main reception hall is filled with silver-framed photographs of rajahs in full dress. Our suite is fit for a nawab, with coal fire going all the time in the grate and a huge tray of alcoholic and nonalcoholic drinks and fruit always at the ready. In the garden, a lovely artificial moon rises so when the real one came up there were two.

PESHAWAR, PAKISTAN, *February 7, 1957*

TUESDAY in Lahore, then drove to Peshawar. Toured Lahore including the Moghul palace fort, the immense mosque, gardens, the Zamzama (an Afghan cannon captured by Ranjit Singh's Sikhs and of which Kipling wrote). It's incredible, but some clubs still bar "non-Europeans."

Had drinks at the home of the former governor, Colonel Nawab Malik, Sir Khizar Hayat Khan Tiwana, KCSI, OBE, DCL (Oxford), as his card reads. Tiwana is tall, lean, with an enormous aquiline nose and a kind of bobbed hairdo. He opposed partition of India and is in the political doghouse. His wife is absolutely lovely, young, dressed in a most becoming white sari and veil setting off black hair and eyes, ivory skin.

Tea with the present governor, our host, Nawab Mushtaq Ahmad Gurmani, a Baluch from the south. He is a rotund, handsome old man with white hair that sets off his coffee-colored skin. We sat in the garden near a huge swimming pool and pavillion, while he smoked a hubble-bubble and played with his puppy.

Lahore, as seen from the top echelon, is a most romantic and lovely city with its polished, handsome aristocrats, its gay tongas (two-wheeled carts) with their plumed horses, and spacious houses and lawns. We drove off yesterday morning in a station wagon sent from Peshawar, with a dashing old Pathan driver who ferociously charged carts and motor vehicles always missing by an eyelash. First, we passed through the great Punjab plain dotted with mud villages and little plots of wheat, buzzards sitting on trees or feeding off carcasses in ugly circles; gaily plumed birds, some, long-tailed and light green, resembling parrots, some, brilliant iridescent blue, perched on telephone wires; herds of water buffalo. In the distant north, the Himalayas of Kashmir including

K-2 (Mount Godwin Austin) covered with snow. This is the traditional highway for the conquerors of India since Alexander the Great. In the wheat fields by the road women lay out long strips of brightly dyed cloth to dry in the sun. Farmers in gay robes stride off to market before their lumbering bullocks.

Drove through craggy, barren foothill mountains of pastel shades, past a convoy of tank carriers and camel caravans, we arrived in Taxila, the last camp of Alexander the Great before he attacked and defeated Porus, King of Jhelum. There is a tidy little (British built) museum. Then on past the grim fort of Akbar at Attock on the upper Indus, set on a cliff overlooking the gray sands and sluggish yellow water. We were delayed crossing the long bridge by a Swati camel caravan. Arrived in Peshawar after dark and put up at Dean's Hotel, which is comfortably Victorian, from the spacious, chilly suites to the little fireplaces in every room.

PESHAWAR, PAKISTAN, *February 9, 1957*

STURDY tribesmen stride in from the mountains before their camel trains, greeting each other solemnly with a "*Stare Mashe* (May you never be tired)," and replying "*Khowar Mashe* (May you never be poor)." In the storyteller's bazaar a bearded, old Pathan smokes a pipe of hashish, and, tears rolling down his leathery cheeks, tells how Alexander the Great searched for the fountain of youth. When he found it and was about to drink, an ancient old cripple hobbled over and warned him against it, "Lest you become like myself, five-thousand years old and neither able to live nor die."

In the gold and silver bazaar the jewelers sell old skulls and coins dug up from Alexander's army passage and make little anklets for parrots and myna birds. A quack herb salesman drums up a crowd by parading a baby otter; snake charmers whistle to vipers, cobras, and pythons; old men sit about smoking hubble-bubbles and sipping green tea.

Kushhal Khan, classic poet of the Pathans, wrote of this region: "How glorious is the spring. Whether from Swat, or from Hashtnagar, or from Peshawar. Everything inclines to it, all blessings come that way. Its young men are stout and healthy, quick are they and active, merry-eyed, fair and ruddy in face, tall in stature to behold."

Yesterday we drove to Swat, crossing a bridge of boats over the Kabul River at Nowshera and turning north. The people of Kaffiristan (between Chitral and Afghanistan) are so primitive they still leave their dead out unburied. The Chitralis, who speak a separate dialect derived from Sanskrit, show traces of Alexander's Greeks in their wine, dress, and vocabulary.

In the village below Malakand are vain old men with beards dyed red and eyelashes shaded black. Swat, on the other side of Malakand, is a pleasant, high valley with green fields and grazing flocks. It is rimmed by snowcapped mountains and filled with orchards of olives and oranges. On the Swat River is a ferryboat of inflated goatskins.

In Mingora a wedding was taking place. A merry gang of men bore the bride to the groom's house in a gaily covered sedan chair on a platform, while trumpeters tootled behind. A man followed with two mongooses led by wires through their noses.

Execution in Swat is curious. A convicted murderer can bail himself out if the dead man's family agrees to accept a fixed sum of blood money. Otherwise one of the murdered man's family is assigned to shoot the murderer—before an approved group of police officials.

At Saidu Sharif I talked with the Wali, Jahan Zeb. He is older and fatter than when I last saw him. He said there was no longer any trouble with neighboring Dir; that no more Russian rifles are being smuggled into Chitral. Kabul radio keeps telling the Swatis to chuck him out and break with Pakistan—but no one pays any attention.

PESHAWAR, PAKISTAN, *February 10, 1957*

SPENT the day in the Afridi country around Kohat pass. Along the Kohat road, once you start climbing, each mud or stone house in the tribal territory is built like a fort with a wall and shot-tower (just in case). The villages are administered by local maliks who arm their own Khasildars. Afridis stroll along the road with rifles slung across their backs.

At the village of Darra is a fantastic "cottage industry" of arms production. They make everything from revolvers, rifles, and shotguns to tommy guns, machine guns, and three-inch cannon. All is done by hand with hand-turned lathes and little bellows furnaces. The steel used to be stolen from railways (possibly still is). In each weapon is stenciled the name of the foreign firm from which it has been copied—British, American, and Russian (often misspelled). I saw a little can of these stencils. Darra makes 250 rifles (303 bore) a day plus other weapons and has been in this backyard business for eighty years. I bought a little Webley-Scott .32 revolver (90 rupees or about $18) made in "Birminoam London." Everything, even the screws and bakelite (from stolen rubber tires) for butts is made here. The eighty-five-year-old chief, Malik Samand Khan of the Zarghun Khel Afridi tribe, told me: "Give us an atomic bomb and we will copy it." We had tea in his yard, surrounded by armed Khasildars, and talked. I asked what he thought of the Faair of Ipi (Pathan rebel). He said: "We revere him as a pious man. But he is misadvised by bad counsellors who intrigue around him." Samand Khan complained the gun business was slipping. Licenses are required now in all nontribal areas. And the Mohmand tribe, once an excellent customer, is no longer fighting the British.

Strolled about the bazaar—each mud stall filled with weapons bearing the labels of world-famous firms. Weapons are "guaranteed" and if they go wrong can be brought back and repaired free. At the top of Kohat pass, we lunched in the fort of the Frontier Corps, while groups of women passed bearing water pots on their heads. These wore no veils (there is no purdah in the tribes). We sat on the roof of a little Beau Geste fort, overlooking the hills and plains, watching the moving caravans of men and camels while bobbed-hair Pathan Khasildars, trim and well uniformed, played a lute called a rhabad, beat a pail in substitute for a drum, clapped their hands, sang songs astonishingly like flamenco, and danced. When we left, a guard of honor drew up in snappy British fashion and saluted while the corporal barked out "Soooo-da arms," as darkness fell over the blue peaks.

This evening in Peshawar, I asked a Pakistan major at the club what he thought of Kohat weapons. "Depends what you need them for," he said. "I've bought some when we've been pinched. Steel's poor. Don't stand up to many rounds. No good for wars or revolutions. But quite useful for the occasional assassination."

KABUL, AFGHANISTAN, *February 11, 1957*

ARRIVED tonight after a twelve-hour drive across the horribly surfaced road through the Khyber pass and the Sarobi and Tanhyguru gorges (via Jelalabad). Passed Fort Jamrud, then entered the Khyber, winding by the Chagai Fort of the Khyber Rifles. The rock faces are carved with regimental insignia of famous British Indian outfits once stationed here; tan, pink, and brown crags, utterly barren; little pyramids of tooth-type tank traps left over from World War II; herders' caves in the cliff side. At Torkham, in a cleft, Pakistani customs is established on a table in the cold sun, little bitter orange trees growing beside it. Passing into Afghan territory, many Uzbek and Tatar faces among the ragged-looking soldiery, somewhat frightening in their long, brown coats and Chinese-type visored caps, with long, prong bayonets. The Afghan trucks all carry mallet-shaped wooden braces strapped on behind to jam beneath the wheels and keep them from slipping backward when it's necessary to stop on a hillside to let the motor cool. Flights of wild pigeons . . . Camels grazing in the arid plain beneath the mountains . . . huge buzzards waiting impatiently for prey. Beyond Jelalabad, plains with grain fields and farms, each built like mudforts with towers and loopholes . . . huge caves in cliff-side where caravan camels and donkeys take shelter.

KABUL, AFGHANISTAN, *February 12, 1957*

ARMIN Meyer, our embassy counsellor with whom we are staying, told me: The only way to decrease Afghanistan's dependence on Russia is to increase its dependence on Pakistan. In 1955, Pakistan blockaded Afghanistan for five months; there was no gas except what the Russians trucked in. The U.S.A. is trying to improve Pakistani-Afghan relations.

Angus Ward, U.S. ambassador until last spring, had a disastrous effect. He disliked the Afghans, thought they were "finished," paid no attention to them, spent all his time traveling in safari trucks. Got himself involved up north and claimed he was arrested when he wasn't.

Peking's embassy here is very active. It puts out lots of propaganda with beautiful books and pamphlets emphasizing the happy life of Muslims in China. Chou En-lai's visit was a huge success. He asked for nothing; just smiled and was pleasant.

Under Hashim Khan, strong-man Prime Minister until just after World War II, there was no inclination to deal with Russia. But Afghanistan got no aid from the West. Then, in 1953, the King's cousin, Prince Daud, took over. Daud inherited 90 percent of the royal family's intelligence and 100 percent of its guts. He is dynamic, and he wants to do things. Russia capitalized on Daud's interest in developing the country. The Afghans say: "By the *Kuran*, Muslims are prohibited from eating pork. But our religion permits us to eat pork if it is a question of avoiding death by starvation." Since 1954, Soviet economic aid has totaled $116,000,000 plus about $25,000,000 military.

Love song—"If you don't give me a kiss I'll break your water pot."

Drinking song—"If you give me a drink in an earthen vessel, make it a vessel made from the dust of a wise man's skull, not a stupid man's."

This morning I had a talk for an hour and a half with Lemar-e-'Ali, Sardar Mohammed Na'im, first cousin of the King and foreign minister. He is tall, slender, aristocratic looking in his early forties with a dark tan skin and hawk nose. He said:

There has been a general awakening of the Asian people and a particular awakening in Afghanistan of a desire to improve living standards. We cannot forget the difficulties Afghanistan encountered in its economic aspirations because of obstacles raised by Pakistan. The Soviet loan agreement is purely an economic matter without any—I repeat any—effects in the political field. Our history testifies that the people of Afghanistan are extremely jealous of their independence. We simply will not accept any limitation upon our independence.

I asked him about the details of Afghanistan's military equipment agreement with Russia. He said:

When I was in Washington in 1949–1950, our government prepared a list of materials required to modernize our army. It was turned down.

On a trip to the U.S. in 1954–1955, I twice saw Secretary Dulles and presented this request to him again. But he showed no interest. Then, as you will recall, came a Pakistan blockade. We felt threatened by Karachi.

As a result, we sent a military mission to Czechoslovakia and the Soviet Union. Toward the end of 1955, we negotiated an agreement under which we received approximately $25,000,000 worth of military material. Allow me to point out to you that Iran received more than $200,000,000 worth of American war-surplus equipment after World War II at cut-rate prices, and since 1946–1947 has been getting about $25,000,000 a year of additional military aid. We are not worried about Iran. But Pakistan has also been receiving an extensive amount of military aid. And, in 1955, Pakistan threatened that their Pathans would invade Afghanistan.

I recalled the 1921 treaty between Afghanistan and Russia included a guarantee by both Kabul and Moscow to respect the independence and territorial rights of Bokhara and Khiva. Did Afghanistan register a formal protest when Russia invaded Bokhara in 1924? He said Kabul did protest. "But objections from a small country such as Afghanistan don't count much against a great power. We did, however, send one battalion and some artillery to help the Bokharans in their fight for independence. Furthermore, we sent people to what is now the city of Stalinabad to bring out the Emir and his harem."

I said I had the impression that Afghanistan's foreign policy during the nineteenth century and until the outbreak of World War II was primarily to try and balance off Russia and Great Britain. If this were correct, wasn't Afghanistan now seeking to have the United States fill in the vacuum caused by Britain's disappearance from the Indian subcontinent. He replied: "Presently there is no power except the United States to create a balance against the Soviet Union."

Na'im sketched a rough map of Afghanistan with the Hindu Kush, Herat, Kabul, and Kandahar. He said:

Herat and Kandahar comprise one of the strategic invasion routes toward India. Afghanistan now proposes to establish a railway link from the Pakistan border to Kandahar and then to Kabul. Later we would like to extend this to Herat. Then finally we would like to link Herat with Meshed on the Iranian railway. Karachi would be the base for this entire network. Then, if you will look on this map you will see that this network would remain behind the curtain of the Hindu Kush. On this basis we could prepare a new and more reasonable defense of both Afghanistan and Pakistan. This is the only sound prospect of means to defend this country. But, much as we press this, we are getting nowhere. The World Bank has so far cold-shouldered our applications for financial backing.

And let me point out another difficulty. In this area the economic situation is critical. You have been to Soviet Central Asia and you know that the people there have been born under the Soviet regime and don't comprehend the actual word or real meaning of freedom. But they see their own economic growth—new cities, new industries, and modern farming methods.

By way of contrast, in northern Afghanistan we still have a totally primitive social system. There the living standards are the worst imaginable. There is a continual comparison by the people of that area with the Soviet economic system to the north—and this creates for us difficulties and complications. The most effective weapon in our part of the world is to achieve a better standard of living. This would do much more than any military equipping of any country to preserve its independence.

KABUL, AFGHANISTAN, *February 14, 1957*

THIS morning I called on Prince Mohammed Daud, Prime Minister, cousin of the King, and strong-man. He has a forceful, intelligent face, long nose, heavy jaw; is very sure of himself.

I had heard from Pakistanis that a branch of the Soviet Godless League had been discovered in Afghan schools and its leaders had been rounded up; was this true? Reply: "As a responsible Afghan leader I can assure you that this is the first time I ever heard such a tale. But we expect the Pakistanis to drum up to Americans the idea that there is communism in Afghanistan. I can assure you that this will be the very last country in the world to become Communist." (Shades of the Emir of Bokhara!)

NEW DELHI, INDIA, *February 18, 1957*

WE are staying in the former Delhi palace of the Nizam of Hyderabad, an official VIP guest house, most impressive; dozens of servants. The bathtub, a combination of British engineering genius and Maharajahs' taste, needs a copilot to operate, with no less than six knobs to turn for various kinds of sprays.

Flew back in a rush to see Nehru. First lap by military attaché's plane to Peshawar. The poor attaché had a cold so every time we prepared to land by losing altitude his eardrums almost burst. Finally it became a contest between ears and fuel reserves. Ears were sacrificed.

By luck we were able to bum a ride onward aboard the tiny blue motor plane of a U.S. construction company building a secret project at Peshawar.* Jammed, sitting on a suitcase, we bumped to a small field near Lahore from where we hailed a rickety taxi. Next day, drove to the border, then switched to an Indian car . . . and on.

* It became the famous U-2 base.

"I SHOULD LIKE TO

WIPE EVERY TEAR

FROM EVERY EYE"

NEW DELHI, INDIA, *February 19, 1957*

S K. DEY, MINISTER FOR COMMUNITY DEVELOPMENT, COMPARED FOR me the Indian technique of rural development with that applied in Communist China. He said:

We are seeking to make up for about two thousand years of steady downhill decline in our thinking, our actions, and our culture. Also for about two hundred years of machine age which simply bypassed us. As a people we remain practically where the world was in the early eighteenth century.

We woke up free, suddenly finding ourselves without any serious restraint. We have to prepare ourselves for the atomic age. And we have to do this fast. Otherwise there is a risk that the large masses of people who are in extreme poverty, ignorance, and disease will not choose to remain wedded to peaceful methods. That might mean the alternative choice of an imposed method—like communism. We are convinced there can be no permanent progress in the life of human beings unless it is evolutionary and conserves the freedom of the individual. And, as a people we prize individual liberty more than anything.

The only country in the world with which India could be compared now is China. They introduced the curtailment of liberty for their people in order to build their reconstruction system. They hope that complete freedom of the individual can be restored later. We believe, on the other hand, that we should use only persuasion and no coercion. Our progress may not be too fast at the start, but we hope that ultimately it will catch up at a rate of geometric progression. We are trying to find out whether it is possible to build a monolithic instrument of action based upon a democratic instrument of decision.

Later, lunched and talked for two and a half hours with Nehru under a peach tree whose pale pink blossoms drifted onto our plates. Afterward, we admired his pet panda. Black, white, and wooly, like an expensive toy, it is kept in a large net cage around a tree. We went in and he fed it dates and bamboo leaves and played with it. Its mate died a few weeks ago. Nehru clearly loves animals. Has a delightful golden retriever pup which he caressed fondly. The only people there were Marina and myself, his niece (Mme Pandit's daughter), and her husband.

Nehru was wearing a white Gandhi cap which he later took off, exposing a sudden bald head much paler than his sunburned face. Also white, tight pants and a buttoned, homespun jacket. A rose was inserted in the second buttonhole.

Nehru just got back last night and goes off again on his electoral campaign. Elections here are very different from in the U.S.A. where radio and television have assumed great importance. Direct contact with the masses, public appearances, and speeches are the thing here. Nehru is astonished at the interest and patience of people who come out in the thousands, wait for hours in the hot sun, and then listen with great attention. I asked if he tried to discuss local issues, he said no; he didn't even know them. He left that to others. He talked about broad things: "Even international affairs, sometimes." The women are amazingly interested in politics. They have set a rule, to encourage them, to have 15 percent of the candidates women.

I asked if he really had written (under a pseudonym) the analysis of Nehru published in a Calcutta review in 1937. He said yes, he had written it for his own amusement then sent it to a woman friend. She passed it to someone else who had published it. Nobody guessed he had written it and Gandhi was even indignant, thinking some enemy was attacking Nehru.

I asked if he would stand by the self-analysis today; that the weaknesses of character he had attributed (tendency to dictatorship, etc.) had not come out in his political administration. He said that, after all, if a man could see such character weaknesses in himself and discuss them, that was proof in advance that he would never succumb to them. I asked if he found time to write anymore. He said no; not for ten years. Of course, occasionally, he wrote papers on such problems as tribal affairs. But this was part of his state work. He was not, after all, a professional writer. He wrote his first book when he was in prison and had little to do. Even so, it took him a year before he sat down to write. Then he thought about it for a month before he started.

He spoke of jail with a certain nostalgia. He was in a group of twelve and they shared the cooking chores. The only thing he ever learned to cook was "various preparations of eggs." Incidentally, he said he usually prepared the salad dressing at home, but today he allowed his niece—for the first time—to do so. Quite good.

Nehru thought Chou En-lai a brilliant man, one of the greatest he ever met. He gives the impression of being very open-minded; whether he is or not, that impression is most important. Of course he is obviously a sincere Communist ("I don't discuss this with him."), but he seems tolerant: "Perhaps, more conservative than the others." Nehru thought China showed more composure and confidence than Russia; that it had a greater cultural tradition and deeper internal roots. I asked if he saw any contest between Peking and Moscow for leadership in Asia. He said perhaps.

Nehru said the Russians could no longer treat their people in a Stalinist way. They were educated despite the fact they had spent forty years under the system. They didn't want a basic change; but more freedom (against secret police) and consumers goods. They had high enough wages and plenty of money; but nothing to buy. They were hungry for education. He was astonished at how much they read—"All heavy books; they have no light books."

He agreed that the Hungarian repression had been terrible. It was too bad it came at the time of Suez. Otherwise, he thought the Russians would have been forced to let go as they did with Poland. Nagy had made a mistake in openly appealing to the West. The Russians were convinced (wrongly of course) that the U.S. had touched off the Hungarian revolt and approved the Anglo-French venture in Egypt. Tito was now on the spot.

I remarked that in his early days Nehru considered himself a Marxist-Socialist but his administrative record certainly did not confirm this. What was his dogma today? He said:

> Marxism or communism or Leninism—call it what you like—first impinged on my mind just after the Russian revolution, when here in India we were in the thick of our own movement. Of course I was completely absorbed in Gandhi. We welcomed the Russian revolution and thought it a good thing. Later on, however, I read Marx when I was in prison. I was much fascinated by his brilliant analysis of the changes wrought by the industrial revolution in England—although I never had much interest in his theory of surplus values.
>
> But we were all so impressed by Gandhi; we thought he was following a more correct path than Marx and Lenin. Later on I said once that if I had to choose between communism and fascism I would choose the former. But that was a reaction to fascism, nothing more. Both communism and fascism have the same evil features: violence, cruelty, and oppression. But communism at least aims at something

better. It is unfortunate, if inevitable, that communism has become so tied up with violence and suppression. As a pure economic theory it would have been more attractive. And we must remember that when Marx evolved his theory in the first half of the nineteenth century, there was no real democracy. He had to think of violent means of upsetting the controlling oligarchy.

I asked him, in the Indian revolution now, what were the relative roles of the individual and the state, of public and private enterprises and ownership. He replied:

In the modern world, everywhere, there is a conflict between an increasing centralization which makes for less individual liberty. It is hard to draw the line. But we would like to preserve individual liberty even at the risk of slower progress in the economic field. I refuse to accept any doctrinaire socialism. Our main objective is that all the people of India should have equal opportunities. And this they certainly don't have yet. It would be absurd to apply to India today the nineteenth century theories of Marx evolved with respect to England.

Ours is a pragmatic, not a dogmatic revolution. It aims at equal opportunity. Gandhi was not a Socialist in the real and generally accepted sense. But he always identified himself with the very poorest. He left with us the idea of identification with the poor and the suppressed. He used a fine phrase about himself once. He said: "I should like to wipe every tear from every eye."

I asked Nehru if he thought of any young man to succeed him in national and party leadership after he retires. He said:

None. I haven't tried to do this—although many people here have asked me the same question. It wouldn't lead to anything. People outside India are likely to take a one-sided view of me, of our organization and our government. It is true that I play an outstanding role, through force of circumstance. But this is not a question only of any ability I may have. Various circumstances have made me extraordinarily popular with the common people—not so much with the intellectuals and others. But I doubt if the same set of circumstances is ever likely to arise again. My popularity is connected with our pre-independence movement, not any actions since independence. And you can't recreate such circumstances.

I asked what, in his opinion, was holding India together; not politically—except during relatively brief periods of strong rule such as the Moghuls—but internally. The concept of India was always there and strong conquerors always thought to subdue India.

Culturally, we are remarkably united. In a sense, it is like the old idea of Christendom in Europe—but even more intense. Political divisions didn't upset the idea of a common culture here. Our chief places of pilgrimage are widely separated—south, east, and west;

there were constant streams of pilgrims coming and going to them from all over India.

Another factor that was very important in the past is Sanskrit. This language has not been spoken since the days of Buddha—2,500 years ago. But it is *still* the language of the learned.

And then, the modern theme of unity was, strangely enough, brought about by Britain. The British enforced their unity. And our opposition to their rule was a unifying force. The Congress party started seventy-one years ago as a small movement, but it was always aimed at *all* India. Today we are politically and intellectually united. But we are not yet emotionally integrated. When something happens, passions break loose. India would be completely united against an external danger. But when we get complacent internally, then we fall out.

I asked what he envisioned as the long-range future for the subcontinent—some kind of federation for India, Pakistan, Burma, Ceylon? He answered:

If you had asked me that question fifteen or twenty years ago, I would have said that certainly we should have some kind of confederation, not federation, of independent states with common defense and economic policies. In theory, this should have been a normal development—something that would have come about this century, within the next thirty or forty years. Just at the beginning of the war I drafted the Congress resolution hinting at just this. But the difficulty in our way now is if we talk about it. This upsets our neighbors because, of course, we are so much the bigger. Nevertheless this is, of course, the logical future path. There should be such a confederation with each member state maintaining its national independence intact.

How about the visit to Eisenhower? Was he impressed by him? Had it helped resolve misunderstandings between our two countries? He said:

I was greatly impressed by the President. He is a big man and very frank. That is a great thing. But I don't understand—from a practical point of view—what your military policies can lead to. I am not suggesting that a country should be weak. But all this talk of strength and problems. Keeping a country strong is all right; but nevertheless one shouldn't speak of this strength too much. It is no secret that you are strong. And the Soviet Union is always talking about its strength also—even in a threatening way.

I mentioned all this to President Eisenhower—with some hesitation. I told him you were giving help to other nations, which was a very good thing. But so much of it was in the form of military aid; and that doesn't really help any country. Giving this aid to some countries merely helps strengthen the feudal and reactionary elements in them, and then you become associated with that in their public opinion. President Eisenhower admitted as much to me, and he said it was indeed a problem.

I noted that in one of our previous talks I had asked him on which side India would be in case of war. He had replied reluctantly that in the end it would be with the West because of a common political tradition and a dependence on maritime commerce.

Did I say that? Really? Well, most of our economic contacts are certainly with the West—our intellectual contacts also. And the mere fact of English being used and known here as a language and in our periodicals and books is important. Furthermore, of course, there is the bond of our governmental and parliamentary system.

But in the event of a war—I just don't know. We would certainly try and keep out of it. And what developments would lead into—I don't know. Geographically we are favorably situated. We are outside the normal way of war.

As he was getting restless, and as I saw my time was up, I then produced the hot one. Many Americans saw a contradiction between Nehru's advocacy of self-determination and his support of the UN—and his actions in Kashmir. How about it?

You must remember that soon after partition there were many things that had to be divided up between India and Pakistan. For example, we had jointly assumed the entire debt of the country and we owed each other a lot of money. We had given Pakistan some liquid cash. Our first fight came on this. We said we would give them a share of cash—about $25,000,000. Then we discussed what they would give us. There was no agreement and the discussions were postponed. Soon after this Pakistan invaded Kashmir; there was tension and anger in India. The question arose about our paying the $25,000,000. They were not only attacking Kashmir but fighting us. Our finance minister saw no reason to pay Pakistan when they were fighting us and there wasn't even full agreement on the rest of the arrangement. But, when Gandhi heard of this he was most upset. He said: "You have agreed to pay them $25,000,000. It doesn't matter what has happened subsequently. You must pay up." He was at that time having one of his fasts. He said: "You must keep your word." We paid. And the money was of extreme use to them in fighting us. They haven't paid us a *sou* of what they owe us aside from their interest on the external debt we assumed.

This is, of course, a most indirect argument. Nehru didn't look very proud of it himself. I asked if he thought the ultimate solution would not probably be de jure recognition of the present de facto dividing line in Kashmir as the frontier between India and Pakistan. He said: "As a dividing line it is a bad line—crossing through villages and that sort of thing. The proper line should have some sort of geographical features if possible—mountains, rivers, something."

While we were wandering and admiring the panda, he said suddenly: "Don't forget. In Russia they admire the United States very much for its techniques. The basic fear, however, is Germany."

NEW DELHI, INDIA, *February 20, 1957*

DRINKS with B. K. Nehru, joint secretary of the Ministry of Finance, a tall, handsome man with agreeable manner and an English education. His wife is Hungarian. They were married in the early 1930s despite the objections of her family who asked, "How can you think of marrying into a family that is always in and out of jail?"

Nehru (a cousin of the Prime Minister) said that if American aid to India continues at the same rate and India gets the loan it expects from the World Bank there will still be a short-fall in financing the second Five Year Plan amounting to $750,000,000. He assumes India will repay all its loans on schedule.

There is a big deficit. The Five Year Plan has to be cut by drastic measures. All projected new developments have already been halted. Imports are being limited to food and vital raw materials. Unfortunately the original planning was based too much on wishful thinking.

Nehru insisted that Pakistan was obtaining weapons from the U.S. only to fight India, not to defend itself against Russia. He said: "I know their mentality. I come from Lahore. When I was in Washington, Amjad Ali, their ambassador, always used to tell me frankly 'Don't think we are getting these weapons for use against the Russians.'"

Nehru thought it curious that the U.S.A. was backing India's social revolution in a race with China, while at the same time crippling the revolution's chances of success by engendering an arms race with Pakistan sponsored by Washington.

Lunch with G. D. Birla, India's wealthiest businessman, an old friend of Gandhi, and one of the most important behind-the-scene figures. In the garden of his house Gandhi was assassinated.

Birla said that whenever Gandhi came they would move all the furniture out so he could live simply; he would eat only vegetables, chappathi, and fruit. Birla first met Gandhi in 1915. He was fascinated by the little man who dressed so simply by contrast with the pretentious bourgeois leaders among Indian nationalists. Nehru was quite a contrast—an impatient, petulant young aristocrat who often quarreled with the Mahatma but always accepted his decisions in the end. Nehru talked too much. Curiously enough, although he was a great charmer, he had no intimate friends.

Birla said: "The old timers are almost gone. In ten years' time we will be able to elect politicians not because they have been in jail but because they can produce goods."

NEW DELHI, INDIA, *February 21, 1957*

GOOD talks with General S. M. Srinagesh, chief of staff of the Indian army and, in effect, C-in-C. He regretted that mechanization has forced out the cavalry saying: "Mastering a horse teaches a man leadership. If he can lead his horse, he can lead other men. He must control himself before he can control a horse."

India had decided to make its big aircraft purchases in the West as a matter of "loyalty." Furthermore, it was difficult to change to new types of arms. He was sure that the bitter argument with Pakistan would eventually pass and then it would be convenient to have arms sources in the West. When Zhukov was here the Russians hinted at weapons offers but nothing precise. Srinagesh contended that although the Russians might be able to offer some kinds at cheaper prices, "price is not the only important thing."

JAIPUR, INDIA, *February 25, 1957*

DROVE to this delightful pink city today. At this season India is green— the fields, trees, parrots, flights of bee eaters. The sun hasn't yet had a chance to burn everything. The shepherds in Rajasthan are brightly turbaned and the women in the fields and villages wear particularly brilliant saris . . . fierce, skinny-legged, brown men with red, orange, and purple turbans and gleaming earrings . . . the country is craggy. Monkeys squat by the wayside, pulling lice from each other . . . peacocks amble by the road . . . Flocks of sheep, goats . . . semiarid landscapes, stark, with pyramidal rocks . . . bullocks, aristocratic Brahma cattle, trotting camels.

Jaipur itself is pink with crenelated walls and palaces, temples with peacocks and monkeys, women in bright orange, red, and gold-fringed saris, elephants with painted foreheads, plumed tonga horses . . . half-naked sadhus wander about. Cows amble through the bazaar, pushing aside women wearing flowers in their hair. Outside, at Amber, an elephant with painted face carries one up the hill to the old Moghul Palace while a lute player and cymbalist play a strange haunting tune. The palace, with glass-inlaid mosaics, overlooks odd Jain temples and a quiet lake surrounded by gardens.

This evening had drinks and a talk with the maharajah of Jaipur and his attractive wife (number three). He had been thinking of going tiger shooting that afternoon; had he known I'd have liked it he would have invited me. (Just as well; I have lousy bronchitis and can hardly see straight.)

Jaipur admits: "There was feeling among the rulers [when the princely states were taken over by New Delhi], but it was in the interest of the country." He himself was made the Rajpramukh of Rajasthan (provincial governor) "for life," but he was eased out of the office last autumn. His only privileges now are his privy purse, special courtesies, and the right to pass on his family title. Most of his former subjects still regard him as a reigning maharajah and don't understand the change. They send him petitions and are puzzled when he tells them to take these elsewhere. He adds: "Many rulers have a difficult time adjusting themselves. Old Kapurthala— I'm sure he died of shock. But once Britain decided to get out of India, the jig was up."

NEW DELHI, INDIA, *February 27, 1957*

CALLED Ajoy Ghosh, secretary-general of the Indian Communist party. Was interested to note in his crummy office three pictures of Stalin. Ghosh gives the impression of being nice and stupid. He says the party has 125,000 card-carrying members (100,000 two years ago), and is strongest in the south.

Ghosh thinks Khrushchev on Stalin "gives an entirely one-sided estimate, inadequate and wrong. He emphasized only Stalin's bad points. Although Stalin committed serious mistakes he remains one of the greatest Marxists of all times. The sole responsibility for all that happened in Russia can't be left on the shoulders of one man."

In India it was necessary to extend "the public sector" of industry; reduce the concentration of wealth in a few hands and break up monopoly capital; transfer land to the peasants in individual holdings. There was no need for collectives—at any rate not yet. Peasants need their own land; later they could be persuaded to join cooperatives. "We are not going in for collectivisation." He adds:

What happened in China will never happen in India. We have a powerful centralized government such as China did not have. Secondly, the tactics of civil war cannot be adopted here. Our people don't desire it, and it would be harmful for our country. If it so happens that in Kerela we can form a left government dominated by our party, then our attempt won't be to establish a "Yenan." We eschew violence. It doesn't conform to the character or the tradition of our people.

NEW DELHI, INDIA, *February 28, 1957*

DINED with H. S. Malik who told me that in 1947, while he was Prime Minister of Patiala, he arranged a secret meeting in New Delhi between his maharajah and Jinnah. Jinnah wanted the Sikhs to join the future Pakistan and promised whatever they wanted. H. S. was mistrustful and asked for some offer in writing. Jinnah said: "My word is as good as the word of God; no one will dare challenge it." He repeated this when H. S. asked what would happen if Jinnah died before the contract was honored. H. S. concluded Jinnah was insane and informed his maharajah. The Sikhs stayed out—and later were either murdered or driven from the Punjab.

KATHMANDU, NEPAL, *March 5, 1957*

ARRIVED yesterday after a flight from Delhi to Lucknow to Benares to Patna. Patna very crowded with Hindu pilgrims returning from Nepal. The last lap was somewhat terrifying as the pilot had been obviously impressed by Russian methods of skimming tree branches atop the peaks. We flew over jungle, forest, and uptilted ranges, into Kathmandu and were greeted by the wreckage of a "near-miss" DC-3. The town is quaint, gay, interesting. To the north are the snow-covered Himalayas on the Tibetan border.

Nepal, as a country in the real sense, is only seven years old. Until 1950, it was merely a vast feudal estate. It had neither budget nor treasury system. The only services provided by the ruling Rana clan were police, army, and tax collectors. The last Rana Prime Minister, opening a school there said: "This is the beginning of the end of the Ranas."

Soldiers are an important export. Several thousand a year go to Britain and India. Some of the money is allotted home; plus pensions. Retired Gurkhas are an element of stability. India, Britain, and Nepal signed a tripartite Gurkha agreement in 1947, which has never been published. This gives Britain and India the right to recruit Gurkhas here. The recruiting season is in the fall—after the monsoon. British and Indian recruiting agents travel the hills and bring prospects to camps where they are medically checked. Agents get a small cut for each recruit accepted.

Nepal signed a treaty of friendship and trade with Tibet (China). There is a Nepalese merchants colony in Lhasa. Clauses in the treaty allow appointments of four Nepali trade agents in Tibet and of Chinese trade agents here in Nepal. The trade agents are specifically allowed to send their messages in diplomatic code and are immune from search.

Mrs. Price, wife of the UN head, says that since lightning is supposed to be a virgin, the many lewd sculptures in the temples here are used to keep away the lightning. She says there is a considerable export of yak tails for use in Santa Claus beards. Gurkhali, says she, is a poor language. There are only five words for differing shades of color; nothing to indicate degree—moreness or lessness, etc.

I went to see Khadgaman Singh, one of the main politicians, in his large house, pitifully furnished and cold. At each end of the main salon were pictures of the King and his father. He served tea and cakes which looked worth their weight in cholera. Singh is a small, wiry man with a red caste mark on his forehead, thick glasses, an amiable smile. He wore a cap and a homespun jacket. He is a nice and undoubtedly fearless little man, but too hard to comprehend—especially as a noisy thunderstorm had just rolled down off the Himalayas and there was plenty of thunderous counterpoint.

He gave me a photo of himself (snapped by a friendly guard) showing him in the cell where he spent ten of his twenty years in jail under the Ranas. He was chained hand and feet. The cell was five by six by ten feet and there were three others in it with him. They died. He couldn't stand upright, and carrying his chains he "walked back and forth like a lion in my cage." In 1951, he was released after the anti-Rana revolution.

The Will Mullers (acting head of USOM) gave us a party. Among those present were Father Moran, a fascinating Jesuit priest from Chicago; Chuda Prasad Sharma, foreign minister; Field Marshal Kaiser Shumshere Jang Bahadur Rana, brother of the last Rana Prime Minister and a relative of the King; a young Indian named Malhotra, in charge of customs at the Finance Ministry; and Tollinton, the British ambassador.

After supper we sat around on the floor. Kaiser is a funny little old man (sixty-six) with a black Nepali cap and coat, white leggings. He was ambassador simultaneously to London, Paris, and Washington. He gave me a long lecture on the use of the kukri. To chop off the head of a buffalo in one shot you need a double-handed grip on a heavy, two-handed kukri. For a human head it is better to use the forehand; but a good backhand can do it. There is also a neat upward disemboweling stroke.

Moran has been here ten years and is very fond of these people. He isn't allowed to proselytize but does seem to manage, in his school, to have the boys cross themselves.

The foreign minister was very chummy, a slight fellow with glasses. He assured me that Hindus (he's a Brahman) simply can't digest beef; that he had it once without knowing in the U.S.A. and was sick three days. He confirmed that it is indeed true that yak tails are exported for Santa Claus beards. (Later I saw some hanging in the bazaar.) He also said Nepalis smoke hashish and drink a sort of dope.

Visited Patan, the capital of a former valley kingdom. Enormous number of coolies in Nepal. Barefoot women walk seven miles into town and back bearing heavy loads of wood—for a wage of two and a half Nepalese rupees (about 40 cents). Even automobiles are carried in over fabulous mountains by coolie.

Patan contains five third-century B.C. stupas erected in Buddha's honor by the Emperor Asoka when he came here. Many of its streets look like medieval European alleys except for the astonishing pagodas and colorful Nepalese people. It contains fantastic red and brown temples, often faced by columns with gold statues. The temple facades contain a congeries of many colored gods and goddesses with amazingly lewd figures at the four eave corners, devilish-looking gods with scowling faces and sexual erections.

Tibetan women from the north wander about with plaited pigtails, gold belts, felt hats, and heavy aprons. Tibetan men, many of them also pigtailed, wear pagoda-shaped hats and colored felt boots. They are bigger and even more Mongolian-looking than the Gurkhas. One wandered by bearing a tray with two silver cups and a bloody sheep's head. Cows stroll about among the toad-like lion statues of the temple. Rows of bare-foot women porters stagger in from the hills under loads of wood. On one temple, above a carved black teakwood fresco, is a colored god happily tearing the bowels out of a demon.

A slaughtered chicken, painted odd colors, was laid before the deity as an offering, and a dog was happily eating it. People in all postures unconcernedly relieve themselves in the gutters beside the narrow street. Families of pigs roam about near Tibetan women squatting in the sun. In a parade ground (with a few Gurkhas) by one of Asoka's stupas—clouds covered Mount Everest in the background—a tough little shepherd boy watches his sheep and tootles a wooden fife.

Visited the foreign minister in the vast Singha Durba Palace (former Rana residence now used as the government secretariat). It is immense—almost on a Pentagon scale—European outside, sordid and dirty inside, uneven board floors, dark, gloomy, underfurnished, ramshackle.

Chuda Prasad Sharma said: "Nepal's policy is neutrality—one word will suffice; nonalignment with any bloc; friendship with all countries regardless of ideology. What else could a small country like Nepal do to stay free?"

Then saw Tanka Prasad Acharya, the forty-five-year-old Prime Minister who said there is still a feudalistic land system which he hopes to reform. He intends to seize large estates without compensation. "But we must watch the situation. The Ranas may try and stir up trouble."

KATHMANDU, NEPAL, *March 6, 1957*

LUNCHED at the Prices'. He is head of the UN mission, a charming American, born in China. Also there were Father Moran and Peter Aufschnaiter, the companion of Hans Harrer (*Seven Years in Tibet*), who now lives and works here; a modest, quiet, elderly man, hard as nails, thin with nice blue eyes. He says the Tibetans claim two portions of Nepal—the Mustang area in the north center and Jumla in the northwest.

Moran said the present King succeeded when his father died in February, 1956. He threw out the politicos who had been dominating his father since the revolution and now he really rules—but well. He is on record as saying when some people criticized Nepal's new democracy but apologized for its corruption, "Don't tell me it's because this is a baby democracy; babies aren't corrupt."

Indian aid here has administrative and economic strings (like ours to India which Delhi doesn't like). The Chinese aid grant has *no* strings at all, making many Nepalese criticize the Indians. One Nepalese observed: "Chou En-lai is winning, but Nehru is dominating."

When the late King Tribhuvana died, the present King Mahendra, to safeguard his father's soul, got inside the body of a newly slain rhinoceros and prayed for his parent. This is an ancient custom.

After lunch, as we sat on the terrace, Mrs. Price suddenly turned her head and said: "Look! Look, here it comes." And as we stared at the immense peaks stretching into the sky we saw, coming through the clouds above them, the breathtaking bulk of Everest, advancing slowly and then vanishing backward into a new bank of mist.

BENARES, INDIA, *March 7, 1957*

LAST night, there was a reception and barbecue for U.S. Ambassador Bunker, who is accredited here as well as India. The meat was buffalo—which can be slaughtered and eaten in Nepal, but not India where it is considered the same as cow. Then we saw a display of Tibetan devil dancers in masks, fifes and drums amid blazing bonfires.

This morning we flew out here to Benares via Patna; a fine, sunny day with a good view of Mount Everest. The Tibetan frontier, by air, is only about forty-five miles from Kathmandu.

BENARES, INDIA, *March 9, 1957*

YESTERDAY we went out on the Ganges in a motorboat to see the bathing and burning. Near the ghats by the riverside are crowds of beggars with every kind of disease and malformation. Brahman priests sit under straw parasols, their foreheads painted with caste marks. Thousands of bathers, men, women, and children, swim and wash in the filthy, oily, brown water, pee in it, drink it, throw wreaths into it. They fill brass pots to take home. If they didn't have this custom I'll wager India's population would be doubled.

Some temples are sinking into the river. A body is stretched under a cloth waiting for wooden faggots to be piled up. The man who runs the burning ghat has a large fake tiger by his platform—a symbol of death. Thirty to forty bodies are burned each day (then the ashes and remnants chucked in among the bathers). A Brahman, stark naked and smeared gray with ashes as a form of penance, sits under a parasol smoking a pipe.

Near Benares, at Sarnath, is one stupa marking where Buddha first met his five disciples and another where he gave his first sermon. Also an ugly Jain temple; printed in English above the portal, "Non-Violence is the Highest Religion."

COLOMBO, CEYLON, *March 12, 1957*

HOT and sticky. There is immense communal tension between the Sinhalese and Tamils who feel they are being treated as second-class citizens. This has crystallized over the language issue. Tamil derives from old Dravidian, Sinhalese from Sanskrit.

The government is Sinhalese and decreed that Sinhalese will be the sole official language. The Tamils demand equal rights for Tamil. A disproportionately large number of Tamils are in the civil service and fear they will have to do all business in Sinhalese.

There are three "Marxist" parties: a regular Moscow-directed Communist party; a Trotskyite party; and a splinter Trotskyite group which supports the present government. They squabble a lot among themselves.

COLOMBO, CEYLON, *March 14, 1957*

VISITED Sir John Kotelawela. He was Prime Minister for three years. A landed aristocrat who represents the conservatives, he has a lovely estate where he grows rice, and you can hear the trumpeting elephants pulling ploughs in the paddies. We sat on the terrace, overlooking a tiny pond where an inhibited swan was trying to swim without success. Kotelawela, a sturdy, brown man, wore a T shirt and white shorts which showed up the varicose veins in his legs.

On the subject of neutrality he said: "For a small country like ours it is ridiculous. God knows where it is going to end. Small countries must have friends and if you are going to be a democratic country you need friends among the democracies."

At one point he said: "Things are going so rapidly to the dogs that we may never again have a parliamentary election. The Communists are so strong that Bandaranaike [present Prime Minister], thinks his only friends are Communists. But nobody here knows anything about Communists. We are going to get a lot more now with the Chinese and Russians coming."

I asked him about Buddhism in politics. He said: "This was what contributed largely to my defeat last year. I am a Buddhist, but it is against all Buddhist precepts for religion to mix into politics. Now the church is behaving scandalously. One prominent woman is being kept by a Buddhist priest. Many years ago the Communists started to infiltrate the Buddhist hierarchy, now they are getting the benefits."

This morning I went to see Solomon West Ridgway Bandaranaike at his comfortable, unpretentious house. On the porch, dozens of hangers-on lounged about, including numerous orange-robed shaven-headed Buddhist priests. We sat in an ugly hot salon. A brown greyhound lay panting.

Bandaranaike, a small, thin man with spectacles and curiously thick tufts of hair emerging from each ear, seems tricky and speaks in pompous, platitudinous English in a lilting, high-pitched voice. He said:

As one of your Americans once said, This is the age of the common man. It is a period of transition in world history. The emphasis is on the needs of the masses. In our country the common man lives largely below the poverty line. I mean to say, he has a very low standard of living. We feel it is not possible to solve the economic question purely on capitalistic lines. We follow socialistic lines of economic development. The repercussions of this situation produce our concept of neutralism. We want to be friends with everybody, to borrow from both East and West, from both capitalism and socialism."

NUWARA ELIYA, CEYLON, *March 16, 1957*

WE came here today after an interesting drive. Lunched at Kandy, where we visited the Temple of the Tooth. The jungle along the roadside is filled with palms, coconuts, bananas. In the rubber plantations a diagonal slit goes down the trunk of each tree where half a coconut shell is hung to collect the latex. Rice paddies and pineapple fields fill out the picture of agricultural wealth. Little bullock carts with hoods of thatch shielding their cargos from the burning sun wind along slowly in the heat. The woods are filled with plane trees, frangipani, tapioca (manioc), and jackfruit trees, cashew nuts, breadfruit and peppercorn vines. Venders sell coconuts from red brown heaps. When the country begins to climb into the hills the tea bushes appear. The British brought in tea plants from Assam in the nineteenth century and it has been planted all over the highlands. Some trees are loaded heavily with thousands of fruit bats hanging upside down and waiting for dark.

Kandy is a lovely little town beside an artificial lake. It was the last independent capital of Ceylon in the sixteenth century and is famous for its sacred Bo tree and Buddhist Temple of the Tooth. The Bo tree is six hundred years old and comes from a branch of the oldest living tree in the world. Its branches are filled with ravens. The Temple of the Tooth, built in 1590, is filled with flowers and incense. Its relic is kept locked up except for one hour a day when people may peer into the shrine.

In the rivers outside Kandy, work-elephants spend the first three or four hours of the afternoon lying on their sides and bathing, squirting water playfully through their trunks. The elephants feel the heat badly so they are allowed their relaxation. Their keepers scrub them while they loll about in the waters. Nuwara Eliya is more than six thousand feet high and delightfully cool and frosty in the winter months. We wore sweaters in the evening.

JUFAIR, BAHREIN, March 21, 1957

WE have been staying with Sir Bernard Burrows, British political resident for the Persian Gulf. He is disappointed that no planning for the future is going on in London. Every time any recommendation is made it disappears into a pigeonhole. I asked if any effort were being considered for some kind of federation so these various states could become more united and play a role in the Commonwealth. He said this was difficult; there are so many jealousies and feuds.

The various rulers want the best of both worlds—Arab emotionalism and independence protected by Britain. Nasserism has therefore caused a sort of schizophrenic strain. Admittedly there are curious anomalies. For example, the official currency is Indian rupees, but most postage stamps are still English with a super-mark. Inland, hard money is the old Maria Theresa taler.

Any British official in this area has the authority to free slaves. If a slave shows up at a residency or consulate and requests his freedom, this can automatically be granted and the slave is given a paper declaring him free. About twenty slaves a year are still freed here in Bahrein. Mostly they are Saudi Arabs. Slavery was abolished in Bahrein decades ago, yet there is still a steady if small demand for slaves in Saudi Arabia. The supply comes either from Baluchistan or from Africa across the Red Sea. A certain amount of opium is also smuggled into Bahrein from Persia.

JUFAIR, BAHREIN, March 22, 1957

THIS afternoon I went to see the ruler, His Highness Sheikh Sulman Bin Hamed-al-Khalifah, KCMG, KCIE. He received me at the entrance to his palace reception room. Outside were various Arab courtiers and some very black gentlemen who looked as if they might once have been slaves. The reception hall is about the size of a tennis court, lined with rugs, rows of chairs around the walls, a sort of divan-throne. The Sheikh is short with a brown smiling face, moustache; dressed in splendid robes, edged in gold, a gold curved dagger thrust into his belt. The Sheikh talked only about hunting, having just returned from a falcon expedition for bustards.

Servants brought tiny cups of bitter cardamon coffee and sweet thick tea; also a ewer of rosewater, poured on our hands, and burning incense.

MARNES-LA-COQUETTE, *March 25, 1957*

YESTERDAY evening Larry Norstad celebrated his fiftieth birthday with a small party. Ismay said he had seen Churchill last week and discussed what Churchill would have done had he been in charge of the British government last autumn. Churchill insisted he certainly would have advised the U.S. before invading and he would have moved directly on Cairo.

Pug thinks it would be extremely helpful to the United States-British alliance if Selwyn Lloyd and Dulles were dumped as foreign ministers. He wants to appoint a three-man committee as arbitrator for the Cyprus dispute. He would like to have Italy, the U.S., and either Holland or Norway represented. They would deal with procedural matters— how to start hearings and an examination of the problem.

After several drinks a large birthday cake was lit. Larry managed to blow out all fifty candles. General Schuyler got up and proposed a toast. First he read a message from Larry's SHAPE friends, headed by Montgomery, predicting that his second fifty years would be more successful and that his golf scores would improve.

PARIS, *March 29, 1957*

DINED at Elie de Rothschild's. Jean Cocteau was there plus a young man who was supposed to be Cocteau's boyfriend and an extremely attractive woman supposed to be the boyfriend's girlfriend.

Cocteau was entirely fascinating. He was strangely dressed in a houndstooth check suit, tan suede shoes, black necktie, and white shirt. He wears his cuffs rolled up in an odd affectation. He has an exceptionally intelligent, sensitive, amazingly young, and curiously innocent face. After a great deal of rather uninteresting badinage, Cocteau really began to talk. These are some things I remember.

"The great tragedy of France is that its politicians are unsuccessful writers and its writers are unsuccessful politicians." Among the former he named de Gaulle and Herriot. He says de Gaulle writes in a perfectly plain but not particularly distinguished French classical style which he does not especially admire.

Among the writers who aspire to politics he named André Malraux. He sneers at Malraux's writing and asks: "Have you ever heard of a *human* reading *La Condition Humaine*?" He said Malraux's consuming ambition was to play a political role. He assured me Malraux had once told him he supported de Gaulle because he thought it was high time that a General Boulanger should succeed in France.

Cocteau thought the greatest craving of children was to be like everybody else. He thought also that the ultimate aspiration of the Communist world was to achieve individual liberty which was now sacrificed to security; the ultimate ambition of the western world was to achieve security which was now being sacrificed to individual liberty. In other words, Cocteau thinks the Communist countries want to become democracies and the democracies want to become Communist dictatorships. This, of course, is distinctly *enfant terrible* talk, but Cocteau says it brilliantly and naturally with a slightly starry-eyed expression.

Cocteau says the trouble with our time is not that this is a lying epoch, but it is an epoch that is lied about. He referred to Napoleon and quoted him as saying: "Any man who thinks is my enemy."

Cocteau said he took a young chauffeur to see a Communist movie. On leaving, the young man said to him: "One recognizes quickly these Catholic milieux."

At one point he was discussing Voltaire. He said Voltaire was "one of those creatures who are insulated against experience and emotion, and therefore unreal."

PARIS, *March 31, 1957*

GOLFED today with Sir Frank Roberts, now ambassador to NATO. At lunch he told me the Jugoslavs didn't mobilize during the 1956 Hungarian crisis and their tanks were never in a position to move. However, there was one forty-eight-hour period when they passed out guns and ammunition to party members. This indicated they were more worried about some kind of anti-Tito uprising inside Jugoslavia than Soviet aggression.

They were embarrassed by Nagy. To begin with he represented Hungarian nationalists and the Jugoslavs don't forget the unvoiced Hungarian claims to Jugoslav territory. Belgrade always wanted to dump Nagy and was embarrassed having him as a refugee in its Budapest embassy. But the way the Russians grabbed him when he was let out of the embassy on a promise of safety was deliberately done to embarrass Tito and rub his nose in the dirt.

The current joke in Jugoslavia now is: "Tito only made three mistakes on Hungary. First he recognized the Gerö government. Then he recognized the Nagy government. Then he recognized the Kadar government."

PARIS, *April 13, 1957*

DROVE to Fontainebleau for drinks with General Speidel, now commander-in-chief of NATO ground forces on the central front. Speidel is living in a little NATO officers' billet—the Hôtel d'Albe. They don't even have a telephone from the desk downstairs up to the rooms. I do hope somebody can get in touch with him if a war starts. We walked out in a cold drizzle to a plain little restaurant about a hundred yards away where we sat and talked.

Both he and Norstad were furious at the British over their white paper on defense. Adenauer is in a rage because it places him in a difficult political position. Above all Speidel was struck by the sentence in Sandys's statement which said Britain could no longer be defended. He wondered what the repercussions of this would be in countries like Denmark which have no pretense to being great powers.

I asked if, as a historian, Speidel could think of any precedent for his present position—a defeated enemy general commanding troops of the nation that defeated him. He said there was none really. In 1866, Prussia fought a war against the combined armies of Baden, Hesse, and Bavaria. Yet four years later, in the Franco-Prussian war, Von Der Tann, a Bavarian general, commanded Prussian troops.

During the Napoleonic wars there were various instances of former enemies suddenly joining up with new allies. But all the nations were continually shifting around at the time.

The Württembergers served as Marshal Ney's rear guard at Viazma in 1812. Speidel himself is a Württemberg. In 1942, he set up his own command post at almost precisely the same spot in Viazma. In 1814, said Speidel, the crown prince of Württemberg commanded a mixed German detachment against Napoleon—having just been fighting on Napoleon's side against the Russians two years previously. He also pointed out that in 1815, Blücher fought with Wellington against Napoleon.

Speidel says glumly: "The Germans and the Americans alone are going to have to defend Europe."

PARIS, *April 19, 1957*

LARRY Norstad told me today it is essential to get the Germans in high NATO command posts before they have their army. This will get them used to the habit of cooperating with the West and "European" rather than nationalistic ideas.

Speidel is very civilian minded. Heusinger would have been terrible, a heel-clicker and strutter. Furthermore, there are hundreds of pictures of him standing beside Hitler briefing him and his staff. Heusinger is more useful in Germany.

The British argument about new weapons permitting force reduction was fallacious. Their effect had already been reckoned in the calculation of present force commitments. NATO had reduced its contemplated strength in the center from sixty-four D-Day divisions, to thirty D-Day divisions while moving its area of strategic commitment eastward from the Rhine to the frontier of East Germany: a bigger task with less forces.

Missiles do not totally change the situation. If you had ICBMs all over Europe, what would be the real difference except a psychological one? What could be done to deter the Russians that is not being done now? Today we have the ability to destroy any and every important objective in Russia in case of war. What more can be done with missiles? Of course we must build missiles because the means of defense are improving just as the means of offense are improving. But missiles will not revolutionize the balance of power.

We will have to assume that when NATO has a full complement of missiles the Russians will also have a complement of missiles. Then, perhaps the only danger of a world war will remain in the chance of some hot-blooded mistake in judgment. That could come most likely on the line in Europe which separates the eastern and western blocs. This is the most sensitive line in the world. The Russians are always presented with the possibility of a chance to "probe" across that line into the NATO area. They could announce that they are merely crossing the line temporarily for peaceful purposes; that they intend to withdraw later. Then what would NATO do? NATO is the cornerstone of the free world. What do we do if the Russians move in that way? Do we start a total World War III, or do we give in and let the Russians' probing expedition remain, with the result that NATO crumbles?

PARIS, *April 22, 1957*

THIS afternoon, Senator Stuart Symington, a Missouri Democrat and a former secretary of air, dropped in for a drink. He wanted to know what effect it would have abroad if we cut the defense and foreign aid provisions of the budget. I told him terrible. He admitted that the British white paper on defense had encouraged our Congress to trim the defense budget, but he blamed Eisenhower for praising "British courage" in doing this. "Why can't we be courageous too?" asked Symington.

Symington, a big, handsome man, does not impress me as being exceptionally bright or one who would stand up for an unpopular cause if he thought it were right but politically harmful to himself.

PARIS, *April 26, 1957*

LAST night we had a rather curious dinner party including the ambassadors from Jugoslavia, Bebler, from India, Panikkar, and from Poland, Gajewski. All their wives were absent. Bebler's wife is acting in a play in Jugoslavia, Gajewski's is in Switzerland recovering from an operation, and Panikkar left his at home.

Panikkar says India wishes to see the development of three large Arab states. The first, the Maghreb, would run from the Atlantic Ocean across Morocco, Algeria, Tunisia, and the western half of Libya, extending to the border between Tripolitania and Cyrenaica. The second state would include Cyrenaica, Egypt, Jordan, the Lebanon, Syria, and part of Saudi Arabia. It would be controlled from Cairo. The third would include the Persian Gulf area of Iraq, Kuwait, the Saudi Arabian eastern coast, Britain's Persian Gulf sheikhdoms, and the Yemen.

He separated this third state from the second for the very obvious reason of Indian national interest. He said India would be happy to see Britain continue its hegemony in the area of the third state as long as Britain was strong enough to do so and still continued to protect Indian commercial interest. But he made it quite clear that if England ever gets out, India wants to gain political ascendency in the area of the third state in order to protect the strategic and economic interests of that area, which were once developed from and run by British India.

Gajewski talked at great length about Poland, especially last October, "When we came within inches of total disaster." He said the joke around Warsaw was: "The Hungarians behaved like Poles; the Poles behaved like Czechs; the Czechs behaved like pigs; and the Jews behaved like Cossacks."

PARIS, *April 29, 1957*

PLAYED golf with Bob Hope. He is exceptionally nice and quite a good golfer. He is over here making a film with Anita Ekberg and Fernandel. He says the French movie industry is very advanced and not too far behind our own. However, expenses here are surprisingly high and everything moves too slowly. One of the large expenses is food and drink for the workers. He is amazed to see technicians and laborers knock off two hours for lunch and eat a four course meal with two wines.

OXFORD, ENGLAND, *May 5, 1957*

WEEKEND up here with Bill Deakin. This morning, Bill had a group of his students over for drinks: a fascinating lot. Wolfgang Leonhard was once a most important East German Communist, although he is now only thirty-two. His parents were Communists and at ten he was taken to the U.S.S.R. where eventually his father was killed and his mother disappeared. He was educated for seven years in Soviet schools and speaks perfect Russian. Neither his father's death nor his mother's exile dampened his loyalty. Nor did the Stalin-Hitler pact: "That was based on actual policy, not doctrinal ideas. And we Communists never give any importance to actual practical policy. Doctrine was and is everything."

It was only when Tito split with the Cominform in 1948 that Leonhard broke. He had been secretary to Walter Ulbricht, the East German Communist boss, and had returned to Germany with him from Russia on April 30, 1945. In Berlin, when he left Ulbricht's office, he taught in the party school, giving lectures on underground activities. As a high party functionary he had lots of money. As a lecturer on how to cross frontiers, he knew just how to do it. He went to Jugoslavia via Czechoslovakia and was taken over the border by professional smugglers.

Leonhard thinks the ideological antecedents of Titoism can be found in two separate bodies of early Bolshevik thinking. The more important was the writing of Shlapnikov on cooperatives rather than collectives and on workers' councils to operate factories democratically. To Shlapnikov's theories should be added some of the ideas of the right-wing deviationists executed by Stalin: Bukharin, Rykov, and Tomsky.

But Leonhard was astonished to find out that Jugoslav ideological writers are not aware of these antecedents. Hardly any have ever even heard of Shlapnikov. The Jugoslavs keep "inventing" new concepts without realizing that practically all of them had already been invented years ago.

Leonhard said that when he arrived in Belgrade from Prague with a false passport, he saw all the Jugoslav big shots. Djilas was fascinated by the idea that Jugoslav Communists were now evolving a brand-new theory of "managerial revolution." "But, Comrade Djilas," said Leonhard, "there's nothing new about that. It was also written by James Burnham fifteen years ago." Djilas was astonished. He had never heard of Burnham.

NEITHER DINOSAUR

NOR BEE

LONDON, *May 6, 1957*

EXCELLENT TALK WITH PRIME MINISTER HAROLD MACMILLAN IN the Cabinet room at No. 10 Downing Street. We sat at the long, green-baize-covered table, where so many famous decisions have been made. He greeted me with his usual courteous urbanity, waved me to a seat, and then pulled up a chair: a large, imposing, handsome Edwardian figure with a shock of gray hair, puffing a slender cigar.

Macmillan impressed me as being the most imaginative and at the same time the boldest, toughest British Prime Minister since the wartime Churchill. In other words, I include the aging Churchill who was re-elected in 1951. He has ideas of considerable audacity and he expounds them in excellent, well-chosen language. He is calm and thoughtful but by no means slow in his thinking processes, and he certainly gives one the feeling that he is a man of decision.

I told him I had heard people describe the philosophy of his government as a "Tory revolution." Did he consider this an accurate statement? He reflected for a moment, puffing his cigar. Then he said:

Yes, I suppose that is exact. Certainly socialism is out of date. It is based on an out-of-date point of view. Likewise, the old capitalism is dying. You in America have already done a great deal toward creating a new capitalism. I think you will agree that this must be both dynamic and creative. We must have equality and opportunity. Privilege must disappear—but not to be replaced with the false privilege of egalitarianism. Everybody must be given equal opportunity to make the best of themselves. But this does not mean leveling people down from the top. It is more important to pull other people up than to let them pull down the rest.

I said the broad outlines of Macmillan's policies of "Tory revolution" were becoming evident in terms of defense and budget reforms. However, would there be any changes in foreign policy? He replied:

No, there will be no change in foreign policy except in this sense— it must be an Elizabethan policy rather than a Victorian policy. During the Victorian age, England, as a leader of the industrial revolution and the richest country in the world, was able to muddle through. We were not very intelligent. But we managed because of our wealth and power. Perhaps we were in the same position as America today.

But during the Elizabethan age we were a small country—only about two million people. The skill of the great queen enabled us to hold an important place in the world.

Of course, you must have a certain size or you cannot be an important power. Thus, for example, San Marino could never be a great country. An ant can never be much of a thing. But mere wealth and size are not necessary for greatness. You can be too big—like an elephant. Man is a reasonable size and perhaps that is why he has succeeded so well. He is neither dinosaur nor bee.

Our great periods have been those when Britain has made its mark not by size or wealth alone. Remember the days of Marlborough, when there were only six or seven million English and twenty million French. The proportions remained about the same during the era of Napoleon. We don't need to be frightened of the Russians or the Chinese just because there are a lot of them.

I asked if there would be any change of emphasis in the Anglo-American alliance. Macmillan replied:

No, I don't envision any change in emphasis. The American people have always wanted a partner in England, not a satellite. And remember this, our defense plan is designed not to make us weaker but stronger. In three years our contribution to allied defense will be greater rather than less. Frankly, the contribution of lots of NATO countries right now is false, not real. What is a Belgian division worth? Lots of tails and little teeth.

We shall be able to get a volunteer army—and our history proves that this is always the best. Of course the Germans never had one. Therefore, they don't understand this. Our tradition is a voluntary tradition. That is the best.

I told Macmillan I remembered a conversation when he was minister of defense and complained about the necessity for Britain of maintaining side by side two military establishments—a modern one for defense in Europe and a conventional one for use in distant overseas positions to fight brush wars as in Malaya. Was this still his view? He replied:

The transport airplane must have an increasingly greater role from now on. Overseas forces will fade out. It is no fun having bases in other people's countries. You have found that you can have floating bases with your Sixth Fleet. Our British fleet, although smaller, will have the same purpose. It will be based on carriers—mobile bases that don't have to depend upon the permanent goodwill of people in other countries.

Then Macmillan told me an amusing story. At Bermuda, when discussing the world situation with Eisenhower,

I told Ike that we have come to the conclusion that colonialism is a bad idea. We have read so much about this in your newspapers that we are convinced of it. Therefore, we proposed now to evacuate all our bases overseas. The President was furious, but I went on and told him that we intended to leave Hong Kong next year. After this background, I persuaded him that we must be supported morally by the United States if we are to keep up our bases overseas. We cannot constantly be criticized as colonialists.

I then asked if Macmillan, in his efforts to link England with western Europe, had any intention of associating with EURATOM. He said:

We would like to associate with it as closely as possible. But we cannot jeopardize our agreements with you people on the military uses of the atom. I spoke to your President about this in Bermuda. We cannot lose our association with you on this subject. Therefore, we cannot share any of our atomic military secrets without your prior consent. And, after all, you must be aware that there really is not any security anywhere except in the United Kingdom and the United States. All the rest is terrible. Everybody seems to read everybody else's codes. This limits the exchange of information.

I would like Western European Union to be worked out effectively on a European defense deal; but everything except nuclear things. We must keep our obligations to you. And security, quite frankly, is extremely important. The Russians are very good at this sort of thing. Nobody has ever broken the Soviet code.

He thought the British expedition against Suez had been useful because it prematurely exploded the Russian penetration plan. Had there been a similar premature blowup in about 1938, there might never have been a World War II. He was sure the Russians had suffered considerably because of this. (I can't buy his argument. Does he really believe it?)

LONDON, *May 7, 1957*

TALK with Duncan Sandys, Churchill's former son-in-law who is now minister of defense. He couldn't have been nicer, but I didn't care for him: vain and ambitious.

I asked if he could explain when the first germs of the revolution in defense policy were detectable in postwar England. Sandys said:

I want you to know that I didn't inherit any scheme. What our white paper does is to take action on previously known facts. We had all understood and seen the change in the world situation as well as in the development of modern weapons. We also recognized the impossibility of defending this country against a nuclear attack.

The white paper came about when we decided that it was both safe and necessary to base planning and the reshaping of our forces upon these known facts. Now we have taken the plunge. The first fact we accepted and acted upon was that this country is not defendable against a nuclear attack. The second one, is that guided missiles are now coming along so well that we can begin to put reliance upon them. We have scrapped all further development of jet bombers.

Britain would certainly hang on to its overseas possessions, but in a more efficient way. For example, with new jet transports the empire was brought much closer. He had just taken a trip around the Mediterranean last week and it took him just under five hours to fly from London to Cyprus in an air transport Command Comet.

At the end of our conversation Sandys observed wryly: "You people would have preferred to have us keep more foot soldiers and give up our nuclear plans. You rather like the idea of having other countries provide the infantry." I commented, with equal wryness, that I presumed we had learned this from Britain, who had done well in this respect during the nineteenth and twentieth centuries.

Sandys continued: "The fact is that we are rather worried about you. We want to have our own nuclear capacity on this side of the Atlantic. After all, we must take into account the possibility that when the intercontinental missile is operational, you may decide to go back to a 'fortress America' policy and defend your interests in Europe from bases in Chicago. We have to be free to look after ourselves in such an event."

Later, I had lunch with Adam Watson of the Foreign Office (a future ambassador). He returned last week from a visit to Washington where he had been sent to discuss Anglo-American policy in the Middle East.

The U.S. now recognizes that Russia has gained a preponderant position in the two oil-transit states, Egypt and Syria. Egypt controls the sea route for oil. The pipelines from Iraq, Kuwait, and Saudi Arabia all pass through Syria. Therefore, the U.S. sees the necessity for extruding Russian influence from those countries.

It has been agreed between Britain and the United States that we should play the hand in the Middle East for the present. The British recognize the necessity for this. But, although we say the 1950 tripartite declaration on Palestine still applies, this is not true. The French are now out in the cold, playing their own game. We have no faith in French security and are not going to tell them anything about our real plans in the Middle East because we are convinced they would leak these immediately to the Israelis.

The next move is to isolate Nasser by achieving a political change in Syria. We have already prevailed upon King Saud to cease financing the left wing—the pro-Communist neutralists in Syria—and from now on to spread his money among more prowestern Syrian elements.

The United States is convinced Nasser can slowly be brought to his knees by economic pressures and political isolation. The world is going to rely less and less on the Suez Canal as supertankers are built, and petroleum is sent in ever increasing quantities by pipeline across a more stable Jordan and a more sympathetic Syria. The U.S. feels that Egypt is economically doomed to strangulation.

LONDON, *May 9, 1957*

NOT very inspiring talk with the Marquess of Salisbury at his Chelsea home. Tall, thin, conservatively but elegantly dressed, with a mobile face and a downtwist at the mouth corners, Salisbury was most agreeable, but some of what he said was tommyrot.

He started by saying the Anglo-American alliance was all important—had been and remained so. He strongly opposed Britain's recognition of Red China, purely because he knew what adverse effect that mood would have in the United States. However, the great difficulty between England and America was that Washington placed too much faith and reliance upon the UN. The UN simply cannot work when its decisions are made only by the vote of power blocs.

He went on to Suez. After Nasser took the Canal, England had led the move to call a conference of Canal users which agreed on a basis for operating the Canal. But its conclusions were rebuffed by Nasser. The government could not then intervene immediately against Egypt because the English people would have said, "You must first go to the UN, which is the obvious court of last resort." This was done. The users wished to force Egypt to accept the principles laid down by the users. But Russia vetoed this proposal.

Unfortunately, perhaps, Israel chose that moment to move against Egypt. France and Britain had to intervene. Their only intention was "to bring about peace between Israel and Egypt." Israel accepted the ultimatum and ceased advancing. "For that reason," it was "unnecessary" to bomb Israeli positions or troop concentrations. Furthermore, even while attacking Egypt, the British took great pains not to kill Egyptian civilians.

This was "only a peace-making action," says Salisbury, and as such it was very useful. And it had an additional value of much importance. The then commander-in-chief of the allied Arab armies (brought together in Egypt), was operating, prior to the Israeli attack, under orders to prepare for a general assault on Israel. These orders were countermanded during the Suez fracas.

If ever I heard a cock-eyed explanation of the Anglo-French-Israeli expedition, this is it. I simply don't understand. Salisbury has one of the sharpest minds in England. He must think I am slightly below the level of a moron if he expects me to believe this one.

He was very opposed to the idea of negotiating with Makarios. After all the Archbishop was a British subject with a British passport and entitled to British protection. Yet he was leading a murder campaign, and many young men had been executed for following his orders. Salisbury appreciated that much can be condoned in the name of nationalism, but facts remained facts.

Later, I had drinks with Eliahu Elath, Israeli ambassador. Eliahu was ambassador in Washington while Truman was President. He said: "Things were easy for us then; no room in any department ever seemed to know what the other was doing. We were able to profit because the White House could always make the decisions, and we knew the White House was with us. Now, of course, things are different. There is the same amount of confusion, but the White House is not on our side."

LONDON, *May 10, 1957*

LUNCH with Geoffrey Crowther at Brooks's. Geoffrey still has his office in the *Economist*, but he is no longer very active editorially, although he is board chairman. He is a member of a government committee drawing up a survey on English education. In England, the tradition has always been to educate an elite and let the great majority sink or swim. In the United States, the emphasis has always been on the majority, with the result that the intellectual elite has had little opportunity to develop. The ideal is to strike a mean.

Geoffrey is not deeply worried about anti-American sentiment here. There was always a certain amount of such feeling on the left. Curiously enough, after the Suez crisis there was a temporary alliance between our own Republican administration and the Labour party on the one hand, and between the Democrats and the Tory party on the other. There has always been a nonpolitical anti-American feeling among some of the right-wing Tories who don't like the way we dress, eat, write. But normally this has not been mixed with political sentiments. It is psycho-

logically entirely comprehensible that the old Tories cannot adjust to
this new age when Britain is no longer the wealthy superpower and depends on the bumptious young United States.

Crowther keeps telling his political friends they should cease having a
complex about how to behave toward America, now that America is a
much greater world power. "The answer is perfectly easy," he said.
"We should talk to the Americans and behave toward them exactly the
way the Australians talk and behave toward us. It is a question of complete equality of attitude, even if the power relationship is different."

LONDON, *May 13, 1957*

ELATH says much of the anger against Eden is based upon the fact that
he exposed how weak England is. These are a proud, formal people. They
dress formally. Even their faces are dressed. And they were exposed by
Eden's policy as a second-rate power.

The British cannot remain for long swayed by bitterness. They are
realistic. Macmillan has been able to capitalize on awareness that this
country cannot survive without the United States in this age of the polarization of power. Macmillan himself was probably the force that brought
Eden down. The day before the cease-fire was accepted, the U.K. had
lost three-hundred million pounds in gold from its reserves. Macmillan
told the Cabinet he had supported Eden, but the question now was one of
possible economic collapse.

Macmillan showed moral courage by this personal shift. Rab Butler
had been against the Suez adventure all the time. Macmillan supported it
but had the guts to face up to his mistakes and the critical situation
arising from them. People respected his courage and that is what produced his quality of leadership in the Cabinet today.

The quarrel is still on between the military and civilian authorities
involved in the Suez adventure. The military complains that Eden gave
them orders to make adequate preparations. At the last minute the original plan—to attack Egypt overland from Libya as well as from the sea
—was dropped.

The politicians accuse the military of being far too slow. The armed
forces should always be ready for any emergency; there was a lack of cooperation between the three services. But instead of sacrificing the service chiefs, London followed the usual tradition and threw out Defense
Minister Anthony Head. The man whose head really should have been put
on a platter was Templer, chief of the Imperial General Staff.

Macmillan needed the Bermuda talks with the U.S. desperately, Elath
thinks. He had to restore a feeling of safety to this country; this depended on the United States. The people of England simply do not believe in a third-power Europe led by England. They don't see how

they could "make" such a Europe themselves without sacrificing their political links with the Commonwealth. Their policy is to remain *in* and *out* of Europe at the same time.

Lunched with Jock Whitney at Buck's. He told me Eisenhower and Macmillan got on very well during the Bermuda Conference. One evening when Macmillan was sitting in his room in his dressing gown, Eisenhower dropped in, also in a dressing gown. They spent an hour and a half together chatting all alone. There is absolutely no record of this conversation.

Whitney says it is much easier to work with Macmillan, who is not nearly so suspicious or nit-picking as Eden. Eden used to read all the papers every day and peruse all the clippings referring to him. Macmillan just doesn't pay any attention to such things.

LONDON, *May 14, 1957*

DINED at Viscount Monckton's charming little apartment in the Middle Temple with Iain Macleod, minister of labor, and one of the brightest young Tories. He confided that Eden had absolutely no friends; nor has he ever had.

Macleod admitted Britain's policy was really to stay "in and out" of Europe. The "grand design" of Selwyn Lloyd was primarily window dressing.

PARIS, *May 16, 1957*

THIS afternoon, I met Ambassador Amory Houghton, our new ambassador. Very engagingly, he started the conversation by saying he knew nothing about France—which is most honest, but not, perhaps, the best advance recommendation for an American ambassador. He told me that if I could find a solution for the Algerian problem he would have my portrait painted and hung on his wall. I told him that when I found the solution I would publish it in *The New York Times*. Houghton thinks France is on the verge of total economic collapse. Algeria is a cancerous drain and there is not the slightest prospect of solution in sight.

Interesting talk with Christian Pineau, French foreign minister. He is the son-in-law of Jean Giraudoux and amuses himself by writing fairy tales for children: very much the French intellectual, a solemn, plump man, with bald head and cold expression. But he is by no means as self-indulgent as his rotund appearance. Pineau was parachuted in and out of France during World War II and has much physical as well as moral courage.

He said France's policy was by no means a question of pure principle, emphasizing the word *pure*. It was just as realistic as the policy of other nations. The events of "last November" had of course retarded the opening of the Suez Canal, "But we were convinced that at that time we were realistic."

France was ready to accept all decisions of the Security Council and the Assembly—provided everybody else did so. But if Russia in Hungary, and Nasser on the Suez Canal, refused, France could not be the only nation to accept. I asked whether the 1950 tripartite declaration of the United States, Britain, and France on Palestinian frontiers was still applicable.

Pineau said: "Practically we do not consult on these things any longer. Secretary Dulles does not think the Atlantic alliance applies outside the Atlantic area. Clearly this does not allow us to deal with problems not directly involved in NATO. From the moment Dulles told me this it became apparent the 1950 tripartite declaration nowadays has only theoretical value."

I asked whether there was any possible solution for the Algerian mess. Pineau replied:

There are many Europeans living in Algeria and they would not be protected unless France remains present as a guarantor. There is no state or sovereign in Algeria to whom independence could be granted except for the chiefs of little bands; therefore the result would be anarchy; the economic situation could not stand total independence. Algeria's economy is wholly dependent on France.

We are entirely ready to leave great powers of government to the Algerians in the domains of culture, social affairs, administration, and economics. But the question of foreign policy and security, diplomats and the army, must remain with us.

He also said it would be very difficult for the French people to accept any form of nuclear disarmament that would permit the three countries today possessing atomic weapons to keep stockpiles of such weapons while forbidding other lands to manufacture and own them. France could not agree to be nonatomic while Russia, America, and England kept their stockpiles. However, if the three countries with nuclear weapons agreed upon a control system and progressive destruction of accumulated stocks, this government could tell the people there is no point in carrying on with plans to manufacture nuclear weapons.

PARIS, *May 20, 1957*

ADLAI Stevenson came for breakfast. Said that during the first twelve days of the Hungarian revolt—when the rebels were largely in control—he thought it shocking that the United States did not send in aid, including troops. We could have gotten away with this and it was our moral obligation. Unfortunately, because he made this suggestion in public during the height of our election campaign, Eisenhower was not able to act upon it for political reasons. Stevenson said any man who makes good suggestions during a campaign automatically negates their chances of success. For example, his ideas on both the draft and the hydrogen bomb were eminently reasonable and sane. Eisenhower would have favored them had he thought of them first.

Stevenson saw Pineau Saturday. Pineau admitted to him that one reason France was particularly interested in saving its position in Algeria was the discovery of large petroleum deposits. He told Stevenson Israel had now become a basic pillar of French policy. Israel was the sole democratic bastion in the Middle East. Furthermore, it was the only potential industrial complex there. The French did not intend to let it be weakened by Arab or other pressures. France intended to test the Gulf of Aqaba with French ships and back them up with French destroyers.

Our breakfast for Adlai was quite an event. We invited Bill and Susan-Mary Patten. Grat, our butler, was exceptionally flustered, even for him. Marina usually takes only toast and tea and I have a cup of hot milk, but we decided to entertain proper American-style: fruit juice, eggs, bacon, coffee, toast, marmalade, etc. Grat started things off by serving one piece of bacon all around. Then came coffee. Then marmalade. Then toast. Then eggs. Then, as dessert, fruit juice. By that time we were all as confused as he, poor fellow. When the phone rang, he rushed off to answer: "Madame is busy. She is receiving guests . . . yes, of course. In this house we receive at any hour."

PARIS, *May 22, 1957*

LUNCH with Vlado Dedijer, here on a unexpected trip. He is furious with Tito's stupidity on Hungary and Poland. He says Nagy and Gomulka represented the logical consequences of Titoism. Yet Tito sold the Hungarians down the river. Everybody in Jugoslavia was seething with excitement during the Hungarian revolt and forgot traditional anti-Magyar sentiments. He added: "We Serbs are the same as the Magyars. Much as we hate them. Give us a couple of good slogans and we will fight anyone." Tito feared a successful Hungarian revolution might spread southward into Jugoslavia. Furthermore, he contends that the

Jugoslav Communist bureaucracy—the entrenched, privileged aristocracy of the Socialist world—fears very much the possibility of losing its privileged position, whether as a result of changes induced by popular upheaval, or as a result of revived Russian influence.

At one point, discussing his own tribulations, Vlado said: "It is wonderful to be a Serb. But oh! What tribulations."

André de Staercke, Belgian ambassador to NATO, was with Spaak when he talked with Stevenson last weekend. Stevenson kept insisting there should be a spectacular idea on world disarmament. He wanted a military evacuation of Europe by both Russia and the United States. Spaak was horrified that Stevenson should be so naive. He kept stressing the Russians could pull back three hundred miles and remain in position to return, while the Americans would have to pull back three thousand miles and never come back.

PARIS, *June 8, 1957*

JOXE told me Molotov recently expressed regret at the departure of Joxe, Bohlen, and Hayter as the western ambassadors in Moscow. He said: "We knew all of these gentlemen were opposed to our system, but we respected them for their intelligence and their accuracy, and we regret their departure."

OXFORD, ENGLAND, *June 29, 1957*

I'VE been spending the last several days with the Deakins, attending a seminar discussing changes in the Soviet Union since Stalin's death. It has been fascinating to meet some of the characters. One is Bertram Wolfe, once an important American Communist during the early 1920s. Wolfe worked for OWI during World War II. When he filled out his application he was asked to name his previous employer. Wolfe had been a free lancer ever since he quit the Communist party. So under "previous employer" he put "Joseph Vissarionovitch Stalin." He got the job.

Bill Deakin told an interesting story about his Jugoslav partisan days. Before being dropped in, one of the many things he was requested to do by the Foreign Office was to keep an eye out for the daughter of the emigré foreign minister, Olga Ninčić, married to a Bosniak partisan named Humo. One day when they were bivouacked not far from Sarajevo, an English medical officer on his mission came back from a tour accompanied by a rather attractive partisan woman dressed in British battle dress. There was only one bed in the shack so Bill gave it to her;

the rest stretched out on the floor. Next day, his radio operator produced a query from Cairo headquarters inquiring once again where Olga Ninčić was. Suddenly Deakin realized this must be the girl. He replied "in my bed." Headquarters bawled him out.

PARIS, *July 9, 1957*

LUNCHED with Adlai Stevenson, who has just come back from his African trip, very tired. "For seventeen years I've been beating it up," he said. "And now to my horror I'm suddenly discovering I am an old man."

We discussed Senator Kennedy's recent speech demanding American intervention to secure Algerian independence. He said Kennedy was a very bright young man and an excellent politician. He thought him first class—although he disliked his father greatly. Adlai had pushed Kennedy's career and it was at his request that Kennedy had tried so hard for the Democratic vice-presidential nomination in 1960. But he did not like the smell of this intervention in Algeria. It was aimed only at American internal politics without the possibility of dangerous consequences abroad.

"I will tell you what I mean," said Adlai. "Just recently Jack went down to Georgia and appeared on a program with Herman Talmadge. My heavens, if I had done that every northern liberal would have wanted to cut my nuts off. But Jack got away with it. Now he is trying to balance things off by getting the Negro and liberal vote and calling for Algerian independence."

I also asked Adlai if he thought Nixon had really accomplished anything on his African tour. Adlai saw no hint of this. All Nixon seemed to do was rush around shaking hands and kissing babies. Nixon saw one African official who was educated in America at Lincoln College. Nixon did not know this and was deceived by the fact that the man was wearing native costume, a very scanty affair. He told Nixon: "You know, you are not the first distinguished American who has been out this way. We also had a visit a few years ago from Adlai Stevenson." Nixon replied in fine pidgin: "Him Democrat, me Republican."

Adlai said:

I spent most of my time on this trip in the Congo. The effort the Belgians are making in that vast country is enormous; in education, agriculture, roads, housing, health. Prosperity and progress is apparent on every side. The policy is based on the assumption that for a successful democracy you have to have an elite who can exercise power and a mass who can decide if the power is being exercised properly. So, having first laid a basis of wide economic opportunity and employment for the Africans, they are now going in for mass education at the primary level, and they are building great universities to further educate Africans for great responsibilities—and educate them not in Europe, but in their country, the Congo.

I can only describe this impression as platitudinous and a blurb for the Belgian government.

Adlai said things in Ghana were not going well. There was an awful lot of incompetence and emotionalism. Also, he was shocked by the corruption in our own pet American baby, Liberia. He said scholarships were being awarded in the U.S. to young Liberians that were worth from $3,500 to $5,000 a year. This made them the wealthiest scholars in the world.

Until now Africa has been silent. It is something like—wasn't it Chesterton who said—"We don't know what the British working classes think because they haven't spoken yet." The Africans haven't spoken yet. The position of the white man in black Africa is changing. Most of those I met were working for the benefit of the Africans. The only forced labor in Africa today is white.

PARIS, *July 11, 1957*

LUNCH with Secretary-General Spaak of NATO. He is optimistic about long-range possibilities for the West—with one exception, Algeria. Someday, French "Colons" may start a terrorist action and wipe out an Algerian village. That would be the end. It would put the argument on a pure racial basis and make it insoluble.

Few French officials really believe in their policy, but nobody dares say so in public. It is ridiculous to claim Algeria is a part of France. Liberals—like Mendès-France—keep saying they should negotiate. But negotiation in itself is no solution. You must know what kind of settlement you would like to negotiate.

The situation is intolerably bad. And there is danger of a revolution in France. The army is a real threat and plays an invisible but increasingly important role in French politics. But he has no idea who "the army" is, that is, who the guiding influences are.

He agrees with me that there is probably no other hope but de Gaulle; and yet he sees no hope in de Gaulle. He saw de Gaulle last week and the General "talked like Cassandra." He was against NATO and against "Europe." He thought there could be no improvement for ten years, until a new and young generation emerged in France.

Spaak said that now that the French Parliament had ratified the European Common Market and EURATOM, England was on the spot. The British were so convinced that this would never happen that they continued to give the idea lip service and talk vaguely of their "grand design" while waiting for the scheme to die. Now they will have to associate themselves in

some way, despite their Commonwealth obligations. Otherwise, in fifteen
years it will be impossible for Great Britain to export a single automobile to the area of the Common Market.

PARIS, *July 15, 1957*

THIS morning I had a talk with Larry Norstad. He said the United States
could never agree not to use atomic weapons in case of war. In such a
likelihood we would have had it. We are hopelessly outnumbered in terms
of conventional weapons and manpower.

He continued:

> The evil is not in the weapons themselves, but in war and the causes
> of war. We have no reasons to apologize for our atomic weapons.
> The only purpose for which we would use them would be to preserve
> our freedom. We are not interested in aggression. Furthermore, the
> only way of making sure that a world war comes is to weaken one side
> so much that the other side is tempted.

PARIS, *July 19, 1957*

THIS morning, I had a long and extremely interesting talk with de Gaulle.*
Before going in to see the General, I had quite a chat with Colonel de
Bonneval. Bonneval, as usual, was extremely friendly and talkative. He
said:

> I want to warn you that the General is going to seem very negative
> to you and to pretend that he is not particularly interested in current
> affairs. But that is just a front. I can tell you that he is seeing a great
> many people nowadays. And he is very attentive to what is going on.
> He may pretend that he isn't interested, but he really is. That is proven
> by the kind of people he is now seeing.

When I went in to see de Gaulle he was most amiable. He has mellowed. He looked a little bit old, pale-faced and somber, with his gray-
tinted, thick spectacles, which he wears now all the time since his operation for an eye cataract. He seemed thinner than last time but always
appears rather puffy.†

We started talking about the subject that was uppermost in my mind.
I said I had heard more and more people talk about the need to settle
the equivocal French situation by bringing de Gaulle back to power. Some
people were saying the road was leading inevitably to de Gaulle and he
should come in before a catastrophe in Algeria. Other people said the
road was leading toward de Gaulle, but he could only come in after a
catastrophe in Algeria. I asked him how he felt about it.

* See de Gaulle's further comments, p. 81.
† See de Gaulle's further comments, p. 81.

He said he didn't think there would be a catastrophe in Algeria. And, it was obvious the present parliamentary parties would never call him in.*

I asked him if President Coty technically and theoretically had the power to call him to authority. De Gaulle said theoretically Coty did not have such power, but actually he could do it if he so wished. But he pretended to think the moment had not yet come. It was perfectly clear, however, that he is considering this more and more and that he is holding himself in what he considers "readiness" to return.†

I asked if he thought the new British defense policy was taking a share in the responsibilities a little more. He said: "Perhaps. But that does not affect France." He would want a new division of responsibility among the United States, Britain, France, Germany, and "perhaps some to Italy. The rest don't matter."

I then returned to Algeria. I said it seemed somewhat paradoxical that the Arab leaders were now openly talking about the desirability of dealing with de Gaulle. Both Bourguiba of Tunisia and Messali Hadj, the imprisoned head of MNA have made public statements to this effect.

De Gaulle was a little cynical on the subject. He said they were just politicians and found it convenient to "deal with de Gaulle as long as de Gaulle is not in power." They use this as an excuse. He thought they would be less apt to talk that way if he were running the government.‡

De Gaulle thought the Algerian stalemate would persist but would get more serious and more tragic all the time. The French army would remain there and keep the Fallagha from gaining control. There would be more and more bombing and murders.

At the same time, he didn't think there would be a real economic catastrophe in France. The situation was getting worse all the time. But it was not catastrophic. He still seems to regard himself as the man of catastrophe, the man who could only come to power after a real cataclysm.§

We talked about his book a little. He said he has one more year of work. He finds it takes him two years to produce each volume. I must say he works very slowly. Of course he is writing it all himself by hand. On the table in front of him were a series of pages which had been laboriously scribbled on in ink, many words being crossed out and changed. I don't know if it was a speech or part of his book. I expect the former.

De Gaulle said one thing of interest when discussing the absence of "giants" from the present political scene. He said this fact indicates a real détente in the world situation because it is only in times of crises that nations throw up "giants." They do not need them in normal times.

* See de Gaulle's further comments, p. 32.
† See de Gaulle's further comments, p. 40.
‡ See de Gaulle's further comments, pp. 69–70.
§ See de Gaulle's further comments, pp. 48–49, 86.

I wonder if he refers at least subconsciously to himself in this analysis, and therefore does not seem to give himself much chance of returning to power.

PARIS, *July 20, 1957*

LAST night, the Schuylers gave a dinner for Al Gruenther, now traveling around Europe. Just before leaving he saw Eisenhower and advised him he expected to see me in Paris. "Double him and redouble him every chance you get," said the President.

LUXEMBOURG, *August 2, 1957*

LONG talk with Walt Butterworth, ambassador to the Coal and Steel Community and chief American diplomatic agent connected with the European federation. He said, in June, 1950, the Korean war broke out and the United States decided Europe had to be armed. We attached the idea of European unification to the rearming of Germany. This was a mistake because German rearmament was Europe's difficult problem. As a result the cause was set back.

When the Suez disaster came, the man in the street began to realize that imports of oil were not going to be enough to supply Europe with industrial energy. The idea of EURATOM grew as a result of this experience of "shoe leather"—when people had to walk because their cars didn't have enough gasoline.

The Germans were not enthusiastic. Above all, German industry mistrusted it. They didn't like the idea of EURATOM's ownership of fissionable materials. But the Germans made concessions in order to get approval of a common market, which they want so much.

Europe realizes that despite its economic recovery it will continue to remain weak politically, militarily, and economically unless it is unified. This era places a tremendous premium on bigness. Today the budget of the Standard Oil Company of New Jersey is larger than the budget of the entire French government. Europe doesn't like to remain indefinitely in an inferior position. Countries like Britain and France simply cannot take drastic action without the backing of either the United States or Russia. Suez not only showed Europe that it couldn't any longer continue to depend on Middle Eastern oil imports, but it also made people aware of the growth of their political dependence upon the United States and Russia. But Britain wants to control an eventual common market or gum it up.

BONN, GERMANY, *August 6, 1957*

LONG talk with Adenauer in the Schaumburg Palais. At eighty-two he still looks remarkably energetic with astoundingly youthful gait. He seemed relaxed and talkative despite the strains of the campaign for next month's elections—a campaign which he intensely enjoys.

The Chancellor began by saying: "Well Mr. Sulzberger, what is going on in Paris?" I replied: "Algeria." He said: "That's something I should write about to Dulles. I have been asked by the French to say everywhere I possibly can—and this is my own opinion, too—that the whole matter of Algeria is not a colonial question but a question connected with communism. The Communists are behind it all."

I noted he believed Khrushchev was a small man who would not remain in power long. How did he feel about the present gyrations in Russia? He said he had had a list prepared for me of all the purges from Lenin's time on. He went on to say,

These so-called purges are invariably connected with dictatorship. Much has been forgotten, but when you read it all again, you see that this is permanent. We still really do not know—at least I do not know—whether Stalin wasn't killed before being purged. That's not established. A process of that nature harbors certain dangers, of course, for the surrounding world, but it also gives rise to a certain hope. Such a system can never calm down internally and people will realize that one day. What lesson can we draw from this? Not to lose patience, to keep on the alert!

I asked if he thought the purges had now stopped and that there might be a further contest between Khrushchev and Zhukov and others. He said: "Suppose you were a dictator, Mr. Sulzberger—that would require a good deal of imagination—and you were together with somebody else who is in command of the armed forces. I feel sure you wouldn't feel altogether comfortable about it."

Only one man since Stalin's death had held military power outside the army—Beria.

That was why they liquidated Beria, but Beria could only be eliminated by the armed forces, by Zhukov. Zhukov could only be eliminated by another marshal. This would mean that the army was split, while in the case of Beria the whole army was against him.

For some time now we have been informed that Bulganin and Khrushchev together stir the marshals up against each other. Zhukov has come to the forefront, but may I remind you of one thing. In *Red Star* there appeared some time ago a picture of Khrushchev and Bulganin on the front page with Zhukov in the background. Shortly afterwards, the editor of *Red Star* was dismissed.

I inquired whether this implied Zhukov was in the background or what? He answered:

For having shown his picture at all! At that time he was not yet one of the top rank. I was in Moscow in Autumn, 1955, and a great reception was given in our honor. One thousand people were invited but not one marshal!

Six months later the French Premier and the French foreign minister paid an official visit to Moscow. When I was there, Bulganin and I occupied the chair in turn, Khrushchev not at all. When the French were there, some time later, Khrushchev occupied the chair and not Bulganin. At the great reception we were given, there were no marshals; at that given for the French, there were many. There had obviously been a change during the seven or eight months in between. This development has not yet come to an end; of that I am firmly convinced.

I asked if he thought Khrushchev or Zhukov would win the fight. He replied:

At present Khrushchev and Zhukov are like this. [The Chancellor made a gesture with his hand to show that they are on the same level.] At the end of the year they will be like this. [He crossed one hand over the other to illustrate that Zhukov will be above and Khrushchev below.] And that is as far as I can see. Who would be likely to come after that? Then we would have a dictatorship of the army! That may well be, but we cannot be sure. Zhukov is in any case no better than the others.

After this I turned to things Adenauer really knows about. I asked under what terms in the Western European Union and EURATOM treaties West Germany could possess or manufacture atomic weapons. He replied: "We are entitled to obtain atomic weapons without the permission of Western European Union. We are entitled to manufacture them ourselves with the agreement of Western European Union. We have renounced the right of production but not that of possession."

Would it be possible, for example, for Germany to start making atomic bombs now if WEU approved? He replied: "We prefer to obtain them from America! It is a difficult matter to manufacture atomic weapons."

I interpreted his policy as being that the stronger and more unified the West became the more cracks would appear in the Soviet empire and it would come apart. He answered:

I am convinced of it. I have heard from Germans who were in Poland or emigrated from there that the Poles—when they converse with each other—emphasize they are western Europeans and not eastern Europeans, that they belong to Europe.

With each loosening of the fetters binding the Poles to Moscow they will come nearer to western Europe. Czechoslovakia is another matter. I was told recently by a non-German, a member of one of these nations, that the Czechs will be the last to join western Europe and I believe that that is so, although Beneš once said to me that Czechoslovakia was thoroughly western in outlook.

I asked whether a reunited Germany would automatically remain in EURATOM and the Common Market, or whether this would have to be reconsidered as is provided in the tie with NATO. He replied:

Please remember: Membership in NATO and membership in the European federation must go hand in hand. A reunited Germany which withdrew from NATO could not be a member of a European federation. That is the nature of things.

I then asked Adenauer who—of all the men he had met during his lifetime—were those, if any, he considered truly great—giants. He replied:

I definitely consider Churchill to be a great man. He saved his country when it was in a very difficult situation. But take de Gaulle for example. He saved his country, but afterward he was a complete failure as head of government. In the United States there are a few men to whom I attach very much credit for having realized—and acted accordingly—that the power that America obtained rather quickly and its wealth create the obligation to be a real leader among the nations.

That is in my opinion the greatest achievement of the United States in our time. History will someday reveal who contributed to this or who played a leading part in it. In general, wealth makes people blind. Thank God that has not been the case with America.

I then asked if he thought any Russian he had met was great or a giant. He answered: "Not even with the best will in the world and with all indulgence." I asked whether he had studied any particular political philosopher or any particular political craftsman to help him in the arts of government or politics. He replied: "No, I did not study anyone. For me the only aim, the guiding aim, has always been freedom."

Was there any man in Adenauer's life who had exercised an important influence on his character and personality? He replied:

I am really not sure. But if I search my mind I have to say that a teacher in our college, our secondary school, who was a friend of Schliemann's, exercised a great influence on me. Schliemann was the one who excavated Troy. This teacher told us a great deal outside school hours about Asia Minor, Greece, and all the developments there. When I look back I realize he had a great influence on me. You may know what kind of man he was when I tell you that he once said to us—at that time I think we were in our final year and that was in the Kaiser's days—that a republic was a higher form of state than a monarchy. And at that time that called for courage. His name was Petit.

I told Adenauer many people including Churchill had compared him with Bismarck. What did he think of Bismarck? He said: "Bismarck was a great foreign politician but a very poor home politician. He persecuted

the Catholics and he persecuted the Socialists, thus preventing the creation
of a large liberal party in Germany. As a result, the German people in
my opinion were not politically strong enough to bear the power
which they suddenly obtained. And that is what led to our collapse."

I asked when he had started his art collection. He replied: "In my third
year of school—with reproductions." I inquired: "How about real original paintings?" He said: "Oh, my wife and I inherited the first original.
The first painting I bought was an Italian one, an old master. That must
have been in the twenties."

I recalled that a few years ago, when Churchill was still Prime Minister, I had remarked to Adenauer that everybody assumed Churchill
would soon retire and that it was believed Eden would be his successor.
I had inquired then who was Adenauer's Eden, but the old man dodged
a reply. Now I wished to repeat the question. He smiled and replied:
"Churchill had no luck in his choice of a crown prince. One should let
things develop naturally; the party will have to choose. Facts must
show where able people are to be found. Certainly Eden did not work
out very well."

BONN, GERMANY, *August 7, 1957*

HAVE been staying with David Bruce, our ambassador to Germany. David
was in London last week for the visit of Foster Dulles who took charge
temporarily of the disarmament negotiations. The great difficulties of the
inspection system we desire have not yet been appreciated. It is possible
to hide the most deadly and secret weapons and not have them detected.
You would need literally tens of thousands of people for the ground inspection envisaged. It would almost mean having large armies of Russians in the western zones and large allied armies in the Soviet and
satellite zones to inspect.

David had great admiration for the way Dulles handled things in London and his great ability as a legal mind and organizer. He presented
the U.S. case brilliantly. Nevertheless, David doesn't think Dulles will
go down as a good Secretary of State. He can never forgive him for
what he did to State Department personnel. Furthermore he messed up the
Middle Eastern situation.

Bruce asked if I thought we should release the remaining thirty-five
German war criminals in American custody. I felt that since Germany
was recognized as independent and as an ally it was folly to retain these
individuals in a U.S. prison. We couldn't retain extraterritorial rights. Admittedly they were bastards, but worse bastards had already been released. I suggested he make a private deal with Adenauer in which the
Germans would agree to lock up and retry the ten nastiest of the lot.

One evening we had a long talk about the great men of our time. Bruce agrees Churchill was the greatest. He doesn't think we have had any versatile modern giants in the United States—with the exception of Teddy Roosevelt. Teddy Roosevelt, had the situation become critical enough, might have shown the same qualities as Churchill. He does not rank Franklin Roosevelt as a giant; he was far too shallow and tricky.

ATHENS, *August 22, 1957*

THIS morning I saw Archbishop Makarios, who is now living in Athens (since his release from forced residence in the Seychelles). He has rented a strange Swiss chalet in the suburb of Psychiko. The house is plainly furnished and adorned with a pathetic stuffed turtle with polished shell. He looked well, unharmed by exile, and in fact said things weren't too tough.

Makarios appeared quite ready to accept independence for Cyprus and a moratorium on Enosis at least as "a basis for discussion," and he was willing to grant Britain base privileges.

ATHENS, *August 23, 1957*

STIMULATING talk with Prime Minister Caramanlis, who just returned from an official visit to Cairo. Nasser insists he is strongly anti-Communist. He says there are only ten thousand Communists in Egypt and he keeps close watch on them. He removed four or five suspected names from the list of candidates in the last elections. But he needed arms because Egypt, with twenty million people, couldn't remain in a position threatened by little Israel. The U.S. wouldn't give them to him; so he turned to Russia. But he didn't intend to lose his independence. He admitted the U.S.A. had been just in its attitude on Suez. But we acted through UN; the Russians were ready to go to war for Egypt. This had more dramatic appeal.

ANKARA, TURKEY, *September 18, 1957*

BOTH Istanbul and Ankara are full of building projects. Why? The country is on the verge of bankruptcy. The lira, officially valued at 2.80, is actually worth 13 to the dollar. There are no spare parts for machines or cars. It is impossible to replace auto tires. And, in the land of Turkish coffee, there is no coffee; imports have stopped entirely.

This evening, I had a long talk with Zorlu, Menderes's *eminence grise*, one of the ablest and least popular men in the country. He is now minister of press, but his office is in the Prime Ministry and he has his finger in every pie.

Zorlu said it was intolerable to leave a Soviet base in Syria. The Russians would infiltrate Lebanon and Jordan from there. It was their old Mediterranean policy. They were soft-soaping Turkey, assuring them Syria wasn't Communist, that they meant no harm. But the Turks aren't fooled.

It is folly to assume Islam is hostile to communism. Albania is a satellite. Egypt and Syria almost are. The wealthy class and devout Muslims oppose communism, but it has infiltrated the poor and discontented; above all the army—through noncommissioned officers.

If Syria isn't changed we risk losing the whole Middle East and isolating Turkey. Tito is now a semisatellite again and backs Soviet foreign policy everywhere. The Balkan Pact is dead.

Zorlu said Turkey advised the U.S. to keep quiet during the Suez invasion until after the British had finished the job. Had there been no Suez fiasco there would be no Syrian problem now.

Lunched at the home of Kasim Gülek, active leader of the opposition. Ismet Inönü, former President, remains titular boss, but Gülek is the mainspring and would possibly be Prime Minister if his party were to win next month's elections. But the government doesn't intend to be defeated. Gülek, forty-seven, was educated at the Sorbonne, Columbia, and in Germany; highly intelligent, he speaks six languages. He has prepared a "prison suitcase" because he thinks a "dangerous" period is imminent. In it he has packed a Russian grammar—to taunt this highly anti-Russian regime, although Gülek is far from leftist—and Churchill's *History of the English Speaking Peoples*.

Gülek complained the government is increasingly dictatorial. It has passed laws preventing the various opposition parties from grouping together for the elections. The opposition is banned from the state radio. The chief justice and eleven judges of the seventy on the high court were retired last year. This warned all others to kowtow. There has been a grave retrogression in democracy since Menderes came in.

ISTANBUL, TURKEY, *September 20, 1957*

YESTERDAY evening I saw Adnan Menderes, the Prime Minister. He was astonishingly affable considering quarrels I have had with him in the past. Zorlu was present throughout our talk. Menderes thinks the Balkan Pact is dead and there is no use even dreaming of reviving it because Tito is again playing a Moscow game. Tito has just sent the Turks a confidential letter proposing a Balkan bloc to serve as a third force, linked neither to the East nor to the West. This is just an effort to break up NATO.

Turkish policy cannot tolerate a Soviet military base to the south in

Syria. From there Russia could infiltrate all of the Middle East and isolate Turkey. But, so far, no one has come up with an idea of what to do about it.

ROCQUENCOURT, FRANCE, *September 25, 1957*

SPENT a couple of hours talking to Larry Norstad. When the NATO chiefs of staff were here for a conference the Turkish general came to see him on instructions from Menderes and read a long statement saying Turkey was very worried about Syria. Turkey wished to know what aid to expect from NATO and the U.S. in case the situation deteriorated into war. Norstad replied:

From a military point of view you cannot expect me to get nervous about Syria. The best thing the Russians could do with their arms would be to drop them in the Mediterranean where they would rust. The next best thing would be to put them in Egypt and Syria where they will never represent a threat because the Arabs don't know how to use them. Egypt showed as much against Israel. You can't pretend to me that Turkey is frightened of Syria. The Turks could beat up Syria just as easily as they could beat up Bulgaria, and they would enjoy it just as much.

I want to warn you as NATO commander that Turkey must be most careful not to obscure the situation. Naturally if Turkey is attacked by Russia she will receive complete assistance from NATO and from the U.S., but if Turkish forces on the Syrian border obscure the issue, that would be another situation.

There would be no Middle Eastern problem if it were not for the existence of Israel. Israel was the one issue that united all the Arabs, but there is no point arguing whether it was right or wrong to create Israel. It is there and it will stay there; and that is a fact. Someday we must face the necessity of imposing frontiers on Israel and then guaranteeing both Israel and its neighbors against attack by each other.

TOKYO, *October 3, 1957*

ARRIVED this afternoon after a magnificent flight from Copenhagen. One unscheduled stop in northern Sweden at Lulea, to take on extra fuel as there was a bad headwind from the North Pole. At Anchorage where we refueled the sun came up.

The navigator showed me the two gyrocompasses necessary to take bearings as an ordinary magnetic compass won't work in the far north. Everything, of course, is south from the Pole. Another instrument allows celestial bearings to be taken on the sun even when it is obscured by clouds.

TOKYO, *October 4, 1957*

DOUG MacArthur, our ambassador, told me there are two things all Asians want: to be treated on the basis of equality and mutual respect; and cooperation in solving economic problems.

Racial troubles in the United States—as exemplified by Little Rock—touch Asia on its most sensitive spot. This is above all true in former colonies—the arc of Southeast and South Asia. There racialism is linked with colonialism.

Segregation hurts our prestige here. There are many pictures and stories in the newspapers which are harmful to us. Racism in any form strikes a deep emotional chord. It can easily be exploited by America's enemies.

There are fifty-six Japanese war criminals in prison, leaving the United States as the only victorious ally which still has Japanese war criminals behind bars. Even the Nationalist Chinese, the Australians, and the Philippines who suffered much more, have paroled theirs.

If the West gives Japan a fair share of world markets everything will be all right. Otherwise Japan would be forced to seek economic accommodation elsewhere. We must not forget that Japan's greatest single market is the United States. Trade is the biggest problem, the very life of the Japanese, and will determine foreign-policy orientations.

TOKYO, *October 8, 1957*

WE returned last night from a two-day trip to Nikko, seat of the seventeenth-century Toshogu shrine for the Tokugawa Shogun, curious equivalent of what one might call Japanese baroque. One ceiling indeed, looks like late Italian Renaissance. All the buildings are situated on the side of the holy mountain amid magnificent three-hundred-year-old Japanese redwood trees called cryptomeria. A little river rushes beneath the mountain spanned by a lovely red-painted, arched bridge. Inside a curious atmosphere is imparted by weird-looking Shinto priests in blue and white robes with high, black, miter-shaped hats. Two were stirring pots of red wax with which holy stamps are made. There are many wooden friezes painted gold, garish blue, green, and white. These are set off strikingly against the dark-red or black backgrounds. The lacquer work is brilliant. On the building that once was a sacred stable there is a frieze of monkeys carved from wood, including the original famous trio which neither sees, hears, nor speaks evil.

FUCHU, JAPAN, *October 8, 1957*

DROVE out to Fuchu, U.S. headquarters, for a talk with Lieutenant General Frederic Smith, commander of American forces. Smith said the

Japanese are apathetic on rearmament. Only about 5 percent of the 1957 budget is for defense—and only 1.2 percent of the gross national product, as compared with 9 percent in the United States.

Smith has no fear that we are creating a Frankenstein monster here. "Japan will never again be imperialistic during our time," he says. But it must play a part in the peripheral defensive ring; it can't be a soft spot. We can't risk "letting this workhouse turn loose to work for the Communists."

There is no assurance that Japan would go to war at our behest. Therefore we must hang on to control of Okinawa, which is the key to the whole area, militarily.

We must hang on to it. The other Ryukyu islands (we also still hold the Bonins) are valuable only for their radar sites. But as for Okinawa, Smith says: "We simply have to make Japan swallow this. We can't discuss it. If Japan wanted administrative control of the island the answer would have to be no. Right now they want to control education there. We say no. We don't want anything like the pink educational system they installed here." (Sic!)

TOKYO, *October 9, 1957*

PRIME Minister Nobusuke Kishi received me in his office near the Diet, rather unattractive but comfortable. He said Japan has no intention of seeking diplomatic relations with Communist China at present. However, Japan would like to promote trade. The best solution to the impasse is the so-called "Two Chinas" formula. This would prevent Peking's control of Formosa—a threat to Japan. However, Chiang Kai-shek and Mao Tse-tung object to the "Two Chinas" formula, and America opposes it.

Japan could simply never permit the communization of Formosa and Korea. It would render this country helpless. Japan thinks it would be desirable to unify North and South Korea. But the reunified country could never become Communist. The best solution would be to have a neutral, unified Korea. It is impossible, however, to solve this problem locally. China and Russia are behind North Korea. As long as the great powers are split, Korea must remain divided.

Kishi thought perhaps the greatest potential threat on the Japanese horizon was not war but a U.S. depression.

TOKYO, *October 10, 1957*

LUNCH with Armand Bérard, French ambassador. He says the Japanese cannot stand the Americans, despite appearances. They have a creditor's complex; they owe us too much: "When Wall Street sneezes, Tokyo has pneumonia."

Realizing they cannot live without us, the Japanese detest us. No country on earth fits the United States democratic pattern so little as Japan. The formula for American democracy is for a rich, underpopulated country with enormous natural resources. Japan is small, overpopulated, and has no resources.

We teach the Japanese how to live with an income they will never have. They can only exist if each citizen accepts the idea of living within the space of 1 tatami—that is to say about 90 centimeters by 180 centimeters. Twenty Japanese live in the space occupied by one American.

Western ideas cannot fit here and American ideas are the quintessence of western ideas. This presents the great problem of the future. At present, in Japan, the right-wing political coalition is strong; the left is weak. Despite fear of communism, there is some Communist influence among the youth. The young people are disgusted with the old regime, tired of political leaders who seem to be remnants from the past.

One must never be deceived by the apparent western facade. You cannot separate Japan from Asia. It is a mistake for the United States to try and make of Japan a bulwark against Asia—above all China. In Japan there is a tendency to assume the external habits of conquerors—but the soul remains the same. If the Japanese, at a moment of history, discover that they are relatively backward, they seize the civilization of another country in order to compete—and, if necessary, to fight it. But Chinese influence in the fifth-century A.D. was the only one which ever took a permanent hold.

Okinawa may soon be a worse question for the United States in its relations with Japan than Cyprus is for England or Algeria for France. America is wrong in thinking it is possible to make a peace treaty as "between equals" between Japan and the United States. This isn't possible. The Russians are better off. They merely seize territory and never promise to give anything back. They have the Kuriles. They haven't promised their return the way we did with the Ryukyus.

There is no fear of right-wing extremism here. The Japanese never make the same blunder twice. The army, for example, learned that Japan was too weak to launch a war by itself.

Democracy is, to a considerable degree, a surface aspect. It is like copying a modern army. The democratic revolution here came from the leaders of the government who imposed upon the people the concepts imported from America. This change was brought about by foreigners— not by Japanese, as the Meiji restoration. This is an American constitution. One day, the Japanese say, they will write a Japanese constitution.

The theory of the Meiji restoration was that it was best to change the system since the system they intended to copy had proven successful in more powerful countries. They copied the German constitution, because Germany at that time had the strongest army in the world. Now, American democracy is being copied because of American strength.

Yet the main foreign interest is in China—not Russia or the United States. Japan owes its religion, its culture, and its way of writing to China.

The Japanese are convinced Japan cannot live forever separated from China. This, in the end, is the main problem. Psychologically, people do not like to be forbidden things. If God had not told Adam he should not eat the apple, Adam might have chosen a pear. In the same way, the Japanese curiosity is increased when we tell them not to talk to China.

TOKYO, *October 13, 1957*

DINED with Prime Minister Kishi and Foreign Minister Fujiyama at Kishi's favorite geisha house, surrounded by geisha girls in lovely kimonos. The menu included gingko nuts, roast quail's eggs, roast chestnuts with sugar, a form of seaweed that tasted like dried fish, lobster, shrimp, rice, soups, hot saki, beer, and whisky. Kishi put away plenty of whisky.

One geisha, beautiful and doll-like in a lovely white kimono embroidered with roses, told me she has fifty kimonos. When she is older she expects to have one hundred. Since each costs at least $100, this is quite an investment.

THE RABBITS

OF QUEMOY

TAIPEI, FORMOSA, *October 15, 1957*

THIS MORNING RIGHT AFTER ARRIVING I WENT OVER TO SEE MY OLD friend, Karl Rankin, American ambassador. He observed that the Chinese situation is still to be seen through a glass darkly. Alone, Taiwan has limited significance, but it is part of the whole picture. Taiwan and South Formosa maintain the only Asian forces which would be worth anything in case of war. By supporting them we help maintain a certain balance of power.

China is the biggest population mass communism has overrun. Taiwan is the only remaining part of that territory which is strongly anti-Communist. How are we to exploit this situation? Militarily, Taiwan, to be of any use, requires a sound economy. Our military and economic aid programs have made much progress.

Chiang is in excellent health and he has quite a few good leaders available—more than most Asian countries. Nevertheless, one man has dominated the scene for years. People hostile to him spread rumors that when he dies he will pass the show to his son, Lieutenant General Chiang Ching-kuo, deputy secretary-general of the National Defense Council, who has a Russian wife and experience. Rankin thinks it improbable the son will take over.

I asked Rankin how we could insure against some internal coup linking Taiwan with China after Chiang dies. He said this was largely a psychological problem. Anything appearing like accommodation by us has a bad repercussion here. We must consider the relative advantages and disadvantages of every step we take.

De facto, Nationalist China dies when the dream of invading the mainland dies. And various things are coming to a head. Political leadership is getting old. Chiang didn't bring many junior officers with him. There is a lack of people to take over when the old man dies and he is seventy. There is an economic strain with three-fourths of the revenue going to defense. They can afford an army only so long as America supports it.

Morale is sustained by slogans of "Back to the Mainland." That is wearing thin. The Taiwanese themselves are not interested in "going back." But now they form 35 percent of the army and the percentage is going up. Many mainlanders prefer independence and remaining on Taiwan to the prospect of going back to Communist rule.

In effect this is a one-party state although in theory there are a few small parties. The Kuomintang rules the show. But there is no feeling of tension and terror, no arrests without warrants. Arbitrary police action has been curbed. In a qualified sense it is a kind of Socialist state.

TAIPEI, FORMOSA, *October 16, 1957*

HAD two enormous Chinese meals—lunch given by Sampson Shen, head of the government information office, and dinner (served in his office) by Foreign Minister George Yeh. In the line of duty we almost died: innumerable courses including fried eel, bird's nest soup, shark's fin, gingko nuts, ginger, roast suckling pig dipped in sugar, all helped down by lacings of dark brown Chinese rice wine served warm.

Yeh told me that under the secret letters he exchanged with Dulles in December, 1954 (eight days after the Mutual Security Treaty was signed) —only the "substance" was published—Chiang agrees not to invade without our prior permission. But we (and this wasn't published) promise to make no substantial reduction in our Okinawa forces without first consulting Chiang. So he has a hold on our Japanese policy.

This afternoon, I had a talk with Defense Minister Yu Ta-wei, and chief of the general staff, General Wang Shu-ming. I asked how many generals there were on Taiwan. Reluctantly, I was told there are 587 generals and admirals on active service; 352 generals and admirals on the retired list drawing 80 percent pay, full rations, and PX privileges.

This evening went out to President and Mme Chiang Kai-shek's for tea and a long conversation. Chiang talked frankly and easily although I had been warned he resented the fact I had written advocating U.S. recognition of Communist China.

I asked if Peking had tried to get him to agree to some kind of peace talks and coalition government during the "100 flowers" period last winter. Yes, he said. The Communists hadn't contacted him directly but had sought to win over many of his high-level officials. Mao had now dropped the easygoing phase and tightened up.

I asked why, since he advocated limited war as the only way of liberating China, he didn't take off. He said: "You know the answer. It is the United States." I asked why he had handcuffed himself by such a commitment. He said the subject had never come up during negotiations for his American treaty. However, after it was signed, Washington asked him to make such an agreement in subsidiary letters so that Congress would swallow the treaty.

I asked if he would have to consult the U.S. before, for example, landing a battalion on the mainland from Quemoy. He said the Treaty wasn't that precise; but he would keep our people advised of everything. Would he be able to move in quickly without waiting for consultation if a rebellion broke out on the mainland opposite Quemoy? Yes, but he'd tell us as soon as possible.

What did Chiang consider as an alternative to coexistence except war, I asked. Nothing, he said. He agreed that the present situation of coexistence was like Trotsky's "neither war nor peace."

I told Chiang I had read his memoirs with interest. Was I right in interpreting his beliefs as seeing only war as a solution. Yes, he said. But he was sure Russia wouldn't come in. Then he leaned forward, always with a grin in which his Hapsburg underlip protruded, and said: "Now let's speak plainly and without hesitation. What do you think? Will the American people support me in a limited war?"

I said: "Frankly, I don't think so. Until 1945, that would have been possible. But since the atomic age began most people don't care to risk a nuclear war which would destroy civilization. They don't think war can be limited."

"I am afraid you are exactly right," said Chiang to my surprise. "That is an accurate statement of the American view."

I said that if a rebellion broke out in China and he aided it, the matter might be different. We would not tolerate another Hungary in China. He agreed and said Hungary had made an immense impression on the mainland. His propaganda had reported the uprising in detail.

QUEMOY, *October 17, 1957*

TOOK off at 6 A.M. in a typhoon for this small offshore island. We had a nice little DC-3 with a crew of three majors, a captain and a sergeant. Also Admiral Liu and Sampson Shen, chief of the government information office, came along to brief me. We had to fly so low we almost touched the waves. Deathly ill, Sampson and two of the majors vomited ceaselessly.

Quemoy is a rocky island of 178 square kilometers. There are pleasant old-fashioned Chinese villages with gabled stone and brick houses and peasants in colored pajamas. The atmosphere is much more Chinese than on Taiwan. The place is honeycombed with tunneled fortifications and absolutely jammed with troops. Chiang told me he had six divisions here. Practically all the soldiers I saw—fit-looking, green-clad youngsters—were busy building roads and planting trees.

Everybody talked of war, but I didn't see a single artillery piece. I was taken to well-built defensive positions which would sweep roads and beaches—but I saw no machine guns. Hardly anybody carried side-arms and only the sentries had rifles. It was a most unwar-like atmosphere.

Quemoy is 220 miles from Taipei, 18 miles from Communist Amoy, and only 1.35 from the nearest Communist position. I scrutinized this through a telescope from one observation point and saw nothing but uninhabited rocks. The civilian population grows sweet potatoes, rice, peanuts, and vegetables and manufactures a drink distilled from sorghum which is 135 proof.

The Nationalists claim that control of the offshore islands is essential to the defense of the Formosa Strait—which I doubt. Certainly, however, Quemoy makes Amoy a dead port. The island is also used as a base for political intelligence and psychological warfare. Both sides fire pamphlet shells at each other.

In one company headquarters, 1,800 yards from a Communist held islet, everything was efficiently tunneled into the rock, but the paradoxically tranquil atmosphere was emphasized by the pet white rabbits loping about in the tunnels. Exotic leaves were growing out of unused gun sites.

TAIPEI, FORMOSA, *October 17, 1957*

THIS evening I dined at the Generalissimo's: most lavish for his Spartan regime. Started off with champagne. Then we had a Chinese dinner served European-style with knives and forks. It was pathetically lousy. The old man is totally disinterested in food and was making an effort, but I will bet he serves the worst meal of any prosperous man on Taiwan, where good cuisine is worshipped.

He has a handsome, intelligent face with an expression both of gentleness and strength. The old man has a lot of trouble with his dentists. He insists on having sparkling white teeth like a child's and they have a hard time keeping him supplied.

He really had little of interest to say but did tell me one thing: the Formosans were very good troops. During the Mainland war five thousand of them came over as a unit; they fought well and not a single one ever surrendered.

When saying farewell, a strange thing happened. Mme Chiang came up, gripped my hand between hers, looked me in the eyes earnestly, and said: "Never trifle, always be in earnest."

"Yes," I said, puzzled. "Did you hear me?" she inquired. "Did you hear what I said? Never trifle, always be in earnest."

HONG KONG, *October 21, 1957*

DINED last night at the home of Sir Alexander Grantham, retiring governor. He thinks we are insanely misinterpreting the Chinese scene. Before explaining his view, he locked the doors to his study, where we sat before maps after dinner. "We have a great security problem," he said, nodding in the direction of his Chinese servants. "You can't be too careful. It is impossible to know what goes on in the oriental mind."

He had no doubt about the firmness of Communist control in China. Whether we like it or not, they are there to stay. They may have trouble if there is another (and third) bad crop year. But there is no chance of organized disorder. He added: "The Communists have Taiwan thoroughly honeycombed."

Today, at lunch at the Shek-O house of Ian Bruce of Jardine Matheson, Bruce said: "Any businessman who can't make 25 percent a year on his investment here must be a damned fool." A crazy situation—before the volcano blows.

HONG KONG, *October 22, 1957*

I HAD breakfast with P of intelligence. He said Chiang Kai-shek's information about mainland China is inadequate. He stands no chance of ever getting back. Even were there to be a revolt, which is most unlikely, he wouldn't be accepted as a symbol. Chiang failed badly in China, and the Chinese respect success.

The Communist regime did very well for five years although now it is in serious economic trouble. But for the first time this century there has been an eight-year period of internal peace. The Korean war did not affect the economy. The regime has built factories, maintained order, and, in 1955, it had one excellent crop year.

There is enormous population pressure. This forces an increase in manufacture of consumers' goods; the people must at least be clothed. And there are about eighteen million more of them every year. Peking has been driven into the very un-Marxist mass sponsorship of birth control.

The Communists have Taiwan well penetrated. We fear efforts to win over Chiang Ching-kuo (Chiang's son with the Russian wife and background). But at this time we are confident he has no connection with Peking. My own belief is that we are insane to back a Chinese emigré regime imposed on the Formosans when we consider an independent Formosa necessary to us. Only the Chinese regime would make a deal to unite with Peking; the Formosans, whom we ignore, never would.

The United States crippled its well-trained China service. Yet it is very difficult to comprehend the Chinese language and mentality. The Chinese think in grays, not in black and white. And they are terrifically realistic. Hong Kong is a center of "manufactured" intelligence. There are plenty of agents for one or another—or both—sides. The Chinese are distinctly able crooks with much experience. They know what we want to hear—and tell us accordingly.

The Chinese really believe they are smarter than other people, including the westerners. They have immense pride. They consider themselves culturally unequaled. They are pleased to be a world power. Overseas Chinese are influenced by any successes of Peking. When the Chinese were beating American troops in Korea, Hong Kong Chinese walked a little straighter.

MANILA, *October 23, 1957*

GOOD talk with Chip Bohlen, now ambassador here. He made the following comments on the Philippines. This is not really an oriental country per se. The people are of oriental stock but they spent three centuries under Spain and almost half a century under us. This has made them more Latin American.

We have successfully infused a deep belief in democratic political forms. But the social and economic forms bequeathed by Spain have been left largely untouched. The question now is: Can we boost up social and economic forms, or will the political forms slip downward?

Had this been essentially a politically unstable country, what would have happened when President Magsaysay was killed while the vice president and principal army leaders were away in Australia? There was not even the rumor of a *coup d'état*. The transfer of power was constitutional to the hilt.

The problem here is basically economic. The country imports more than it exports. Existing commercial controls are not very effective. There is too much leakage. There is not enough social or administrative discipline.

Mayor Lacson of Manila is a tough, crude, forthright man. The first time Chip met him was at a mixed (men and women) luncheon, Lacson, an excellent mimic, was recounting the tale of his trip to Tokyo last year when Premier Hatoyama was still in power. Hatoyama inquired if the feeling toward the Japanese was any better. Said Lacson: "We still think the only good Jap is a dead Jap, and even when he's six feet under the ground he stinks." Hatoyama, taken aback, said: "So solly atlocities commited by Impelial tloops." Said Lacson: "Bull shit."

MANILA, *October 24, 1957*

LUNCHED at Malacañan Palace with President Garcia, very dark-skinned man with an oriental face. He has intelligent, bland features and a slightly cynical twist of the mouth. He talks like—and is—a weather-beaten politician.

SINGAPORE, *October 27, 1957*

AT Singapore our first evening was marked by a big reception in Raffles Hotel. I was intrigued by the names: Mr. and Mrs. Run Run Shaw (sic), R. B. Ooi (a newspaperman), and the United Press correspondent, Wee Kim Wee—I hope he drops the middle name in his byline.

SINGAPORE, *October 28, 1957*

LAST night, Freddy Reinhardt, counsellor of the State Department who is here on a quick tour, assured me Malaya remained in the secret (1952) ANZAM combination which is still effective. But the British have stopped thinking in terms of defending this region by a line across the Kra Isthmus in south Thailand; they are now more confident of SEATO.

Lunched with Lim Yew Hock (Singapore's chief minister), and Tengku (Prince) Abdul Rahman, first Prime Minister of Malaya, down on a one-day visit. I asked the Tengku about ANZAM. He was astounded; had never even heard of it. Abdul Rahman met Chin Peng, the guerrilla leader, in December, 1955. Chin impressed him as an idealistic, brave man; but an uncompromising Communist. The Tengku told him: "We can't coexist; one or the other must conquer and destroy the other." Then they parted—without shaking hands. Chin is now hiding in south Thailand.

BANGKOK, *October 29, 1957*

RODE here with Assistant Secretary of the Navy Norton on his plush DC-6. Norton told me that for years—starting now with the Democrats—he has been arguing for freer exchange of scientific knowledge with our allies. Fortunately Sputnik has now made us wake up and see the need.

Europe's abstract scientists and researchers have always been ahead of ours. Look at the men responsible for the atom—Einstein, Teller, von

Neumann, Bohr, Szilard, Fermi. We just can't afford to cut ourselves off. The British are ahead in infrared research, the French in electronics, the Germans in isolating isotopes. The Norwegians wanted a proximity fuse from us and we couldn't give it to them—security. So they invented and produced a better one.

Norton says he had a Billboard radar in north Turkey tracking Soviet rockets for three years. Its range was about three thousand miles. It is a huge apparatus. At one time Kresge's Department Store was thinking of opening a Turkish shop and we wanted them to put up a sign to camouflage the radar. But they couldn't use the site the technicians needed; so the disguise was dropped.

ANGKOR VAT, CAMBODIA, *October 30, 1957*

FLEW off at dawn to Siem Reap in Cambodia, a few miles from the fantastic, huge cluster of ruins at Angkor: vast temples and palaces of gray sandstone rising from the bright-green jungle. They are covered with friezes of dancing girls with intricate, towering headdresses, burnished breasts and faces. The collapsing altars, where Buddhists still place incense sticks before idols, are covered with bird and bat dung and you can hear and see the leathery and feathered creatures fluttering inside the towers overhead. The wide moats around the main edifices are green with slime. No animals were in sight, but you could hear the restless jungle. Oddly enough, while we were picnicking beside a lake at Angkor Thom, who would arrive but a large official party in honor of Richard Casey, Australian foreign minister, dapper as ever.

BANGKOK, *October 31, 1957*

THIS evening Rivett-Carnac of the British embassy came up for drinks and a long talk. He speaks excellent Thai and knows the country better than any foreigner. He assured me that it was all right for Thais to be immoral and corrupt; "after all" said he, "it isn't as bad as things were in Egypt." When I asked "What does that prove?" he said: "I hope you're not going to read me a moralist lecture like Mr. Dulles."

I have a feeling that under our benevolent protection Bangkok smells like Saigon under the French or Cairo under the British—the same musty odor of corruption and decay. Bao Dai sold the prostitution racket of Saigon to a gang. Phao's rackets here have been taken over by the lieutenants of his successor. I wonder if Angkor Vat smelled this way in the fifteenth century before disaster came. They say Pibul, the former dictator, was honest—but his pals were crooks. The same is said of Diem in Saigon—that he is fine but his brothers are corrupt. I can't accept the idea that these people don't care about morals. It isn't logical to expect that those who produced Buddha, Confucius, Milarepa, and Gandhi, should have inferior ethical codes.

BANGKOK, *November 2, 1957*

WENT with Ambassador Bishop to call on Field Marshal Sarit Thanarat, the dictator. A couple of generals interpreted (although Sarit speaks English). In the next room were tough-looking guards wearing bandoliers of cartridges and sporting bone-handled revolvers. In the place of honor, between two mounted elephant tusks, was an inscribed photo of Pibul Songgram, the dictator Sarit ousted.

Sarit is a tough-looking little man with high cheekbones, a shrewd expression, sensual mouth. He was wearing a gray suit, white shirt, striped tie, and bright yellow shoes and socks. While we talked the ambassador (who came along uninvited by me) listened raptly and his military attaché (also uninvited by me) took notes. It certainly made it appear that I represented the U.S. government and I can't blame Sarit if he thinks so. But there was nothing I could do. He had a couple of generals also taking notes.

Sarit assured me that regardless of how elections come out next month: "I won't allow anyone who is a neutralist or antiwestern to be named premier—no matter what the results of the vote are." He claimed many "outsiders" were misrepresenting his own activities. It was a "lie" that he had contacts with China.

BANGKOK, *November 3, 1957*

DINED at the Bishops' with an interesting fellow named George Hellier, deputy director for the Far East of USIS. He was a young air force lieutenant with Wingate's chindits in Burma and tells a tale about my friend Bernard Fergusson who commanded a brigade there. Fergusson wore a heavy black beard and always retained his monocle. One of his men was a slacker. Fergusson summoned him and offered him a choice— either be shot or flogged. The man selected flogging. "Good show," said Bernard. "If you had asked for shooting I'd have had you flogged first anyway." After the flogging, the man's offenses were forgotten and he did well.

RANGOON, *November 4, 1957*

ED Law Yone, editor of *The Nation* (best Rangoon paper) dropped by for a drink. He said there are still numerous civil wars going on with the following insurgent groups: the Pa-O's in the Shan states, the Red Flag Communists, the White Flag Communists (of the Burmese Communist party), the Karens (KNDO—Karen National Defense Organization), the Peoples' Volunteer Army (remnants of the resistance groups), the Mon National Defense Organization (a minority in the south), remnants of the Kuomintang Chinese forces in the north, the Mujahids—Muslims on the East Pakistan border. The Karens and the White Flags are the most important. But all are still fighting and sabotaging communications.

China is pressing claims for part of the Kachin area. The border has been a subject of dispute since the nineteenth century. In 1955, the subject was raised again and the Chinese sent troops across into the Wa state (near Laos). It is so remote that nobody knew the Chinese were there until there was a clash with a patrolling Burmese unit.

Ed says there is a real "love affair" between Burma and Israel. Both states began the same year. They have the same approach to socialism.

RANGOON, *November 7, 1957*

THE last several days have been a nightmare. Monday a dinner party was given for us by Walter McConaughy, American ambassador. After dinner, I noticed that Uncle Arthur kept holding a handkerchief to his right eye and was clearly in pain. He seemed a bit sleepy also. We left early—around 10:30. In the car Uncle A complained that he had a sinus attack. I told Marina, when we were alone, that I was worried; I feared he had had a stroke.

Next morning, we were to visit the Shwe Dagon pagoda. Aunt Iph came downstairs at 9:20 and said: "Arthur isn't feeling well. Something happened during the night and he says his left hand isn't working right. Would you go up and see him?"

I found him sitting in an armchair in his dressing gown. It was perfectly apparent he had had a stroke. He was even more ruddy of complexion than usual (he has high blood pressure). His speech was thick; he couldn't articulate properly. His left arm and hand were weak and he had lost much of the feeling in them. His left leg wasn't functioning right and when he walked he staggered. He insisted on trying to walk about—tottering—and did strange, useless things such as getting up, picking up two ashtrays, carrying them weakly to the bathroom, washing them, and then placing them neatly on a table. I tried to get him to sit down and when he did so and promised to stay put, I went down to call the ambassador in search of a doctor (this being Rangoon, the room telephone didn't work).

I sent Aunt Iph and Marina off to the pagoda with a guide and whispered to the guide to keep them away for at least an hour, assuring Aunt Iph I'd get a doctor for a check. I called McConaughy and told him I was certain A had had a stroke. He sent over the embassy nurse, an American woman. He also sent his car for a doctor, an Indian named Dr. Suvi, a graduate of Edinburgh University.

I then went back upstairs to wait. Uncle A was an excellent sport, cracking jokes weakly. Soon the nurse arrived and helped persuade him to stop moving around. Then Dr. Suvi, a dark, handsome gentleman, showed up. He examined him and told him he'd had a stroke, a blood clot on the right side of the brain. We booked a room at the Prome Road Nursing Home and the ambassador's car came for him. Bernie Kalb, *New York Times* correspondent, and I carried him to the elevator in a chair and then from the elevator to the car. Aunt Iph and Marina returned just in time and we rode out to the home, quite a nice hospital on the side of the lake—but not air conditioned.

During the past two days he has been immobile and cared for by nice Burmese nurses. He doesn't look well but the doctor says after the first seventy-two hours (twenty-four more) he will be over the hump; rest is the key.

The complications of this place are something. We have hired one car just to transport nurses back and forth—one has to hire one's own nurses; and another car to transport ourselves to and from the nursing home, which is a twenty-minute ride.

The first night A was in the hospital was the evening of the Buddhist full-moon holiday; there was singing and dancing all over (the whole city was hung with lights). He didn't get much sleep.

RANGOON, *November 9, 1957*

NOVEMBER 7, went to the Soviet embassy party celebrating the fortieth anniversary of the October revolution. The Russian diplomatic group is about the nicest I have ever met: well dressed in white dinner jackets, all speaking excellent English, friendly, courteous. I was introduced to U Nu's chef de cabinet, a quite tall Burmese named U Ohn with a lean, passionate face and fanatic's eyes. He greeted me saying: "Ah, I am glad to see you, Mr. Sulzberger. I am the 'naive, little Burmese ambassador.' " "My god," I said. "It's you." In Moscow, Chip Bohlen had told me that the Burmese ambassador said the Americans should encourage the Russians, who were timid like a certain kind of Burmese lizard which the people entice out of its lair and then kill. I wrote this and the ambassador was furious at Bohlen. Said U Ohn: "I don't mind you calling me naive. But am I little? I'm almost as tall as you are."

This afternoon, I visited U Nu, the Prime Minister, at his house. U Ohn was there—very friendly.

U Nu is well protected. He and the other ministers live in a compound surrounded by barbed wire and sentries armed with tommy guns. This is practical in a country at present engaged in fighting eight civil wars and where murder and violent robbery are the norm. In 1947, a Prime Minister and almost his entire Cabinet were wiped out by tommy gunners at a routine Cabinet meeting.

U Nu is a nice-looking man of medium height and sturdy build, affable, poised, speaks good English.

I started off by asking for his views on the theory and practice of neutralism.

Neutralism is a very simple thing. It means that you don't join any power bloc, but at the same time you try your level best to bring the two blocs together as quickly as possible. This we are trying to do in our own humble way.

When I visited China I told the Chinese how good the Americans are. When I visited the United States I told the Americans how good the Chinese are. These simple facts are of course known in China and in the United States. But in the heat of the moment, if I may say so, some people are apt to forget things about each other.

When I met Secretary Dulles in Washington [July, 1955], it was I who suggested that the level of diplomatic talks between the United States and China should be raised. He agreed—and the level was raised. The result has been the ambassadorial conversations with Mr. Dulles.

War won't solve problems. I have become more and more firmly convinced of this particularly after World War II. The democracies won that war. But they lost the peace. They lost China, Poland, Czechoslovakia, Hungary, Rumania, and Bulgaria. And they will lose even more territory if there is another war. I am convinced that they would win another war—and lose the peace. And war would bring with it misery, poverty, and disease—the very thing on which communism thrives.

I asked if he wished to use capitalism and the profit motive to bring about an evolution permitting gradual development of socialism. Yes, this delighted him; that was exactly it.

He said America was now going to send Burma arms. Also, a small U.S. military mission was coming soon. U Nu then added: "Now you see the practical political value of neutralism as a policy. If we weren't neutralist the Chinese might be aiding the rebels. But they are not. Of this I am positive."

I reminded him he had written that "a man who wants to rule must learn to be tough." How did he plan to get tough with the guerrillas? He said:

We will fight them in a guerrilla way. Before it was only a game of hide and seek. But you can't keep forces all over a country like this with its mountains and its jungles. And when you send up troops, the guerrillas disappear before they arrive. Now we are changing our tactics. We are organizing special commando units. Some of them are already working in the field—and working well. These new forces are scaring the rebels.

I never believed the Americans were warmongers. They shed their blood twice in two world wars to save the world from two tyrannies. They did this at a tremendous sacrifice. How can we say that people who sacrificed so much for the world want war? And, after all, the Americans are the most prosperous people in the world. How can one expect that they would seek to bring about their own ruin. There cannot be any survivors in a war in this atomic age.

RANGOON, *November 11, 1957*

TODAY, Ambassador McConaughy told me a very secret American military mission is arriving to explore possibilities of aiding Burma against the rebels. The mission is masquerading as economic specialists. Burma is coming our way slowly. U Nu says there is no point in seeking Communist arms to help against Communists.

RANGOON, *November 14, 1957*

So busy, thanks to Uncle Arthur's illness, that I haven't had a chance to see a thing. This afternoon at sunset, therefore, I went for a quick glimpse of the Shwe Dagon pagoda. It was especially lovely with the enormous golden steeple in the center catching the last rays, set off against gathering clouds. Before the gilded Buddhas (the gilt covering the secret relics including the Buddha's hairs, his staff, and water filter), women sat with their eyes closed muttering silent prayers, hands folded before them. Puppies lay fast asleep on the steps of idols. An old woman, having paid alms, struck a silver gong three times with the base of a stag's horn.

Beside the main steeple rose dozens and dozens of steepled gold shrines, silver shrines, red-trimmed shrines, white shrines, most of them with filigree edges, all the towers decked with little bells which tinkle when the wind blows. The smaller shrines, put up by prosperous families, contained Buddha idols and dragons, and colored, life-size, human figures.

Orange-robed bonzes (monks) and pink-robed nuns, indistinguishable with their shaven heads and flat chests, sat about praying. Candles and oil lamps flickered outside the shrines and inside were vases filled with gift offerings of flowers that are sold in the shops lining the entrances.

In one corner was an immense banyan (peepul or bo) tree, the holy tree of Buddha. Chanting priests doused idols with holy water. Despite dog dung, dust, and rubbish about there was peace and loveliness.

LONG talk with Dulles. I started off by asking how we were to avoid the
dilemma of the relative importance of our alliances and of our different
allies. What would we do to resolve this?

He answered:

Maintaining alliances is quite an art. There is no simple formula.
The miracle is actually that they are maintained at all. In the Federalist Papers our early leaders contended that alliances could not be
kept up except during wartime. Of course it's hard to keep alliances
alive. There are many stresses and strains. But, I'm glad to say, nothing has actually cracked yet—touch wood. [Here he deliberately
leaned over and rapped his knuckle on the table.]

Issues must be resolved in general terms. Thus, it is obvious the
United Kingdom is the most important ally we have. But we even
went against Britain on Suez. We felt it would destroy UN if they went
on; that it was better to strain our relations with the U.K. than to
accept the destruction of UN and get into the morass of war in the
Middle East, from which none of our people could see a possibility of
extricating ourselves without the loss of much money and prestige.

We must decide each question on its merits. There was the question
of relations with France and sending police arms to Tunisia. France
is more important than Tunisia. But we had to consider the issues. Everyone felt the Tunisians were entitled to get some arms; this even
included the French. We could not repudiate the concept of independence and throw North Africa into the arms of the Soviets.

Each issue must be faced separately. You can't operate on the theory of big allies and little allies. You would lose each ally one by one.
Look at Greece and Turkey on the Cyprus issue. If you favored one,
you would lose the other. Each problem must be appraised. It is not
just a question of who you love the most or who can help you the most.

I told Dulles I understood the Pentagon doesn't want to make ICBMs
at all; that it felt we could rely on IRBMs indefinitely with our present
base system. If this were true, did we have enough bases? Dulles said we
are developing IRBMs, which are now going into production. We were just
not sufficiently advanced yet to go into production with the ICBM, but he
had heard of no Pentagon decision. "I am unaware of that viewpoint,"
he said. "But the Pentagon can say anything. It depends on whom you
talk with. That place is a tower of Babel. You can get any opinion on any
subject. Of course we need as many bases as we can get until we can depend more on the Polaris submarine. That is movable."

I asked if, in line with the consultative aspect of NATO, we had consulted with our allies before sending the Sixth Fleet to the coast of Syria

this autumn. After all, wasn't the Sixth Fleet under NATO command? Dulles said the Sixth Fleet was not under NATO, but,

It is a detached position. It is only contingently under NATO. Washington directs its movements—except when it is specifically assigned to NATO maneuvers.

Therefore, there was no consultation on that issue. Action was taken by us on extremely short notice in order to offset a Communist probing operation. If you don't react immediately to that kind of probing operation the situation becomes highly dangerous. You must react quickly. What you do is in line with basic policies. But there is no time to consult. That situation called for extremely quick action.

WASHINGTON, *December 5, 1957*

THIS morning, I had breakfast with Adlai Stevenson, Bill Blair, his secretary and friend, and Chet Bowles. Every time I got Stevenson talking, when he stopped for a sip of coffee, Bowles would interject something like "Well, what do you think about India?", or "Why don't you come up to Connecticut and refresh your mind?", and Adlai would lose track of what he had been saying.

When the subject of his participating in our planning of NATO first came up, Stevenson had been asked to be second man on the U.S. delegation—that is to say, just below President Eisenhower and above Secretary Dulles. But he did not wish to accept that position because it implied too much responsibility in our foreign policy. He wished to have elbow room for attacks on elements he opposed.

The subject of his going had only been brought up in a backhand way. At the White House the President had casually asked, "Don't you want to go over with us?" Stevenson said no and the matter was then dropped. He felt the emphasis of our program was far too much on military rather than on peaceful things. It had been made clear that his only role in the delegation would be to sit there and not make any speeches.

He felt there wasn't enough urgency about our approach to this NATO meeting. There was going to be a "declaration of Paris." But it was already being vitiated. Spaak had sent over a first draft which was crisp and effective. Now a committee has been established to rewrite it— "sort of like setting up a committee to write the Gettysburg Address." It was getting long, turgid, and confused.

The thing we should stress was peace and our desire to negotiate, "not just weaponry." But when he had tried to insert things along these lines in the Eisenhower speech, they had been taken out. Instead there was the kind of stuff Churchill used when he warned the Germans, "We will fight on the beaches." This was the wrong approach.

WASHINGTON, *December 6, 1957*

LAST night went to a party at the Dillons. Walter Robertson bent my ear about how good our China policy was. He assured me Mao Tse-tung did not represent the Chinese people any more than William Z. Foster represented the American people. The nearest Washington taxi driver was more representative of China than Mao!

WASHINGTON, *December 7, 1957*

LUNCHED with Senator John Cooper. He told me the plan now being considered by the administration to aid India is the one he and I cooked up in Paris last summer.

He is desperately worried about the world. Thinks Eisenhower is not providing the necessary leadership. Dulles is foolishly minimizing the gravity of the situation; Walter Robertson is wholly idiotic and unrealistic; Stevenson is not facing up to his responsibilities as an opposition leader, and anyway, he has no original ideas to offer.

This afternoon, Scotty Reston told me that when Foster Dulles's name was coming up for confirmation as Secretary of State, Senator Knowland came to him and said he had read in his book, *War or Peace*, Dulles's views that whether we liked it or not Communist governments ruled a third of the world's population; that we had to recognize them even if we didn't approve of them; that we would have to let China into the UN if we wished to have it a true world organization. Knowland wished to know if Dulles intended to pursue that policy if he were approved as Secretary of State. Dulles said no. Furthermore, he was prepared to give a guarantee by letting Knowland select a man he trusted as assistant secretary for Far Eastern affairs. He, Dulles, would earnestly consider recommending to the President that Knowland's candidate be named. Walter Robertson was selected. Ever since he had influenced Dulles to carry out a policy precisely opposite to the one in *War or Peace*.

NEW YORK, *December 9, 1957*

THIS afternoon, I called Averell Harriman at Albany to say hello. He sounded like the voice of doom. Everything is crumbling. Nixon is the only man who has tried to give any leadership and that not enough. Even Nixon talks delusions.

Averell was distressed by recent statements by George Kennan. He said: "George always has some strange ideas. When he was with me in Moscow in 1944, he strongly advocated that we should drop all thoughts of free elections in Poland and elsewhere in eastern Europe because it would be impossible to achieve this when the Russian armies entered that area and we would only irritate Moscow unnecessarily. Of course I did not accept this suggestion and I reminded him that the war had started over Poland and that this was not the question of a Polish vote, but a moral principle."

NEW YORK, *December 11, 1957*

HARRIMAN invited me to a lunch for the King of Morocco. There were about twenty-eight guests. Before the King showed up we were all given a couple of quick shots of liquor since nothing was served in the King's presence.

After lunch, the King made a correct little speech which was read out in English by an interpreter. Then Harriman made a really nice reply. He told the King how delighted everybody was at Eisenhower's recovery because Eisenhower was President of all the American people and although Democrats and Republicans vote against each other they are all presided over by Eisenhower and all rejoice in his recovery.

PARIS, *December 20, 1957*

LAST night, saw Dulles at the embassy residence. He said Eisenhower had re-created an esprit de corps at the NATO summit. He has a great gift for making people feel he understands their problems.

Dulles made a rather odd observation. "I don't think the relative status of our missile power has much to do with the status of negotiations with Russia. If there were a war we could devastate Russia now. For two or three years we have been assuming that the Soviet Union could devastate much of the United States. There is not much difference now that they have the missiles. Our estimate of damages hasn't altered much; the same estimates of power prevail today."

He admitted it would be impossible to insure against surprise attack. The question is how big a risk we would have to take. The Russians just don't want foreigners prowling around. This is partly suspicion and partly centuries-old prejudice. In other words, part of it belongs to their Communist system and part of it belongs to Russia's heritage.

He is going to visit Franco because the United States has important relations with Spain. As a matter of fact, we would be happy if Spain were a member of NATO. It is appropriate that the Spaniards know our thinking and what is going on and what risks they are taking—what insurance there is for them. The countries with the most "socialistically inclined" governments, particularly Norway and Denmark, were those which most strongly opposed Spain's entry into NATO.

LUNCHED today with Spaak. He considers the NATO summit conference a great success. The most significant result was establishment of a new relationship between the United States and its European allies. He was struck by Eisenhower's insistence on refusing a suggestion that special thanks to the United States for its aid be included in the terminal communiqué. The President wished to stress equality of all the allies. Cynical as many people were by inclination, they were all very moved by Eisenhower's request for thirty seconds of silent contemplation at the end of the meeting and for the aspirations of NATO being "the welfare" of all allied peoples. But he whispered to someone next to him: "My God, we are not for the welfare state." This reverberated around the room.

THIS morning Norstad told me England and Turkey are the two main initial centers for IRBMS. In order to cover the heart of the U.S.S.R. you would have to go outside the NATO area and use either Iran or Pakistan. His aide brought in a chart showing arcs swung at a fifteen-hundred-mile range from various potential NATO missile bases. The bases marked were England, France, Norway, Italy, Greece, and Turkey.

I asked what Larry thought about the Rapacki Plan to take nuclear weapons and missiles out of West Germany, East Germany, Poland, and Czechoslovakia. He said this was bad because it would discriminate against the West Germans. How would it relax tension, he asked, or help in any way to unify Germany? It was too small a project to have any real effect. The Russians again would be able to build an atmosphere of sweetness and light and lull us to sleep.

The time might come someday when we could make "the big offer" to Russia. To counter the big-lie technique we should use the technique of a big offer including many elements which really would be useful in stabilizing the world situation. There was no point in frittering away any possible details of such an offer. The West is still reasonably strong. There is too much gloom at home.

He was very disturbed about the lecture George Kennan had just given in England. He was astonished when Kennan in one lecture gave his "personal assurance" that there would be no war if his plans were carried out. This was the height of egotism. "What is his personal assurance worth?" he asked. "What authority does he speak with? Is he speaking of the divisions of the Princeton School of International Studies?"

LECH, AUSTRIA, *January 3, 1958*

WE spent the last four days at Cannobio, in northern Italy on Lake Garda, at the home of André de Staercke, Belgian ambassador to NATO, with the Norstads. Flew down on Larry's personal plane. Italy was socked in. We had a beautiful flight over Mont Blanc, passing the peak, it seemed, close enough to scoop off handfuls of snow. When we got down, the Po Valley was completely covered. At Turin, we could see a smokestack sticking out of the fog and puffing away. It was New Year's Eve and, disconsolate, we thought we would have to go back to empty houses and cold suppers in Paris. Then the wind opened a patch the size of a football field and we came down in a hurry. By the time our engines had stopped the field was covered again and you couldn't tell one wing tip of the plane from the other.

At Cannobio, Larry gave me a verbal portrait of Montgomery: a lonely, crotchety man. He has been eased out of the château which the French government let him have for years, and he now lives in a suite of the Trianon Palace Hotel at Versailles. There he has the same meal every night—lamb chops. Often he eats alone, but occasionally he invites an aide. The only thing Monty does at SHAPE now is to run the annual Command Post Exercise (CPX).

When Al Gruenther was commanding general he had a lot of trouble with Montgomery who kept traveling around making foolish statements. He is pretty well out of things now and simply doesn't realize when he is saying something in public that is totally contradictory to SHAPE policy. Once Gruenther was going to send him a sharp note, and he showed it to Norstad first. Larry got him to tone it down, but even when the modified version was sent to Monty, the old man burst into tears.

LONDON, *January 12, 1958*

DURING the last few days, I have been conferring with about twenty of Prince Bernhard's "Bilderberg Group," including Bernhard, General Sir Colin Gubbins (British chief of SOE during the war), Denis Healey, E. N. van Kleffens (now Dutch ambassador to NATO), Pietro Quaroni (Italian ambassador to France), Otto Wolff von Amerongen, Arthur Dean, and Nuri Birgi (Turkish ambassador to London). Gubbins, to my amazement, came up to me right after we met and recalled that it was he who had prevented me from being parachuted into Jugoslavia during the war. Some memory!

One doesn't discuss the actual meetings, but I had some fun on the peripheries.

Arthur Dean, over drinks, talked at length about his negotiations for the Korean armistice and a curious party he attended in New York given by Vyshinsky in October, 1953. After dinner, Vyshinsky took Art aside and made a blatant offer for Russia and the United States to divide the world into spheres of interest. He even brought out a map to illustrate his ideas.

Dean told me some stories about Dulles, who is senior partner of Sullivan and Cromwell. He is clearly fond of Dulles and thinks him highly intelligent, but he gets into unnecessary jams. For example, when World War II started, Dulles sent a memorandum around telling everyone it was more important to continue working for Sullivan and Cromwell because of its objectives than to join the armed services. Dean was horrified and gathered up the papers. He told Dulles he knew his mind well enough to realize that this wasn't what Foster meant, but nobody could fail to interpret this note as a plea not to allow the war to interfere with the working of his law firm.

Wolff von Amerongen said Ambassador Smirnov (to West Germany) offered him—and asked him to pass on to the Bonn government—a fifty-fifty split for a West German-Russian financial undertaking to invest in underdeveloped countries. Smirnov warned that if West Germany did not join Russia on this, Moscow would do it alone on its own terms, which the Germans would not be able to meet on a commercial basis.

Van Kleffens said the Russians are like cuckoos. They get into the other bird's nest and lay eggs there. They take democracy and liberty and extract all the real meaning from these words and then sell them in order to secure others. They say, "We are the champions of democracy, liberty, and justice." But there is a misunderstanding of these terms.

PARIS, *January 15, 1958*

SPAAK has prepared a long "reply" to George Kennan's argument in favor of a neutral zone in central Europe, and he showed it to me asking for criticism. I didn't cheer him up. It was a mistake for the NATO secretary to engage in debate with a former American ambassador. He should make public pronouncements rarely and not, like Dulles, shoot off his trap all the time. He was planning to squash a mosquito with an atom bomb.

Spaak said his temperament favored engaging in arguments. I cautioned him against this, adding that anyway his paper was too long and lacked pungency. He didn't like that terribly well and said that as a matter of fact it was his own feeling that "the last twenty-five pages" were much too short.

He is very concerned about the propaganda situation. Dulles has succeeded in uniting the whole world, including all Americans, in the erroneous belief that he is just a "no man."

LUNCHED today with Pierre Courtade, foreign editor of *Humanité* and a member of the Central Committee of the French Communist party. He was in Moscow recently and says that if Molotov had been either a brutal dictator or a good politician he would have licked Khrushchev. When the Presidium met at Molotov's behest to bounce Khrushchev in 1957, two-thirds of the members present supported Molotov. Molotov intended to become secretary-general of the party or Prime Minister, and he had drawn up his Cabinet list. Shepilov was to be foreign minister and Khrushchev had been assigned as minister of agriculture. But Molotov had no pipelines to the party apparatus in the countryside. Zhukov placed his planes at the disposal of Khrushchev who flew in a stacked Central Committee which supported him two to one over Molotov.

Zhukov had backed Khrushchev but Bulganin did not. Shepilov also backed Molotov. Shepilov is an ambitious man who let down his "liberal" friends because he thought Molotov would win. Khrushchev destroyed all the others except Bulganin. He needed a figurehead Prime Minister, and since Bulganin had opposed him and then recanted, he no longer had influence but was a good front man. As for Molotov, although Courtade despises him personally as a Stalinist, he admires his courage. Khrushchev offered him a considerable choice of jobs all written out in a list ranging from president of the Academy of Science on down. Molotov personally selected the position of ambassador to Outer Mongolia—the least important job on the list.

Courtade says Zhukov supported Khrushchev in the whole fight. But Khrushchev fired him because this was Russia's "MacArthur case." Zhukov was getting too big for his boots and Khrushchev had to reestablish civilian control of the army. None of the generals supported Zhukov for precisely the same reason that no American generals resigned to support MacArthur. One less marshal meant more room for promotion at the top.

Courtade doesn't think Khrushchev is a great man, but he is a very skillful politician. He is a Russian Truman.

Courtade thinks that in twenty years the U.S. will still be way ahead of the Soviet Union in its level of living, but both the political and economic systems of the U.S.S.R. and U.S. will be closer to each other than either one is to France. Russia and America by then will be natural allies.

Pierre said I was crazy to think there would be a *coup d'état* in France. It wouldn't come next year or two years from now or ten years from now.

PARIS, *February 8, 1958*

YESTERDAY evening, I spent an hour with Prime Minister Gaillard. He is very youthful looking, tall, with black hair, black eyes, pink cheeks, and with a pleasant, professorial manner. I know he is extremely bright, but with the exception of the famously stupid Laniel, he is the dullest French Prime Minister I have ever talked to.

He said it was impossible to govern France without constitutional reform. De Gaulle had tried to introduce a new type of constitution but failed. The first Constituent Assembly after the war had operated under a constitution which gave the Assembly virtual control of the government. This system had been pushed through by Communist influence. The second Constituent Assembly was better balanced. But it still drew up a constitution which left Parliament in a position where it was tempted to substitute itself for the executive.

This, said Gaillard, "gives a certain incoherence" to the administration of France. Parliament is tempted to move into the executive field and at the same time it does not do enough of its own legislating work in things like fiscal affairs.

Right now, the government is virtually helpless. It cannot even pose a question for debate in Parliament if Parliament does not agree to accept it. I asked Gaillard if he thought that in the absence of any real reform there would be a *coup d'état*, either from the left or from the right. He said certainly not. The French people were too balanced; the present weak system would continue indefinitely without grave consequences.

PARIS, *February 14, 1958*

THIS afternoon, I saw Houghton, U.S. ambassador. He is up to his ears in the present Tunisian crisis, which resulted from French bombing of the village of Sakiet.

Twice during the last few days Washington has tried to push an overall settlement on France. But Houghton is advising Washington there is no sense in this; it is premature. The urgent thing is to keep the crisis from getting worse.

The French army won't tolerate any effort to push France out of Bizerte. The French can no longer dodge the fact that the Algerian war has been "internationalized"—thanks to their mistake at Sakiet. Even before the Sakiet incident, Houghton had asked General Norstad whether he thought NATO could provide a force to police the Algerian-Tunisian border. NATO replied in the negative.

Nobody is really governing France. All the present leaders talk one way

to Houghton and another way to each other. Nobody is really in power
and everybody is fed up. The political situation is steadily decaying.

PARIS, *February 20, 1958*

THIS morning, I had a good talk with de Gaulle in his office at 5, rue de
Solférino. The General was as haughty and disdainful as ever. He is almost sixty-eight years old now and is beginning to show it. But he is
not exactly decrepit and behind a mild and withering exterior he is still
the vigorous prophet of doom.

I told him I had the impression that France was heading slowly but immutably toward disaster. Was there any way of stopping this trend? He
replied: "I don't know how to stop it. If I were in power—without this
type of regime—something could be done. But the only thing that can
be done is to give this country back its independence."*

I reminded de Gaulle that the last time I had seen him a few months
ago, many people were talking about the chances of his return and he
referred to *coups d'état* he had engineered in the past. What were the
chances now of his return? Was the situation bad enough to warrant this?
He replied:

> The situation is worse now than it was a few months ago. But it is
> not yet dramatically bad. The French people eat well. They are con-
> tented. They do not suffer. That is the trouble. Because, in the mean-
> time, if this regime [meaning not just the Gaillard government, but
> the entire system now prevailing] continues, France will lose all
> North Africa.†

I asked how he thought the countries of the West should stand up
against the Russian menace. He replied:

> The countries of the West must be for themselves, each should be
> for itself. France must be for the French. Nations cannot be suppressed
> as individualities. But NATO suppresses them as individualities. One
> reason for the success of Soviet pressure now is that the Russians have
> changed a lot internally. They are no longer the Bolsheviks of other
> times. They keep communism in an economic sense. But in an intellec-
> tual or perhaps a spiritual sense they are no longer Communists. There
> is an internal trend within Russia that is going toward liberty—
> above all liberty of the spirit. Russia used to be an ignorant country.
> But now it is educated, even if it is not impartially educated. And
> the educated people—above all the elite—are working toward liberty.
> This fact alone is incompatible with the old-fashioned Bolshevism.
> The Russians are pushing toward liberty, pushing toward the sun.

* See de Gaulle's further comments, pp. 61–62.
† See de Gaulle's further comments, p. 33.

They crave contact with the West. This is no longer the Russia of twenty years ago, or even of ten years ago.

They have kept the economic and social system of communism. This won't change and we should realize it will not change. But in terms of the spirit, they are seeking and obtaining more freedom. Their politicians—and we should never forget that they are politicians—represent this trend. This is the current of the moment.*

I asked what he thought about the Rapacki Plan. He replied:

That is not a big thing. The Poles are obviously in accord with the Russians over it. For them, of course, it is in good faith—they want to neutralize a zone in Europe. The West should not reject such projects immediately. It is not a monstrous thing for the Poles to propose that a part of Europe should be de-nuclearized. It is not a monstrous thing for the Poles to wish to be specially treated and not to be lumped together with the Russians in all our considerations. We should examine their project.†

Did he think Bourguiba's references to the possibilities that it might be easier for Tunisia to deal with a de Gaulle government were not really a *blague politique*? He replied that probably this was the case. But he thought also that Bourguiba considered that a France which was sure of herself could be treated with. It was much easier to treat with a decisive France than with an indecisive France.

I asked if he thought that the future of North Africa did not lie in a completely independent set of states which were linked only vaguely with Paris by a commonwealth like the British Commonwealth. He replied that such indeed was his view. It had been his view since a speech he made in Brazzaville in 1943. De Gaulle said the only reality would be to have a commonwealth of independent States. That was how things stood. There should be reciprocal engagements; economic, military, and in foreign affairs between France and the members of the commonwealth. It should be like the British system.

He said the current regime is incapable of taking any responsibilities or military decisions. If it did seek to take responsibilities it was immediately thrown out by Parliament.‡

But de Gaulle did not think an Algerian disaster would in itself aggravate things sufficiently to bring about a change of regime. He thought perhaps it might but by no means necessarily. Perhaps enough people would not suffer by such a disaster to cause a revolution or a *coup d'état*. All that would happen, he ventured to predict, was that a man like Gaillard would be thrown out and a man like Mendès-France would be voted

---

* See de Gaulle's further comments, p. 49.
† See de Gaulle's further comments, p. 62.
‡ See de Gaulle's further comments, p. 33.

in. But it would be the same regime. "I told this to Mendès-France my-self," said de Gaulle.

He continued: "There are many people in the regime who have good qualities and ability. But they are paralyzed and helpless. They stay in the regime for the sake of their own careers. But they can do nothing."*

BELGRADE, *February 27, 1958*

YESTERDAY I lunched with Iveković, one under secretary of foreign af-fairs, and today with Vladko Velebit, another. Iveković said the Jugo-slavs had been very irked and worried by the way Khrushchev fired Zhukov while he was visiting Tito. It left a nervous taste. Unsettling things may be occurring in Russia. He also was restless about the frozen situation in Albania and the shadow of that old Stalinist Tchervenkov again lengthening over Bulgaria. The only neighboring Communist country that looked good was Rumania. But, I remarked, the Rumanians have no guts. "Yes," said Iveković, "that is the trouble."

Velebit talked about his bourgeois position: he owns a small house on a Dalmatian island and another in Zagreb. He looks forward to retiring at fifty-five (he is now fifty) and writing, living a few months in Zagreb, a few on his island, and traveling. His grandfather was a Hapsburg gen-eral. His father became a (royal) Jugoslav general. Vladko determined to be a civilian and got a law degree, but ended up a partisan general. "All Velebits become generals," say his friends.

He became a Communist while studying in Paris around 1930. But when he came back to Zagreb he became a prosperous lawyer and lost contact with the party. Together with some leftist intellectuals, he or-ganized a "wild" Marxist group. He met Tito knowing neither his exact position nor name, and in 1939, he went to Istanbul on special assign-ment to confer with him.

In 1941, Vladko was drafted as a cavalry lieutenant and his unit fought well for four days on the Austrian border. When they retreated they found themselves cut off. The Germans disarmed and released all soldiers and sent the officers to prison camp, but Vladko escaped in the con-fusion, walked to Zagreb, changed to civilian clothes, and went under-ground. The party found him.

V thinks it is high time we got new definitions to describe political situations. Communism, capitalism, Titoism, etc., are useless. There is plenty of socialism in the U.S.A. There are both socialism and feudalism in England and Russia. There is a larger segment of privately owned arable land in Jugoslavia today than before the war; and at the same time not much private manufacturing. I must say V, well dressed, well

* See de Gaulle's further comments, p. 81.

set up, looks and talks like what we in America would call a capitalist; although he is no more that than I am a Communist.

BELGRADE, *February 28, 1958*

WENT over to Vlado Dedijer's house for lunch. "You are a good Serb," said Vlado on the phone, "so come over and have Serbian beans." He reminded me that when we saw each other in Paris last year I had written a column on him—"How to Prepare for a Diet of Beans"— referring to the traditional Jugoslav prison menu. The beans were good.

Vlado showed me the schedule he makes out for himself each week. He works and reads in the university and public libraries, is now teaching himself German, writes reviews and articles for foreign Social Democrat publications; extensive correspondence. He grades his own efforts. He earns a small free-lance income. He has no special trouble with the police; merely can't get a job or passport.

Tito is moving steadily eastward, says Vlado. He gets no intellectual stimulus. He is surrounded by "bureaucrats." Even Kardelj, theorist of the movement, has been eased out. Tito's greatest enemy is Khrushchev— who can't permit the Titoist theory of separate roads to socialism. But Tito doesn't realize this. Jugoslavia is drifting because it has lost its ideology.

Djilas is badly treated in jail; inadequate food and heat. But he is fearless. Most of his immediate male relatives were killed for independent views in the past. Djilas won't recant. When he was in prison, before the war, Djilas tried to commit suicide with a knife. V thinks they're trying to drive him to that again. Yet they let him have books, paper, pencils. His wife and mother can visit him.

Dedijer got so discouraged when Vera found she was sick that one day they were talking and forgot the kids could overhear. Vlado said: "Well, if you fall ill, I guess there's nothing to do but take poison, all of us." The little girl rushed out and told the others: "We're all going to take poison and die." One boy complained: "But that hurts your belly. It's better to jump out of the window." Vlado explained it was just a joke. "But it's hard to watch oneself," he adds.

HOW TO GET HELP

FROM BOTH SIDES

BELGRADE, *February 28, 1958*

THIS MORNING, I VISITED MARSHAL TITO AT HIS HOME. MADAME Kveder, wife of the former ambassador to West Germany, interpreted and a private secretary took shorthand notes. We sat around a low table in the President's study. Turkish coffee, *šljivovića*, and a fruit juice were served. Tito smoked cigarettes in a gold and ivory holder.

I started by asking why Jugoslavia had requested termination of U.S. military aid. He said relationships were good. The fact that Jugoslavia had decided to accept no more military aid had no effect upon our cooperation. Military aid was no longer necessary; Jugoslavia felt no longer threatened.

Furthermore, American military aid had become politically inconvenient. The U.S. Congress insisted on scrutinizing Belgrade's foreign policy in connection with the aid program—and especially relations with the Soviet Union and the eastern countries. "This was often embarrassing and insulting to us," Tito said. "But that was not the primary reason for terminating aid. American military assistance was simply no longer in keeping with our foreign policy."

I asked if Tito considered the Balkan Pact linking Jugoslavia with Greece and Turkey still valid and active. He replied:

From the military side, the pact no longer exists. The threat which occasioned it no longer exists. The main importance was that it helped us establish close cultural relations with Greece and to improve relations with Turkey. Of course, relationships between Greece and Turkey are not of the best at present and this makes the pact invalid from a tripartite point of view. It only exists now as a factor that makes possible the best relations between Jugoslavia and Greece and good relations between Jugoslavia and Turkey. In this sense it contributes to peace in this part of the world.

I asked if Tito wanted a neutral, demilitarized zone in Europe and whether he favored a neutral bloc as a diplomatic force in international affairs. He said it would be unrealistic to feel that the creation of a neutral zone could be achieved in the sense that member countries would renounce their existing alliances. The only realistic possibility would be to create a denuclearized zone. Such a zone would include countries belonging to the two alliances. We could not expect Western Germany or Italy to leave NATO, but they could be included in a denuclearized zone.

A denuclearized zone would be an important step. Jugoslavia feels itself deeply affected by this as an uncommitted country. For example, Italy has agreed to the installation of rocket bases. Even in a war in which Jugoslavia was not involved, these rocket installations would be turned in our direction and would violate our integrity. We keep thinking about this and I think we will have to take a concrete stand. By this I don't mean military arrangements with anybody, but rather a diplomatic stand and public statements.

I asked why Jugoslavia had recognized East Germany. He replied:

This was decided on the basis of facts and also on the basis of our foreign policy of coexistence and cooperation with all states. One cannot ignore the fact that historical circumstances after World War II created two Germanies. We wanted relations with both of them. If we recognized only one, this would be contrary to our principle of diplomatic relationships with all states. [This, of course, is not true because Tito does not, for example, recognize Nationalist China.]

We did not believe that our recognition of East Germany needed to prejudice the question of German unification when the time arose for this. We were very sorry that West Germany took our step as a hostile gesture. This was most unfair. We were willing to have the past forgotten.

Finally, it would be absurd for us not to recognize East Germany, which has a political system similar to ours, and only to have relations with capitalist West Germany. This would make it difficult for our relationships with other eastern European countries.

I asked if he thought it possible for a Communist state to be as neutral in world affairs as a non-Communist state considering, after all, the close ideological ties of communism. He answered: "It is impossible for any country, including a Communist country, to be neutral. All countries are members of the world community. It is not possible for any country to be indifferent to the world situation. There can be no neutral countries today. But a Communist country does not have to be a member of a bloc. It can cooperate with anyone—even though abstract neutrality is impossible."

I told him I knew he objected to the American distinction between "national communism" and "international communism," but that some form of differentiation is necessary. What did he think of the future of national versus international communism in this sense? He laughed heartily. He answered:

National communism simply doesn't exist. Jugoslav Communists are international. Our point of view is that communism in various countries builds socialism with different methods. We have our own methods. We don't have different systems, but we do have different ways of building systems. We have our own point of view here on how socialism should be built and we don't try to force this on other countries abroad. Jugoslav Communists don't shirk from the general aspirations of communism. *We have never renounced* the international obligation of communism, but we don't interfere with other countries.

Did he think, as some people say, that "national communism" had now been introduced in Russia? "No, no, no," he replied with a smile. "That is not true. But in Russia things have gone forward quickly since Stalin's death. It is not national communism, but there have been big developments in agriculture, in industry, and in scientific achievements. Also there have been big developments in foreign policy. Moscow, in seeking to settle international problems, has put forward propositions which are meeting with a positive response even in Washington and London."

I then asked what were the main differences between the ideology of communism in Jugoslavia and Russia. He answered: "There is no difference in ideology. There is only a difference in method."

I had the impression that philosophically all revolutions throughout history had eventually matured and moderated as they grew older. Did he think such had been the case in Jugoslavia? He answered that this revolution had occurred in the middle of war, during and immediately after the fighting. Now with the revolution in the process of internal development, it became more moderate and more democratic. There were evident changes; things like decentralization, creation of workers' councils, the handing over of factories to the workers, the growth of democratic rights. This showed a trend toward internal moderation.

As I often inquire of statesmen, I asked him who were the greatest men he had met during his life and who had influenced him most, either through personal contact or through their writings. He said:

It is very difficult to answer, to set one man apart from other men. When you do find a great man, you find that he is not alone. It depends upon the group of people around him.

I would not like to speak in any great detail concerning living leaders. Certainly Churchill was very great for England, both as a

political leader and a war leader. I have much respect and esteem
for President Eisenhower as a soldier and as a statesman seeking
peace. Of course, I met and admired Stalin. No, I suppose the word
would be *esteemed* not admired. I still esteem some of his qualities. I
also respect Khrushchev, who has many bold ideas on internal policy. I have great esteem for Nehru, who has gathered together the elements of India and welded a nation as well as being a great champion
for peace. I respect him as a political and philosophical leader. I
also respect Nasser, who has recognized the aspirations of his people
and is trying to unify the scattered Arabs.

At this point, I told him Nasser had once said to me he considered
Tito a great man because "He has shown me how to get help from both
sides without belonging to either." This delighted Tito. He continued,
referring to great men of the past, "I have a strong admiration for Marx
and Engels and especially for the persevering work they did on social
changes through the centuries and for analysis of the social systems of
their time. Lenin, of course, was one of the greatest of all men. This is
especially true in terms of his application of Marxism to practical
realities."

I told Tito that when I last saw Molotov in 1956, I asked him who
was the greatest diplomat he had ever met and Molotov answered "Eden."
Tito remarked, with a sour smile, "I am surprised he didn't say himself."

I then had a really tough question to put forward. Eight years ago,
when Archibishop Stepinac was imprisoned, I had asked Tito for permission to visit him. He agreed. Now I would like to visit another man
in prison, namely Djilas. How about it?

There was no warmth in Tito's smile. He said:

Why, that certainly is a tough one. But there is a big difference between Stepinac and Djilas. After all there were many Catholics in the
United States who were very interested in Stepinac. When I told
you you could go and see Stepinac, I knew he was popular with
American Catholics and that rumors were being circulated that he had
been tortured. Therefore, I felt justified in letting you go see him. But
I would not advise you to make this request concerning Djilas. His
case is entirely different. People would not look upon it with favor if
you were to visit him. My associates would disapprove if I gave you
such permission. And it would create a precedent.

BELGRADE, *March 2, 1958*

DINED with Vlado and Vera Dedijer in the Dva Jelena restaurant. He
told me the son of Vilfan is an original character. A couple of years ago
in school all the students were told to write an essay in Serbian. The
theme of his was as follows: "In Jugoslavia there are two classes. There

is the governing class, to which my father and his associates belong. And there is the working class." Vilfan is president of Tito's Cabinet.

Once Vlado drove with Pijade and his bodyguard to Paris. When they got to Zurich, the bodyguard was impressed by everything in the shops. Said Pijade: "Just you wait. Someday we will introduce socialism here too and then there won't be anything in the stores." Another time, a newspaperman met Pijade in the men's room of a little hotel in Slavonia. As usual it was filthy. Pijade grumbled: "Why can't these people learn that you can have socialism and clean toilets at the same time?"

When Dedijer spoke to a group of Labour MPs last summer he told them Djilas was suffering from the cold in his prison cell. He recommended: "When you people win the next elections the first thing you had better do is put radiators in your prisons. You may need them later."

PARIS, *March 7, 1958*

LAST night, Pam Churchill told me Winston, when he became Prime Minister in 1940, held a family dinner in which he promised he would resign as Prime Minister the day the war ended. Unfortunately, said Pam, even the slightest taste of power corrupts.

De Gaulle in London had written her a charming letter in his own handwriting sending his copy of Churchill's *Life of Marlborough* to give to young Winston when he grew up and to tell him it was a gift from a General who had brought it with him from France and who was proud to serve under Marlborough's descendant.

Pam is obviously fascinated by her ancestor, Lady Ellenborough. As a little girl, she was always impressed by pictures of that great beauty, but nobody would tell her anything about her except that she was "very wicked." Later, when studying in Germany, she was told "this is the most wicked Englishwoman who ever came to Germany." Lady Ellenborough was involved in the first divorce case in the House of Lords, then lived in London with an Austrian prince who could not marry her because he was Catholic. She was successively mistress of the King of Bavaria and his son, then married an Arab sheikh, having children by all of them. She kept an intimate personal diary which had been locked up in the family safe. Unfortunately, Pam's very proper father tore out and burned all but the first twenty and last thirty pages.

PARIS, *March 8, 1958*

DRINKS with Bob Murphy. He is handling the U.S. "good-offices" mission between France and Tunisia. He asked if I would take a leave of absence and take over the second (Algerian) phase of the negotiation. I told him it was more fun to write about the mistakes diplomats make.

Bob is convinced the only solution is Algerian independence. But no French dare face the issue and the lobby of the *colons* is powerful in Paris. The French have told him they are holding Ben Bella and his pals in order to have people to treat with (like Bourguiba, who was once under detention here).

The U.S.A. has no crystallized policy. We are still pro-French. But we can't lose North Africa. When the French warn Murphy they'll quit NATO if they are not satisfied, he tells them to get out. NATO isn't a device only to protect America.

PARIS, *March 17, 1958*

PLAYED golf yesterday with Air Chief Marshal Sir William Dickson, chairman of the British Chiefs of Staff Committee (equivalent of our chairman of the Joint Chiefs). He assured me a revolution was coming in France and would be accompanied by bloodshed.

PARIS, *March 18, 1958*

LUNCHED with Jean Laloy. He is very worried about de Gaulle. He admires him as a man but considers him an imbecile as a statesman.

Just before Dulles went to Manila for the SEATO talks, he received Hervé Alphand, French ambassador to Washington. He told Hervé France had only one year in which to settle the Algeria problem. If it could not achieve a settlement by then, the U.S. would have to take steps to insure that North Africa doesn't slip out of the western fold. Dulles was convinced that no military victory could succeed in establishing French sovereignty in Algeria on any firm basis.

PARIS, *March 20, 1958*

LUNCHED with the local head of the CIA. The CIA feels this place is going to blow up very, very, very soon. De Gaulle is getting stronger by the day. The war veterans organizations are well organized and have quite a lot of small arms. President Coty is a weak man and could well be prevailed upon to ask de Gaulle to form an unconstitutional government.

All the police forces including the gendarmes, the CRS (security police), and the gardes mobiles are under the command of the minister of the interior, Bourgès-Maunoury. But he is confused. And Chaban-Delmas, minister of defense, is detested.

The only thing that the extreme left and extreme right mobs would agree upon if serious trouble starts would be anti-Americanism.

NASSER:

"MY INTELLIGENCE

SERVICE WOULD BE

ANGRY WITH ME"

Cairo, *March 23, 1958*

L AST NIGHT, I TALKED WITH NASSER FOR TWO AND A HALF HOURS IN his home, a comfortable and quite luxurious villa on the road toward Heliopolis.

I have certainly been given the red-carpet treatment. A man from the information department met me yesterday at 1 A.M. when my plane came in. Waiting at the hotel was a car with a driver from Nasser's office—at my disposal for the duration of my visit. In the morning, just as I woke, a call came to advise me that the President would receive me in the evening.

Mohammed Heikal, a great friend of Nasser and editor of *Al Ahram*, obtained permission for me to take a stenographer along. I got a girl from the embassy and Heikal drove us out himself, remarking (correctly) as we sped along: "I am a very bad driver, I believe."

On the way out, Heikal had told me Nasser's only relaxation nowadays is tennis three times a week and occasional furious private movie showings for his friends; three films on top of each other, until most of the watchers are dizzy.

Nasser certainly looks fit although he has put on weight. Massive, strong, he was dressed in a gray suit, black shoes, white shirt, and wore a nondescript necktie. He is beginning to show gray patches around the temples. Turkish coffee was served and he kept handing around filtered cigarettes. He smokes a lot.

This is Ramadan, and, being a good Muslim, he fasts all day until after sundown. Despite this, he obviously has incredible energy. He talked nonstop until long after midnight, being interrupted only once by a brief, late phone call. Heikal was getting a bit nervous as I kept pouring questions on. But Nasser was easygoing and patient, although elusive as an eel on some questions. He makes an impression of being bright, self-confident, ruthless, charming. Under the bluff exterior he can strike with the rapidity of a cobra. His massive body moves with a certain feline grace. He has bright teeth and luminous eyes: a handsome, aquiline-featured man, with mobile expression and broad, easy gestures.

He says he reads American papers carefully every day (including *The New York Times*); also reads some American history, especially on the career and presidential administration of Washington with whom, by inference, he seemed to compare himself. He said Washington preached nonalignment (like Egypt) and opposed a two-party system (which I don't recall).

> We are a simple people. Our historical background is based on morality and sincerity. Christianity came into this area—based on moral and material action. Then Islam came by just moral actions. The three main religions in the world came from this area.
>
> Saladin, a Syrian, came from Syria with a Syrian army to help Egypt overcome the crusaders when they reached the outskirts of Cairo. After that he was appointed here as a minister.
>
> When Syria was in trouble after that, Saladin helped Syria with Egyptian troops and his object was to protect the area from foreign domination. This is the same objective everyone in the area now seeks.
>
> If there is a comparison between Saladin and myself, it is a comparison in the meaning of our actions. I expressed that in my last speech—I said that during the troubles in this area we must develop an organization for unity between Syria and Egypt, the only defensive line against outside aggression, just as it was against the Christians and later against the Tatars.

I asked what was the present condition of relationships between his country and the U.S.A.? He replied:

> Well, on the governmental side, we are now past a period of hesitation. I have said many times that our object is not to be opposed to the U.S.A. Our object is only to be free. We are ready to do anything except to give up our sovereignty or our dignity. The U.S. is a big power. We are a small country. But although we are a small country, we give great consideration to our dignity. So if our dignity is affected by a big power, we cannot accept this.
>
> The Baghdad Pact was a turning point in our relations with the

United States and with the West. We believe defense of the area must depend on its people. We are not the same as western Europe. The historical development of the West was different. When Hitler invaded, the U.S. helped western Europe. Again Europe faced the danger of the threat of communism after World War II. It was clear the danger was communism and that there must be an alliance with the U.S. for defense.

But in this area we were suffering from western colonialism. There was the British occupation, and the French. Then after World War II, France left Syria and Lebanon, but Britain continued to occupy Egypt. Our main object was to get rid of the British colonialists—western occupation. Therefore, any new form of defense which constitutes any sort of western influence will be a new sort of colonialism.

This affects the internal front, inside the Arab countries. And that is why we put in front of the West the idea of defense without the help of any great power. We must convince the people they are really independent.

The Baghdad Pact, as was said by Mr. Eden in April, 1955, was an instrument to increase British influence in this area. That's why we opposed the idea. Appeals to other countries to join the Pact were appeals to pressure. This involved the area in the conflict between East and West.

The second thing was the Israeli aggression in February, 1955. This was also a main turning point. From 1952, when we took power here in Egypt, to 1955, there was no tension on the borders. Everything was quiet. We felt we were perhaps in a period of peace. But suddenly in February, 1955, there was this Gaza incident. Many people were killed. We felt the danger of Israel. Then after that there was the election campaign in Israel. The Herut party demanded expansion. This was headed by Menachem Beigin.

They said in election speeches that their Holy Land extended from the Nile to the Euphrates. This meant that if their party ever took power, the result would be war. Mr. Ben Gurion's policy was based on forcing settlement. But to force a peace also means war; you will begin by war and try to defeat your opponent before you can reach peace. This, to us, is also a threat.

Israel claimed it had been able to fulfill two-thirds of its armament program by supplies from the West—when we were not able to get any supplies from the West. This led to our arms deal with the Soviet Union. That was the second turning point in our relations with the U.S. There was a blockade against us—and the press campaign, especially in *The New York Times*. They say Nasser is a Communist, that Nasser works with communism.

But these are not Communist arms. Any weapons we receive from the outside become Egyptian weapons when we receive them, when they reach our ports. And we look to the Israeli danger with more concern than ever. We sought arms because we were facing a threat.

There were various pressures after the arms deal—until we were faced with the withdrawal of the High Dam offer. It was said in the newspapers that Nasser was playing the East against the West. We were not. We were working for the interest of our country. We asked the West for arms. We got none. We were negotiating with the West for the High Dam when the East came to us and offered help. I said no thank you.

It was the withdrawal of the High Dam offer which led to the nationalization of the Suez Canal. It was not because of the withdrawal itself. This was your right. It was because of the way it was done. The meaning of Dulles's statement was clear—to undermine the government. He also said something about our economic position. But this was not the real reason. So we nationalized. We feel that in spite of being a small country, we must not accept anything against our dignity. Then came the Eisenhower Doctrine. This means that the U.S. wants to influence this area and to have agreements to defend the area against aggression from the Soviet Union. But we had seen, all of us, that aggression was not from the Soviet Union but from Israel and the West. Its object was to isolate Egypt.

I then asked if Nasser could tell me anything about relations with the Soviet Union. He said:

There is no problem between the Soviet Union and Egypt. They have helped us greatly during the last two years. First, they helped us with arms supplies. Then, when we faced economic pressures and really needed help, they gave it. Our money was frozen in Britain and the United States. When we asked Russia to help us with petrol, they agreed at once. When the U.S. refused to supply us with wheat, they agreed. When we asked for a loan, they gave us a loan of $200,000,000. They haven't made any political request. It may be strange, but that's what happened: no single political request from the beginning of our relationship until right now. We asked them for so much help, and they were always agreeable to all we asked. There have been many articles in the American newspapers about troubles in relations between the Soviet Union and Egypt. This is all nonsense.

I then said I wished to return to the general subject of foreign policy within the Arab world. First of all—in terms of Arab federation of all the Arab countries—what were the maximum boundaries? For example, part of Turkey, the Sanjak of Alexandretta, had been a part of Syria. Part of southern Morocco was a disputed area in the southern Sahara. Does the Sudan come in? Is there a broad area which logically should be included in the overall Arab federation? Nasser smiled and said:

The Arab countries are those which speak the Arabic language, from Morocco to Iraq. Some are members of the Arab League. Some are not members because they were not independent; or they are independent but still suffering from French occupation, like Tunisia and Morocco.

We speak about Arab solidarity more than the solidarity of the Arab League. This means political agreements and military agreements for defense developed since the Israeli aggression. There were two ideas on how to defend the region: the Baghdad Pact and an alliance among only Arab countries. We formed an alliance among Egypt, Jordan, Syria, and Saudi Arabia. After that we faced the Suez aggression. And then American policy sought to isolate Egypt.

Syria was facing severe pressures, and this led to our present union. The Syrians asked for unity. It was not on our initiative. We had not anticipated this demand. We were forced to follow the will for unity between Egypt and Syria. But I don't think anyone can complain.

In Egypt, we had Communists and communism. The parties were all trying to get rid of these strings. But at the same time they were accused of being foreign agents. The extremists and the Communists can always adopt the nationalist line. They can inflame the big bloc of innocent people in the country—the masses who are always hesitant. We cannot permit the extremists and the Communists to act. The result would be internal instability. Some people can take advantage of such a position. Our problem is only to raise the national dignity of our country. At the same time we must convince the people we are not foreign agents but are working to fulfill our national line. In that way we will be able to isolate the Communists and extremist elements.

You Americans say the aggression will come from the Soviet Union. In such an aggression, of course, we will expect the West to help us. I said that to Mr. Eden in 1955. But what about aggression from the West? We'll ask for the Soviet Union's help. The West said it is impossible—aggression from the West. This was said to me by Mr. Eden himself. But what happened? The Big Three made a guarantee in 1950. And two of them joined Israel to break it.

I inquired: "What is your ultimate policy toward Israel? Do you think it should exist as an independent state and in what relationship to its Arab neighbors?" He said:

Until 1955, we thought time might solve these problems. This is not something that can simply be decided on paper: that Israel must be liquidated; or that Israel must stay. We are not the only power to decide that.

Certainly, we feel that aggression cannot lead to any result. Aggression can only be the beginning of something. Anyone can begin aggression. But nobody can know what will be the end of this aggression. Today the world is not the old world in which one was able to isolate part of it and deal with it apart. Today the world is connected.

Any situation could create a world war. Any action could affect the ultimate security of the world. So our policy is based on a period of peace in this area and stability. That is why we accepted the UNEF [UN Force].

But what about the future of Israel? What I feel important is the rights of the Arabs of Palestine. As long as the Arabs of Palestine are deprived of their rights there will be a problem. They were expelled from their homes, property, and land. Now they are refugees. One million live around Israel, while Israel receives 100,000 Jews a year from abroad.

The second question concerns our security—Arab security. Israel needs $1,000,000 every day just to continue. Suppose this aid ceases? What will be the result? The result will be expansion. We have to prepare ourselves to face any ideas of expansion.

I asked whether, over the long range, some kind of relationship could be worked up between Israel and neighboring states. He answered:

Every day we wait for news that Israel has invaded Egypt. On October 28, 1956, we were celebrating the birthday of one of my children when they brought in a message. It said Israel had invaded Egypt. This was 1956. One year later, on October 28, 1957, they again brought me a message. My first impression was that this must be another invasion. But it said there had been a bomb attack against Ben Gurion in the Knesset. Every day I wait for news of another invasion. This is the condition today—fear, no trust and no confidence. Tomorrow I wait for invasion.

"As long as Israel exists there is a danger?" I inquired. He said: "Yes, that is what we feel. That is the lesson of history. The turning point came in February, 1955. Since then we have had to spend a big part of the budget for arms instead of internal developments."

"Don't you think there is any form of insurance?" I asked. "No," he said. "There was the tripartite declaration to guarantee the borders, but two of the guarantors joined Israel to invade us. Even before that I said I had no trust in the tripartite agreement. From 1952 to 1955, I was an officer. The army asked me to give them all the arms they want. I was against this argument, but after the Gaza raid, of course I felt their fears."

I was puzzled about one thing. Everyone knew Nasser's concern with the Islamic world. Why had he no interest in the Muslims of Soviet Central Asia, whose religion was taken away from them. Nasser said:

I am a religious man. But I think mixing religion with politics may cause trouble. I suffered from this in Egypt. As for Muslims inside Russia: We sent some of our Islamic leaders to visit their areas. They visited Tashkent, Bokhara, and Samarkand. They told me the Muslims there have full freedom. I will visit these areas when I visit Russia.

How many people in the Soviet Union are members in the Communist party? I think less than ten million. These are the people who must follow the religious philosophy of Marx. But the others are free—those who are not members. That is according to what I know. I will get the opportunity to see for myself.

I asked if he had any program for establishing peace in Algeria, or peace in Palestine? He replied:

Of course we support the Algerians. They said we were training them. I told them we were not training them. If we wanted to train our people for guerrilla warfare, it would be the other way around. We would send them to learn in Algeria. They have the field there.

As for Israel, I told you at the beginning, it is not an easy question. In order to solve the question of Israel we have to solve the question of the refugees. This is the main problem. And as I told you, I think every day about a possible Israel invasion. We try and hope we can have a period of peaceful conditions. But in spite of that, any day there may be another Israeli aggression.

American newspapers always mention Israel's demands—Aqaba and Suez. They say Nasser is stopping Israel; Nasser is not permitting Israel to use the Suez Canal. No one mentions in American newspapers the rights of the Arabs of Palestine, who were expelled from their land, leaving all they owned. Aqaba and the use of the Suez Canal—these are the demands of Israel. The demands of the Arabs—the rights of the Palestinians to return to their land and to have their territory; the question of the frontier as decided in 1947; these are forgotten.

I said many Americans were concerned about Nasser's radio, the Voice of Free Africa. There was great emphasis on antiwhite, racist propaganda; racism is an evil thing and all good Americans are against it. Nasser was coy. Perhaps Free Africa was broadcast from Cyprus, he suggested. "Is it from Cyprus?" I asked. He replied:

There are nine secret broadcasting stations which started after nationalization of the Suez Canal—from France, from Cyprus, from Aden. A new one began last week adopting a line of black propaganda. We are sure these broadcasts are administered by the French. We have several of our own people working in these stations. So we know. They broadcast black propaganda against me and my government. I warned them if it does not stop, I will retaliate; that I would set up ten broadcasting stations; that I can do the same to them. I fixed a date, May 25 of last year. I said if they didn't stop their black propaganda, I would go into the field. Of course, you had better not write I said we have secret stations. Better not say this, my intelligence service would be angry with me."

I asked: "What is the position in the U.A.R. on non-Muslims?" He said:

There is no discrimination at all. They are equal in all rights because the law stands for all citizens, whatever their religion. In the Constitution, all people are equal whatever their color or religion.

We don't distinguish for minorities. For instance, we have Jews. We cannot expel any Jews because of the Constitution. But they can leave Egypt and go to Israel. They can have visas to go to Italy, thence to Israel. After the aggression we arrested some Muslims, some Christians. This was because they were dangerous elements. We arrested some Jews as fifth columnists. But we don't have questions of minorities.

I asked how long he planned to continue a one-party system in the U.A.R. He said:

In order to give an answer to that, we must see the background of the system. What is democracy? What is a police state? What is a dictatorship? Before the revolution, there were six or seven parties here and what you call democracy. But I think democracy is something subject to the social status of any country.

In this country, democracy represented the liberties of the landlords. They dominated the country. The farmers, who represent the majority of the country, were slaves of the land and the landlord. No one of them was able to say yes or no. If he said no, against the will of the landlord, he could be expelled and lose his daily livelihood. So democracy was a sort of system in which the landlord and the corrupt capitalist dominated the country.

After the revolution, we tried to keep the country under the old system of the parties. But we asked to have social reforms; first of all we put an end to feudalism and limit ownership of land and the influence of the corrupt capitalists who influenced the government. I felt the parties interfered. Therefore we discontinued them, liquidated them, put their leaders in prison, put into effect land reform, limited ownership of land, and redistributed the land to the people. We were therefore a free society in which a man could say yes or no. After that of course we were in a position to work for a free democracy.

I asked Nasser's views on communism. He said:

I have read all the books about communism from Marx to Engels to Stalin. And I have read all the books about Islam from the days of Muhammad until now. There are some things I like about communism —the planning, for example. But I don't like the materialist system. I don't like a government to be only capitalist. I don't like all the people to be workers, not owners. I want to have more owners in my country. I want to have some of the workers become owners. But I don't want to change owners into workers. This is part of the Communist system and Communist theory.

We give great consideration to the spiritual side. For instance, I cannot say that there is a God through materialism, but, through spirituality, I am convinced there is a God. I like materialism to work in connection with spirituality. This is our system. We have a planning system. But we work to give ownership to the people. We give great consideration to the spiritual side.

We are now working against feudalism, the landlords. We want to liquidate the landlords, to free people to say yes and no. If they all work for me, I am the only owner in this country. They would not be able to say yes or no. That is no answer, no freedom. The people must be sure no one will be able to take their land from them and that they have freedom to say yes and no. If I were to be owner of all the factories and industries, I could dismiss any worker and he would not be able to say yes or no. I like to have owners and workers. I like to secure the owner against the worker and the workers against the owner. The workers should not be able to strike before coming to a sort of agreement or discussion with the government and the owner. At the same time, we must secure the owner and the worker. Then we can have a free society in which anyone will be free. This is really my idea as a result of reading communism and reading Islam.

I asked why the Communist party is illegal in Egypt and Syria. He said: "All parties are illegal. The Communists before the revolution were banned. All parties are illegal now." I said: "But now you talk of two parties in five years' time. The Communists will say they want a party." He said: "This will depend on our understanding of democracy. In some years, there will be a party which will favor nonalignment; another party will say we must have alliance with the West; the Communists will want alliance with the East. This will be a real democracy—all points of view in the country. We are adopting nonalignment."

I asked how many bloc technicians were here. He said:

I don't think there is a large number. We ask for some special jobs. And we pay for them. But there are no conditions from Russia such as you make in your Mutual Assistance Security Act. This was what we disagreed about with you.

And I want to add—about technicians—we are a suspicious country. But their technicians work from 6 A.M. until 8 at night without discussing politics. There were, at the beginning, many technicians for the assembly of airplanes. None of them tried to interfere, but they gave our people a good example of their hard work. We sent some of our people to Russia—military people. None of them met with any discussion about politics. I think the main idea of the Russian line is sincerity. They are sincere in all relations with us.

I said I heard General Naguib had been sentenced to ten years' house arrest. Nasser said this was true. Naguib had conspired against the state. He was now "under house arrest. No, in his palace: palace arrest."

CAIRO, *March 26, 1958*

DINED with Ambassador Ray Hare, just back from Damascus, which is now part of his embassy. He says Nasser doesn't have an original mind. He doesn't act; he reacts.

He isn't so strongly pro-Russian as he seems. He'd like to balance things a bit by getting somewhat cozier with the U.S.A. At least that would give him a better trading basis.

Ray thinks the U.S.A. must realize that Nasser is a symbol of Arab nationalism. If he weren't there, it would be someone else. We should stop our totally negative attitude, which drives him toward Russia. There can't be any grand new plan at the moment. But we should behave like a big power, sit back blandly, talk politely, make no declarations, and play poker. The Israelis are showing a much more grown-up and mature attitude on Arab federation these days than the U.S.A.

DAMASCUS, SYRIA, *March 28, 1958*

LAST night, I had drinks and a talk with Charlie Yost who was ambassador in Syria, but who is now going since Damascus has become a consulate general in the U.A.R.

Charlie says that Nasser laid down tough conditions for Syrian union. But they were accepted. He stipulated that the army must be removed from politics and that all parties must be banned. The Syrian leaders, fearing an outbreak of internal strife, agreed.

This, says Yost, is the moment for a mild U.S. gesture of approval for the Arab Republic; to show they don't have to go to Russia for all their aid. These people need both help and psychological sympathy. But we can't go too far. We must continue to support the Iraq-Jordan federation, building dikes so the Egyptian-Syrian bloc doesn't flow onward unchecked.

BEIRUT, *March 31, 1958*

THIS afternoon, I visited Charles Malik, Lebanese foreign minister, a large, hook-nosed man with the face of an Italian condottiere. He is an historian (American University of Beirut), and a Greek Orthodox (in this largely Muslim country). He seems to fear Nasserism will spread to the Lebanon if the West does not smash him in Syria.

Nobody knows what U.S. policy in the Middle East is. Malik has been trying to find out—without success. Few people talk any more of either the Baghdad Pact or the Eisenhower Doctrine. There has been "lack of courage" in dealing with this area. The West keeps swallowing bitter pills and postponing the day of reckoning: one retreat after another; no backbone; no stand anywhere.

The most important decision to be taken is against Nasser. But the U.S. is dillydallying. There is a disturbing parallel now between the spread of Nasserism and Hitler's growth in Europe. Hitler was given a chance largely because other countries thought he might bulwark central Europe against communism. Today, many voices say the Syrian-Egyptian union stemmed communism in the Middle East. This is nonsense.

The entire existence of Nasser depends on Russia. At least Hitler had his own industry and economy. But Nasser gets his arms, his diplomatic support, his economic aid from Russia—and probably has secret understandings with Moscow. He is totally dependent.

There should be a frontal assault on Nasser's realm at its weakest point, Syria. Since 1949, Malik has been saying that *the* problem in this area is Syria. There is a vacuity of spirit and purpose in facing this.

He added: "For nine months, I have been telling the West that the order of priority has changed in the Middle Eastern problem. The Arab-Israeli question is no longer first. Now, and for a year, the primary problem is the eruption of Nasserism beyond the African continent. The second problem is the entry of communism into this area. The third is Israel."

Malik describes Nasserism as a "long-delayed reaction of Muslim-Arab spirit in the Middle East against the West." Islam itself was a self-conscious rejection of western thought and the Christian tradition. And the western nations were always rivals here. The last example was the Suez fiasco. The West is never in agreement on aims and methods. Europe, which is the natural representative of the West in this area, was weakened by two world wars. It can no longer stand on its own. And the inexperienced U.S.A. fumbled and erred.

And Communist influence has achieved some good in its social vision. Nasser has been influenced by this vision, which has reached him through Moscow.

These make up the phenomena of Nasserism. If the thing continues, Egypt will be dewesternized in six more years. Ever since Mohammed Ali—for about 150 years—Egypt has been half-heartedly opening up to the West and its ideas of freedom, intellectual thought, travel. Now, the only European influence to which it is open is communism. We face a new proletarianization in Egypt. There is no more interest in western thought, art, or philosophy. It is abhorred.

Nasser's only ideology is power, hatred, and nationalism. He has no concept of truth. There is no intellectual in his entourage. He exists on phony, bankrupt thoughts. His movement is inspired by emotionalism, nationalism, and an inferiority complex.

BEIRUT, *April 1, 1958*

FAREWELL drink with Rob McClintock, U.S. ambassador: a bright, charming man. He considers the function of a diplomat is to represent his country's strength in a polite way.

Says Malik is a handicap. He represents only the U.S. viewpoint and therefore draws all criticism to us like a lightning rod. You can't defeat the new with the old, no matter how good. And what a "galaxy of octogenarians" we have acquired. Malik, says Rob, is so nervous he recently called up and asked if we could get tanks over here from Cyprus within forty-eight hours.

McClintock was horrified when Don Heath, our ambassador in Saudi Arabia, and no Talleyrand, sent a telegram to the State Department this week quoting as the source of his information "the master of the royal garage."

OOSTERBEEK, HOLLAND, *April 25, 1958*

PRINCE Bernhard only drinks bourbon whisky. I asked why. He said he had laid in a wonderful stock of scotch just before the war. When the Germans occupied Holland he knew they would drink it all up so there and then he resolved to drink only bourbon.

Bernhard has recently come back from a hunting trip in Tanganyika where he got blood poisoning. He was afraid it was an infection in his back, where he has eight ribs missing after a lung operation in his youth. He showed me, to my horror, how he could push his hand through his shirt right into his back, as if—on the right side—it were a soft balloon.

BONN, GERMANY, *April 28, 1958*

TALK with Brigadier General Werner Panitzki, chief of staff to General Heusinger, inspector-general of the army. Panitzki is a big, blond, brutally handsome fellow with a thick scar on his forehead. He was a Luftwaffe bomber pilot. Now forty-seven, still air force, he looks like a bad dream in his gray uniform.

His office is in the compound that has mushroomed up around the old barracks which was the original defense ministry. It is symptomatic of the times—when old decorations, minus swastika, are again worn, when cemeteries are labeled "hero's" rather than "soldier's" graveyards again, when "war criminals" are now referred to as "war convicted."

Panitzki told me the Bundeswehr is part of the overall NATO force; therefore it has no strategy of his own.

To fulfill its role, Germany will and must have tactical atomic weapons. It would be impossible to equip this force differently from the allies fighting beside it. The enemy would break through at any point where it realized it was not being opposed by tactical nuclear weapons. This would split the front and make inevitable the use of strategical nuclear bombs on German soil.

BAD GÖDESBERG, GERMANY, *April 29, 1958*

DINED at the Bruces'. David is furious about the scandalous use of American counterpart funds by congressional junkets. They come abroad on missions, draw funds in local currency, and spend them on nightclubs, poker, presents. They don't have to account for this. The embassies are instructed to make money available and these "missions" abroad are classified so nobody is able to check.

COPENHAGEN, *May 2, 1958*

EXCELLENT talk with Ambassador Val Peterson, the former governor of Nebraska. Peterson thinks Eisenhower made two big mistakes. He failed to realize the need for a President to be an active leader of the party and he appointed to his Cabinet a group of men inexperienced in politics.

Peterson thinks we pay far too little attention to the heads of small countries. We should invite them to the U.S.A. more and roll out the red carpet—the way Russia does. We should invite people opposed by minorities—like Tito—and also the heads of small allies we take too much for granted. Peterson continued:

> Maybe Eisenhower is too tired to see them. Maybe Dulles is too busy and tired. I don't care. If the Russians have time to do these things, we should have time—no matter how tired the President and the Secretary of State are.

PARIS, *May 10, 1958*

WENT over to the embassy residence for a talk with Foster Dulles, here after the NATO meeting. Dulles remarked that no Secretary of State had been President since the early days of the republic. It was not a place from which to find higher office.

He thought perhaps his position had been misunderstood—"partly through my own fault." Now people realized he was neither as belligerent nor as rigid as he sometimes appeared. Dulles added:

> I don't expect to change my views on basic principles such as the nature and the rights of man. There is a permanent conflict in doctrine between ourselves and communism. This cannot be reconciled by any compromise. On this I must be steadfast. But this is a world of changing conditions. The application of principles changes. The situation varies. For example, the speech I made two days ago in Berlin was a tough talk. But that is a beleaguered city. You can't speak in terms of

mildness there. Berlin only keeps going because its people reflect a certain martial spirit. This spirit must be kept alive.

I asked whether there had been a shift in our Middle Eastern policy. He replied:

The situation is so changeable there that it is difficult to formulate a long-range policy. Our policy today is more on a day-to-day and place-to-place basis than in terms of a big overall program. The only stable element perhaps, is Nasser's popular appeal in terms of a Pan-Arab movement. But this does not have the necessary consolidating element behind it to be a successful policy. We must operate a good bit in terms of taking into account the developments in time and geography as they occur. It is a shifting situation.

I must say, Israel is relatively calm in the face of what is going on. I think theirs is a sound policy and I don't get the feeling that what is going on in the Middle East right now will be disastrous. I don't think the Soviets will take over in any way, like they did in Czechoslovakia. Such an overt take-over is too contrary to the visage that Russia is trying to present to other countries. It would be contrary to Moscow's own interests to rush in brutally. It will be quite a while before the Russians are ready to assume the oil interests in the Middle East. They have no marketing facilities. Middle Eastern petroleum would be a dubious asset to them. The Soviets themselves are exporters of oil. They can't pick up a billion dollars just by grabbing the wells. Iran found this out when they seized the petroleum. They had no market for it. And there were alternative supplies in the world which destroyed their bargaining position.

I asked what the U.S. attitude would be if the Russians came out and promised Nasser that they would support the 1947 frontiers for Israel. Dulles replied:

Nobody wants to go back to the 1947 settlement. Those were impractical borders. For example, the 1947 settlement gave all the Negev to Israel. But Egypt wants a land connection to the Arabs in Asia that goes across the Negev. Saudi Arabia likewise wants to do away with the Israeli port of Elath which is in the Negev. They would not get this by a return to the 1947 boundaries. Nobody can win Arab favor by asking for the 1947 settlement today. It doesn't give either Saudi Arabia or Egypt what they want.

I asked if the United States still felt bound by the 1950 tripartite agreement with Britain and France to preserve the status quo in Palestine. Dulles said: "We consider that the United States is still committed by the 1950 declaration. But the position of France and Britain is dubious. The British are equivocal and the French consider the declaration dead."

I asked if Dulles thought it might eventually be useful to have direct bilateral negotiations between the U.S. and Russia. He answered:

We must distinguish between exploratory talks and negotiation. The United States should never *negotiate* on behalf of other countries. Many of the matters which must be discussed involve several countries and many interests—for example in Asia or Australia. Too many countries are interested and involved. It would be a dangerous position for us to get ourselves into.

It is useful to be able to talk bilaterally in informal conversations, which are designed to ascertain whether there is a change in the Soviet viewpoint. For example, the end of the Berlin blockade came after an almost accidental and occasional conversation between Phil Jessup and the Russian envoy in the UN lobby. I see a value in such contacts. But this is quite different from formal negotiations.

I asked if Khrushchev were in real difficulty with the Stalinists in Russia. He replied:

We have no solid information that Khrushchev is in trouble, but we can draw inferences. For example, why does he keep beating the dead horse of the people he has already thrown out of office like Malenkov and Molotov? A logical answer is that he wants to warn others they face a similar fate if they oppose him. Khrushchev is the type of man who might not be easy to get along with for his associates. He is a jumping-jack sort of fellow, not cool and calculating in his mind. He is more of an impulsive type rather than a man given to cold logic. It is difficult for people to follow a jumping jack.

PARIS, *May 12, 1958*

SPENT yesterday with Tommy Thompson, ambassador to Moscow, golfing and lunching. Tommy said Khrushchev boozes much less in public now and is calling for a campaign against too much vodka drinking. He is extremely sensitive to public opinion.

Khrushchev is certainly still the boss. But many party leaders disliked his plan to dissolve Machine Tractor Stations. At this moment, it is an ideological step backward. Moving from state ownership to collectivism is a retrograde step in Communist ideology.

Khrushchev cannot let liberalism continue to grow without an eventual blowup. The intellectuals have become bolder in the new atmosphere. Many writers summoned to recant have obviously done so with tongue in cheek. Liberalism cannot be rationed and someday Khrushchev will have to crack down on it and move back in the direction of Stalinism.

The reason for the attack on Titoism is that Khrushchev now realizes he can no longer tolerate the heresy of a Communist state making independent decisions without first clearing them with Moscow. When Khrushchev was in Hungary, he became acutely aware of where this ultimately leads. He found himself forced to hit Tito who had often boasted that China backed his ideas. Khrushchev resolved to use China to smash Tito.

PARIS, *May 15, 1958*

LUNCH with Randolph Churchill. He says his father is very old and tired and really doesn't follow anything nowadays. It might be better if he died. Yet, although failing and fatigued, he is in excellent medical health.

Henry Hopkinson told Randolph he spent the weekend with Eden, and he suggested it had been a mistake for England to go into Suez; it would have been smarter to let the Israelis get there on their own. Eden was horrified. Next morning at breakfast he said: "I couldn't sleep all night. You know, I don't think you are right about what you said, but I must admit the idea had never occurred to me." Both Hopkinson and Randolph were appalled.

Dulles told Randolph the real reason for the American attitude at the time of Suez was not fear of Soviet rockets and war, but Britain's financial crisis. Capital was flowing out at a tremendous rate. Harold Macmillan called Washington and asked for $1,000,000,000 to be made available immediately in order to prevent a catastrophic devaluation of the pound. Dulles said it would be politically impossible to provide emergency help without an immediate ceasefire. Eden accepted his terms. "Thus," says Randolph who calls Eden the Jerk, "the Jerk ordered us into Suez and the Jerk ordered us out again."

Randolph recently saw Aristotle Onassis, who says the leaders of the West are floundering in ineptitude. He adds: "If you gave them Aladdin's lamp they would be afraid to rub it and tell the genie what to do."

DE GAULLE

MARCHES BACK

PARIS, *May 15, 1958*

D E GAULLE WILL BE THE LEADER OF FRANCE WITHIN A VERY
short time—I should say a maximum of seventy-two hours. I
went over to see Ambassador Houghton at 3:30. The poor chap
is perplexed. He was kind enough to recall our conversation of a couple of
months ago when I predicted de Gaulle would come in and said one possible means would be when the army ceased to obey the government. I asked
why the State Department had put out to Washington correspondents last
night their impression that de Gaulle would fail? He said "Lord knows;
they didn't get it from us."

He had heard a rumor that General Ely, chief of staff of the armed
forces was contemplating resignation. General Ganeval, President Coty's
military aide, is saying that if the government cannot establish its prestige
rapidly, Coty will have to summon de Gaulle. Houghton promised to
find out two things for me; namely whether Ely was loyal and in office,
and whether the air force was loyal. We would refer to Ely as "Smith"
on the phone and the air force would be "those guys."

Next, I had coffee with Raymond Laporte at a café outside the National Assembly. Laporte is now chef de cabinet for Maurice Faure, minister of the interior. Raymond looked up at the cloudy sky and said:
"Thank God for the weather. This will make an airborne assault on Paris
difficult."

He told me the following: General Ely, chief of staff, resigned this
morning. The security forces last night tried to arrest his two principal
assistants, General Challe and General Martin, without even advising him.
So he resigned. There is no commander of the French army at this moment.

Nobody knows whether the air force is loyal, but it appears dubious. General Chassin, a leading air force general, is in hiding.

The Ministry of the Interior does not know who precisely started the plot. There is no evidence that de Gaulle promoted it, but he is fully aware of it, although no one can say whether he gave it his blessing.

Paris is safe as far as street fighting or a putsch are concerned. The police and the security forces have been mobilized to protect key points. But in many arrondissements the commissariats of police have been shut with signs outside saying they are closed in order to send every available man to essential places.

De Gaulle is under protection of security forces, on the grounds that his life has been threatened by the left. I asked Laporte if either the Communists or the Gaullists had arms available for fighting. "Everyone has arms," he said sadly.

It would be easy for the military rebels in Algeria to send four or five thousand paratroopers to Paris because almost the entire Air Transport Command is down there. The crowd, including the police, would go wild over them.

Laporte thinks General Ganeval is probably in the plot. There is only one choice now and that is between de Gaulle and the Popular Front. Raymond adds: "I will do everything against the Popular Front."

I telephoned General Pierre Billotte. He told me de Gaulle has no paramilitary organization now. But he added: "Why would he need it? All the troops are for him. De Gaulle is the only reality whether you like him or not. The only choice is between de Gaulle and a Popular Front. That means de Gaulle. The police and the army won't fight for a regime that doesn't exist."

Later Laporte dropped in for a drink. He said hoarding of food has started in Paris. The grocers are sold out. He claims the French are crazy; this coup has had no more effect on Parisians than a coup in Paraguay. But it is really so serious that Maurice Faure, minister of interior, sent his children out of Paris for safety this afternoon.

Tomorrow, Faure will be replaced by Jules Moch, a tough Socialist.

The story of General Ely is fascinating. Yesterday evening, Mollet, as vice premier, summoned General Challe (one of Ely's two right-hand men) to ask about the condition of the forces. Challe told him they were all behind Massu and de Gaulle. Mollet said nothing. But shortly afterward, he had Challe sent to fortress arrest in Brest. The same thing happened to General Martin, the other right-hand.

Early this morning, Ely stormed in to de Chevigné, minister of defense, raised hell, and resigned. But this afternoon, around 6:00 P.M., Ely was prevailed upon by Coty and Prime Minister Pflimlin to resume his old post.

PARIS, *May 16, 1958*

THE last time de Gaulle threatened to come out of retirement and seize the helm one of his supporters complained: "He marched us to the Rubicon; and then he told us to take out our fishing rods." This is no angling party. On the surface, Paris appears *insouciant*. But danger rumbles underneath.

Revolution and counterrevolution are curiously permanent realities in France. And, as the faltering republic strives to defend itself, each faction that would destroy it speaks of national honor. National honor is an acetylene torch that can be set to anything.

France lies helpless before those who would employ unconstitutional methods. This is increasingly a struggle between the extreme left, which clamors for a Popular Front, and the Gaullists, over the Fourth Republic's sickened body.

Trade unions have ordered labor to prepare to protect democratic liberties. The Socialist party announces: "The republic is menaced." And in three successive directives, the Communist Politburo has commanded workers to rally in factories, towns, and villages and not to allow "factionalists" to gain control of the streets.

The government has decreed dissolution of a handful of ragtag and bobtail hoodlums' groups that specialize in chalking up provocative slogans and baiting the gendarmes.

But the real right, to which the center is rapidly gravitating, backs de Gaulle, who sits quietly under a "protective" security watch in his distant country estate.

For the record, the military coup in Algiers would seem to have been an unplanned putsch led by a bunch of disheartened desperadoes.

Its leaders are impressive bully-boys. General Massu rejoices in the nickname "Roughneck." One of his colleagues, Colonel Thomaso, is known as "Leather Nose."

Did these men alone decide to seize the helm? That is hardly likely. Massu has the political brain of a pumpkin. But behind him and beside him are shadowy agents of civilian leaders who owe allegiance to de Gaulle.

This is undoubtedly a deep conspiracy. Mysterious arrests are taking place. De Gaulle's old hatchet man, Soustelle, is under surveillance. Thanks to efficient police dispositions, Paris has been rendered safe, although many political cliques have arms. But what about France? The bulk of the army and all its striking force are in Algeria. So are the Air Transport planes.

PARIS, *May 17, 1958*

DURING its eleven years of existence, this unsteady Fourth Republic has reflected almost every weakness of its unhappy predecessor, the Third Republic, in whose image it was created. The position of postwar France, liberated from tyranny and occupation, has curiously followed the pattern of another France, the First Republic of the revolution, which endured until Napoleon's *coup d'état* of the Eighteenth Brumaire.

The *coup d'état* in Algeria pretends both to consummate and, in effect, to abolish the republic. And, like the maneuver that produced Napoleonic rule, this plot was evidently organized from within the government as well as from without. Like Bonaparte, de Gaulle had evident supporters among those in power, above all in the army.

The shock has come from Africa. The force that brought Franco to Madrid was generated in Morocco. The force that seeks to push de Gaulle back to Paris was generated in Algeria.

Already, before the coup began, Jean-Paul Sartre, speaking of democracy's degradation, warned: "The real government is in Algeria." Georges Bidault, a former Rightist Premier, told his countrymen: "Let the republic perish rather than French Algeria."

PARIS, *May 18, 1958*

THE French drama has assumed the aspects of a ritual play in which all principal actors seem obligated by some code to deceive both themselves and the audience. The reason for this pretense is a desire to avoid provocation and fratricide, but the spectacle seems strangely sham.

The government pretends to believe the military putsch in Algeria is not a coup against itself. Yet every leader of that action has been making totally seditious statements. The heads of the insurrection that is officially not an insurrection seek to bypass Parliament along clearly unconstitutional lines.

No official from the Premier on down has dared brand the patently rebellious leaders as rebels. And the Communists, who have been issuing manifestoes ordering protests in the streets and factories, managed only the pale imitation of a strike.

General Salan in theory acts for the government as commander in Algeria. He solemnly insists the coup "is not a coup or an action against the republic." Nevertheless he associates his person with demands for a de Gaulle administration.

De Gaulle himself emerges from self-imposed isolation only to utter cryptic statements that might have been the envy of Delphi's enigmatic oracle. He blesses the Algerian conspirators who wish to upset the will of Parliament. Yet he speaks, as it were, in the name of the republic.

De Gaulle sets himself up as a neutral arbiter. Is he truly neutral? Is it coincidence that Lieutenant Neuwihr, military spokesman of the Algerian Committee of Public Safety, visited the General just before leaving for Algiers? Is it accident that those who claim to act on de Gaulle's behalf, without his knowledge, should demand that he "arbitrate" the day before he offers to do precisely that?

The French army is the real fulcrum of the forces playing in this almost oriental ceremony. It prides itself on a tradition of avoiding politics. It teaches its officers allegiance to the republic. Yet even Marshal Juin, France's senior officer, announces he has "no more confidence" in the regime.

The Praetorian Guard is the elite of parachutists. This provided the backbone for the Algerian putsch. The government worries almost every night when rumors start about a sudden airborne descent on Paris.

The only forces maintaining security around the capital are the police deployed beneath the chestnut trees. But just two months ago, some seven thousand of these same police, wearing mufti, marched on the Assembly hollering "Into the Seine with the Deputies."

The greatest paradox in this paradoxical crisis is the position of the army. It argues it is not involved in conspiracy against the republic. But it endorses de Gaulle's implied conception of that republic: "La République c'est moi."

Operating as a power within the state that in effect seeks to reform the state, the army insists it is not plotting. But, in the same breath, it specifies its own conditions for settling the impasse. Today the only solution it considers acceptable is de Gaulle's return.

Neither by sentiment nor by recent tradition has the army been Gaullist. But it has suddenly swung its influence behind the General. It now considers his person, his prestige, and his concepts the only logical answer to the problems of France and Algeria.

PARIS, *May 19, 1958*

THIS morning, I dropped in to see Colonel Jean-Louis de Rougemont, one of the closest friends of General Ely and now a professor at the French War College. I asked him where a soldier's duty lay when there was a civil split in his country. He said he has just been lecturing on this. He has given "two" lectures on military honor. The first was easy because it dealt with battlefield honor. The second is an infinitely more difficult problem.

He told the officers in his class that their allegiance is always to the government except when the structure of France itself is endangered. By this he meant some form of Communist administration or an administration influenced by Communists. He had not foreseen development of the present situation.

The last time the French army interfered directly in politics was in 1830, when two thousand officers considered it necessary to resign *en bloc*. The War College desperately hopes the army can now stay out of the political dispute. I showed Jean-Louis the order-of-the-day sent out yesterday by General Ely. It asks all troops to maintain "cohesion and unity," but it does not mention the republic.

PARIS, *May 22, 1958*

THIS afternoon, I went to see General Ely in his apartment in the Ecole Militaire. An extraordinarily nice and noble man, he looked old and tired. He was wearing a blue suit which hung loosely on his skeleton figure. He has a bad right arm and of course shakes hands with his left arm. His face looked pale and almost like a skull.

He thought men like General Massu, if involved in the conspiracy, had become involved only at the last minute in order to prevent bloodshed and in the sense of general discipline. Ely continued: "I was in contact with General Salan in Algiers several times by telephone directly from Premier Pflimlin's office on the night of Tuesday–Wednesday. [Just after Pflimlin's formation of a government, also the day of the Algerian coup.] I asked Salan to avoid bloodshed and restore order. I did this in Pflimlin's presence. Several times from Pflimlin's office I spoke to Salan. General Salan is following my instructions."

Ely said Massu had been fighting for a long time. He was a tough man but nevertheless wise. As for General Salan, he was obeying the government and at the same time crying long live de Gaulle. He was obliged to do this. Massu was nearer to the people than Salan. Therefore Massu had to "appear more ahead," to use Ely's own words. Ely added:

In such a revolution, one must place oneself in the spirit of what is taking place in order to understand it. There is a very peculiar psychological situation in the world. This psychological situation had included such incidents as Indochina, Suez, and our war in Algeria. They are all provisional stages of permanent psychological war. It is a revolutionary war. We have pushed our cadres to learn this war. Our generals in Algeria are well versed in it. They feel it. They feel something new in it. There are different methods of acting in this kind of war. One must command the mob in a different way from in the past. We in the West do not understand this kind of war very well yet. It is a big development for our age.

The Suez campaign is an interesting example. One cannot deny it showed that Nasser, by psychological force, transformed a military defeat into a political victory. The Russians and Arabs would comprehend well the situation now taking place in Algeria. Nasser triumphed by lies. He decorated officers for "sinking" the battleship *Jean Bart*. Now it is a "fact" that the *Jean Bart* was sunk. Of course it was not sunk. But if we were to send the *Jean Bart* through the Suez Canal now, Nasser would say we had rebuilt it in a hurry in order to demonstrate that he had not sunk it. Psychological war is a lie, and we in the West do not know how to lie.

We talked about Ely's resignation. He said: "I resigned not only for the little but serious incident of Challe and Martin. I also resigned in order to maintain cohesion and unity in the army. Young officers of the metropole might think in this sense that General Ely was not with them in Algeria. That would have created a schism in the army. That had to be avoided at all costs."

Ely is convinced General de Gaulle is coming to power. He said: "I esteem that today there is no other solution. Eight days ago there was. Now it is only a question of de Gaulle."

I asked Ely if the army was behind de Gaulle, behind Pflimlin, or split in its opinions. He said: "The army is for de Gaulle as the only solution. This is not for reasons of sentiment, but for reasons of logic. The army was not especially Gaullist before. But de Gaulle is the only man now who can heal the break. He would only come in for a few months, but he could do it in that time."

Ely continued: "De Gaulle must come quickly now. The Algerian situation cannot be reversed. You can change men, but you cannot change fact. The Algerian situation is a fact. Therefore the only place to act is here in Paris, the solution of the problem must come here."

After leaving Ely, I rushed out to see Norstad at SHAPE. He said:

The armed forces in Algeria have been increasingly upset. For eight years, they have been being killed. And they saw no policy in Paris. They had no chance of victory or success. Why? Because of a weak government which was only interested in keeping itself in office. Many of the highest French officers have said to me: "We have been killed and have been killing. And it makes us sick. There is no solution."

The army did not conspire. But like all armies, it responds to strong leadership. In Algeria the army only had two choices. It could shoot at the rioters, or it could join them. It did the latter.

I asked what would be the position of NATO when de Gaulle came to power. He said:

There are reports that to establish the position and prestige of France, de Gaulle might try to deal directly with the Russians. This frightens me. But within the last five days an increasing number of people have gone out of their way to assure me de Gaulle is not anti-

American and anti-NATO. They tell me he has progressed beyond the point of feeling that he could safely deal with the Russians outside NATO. I hope this is true.

There can be no plans for a NATO minus France. It is a mistake to even think in those terms.

No one can be so stupid as to think there is a future for France outside of the alliance. I will put all my marbles on that one.

De Gaulle, he said, might want to be tough. But NATO also could be tough. It could be tough back at de Gaulle. The Germans said de Gaulle's coming to power was the last solution Adenauer had wished. They recalled: "We Germans had a corporal who came to office legally also."

Norstad foresaw that de Gaulle would "yap about commands in NATO, but he will have to deal with me. I am the commander of NATO and it is for me to make the commands. If he wants to complain he can complain to me. I'll tell him he can fire me if he wants to, but I am not going to change my commands unless I wish to do so."

PARIS, *May 26, 1958*

LUNCH with Gajewski, the Polish ambassador. He thought the situation was probably even more dangerous than 1956, at the time of Suez. Too many unknown people might change the present French crisis into a world crisis leading to war.

France's Communist party was floundering and worried. The Communists remembered the 1939 Hitler-Stalin Pact, which had left them isolated. Many were afraid Moscow really wanted to have de Gaulle in and was going to sell them down the river. Vinogradov, the Soviet ambassador, has seen de Gaulle several times.

De Gaulle told Gajewski that when he went to Moscow in late 1944, he told Stalin Russia must give two things to Poland—the Oder-Neisse frontier in the west and internal freedom. He said, "Together, we [meaning de Gaulle and Stalin] can give peace and freedom to Poland and Europe." Gajewski sneered in an amused way, saying that France was even weaker then than it is now. De Gaulle's argument was that no Polish government could afford ever to be anti-Russian if it knew that Russia had imposed the western border, giving Poland a large piece of Germany. But Russia did not give freedom.

Ambassador Houghton is pretty glum. He now hopes de Gaulle can come in legally and quickly. However, he is terribly afraid civil war may break out. Every day that goes by, army hotheads gain in ascendency. It would certainly be much more difficult to deal with a man like Massu than de Gaulle.

There is an absolute air of unreality at the Quai d'Orsay, which is so out of touch with events. It is no longer possible to distinguish between fact and fiction. For forty-eight hours the embassy has been getting reports that places like Marseille, Toulouse, and Pau had been taken over by Gaullist "Committees of Public Safety." But every time the embassy checks, these stories prove untrue.

PARIS, *May 27, 1958*

EVERYTHING seems over with the Fourth French Republic save for the shouting—or the shooting.

Today, while Pflimlin and his legally constituted government were still in office, de Gaulle was already issuing a statement of far more significance and impact than anything promulgated by the Assembly or the Premier. The first act draws to an end.

During a confused fortnight, whatever initiative Paris might have gained by ruthlessness was dissipated by inaction. For the sake of avoiding bloodshed the regime chose to appear as if it supported the intrigue against itself. Premier Pflimlin was in the position of a man who finds a burglar rifling his safe. At gun's point, he tells the intruder to continue. Later he announces: "I wasn't burgled. The man was acting on my instructions."

Jules Moch, the Socialist who once broke Communist riots, was minister of interior, but his famous will power seemed paralyzed. No organization was rallied to fight for the republic. Only the Communists, somewhat frightened and half-hearted, talked tough.

Helmeted gendarmerie are still under the chestnut trees. But they are unlikely to battle for this government against anyone but Communists, certainly not against de Gaulle.

For days, the Assembly has been passing ritual resolutions. For all their significance these might have been endorsing motherhood. One of Parliament's rare unanimous votes expressed gratitude to the army—already engaged in insurrection.

Some politicians commenced acrobatic swerves in an effort to catch the accelerating Gaullist bandwagon. The day before he fled to Algiers, Pascal Arrighi, a Corsican deputy, told friends he was off to Taiwan. He showed his passport with a Chinese visa. That same passport included a wad of American dollars. "Why do you need so much money on a free official journey?" he was asked. Arrighi had the grace to blush. Today he is in secessionist Corsica.

The Communists are in an odd position. Like their brethren in Germany at the time of the Hitler-Stalin deal or like their own fathers they are between two millstones. One is the long-range Kremlin game played in Russia's own interest and happy to see de Gaulle shatter the present regime. The other is the anticommunism of de Gaulle. The local party may have its brain in what it does during the ensuing days; but not its heart.

PARIS, *May 28, 1958*

IT looks as if de Gaulle will be in power by midnight. Lunch with Billotte at Lucas-Carton. Alex Allegrier-Carton (the proprietor) came up for his usual chat. De Gaulle for the past several years, has always stayed in his hotel, the La Pérouse. "He will no longer be my guest next time," said Alex. "He will have different lodgings—but cheaper for him."

Before meeting Billotte, I had a talk with Jean Laloy. He is furious at Dulles, who said he was glad to see France, as an independent country, have a fully independent government produced by independent choice. "What kind of a government does Dulles think we have had during the last twelve years?" he asked. "Does he think we have been satellites? Does Dulles think *I* have been working for *him*? I have been working for France and for the cause of the whole western world."

Laloy was distressed by all the sneering remarks now being made about the Fourth Republic. "It is ridiculous," he said, "to say that the Fourth Republic did nothing. The republic did many things. It achieved positive results in an economic sense and with its foreign policy. It even created an army so strong that this same army is now in a position to destroy the republic."

Moscow hopes de Gaulle will come in—no matter how many French Communist heads are cracked—in order to destroy the republic. Moscow then calculates de Gaulle will be a French Nasser who will play a policy of neutrality and balance of power. Since this would destroy the real balance of power that now exists, it would benefit the Kremlin. Then, later, the Russians would hope for a new round of chaos, a failure by de Gaulle, and the eventual take-over of a Popular Front government controlled by Communists.

Billotte said both Houghton and Burgess (our ambassador to NATO) had told him in detail of my last conversations with de Gaulle, including what the General said about *coups d'état*, the role of the army, policy towards EURATOM, and European Union, etc. This horrifies me. Houghton had promised to keep it all superclassified. I said to Billotte: "But I never see Burgess and I know damned well I never told him anything." Said Billotte with a smile: "But Houghton did."

PARIS, *May 30, 1958*

A MIASMA of incipient terror has lifted. The capital is still glutted with leaden police concentrations. Secondary airports are blocked by barbed wire. There is a surly undertone of grumbling in the Red belt. And the unhappy Parliament, so fittingly decorated with that style of mural painting known as *trompe l'oeil* or illusory, echoes failures. But the nightmare of violence has been swept away by a Gaullist wind.

The splendid Place de la Concorde, where hard-bitten Frenchwomen knitted beside the guillotine during this country's great revolution, presented a different aspect last night. No grim harridans clacked needles to the slicing off of heads. Instead, automobiles massed, tooting frenetic horns in honor of de Gaulle. The noise violated a strict city ordinance. And the sentiment violated the Fourth Republic.

In effect, what this noisy sentiment meant to indicate was sudden endorsement of the *coup d'état* in favor of the General. Everybody has chosen, with remarkable self-deception, to avoid use of the embarrassing phrase. Yet it was a coup that ended the regime.

PARIS, *May 31, 1958*

LUNCH with Pierre Courtade today. He assured me that the party intended to act only in a legal way and begged me to see Thorez as soon as possible.

Pierre gave me a rather labored explanation that in all probability, he would be a liberal Democrat if he were an American. But in France, there was no way of expressing opposition except by being a Communist. I told him: "I am against dictatorship in any form and any country. I don't care if it comes from the left, right, or center. You get your orders. I don't get mine."

Courtade resented that I had written that the French Communist party today was in the same psychological position as in 1939, when Hitler signed his pact with Stalin. But he grudgingly conceded that it was to Moscow's interest to have de Gaulle in power in order to break up NATO.

He confided to me ("Mais tu jures que tu le gardes toujours secret") that there was a deep and bitter feeling in the "highest quarters" of the French Communist party against Moscow. He said: "You will see. We are not going to follow them forever. We represent the left. We are French. We will not be their slaves." I inquired, "You mean you are becoming Titoists?" He changed the subject.

Pierre is filled with historical references. He recalled the cynical remark of the Abbé de Sieyès about Robespierre: "He will go far; he believes what he says." He recalled that Napoleon had described Talleyrand as "a silk stocking filled with shit." He was implying this when he wrote a few days ago about the paratroopers; that their aims were disguised in the silk of parachutes.

PARIS, *June 2, 1958*

LONG talk with Jean Monnet. He could not mask his concern about the possibility that de Gaulle would reverse the trend toward European integration.

He had no doubt that Couve de Murville "is with us" on basic policy. "But," he added, "de Gaulle is the boss. Much will depend on how long de Gaulle stays in power and on the form of the new Constitution. I am not too worried about what de Gaulle has told you concerning his attitude on European integration. De Gaulle's tactic has always been the same. He says no first; then he adjusts to yes later."

Monnet thought de Gaulle the best solution for France's critical problems and that he was not a dictator. He added:

He is an artist, an artist in power. He is not a dictator in the conventional sense of an organized party with all its trappings. He wants to renew the bonds with the past, the ties which he thinks have been destroyed. He has the greatest authority of anyone in France and can therefore solve the North African problem better than anyone else. He has the necessary prestige and he is a great chief. I think he means to settle the North African mess. And I think he will put the army in its place. He is not a faction or a party, he is France, historic France.

He is against any indiscipline. This is not because he is a general and therefore understands discipline. It is because he has a sense of proportion. Furthermore, he is fully aware that North Africa is not France. Both North Africa and the army can better be put in order by him than by any other Frenchman. De Gaulle must be considered as a common denominator among many people and many currents of thinking who can find no other common denominator.

If de Gaulle were alone, because of his authoritarian temperament, he might make bad proposals. But he is aided by men like Mollet, Pinay, and others. There are some things those men will not accept. There is a good chance of really good proposals to modify the Constitution resulting from discussions among these men. I am hopeful.

De Gaulle is not a dictator. He is French. You can argue with him. The people he has chosen to be around him will serve as a security against arbitrary decisions. I say this even though he does not respect them too much.

PARIS, *June 3, 1958*

LUNCH with Jean-Louis de Rougemont, happy as a clam in full uniform with all his decoration ribbons. General Ely has just been reappointed chief of staff for all the armed services. Jean-Louis says he had access, in the War College, to reports on previous students which are kept secret while these officers are alive. When de Gaulle was a young captain there his professor observed that he behaved "like a king in exile."

PARIS, *June 4, 1958*

LUNCHED with Bertrand de Jouvenel, a real French intellectual, who lives in a country chateau, writes, and runs an economic news service. He says it is impossible to consider a constitution "sacred" in this country because there have been so many. One can only consider a constitution sacred in the U.S., where there has been but one, and in England where there isn't any at all.

He claims—and this I have never heard before—that Léon Blum deeply desired the restoration of the monarchy because he thought it provided a stable system under which you could alternate between left-wing and right-wing governments. Vincent Auriol saw to it that the law exiling the Orléans pretender's family was repealed, thus permitting the return of the Comte de Paris, because this had been "Blum's death wish."

On the way out, Alex Allegrier-Carton, who owns the hotel La Pérouse as well as the restaurant Lucas-Carton, told me de Gaulle is staying in his hotel. He moved officially to the Matignon yesterday but still sleeps in his four-room apartment at the La Pérouse.

PARIS, *June 9, 1958*

YESTERDAY dined at the Billottes'. Pierre says that four months ago Soustelle called at de Gaulle's office and asked to see the General. Colonel de Bonneval said de Gaulle could not receive him because he was too busy. Soustelle was furious. "What," he said, "de Gaulle will not even say a word to his old friend Jacques Soustelle?" The door opened and a long nose stuck out. "Monsieur Soustelle is quite correct," said de Gaulle to Bonneval. "I would not refuse to see him without a word." Then he looked at Soustelle and said, "Adieu."

When Billotte first met de Gaulle in London in the autumn of 1941, de Gaulle eyed him coldly and said: "Why were you a prisoner? I have no respect for prisoners." Pierre reminded de Gaulle he had been a prisoner during World War I and had not even managed to escape—as had Billotte. He himself had been taken prisoner because his tank blew up and every other member of its crew killed. He was so angry that he turned down de Gaulle's invitation to dinner. Immediately afterward he became his chief of staff.

De Gaulle was very worried about the outcome of World War II, until Pearl Harbor. However, when he learned that Japan had attacked the United States, he was deeply relieved. He began to speculate about the contest for authority in the postwar world between America and Russia.

LONG talk with André Malraux: terribly tense, pale, and electric. He grimaces constantly and speaks faster than any man I know. Since he thinks even faster than he speaks, his tongue is always racing to catch up with his mind. After five minutes with the brilliant Malraux, who by then is speaking a kind of French shorthand, I long for the composed paragraphs of de Gaulle.

I gathered from what he said he is a combination of orchestra conductor and stage manager, a sort of super P. T. Barnum. As he says: "I orchestrate," in the new government.

He said there were "two capital things" he is working on, scientific research and housing. "We must put an end to our absurd backwardness in these fields," Malraux said. "This is a serious challenge."

As far as appeals to the left went, the government wanted a much greater participation by the workers in the national life. "We want a modern France with full participation by the workers." It would be a great mistake to imagine that the present regime was merely a legatee and executor of the Fourth Republic. He said:

> The Fourth Republic is dead. It did not die as a result of an Algerian or military conspiracy. That is a legend. It died of Dien Bien Phu and Sakiet.
>
> General de Gaulle has made a government designed to reform the institutions of France. These reforms will be presented to the people. And if the people approve—that will be the Fifth Republic. But in between, we are not the executors of the Fourth Republic. We are a government of public safety. In a few months we want to save France and enable France to make her own decisions.

Malraux said de Gaulle would prepare a "presidential constitution something like the American Constitution," and a "social reform something like the American New Deal." Above all, he said there must be a swift and extensive improvement in workers' conditions. I asked him about de Gaulle's old idea of labor-capital *associations*. He said, "That idea, that word, has not been mentioned from the government camp. Algeria, peace in Algeria, is the only question of the moment."

Malraux said:

> The RPF was a movement just to gain power. Now we have power. The RPF is not needed now. It is finished. As for the political parties? What are the chances of the parties? This depends upon how the people accept the new constitution. Right now, there is no question of new parties. Right now, it is a question of saving the country first and the country is menaced by both the left and the right.

You can't talk of democratic parties or a democratic party system when you have established in the midst of them a powerful Communist party like that in France. A party system is doomed the day a party which does not play fairly, like the Communist party, gains a position of strength such as the Communists have here. The reality of democracy ceases to exist.

We must weaken the Communist party. But that doesn't mean we have to go to dictatorship.

I said I was astonished at how weak the Communist party had proven during the crisis, and I asked him why he thought this had been the case. He said: "Budapest was the first reason for weakness. Then there was the lassitude of the working class. Despite all the slogans, they saw no change in their status. And, apart from the hard core of the party, most of the people who vote for it are genuinely French. As Frenchmen, they saw hope in General de Gaulle."

Malraux made the odd remark: "Communism destroys democracy, but maybe democracy also destroys communism. We will beat the Communists by doing what they didn't do. But if we don't do this, we won't beat them."

In the end, I reminded Malraux that he had once told me he considered the two real "giants" he had met to be de Gaulle and Maxim Gorki. "Ah no," he said. "Of course Gorki was not a political figure. Maybe he was a giant in the way he ignored little details. Of course I have known very few of the big leaders of the world. Really only de Gaulle, Stalin, and Nehru. I think Nehru and de Gaulle are the giants I have known."

As I was leaving I remarked to Malraux that I presumed he wasn't writing these days. "No," he said. "This is no time for literature."

PARIS, *June 17, 1958*

TODAY, Maurice Thorez, the French Communist boss, received me in party headquarters, a large building on the edge of the banking district, almost a fortress. Even the front door is opened by a tough character who regards you carefully before he unlocks. You walk up one flight to a grilled gate which is opened only after scrutiny. Then, there is an elevator to Thorez's third-floor office. Thorez looked surprisingly well despite the stroke he suffered a few years ago, which has completely crippled his right arm. His face was ruddy and healthy.

I asked why the Communists called de Gaulle a fascist. He replied:

We do not call him a fascist, although he formed a government, in abnormal circumstances and on an illegal basis, which is in reality a personal dictatorship. He came in by force and is maintained in power by the military. Such a situation can lead only to fascism. But it is not yet fascism. Fascism is a regime of open, violent dictatorship that is at the same time demagogic. It is a dictatorship of capital. It openly denies democracy and destroys the democratic rights of everyone, the bourgeoisie and the workers. It is the negation of all liberty. Such conditions of fascism do not at present apply. But we fear this government is heading toward it. Indeed, de Gaulle himself speaks against the "regime of parties."

I knew de Gaulle, of course. And I am convinced that he does not have the same conceptions as other people of the republic or of democracy. All his ideas are different from those of bourgeois and worker republicans. And his ideas and methods can only lead to fascism.

When de Gaulle relinquished power in 1946, he summoned all his ministers one day to the Matignon. He said: "Sirs, I am going." There was no explanation. That was all. Since that moment I have been convinced that de Gaulle would never suffer the control of any group, not even the Constituent Assembly of that time. You can see right now his very first gesture has been to give the deputies the gate. He is used to bossing a team, not leading a government. He is not a *chief* of *government*. He cannot tolerate such a position. Because of all this we are more than mistrustful.

How would the party react if the government tries to outlaw it. He said:

We will defend ourselves. We are already doing this. The working class and the unions have declared themselves against personal dictatorship. It is hard to smash them. And our party has a solid connection with these masses. We count on the masses. We count on the Republican Committees of Defense. They will find arms if necessary. The FTP partisans had no arms during the war when they were first formed. But they found them.

Thorez said the French army had joined with the rich capitalists and the Algerian "ultras" because it was suffering an inferiority complex after a long series of defeats and wanted a military victory. The French army had not even done as much for victory during World War II as the Maquis. By seeking to defend the grandeur of France in Algeria it hoped to end its inferiority complex.

I asked why the Communists had not shown more vigor in efforts to prevent de Gaulle from coming to power. He said: "The reason we did not try violence was because we did not wish to give de Gaulle the argument that the Communists were seeking a putsch."

PARIS, *June 18, 1958*

LAST night, at dinner, George Ball told me a fascinating story. During the 1956 presidential campaign, the Democrats wanted General Mac-

Arthur to come out for Stevenson. Ball and Chet Bowles called on him in his suite at the Waldorf Astoria and spent the better part of two days trying to arrange this. MacArthur was just as sweet as pie. He said: "If Eisenhower is reelected President it will be the greatest disaster in American history. I know just what will happen. He will go off to the golf courses and the trout streams of the country and then he will just disappear. There won't be any American government at all."

MacArthur had a high regard for Stevenson. He had never met him but agreed with his stand on almost everything. Stevenson was quite right to come out against atomic testing. His ideas on strategy were sound. He was correct in saying we should end selective service and create a small professional army.

But MacArthur simply did not see how he could publicly endorse Stevenson. After all, he had been the keynote speaker at the 1952 Republican convention. Despite the way he felt, he could not become a renegade. His friends and supporters would never understand this. He knew Eisenhower well. Eisenhower had been an idle, useless major on his staff. But he could not publicly endorse Stevenson.

Ball told me he had seen Guy Mollet after the Suez debacle. Mollet said he had made two miscalculations as Prime Minister of France. He had not realized how sick Eden was. And he had not realized before that no British Prime Minister can last twenty-four hours without American support. France had been willing to continue the venture alone. But Britain folded.

PARIS, *June 19, 1958*

THIS afternoon, I had a good talk with Couve de Murville, now foreign minister: quiet, dignified, friendly, elegant, and intelligent. We sat in a corner of his office, smoking and chatting.

Couve assured me there was absolutely no change in France's basic foreign policy. I asked if, as far as France is concerned, the 1950 tripartite declaration on the status quo in the Middle East still applied?

He replied: "Yes, of course, the declaration is still valid. It was not changed by Suez. France is still just as bound by its terms as it was in the 1950 declaration. It is much in our mind these days in connection with the Lebanon." (The 1950 declaration pledges the U.S., Britain, and France to promote the establishment and maintenance of peace and stability in the Middle East and to take action, both inside and outside UN, to prevent violation of peace.)

I asked, if the UN decided to send a force to the Lebanon, would France endorse such an attitude and send a military contingent? He said: "We would certainly back such a policy and, if asked, we would send French contingents. But the probability is such a force would be drawn from neutral nations."

France intended to honor NATO and all other treaty commitments. He presumed that if there were any French desires for a change in emphasis involving French relationships with NATO, this would merely affect things like commands and would be discussed inside NATO and SHAPE. Couve commented: "We haven't even discussed the prospect of any such changes."

FONTAINEBLEAU, *June 20, 1958*

LUNCH with General Hans Speidel. At last he has his own house in Fontainebleau—after having long been given the cold shoulder. Speidel was in full uniform with ribbons for the campaigns and honors he had earned fighting the Allies—all minus swastikas. He had three signed pictures above his desk: Hindenburg, General Beck, and Rommel. Speidel was Rommel's chief of staff.

He told me that in 1937, he had arranged a private meeting between General Beck and Marshal Pétain. At that time, Speidel was back in Berlin on the general staff, having been military attaché in Paris. Beck and Pétain sought to work out a deal between the German and French armies "to preserve the peace," the inference being that they wanted a secret, anti-Russian arrangement. The project was stillborn. Pétain couldn't sell it to Daladier, for whom he had contempt, and Beck got nowhere with Hitler.

As a young officer, in 1932, Speidel was present at German maneuvers, which Marshal Tukhachevsky and a group of high Russian officers attended. He was immensely impressed by Tukhachevsky, one of the best military men he ever met. Tukhachevsky had been a lieutenant in a Czarist guards regiment. He was only in his thirties when he came to maneuvers as commander of the Red army. An insolent German general asked him how old he was. According to Speidel, Tukhachevsky replied: "Old enough to lead my armies to victory if necessary."

Tukhachevsky spoke excellent French and quite a lot of German. He and all the other Soviet officers drank like fish, but Tukhachevsky never showed it—although the rest were staggering around.

After an alcoholic dinner, Tukhachevsky said to Speidel that he wanted some sherry. Speidel swiftly produced a glass of sherry. "No," said Tukhachevsky, "I mean cherry brandy." Speidel substituted a glass of cherry brandy. "No," said Tukhachevsky sternly, "I want a bottle." Speidel produced a bottle. Tukhachevsky drank it all, using a large whisky glass.

Speidel says de Gaulle is now insisting that a French officer be given either the job of Norstad as NATO commander or that of Schuyler as chief of staff; that de Gaulle is also demanding that a Frenchman be given the NATO Mediterranean Command based on Naples. Speidel sneered, "It's preposterous. I have only a division and a half of French troops. Let us first have more French troops before the French ask for greater positions. They had better be careful or we Germans will be demanding more commands."

PARIS, *June 25, 1958*

LAST night, Gladwyn Jebb told me he was going to see de Gaulle today, his third talk since he came as British ambassador four years ago. When he saw de Gaulle last March the General read certain excerpts from his *Mémoires*, including his observations when Churchill was voted out of office in the 1945 elections. "I will never let that happen to me," he said. Jebb said his impression then was that de Gaulle had no political aspirations and entertained no thoughts of returning to power.

Prince Paul of Jugoslavia was at dinner: very civilized and polished if not the tough guy needed to rule the Serbs. He confided: "Maybe it is not very discreet of me to say this, but I think Tito is doing wonderfully."

Paul told me about his negotiations with Hitler. His government advised him to go to Berlin in 1941, because Hitler might possibly be seeking his mediation to make peace with England. He was received by Hitler alone with Ribbentrop. The conversation was in German. Occasionally he had to use an English word which Ribbentrop translated. Hitler wanted Paul to sign a proclamation urging peace, together with Mussolini. Paul said: "How can you expect me to sign anything together with that Italian who murdered my cousin, King Alexander?"

Hitler made a long speech about how tragic it was to have the Germans fight the British and how it disturbed him to think of a "pretty" English boy lying dead on the battlefield beside a "beautiful" young German. Paul was amazed. After he left Germany, he rushed to his cousin, Princess Bonaparte, who was Freud's best pupil, and told her the story. She said obviously Hitler was a thwarted homosexual. Later she confirmed this with Freud himself.

PARIS, *June 26, 1958*

MARINA and I attended a regal lunch party today: Prince Paul of Jugoslavia (host), Princess Olga, Princess Elizabeth (their daughter), ex-King Umberto of Italy, the Duke of Verdura, and Marie de Rothschild.

After lunch, Prince Paul produced some remarkable hundred-year-old white Chartreuse and told me he made a practice of asking people who was the greatest man they had ever met. Berenson was his number-one nomination. That shows a pleasant originality. Eden, whom he doesn't like, nominated Stalin.

He went back to our conversation of the other night. Although he hated Mussolini, he had to admit the Duce was at least human. He met him first in 1923, and Mussolini told him then there were two mysteries he couldn't understand: the first was the Holy Trinity; the second was Italian finances. He thought Mussolini had coarsened through the years and suspected this was the result of syphilis.

Hitler was a man without the slightest attribute of charm. Paul is convinced he was a homosexual and never believed there was anything in the Eva Braun affair. Furthermore, Paul said he had no use for a man who didn't smoke, drink, and ate only mashed vegetables. When he met Hitler, he asked him if there were any good writers in Germany at the time (1941). Hitler reflected. "No," he said. "But then, of course, there are my speeches. Some of them are like those of Martin Luther and will live at least as long."

I called up Larry Norstad to say good-bye. He was extremely encouraged by his meeting with de Gaulle this week, the first time de Gaulle impressed him: gentle, reasonable, well informed. "Things are moving," said Larry.

NEW YORK, *July 9, 1958*

THIS afternoon, I had a long and satisfactory talk with Dag Hammarskjöld, UN Secretary-General. Ralph Bunche sat with us. Both Hammarskjöld and Bunche were delighted with the column I wrote from Oxford two weeks ago, in which I lambasted the project for military intervention in the Lebanon. I gathered from them that this had considerable effect in helping change American policy.

Hammarskjöld saw Dulles yesterday. Dulles has swung around, and American policy has become almost parallel to that of Hammarskjöld, "except for some rather slight differences of nuance." But both Hammarskjöld and Bunche said that not too long ago we appeared on the brink of intervention, which would have been, they observed, totally insane. The information concerning U.A.R. intervention in the Lebanon had been greatly exaggerated.

Hammarskjöld's objective in his recent trip to Egypt and Lebanon was to try and reduce meddling by Nasser, and to arrange for a cooling-off period during which a compromise might be prepared. Had there been armed intervention, there was serious danger of Soviet riposte and war. The UN would have died in the process.

I asked Hammarskjöld how he reconciled his personal views, which were evidently liberal-democratic and western, with his position of having to serve two mutually irreconcilable masters, the Soviet and NATO blocs in UN? He said:

In this position, a man must distinguish between his private views and his official role. The official position of secretary-general has its own specific ethics and code laid down by UN itself. The secretary-general, as a private individual, must adjust himself to this. If I stick to the official facts and principles prescribed, I am bound, whenever there is a crisis, to run into conflict with one or the other side. I do. But this fact and my insistence on adhering to the prescribed code is now respected by both sides.

I make it perfectly clear to everyone what my personal ideology is. Both blocs understand this, and, of course, the United States likes my private views. The Russians have a curious reaction. On one particular issue, when I was fighting for the UN line to insure peace. Vyshinsky confided to me Moscow did not want a secretary-general with whom the Russians would agree, but one with whom it was possible to reach agreements. This attitude has been strongly reflected in their private talks. They now realize that objectivity and integrity, not neutrality, are the essential qualities needed in this job.

I have had many conflicts with the Russians behind the scenes. I have made it plain to them that I don't care if they approve of my stand, but they must understand my motives. These are clean and they must realize, as I think they do, that I play no tricks. They accept this. They recognize that although they cannot kick me around, I also will not allow myself to be kicked around by others. There is one added essential to this job, and this is discretion. I can be frank and blunt in private talks but not in public.

Hammarskjöld admitted the structure of UN was built about one man, the secretary-general. If there was no secretary-general, the organization would get stuck. It was a one-man executive. If he were killed or resigned, it might take an incalculable time for East and West to agree on a successor. He could only consider resignation as a last trump, when he thought UN would be more harmed by his passivity and would consequently fade out and vanish.

The job requires someone with a liberal European tradition. You can't have a card-bearing member of any church. The position requires a man who does not have a personal loyalty that might transcend his loyalty to the charter.

NEW YORK, *July 19, 1958*

CHARLES Malik, Lebanese foreign minister, called up from Washington to congratulate me on my column. I had been taking the State Department to task for its Middle East policy but said that now that we were stuck with a bad deal we had better follow through.

Nuzhet Baba of the Turkish delegation to UN came in to see me. Nuzhet, a friend for almost twenty years, told me he had come on his own initiative to ask me to write another column about Cyprus because he thinks if I bawl out the Turks, the Greeks, and the British, I may be able to promote a Cyprus settlement at this time. I don't know whether Nuzhet *was* acting on his own initiative or whether his government put him up to this.

WASHINGTON, *July 23, 1958*

DINED last night at Wisner's. Allen Dulles boasted to me the CIA had been seeing de Gaulle regularly before he came to power, through a French contact. He also said they had an excellent agent among the ultras who plotted in Algeria. Maybe, but it seems indiscreet to say as much.

Lunched today with Sammy (Lord) Hood, chargé d'affaires of the British embassy. He thinks now is the time to get a Palestine settlement. In the past, we've always been afraid of irking our Arab friends, like Nuri. We don't have friends anymore. We have to make a deal on Arab refugees and Israeli borders and then get a great power guarantee (including Russia). But we cannot let Russia have any voice in disposal of the British oil sheikhdoms. Britain insists on keeping them—by force if necessary.

It is impossible to make a real settlement with Nasser. He must keep his momentum and expand; in this sense he is like Hitler. He thrives on crisis. He has internal problems (like Syria), which can only be obscured by new emotional headlines. He wants Britain's oil possessions—actual ownership of the petroleum. And Britain cannot afford to let this go.

It was folly to suggest Khrushchev should come to New York for a summit. Why give him such an enormous television tub to thump? Although the UN has means for secret negotiations (for example, in Hammarskjöld's offices), Khrushchev certainly isn't going to miss the opportunity for propaganda.

WASHINGTON, *July 24, 1958*

DINED with Allen Dulles and Senator Fulbright. Tomorrow, Fulbright's committee investigates Dulles's CIA. They were polite and friendly with each other, but Fulbright made no bones about his intentions to make Dulles squirm. He felt CIA should have known more about the Iraqi coup in advance.

Dulles told me Arif, the deputy premier, seems to be the Nasser of the Iraq cabal; Kassem, the Premier, seems to be the Naguib. He says, by the way, that Naguib (always a prisoner) has been encouraged to drink himself to death by Nasser. He likes booze and is given plenty.

The military information and plans of the Baghdad Pact that are now available to Nasser (and Russia?) are admittedly embarrassing. Also the plans Iraq had drawn up for mixing in Syria will be useful to Nasser's propaganda.

Dulles thinks the way our intelligence is set up is more logical than Britain's. We have in one organization what they have in three and a half. It is better that way, and better to have the organization known. The best agent he ever had, in Switzerland during the war, was a German who offered aid to the British military attaché, was rebuffed, then came to Dulles (whom he didn't know) merely because he knew Dulles headed our spy operations there.

NIXON: "PEACE AT

ALMOST ANY PRICE"

WASHINGTON, *July 25, 1958*

THIS MORNING, I HAD A LONG TALK WITH VICE PRESIDENT NIXON. We started the conversation in his formal office in the Capitol, and then he drove me in his air-conditioned Cadillac to the Metropolitan Club, where I had a date with Dean Acheson.

Nixon was sitting at his desk when I entered. He was wearing a gray suit and black shoes. He has a curious, heavy jaw which gives him a puffy appearance. I found that when I looked down at my notebook and did not look at him, his personality came through more strongly. For he has a resonant, good voice, and what he said was sensible and well phrased.

I started by asking him what he considered to be the aims, basically, of U.S. foreign policy. He replied:

> I would say that our foreign policy begins with the major consideration of protecting the independence of the U.S. We recognize that the independence of our nation and the freedom of our people cannot be considered as separate from the independence and freedom of other nations.
>
> Therefore, especially since World War I, we recognize that when the independence of our allies is threatened, we have a stake in helping them to defend it. This was a primary consideration in both world wars and in the Korean War.
>
> Up to this point, you will find general agreement among most American people: that the U.S. must help other threatened countries when the threat is of a military character.
>
> Until the time when the imperialist Communist movement began to be effective—since the latter part of World War II—I think this kind of policy was relatively adequate to protect our security. But now

we find that the Communists have developed to a degree never before reached, the tactics of indirect aggression. Therefore, we must expand our concepts.

This is why we have interest in mutual defense pacts in Europe and Asia and why we have supplemented the military aspects of these pacts with arrangements for foreign economic assistance on a massive scale.

This foreign economic aid is often misunderstood and misrepresented. Its fundamental purpose is to enable countries abroad to become economically strong enough to maintain political stability and to resist the political and economic infiltration of forces in nations whose ultimate purpose is to dominate them. This is the greatest danger faced by the U.S. and the free world, and in this particular area our policies are most inadequate. In both administrations, the leaders of our government have been unable to develop enough public support to enable Congress to vote sufficient funds for these purposes.

Let me summarize my ideas of policy. First of all, we should protect the independence and security of the U.S. Secondly, we should give military support to those nations who will stand beside us. Thirdly, our economic program should shore up the independence of other countries. And fourthly, we must recognize that any world war would destroy or warp our freedom, and, consequently, we have the obvious objective of finding useful solutions to international problems; that is why we support UN.

The people of this country and perhaps its policy makers cannot stress too much that we are devoted to peace at almost any price. And there is an important ingredient of our foreign policy which we have not adequately conveyed abroad: We are not wedded to the status quo. We recognize that the world, above all the world outside the West, is in a process of change and that the popular masses want a better way of life. Unfortunately, the image we present to many people abroad is precisely the opposite of this desire on our part. We are not for change merely for the sake of change as Russia is, but we do not oppose change.

In the Middle East, we are presented as taking a position of opposing change in the status quo and opposing Arab independence and economic improvement. This is not true. Regardless of ideology, I think we should aid any independent nation. The security interests of the U.S. require this. Therefore, for example, I am for helping Spain and Jugoslavia. My own view is that we should take chances like granting economic aid to Poland to encourage the independence forces in nations that are not really independent.

I then asked Nixon what he thought was the proper role of an opposition party in the nation's foreign-policy decisions. He said:

An opposition can bring about changes in two ways. First of all, it can have an influence on public opinion. Key senators can speak out and influence public opinion, and in its turn, public opinion will influence the administration. Secondly, the opposition can exert influ-

ence through direct consultation. In this way, we have seen Senator
Humphrey discussing the Middle East with Dulles. The administration
hopes to gain bipartisan support on these matters. Thirdly, the opposition can exert an influence through legislative control of the purse
strings. For example, one can see this in terms of foreign aid. The
tools with which an administration implements its foreign policy can
be denied by Congress.

I asked if Nixon would give me three names of men he would con-
sider eligible for the position of Secretary of State if he should be elected
President in 1960. He looked a bit coy. He said: "It would be pre-
sumptuous of me to comment on anything I might do if I were elected
President. I don't even mention such things to my wife. In those terms,
I can't answer your question. I don't like to speak of names."

But then, somewhat to my surprise, he went on and answered: "As a
Secretary of State I think that first of all, a man should be able to talk to
various people and get their various views on foreign policy, even though
the Secretary of State should have the final word." (I took this as a jibe at
Dulles whom Nixon dislikes.) He continued:

A President should have several broad-gauge men sophisticated in
international affairs in his Cabinet. There is a continual and extensive
political campaign in the world. The propaganda and political struggle is constant. Therefore, just as in wartime, when several members
of the War Cabinet participate in making decisions, a President nowadays needs to call on the best men in his administration to help guide
his decisions on foreign policy. For example, such ministers as the
Attorney General, the secretaries of Commerce, Treasury, and Defense, should join with the Secretary of State, the head of the Atomic
Energy Commission, the head of the CIA, and others in making decisions. All of them can contribute something to the thinking of the
chief executive.

(I was very interested to see Nixon put the Attorney General at the
head of the list. His own closest personal friend in the Cabinet is Bill
Rogers, the Attorney General.)

Nixon continued:

It is dangerous for an administration to confine itself to too narrow
consultations in the field of foreign policy. [I took this as a dig at Dulles
also.]

I would not venture to suggest who would be a good man to follow
Dulles, but he would have to have a basic understanding of the world
struggle and how the international Communist movement operates. He
would have to be able to work with the people in the foreign service
and inside the State Department.

As much as anything else, we need a man with initiative, creative-
ness, and a recognition of the necessity to break out of old patterns of

thought. It is easy to say that we need a bold new program in foreign policy today. But Dulles is extremely able and a tower of strength.

Nevertheless, as we move into the period ahead, I do not think that the struggle will be determined by the military strength of the U.S. and Russia. It will be decided by things like the Middle East today and what I saw in Latin America on my recent trip. Therefore, we must have people who understand the political and economic aspects of this struggle. I must emphasize foreign economic aid.

At this point, we had to take off in Nixon's car and my notes are less complete. He said he thought there was a definite need for a longer range system of budgeting instead of the present year-to-year basis and that Congress must recognize this. He also said it was very difficult for us in analyzing foreign movements to distinguish "the voice of the mob from the voice of the majority."

He thought our propaganda was inadequate. The crux of the problem was in the very name of our government radio, the "Voice" of America. This voice tells people abroad how we live, etc. But instead of trying to be the voice of America, we should seek more to be the voice of other peoples. The Communists have done this. They have identified themselves with the aspirations of other peoples, but we only speak for the Americans. Our propaganda should associate itself with the voice and aspirations of peoples like the Tunisians.

We are inept in presenting a true picture, even of ourselves. We do not adequately let other peoples know that we do not want to dominate them and that we believe in their economic progress for their own sake as well as for the simple reason that it is in our own best interest. We should be the voice of others, not of Americans. We must get across to other nations that ours is the true revolution. We should talk more of the *promise* of the American revolution and less of the menace of the Communist revolution. But we must make it plain that we do not expect other peoples to share all our views and to imitate us in all their action.

At this point, the car deposited me at the Metropolitan Club and inside thirty seconds I was beside Nixon's worst enemy, Dean Acheson.

Acheson and I had a stimulating lunch. He was bland, witty, very bitter about Dulles and the administration. Thinks our Middle East policy has been a total disaster and that now we are risking grave division with Britain and France, which would be disastrous.

The two men he most dislikes and distrusts in the world are Dulles and Selwyn Lloyd. It was natural that there should be misunderstanding between Britain and the U.S. on the recent notes to Khrushchev and that the two men had differing recollections of their agreements in Washington. They're a pair of slick lawyers who are trying to outsmart each other. Acheson knows Lloyd well. When he went to London to discuss a Korean armistice he told Eden he would simply refuse to deal with Lloyd; that he would only deal with Eden. If Acheson were suddenly made secretary of state (a sour joke), he would promptly go to London and tell Macmillan that he would deal only with Macmillan, never Lloyd.

He thinks the Middle Eastern situation hopeless. We have no policy. We began to elaborate one vaguely under Truman during the Iran crisis (in which we prevailed on the British not to send troops to Abadan). But there has never been a long-range, coherent policy. We must recognize the area is a peninsula whose base is the Soviet Union and which connects Eurasia with Africa. The only comparable area is Central America, linking two continents. (There are canals in both regions.) We showed our extreme nervousness when a Communist regime came in Guatemala—and ousted it. Russia's interest in the Middle East has always been strong and for logical reasons.

There is no real "country" there apart from Iran, Turkey, and Israel. The rest of the area is inhabited by a people linked by Semitic blood, the Arabic language, and the Muslim religion. They have been part of one or another empire for thousands of years. They have been kicked around so much that they have immense pride and fanaticism. There are no borders or status quo and only the nationalist movement symbolized by Nasser. Plus oil. This is the region's wealth. And its only natural market is western Europe. We should seek to base a policy on neutralizing the area and arranging a satisfactory petroleum link to Europe. Unfortunately Israel intrudes. And Israel is an unsolvable cancer. Acheson always opposed its creation.

Each power bloc can deny the Middle East to the other, but neither can hold it. Our present posture is ludicrous. One can do everything with a bayonet but sit on it—even ten thousand bayonets as in Lebanon. And Nasser needs a whipping boy for propaganda. We, unnecessarily, make ourselves that—and the British have skillfully benefited. Nasser runs against us the way Big Bill Thompson "ran" against King George V in Chicago.

To bargain with Nasser we must establish a better bargaining position. The military helps its aims with science. Why doesn't diplomacy?

We should use new scientific methods of transporting oil (such as by submarine-towed plastic sausages) and storing it (as in abandoned coal mines in Britain). If Europe has an emergency supply of six or twelve months, it is not so easily subjected to Nasser's blackmail of cutting the supply. We must start preparing for this right away.

We should gently begin to reduce our commitments and public attentions to the Middle East. It is not nearly as vital an interest to us as to

Europe; let them take the diplomatic lead—and also get prior propaganda attention from the Arabs.

Acheson said he had no use for Nye Bevan, who is a thoroughly untrustworthy man, and he bemoaned the death of Ernie Bevin. He thought Hugh Gaitskell was all right but weak. The only Labour leader he considered first class and reliable was George Brown, and he wished he could be slated for the foreign instead of defense ministry job. The English Tories are still pretty antediluvian. Acheson recalls a long chat he had with Lloyd and Lord Salisbury which discouraged him immensely. "It wasn't that their attitude was nineteenth century," he said. "They hadn't even reached the nineteenth century."

WASHINGTON, *July 28, 1958*

GENERAL Howard Snyder, Ike's old friend and physician, told me that unfortunately Eisenhower is very tense now. In addition to all the problems of the world, the Sherman Adams affair was dumped in his lap.

"I am worried about this tenseness," said Snyder. "He might blow a valve again. But I must say he gets a good day's work done. When he sits down at his desk he works quickly and intensely. He is very fast. The Canadians were most impressed with the fact that he is really a strong leader despite what they have been reading in their own and the English press that he was a sick man."

Snyder told me he checked Eisenhower physically every day at noon. This is a pretty careful watch. I asked if Ike gets much benefit out of his weekends at Gettysburg. I recalled to him what a fool I had been when, about seven years ago, Eisenhower had offered to sell me the neighboring farm at Gettysburg and I, like an idiot, turned it down. Snyder said Gettysburg was really too hot. Ike originally had wanted to buy a farm near Warrenton, Virginia. But Mamie had fallen in love with the Gettysburg region during the war when she was staying near there. Ike had ordered George Allen (the fat one, not the diplomat) to look around and find a place. It was pretty cheap, but it has cost a small fortune to fix up.

Snyder took me up to see Mamie. She was sitting up in her large double bed in a pink jacket, talking with her sister. I noticed, on the windowsill right opposite her, a picture of her grandson David in a pose remarkably like Ike looking puzzled at a bridge hand. Beside Ike's bed table were some Wild West stories, including one called *Wyoming Jones*—not very intellectual reading for the President of the U.S. Mamie showed me a trick green Swedish telephone she has, which is very light and in which the earphone and the mouthpiece are one gadget.

Mamie said she had lots of work as First Lady. She likes to plan her own menus, such as today's for the Italian Prime Minister. She answers all letters herself from friends, from people more than ninety years old, from children, and from people who send wedding announcements or presents; and this, sometimes, takes two and a half hours a day.

Later, I had an extremely interesting lunch in the office of Senator Clark with senators Fulbright of Arkansas, Humphrey of Minnesota, and Sparkman of Alabama.

Fulbright spoke most. He said there were a lot of misconceptions about what we could do to bring pressures on Nasser. We could not destroy the position of Egypt's cotton in the world market. We had a great surplus of cotton, but it was almost entirely short-staple cotton which could only be used for stuffing, not spinning. There was actually a shortage of the excellent long-staple cotton Egypt produces.

Fulbright was much concerned about the attitude of our military leaders. He said both General Twining, present chairman of the Joint Chiefs, and Admiral Radford, his predecessor, favored preventive war against Russia. They felt that the balance of power was still in our favor, but in a few years time it would be in Moscow's favor and therefore we should strike now. Fulbright thought it most significant that the only military man Eisenhower consulted before going into Lebanon was Twining who "wants a war anyway."

He said it was impossible to discern either a Democratic or a Republican view on foreign policy. Democrats, such as the group assembled at this luncheon, were hammering away at Dulles for his intransigence and for always getting us to the brink of war. But Republicans, such as Knowland, Bridges, Jenner, and Capehart, almost implied that Dulles was soft and was not doing enough against the Communists. In the meantime, the great mass of people was not really concerned with foreign issues at all. If you could just pass a slogan on saying that any action was "anti-Communist," that was enough. Back in the sticks, people did not know where Lebanon was and they didn't give a damn whether our Marines were there or not.

The only influence Congress had on foreign policy was in terms of appropriating necessary funds. It was highly desirable to reform our present system in order to budget for five years on such things as defense and foreign affairs; but no headway was being made on this. And foolish men, such as Representative Rooney of Brooklyn, a Democrat, were able to hamstring the necessary appropriations. Fulbright offered the suggestion that if Lyndon Johnson were in the White House with Adlai Stevenson as his secretary of state they could get around such problems because Adlai could make policy and Lyndon was a wise enough politician to know how to apply pressure on Rooney and shut him up. The trouble was that Eisenhower was not expert enough in the field of politics.

Fulbright complained that our system of government could only work in the present world when a really strong man was President, and yet it was a total accident if a strong man were elected, because the best-qualified candidates in terms of getting the nominations were those who had never taken a stand on any controversial issue.

Humphrey is a bitter, intelligent man with an incisive mind and not in the least disturbed by the fact that many people call him "leftist." He has black hair, a pale complexion, sharp eyes, and a strong mouth and chin. He talks a lot and well.

He complained that during recent days *Pravda* had been printing more truth than the American press about aspects of the Middle East crisis, much as he regretted saying this. Our press has been misled by the lies put out by the State Department. But he agreed with Fulbright it was impossible for the Democratic party to express an effective oppositional voice that might alter our policy. The best thing to achieve change would be to oust Dulles. That simply cannot be done. The most that could be hoped for would be for the Senate to censure Dulles. But that would have no effect and would be very difficult to achieve. Humphrey added: "Dulles has it all in his hands; nobody else in the State Department knows what's going on. And the whole apparatus of our diplomatic service funnels up to him. This produces a situation like a man with a fainting spell. The oxygen is choked off before it reaches the brain."

Clark said one of the tragedies of the present situation was that the administration is totally divorced from the country's intellectual life. Humphrey said this doesn't matter because the intellectuals really had very little influence as he found every time he went back to Minnesota. The people of this country just don't care about foreign policy. As long as you can't accuse Dulles of being pro-Communist, you can't build up any public opinion demanding that he be fired. You can't fire a Secretary of State or get the public to request it just because his policy is wrong. The thing that hurt Acheson was that he was accused of being pro-Communist, not matters of policy.

Sparkman brought up the point that the Policy and Planning staff of the State Department is now nothing but a sad joke. It had been started off with George Kennan as its head. Then came Paul Nitze, then Bob Bowie. They were all intelligent men, but every time there was a change, it was for the worse.

On the whole, it was a pretty sad, if stimulating, performance. They all agreed the Democratic party could have no influence in changing foreign policy. The only way it could act would be by rousing public opinion to demand a change, but public opinion did not give a damn.

They also all agreed that there was no substitute for the present system except by rectifying the American governmental method (which both Clark and Fulbright advocate). Fulbright said he had learned a lesson. He is not going to demand parliamentary government as in England anymore, because when he did this once the only result was to provoke a storm of criticism recalling that he had been a Rhodes scholar and had "sold out" to the British.

In a nutshell, these four distinguished Senators think the situation stinks but nothing can be done about it and they don't intend to stick their necks out.

WASHINGTON, *July 29, 1958*

THIS morning I talked for an hour and a half with Senator Jack Kennedy, who, at the moment, is way in the lead as Democratic candidate for President in 1960. I have met Kennedy a few times before, starting as far back as Belgrade during the war, when he visited the late Arthur Lane, then our minister. Kennedy has a good politician's memory and promptly reminded me of our very first meeting.

He looks extremely youthful, although he is now over forty. Tall, thin, with a boyish expression and a shock of brown hair, he is nice looking and clearly bright. He talks glibly and easily but without particular lucidity, and I must say I would hate to see him President of this country.

I started off with my standard question: What should be the essential aspirations of U.S. foreign policy? He answered:

> Our policy should obviously sustain countries and help them to maintain their independence of the Communist system, at least as it is controlled by Moscow or Peking; by doing this, we can preserve the security of the U.S. Within these broad terms of reference, I think we should support countries regardless of their ideology. I would like to see American loans to nations behind the Iron Curtain in order to lessen their dependence on Russia. Those countries don't have to associate themselves with us. That would be self-defeating. Neutrality is the best that some of them can hope for. [This sounds perfectly reasonable, but I can see Kennedy's mind pondering these ideas in terms of the minority vote in the U.S., above all the Poles.]
>
> I opposed both Suez and our landing in the Lebanon; I did not think either policy would attain our objectives. I don't think the problem in the Middle East is external.
>
> If we guarantee the government in Iran, we can sustain them against Soviet pressure. But I never thought the Eisenhower Doctrine was useful. On the other hand, it would have been worse for the U.S. if the Senate had rejected that doctrine.
>
> I assume that Jordan will sooner or later fall to Nasser. But the Lebanon might be sustained. I am also concerned about Tunisia and all North Africa. I don't feel that de Gaulle is making any approach to Algeria that can succeed. He is now pressing a vigorous policy, but it is too late.
>
> There is some feeling around about doing business with Nasser. I

supported the idea of helping him with the Aswan Dam. And we should have given him some arms. But I doubt if now we can reach a very happy solution with him. A lot of western positions are going to be lost and these may include Tunisia and Morocco as well as British exploitations in Kuwait. I am not optimistic about reaching a solution with Nasser. But I think we should wait to see what we can do.

I asked Kennedy why it was that the Democratic party seems so strongly opposed to our foreign policy while at the same time totally unable to exert any influence in order to change that policy. He replied:

We have no organization in the Democratic party. We are split. It is impossible to present any uniform argument on behalf of the party. Furthermore, most of our foreign policy is based on day-to-day positions. There is no basic argument between the Republicans and the Democrats like the old argument about tariffs. The executive decisions which make up our foreign policy are too swift to allow for any influence to be exerted by the opposition. Policy on such matters as Aswan, Suez, and the Lebanon is made on a day-to-day or hour-to-hour basis. How can the Democrats take a stand on such things?

We do not have the party organization for this. For example, we have not had a caucus of the Democratic Senators since January, 1957, and this was just to organize the Senate. Under our system of government, the executive can go as far as he wants in foreign policy by executive agreement. He does not have to refer such things to the Senate. And even if he did, we don't have a unified opinion on foreign-policy matters in the Senate. Not even the Democrats on the foreign-policy committee try to get a unified consensus of party opinion.

Once both the Republicans and the Democrats had accepted the idea of mutual security, the administration's hand was strengthened to take executive action. Since that basic decision, not nearly so much has to be cleared by the Senate.

Furthermore, in this day and age, it is almost necessary for the Secretary of State to be freed from having to drag us Senators along on these decisions.

The Senate is playing an increasingly secondary role in foreign affairs. This is unavoidable. Our political parties don't divide up as parties on foreign-policy issues. For example, the Democrats themselves are split on reciprocal trade and foreign aid.

Everything conspires against an effective role by the opposition party in foreign affairs. And you must remember that the President maintains a good deal of general support in the country on his foreign policy. It is not like internal political questions.

In 1954, Congress did have a real effect on foreign policy, when a few leaders actually prevented our military intervention in Vietnam during the battle of Dien Bien Phu. Senators Johnson and Russell strongly discouraged such an intervention in their emergency meeting with the administration.

The upshot was, in my mind, that the President of the U.S. is now in a position to get us into war or to involve us in treaty obligations without the necessity of Congress declaring war or the Senate approving a treaty by ratification. And Kennedy seems to think this is a good thing. Maybe he feels that way because he hopes so much to be President in 1961. He told me the Democrats are going to win the 1960 election by a real landslide.

NEW YORK, *September 22, 1958*

TALK with Couve de Murville at his suite in the Waldorf Astoria. He is a pleasant man to do business with because you can swiftly get all the answers you ever are going to get; there is no waste of time.

I said de Gaulle had told me several times he wished to see a change in France's NATO role, with greater responsibilities and powers for the French. Had there been any development in that direction? There had been no change so far, but Couve was sure there would be discussion along these lines during the autumn. He added: "Certainly one of the major problems from our point of view is that of avoiding being led into war without knowing about it."

What did he think about Khrushchev's statement to *Pravda* denouncing de Gaulle as a fascist? Couve smiled sourly, saying:

I believe Khrushchev's statement was intended in part to support the position of the French Communist party before the referendum. But I think primarily it was the result of Adenauer's visit to de Gaulle. The Russians have now given up all hope that their blandishments would have any effect upon de Gaulle's government. Therefore, they are being frank. The declaration signed by Adenauer and de Gaulle expressed the hope that Europe would be enlarged which, of course, meant they hoped the satellites of eastern Europe would gradually join with the western bloc. Obviously, the Russians cannot tolerate such an idea.

I asked whether there had been any developments in France's views concerning China. Couve answered:

We think it would be logical to recognize the Peking government. We should have done this ourselves at the same time the British did. But then we were really at war with China in Vietnam. And after that conflict ended, it was too late. We have no intention of taking the initiative now. Although we think it logical to recognize, this is not a matter of sufficient importance to risk a major crisis in relationships with the U.S. Therefore we will continue to support the U.S. position in the UN—although we think recognition would be wise.

PARIS, *October 3, 1958*

LUNCH with Raymond Laporte, on leave from the Quai d'Orsay; he has held no job since Maurice Faure disappeared together with the Fourth Republic. Couve offered him the post of French consul general in Damascus. Laporte said: "I am not a French Lawrence of Arabia." Couve was not amused.

He told me of the final meeting of the last Cabinet of the Fourth Republic on May 27—five days before de Gaulle became Prime Minister. Laporte's information came directly from Faure's notes:

> The Cabinet Council presided over the resignation of Pflimlin last night. After discordant voices had been heard in favor of or against the resignation, Pleven was the last to take the floor. "We are, gentlemen," he said, "a government of phantoms."
> Mutter, minister to Algeria, has no contact with it.
> Corniglion-Molinier doesn't have much more with the Sahara.
> Chevigné, minister of national defense, doesn't command fifty soldiers.
> Jules Moch knows that he cannot count on the police.
> Maurice Faure, minister for the European Community, can only hold back its realization.
> As for myself, I am a strange minister of foreign affairs, whose only job is to receive friendly ambassadors who come to me and express their pity.

PARIS, *October 6, 1958*

I WENT over to see Michel Melas, Greek ambassador to NATO. When he returned to Athens to report last week, he thought the odds were three to two that Greece would quit NATO because of Cyprus. Caramanlis is on the verge of resigning. If he does quit, it is certain a leftist government will come in—controlled by the Communists—and will vote for Greece's withdrawal from the alliance.

The Jugoslavs have been strongly urging Athens *not* to weaken NATO.

Melas suggested to Burgess, U.S. ambassador to NATO, that the United States should take the initiative in proposing capitulations in Cyprus for the Turks. Burgess didn't understand what the word meant. Consequently, everything is stalemated. The Melas theory is that the Turks could present to their people as a "victory" the grant of "capitulations" because they know the meaning of that word so well, in terms of allied protection of minorities in Constantinople.

Melas asked if I could help out. I said perhaps I could. Maybe I would be able to arrange a meeting with anyone who might at least understand.

I dropped by at the embassy and told our CIA man adding: "For God's sake, you have to keep me out of this. I don't want Melas or anybody else to think I work for you of all people." He said somebody was coming from Washington tomorrow who could help.

PARIS, *October 7, 1958*

C, WHO handles Greek-Turkish-Cyprus affairs for the CIA and was on his way back to Washington from Greece and Turkey, came by and I introduced him to Melas. I had explained the delicacy of the situation which amounted to bypassing Burgess, our ambassador to NATO, and that I was merely acting as a friend of all parties and had nothing to do with CIA. I then left the two together.

Afterward, C said he thought he might be able to get something done. We will see. What Melas is after is really to combine the Makarios plan for Cypriot independence with the establishment of a mixed court system such as existed in Egypt for many years. He also wants acknowledgment of Turkish right of capitulations for the Turkish minority on the island.

PARIS, *October 13, 1958*

LONG talk with Jacques Soustelle, present minister of information and an important figure on the French political scene. He has formed a new party and hopes perhaps to be de Gaulle's first Prime Minister.

I asked if there was any truth to the rumor that Soustelle has been converted from his old ideas on Algeria to de Gaulle's present thinking; that he envisages eventual participation of moderate FLN leaders in an Algerian administration.

Soustelle replied: "While I was governor of Algeria, the first proposal for reforms there was made by myself. I suggested the accession of Muslims to the civil service, land reform, Muhammadan municipal officials, women's suffrage, industrialization. But I am completely against the FLN because I know they are murderers and fanatics and nothing serious can be achieved with them."

I said: "Your enemies say you are a fascist. How would you define a fascist and, according to that definition, how would you explain that you are not one?"

Soustelle smiled. He said:

A fascist is a man who is against freedom of opinion and expression and who wants to establish a dictatorship with a one-party system and who has built-in prejudices like anti-Semitism or racism.

I am on record as saying that France cannot even have a two-party system, much less a one-party system. French history and French psychology present reasons which make it necessary for us to have several parties. I have always advocated a presidential system such as exists in the United States. Certainly the United States system cannot be considered fascism.

I approve of our new Constitution, of which I am one of the authors, and I think it is reasonable compromise between the traditional parliamentary system and the presidential system. For years I have been a vigorous enemy of racism and anti-Semitism. I am president of the France-Israel Committee. These tales about alleged fascism are put out by the Communists as a deliberate smear campaign.

I am and always have been a man of the left of center. This, by the way, is the position of my seat in Parliament. But apart from this purely material and geographical situation, it is how I would describe myself.

I am a working-class man. I rose up to my present position because we are a democracy, because we are a country where the poor can be educated. I know the real situation of the working class and their hardships. My stepfather is still a factory worker. I don't have to dive into unknown depths of a social abyss in order to know these things. I know them right in my own home. I am not like the so-called leftists of the 16th arrondissement who only know workers in order to push them around.

Furthermore, I am a republican. I am in favor of social progress and justice. And I am a Protestant. I don't favor any intrusions by religion into state affairs. I suppose that with the same ideas I would be on the right of center if I went to Mass every Sunday.

I remarked that many people said Soustelle was anti-American. He replied:

I am not anti-American or pro-American. I am pro-French.

In the long run, you never profit by having a weak ally. As a friend of the United States, when you disagree you must be blunt. The pretext used for calling me anti-American is that I disagree with the Arab policy of the United States. But this is not enough to label me anti-American. I think it was a foolish mistake of the United States to oppose the Suez expedition. You never get anywhere by appeasing would-be dictators and warmongers. But you can disagree and still be a good friend.

The Russians are trying to isolate Europe from Africa by driving from the Middle East across Africa. It would be a disaster if they succeeded in this. It is in the interest of the entire free world to keep France in North Africa. The moment Europe is isolated from North Africa, it will fall like a ripe fruit.

PARIS, *October 20, 1958*

LUNCHED with Averoff, the Greek foreign minister, and Seferiades, Greek ambassador in London (who, as the poet, Seferis, later won a Nobel Prize). They are both here for the NATO council meetings on Cyprus.

Seferiades warned the British that a Cyprus settlement must be reached soon because there is a distinct threat of a "Baghdad solution" in Greece itself. The Greek government may be seized by *coup d'état*. He complained that the United States favors the Turks because of Pentagon influence.

Averoff said Tito has been urging the Greeks not to quit NATO under any circumstances. It would be a disaster to weaken NATO. The reason neither Jugoslavia nor Greece has denounced the moribund Balkan Pact with Turkey is to avoid the logical consequences of such an act; namely, bilateral military alliance between Jugoslavia and Greece. Tito would find such a commitment of a specific nature very embarrassing vis-à-vis the Communist world.

PARIS, *October 22, 1958*

THIS afternoon I saw Malraux. We huddled in a corner of his office smoking and scattering ashes all around the little ash tray he put on the sofa. He said the next step needed to continue the psychological momentum of de Gaulle is to remove the burden of the Algerian war. Then France will regain confidence in herself.

It is hard to envision economic development that can have visible results. The soundness of the currency must be reestablished, but this is a difficult task and even when it succeeds it will not have any immediate spectacular value. The housing program is going on and "we attach immense importance to it," but it will not move on a massive scale until the Algerian war ends.

A vital necessity is to reduce the strength of communism, to pare off the fellow travelers. It would be romantic folly to imagine that all this can be done swiftly. Both Algeria and France itself must be modernized and it will take considerable time to produce economic results. Furthermore, there are no *guarantees* of success. "But we must try," said Malraux.

He claims the modern world is no longer influenced by Marxist tenets. And, although France cannot be remade with a bad financial and economic system, it is possible for a state to have a national renaissance without a financial or economic renaissance. "The renewing of a state has little to do with statistical figures," said Malraux. Even in China, the "partial success" of the Communist government was not essentially due to Marxist practice. Other things such as nationalism played a role.

Malraux predicts that France will soon have something equivalent to a two-party system. There will be a moderate bloc of parties like the Tories in England and a Socialist bloc like the Labour party. In between, there will be a center with two wings, left and right, but the polarization will be toward the two blocs.

PARIS, *October 24, 1958*

LAST night at dinner, I saw Georges Pompidou, de Gaulle's directeur de Cabinet (later Prime Minister, then President): a quiet, intelligent man with a sense of humor. He told me de Gaulle himself forecast that he would have a 72 percent backing in the September referendum. The actual figure was 80 percent. Nevertheless, de Gaulle's own guess was higher than anyone else's in the government.

The General really has no close friends. There are few old friends from prewar days whom he sees from time to time. For the rest, he has no intimates, outside his family.

Pompidou told me de Gaulle had a great admiration for Roosevelt, although he preferred Churchill as a man. He agreed there was a certain resemblance between the present emergency period and Roosevelt's One Hundred Days, and said de Gaulle had studied Roosevelt's techniques.

Pleasant chat with Norstad. I asked what commands de Gaulle had requested. Larry said no formal requests had been made. Nevertheless, the French feel they should have a greater role in the alliance and greater participation in its direction.

De Gaulle told Norstad he definitely would like to get rid of Speidel. Larry pointed out that Speidel had been selected because of his extremely excellent qualifications. He was no heel-clicking Prussian. De Gaulle repeated he didn't want him. He didn't mean to make an attack on Speidel as a person; but nevertheless, because of the situation, he would like him to leave France. His wartime associations with this country made him vulnerable.

The French want a greater voice in world policy, full equality with the United States and Britain, more influence in global strategic direction and especially in atomic matters. They feel that a balance must be struck between nationalism and "alliancism." They argue, and quite rightly says Norstad, that a solid foundation for an alliance can only be built on a proper balance of national strength.

They apparently want to see created an informal political standing group. Yet they know this is not in the cards. They fear that there is a secret United States-British planning group from which they are excluded. They want to join what Churchill calls the "atomic club." They remember that Macmillan said it was necessary for Britain to have nuclear weapons in order to impress the United States.

PARIS, *October 30, 1958*

RATHER interesting talk with Guy Mollet, head of the French Socialist party and vice premier in the Gaullist government. In some ways, he bears a slight resemblance to Léon Trotsky. He wears his hair in two little horns on either side of his high brow. If he allowed it to grow more, it would resemble a Trotsky hairdo. Of course, he doesn't have a moustache or beard and his glasses are rather different.

His political analysis was as follows:

Apart from the Bolsheviks, I think there will be three main party groups: the workers [Socialists], the conservatives, and between them the liberals. These are the three parties that one can have in France. The small parties will have to choose among them.

I asked Mollet if the Socialists would agree to the banning of the Communist party or, at any rate, to the discharge from all governmental positions of practicing Communists. He answered:

Certainly not. We are in favor of ousting from any official position all men who commit misdemeanors. But we would do this only because of their misdemeanors, not because of the party to which they belong. If a man betrays the government or spies, he should be discharged. But he should not be discharged just because of the party he is in. And I am certainly not for banning the Communist party as a party. We cannot apply the jungle law to the Communists just because they would do as much to us. We must defend freedom.

Also, in a practical sense, you do not end the Communist problem merely by banning the party. The Communists would get influence and express this in many other ways. I am not at all sure that the Communist influence in England is not as great as it is today in France, although they have no deputies in Parliament. They have managed to penetrate all kinds of positions, such as trade unions.

I asked if he thought a loyal opposition could be developed in the next French Parliament similar to "Her Majesty's loyal opposition" in the British Parliament. He replied:

This is what I hope for. This is my objective. Already in the last Assembly of the Fourth Republic, I proposed to my political friends that we should not be in the government, but that we should permit the government to apply its own policy even if we did not support them actively.

The problem in France is rather difficult because we have an extreme right of fascists and Poujadists and an extreme left of Communists. It is hard to play a role of loyal opposition when you have such groups in a position to sabotage the system. In England or in the United States, the opposition can eventually overthrow the government. Here in France the disloyal opposition of the ultras on the left and right make it difficult to establish a loyal opposition. My party agreed to try the role of loyal opposition at the end of the Fourth Republic, but within fifteen days the republic had failed.

I asked Mollet if he thought the Prime Minister of the Fifth Republic would be a weak figure always in the shadow of the President. He replied:

There are two problems, problems of men and problems of the Constitution. The character of one man or another will play a role of great importance. Obviously, if de Gaulle is the first President of the Fifth Republic, it will give the position of President enormous importance. The comparative role of the Prime Minister will therefore be diminished under him.

Mollet added there was no doubt whatsoever in his mind that de Gaulle was a man of the left.

PARIS, *November 3, 1958*

THIS afternoon, I went over to see General Ely in his office in the Cour d'Honneur of the Invalides. He said:

NATO actually has succeeded in Europe and halted the danger from the East. But in the same sense, NATO succeeded in pushing the adversary elsewhere. The adversary is moving into the underdeveloped countries to try and turn our flank through the Middle East and Africa.

What I am concerned about is how to defend our position and the interests of the West in the Middle East. I have spoken of the axis running from Paris to Algiers, through the Saharan oil to Brazzaville and Black Africa. This is a French axis. It is important to the entire occident, not just to France, above all because of the petroleum.

In the Middle East, we allies have been disunited and in disorder in that area while the Soviet has pushed in. It is difficult for us to act in that area inside NATO. We cannot increase NATO's responsibilities in the world. Allied countries like Norway and Denmark would be unhappy if NATO sought to assume new responsibilities.

I think that all countries interested in the region should concert their policies there. It is not necessary to have a common policy and a common action, but it is necessary for us to cease opposing each other. Maybe this can be done inside NATO or maybe outside the alliance.

PARIS, *November 10, 1958*

LUNCH at (Lady) Diana Cooper's with the Jebbs and the Roberts. Jebb (British ambassador) said de Gaulle still thinks in terms of the nineteenth century. He says France has one man, de Gaulle, and one problem, Algeria. Jebb says he suggested to Mollet that de Gaulle should stay on as Prime Minister, keeping Coty President.

Roberts (British ambassador to NATO) said if the French refuse to compromise with Britain on the free-trade area, London will not keep its troops in Germany unless it has equal access to the German market.

Roberts says Italy is now imitating France, seeking a freer hand in NATO. Gronchi and Fanfani are copying de Gaulle. They have just finished demoting or retiring the Italian ambassadors most closely associated with NATO.

PARIS, *November 18, 1958*

I WENT over to the Ministry of Justice to see Michel Debré. He is one of the most ardent Gaullists in the Cabinet and a leader of the right wing. Debré, who has been a senator and is at present minister of justice and keeper of the seal, is much talked of as Prime Minister of the next government. He is a small, delicate-looking man of forty-six, pale with somewhat unfinished features, intelligent and filled with nervous energy.

Debré has written several political tracts. I brought with me the latest called *Ces princes qui nous gouvernent*, to ask what influence this had had upon the insurrectionists of May, 1958, and what influence it had had on the thinking of General de Gaulle. He replied:

"The book was a big success and did bring a spark of intelligence to electrify many people and many officers who were discontented with the old system. I think it fairly represents what these people had been thinking for many years. It expressed these thoughts rather than producing new thoughts."

I noted that Debré had written that there were between one and three thousand "princes"—leaders in politics, industry, labor, science, the army, etc.—who ran France under the old system and that it would be necessary for at least three to four hundred of them to join together in order to overthrow it. How many "princes" actually joined in the May upheaval? He said:

"I was struck at the time by the degree to which the directors of the old regime rallied to the authority of General de Gaulle. One has only to take the instances of Pflimlin and Mollet. And by rallying to the General they have today become different from what they were. They have now profoundly realized how necessary it was to change their past attitudes. Some of the 'princes' understood what was necessary."

He said the destiny of France and Germany was to be allied "like both sides of a hand" since "there could be no security for one without the other." Nevertheless, Debré thought it would be a catastrophe if a united Germany were to end up in the Soviet camp; it would be a happy event if a unified Germany were to end up in the western camp. And there was no doubt that any kind of "neutral" Germany meant running the risk that such a Germany might go with Moscow.

The French should never forget what the Germans had done to them. "We must pardon the Germans, but we must not forget their crimes."

I asked how, under the Fifth Republic, a new batch of "princes" could be prevented from taking control of France. He said the electoral law and the mode of elections would tend to restrict the number of real parties. In England there was a Labour party, but this was not entirely necessary here any more than in the United States. American workers benefited from a particular structure of society which offered them an opportunity for rising in social position. A New York taxi driver could aspire to become a lawyer or a city councillor. This allowed for a steady refreshing of the administrative machinery of the government. The same sort of thing was evidently needed in France.

Debré quoted Machiavelli, saying that when a republic is menaced with corruption it must break with legality or be lost. I asked if he favored dictatorship in France. He said he favored dictatorship in a "Roman" sense, which gave great power to a leader who had been democratically designated and awarded this power only for a period as long as necessary.

He cited Cincinnatus as an example. Debré had tried to explain this approach during the very last session of the council of the Fourth Republic. This kind of dictatorship in the Roman sense was not the same thing as tyranny.

I asked Debré if it was fair to say he was the author of the Constitution of the Fifth Republic. He replied: "You might say the Constitution was edited here, and to a large degree by me."

In principle, he was opposed to the idea of a Common Market, but he would accept it if, in exchange, Germany and Italy supported France in North Africa. "We will never accept the Common Market except in return for German and Italian agreement with our wishes in Africa, and German and Italian financial investment in Africa."

I asked if the new Constitution provided sufficient executive power. He replied: "The government will be as strong as General de Gaulle—and no more. First there will be General de Gaulle; he is doctor and it is necessary for him to apply medical treatment. France's divisions remain acute, above all the Algerian question. But I hope that in coming years he will bring unity and leadership and that under these conditions we will find that the executive has been given sufficient power by the Constitution."

Did he still think France's participation in an integrated Europe was synonymous with renouncing the idea of France as a nation—which he had written in his book. He replied: "I don't think you can renounce nationalism in Europe. Therefore, no integration is possible in Europe—only association."

He added that the English must realize that they cannot remain apart from Europe. They will find out, despite the present halt in negotiations with France, that they will be coming back for negotiations in a few months.

I asked what he thought of Mollet's idea of leaving Coty at the Elysée with de Gaulle continuing as Prime Minister. This horrified Debré. "The French want to be governed by de Gaulle. They want him as their director and don't want Parliament to take back authority. De Gaulle must remain above all parties."

ROME, *November 21, 1958*

DINED last night with Luigi Barzini, now a Deputy for the Liberal party. He views his role as that of public relations man for the party.

Luigi says the ruling Christian-Democratic party is a makeshift that came to power with the Vatican after the war, and it is the church's political machinery replacing that of the monarchy (and, although he didn't say this, fascism). The parish priests and lay organizations created an electoral machine. The party had four main tasks: to fight communism; to reconstruct the state and establish a rule of law, ending corruption and favoritism; to produce economic stability and prosperity; to create a national defense.

The party has failed, and Fanfani, a slick, party operator of the American party boss type, is playing with Gronchi and left-wing Christian-Democrats seeking "an opening to the left." In this, he is encouraged by Mattei, the oil king. He will fail to win the support of Nenni and the left Socialists, thus creating a serious crisis.

Fanfani doesn't dare really fight communism because when the disease disappears the doctor (Christian-Democrats) will no longer be necessary. The only concrete move against communism here was American-inspired: Mrs. Luce's program of withholding U.S. financial aid from factories where the workers had a Communist majority. Even papal excommunications have been carefully worded to outlaw atheist, materialist Communists, thus leaving a loophole for Communists who claim to be Catholics.

The Catholics, like the Tammany organization in New York, work on the political bases of brotherhood, help, and favors. Priests continually interfere in operations of the state, seeking jobs or favors for friends and supporters. In this setup, the party comes ahead of the state. The philosophical roots of the party thus negate the old democratic principles of Italian democracy as set out by Cavour.

Christian-Democratic economic theory mixes a vague kind of New Dealism with medieval guild traditions and some remnants of fascism. It fears a truly free society where able men emerge and incompetents sink to oblivion. It tries to build a static system such as in Spain. Italy is at present prosperous, thanks to the momentum of Europe's boom. But the system is top-heavy. State-owned enterprises, for example, cannot fire surplus workers without paying enormous recompense. Industry is saddled with charitable obligations for which the state and the taxpayer must pay.

Italy is weak and must depend on NATO. But Fanfani also seeks a private and somewhat neutralist policy in the Middle East, which would run counter to NATO. He tries to have his cake and eat it too. Thus, Fanfani went off to see Eisenhower and got a lot of local kudos. Now he plans to visit Nasser.

Fanfani's game is simply the old Gronchi plan of detaching Nenni from the Communists, getting him to join a coalition government with the Christian-Democrats that would then have 60–65 percent of the Parliamentary votes and could rule Italy for years.

ROME, *November 23, 1958*

DINED last night with Alessandrini. He has just been canned as head of the Foreign Office and is going off to Canada as ambassador—with no enthusiasm. Of course, he detests Fanfani, who did this to him, and the "Mau Maus" of the Fanfani wing of Christian-Democrats.

Fanfani is ready to loosen NATO bonds if he can gain Nenni's support. Nenni, at the same time, can tell Togliatti not to worry because he is achieving the prime aim of the Communists, neutralism.

Yesterday afternoon, I spent two hours with Enrico Mattei. Mattei who heads the fuel trust (ENI), is certainly one of the most powerful men in Italy and is reported to have a bloc of seventy Christian-Democratic Deputies who vote as he wishes. He also owns the paper *Il Giorno*, oil wells, gas, pipelines, service stations, ships, steel plants, bridges, technical schools, and has negotiated important foreign contracts, notably in Iran, Egypt, and Morocco.

He speaks moderately bad French, is tall for an Italian, lean, very fit (fifty-two), handsome, with sharp, intelligent features, wise, brown eyes and a sensitive, cruel mouth. Clearly he is most vain.

Mattei said although he was no longer a Deputy, he is still a "militant member" of the Christian-Democratic party. The only contributions he makes to it are "small, personal" gifts, and, though his enemies claim otherwise, he gives no funds to the Socialists. He admitted he sent some fifteen gunners to protect his Sinai fields during the Suez war—but "only against Bedouin marauders." He proudly added: "They wore ENI—not UN—armbands."

He thought Italy should be friendly with Nasser "because we're in the same lake, the Mediterranean. Italy's role is in this sea—but not, as Mussolini advocated, through the use of force. Our policy must be based on friendship with *all* Mediterranean countries."

Mattei was an industrialist. In 1943, he left his home in Milan and became a (non-Communist) partisan wartime leader. He says he had 160 brigades of 82,000 partisans under him at the end, mainly around the Gothic Line. He lost one out of three men. "It was cruel," he said, looking cruel. "There was no quarter on either side, no prisoners. I never talk about it."

ROME, *November 25, 1958*

YESTERDAY, I attended a meeting of diplomats, businessmen, politicians, and journalists discussing the East-West economic contest and the implications of foreign programs. Following are some observations made:

The Communist bloc's rate of growth in productivity is much more rapid than our own. If this difference continues for the next ten or twenty years, and the West does not accelerate its own rate of growth, the world power situation will be completely altered. What would be the effect when Communist countries become richer than the West and have a higher living standard?

The underdeveloped countries must be developed and we must do our share. They represent more than one-half the world and we must show dramatically our concern about improving their situation. This cannot be achieved merely by private enterprise or by sticking to such nineteenth-century commercial criteria as "soundness."

China is increasing its productive growth and raising its standard of living at two or three times the rate of its obvious democratic competitor, India. We must face this problem if we are to avoid the possibility that underdeveloped countries will consider the political attraction of communism invincible.

We are used to expecting gratitude from those we help, but it was Strindberg who said, "Why does he hate me? I have never helped him."

This afternoon Barzini came to see me. Claimed his telephone was tapped and that is why one of the numerous papers attacking me today for a column I wrote about the Italian "Mau Mau" said not only that I was a French hatchet-man, but that I had consorted with a "few Italians" who were not Italy. Luigi took this as an indication of himself, and a tapped phone.

He said General Di Lorenzo, chief of intelligence, is most nervous lest I mention his name in a column, as I had planned to do tomorrow (saying he was due for replacement and many feared the Mau Maus would put in an anti-NATO man). Di Lorenzo begs me to keep his name out.

Last night, I dined at the French embassy where Palewski is now ambassador. A fantastic building, the Palazzo Farnese. The dining room, with a Caracci ceiling, is the loveliest I have ever dined in.

Ivan Mattei Lombardo, a right-wing Socialist who was there, says Italy is heading for disaster; that Fanfani and Gronchi are trying the dangerous pro-Nenni game, that Mattei is the real boss of Italy and will someday seek to become dictator. He says Valletta, the boss of Fiat, has sold out to Mattei (politically) "because Valletta is a whore" and the famous *La Stampa di Torino* is now a Mattei organ.

Il Giorno, Mattei's paper, attacked me as a Jew and said I'd written my piece out of concern for Israel vis-à-vis the Arabs. This is the first time since fascism that such anti-Semitic innuendos have appeared.

Senator Kefauver was at Palewski's. Afterward, we went out and had some drinks at the Excelsior; then Kefauver wanted to "find women." We joined some American girls and two Sudanese diplomats at the Brick Top nightclub.

Before the carousing, Kefauver talked well. He said Faubus had been a decent liberal who got into integration by accident and had made a fetish of segregation. This was the way McCarthy got into "communism in the State Department." Senator Wherry had prepared a speech on the subject for a West Virginia audience. Wherry fell ill and asked young McCarthy to substitute. McCarthy made the speech on which he catapulted to fame—having no advance idea of what was in it.

Kefauver says Stevenson is still running hard for the 1960 nomination. He makes no bones about running himself. He says Symington stands the best chance; Kennedy is running too fast on these early laps and will lick himself.

BONN, GERMANY, *December 6, 1958*

LONG talk with Franz-Josef Strauss, German defense minister. I find him both the most impressive and depressive individual in Germany today. Someday, he is likely to be Chancellor. He could be a fine democrat, another autocrat, or even the man to make a nationalistic deal with Russia. As it is, he is an attractive, shrewd, forthright fellow, of medium height, very overweight, but healthy and dynamic.

I started by asking what was Bonn's attitude toward de Gaulle's proposal for a Big Three "directorate" in NATO to handle political strategy. Strauss replied: "Obviously there is a great difference in the political importance of various members of NATO. You cannot, for example, compare the United States and Iceland, or Great Britain and Luxemburg.

"Nevertheless, a directorate, such as that suggested by de Gaulle, would touch upon the legal status of NATO. We are afraid this would bring about a system of first-class, second-class, and third-class members. This would add to the tensions and controversies in NATO and would sicken its internal structure."

I asked what orders Strauss would give the Bundeswehr and/or the militia in case of another uprising in East Germany. He replied: "We will do all we can to keep the people quiet. For there is *nothing* we can do if they arise. That is to say, there is nothing we can do unless there is a NATO decision to act. There will be no special and specifically German action. Furthermore, any kind of armed interference would risk war."

I asked on what conditions West Germany would agree to forgo nuclear rearmament. He said: "We didn't ask for atomic arms until there was a NATO decision to equip all alliance forces accordingly. If there is a political solution for international disarmament in stages we will, of course, accept it. But we took no national decision about rearmament and we are taking no national decision about disarmament. This is up to the alliance. If the whole alliance is to be equipped with nuclear arms, as NATO decided, we cannot exclude ourselves."

BONN, GERMANY, *December 7, 1958*

DRINKS with David Bruce. He said the present condition of Europe with a divided Germany and an occupied Berlin has existed for thirteen years and cannot go on indefinitely. A new effort to negotiate with Russia must start.

Actually, from a strictly legal point of view, if the Russians turn over their *full* powers in East Berlin, the western Big Three have the technical right to rush in and fill the vacuum. But Russia may not turn over full powers, and such an act by the West would start a war.

Bruce thinks the West must reaffirm that any attack on Berlin is an attack on all the West. But what guarantee can we give if there is no open attack, merely a gradual strangulation? The Russians can throttle access to Berlin, which would also hurt West Germany's economy. How far can we go in protecting this?

Hitherto we have *never* been cut off from access to Berlin. A decade ago, we had to depend upon the airlift, but there was no military interference with this. Now the East German government announces it is the sovereign of its own air space and that it will assert this authority. We must decide where and how we will use our air force.

The United States believes that a lack of German unity represents a great danger for the future in Europe's heart, though Bruce admits he is not personally convinced this is true. Nevertheless, we must show full fidelity to an ally, Bonn, who desires unification.

Bruce thinks the United States should not *risk* anything for the sake of German unification. He cannot imagine the Russians giving up East Germany, their greatest satellite prize. It is economically valuable, offers a superb strategic situation, and is run by a totally subservient government.

One reason Khrushchev raised the Berlin question now is that East Germany is being crippled by a flow of refugees fleeing to the West. There is an increasingly high intellectual level—doctors, professors, teachers. The brains of East Germany are quitting. Ulbricht is pressing Russia to put a halt to this. Also this is a lovely opportunity for Khrushchev to try a probing operation. We must never forget that Russia is scared stiff of Germany's military revival.

PARIS, *December 17, 1958*

EDDIE Tomkins (British embassy), says a Swede remarked to him after the OEEC meeting: "The Germans always win battles and lose wars. The French win arguments and lose negotiations."

PARIS, *December 18, 1958*

THIS evening, I saw Dulles. The poor fellow looked pale, thin, ill. His voice was tired and it seemed to me he talked more slowly. Some of the electricity has gone out of the man. I must say he has guts and I feel sorry for him. I think he has cancer.

He said the geopolitical situation has changed greatly since NATO started. The problem raised by de Gaulle is very real. There has been *no* French assurance on IRBM ramps here.

On Germany, we still stand by our 1955 offer. This told the Russians that if a united Germany was produced as a result of free elections and it decided to stay in NATO, the NATO forces would not be stationed in East Germany and there would be no increase in the scheduled German military strength. Furthermore, we are prepared to give the Russians specific security guarantees that if a united Germany attacked Russia, all the NATO countries would help Russia against Germany, despite the fact that the latter was a member of our alliance.

PARIS, *December 19, 1958*

GOOD talk with Ambassador Am Houghton. Dulles has made a remarkable recovery, but is still in pain. He has been on a diet—which explains why he is pale and thin. He only ate at the embassy while he was in Paris and for all but two meals was served on a tray in his room: boiled chicken and rice. At one larger meal a bisque of lobster was served.

Dulles said: "The hell with it, I am prepared to accept the consequences," and took two helpings.

Houghton told me the story of Dulles's reception by de Gaulle. Dulles outlined his views on Berlin and his insistence that Khrushchev's ultimatum be rebuffed. De Gaulle was in complete agreement.

The next matter raised was de Gaulle's request for a United States–British–French political *directoire* to coordinate global strategy. De Gaulle pointed out that the world situation had changed greatly since NATO was founded. He had no intention of smashing NATO, but it must be modified. Only recently the United States—without consulting Paris—had voted for Guinea's admission to the UN, and had abstained from the vote on Algeria instead of supporting France.

Dulles appreciated the General's position. Nevertheless, he considered it impossible to have any formal organic committee inside NATO, such as that suggested by de Gaulle. The matter might be approached by more extensive ad hoc consultations on various matters as they arise. There were certainly some areas where it was both possible and desirable to coordinate Big Three viewpoints outside the NATO treaty limits. One such obvious area was Africa, which is probably the only uncommitted continent left in the world. De Gaulle said Africa was precisely what he meant and then, to Dulles's discomfort, hopped right back to Guinea and Algeria.

De Gaulle made it perfectly apparent that France would drag its feet in NATO until he was satisfied France was being given a greater role in allied strategy. He said, that as it is now constituted, NATO is an arm of U.S. policy. It is dominated by the U.S. and has an American commander-in-chief.

PARIS, *January 2, 1959*

HOUGHTON read me the memorandum of a conversation last month between Debré and Bob McBride, head of the State Department's Western European Division. Debré said he is 100 percent committed to a "French solution for Algeria"—but not necessarily integration. He is determined to kill the Common Market. He thinks France must honor its commitments, but this doesn't mean those cannot be replaced by others. He wants an agreement with England, in two or three years, designed to nullify the Common Market. This is his "number-one objective." Debré is firmly convinced the Common Market is an instrument of United States policy and was virtually imposed upon France by Washington. He makes no secret of his anti-American views.

PARIS, *January 20, 1959*

INTERESTING lunch with Reuven Shiloah. He has summoned a meeting of Israeli diplomats to coordinate their approach on the current contest between Nasser and el-Kassem in the Arab world. The Israelis support el-Kassem. They are doing everything possible to block friendship between Nasser and the West.

Shiloah has the rank of ambassador and continues as Ben Gurion's hatchet-man. Any diplomatic problem that cannot be handled through one of the normal Foreign Office desks is handled by him. I gather he is also still liaison between Ben Gurion and Israeli intelligence.

Shiloah told me when Fanfani was in Cairo, he offered Nasser aid on the Aswan High Dam, not money but technicians. Nasser turned him down because in the Soviet-Egyptian agreement on Aswan there is a clause stipulating that during the first stage of the dam's construction the only non-Arab technicians to be employed must come from the Soviet bloc. The French have a copy of this agreement, which ties a much tighter string to Cairo than all the so-called western "strings" of which Nasser complained.

Later, Averoff, the Greek foreign minister, told me a Cyprus solution appears to be in the offing and will be incorporated in an overall Greek-Turkish arrangement, reaffirming the alliance between the two countries, reestablishing the Balkan Pact, and settling several basic problems including new guarantees concerning the Greek Orthodox patriarchy in Istanbul. According to Averoff, either all this will work out or the alternative will be chaos and possible war.

Averoff asked me if I would be prepared to go to Cyprus and secretly contact Colonel Grivas, head of the EOKA underground, who has been hunted by the British for the last four years. Averoff has no direct or sure contact with Grivas and thinks the reports he sends Grivas by present, uncertain contacts are watered down by extremist Cypriots (pro-Enosis). Would I be ready to go and see Grivas? He stipulated as a condition that I should first see Averoff in Athens for a briefing. Averoff would advise the British of my trip in advance and said he was in a position to guarantee they would not use me as bait to capture or assassinate Grivas.

I expressed scepticism and recounted how I had spent a night with EOKA in September, 1955. Averoff said: "I can assure you I shall be able to arrange this with the British." I think Grivas is too wise a guerrilla warrior to risk his neck on Averoff's promise.

Nevertheless, I agreed to go. I told Averoff to get a message to me through his embassy stating he is anxious to see me in Athens. I would drop everything if I get such a message. I am not going to tell anybody in advance concerning this plan. But knowing how ruthless the British can be when necessary and how bitterly they feel about the numerous murders accomplished by Grivas, I don't bet much on any assurance they might give Averoff.

Averoff told me something about the secret negotiations on Cyprus between Greece and Turkey. He said he is sworn to secrecy (immediately telling me everything) and that only four people in the world know what is taking place—Caramanlis, and Menderes, prime ministers of Greece and Turkey; and Averoff and Zorlu, respective foreign ministers. They haven't even told their ambassadors to NATO. No representative of Spaak or any Englishman took part in the talks, which ended today with Zorlu's departure.

The basis is as follows:

Greece will not accept partition of Cyprus. Turkey will not accept Enosis. Both Athens and Ankara agree that, in an independent republic of Cyprus, Britain can retain military bases, including the Akrotiri Peninsula, Nicosia, and Famagusta. The Greeks agree that Turkish Cypriots must have full religious, educational, and legal rights. The ultimate settlement will be incorporated in a treaty signed by Turkey, Greece, Great Britain, and the Republic of Cyprus, granting territorial integrity and forbidding it ever to join any political group to which both Greece and Turkey do not already belong. In other words, it would be incorporated within the NATO framework.

The Greeks are not yet certain EOKA will agree and this is why Averoff wants me to sell Grivas a bill of goods. He will conceivably— if I may be cynical—try to use me as a trap so the British can kill Grivas and solve the problem a priori. Averoff frankly admitted Grivas was in a position not only to scotch possible agreement but to bring about the downfall of the Greek government.

He said he could guarantee that Archbishop Makarios would accept an independent Cyprus. (I am sure Makarios would like to be its first chief of state.)

PARIS, *January 22, 1959*

AT dinner, Henri Bonnet, former ambassador to Washington, told me that in 1955, when Sainteny was French "commercial representative" in Hanoi, Paris was hoping not only to develop relations with North Vietnam, but also to make of Haiphong a French Hong Kong, through which massive trade could be developed with southern China.

GAULLISM'S

D'ARTAGNAN

NTERESTING TALK WITH CHABAN-DELMAS, FORTY-FOUR-YEAR-OLD
president of the National Assembly, who under French protocol is
number-four man in the Fifth Republic, but who, in terms of actual
authority, is possibly as important as the Prime Minister. (Later he became
premier.)

He is youthful looking, slender, pale, dark, elegant, very friendly, obviously ambitious, vain, and self-centered. He had a fine record in
the war. He was commissioned a brigadier general by de Gaulle before
he was thirty, acquiring a dazzling series of decorations, including the
British DSO. He was once an international Rugby player and is quite a
hand with the ladies. He has been described as the "d'Artagnan of Gaullism." Under the Fourth Republic he was once defense minister. By training, he is an inspecteur des finances, which proves his mental brilliance.

De Gaulle, he said, relies totally on a very small group of devoted
followers. "There are perhaps five of these," said Chaban, and then
added, "No, I cannot even think of five." At any rate, the group includes
Debré and Chaban-Delmas. Malraux is an intimate of de Gaulle's but absolutely without political influence; he is merely the "singer" of the
movement. Soustelle was in the group but has had too many sharp rows
with de Gaulle. Chaban has tried to patch up relations between de Gaulle
and Soustelle and between Debré and Soustelle. Now they are again working together, and Chaban meets with Soustelle and Debré every evening.

De Gaulle is extremely sensitive "despite the fact that he gives the appearance of being a machine." He was hurt by Soustelle's obstinacy. De
Gaulle recognizes that it is a function of politics to be opposed by those
who disagree, but he cannot accept the disloyalty of his intimates. The

General's technique is to listen to everybody's views, then finally, to make categorical decisions. Debré accepted this even when the decisions did not agree with Debré's views. But Soustelle did not. The quarrel stems essentially from the Algerian question. Soustelle feels that de Gaulle and Debré are deceiving themselves on Algeria.

Chaban said:

Under the Fourth Republic, Parliament substituted itself progressively for the government. The government became more apparent than real. The ministers were not ministers but representatives of political groups in the Assembly. These groups were led by the different parties, represented various special interests, including labor, the *patronat* and, in the case of the Communists, Russia. In reality, the government was teleguided by the National Assembly which itself was divided into political compartments which were in permanent opposition to each other on many issues. Consequently, in order to survive, the government simply ignored or failed to act on important problems. Or else, when it attacked serious matters, it exploded when the ministers resigned, or it was overthrown by the Assembly.

Today, under the Fifth Republic, there is a clear separation of powers and a distinction between the various arms of the state. Consequently, the government has a free hand to govern. And Parliament has the right to control this as foreseen by the Constitution. Parliament can overthrow a government by a vote of censure. But the government does not depend upon Parliament in order to be formed. The Chief of State nominates the Prime Minister and approves his Cabinet. But the government remains responsible before the National Assembly. Thus France has a parliamentary regime and not a presidential regime. And it is certainly not a dictatorship.

Right now, public opinion still tends to distrust Parliament. I remember twelve years under the Fourth Republic, when the Assembly practically paralyzed the government. But after a certain time, when stability is restored, public opinion will appreciate again the extreme importance of being a parliamentary regime and the suitability of such a regime to a liberal people like the French. Parliament is the *only* guarantee against an arbitrary administration. This guarantee is essential to our national life. Each Frenchman must know that *his* deputy can question the acts of the government on any issue. This is a right of every citizen and a most important right.

I asked Chaban my usual question: Who, during his life, had most influenced his personality and development? He replied without hesitation, his mother.

She influenced me profoundly from the time I was three until the time I was eight, when I lived entirely under her influence. She showed me only the noble and great things. As it were, I was brought up by Joan of Arc. I didn't learn to read from ordinary primers. I learned to read in *La Grande Guerre Illustrée*, a volume of pictures showing the photos of our French soldiers. When Lord Kitchener died I was only two and a half but it was a big thing for me; I wept.

I asked about his future ambitions. He said: "I only hope profoundly that the rest of my life can be useful to the nation. Everyone has a vice. Mine is to serve the people. If, for example, I had a choice between retiring and being offered a big position, and I thought that it was in the public interest for me to retire, I would retire. I am an instrument of the public."

Lunch with Gajewski, the Polish ambassador and his wife (together with Marina). As usual, incredibly lavish—caviar, smoked salmon, vodka, truite aux amandes, an excellent Moselle wine, duck, peas, Chateau Haut-Brion, cheese and a fine Burgundy, a sweet, a first-class Veuve Clicquot, followed by coffee and Napoleon brandy. Latest Warsaw jokes: Why do the Poles like the Russians so much? Because they want a buffer state between Poland and China. What is the difference between capitalism and communism? Capitalism is a system under which man is exploited by man. Communism is just the opposite.

I don't understand the game. Gajewski, just back from Poland, emphasized its intellectual vitality. He said there were twenty-three theaters in Warsaw now; there used to be ten. Everybody is reading Pasternak. There was a recent election in the writers' association and not a single member of the Communist party was admitted to office. Last year, when the Russians invited the Poles to send a painting exhibition to Moscow, they deliberately selected their most avant garde and abstract paintings, which caused confusion in Russia.

Voroshilov went to an art exhibition in Warsaw and couldn't understand the painting. He asked for an explanation of an abstract work. He said: "Why does the state support and finance such painting?" He complained nobody could understand it, certainly not a worker. The Poles replied it was their aspiration to bring workers to a level where they could understand such painting.

He said Gomulka was a simple, earthy man without any sense of humor. In this respect he is like Khrushchev. He had no intellectual pretentions. Socialist-realism was an acceptable art form with him. He considered painting in the light of colored photography; he wanted a tractor to look like a tractor.

Khrushchev had made it clear that the Poles could have anything they wanted provided they didn't talk too much about it. They didn't have to collectivize their peasants and they could have a free church. But they shouldn't talk against Russia and against Socialist realism.

Gajewski insists that both for Poland and the world it would be a terrible thing if Khrushchev fell from power. He genuinely wants peace because he thinks this is the way communism can triumph. If he is replaced, it would probably be by a faction that would clamp down on the satellites, be opposed to any accommodation with the West, and be prepared for war. But Khrushchev is not popular with the Russian people. They hated Stalin, but they respected him as a boss. They make jokes about Khrushchev, even though they are happier.

Gajewski thought the only world capitals interested in German unification were Washington and Pankow (East Berlin). He said: "I wonder if you dislike the West Germans as much as we dislike the East Germans."

ROCQUENCOURT, *January 30, 1959*

SAW Larry Norstad just before he went off to Spain and Morocco to see our military bases. He said: "As longer range aircraft and missiles— either IRBMs or ICBMs—come in, we become less dependent on intermediate-type bases. Nevertheless, now and for a considerable time, they continue to be highly desirable, and I might even say essential for at least the next three to five years."

Norstad admitted he was not thoroughly sold, back in 1951, on the necessity of bases in Spain. But it was required to have additional bases to handle the range of B-47 bombers. North Ireland was one alternative site considered. Finally, Spain was selected since Spain would also serve as a political hedge against the possible loss of our bases in Morocco.

By about 1965, air defense would be largely accomplished by missiles. Some short-range operational tasks will then be divided by the aircraft and missiles. But for close support operations a "missile with judgment"—that is to say, a manned aircraft—will continue to play an essential role.

PARIS, *January 31, 1959*

THIS evening, I had a good talk with de Gaulle, the first since he became President of the Republic. I saw him in the Palais de l'Elysée, France's White House, which is busy as a beehive nowadays. I have been there when it was inhabited by Auriol and Coty, but for the first time today, I had the impression it was truly the center of the French government as well as the residence of a chief of state.

I entered through the gate on the rue Faubourg St. Honoré, outside which stand ordinary gendarmes in dark-blue capes and képis as well as

Gardes Républicains in their nineteenth-century uniforms with red-plumed shakos and bayoneted rifles. A Garde Républicain escorted me from the gate to the main entrance of the Palais where I was taken up-stairs and passed into an antechamber, with high ceiling, high windows, brocade curtains, Aubusson carpets and tapestries, a huge crystal chande-lier, and a couple of azalea plants. Tail-coated flunkies slid in and out. Some were red-vested and others had ceremonial chains around their necks.

While I was waiting, Colonel de Bonneval, his aide, came out to say hello. I noticed that, in contrast to his long years of waiting at 5, rue de Solférino, he was wearing full uniform. Then Couve de Murville emerged and we talked while Prime Minister Debré went in to see de Gaulle. Shortly Debré came out, looking tired, rather depressed, and in need of a shave. The bell sounded and in I went.

De Gaulle came halfway to the door to greet me and then motioned me to a chair across from him before he sat himself down behind his desk.*

(Incidentally, I was quite fascinated to observe that nobody referred to him as "Monsieur le Président." They all referred to him as "le General" or "General de Gaulle." When I shook hands with Debré, I said, "Bonsoir, Monsieur le Président." This produced a merry chuckle from Colonel de Bonneval, who said, "Non, non, 'Monsieur le Premier Ministre.' Il n'est pas le Président." In the past, the Prime Minister of France was known as the "Président du Conseil." Now he is specified in the Constitution as the "Premier Ministre." This, I may say, is more than a question of protocol or semantics. For it was perfectly evident to me today that the President of France is Charles de Gaulle. It is fully evident from a couple of hours in the Elysée that the French White House has undergone even more of an organizational revolution than our own White House did in 1933, when Roosevelt began his New Deal.)

I told de Gaulle I had several questions I wanted to ask, particularly concerning foreign policy. I would appreciate it if he would clarify for me the desires of France vis-à-vis the United States in terms of our alli-ances. He replied:

> I told the United States and British governments that we must con-sider our relationships in terms of world security. NATO only covers the North Atlantic area. Together we must organize something for the whole world. This must be done by our three countries, as the three leaders of the free world which have global interests. These three leaders must organize world security both in a political and in a stra-tegic sense. In this respect, NATO is a secondary question. It comes below and after the global problems.†

* See de Gaulle's further comments, p. 81.
† See de Gaulle's further comments, p. 62.

I asked him if he thought there was now more United States comprehension of these views than there had been in the past. He said he thought there was, but that it was a slow affair, and conversations were just starting.

I asked if he thought the United States should or could grant more aid to France in connection with atomic weapons. He replied, lifting his shoulders in a shrug, stretching out his long arms, and raising his eyebrows: "That is up to you. Certainly France thinks there could be more such help. Of course, we do not know how this could be arranged with your Congress; but if there were better cooperation from you on this, it would save us much time and money."

I asked him if France intended to go ahead and explode its own test bomb. He replied in the affirmative. A bomb would be exploded "soon" but there had been "some delay." He added, however, "But we will do it."*

Then he added a threatening phrase, almost menacing, if one ponders it. He said: "Only, if there is no comprehension of our viewpoints, if there is no other way than war [meaning an intra-allied political dispute, not an armed conflict], will we join in the battle. We will take back our liberties. But I don't foresee this. All logic points toward an accord."

I then asked him if he could see any basis for compromise between the Common Market, as advocated by the French, and the Free Trade Area, as advocated by England. He replied:

The Common Market exists—not that it has had many consequences so far. But the Free Trade Area does not exist. Obviously there should be an economic accord between the two ideas. But Britain exaggerated greatly. They said that all Europe would be split on January 1, when the first phase of the Common Market began. But it did not split. There was no revolution in commercial exchanges. Then Britain wanted to support the Common Market but this we refused to do.

(This was also interesting in terms of de Gaulle's previous indications to me to the effect that he wanted to drop the whole idea.)

I asked if he had any plans to accept the invitation extended through Dulles last July for him to visit President Eisenhower in the United States. He said he didn't know what would happen. He added: "Maybe Eisenhower will come to Europe."

I asked if he had extended an invitation to the President to pay an official visit. He said: "Not yet," adding: "One cannot foresee these things. Nothing has yet been arranged. But I would like to see President Eisenhower. He has always been my friend."

I then said I had heard a rumor that the Russians had suggested to him he should have a meeting with Khrushchev. Was this true? The reply

---

* See de Gaulle's further comments, pp. 62–63.

was surprisingly imprecise. He asked: "Did the Russians say that? I don't know what the Russians said. I have not heard this. This is the first time I have heard it."

I asked if he would agree to such a meeting. He shrugged his shoulders. On that note we terminated the conversation. I thanked him. He rose and came to the door with me and he shook my hand and wished me well, he leaned over a bit and said in a somber voice, "Remember, je n'ai rien dit."*

MADRID, *February 1, 1959*

THE evening we arrived, Ambassador John Lodge invited us for dinner. Lodge has huge political ambitions (a former Republican governor of Connecticut). He is a tall, handsome, hearty man, much like his brother Cabot, but no quiz kid. He hates Jack Kennedy and seems to have an inferiority complex vis-à-vis him. He says that it is U.S. policy to get Spain enmeshed in so many international entanglements (such as UN) that it cannot escape again into isolationism. He claims we simply do not understand Spain. He is proud that this is not a "totalitarian" regime, only "authoritarian." (An odd boast in the U.S. embassy.)

MADRID, *February 3, 1959*

BEN Welles arranged a most interesting lunch for me today. It included Fernando Maria Castiella, the foreign minister; Lieutenant General Antonio Barroso, the war minister; Manuel Arburua, former minister of commerce.

Castiella is a big, friendly Basque, who fought as a private in the Blue Division against Russia (after having been a captain in Franco's army), was ambassador to the Holy See for several years, and was refused as ambassador to London because the British disliked his claims on Gibraltar. He said Spain plans soon to raise the issue of the Spanish Republican gold in Russia (for which they received the claimant documents from Negrin's son late in 1956) at the UN or the Hague International Court.

There are *no* more negotiations with Moscow. The Russians did negotiate on recognition for a while. Madrid had sent a note to Vinogradov (Soviet envoy in Paris) through Casa Rojas, ambassador in Paris, in late 1956. Then Vinogradov called on Casa Rojas. The Russians wanted recognition before discussing the gold. Spain refused. Everything lapsed, although the Russians hinted they want recognition and claim it is "unrealistic" not to exchange embassies. The Russians now claim no more Spanish gold is left; that Spain, in fact, owes them money.

* See de Gaulle's further comments, p. 87.

Spain is eager to join NATO but won't take the initiative; she must first be asked. Madrid knows Norway opposes. Belgium used to, but since Spaak has become the alliance's secretary-general, Spaak and Belgium have both undergone a change of mind.

Castiella and Arburua assert the U.S.A. must help Spain build up its economy. They complain Spain got no Marshall Plan aid because of our previous policy.

Barroso, a pleasant little grandfatherly type in grandiloquent uniform with decorations, adorned with large paunch and gray hair, is supposedly the general closest to the Monarchists. He desperately wants Spain in NATO.

MADRID, *February 4, 1959*

TODAY, I spent more than an hour with Franco. At the Pardo Palace I was met by Martin-Gamero of the Foreign Office, all dolled up in cutaway. We sat about, chatted, and regarded the magnificent tapestries (cartoons by Goya) in the antechamber: scenes of Spanish life in vivid colors; stilt walkers, bowlers, peasants caught in a snow storm.

Martin-Gamero told me of Franco's famous capacity to sit for hours at Cabinet meetings, never smoking (he does not), never even leaving the room to pee. The ministers go out often for a smoke or relief.

Franco greeted me in very friendly fashion, shook hands with a firm grip while his official photographer snapped pictures, waved me to a chair across from him, Martin-Gamero beside me. The desk was piled two feet deep in papers. I noticed in a corner a signed photograph of Eisenhower.

Franco was wearing full uniform with a red sash about his middle. He's almost sixty-seven, plump, with delicate features, amazingly soft, warm eyes for so hard a character, olive complexion, quiet smile, soft, high-pitched voice.

To start things off on an easy basis, I asked about his relatively new hobby of painting. He said (always in Spanish through Martin-Gamero) he had taken it up twelve years ago and enjoys it "when I find a free moment." He likes to paint wild animals and landscapes. In the country, he makes sketches and then paints from them on rainy afternoons later on. He also admitted to having taken up golf. But he is clearly no enthusiast. He said: "It takes up too much time."

Franco said the U.S.-Spanish bases agreement was working out "very smoothly and well." I asked if it were correct that Spain, through the Portuguese alliance (and consequent tie to NATO) and the U.S. agreement, could still be considered a neutral. He replied: "Obviously Spain is no longer neutral; and for the reasons you point out. Nowadays neutrality is impossible for any country on the continent of Europe. This is especially true for a land with the strategic importance of Spain."

I asked if he considered the Spanish-U.S. accord "an alliance." He replied: "Up to a certain point, it is an alliance. It is certainly an alliance from the standpoint of our agreement to oppose a common foe, Russian communism."

I then inquired if he would consider it as a sine qua non for any government that should succeed him, under the 1947 Act of Succession, that it must accept the provisions of the bases' agreement. He answered: "Yes, of course. Naturally."

I told him I had heard that, although the bases' agreement provided that Spain would publicize our help, this had not been done. He said: "I consider there is no foundation for such a complaint. We have given this enough publicity and shall continue to do so."

I inquired about the rumors that Spanish arms were being used by the Riff rebels in Morocco. He said: "That is entirely false. The people of the Riff, as a matter of fact, are very badly armed. The great majority of such arms as they have were captured either from the Royal Moroccan army or the police. They have a certain amount of other equipment, I understand, that has been smuggled from Algeria. And they have some stuff received from deserters from the royal army and the army of liberation."

I asked if Franco thought Nasser was stirring up the Riff by using the prestige "of your erstwhile opponent" Abd-el-Krim. He said:

Abd-el-Krim is too old. He is removed from the Moroccan problem these days. As a matter of fact, his sons are in Rabat and are working with the King and his army. Personally I consider the rebellion now taking place is a natural process, a reflection of the special problems of the Riff. The Riffians felt themselves persecuted.

The only thing we fear and fear gravely, is the penetration of communism in that area. Communism is working hard there and it is favored by prevailing economic conditions. Infiltration by the Communists is a serious danger and should be recognized. For us, as neighbors, we consider peace and stability absolutely essential in North Africa.

I asked if Spain desired to join NATO. He replied with arrogance:

Spain would study the question if we received an invitation. Every time the matter has been raised in NATO [by Portugal], it produces the criticisms and vetos of certain members. Spain does not like to provoke such discord. And the matter is not urgent. We are in a position always to align ourselves with the NATO lands in case of war, thanks to the U.S. agreement. For this reason, in our conversations with the United States, we point out that we fulfill practically the same role as NATO members and that therefore we want the same amount and kind of aid.

I wondered if Spain would be willing to discuss diplomatic recognition with Moscow if Moscow agreed to return the gold. He said: "No. Definitely not." He went on to say that in several countries around the world (I believe he meant France, the U.S., and Morocco), Soviet representatives "had contacted our own representatives and asked that at least commercial relations should be established between us. We always stated that a necessary precondition to continuing such talks was the return of our gold. Nothing ever happened."

I said there was a rumor that Franco intended to proclaim on the twentieth anniversary of the Civil War's end a general political amnesty. Was this true? He answered:

Such an amnesty would be quite unnecessary. After all, who would benefit? Why, the total prison population in Spain today is only half what it was under the Republic. The immense majority of these people are common criminals. The question of the Civil War is all over, finished. There have already been various amnesties and measures of clemency. There is no need for any more.

I then inquired whether, thanks to Soviet aid and propaganda, communism was spreading underground in Spain. He said: "Periodically the Russians make new efforts. This is a regular occurrence. About every two years they organize a new attempt, then we squash it. Then, after a time, they begin another endeavor. They always look for the slightest opportunity to foment strikes or other troubles here, the slightest excuse."

I asked if, under the 1947 Succession Act, Don Juan was "the obvious and only heir to the Spanish throne." Franco said that undoubtedly Don Juan could lay valid claim to "all the rights of inheritance" of the throne. "He has the most natural rights and claims." But then he went on to say, "Naturally whoever succeeds to the throne must first accept all the conditions and stipulations of the Act of Succession. The monarchy would have to rest upon our prevailing laws. After all, they were accepted by more than 90 percent of the people in a plebiscite which established them as the laws of the country."

(This would certainly hang quite an albatross around Don Juan's neck.)

Finally, I asked him if he still felt—as he had told me in 1948— that socialism and communism were one and the same thing. He answered:

You foreigners must understand that Spanish socialism is entirely different from such other kinds of socialism as, for example, British socialism. Here it is far more primitive and revolutionary than elsewhere.

From our experience, we could not help but see that socialism and communism in Spain were practically the same. One of the tactics of the Communist party here was to penetrate socialism, to attract Socialist party leaders to communism, letting them appear to remain Socialist, but actually using them as Communists. That is why, in

1936, communism spread so rapidly and so widely. Both parties had Marxist roots. Believe me, if you ever establish a Socialist state in Spain you will end with a Communist state.

MADRID, *February 6, 1959*

DROVE out to the "Valley of the Fallen," a massive Civil War memorial Franco has been building more than fifteen years, carved out of a granite mountain a few miles from the Escorial. Rather beautiful despite its incredible scale; must be the most enormous funerary undertaking since the days of Pharaoh. In the heart of the mountain is a vast chapel, hung with wonderful Flemish tapestries and domed with a modern (ugly) mosaic right beneath the cross outside. The rumor is Franco will be buried on one side, José Antonio (the Falange martyr) on the other. José Antonio, to the horror of Monarchists, is at present lodged in the floor of the Escorial above the royal family's chapel. So far there isn't a bone of either a Nationalist or Republican soldier in the memorial. Will there ever be?

ESTORIL, PORTUGAL, *February 10, 1959*

LUNCHED at his home with Don Juan, Count of Barcelona and (he hopes) future King of Spain. Among those present were his wife, the Duke and Duchess of Alba, and his secretary Padilla. The house, in Estoril, is a suburban mansion, white, comfortably furnished, the hallway filled with heads and tusks from various hunts in Africa, the stairs containing a few ship models.

Don Juan's wife is a tall, fat woman with sad Bourbon face, like that of her ancestor, France's Louis XVI, extremely pleasant and cozy. Complained that Portuguese sounds to her like Spanish spoken with a mouthful of boiled potatoes. Don Juan is a massive fellow, about six foot one, huge, broad shoulders and chest; must be strong as a bull. He looks like a former all-American tackle; beak of a nose, heavy jaw, thin lips, a not-too-high forehead that slopes sharply backward.

He served very happily in the British navy, getting a royal commission from his uncle, King George V. He had eventually to resign this commission as Lieutenant Prince John of Spain because of a regulation introduced by Ramsay MacDonald's Labour government that only British subjects could command ships. He went back to England from India and sat up one evening with King George, drinking highballs, while George cussed out the "bloody Socialists," but could do nothing about keeping Juan in. After the Spanish Civil War started, Juan slipped across from Portugal to join a Franco unit, but when it was discovered by higher echelons and referred to General Franco, he was sent back. Nobody wanted to (a) assume the responsibility for his life; (b) be stuck with the monarchic question.

Don Juan talked freely and at length. He said: "Portugal is a republic where if you mention the word 'republic' you are clapped into jail. Spain is a monarchy where if you mention the word 'monarchy' you are clapped into jail."

He is discouraged about the future. Franco keeps talking about being a Monarchist, but he does nothing to pave the way. He obviously intends to sit out his own life in power, come what may. "A real case of 'après moi le déluge.' " Don Juan asked him if he wouldn't at least form a "government" with a prime minister. Got nowhere. Franco *is* the whole government. If he dies suddenly, Juan figures the only thing to keep the lid on is the army. He admits that "it will be a ticklish moment for me." The army would have to invite him back; but he has little faith in its generals. Garcia Valiñõ, he says, is intelligent and highly ambitious. He hates Franco and told Don Juan, "I'll kill him if you give me the word." But Don Juan doesn't trust him. Muños Grandes is colorful but a symbol of the regime and content to live it out. "I place my reliance on the colonels, not the generals," said Juan. But he didn't know which ones.

He said the Foreign Office and diplomats were Monarchists. But they would make no move to aid him; they were content to serve Franco. He complained the U.S. sent a few million dollars in aid every time it looked as if final collapse was coming; thus we kept Franco in. He recalled telling me a few years ago that America had "gummed me up" in 1946.

The Communists were growing in strength as Franco continued to squash other, less conspiratorial forms of opposition. Don Juan said some Socialist elements were backing him, and "this is necessary." But he said this without conviction and gave the impression he didn't much care for any brand of socialism—above all "Marxist."

When he was in Washington last year, Don Juan said he was received by Herter at the State Department. Being in an unofficial position he said he could not be received by Dulles. Herter told him the United States would like him to guarantee full liberties for Spain—and *immediately* upon his accession. Don Juan said he could not do this; it would create anarchy and chaos. Such things had to be done gradually. It would take a generation. And some aspects of the present regime could be kept and developed—the syndicates, the Cortes.

His idea of his future regime would be to install a system similar to the British monarchy, "not the Scandinavian [which is Socialist]. In England nobody ever mentions the royal question. Even the Socialists accept the queen. She never—or very rarely—has to intervene in anything. That is what I should like, what I would aim for, but it will take a generation to bring this about. We must move slowly to avoid chaos; Spaniards are anarchic people."

He would flatly refuse to sign "any contract" with Franco to continue the present ideology and system, including the 1947 Succession Act and all its implications. "There is no point in accepting this," he said. "Franco himself told me it doesn't matter, when I explained to him that nobody can decree the kind of system that will prevail in the future." But Don Juan sadly admitted he was sure Franco wants to stay on as boss until he dies.

Don Juan, somewhat cynically, said Franco was "entirely pragmatic." He changes continually as the world changes. He has no real ideals. He is just a dictator. "I like him as a successful general; but how can he attempt to impose terms on me? History is with me; history and the tradition of monarchy in Spain."

LISBON, *February 11, 1959*

LAST night at a dinner party, I met the owner of the Aviz Hotel who told me about Gulbenkian, the Armenian oil billionaire. In 1942, Gulbenkian came to live in the hotel, taking eight rooms and remaining for the rest of his life. Once the government requisitioned the Aviz for a meeting—and Gulbenkian refused to move out. He was arrested, carted off in a Black Maria, and jailed for thirty-six hours. But, as time went on, he became a fixture. He was the only resident not expelled for the 1952 NATO Conference, when the hotel was taken over by generals, admirals, and ministers.

He always ate at the same corner table, enjoying the whispers and stares of other guests. He had a phobia about being poisoned. He ate fish almost exclusively; every day the chef would bring several to his suite. He would take these to the bathroom and examine them, choose one, make a tiny incision with a penkife, and return it to the chef to be cooked. If he could not find his secret incision in exactly the expected place, he would refuse to eat the fish when it was served.

He was incredibly stingy, never tipped, never gave the staff Christmas presents. They hated him. He had the same valet fifteen years, a man who dressed him, massaged him, looked after him. He didn't leave him a nickel in his will. A remarkable, detestable man.

RABAT, *February 15, 1959*

ARRIVED yesterday by car from Tangier, shabby and run-down since its absorption into the new state. Last night, Charlie Yost (our ambassador, with whom we are staying) had Les Squires, his public-affairs officer, and his CIA man over for dinner. I received the following impressions.

Morocco is free—but, although the protectorate is officially over, it is still "protected." French and Spanish troops are dispersed about the country. We maintain our forces at the bases—although "illegally" from a technical viewpoint.

This is still a feudal, medieval land. There is not one single popularly elected official of any rank. All, even the Consultative Assembly, are appointed. The King is an absolute ruler. The Crown Prince, in his late twenties, bright, quite well educated, and commander of the army, is a playboy.

There is a shortage of administrative talent. At the very top are a few competent, well-educated men who were in the old Istiqlal. But there is nobody able to handle things efficiently "from colonel on down." And now the number at the top has been virtually halved by the sharp split in left- and right-wing halves of the Istiqlal, causing available right wingers to refrain from working for the new government.

There is no fixed border. Extremists (geographically) claim all North Africa up to the Libyan border and down to Senegal, the extreme limits of the old Sheriffian empire. All factions claim Mauritania. Some object to French atomic experiments in "Morocco's Sahara."

The King says: "It is harder to fight my people than the French. I want to go with the West, but I think my people want to go with the East. If I am convinced of this, I won't stop them. If it is apparent that my being king will prevent them, I shall abdicate." He makes increasingly frequent reference to the possibility of his abdication "If the people want a republic."

Our agreement on air bases here with France was signed December, 1950. In 1952, Norstad came here and invited the King to visit the bases. He replied "Inshallah" (God willing), but instructed the interpreter to explain this was a polite no because he had no "official knowledge" the bases existed.

RABAT, *February 16, 1959*

THIS afternoon, I had a talk with Allal al Fassi, head of the Istiqlal party. Al Fassi is a short, plump man with fat, pale face, blue eyes, fringe of beard, a dab of moustache. He has a sulky, passionate expression, perhaps typical of the fanatical Fez (Fassi means "from Fez"). He is an old-fashioned, conservative nationalist who led the fight against the French.

It is difficult here to speak of left or right. The climate is different than in Europe. Our party, for example, has a progressive economic program, but is not Socialist. We are in a transitory period. We don't want to remain too dependent on the French economy.

Soviet propaganda is effective. It pretends that Islam is well treated. The truth is not sufficiently realized throughout the Islamic world.

Most people are not aware that all the Russians want is to colonize the Muslim lands with European (white) Russians. Our people are still familiar only with western colonialism.

Fassi showed me on a map what he considered the rightful boundaries of Morocco—down to Senegal in the south and including a great chunk of Algeria to the southeast. (The Tunisian envoy here observes: "Soon he'll be having a border dispute with the Union of South Africa.")

RABAT, *February 17, 1959*

THIS afternoon, I visited Parodi, the French ambassador. He admits everyone dislikes the Crown Prince but says he is intelligent.

In the morning, I saw Mehdi Ben Barka, head of the left-wing Istiqlal faction that broke off from al Fassi's conservatives. Ben Barka, president of the Consultative Assembly, is extremely short (less than five feet), with a merry, pert face, and messed, curly hair. He obviously loves to talk, and he speaks fluent French. However, I didn't get one clear answer on anything. (Ben Barka was later murdered near Paris by French and Moroccan agents.)

He said:

We have to build a state, not just run it. Morocco was three hundred years behind the rest of the world. The colonial heritage must be eliminated. Morocco had been skipped by the industrial revolution. As a result, our job is different from that of a Socialist party in Europe or a Communist party in Russia. The conditions for class war simply do not exist. We have three tasks: Form the citizen, not his children, him; give him a civic sense of his duties and rights; mobilize the nation; each citizen should be taught to feel what he must *do* for his country. Prevent the growth of the maladies of independence: nepotism and corruption.

RABAT, *February 18, 1959*

THIS morning, I was received by King Mohammed V. The tiled palace is done in the style of a Turkish bath—except with less taste and comfort. It is picturesque, outside, to see the red-uniformed royal guard marching about.

Inside, the King's large sheep dog was barking furiously at two servants who were squirting the drains with disinfectant sprays. The entire Cabinet was assembled in one anteroom waiting to have a session with the King. The ministers were all in overcoats (it was colder inside than out) and hats or fezzes. Several had on dark glasses, although there was little light.

I was put in the charge of Moulay (Monseigneur) Ahmed Alaoui, the King's press attaché and cousin, which appears to be his only qualification. He is unpopular, unattractive, and rude. He was with the King in the U.S.A. "Did you enjoy your trip?" I asked. "No," he said. "I don't like your country."

Mohammed V is short (about five foot seven), in his very late forties, rather handsome with sensitive features and a cruel mouth. Our conversation was dreary. To begin with, although in New York where I saw him last I spoke to the King directly in French, this time he went through the oriental protocol of using an interpreter, no less than Alaoui. Alaoui drew himself up, flung out his tiny chest, and declaimed in rather bad French and with flourishes everything "His Majesty" said, staring straight ahead with his one good eye.

The King started by thanking me for coming here as he had suggested, wished me a pleasant tour, and described the beauties of Marrakesh. All this took time to translate and a photographer kept banging away. The King then said how much he had enjoyed his trip to the United States, how friendly he felt toward Eisenhower and the American people and would I please transmit this message through my newspaper. (I could just see the front page: Moroccan King Likes Yanks.)

He expressed concern over the Algerian situation. Morocco felt friendship for the French people, but this was "an age of liberation" and colonialism simply did not fit in it. The basis for any solution must respect the desires for independence of the Algerian people, the economic and military interests of the French, and the status of the French people living in Algeria. Both in Morocco and Tunisia it had been demonstrated that such a basis could work for solution; why not Algeria?

Today, Abdel Khalek Torres, former head of the independence movement in the Spanish zone and now ambassador to the U.A.R. came to lunch with Mehdi Bennouna, at Yost's house. Mehdi brought a copy of the book he had published here on an underground press in 1951. Although he's a Muslim, he loves whisky, and tiny and frail, he got merry on two highballs.

Torres is a nice fellow with excellent manners and looks more Spanish than Arab. He is clearly on the western side. He said "nondependence" was used to describe policy here because Nasser had spoiled the meaning of neutrality by using his "positive neutrality" to favor Moscow. I suggested that "nondependence" meant "neutral neutrality." Torres loved that. He said it was hard to use "nondependence" anyway when Morocco still depended so much on others and had French government employees; French and Spanish workers and farmers; French, Spanish, and American troops; and sizeable American aid.

NOUASSEUR, *February 18, 1959*

THIS afternoon, I visited Nouasseur air base, where we have some of our best H-bomb retaliatory power. There are four bases in Morocco, of which Nouasseur is the most important. It takes orders from Torrejon in Spain. I drove around looking at immense B-52 eight-jet bombers and the new 1,500 mph fighters.

The approximate Moroccan dollar payroll injected annually into the local economy from these bases is $30,000,000. They will be vital for five to eight years and will always be of great value as long as we have units in Europe. The weather is so good in Morocco that it is ideal for training and alternate landing fields for units coming from America.

MARRAKESH, *February 19, 1959*

ARRIVED yesterday evening in time to have coffee and brandy with Churchill on his last night in Marrakesh. We sat at his table in the corner of the Mamounia Hotel dining room. He was with Lady Churchill, Diana Sandys (his daughter, Duncan Sandys' wife), Anthony Montague Browne, the Foreign Office fellow assigned to him as secretary, and the British consul general in Tangier and his wife. Tomorrow, they plan to motor down to Safi where they are boarding the yacht of Aristotle Onassis for a trip to the Canary Islands.

He looked older: his skin is no longer pink but whitish and blotchy. His eyes are watery and dim. His hearing is even worse (as usual he wouldn't wear his hearing aid), and his voice is very faint. He is now really weak and can't get up without massive effort, has to be half-supported when he walks upstairs. But he wasn't "ga-ga" as so many people have said. I think he has difficulty, because of his hearing, in following things. So he seems to miss part of what's going on, above all when he's tired. But he had moments of his old self.

He offered me some marvelous brandy which Lady Churchill, with glee, said they had been permitted to bring in with them "duty free." When the servant offered me a cigar, I said I didn't smoke them. "That's a serious mistake," said Churchill.

He had painted three pictures while here and was "quite satisfied" with them. Lady Churchill, who gasses merrily in a low voice so he won't overhear, regretted that she's been stuck here and not even able to go to Fez, but said he was too weak for her to go away from him.

He said he was going to America on May 4, for about ten days. First he will stay at the White House, then at the British embassy, then with Barney Baruch, who, he said, was still in excellent health. "Probably better than Eisenhower's," I remarked. "Oh, I don't know," murmured Churchill. "The President seems to be on the golf links every day."

He told me he had first come here for two days after the Casablanca Conference, motoring down at the suggestion of "the President" who had a "very nice villa here."

I told him I'd just been at our base at Nouasseur and had seen new fighters that go 1,500 miles an hour. "Ah, that's very swift, very swift," he said. "When I go to the United States in May, I shall attempt to find a plane that proceeds just rapidly enough, so that I can accomplish the journey entirely in the night and have my accustomed amount of slumber."

While talking about airplanes, I remarked that it had been a miracle that Menderes, the Turk, had lived through the recent air crash. Churchill said he was sure the percentage of fatalities in air travel had not increased; on the contrary, they had decreased. "Otherwise I should have to reconsider," he added. It was odd to think of this old hero on death's doorstep talking about "reconsidering" travel means, in terms of safety.

At another point, we were talking about space rockets. I said I supposed in a few years men would be projected to other planets. "Oh, no," he said with some horror. "Why would anyone wish to leave this planet? That would be foolish. I cannot believe that."

He said Eden would never go back into politics although he could easily regain his parliamentary seat. That would unleash upon him a torrent of Suez criticism, hitherto held in restraint. Lady Churchill thought Eden had lost much of his energy; that he was no better.

Churchill was unexpected on Molotov. We were talking about how the Dutch had rejected him as ambassador. "I like Mr. Molotov," he said. "I think he is a fine man, a nice man, a very able man." "Oh, surely you can't call Molotov nice," said his wife. "I do," he insisted. "I think Mr. Molotov is a nice man."

He asked me what I thought of the King (whom he still calls the Sultan). I said, noncommittally, it was hard to tell through the barrage of interpretation. "He has sentenced six people to death," said Churchill. (I don't know to whom he was referring.) "One of them was staying with him as a guest in his own palace. It will be interesting to see what he intends to do about that sentence."

Churchill told me the first time he went up in an airplane was 1912, and that he often flew during World War I "as a means of transportation, you know." He boasted with pleasure: "I used to take over the controls in the air. But I was never alone in a plane; I never went up alone."

He was looking forward to going to the Canary Islands, where he had never been. It was a twenty-eight-hour sail. After that, Barcelona. Lady Churchill told me Randolph had just gone to Moscow for Beaverbrook, two days ahead of Macmillan, to cover the Macmillan-Khrushchev talks. Before going he went to No. 10 Downing Street to ask permission to go on the same plane as Macmillan, offering to pay his own way and saying, "This will save money for the British tax-payer." Macmillan gave an unamused no.

I noticed Churchill had eaten a goodly meal, laced as usual with champagne, and puffed contentedly on his cigar, produced from a box of two varieties he had with him. He and the other men wore dinner jackets, even here. Lady Churchill had on odd blue-tinted glasses.

MARRAKESH, *February 20, 1959*

WENT around Marrakesh this afternoon and dined in an Arab restaurant. Streets are lined with lovely, neat rows of bitter orange trees. The old royal palace has immense olive groves and numerous ponds filled with ducks and frogs. Daggered Berbers wander about ignoring the women with veils up to their kohl-painted eyes.

Then saw the Saadi dynasty graves, set in chapels with arabesqued plaster, tiled floors, and huge cedar doors, all smelling of incense. Hundreds of women and children claiming descent from the Saadis were visiting their ancestral tombs. An Arab told me there were still some slaves in Marrakesh (born into slave-holding families, but there are no more sales or purchases). Several of the Glaoui's slaves were freed when he died.

At the Djemaa el Fna, Square of the Mosque of Annihilation, black Berbers (called Gnawa) were dancing to the beats of drums pounded with curved sticks. The dancers wore black, pointed skull caps to which were sewn cowrie shells; some played cymbals.

Water sellers strolled around with brass studded leather aprons, brass cups, huge, broad hats, ringing bells. Chleu tribesmen (also Berbers), wearing white turbans danced to the music of tambourines; other groups of Chleu lute singers, wailed away. Nearby, Hajjah (storytellers) were spinning great tales to squatting old men and boys. Acrobats did cartwheels. Scribes squatted with old pens and ink pots, waiting to take down letters.

In the souk (market) peddlers sold kebab and flat bread, while women shopped with babies tied to their backs. Apothecary stalls displayed talisman verses of the *Koran*, wrapped in gilt paper; dried chameleons, bats, lizards, mandrake root, asphodel bulbs, snakeskins, weasels, and fake amber and live tortoises. The dried specimens are burned to produce healing vapors.

ALGIERS, *February 23, 1959*

THIS afternoon, I spent an hour with General Massu at his headquarters in the Caserne Pelissier. The building is rather crummy; surrounded by soldiers in jeeps. (Algiers itself looks like an occupied town with all the helmeted troops and police with tommy guns.)

Massu's aide, a lieutenant of paratroops, told me Massu (who is fifty-one) only began jumping after World War II. He is very fit and a good tennis player. Massu, who comes from Châlons-sur-Marne, is a great-grand nephew of Marshal Ney. He graduated from St. Cyr in 1928, was with Leclerc during the war, coming up to the Mediterranean from Chad, then joining Patton's force in France helping liberate Paris. He went to Indochina with Leclerc, then to Tunisia. He commanded the Tenth Parachute Division at Suez, and he was in charge of clearing up Algiers in 1957.

He is tall, about six foot one, has a thin face, enormous arc of nose, long moustache, prognathous jaw, a few gold front teeth, large ears, thin-lipped mouth, rather brown eyes, low brow; an ugly man, not very intelligent looking, but with a pleasant smile. He was wearing jump boots and a regular uniform with a dark blue vest, the front of which was covered with a long row of gold buttons, sewn closely together, rather Edwardian.

He started things off cozily by assuring me he mistrusted journalists. I told him there was a permanent cold war between newspapermen and generals, adding that he should realize there were newspapermen and newspapermen just the way there were generals and generals. I said if he doubted my recommendations he should call Colonel de Bonneval in the office of de Gaulle whom I had seen the night before I left Paris.

"I'll take your word for it," said Massu without enthusiasm. "But who have you seen here? Have you seen Challe [commander of all Algeria]?" I said no; that I had wanted to see Massu because he had a certain renown in the U.S.A. as a paratroop commander at Suez, because of his activities in Algiers, and because of his role in the May 13 Algerian uprising that produced de Gaulle. Then I whipped out a list of questions. Begrudgingly he answered, with neither enthusiasm nor brilliance.

I inquired first what lessons in the art of fighting guerrillas he had learned in Indochina and from studying Mao and other Chinese partisan tacticians. He said:

> The experience I drew from that adventure was that what we most lack is adaptation of our legal system to a situation that juridically is not war.
> Everyone knows I won the battle of Algiers by being illegal. The system of justice must be adapted to the prevailing situation and to the mentality of the population. Technically, we fight a war in the regular way, using helicopters and other modern methods.
> A second observation I can make, after analyzing Mao's writings, is the need for double action against the political administration and organization of the rebellion as well as against their armed bands,

the rebel companies. These are very different actions. Against the
bands we employ classic means—night combats, ambushes; we have
to surround the adversary before attacking and this requires sufficient
numbers, artillery, and air power.

But against the political-administrative organization—against its
political commissars, saboteurs, and terrorists—we are limited to the
police action. We need *all* the police powers we can get. The military
and police must be under one chief. We have to adapt ourselves to
subversive war. We are not juridically at war; but we need court
martials. Yet people speak less of this phase of the struggle than the
helicopter phase.

I asked him what operational techniques he had been able to borrow
from the Communists (in Indochina) to use against the FLN. He replied:

It is a question of diplomacy. One always, of course, needs large

I defend western civilization. Therefore I cannot use totalitarian
methods. But I must employ efficient means of action. It is essential
to organize the population in a defense against the OPA [political-
administrative organization]. We have developed a home guard somewhat like that in Switzerland or like in Britain during the war, but
with modifications on the basis of our Indochina experience.

I asked Massu how it was possible to defeat a guerrilla operation, regardless of one's material superiority, citing the cases of China, Jugoslavia, Greece, and Indochina. He said:

It is a question of diplomacy. One always, of course, needs large
effectives against guerrillas. But in the end, it is diplomacy that
counts. The Greek rebels were crushed when the border was closed and
they could get no external supplies. We have the same problem here.
The FLN depends upon its bases in Tunisia and Morocco. It is a question of diplomacy.

Did Massu think torture was still necessary in fighting the OPA aspect of
the war?
He said:

It is necessary. One can get nowhere with mere polite questioning.
But I have given orders that neither the physical nor the moral integrity of a man should be damaged. Naturally, it is different with
their fighters; like Azzedine, for example. I talked directly and politely to Azzedine. That was different. He was a fighter. But against
the OPA, tough interrogation is necessary. I have ordered that this
should leave no moral or physical trace on the person of the individual. [A curious phrase.]

Was it true, as Italian and other papers have reported, that he had
submitted himself to the same tortures, or "tough interrogation" as his

captives? He was reluctant to discuss this. He said: "We never beat anyone; not blows. But we keep them in a state of tension. I, myself, and
my officers, we watched this, to see for ourselves. We wished to see how
a man's resistance could be diminished this way. We tested ourselves, in
a sense. But of course we were in a different psychological situation."

He then got quite huffy and said he saw no reason to discuss this with
me; that I had no right to ask such questions. He got quite worked up and
said it was highly improper. I said Henri Alleg in *La Question*, had mi-
nutely described real and cruel tortures. "All lies," said Massu, "totally
false."

I asked what had become of Azzedine, the rebel chief who had become a go-between, seeking to ascertain peace chances with the French.
Massu said: "I sent him out three times and three times he came back.
The fourth time he didn't return. That is all I know. That was December 8, the last I know."

I asked if there was one outstanding guerrilla leader, a Tito of the
FLN.

> No. There is no such man. The best known is Amirouche. He has
> killed so many; that is why he is known. Some months ago he con-
> ducted an extensive purge because he feared treason among his fol-
> lowers. He himself has killed many. He is very cruel. But his only
> real talent is the talent of escaping us. He is an authoritarian. He
> rules by terror.

I asked how effectively the frontiers with Tunisia and Morocco were
now sealed off. He said Tunisia was now quite well sealed and that
"my paras have caught many rebels on that border." He added that at
present less of a rebel effort was being made from Morocco.

He said he had captured no Soviet or Chinese arms, but that a good
deal of rebel equipment did come from the other side of the Iron Curtain.
"It is difficult," he said. "There has always been a big arms traffic in the
Mediterranean." I asked him about rebel strength. He said I should not
quote him, but that, without OPA, it was between 25,000 and 30,000. But
the quality was worse than a couple of years ago, although the total
figure was unchanged. Also, the armament was less plentiful.

I asked, apropos of May 13, what he thought was the proper political
role of the French army. He said:

> An army must have its peaceful formation. It makes sacrifices. It
> should have the right to express its viewpoint. I cannot precisely
> define this, but an officer surely does not give up all his rights as a
> civilian. There is no political formation of the army. But we have been
> forced into political choices. We have made political-military war
> ever since Indochina. In Indochina politics were more important than
> arms.

ALGIERS, *February 24, 1959*

LONG talk with Hans Imhof of the U.S. consulate, a highly intelligent young man. Every move made by Paris is vitiated here because the local press, controlled by ultras, explains that these moves mean nothing, that in reality there has been no change.

Now, for the first time, Paris is the boss; the dog wags the tail. Before Delouvrier, new delegate general, the head men were always politicians who sought to use Algeria as a personal steppingstone. Delouvrier says he is here to take orders, that he is only the agent of Paris, that if people dislike policy they should go to Paris and get his orders changed.

The ultras are mostly Pétainistes. They have no illusions about de Gaulle. They are ready to have another May 13. But they are helpless without the army. The army criticizes certain Gaullist measures—like clemency and his refusal to come out for integration.

Nevertheless, there is a basic feeling of trust.

The army recognizes de Gaulle as a "chief." And they see in him the biggest drawing card as far as the Muslims are concerned. Therefore the army is unhappy about extremist demonstrations here which, it feels, weaken French prestige.

The French army is not a South American army. After all, May 13 was not a revolt against authority but against the absence of authority. Massu adheres to the military hierarchy and is loyal to his chiefs. But if the war drags on for another eighteen months, de Gaulle will lose prestige. Then a frustrated army might move.

ALGIERS, *February 25, 1959*

DINED last night at the residence of Delouvrier, French boss in Algeria. His wife, and a young couple named Poincaré were also there. There was excellent food, interesting informal conversation. Delouvrier was very frank. He said Massu is a first-class general and adored by the Algérois, above all the women, for having put an end to the terror in 1957. In the last three or four months, there have been only four bombs in the city, only two killed. Massu is not overly intelligent but a brave, loyal man who takes orders. He is not a plotter by nature. He had to use torture, the only thing possible. Delouvrier himself during the resistance was forced to do things he desperately disliked. Now the army doesn't use torture or mix up in things primarily handled by the police.

The situation here is tragic and confused. There is NO visible solution. De Gaulle has avoided committing himself to integration or anything else. He will sponsor no solution that divides instead of unites. He would rather, in case of new divisive situations, retire to Colombey.

The only thing to pray for is time in which to spread the effects of the new social and economic reforms. And it is possible the army may again get fed up with the impossibility of chasing the rebels back to Tunisia—and, in time, stage a new uprising prompted by the ultras.

One must remember that in a sense every one of the one million Europeans is an "ultra." The "liberals" only oppose undemocratic means and torture; but they also want a French "presence." The French have seen what happened to their compatriots, expropriated in Tunisia. They have absolutely no racist feeling. But they see—and it is true—that the bulk of the Arabs are backward, medieval people, incapable of running a modern, twentieth-century state. One cannot compromise between the present and the distant past. So, in the lack of any other solutions, it is better to have the army still here, fighting, giving its protection.

TUNIS, *March 2, 1959*

I DROVE down to Sousse with Ambassador Lewis Jones, our host, to attend the opening day of the Neo-Destour party congress. This was dominated by a speech by Bourguiba, lasting three hours and eighteen minutes.

Bourguiba stood on the platform, a short man dressed in dark blue double-breasted suit with blue tie and white shirt. When he speaks his arms gesture in writhing, serpentine fashion. His voice is soft and high with a fanatical quality. He uses his eyes and teeth effectively. I was amused to see a heavy, dumb-looking brunette, who I know is a friend of Bourguiba's, sitting in the row behind me and staring at him goofily, her lips half-open.

TUNIS, *March 5, 1959*

LAST night, I dined with President Habib Bourguiba at his home in Monastir, about one hundred miles away. Monastir is an old walled town where he was born. When I arrived, with typical Arab confusion, nobody knew anything about the arrangements.

While waiting, I chatted with Madame Bourguiba, Cecil Haurani, his Lebanese-born aide, and other hangers-on in the sitting room of his home, enlarged and modernized by the party as a special gift. It used to belong to his father, an officer in the Beylical army, whose photograph in old-fashioned military costume still rests on the radio.

We sat on a taudry, gilt-trimmed sofa with Madame Bourguiba, a large French woman, older than her husband. She told me how her romance began. She was working as a clerk in the Paris ministry of finances. A French teacher went to Monastir to teach and got to know young Bourguiba and told him to look her up when he came to Paris to study law. Bourguiba discovered a Tunisian nougat merchant from whom he borrowed enough money to reach the young lady's house. She invited him to dinner, and he, starving, admitted later this was one of the most welcome meals of his life.

Madame Bourguiba said she had a hell of a time bringing up her children and nephews in Monastir because her husband was in jail or exile most of the time as a nationalist agitator.

Bourguiba came in around 8:30 with some friends and, after shaking hands, summoned us to table. With his fez off he is quite nice looking although very short, which suits his name ("Habib" means "beloved"; "Bourguiba" means "short-necked"). He has a square jaw, good features, and light blue eyes.

We were about a dozen. Bourguiba sat at the head with his wife at the right and me at the left. A manservant brought in a steady series of bowls which were left upon the table and from these we helped ourselves— soup, grilled fish, pilaff, chicken stew, tangerines. There was flat Arab bread and nothing to drink but water.

Bourguiba talked a lot, starting on Algeria which overshadows everything in this part of the world. He said:

> The situation is not ripe for settlement now. It will ripen; eventually it will have to ripen—but at what price? The French live totally apart from reality. They are fighting a full-scale war in Algeria with all their power just exactly as they did in Indochina and the result will be just exactly the same.
>
> They imagine they will win this war. They say it is a question of honor and prestige. They say that by winning it, they will be able to diminish the impression made on the world and on their own people by their having to leave Indochina, Syria, Tunisia, and Morocco. They still seem to consider the liberation of these countries as due to the treason of the *système* of the French regime.
>
> They don't yet recognize that this liberation movement is a natural phenomenon. After all, it happened to the British and the Dutch. It should be faced coolly and logically. The French think they are stronger and smarter than the British. How unclever they really are.

Bourguiba thought French insistence on continuing the uncompromising war will doom the only logical future plan for North Africa—a Maghreb federation closely linked to France. Even if Tunisia remained prowestern in its thinking, this continuing war was pushing Morocco toward neutrality and the Algerians toward communism.

I recalled to him that last time I had seen him he expressed interest in Tunisia's joining NATO after Algeria was independent. He remembered. "But," said he, "today I am much less interested."

He attacked Nasser, saying he had a "childish mind" and his regime was "doomed." He was no longer gaining in the Arab world and had been defeated in Iraq, Saudi Arabia, in the Lebanon, in Jordan, in Tunisia, and in the Sudan. He was perhaps still strong in Libya, but was losing out in Syria. While Nasser kept thinking of lavish gains abroad, the Egyptian people were impoverished and hungry.

Bourguiba complained that there is a ridiculous situation in the world today. Dictatorships, such as Russia's or China's, which deny human rights to their own people, appear before the world as the champions of liberation, while the countries where true freedom reigns oppose such colonial liberation. He added:

If by the end of this year the Algerian war has not yet ended, there is great danger. You will see the same end of the Fifth Republic as of the Fourth Republic. This is a fatal logic. The ultras control the army and the army will impose its decisions. A year from now big things will happen. There will be a sharp movement to the left. Soustelle and company will use force to prevent this if it occurs. That will mean civil war.

CARTHAGE, TUNISIA, *March 6, 1959*

ON March 4, I spent about eighteen hours with the FLN, the Algerian rebels. I had made my arrangements through Boumendjel, their permanent representative in Tunis. Some of the time I was with them in Algeria, across the border; some of the time at posts in Tunisia itself.

I was accompanied by Ait Ahcene, FLN envoy in Bonn, who was shot there in the street by a French assassin and wounded three times in the head; also Omar Ousseidik. Ousseidik is under secretary for administration of the provisional government of the FLN: a fanatical youth with a wispy reddish moustache and curly hair, who talks like a professional agitator.

Also along was Adelbert Weinstein, military editor of the *Frankfurter Allgemeine Zeitung*, who has an international reputation as a military expert.

He was a lieutenant colonel during World War II and useful in judging the efficiency of FLN training, discipline, and armament. He was most impressed. Although the West Germans keep kidding the French along in Paris, they are obviously on very good terms with the FLN.

Weinstein and I drove in a little Peugeot chauffeured by a madman. He had souped up the carburetor so we were able to go 150 kms an hour on the bad, narrow Tunisian roads. Sitting next to the chauffeur on the front seat was a big FLN lieutenant armed with a machine pistol. We were never stopped or questioned by the Tunisian police.

With us was the FLN hero, Major Azzedine, wounded six times within thirteen months. He has twelve or thirteen holes in him, and six bullets still in his body. His right arm is gnarled; it contains an American explosive bullet fired from a B-26.

When he was captured for the second time by the French, de Gaulle sent a certain Captain Marion of the psychological warfare services to Algiers to seek his help in arranging a cease-fire.

Azzedine woke up in a helicopter on the way to Algiers. When there, he was visited in hospital by General Massu, whom he refers to as "the massacrer of Algiers." Massu told Azzedine: "We've been looking for you a long time." Azzedine told me: "I could understand this. I defeated Massu's men in the field. He had to write one of his defeats into his battle book."

He continued: "Massu said: 'I've been looking for you. You're a brave man. Your bravery is written on your body. I am happy to have seen you. At last I see you. But you can't win. We will win. The people are with us.' "

Azzedine said he pretended to agree with Massu. When Captain Marion visited him in hospital he made certain proposals and said the French would release Azzedine so that he could return to his headquarters and arrange a cease-fire.

Azzedine replied he would transmit any proposals. He was released and went back to a rebel command post which joined in the game, telling him to give the French certain information, but not of a military nature. He went back to Massu who said: "I am happy to see that the confidence we placed in you has been merited. You came back."

Azzedine told Massu his colonel was not at the command post but was attending a conference of colonels. Therefore he was not able to arrange anything and would have to go back. When Azzedine returned, rebel intelligence warned him he had better stay this time. So he did. The French proclaimed they didn't know what had happened to him.

The ALN (Army of National Liberation) has several organizations. Their paramilitary organizations include the "Fiday" or "Sacrificers" for sabotage and the "Moussebel" for security protection of nationalist civilians.

Azzedine was originally both in the Fiday and the Moussebel. He boasted: "We, a company, captured arms from a French division. What kind of morale do you think the French have? Their morale must be terrible. It is only the colonels who keep them going."

Azzedine claims the best troops opposing the rebels are Foreign Legion paratroopers, the green berets. They are the most courageous and use the terrain best. The worst troops facing them are the conscripts. He says: "We call them *gateaux* [cakes]. At the first shot they quit." The French are still using Algerians in their units; about forty out of each four hundred men. Azzedine said: "We like this. Sometimes when there is a battle they fire on their own troops. The French are caught in Algerian cross fire. They don't realize their own men are shooting them." He said French troops often try to surrender and are shot down by their officers.

Azzedine said there are a few German, Spanish, and Arab volunteers in the ALN: former Foreign Legionnaires. Mao Tse-tung is the ALN's most admired expert on guerrilla warfare. However, FLN officers claim Mao wrote for China, where conditions were different from those in Algeria. They say, "We don't accept Mao's ideology. We have had to change his tactics to suit our own special circumstances."

There is no general in the ALN. The highest rank is colonel, one for each wilaya. Under him there are three majors; one for intelligence, one for political administration and supplies, and one for operations.

They say: "The mountains belong to us. We have a political infrastructure in the cities and the plains." This infrastructure helps feed the ALN, and it also sees that the local population gets enough to eat. Each region has its economy directed by the command of each wilaya and its political officer. When the colonels of the different wilayas meet, they coordinate the administrations of the different regions. There is a general staff in the interior which keeps moving.

The troops I saw were very fit looking. There were quite a few machine pistols. Apparently, the minimum training before they are sent into action is two months. I noticed a few English-type helmets (probably from Egypt's Suez stockpile) on sentries, and one or two World War I machine-guns. Their main artillery seems to be 45 mm and 81 mm mortars. For rifles, they prefer the German Mauser.

Azzedine claimed 80 percent of ALN losses were due to American equipment. He said:

> When one sees Sikorskis or B-26s, we place the responsibility where it is. My people say we would have had peace long ago if it hadn't been for American aid to France. It's America that keeps the French going and keeps the war going. I think my people are right. We have had a million victims now, of whom only twenty thousand are military. Think of the poor Algerian people. It is American arms and money that keep this tragedy going.

Omar said the war has been going too long to ever imagine friendly relations between the Algerians and the French again after peace has come. Furthermore, he said that because of our close connection with the French it appeared almost inevitable to him that the Algerians would have to break their previous friendship with the United States. Here Azzedine added: "I liked Americans. I used to work in an American factory. But when you have as many bullets in your body as I do and they are all American, things change."

They claim communism is not important in their own movement. One officer said: "The Communists did nothing for us in France. When they sent planes to bomb us in 1945 there were three Communists ministers in the French cabinet." Another added: "We fear a French Communist government might be even worse for us than what we have now."

PARIS, *March 19, 1959*

LONG talk this afternoon with Ambassador Am Houghton. He is perplexed because no one can do business with de Gaulle except another chief of state. However, were he to try and do his business with de Gaulle he would lose his present contacts with Prime Minister Debré and Foreign Minister Couve de Murville. Houghton thinks it is extremely important to arrange an Eisenhower–de Gaulle meeting, and this week he cabled Washington recommending as much.

He hears that all the members of de Gaulle's Cabinet, except Debré, opposed the General's policy on the French fleet, but he told them: "You will see that I have been right." Am saw Couve a couple of nights ago, and Couve assured him this was a tempest in a teapot. Houghton replied: "You wouldn't think so if you had been reading my cables."

Am thinks this move was a disaster and is going to put an end to France's chances of getting the atomic submarine Dulles promised last July, no matter what pressure the administration puts on Congress. It is also going to make it much harder for de Gaulle to get the commands he wants in NATO because the other NATO countries are up in arms.

PARIS, *March 20, 1959*

DAVID Bruce came for lunch. Most agreeable and talkative. He is here for a Berlin strategy committee meeting.

He told me his embassy in Bonn had chewed over my idea of turning over our rights in West Berlin to the West Germans. They had finally come down against it on the grounds that neither the Russians nor the West Germans would accept it. I argued that if the Russians didn't accept it, at least, it would put the onus where it should be put and that, far as the West Germans are concerned, it is high time we made them face up to their responsibilities; that they should cease getting a free ride. David agreed in principle but added that they were desperately counting on American protection. Willy Brandt, mayor of West Berlin, admitted to him that Berliners count only on American protection, not in the least bit on Bonn.

Bruce said Adenauer's system of government is precisely like de Gaulle's—one-man government. Brentano, the foreign minister, recently admitted as much to him. David feels Adenauer is a noble man with a true sense of Germany's obligations to the world, that the Germans must make retribution for past sins. He has gone farther than anyone believed possible in applying this belief toward Israel.

The other aspect is his policy toward France. He feels that no matter how unreasonable the French are, Germany must be able financially and in every other way to support France's claims and desires. France has suffered generations of sorrow as a result of Germany's aggressions, and he is determined to rectify this. As a consequence, despite the grumbling of ministers like Erhard, Adenauer will brook no criticism of his French policy. In a way, he even seems to put his ahead of NATO.

There is a deep personal feeling between de Gaulle and Adenauer. Nobody knows what goes on when the two men talk except the interpreter. But Adenauer considers de Gaulle a "noble" Frenchman, using one of the few English words he knows. He says it is too much to expect a true friendship between France and Germany, but at least he counts upon a "rapprochement." He is prepared to go ahead supporting France in Algeria and North Africa and investing money even when his ministers say it is unreasonable.

PARIS, *March 22, 1959*

PLAYED golf with Frank Roberts and Wassard, Danish ambassador to NATO, a charming and amusing old man who kept insisting on two points. Almost every member of NATO has at one time or another been a great power. Denmark was a great empire and once ruled England. Portugal, Greece, Turkey, and Italy (through ancient Rome) were imperial powers. Therefore, the allies have it in their nature to comprehend the rise and fall of international influence.

The western nations must get ready for the obvious coming period when Russia will be their ally against China and when racial ties will be more important than ideological differences.

LONDON, *March 23, 1959*

LATE this afternoon, I spent an hour and a half with Aneurin Bevan. I met him in the visitor's room of the House of Commons, and he took me outside on the terrace where we walked up and down, up and down, as he talked. Although his breath smelled heavily of whisky, he seemed stone sober, and, for him, spoke moderately.

I asked Bevan what, if he is named foreign secretary under a Labour government, he would do about the Common Market and the British Free Trade Area Plan. He replied:

> What does the Common Market aim at achieving? Its supporters are impressed by the notion that the economic difficulties of Europe derive from the fact that there are too many fiscal barriers in Europe

itself. How valid is this theory? It is merely the application of over-simplified continentalism. The United States has had an immense industrial and trading area on its continent since your revolution. But even there, the poverty in the South continues. And at no time during the crisis of 1929 and the early 1930s were there less than nine million unemployed in America. Obviously a continental market is not necessarily a solution to the problem of an area.

The theory of the European Common Market is based upon the competitive conditions of the nineteenth century and the early twentieth century. But with today's huge cartels and syndicates these conditions no longer apply. Cheap goods do not necessarily emerge. Businessmen are trying to capture markets. Instead they should concentrate on creating customers to purchase their goods. Trade is exchange.

I have always contended that the Common Market is letting loose the giants of the Ruhr and some of the giants of French industry who will create national pacts and raise the level of unemployment by their protective trading methods. This will produce the resurgence of nothing. Look at Belgium. Already unemployment is increasing in its coal area. The only way to improve the conditions of modern society is for more social expenditure. This is needed to maintain the purchasing power of the masses. And state expenditures are essential to it. Right now, the purposes of this are to a degree being accomplished by armaments expenditures, which are serving as a temporary substitute for a public-works program. But I maintain that the economic problems of the West derive directly from the lack of economic planning. And it is impractical to bring about adequate economic planning because there is still insufficient public ownership in the West. One of the purposes of the Common Market, indeed, is to bring about unemployment in inefficient areas. This is no answer to our problem.

I asked what his policy toward the Arab world would be if he were foreign secretary. He replied:

I have never accepted the British attitude toward Egypt. There is a ferment of mutually contradictory elements in the Middle East these days. There is a revolt against imperialism. There is an effort to cooperate under the broad idea of pan-Arabism. But this in itself is modified by Arab nationalism. There is a rise of the bourgeoisie which depends on oil for its wealth.

The Russians face this growing power of the bourgeoisie in countries like Iraq and Kuwait and Saudi Arabia where these newly prosperous classes are not prepared to jeopardize their position by severing their connections with the West. The Russians cannot supply the Middle East market for oil.

This checks the Middle East from going too far toward Russia. They need to continue commercial connection with the West. But the West must try and establish its oil requirements on a just commercial basis. The Arabs are not prepared to substitute Egyptian hegemony for western imperialism.

It is absolutely essential to provide a plan for the economic development of the Middle East on a very big scale. The Arab peoples should be able to look to the development of their own reserves. The oil companies should be brought into this picture. They should get together with the oil-owning governments and arrange to put new royalties on more favorable contracts with the Arabs into a development plan for that region. And the oil states should contribute to the nonoil states to bring up the entire regional living standard.

Israel is guaranteed by UN. The Arabs must be told that they have to accept the existence of Israel. Otherwise they cannot have the development plan, because the chances of its working out would be nullified unless Israel and the Arabs can cooperate. And we must settle the refugees. There is plenty of room in Iraq and Syria for the Arab refugees from Palestine. This is the fundamental policy I would seek.

I then asked Bevan what his policy toward NATO would be. He replied:

The alliance is based upon a false premise—on the assumption that the Soviet Union will attack us sooner or later via military aggression. As a consequence, we can never take a positive policy because we were always on the defense. By bringing in West Germany, we brought about a crisis in France. The EDC was destroyed by Mendès-France. We do not yet have the twelve German divisions that were envisioned under EDC. And we have been talking about them since 1951.

I do *not* want to denounce the NATO alliance. We should maintain it. If the Russians say they are ready to abandon the Warsaw Pact, we should not fall for that bait because obviously they could reactivate the Warsaw Pact at a moment's notice. But we should aim at superseding all regional alliances by NATO itself. We should end atomic tests and start means of inspection in a central area of disengagement. And this could be accompanied by the beginning of arms reduction. This would change the climate of world opinion and that is very important.

LONDON, *March 24, 1959*

THIS morning, I had a chat with Harold Macmillan. Macmillan was his usual bland self, and sipped sherry while informally reviewing the world situation. He sat on a sofa in a reception room at No. 10 Downing Street, a Guardi painting of Venice behind him. He was wearing a fawn-colored Edwardian vest, a handsome, distinguished Edwardian figure himself.

Macmillan started by saying he had taken his grandchildren to the theater. It was difficult to find the right sort of play for children nowadays without too much sex or horrors. He regretted the disappearance of the old music-hall entertainment. This was symbolic of the change in our time. For example, it was now the fashion in the House of Commons to give short speeches. Gladstone would have spoken for four hours, but nowadays nobody would listen to him.

Khrushchev had spoken seven hours at his party congress. This really showed how old-fashioned the Russians still were. He was advised by the experts that the Russians considered short diplomatic notes to be simply rude.

During his trip to Moscow, he was glad Khrushchev had been impolite, failed to go to Kiev with him, and said he had a dentist appointment. Prior to then, he felt he was Khrushchev's guest and could not speak too sharply. After the affront, Macmillan felt he had a chance to be more blunt. When he was in Kiev, Khrushchev sent a message saying the dentist had used a new English drill on his tooth. Macmillan simply was unable to figure out whether Khrushchev was trying to be funny or to pay a compliment. He said: "I suppose if I am ever admitted to the House of Lords I shall have to take a drill as my coat of arms."

Macmillan did not feel Mikoyan was very important in the Soviet hierarchy. Mikoyan had been in all Soviet governments and was a bright, successful man. It was an accident that he had been born in Odessa and therefore became a Bolshevik. Had he gone to Cairo, he would have been a carpet dealer. Had he gone to New York, he would have been a successful stockbroker.

If there is a summit meeting, Macmillan feels it should be a small, informal session held in a secluded place. This kind of procedure had worked out very well during his talks at Camp David with Eisenhower. The two would talk for a few hours and then leave their assistants to do specific work while they drove around and visited Eisenhower's farm. In the evening they might see a western movie instead of continuing their conversations.

Macmillan personally had a horror of Geneva. He had attended the Geneva Summit Conference as foreign secretary for Eden and remembered how dozens of delegates sat together in an enormous room with their advisors in serried rows. Everybody got up and made propaganda speeches. The only business ever done was in a few face-to-face talks at dinner parties.

I asked if at any time Khrushchev had hinted he would be prepared to make a deal on the Middle East in exchange for a status quo on Europe. Macmillan said definitely not, and that he would have nothing to do with such an idea because it would allow the Russians to "blackmail" us too much.

Macmillan indicated he was perfectly prepared to accept a status quo as between East Germany and West Germany and de facto recognition of East Germany. Khrushchev would be satisfied with such a deal and had even used the words "de facto recognition" for East Germany.

If there was a new Berlin deal, it would be easier to lower pressure in the area if there were an agreed force reduction, in a region perhaps a hundred miles equidistant in all directions from Berlin, subjected to rigorous systems of inspection.

Macmillan was convinced the Russians were genuinely afraid of an American attack. He said they don't understand the workings of democracy. They read in the papers how some general or some admiral will get up and say it is best to hit the Russians now because they will be stronger in three years. They think this is an indication of serious American policy.

In terms of how a summit conference should work out, he cites the Berlin Conference of 1878, Bismarck and Disraeli sat down to dinner where they did serious business. Afterward, they issued instructions on how their agreement should be formally ratified. There should be similar informal meetings at the summit and then a plenary session to ratify the deals agreed to.

It is useful to get the Russians more and more into the idea of playing a role in the outside world. Khrushchev, he thinks, is a very different personality from Stalin. In some ways, he is almost a democratic-type figure. He could certainly be elected to office in an honest, democratic vote.

Macmillan admits that Adenauer is very unhappy about what's going on but, "Where the tree falls, there the timber lies." What he meant, of course, was de facto recognition of East Germany.

LONDON, *March 26, 1959*

THIS afternoon I had tea and pleasant conversation with T. S. Eliot in his office at Faber & Faber on Russell Square, Bloomsbury. He has a very small, cluttered-up office filled with snapshots and other little mementos. There was an electric heater burning although it was not cold. He served me with tea and biscuits.

Eliot moves like an old man now, but he really doesn't look much older than he has for years. His hair has not yet grayed. He still has quite a lot of it and seems to have his own teeth. He has a sallow face and quizzical owl-like appearance behind his spectacles, over which he peers from time to time.

I had written Eliot, whom I have known on and off for more than twenty-five years, stating that I wanted to ask him questions concerning the role of the writer in today's Cold War propaganda contest. He said today:

20-1-60

Pour M. Cyrus Leo Sulzberger,
Bien cordialement!
C. de Gaulle.

Autographed portrait of Charles de Gaulle.

Visit to Cracow with Polish
government officials, 1956.

With Janos Kadar (*on the right*), Communist boss of Hungary, and an interpreter.

With Abd-el-Krim (*left*), chief of the Riffian rebellion against Spain and Morocco in the 1920's.

With the chief of a Pathan village in the no man's land between Afghanistan and Pakistan.

With King Hassan of Morocco.

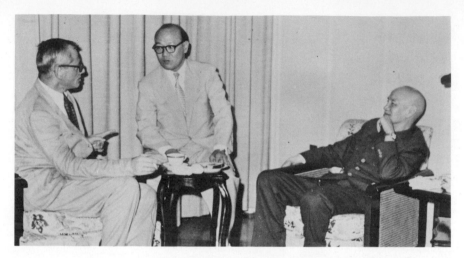

With Chiang Kai-shek.

Party with President Sukarno of Indonesia (black hat), 1959.

Autographed portrait of Dwight D. Eisenhower.

THE WHITE HOUSE
WASHINGTON

January 31, 1959

PERSONAL

Dear Cy:

Your column in the TIMES on Thursday morning of last week
interested me greatly. It concerned, of course, Pope John's
suggestion to convene an Oecumenical Council.

I personally support the idea because I believe that much good
can come out of it provided that the objective is simple, clear-
cut, and one that can achieve unanimous approval.

There is no need to dwell here upon the obvious difficulties that
would be encountered in an attempt merely to convene a council
of all faiths. But assuming the convening of such a great body of
religious leaders, I believe that if all factions could direct their
attention to a single main point -- namely that of insisting upon
the supremacy of spiritual values and thus demonstrating clear
kinship among themselves -- there would develop a more unified
and stronger purpose among free peoples to yield no single inch
or advantage to atheistic communism.

My fear would be that zealots would introduce so many questions
and argumentative subjects into a convocation of such a kind that
most of the discussion would revolve around relatively unimportant points. On the other hand, the need, in my opinion, is
for recognition of the ascendency of spiritual values and a ringing
declaration that it is because of their importance that free men
always stand ready, individually and collectively, to defend them,
support them and advance them. Such a declaration, I believe,
would do much to alert us to the threat posed by Communist imperialism, and to unite us better in the search for peace.

Most of this I wrote to Arthur, but I also wanted to tell you personally how much your column appealed to me.

PERSONAL

A letter from President Eisenhower.
USED BY PERMISSION OF AMBASSADOR JOHN EISENHOWER.

THE WHITE HOUSE
WASHINGTON

- 2 -

PERSONAL

Here in Washington things go on much the same, though
the problems that occupy every twenty-four hours change.
At the moment, of course, Berlin occupies most of our
attention on the international scene -- and the fight on
the budget is shaping up as the predominant topic as
far as domestic matters are concerned.

Al and I are, of course, undisputed bridge champions
whenever we get an opportunity to play. That opportunity
doesn't come too often, primarily because he seems constantly to be on the speech-making trail.

With warm regard to you and Marina, and congratulations
on an excellent article,

Sincerely,

D. E.

Mr. C. L. Sulzberger,
THE NEW YORK TIMES,
37 Rue Caumartin,
Paris, France.

PERSONAL

Marina with Greta Garbo and Stavros Niarchos during a summer holiday in Greece.

MEMORANDUM OF A BET

Munich
April 14, 1961

Cy Sulzberger bets Franz-Josef Strauss one case of French champagne payable in the year 1970. CLS bets that by January 1, 1970, Strauss will either be Chancellor of Germany or will have been Chancellor of Germany. FJS bets the contrary.

A bet with Germany's then defense minister. (The bet was subsequently lost and paid off.)

(LEFT)
Visiting Israel's founding father, David Ben Gurion, at his kibbutz in the Negev.

(RIGHT)
Helping Mrs. John F. Kennedy (now Jacqueline Onassis) ashore in Italy, 1962.
PHOTO BY GILBERT GRAZIANI.

(BELOW)
With President Nasser of the United Arab Republic.

Dear Cy — What would the Herald Tribune say
This shows we both believe in "when in Rome etc"
With happy memories of Ravello —

My regular golfing companions with some distinguished
company (Ben Hogan, *second from right*). My fellow players are
Indian Ambassador Sardar (*left*), H. S. Malik (*second from
left*), Sir Christopher Steel (British Ambassador to NATO, *third
from left*), and General Lauris Norstad (*extreme right*).

Talking with Chairman Khrushchev in the Kremlin, 1961.

With Khrushchev in the Kremlin, September, 1961.

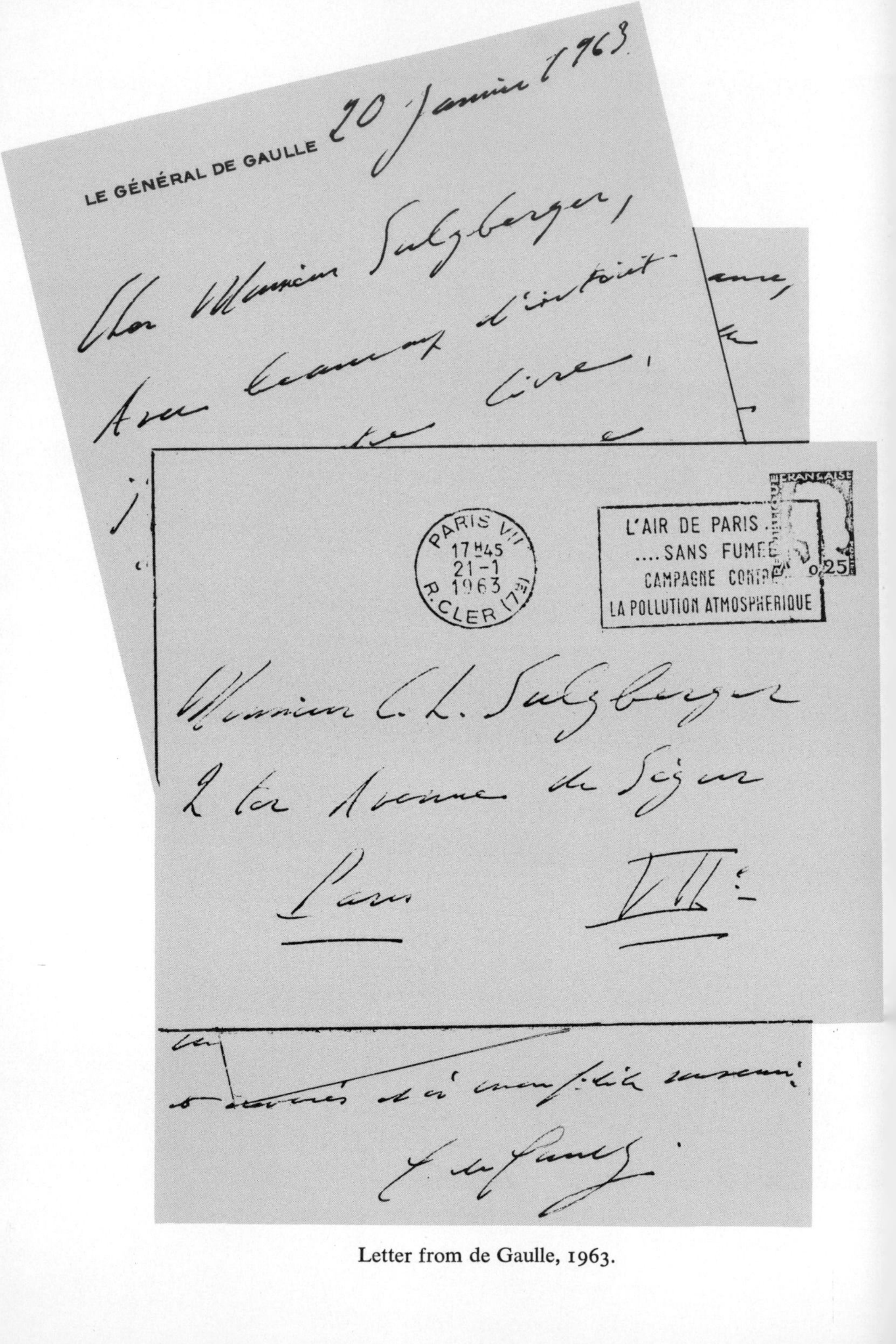

LE GÉNÉRAL DE GAULLE 20 Janvier 1963.

Cher Monsieur Sulzberger,

Avec beaucoup d'intérêt ... livre,

PARIS VII 17H45 21-1 1963 R. CLER (7e)

L'AIR DE PARIS ...
.... SANS FUMEE
CAMPAGNE CONTRE
LA POLLUTION ATMOSPHERIQUE

FRANÇAISE 0,25

Monsieur C. L. Sulzberger
2 bis Avenue de Ségur
Paris VIIe

... et à mon fidèle souvenir.

C. de Gaulle

Letter from de Gaulle, 1963.

Autographed portrait of John F. Kennedy.

With King Hussein in Jordan, 1963.

Bet with Stash Radziwill, December 9, 1963.

The role of the writer, of course, depends on his own political and ideological views. I presume you are referring to the creative writer, not the political or ideological writer. Isn't it very much like the role of anyone else? A writer should not use his influence as a writer in an irrelevant way. There is a danger of his misusing his prestige.

A writer like myself is constantly appealed to in general appeals for letters to express views on various public problems. The writer is asked to sign letters and to lend the weight of his name for various causes. This must be approached with extreme caution. I do not lend my name to appeals on things about which I don't know enough. I try and limit myself to sponsoring appeals on things with which I am generally concerned. Very often, if you stop to ask what good a public statement will do, you hesitate to sign it. General statements on such things as peace or against race discrimination are what I refer to. One does nothing by signing these. Everyone of goodwill feels the same way on such matters as peace.

Of course, we all wish to write about things that we feel strongly about and have thought about. Some of my attitudes have been expressed in some of my longer prose essays. But I am perfectly aware that certain sociologists have resented the intrusion of amateurs from the outside. And I understand their viewpoint.

The writer really has the same duties as the ordinary citizen. One should have feelings—as most of us have—on the side of liberty, in such things as the Pasternak case. Naturally we feel that greater scope should be given to the opinions of people who disagree with us than is permitted, for example, by the Soviet authorities.

An ineffective protest is certainly better than silence. The man of letters, of course, has a particular interest in other writers and in seeing to it that they enjoy the same liberties as he himself has. But otherwise, our protest should be limited to those of any other citizen.

Acts of tyranny—whether on racial or religious persecution—invite the protest of anyone.

Of course, there is always this question of how far it is right to interfere in other peoples' affairs. But one cannot allow this approach to serve as a pretext to avoid one's moral responsibility. However, there are some issues we cannot easily comprehend. During the Spanish Civil War, I felt that the less foreign interference there was on one side or the other, the better it was.

That point of view now seems rather out of date. So many fictions have been given currency. I refer to fictions such as that which Moscow has sought to create—that the Russian army in Hungary was only there to support the legitimate government upon its request for help.

I wonder if there are people who really want war. I am thinking of all these petitions in favor of peace. Perhaps miscreants would like to gain their aims by threats of war—but without fighting. Nevertheless, I think everybody wants peace, although some people want peace on their own terms.

In the seventeenth century, Jonathan Swift wrote brilliant essays on particular things—like the "Draper's Letters"—against depreciation of currency in Ireland. This became a national issue. But Swift had proven his qualifications in advance. It is not good enough for a writer simply to sign letters drawn up by someone else. That is a cheap way out.

I then asked Eliot if he could explain why so many American writers, including himself, during the last thirty or forty years have chosen to live abroad. He replied:

I don't know if there is any particular reason. I don't know, for example, what Prohibition had to do with it. I have got a clean bill because I was living abroad before Prohibition was even thought of. I was encouraged to stay over here by Ezra Pound, who was the first man who managed to get any of my poems published, and was enthusiastic about them.

At that time, there were certain advantages for a young man in staying abroad. For example, I had to earn my living because I had no private means. It was easier for me to earn my living abroad. I never looked very far ahead. One doesn't when one is young. But I had a good job. Eventually I worked in a bank in the city. Then, when I found that I was going to stay on over here, because I married here, I decided to take full responsibilities and become a British subject.

I can't think of any general reasons for having done what I did or for having other Americans live abroad. I don't know if I could have gotten a job in New York and lived there when I was a young man.

Also, the American literary scene at the beginning of the century didn't seem to offer much encouragement to young men, especially for poets. You know, that was a very dull period with poets like George Cabot Lodge and Trumbull Stickney. There were no particular literary groups or societies for the young poet to mix with. Things have changed now.

The influx of Americans into Paris came after the World War I. I don't know exactly why. In many cases, it was just a question of a good deal of drift. You just go and find yourself in a certain position and then you find you are earning your living there.

Ezra Pound had no prospect of gaining a livelihood at home except by teaching. He had had an unfortunate experience and was thrown out of a midwestern college.

There was a dull intellectual period then at home. This helped to push people abroad. But over in Europe, I met established literary people. Pound introduced me to Yeats. I got to know Virginia Woolf. People were interested in my poetry. I had never experienced that interest before.

That there is a definite moment of choice or a reason for emigrating in this way is an illusion. It is more a question of drifting along and a gradual readaptation. I don't think there is any single brilliant clue to my story, for example.

Eliot said that both economic factors and the intellectual receptiveness of the community in which they live are important to young writers. He added: "I solved this by going into a bank. Wallace Stevens was with an insurance company for years."

LONDON, *March 28, 1959*

PLEASANT luncheon and long talk with Ambassador Jock Whitney, just back from the United States. I saw him at his house in Regent's Park, where, most of the time, we discussed some important personal matters. He again invited me to become editor of the *Herald Tribune.* I said I could not consider this while Uncle Arthur was alive.

He said Nye Bevan is extremely fond of painting and knows a good deal about it. Every time he comes to Jock's house he says to him: "I don't come to see you; I come to see your pictures." And he spends a lot of time looking at them.

PARIS, *April 3, 1959*

At dinner I asked Norstad if Hawaii wasn't now included in NATO since it has become a state. He was a bit puzzled, then said yes. Air Force General Lawrence Kuter chimed in by pointing out that Midway was a part of the state of Hawaii (which I didn't know) so that NATO now extends close to Japan. Kuter said: "Come to think of it, it is strange that the headquarters of our Pacific air force is now in the NATO area."

PARIS, *April 10, 1959*

USEFUL talk with Couve de Murville. He wastes no time but never gives the feeling that he is in a hurry.

He told me the Washington meeting of the NATO Big Four had not been much of a strain. Herter made a good impression and seemed very au courant, although lacking Dulles's force of character.

I asked how he interpreted Adenauer's decision to give up the Chancellorship in order to run for President of the Federal Republic. Couve answered: "I think Adenauer's explanation is true. I think he is looking ahead and wants to organize a succession. We cannot forget that he is eighty-three years old."

Couve would not "exclude" the possibility that the precedent of de Gaulle's presidency in France had psychologically affected Adenauer's decision. "Certainly he will play a bigger role as president than Heuss," Couve said. "After all, he has a different personality and he takes the authority of ten years with him."

I asked how serious the NATO split was on dealing with Russia over Germany. He said: "The division is not on the basic issue, but it is on the spirit of the negotiations and primarily on disengagement." Canada, Denmark, Norway, and Belgium were supporting the British viewpoint.

The real argument was on disengagement, not on keeping control of West Berlin. The British idea was to try to sell their thin-out plan to the Russians in exchange for a deal on Berlin.

"It would concede something to the Russians in advance," Couve said, "and I can't see the need for it. Of course, Macmillan is thinking of his election. Also he wants to pull out the last of the British army of the Rhine. Finally, we can't forget that there is a considerable amount of ill will toward Germany in England. They resent German trade competition and they resent German friendship with France."

I asked if de Gaulle's reference to the East German frontier with Poland as a final border for a unified Germany had been a deliberate statement and the result of a Quai d'Orsay decision, or if it had slipped out inadvertently. Couve said it was deliberately done. I asked: "But isn't that a concession to the Russians in advance of negotiations?" Couve said, "No." He continued:

After all, we won't be discussing a peace treaty with the Russians. Nobody wants to discuss a peace treaty now. Therefore, this is not at present a material question. De Gaulle merely wants to be honest. He wanted to state his entire position on Germany. We didn't sign the Potsdam agreement which made the Polish German border a de facto —if theoretically temporary—frontier. But *you* people don't dare say that this is really the final frontier, although you know it is.

I asked whether there were any major reforms in NATO shaping up. He said:

France thinks that what should be changed is in the Mediterranean area. That area, to the south, is not wide enough now that the Russians are in the Middle East. And the defense area should include Dakar, West and North Africa, Libya, and Egypt. That area is not yet in NATO and we must do something about it. But we must start with an agreement in world political and strategic approaches, then get down to precise questions.

PARIS, *April 11, 1959*

LONG lunch with René Brouillet, directeur de Cabinet for General de Gaulle. Brouillet said de Gaulle is timid and nervous about press conferences. He said: "I dined with him alone the night before the famous March conference and found the General very uneasy, but once he gets before the audience he pulls himself together."

De Gaulle likes to read a lot and reads the press and magazines of opinion quite faithfully. He quits work at 8 P.M. every evening and doesn't start until 10 A.M. the next morning, which gives him a considerable amount of time for reading. He can read English quite easily and can actually speak it haltingly. When Macmillan was here, they talked to each other in French. De Gaulle used to know German, which he learned for military purposes and which he polished up as a prisoner during World War I, but he has pretty well forgotten it. When he and Adenauer met, they talked through an interpreter.

PARIS, *May 1, 1959*

LAST night at dinner, I met Allen Tate, the poet: a wispy, thin little man with a slight moustache. He is a professor at the University of Minnesota. He has been at All Souls in Oxford since September on a Fulbright fellowship. He told me Ezra Pound had already shown signs of insanity as far back as 1926. Pound was a great teacher and a great discoverer of new talent. One could learn much from him about meters, length, and line, etc., but Pound was not really a first-class writer himself. Tate described him as a pre-Raphaelite, lingering on into the twentieth century.

This afternoon, I had a pleasant talk with Chris Herter, my first since he became Secretary of State: very relaxed and agreeable. He makes a good impression and has the advantage of enthusiastic backing in Congress. He looked well and healthy although, of course, he had his half-crutches with him. His six-foot-five height is very stooped.

Herter said we didn't want to accept the Poles and Czechs as Geneva participants, but were prepared to allow other countries to participate if matters directly concerning them arose. If the Russians wanted the Poles and the Czechs we would have to insist on the Italians, and that might get the Russians to request the Rumanians, and it would turn into a very large conference.

I asked why we didn't dodge this by suggesting reconstitution of the four-power Council of Foreign Ministers. After all, it had never been disbanded formally. Herter said this had never occurred to him, but he thought the council was pretty well outmoded because it hadn't met for years.

He said there had been no discussions here on what the allied "fall-back" position should be at Geneva. Obviously, this would have to be elaborated on a day-to-day basis and as negotiations developed. It was impossible to prepare a real "fall-back" position now because that would automatically make it part of our initial position when discussions begin.

It was strange that so many people seemed to assume this was not a genuine crisis with a danger of war. For a time, the May 27 ultimatum had worried everybody. Then Mikoyan first said the date was not essential and later Khrushchev made several statements in which he said he had "reached for the ceiling" and produced that date, but it could be extended by a year or two if necessary. May 27 gave a feeling of crisis which has perhaps now been dissipated, but the United States still feels this is a very serious situation.

I asked him what was the maximum and what was the minimum he expected from Geneva. He said it was impossible to state a maximum. "As for a minimum, that would be the maintenance of the status quo in Berlin. Of course, if the Russians want to get out of East Berlin, that is their privilege."

WEST BERLIN, *May 2, 1959*

I FLEW up here today and, as far as Frankfurt, had the benefit of the Bruces' company. David said the cleverest Soviet tactic in coming negotiations would be to try and gain concessions from the West everywhere *except* in Berlin, finally appearing to concede in Berlin—leaving the status quo. Moscow would, of course, have to clamp down on the East Germans who would be disappointed; but Ulbricht isn't much trouble for Khrushchev. The allies could boast of a diplomatic victory on Berlin—having made big yields elsewhere. At another time, Moscow could put the squeeze on Berlin all over again.

We must take a stand and be ready to fight if necessary. And, with a two- or three-year missile gap coming up, during which we will be weaker than the Russians, perhaps now is the best time to be tough. The UN could be only of limited help in the Berlin crisis. It could police the access lanes to West Berlin, but our troops must remain there and cannot come under a UN commander.

West Berlin is a tragically impossible position. Someday, *all* Berlin will have to be internationalized; or Berlin will have to again become the capital of a unified Germany. And that won't occur for years. The only way we can keep West Berlin now is by the menace of war. The majority of West Berliners think we will fight for them—unlike the majority of West Germans, who don't.

EAST BERLIN, *May 2, 1959*

WENT straight from the airport to keep an appointment with Walter Ulbricht, secretary of the communist party and boss of East Germany, at Central Committee headquarters, an ugly, massive affair.

Ulbricht, a short, solid man, was wearing a gray suit and tie. A pointed beard (Leninist fashion) covers a slightly receding, half-stubborn, half-weak chin. He wears rimless glasses, has a long nose, suspicious blue eyes. He was very friendly. Gerhard Eisler, his propaganda chief and a well-known refugee from America, translated.

I asked Ulbricht what his reaction would be if the West turned over control of West Berlin and the access lanes to Bonn's forces, replacing those of the Big Three, when Russia hands East Berlin to the East Germans. He became indignant and said:

There are no Soviet rights here in East Berlin; just the rights of the German people. We have a treaty with the Soviet Union. We have full sovereignty. Of course, we have accorded to the Soviet Union certain rights of transportation to handle the requirements of its military forces.

The western allies have NO rights to hand over to Bonn in West Berlin. West Berlin is in East German territory. Any changes will have to be talked over and decided by four-power agreement with us. What you suggest is that West German tanks supported by the western allies should come to Berlin. That's no good. There is no question of what kind of West German troops should be in West Berlin. I can't imagine an American actually wanting them there. You know perfectly well it would mean war. Your theory leads me to the conclusion that you want foreign troops on our soil. West Berlin doesn't belong to West Germany and never has. You want to establish there a base for West German militarism.

This question has only been made difficult by your refusal to recognize us, by the assertion that there is no German Democratic Republic. Yet anyone seriously wanting reunification would want talks between the two Germanies. Moscow has diplomatic relations with Bonn. The West should have diplomatic relations with us. Much can be done by such sensible relationships and the United States should help by making the first move.

European tension should be relaxed and relations between the two Germanies encouraged. This should start with questions that are immediately solvable. The obstacle is not representation on a basis of Länder. It was West Germany, not East Germany, which began an atomic army. The first question is that of atomic weapons in West Germany. The second question is to arrange an agreement on a non-aggression pact between NATO and the Warsaw powers. At the same time, West Berlin should be demilitarized.

I asked Ulbricht what he considered the frontiers of a reunited Germany should be. He said the existing ones, adding: "I can't imagine that Truman, Attlee, and Stalin agreed on these borders at Potsdam just to have them altered later."

I asked him if there were any nuclear warheads or dual-purpose weapons on East German soil. He said:

Neither one nor the other. I'll tell you why. We have none because we still sincerely hope the western governments will see that it is possible to limit armed forces. We want to safeguard the peace. We hope understanding on this will be reached at the summit. We have NO intention of acquiring such weapons.

Let us have the Americans, British, French, and Soviet Union and the two Germanies sign a peace treaty. The result would be a limitation of arms. Then the Americans will no longer be in danger of being dragged into war by West German militarists. But the basis would have to be equal between the two Germanies. Both must have NO nuclear weapons or rockets. We will undertake any pledges desired to apply no pressures or force on West Berlin. And this can be insured by either the UN or the Big Four powers. Thus, there would be no real change in the situation—except that the presence of foreign troops and Cold War agencies would be removed from West Berlin.

WEST BERLIN, *May 2, 1959*

THIS evening, I went to see Willy Brandt, mayor of West Berlin, at his comfortable, modest suburban home. Brandt had a mild case of grippe but is a pretty sturdy-looking character: a big, open-faced, hefty man who was a refugee from Hitler in Norway and came back to Berlin after the war as press attaché for the Norwegian Berlin mission.

The only thing distinguishing Brandt's house from its neighbor's was a uniformed policeman at the door standing beside a child's bicycle. Brandt was wearing a cardigan and jacket. Although his collar was buttoned, he had no necktie. First we sat in his book-lined study and then moved into the little sitting room where he served whisky as we talked. He said:

Politically, I have always been doubtful about the West's position on Berlin's relationship to East Germany. I have never accepted the way the allies interpreted our reservations on West Berlin's position as a member state of the Federal Republic. The West says Berlin cannot be a *land* of the Federal Republic. But the GDR has incorporated East Berlin as part of the GDR. Therefore, there is no more reason for the allies to exclude West Berlin from being a portion of West Germany on the grounds of the Potsdam agreement.

However, I don't believe in substituting federal German troops for the allied garrison here. The danger would be much greater that trouble could break out if you had East German troops on one side of the Potsdammerplatz and West German troops on the other side. And politically speaking, the allies *have* rights of access to West Berlin despite Russian arguments to the contrary. There would be no similar legal basis for federal German troops to claim a similar free access.

I asked if Brandt thought there was anything the West could yield in its West Berlin position for the sake of negotiations—and against what concessions by the Russians. He answered:

A good mayor has to think his city is the most important in the world. I cannot say what is just or necessary and what might be the outcome of any concessions. But remember that the military forces now here are already only a symbolic force. They represent a tripwire defense.

A few days ago, a British MP had a general discussion with a Russian officer in a private home here. The Englishman said: "If you chaps start any nonsense we can give you a tough time for about two hours." The Russian replied: "No, only ten minutes. But we know this would lead to serious trouble."

There are perhaps ten thousand allied troops here now, and perhaps only half as many troops could serve the same tripwire purpose. But any reduction in allied strength might lead to a misunderstanding on the Soviet side.

There are, of course, other aspects of the Berlin situation; for example, propaganda, intelligence, and subversive activities. But even if the West closes such agencies, the Communists would still complain; because our newspapers continue to print stories which the Communists would consider hostile, and if we closed RAIS [Allied Radio], there would still be an ordinary Berlin radio station whose broadcasts the Russians would dislike. And they would continue to dislike the fact that East Berliners can come over to West Berlin to theaters and lectures and can compare our life with theirs.

We can't help out there. We can't change these things unless we give up what we stand for. The fact is, the Communists are genuinely afraid of competitive coexistence. As for intelligence activities, it would be quite unrealistic to believe that West Berlin should be the only place in the world without intelligence. Intelligence exists everywhere else. If East and West make an agreement that there should be no intelligence activities in Berlin, all the world would know that this is nonsense. Intelligence would continue.

I can't agree to refuse to help a fellow countryman who finds himself in a difficult position. A refugee who comes to West Berlin, for example, deserves aid. If someone from East Berlin comes over here and wants to buy newspapers and books, I am prepared to let him have them. If a teacher from Dresden wants books, why shouldn't he have access to them? It's his own risk.

BAD GÖDESBERG, *May 4, 1959*

LUNCH conversation with my old friend Pietro Quaroni, now Italian ambassador here. He says the allies are insane to think that by offering something vague to Moscow in other fields we can distract the Russians from their main aim—to make a separate peace with East Germany.

The Russians, in their way, are as legalistic as Dulles was. They calculate that after such a separate peace it will be juridically clear that there can be no more question of German reunification. We can't *prevent* a separate peace and it is impossible for us to talk of going to war to prevent it.

What is really of vital importance to the West, unlike Berlin, is the military setup of NATO. This would not in any way be endangered by allied recognition of Pankow (East German capital). The question of recognition is a matter of political sentiment only. Militarily speaking, West Berlin is a negative, not a positive factor for the West. We maintain soldiers there who would be wiped out on the first day of any fight.

We cannot let the idea of neutrality spread. If, for example, all Germany is neutralized, Norway and Denmark will want a similar status, then Italy, then France. When the chain reaction sets in, it cannot be stopped. One cannot make any concessions in this realm without beginning to break up NATO itself.

"In virtue, only the first mistake counts."

Right now, West Berlin gets 3,000,000,000 marks a year from the federal government and the U.S.A. The profession of being a Berliner is even more profitable than it once was to be a Triestino. Each Berliner gets 1,500 marks a year. But a *free* city, as Khrushchev sees it, must be independent of Bonn. Therefore, the economic life of West Berlin would fall into the hands of the GDR.

The best way for us to worm out of an impossible situation is to pass the buck to UN. When you want to yield with a minimum loss of face, UN is the formula. And we can make it clear to our populations we haven't given an inch on the essentials, NATO itself. Khrushchev knows he can't break up NATO. He sneered to Carlo Schmid: "You can remain in NATO if you want. We know that without Bonn there would be no NATO. And it is better for Russia that you have such large military defenses instead of being more free to compete economically."

At the beginning of 1945, an important Russian told Quaroni (then ambassador in Moscow) that Germany could have been democratic in the past but had always been stamped down by Prussia, Brandenburg, Pomerania, and Mecklenburg. By taking these provinces away, said the Russian, the Germans would be given a chance to become democratic; and if they did not do so it would be only because they were fascists. Quaroni adds, "He really believed this."

There are no hostile feelings toward France in Germany. There *is* a large suspicion of de Gaulle, not because it is feared he is anti-German, but Germans remember they were brought to ruin by a German madman and they don't want to be brought to ruin again by a French madman. They see that the French are aspiring to a *gloire* quite beyond their capacities. In their Common Market policy, they see that the French want placed at their own disposal Germany's hard-won money, the result of work, of a wise economic policy, and a wise foreign policy. France is merely seen as an adorable old lady, incurably foolish, going along a way that can lead only to ruin.

The U.S.A. is asinine not to adopt the idea of using the West Germans as proxies. We should do for Berlin what we did for Formosa where we used Chiang Kai-shek's troops, not our own, against China. We should put the West Germans in West Berlin. The West assumes Russia is bluffing and playing on allied dissensions; that if we show a united front, the Russians will give up. This is wrong. The Russians don't really care about western unity. They are only concerned about what America will do.

The Russians don't want a war any more than the U.S. does. But they see they have challenged the U.S. on a ground strategically favorable to Russia. The U.S. is essentially a sea power. It had a favorable ground in Quemoy and the Lebanon; but not in land-bound Berlin.

BAD GÖDESBERG, *May 5, 1959*

LONG lunch and pleasant conversation with David Bruce. He says Adenauer boasts with pleasure that Johnny Walker, head of the Washington National Gallery, told him if he ever quits as Chancellor he (Walker) will resign as gallery boss because Adenauer is the most qualified living man for the job. (His other passions are Rhine and Mosel wines and gardening.)

Our position in Berlin is tragically bad. Our best hope is to play the summit card right. Khrushchev really wants a summit meeting and we can insist this won't take place unless he is reasonable on Berlin. He wants to see Eisenhower and the summit is his only way. The only negotiating card we have is the question of the summit.

Bruce believes we should enter into a series of negotiations, what he calls a "rolling conference," like the Korean talks. He has often spoken informally to Adenauer about this idea and was embarrassed last time Dulles was over when Adenauer suddenly turned to Dulles and said: "You should pay attention to the Bruce plan." Dulles didn't know what he was talking about. But when it was explained, he nodded and said there was much merit in it. That was the last David ever heard on the matter.

Last week, Adenauer wrote a long personal letter to Dulles and showed it to Bruce first. He has a real fondness for Dulles and is deeply affected that a man so much younger than himself is now facing death. The letter spoke warmly of the great "spiritual support" Dulles had given him. There was a real religious bond (despite their different creeds) and the same fanatical detestation of communism as an evil dogma.

Adenauer is no intellectual. He is a fine politician. Also, he has a few simple, major ideas to which he adheres through thick and thin; these are the essence of his statesmanship. He is lazy on reading documents and badly informed because he chooses to believe gossip rather than what his ministers tell him.

Long ago, Adenauer decided that there are only two real powers in the world, Russia and America. He decided to choose one, us, and having done this, he built his policy on tying himself as tightly as possible to Washington. Adenauer continued to count on Russian fear of China and a consequent desire to do business with the West.

BONN, *May 6, 1959*

TALK with Ludwig Erhard, vice chancellor and economics minister and probably the next Chancellor of West Germany. He is a very broad man who looks enormously fat, having a round face and small features so that his face is really more swollen than his body. He has white hair, pleasant blue eyes, a look of efficiency. His hands are aged and spotty.

I asked Erhard why Adenauer opposed him as next Chancellor. He said: "He is not opposed to my succession and the reasons sometimes given—that he fears I might change his French policy—are untrue. But, on the Common Market—the issue so often discussed—I feel this should not be limited to the six members. There are other countries in free Europe and we must be careful to avoid a split." (Erhard will do everything possible—if he is Chancellor—to arrange a compromise between the Common Market and Britain's European Free Trade Area.)

"Permit me to say that Adenauer is eighty-four now and maybe he is not quite happy that another, younger man has also gained a wide prestige. It is a human consideration that is nevertheless quite comprehensible."

I asked Erhard how he would negotiate with the Russians on Berlin and reunification. He said:

I think we must accept that the chances of a solution on Berlin might come sooner than anything else. You can't reunite Germany in one jump. A confederation of the two Germanies cannot be attempted yet. But it is possible to begin on technical cooperation and such things as freedom of movement.

Nevertheless, you must remember that we can't combine dictatorship and freedom, slavery and liberty, in the same country. And, furthermore, you can't put off free elections until the end—after everything else has been frozen. The right of self-determination has been acknowledged for every black tribe in Africa; surely it should be allowed to the people of Germany.

IT'S BETTER TO
PRAY WITH BOMBS

GENEVA, *May 12, 1959*

HERE SINCE FRIDAY EVENING, HAVING DRIVEN DOWN FROM BONN. A very dreary assemblage of diplomats and reporters for the foreign minister's conference.

Sunday I lunched with Luigi Barzini and his first wife, Giannalisa Feltrinelli (mother of the young Milanese publisher who had the great scoop of obtaining the only "refugee" manuscript of *Doctor Zhivago*). Luigi told me Fanfani was now finished; that after the "torpedoes" of my three columns he never recovered; that the new government is beginning to let go at Mattei. Fanfani's gang, while trying to save themselves, had publicly accused Alfio Russo (editor of *La Nazione* in Florence) of staging a secret dinner at his home for Scelba and myself to arrange to ruin Fanfani. Russo, at lunch here Monday, repeated the same tale. The only wrong fact is that Russo did indeed have Scelba for dinner—but not me.

GENEVA, *May 13, 1959*

DINED tonight with Tommy Thompson and Jean Laloy, two Russian experts who frequently disagree. Tommy thinks we can probably work out a deal on Berlin here at the summit because Khrushchev needs a diplomatic success, having failed in Hungary, Jugoslavia, and Egypt; because Khrushchev is worried about China; because he is worried about his Seven Year Plan succeeding and wants U.S. credits and needs to cut down on arms costs.

Laloy and I argued that East Germany is a key to the Seven Year Plan and he must hang on, rather than permit any reunification; that his success, diplomatically, is ready-made in Berlin because of our own uncom-

571

fortable position; that he can get a summit as easily by being nasty as by being nice.

Tommy suspects Khrushchev wants a big deal at the summit; might suggest *total* disarmament, discuss a secret deal against China, or a Middle East deal settling the Israel-Arab question.

Laloy says Vinogradov (Soviet ambassador in Paris) said today, for the first time, that if France were more "reasonable" to Russia perhaps Moscow could help protect French interests in Africa. He asked Vinogradov how many western troops would be considered a "reasonable" garrison in West Berlin under a new arrangement. "About twenty from each country," said Vinogradov.

Tommy says Khrushchev told the Swiss ambassador: "If I go to a cathedral and pray for peace, nobody listens. But if I go with two bombs, they will."

GENEVA, *May 19, 1959*

THIS morning, Chris Herter said our position here is that the peace of Europe depends on settling the German problem; not on two treaties with two Germanies or a Berlin arrangement.

Khrushchev may want a summit to please his own ego. Yesterday evening, the French told us de Gaulle wouldn't go to a summit in the U.S.A. for three reasons: he wants it on neutral ground; since European problems are the principal matters, it should be in Europe; he doesn't want Khrushchev propagandizing in the U.S.A.

This morning, I called on James Wadsworth, a tall, large man with glasses, a big jaw, and a friendly face, who is our special ambassador for the nuclear talks with Russia and Britain. He said one reason Russia wants a nuclear treaty ending tests is to prevent other countries from joining the club, especially China.

But China would have to come under any world-inspection system to make that effective. China would thus have to adhere to the treaty. It is not necessary to have diplomatic relations.

The treaty could become operative without China's signature, but it wouldn't work out fully. It would leave a major physical gap in the inspection system. We think twenty-four inspection posts would be needed in Russia, which is bigger, and only about ten in China.

Tsarapkin, the Soviet delegate, keeps telling Wadsworth (who says they are real friends): "If we can obtain an accord we will become famous men in our own countries."

NEW YORK, *June 1, 1959*

LUNCHED with M. C. Chagla, Indian ambassador, who was governor of Bombay state before he came to Washington. The Dalai Lama stayed with Chagla in Bombay. New Delhi had briefed Chagla on the Dalai Lama's habits and warned him, for example, that he did not like meat or women. Nevertheless, the Dalai Lama demanded sausages and kidneys for breakfast and went out of his way to shake hands with all female guests at receptions instead of the usual Buddhist greeting of a slight bow with two hands folded as in prayer. He also skipped out one evening to attend an American movie in Bombay, incognito.

NEW YORK, *June 4, 1959*

LONG talk with Governor Nelson Rockefeller. He complained that the people of New York State and especially the legislature in Albany are far too provincial and display absolutely no interest in foreign affairs. The same is true of the party apparatus and the entire Republican mechanism. The legislature has absolutely no appreciation of the relationship of New York State to tremendous events taking place in the outer world.

I asked him what kind of man he would like to appoint as Secretary of State if he were elected President. Rockefeller replied:

He would have to be a man with some political judgment and deeply human understanding. Increasingly, our relations in the world are of a political nature rather than the formality of traditional diplomacy. International political relationships involve people and human forces. The Secretary of State must be aware of the hopes and aspirations of different peoples.

It seems to me that increasingly international meetings are like political meetings. Statesmen are motivated by the same human forces from which they cannot disassociate themselves. Like the politician, the statesman cannot divorce himself from his own constituents—even in a totalitarian system like Russia's.

This doesn't mean I discount the importance of diplomatic procedure. But personal relations in international affairs are far more important than the public may realize. If two states are represented by two men who trust each other, that certainly facilitates the establishment of good relations between these states.

I asked Rockefeller what sort of background and training he considered desirable for such a Secretary of State, pointing out that I thought too many of our secretaries had been lawyers. He said he thought

Herter's training had been ideal. He was not trying to evaluate Herter as a Secretary of State but merely as a product of a certain background. Herter knew politics, having been in Congress and having been a governor. Thus he knew both federal and state affairs. He had also lived abroad. He had had a lifetime interest in international affairs. All this together made the ideal combination.

Lunched with Tom Dewey, and for the first time in the years I have known him, he left an extremely favorable impression. He is deeply concerned about the paralysis creeping into our governmental system and thinks the British formula for democracy is considerably more successful than our own. Our civil service, by its very nature is mediocre.

Today, only princes or paupers can afford to go into government service. Few men are willing to sell their accumulated security holdings, agree to go to Washington to lose money by having to spend more than they are paid, and be badgered by Congress. Congress is beginning to paralyze the executive. Representatives and Senators find that the best way of attracting public attention and thereby assuring reelection is to dragoon some distinguished Cabinet minister before some committee and then hector him—if possible in front of television. It is an appalling waste of time that generals and Cabinet ministers have to spend so much time answering legislator's questions. Furthermore, it is ridiculous that a legislature should have the right to approve all appointments from postmaster to ambassador to general to Cabinet officers. The only right of approval Congress should have is over Cabinet officers. How does Congress know whether Colonel Jones is or is not qualified to be made a one-star general? Dewey would rectify this by amending the Constitution and striking out the word "advice" from the phrase "advice and consent of the Senate."

The system is in itself paralytic, but it could be less damaging if the President were prepared to assume political leadership. But Eisenhower is not a political leader. He himself admits he is not a politician.

Dewey expressed great admiration for Nixon. He had sold Nixon to Eisenhower in 1952, as the vice presidential candidate. Already in 1952, he was an admirably equipped political leader and has grown steadily ever since. It was perfectly obvious that Dewey hopes Nixon will be the nominee in 1960.

NEW YORK, *June 6, 1959*

LUNCHED at Laporte's, French consul general. Armand Bérard was there. He is now France's new ambassador to the United Nations. I last saw him in Tokyo and so we discussed Japan.

He told me how the marriage of the Crown Prince was arranged. When the highest court officials finally decided it was time for the twenty-four-year-old Akihito, who had never shown any interest in women, to get married, they went to work. They investigated two thousand young women and ended up with a list of four, two princesses and two commoners.

The two princesses were discarded as old-fashioned, unintelligent, and not particularly healthy. Health was a matter of primary importance because the Crown Prince's grandfather was weak minded. As a consequence, the present Emperor Hirohito had been carefully married off to the Empress, who was regarded as a good breeder. It was felt essential to follow up this improvement in the blood line with another very healthy spouse. Michiko was seen as extremely satisfactory in this respect. She also meets Japanese ideas of beauty: flat-chested, with big thighs and thick legs, calculated to excite the Crown Prince.

Finally, Michiko's family represents the big trusts; she is related to the Mitsuis. It is a tradition that when possible the royal family should be tied by marriage to the most powerful element in the country. This used to be the military aristocracy. Now it is the trusts.

Michiko met all qualifications. The Empress objected and wept, but she was overruled. The nobility was infuriated and has already begun to do everything possible to make life difficult for Michiko (such as appoint a lemon as her lady-in-waiting on the grounds that, after all, Michiko is only a commoner).

Akihito had only seen Michiko once or twice and barely knew her. But it was arranged that he should see her often, preferably in brief tennis dresses. The lonely little Crown Prince eventually fell somewhat in love with her and the grand illusion of the love match between prince and commoner was developed.

WASHINGTON, *June 18, 1959*

DINED last night (at his Maryland farm) with Dean Acheson. Acheson was, as usual, charming, suave, witty, cynical, and somewhat bitter. I was no advocate of Dulles's policy, but I did find it offensive when he said, "Thank God Foster is underground." He regaled us with one story after another terminating "Balls, balls, balls," and described Sumner Welles's conversation as sounding like "a fart in a bathtub."

We and the British had quite sensibly divided up the French effort during the war. The British backed de Gaulle and we backed Vichy. The trouble was that Hull, "in his Presbyterian way," convinced himself that Pétain was right and was perfect.

Acheson detests Selwyn Lloyd as incompetent and unreliable. He likes Macmillan. Macmillan told him, after the Cabinet meeting when Britain decided to send troops to Jordan as we went into the Lebanon, that his Cabinet was useless and dodged issues because they represented "the intellectual middle class." Macmillan claimed, says Acheson, that the aristocracy and the workers were OK because they would face responsibility and go along. "I represent both of these," he said to Acheson.

Averell Harriman called him up before going to Moscow to ask him to represent Harriman as his lawyer in obtaining State Department approval for a Chinese visa. Averell added: "But please keep your price reasonable because I have a lot of expenses these days."

Dean called Bob Murphy and got a meeting arranged at the State Department. Murphy, Walter Robertson, the head of security, and others were there. Robertson objected. Acheson argued journalism was now Harriman's sole means of earned income and therefore Washington should approve his visa as a journalist. Robertson said other Asians might protest that Harriman was being secretly sent to negotiate with Peking. "You don't mean to say," said Acheson, "that you believe people abroad would think you fellows were really sending a Democrat to negotiate for you?" Robertson subsided.

WASHINGTON, *June 19, 1959*

THIS afternoon, I had an excellent talk at the White House with President Eisenhower. Invited for drinks, we arrived early and were taken to Ike's private elevator and conducted up to the second floor.

The President was waiting at the door of the elevator. He shook hands warmly and took us into his private sitting room just off his bedroom. Mamie was still getting dressed for the theater, and he was going to a formal dinner marking the twenty-fifth anniversary of the Federal Housing Administration. Ike was wearing a summer dinner jacket, cream-colored linen coat with black trousers. When Mamie came out she was most becomingly dressed in a black lace evening gown.

During our talk, Ike had two old-fashioneds and I had two highballs. I remembered how General Snyder, his physician and friend, confided that he always liked to make Ike take a couple of drinks—and sometimes more—at the end of the day because it helped him to relax.

He looked better than any time I've seen him since he went to the White House: thin, hard, tanned, relaxed, and full of beans. Even when he got irked—when I brought Symington's name into the conversation—he did not display his familiar tendency to get all red in the face and neck. He seemed composed, well rested, and full of confidence. He complimented me on having lost weight (which isn't true unfortunately). He told me what a hard time he had keeping his weight down, as his doctors ordered him to do after his stroke, his heart attack, and ileitis. At one point, he took me into a little room, which he has turned into a studio. He showed me the paintings he is now working on and dozens of others hanging on the walls that he had recently completed. He gets a tremendous bang out of this.

Mamie, incidentally, looked just as flourishing and gay as Ike. She kissed both of us and then sat down on a little sofa with Marina while they chatted happily. She spoke eagerly about the plans the two of them were making for the day when they could retire. That will be in January, 1961. Said Mamie: "Oh how nice it will be to be free and to rest and do as we like. That is, if we have any money left."

She talked about the arduous job of entertaining. The Queen of England and Churchill had both stayed in the White House, but this was only because they were old personal friends. For the most part, official visitors are put in Blair House after one night. The White House is so constructed that it is too inconvenient because there is no privacy. When the Queen of Greece came for a brief stay before moving on to Blair House, she had eighty-five trunks and they had to be distributed all over the place, including the private sitting room where we were talking. All official visitors have an enormous amount of luggage because if a woman wears the same dress twice this is immediately commented upon. The Queen of England wore the same yellow dress she had had on for good luck at the Derby and all the papers were full of it.

Mamie said she hardly ever knew which of the ladies she entertained was a Democrat and which a Republican. She said she had learned the one cardinal rule was never to discuss politics or religion. She never smokes in public. She hardly ever uses the Presidential loge at the theater. When she goes unofficially, like this evening, she leaves as the last curtain goes down, departing through a side door.

The President said that on the whole his personal relations with political leaders were very good. He spoke warmly of Lyndon Johnson and Sam Rayburn as friends who were cordial and amiable when they came to the White House no matter what debate had been taking place at Capitol Hill. "As for Hubert Humphrey," he added, "why, he practically salaams when he comes through the door." But he had absolutely no use for Symington. "I don't even want to hear that man's name," he muttered. I told him I had urged Symington to take up my idea of a civilian draft, but the Senator had refused because it was "too hot." Ike nodded with a grim smile saying: "That's just like the guy." I told Ike about my idea and he smiled. He said: "Go ahead and write that. It's a damned good idea. I'd like to see that idea debated in public."

He said he had tried to have good relations with Truman (which wasn't Truman's version), but that the former President had always spurned these efforts. He felt that a former President could always be of help to his country as an elder statesman and that he would like to value their advice. But the trouble with Truman was that he simply wasn't intelligent or competent and the counsel that he gave in public just wasn't useful.

Ike said he had now come to realize that the constitutional amendment preventing any President from having more than two terms was a good thing. For some years he had not thought so. He had thought it weakened the political position of the Chief Executive. But he saw now that this wasn't true. In fact, in a sense, it freed him by removing him from the political arena and allowing him to speak more freely for the entire country. He noted in this respect that as his own popularity seemed to increase in the polls taken, the popularity of the Republican party decreased.

He felt automatically that any man who *wanted* to be a candidate for the presidency was not qualified for the job. No man of any sense would aspire to the job; it had to be thrust upon him. He was inclined to oppose anyone who sought the job. He remembered how long it had taken when people worked on him to persuade him to accept the Republican nomination.

He got back to Truman and said he had never respected him on an intellectual basis. Truman had put out a story that when Eisenhower was in Kansas City, he (Truman) had called him up at the Hotel Muehlebach because he wanted to pay his respects and Eisenhower had never even acknowledged the call. Ike said he had personally never heard of the call. Then, when the story was published, he inquired of all his secretariat and none of them had ever heard of it. He had an investigation made checking all calls on the Hotel Muehlebach switchboard during the few days he was in Kansas City and found no trace of such a call. "It was a damn lie," he said.

He said the first talk of running him for President started in 1943, and that in 1948, Truman had offered to him to run for Vice President on any ticket headed by Eisenhower (as a Democrat). He said that when the pressure built up in 1951, he had finally gone so far in January, 1952, as to announce that he was a Republican.

He and Foster Dulles often used to talk informally after they had finished some particular business discussion and the subject always came around to government and the problem of keeping democracy going as a system—yet making it effective during the pressures of the Cold War. He remarked: "I was always fond of Foster Dulles."

He made a passing remark about Secretary of the Treasury Bob Anderson as "the brightest man in our government today." (This contrasts curiously with the belief of many Washingtonians that it is George Humphrey rather than Anderson who has the inside track with Eisenhower.) I also remembered the last time I had this kind of a talk with Ike. He observed that the three most competent men who should be considered as Republican Presidential nominees were Anderson, Gruenther, and his own brother Milton. He was referring merely to his estimate of their abilities rather than their political chances.

He talked a lot about Churchill, who had visited him some weeks ago. He always refers to him as "Winston." In all of my conversations with Churchill he has always referred to Eisenhower as "the President"—since he was elected to that office.

He said old Churchill was not really in very good shape and had seemed to be in a fog a considerable part of the time, although now and then he would emerge as his old self. He refused to wear his hearing aid so that he suffered a lot from deafness.

When Churchill's paintings had been exhibited in the United States, Churchill had written to him and told him to pick one out that he liked best as a gift. He had done so and had written Churchill. The exhibition went on around the country and on to Australia, but Churchill had not forgotten and had brought the painting with him.

At this point, he recollected that among the pictures hanging in the hall on the way to the room where Churchill slept (they always gave him the same room—the one he first had when he stayed in the White House as Roosevelt's guest) was one of Field Marshal Montgomery. He felt very strongly that despite the criticisms of himself uttered by Montgomery there was no reason to take his picture down. As he was conducting old Churchill down the hall of his bedroom one evening, Winston looked up and saw the painting of Montgomery. He suddenly came to life, emerging from his fog and said in a low voice, "Aha! I see you still have that picture." Ike was clearly irritated by Montgomery's television appearance during which he had made unkind remarks about Eisenhower and he added: "I can't stand that gangster [Ed] Murrow. I can't stand looking at him. I have no use for him. He always looks like a gangster with a cigarette hanging out of his mouth."

He said his golf varied a great deal. General Snyder kept urging him to play but wanted him to use an electric cart. Just today Eisenhower had played but was terrible. On the other hand, the previous time he played he was pretty darn good and made a 38 for nine holes. He still loved fishing, but he was afraid he couldn't go up into the high Rockies any more—not above six thousand feet.

I asked about his painting. He said he still worked whenever he got any spare time and at this point he took me into the studio. On the easel Ike had a painting of a golf hole on the Augusta National course—a short water hole. On top of a bookshelf to the left was a color photograph of the same hole from which he was working. Ike, who is no genius as a painter, always requires colored photographs as models.

Ike said he thought he had a pretty good memory for color and was not forced to depend on the tint of the photograph itself. He found it hard to work on colors except in daylight, but at night he often dropped in and tried to paint the design aspect of pictures after he had finished work.

It is endearing to see his enthusiasm. He told me one of his paintings has been included in the American Exposition opening next month in Moscow.

When we returned to join the ladies, Ike complained about the loneliness of his job. It was absolutely impossible to lead a normal life. The Secret Service is assigned to protect him and his family and, of course, he couldn't interfere with their job no matter how inconvenient it is.

The Secret Service more or less had to isolate him and if, for example, he ever went anywhere for dinner they had to completely search the place first. It was very hard for him to go to the theater and he rarely did because the Secret Service had to case the theater in advance. One time, when he was in New York, he wanted to play golf at his old club, Blind Brook; but his own friends and golfing partners urged him not to. If other people who had been trying to play golf with him and who were big party contributors heard about it, they would be offended. The big fear of the Secret Service was the possibility that the grand-children might be kidnapped.

Eisenhower said he had been educated with a smattering of Latin, French, and German but really doesn't know any of them now. His son John had had the advantage of learning French pretty well when Ike was assigned to Europe in the 1920s and as a child he used to translate for the family.

At one point, when we were discussing political figures, Eisenhower said: "It's a point of religion with me never to denigrate other people. I never try to pull others down no matter how I disagree with them. This is my religion."

I said I thought it was high time we tried to bring about a change in the rules of Olympic competition. The Russians make no distinction between amateurs and professionals and, indeed, under their social system, they can't do this. It was idiotic for us to expect them to do this and we should bring about a change so we could send around the very best American teams in a competitive sense, regardless of whether they were professionals or amateurs. Ike didn't think we could alter the amateur rules of competition.

He told me that recently he had made a speech at the Foreign Service Institute. He invited the young men attending for a drink. He was very impressed by the fact that there were seventy-five youngsters specializing in Russian who seemed very familiar with that language. But there ought to be about 75,000, he said sadly. He expressed great pleasure that four of the seventy-five were Negroes.

He complained that he was frequently attacked for conducting a "government by veto" and then at other periods he was criticized for lack of leadership. He had learned that a man in his position simply had to let these things roll off his back. For example, on topics like foreign aid there were some people who criticized "give-away" programs of economic aid and others who didn't want any military aid but were prepared for anything else. He was absolutely determined to defend the value of the dollar against pressure and to prevent inflation.

At various times, the talk dealt with foreign affairs. He was disturbed by the obstinacy of the Russians on Berlin and said they seemed to think they could have the summit conference anyway even without agreement at Geneva. They hoped to come in through the back door for a summit conference even though they ignored the front door of the foreign ministers conference. But he wouldn't do it. Nevertheless, he implied that he assumes there will be a summit conference because he said he thought he would see de Gaulle when he stopped over in Paris on his way to such a meeting.

He showed great understanding of and sympathy for de Gaulle. Roosevelt had mistreated de Gaulle during the war and hadn't understood his pride and his determination to represent the noble things in France. This had given de Gaulle a complex toward us and it made him difficult to deal with now. But he liked and respected de Gaulle (which, I might say, is a contrast to some of the things Ike has said to me before and some of the things he has written about de Gaulle).

He acknowledged sadly that there were many difficulties in keeping alliances among the democratic powers going because they all had to respond to their public opinion and this was not an easy thing to resolve among many nations.

There was absolutely no doubt that Nehru needs aid in India and we must give it to him. He had been told the Russians were now offering Nehru between $600,000,000 and $1,000,000,000. This was a vitally important sector and we had to react in our own interest.

Eisenhower came to the elevator to see us off. I had the sad feeling that he really enjoyed old friends with whom he could discuss all kinds of problems—from golf and family to national politics and foreign affairs—and that perhaps, all too often, he is limited to the frivolous things with some groups and to the serious things with others. I left with the reinforced conviction that he is a fine, decent man who is doing the best he can.

This afternoon, I had a long talk with General Lyman Lemnitzer, who will become army chief of staff this month. I knew him in the Far East: a friendly, big man.

I said it seemed lunatic to me that we were talking so tough on Berlin without making any evident military preparations to back up our talk. Lemnitzer smiled happily, and said:

You won't hear any argument about that in this office. Since November 27, when Khrushchev announced his first ultimatum, we have been looking at the Berlin situation. Khrushchev is so erratic that it was hard to predict what he would do after the 27th. I was in the Far East last April for three weeks and I told a group of our officers that May 27, the expiration date of the ultimatum, might come with a major military hassle or it might pass just like any other day. As a matter of fact, the only thing that happened was Dulles's funeral.

But let me tell you, you give me a cold chill if you mention the possibility that we might run another airlift if Berlin is cut off again. The consensus here is that this would be a last resort and attempted only as a dire necessity.

In 1948, we conducted an airlift under other conditions. In 1948, our power position was different. We had dismantled our army and air force. Our allies had virtually no power; and we had little. We were at a low ebb in strength. We didn't want to take the risk of testing Russia on Berlin.

Most of us are studying the possibilities of action in case of a crisis now. We believe we should never start an airlift without first testing the Russians vigorously. I mean testing them on the ground. And if the Russians stop us, we won't meekly turn back or immediately start an airlift. We should show our strength. We won't just let them lower the bar on the Autobahn, preventing our access.

What happens if they do this? OK, you start by sending out a couple of scout cars along the road at Helmstedt in the British zone, which is the terminus of the Autobahn. The scout cars go. Maybe the Russians raise the barrier. Or maybe they shoot at the tires of a car. What do we do then? Maybe there will be a small-fire fight. Or maybe the Russians let the scout cars go and a couple of miles further on there is a roadblock, and the scout cars return and report that there is a big block ten miles down the road that they can't penetrate.

Then we might send a couple of tanks and supporting troops letting the Russians know we intend to force our hard-won rights of access. And this tank outfit removes the roadblock. Then we find the Russians have taken the bridge out still farther down the road. This forces us to move in a battalion with emergency equipment to build a new bridge.

We can play this game by ear as long as we know that our *policy* is strong. In this way we can see how far the Russians are ready to go.

The British tend to simplify the problem and point out the complications presented by the Russians bringing the East Germans into the situation. But if the Russians sign a treaty with the East Germans and turn over their rights to them I would consider this the most insulting step the Russians could take. We are in Berlin as the result of winning a hard-fought war with heavy losses. It is unspeakable that the Russians should be permitted to turn over their rights to our former enemies. The British point out that the Russians threaten to turn over their rights to the East Germans, who would make us show our credentials to them. But we can't condemn the Russians' right to do this. If the East Germans ask to see the triptyque of an American vehicle we are up against a hard issue. Do you recognize this authority?

Most of us feel we can't accept this. It would be the first step along the long road of harassment that can eventually force us out of Berlin. But if we don't condemn the East Germans' right to inspect, this will get us into some kind of a hassle. Maybe the Russians will put it differently and more subtly. There are a thousand angles.

From a strictly military view, it is a tough problem. The road lies more than a hundred miles through enemy territory, so that militarily we are in a bad fix. And, after all, our troops in Berlin are a mere symbol. Suppose the Russians put a little more resistance up against us as we press our lines. That is a nasty situation. Do we fight our way through or not? We would have to develop the Russians' intention to resist and the degree to which they will resist on the grounds that they have more forces than the allies.

This is a complicated situation and must be played very carefully and with much firmness. No one can foresee the outcome. We could fight a tactical nuclear war on the ground without calling in strategic forces. But one of the hardest things in atomic warfare is to detect a small atomic burst. When I was in Korea, I saw the Reds in the neutral area explode an atomic simulated burst which was very convincing. It is hard to tell the difference between the real thing and a simulator. It is hard to say categorically whether a seminuclear war—you might say a semiconventional war—could be fought around Berlin; but I think it *is* feasible.

If the Russians support a war in Europe with missiles and their air forces, will we consider the U.S.S.R. a privileged sanctuary that cannot be attacked by our strategic weapons? This would involve bombing in the satellites and in Russia itself. Will the Russians try to sweep us out of Europe or only to throw us out of Berlin? And if they try the latter, could it be held to a little hassle, or would it grow? Or might they try to stall us off from Berlin to prevent our entry without a major effort?

Obviously, if they try to overrun western Europe, this will mean all-out war, and we must face the fact that the advantage of strength in Europe is with them.

In all these considerations, the French are being tough, but they don't have any forces on the scene, and the British prefer to show the triptyque to the East Germans, as they put it, rather than having a nuclear war. They don't admit that there are intermediary steps.

LUNCH at Joe Alsop's. Others present included Stew Alsop and Mrs. Longworth. Both Joe and Stew consider Lyndon Johnson a great man and the best candidate the Democrats could nominate in 1960. Joe compares him with Churchill. They both say he is really larger than life-size. Stew thinks that among all the candidates, those with by far the highest IQs are Johnson and Nixon. Next he would rate Humphrey. He put Stevenson and Rockefeller well down on the list.

Stew says the doctors have ordered Johnson not to drink any liquor except between 5 P.M. and 7 P.M. As a result, wherever he is at 5 P.M., he starts pouring it in in enormous quantity and with great rapidity. Stew was once riding in a jeep with him on his Texas ranch, together with Mrs. Johnson in the back seat. Five o'clock came and the Senator hollered to his wife, "Lady Bird, it's time."

"I know it's time," came a voice from the back seat, handing him a ready-made scotch and soda which he downed in one gulp. After three destroyed this way, he drove on fixing his fourth drink in a special holder he has rigged up in the driver's seat. He took about nine before 7 P.M. came, but it had little effect on him.

LBJ: "I CAN PROVE
MY OWN IQ"

WASHINGTON, *June 22, 1959*

ARLY THIS AFTERNOON, I WENT UP TO THE CAPITOL FOR A TALK
with Senator Lyndon B. Johnson, majority leader of the Senate and
one of the more obvious Democratic candidates for the presidential
nomination next year, although he denies this. Johnson is tall (about six
foot one and a half), rangy, active, filled with energy. Once he opens his
mouth, a hailstorm of words and ideas pours forth. He is an engagingly
informal Jacksonian man, and several times during our talk, he tilted back
in his chair to reach under his shirt and scratch his belly. He was neatly
dressed in the Esquire manner, with striped shirt, white tie, slacks, and a
gray coat; a rugged, tanned, handsome man with spectacles. His hair is
thinning and graying a bit at the top. His expression changes with a varying assortment of wrinkles and I noticed that he has large ears. He talks
with extreme rapidity, but his Texas drawl is not overdone. He is certainly
intelligent and charming, but I did not get the picture of a dominant mental
giant such as the Alsops gave me. Obviously, he is an extremely clever
political manipulator and has a remarkable reputation for handling the
Senate. He is not overwhelmed by modesty and took pains to give me a
photostatic copy of an honorary degree and citation he received on June 1
from Brown University which said: "Your skill as a politician has been
notable, but you have subordinated politics to national interests, the service
for which you will be best remembered."

Johnson started off in response to a question of mine on what he thought
of the foreign-aid program not as a Democratic politician, but in terms
of the national interest. He replied:

The most important thing is to underscore the system. The President must at all times be free to deal as our spokesman with foreign

nations without having the country divided behind him. We ought to do things because they are right and not because they are expedient or in order to tide over an emergency.

New nations are being born all the time. Therefore status quo and laissez-faire attitudes are not sufficient to deal with a changing world. If we believe in free enterprise we must believe in this for everyone—for Asia and Africa, for the Philippines, etc. But we can't do this on the basis that "If you don't do something for Texas, Texas won't do something for such and such a foreign country." We have to meet the Soviet challenge and we must educate the public to this problem and produce some specialists on our own.

The Soviets have developed a new system that is really attracting people who need help and hope. We must make our own more competitive, and this is particularly true in terms of our foreign trade. If we do not compete more successfully in attracting the people of these nations they will look upon us as decadent. I have confidence that we can do this. I would hide in a cave if I didn't have confidence. Let's have an open-curtain policy. We have nothing to be ashamed of.

Why, when Mikoyan was over here he wanted to see people and no Senator agreed to see him. But I wanted to be as close to him as I could. I can prove my own IQ. I welcomed him. I told him he should come to Texas and told him he should see San Francisco; he should see what we have and see what we do, take a look at our mines and cotton fields and our supermarkets. But he was pretty vicious. He said he'd been invited to see all kinds of glorious things, but that we didn't even want Russian children to have milk.

I wasn't entirely clear what Johnson was trying to prove either to himself or me. He continued.

I think that the more our people see of Khrushchev, the more they will like our system. [Again, Johnson talked like a machine, going in eighteen different directions.]

I think it's goddamned unfortunate that the Republican National Committee and Nixon lead Eisenhower around by the nose. Eisenhower won't take on a housing bill unless it's exactly as he wants it. I've narrowed the gap between his view and the Senate's, but he'll find some damned little excuse to veto it. I'm a compromiser and a maneuverer. I try to get something. That's the way our system works, not by all-or-nothing vetoes.

At this point Johnson had a telephone call and when he hung up, amiably scratching his belly again, I tried to redirect the conversation to foreign affairs. Johnson said:

It's damned dangerous when a President takes on the Senate. Wilson and Roosevelt found this to be the case. Wilson lost out to a handful of willful men and that handful kept us out of the League of Nations and helped build the basis for World War II. Roosevelt lost out on his Supreme Court Bill, and after that he was only tolerated by the Senate through the war. Eisenhower should know that it's wiser to let dead dogs lie.

In our foreign relations, no man speaks for the Democratic party, but one man speaks for the United States. Herter and Dillon are good men. Herter is crippled like I am [referring to Herter's arthritis and to Johnson's own heart attack], but he can work eighteen hours a day. When he came up for confirmation I got him confirmed unanimously. [I must say Johnson is perhaps endearingly vain, but I don't quite know how endearing that quality would be if he were President of the United States.]

But you can't get this attitude of a united American opinion over to the outside world when your President is spoon-fed by Nixon and the Republican National Committee. We confirm Eisenhower's appointees except when honest men in the U.S. Senate think these appointees are not qualified, like Lewis Strauss [refused as Secretary of Commerce]. The U.S. Senate is not for sale.

Nevertheless, we can't have paralysis or stagnation in our foreign relationships. The President must have convictions and express them. However, he must also recognize that compromises are necessary in our political system. Take the question of the debt limit. Certainly it must be raised. Personally I think there shouldn't *be* any debt limit.

Our free enterprise system must compete with Russia's. Long-range planning is needed and we can't go ahead always budgeting on an annual basis. Why Eisenhower recommended the same thing as Fulbright two years ago—and then he ran from it. He is still under the influence of Humphrey [not the Senator, but the former Secretary of the Treasury] not Anderson, as you imply. George Humphrey is the most important man in this town—and he lives in Ohio.

I asked Johnson what type of man he would consider would be the best Secretary of State if he, Johnson, were ever elected President of the United States.

I'm not a candidate, nor will I ever be. But answering your question, I would like to see Dean Acheson Secretary of State if he were elected to Congress for two terms. What I mean is that you want a man who knows the world and knows politics and believes in the golden rule that you should do to others as you would have done unto yourself. You must remember our own history and use it as a guide line in dealing with others, like these new nations. A knowledge of political realities and human nature is necessary for a Secretary to make himself effective. He must have at least some practical political experience to deal with Congress.

I don't think any man should be in the Cabinet who is unable to obey the Supreme Court and also to deal with Congress. There are three coequal branches of our government and it can't be otherwise. Just you take the example of Strauss. He couldn't deal with Congress. He was a troublemaker in every place he's been.

I asked Johnson what he considered to be the Senate's role in foreign affairs, apart from giving its "advice and consent" to Cabinet and diplomatic appointments and ratifying treaties. Johnson replied:

I suppose the first thing is molding public opinion. The Senate mustn't be a "yes-man and me-too" outfit, but it must recognize the constitutional powers in this country. The President alone is our spokesman in our relations with other nations. I always try to put myself in his position. I try to figure how it would be necessary to keep a man in my position advised and informed and to consult him. Eisenhower is a good and decent and moderate man. But he'll go down in history as bad as Grant if he don't stop this stuff like the Strauss business.

The United States Senate won't be threatened by lobbyists. Why they used every trick in the business in this Strauss case. My wife was invited to a party by a woman she knows. The first thing that happened was that another woman came up to her and said, "Lyndon won't get any votes from any Jews if he doesn't vote for Strauss." They used every kind of threat and pressure. John L. Lewis was calling up the Senators from West Virginia saying that the miners wouldn't vote for them if they didn't vote for Strauss. I tell you Roosevelt was bashful compared with what happened here on the Strauss case. There were two White House lobbyists standing outside the Senate door applying pressure. If this is the way the Republicans keep operating they are going to divide our country.

At this point Johnson had to go off to a meeting. I left, with a firm grip of the hand, interested—if not, in a sense, fascinated—but not thoroughly enlightened on the foreign policy of Lyndon Johnson.

ROCQUENCOURT, *July 8, 1959*

I SPENT two and a half hours this morning with Larry Norstad. He had talked to Eisenhower three months ago about de Gaulle and found him very tough. It is high time Eisenhower should read de Gaulle a lecture.

Nine U.S. fighter-bomber squadrons are being moved out of France to England and West Germany as a result of de Gaulle's insistence that we cannot store nuclear weapons here unless they are under French control. The planes have to be near to accessible arms and fully under our control.

Norstad says French fighter forces have not been withdrawn from NATO. No final position on this has yet been taken. De Gaulle is obviously being very balky. It is even possible that he could pull his army from SHAPE control, but Norstad thinks this is unlikely. The fleet picture was not too significant.

De Gaulle simply doesn't understand the problems of air defense. By this fall, it will have to be decided whether the French fighters are integrated with the rest of the force. French ground forces remain assigned to NATO. They are quite effective and comprise two good divisions. Furthermore, France remains committed to contributing more when the Algerian situation allows.

It was a very wrong conception to think we should be too tough at present in the Berlin crisis. It's a popular line to be tough. But we must take any action that we find necessary in Berlin calmly and deliberately. There should be no quick, crash reaction to developments there. We don't want a war; we want to prevent a war. Therefore it is imperative we should not fly off the handle. And we should confine ourselves to doing things we can do and not try to do things we cannot do.

I was puzzled by arguments in the press that it was possible to have a small atomic war, limiting it to the use of tactical weapons. Norstad said, "I agree entirely. It is absolute nonsense to think you can have a limited war; it can't be done. Always a country will use every weapon it has when necessary. You can't keep an atomic war limited. That is the great danger and you can't forget this."

He said that as far as NATO relationships went, we must stand by our alliance philosophy which endorses the moral equality of small countries. It is no longer a curse to be born a Belgian, a Dane, or a Norwegian. Those countries now see that they can have influence in the free world. It is a great thing that the United States insisted on this philosophy and has made it stick for ten years. We can't go back on this to the law of the jungle and have three big top powers dictating to the West.

GENEVA, *July 13, 1959*

DINED last night with Laloy and Reinhardt (State Department counsellor). Laloy says Khrushchev has discovered the sword of Damocles (threats) is more useful here than the sword of Caesar. Our only sword is enormous, double-edged, and suicidal, as well as murderous.

Lunched with Andy Berding. When the four foreign ministers were flying back here on the same plane after Dulles's funeral, Lloyd said to Gromyko (after a disagreement): "Well, I guess you'd better get off the plane." Gromyko replied: "That is a subject on which I wish to make it clear that a majority decision will not prevail."

Pleasant talk with Chris Herter, just before the plenary session of the Big Four Foreign Ministers Conference resumed.

I told him I was going to the Antarctic in the autumn and wanted to know what he considered the diplomatic importance of that area to us. He answered:

We've never filed any claims to territory there. We operate in the area of other peoples' claims [largely Norwegian and Australian] and in unclaimed regions. The Russians haven't filed any claims either. We hope to keep the area free from war, to neutralize it. As things are, no nation is in a position to enforce its Antarctic claims.

GENEVA, *July 14, 1959*

DRINK with Armand Bérard, French ambassador to UN, here for a consultation with Couve. Armand says Spaak, when he last saw de Gaulle, pompously began: "My General, there is no longer any German national air space, or a Belgian national air space, or an Italian national air space . . ." "Don't trouble yourself," said de Gaulle, "there *is* a *French* national air space."

ROME, *July 20, 1959*

IN the gloomy old Viminale Palace, I saw Prime Minister Segni, a distinguished old Sardinian country gentleman with thin aristocratic features, a rather eighteenth-century face, pale skin and white hair, birdlike, gentle, but with a hidden quality of tensile strength. We chatted in French. His heavy Sardinian accent is almost incomprehensible.

I asked him if there were still a strong movement in the Christian-Democratic party for what Fanfani used to call (and Gronchi still calls) an "opening to the left" (a deal with the Nenni Socialists). Segni said: "The problem—as such—does not exist."

I asked Segni what he thought was the chance of a "Gaullist" experiment or a "new form of democracy" in Italy. He replied: "There is no feeling for this here. There is no need for a new democratic form. As far as Italy is concerned, there is no need for such a development; everything is clear and quiet."

ROME, *July 21, 1959*

ENRICO Mattei, the mysterious *eminence grise* of Italy is, I admit, a highly agreeable person. He gives the appearance of talking with great sincerity and openness; but one must not be deceived. We began with a long and amicable discussion of fishing. He is a great dry-fly man and invited me to let him know next time I come to Italy so I can fly up to the Dolomites where he has a couple of private lakes stocked with brown trout.

We chatted along in French, which he speaks with limited fluency. He was exceptionally friendly. Said the article I wrote about him last time was so much less hostile than those I wrote about Fanfani that people accused him of paying me. Also said I exaggerated his power. I told him his paper, *Il Giorno*, had attacked me with a front-page editorial. He pretended to be surprised. He said:

I have only one ambition in life, and that is to give my country complete independence in sources of energy. I have NO political ambitions. I merely seek to develop natural gas in south Italy; oil in Sicily, Egypt, Morocco, and Iran; and to spread this energy with pipelines.

Private industry in Italy and Germany were unable to do the job and they lagged behind in the world race when private industry in the U.S.A. and other countries spread out and developed world petroleum. Our private firms simply never ventured abroad. This was the fault of the previous generation. By that I don't mean my father, who was only a subofficer in the gendarmes. But the industrialists of his generation did not keep up with those of other lands.

I asked him about his political views and allegations that he was playing ball with the Nenni Socialists. He said:

I am only a member of my own Christian-Democratic party. Of course, everyone knows I am not for a right-wing economy. But what does this mean? I was very impressed, when I was in the United States, to see the way democracy applies. The boss sits down and eats the same food with the workers. There is not too big a gap between the rich and the poor, as there is in Italy. I know what poverty means. When I was a child, I did not get enough to eat.

He had been impressed in Moscow, despite some of its ugliness, by the fact that everyone had work and a place to live, even if most families lived in one room. "After all," said he, "compare the poor of southern Italy; there are houses without any windows, where six or eight people live in one room. We can't stay like that. We must work to improve conditions."

Later, I lunched with Alvise Savorgnan di Brazza. He has just inherited a large estate from a rich aunt so he has quit Mattei's employ but remains a consultant. Prince Pignatelli of Gulf Oil was also present.

Pignatelli believes Italy's future is now being decided in Sicily, and the Communists hope to establish a bridgehead there, turning it eventually into another Algeria. The armed forces won't be able to put down an insurrection if one judges their ineffectiveness in squashing the bandit Giuliano.

Brazza told me interesting things about Mattei's political operations. He remains very close to President Gronchi. When Fanfani fell, Brazza and other confidants urged Mattei to move in and tell Gronchi to make him (Mattei) Prime Minister. Mattei refused and claimed he didn't want to get openly into politics.

Mattei has two "operating" assistants: Brazza and Falaschini. Falaschini was originally Brazza's boss; now he is also a "consultant." When Fanfani came in, Mattei took Brazza and Falaschini personally down to the Foreign Office to see a leading official of Fanfani's old Mau Mau gang and said: "I want to introduce you to these two men. They represent me. Henceforth they will speak for me."

X, a brilliant operator although an unattractive man who drinks too much and chases whores, was Mattei's principal payoff man. He was charged with buying deputies. This was done by offering a man a highly paid job on a state enterprise, a job in which he had nothing to do. And X would see to it that he voted correctly. Likewise, X did the actual payoff part of Brazza's diplomatic and public-relations job, sugaring the Nenni Socialists and acquiring the paper, *Il Giorno*. On the whole, an unsavory but fascinating operation.

VIENNA, *July 23, 1959*

EARLY this afternoon, I saw Chancellor Raab. He chatted away informally in his guttural Austrian accents, saying: "There are some south Tirolean neofascists and nationalists in Alto Adige, but there won't be any partisan operation there.

"Austria wants to settle this by negotiations, but the new Italian government has such a slim majority, depending on the right wing, that it is difficult to negotiate. Because of this, things have reached a stalemate."

I asked him if there were much subversion and espionage still in Austria. "Yes," he said with mild cynicism. "Both sides are still up to funny business. They are equally bad. They spend all their time watching each other; they're not interested in Austria."

Raab talked mockingly of Tito. He said: "Tito's lifelong dream is to come to Vienna and stay at the Hofburg [the old imperial palace]. I'll invite him—when he signs the commercial agreement we're negotiating; not before. I'll even put him in the imperial apartments. After all, Tito was on guard duty at the Hofburg [when as a young man, he was in the Austro-Hungarian army]." At this point, Dr. Meznik, who was translating, said Tito had once been a Feldwebel (sergeant). "Not that," said Raab. "He could never get that high. He was only a private first class."

Fritz Molden, young publisher of *Die Presse* and *Express*, came for a drink. Fritz was instrumental in joining together the publishers and editors of the ten non-Communist Vienna papers to boycott the Communist-front Youth Congress opening here in three days.

In July, 1958, the Austrian press agreed to boycott this year's Youth Congress. Its program of events isn't announced, so the Viennese aren't informed and won't drift out to its stadium to give it a propaganda success. The press won't even mention the Paul Robeson concert or soccer games between the best Russian, British, and Vienna clubs—so people won't go. They'll merely print scores afterward, not saying where the games were played. The government radio has also pledged silence.

Molden said: "The Communists want to start a debate with the free world here trying to show that youth wants peace. But they won't find anyone to debate with. We're putting their operation in the deep freeze."

Molden argues that his paper tries to publish "all the news that's fit to print," but this "isn't fit to print. It's an immoral operation seeking to camouflage the immorality of Communist dictatorship. We would only be acting as the agents of an immoral cause. If an Austrian Communist makes an important statement, I'll publish it as news. But I won't publish propaganda speeches not containing news. And this Congress is just pure propaganda."

VIENNA, *July 24, 1959*

LAST night, I dined at Princess Hohenlohe's. The only people there were Bruno Kreisky, the foreign minister, and Gastone and Raffaella Guidotti. (Guidotti is Italian ambassador.) It was totally informal; no servants. She has a tiny, simple flat (although she is suing the government, as granddaughter of the Emperor Franz Josef, for the entire Albertina Palace and art collection). We had drinks first in the small sitting room, then dined in the kitchen on goulash with dumplings that she had cooked herself. She is a merry, fat woman with glasses and bobbed hair, clever and nice, but she looks more like a Bohemian cook than a princess.

Kreisky is a droll-looking fellow with kinky, reddish hair like Harpo Marx, a sharp, long nose, humorous, bright eyes, and a very short upper lip. He is bright as a whip. He is a Jew (the first Jewish foreign minister in a Teutonic country since Walter Rathenau), the son of a wealthy family, number two in the Socialist party. He was jailed under Schuschnigg and again under Hitler. When he got out, he escaped to Sweden where he married and where both his kids were born. They still speak Swedish at home. After the war, he came back, went into the diplomatic service, then entered politics.

Kreisky considers Adenauer a simple, stupid, provincial man. He is uncultivated and has read scarcely anything. He believes any rumors and has no political wisdom. But he has a politician's instinct and massive confidence. He destroyed Erhard. Erhard is nothing—a weak, ineffectual man who merely came to symbolize (but did not inspire) West German recovery and prosperity. Adenauer had contempt for him, and, to Kreisky, refers to him as "Erhardchen" (little Erhard).

It is frightening, fourteen years after the war, to find both France and Germany on the edge of dictatorship. Neither de Gaulle nor Adenauer are dictators, but both use very high-handed methods and the people are content to let them do so.

Adenauer was a provincial Catholic who wanted to tell God when he went to Heaven: "See, I made a Catholic Europe." He is "naively" convinced there is a deep split between Russia and China "because Khrushchev told me so." He doesn't realize that Khrushchev deliberately feeds such impressions. Adenauer claims Khrushchev wants two Chinas and two Koreas.

Kreisky says Adenauer doesn't want a united Germany at all. He realizes this would be a Protestant Germany—which would offend his deep Catholicism.

Khrushchev joked to the Austrians in 1958. He said: "Mikoyan is a great theoretician, you know. He wrote a cook book. But all we had was salt in those days. The only use for Mikoyan's book was to burn its pages in order to cook the salt."

ATHENS, *August 1, 1959*

I ARRIVED this morning from Belgrade and just had time to bathe and shave before going for an interview with Prime Minister Caramanlis. He seemed suspicious and reticent.

The Cyprus settlement is due to come into operation in February. But Caramanlis is trying to have Cyprus become independent by November or December, because as long as Cyprus remains an active problem, there is a possibility of trouble.

Caramanlis said: "I do not *foresee* any abnormal developments, but I wish to expedite the establishment of the new state of Cyprus as an elementary precaution that any wise person would take. I wish to avoid any chance of interference with a final Cyprus solution."

Caramanlis said Greece's relations with NATO have never been disrupted "despite the fact that all NATO members always voted against Greece in UN." The Greek fleet had not participated in maneuvers with the Turks and the British "because of our fear of incidents." Caramanlis then complained with considerable indignation:

Nobody asked me during the last four years how I kept the alliance and how I kept my country out of communism.

We remained faithful despite four years of maltreatment by our allies. Countries like Iceland and France were ready to quit the alliance whenever they were pricked. But we withstood the strain. There is no nation that has shown such tenacity in its obligations and friendship as has Greece. I have fought against a popular front in two elections, but I was able to persuade the people to follow my policy.

I won't allow [General] Grivas to upset the Cyprus settlement. And if he goes into politics, he *must* follow the normal rules. I doubt if he will get 2 percent of the vote. We have a stable and strong government. Our people are satisfied with their economic and political stability that now exists. The people do not want an experiment of military leadership in politics, the kind of experiment for which they have paid dearly in the past. They do not want a messianic military leader like Plastiras or Papagos. The Greeks tried this theory before and they know it is no good.

ATHENS, *August 3, 1959*

LUNCHED with Averoff, the foreign minister. He says the Turks are "tough guys" and good bargainers. They feel the Greeks are embarrassed by the present Grivas political insurrection in Greece, and they intend to drive home a tough deal because they feel the Greeks are in a hurry to get Cyprus launched.

Averoff, by the way, said that the Communists had been making a serious effort during the last four years to inveigle Greece into abandoning the NATO camp and have offered all kinds of inducements.

After lunch today and again at dinner (which Averoff gave in Adlai Stevenson's honor), I had long chats with Adlai, who is over here on a trip. He insists it is necessary for the United States to modify its attitude on Germany and to get out of the present deadlock. We simply have to make a more realistic assessment of the fact that there is not going to be any German unification and that the people in control of Western Germany themselves are not too eager for it.

YESILKOY, TURKEY, *September 20, 1959*

FOR the past three days, I have been attending a Bilderberg Group Conference here. Air Chief Marshal Sir John Slessor told me over a drink that the U.S. had offered the French the B-47 as an inducement to call off its A-bomb. Paris refused.

Klaus Mehnert, German editor, said during thirty years the Soviet people have changed remarkably, drifting away from Bolshevization as they urbanized, industrialized, and educated. Intellectualization works away from Khrushchev. People are more independent minded. In the long run, this is bound to affect the leadership.

Yesterday evening, I had a pleasant chat with Zorlu, the Turkish foreign minister. He talked rather mournfully about the fact that Turkey, which does so much for NATO, has no atomic weapons of its own. (Randolph Burgess, U.S. NATO ambassador, argues we have given the Turks atomic weapons; but, of course, these remain under our troops.) Zorlu says a country such as Turkey cannot indefinitely accept such reliance upon another ally and the dependent psychology it brings with it.

ISTANBUL, *September 23, 1959*

NURI Birgi, Turkish ambassador to London, took me to the Töpkapi Palace of the Ottoman sultans where, among other objets d'art, I was surprised to see the silver-covered arm of St. John the Baptist (with the back of a gnarled hand exposed), as well as the Saint's jewel-encrusted cranium. In another room, covered and invisible, are some relics of the prophet including hairs of his beard.

This evening, I had a long and excellent talk with Adnan Menderes, the Prime Minister. He is a pretty tough customer, politically, and has been rough on the opposition and on the press. But it is still impossible to run Turkey in western democratic terms. And one cannot forget that the opposition was even rougher when it was in power (until 1950).

I saw Menderes in the Vilayet (office of the governor of Istanbul province). This is a large, ramshackle building which used to be the office of the Sultan's Grand Vizier. It is the old Sublime Porte, once as famous as the Quai d'Orsay or Whitehall.

Menderes is a smooth, soft-spoken man. He speaks quite good English, very slowly and deliberately. He learned this as a youngster in the American College at Izmir. He appears very calm and has an old-world politeness masking an obviously shrewd mind. He is married to a cousin of Zorlu's wife who, in turn, is the daughter of old Tewfik Rushdü Aras, Ataturk's famous foreign minister.

He said:

The situation in Iraq is not favorable for the West. Kassim, the new boss, is playing both sides. He seems to be more favorable to Russia. The Soviets continue to send in arms and agents, disguised as specialists.

Russia is also intensifying pressure on Iran. And the Shah feels there are no sincere links with the U.S., despite the risks he assumed by joining the Baghdad Pact. [I noted that Menderes always spoke of the "Baghdad Pact" and never of "CENTO," its new name.] Russia is trying to get Iran into its orbit. It is therefore imperative to improve Turkish-Iranian communications to induce Iran to lean westward through us instead of northward to the Caspian and Russia.

You must remember that Turkey and Iran form a dam together

against Soviet access to the wealth of the Middle East. But Iran is disenchanted; it feels lonely and in danger. It wants to be cared for. Russia is now applying stiff, new pressure.

BURSA, TURKEY, *September 25, 1959*

CAME here yesterday via Iznik (the ancient Nicaea). Nicaea was once a large city and its wall, starting from the shores of Iznik lake, studded with 366 towers, still stands. Now it's a sleepy village of less than five thousand. Aya Sophia, the church where the Council of Nicaea (325 A. D.) was held (later a mosque), is a total ruin. There is an open sarcophagus containing bones said to be those of the clerics who defended Arianism against the Athanasian creed.

Bursa is a lovely old city, capital of the Ottoman sultans until they took Edirne (Adrianople) and later Constantinople. Built on a mountain side, fertile because of underground springs, a spa and cure center since Greek days, it was once the capital of Bythinia.

SINGAPORE, *September 30, 1959*

PICKED up Marina on a plane from Paris and flew to Singapore. First thing, went over for drinks and a long, interesting talk with Sir Robert Scott, British High Commissioner for Southeast Asia, an exceptionally intelligent man. Scott behaved beautifully during the war as a Japanese prisoner, despite innumerable tortures. He is leaving here soon to become first civilian head of the Imperial Defense College in London.

He said it was essential to ascertain what happened in Laos, why, and what to do about it. It appears that North Vietnam furnished support to the guerrillas. The guerrillas themselves are Pathet Lao nationals, not Vietnamese. There is some resemblance to the Greek rebellion after World War II, when Greek Communists were supported by Bulgaria, Jugoslavia, and Albania, and moved through those countries back into Greece for operations. It is essential for the UN to get into the act and scare off the Communist attack. If SEATO alone were involved, it would become a guerrilla war, extremely difficult to fight. In Malaya, which has no common frontier with any Communist state, it took ten years to defeat the guerrillas, and the process is still in its final stages. A guerrilla war in Laos would last at least seven years. There is a frontier of up to four hundred miles with North Vietnam and another one hundred miles with Communist China.

If Laos were to fall to the Communists, both Thailand and South Vietnam would be outflanked. It is militarily impossible for the North Vietnamese to invade South Vietnam across the military frontier now fixed between the two states, but the traditional invasion route is through Laos and if that country were to fall, Vietnam would be finished.

Ultimately, this is a contest between the United States and China rather than between Asian Communists and anti-Communists. A threat from China hangs over the area. But people here are not well informed. They know much more about distant parts of the world than they do about their own neighbors. For example, Malaya knows more about Detroit and the fluctuation of the automobile industry and rubber-tire markets than they do about states on their own border, such as Indochina. The people of Indonesia are still riveted by Holland and in Cambodia they are deeply affected by developments in France.

India has a much bigger political and propaganda role outside Asia than inside Asia—above all in Europe and America. The West tends to think of a great contest between India and China, in which India must be developed as an example of successful democracy to impress Asians that communism, as expressed in China, is not the only successful way of national development. But in this part of the world, unlike the West, people think of the present struggle for power not as a struggle between China and India (as an example of democracy), but as a struggle between China and the West; in fact, as a struggle between China and the United States.

There as been a miscomprehension of the entire border dispute in the Himalayas between New Delhi and Peking. The Chinese want to "liberate" and modernize Tibet in approximately the same way the Russians wished to "liberate" and modernize the archaic civilization of Muslim Central Asia—for example, the old feudal emirate of Bokhara. The Chinese tried to lay down a uniform type of Sinification in Tibet, but they struck more trouble than they had expected. Therefore, they decided to go after local Tibetan centers of population that might support potential elements of resistance. This brought them to the frontier areas of border states in the Himalayas like Assam.

Communism is *not* recoiling in Southeast Asia as certain people seem to believe; nor is it advancing. During recent years, neither trend has been evident. Peking's has been a quiet, long-term policy. We in the West assume the Chinese are more active than they really are. The Chinese are fundamentally preoccupied with internal problems. And their big external fear is the United States, nothing Asiatic. What prompts them to move into adjacent countries is the fear or suspicion that American bases might be established there. They base their policy and make their calculations on information that is frequently erroneous.

China's policy is to establish neutral, friendly, and *indigenous* governments in Southeast Asia. They want "native" and not overseas Chinese governments for the present. This—and no more than this—may remain Peking's policy for the next two generations. At present, the local

Communist parties in this part of the world are regarded as experimental by Peking. China wants western influence expunged from this part of the world and thinks the best way to do this is to bring about the establishment of "native" neutral and sympathetic governments. These should not be dominated by overseas Chinese because this would scare the other inhabitants of Southeast Asian lands.

In the long run—after a generation or two—there is only one outlet for future Chinese expansion, and that is Russia. Someday, the Chinese must push into the Soviet prairie lands of Mongolia and Turkestan. But this is not yet an acute problem.

In South Vietnam, Diem is trying to establish a kind of Confucian-Mandarin system of government. But in Laos and Cambodia, there is a different trend. It is more of a Buddhist and Indian trend. Sihanouk in Cambodia likes to call the people together and have them address their grievances directly to him in an old-fashioned paternalistic way.

The West has imposed alien traditions of parliamentary government on Asia, just as it has imposed artificial frontiers. Many of the existing borders between Asian countries were established by the acts of the war in Europe, starting with the present frontier of Russia and China.

One cannot ascertain the exact role of SEATO during the past five years, but history shows that the Vietnamese arrangement *did* stick and war did *not* break out again—even if SEATO's role in all this cannot be precisely assayed. It was hoped that other Asian countries would join SEATO but none have; they were afraid. Despite this weakness, however, SEATO has remained part of the Asian political landscape. It now constitutes a certain guarantee that if there is an *open* armed aggression there will be an *American* reply.

We must demonstrate to the people of Southeast Asia their future is in their hands. We will keep the aggressor out, but they must keep their own backyards tidy. It is impossible to meet every kind of Communist threat with SEATO, even if that now rules out open external aggression. We cannot, for example, send American guerrillas into the jungles of Laos. But we have assured these people that any prairie fire will be stopped, even though it remains up to them to put out brush fires. If we can hold the region on this rather unsatisfactory basis for another generation, the people of Southeast Asia will get a feeling of their own personal investment in continuing their own political integrity and economic comfort.

De Gaulle has an extraordinary and interesting influence out here. Britain always considered herself the mother of parliament and law; the United States always considered herself the great anticolonial power, but France is seen as a great political innovator. Democracy stems from the French revolution. The ideas of the French revolution are now shaking Asia and will soon shake Africa. Vietnam, Cambodia, Laos, Thailand,

and to some extent Burma, Indonesia, and Malaya see France today discarding one pattern of democratic government for another. They have already tended to develop their own applications of political theory like "guided democracy." Now they see a new theory being developed in France and rejuvenating France. They feel this gives a certain respectable western intellectual example to themselves.

In 1958, Field Marshal Sarit of Thailand was operated on in Washington and then went to England to recuperate. When de Gaulle's new Constitution was published in France, Sarit cabled Bangkok to send him a translated copy. Within a few weeks, after he had read it, he flew back to Thailand and staged a *coup d'état* to take over. France's intellectual example and now its constitutional example is of far more significance in Asia than France's limited power.

SINGAPORE, *October 5, 1959*

SPENT the last three days in Malaya, staying with Ambassador Homer Byington in Kuala Lumpur, then driving back via Malacca and Johore Bahru. K.L., as everybody calls it, is a pleasant, sprawling town of about a quarter of a million, with modern buildings built over old tin mines. The jungle is still filled with crocodiles, pythons, cobras, elephants (in the north), and tigers.

One big problem is to persuade the Malayans it is to their advantage to keep the world rubber price below $1 Malayan (33 cents U.S.) because synthetic producers can make and sell at a profit about that price, killing the natural industry. The population balance is about 50 percent Malayans, 40 percent Chinese, and 10 percent Indians (and Pakistanis). The government's major effort is to build a "Malayan" nationality including all but to keep the Malays in the majority.

Malacca, a drab port on the straits opposite Sumatra, was the key to the Orient trade, first under the Portuguese, then Dutch, then British. St. Francis Xavier used it as a missionary base. It has two tiny forts and a ruined Portuguese church with lovely old gray tombstones from the seventeenth-century Dutch period, containing coats of arms; huge, thin, rectangular slabs about 8 feet high.

DJAKARTA, *October 7, 1959*

AMBASSADOR Howard Jones, our host, told me Sukarno was in the first university class of Indonesians to graduate under the Dutch, a brilliant pupil. He organized a political party six months after his graduation.

Sukarno has a great hold over the masses and a skill in balancing power groups. In 1953, he saw the right-wing parties gaining strength, so he helped the Communists grow stronger as a counterweight, although only a few years earlier he had ordered the army to destroy the Communists.

Tea with General Abdul Haris Nasution, army chief of staff and defense minister. He is reputed to be anti-Communist and pro-American. Nasution, who speaks quite good English, is a clean-cut, handsome man who looks even younger than his approximately forty years.

He said:

Our army was born from the proclamation of our independence. The army considers itself as a force of the center. That is our ideology. Our principal formula might be described approximately as follows: The army is one of the functional groups of Indonesia—like labor or the farmers. We are only one of these groups and not the only one as in certain South American countries.

During the first period of our history the army was building from the young fighting organizations. We didn't look at a man's political roots. Some of our people were leftists and some of them were rightists. But the majority, even then, was brought from the nonpolitical youth and resistant forces of the Japanese period. We have been *de*politicalizing the army. It is now forbidden to be a member of any political party.

Both the extreme left and the extreme right wings have made efforts to infiltrate, but we discovered them and cleared them out. Now such efforts are decreasing. If it is proved that a soldier or an officer is a member of the Communist party, he is fired.

I asked if he had any reason to believe the United States had given backing to the present rebellion. He said:

I have proofs and documents certifying that there has been help from abroad, but for political reasons I have restricted publication of these facts. However, I did show one of your admirals a diary we captured and actual orders issued in Okinawa to one of the rebels. We have taken crates of new American equipment stamped certifying their origin as Clark Field in the Philippines and on Formosa.

Our army supports a foreign policy of "active independence." We don't want to be exploited by either side in the Cold War, and we resent interference from either side. During the first phase of the rebellion, it was perfectly evident the United States sympathized with the rebels. During the second stage, when war really began, there was physical assistance from your side. This included not only arms, but the training of cadres in the Philippines and Taiwan. But we spoke to your officials and gradually they began to realize that our policy was not pro-Communist. After we took central Sumatra in May, 1958, outside aid to the rebels ceased.

I speculated that if (God forbid) a world war came, Indonesia would be forced, whether it wanted to or not, to be on the side of the free world because we included the great maritime powers and Indonesia would depend on overseas transportation for supplies of arms, etc. Would he not agree? He said: "We won't change our policy, but it would be very difficult to maintain neutrality. All I can say is that if a big power interfered we would consider it an enemy. The first one to interfere would be the first enemy. But there is something in what you say about sea power."

After seeing Nasution, I had a good talk with Dr. Djuanda, the Prime Minister, a small man with glasses and rather Chinese countenance.

I asked if Djuanda saw any friction between the Soviet Union and China. He replied: "We don't feel it here. We are getting Soviet technicians now for specific projects. My own impression is that Chinese national pride would never allow the Chinese to accept an inferior position to that of the Russians."

When I asked what he thought of U.S. relations, he said:

Permit me to speak frankly. The first thing you must do is to stop accenting anticommunism too much. Most Indonesians don't like to be reminded constantly that communism is dangerous. Our approach is different. We act against propaganda from any and all outside countries.

Another big difficulty, I must admit, is caused by the different living standards of your country and mine. It is difficult for us to mix with Americans here. Even our Cabinet ministers are not paid enough so that they can afford to give parties like yours. This is not a matter of jealousy. It is merely embarrassing not to be able to return hospitality and it puts us in a difficult position. Americans here have cars and air conditioners and refrigerators. But even for one of our ministers it is a great luxury to have a Chevrolet.

I asked why Indonesia seems to avoid big decisions at the United Nations on human and moral issues such as Tibet and pointed out that Malaya had taken a fearless attitude. He said: "For centuries we have been under foreign rule. Therefore, we don't like to express ourselves on the policy of other countries as long as they keep their hands off us. Secondly, we frankly want to do what is most advantageous to us. We need and want aid from both ideological blocs. If we mix in these things too openly we might jeopardize our aid. It is better to mind our own business."

I asked him what he thought was the true meaning of the phrase "guided democracy." He said:

General de Gaulle in France seems to be applying certain underlying ideas that resemble ours. There is some similarity. I have been reading as much as I can on the de Gaulle system. I am also very interested in Salazar and what he is doing in Portugal. He has been dictator there for years. There is obviously something for us to learn from that experience.

DJOKJAKARTA, INDONESIA, *October 10, 1959*

DROVE during the past two days from Djakarta to Tjirebon to Salatiga and here, stopping off en route at Prambanan and Borobudur. Central Java is hot and steaming along the coastal plains and only relatively less hot—equally steaming—in the hills. For a rich area, it shows great signs of poverty. But there is a benign climate and enough food. One of the four civil wars still going on (central and west Java, Sumatra, Celebes, Moluccas), empties the roads and fields long before sundown, when the rebels take over everything except the towns and bamboo-fortified villages. People appear happy, lazy, and teckless. A landscape dotted along the seashore with old Javanese piratical canoes, with viking prows; bamboo groves, water buffaloes, sugar cane, rubber woods; and, in the hills, teak forests (tall, straight trees) and, higher up, tea plantations. Streets jammed with betjaks (bicycle rickshaws) and two-wheeled and four-wheeled horse-drawn wagons and carts with huge wheels drawn by braces of oxen.

Prambanan is an old Hindu temple with a magnificently carved, larger-than-life-size stone bull (tenth century). Borobudur, the famous Buddhist temple monument, has hundreds of Buddhas rising in bell-shaped covers resembling tea-caddies. These are on the terraces of a vast pyramid that resembles a Mayan or Aztec temple, set against the jungle and volcanic peaks; gray sandstone, massive, cruel.

In Djokjakarta, the intellectual capital of Java and first center of the anti-Dutch republic, I saw the Sultan, Kandjeng Sultan Hamengku Buwono Senapati Ing Ngabdulrachman Sajidin Panatagama Kalifah Allah Ingkang Djumeneng Nata Kading IX Ing Ngadjokjakarta Hadinigrat, usually called (thank goodness) Hamengku Buwono IX, or still more simply, the Sultan of Djokja. He is the only important royal figure left in the republic, which he supported from the start. He reigns as a kind of local governor.

The Sultan received me in his office, quite simple, dressed in half-Javanese, half-western clothes. His pleasant appearance was marred by his upper jaw, which lacks all but the central two large front teeth, giving him the appearance of a smiling, earnest beaver.

He was gloomy. Expects serious trouble within the next three months. Says Sukarno isn't administering urgent executive problems. Skeptical about the potential ability of General Nasution because too many battalion commanders oppose him. Says the economy is sagging. Feels that most leaders are scared to stick their necks out.

Driving back as evening fell, we ran into a massive water buffalo. He smashed our Chevrolet and for a time I thought he was dead. But, after fifteen minutes, he rose, shrugged, and stumbled off into the paddies. Because of guerrilla fears, there was no traffic to give us a hitch to the nearest town with a telephone. Finally, a rattling little truck with a cheerful Chinese driver came along. On its sides were the letters "Moscow Biscuit Company."

DJAKARTA, *October 13, 1959*

PRESIDENT Sukarno came for lunch at Ambassador Jones's country house in the Puntjak hills. Two platoons of soldiers, garbed in black jackets, helmets, full field equipment, and paratroop boots, showed up, carrying Sten guns. They took positions all around the house; somewhat creepy, as they disappeared in the bushes, camouflaging their "strong points" and doing everything but digging foxholes in Mrs. Jones's beautiful lawn. Then, assured by this, the "highly popular" President arrived.

Sukarno is about five feet seven, well built, somewhat pockmarked, with a tricky and slightly evil face. (Ambassador Jones describes him as "a combination of Franklin D. Roosevelt and Clark Gable; the greatest charmer I have ever met.")

He brought his current favorite wife, Hartini; the head of the foreign office's American section, his wife, and beautiful twenty-year-old daughter (on whom the President had an evident eye); also present was Mrs. Subandrio, wife of the foreign minister (an intelligent, nice, forthright woman with a beautiful voice, who sang after lunch).

The ambassador, a friendly, sincere, benevolent man, had assembled the leading lights of our mission plus wives. The first hour was devoted to drinks and small talk. Then lunch. (Sukarno had a neat shot of Cointreau first.) After lunch, a brief toast by the ambassador; then one from Sukarno to "President Eisenhower and the prosperity of the American people."

There was music (following songs from an embassy clerk and Mrs. Subandrio) and Moluccan tunes from an orchestra. The President got ants in his pants to dance. Started to do so in the house; then we all moved to the terrace; then the lawn. (I kicked my shoes off.) Moluccan dances (a gay version of the Portuguese fado) with the orchestra ranging from an electric guitar to kitchen pots, these latter were pounded so hard that in the end they were beaten flat. Sukarno, delighted with his dancing skill (he is graceful, but the dance is a kind of mild cha-cha-cha), kept us going, in couple and circle groups, for more than an hour. I saw the soldiery filtering away (to protect their beloved leader as his car approached the main road); then he left.

I didn't care very much for Sukarno, having perhaps been put off by exaggerated tales of his enormous charm. He is around fifty-six, although he looks younger (which some attribute to hormone injections or "bull venom"). He wears the Indonesian black fez and a khaki military tunic (he was never in anybody's army). There is no insignia of rank but several rows of ribbons—decorations given by foreign countries, nothing for valor.

He is immensely pleased with himself, vain, cocksure that he can charm anyone (especially females). He is fond of music and painting, and he pretends to be intellectual and clearly read quite a lot at one time, although he admitted to me he hardly ever reads now. Speaks quite good English, says he speaks French and German, Indonesian (a somewhat contrived language), Javanese (although his mother was Balinese), and, of course, Dutch. Mrs. Subandrio said when they are all together en famille with the President, they speak Dutch—especially when they're angry; it's good to swear in.

He told me the three persons who had most influenced his life were Jean Jaurès, the French Socialist (whom he never met), his mother, and Tjokro Aminoto, his foster father and first wife's father, with whom he went to live at fourteen. Tjokro Aminoto was a Surabaya businessman and nationalist often regarded as the grandfather of the independence movement.

Sukarno is a remarkable orator, everyone agrees, and loves to shoot his trap off. I asked him who he considered the great speakers of modern times. One by one, he dismissed Trotsky, Khrushchev, Hitler ("Goebbels was much better"), Mussolini, Churchill, and de Gaulle. Said Jaurès was the finest orator (he had read his speeches). Left the implication he considered Sukarno even better.

He's obviously fond of painting and the Chinese have published a marvelous two-volume set of reproductions from his collection. Sukarno stuffs his palaces with pictures which he either gets free or with public funds. (There is no audit of his expenses.) Mrs. Subandrio explained he is deliberately making the collection in the hopes of being able to hand it over to an art museum here someday. He claimed to have read Dante in translation (both in English and German). He drops names—such as Hammurabi—seeking to impress.

He is clearly arrogant and surrounded by toadies: intelligent, power loving, vain, reputed to be a coward; a terrific tail-chaser (on the islands he sometimes sends out officials to pimp for him in a helicopter), confident that he is among the world's great. Undoubtedly, he can give the Indonesians a much-needed feeling of nationhood and importance and often tells them: "Without you I would be nothing; I am only your voice, only what you make me." He loves splendor; lives in fine style in a Djakarta palace and has another magnificent palace at Bogor (designed by Stamford Raffles), which I saw driving to Djakarta, its great, green, deer park luxuriant in the rain; like a splendid White House.

Sukarno, by the way, studied to be an engineer and still claims to have a hobby of architecture. I asked him if he ever painted. Said he had painted one picture, that was all.

He appears to be a lazy, self-indulgent, fun-loving, undisciplined man with obvious native intelligence and immense ambition.

WINGLESS EAGLES AND

WINGLESS MOSQUITOES

DJAKARTA, *October 14, 1959*

THIS MORNING, I DROPPED IN TO SEE RUSLAN ABDULGANI, VICE chairman of the Supreme Advisory Council (Sukarno is chairman). His office is next to the presidential palace. He told me that Sukarno had been named Jusno as a child, changed later to Sukarno ("beautiful ear") as is Indonesian custom.

We hadn't been talking long when Sukarno came in and joined us. He was exceedingly friendly and we had a long conversation (about an hour and a half). What pleased me most was that he made an infinitely better impression: no more clowning or wisecracks. He took off his black fez, scratched his almost bald head, wiped his spectacles, sipped tea, ruminated, asked questions, thought aloud. But I found it possible to talk easily with him, interrupt, discuss anything, pose questions. And he seemed to enjoy it. Here is a summary of what I remember (I took no notes).

We discussed how statesmen relax. He said he never shoots. As a boy he had a shotgun. Later on, as an exile under the Dutch, he once shot an eagle (I think he means hawk) and brought it down. A friend who was with him cut off both the eagle's wings while the bird was alive. "I can never forget the look in that eagle's eyes," said Sukarno. "I can't kill anything. I won't even fish." He made his finger into a hook shape and jerked it up. "Of course, I eat fish and birds," he added with a grin.

He doesn't play cards, tennis, or swim. For exercise, he walks or dances. He doesn't paint, much as he loves it. He once painted a portrait of a Balinese woman; this hangs in his Bogor palace. But never again "because I have no time, like President Eisenhower. When I get three or four hours a week [clearly a minimization], I like to talk with my friends, to exchange ideas. Or I like to go to one of our shadow plays. It sometimes lasts all night and tires me out. But it clears my mind."

He claimed that his political ideas were different from those of any other leaders, suited to Indonesia. "There are points I have taken from Tito, Salazar, de Gaulle, Eisenhower, Nehru," said he. (This is baloney.) He said he had likewise been influenced by Marx, Engels, Jaurès, Sun Yat-sen, Gandhi, Jefferson, and Paul Revere, all of whom he had read. "What did you read of Paul Revere?" I inquired. He skipped deftly on to other things. He said he had taken "what I wanted" from other ideologies and writings. He brought up West Irian several times and said relations with the U.S.A. could never be really good until we accepted Indonesia's claim as "just." He said there was oil and uranium there. Australia was foolish to back the Dutch (because they feared East Irian— New Guinea—would go then), and the Dutch were absolute fools to obstinately hang on there and ruin any chance of good relations.

He did admit that U.S.-Indonesian relations were now better. He was satisfied with our training of Indonesian officers and they came back liking us. But we still failed to understand this country's national aspirations. Because of this, Eisenhower should come here. He had invited him directly and also through Nixon. "He should come. It would do him good. Why it would even do him good to dance. After all, Voroshilov was here and he is over seventy. You should not let the Russians always take the lead."

Sukarno didn't like Dulles. Things were now better under Herter. Dulles always considered anyone not actively allied to the U.S. as a Communist. He had to be pro-American or a Communist. Sukarno liked Nixon a lot. He was a good, direct man to do business with. He didn't care too much for Adlai Stevenson (despite the theory among liberals that Adlai appeals to Asia). Sukarno thought him too vague and "philosophical." He didn't think Adlai really understood things. He preferred Nixon.

We talked about art. Sukarno was delighted with the two volume book of reproductions of his collection (two more coming soon) printed in China and given him. It is a truly magnificent job. Why could not the U.S. do such a thing, why just China? I said we had no state publishing house, only private. It's the same in China, he said (obviously not really believing it). He told me how he hoped to make a national gallery of his paintings, now in his palaces.

When he complained about us on West Irian, I said, after all, he must realize we were allied to the Dutch and it was impossible for any state to take a clear-cut stand for all that was moral, everything either right or wrong. Look how Indonesia had voted against Tibet in UN last week. Surely Indonesia would have wanted to vote for a just cause but also wanted to continue getting aid from Russia and was scared of China.

He gave me a sophistical argument about it doing no good to bring Tibet before UN; it would settle nothing and not help the Tibetans. Besides, what was truth? Was the Dalai Lama any better than the Panchen Lama? Were the Tibetans to be doomed to medieval lamaism? How about Hungary, I asked (where Indonesia voted with Russia). He claimed nobody really knew the truth there either and he had been in Vienna a year before the uprising and had learned trouble was coming (the implication being the West cooked it up).

He said he had told Dulles Indonesia's friendship for the U.S. would warm up as soon as we backed them on Irian as a good anticolonial power. Dulles said we had to have a global policy. Sukarno replied we should have one policy for Europe, another for Asia. Americans still didn't appreciate just how nationalistic and sensitive Asia now was.

He spoke of Tito as "a friend of mine." He said he'd been accused of collaborating with the Japanese, "but I don't care. I was preparing our young men for the revolution. I gave orders for them to join the Japanese forces and learn as much as they could about weapons. As a result we had 100,000 soldiers when our revolution started. We would never have won otherwise." He said the Japanese were so short on man-power that they had to take them, even if they mistrusted them.

He described himself as a "historical materialist, not a philosophical materialist or a dialectical materialist." (All this means, I guess, that he isn't a Communist. Obviously he never did the intellectual homework of Marxism or Leninism.)

DJAKARTA, *October 15, 1959*

DRINKS at Ted Newton's (the Canadian ambassador). He told me that on one of his plane trips with the ambassadors, Sukarno turned, as he frequently does, to sex. He asked each envoy how long he could do without a woman. The Russian, whose English is fluent but imperfect, said, "Two years." "Ah," sneered Sukarno, "you can't call yourself a man." The Russian, in a huff, retired early. The Pole was delighted.

CHRISTCHURCH, NEW ZEALAND, *October 20, 1959*

HURRIED down here via Australia to slip onto a flight to Antarctica while the relatively warm season is on. This morning, Captain MacDonald of the Navy talked about our present Antarctic plans. Lately, it has been very cold at our polar station, which is 9,200 feet high. The last week of September, the temperature at the pole has been 114 below zero. The Russian station at the pole of inaccessibility has registered the record low of 130 below zero.

The United States would like to build an airfield at Marble Point. This would take seven years and would cost between $120,000,000 and

$150,000,000. Marble Point is less than fifty miles from McMurdo. It is one of the few spots in Antarctica where it is possible to construct a permanent earth field. The ground is eternally frozen, perhaps down to a depth of 700 feet, but an all-year field could be constructed with a 10,000 foot cement runway.

We hope to install three atomic power plants in the Antarctic. The first would be at McMurdo. Each will cost $3,000,000. The other two would be at the Polar station and at Byrd station. MacDonald points out there will be a huge saving in oil because each gallon of fuel brought down costs $5.

If the United States has an earth airfield in Antarctica, says Mac-Donald, we will be the dominant power on that continent. And Antarctica is very important for air routes; because of the tremendous effect of that region on the climate of the southern hemisphere; because it provides fixed points from which satellites can be observed; and because it might be a good launching point for rockets and satellites.

McMurdo Sound, Antarctica, *October 23, 1959*

FLEW here yesterday from Christchurch. Tried on the previous day, but we were turned back almost halfway. The weather in Antarctica is still poor: yesterday the wind was so strong we had to tack up and down. Five minutes past the point of safe return, McMurdo wanted to send us back again. Couldn't. We came in on the ice with 100 foot ceiling, 300 foot visibility, in a 45-mile-an-hour wind: a beautiful GCA landing. The plane, a superconstellation from naval air support, was lousy with brass, including Admiral Hopwood (commander of the Pacific fleet), Vice-Admiral Beakley (from the CNO's office), Bill Martin (chairman of the Federal Reserve Board), and Edward Bacon (assistant secretary of the army). The seats are set backward (an extra crash precaution) and it's pretty gloomy with few, small windows, crisscrossed with bars so no cargo lurches can smash the glass.

An eerie flight. The *U.S.S. Peterson*, a destroyer escort working as a weather ship, is halfway down from New Zealand. Hopwood made a radio speech to them (they tuned us in on most of the stuff including the GCA landing) and the *Peterson* reported 35-foot waves, ice all over. En route, they turn off the heating gradually in the plane to acclimatize the passengers and prevent dashboard instruments from snapping. It's spring now and relatively warm—minus 15°F. Daylight all the time, the sun sets briefly around 1:00 A.M., but it's still light enough to read a paper. When everything isn't obscured by snow or blowing clouds, it's incredibly beautiful—a flat sheet of ice covering the Sound (the airstrip is on seven feet of ice and will break up around January), stark mountains rising behind, their rocky peaks bursting through the snow. This base is on

Ross Island, a volcanic formation in the ice. Mount Erebus, some miles away, is still a live volcano.

Strange things. There is a snow mine—the place they dig out snow and bring it to the camp by machine to melt for drinking and washing water. This is rationed—only one shower a week. Men work always in silken gloves, and work ten minutes, warm their hands five. The silk keeps the hands from freezing to metal. My garb in this protected camp: two suits of underwear, one set of long-woolen; three pairs of socks; heavy, lined, rubber boots; heavy woolen pants; lined outer pants with waterproof exterior; double-thickness woolen shirt; woolen sweater; fur-lined parka with two hoods (over my woolen balaklava face helmet); either silk gloves plus woolen mittens plus leather mittens; or leather, fleece-lined mittens extending above the elbow and tied around the shoulder by a strap so as not to lose one when it's off; sunglasses, day and night, against snow blindness.

Billets, in Quonset huts, are excellent. A New Zealand artist in our billet got frostbite on both hands and face. Johns rather primitive. Beer in the officers' club. Food astonishingly good and devoured in vast quantities.

Hopwood, a jolly, short, plumpish man with amiable face, told me he was making a tour largely to cheer the men up and show them they weren't forgotten. Says the continent has no strategic value now except as a satellite observation point. He hopes a Marble Point permanent airfield can be built; this will be needed by commercial airlines some-day, halving the distance between Australia, Africa, and South America.

There are four poles, three at the North Pole: here, geographical, geomagnetic (marks earth's axis), magnetic (off the axis, center of com-pass attraction), and inaccessibility (point furthest from water on all sides). There is no inaccessibility pole in the Arctic, which is water sur-rounded by land, the reverse of the Antarctic.

Beer in the officers' club is kept in a refrigerator (a blood refrigera-tor)—to prevent it from freezing. The officers' club was built by six officers long after the ratings had their club; they couldn't ask enlisted men to work on it.

The sick bay bears a sign: "Texas Immigration Service—Antarctic Branch." Everyone talks of the "head shrinkers," the psychoanalysts who give Rorschach and other tests to those volunteers or draftees who have already technically and physically qualified. They weed out those who might not get along. The officers in command of isolated stations like Byrd and the Pole are navy doctors. Thus they can take charge of health as well as supervise the station.

Shackleton's 1908 hut, nearby, still contains cans of food he brought—rusted only because of the sea voyage in. A New Zealander baked good bread recently from the fifty-one-year-old flour.

A biologist has found that a certain kind of wingless mosquito at

Hallett station seems to hatch out of thousand-year-old eggs. He puts a plexiglass globe over it. After several hours of sunshine, the insects appear underneath wiggling by the hundreds.

Today, I attended a series of briefings arranged by Admiral Tyree, commander of our Antarctic installations, for Hopwood. Tyree is a short, stocky man with big ears, long nose, and twinkling eyes. Roly-poly in his Antarctic gear, his appearance is more that of a humorous college professor than professional naval officer.

Tyree said 85–90 percent of the world's ice is on this continent distributed over five-million square miles. It is the highest continent in the world, largely rimmed by mountains. The vast plateau in its middle is the world's most barren desert; also the coldest area on earth.

Although U.S. sealers came down as early as 1820, our interest in the continent was only revived by Admiral Byrd in 1928, when he brought mechanization and the air age. The army and air force work together with the navy, although overall responsibility is the navy's.

The installation of nuclear reactors for heat and power would save on fuel costs and add to the water supply. The building of an all-weather airfield at Marble Point would cut the distance from South America to Australia and New Zealand by 50 percent and speed up development of the southern hemisphere.

We have to take care of the ice to keep the airstrip going. Dark objects left on the ice melt it. A black pipeline stretched out for fuel will gradually work its way down. Water temperature around here is below freezing point, even when it is liquid.

Land at the South Pole is probably 9,000 feet below the surface of the ice. At Byrd Station, we know that the ice goes down 5,000 feet below sea level and there is another 5,000 feet above sea level. There is probably more coal, although very low grade, than on any other continent.

SCOTT BASE, ANTARCTICA, *October 24, 1959*

A FINE and relatively warm day with glowing sun and little wind. There are husky dogs at this station: strange contrast with the massive Globemasters down on the ice airstrip and the luminous orange helicopters outside camp.

Scott is a New Zealand base near McMurdo in what the New Zealanders meticulously call the "Ross Sea Dependency." Rode over in a Sno-Cat. Afterward, went out on the ice and watched three sled teams (Greenland huskies weighing about 110 pounds each) come in from a long trip (thirty-five miles a day), their leaders' beards white with snow. The ice was magnificent. It was windless but 25° below zero; so cold that your nose froze, despite parkas and woolen helmets, and your hands hurt within seconds if you took a pencil out. Wandered around the ice with a New Zealander testing the way with a long pick, looking for crevasses in the snow. Whenever it whined through we went around the cracks, heading toward two enormously fat seals lying sluggishly against the white background and mauve, blue, and rose mountains in the distance.

Admiral Tyree had invited me to dinner and sent a Weasel for me. I clambered in a tiny window entrance, hard to squeeze through in furs and boots. Arrived at McMurdo in time for drinks, looking through a picture window at the magnificent snowscape, the most beautiful sight—and the most terrifying—I've seen. Hopwood, Beakley, and Bacon were there.

Tyree talked about the "thousand-yard stare," a form of snow madness; also "the big eye—a ten-yard stare in a five-yard room," when men are bothered by perpetual daylight (in the summer) and can't sleep.

All were opposed to a policy of uncontrolled internationalization of Antarctica. They want condominium with Australia and New Zealand—which would take charge of the largest continental slice—but they realize it would be impossible to oust the Russians from their sector.

McMurdo Sound, Antarctica, *October 25, 1959*

Everyone works twelve hours a day, seven days a week. Church services are held on Sundays, and men attend only when possible.

Seven nations have made official claims to Antarctic territory: Britain, Argentina, Chile, New Zealand, France, Australia, and Norway. The United States makes and recognizes no claims. We reserve the right to go anywhere. Russia has a similar position.

There is an idea of tunneling under the snow to build an underground city. Another is to pull buildings around in sections on sleds from McMurdo. These buildings could then be moved each year before they become too covered by drifting snow, which endangers the roof by its weight. As things are now it is very expensive to rebuild existing stations every four or five years.

South Pole, *October 26, 1959*

The South Pole is marked by a circle of fuel barrels about fifty yards in diameter, set amidst an enormous, flat, empty plain of snowy waste, pockmarked and rippled by the wind. I spent an hour here this morning, circling overhead in a cumbersome C-124. We dropped fifteen tons of fuel products by parachute to our seventeen-man Pole station and then waited while another C-124 dropped an equal load. They had trouble after their first drop; the loads got snarled up. All told, we circled the Pole eight times, thus making eight trips completely around the world.

I flew up with Hopwood. We, the only "tourists," sat happily side by side, strapped onto a crew bunk behind the cockpit, chatting. A C-124 is like a ferryboat. It's a double-decker (when used as a troop transport), but the deck was out today. Huge piles of gasoline barrels were heaped up on the ramp of rollers in back, bound with straps and ropes to parachutes. When the plane was finally emptied, a process which jolts the ears because of suction as the immense packages drop through the bay, the entire rear looked almost as large as a basketball court.

The drop master and his crew were all wearing parachutes, unlike the rest of the crew. It is easy to get caught in the tangle of straps and be whisked out by a one-ton load. I went down for the second of our drops and watched the vast bundles thunder down the rollers and fall through the gaping bay. It was —57°F. at the Pole below us, and, I presume, colder in the air above.

The flight lasted ten hours. We had good, full sunshine all the way. It is now six months continuous daytime at the Pole, where there is only one day and one night each year. We flew along the frozen Ross Sea by volcanic Mount Erebus and tranquil, snowcapped Mount Terror, up the sloping flat plateau to Beardmore glacier, then up the glacier for about an hour, between its towering borders of harsh, craggy mountains rising high above us on either side. We then reached the high polar plateau, extending, it would seem, infinitely to the Pole itself, 9,200 feet above sea level. We were high enough so that we had to breathe oxygen from masks every few minutes. Exertion was difficult.

The Pole is on a great, flat ice desert; totally featureless except for pocks and ripples whipped into the snow by the howling wind. It looks like a perfect, incalculably large airfield (surely bigger than all France). The Polar station is hard to discern—a few Quonset huts half-buried in the drifts.

CHRISTCHURCH, NEW ZEALAND, *October 27, 1959*

FLEW back last night, arriving at 9:30 A.M. We left at 11 P.M. and just after midnight—when my birthday set in—I broke out a bottle of scotch and had a little party with Hopwood, Beakley, Bacon, and Martin. Fortunately, Martin is a teetotaller so the bottle went far. Hopwood called for steak and we had a merry time.

Hoppy had a cruiser during the latter part of the war and transported MacArthur on one Pacific campaign. Mrs. MacArthur gave him meticulous instructions ahead of time on how the General should be treated. Among other things, MacArthur required eight pillows on his bed. These were carefully laid out under his head, knees, and elbows.

WELLINGTON, NEW ZEALAND, *October 30, 1959*

WENT with U.S. Ambassador Francis Russell to have coffee with Viscount Cobham, Governor General. Cobham is a nonintellectual, John Bull type

English aristocrat: large, heavy set, hearty. He told us about the cruiser *New Zealand*, contributed in 1913 by this (then) colony. A Maori chief gave a grass skirt to the Captain and told him as long as he wore it in battle there would be no casualties. The new skipper was horrified when an aide brought him the skirt as they entered their first action. He demurred, but the aide said the crew would refuse to fight if he didn't wear it. The ship was in several major battles, only hit by one shell, and suffered no casualties.

Cobham said the country lives in a dream of isolation from world problems, an agricultural paradise. They don't want investment or industrialization.

This is a welfare state and everyone is taken care of—which deprives people of incentive. There is NO industry of importance. Death duties are punitive and force dissolution of big farms.

CANBERRA, AUSTRALIA, *November 5, 1959*

EXCELLENT talk with Robert Gordon Menzies, the Prime Minister, at his office in Parliament House, a pleasant building that looks as if it had been put up in Kipling's India. We chatted for an hour; then he invited me into a neighboring room where we had drinks and more conversation.

There was a selection of bottles, ice, soda, and glasses on the table, and I gather the Cabinet always has a quick one in there after sessions. There was a long, tough meeting today on defense questions. I was amused to notice that despite his Scottish name, Menzies disdained the decanter of scotch and mixed himself two strong dry martinis or, as he said, "gin and French."

Menzies's office is a large, informal, old-fashioned room with a big mahogany desk, books, pictures, and knickknacks. He sat behind his desk, puffing a cigar; a massive man with white hair and a strong face. He was wearing a dark well-cut suit.

We began by talking about China. Menzies said:

If a "Two China" idea could be worked out—and accepted by Peking—we would think that a happy solution. We have gone to pains not to part from the United States on China. We do not want to concede anything that might look like a Communist diplomatic victory by switching to recognition. After all, one of the terms Mao wants is Formosa. This is intolerable to us.

We are very conscious of Chinese pressure to the south and the southeast. There are disturbing possibilities in Malaya and Singapore, with their large Chinese minorities, to say nothing of Indonesia. The overseas Chinese would undoubtedly interpret recognition of Peking as a Chinese victory and this would certainly affect their attitude toward the free world.

We won't break the line with the United States; we won't see Formosa handed over to Peking. We are anxious about the effect on the overseas Chinese if recognition is granted on any terms that might appear to concede a victory to Red China. This is not a juridical problem. It is a hard, current, political problem.

I asked him about ANZAM. He said this was "only a survival." It started during the war when the line of defense ran up through the Malayan Peninsula. After the war, it fell into desuetude, and ANZUS and SEATO developed. The ANZAM machinery was revived a bit. There were, for a while, plans to defend Malaya at the Kra Isthmus. But SEATO has replaced these. Now, ANZAM is a consultative mechanism which allows Australia, New Zealand, and Britain to sit down and discuss strategic matters.

He feared "a crashing chaos" might develop on the borders of Australian New Guinea if Indonesia took over West New Guinea (West Irian). He added:

Such a position would give every opportunity to infiltrators. There is always a danger that Indonesia might become Communist. And he who holds New Guinea sits on top of Australia. This was burned into our consciousness during World War II. New Guinea can never be in enemy hands. Our attitude on this is like the attitude of Britain on Belgium. We told Dulles he should warn the Indonesians that if they tried to take West New Guinea by force, we would regard this as an act of aggression. We want the United States also to regard it as an act of aggression.

Sukarno, on the subject of West New Guinea, is a rabble-rouser just like old Musso was on Albania. I am going to Djakarta soon to try and cultivate a closer knowledge and understanding and to make it plain that we have no differences with the Indonesians—except New Guinea.

He said that Australians had never hated anybody as much as they hated the Japanese during the war. They had no similar feeling against the Germans in either world war. However, he continued: "We concluded that we have to live with Japan. Japan could not be ostracized by the free world and it had to be kept out of the Communist orbit. Therefore, without embracing them, we decided to behave with warm friendliness. We don't *trust* the Japs. But American opinion has modified enormously and it now accepts that this is the right way to treat them."

I asked if there were any difficulty for Australia in contrary policies by London and Washington, which made it hard for this country to satisfy both its principal friends. He replied:

Of course old Churchill was very annoyed by ANZUS. He thought Britain should have been a party to the agreement. Nevertheless, we are British to the boot of our heels in this country. There is never a question of our turning our backs on Britain and there never will be.

But we know two things. The United States is very friendly to Australia and wishes Australia well. And we are very friendly to the United States and we recognize that, situated where we are, the United States would be our nearest and most powerful friend in case of trouble.

Over drinks, I asked Menzies why he pronounced his name as he does; I thought any good member of that clan called it "Min-gis." He said his grandfather had given up trying to teach the Australians how to pronounce a Scottish name, but whenever he went "home" he called it "Min-gis." At one reception in England the butler came up to him with a good Scottish burr and asked, "Sir, how shall I announce you—by your real name?"

He was determined the "white Australia" policy for immigration must continue to avoid race prejudice and the complications of miscegenation. There is no race prejudice and a Negro, he assured me, would have no trouble in going to an Australian hotel or restaurant. Before the war he discussed this with a Chinese minister and asked him: "How would you like it if three million Europeans were to settle in the Yangtze Valley— with all the social and intermarriage problems?" The Chinese admitted he had never thought of it that way.

MELBOURNE, AUSTRALIA, *November 9, 1959*

SIR John Latham, eighty-three, former chief justice of the High Court, minister for external affairs, and last Australian envoy in Tokyo just before Pearl Harbor, told me there is no snobbism in Australia based upon early colonial antecedents as in the United States, because the earlier your ancestors established themselves here, the more likely that they were criminals sent to the convict settlement.

The first serious social dispute was between the "diggers" and the "squatters." The diggers came here during the gold rush in the middle of the nineteenth century and later sought to establish themselves on lands occupied by the squatters, with their huge sheep herds. The squatters at that time had no legal title to their lands but merely moved their herds whenever they desired. Eventually these great sheep herders became what is now known as the "squattocracy," a powerful, "county," land-holding aristocracy. The "New Australian" immigrants do not get into that society, no matter how successful they are, but their children can.

KOROLEVU, FIJI, *November 11, 1959*

FIJI is lovely. The people are Melanesian: tall, extremely sturdy, with muscular legs and enormous feet. The climate is astonishingly cool but humid; it rains virtually every day. There are no native animals but many wild pigs descended from those brought by Captain Cook. Plenty of birds, including mynas and small green ones with red crests and tails. Gaudy and innumerable tropical fish and sharks cruising inside the coral reefs. Well-built thatch huts lined with tied bark cloth and bamboo.

Fijians ride horseback along the beaches just like Gauguin's painting of the Tahitian boy on a pink horse. The sea is filled with magical beasts and shells; the air is redolent with heavy flowers; and the moon seems larger and nearer than in other places.

PEARL HARBOR, HAWAII, *November 14, 1959*

THIS morning, I had a series of conversations and briefings at navy headquarters, starting off with Admiral Ramsey, chief of staff.

The United States needs seventy-seven critical items from abroad every day of the year. Each day 2,500 ships sail in the Pacific under all flags; 99.5 percent of the goods transferred around the world, including the seventy-seven critical items we need, must be brought by sea, not air.

The Russians appear to be doing to Mao what we do to Syngman Rhee. They give Mao enough equipment to defend himself well, but not enough to take off on his own in a war that would involve the United States.

WASHINGTON, *November 23, 1959*

ARRIVED this afternoon and went over to Chip Bohlen's for a drink. He has been home less than a fortnight and is just getting back into the "Russian business," reading up on the record of the past few years. He sees no fundamental change in Soviet policy or in Khrushchev's tough intentions. Therefore, he worries about the euphoria growing here.

The present division of Berlin, says Chip, is precisely according to a British plan of 1943—except that this was not postulated on a divided Germany. But, unlike Austria where there was a central government to deal with, there was no central German government.

Chip has great faith in Chris Herter. Says he *is* tough under his courteous manner and has "done his homework well." But he thinks today's is an "Eisenhower policy," not a "Herter policy," because Ike has reasserted leadership. However, Ike takes off long holidays. Full-time leadership is needed to prevent a drift.

WASHINGTON, *November 25, 1959*

SPENT the better part of an hour with Secretary of State Herter. I asked whether the United States had resolved upon a policy toward France that seriously took into account de Gaulle's noncooperative attitude. He replied with a slightly sad smile:

The trouble is, we can't really find out what de Gaulle's peeves are. We have backed him faithfully on Algeria [his major preoccupation], when we were suddenly thrown by the thinking of Debré on the question of issuing visas to Algerian rebels coming to the UN and the effect of this on the use of the French fleet in the Mediterranean. I just can't understand this.

Surely, the French realize we cannot refuse visas except under our law. And these Algerians were neither Communists nor anarchists, nor could it be demonstrated that their arrival in the United States was detrimental to our interests.

Two days ago, there was an interesting development when one of Adenauer's close associates talked about paying a further price for the fact that Germany had lost the war. Obviously this meant, by implication, formally acknowledging the loss of the provinces to the east of the Oder-Neisse line. The last we heard is that the Bonn Foreign Office wants to get out of the position of being accused by the Russians of *revanchism*.

I asked what was the U.S. attitude to the Chinese-Indian border dispute and what had been the U.S. attitude since the McMahon Line was first drawn between India and China in 1914. With mild embarrassment Chris said:

You know, the issue has never come up before. We were never asked to pass judgment. In the Ladakh area, there is the darnedest confusion. This is a territory claimed both by China and India. Yet the Chinese built in it a road 150 miles long that the Indians never knew anything about. Nehru doesn't even know if there is an air strip. And Pakistan *now* claims it as a part of Kashmir. I must admit that the old maps, including the British maps, show that the Chinese have rights in that area. And, although they don't say this publicly, Taiwan backs Peking on the issue because the Chinese Nationalists also used to claim it.

WASHINGTON, *November 26, 1959*

THIS morning, Thanksgiving Day, I had an excellent talk with Bob Amory of the CIA. He says there is a strong split on Algeria between Moscow and Peking. China wants to pour in massive aid, trained guerrilla fighters, as well as aircraft which would fly across Russia, Iraq, and Libya and operate from secret Libyan bases to stage sneak raids on Algiers and other points. But Russia has categorically refused to play.

Bob is pessimistic about de Gaulle and NATO on a long-term basis—although he is careful to point out that his views are not shared by the

State Department and the Pentagon. (I agree with Bob.) He points out that already the concept of an integrated defense force has been forgotten in France. If this idea is pushed through, it might precipitate in the United States a new policy of relying only on a tripline defense in Germany and pulling everything else back, relying fundamentally on strategic air command.

Khrushchev is in a fine position to butter up de Gaulle. However, Khrushchev will keep an eye on the summit, where he wants to deal with Eisenhower. Therefore, we assume he won't antagonize the United States too much in March when he goes to Paris because he doesn't wish to jeopardize the real coup he looks forward to in April in Geneva. *No* French deal he could make alone with de Gaulle, says Bob, would be big enough to justify this.

Later, I had drinks with Herman Phleger, who used to be Dulles's counsellor and now has been charged with negotiating the forthcoming treaty on Antarctica. I wanted to find out whether the State Department was consciously relating its policy on Antarctica to future policy on outer space.

My theory is that we had better try and tie up the Russians now in legal obligations on Antarctica. There, we are way ahead in terms of our presence and have an immense advantage, but in outer space, we are equally far behind and have an immense disadvantage. To my regret, Phleger indicates that not one whit of our policy thinking on the Antarctic treaty is linked to future policy in outer space.

We say there has never been effective occupation in any Antarctic area and that there cannot be. In 1956, Russia moved into the Antarctic. They went into the Australian sector without even asking Australian permission and began an extensive exploration. The Russians are now in a physical position to damage the entire southern hemisphere from their Antarctic bases if they put modern weapons there.

Phleger said both Washington and Moscow appear to accept the conception that Antarctica (and presumably outer space) was terra nullius or no-man's-land. In other words, it was the opposite of the seas, which are everyman's-land. Because of this joint conception by the United States and Russia, they agree on effective military inspection of Antarctica. Both, as nonclaimants, consider that inspection violates nobody's territorial sovereignty. Phleger argues that this concept can be translated into outer space, where certainly, at the moment, no nation has any sovereign claims.

Furthermore, on Antarctica, there is agreement that the continent should be used for peaceful purposes and exchange of scientific information. We think the moon is like the Antarctic continent and that for the foreseeable future no effective occupation is possible. Likewise we feel the moon should be open to free exchange for scientific purposes.

I told Phleger that General Thomas White, chief of staff of the air force, believes that any nation controlling the moon, in a military sense, can strategically control the earth. On this basis, I asked if Phleger thought our projected Antarctic treaty draft would serve as an adequate precedent to seal off the moon from Soviet control. He hoped so.

But no body of law exists concerning potential legal rights of this world's nations on the moon or Mars. The only law governing outer space is still old Roman law—a line drawn from the earth's center to the surface of the earth and projected upward to infinity represents a borderline for property claims. I pointed out that Roman law was based upon the assumption the earth was flat. Any global extension into outer space meant that projected cones would overlap and that no country could possibly establish a better claim than any other country—above all since the relative positions of the earth and the moon were changing constantly.

Phleger said air space never became an issue until World War I, when airplanes became a military instrument and were able to fly over the territories of foreign countries. There is considerable agreement among lawyers that sovereignty in the air ceases to apply. But there is no definition of "air," and the gravity concept is not yet legally agreed on. To avoid any argument about this ticklish issue, we took pains, when we launched our first earth satellites, to orbit them around friendly areas. In other words, we tried to keep them from orbiting over Soviet and Chinese territory.

NEW YORK, *November 28, 1959*

LUNCHED with M'hamed Yazid, minister of information in the so-called Algerian Provisional Government, and Ahmed Boumendjel, who has just arrived from Tunis as an Algerian lobbyist.

Yazid and Boumendjel admit Russian support is softening because of Khrushchev's effort to court de Gaulle, but they don't think this will last. They claim it is not necessary to get massive arms supplies from China, but two or three airplanes passed onto Libya by friendly nations would do them a lot of good.

NEW YORK, *November 30, 1959*

DINED with Averell and Marie Harriman. Averell resents the political power of charity trusts and claims Rockefeller is using such funds to further his own political ends.

He said he saw Khrushchev for eleven solid hours last summer. At one point, when Mikoyan was lunching with them, he said to Khrushchev:

"You should send Mikoyan to the United States where he would become a millionaire." Khrushchev replied that Mikoyan had been born a generation too late, otherwise he could have made a fortune. Mikoyan interrupted and said to Khrushchev: "You can't send me anywhere now. Those days are over."

When Khrushchev was here, Harriman invited him to meet several leading bankers and industrialists. Khrushchev had told him he considered our two parties didn't differ from each other and were run by the "ruling class." Khrushchev didn't seem to like it when Harriman introduced the group as the "ruling class" but assured him, regardless of party, they all stood behind the President on foreign policy, defense, and Berlin.

Harriman is irritated that American policy is always described today as safeguarding free enterprise from communism. The real issue is not between free enterprise and communism but between freedom and dictatorship.

He thinks de Gaulle is very useful to us by delaying the summit meeting, and because he is a tough bargainer and won't fall for anything Khrushchev offers.

To my astonishment, Averell recommends recognizing East Germany in exchange for another Berlin deal.

NEW YORK, *December 1, 1959*

SAW Jack Kennedy for lunch today. He is an attractive man but, I must say, he continues to look awfully young. He admits that is one of his big political difficulties: People say he is too young to deal with the men who now dominate the world scene.

He indicates that Catholicism doesn't bother him too much politically. It is a disadvantage in many ways, but an advantage in others. The political climate is more tolerant than in the days of Al Smith and, realistically speaking, there are more Catholic voters.

He will formally announce his candidacy in early January. If he runs ahead in the primaries and maintains his lead in the public-opinion polls, he thinks he can get the nomination, but the tough thing is dealing with the politicians, not the public. He will not accept the vice-presidential slot if he goes into the convention with a substantial lead and is merely jockeyed out of position by the politicians in a smoke-filled room. He says the only other obvious candidates now are Stevenson and Symington. Humphrey and Johnson are out.

He is confident he can lick either Nixon or Nelson Rockefeller, but would still prefer to run against Nixon.

He thinks the Catholic bishops made a mistake raising the birth-control issue on foreign aid. He is opposed to sending an American ambassador to the Vatican because this would help to divide the country just as the birth-control issue makes the foreign-aid program more difficult to pass politically. One must make compromises in a multilateral society such as ours.

He thinks foreign policy will be the main electoral issue in the sense that the Republicans will be attacked for letting the United States slip backward in the power race. He thought any Democratic nominee if elected (provided, of course, that it isn't Stevenson himself) would be delighted to have Adlai Stevenson as Secretary of State. Kennedy said Adlai was certainly the outstanding candidate for the job if the Democrats win.

PARIS, *December 11, 1959*

GOOD talk with Jean Laloy at the Quai d'Orsay. He thinks U.S. policy allowed Khrushchev to gain everything he wanted without having to make any concessions.

The reason for Khrushchev's long stay in France is in order to visit this country for the same length of time that he visited America; another sign of grandeur. Khrushchev will not, however, be able to break down France in terms of the alliance, no matter how hard he tries. What has he got to offer? He can't make the Algerian rebels yield to the French because he doesn't control them. He cannot offer de Gaulle fifty atomic bombs. De Gaulle's policy is tied to Adenauer and opposes any deal on Berlin. No matter how skillful Khrushchev is, he just doesn't have the power to influence de Gaulle despite de Gaulle's bad relations with America.

De Gaulle has long tended to regard the Soviet regime as more "Russian" than "Communist," and therefore, he hopes this Russia will someday reassert its ties with the European family of nations. But the General will not find Khrushchev as appealing as did Eisenhower because Khrushchev is certainly not a cultivated intellectual.

PARIS, *December 15, 1959*

ONE by one, our friends in the French army are quitting. Ely is finished with de Gaulle, who regards him as a NATO propagandist, and he will quit as chief of staff in about six months. He will be succeeded by General Challe, provided Challe doesn't queer his pitch in the Algerian campaign during the intervening period. Challe recently reported to de Gaulle that France was winning the Algerian war militarily, but that the French army is totally confused about the political position.

Everybody is convinced there will be no regular succession when de Gaulle dies. If the army is not too fragmented, it may seek to take power, possibly opposed by a popular front. Otherwise, a popular front may move first.

The minutes of the Eisenhower-de Gaulle meeting last September were so secret that our embassy here never knew what happened, and was extremely embarrassed whenever the French referred to that meeting in discussions. The first details the embassy learned was when Ambassador Houghton was recently in Washington and found out from the White House. From our point of view, no specific commitments were made. However, the French consider we promised to support de Gaulle on North Africa— and that we have reneged.

De Gaulle reasons that an alliance must mean what it implies. He argues that the U.S. has to back France in North Africa. The alliance is worthless if the U.S. does not back France in North Africa, and he is prepared to get out. Just before Eisenhower saw de Gaulle in September, General Ely prepared a paper for de Gaulle purporting to prove that the U.S. was helping the FLN.

This evening I saw Jean Monnet. I told him I had been away six months and was alarmed by the pessimism I now found; people talking of the chaos and civil war that would follow de Gaulle's death, of the crisis in NATO. Monnet said he thought this was usual Paris alarmism. It was impossible to go to a dinner party in this city without hearing negative conversation. As for what happens after de Gaulle's death, "Well, after all, he is still alive. I doubt if anything dramatic would happen. Why, Pinay would probably be elected to succeed him."

Monnet regretted de Gaulle's "fool ideas" on NATO, but added, "The man is, however, not by any means a fool." Despite the present situation in NATO, the relations of the East-West balance were unchanged because Khrushchev thinks only of the U.S. and the U.S. military strength. As long as that remains, there is nothing to worry about.

The economic aspect of the western alliance is more important than military unity. The United States still gives military protection to Europe, but we should cease focusing our attention only on defense. American economic aid has been faced with a crisis caused by America's own problems. The U.S. has been hit by its balance-of-payments problems and the increasing need to aid underdeveloped countries. Europe is in a position to help in this respect, and today we must stress the economic basis of the alliance.

In 1952, when he, Harriman, and Plowden comprised the NATO wise men's committee, General Abe Lincoln said: "It is simple for the Russians to win a war. All they have to do is fire one shot. Then the western armies will move. They can only move in one direction—forward. And their equipment is so mixed up and their instructions so confused that they will get inextricably tangled and dissolve into chaos." Monnet made the point that the integration of the last seven years has put an end to such confusion.

Monnet thought de Gaulle's attitude on Algeria was remarkably correct. Furthermore, he was right on the colonies. He was working to shed them without war. No Frenchman was going to die for Dakar. De Gaulle is being intelligent on Africa. Therefore, we should not assume he is being stupid elsewhere. One consequence of a liberal policy in Africa will be a return to Europe of at least part of the French army. The purpose of de Gaulle's famous speech to the military school was to give new psychological objectives to the army when it returns, to galvanize its soldiers. Integration, says Monnet, is not a sufficiently national slogan for such purposes.

He concluded: "Don't worry too much about the present period of alliances. I have known de Gaulle for years and I don't like him. He has an odd technique. He always creates problems in order to solve them."

PARIS, *December 16, 1959*

LUNCH with Chip Bohlen. The only real U.S. objective at the present NATO meeting, he says, is to obtain de Gaulle's assent to the integration of Europe's air defenses—including France. We can't see the logic to his opposition to integrating air defense even though we can at least understand—if not agree with—his views on ground and naval forces.

Chip has been studying Chinese-Soviet relationships and is convinced there are major centrifugal forces in their alliance. After Khrushchev's visit to the United States, the Russians made a documentary movie which was shown all over the U.S.S.R. and which was sent to China. After some days the film was taken out of all Chinese theaters.

China is now in the same position Russia was in when Stalin was collectivizing the land—only worse. Stalin needed a whipping boy to divert public attention in those days. China needs a whipping boy now. But Soviet society has evolved, and Khrushchev no longer requires one. In fact, because of nuclear arms, he probably thinks it undesirable to excite people too much, although he still pursues the Cold War. In China, on the other hand, they want to keep people stirred up. Thus, there is a basic conflict in everything that goes to make up the fundamentals of Soviet and Chinese policy.

Chip thinks de Gaulle is already trying to build up a new system that will succeed NATO. He thinks of all Europe and doesn't want to freeze out eastern Europe. He thinks above all of Poland. And he has never lost his 1944 regard for "puissante et chère Russie."

The trouble is that this may be a fine thing for the future but we must face present facts on NATO. De Gaulle dreams of a Europe headed by France, which does not include America or England. This would more or less be the ultimate fruition of our own ideas, starting with the Marshall Plan. But the world is not yet ready for it.

PARIS, *December 20, 1959*

CHIP Bohlen came for lunch. He insists there is an inherent Chinese-Russian split because they are at different revolutionary stages, which is one reason Khrushchev is trying to quiet the Chinese-Indian quarrel. Both the Moscow and Peking regimes suffer from a delusion that the popular masses of the free world support them. They made this mistake in Korea and in Hungary. In a sense, they *have* to make it because they could no longer retain faith in their own international revolution if they were convinced the masses opposed them.

PARIS, *December 28, 1959*

LAST night, Norstad gave a party for Stu Symington. It was loaded with brass, from "Lightning Joe" Collins down. Symington had been traveling around with a Kansas City lawyer named Fowler Hamilton, visiting U.S. air bases.

Larry told me Eisenhower's talk with de Gaulle was too short and too sweet. He had hoped that Ike would get tough. In fact, nothing happened.

Collins has still not been able to find out who was responsible for the decision allowing the Russians to take Berlin and fix the demarcation line between East and West on the Elbe. He says: "I have read all the memoirs and I don't know the story yet. I know damned well I could have moved right on to Berlin and nothing could have stopped me."

Lunch with Symington, Fowler Hamilton, and General Martin, sent by the air force to look after him. Alex Allegrier-Carton (owner of the restaurant) put us at the "President's table." I told him my guest had aspirations in that direction. I asked which seat de Gaulle once occupied and put Symington, as an aspiring candidate, there.

Later, Alex invited us downstairs to his *cave*. Before Symington escaped, he had had too much 1943 Marc de Bourgogne plus several shots of a superb Napoleon brandy. To my horror, until I stopped him, Stu poured his first priceless cognac on the concrete floor of Alex's *cave*, behind his back. The appalled *sommelier* watched.

Symington says he is not going to announce for the Presidency yet. He was Missouri's "favorite son" last time when Truman was out to lick Stevenson, and the state organization chose him. He can't announce soon because he wants to do some telecasts and if he were an open candidate he would have to pay for them himself.

PARIS, *December 29, 1959*

LAST August, General Ely, chairman of the French Joint Chiefs of Staff, sent a position paper to de Gaulle, arguing that it was in the common interest of the West to keep Algeria tied to France. The Saharan oil is of vital importance. Furthermore, unless France held Algeria, NATO would be outflanked. General Ely's paper ruled out the possibility of Algerian independence and said this was incompatible with France's interest.

Ely insists the U.S. must be brought about to fully support France and made to see the dangers of Algerian independence. Ely said all French military leaders agreed with him on this. But the paper was prepared just before de Gaulle's famous September 15 speech, in which he promised self-determination for the Algerians.

Last October—after de Gaulle's self-determination speech—there were rumors of a new military conspiracy. These proved to be exaggerated. Nevertheless, many army leaders feel the military esprit de corps will be permanently damaged if Algeria is lost, and they insist that the army must have a strong say in Algeria's future.

Late last summer, extremists contacted the generals, seeking support and aid in another antigovernment plot; but few responded. It does appear that General Lecomte, commander of the army corps in Germany, has maintained contact with these malcontents. So has General Faure, commander of the 27th Alpine infantry division in Algeria. General Zeller, now retired and former deputy chief of staff, has similar contacts. On a farewell visit to Algeria before retiring, Zeller spoke against de Gaulle. Marshal Juin, also retired, retains contacts with the malcontents. The real test between de Gaulle and the army will come when there are actual negotiations with the FLN on the modalities of a political solution.

PARIS, *December 30, 1959*

DINED quietly at the Norstads; just the four of us. Larry said the French aren't making things easy. Without consulting him, they submitted to the Standing Group in Washington a plan for revising the Mediterranean command in order to give France greater power—despite the fact that the French Mediterranean fleet has been withdrawn from NATO.

He sent word to General Ely expressing his irritation and warning that he intended to take the matter up with Prime Minister Debré. Ely begged Norstad not to do this because it would only enrage Debré and Ely belived there was a slight easing in the French attitude on NATO.

Larry said the French army hates de Gaulle but agreed to back him in 1958 because it was the only alternative to civil war. Nevertheless, despite schemers like Lecomte and Faure, who really have no importance, de Gaulle has nothing to fear from the military now. The army was in politics in 1958, and if it dabbles in them once again its reputation will be ruined.

PARIS, *January 2, 1960*

POMPIDOU told Cecil Lyon that de Gaulle is half-blind without glasses, which he refuses to wear when in uniform. On a tour, he turned to Pompidou to ask him if there was anybody lining his route, which was packed with people. Recently he put his hand through a glass door.

HOW BRITAIN COOLED

OFF JOE KENNEDY

PARIS, *January 15, 1960*

Y ESTERDAY, I SAW RANDOLPH CHURCHILL TWICE—FOR LUNCH AND
again in the evening. He had the following story about Joe Kennedy, Jack's father—and he swears he can confirm its truth.
In 1933, Jimmy Roosevelt came over to London just before the inauguration of President Roosevelt, together with his friend Joe Kennedy
(who paid for the expedition). Randolph took them to his father's for
lunch, little knowing what the purpose was. He soon found out.

Kennedy got in touch with all the biggest whisky distillers, told them
he had given $50,000 to Roosevelt's campaign (before the convention),
and was in the middle of things. He could assure them Prohibition would
shortly end and he wished to line up contracts to represent the best firms.
He got a fistful.

The next time Randolph laid eyes on Kennedy was after he came over
as ambassador in 1936, to represent Roosevelt at the Court of St. James's.
Word was passed around (before his arrival) to be nice, consequently the
establishment went to work. He was invited to house parties, dinners, golf,
and shooting by dukes and earls.

However, war came, and it soon became apparent that Kennedy thought
England was dilapidated and done for; he indicated a private personal
preference for the Germans. This became quietly known and the government told the establishment it was no longer necessary to be nice. Suddenly Kennedy found himself isolated and alone.

In 1940, Clare Luce came over to stay with him in London. The Luces
were busily organizing a campaign to prevent Roosevelt from getting a
third term. They secretly arranged with Kennedy, who had been telling
people that he didn't think much of Roosevelt, for Kennedy to fly over

to the United States and, in a surprise move, come out in public opposition to a third term.

Kennedy flew home as planned. A delegation of Luce's henchmen was waiting at the airport, but they could not find their man. They were supposed to whisk him up to the Luces, but Kennedy had disappeared. The next thing heard of him was when he emerged from the White House at the end of that same day and made a statement to the press endorsing Roosevelt's candicacy.

What had happened? The British were very anxious to get rid of Kennedy and to get Roosevelt back as President. Therefore, the Secret Service, which had been tapping Kennedy's wires and found out he was anti-British and also that he was certain they were going to lose the war, consulted Winston Churchill and other Cabinet members on what to do. Brendan Bracken amassed a sheaf of tapped conversations of Kennedy's in which he expressed critical opinions of Roosevelt. These were given to Harry Hopkins, who was infuriated and showed them to Roosevelt, who was even more infuriated.

The British knew about the Luce plot. So they tipped off Hopkins, and the White House arranged to have a jeep waiting on the airfield when Kennedy's plane came in. In the jeep was a representative of the White House and Kennedy's wife, a very devout Roman Catholic. Kennedy was disembarked before the plane reached the regular ramp and was whisked onto a small plane, which flew to Washington and landed at a military airfield. He was taken to the White House where, in addition to Roosevelt and Hopkins, Jimmy Byrnes was waiting. Byrnes was an example of the former Catholic who had left the church and, as a consequence, had had his political career wrecked because he had lost the Catholic vote and had never gained the anti-Catholic vote. Mrs. Kennedy pointed out to her husband that if he got into trouble with the Roosevelt machine, he would be finished in politics, because the Catholics would turn against him. He cracked, and backed Roosevelt.

Randolph's story reminded me of an experience I had with Kennedy in 1938. I was asked by the *Ladies' Home Journal* to write a piece about the Kennedys in London. Joe, whom I had known in the SEC and Maritime Commission in Washington, was very helpful. He only asked if, in exchange, I would let him see the manuscript before it went on to Curtis Publishing Company. He said: "Of course, I don't want to censor. But I might be able to prevent minor errors." I agreed.

I showed him the manuscript and he was furious. He said that if I didn't change my piece he was going to have the company kill it. I sent it.

Weeks later, in Prague, I got galley proofs. It had been completely rewritten—in saccharin instead of ink. I cabled Curtis Publishing to take my name off it. They wired back that it was too late; the article was already in print.

I append, on Kennedy, some excerpts from the original article:

A letter from an important Roosevelt aide:

"You probably know all about him because of his gift for charming newspapermen into writing such reams as are usually reserved for occupants of the White House or the electric chair. So far, he has evinced no public aspiration for either. However, he had received a great number of letters from Americans announcing they will vote for him if he runs for the Presidency in 1940. He has also been sounded out by certain political sources. He told a friend of mine he wouldn't dream of taking such a job because it would be too tough on his family.

"Joe is intensely interested in public affairs, but equally interested in his own power, position, and promotion. Generally speaking, he likes to do a spectacular job and move on as he did with the SEC and, less successfully, with the Maritime Commission. I think he has had his eye on a Cabinet post in Commerce or, preferably, in the Treasury.

"Neither seemed to be available when he was receptive. Then his mind turned to an ambassadorship. He probably sensed the possibility of war and increasing importance and popular interest in foreign developments. The social prestige of the position probably weighed significantly with him.

"I think he did feel that the position would mean a great deal to his wife and children. Joe seldom plans to stay in any position long. But I don't know that he has set any time limit [on London]. That might depend upon his being asked to take up an equal or higher post here—his accomplishing something definite in his job abroad. From his early experience as a speculator, Joe has learned that it is a good thing to get out as well as sell out when your stock is riding high. Joe has been written about as a possible candidate in 1940 but is too smart to get out on a limb. Yet he is smart enough to seize an opportunity if it comes his way. I am by no means trying to run him down. But I think one must make an emotional rather than an intellectual analysis of Joe. And a psychoanalysis of the greatest of men is likely to find explanation in the simplest emotional forces."

PARIS, *January 18, 1960*

THE army is now conspiring more and more openly, but it is politically weak. Bidault is the only well-known political man more or less linked with its aspirations. Nevertheless plotting increases. There is not likely to be any army uprising in metropolitan France. But the chances of such a coup in Algeria are waxing.

The reformed Provisional Algerian Government is still probably willing to negotiate with de Gaulle, but it insists on even stronger political guarantees. However, it is impossible for de Gaulle to accept these because they would provoke another military revolt.

Delouvrier recently said de Gaulle has transferred a whole series of suspected generals and colonels from Algeria, but the new ones are just as bad. Little more than a month ago, de Gaulle wanted the army to punish a lieutenant who was responsible for a murder. However, he is still on active duty. This is the first clear confirmation that de Gaulle has lost the power to discipline the army.

There will be troubled times during the next few years. Probably, at most, six months' grace remains. During that period, de Gaulle will have to win a settlement in Algeria.

De Gaulle has made no substantial dent in the professional officers' corps. And these officers increasingly want a Socialist nationalist solution. They are dead set against any kind of liberal Algerian formula.

LONDON, *January 20, 1960*

LUNCHED with Julian Amery and his wife (Macmillan's daughter). Lovely set of huge Persian paintings all around the hall and dining room, collected by Julian's uncle in Cairo. Julian is now up to the ears in Cyprus and Africa.

He says the United States made too much of Tom Mboya on his American tour. American trade unions are naive about throwing aid and money around to African groups calling themselves unions but which are really political organizations.

The reason West Africa is ahead on independence is that its climate is worse than in the east and it is farther from India; smaller white and Asian minorities; i.e., fewer racial problems.

The Central African Federation must hold together. If it splits, Southern Rhodesia will join the Union of South Africa and bring apartheid north. Britain wants a coffee-colored Africa between white and black Africa. There will be none if federation fails.

George Brown came to drinks this evening. (He is defense minister in Labour's Shadow Cabinet.) Very worried about France.

Says Bevan is dying and this comes as a terrible blow. The Labour party is in bad shape. Only about 10 percent still follow Gaitskell (whom Brown doesn't like and who "is always away when trouble comes"). Now the party will have, simultaneously, to find a new leader for the left wing, deputy leader, and a Shadow Cabinet foreign secretary.

He says Macmillan and Eden both detest Gaitskell. They consider him not only a "traitor to his class," but also "unreliable." Gaitskell, at the time of Suez, first supported the government on a Saturday and then attacked it on the next Monday.

LONDON, *January 21, 1960*

INTERESTING talk with young David Ormsby-Gore (later Lord Harlech), minister of state in the Foreign Office, a youthful, easy talking, bright fellow with glasses, obviously sure of himself, a member of the Cecil family that has influenced British policy for centuries.

Ormsby-Gore has been specializing in disarmament. He said the Russians had taken pains to launch rumors that if the French exploded their atomic bomb Moscow might have to reconsider its position. But in fact, Russia continues to maintain the same attitude it has always had, while confident that a French explosion won't really change the situation. The Russians know a large body of American opinion wants to resume nuclear tests. Therefore, if they want to use the French explosion as an excuse, the Americans would be happy to resume testing. The Soviets surely don't believe that the French atomic program will in any sense affect the existing balance of power.

Moscow appears convinced of the wisdom of stopping a spread of the nuclear program and preventing other states from spending billions in order to prepare their own atomic weapons. The Russians have made it clear time and again that they don't want China to get the bomb. They would like to restrict the atomic club and the French experiment will not change the Soviet attitude.

Ormsby-Gore agrees that de Gaulle is already pursuing a policy in Germany which is similar to that of Russia's—the Oder-Neisse frontier in the East, and a divided Germany. Likewise Khrushchev is already pursuing a policy acceptable to de Gaulle in Algeria—not backing the FLN. So Khrushchev really has very little concrete to offer de Gaulle.

Ormsby-Gore is worried about the recrudescence of French nationalism, which he thinks is bound to be mirrored in Germany. Eighteen months ago, Adenauer was already frankly warning about the possibility of a dangerous German nationalism.

Ormsby-Gore said, "You cannot change de Gaulle's character." He has chips on his shoulders from his treatment during the war—for example General Spears's activities in Syria when Spears tried to get Britain to replace the French in the Levant. De Gaulle will never forget this and it makes for an awkward situation these days. "We will have to use palliatives during his reign as emperor," he added.

PARIS, *January 24, 1960*

LAST night Colonel Jean-Louis de Rougemont, now in de Gaulle's office at the Elysée, told me rigid orders had been handed down that no officers were to speak on any subject to newspapermen. This is, of course, a consequence of General Massu's foolish interview with a German reporter, in Algiers.

Jean-Louis says Massu is not too bright; however, he had done a remarkably effective job in cleaning out terrorists in Algiers and restoring order.

Larry Norstad expresses relief that de Gaulle moved so promptly in the Massu case. Had he waited a week, as many French officers were advising, we would have had a new army uprising in Algeria.

PARIS, *January 25, 1960*

LUNCH with General Pierre Billotte, former minister of defense. Billotte is an old Gaullist, and at present heads a center-left Gaullist party called Union Démocratique du Travail. He seems to have taken it upon himself to act as a kind of unofficial liaison between de Gaulle and Washington.

Pierre told me he had sent a memorandum to de Gaulle advising that he must assert governmental authority in Algeria more strongly and take the following steps:

1. The ultras had to be reduced in strength, and some transferred to metropolitan France in fixed residence.

2. Those Algerian terrorists sentenced to death should be executed.

3. Weak men in the administration of the Fifth Republic should be cleaned out. Among these, Billotte included General Challe and Guillaumat, the minister of defense.

4. Politicians like Bidault must be warned they will face punishment if they conspire seditiously.

5. The FLN must know that France is determined to pursue a logical and tough policy, ready to negotiate but not indefinitely.

Billotte thinks de Gaulle must discipline army conspirators. The most important are Generals Lecomte and Faure, and Colonel Godard.

Challe behaved suspiciously prior to the Massu interview incident and his loyalty has been wobbly. Soustelle has also been indirectly involved with the conspirators, but Soustelle is too clever and has too much secret-service experience to be caught.

Pierre saw de Gaulle last at the beginning of the month and asked him what preparations he had made in case of his own death. De Gaulle appeared horrified and said nobody had ever mentioned the subject to him.

Since the summer of 1958, de Gaulle has reluctantly agreed to see his physician once a week. It took a lot of pressure to induce him to do this because he previously considered it immoral to see a doctor except if a man were on the point of death.

Billotte told me an interesting story concerning the Suez war, which he strongly opposed. He said that at 9:30 A.M. on the day the intervention began, he was summoned by President Coty. Coty inquired of Billotte what he thought about it. Billotte said he was against the campaign but asked what the idea of the Americans was. Coty replied that Washington didn't know anything about it yet.

Billotte said: "Then you are finished. If you don't have the benevolent neutrality of the United States there is no hope. Russia and America together will insist on keeping the peace." Coty was horrified and surprised. Billotte says he stayed with him until 7:30 P.M. and that he suggested to Coty that the best way out of it was to pretend that France and Britain were intervening on behalf of UN to keep the peace. Coty got his government to sell this idea to Eden that same day.

He said that from a French point of view, the Suez conspiracy had originated with Bourgès-Maunoury and his staff. Bourgès' directeur de Cabinet, Abel Thomas, assured Bourgès that if the French marched into Suez, Bourgès would soon be Prime Minister of France.

Today was a tense, taut day; nerves are stretched.

The situation in Algeria is materially worse, and within the next twenty-four hours we will probably know whether there is or is not a Fifth Republic. The Cabinet is now (5 P.M.) meeting with General de Gaulle to figure out how to act with a minimum of bloodshed. So far, the army appears to be on a sit-down strike. There is complete censorship in Algeria and it is impossible to know precisely what is going on.

Nevertheless, this appears to be what has taken place since the trouble began yesterday morning. The insurgent ultras are still barricaded in two key buildings in the center of Algiers. The army has failed to go into action against them. So far we cannot tell whether orders were given for action or not. Anyway, for the past twelve to twenty-four hours, the insurgents have been receiving arms, food, messages, and possibly reinforcements from the European population of Algiers. The army has been letting these things pass through the lines to the insurgents and troops seem to be fraternizing with the insurgents.

General Challe has called for reinforcements to be sent up to Algiers from the hinterland so that he can get soldiers not yet infected by the virus of the ultras. So far, neither the parachutists nor the Foreign Legion have been used—either because the government fears to order them into action or because they have already refused to obey orders.

There is a rumor that the government intends to pull back the army from the two barricaded buildings and send in the CRS (armed police). Yesterday the Foreign Legion started down the grand open staircase in the center of Algiers, but when it was halfway down, it was recalled, and the CRS was used instead. This was followed immediately by bloodshed.

If de Gaulle doesn't successfully send in the army within twenty-four hours, I fear a militarily autonomous state of Algeria may de facto be established; this could invade Tunisia within a fortnight, and then the

Fifth Republic would fall with chaos, bloodshed, and probably civil war in France.

PARIS, *January 26, 1960*

BILLOTTE says the situation is "tout à fait ridicule." New paratroopers from Constantine have been sent to Algiers, but they are doing nothing, even though they are supposed to be more reliable. The army appears loyal, but it gets no orders. De Gaulle is firm but doesn't seem to have any firmness in his government. The situation cannot continue as it is for twenty-four more hours. Momentum is being lost. Billotte says that logistically there are enough stocks in Algeria for a rebellion to survive quite a while—food, fuel, ammunition, aircraft. There was also enough in May, 1958.

I just spent an hour with Ambassador Houghton, who is very gloomy. He knows little because he has no contacts with the Ministry of the Interior or directly with de Gaulle.

Washington told Houghton to offer any assistance we could. All he did (wisely) was to tell the Quai if the government could think of any way we might be useful, to let us know.

He thinks the army is gradually losing its disciplinary link with the Elysée and de Gaulle can do nothing if the army moves, because General Lecomte, in Germany, is part of the plot.

PARIS, *January 28, 1960*

GEORGE Ball (Adlai Stevenson's partner) says Stevenson still wants to run this year. He pretends not to, but then adds: "I don't want the job, but goddamn it, we have got to organize a team now just in case I have to run."

Ball thinks the only possible combination for the Democrats that would have any chance of beating Nixon is a Stevenson-plus-Kennedy (for Vice President) ticket, and he doesn't think there is any more than a minimal chance of getting Kennedy to join in.

He said it is certain now that Chester Bowles would be Kennedy's Secretary of State. It was a smart move by Kennedy to choose Bowles as a foreign-affairs advisor, because Bowles can attract some of the East Coast liberals and he was very strong in Los Angeles. Kennedy must win the California primary against Brown in order to get the nomination himself.

Lunched today with Spaak.
Spaak has just read the entire text of Khrushchev's supreme Soviet

speech and concludes that a tremendous change in Soviet strategy is taking place. In effect, Khrushchev has adopted the NATO strategy of the
sword and shield. The sword comprises long-range missiles scattered
around Russia and the shield is being reduced into a defensive Soviet
army. Khrushchev indicates he expects problems with the demobilized
officers who, coming back from Europe, may be psychologically as mal-
adjusted as French officers coming back from Algeria.

Such things as disengagement and the Rapacki Plan are already outmoded by these developments. But it is extraordinary that Khrushchev's
announced intention is to imitate and surpass America. For the first time
in this speech, he talked about the "rights of man" and said that communism
is the only way to achieve these.

He told me the great problem of NATO now is that West Germany
is trying to make a secret military deal with Spain, above all to help its
air force. Spaak was surprised when he realized I knew about this and
said, "But it's top secret." NATO and SHAPE are trying to squash it because
Norway and Denmark especially are enraged.

Spaak said de Gaulle "is unsupportable—but a great man." Everyone
in the international world who has been quarreling with him is now behind him. But if he wins this test, it will mean that he will also settle the
whole Algerian affair right away. If his authority is sufficient to end the
present insurrection, it will be sufficient to impose a solution on the FLN
rebels, who have faith in him. Then, he will no longer be needed by France.
All the old reasons for friction between de Gaulle and the allies will revive
and de Gaulle may very well be out of office six months after Algerian
peace.

Spaak suggests that the present insurrection was timed to explode now
because the army had received confirmation of secret negotiations between France and the FLN and feared that a peace was about to be arranged.

Yesterday's Cabinet meeting was extraordinary. De Gaulle was in a
cool rage and announced his absolute intention of restoring discipline and
carrying through his policy without any deflection from his purpose. Some
ministers are still wobbling and want to get out. De Gaulle will brook no
argument. When he summoned Challe and the other generals earlier in the
week, he read them a brutal riot act. He is almost ready to go down himself and storm the barricades.

PARIS, *February 1, 1960*

LUNCHED with Pierre Courtade, my Communist friend. Pierre admits
that de Gaulle's speech was courageous and moving, but he thinks it will
get nowhere. He said, "Nobody has spoken like that in France since
Louis XIV."

PARIS, *February 2, 1960*

LUNCHED today with Simonne Servais, now attached to Roger Frey. Pompidou had originally tried to bring her to the Elysée, but Madame de Gaulle said she would not have a divorced woman in the Elysée.

Simonne told me de Gaulle had written the third volume of his *Mémoires* in his own handwriting. He had reworked the manuscript scribbling in corrections until it was an awful mess. Then he insisted on copying it all over himself because he wanted to leave an "original manuscript for history" and thought the first one too sloppy.

Incidentally, Pompidou has kept notes of his conversations with de Gaulle. Someday he will write memoirs equivalent to Saint Simon's classic.

PARIS, *February 3, 1960*

LAST night at dinner, Sir Evelyn Shuckburgh, once Eden's principal private secretary and now an ambassador and head of the political section at NATO, told me some extremely interesting things about Eden. He knows all his faults but, despite this, likes the man and feels very sorry for him. Eden is a petty fellow with a very quick temper and extremely vain.

Once he flared up at Shuckburgh, saying: "Like all the others you are not loyal to me but are working for Rab [Butler]." For the rest of that day, Shuckburgh refused to speak to Eden.

Once, when he was ill out in the country, Shuckburgh spent a couple of days with him to keep him in touch with the Foreign Office. Eden took him for a walk in the garden one afternoon and to Shuckburgh's astonishment, Eden talked to the flowers like a little boy. He would say looking at a flower bed: "Peony dear, you need a little water, don't you?" Then he would turn to Shuckburgh and say: "Evelyn dear, do get a little water for Peony."

Shuckburgh found this tragic but somewhat endearing. Perhaps. I find it horrifying to think that this man had such a large share in the world's destinies. Shuckburgh said Eden's whole life was devoted to the aspiration to succeed Churchill as Tory Prime Minister. The tragedy was that in the end he did succeed him and was such an abysmal flop.

Eden is famous for his pedestrian literary style. Many years ago, Churchill said about him: "Poor Anthony, he used every known cliché, from 'The situation is fraught with consequences' to 'gentlemen will please adjust their dress upon leaving' [the sign in all English men's rooms]."

PARIS, *February 4, 1960*

THIS morning, I had a long talk with the Comte de Paris, Bourbon claimant to the French throne.

He is slender, of medium height, with an over red, somewhat petulant, nervous face. He spoke in a soft voice, shifting between French and English. He said:

> In France today, there is a king but no monarchy. There is no pro-vision for succession. De Gaulle has transformed many things and he is giving the habit to the country of needing a chief. There is increas-ingly wide consent to this delegation of authority. Of course, the work he has started here and in Africa requires a chief to complete the task.
>
> I don't think we will return to the parliamentary system and to the election of a president and the party system. Neither the right nor the left (which has some undoubted men of quality) can assert itself. And no man can be produced by the competition of right and left who would have the freedom to speak for France as a whole.
>
> France needs a man above parties. And even men like [former President] Coty and [Marshal] Juin are not suitable anymore. People are looking for someone above parties and also qualified by reasons of age and historical role.
>
> Of course, it is difficult to foresee events now because everything is moving too rapidly, but the need for an intelligent man above factions will remain. And there are very few among whom one could possibly choose. Nevertheless, opinion is beginning to think of these problems. This is a new phase in French history and it permits me to think in-creasingly of the possibility of a return to the monarchic form.

I asked if he had ever discussed these things with de Gaulle. He said he had had rather frank talks with him before he returned to power in 1958, but had not seen him since. However, he had been much impressed by the phrasing of de Gaulle's letter to him on the occasion of his son's marriage, "because de Gaulle chooses his words most carefully." He said: "There is no powerful antimonarchic feeling in France today. No one would raise barricades against the return of a king."

Later, lunched with Jean-Louis de Rougemont. He thinks the army did well during the recent crisis, showing restraint and sangfroid. It delib-erately moved step by step in order to remove all risk of bloodshed. In 1934, when Rougemont was a lieutenant, he was sent by his commander to protect one of the ministries against the mob during a Croix de Feu riot. His colonel handed out ammunition but ordered that the bullets be sewn in "sachets" and be returned still "sewn" at the end of the day. In other words, orders should be followed. But French soldiers should not fire on French workmen. Jean-Louis said that both he and his colonel were "of course" on the side of the Croix de Feu.

He said it was difficult even now for a Frenchman to become friendly with Germans, adding that although he had a German cousin who was a very decent fellow: "The only time there has ever been a German in our house was after the 1914 war, when my parents had in the Prince of Reuss. There was a great deal of discussion before he was invited."

PARIS, *February 9, 1960*

PLEASANT chat with Louis Joxe, now minister of education, former ambassador to Moscow. Joxe sees increasing troubles between Russia and China and says he has always felt that Khrushchev's Siberian population program is founded on political rather than economic reasons—the fear of China.

Khrushchev's great aspiration is to stabilize the world now along its present ideological lines. He may offer to de Gaulle to tranquilize the French Communist party, but this is not of much interest to Paris because it is a French problem and the regime intends to keep the Communists isolated. The big offer Khrushchev is likely to make is to recognize western preeminence in Africa; and this might be tempting. But Khrushchev has no influence on the Algerian war and probably not much among the Arab states.

PARIS, *February 11, 1960*

POLISH Ambassador Gajewski told me the following story. After de Gaulle took power in 1958, he went down to Algeria. One of his aides whispered that he had ignored General Massu and reminded de Gaulle that he should perhaps say something to him. Before everybody, de Gaulle tapped Massu on the back and said, "Alors, Massu, con comme toujours?"

This is a fine story, but I had already heard it otherwise. According to the original version, Massu drew himself up, saluted, and replied, "Oui, mon General, toujours Gaulliste."

This morning, I had an especially interesting talk with Pompidou, de Gaulle's former directeur de Cabinet. He said there was an unfortunate misapprehension in America concerning Algeria. The man in the street seemed to imagine there were just a few hundred Frenchmen there protected by the army and sitting on the Arabs.

The entire French army is convinced the Algerian Muslims would vote for France if given a fair chance. Unfortunately, race and deceit play a large role, and General de Gaulle himself knows the army's impression is not true.

Pompidou said the recent "ultras" plot in Algiers had been brewing a long time and it had been exploded prematurely by General Massu's indiscreet interview with a German newspaper and the resulting brouhaha. He has come to the reluctant conclusion that Pinay was indirectly involved in the plot. Pinay had definitely arranged his own discharge from the government by an openly insolent attitude on Algeria. Pinay several times said to Pompidou, "Don't you think something is about to happen in Algiers?" Pinay clearly wanted to get out and hold himself in reserve as a pacifier after the crisis.

Then as a bombshell, Pompidou told me that to his deep distress—"but I assure you this doesn't come from the Elysée"—there was a very serious plot to oust de Gaulle, a plot backed by American money. The scheme was to form a government, including Bidault, and eventually to bring in Pinay as President. The most fantastic aspect of the story is that Alain de Sérigny, an Algerian French leader and editor, was supposed to be one of the principal conspirators and money raisers. It is not forgotten here that de Sérigny actively conspired with Bob Murphy prior to the North African landing and had close American contacts. Pompidou said it is apparent de Sérigny would not have been arrested and imprisoned recently merely because he attacked de Gaulle in his newspaper and called for an Algérie Française. He is suspected of something infinitely more important, and now the government is in the process of ascertaining the truth.

Pompidou didn't tell me what the alleged source of the money is. It was clearly not the oil companies because, of course, "the oil companies are always for peace anywhere and are totally amoral in terms of whom they help, whether in Saudi Arabia or elsewhere. They need peace to make money." He never even inferred that he suspected the CIA, but I had a feeling that this was what he was getting at.

According to his story, important circles in America had become so distressed by de Gaulle's attitude on NATO that they had resolved to oust him and bring in a pro-NATO government. Pompidou saw de Gaulle just before he went to the United States last month and said he was going to be asked many questions about France's NATO attitude. He told de Gaulle he had to know what was correct so he could speak the truth. "I was entirely satisfied by what the General told me on NATO," he said.

PARIS, *February 12, 1960*

INFORMATION from the insurgents in Algeria (the ultras) says General Allard and General Lecomte were ready to move on Paris from Germany with their troops but the crisis broke too soon for the plotters. The plotters also counted on Generals Maisonrouge, Lennuyeux (commander of the 7th Mechanized Division), Gracieux (10th Paratroop Division), Faure, and de Courneau (25th Armoured Division).

There is a report from Algeria that General Allard and General Zeller have been implicated in the conspiracy by tape recordings now in government hands.

Yesterday evening, I told Houghton what Pompidou had told me. He was very alarmed and recalled that he had written a letter to Alain de Sérigny some time ago saying he would be glad to see him next time he came to Paris. He buzzed his secretary and asked her to find the letter, but when I left one and a half hours later, much to Houghton's distress, it had not been found. I told him I calculated this document would provoke some interesting questions when they applied the thumbscrew to Sérigny. It could add to the French fit of pique being built up against Houghton on the grounds of his friendship with Pinay. He smiled sourly.

He asked if I could arrange a very confidential luncheon with Pompidou because he is worried. (I am dictating this on Friday after having arranged said luncheon for next Wednesday.)

Houghton has a very good idea. He is now drafting a telegram to the State Department suggesting that the *directoire* de Gaulle wishes among the western Big Three should be established within NATO as a kind of alliance security council. There should be a five-man policy committee with three permanent members, the United States, Britain, and France, plus two rotating members from the other countries: The first to be chosen from among West Germany, Italy, and Canada; and the second to be chosen from among the smaller states. This could satisfy both de Gaulle's aspirations and the worries of other NATO countries. As the same time, it would reassert the value of NATO in de Gaulle's mind.

Lunched with Brouillet, who talked about the "conspiracy of silence of the press" during de Gaulle's self-imposed exile, attributing this to the tradition among French intellectuals that a man in a uniform could not be an intelligent or successful man.

De Gaulle's curious phrase about representing legitimacy since 1940, and the speech he made at the Conseil d'Etat on that same January 29, in which he talked about his representing legitimacy, were very important. The idea was to warn army conspirators now that they were not in a position to imitate what de Gaulle had done in 1940.

In his intellectual formation, de Gaulle is much more fifth-century B.C. Greek than he is Latin, "although the envelope is Roman," said

Brouillet. De Gaulle's parents played a remarkable role in his intellectual formation. He had recently seen an old man who had taught de Gaulle as a youngster and who said he was a first-class classical scholar.

PARIS, February 17, 1960

LAST night, at the Alessandrinis', Frank Roberts expressed surprise that the German-Spanish deal has not yet leaked out to the public. France offered Bonn equal facilities to those desired in Spain, but Germany has stuck to its Spanish intentions.

Alessandrini, in his cynical Italian way, considers de Gaulle merely "another dictator. I should know; I remember Mussolini." The only difference is that de Gaulle is a military man and Mussolini, despite all his pretensions, was not.

Lunched today at Ambassador Houghton's with Pompidou, just the three of us. I acted as interpreter. Houghton wanted it so secret that his own staff wouldn't know. Houghton reassured his guest that U.S. policy remained firmly behind de Gaulle.

Pompidou again gave an account of the rumors of a conspiracy aided by American money. He said it was now evident that the political plot involved in last month's crisis was far more extensive than anybody had believed. Everything was supposed to go off in March or April but was prematurely exposed.

According to the rumor, Pinay would have been made President to placate the Americans. The idea behind the conspiracy was that France would impose a policy of integration on Algeria and gain American support in exchange by reaffirming close ties with NATO. Alain de Sérigny was supposed to be a money-raising agent.

Pompidou advised Houghton to do nothing about knocking down the rumors. He thought it was easier to let them die a natural death. The only thing required was for the U.S. to officially reassert its support for de Gaulle. Our abstention in the last Algerian vote in the UN had raised serious doubts.

The FLN was counting on producing such a desperate situation in Algeria that the U.S. would eventually have to intervene and then come out for an independent Algeria. The U.S. was emotionally involved in an "anticolonial" attitude and unfortunately we were likely to be misled by any man who gets dressed up in a burnous.

He argued that it is now necessary for France to push swiftly to establish a new kind of organized opinion in Algeria. It could be freely elected and then could freely choose its own future. The recent crisis had awakened in France itself a great realization of the problems of the unfortunate

Europeans in Algeria. It had also created a new faith in de Gaulle among the Muslims. France had to capitalize upon this new situation and swiftly.

Pompidou was interested in American reactions to France's atomic explosion. He thought it useful for the entire West to have a nuclear military capacity in Europe. Without such a capacity, were Russia to bring immense pressure on western Europe, wouldn't many Americans repeat the old slogan, "Is it worth while dying for Danzig?" Of course, in case of a direct attack, the U.S. would retaliate. But would it retaliate for anything short of a direct attack? This dilemma was being eliminated by Europe's own nuclear arsenal.

He admitted it was embarrassing having Khrushchev on hand for two weeks, but he didn't think it would help the popularity of the Communist party here. Khrushchev would have a "succès de curiosité"; but not a popular success.

It was silly to imagine that Khrushchev could offer France nuclear warheads, as Paul Reynaud had recently suggested in a statement warning the U.S. to share its secrets quickly. Russia could not do for France what it doesn't dare do for China.

PARIS, *February 18, 1960*

LARRY Norstad filled me in at length on the secret Spanish-German negotiations. Last autumn the Spanish foreign minister, Castiella, visited Bonn, and the Germans told him they were interested in special military facilities in Spain. Castiella agreed and negotiations were begun by military experts. When Norstad first heard about this at the time of the NATO meetings, last December, he discussed it with General Heusinger. He expressed regret and said the matter affected NATO. The negotiations were temporarily suspended.

The Germans say they want special help for training their new air force, for supporting it, and for practicing with new missiles. Spain would afford useful facilities for such things as long-range practice flights. Norstad and the Germans prefer to call these "facilities" rather than "bases." The French (and in a minor fashion, the Portuguese) offered the Germans similar facilities, but the Germans complained that it takes far too long to negotiate anything with France, that France was unreliable, and the Germans felt they were likely to lose their shirts in negotiations after perhaps three years of talks. They wanted something in a hurry.

Norstad offered to send some of his own experts to Bonn to discuss the negotiations. He met Defense Minister Strauss who was agreeable but firm.

Larry is very worried about the propaganda and psychological implications. While Germany can cite the special agreement of the United States with Spain as a precedent, it is treading on delicate ground.

I showed Larry the memo of my conversation with Adenauer on October 19, 1953, suggesting that Germany might someday hope to sign a special alliance with Spain. He found this most interesting but feels Bonn really isn't seeking such a secret alliance. The situation is still pending. I told him I was going to write about it and I thought my column might very well raise enough reaction to kill the entire project. He smiled.

He suggested I should look up the Paris Treaty of 1954, under which Germany came into NATO and study the references to logistics. These logistical clauses necessarily brought the whole matter of the German-Spanish deal into SHAPE's sphere of interest and he had told the Germans as much.

He said the French argument that they should have a nuclear trigger of their own on an independent basis ("and there is no doubt that they are establishing their independence") because of a fear that the United States might not retaliate to Russia's threats, might have logic to other countries, but was a ridiculous approach to make us Americans. This argument, in a nutshell, is that the United States should give France a trigger to force us to do what we don't want to do.

PARIS, *February 19, 1960*

How France is governed nowadays is a mystery. Here we have the "strongest regime" in years and yet nobody seems to venture to tell de Gaulle anything. The old General works a limited number of hours each day and spends at least part of them in personally answering letters from unimportant people—like a note I got from him.

Interesting lunch with General Jacquot, inspector general of the army. He is fifty-seven, a St. Cyrien, and the son of a professional officer, but still very much a man of the people and has none of the elegance of the old aristocrats. He eats clumsily and talks with a richly vulgar vocabulary. I like him. He is bright, tough, sincere.

He said the situation in Algeria, militarily speaking, is much better. The weight of France's effort is gradually grinding the FLN down. The barrier erected along the Tunisian and Moroccan frontiers had created a Maginot-line complex among FLN units in Tunisia and Morocco. They are contented to stay where they are.

"Total French army discipline" has been reestablished. De Gaulle has efficiently and effectively purged the uncertain elements. It was only a question of the professional corps of officers and NCOs.

It is out of the question that any army should have a political role. "France," he said, "is not like Spain after the loss of South America, when the army kept mixing in politics. And it is a mistake to exaggerate the influence of the Indochinese experience on the French army. The function of the French army is to win wars as ordered. If the war is difficult it should win it anyway. It has no political function."

We discussed the 1958 and 1960 conspiracies. Jacquot called in all the senior officers in his German command one day after the May 13, 1958 (pro de Gaulle) uprising and told them he expected total discipline. He also reminded them they were guests on German soil and therefore the discipline would be exceptionally rigid. That is all, he said. Any individual who in the slightest way violated his orders would be *bouclé*, (locked up).

It was very difficult for France to replace the heavy losses in Indochina. It was increasingly hard to recruit young officers. The best, the elite, had been lost in Indochina. Furthermore, French officers were marrying much younger nowadays and had greater family and financial problems as they were transferred around.

He talked at length about his experiences in the resistance during the war. He said: "The Gestapo and forced labor drafted by the Nazis were what made the resistance. If they had left France alone, the resistance would have comprised only 5,000 idiots like me."

When French defenses collapsed he ended up in Bergerac in the Dordogne with four hundred of the eight hundred men in his battalion— "not bad for those days." He established contact with André Malraux (whom he had known in Spain) and Aragon. His first link with the English and de Gaulle was arranged through Malraux, who was then hidden in the Dordogne. Jacquot said: "Malraux has a genius as a condottiere. He might have been the captain of one of those late fifteenth-century mercenary groups. He doesn't know anything about the techniques of soldiery, but he is a real *chef de guerre*. With him it is instinct and art—not knowledge."

He evolved an extraordinarily strange theory: "Every large rebellion [insurrection] lasts seven years," he said. "This is a mystical law. I don't know why, but it is true. The Indochina affair lasted seven years. The Carlist war in Spain lasted seven years. General Markos's war in Greece lasted seven years. [Here he is wrong.] And the FLN started in 1954. Sometime next year it will end in Algeria." He thought there was something strange and inevitable in this that had to do with the number seven, similar to the old Hebrew seven days of the week.

I told him that it was my belief that only two kinds of war were possible at the present time—atomic war and guerrilla war. Since atomic war was probably to be excluded, guerrilla war was the only type for which one should prepare. He agreed. I then went on to ask if guerrilla warfare were really being taught in the French army and how. He answered: "Unfortunately it is impossible to *teach* the work of a maquis. When I was in the resistance, I only kept with me the few who were really clear on and understood the work of a maquisard. The other types I sent on to Spain and Africa."

Jacquot said that the only way to give the army faith in France when the army leaves Algeria—as it will have to do—was by building its faith in France's nuclear weapons future. This was a psychological fact of immense importance. The United States should understand this in approaching the entire problem. He added: "General Ailleret [in charge of the special weapons section] is one of my colts." (Ailleret subsequently became chief of all forces.)

He recalled a statement by Bismarck, whom he considers a very great man: "Laissez le coq gaullois gratter le sable du Sahara." Bismarck thought if the French spent their energy in North Africa, they would forget their claims in Alsace and Lorraine. "But," said Jacquot, "the Sahara is of immense importance. This is not just the need for oil. The Sahara is far more important to France as a laboratory for atomic experiments."

Jacquot regards Germany's General Heusinger as especially intelligent. "After all," said Jacquot, "a man must be pretty crafty to be chief of staff to both Hitler and Adenauer in the same lifetime."

DE GAULLE: "THERE IS NO QUESTION WE CAN SOLVE WITH THE RUSSIANS"

Paris, *February 20, 1960*

THIS MORNING I WENT TO SEE DE GAULLE AT THE ELYSÉE. FIRST, I was received by Brouillet, director of his Cabinet, who said there had now been a definite decision that de Gaulle would not give me an interview, but I could ask him any questions I wanted in a private capacity. Brouillet asked me to be very discreet and not to let anybody know I had seen the General; he was continually refusing hundreds of such demands, but liked to see me as a friend.

De Gaulle looked particularly tired, paler, and older. Nevertheless, I found him in excellent health and extremely talkative. He was wearing slightly tinted glasses. He reminded me this was *à titre privé*. I told him Brouillet had told me so but I wished to ask him questions.

I began by asking what his reaction had been to Ferhat Abbas's speech offering Europeans in Algeria full citizenship in an independent state. De Gaulle said:

This was not a contribution to peace. He said nothing about self-determination. Ferhat Abbas obviously doesn't want self-determination. He wants only *his* solution—independence. And he continues the *égorgements* [throat-cuttings] he calls war so long as his solution is not accepted. This is a dictatorial and totalitarian approach. I don't want a dictatorship of any sort in Algeria.*

* See de Gaulle's further comments, pp. 55–56, 70–71.

I asked if there was a better chance of an allied Big Three agreement now that France had exploded an atomic device. He said:

> If our wish in this matter is not granted, we will no longer support the Organization of the North Atlantic Treaty. We have taken back control of our fleet and certain other things. We will take back our liberty in other respects also if this is not granted. We will take back our complete liberty. We will, of course, remain allied; but we will only be an ally and fully independent.*

I then asked de Gaulle what he thought was necessary to make a success of the May Summit meeting. He replied:

> I don't expect any important positive results. Perhaps I deceive myself, but I doubt it. The only thing that could possibly happen would be an acceptance on both sides not to attack each other and, in the same sense, to keep a certain armaments balance. But I doubt if any solution can be reached. Clearly Khrushchev is applying more pressure in Berlin now. That is his game. He tries to get what he wants. But there is no sense in giving him what he wants.

Did he think there was any means of assuring Soviet good faith in coexistence? He answered: "The Russians cannot be of good faith, nor can we. Russia can think that it is in its own interest not to continue the Cold War and to pursue a temporary détente. Perhaps, at that moment, it is in their interest; but they won't give up on major, long-range aspirations."

I then asked what Khrushchev expected from his French visit in April. He said:

> Propaganda. Khrushchev makes propaganda. Perhaps also he hopes this might aid him in his present relaxation policy [*politique de détente*] and perhaps it is now in Khrushchev's interest in many respects to start détente. He might need this in terms of his internal position in the Soviet Union as well as in terms of his relationships with the satellite countries of Poland and Hungary. Perhaps he sees it as desirable to pursue such a détente for the moment. And a tour of this sort—his visit to France—helps propaganda. Of course, I will talk with Khrushchev. We will chat. But I don't expect anything. There is *no* question that we can solve with the Russians. There is a need for all of us to act together to solve any question, not just France.

This certainly stresses his intention to remain allied to the West even if he doesn't join in the pro-NATO philosophy of integration.

I asked if he thought there might be any reason to revive the Franco-Soviet treaty of 1944, denounced by Russia some years ago. He said: "There is no more reason for such a treaty. In 1944, Germans were still in the war and we didn't know what our future alignment would be. But

* See de Gaulle's further comments, pp. 54, 63.

we are not menaced by Germany now; nor is Khrushchev, despite what he says."

De Gaulle said he was happy to go to the United States on his projected visit and glad to see Eisenhower, but he didn't expect any negotiations there. He called it merely a visit of friendship. "Naturally we will talk, your President and I," he said. He also admitted that he would like to see a settlement of the so-called *directoire* question and perhaps it could be brought up there. "This must be settled," said he. "There perhaps it is possible."

This concluded the questions I had to raise. De Gaulle then turned to me and said: "How do you see things?" I said I was pessimistic about the world at large but optimistic concerning allied relationships, repeating what I had said earlier about the ultimate implication of the French nuclear explosion. De Gaulle observed: "That is not important for the moment. It will take time for us to make nuclear arms. In terms of the immediate present, the United States is certainly not disposed to change its attitude toward us."

We then talked about disarmament. I asked de Gaulle if he thought that France could play a more important role in disarmament talks. He came up with an interesting idea. He said:

> There is only one subject on which it is possible to make a practicable disarmament arrangement today, and that is in the field of missiles. Perhaps a reciprocal control on missiles could be worked out. After all, missiles cannot be hidden. They are localized and can be inspected. [I am afraid de Gaulle missed the point of the new mobile missiles presently being developed, such as our Polaris submarine.] If an agreement on missile inspection can be worked out, atomic arms will become less important. One can do something in this field. But I don't know if anybody *wants* to do anything.
>
> All this talk about stopping tests is unimportant. Stopping atomic tests wouldn't stop atomic arms. The United States and the Soviet Union already have enormous supplies of weapons and they will continue to make arms if they stop testing. A cessation of testing will only hurt France, which has not yet got its weapons. There can be no nuclear disarmament unless stockpiles are liquidated and I don't believe this will be done. The only field is that of missiles. The only possibility of making things a little easier is in the realm of missiles.

I had no more to ask him, although de Gaulle seemed disposed to chat a while. I am afraid I looked at him rather blankly. Finally, I said I would like to ask a nonprotocol favor. Many years ago he had given me an inscribed photograph of himself in his wartime uniform. Would he do the same as President of France. "For you I will be happy to do this. I shall leave instructions." Then he arose and in a fatherly way conducted me to the door, shook hands, and said good-bye.

PARIS, *February 22, 1960*

LUNCHED with Alessandrini. He is desperately worried about the Italian political crisis.

He says the special tragedy now is that President Gronchi had really woken up during his recent Moscow visit and realized the Russians were tougher and more disagreeably inclined than he had thought. February 17, Alex reported on the Gronchi trip to the NATO council and said, "It was the most brilliant speech I ever gave. I can say that fairly because it was not my speech. It was sent to me from Rome."

Gronchi was deeply shocked by Soviet unwillingness to compromise. Khrushchev had offered him the following bargain: Russia would withdraw its garrison from Hungary if Italy would close its NATO IRBM bases. Gronchi explained to Khrushchev how impossible this was because Italy would remain true to its allied obligations. This provoked Khrushchev's famous sneers about "spaghetti people."

We closed a pleasant lunch with Alessandrini muttering, "For God's sake, why don't you Americans send us a decent ambassador to NATO? We have had Hughes, Perkins, and Burgess. Mrs. Burgess at least could be a good ambassador."

PARIS, *February 25, 1960*

VISITED Walter Eytan, now Israeli ambassador, for the past eleven years secretary-general of the Israeli foreign office, an Oxford graduate, a classicist, and a nice, impressive fellow.

Eytan assured me Nasser has had about 1,400 of his officers trained in Russia. Soviet instructors have inculcated a new morale and sense of duty in these men. Therefore, Israel's great "human" advantage in the quality of its army has been reduced. And the situation will become increasingly unfavorable with time. "The more the Russians put a backbone into the Egyptians, the worse things will be for us," he said.

"Furthermore, extensive new Soviet arms have reached the U.A.R. The situation is now very disquieting," although Israel does not think an attack is yet imminent. "The bulk of the Egyptian land forces are disposed in the Sinai Peninsula facing Israel, and at the same time, the whole Syrian army has been mobilized near the Israeli border."

If Russian aid to Egypt continues, Israel won't be able to keep its present relative advantage. "Therefore we must look ahead," he said. Israel had to secure new arms. (I have heard a report it is buying French Mystère jets.)

Eytan insists there is no secret mutual-defense agreement with France. However, he said, "There is an implicit understanding which I imagine

also extends to the West in general. We won't expect to be left in the lurch
if we are attacked. However, French interests are more directly menaced
by Nasser than those of Britain and the U.S. They must realize that if
Nasser gets his way in Israel, he will become irresistible, not only in the
Middle East but in all Africa."

I asked if Israel were alarmed by Nasser's denunciation of the 1950
Big Three status-quo guarantee in the Middle East. "Not at all," said
Eytan. "He is just flogging a dead horse. Everyone has considered this
nil since 1956 [Suez]."

Israel would welcome a treaty guaranteeing the status quo—either by
the West or by the West and Russia. Furthermore, Jordan knows its own independence is linked to that of Israel and that if Israel collapses, so
will Jordan.

Israel felt Russia was pressing Russian interests in the Arab world,
whereas China was pressing both Chinese and Communist interests,
above all in Iraq.

I have the feeling Israel regards Paris as perhaps its most important post now, in terms of military bonds with France, and that is why
Eytan is here.

Alessandrini dropped in. He had received a cable from Rome giving
him the details of my column on Spain and Germany; he wanted to find
out more. At today's NATO council meeting, the German ambassador, von
Walther, passed out mimeographed copies of the official denial put out
by the German Foreign Office on my column, saying a secret bilateral
military deal was being negotiated, despite allied distress.

He wants to know why the Germans did not tell the rest of the allies.
I told him not to worry because not even the German Foreign Office
knew. He said, "Thank God you wrote about it before the Germans signed
anything. It would have been a disaster. They are such fools."

PARIS, *February 26, 1960*

SELIM Sarper gave a farewell cocktail party; he is leaving to become
secretary-general of the Turkish Foreign Office. I was immediately buttonholed by diplomats because of my Spanish-German bases column.
Frank Roberts asked me, "Why didn't you write this earlier? You have
known about it four weeks. What were you waiting for?" I told him I was
waiting for the Germans to make up their minds to give it up on their
own account; but since they hadn't, I decided to put an end to it. Frank
admitted it was probably a good thing.

I noticed Roberts spending a lot of time in a huddle with Dr. Schwoe-
bel, deputy to the German NATO ambassador, and a fat, unpleasant-
looking character with an oily smile, a face like a pig. He came up

oozing friendship, saying, "Ach, don't you remember me? From Athens. 1941?" I did indeed remember. He was a Nazi press attaché at the German legation when the Nazis attacked Greece. I told him I recalled a sea voyage from Greece to Turkey (my escape) as a consequence of those memories.

Another German diplomat said, "I used to work with your old friend, Seiler. I believe you sent a letter to Seiler after the war helping to exonerate him with the allied authorities." (Seiler was a press counsellor in von Papen's embassy and a good friend of Julius Streicher—the worst of all German Jew baiters. He kept Streicher's picture in his office after Streicher's disgrace, when even Hitler found he couldn't stand his perversions.)

I told him, "You must have that mixed up. Frau Seiler wrote me asking for such a letter, but I replied I didn't feel free to grant her request."

PARIS, *February 28, 1960*

LUNCHED with President Manuel Prado of Peru and his wife. Spaak was there. He thought it was a good thing that the Spanish bases story had come out now rather than after the deal had been made. When he came into the room, he winked and said: "I see the Spanish say I gave you the information because I am a militant Socialist who hates Franco."

PARIS, *March 1, 1960*

PIERRE Billotte, at lunch, showed me the official minutes of the first secret meetings exploring the possibility of creating an Atlantic alliance. Pierre originally went to Washington at the time of General Pershing's death as de Gaulle's representative, then was coopted to discuss a projected alliance with the British and Americans. As far back as 1947–1948, the French wanted a global Big Three directorate, even though the British and Americans didn't agree.

PARIS, *March 3, 1960*

ALESSANDRINI came in for a drink. He told me von Walther flatly promised yesterday's NATO council meeting that Germany would not negotiate any agreement with Spain without *first* reporting this in the NATO council and obtaining its approval.

PARIS, *March 4, 1960*

GOOD talk with Jacques Soustelle in his pleasant, typically French, bourgeois flat. He received me in a sitting room lined with books, Aztec objets d'art, and a copy of a prehistoric cave painting from North Africa.

We started off chatting about the Toltecs. I mentioned my old favorite Nezahualcoyotl ("Hungry Wolf"; *coyotl* is the mother word for coyote). Soustelle shares my admiration and has been toying with the idea of writing a book on him to be called, *Hungry Wolf—the Story of a Mexican Gentleman.*

Soustelle claimed his position on Algeria was shared by nine-tenths of the members of the Gaullist party.

But I don't wish to force a showdown. Events will show I am right. There is no need to precipitate a test of force.

If I had said one-tenth of what de Gaulle said in his speech yesterday, I would have been expelled from the party. He is after peace; that is also my aim. The trouble is that in the party leadership there is immense ignorance. People simply know nothing about Algeria. And this harms de Gaulle, letting it appear that he is willing to liquidate the Algerian problem at any price. That isn't true. Some of these people go much further than de Gaulle himself. We also want peace—but not peace at any price.

Any system leading to a so-called solution in which the FLN could claim domination, would only bring a protracted, interracial war. What would be the situation of any French regime having withdrawn the French army? Algeria is next door to France—not some distant country. What would any French government say or do if a civil war broke out in Algeria, with one million Europeans fighting the Arabs and with thousands of Jews being massacred by the anti-Semitic killers of the FLN? The Europeans would forcefully expel the Arabs from areas like the casbah. On the other hand, Europeans would be massacred in the villages. No French government could sit tight and watch this. France would have to go back—and quickly.

You cannot compare Algeria with other problems. The Algerian problem is entirely sui generis. The U.S.A. and the UN simply don't understand this. They keep talking in meaningless clichés. They seem to have the idea that it is only a question of a handful of settlers or French civil servants against a unified Algerian population. That word "settlers" makes my hair stand on end. The Europeans lived there since long before there were any Americans in, for example, Nevada.

The January upheaval was a very foolish move. But it proved that even leadership of brainless men could gain a following. Why? The leaders had no real moral and intellectual value. But the people of Algeria make the most of every occasion. They will never agree to become displaced persons.

Most of Algeria is a mixture and no definite territory belongs to any single group. It is mixed up like a salad dressing and you cannot separate the various elements except at great expense of human life— like Palestine in 1948. That may happen, of course. The Arabs can sweep the Europeans out of some regions and the Europeans can sweep the Arabs out of others. But what's the use?

PARIS, *March 7, 1960*

YESTERDAY, I played golf with Frank Roberts. He told me Macmillan had wanted to have the de Gaulles overnight at Chequers during de Gaulle's official visit to the Queen next month. But de Gaulle did not think it was suitable for him, as chief of state, on an official visit, to accept the hospitality of a low character like a Prime Minister. So Macmillan asked if he could come over here.

Maurice Macmillan, the Prime Minister's son, has been spending the weekend with us. He says his father is fascinated by de Gaulle in a literary sense and loves to talk with him. He is much impressed by de Gaulle's grave courtesy, likes and admires him. Incidentally, Maurice says his father's French is perfectly good enough—despite an appalling accent—to handle conversations without an interpreter.

Lunched today with Gebhardt von Walther, German ambassador to NATO. He has been patching up the scars of the German-Spanish uproar and he tried again to find out where I had gotten my information. I remarked that I was quite fascinated by the authoritative newspaper articles I had read, explaining how and why, in great detail, the British had told me, the Americans had told me, SHAPE had told me, and Spaak had told me. Walther admitted three German generals had been in Spain at the time my column appeared, but added, "Of course, as you know, this had nothing to do with the bases deal."

LONDON, *March 15, 1960*

THIS afternoon, saw Selwyn Lloyd. Our conversation began with his remark: "Well, you are the man of the Spanish bases story." He thought the piece had done some good and said Britain's relations with Spain had, strangely enough, been improved by the affair, that Strauss had been a thick-skinned fool, ignoring all advance warnings of trouble.

I asked if he thought Cyprus, when it becomes independent, should join NATO. He said: "Of course, Cyprus is geographically eligible. But what would Cyprus do? Do not forget that an independent Cyprus excludes the area of British bases. Britain would not accept any NATO veto on how these bases should be used. And they could support CENTO or serve as a Middle East deterrent."

I would like to see a code of conduct approved for peaceful coexistence. Khrushchev now continues to try and subvert and undermine the West wherever he can. That is Cold War, not peaceful coexistence.

I wonder if you can establish a series of self-denying ordinances, doing such things as controlling propaganda and subversion.

The only possible agreements he could envisage at the summit would be agreement to meet again and acceptance of a code of conduct. If such a code of conduct were accepted, Berlin would be an important element in it, because Russian threats against us in Berlin would violate such a code.

He added: "Both sides see that another world war would mean mutual suicide and a continued Cold War leaves an unsettled and unstable world. But I think Khrushchev has a more open mind than Molotov, and perhaps a summit can remove the risk from peaceful coexistence. Soviet handling of the Algerian problem has indicated that Moscow is prepared to consider a new and more open approach."

PARIS, *March 19, 1960*

JEAN Laloy wants the West at the summit to proclaim to Khrushchev (and get his acceptance) that what is desired is not "victory without war" but "peace without victory." Couve de Murville, with his "cold Protestant mind," does not like the idea of this slogan, but Laloy is pushing it hard because it could have profound effect on western propaganda among neutralist nations.

Bidault had very good relations with de Gaulle when he was his foreign minister and they used to dine together and discuss all kinds of things. Bidault learned a lot in 1947, during the Moscow Conference when he dealt with Stalin. Stalin received him rudely, doodled persistently on a pad, only looked up briefly to shake hands with him, and from then on, ignored him, talking only to his interpreters. Stalin tried to make a deal to support French control of the Saar in exchange for Russian participation in control of the Ruhr, but Bidault staunchly said the Saar question was settled and Russian help was not required.

In December, 1944, de Gaulle was not as successful with Stalin as he says in his *Mémoires*. Laloy was de Gaulle's interpreter. "After all, de Gaulle sent an agent to the Polish Lublin government when neither England nor the United States did." De Gaulle demanded Russian support for control of the German left bank of the Rhine. Laloy was horrified, although he was then a devout Gaullist. He pointed out that this would permanently poison Franco-German relationships.

PARIS, *March 27, 1960*

LUNCHED and golfed with Norstad and Roberts. Roberts said General Valluy, commander-in-chief of the NATO central front, says the one essential thing for France is to get rid of de Gaulle before he wrecks the alliance.

Roberts says Montgomery visited Jugoslavia while he was ambassador there and attended a luncheon given by Gošnjak, defense minister, including some eight or nine Jugoslav generals who had fought Franco in Spain. Monty criticized NATO saying: "They saw nothing wrong with my visiting you people, but they're dead against my going to see that other great soldier-statesman, Franco." He was surprised at the sour silence.

PARIS, *April 5, 1960*

BREAKFAST this morning with General Paul Grossin, head of French military intelligence (SDECE).* Grossin has five stars and will be the senior general when Salan retires as military governor of Paris in a few weeks.

He says the FLN has no need for heavy equipment and aircraft now, but some of their pilots have been trained in China. China gave the FLN considerable money with which to purchase arms in Czechoslovakia. Czech arms are sent through Hamburg, which is a free port. Many West German arms dealers sell to the FLN, although the Bonn government tries to stop it. The French terroristic Main Rouge hires professional killers for special murders of arms merchants in Germany.

Since 1956, the Russians have been warning the French that they had better settle the Algerian war soon. General Jougov personally said this to Grossin. Grossin asked him, "How?" Jougov said: "That is your business."

Grossin says a purge of anti-Gaullists is now taking place among French commanders. Grossin himself, who has the reputation of being a Socialist, spoke freely of the *défauts* of de Gaulle and said people expected him to come in like a black sorcerer to settle everything—and he has settled nothing.

General Cherrière had hoped to take over the government of France in 1958, but the Gaullists outwitted him and General Chassin. A serious conspiracy was brewing late in 1959, and early this year. Intelligence found an enormous increase in exchanges of mysterious telegrams and telephone calls. Grossin had expected the plot to go off in April when de Gaulle was in America, but the Massu incident exploded it prematurely. Undoubtedly, the conspiracy is continuing, but it is very clandestine now and hard to spot. He didn't think there was any single head, but all the various groups are in touch with one another and plotting something again. If ever they agree on a single head, it will be a dangerous moment for France.

* Service de Documentation et de Contre-Espionnage.

PARIS, *April 7, 1960*

DINNER with Prince Paul and Princess Olga, former ruler of Jugoslavia. She says King Peter was a nice little boy but never had the character to be king. King Alexander, his father, was tough and manly and had no use for his son because he was timid and afraid of guns. This made Peter slightly tricky.

When the March 27, 1941 *coup d' état* took place, young Peter was with Paul and Olga all day long, although history says he made a broadcast to his people. In fact, they found another boy and put him on the air. When he was trying to get parachuted back to Jugoslavia during the occupation, Churchill blocked him. He never would have been able to block Peter's father.

Paul said he was in England at the time of the crisis before the abdication of King Edward VIII. Prime Minister Baldwin called Paul in for his advice and asked: "How can I save the boy?" Baldwin claimed the Australian Prime Minister had sent confidential word to him that Australia would leave the Empire if the King married "that woman."

Paul considers monarchy an outmoded form of government and is sure it will disappear everywhere eventually. It still was a success in England and Scandinavia because they had long traditions and fine discipline. He didn't think Don Juan had any chance in Spain; and the Comte de Paris is an insignificant fellow who will never regain the throne of France.

Under the influence of Queen Frederika, King Paul of Greece is preparing young Prince Constantine badly for kingship. He is giving him an old-fashioned education, which is no good nowadays. A prince, to have any chance as king, should be stuffed with knowledge and should mix with all kinds of people to know what they are like and what they want. Furthermore, at an early age, he should attend crown councils and read state telegrams to see how government works.

Paul said he had had a very unhappy childhood himself and suffered by being a prince. He couldn't mix easily with other boys and, although he had an interest in art, this was discouraged. His school teachers were more severe with him than with other boys because they wished to demonstrate they were showing no favoritism.

Paul expressed admiration for Tito. He says: "We must never forget that he was the only man to stand up to Stalin. Also he has held together the artificial nation of Jugoslavia, which was a chance creation of the Versailles Treaty. He saved the country and the world owes a lot to him—even though Jugoslavia may fall apart when he dies."

We talked at length about de Gaulle, who, he thinks, is a great man, but says history cannot judge him until he settles the Algerian war. De Gaulle's literary style (which he considers magnificent) has changed immensely since he wrote *Le Fil de l'Epée* more than thirty years ago. Gaston Palewski once told Paul that he had introduced Saint-Simon's writings to de Gaulle. Afterward, de Gaulle's style improved tremendously.

PARIS, *April 8, 1960*

LUNCH at Spaak's. Gardner (Mike) Cowles, who was there, thinks it is an even-money bet that Kennedy will be stopped. In that case, the most likely Democratic Presidential nominee would be Symington. Stevenson has no more chance.

Cowles has heard an interesting tale. Some weeks ago, a very secret dinner party was given in Brooklyn by outstanding Catholic leaders of the east, including Cardinal Spellman. Johnson was there. The purpose was to advise Johnson that the Catholic hierarchy did *not* want Kennedy as the Democratic nominee (presumably to avoid a sectarian rift). They wanted Kennedy on the ticket as a vice-presidential nominee only.

Pinay, who was also at lunch, talked with great bitterness about de Gaulle. He is convinced de Gaulle will be out within a year. The army is not planning a *coup d' état* because it doesn't want to take over, but it wants to prevent a left-wing government and is furious with de Gaulle because of his Algerian policy.

He lambasted de Gaulle on his European and NATO attitudes. He said Cabinet meetings are ridiculous. Debré presents all the disagreeable news and de Gaulle all the agreeable news. Once the General has made up his mind and adopted an attitude, nobody ventures to disagree. De Gaulle told Pinay, "I, and I alone, make French policy."

Spaak claims that Furtseva is Khrushchev's great friend and saved Khrushchev's scalp when he was almost thrown out by the Politburo. She allegedly got hold of Marshal Zhukov who sent military aircraft all around the U.S.S.R. to gather up loyal Khrushchev men on the Central Committee and beat down the opposition. Khrushchev paid Zhukov back by firing him when he was on an official trip to Albania. He showed up at a long-delayed Kremlin reception, talking about how sometimes men had to accomplish certain disagreeable tasks. Bulganin kept trying to shut Khrushchev up, but without success. Nobody knew what was going on until next day's newspapers announced Zhukov had been retired.

This afternoon, I visited Georges Bidault, former foreign minister, Prime Minister, MRP leader, and now one of de Gaulle's principal opponents, in his home at St. Cloud. It was watched over by two agents with tommy guns. Inside, the house was dirty, untidy, and smelled heavily of illness and fear.

I must say to Bidault's credit, it is very simple, filled with books, and gives evidence of being the residence of a cultivated, unpretentious intellectual. Nevertheless, you could see the deterioration of the man by the setting. When I rang the bell, a dowdy servant was raced to the door by an even dowdier looking police dog. I waited in the sitting room, which smelled as if it had not been opened since last summer—a bit like an undertaker's establishment. Then a door opened and Bidault entered, greeted me with considerable warmth, and invited me into his study.

The entire conversation was incoherent, emotional, and illogical. He was extremely difficult to understand and spoke with savage bitterness and rancor, hating almost everyone.

He offered me a cigarette and then picked up a dead cigar that must have been lying there for hours, which he lit and began to puff. He must have noticed my face and asked if I would like the window open. I suggested it might be a good idea, and he did open it—for about two minutes. Then he closed it again and sealed us in with the odors of his psychosis.

I can't imitate his rambling conversation. He called de Gaulle "crazy." He says France is "finished" and "the game is over." He talked about being locked up behind machine guns (referring to the guards outside). He said he did not know whether he was going to be shot or whether I would be shot. "Of course they took your picture as you went in the door. They take the picture of the butcher, the baker, and the grocery boys as they deliver things." Later he said the policemen were there to protect him from assassination by the FLN. Still later, he said he was entirely free and could go wherever he wished. At one moment, he said he wanted to make a strong political speech but the Elysée had prevented it. But he admitted the press was "fairly free" and that his articles in *Carrefour* were uncensored. He expressed contempt for everybody, saying France was being governed by a "madman" (de Gaulle) and an "idiot" (Debré).

There were continual hints that he is on the extreme right now. He complained: "There is no right in France any more." He sneered at Eden and said his memoirs were filled with lies. Eden had it all wrong: "I didn't ask Dulles for an atom bomb at Dien Bien Phu; Dulles proposed that the U.S. should drop an atom bomb and I refused, saying this would lose the support of the world."

He said de Gaulle had destroyed the French army. Six months ago, there were two real forces in France—the Communist party and the army. Now there are only the Communists, and Khrushchev's visit had built them up. There was such hatred for de Gaulle in the army that Bidault felt relief when Khrushchev left. He was afraid the army might use the excuse of the visit to assassinate not Khrushchev, but de Gaulle. But shortly afterward, he said the Communist party was "*applati*" and the army remained an important force. There were no generals ("and if I mentioned the name of a general, they would consider that proof of conspiracy"). But the army was represented by the captains and the majors and they didn't dislike de Gaulle—they "hated" him.

He said: "I am the only man who has contacts with the army and in whom the army has faith." I asked him how about Pinay. "Pinay isn't behind machine guns in the midst of the city; I am," he commented.

He had no idea what would happen after de Gaulle left, "because if I said anything, they would accuse me of conspiracy." He indicated he had nothing more to do with the MRP and mentioned Robert Schuman only to say, "Poor Schuman, who has vanished into thin air."

I suppose I could go on recapitulating at length, but it would be pointless. He was almost more than cordial and told me to please call up and come out again, "now that I know it is safe for you." Poor man.

This was the wreckage of a man who had once been one of Europe's leading statesmen. I suppose a psychologist would say that he had to find a courage that was not in his system in order to play a very brave role during the resistance and that the additional strength he sought in alcohol at that time proved too much for him. He looked thin and frail and almost a bit hunchbacked, although the slight flush and the resonant voice with which he pronounced his views would have been deceptive to an observer who saw him for perhaps only ten seconds.

PARIS, *April 14, 1960*

LUNCHED with Jacques Soustelle, extremely friendly and pro-American. He was amazed on his last trip to the United States to find how strong pro-French sentiment was. He had never seen it so strong before. The U.S. remained confused because it simply could not understand France's policy in Algeria.

But there had been other waves in history. Somebody had to stop them. The most astonishing historic wave had been the spread of Islam, a bunch of uncivilized Arabs who conquered the Byzantine empire, much of Asia, Africa, and Europe. And then they were met by Charles Martel, a man who could probably neither read nor write, much less understand the significance of "historic waves." He turned back the tide. Today, there were only two forces against this new "historic wave"— Israel and France.

It is impossible to argue with the new de Gaulle. Prior to 1958, when he regained power, and during the first weeks of the Fifth Republic, one could discuss things with him reasonably. But all that was finished. De Gaulle refused to permit anyone to exchange ideas with him. Soustelle had sought, before his expulsion from the government, to reason with him that the only two logical solutions were "integration" (now called "francisation") or independence. He told de Gaulle that Ferhat Abbas was quite right in asserting that "association" meant complete independence within two weeks. He argued this would produce nothing but chaos and bloodshed and, in the end, an explosion of violence similar to Pakistan and India, ending up with partition into a French state on the rich Mediterranean shore and Muslim control of the hinterland. This presented no hope for the future. But de Gaulle wouldn't hear him through.

He has had several letters from Debré, warning him to keep his mouth shut on Algeria, and in the last one, telling him he could no longer consider himself a member of the Gaullist party (UNR). Soustelle has written saying that there was a specific statute in the UNR Constitution providing that members could be expelled by majority vote of the central committee, approved by a special supervisory committee. Until this was done, he saw no reason why he should not continue to consider himself a member. I commented: "You are trying to give Debré a case of schizophrenia." He smiled with murky sadness and said: "Michel and I have been very good friends, and I used to have lunch with him once a week. I spent most of my time keeping him from being too extremist. He is a nice fellow, but he is very excitable and he is also very ambitious."

Soustelle implied that although he has no intention at present of organizing a new French political party ("There is no meaning to political parties in France today"), the new center of information on Algeria (Centre d'Information sur les Problèmes de l'Algérie et du Sahara) might serve as a nucleus. He didn't intend to get out of politics and spend all his time during the next year "writing about Nezahualcoyotl."

It was absolutely necessary for the French government to announce a precise Algerian policy that everyone, Frenchmen as well as Americans, could understand. Something had to succeed a cease-fire.

Soustelle said that in addition to two armed agents in uniform outside his apartment, his home was surveyed regularly by two plainclothes detectives, and, "I am followed a lot of the time—but not always—and my telephone is tapped." I told him of my recent experience with Bidault. He said he had also heard that Bidault was now a wreck.

It was possible he might be arrested, he had no way of knowing. The Constitution was no longer applied. De Sérigny, after all, had been held for more than two months without any regard for the Constitution, although the only charge was that he had written articles the regime didn't like.

Soustelle kept insisting he had no use for conspiracies and that he would never tarnish himself by plotting. Papers like *L'Express* sought to mix him up in every rumored plot.

Soustelle said the French army desperately needed a clear policy on Algeria for which to fight and was confused and lethargic because such a policy had never been laid down. It would be disastrous if the army took things into its own hands and invaded either Tunisia or Morocco in order to extirpate FLN concentrations there. This would only spread the war and would not secure victory.

PARIS, *April 16, 1960*

LONG and pleasant evening with Chip Bohlen and Tommy Thompson. We destroyed half a bottle of 1820 brandy. Tommy insists: Mattei is the most important man in Italy and he is against us. He was, as it were, "for sale." But Mrs. Luce went out of her way to irritate and oppose him, and we must now reckon him as an important opponent.

Tommy is very worried about Berlin and sees nothing we have that we could give to the Russians to keep them quiet there after Eisenhower's trip. They very much want his visit. Tommy also says it would be a mistake to underestimate the seriousness of the growing trouble between Russia and China.

Chip believes we ought to tell Khrushchev he either has to leave Berlin alone or, if he grabs it, we will pass a $100,000,000 defense budget. We must make him see that a "Munich" deal by the West over Berlin would ultimately produce disaster for him.

He told me Dulles went with him to see Eisenhower just before his assignment as ambassador to Moscow. Dulles pompously turned to Chip before the conversation began and asked if Chip wanted him to leave the room. Chip replied that he had nothing to say to the President of the U.S. that he did not want the Secretary of State to hear also. Chip told the President that as an officer in the Foreign Service Association, he felt obliged to call to the President's attention the terrible damage that had been done by McCarthyism to the Foreign Service, and that many officers were thinking of resigning because of the way policy was being applied by an officer in the State Department.

After his opening remarks, Eisenhower said: "I suppose you are referring to Scott McLeod. It was a mistake for us to have taken him, but now that he is there, I think it would do more harm to get rid of him."

PARIS, *April 21, 1960*

AN extensive talk at SHAPE with Norstad. He spoke sharply about de Gaulle and said it is impossible to get him the kind of Big Three directorate he wants, observing: "We can't give de Gaulle a veto power over our own actions." He said Britain and the U.S. no longer had the formal strategic relationship they had during World War II. De Gaulle can never gain our confidence—which is necessary for any closer cooperation—while he keeps talking about France first at the expense of everybody else. If de Gaulle wants to play poker over these things, he should recognize the facts and see that he is in a tough game where, in order to win, you have to have aces up your sleeve; "and he doesn't even have a sleeve to put aces up."

I said this might seem all right from an Anglo-American point of view, but a different psychology was involved. The French don't do things the way we do them. We fight with our fists and they fight with their feet. The British have no constitution; we have had one; the French, with their passion for spelling things out, have had fifteen. De Gaulle wants to get things spelled out again on this directorate.

PARIS, *April 27, 1960*

LAST night at dinner, Pompidou had the following things to say:

There are no real problems—no problems of substance—between France and the U.S.A. France has problems with Russia, Germany, and England—but not with America.

Debré never reads the newspapers, fortunately, and therefore has no idea how much he is mocked. Couve de Murville happily has a good sense of humor and doesn't mind being kidded.

De Gaulle told Khrushchev that both Russia and France were happy to have Germany divided. Neither was afraid of his own Germany. Therefore they should agree to let the Berlin crisis alone and to discuss other things at the summit.

Pompidou was amazed at the frenzied reception given by the United States to de Gaulle. He thought there was something strange about it—it was like a funeral paean; we seemed to speak about de Gaulle as if he were already dead and a figure of history.

De Gaulle is perfectly aware that neither Moscow nor Washington will accept his idea of East-West cooperation to help underdeveloped lands. But he needed to put forward this idea politically because of France's relations with its community.

Pompidou had an odd observation about Algeria. I said I thought that someday it would be associated with France perhaps the way Canada is associated with England. "More like Scotland," said Pompidou.

Pompidou said de Gaulle reasons (and told Khrushchev): The world can have either war or peace; if it isn't war, it is peace—and that means negotiations.

PARIS, *April 28, 1960*

LUNCHED with Billotte. Although de Gaulle waited too long, he has now succeeded in reestablishing firm discipline in the army. Challe was quietly opposing de Gaulle in Algeria but Challe has been replaced. Also the heavily overstaffed headquarters has been moved out of Algiers, thus taking the officers away from the conspiratorial atmosphere.

Pierre says Soustelle is working hard on the army. He has a talent for conspiracy developed when he took over the secret service from Billotte in 1943. He may be expected to group around him the Bidault faction of the MRP, and the right wing of the UNR. This will be a formidable opposition.

PARIS, *April 29, 1960*

LAST night, Chip Bohlen came for dinner, and today we golfed and lunched. Here are some of the things he said as the result of a ten-day visit to Russia, where he was trying to figure out what should be the main trend of the speeches Eisenhower makes on his tour in June. (Chip is going along.)

Bohlen is strongly convinced that in dealing with Russia the U.S. must "prepare for the worst and act for the best." He argues that one cannot have the confidence to act boldly in a diplomatic sense if one is not first prepared for the worst.

He is worried about the effect on our diplomatic position of the missile gap between 1961–1963. We not only have fewer sites, but the Russians know precisely where they are. Khrushchev appears now to be convinced that no *big* countries can be knocked out by surprise attack. This is probably a very important element to be considered in our diplomatic dealings.

Chip says the split between Russia and China is real, but the big question is on timing. When will the two countries really divide? The West cannot act now as if the break that may not come for ten years is already here. That might lead to catastrophe.

And Khrushchev himself is more on the spot than we realized. There was a very tough meeting of the Central Committee in 1959, before his trip to the U.S., in which it was strongly expressed that the idea of such a trip would be undignified because the leader of world communism seemed to court favor in the capitalist citadel.

However, the essential argument is not on policy but on Khrushchev's method of applying policy. There is a feeling that he is too personal. There is resentment against his role of traveling salesman for communism, which is considered unworthy of a Communist leader.

There has been a steady and constant Soviet policy line since the death of Stalin. This started with Malenkov and has been carried on by Khrushchev. We should never forget that only one crisis has been deliberately created by the Russians since Stalin's death; that was over Berlin, and started in November, 1958. All the others—Suez, Hungary, the Lebanon, etc.—sprang from events outside Russian control and were not promoted by the Russians.

We should make very certain Khrushchev realizes that a Russian policy whose success would ultimately be catastrophic is unwise. Thus, Khrushchev could undoubtedly take over West Berlin by nibbling it to death; but when he has Berlin, we will be forced to rearm and war will become probable. Khrushchev doesn't want war.

The only logical explanation of Khrushchev's Berlin maneuvers is that he wants to keep the crisis alive for blackmail purposes, to chisel out such things as the summit conference and the Eisenhower visit, and to be used to apply pressure for other areas. But in his Baku speech this week, Khrushchev behaved very dangerously in dotting the i's on Berlin to a degree never before attempted by him. He seems to have placed himself in a position of being forced to do something on Berlin before too long, or becoming the laughing stock of the Communist world.

If Khrushchev only had Russia to run, we could probably manage things with him. But he is also boss of the nervous Communist bloc. Even Russian leaders have admitted to Chip that only 10 percent of the Soviet population is affected by ideology, and Chip himself says he thinks the figure is nearer 1 percent. We could deal with Russia as Russia, if there were not also the problem of Khrushchev's relationship to external Communist movements.

Stalin told Harry Hopkins that the U.S.A., not Russia, would have to worry about China. He thought it would be our problem because he thought Chiang Kai-shek would head the postwar regime. He underestimated Mao.

One of the great contradictions existing in Moscow's thinking today is that between the assumption that there will be a world triumph of communism and the desire for a bilateral deal with the U.S. to split up the world.

It is important for our policy that we stress that we have no quarrel with Russia as a country. We should emphasize to the Russians that they are subordinating their national interests to a world ideology.

Every society operates on an image of itself at least fifty years out of date. Thus, we find a big contradiction in Russia between the developing Soviet industrial society and the anachronistic system of party rule perfected under totally different circumstances.

The real Russian fear of Germany, although they will never admit it, is the fear of instability in East Germany. West Germany is now getting nuclear arms. If East Germany erupts, the Russians fear the West Germans could not resist the call of *Brüderschaft*, and world war would result.

Chip said that what ended Marshal Zhukov's career and forced his premature retirement was the fact that he had backed Khrushchev. At the famous Presidium meeting where Khrushchev almost lost his power, Zhukov guaranteed him the support of the army. Khrushchev pondered afterward on the fact that one man was in a position to pledge support of the army. He could not afford to let that situation continue.

PARIS, *May 9, 1960*

LUNCHED today with X, who presented me with an interesting thought. U-2 planes, such as that shot down over Russia on May 1, have been overflying the Soviet Union for the last four years. It is possible that, with the Summit coming along and conceivably producing some disarmament agreement, we wanted to have one more extensive mission accomplished before it became impractical to continue in an atmosphere of disarmament.

The Russians have spotted our planes before but were helpless to do anything about them. Their fighters didn't go that high (over twelve miles). We don't seem to know whether the rocket that hit our plane was ground-to-air or sent from a fighter. If it was ground-to-air, it is very worrisome to SAC, not only because it can hit aircraft at such an altitude, but also because there must be lots of them if they had one as far inland as Sverdlovsk.

PARIS, *May 11, 1960*

GOLFED and lunched with Tommy Thompson. He says Khrushchev genuinely thinks we are foolish not to accept his Berlin offer. He reasons that it is impossible for us to hold onto Berlin indefinitely and that by accepting his offer we can gracefully pass the buck.

It would be dangerous for either the West or Russia to have a complete victory or a complete defeat on Berlin. It is imperative to get a compromise that saves face on both sides. We have advertised the importance of West Berlin for so long that we can't just give it up. Khrushchev has recently stressed his intentions to hand over to the East Germans if he can't get a deal, so that he is forced also. Tommy thinks that either an oral compromise or a temporary agreement can and will be worked out at the Summit, and that Eisenhower will go to Russia as planned. The Russian people are terribly excited about the Eisenhower visit.

He doesn't think the Powers U-2 incident will delay it. Although the Russians are advertising it extensively in external propaganda, they are playing it down in internal propaganda. Khrushchev told him a U-2 spy plane flew over Kiev the day after General Twining ended his official visit to the U.S.S.R. in 1956. On April 9, of this year, there was another U-2 which Khrushchev claims they followed on Soviet radar but didn't shoot down. At that time, Khrushchev gave the order to shoot the next one down.

Tommy is disturbed by the military implications of Khrushchev's announcement on the U-2. All the important marshals were assembled in a row behind Khrushchev when he made his disclosure, and they looked grimly satisfied. The marshals are in a tough spot because they dislike the recent Soviet demobilization, which deprives them of the military strength they want and of a certain political influence. Demobilization is unpopular in the army, which hopes to reverse the trend, as a consequence of the U-2 incident.

I asked Tommy why Khrushchev had seemingly gone out of his way to wallop Nixon. Tommy answered, and this was most interesting, by saying that Eisenhower had written Khrushchev a courteous letter explaining that he had an engagement in Portugal and would have to go away at the end of seven days, although he could return to Paris again, and that Nixon would substitute for him. Although this was well intended, it probably wasn't too bright, because we would be a little offended if Khrushchev left Kozlov at the Summit and went off for a few days to Albania.

Nevertheless, Khrushchev saw this as a great opportunity to interfere in the American elections. He doesn't like Nixon anyway and prefers that Rockefeller be the Republican candidate and elected. He values the name Rockefeller as a symbol for the presidency of the United States representing the idea of capitalism. Furthermore, he is still genuinely convinced that Rockefeller represents the real "ruling circles." Also he has the impression that Rockefeller is relatively liberal.

PARIS, *May 12, 1960*

GOLFED and lunched with Tommy Thompson. He believes Khrushchev has decided to escalate the Cold War again and no longer wants Eisenhower to visit Russia. That is how he interprets developments of the last few days in the U-2 case. He is even afraid Khrushchev may come here and talk so sharply that Eisenhower and de Gaulle won't take it and the Summit will break up within a day.

PARIS, *May 13, 1960*

DINED last night with the Thompsons. Khrushchev now seems definitely to have swung to a tough line. There have been two schools in Russia— the tough boys and those who want relaxation. The tough boys have won. These include the army, the so-called Stalinists, and the pro-China group. Khrushchev presumably made his decision because he thinks that in the United States, those who oppose coexistence have come out on top. He interprets the spy plane and the resumption of nuclear tests as confirming this impression.

PARIS, *May 16, 1960*

PARIS has filled up with diplomats, statesmen, journalists for the dramatic Big Four Summit meeting that may, because of U-2, be a bust.

This morning, I had a talk with Yuri Zhukov at the Soviet embassy. Zhukov says the situation is very grave. Khrushchev had come back from America favorably impressed, saying he was an "incorrigible optimist." He was convinced the American people and government wanted peace. The Camp David talks had been successful, and they had even coolly discussed Berlin at length. Furthermore, Khrushchev became persuaded that American "big business" opposed war and accepted the fact that the competition was now economic, not military.

Therefore, the Russians were especially angered by the U-2 incident. They could not understand why May 1, their big holiday, had been selected for the flight. Zhukov asked how we would feel if a Russian plane had been shot down in Texas on Christmas day. In the beginning, Khrushchev deliberately played down previous U-2 flights and isolated this one. He tried to leave a way out for the President by stating he was sure Eisenhower knew nothing about the flight. Therefore he was appalled by Herter's statement that the flights would continue as a matter of policy.

Zhukov says that unless Eisenhower makes a statement reversing that policy and apologizing for the flight, there will be no Eisenhower trip to Russia, and the situation will become even more serious. Khrushchev is furious. He cannot understand why Eisenhower made no effort to see him yesterday before the Summit began.

Tommy Thompson told me yesterday that Zhukov is quite a dangerous figure because he always makes a point of seeing to it that Khrushchev gets the most hostile and inflammatory American newspapers to read.

PARIS, *May 18, 1960*

KHRUSCHCHEV had an extraordinary press conference which resembled a mass political meeting more than anything else. Apart from the microphones and cameras there were about three thousand people present, and it is a tribute to the engineering of the temporary Palais de Chaillot structure that the floor did not collapse.

Khrushchev put on a very good performance. He is a remarkable actor. He got immensely excited and red in the face, shaking his fists, stamping, recalling how his mother used to punish cats who stole cream and saying this had to be done in the U.S. But at other times he was humorous and good natured. Despite his bluster, he didn't stick out his neck, said Russia still desired peaceful solutions to all problems, that West Berlin could remain capitalist, and that although he had a prepared draft for a separate peace treaty with East Germany, it was his secret when he intended to use it. He kept using our peace treaty with Japan (minus Soviet participation) as a precedent.

PARIS, *May 19, 1960*

LUNCHED with Spaak. This morning Couve de Murville, Herter, and Lloyd reported to the NATO council on the abortive Summit. Everybody agrees that NATO is stronger because of sudden new unity. Spaak thought it paradoxical to have Khrushchev responsible for the resurrection of NATO as a result of his press conference given in what was recently NATO headquarters, the Palais de Chaillot.

Spaak thinks a combination of Chinese, Stalinists, and Soviet army pressures forced Khrushchev to change his policy when it became evident he would get nothing from the Summit. The West had made a great mistake in announcing too early that Khrushchev would not get anything. As a result, his enemies were strengthened, and he decided it would be easier to break off the meeting on the excuse of the U-2 incident instead of the excuse of no compromise on Berlin.

We must remember that Khrushchev is a bland and total liar. For example, when he announced his partial demobilization policy he told the Russians that the reason for this was that it would make the Soviet Union militarily stronger by reequipping the smaller army with new weapons on a more effective basis. But when he announced the partial demobilization to the Warsaw Pact allies, he advertised the move as a peace move and a unilateral step toward disarmament. These statements contradict each other completely.

Spaak is convinced that Marshal Malinovsky is here as a kind of watchdog for the army. He never let Khrushchev out of his sight. When Khrushchev went to see de Gaulle, Malinovsky went along. Khrushchev was unable to say anything to anyone that was not heard by Malinovsky.

KHRUSHCHEV

IS ON THE SKIDS

PARIS, *May 20, 1960*

PLEASANT TALK WITH CHRIS HERTER IN THE UPSTAIRS SITTING ROOM of the embassy residence. He looked well considering the strain he has been under. He is a true gentleman and I like him a lot, but I don't think he is a very good Secretary of State.

I asked whether the Summit failure and the new Soviet attitude would affect our approach on disarmament and nuclear testing. Herter said no; our policy remained unchanged. The arms talks in Geneva are supposed to reconvene June 7.

There is no legal distinction between photographic satellites and U-2 reconnaissance. De Gaulle observed to Khrushchev, when the latter was yammering about the U-2, that the latest Soviet satellite crosses France eighteen times a day.

The Russians never brought up our U-2 aerial reconnaissance at any time before this incident. They have made several protests about American overflights, but never the U-2. We had always replied we were prepared to put any of those protests before the Hague World Court.

Herter said de Gaulle was extremely angry with Khrushchev. Both de Gaulle and Macmillan had suggested in their bilateral talks with Khrushchev, after the single explosive Big Four session, that everyone should wait twenty-four hours and try to patch things up. De Gaulle requested that nothing should be given out to the public about what took place, but Khrushchev insisted everything should be made public because his people had to be informed.

Herter told me de Gaulle had talked about the so-called *directoire* during his trip to America, a fact that has not yet emerged publicly. "Also," said Herter unhappily, "I am afraid we are going to hear more about that." Washington wants close consultations among the Big Three but simply cannot put anything on an institutional basis as the French want. The various NATO countries are very much against this.

Gajewski called, very anxious to chat about the Summit. He said the situation is bad in the satellites. If the hard line in Russia becomes stronger, Poland and other eastern European countries will have to go along or else be crushed. Pressure is bound to increase and it is better that this pressure should be applied by Gomulka and Polish leaders rather than Russians. The Poles are in for a very thin time.

It looks as if Khrushchev is now slipping or is on the skids. He has been forced by events to change his policy, and in the hard-boiled world of communism, a man is usually finished when his policy is finished. Nobody can say precisely what was the strongest factor producing this change, but there is certainly no doubt that Chinese influence is growing.

Khrushchev received Gajewski with the other satellite envoys before leaving here. Although it was a private conversation, Khrushchev got so angry when talking about the Americans that he became red in the face and used incredibly foul language. Gajewski had a feeling the man was just a bit unbalanced emotionally: this worries him.

PARIS, *May 23, 1960*

GOLFED, lunched, and dined yesterday with Jock Whitney and Tommy Thompson. Jock told me the American delegation had been extremely worried about Macmillan during the Summit meeting. Macmillan, who seemed to get very emotional and overwrought, was pressing to keep things going when this was obviously no longer possible, and he also wanted Eisenhower to make some kind of apology.

The President took a long drive with Macmillan to visit the village he used to live in, Marnes-la-Coquette. When he got back, Jock asked if he were worried about Macmillan's attitude. "Not at all," the President replied. "I know Harold well and that's just an act he puts on."

Jock said Chip Bohlen, in fact, "ran the show" when the Americans were conferring on policy. Herter relied on him quite openly, and Chip set the policy line including the necessity for restraint and avoiding a slanging match.

PARIS, *May 27, 1960*

FAREWELL lunch with Thompson who goes back to Moscow tomorrow. On May 6, the Russians yanked a pro-Eisenhower article from the scheduled publication of their magazine *U.S.S.R.* (an English-language journal circulated in America). This confirms that the change in policy took place before then. On May 4, there was a meeting of the Central Committee. Obviously the new policy was decided then—to abort the Summit.

Khrushchev is still running the show but is increasingly subject to pressures. Tommy seems more skeptical about his chances of surviving. The big thing now is to find out who controls the police. There is still a very extensive apparatus, although they no longer have their own armored divisions as in the days of Beria.

The boat that Eisenhower was going to give Khrushchev as a gift on his official visit is already in Moscow: a tricky new gadget with no propeller. Tommy would like to use it for the embassy, but there is no chance. The naval attaché was refused permission to have a boat on the river, and there would be even less chance of allowing one that was supposed to belong to Khrushchev.

Tommy said he once talked to Khrushchev about the desirability of having one golf course in Russia, pointing out that apart from the fact that diplomats like to play, it was useful for prestige reasons, since golf was such a well-known game. Khrushchev said he would think the matter over.

PARIS, *June 1, 1960*

LUNCHED today with Maurice and Katie Macmillan. They say with great emphasis—and I suspect this reflects Papa's opinion—that the British Conservative party desperately hopes Adlai Stevenson will be the next American President. If he is not President, they hope Kennedy will be, with Stevenson as Secretary of State. They have a feeling that Stevenson has worldly experience and also values the approach of "understatement." They have no use for Nixon, whom they consider unsubtle and, in a worldly sense, unwise and likely to make wrong decisions and to be influenced by the wrong people.

CADENABBIA, ITALY, *June 4, 1960*

THIS morning, I spent two hours with Adenauer, who is vacationing here in a villa above the lake. The property is very pleasant, but the villa itself is quite simple. His life seems agreeable and rustic—if one can forget the secret-service men hovering around. We sat on a terrace looking down over Lake Como, where we had coffee and chatted away. Weber acted as interpreter. Adenauer explained this was a good corner "because nobody can hear us."

Talking about Khrushchev, he said:

Khrushchev has lost his mind. That happens to all dictators. [He was referring to the Soviet Prime Minister's recent crude remarks in which he suggested Adenauer should be put in a straitjacket and Eisenhower should be placed in charge of a kindergarten.]

Khrushchev is a good man. He always helps us. And he helps you too. Now you Americans will be in a position to get over the dangerous months while you are choosing your new President. I always fear that period. Thanks to Khrushchev's hard line, we don't have to worry anymore. Now you should just let things take their natural course. Don't try to push things; let them settle down.

I remarked that there were many people who consider that the only "winners" from the Summit failure were Adenauer and Mao Tse-tung—the two men who were not there. Adenauer made no effort to deny that he himself was a "winner." "But," he said, "I don't think Mao won. Soviet policy hasn't changed."

Adenauer thought the influence of the army on Khrushchev was more important than the influence of China. He said with a cynical smile: "I think high-ranking officers in any army are opposed both to war and to disarmament. That is true in all countries you can name, and of course Russia."

He explained Khrushchev's decision to torpedo the Summit meeting accordingly:

I think it was a combination of things. To begin with, American planes had been carrying out flights over Russia for several years and the U.S.A. had good pictures of all Soviet military preparations. This fact shocked Khrushchev and his army. Therefore, he wanted to show the army that in spite of this situation he was not afraid of the Americans. Possibly, fright played its role in Khrushchev's attitude. One doesn't know this because he is such a good actor. In fact, he is the best actor I have ever seen. But we can be sure that he and the army were impressed by the fact that the U.S. could take those pictures.

However, Adenauer doesn't seem to think Soviet policy has changed in any serious sense, and he takes a rather reasonable view of Khrushchev's new disarmament proposal. It would be a mistake just to dismiss the new Soviet plan as another bit of propaganda. It contained some useful new points of departure.

"For months," said Adenauer, "I have been in favor of controlling the means of delivery of atomic warheads. The military and the scientists don't like this approach, but, in fact, it can be very easily effected." (Of course, this is de Gaulle's idea. It is interesting to note how close Bonn and Paris work together nowadays.)

Adenauer continued: "In making his new proposal, Khrushchev inherently implies he is ready to accept controls of disarmament. If you reach that point, the force of reality will help in the end to make serious disarmament progress possible."

Adenauer was also struck by the fact that Khrushchev had, for the first time, conceded that a UN police force might be desirable and had mentioned that even after disarmament Russia might make available units to such an international peace force.

"These are all interesting points," said Adenauer. "There are undoubtedly some kernels in Khrushchev's plan that can be picked out. We should study these carefully, but we should not try and go too fast. We don't really have to do anything until after your presidential elections because Khrushchev has given us time."

I asked Adenauer whether he thought Khrushchev was really a big man or not. His reply was this: "Every dictator knows only his own country and he looks at the world from a misleading angle. We had this experience ourselves with Hitler. And this is true in the instance of Khrushchev. He is not a man of foresight and vision. Of course, from a Russian point of view, he tries to build up Russia and to strengthen his country, but in a world sense he is not a big man."

I asked Adenauer why he thought Khrushchev had such a personal hatred for him. Adenauer replied: "I think it is rather a mixture of hatred and liking, although I fear hatred is predominant. During my Moscow visit, at first we had a good quarrel, but later on Khrushchev gave me the feeling that he had a certain trust for me, even if it wasn't really a liking."

We then went on to a discussion of European unity prospects which Adenauer thinks have been helped by the new Khrushchev tough line. During the past two years, "essential progress" had been made toward European unity. De Gaulle's recent speeches favored it. He had been worried about de Gaulle as an opponent of this cause, but there was no doubt that since he had taken power in 1958, de Gaulle had become a powerful ally of the cause.

I asked him what would be England's role in this new Europe. He said: "Of course, that is England's affair. But we would be highly pleased if she came in with the Common Market powers. We must be cautious not to disturb things in Europe; we must grow organically from within, and nobody should be pressed to play a particular role."

I asked about the relationship of a unified Europe to Africa. (It is clear Adenauer has given certain promises on Africa to de Gaulle in exchange for promises by de Gaulle to Adenauer on Europe.) Adenauer said: "Africa is a vital necessity to Europe. I hope truly from my heart that developments in Africa will promote close ties to be established between that continent and Europe."

I then asked how he thought Germany, which had, after all, lost all its colonies two generations ago and was therefore no longer tarred with anticolonialism, could help. Couldn't Germany send experts and technicians while French and British and Belgians might not be welcome?

Adenauer complained there was a shortage of manpower in West Germany and there were simply not enough men in the age group providing technicians to send any great quantity. This is the age group from which so many were lost during the last war. "We are prepared to help," he said. "But this must be done within the limits and possibility of reason."

During the whole conversation Adenauer paid special tribute to de Gaulle. He thought his twelve years in Colombey had done him immense good and that now he was the ablest statesman in the West.

When I was about to leave and the old man came to the steps with me, I asked him what music he was playing here because I knew he had brought quite a collection of discs along. He replied that far and away his favorite composer was Haydn. After that, he liked Beethoven, Schubert, Mozart, and Vivaldi. Oddly enough, he didn't like Bach.

GENEVA, *June 6, 1960*

LUNCHED today with Frederick Eaton, the lawyer in charge of our disarmament-negotiations delegation. James Wadsworth, U.S. delegate to the nuclear negotiations, joined us afterward at Eaton's villa in the country. Eaton said the Soviet disarmament plan announced by Khrushchev is not really new but the only sensible way to treat it is as if it were a move toward the western point of view. We must probe it.

Eaton said there is no doubt that the Russians really *fear* the Germans and are afraid Bonn could assume a provocative leadership in the western world. For this reason, the Russians are especially eager to disarm the West Germans. We could get concessions from the Russians if we refused nuclear arms to Bonn. The Russians are also eager to keep China out of the nuclear club.

During previous negotiations, as in 1958, the Russians were genuinely afraid that the U.S. would give nuclear aid to France and thus force Russia to give aid to China. That is why the French put up a counter-proposition they knew we can't live with—the control of the means of delivery. We can't take this because our deterrent would be crippled. The French deliberately wished to throw everything into a stalemate when we brought up the ideas of an atomic cutoff and manpower reductions (which they can't afford because of the Algerian war).

GENEVA, *June 7, 1960*

THIS afternoon, I had a long talk with David Ormsby-Gore, Katie Macmillan's brother and head of the British delegation to the disarmament talks. He said Russia is interested in conventional disarmament and will have to do it unilaterally anyway. In the early days of disarmament negotiations, Moscow wanted to ban the nuclear bomb because it felt an inferiority; it no longer feels this.

The Russians have a good all-round defense position with both conventional and nuclear arms. This gives the Russians a base for a flexible negotiating position.

The French don't want conventional disarmament discussed because of Algeria. Previously they were committed to cutting their own forces to 750,000 and eventually 650,000. (They are now over a million.) The French use the argument that conventional forces are not important in a nuclear world.

We have all said that once the development of nuclear weapons has continued for years without control—as at present—there is no means of *knowing* if stockpiles have been eliminated under any international agreement. You can't control the elimination of stockpiles without thousands of men searching all over the Soviet Union and other countries.

We must be careful not to let the Russians try to eliminate our deterrent before there is an effective balance of terror and a stable situation. Also, it would do no good merely to eliminate nuclear weapons and restore the unhealthy situation of the 1930s, with large conventional forces. Any so-called conventional war of the great powers would start a nuclear war eventually. Even if you eliminate all nuclear weapons, you cannot eliminate the scientists who know how to make them, and within a year these weapons would be back in production. The essential is to preserve a general military balance.

Russia has given China no nuclear arms. All four of the big powers want to keep China out of the nuclear club.

PARIS, *June 20, 1960*

SPENT the weekend at Diana Cooper's. André de Staercke, the Belgian NATO ambassador was there. De Staercke indiscreetly says he has seen the basic U.S. war plan which provides that in case of a nuclear war we shall destroy China first. In other words, there isn't going to be any chance of Peking's dream that the U.S. and Russia will knock each other out and China will inherit the earth.

André says there is an unholy row going on in NATO about missile defense. Under the 1957 plan, it was agreed that IRBMs would be established in Europe in sufficient numbers to serve as a deterrent. Since then, details have been worked out and the Polaris is the desired weapon because it is a movable, solid-fuel missile, with sufficient range and can be shifted around constantly on railway cars, trailers, and even canal boats.

It was furthermore agreed that three hundred IRBMs should do the trick. One hundred and fifty of these should be based in France. Messmer, French defense minister, says that France would agree only if one out of three of the one hundred and fifty Polarises here were made available to France as apart from NATO. France would supply its own nuclear warheads for these fifty missiles. But the U.S. doesn't want to give any missiles to France on a bilateral basis because it doesn't want to lose control of the warheads. It wants a NATO striking force, not a French striking force.

PARIS, *June 24, 1960*

THIS morning, Allen Dulles said we don't believe the Russians are planning a war for any particular date, if at all. However, they are developing a substantial nuclear missile capacity and are not giving up on the production of bombers, although they are not making as many as we had thought they would.

They are beginning to have a potential in the long-range missile field. We think we have monitored *all* their missile tests so far. They have plenty of range and can reach all of the U.S. from central Siberia. We are approaching a period of nuclear-missile stalemate.

The Russians are too smart to put bases in Cuba. They realize these would be strategically indefensible. They seek an economic hold and they hope to develop trade, like oil and sugar. We don't consider Castro a Communist, although he is playing the Moscow line. Che Guevara is a Communist.

Dulles is sure Gary Powers was not shot down at normal altitude (above 70,000 feet). The U-2, when it reaches rarefied altitudes, tends to get a flame-out. We think Powers glided down to try and restart his motor. He was then shot down around 30,000–40,000 feet. Present Soviet defenses don't go above 60,000 feet. We think Powers parachuted. He *never* broke radio contact.

Dulles explained the ideological quarrel between China and Russia in these terms. Peking thinks coexistence is dangerous to the Communist system. Stalin thought this; so does Ulbricht of East Germany. The Chinese feel they cannot maintain needed controls if it becomes official Communist policy to say that both systems are good, theirs and ours. This makes for fundamental cleavage with Russia.

The Russians were debating what to do about the U-2. They knew the U-2 had been shot down by noon on May 1, Soviet time, yet until May 5, they didn't say a word, only that a plane had been shot down. On May 7, the first big blast came. Mikoyan wanted to shove the whole thing under the rug and just send a diplomatic note, but he was overruled. Perhaps the reason was that this incident helped to dodge the Berlin question at an inconvenient moment. It also helped Khrushchev in his quarrel with the hard-line boys.

Dulles suspects that China has a long-range policy of wanting to plant colonies of five to ten million people in different places around the world, such as Algeria or Latin America. This would help get rid of their surplus population and would also increase their global power. Human beings are the greatest Chinese product. Overseas Chinese colonies could be established all round to help take over world power later on.

PARIS, *June 25, 1960*

LAST night at dinner, I had a long talk with Bourgès-Maunoury, former Prime Minister and defense minister, now up to his ears in Soustelle's Algérie Française group. He had seen Allen Dulles this week and, to his astonishment, Dulles was very optimistic about Cuba, saying that if things got worse there the people would throw out Castro and come back to our side.

He had two good talks with Ben Gurion during Ben Gurion's visit here. (Bourgès was one of the key figures in the French plot to help Israel in the Suez campaign of 1956.) Ben Gurion said Israel would be wrecked if it were not surrounded by hostile Arabs. Enmity of the Arabs produces greatness and vigor among the Israelis right now. If Israel were suddenly friends with all its neighbors it would lose steam and be absorbed.

Bourgès is terribly gloomy about Algeria. The ultimate result will be independence and a great many of the Europeans, plus at least two million pro-French Muslims, will be driven out. Almost inevitably this will be followed by a revolution in France.

LOS ANGELES, *July 12, 1960*

INTERESTING talk today with George Weaver, a Negro labor leader working in Stu Symington's campaign for the Democratic nomination. He saw an analogy between the American Negroes' reaction to African freedom and American Jewish feelings toward Israel; "Negro Zionism" was of a broader variety. African independence had stimulated pride among American Negroes and identification with and interest in Africa.

African leaders are fascinated and repelled by the United States—fascinated by the standard of living and repelled by discrimination. There is a growing interest among American Negroes in geneology. The new young generation for the first time takes pride in being black.

The African independence movement had a direct effect on the American Negro sit-in movement. This, based on a kind of distorted Gandhi philosophy, sprang up spontaneously after the 1956 Montgomery, Alabama, bus strike, and was the original inspiration of Martin Luther King. The present movement was primarily conducted by college students from successful, middle-class Negro families, and the youngsters are strongly supported by their families. The Negro protest movements of the early 1930s were essentially led by poor elements and centered primarily on economic injustices. Now the middle class is in the van. The kids feel this is to be a part of a world-wide students' movement.

Hitherto, the American Negro middle class had, in fact, possessed a vested interest in segregation. The doctor, lawyer, dentist, teacher, minister all had a ready-made market, thanks to segregation. The eighteen million American Negroes have a population and purchasing power larger than that of Canada.

Long talk with Symington in his hideout at the Sheraton-West. He was lounging in a dressing gown and we spent a couple of hours drinking and chatting, while his wife, in the next room, answered the telephone.

Stu assured me he would rather stay in the Senate than run for the vice presidency (which I don't quite believe). He was still running hard for President. I said I didn't want to be impolite, but it did not look as if he had any chance. He commented ruefully: "It is never impolite to tell the truth."

In the lobby coming out, I ran into George Ball, who is working hard for Stevenson. He took me up to Adlai's rooms, which, rather pathetically, had a brass plate on the door marked "Presidential Suite." There I saw Bill Blair and Tom Finletter. Ball claims there is still a slim chance of holding Kennedy; that Kennedy is like Nixon: a cold, efficient man with a methodical machine, but the applause of the people is for Adlai.

Ball says Bowles is working very hard to be Secretary of State if Kennedy wins. Many people are now confiding to Kennedy that Adlai would be a bad Secretary of State.

LOS ANGELES, *July 14, 1960*

JACK Kennedy got the nomination and today I spent three fascinating hours in his suite at the Biltmore while the Democratic bigwigs and bosses were consulted, some in groups, others one by one, to decide on who would be the nominee for Vice President. The business was transacted in the next room. In the larger sitting room where I sat, the bosses, governors, senators, and mayors waited and talked with each other, drinking gallons of coffee until Jack called them in. Jack himself came out several times. I was the only newspaperman present. Originally, I had an appointment to see Kennedy at 12:30, but my date got lost in the rush.

I was there from 12 noon until 3:00 P.M. Earlier that morning, Jack had gone to see Lyndon Johnson in his suite and had offered him the vice presidential nomination, which Johnson accepted. But I did not know this while sitting there, nor did any of those around me. Among them were Adlai Stevenson, Senator "Scoop" Jackson, Chet Bowles, Senator Smathers, Governor Abe Ribicoff, Governor Loveless, Governor Combs of Kentucky, and Governor Dave Lawrence of Pennsylvania.

Jack had his own team of young hatchet-men scurrying about, including his brothers Bobby and Teddy, his brother-in-law Sargent Shriver (a handsome young man who looks like Ribicoff), and Larry O'Brien, who is one of his oldest and most intimate political operators. I asked Larry who was the oldest member of this Kennedy team, and said: "I guess me; I am forty-three, the same age as Jack."

Jackson assured me at about 12:30 (at least two hours after the deal had been made with Johnson) that the vice presidential choice had narrowed to a contest between himself and Symington. Little did he know.

Poor Loveless was kept cooling his heels for two hours and then went in to make a pitch for the vice presidential nomination. He was the last. By the time he got in, there was only one other fellow besides myself and a Mexican waiter serving coffee and cookies. I turned to the other fellow, commenting: "I wonder what Loveless is doing in there; the race is only between Johnson and Symington." The young man said: "Don't forget Loveless. I am from Iowa and I work with Loveless. He wants to be Vice President and he has a good chance."

As soon as Adlai Stevenson came in, accompanied by Bill Blair, who was limping with a bum knee, a phone call was placed for Mrs. Roosevelt, and both Adlai and Jack spoke to her. Kennedy is obviously trying to pull the party together again after the nomination fight.

There was an impressive atmosphere of youth, with the kids taking over from the old party bosses. Jack himself gave an impression of calm, decisive, efficient politeness. He looked amazingly healthy, considering the strain he has been under.

O'Brien remarked to me, "The old generation is gone—Mrs. FDR, Truman, Stevenson. Look around you and you will see the new generation that will be running the party."

Later, I had another long talk with Chet Bowles. I had breakfast with him two days ago and saw him again yesterday. We had argued the foreign-policy plank at length. He was very angry with a column I wrote on this.

He frankly admitted he would like to be Secretary of State and would *not* like to be ambassador to UN, because "I am no good at debating." He wants to reassure the Russians that we are prepared for exploratory talks on ways to solve mutual problems. We must strengthen American military

power but assume an easier attitude on bases and slowly begin to replace them with new defense methods. We must understand how the
Russians feel with a ring of American bases around them close to their
borders. While we take a tougher military position, the Russians should be
reassured of an easier American policy on bases.

We must recognize there are three influences at work in Communist
China: communism; national-independence feeling; and resentment toward
"have" countries by a "have-not" country. The last two points would
have existed even if Chiang Kai-shek were running China. The people of
Asia understand this. We should stress these last two points in our approaches, and stop harping on communism.

We must get India associated with us in some kind of Asian Monroe
Doctrine type of guarantees. This is a five- or ten-year program.

This afternoon, I had a nice but sad talk with poor old Adlai in his
"Presidential Suite" at the Sheraton-West. He was drafting a statement on
Lyndon Johnson's nomination for the vice presidency.

When he arrived at Los Angeles airport and was greeted by a huge
and enthusiastic delegation, this was "a most shattering experience, the
best of my political life." He kept stressing that he hadn't actively
sought the nomination here and had no delegates. But he "realized"
now that if Kennedy had not been able to get the nomination on the first
ballot, he would have begun to lose votes, would have been blocked,
and the Stevenson movement would have won.

I asked if he would agree to serve as Secretary of State should Kennedy win. He said he would first like to have a briefing on a number of
Jack's views on different issues. Jack has never asked him to be Secretary, but he has made several public statements to the effect that any
Democratic President (candidate) would want Stevenson for that job.

"But he never said this to *me*," said Adlai, "although there have been
many indirect messages sent through governors or other people."

Adlai said, apropos of his candidacy here (now you see it, now you
don't):

I thought it would be impertinent of me to seek a third nomination.
It would have been immodest and selfish to presume. At least Bryan
let eight years go by between his second and third nominations. I don't
have that much time.

I told everyone this year that I would not come out for anyone.
Neutrality is the best position for the titular leader of the party. And
now that the choice has been made, I am glad to leave the scene to the
accompaniment of applause.

I asked if he would tell me who he had in mind as the Secretary
of State in 1952 and 1956. He hesitated a moment and then said: "I

will tell you this in strict confidence, but you are the only person who has ever known. I was thinking of Bill Fulbright, for whom I have great admiration, but I never even told him—then or now. I am sure he would not have accepted in 1952, because he wanted to solidify his position in Arkansas and insure that he could be reelected so as to establish the basis for a career. Of course, Chet Bowles has always been hungry for the job, and he still is."

I asked if Adlai should become Secretary of State in January, would he try and guarantee that our ambassadors to Paris, Rome, Bonn, Madrid, and similar capitals would speak the local language. He said it was difficult to find men for these jobs under present laws and appropriations, because, as things are, personal wealth was required. But in other areas, he would favor career diplomats. By and large, professionals were the best.

Stevenson said he had found in Latin America a general feeling that a revolution was overdue in Cuba, where big business, as throughout Latin America, has been working for selfish U.S. interests. He thought the Eisenhower administration has been doing all right in handling the Cuban crisis. During his Latin American tour, he had been depressed by the insensitive attitude of American businessmen and Washington tactlessness. We had decorated Latin American dictators for their bloody threats.

Eisenhower had not realized on his South American tours that he was played up as a hero simply because instructed crowds had greeted him. The American press had erred in giving a distorted picture and reporting that everything was hunkydory and Ike was loved. Stevenson had contempt for Milton Eisenhower, who "ran around Latin America seeing little, learning nothing, and reporting to the President that all was well."

LOS ANGELES, *July 15, 1960*

THIS afternoon, I had a talk with Jack Kennedy in his hideaway at the Beverly Hilton, where he was resting and preparing to make his acceptance speech this evening. Jack has hotel suites scattered all over this sprawling town.

This morning, he asked me to come out to the Beverly Hilton ($6 cab money each way). I rode out with three members of the New York Liberal party: Arthur Goldberg, lawyer for the AFL-CIO; Paul Hayes, chairman of the Liberal party; and Alex Rose, clothing union president. They were perturbed by the addition of Johnson to the ticket. If the Liberal party had to make up its mind today, only 50 percent would back the Democrats. But they have a party convention in September, and they hope to reduce the opposition to Johnson.

Kennedy received us at the door of his suite, and I sat in the bedroom while he talked to the Liberals. Congressman Torbert MacDonald, former Harvard football player and Jack's close friend, joined me. In another room, a couple of guys, including Larry O'Brien, were working on the final draft of Kennedy's speech.

When the Liberals left, Jack came in and sat on the bed across from me. He was exceptionally friendly. I must say he is impressive (looking much younger than forty-three years): about half an inch taller than six feet, slim and athletic in build, and remarkably fit and healthy looking considering what he has been through this week. He is clearly a man who can make up his mind (unlike Adlai), and he does so quickly without the slightest hesitation. He is bright and self-confident, and I think he is willing to learn. He is frank to admit there are lots of things he does not know yet. He has a high, nasal Bostonian twang and speaks quite rapidly. Our conversation was limited to foreign affairs.

He told me he does not plan any trips abroad either before election day or, should he win, before inauguration day. I asked when he intended to announce his choice as a potential Democratic Secretary of State. "Right after the election," he replied. I asked if it were a fair assumption that either Bowles or Stevenson would be his choice, and he said this was "sound speculation." I feel he will probably be using Adlai as much as he can until the elections; but in the end, Bowles, who is a tougher character and got on the bandwagon earlier, will be the choice.

He was determined, if elected, to choose the best possible ambassadors. These would not necessarily be diplomats from the foreign service, but he favored maximum use of career men. In any case, he would certainly try to get the best available. This would not mean the men who had made the largest political contributions, but the best available for the particular post. Experience and linguistic ability would weigh heavily in these choices. It was especially desirable to have a really good envoy to NATO. But he did not elaborate.

He strongly favored lengthening the period of budgeting to permit the United States to accumulate larger sums for longer periods than one year for foreign aid, so that other countries we wished to help could plan on a long-range basis instead of a year-to-year basis. He had vigorously supported the idea of the Development Loan Fund, and would like to push the idea further. He would suggest enabling legislation to this effect.

I told him that once I had suggested to President Eisenhower that it might be of great help if the government were legally in a position to draft civilians for special service abroad; that Ike had heartily endorsed the idea, but had never done anything with it. What did Jack think of it and would he do something? He dodged this and said only that he thought Senator Humphrey's plan for students to work abroad for a year after graduation was a good idea.

I then asked if he did not think that in this nuclear-missile era, it was wise to shorten the period of U.S. political campaigns in order to have a much briefer lame-duck period of government. Jack gave a practical politician's answer. He did not wish to see us give up our system of primaries and did not see how we could reduce the period without so doing. And, he added, a grin on his face, if it had not been for primaries, he would not have gotten the nomination.

He pointed out that in our country, "Parties are not everything as in England. What is most important is the man himself and what the man thinks and does. For this reason, I do not see how we can change things." Before going, Jack suggested I get in touch with him later in the summer so that we could talk at greater length. "We need ideas," he said. "If you've got any, please pass them on."

CHICAGO, *July 19, 1960*

LAST night, I went out with Senator John and Lorraine Cooper. John was immediately tied up in politics, so I took Lorraine to dinner, and he joined us afterward. He is in charge of the foreign-affairs plank for the Republican platform committee.

John wants to face the problems of the 1960s, not recriminations for the 1950s. I strongly urged him to include in the plank one item on indirect aggression (I recommended that he study the treaty draft offered by Russia to France and England in August, 1939); also another section defining free air and territorial air limits and pledging an international conference on this. These things were basic to the coming decade and needed attention. Foreign countries paid attention to our political platforms even if the American people did not.

He expressed discontent and disgust with the Eisenhower administration and its lazy lack of leadership; he hoped Nixon would do better. Chris Herter had been a great disappointment as Secretary of State. He is sure Dillon would be Nixon's Secretary of State and first class.

Before he joined us, Lorraine said that while they were in India, when John was ambassador, they had visited a female Swami who believed in reincarnation. The Swami persuaded her that John, in prior lives, had once been a red Indian and another time "a powerful and evil force in old Egypt."

CHICAGO, *July 22, 1960*

RAN into Harold Stassen so I brought him up to the room for a drink. The poor guy wanders around "lonely as a cloud," totally ignored by his Republican colleagues.

Stassen said he had affection and respect for Foster Dulles, but they had disagreed on many things and Dulles opposed *all* agreements with Russia. Adenauer egged him on. As a result, when Stassen was leading our delegation at disarmament talks in London, Dulles flew over and ended the talks, pulling the rug out from under Stassen.

Cooper called to say cheerily that he had gotten through his subcommittee the ideas we had discussed for the platform. This afternoon, he will meet representatives of Nixon and the State Department, but he is sure they will accept his draft. He told me to call at 6:30 at the committee meeting room and not to give my name (because they are pledged against leaks) but to say that it is urgent. Then he will tell me whether everything is OK, and I can write a column on it. At 6:30 he called and said there were "complications."

CHICAGO, *July 24, 1960*

GOOD talk with Governor Rockefeller. On foreign policy, he said it was hard to tell whether Nixon had in any way changed his mind by accepting the fourteen-point platform agreement the two men worked out yesterday in New York. Certainly Nixon had agreed with Rockefeller on the essential points needed to face the challenge of a changing world. But there were basic disagreements.

On their military plan, the only remaining question is the sum needed to meet the needs. Both men say no budget ceiling should be allowed to determine our defense needs. They agree on the need for a retaliatory (second-strike) force and civil defense. Rockefeller again stressed how lack of adequate civil defense weakens a country's international position and therefore its policy effectiveness.

He said Nixon accepted his idea of large regional confederations. This would, if carried out, inspire people both abroad and at home with the reality of our leadership and give them new confidence. It reaches into the political aspect of our foreign policy, which has recently been stressing only the military and economic aspects.

He'd like to see a start made "immediately" in the western hemisphere. "I'd like to see us call for a conference on this next month, to discuss common objectives and goals. And I'd like to see the next Congress approve a kind of Marshall Plan for the Americas. I would like to see a common market among the OAS nations. When all this was accomplished, we would be strong enough to meet the Castro problem."

Rockefeller thought NATO could quickly be transformed into a confederation also. And eventually Africa, the Middle East, South Asia, etc. (What an optimist! What a simplifier! But maybe this kind of bland overconfidence would be helpful.) "There is," he said, "a need for nations to join together. The old structure of empire is gone. The Soviets have offered a new structure and the free world hasn't met the challenge yet by offering anything new of its own."

ASPEN, COLORADO, *August 17, 1960*

DR. James R. Killian came to dinner with his wife after we had had an unsuccessful afternoon of fishing. He said Eisenhower will make a summary of his administrative experiences and a series of recommendations concerning the practice of government at the end of his term. He will recommend creation of a new post—First Secretary of Government—to coordinate all branches of defense and foreign policy. (This sounds almost like creating a Prime Minister.)

NEW YORK, *September 16, 1960*

CARL Sandburg, a fine, salty, immodest octogenarian, had three amusing stories to tell:

One of the current presidential candidates (guess which) was asked, "Were you born in a log cabin?" He answered, "No, that was Abraham Lincoln: I was born in a manger."

Old Man Scripps left instructions that since he would probably die while voyaging around the world on his yacht, he wanted to insure that he was buried at sea. This is just what happened. When the news came in, a linotypist on one of his papers commented sourly, "You know why the Old Man did this? So that nobody would piss on his grave."

Sandburg swears the following is true, but he couldn't put it in his book unless he bowdlerized it. It was told to him by one of the Hay family, Milton Hay. Lincoln, as a young man, was defending a man in court. His opponent attacked the sanity of Lincoln's client saying: "He is a strange man. Why he even stands in his house and pisses in the street." Lincoln got up in rebuttal and said: "What's so strange about that? Wouldn't it be even stranger if he stood in the street and pissed into his house?" The case was dismissed.

Saw Averell Harriman, who got back this morning from Africa and France. I'm convinced he is running hard to be Secretary of State. He said Stevenson doesn't have a chance, that Bowles is well ahead in the race. Then he proceeded to knock Bowles. "He doesn't know anything about Africa and his ideas are crazy," said Averell. "It is appalling that in the eight new countries applying from Africa for membership in UN, the entire American diplomatic representation is comprised of two consul generals." He is dead right.

He says the Russians have given sixteen aircraft and quite a few trucks to Lumumba to transport his army and have surrounded him with advisors. However, if we take a tough line, Averell thinks the Russians will recognize a lost cause and get out. He warned the Soviet ambassador in Léopoldville that the U.S. would not allow the Congo to become a Russian satellite.

NEW YORK, *September 20, 1960*

DRINKS with Bohlen. Chip thinks Nixon is prattling when he says the country is doing beautifully in the international power race and that we never had it so good.

Khrushchev's main desire here is to demonstrate to the entire Communist world the diplomatic strength and power of the Soviet Union, so that all Communists will recognize that only Russia is orthodox and only Russia is the boss in the Communist hierarchy. The idea is to put China in its place.

The fight between China and Russia is the most important aspect of Khrushchev's visit. China needs a foreign devil and a tough line because of its internal problems, but this is not required by Russia. The Chinese don't like to see the Russians aiding bourgeois nationalist governments in Africa and other areas.

Bohlen is convinced Russia will risk a break with China if Peking doesn't knuckle under. The recent exchanges are strikingly similar to those between Moscow and Belgrade before the Tito-Stalin break.

NEW YORK, *September 22, 1960*

DINED with Bohlen. On August 22, 1956, General Kenneth Strong (British military intelligence) told him: "If you ever hear that we have mounted an expedition against Nasser, pray for us because we haven't got the stuff to do it properly."

He says the big question between Moscow and China is: Should one put peace ahead of revolution?

NEW YORK, *September 24, 1960*

LUNCHED with Selim Sarper who, as foreign minister, heads the Turkish UN Assembly delegation. Trials of the leaders of the previous regime will probably start next month. The principals, including former President Bayar, former Prime Minister Menderes, former Foreign Minister Zorlu will be liable to the death penalty. Sarper asked me what the reaction here would be if they were executed. I said it would be better if the sentences were commuted.

Sarper says Bayar is the real villain, that Menderes is emotionally unbalanced, and Zorlu is a schizophrenic. Menderes was planning to fire Zorlu and replace him with Sarper. Lucky for Selim that this didn't happen too soon. (I remember the times in the past when Sarper told me what great guys Menderes and Zorlu were.)

He has intense distrust for Nasser and says the British and the French were fools to intervene in the Suez war, because the Israelis alone could have finished the job. It is unfortunate that Russia is in a position to intervene or we could tell Israel to take a second crack now.

NEW YORK, *September 27, 1960*

LUNCH with Aleksei Adzhubei, editor of *Izvestia*; Pavel Satyoukov, editor of *Pravda*; and Mikhail Kharvlamov, head of the foreign ministry press section. A futile exercise in polemics. Adzhubei, Khrushchev's son-in-law, a broad, stocky, powerful man, held forth with brutal, foolish, aggressive propaganda, almost in the Orwellian sense of "doublethink."

He insisted that Russia and the United States should, in effect, divide up the world on a 50-50 basis. I asked: "How about the countries that have no use for either of us?" He said that didn't matter. He harped along the old line that the future belongs to Russia; that we could make seven million automobiles here if we wanted, but that they were producing twice as many scientists.

NEW YORK, *October 1, 1960*

DINED last night at John Gunther's. Tom Finletter was complaining about the influence of Arthur Schlesinger in the Kennedy campaign. He was most distressed by Arthur's behavior in dropping Stevenson much too early. Ken Galbraith was far more open about his support of Kennedy. Galbraith told Finletter, "I am a Massachusetts Democrat who is interested in politics, so obviously I was in Jack's camp from the start."

Finletter thought it unlikely Stevenson would be Kennedy's choice as Secretary of State, because Kennedy would not want a man who is better known abroad than he.

This morning, I had a long talk with Lord Home, the new British foreign secretary, in his Waldorf Towers suite. It was most informal and easy. We sat on a large sofa, from which he removed a litter of documents. He is a thin, tall man who, underneath his easygoing courtesy, gives an impression of intelligence and a certain tensile strength.

Home thinks Khrushchev's basic objectives in this UN meeting are, first of all, to fight for the Congo and, secondly, to restrict the powers of the Secretary-General. If he can get Lumumba back into power, then he can push Lumumba into an attack on Katanga and we will have a Korean situation right on the borders of British central Africa. If he can force a change in the powers of the Secretary-General, it will be much easier for him to achieve his Congo aims.

Khrushchev explained to Macmillan that he thought the Secretary-General of UN was too powerful. He implied that he fears he might one day become as powerful a man in the world as the President of the United States or the Prime Minister of Russia.

Khrushchev has by no means given up his aspirations in the Congo. Home was astonished at the effectiveness with which the Russians got their agents there so speedily. They had hundreds there at the time they were turned out and hundreds more were actually on the way.

Not only would Khrushchev's Congo efforts become easier if he could clip Hammarskjöld's wings, but it might also facilitate his position later on in Berlin. If the Berlin problem is eventually turned into a UN operation, it would be much more difficult for the Soviet position if UN were an effective, strong force.

Khrushchev is willing to have inspection of the actual process of disarmament. That is to say, if each side agrees to destroy one thousand rockets, Khrushchev is prepared to bring the thousand rockets to Moscow and let the inspectors watch him burn them. But he is not willing to have inspection of what remains available after these rockets are burned. He claims that he is ready to have complete inspection after there is complete disarmament; but he won't agree to anything in the middle.

Home expressed confidence that Nkrumah can be brought back to a more prowestern attitude. He said:

> Nkrumah does not want communism in Africa. After all, he is a good, old-fashioned, imperialist himself. He wants to be a big noise in Africa. And communism would defeat this aspiration. Nkrumah wants to create a system under his leadership which can balance off Nigeria both politically and economically. He tried to join up with Guinea and this failed through incompetence. The same thing happened vis-à-vis Togo. As a result, he has now been trying to build up Lumumba as an ally. What he wanted was to have Lumumba take over Katanga and nationalize the copper mines, giving Ghana a share.

Nkrumah is an extraordinarily conceited man. Home had been appalled by the inscription on the statue of Nkrumah erected in Accra. It says: "Seek yet first a political kingdom and the rest shall be added unto." Nkrumah "allows" the controlled press of Ghana to refer to him as "the Messiah." It was Nkrumah's vanity that led him to think that the placing of Soviet technicians in the Congo would help him and therefore he allowed the Russian planeloads through. His egotism encourages him to believe he can control the Communists.

Home said the Russians and the Chinese were making a "dead set" at Africa and that Chinese penetration is "very serious" in both the Middle East and North Africa. He simply doesn't know whether the Russians are worried about this or not. However, he added, "There is a real Chinese-Russian row on now."

NEW YORK, *October 3, 1960*

CHIP Bohlen sees a frightening comparison between the present situation and 1938. Khrushchev is trying to scare all neutral nations that the choice is between peace or war, the way Hitler turned the heat on Chamberlain. We should make it plain that if there is a 1938, it will be followed by war as in 1939, and there can be no yielding now. Khrushchev's tactic is to use fear, deceit, and the example of swift, economic development to attract neutral support. Ideology is *not* the magnet.

Khrushchev can and will wreck UN if he doesn't get his way. At this stage, he won't walk out of the Assembly, but he will simply not obey UN resolutions. Time and time again, he talks of the "correlations of strength," and his whole point is that the world balance has changed and must be recognized by giving Russia greater say.

The Congo is his big ploy in the game to wreck UN, but it didn't start off on the Congo issue. In fact, last July, Khrushchev was already indicating that he considered the Security Council a "dishonest" group of judges to consider the U.S.-U.S.S.R. dispute.

NEW YORK, *October 4, 1960*

LORD Home, at lunch, said that if it were not for American pressure, Britain would certainly vote for China's admission to UN. Its exclusion makes no sense and offers Khrushchev admirable opportunities for propaganda. It would make it much easier for India to have China in. As it is, Nehru is absolutely helpless to counter Chinese encroachments except by bombing, which he dares not do. Furthermore, it would be useful to exploit the theological row between China and Russia in UN.

He thought Nixon had done better than Kennedy in the TV debate, although Kennedy made a better appearance. It was silly for Nixon to participate in such a debate. "When you have power, it is foolish to agree to debate such power on a basis of equal limitations for debating rules. They would never do this in the U.K. After all, Nixon, who holds office in the present administration, allowed his opponent fifteen minutes to hit him and he had only fifteen minutes to hit back. This was political folly."

NEW YORK, *October 5, 1960*

LUNCHED with David Bruce. The big issue in this campaign between the two "cool kids" is Kennedy's Secretary of the Treasury vis-à-vis Nixon's Secretary of State. He thinks it virtually certain that Nixon would choose Dillon, a good, tough man, for State although he will start out unpopular with the British and the Afro-Asians.

The most likely candidate for the Democratic Secretary of the Treasury is Harriman. As always Averell is trying hard for three jobs: State (no chance), ambassador to UN (little chance), and Treasury. This would raise a tremendous howl on Wall Street. But in the end, Averell would probably do a very effective job, and he would assuredly be most loyal to the administration.

Adlai Stevenson stayed with Bruce in Hyannis this summer. Before he went to see Kennedy, he told David he would "very much" like to be Secretary of State. When he came back from his talk with Jack, Bruce asked if he had mentioned his desire. The answer was no. Kennedy is too tough for Stevenson. Bruce agrees that Adlai would not be a good Secretary of State but would be an extremely good ambassador to UN.

Bruce thinks the next Democratic Secretary of State must have real influence in Congress, the way Cordell Hull had under Roosevelt. Fulbright would be a lousy Secretary. Kennedy is a tough cookie and won't give any commitments in advance. At this moment, Kennedy has only one aspiration—to win the elections.

Bruce says Jean Monnet is still working, in a subtle way, to establish a Europe dominated by England. The original Marshall Plan policy was to establish a Europe dominated by any European country so long as it wasn't Germany. This meant France or England; but France is clearly out.

NEW YORK, *October 6, 1960*

LATE yesterday afternoon, Gomulka gave an off-the-record talk: exceedingly interesting, although a cold, calm defense of the Soviet line.

What he said, in fact, was that Poland could apply its own interpretations of socialism in internal policy, but she was helpless to do anything but faithfully echo the Soviet line on foreign policy. Basic policy today is made only in the great-power centers of Moscow and Washington; for geographical reasons it is not possible for Poland to have a policy independent of Russia's.

Gomulka is a short, strong man with seamed face, glasses, and a deadly hard look. He spoke in a low, well-modulated voice.

These are realities, and no one should delude himself. Poland's ideas of peaceful coexistence are identical with Moscow's. Poland has a tragic experience of war and knows that peaceful coexistence is the only formula for mankind, because war would destroy our civilization.

If the present arms race continues, war is absolutely inevitable and that means nuclear war. Therefore there must be a move toward international disarmament. Disarmament must start before controls and not vice versa, as the West wishes. Western policy is perfectly understandable in terms of old-fashioned prenuclear days, but it is hopelessly outmoded. Everybody on both sides knows that there is no method of control which will insure that secret stocks of deadly weapons are not hidden away. By controls first, the West indicates a desire to find out how much strength Russia has; and if it discovers that Russia is ahead in the arms race, the West will try to establish a balance by catching up before disarmament starts. This is a hopeless, vicious circle.

It is impossible to have either a valid United Nations or disarmament without the participation of Communist China. This is a reality. Nobody can seriously talk about disarmament without including the largest nation on earth. When the UN was established in 1945, it reflected a world situation in which the United States had an atomic monopoly, there was another regime in China and the world balance of power was different. These are no longer realities and UN must be changed. The west is following an outmoded policy of "hoping to liberate" the Russian satellites. Today, it's impossible. The West must recognize facts, change its policies, change UN, and change its disarmament formula in order to admit to conditions now prevailing.

West Germany is the strongest and most dangerous power in Europe. It is not only militarily the strongest power on the continent, but also it has passed Britain as the second greatest producing power in the West. Furthermore, West Germany is the only European country with territorial claims and an ambition to expand. This ambition is aimed directly at Poland and Czechoslovakia. Poland is desperately worried and the West should recognize this. Talk of a united Germany is foolish.

Last night at dinner, Costi Stavropoulos, legal counsel for UN, said that when Ralph Bunche went to the Congo, he was distressed because time and time again Congolese came up to him and asked: "What tribe do you belong to? Are you a member of the same tribe as Hammarskjöld?" The gap between Congolese experience and our experience is overwhelming. Bunche got into a terrible personal row with Lumumba and the two men cannot bear each other.

ARRANGING TO BE

KIDNAPPED IN

ALGERIA

NEW YORK, *October 6, 1960*

LUNCHED WITH M'HAMMED YAZID, MINISTER OF INFORMATION FOR
the Algerian Provisional Government, and Abdel Kader Chanderli,
their permanent representative to UN (as an observer), at the most
expensive restaurant in New York, La Côte Basque. They explained that
FLN diplomats are under orders not to drink on diplomatic mission; presumably so they have their wits about them and so they respect the virtues
embodied in the *Koran*. Nevertheless, we all had cocktails, shared an excellent bottle of rosé and ended up with an exceedingly good Calvados.
We also ended up calling each other Abdel Kader, M'hammed, and Cy.

The big gimmick of the luncheon was this: I said I would be prepared,
despite my dilapidated condition, to spend a week in FLN territory if
they could arrange it on my terms. I couldn't spend more than a week
because of my regular column commitments.

They agreed. Yazid said they could arrange for me to go in from
Tunisia or Morocco and make a "deep penetration." I said I was more
intrigued by what Ahmed Boumendjel had suggested in early 1959: They
could pick me up at the St. Georges Hotel in Algiers and get me out of
the country without killing me. That would be a test of their ability to
show they really ran the hinterland. After a week, they would have to
get me to a communications point in either Tunisia or Morocco. Yazid
said he would fix it up for some time during the month of November.

I said I respected their conspiratorial ability, but judging from French
documents that had been shown to me, they were heavily penetrated

and the fewer persons he discussed this with, the better it would suit me. He protested that they were in great shape from a security point of view, but that he, as a conspirator, understood. "Furthermore," he said, "I don't want the U.S. Marines called out to look for you in Algeria. That would be embarrassing."

He asked me if there were anybody I could appoint as my confidential agent in the negotiation. (This began to smell like EOKA days in Cyprus.) I said: "You must call my Paris office where I have a secretary named Nancy Ross. But you will have to have an agreed means of communication. She shares an office with another secretary who might answer the phone. You must have somebody on your team call up and say, 'Hello, Nancy.' "

He had to decide on a name for his agent (and himself). The agreed name is Gilbert. Somebody from their outfit is to call up and say, "Hello Nancy, this is Gilbert. Can you meet me for a drink at such and such a place?" Nancy will then arrange the next step along this labyrinth. We will see what works out.

Yazid said the Russians have not changed their policy toward Algeria but *have* changed their policy toward France. He warns that the French had better make their final settlement with Algeria now because today the people who lead the FLN are "the last generation of Frenchmen in Algeria."

NEW YORK, *October 9, 1960*

YESTERDAY afternoon, Evariste Kimba, foreign minister of the independent republic of Katanga, came in to call upon me, introducing himself as. "Mon Excellence, Monsieur Kimba." With him was a Turk named Arsin, who calls himself private secretary. Kimba, a powerful Negro, about six foot one, would make a handy tackle for Notre Dame. Arsin, short and with a slight bay window, is white.

I asked Arsin where he came from, and he answered Katanga. I then asked where he was born and he told me Istanbul. He left Turkey in 1943. I gather he is somewhat an adventurer, Kimba's bodyguard as well as counselor.

Kimba said that he had visited Belgium often, explained that Katanga was an independent republic which *might* agree someday to political confederation with the Congo republic, but which, for the present, was only interested in economic unity.

(Kimba was later hanged.)

WASHINGTON, *October 10, 1960*

DRINKS with the Gruenthers. Al told me of a recent weekend when he played bridge at the White House with Eisenhower from 4 P.M. to 11

P.M. and then again from 2:30 P.M. to 8:30 P.M. the next day. (This doesn't give me the feeling that our President is working overtime.)

Al agreed that we had not put our best face forward at UN meetings. He referred to my column complaining that we hadn't done enough about the neutrals. He had passed on this criticism to Eisenhower, and I gather this contributed to the President's decision to invite fifteen African leaders to see him Friday.

I told Al I wanted to ask Eisenhower to break his rule and give me a publishable interview. Al was doubtful. "After all," he said, "in all the years he has been in the White House he has never even seen Scotty Reston once."

NEW YORK, *October 11, 1960*

JACK Kennedy very kindly came in to see me today for a first-class talk. He was most relaxed and looked fine. Before going into the serious conversation, I will recollect a few tidbits.

Stash Radziwill, now his brother-in-law, is campaigning for him, making speeches in Polish to American Polish communities. Stash almost faints before each speech because he is so terrified, but it seems to be working out all right. Jack says, "I haven't the vaguest idea what he is talking about, but I only hope it is helpful."

Jack thought Nixon "was a damn fool to agree to debate with me on an equal-time TV basis." He could easily have prevented it by applying pressure to the big TV and radio chains. Now it is too late. It is a tough ordeal. Says Jack: "Just imagine if Eisenhower had had to do this against Stevenson in 1952 and 1956. He would have looked silly."

Nixon tried to use all kinds of tricks. For example, last Friday the studio temperature was down to 65° so that Nixon wouldn't sweat before the camera the way he did the first time. Jack said there were little tricks with the lighting designed to operate against him and for Nixon. But he thinks basically it was an enormous break for him to have this debate. The press is largely pro-Nixon and has been building Kennedy up as a naive, inexperienced young man. Now he can come before the whole nation and show his true colors.

I inquired at length about foreign policy. Since he implicitly foresaw a period of crisis for years to come, would he bring Republicans into the administration in important offices and in the interests of national unity. "Definitely," said he.

He criticized the Eisenhower administration for failing to do this. To the best of his knowledge, David Bruce was the only Democrat who got any post under Eisenhower. Kennedy would like to do what Roosevelt and Truman did, and use Republicans whose basic thinking was close to his own in positions affecting foreign policy and national security—

men like Douglas Dillon, Cabot Lodge, Jimmy Smith, and Harry Labouisse (who is *not* a Republican).

He would strongly urge Dillon to stay on if he were elected, but he
didn't want to embarrass him politically now by talking too much about
it because Dillon has contributed heavily to Nixon's campaign and many
people say he is being tapped as a Republican Secretary of State.

Jack said:

> There is no partisan division or party label on national security or
> foreign policy. I have worked closely with Dillon, for example, on
> changing the Battle Act and the World Bank mission to India. There
> is no division between most intelligent people on national security or
> foreign policy.
>
> Look at the way Franklin Roosevelt brought in Republicans, some of
> whom later stayed on with Truman: people such as Stimson, Lovett,
> Forrestal, and McCloy. It is too bad the present administration doesn't
> continue this tradition [with the exception of David Bruce]. There is
> no party split on these issues.

I asked what kind of a Secretary of State he was thinking of and
whether he considered national legislative experience as a necessary
prerequisite. He said this was too tricky to answer. Naturally, there
were political considerations, for example, of such men as Stevenson
and Bowles (he specifically mentioned both names). He said: "I consider
it essential that the Secretary of State should be able to get on well with
Congress. However, prior legislative experience isn't necessarily essential and could not necessarily guarantee effective relationships with
Congress."

I asked if he favored the idea of a separate foreign-affairs advisor
or agent like Colonel House or Harry Hopkins. He replied negatively:
"The Secretary of State should be the President's agent. Only when there
is no harmony between the President and the Secretary of State—as with
Lansing and Wilson, and Hull and Roosevelt—do you have these special
agents or advisors. The President and Secretary of State should be on
an intimate personal relationship and have full confidence in each
other."

He thought the next Secretary of the Treasury must have a comprehensive view of the world. He should also understand the importance
of foreign affairs. For example, when Humphrey was Secretary of the
Treasury, he was so strong that despite Dulles's own influence, Humphrey
was able to adversely affect the implementation of foreign policy.

Kennedy said his head of ICA (foreign aid) "must believe in the
foreign-aid program. This is a much bigger job than it has been given
credit for being. The same applies to the administration of the Development Loan Fund. Both are very big jobs, and I would like to see them
well filled."

He said USIA should be souped up, and his own impression was that, for example, our libraries in Latin America failed to attract the young intelligentsia. The new head of the USIA should be a "hard-headed but imaginative man having the strength of character to persuade Congress."

He would like to keep Allen Dulles on "for a while" in CIA, but then replace him. There is no way of checking up to see how well CIA is going. A new man could give a new perspective to the job. He hoped to persuade General Max Taylor to take it over after Dulles.

He had no opinion on whether he would ask Norstad to stay on or not, but said he would very much like to persuade both Taylor and General Gavin to get back into uniform. It would be very hard to get Gavin back because he has an extremely good job now.

The post of ambassador to NATO was "tremendously important. I hope we can attract talent to the government, not only in the major jobs, but also in the administrative jobs." But getting back to NATO, he said, "We are going to try to put a great deal more emphasis on NATO, its economic and political potentials. Our ambassador to NATO should be a key figure in our policy." He definitely intends to name to all the main ambassadorial posts men who speak the local language—French, German, Italian, etc. He hopes it will prove easy to find competent men who do speak these languages.

He intends to revitalize the Policy Planning staff of the State Department. He would like to bring back into active service men like David Bruce and urge Chip Bohlen not to retire. I asked about George Kennan. He has been in correspondence with him and eventually hopes to get him back. But since George is involved with things like disengagement, he wouldn't want to mention his name at this time.

He repeated he was definitely in favor of longer range budgeting for foreign aid so that other nations can plan ahead and our money will be more effectively used.

I asked about drafting civilians for special jobs. He said: "I would be delighted to see this done. But I don't think it is politically feasible; we probably will have to continue trying to recruit people through some such agency as volunteers."

WASHINGTON, *October 12, 1960*

LUNCHED with Dillon in his office, munching sandwiches and talking. As usual he was quick and to the point.

We have done nothing and will do nothing about the *directoire* business, and de Gaulle himself never raises the issue of his September, 1958, letter. Indeed, we keep saying to him, O.K., you want to reform NATO—how? He doesn't answer.

The substance of what de Gaulle wanted—Big Three talks—has been granted. There are regular consultations among the foreign ministers and at a lower level. But we can't grant him the binding commitment he desires for grandeur's sake. And now he is embarked on a costly nuclear arms and missile program which England, although its economy is at least as strong as France's, had to abandon as too expensive.

Doug is concerned about the Quemoy-Matsu issue becoming so crystallized in the political campaign that whoever wins will seem committed a priori (like the "liberation" business in 1952), and the whole Orient will judge us by it. Dillon talked to Bowles about this and tried to keep it out of the TV debate. But Bowles insisted and was responsible for getting Kennedy to inject the offshore islands into the contest.

This afternoon, saw Allen Dulles in his CIA office. On the wall a map shows the route of the Soviet ICBMs to the Pacific from the general region of Kirghizstan. Allen said the takeoff point was deliberately changed on the map for security reasons.

We talked about Gary Powers. The CIA has a theory that no man should ever be ordered to commit suicide if captured and this was not in contracts with agents. The CIA thought there was more chance of a man's individual nobility prompting him to such an act if there were no such advance order.

Allen said Powers had done nothing wrong and probably would have had a hard time committing suicide either by pistol or with his poison needle, even had he wanted to. First he was parachuted out and secondly he was in a cumbersome pressure suit. Thirdly, he was captured pronto on landing.

Nevertheless, Dulles left me with the impression he thought Powers should somehow have knocked himself off. He said Powers had been brainwashed or brain-conditioned prior to the trial. It was clear he had told the Russians more than emerged, because his previous "testimony" was always referred to.

I gather Dulles is unhappy with Powers' behavior but doesn't like to say so. Powers had a specific, short-term contract with CIA and was paid between $25,000 and $30,000 a year, about what a good, civilian jet pilot gets. Under the law, he must be paid as long as his contract runs, even though in jail. Funds are given to his wife, taxes are deducted, and the rest set aside. But no decision has yet been taken on what to do when the contract expires; or how he should be treated when released.

WASHINGTON, *October 13, 1960*

HAD breakfast with Chet Bowles. He says he'll try and help get a "private bill" started in Congress so Milica Dedijer (Vlado's daughter) Mihić isn't bounced from the country.

He claims he never discussed Quemoy-Matsu with Dillon. Says he wrote

Herter last May urging him to negotiate evacuation of the islands and guaranteeing the Democrats would not attack him for it.

He wired Kennedy yesterday urging him to state that if Mao attacks the islands the country will be united on policy, regardless of party. Deplores the issue as a political controversy.

Drinks with Harry Labouisse, who has been helping Hammarskjöld. Bunche told him when he got back from the Congo, "They asked me if I was a Swede. Maybe I looked like one. I was scared enough."

WASHINGTON, *October 15, 1960*

DINED with the Herters. Chris bet Chip Bohlen $5 that *The New York Times* would support Nixon—poor fellow.

Chris was indignant when I told him Bowles said he'd written him in May urging that he negotiate us off Quemoy and Matsu and promising there would be no Democratic criticism if he did. "If Bowles is going to be so indiscreet about his letters, I will too. He wrote me a lot more recently than May. And he concluded his letter by promising to support our position there if the President decides the two islands are strategically necessary."

He agrees there must be extensive underground communism in Spain and expresses full backing for Don Juan. I opined Juan was lazy, preferring to leave everything to his advisors while he played golf. "Precisely what we want for a constitutional monarch," said Herter. I couldn't help thinking of parallels closer to home.

WASHINGTON, *October 16, 1960*

WE have been staying with the Bohlens. Chip argues that the Cold War suits the Russians better than the West because they need psychological pressures to keep their disciplinary system going and also to keep China from breaking loose. Détente suits us. After the Geneva Conference in 1955, there was a relaxation in Europe and the result was explosions in Poland and Hungary.

NEW YORK, *November 7, 1960*

YESTERDAY evening, I had a talk with Ken Galbraith and Arthur Schlesinger at Marietta Tree's. Arthur thinks Kennedy's Secretary of the Treasury will be either Galbraith or Averell Harriman. I told Galbraith there would be more suicides on Wall Street if he were named than if Averell were named, because they regard Harriman as merely a traitor to his class, but they think Galbraith is mad.

Arthur thinks Kennedy will be forced to choose between Stevenson and Bowles as Secretary of State, although he doesn't really want either of them. If this happens, he will name Stevenson. Practically all Presidents this century have been forced by circumstances to take Secretaries of State whom they really didn't want—like Wilson and Bryant, and Roosevelt and Hull.

Galbraith says what Kennedy is after is "a government of the rich by the clever for the poor."

PARIS, *November 13, 1960*

AM Houghton says that since de Gaulle's press conference of September 5, 1960, the situation has deteriorated steadily. There are continued rumors of plots, *coups d'état*, and assassinations. Just the other day, Houghton heard a story about forty officers who had banded together in a secret society determined to break into the Elysée and murder de Gaulle.

Houghton nevertheless counsels Washington there is no likelihood of any "immediate" upset. De Gaulle remains immensely popular. The Ministry of the Interior is better informed about plots than last January. It is hard to beat somebody with nobody, and there isn't any real leader among the conspirators.

There is much gossip about the military plot. If de Gaulle moves any farther in Algeria there are three alternative steps the army could take: invade France; invade Tunisia and Morocco to internationalize the war; or sit on its hands while riots break out in Algeria, letting events assume control.

PARIS, *November 17, 1960*

SAW Larry Norstad for the first time in months. To my delight, he said that by far the best Secretary of State would be Chip Bohlen. Chip was brilliant, tough, imaginative, and never made a mistake. The fact that he had been pilloried by McCarthy would "gain him another million votes." He has an immense reputation in Europe.

I asked if it were true that SHAPE had advised the French government that it would use military means if necessary to prevent Communist intrusion in Algeria. Larry asked his aide to bring in a memorandum he had dictated. This said (in part):

"Until 1955, Algeria was a part of Allied Command Europe. It is still a part of NATO Europe, although not a part of my command. It is quite clear that it is a part of NATO, and, if there were an external attack on Algeria, there would be a responsibility on the Alliance."

The presidential order that dependents of the armed forces overseas should be sharply reduced irritated Larry, although he recognizes the gravity of the gold-outflow problem. The very first he heard about it was in a message from Washington at 11 P.M. last night. It has created a furor among American commanders in Europe.

American soldiers resent the words used by Defense Secretary Gates when he referred to the necessity of "sacrifice." They reason that it is civilians who should make these sacrifices and they are bound to "holler" at American tourists coming to Europe: "Yankees go home!" It would be much more effective if the administration were to limit tourist expenditures.

Larry would like to bring over a bright, young general sometime fairly early next year and train him for at least a year, taking him around Europe as a chief of staff so that he has sufficient prestige when he finally inherits as commander—perhaps the last American commander of NATO forces. Norstad already has his eye on the man: Lieutenant General "Bus" Wheeler, at present secretary of the Joint Chiefs of Staff.

I then asked Larry to outline his proposal for turning NATO into the fourth nuclear power. He gave me a long briefing. First there is the requirement for IRBMS and MRBMS to supplement bombers. This is part of the continual process of keeping NATO forces up to date as weapons develop. It is increasingly difficult for manned aircraft to penetrate enemy defenses. Because of this, we started a missile program over here and installed Jupiters in Italy and Turkey. There was talk of putting land-based Polarises in Europe on transportable launching pads, but this got hopelessly confused. Washington is now considering commitment to NATO of a fixed number of Polaris submarines.

Secondly, there is the question of a NATO strategic force. Thirdly, the U.S.A. should tell the alliance a certain minimum number of nuclear warheads is essential to the direct defense of Europe. The U.S. would make those warheads available and guarantee their availability "for the life of NATO in its present form." These weapons could be used *only* as NATO directs.

We would provide U.S. custodians to secure these warheads and hold "the key to the box." Each custodian, however, would be responsible only to NATO, directly, and not to any control by national authorities, including the U.S.A. By this system, NATO would be turned into a "fourth nuclear power."

PARIS, *November 18, 1960*

LUNCHED with André de Staercke. The importance of the Norstad plan is that if NATO were given its own deterrent power, this fact will end the question of "American bases in Europe." If the Russians insist we get out of Europe, it won't matter because NATO will have its own military force and even if the "Yankees go home" there will be a nuclear power in Europe.

This idea took shape two months ago (last September) at an informal meeting in the home on Lake Como of Stikker, Dutch ambassador to the alliance. Present were Norstad, de Staercke, Adenauer, and Herbert Blankenhorn, West German ambassador to France.

The French are alarmed that the Norstad plan may go through because this would sink de Gaulle's idea of a French nuclear striking force. As a result they propose a six month NATO "truce"—meaning there should be no change in plans, but all the allies should cease criticizing each other.

PARIS, *November 21, 1960*

LUNCH with Herbert Blankenhorn, West German ambassador to France, former ambassador to NATO, and the German diplomat closest to Adenauer. He said Bonn would be upset if Stevenson were named Secretary of State. Adlai spent an evening with Adenauer, who found him a "dangerous theorist" and a highly impractical intellectual.

Blankenhorn had a little typewritten timetable in his wallet which he whipped out to give me the exact dates of diplomatic events last summer. On July 29 and 30, Adenauer met de Gaulle at Rambouillet. De Gaulle indicated that he wanted to create a "Europe of nations." August 6, Adenauer sent Blankenhorn and Hilger van Scherpenberg, state secretary for foreign affairs, to see Couve de Murville and discuss de Gaulle's views. Couve said that de Gaulle wanted to reform NATO and revise the Rome treaties in order to produce a "nationalistic Europe." The Germans refused.

On August 10, Macmillan visited Bonn and on August 15, Adenauer wrote de Gaulle reporting on this visit. Macmillan wanted to overcome his own difficulties with Europe and favored a rapprochement between the Six (Common Market) and the Seven (Free Trade Area). Adenauer agreed and, said Blankenhorn, "This meeting buried Anglo-German differences."

Adenauer urged de Gaulle to leave the Rome treaties untouched and cautioned that it would be best to wait and see what the Americans wanted for NATO. On September 9, Adenauer was in Cadenabbia. At luncheon, at Stikker's, Adenauer insisted on continuing NATO in its present form; in fact, the Chancellor wanted even further integration. They discussed the world consequences should the alliance be loosened (as de Gaulle wants) into a defensive coalition among national allies. Adenauer said this would pave the way for German national rearmament and that the latter in turn might very well become unbearable to Germany's neighbors. Adenauer said we had to think about how to win de Gaulle over and bring him closer to NATO. He asked if it would not be possible for the United States to make concessions in the nuclear field. At this point, Norstad developed his thesis about the U.S. relinquishing its nuclear monopoly and putting warheads at the disposal of four or five powers in NATO. This delighted and impressed Adenauer.

Debré visited Bonn on October 7 and 8. The Germans said that they would not go along with French plans to change NATO.

Debré was sensible enough not to try and convert Adenauer.

The Como meeting was of special importance. Norstad said he would push the U.S. to take an official decision, and Adenauer said he would try to convince de Gaulle to accept such a decision, if it comes.

PARIS, *November 22, 1960*

I SPENT an hour and a half with Soustelle this morning. Near the door were a couple of cops but neither bore a tommy gun.

I noted the courtyard through which Soustelle escaped from the police in May, 1958, and got to Algeria. A half-Brazilian woman who lives in the same building agreed to drive him out. He huddled on the floor in the back seat with a rug thrown over him.

He thought de Gaulle had changed his policy enormously and was now preparing to abandon everything including Algeria. As Soustelle analyzes this, de Gaulle thinks general war unavoidable, a great cataclysmic shock between the two power blocs. He therefore believes France should have its own nuclear force to warn both opponents: "Don't touch our territory or we will react automatically." However, this armed neutralism is designed to cover France only in Europe.

What de Gaulle, in fact, is trying to do in Algeria is to apply a Bao Dai policy such as the Fourth Republic attempted in Indochina. That didn't work in Indochina, but here in Algeria there isn't even a Bao Dai. De Gaulle is looking for—but cannot find—a Muslim head of the executive he plans in Algiers. "De Gaulle's idea leads only to a political no-man's-land in which each one stands to lose," said Soustelle. Furthermore, he pointed out that, "Algeria has always been a land of plots."

Soustelle said he intends to quit politics entirely if Algeria is lost and if France becomes a country no longer worth living for, a dictatorship. He fears that moment is coming.

Saw Sir Pierson Dixon, the new British ambassador. Until last week he had felt the Algerian mess was so insoluble and de Gaulle had lost so much popularity that he was doomed. He now thinks that probably one way or another, de Gaulle will survive and get some form of Algerian settlement. He has slowly, almost like a pope, preached the people around from French Algeria to Algerian Algeria to accepting the idea of an Algerian republic.

The provincial press wholeheartedly supports de Gaulle and just wants to get rid of the question. It is the Parisian press which is confusing; and the debate continues here. But there don't seem to be any leaders in the army, which makes an army revolt less likely. There is no crisis atmosphere.

De Gaulle wants to use his atomic striking force to put pressure on his allies. Dixon recalled that in his *Mémoires* de Gaulle says that it is an "iron rule" among nations that no nation ever gives anything without getting something in return. We may have to face the fact that de Gaulle has to be given something; and if we do face this fact, we can probably change his attitude toward NATO.

PARIS, *November 24, 1960*

LUNCHED with Billotte. He told me that in October, 1955, as minister of defense, he had issued orders to both General Lecomte and Marshal Juin of the sort de Gaulle should issue today. According to Pierre, he told Lecomte: "You must either remain in the army or give up politics; and if you prefer politics, you must resign from the army. I will give you five minutes to decide." Lecomte agreed to give up politics and Billotte made him his commander of the French military college, where he served brilliantly. However, as soon as Pierre was replaced as defense minister, Lecomte resumed his political activities.

Likewise, Billotte saw Juin at a dinner party shortly after Billotte was named as minister. He said to Juin: "You will either give up politics or resign from the army. If you do not answer me within five minutes, I will incarcerate you in the fortress of Vincennes. Furthermore, I want the people of France, whom you serve, to know that you accept this decision. Therefore, I want you to call on me every Wednesday afternoon so that people will know you are accepting instructions from the minister of defense and from France. If I have nothing to tell you, I will give you a cup of tea." Billotte says the following French generals are involved in conspiracy against the state: Marshal Juin, Generals Zeller, Jouhaud, and Salan. Pierre thinks that by February 1, there will either be a complete end to the continuing drama of plots and an imposed settlement of the Algerian conflict, or civil war in France.

Drinks with Am Houghton. He went to see de Gaulle with Lyndon Johnson. De Gaulle told Johnson he had worked with several American presidents; with Franklin Roosevelt, although he admitted with a wry smile there had been difficulties, with Truman, and with his "great friend" Eisenhower. Now he hopes to be able to work on a friendly and effective basis with President Kennedy. He then got back to his old favorite subject—the need for tripartite cooperation.

Johnson made a good impression, quiet and respectful. He told de Gaulle what a privilege he felt it was to meet the renowned French President. Afterward, as they were riding back to the embassy, Johnson explained that he had talked perhaps too long because he wanted to avoid any possibility that de Gaulle might bring up Kennedy's 1957 speech on Algeria.

PARIS, *November 25, 1960*

LAST night, I got a call from Lyndon Johnson's aide. Johnson wanted me to come around this morning to tell him a bit about Spaak and NATO, before he went to see Spaak. I had to take my dog, Benjamin Beagle, because Marina was away and the servants were out. Johnson was not in the least bit garrulous. He only wanted to listen. He sat there glumly pulling his long ears, but from the questions he asked I deduced that he was browned off at Norstad. Twice Mrs. Johnson joined us briefly: a trim, self-possessed, friendly woman.

He asked: "Don't you think a man like General Norstad should have consulted Democratic leaders before explaining this plan here?" I blew my top, saying that after all, Norstad was a nonpolitical general. Obviously he was a member of the Eisenhower dynasty and close to the President, to whom he was responsible, but he had no politics. Furthermore, his principal responsibility was as a commander not just of U.S. troops but of all the allies. Spaak could fly off to the States to sell ideas, but it was not easy for Norstad to shrug off his command responsibilities and fly home after election day. Johnson grunted.

He asked what I thought about keeping Norstad on here as commander. I thought it would be fatal to remove him. Furthermore, he should be kept here for at least eighteen more months so that a new general could be trained as his chief of staff to succeed him eventually.

Johnson asked me if I would please tell him how I interpreted the Norstad plan. I said: "Really, I would feel like a lunatic telling you what the Norstad plan is after you have spent the entire week being briefed by General Norstad himself." "No," said Johnson. "I would like to know what the thing means."

I really had a feeling he didn't understand the plan and wanted it explained in kindergarten language. He sat there listening with an absolute poker face, and I couldn't tell whether he was testing me, trying to get elucidation, or what.

It was an odd meeting and Benjamin's presence brought about a rather curious insight into his character. He told me he had eight beagles, that the first one had been purchased nine years ago in Virginia. When he had his heart attack in 1955, that dog, whose name is simply Beagle, sensed there was something wrong and used to put its head up against his to comfort him.

A friend of Johnson's told him that when somebody is unhappy, a hound's olfactory organs smell a special secretion and the hound comforts his master or friend. Then Johnson said an extraordinary thing. He said: "Beagle always sleeps under my bed. But when I am sick or unhappy or feeling sorry for myself, or when I cry, he comes up on the bed and comforts me."

"My God," I thought, "only a heartbeat keeps this man from the White House." I was really rather struck by the big Texan casually saying, "when I cry."

Drinks with Doug Dillon, who spent two days in Paris after his strikingly unsuccessful mission with Treasury Secretary Anderson trying to get the Germans to fork out more for the U.S. defense costs in Europe.

The Germans had drawn up a detailed program, offering to prepay a thirty-five-year-old debt right away plus a big one-year foreign-aid program. However, Anderson dismissed the proposal, saying that if the Germans did not agree to a long-range effort, the only solution was for the meeting to break up. Anderson had always been telling the State Department, "You guys aren't tough enough," and he was trying to prove his point.

I said Europeans were struck by the parallel between Eisenhower's decree on withdrawing military dependents and the simultaneous purchase by Ford of minority stock in British Ford. The amount saved by withdrawing U.S. military dependents was approximately equal to the capital exported to purchase the Ford minority stock. Dillon smiled sourly. He said that unfortunately we can't stop Ford from such a move without legislation. If the problem of payments continues, the U.S. will simply have to enact laws to change the climate of American investments in developed countries abroad and to make it less attractive. Our initial postwar drive had an entirely different philosophy. It sought to help Europe master the problems of the dollar gap. Now this had to be reversed.

I asked whether Dillon was ready to join the Kennedy administration. He said he had read my interview with Kennedy and certainly there was no difference between him and the Democrats on foreign-policy aims. Indirect indications had been sent to Dillon that Kennedy wants to talk to him about this next week.

Doug said the Norstad plan was undoubtedly good for SHAPE, but it was not good for the U.S. government. It would involve a substantial change in the Atomic Energy Act and "could trigger off a constitutional debate on how U.S. troops are ordered into war." At some future date, a NATO commander who was not American would be in a position to order our troops into war under this plan and the U.S. government "cannot and should not propose this."

Very sadly, Doug said the trouble with de Gaulle was that he always returned to his September, 1958, letter on the *directoire*. On this, de Gaulle really wanted the form and not the substance, while his government—such as Couve de Murville—wanted the substance and not the form.

PARIS, *November 28, 1960*

CYRUS Eaton and his wife came for lunch accompanied by Lady Jean Campbell, Beaverbrook's granddaughter. All three bound for Moscow and an appointment with Khrushchev.

I was much taken by the Eatons. She is charming and intelligent, although crippled. She has to be wheeled about in a chair, but she is cheery and particularly useful as an interpreter, because her husband is so deaf that, although I found myself screaming, she had to more or less translate. He is used to reading her lips.

He was a Republican way back and indirectly helped the nomination of Warren Harding for the presidency. Mrs. Eaton was a delegate to the last Democratic convention. They both seem moderately optimistic about Kennedy.

Eaton saw no reason why we should not do business with the Russians. He said one of his most prosperous interests had been a paint company in Cuba. He could have made a deal with Castro, but his colleagues on the board wouldn't go along because they thought this would be letting down capitalism.

Chat with Spaak this afternoon. He thinks the English will do everything they can to prevent nuclear sharing so long as they don't have to take the rap themselves. They would like to see de Gaulle the fall guy. They keep talking of the dangers of giving Germany nuclear weapons without realizing that the real intention of the Norstad plan is to prevent Germany from having nuclear weapons of its own.

PARIS, *November 30, 1960*

LUNCHED today with Maurice Faure, several times minister of the Fourth Republic, healthy, intelligent, energetic, young (thirty-eight) deputy from Cahors in the southwest.

Faure is very pessimistic. He thinks while there will be violence and bloodshed in Algeria next year, it won't come to metropolitan France; the French people will rally behind de Gaulle just because of the bloodshed he foresees.

Many will vote yes in the referendum merely because there isn't any alternative—not because they back de Gaulle. De Gaulle has compromised both France's institutions and alliances. If you vote yes for de Gaulle on his Algerian policy, you imply you support him on everything else—even where you oppose him.

De Gaulle has taken far too long to move on Algeria: eighteen months to shift from a policy of "Algérie Française" to his present liberal approach. The reason is almost certainly because de Gaulle, realizing that he split France in 1940, doesn't want to split France again. Every time he makes a move hailed by the right, he immediately follows it up by another move hailed by the left.

PARIS, *December 1, 1960*

ROBERT Abdesselam came to my house for lunch. I had invited him to a restaurant but he didn't dare. He said: "It is too dangerous." He was shot six times by the FLN so I can't entirely blame him. During lunch, his car with chauffeur and armed bodyguard waited outside.

Abdesselam is small, wiry, forty years old, an Algerian deputy, descended from a noble Berber family of the Kabylie. He was an officer during World War II and considers himself a Frenchman. What he would really like is to keep Algeria bound to France.

I complained about the lack of new ideas on an Algerian solution and asked, "Why doesn't one of you propose for Algeria the solution Churchill offered France in 1940: union of two independent countries with one parliament?" Abdesselam was very excited about this and said he would.

PARIS, *December 6, 1960*

EXCEEDINGLY interesting lunch today with Pierre Mendès-France. I must say he is a remarkable and admirable little fellow. He looks like a very tough, shaven, tiny, eastern European rabbi. He has little grace but great earnestness. He is a brilliant economist and a sincere patriot. He survived eighteen months of occupation by the Nazis in France and then, when he escaped to England, instead of taking a desk job in the miniature Gaullist Free French government, he joined the air force. He was no schoolboy when he did this either.

We had no small talk apart from the subject of booze. I made the customary offer of an apéritif and then again of wine, but he steered off meticulously. I offered a glass of milk, and he didn't even smile when he replied, "I don't even want a glass of mineral water." He did remark that the present Fifth Republic seemed in a mild way to be trying to emulate his own campaign against alcoholism in France.

Mendès-France is convinced that there will be a major crisis in the

very immediate future. If this materializes, he thinks the left has absolutely no chance of asserting itself at present. It is entirely possible that
there will be a crisis exploding in Algeria at the end of the week when
de Gaulle goes there—or a crisis exploding in France while de Gaulle is
in Algeria. He does not exclude the possibility of an assassination attempt
against the General.

There were probably only three possibilities for settling the fate of
France as the question is now posed.

1. De Gaulle would face the crisis with complete determination, ruthlessly resolved to squash opposition to his intention of making peace in
Algeria (in this case the great majority of the country, including the entire left, would rally behind him).

2. De Gaulle would keep the shadow of power but cede the substance
to the ultras and the army, as in fact he did after the January, 1960, putsch
(this would lead to inevitable, ultimate civil war and disaster).

3. De Gaulle would either be murdered, ousted from power, or quit
and go back to Colombey (in that case there would be some form of
right-wing government, probably fascism, and again ultimately civil war).

The only thing the left could hope for was point 1.

I asked Mendès-France if he thought, considering that all the generals
seemed to favor the right, a popular front was the answer. He said he
sincerely hoped not. He said that if point 1 were to come about, the
left would throw its weight behind de Gaulle. But if fascism, real fascism,
came to France, the only reaction would be a popular front. The more
right-wing the government that succeeded de Gaulle, the more left-wing
would be the ultimate reaction.

Mendès says it is absolutely and immutably evident that Algeria will
become a totally independent republic without any connection with
France. One cannot escape history.

I asked what the United States could or should do to help France
during its present period of tribulation. He said: "You can do nothing—
absolutely nothing—until after we have had our crisis."

I asked what he would do if, by hypothesis, he were suddenly projected
to power tomorrow. How would he seek to emulate his sixty-day formula of 1954, under which he stilled the Indochinese war? He said the
answer was obvious. The first thing necessary was immediately to mobilize French opinion, which was clearly in favor of a settlement. This
could be done very rapidly; and then shock treatment was necessary. The
first step in the shock treatment was to open prompt negotiations with
the FLN. The result of this would be the swift establishment by the
colons of a rump French republic in Algeria. But, even with army sympathy, such a republic could not survive economically more than two
weeks. It was probable that, concurrent with the creation of such a rump
republic, there would be an armed insurrection around Toulouse and a

few minor attempts at *coup d'état* in Paris. But these could be put down easily. There would indeed be bloodshed; this was inescapable. But the bloodshed would be minor, and, in the end, the army would reluctantly refuse to intervene once it had been clearly demonstrated that the great mass of French people were mobilized behind the state.

He complained sadly and bitterly that de Gaulle has always given way to the army. It is a mistake to think that the General has had a clear idea in mind concerning his Algerian policy and has used Machiavellian tactics shifting generals around in order to pursue his ultimate aim. On the contrary, de Gaulle has proved himself to be the prisoner of the army.

Mendès-France told me an extraordinary thing about de Gaulle. He said that once when he was having a private conversation with de Gaulle during the war, the General had confessed to him: "One of my brothers, Xavier, is crazy. The other of my brothers, Pierre, is thoroughly normal. I am in between."

In February, 1942, Mendès-France escaped from occupied France to London and as soon as he arrived he was invited to dinner with de Gaulle. He said he was very impressed and embarrassed by the invitation because "We in the resistance thought of de Gaulle as God and this was a startling invitation. There was I, penniless and extremely badly dressed, and de Gaulle said he would send a car for me. I went very timidly."

The only people present in addition to himself and de Gaulle were René Pleven, who as "minister" of de Gaulle's provisional government was the General's principal man of confidence at the moment; and Claude Serreulles, de Gaulle's ADC. Mendès-France told de Gaulle that he intended to volunteer immediately for service in the air force, and de Gaulle, ignoring Pleven's embarrassment, said: "Yes, that is the obvious thing to do. There are too many people who sit at desks."

Then, to Mendès-France's embarrassment, the great god spoke to him about nothing except his troubles with the Allies. He complained far more about Roosevelt than he did about Hitler. He asked Mendès if the latter agreed with de Gaulle's intention to take over the islands of St. Pierre and Miquelon off the Canadian coast. Mendès-France recalled: "Most people in France had never heard of St. Pierre and Miquelon. I was astounded."

Then de Gaulle complained about British activities in Syria and asked Mendès-France if he himself had been right to go to Syria. Finally, he got down to the burden of his thinking and wondered if he had been right to stage a mutiny in June, 1940. Mendès said he could never forget this experience because, while 100 percent of the resistance people in France venerated de Gaulle and thought he was infallible, on his very first meeting with the General he found de Gaulle himself wondering whether he was right.

PARIS, *December 9, 1960*

LUNCHED with Jean Laloy. He thinks Mao Tse-tung is for militant co-existence; Khrushchev is for dynamic coexistence; Tito is for truly peace-ful, or rather passive coexistence.

Last time he went to Bonn with Debré and Couve de Murville, Aden-auer took him aside and said: "For heaven's sake, be tough with *my* delegation; they don't understand things. You must tell them the reali-ties."

PARIS, *December 12, 1960*

DE GAULLE has won a great victory and has simultaneously suffered a great defeat. The victory was assertion of firm discipline over the French army in Algeria. The defeat was the disappearance of any chance for his plan of an independent "Algerian Algeria" in "association" with France.

Thus we see the strange paradox of a man who fought almost alone in 1940 against world historical tides and French public opinion to achieve the restoration of the French empire; and twenty years later, has again fought against French public opinion to dissolve that empire which he, virtually alone, established. He has given away all of Africa except Algeria, and is trying to keep that toehold. The toehold is gone.

I make these statements largely as a result of a luncheon I had today with Philippe Baudet, number-one civilian in the office of Gen-eral Ely. Baudet thinks there is a serious chance that within the next few days FLN agents in Paris will try to stage a bloody uprising.

The situation is very strained. There is complete censorship in Algeria now. The only thing he could tell me was that at noon today the crowd seemed to be forming up for further trouble. Nobody knows what de Gaulle intends to do. De Gaulle is a magnificently courageous man, but it is dubious whether courage is enough.

The U.S. must do something to help de Gaulle in his present desperate straits. There is no blinking the fact that the alliance with Washington has been working badly. De Gaulle's "force de frappe" plan was intended as a lever against the allies rather than against the possible adversary.

De Gaulle had gambled on two hopes. He had hoped to be able to work out a deal with France's traditional ally, Russia. "Note that I say Russia and not the Soviet Union," said Baudet. But this failed, and the Russians have now pretty well declared themselves on Algeria. Ferhat Abbas, who had been a friend of the West, has not been able to withstand the pres-sures. It is an historical law that the extremists always win, and Ferhat Abbas has been conquered by the extremists. The other great gamble was to build a really firm alliance with West Germany based on de Gaulle's friendship with Adenauer. But this too has failed.

PARIS, *December 13, 1960*

PLEASANT talk with Am Houghton. When he saw Eisenhower, the President complained: "All these fellows around me want to resign. [He was referring to McElroy's decision to quit as Secretary of Defense.] I can't resign my job; I don't see why they should be allowed to resign theirs." Houghton said this had impressed him deeply. Therefore he intended to stay here until the last moment now that the presidency is changing.

PARIS, *December 15, 1960*

LAST night, dined at Birgi's, the Turkish ambassador to NATO. Freya Stark was there looking as strange as usual, but cheery and nice. She is one of those marvelous screwball English women who fear nothing and go everywhere. They do adventurous things and manage to write beautifully about it. I think NATO should employ about two divisions of English women as an Amazon corps.

Agreeable talk with Pompidou at his office in the Rothschild bank. He is the greatest chain smoker I have ever known, letting long ashes form on the cigarette in the corner of his mouth and disregarding the fact that they dribble all over his suit. When one cigarette burns out he lights another.

He said de Gaulle's Algerian trip had clarified certain things. The General asserted true control over the army and smashed the last hopes of the ultras. Another illusion destroyed was that there was any Muslim opinion behind the Algérie Française slogans. Despite all difficulties, it will be possible to stage a referendum in Algeria.

Pompidou thinks that in 1961, formal negotiations will result in the creation of a fully independent Algerian republic without any official ties with France—but with friendly relations. Both the FLN and the French government think the worst solution of all would be partition and the creation of a French "Israel" along the seashore between Algiers and Oran.

Pompidou assured me Ferhat Abbas isn't the real chief of the FLN. The real chief remains Ben Bella. I said, "In that case you are in a good position for the English formula. You have him locked up, the way the English had Nkrumah and Makarios." "I fear they are a bit disappointed with Nkrumah these days," he said.

He reflected de Gaulle's old belief that the big clash this century would be between the white and colored races and that Russia would gradually incline toward our side. He also thought there would be a U.S.-U.S.S.R. nuclear agreement in 1961, because Moscow fears letting China have atomic weapons.

PARIS, *December 18, 1960*

TONIGHT, I had a first-class talk with Chris Herter at the embassy residence, together with a couple of first-class martinis. He is an admirable man, even though not the most successful secretary in history.

Chris said he wanted to ask me a question: namely, whether I had actually known *The New York Times* was going to come out for Kennedy the night we dined in Washington and I bet $5 with Bohlen. I said I had. "You are a good liar," he said with a grin.

He had been most impressed by the guerrilla warfare school the army is now running in South Carolina. The State Department had urged its establishment against a great deal of army resistance, but fortunately it was beginning to produce excellent results.

The army was very old-fashioned and hated the thought of doing something so novel as going into guerrilla warfare.

I asked if Herter really knew what was happening in Laos. He said we have evidence there have been between thirty-five and sixty-five flights to Vientiane of Soviet Illyushins which, in addition to gasoline, brought in guns and ammunition to the Communist rebels. We have photographs of the unloadings.

We do not yet precisely know what the North Vietnamese have been doing to help the Communists in Laos. One report says that a North Vietnamese division has crossed the frontier. Another very curious report says that two North Vietnamese divisions are moving toward the frontier without permission of their government. Laos is protected by a special annex to the SEATO treaty, which obligates the allies to defend Laos.

In terms of international law, it is hard to define the status of the present government. It is a "provisional" government named by the King. But it has not yet been confirmed by the National Assembly, and under the Laotian Constitution, no government is legitimate until it has been blessed in a particular temple.

We are very near to conditions of brush-fire war in all of Southeastern Asia. It is a very grave situation. Laos itself isn't worth a damn, but it leads right down into the heart of Southeastern Asia.

The Congo is also in a mess. The U.S.A. has leaned over backward to play the game with UN. Our aircraft furnished to UN have only taken troop contingents to places designated by UN. The only armed forces people we have there are traffic control experts.

The French have now turned their Algerian policy into an unloading operation. The only remaining problem is how to unload gracefully. There is nothing more we can do to help on de Gaulle's *directoire* request. We have done our best to satisfy him without institutionalizing Big Three partners. The night before this last NATO meeting began, Herter, Couve de Murville, and Lord Home sat up until 1 A.M. conferring on world problems. Livy Merchant, Hoyar-Miller, and Lucet have formed a regular committee to meet and talk things over. But much as the French want us to consult them, they refuse to consult with us.

PARIS, *December 19, 1960*

LAST night, Jimmy Smith came for dinner. When Jimmy was here ten years ago it was primarily to negotiate establishment of U.S. bases. But his dream always (as assistant secretary of the navy) was to establish some kind of mobile NATO force that would not depend upon fixed land bases with their attendant political complications.

The only way he could envision this would be for some kind of seaborne, medium-range missile base, and he thought of submarines. He talked to Admiral Rickover about this and Rickover was entranced because he saw the possibility of using submarines as underwater satellites continually on the move, less visible than satellites in the skies.

At that time, the navy was working with the air force on a missile and Jimmy wanted to call it Polaris after his own North Star Ranch in Aspen. But navy experts advised that it was going to be a flop so he should hold off his pet name until another program was worked out.

There were all kinds of problems involved. It was necessary to devise a small enough warhead. The navy would have to reckon on using liquid-fuel missiles unless it found a solid-fuel propellant. The storage of liquid fuels on submarines presented immense dangers. Faced with the alternative of dangerous explosive liquids, the navy mastered its own solid fuel.

We had to build a submarine small enough to be workable and still house the missiles. When the plan was first conceived the submarine would have had to be about as long as the Queen Mary. But as warheads shrunk and nuclear engines were reduced in size, submarine planning advanced.

The next thing was to devise a system whereby a submarine could navigate underwater by new methods. The air force was largely instrumental in designing the *Albacore*, which operated like an airplane under water by driving a very powerful stream of water behind the fins so that the submarine could be operated with only one control, like an old-fashioned plane with a joy stick.

The navy, at that time, had no system of figuring out just where its vessels were with exact precision. The new navigational system devised now permits the chief of naval operations to know within one hundred yards where any vessel is.

When Smith was first dreaming of this, he thought the ideal place to base missile submarines would be in the caves of Bizerte, but it became apparent that for political reasons these would not be available. The alternative was the polar ice cap, but nobody knew anything about it, whether great stalactites hung down beneath or whether it was flat. The primary job of Commander Beach and other nuclear submarine commanders who voyaged in the Arctic was to investigate the undersurface of the ice cap and also to map a way beneath the ice so that missile vessels would have an exact fix for potential targets. Finally, a new satellite system had to be devised in order to improve both navigational accuracy and communications facilities between vessels and Washington.

Marcello Mathias, Portuguese foreign minister, asked me to join him for a drink with his ambassador in Paris, Antonio de Faria. Mathias is a thin, slightly misshapen, little man with a passionate El Greco face.

He apparently felt I could be induced to put out a propaganda argument for Portuguese tenure of its colonies—which are now called "overseas provinces." If the kind of chaos in the Congo were to spread to Angola and Mozambique, it would hurt the cause of civilization and humanity. He made an incredibly impassioned speech, slipping forward on his armchair, down on his knees waving his arms around and addressing me as if I were an audience of fifty thousand people.

He said Portugal would fight against any incursion on its territory, "Even if we have to use bows and arrows against Russian tanks." Mathias said Portugal is seriously considering quitting NATO and becoming neutral, because it is so angry at the lack of allied support.

PARIS, *December 22, 1960*

LUNCHED with Spaak. He is desperately worried about NATO and thinks it is coming apart. Unless the Kennedy administration names a really remarkable envoy to the NATO council the dry rot will rush along.

There was absolutely no U.S. leadership evident at present. Herter had been an "insignificant" figure—above all, at the last meeting. Couve de Murville is, of course, playing de Gaulle's game of splitting the allies in favor of a Europe dominated by France. Brentano in Germany and Segni in Italy were also "insignificant." Nobody knows about British policy. Green, the Canadian foreign minister, is an absolute disaster. "I can't continue to lecture all of them," said Spaak. "They simply won't take it and, after all, I *am* their servant."

Spaak thinks NATO should arrive at a compact that in all UN votes, if an ally is involved in an argument, the other allies should either vote with him or, if they cannot agree, at least abstain; not vote against him. Furthermore, NATO should discuss important UN votes in advance at council meetings. The present situation is lamentable. The Greeks voted against Portugal in UN because Portugal had backed Turkey previously in UN votes on Cyprus. Compare this attitude in UN to that of the members of the Warsaw Pact, all of whom always vote as a bloc.

Germany has become the most important continental power and, after Adenauer fades away, there is a grave possibility that German nationalism may assert itself again. The French have been deliberately weakening NATO. And while the British have played a NATO role, it has always been in order to oppose the French.

PARIS, *February 11, 1961*

LUNCHED with Fritz Nolting. He had just come back from Washington where he had two long talks with Acheson. Dean told him that when Kennedy visited him and asked him if he would accept the post as ambassador to NATO, Acheson inquired, "Did you get this idea from Cy Sulzberger's column?" Kennedy replied, "Yes." Nolting said, "You guys don't realize how much influence you have." (Acheson declined the job. He preferred to stay in Washington and keep his finger in the pie.)

DE GAULLE:

"U.N. IS AN AUGMENTED

BABEL"

PARIS, *February 14, 1961*

THIS MORNING, I HAD A ONE-HOUR TALK WITH DE GAULLE. I ARRIVED about twenty-five minutes early at the Elysée and de Gaulle was in the process of receiving letters of credence from the Cuban and Argentine ambassadors. I sat chatting with Colonel de Bonneval and a naval aide, who apologized that I was kept waiting, but the President wanted to change into more comfortable clothes.

De Gaulle was in very good form. I sat across from him at his desk and exhausted my entire list of questions, writing down the answers. When I had tucked my questions and notebook in my pocket, he leaned back and said with a faint smile: "Well, how are you and how do you see things?" I said I was pretty unhappy about the world. He advised me not to be so sad because if people and nations had resolution they could face difficulties whatever they were.

De Gaulle said it was perfectly apparent that during our age nations needed greater direction by their governments. Eisenhower had not given the United States sufficient leadership. Whatever his intentions, President Kennedy would find himself increasingly pushed toward strong government and the U.S. economy would find itself increasingly pushed toward dirigisme. This was a necessity of our times. The United States would simply have to abandon its shibboleth of free enterprise and accept ever greater government controls for its economy. There was no escape from this. The problems and pressures of our era are simply too great to permit the luxury of laissez-faire. We were all finding this out and we all had this reaction to the enormous events of our time.

Incidentally, I asked de Gaulle if there were any truth to the tale that he was a friend of General Gavin, our new ambassador. "Absolutely not," he said. "I suppose it is possible that I could have met him at some time or another and perhaps shaken his hand; I met many American generals during the war. But if this is the case, he made absolutely no impression because I surely don't remember him." (Before I went in to see the President, Bonneval had told me with a sardonic smile: "We hear that your General Gavin is taking a cram course in French.") I expressed the polite hope that at least General Gavin might be a friend of de Gaulle's by the time he left. "On verra," said the President without any particular interest.

De Gaulle expressed mild curiosity in why Gavin was chosen as ambassador. I said the post had been offered originally to Chip Bohlen, who would have been excellent. De Gaulle agreed. However, he (Bohlen) thought it would be better for him to remain in Washington because of his great experience in Soviet affairs. De Gaulle also agreed that this had been wise.*

I was very much struck by one thing throughout our conversation. De Gaulle continually spoke of Algeria in terms of a fully independent republic which could decide freely on its own whether it had any links with France or not. In other words, he has gone whole hog. Other points will emerge in this account of our conversation which clearly will produce troubles in negotiations that have now started. But there isn't any doubt that he has taken the major step.

I then asked de Gaulle what kind of guarantees concerning the status and rights of the European minority would be satisfactory in case Algeria finally opted for complete independence.

To my astonishment, he replied:

> We are not asking for anything, for any guarantees. That is up to the Algerians. Obviously the Europeans are very useful to Algeria. It is the Europeans with their abilities, their techniques, and their capital who can make Algeria work. Without them there would be economic misery. It is clearly in the interest of Algeria that the Europeans should remain. But it is up to the Algerians to make the decision. *They* must make the decision and they must offer the guarantees and conditions which persuade the Europeans to stay on.†

I said that I remembered an offer made by President Bourguiba of Tunisia more than an year ago in which he said he would be willing to extend the lease of Bizerte as a French base in the event of an independent Maghreb state including Algeria and suggested similar bases in the Algerian portion of such a state. How did de Gaulle feel about this?

* See de Gaulle's further comments, p. 71.
† See de Gaulle's further comments, pp. 72–73.

He answered: "We will have to see about that. Unquestionably Bizerte is very important to us. If the Russians were in Bizerte it would be extremely serious. And yet the Russians could come very swiftly with paratroopers and submarines. Therefore, the matter of Bizerte is of real importance. Also we will have to keep Mers el-Kebir. There is no question about that. And there may probably be other strong points we will require."

This is going to be difficult to talk out in negotiations. It doesn't quite jibe with the idea de Gaulle expressed about total freedom of action for the Algerians.* He saw no chance of a deal between Adenauer and Moscow. About Adenauer he said:

He won't treat with the Russians. Furthermore, nothing will happen of any sort before this year's West German elections.

But after Adenauer, things may change. Russia may work out a deal on Berlin and a federation of East Germany and West Germany as the basis for such a realignment. It is not possible to envision this after Adenauer. That is why we must have a strong Common Market Europe.†

I then told de Gaulle I had heard that France had requested the Spanish government to return to this country General Salan, Lagaillarde, and the other ultras who fled to Spain; and that the Spaniards had said they would do this if France would return the leading Spanish political refugees here.

De Gaulle answered:

This is untrue. We never asked for Salan, Lagaillarde, and the others. We are totally indifferent. We only asked the Spaniards not to let them go to Algeria. And the Spanish kept them under surveillance. In fact they prevented Lagaillarde from going to Algeria.

The Spanish are, of course, very attentive to the activities of our political emigrés. But they recognize that they are political refugees and that France is a haven for political refugees.

I then asked de Gaulle if it were true that he was contemplating the advisability of changing the French Constitution to provide for a Vice President, an idea he often entertained and then discarded.

He said:

No, such reports are not true. I have taken no new position on the Constitution. It doesn't work badly. It assures our political stability, and I don't see any reason to change it now.

But after me [après moi], I don't know what.

After me, I think it would be wise to create a formal presidential regime like that of the U.S.

* See de Gaulle's further comments, pp. 41, 45, 63–64, 75.
† See de Gaulle's further comments, pp. 54, 54–55, 77.

After me, I think it would be best to have an outright presidential system like yours which would include a Vice President.

But that is not for now. That is for after me.

(I was extremely interested in the number of times he successively used the words "after me.")

I will here add a little postscript to what I dictated at the very beginning apropos of de Gaulle's view that we would need an increasingly strong government. I said I agreed and that it was rather interesting to note the increased recognition in the U.S. of a strong hand at the helm. For example, there was a striking contrast between the American people's view of de Gaulle today as compared with two years ago. Originally it feared too strong a hand at the French helm; now it was grateful for it.

De Gaulle asked me what I thought about the referendum. I said I considered the most important thing was that it had destroyed all chances of an effective alliance between the extreme right and the army. It had already been clear that de Gaulle had broken up the left—even including the Communists who were in relative disarray. But I had felt the experienced, clever politicians, like Soustelle, Bidault, Pinay, and others, were capable of organizing a considerable right-wing bloc which might present potential dangers. The referendum had shown they had failed. De Gaulle agreed.

I then said the party system in France was ineffective at present. I asked if he thought, nevertheless, that when the kind of post-de Gaulle government he talked of, with an American-type presidential regime, came in, it would be possible for France to have only two or three major political parties instead of a wide split of small parties.

He shrugged his shoulders and said he thought not. Only the Communists had any kind of a party organization in France today. He could not really imagine major parties growing up here. The French were by nature too precise in their political ideas and tended to split off from each other. This was difficult, but it was a fact.

ANKARA, TURKEY, *February 20, 1961*

THIS afternoon, I spent two hours with Selim Sarper, foreign minister almost since the *coup d'état* last May and one of three surviving members of the original Cabinet. He said: "I noticed in a column you wrote last week a reference to a Turk working in the Tshombé government of Katanga. Do you know his name?"

I replied I could not possibly remember (later I checked: Arsin). He then asked: "Was his name Kabibay?" I said I couldn't recall. He then went over to his desk where he had laid out a series of pictures of Turkish officers in uniform, and brought back a picture. "Was this the fellow?"

he asked, showing me the photograph of a colonel. I thought not. "What's it all about?" I asked.

He told me Colonel Kabibay was one of fourteen members of the military junta who were put on the shelf last November. He had been sent to Brussels. Kabibay wrote Sarper saying he had been offered a job by the Tshombé government and was tempted to take it. Selim recommended that he should turn the offer down. However, Kabibay had not replied and Sarper was worried lest he might have sneaked off to the Congo. "You can see how embarrassing it would be for us after the murder of Lumumba was announced," said Selim. I was astonished that the Turks seemed to have such a loose check on their own dissidents.

I pointed out that eight years ago the pact of Ankara had been signed among Turkey, Greece, and Jugoslavia. It was supposed to be a five-year treaty. What was the status of that alliance today?

Sarper said: "You might say it is in a deep freeze. It has never been renounced. But today none of the three signatory powers is very enthusiastic about it. It still exists on paper. We are leaving well enough alone."

ANKARA, TURKEY, *February 21, 1961*

USEFUL talk with President Çemal Gursel at the Presidential Palace of Çankaya. Gursel (chief of the provisional government) received me in an ugly high-ceilinged, brown-paneled room. He sat on a small sofa in front of which was a table with three chairs around it. He is heavyset and overweight, with a humorous face, a huge nose, egg-shaped, bald head with a white fringe in the back, a ridiculous little white moustache, intelligent, brown eyes, and a musical voice. He speaks only Turkish.

He suffered a stroke some months ago, and although his mind functions well, he moves in a cumbersome way. His left arm is clearly not working. He had difficulty ringing a bell for his secretary. I asked whether he would run for the presidency whenever elections terminate the present martial law. He replied: "For the moment, I have no wish to do so. But if during the pre-electoral period, people continue to ask me to stay and their number grows; and if the interests of the nation require that I should, then I will stand. To constitute a democratic system here we must have a wholly impartial chief during the transitional period. If there is no other wholly impartial chief available I may stay in office."

I deduced that he has every intention of staying in Çankaya Palace even if he has to be carried there stuffed. I asked whether his health was good enough for him to continue. He said: "My doctors say my health is plenty good enough. Even today they say I am plenty well enough to fulfill the functions of chief of state."

I said that I had been interested to read several times his words—uttered before and again after the revolution—to the effect that the Turkish army must remain out of politics. Did he still feel this was necessary? He answered:

"Indeed I do. We have already put the army out of politics. We have isolated it by specific orders which are followed in the sense of rigid discipline. The army is out of politics." This is not strictly true because he, a general, is chief of state; a prominent member of the military junta remains commander of the Ankara district; and several others retain commands.

Gursel continued: "The military Committee cannot return to the armed forces again. Its members have been too deeply involved in politics and we will make it impossible for them to return to the armed forces. Instead, the new Constitution will give the members of the Committee seats in the Senate. I also will be entitled to a seat in the Senate. I am finished with the army."

I asked what had been the reason for his revolution, why had the junta considered it necessary to throw out the previous regime? He said: "The revolution took place because the political situation had degenerated beyond repair. We were headed toward a dictatorship: a sectarian, party and class dictatorship. Furthermore, the economic life of the country was stultified. The people of Turkey were rapidly dividing into two camps preparing to fight each other in a civil war. Is that not adequate reason to justify a revolution?"

I asked if he could describe the revolution's philosophical objective. He answered: "This is easy. The philosophical objective was to install an authentic democracy and to order the pattern of our life in a democratic way."

I noted that after the *coup d'état*, the junta said it would turn back the dictatorial authority to the people in a real parliamentary democracy in three months. That the deadline had expired about a half a year ago. How did he explain the delay?

He answered:

First of all, the trial of the members of the preceding government has taken much longer than we realized it would take. A legal process of this sort is not easy. Secondly, we soon became convinced that it would take a long period of time to reestablish the basis for normal political life. We had to wait and allow enough time for new parties to be developed. Thirdly, we found that it is really quite difficult to establish a new Constitution and electoral law.

But don't make any mistake about exaggerating the amount of time it will take before we get back to a normal system. You asked me if I can guarantee that we will again be a parliamentary democracy by the end of this year. I assure you it will be much sooner than that. We will be a full, peacetime, civilian democracy, a normal democracy in which the only role of the army will be to protect the nation.

I then asked my favorite question: Which man, alive or dead, had most influenced him? I expected him automatically to say Kemal Ataturk. To my astonishment he perked up and replied without a moment's hesitation, "Bergson, Henri Bergson." He went on to explain that he had been fascinated by Bergson's writings as a young officer, adding:

"Bergson is the foundation of my political thinking because Bergson accepts liberty as an indissoluble part of life. He says the evolution of life can only develop in an atmosphere of freedom. According to Bergson, only a life evolving from freedom and in freedom become creative. That is the basis of my thought."

I was particularly interested because de Gaulle was also profoundly influenced by Bergson. I then added that one aspect of Bergson's philosophy had always fascinated me and this was that Bergson considered intuition an essential part of true wisdom. "Yes," he said, "intuition must play a major role in one's decisions. I have felt this since I first studied Bergson. I am a soldier, but I have studied much, I have read much."

I asked if he thought his final decision on whether to stand for the presidency would be in any way affected by the Bergsonian theory of philosophical intuition. He smiled and answered: "I might use intuition as an important factor in making up my mind."

ANKARA, TURKEY, *February 22, 1961*

DINED with Jasper and Nermine Streeter. Nermine (ex-Menemençioglu) is from a famous family of diplomats and intellectuals. She hates the former regime with venom. Claims they interrupted progress, catered to reactionary Muslim church elements, tolerated the ghastly illiteracy problem by closing down village institutes. Jasper says Zorlu was far more crooked than has yet come out in the trials; Menderes also. Both admire the guts of ex-President Bayar, who shows no fear; and both have contempt for Menderes, who is cowering.

Nermine says a strong, reactionary religious movement still fights the new regime and demonstrates for Bayar and Menderes. Unfortunately, Islam has a reactionary influence on political development and this is the reason no Turkish or other Muhammedan revolution has followed through in the economic sense.

A rumor has been circulated by the backward Mullahs that Menderes, who is supposed to be touched with immortality as a consequence of escaping from an air crash, rides off from Yassiada Island prison every night on a white horse (like Muhammad) to say his prayers at Eyub mosque in Istanbul, a very holy place.

ANKARA, TURKEY, *February 24, 1961*

SARPER invited me for lunch at Suraya's. He told me that when the fourteen "rebels" in the revolutionary Committee were rounded up by Gursel, one came to the door in the pyjamas in the middle of the night. He insisted that, as a proud Turk, he would rather be shot than taken in that condition. He was permitted to go back, change into uniform, and put on his gun. Then he came peaceably.

ATHENS, *February 28, 1961*

I HAD a talk with Prime Minister Caramanlis, sipping Turkish coffee in his office.

He thought NATO should be made a fourth nuclear power and this would strengthen its solidarity. A NATO summit should be held to discuss this. Unfortunately, right now there was confusion in NATO, which gave the Russians the impression of allied disunity.

Caramanlis said the Greek economy was good in comparison with the past but bad vis-à-vis developed Europe. Much remained to be done. There was a need for rapid action because the contrast between wealth and poverty created a social danger.

The big problem is that no private capital is available and the job must be handled by foreign Greek and government investment. The state is obliged to build everything from ships to hotels. Nevertheless, he is pleased that in his budget during the last four years he has shown a surplus after fifty years of deficit.

Caramanlis complained that he cannot get more money from Greek ship owners living abroad because if they are bothered too much they will sail their ships under other flags. Three years ago, Greece had 1,500,000 tons in its Merchant Marine and it now has 5,500,000 tons.

He boasted that the Greek currency was the second most stable in Europe—just after Switzerland; that the cost of living here is the most stable in Europe. It has risen 10 percent in five years as compared to 14 percent in the U.S.A.

ATHENS, *March 1, 1961*

LUNCHED with Evangelos Averoff-Tositsas, foreign minister of Greece for five years. Averoff says Hoxha, the Albanian boss, has always been a fanatical Stalinist. Khrushchev went to Tirana in 1959, to try and convert him but failed. Last summer in Bucharest, when there was an international Communist meeting, Albania supported the Stalinist line, thinking this would either force Russia to get more friendly or would attract

Chinese support. China took the bait. Despite its own serious famine, China has shipped wheat to Albania.

Averoff began talking about Spaak's successor as NATO secretary-general. He was ambitious for the job himself because it would help him politically and help Greece nationally. He claims he would have gotten the job if the U.S.A. had not backed Stikker "who has a bad heart and is a Dutchman with a colonialist taint."

I asked him about the 1953 Balkan Pack of Ankara. He said: "In reality this does not exist." Neutralist Jugoslavia could not afford an indirect link with NATO but did not wish to renounce the treaty. Greece's relations with Belgrade were good and military exchanges continue. Through Greece, Jugoslavia is able to breathe and has an opening toward NATO.

I recalled his request, before the Cyprus peace, that I take a letter down to Grivas—which I undertook to do as a journalistic experience. He told me he had not gone through with this for the following reasons. At that time Grivas was holed up in a house near Limassol. He was afraid that if I established contact with him the British might be able to trace Grivas because they had a good idea of the neighborhood he was in and it would have been disastrous for the Greek government to be linked with this.

Averoff claims the Russians are still trying to win over Greece in order to outflank Jugoslavia and Turkey and establish a bridgehead aimed at the Middle East. This is a permanent aim even if tactics change. There are no armed threats because the Russians know NATO would intervene and also the Greek army and police could squash a guerrilla uprising. The tactic now is to concentrate on propaganda. The Russians are helping EDA (the extreme left) and in the 1958 elections EDA spent more than any other party.

ATHENS, *March 4, 1961*

YESTERDAY evening, I had a long talk with General George Grivas who, under the pseudonym of Dighenis, headed the EOKA uprising against the British in Cyprus. He was then a colonel, but when he returned to Greece he was promoted to three-star rank. Although born in Cyprus, he has made his career as a professional officer in the Greek army. He is now up to the ears in politics and would like to overthrow the present government and become Prime Minister.

Grivas is sixty-three, was born in Nicosia, and brought up in the nearby village of Trikomo. He graduated from the Athens Officers Academy in 1918, and in 1920, he fought the Turks in Asia Minor as a lieutenant. Later he graduated from the Paris Ecole Supérieure de Guerre. He is married and has no children.

He received me in his neat, little office, filled with ugly carved furniture. In his pictures he looks like a diminutive Groucho Marx but in reality he is not ridiculous. He is about five foot six, trimly built, bald with tufts of black hair on the sides, huge moustache, tough face, and piercing eyes. I asked if he had been among those present when I saw EOKA leaders briefly in 1955. He said no, he had been near Limassol then.

He said in guerrilla warfare no system that works in one country is of any use in another. Flexibility is all-important. His permanent EOKA force in the mountains was never larger than two hundred, but the towns and villages were filled with hidden guerrillas. Grivas himself went back and forth between mountains and villages. During the struggle there were 40,000 British troops in Cyprus, which has a population of less than 500,000. The one essential for guerrilla success is to have widespread popular support.

I asked what his foreign policy would be if he ever became Prime Minister. He said: "We are with the West. There is no other possibility. And it would be inconceivable for Greece not to stay in NATO."

He said he was strongly anti-Communist and had begun fighting the Communists since 1941. But the West was not choosing the best way of fighting communism. It gave too many small countries the impression that it opposed their aspirations; the Arab lands for example. Colonies want their freedom and will take help from anyone. The West gives the impression that it never helps them and Russia does the contrary. Even in Cyprus, an impression was left behind that the only real support the independence movement got in UN was from Russia.

Grivas said he had absolutely no understanding with the Communists here and, "I would defeat communism or be defeated. I am trying to draw strongly from the Communists and their supporters, but I will never collaborate with them." There was a strong feeling here that Greece's policy on communism was wrong and the government only used violence against the Communists. "The Communists cannot be beaten by violence alone. Social measures are needed. When I talk to the Communists, I say I disapprove of all the government dossiers filed away on them. I would burn them and give the Communists social justice. But if then they worked against the state I would hang them."

I asked Grivas how he would describe his ideology; was he a liberal, Socialist, or what. He said: "I give no importance to labels. I am a Greek and a humanitarian. I am a nationalist and I want to help the masses. I am for justice."

He said that Greek nationalists had foolishly abandoned all the best slogans to the Communists. I asked him if he favored a monarchy or a republic. He said monarchy was the best thing if the King served as a real king and not just as a party chief. He added, "I have been England's enemy but their system is excellent." He also added that if he were Prime Minister he would have no feelings against the British or Turks in NATO but would like to speak freely to them. He added, "Good opponents make good friends."

I asked the usual: What individual had most influenced his life? He replied, "Perhaps it was my village teacher in Trikomo. This village atmosphere of honesty and family life still governs my thoughts. Only recently, I saw my eighty-five-year-old teacher and I kissed his hand. He helped form my character. All my philosophy comes from my village."

Grivas said he had taken great care of himself all his life and had lived by rigid discipline. He had never even visited a coffeehouse until he got married at the age of forty. He had no amusements or relaxations.

ROME, *March 9, 1961*

AT 11:30 last night, Averell Harriman, who is staying in my hotel, asked me down for a drink.

Averell had a good talk with de Gaulle, who did not bring up the *directoire* issue, contrary to newspaper reports, or ask for nuclear secrets. Indicated a real desire to get going on Algerian peace with NO preconditions. Wants to work out some sort of condominium basis for the Sahara and its oil. "Why should we hand that over to the Arabs?" asks Harriman. After Rome he is flying off to Teheran to stiffen up the Shah. Harriman doesn't yet know what his function is to be. Will he be a Hopkins or a Colonel House? He thinks he has been very useful to Kennedy on this trip ("much more useful than he will ever know").

It's too bad Acheson didn't take the NATO post. Max Taylor was offered Paris and turned it down. Chip Bohlen should have taken it (although, in fact, it was never "formally" offered to him). Bill Walton in the end suggested Gavin to JFK. Harriman thinks it was a lousy choice.

It's hard to know how Rusk will do. Rusk thinks he knows it all on the Far East. Harriman admits he "does know a lot" on this and respects him. The chain of command isn't too damned clear yet, however, and anyway, Kennedy expects to be his own Secretary of State. Kennedy is bright, impressive, tough; but he has lots to learn.

Averell has no use for Lyndon Johnson and is sad that his office has been moved so near the White House. Averell regards him as a stultifying, illiberal force. He is impressed by Kennedy's energy and says, "He really reads the newspapers. He has caught me up several times on things I had missed." Harriman is deeply depressed about the Eisenhower era. Says: "We wasted eight full years."

One big policy change has been in Laos. The Kennedy administration has retreated from the previous tough position. Now we seek a neutralist government there, backed by popular support, and not penetrated by communism. This is our aim; but it may already be too late to achieve it.

I asked if Kennedy had any preconditions for a meeting with Khrushchev. Harriman said no; he would meet when he thought the prospects were worthwhile, but he would not be bludgeoned into it.

Averell keeps saying: "Kennedy doesn't know how much good I'm doing him over here. People simply didn't know him. But they accept it from me when I tell them how competent he is."

CAIRO, *March 26, 1961*

YESTERDAY, I had lunch at Gigi (Bechara) Takla's still listed as vice president of *Al Ahram*, the paper his family used to own. He goes to his office every day but has nothing whatsoever to do. Mohammed Heikal runs the paper. Takla is going to be paid off in government bonds but hasn't received them yet. One reason he goes to the office is to protect his interests.

The press was nationalized in May, 1960. Takla is bitter about the regime but used to see Nasser often and supported his ideas. Now he and other young intellectuals (Gigi is thirty-three) feel Nasser has betrayed the revolution by turning Egypt into an authoritarian state which is slipping more and more toward communism.

Takla is not living in poverty. We had a splendid lunch at his house in Garden City—together with his mother, who has resumed her Lebanese citizenship, Mohammed, and Laure Sultan. After lunch, Takla asked if he could drive me home. I was astonished to find seven cars in his garage. Gigi told me that I could rest assured all my telephone calls were tapped. So were his. They had built up a large dossier on him but so far had done nothing with it.

This evening, I had a talk for two and a half hours with President Nasser at his home in Heliopolis. I drove out with Heikal. Nasser's house is still the same he lived in as a young lieutenant colonel, but it has been steadily enlarged and is no modest villa. In fact, at one point in our conversation, Nasser pointed out that the large office where we were sitting had formerly been a tennis court. It is exceedingly well protected by armed security police and soldiers.

Together, Heikal and I went into Nasser's new office, comfortable, but not ornately furnished. We smoked filtered cigarettes and drank Turkish coffee.

Nasser was well dressed in a striped, gray flannel suit, white shirt, and conservative necktie. He looked thinner than when I saw him last, and his hair is graying on the sides. But he appeared fit despite reports that he has a bad case of diabetes.

I asked him to start things off by listing points of agreement—rather than disagreement—between the U.A.R. and the U.S.A. He said:

I suppose we agree on some principles, but even then we often disagree on their application. For example, we are against colonial domination in Algeria and we have always wanted Algeria to be independent. This was once the feeling of the U.S.A., and Franklin Roosevelt strongly supported self-determination. But from that point on, the U.S.A. has changed and we have disagreed with your approach. You have your alliances and sometimes you are restrained by them.

We are certainly in disagreement on the Congo. The U.A.R. supported the legal Congo government and the desire of the Congolese people for full independence. We were against bringing the Cold War into the Congo.

In some ways, there has been help from your country. We have had some loans from the Export-Import Bank of the Development Loan Fund. But these have been small loans. We have also had food surplus. These things have been going along in a cordial and friendly way and have not been affected by political questions. Economic and cultural relationships have not been interfered with.

I asked what was needed to improve relationships. He answered:

One of the main obstacles is Israel. We want to see the U.S. fair on this. But if the Arab people see the U.S. taking sides and neglecting our own views, then naturally they get angry. Nobody can neglect the Arab viewpoint and questions affecting the sentiments and emotions of our people.

The American newspapers are not fair in discussing this problem. The U.S.A. must be fair; but it isn't. And our reaction is bitter. I have myself attacked *The New York Times* on this point in speeches. I am trying to direct your attention to the problem.

I said I knew his policy was what we called "neutralist" but that, in reading his newspapers and listening to his radio, I felt it was extremely *un*neutral toward the U.S.A. He answered:

Neutrality is not an exact description of our policy. Neutrality applies only during war. Ours is a policy of "nonalignment."

And our policy is perfectly fair. There is a plain reason for the fact that we do not attack the Communist bloc. We never read any attacks on us in the Soviet press or by Soviet statesmen. But the U.S. press attacks us and U.S. politicians attack us. I keep reading of American senators who want to blockade us because we don't allow Israeli ships to go through the Suez Canal.

I said he should remember that America was a land of free speech and that every statement by every politician and newspaper did not necessarily represent official policy. Nasser then referred to Secretary of State Rusk's testimony before a Senate committee as highly unfriendly and added:

Whenever we read of a hostile action or article or statement, that produces a reaction here. But there are no such hostile actions or statements on the Communist side, and that explains why there are no angry reactions in our press. When the Russians attacked us in 1958, we answered back sharply. They criticized us for arresting Communists. But when they stopped, we stopped. We don't attack without reason.

And we cannot isolate the opinions of your newspapers and politicians from the opinions of your government. We are a new country and we are very sensitive. We value our dignity. Our public is impressed by speeches and articles abroad. It is angered when it sees threats in the American press and menaces in the speeches of American politicians, when it reads that some senator has warned what you will do if Israel cannot use the Suez Canal; when it feels that the U.S.A. is trying to create pressure. How can we tell people that this is not American policy?

I said I was appalled by the shortness of memory around here. After all, in 1956 the U.S.A., which is always being attacked as "run by Israel," turned against its two closest allies, Britain and France, and forced Israel to retreat to its own borders. Surely this showed that we mean what we say, that we oppose any kind of aggression and that we are a fair-minded people. And yet we received no credit from this "nonaligned" government and "nonaligned" press and radio.

Nasser replied rather lamely that they had praised our stand against aggression following the Suez war and again in 1958. But that our Suez stand was "almost immediately followed by the Eisenhower Doctrine which ended all understanding with Washington. We felt this was an effort to isolate Egypt from the other Arab countries, and naturally we opposed it."

I asked why he was so strongly opposed to the Congo confederation scheme which, it seemed to me, showed at least some chance of producing peace.

It is for the people of the Congo to decide on their future and not just for a few personalities. That is why we want to see the Congolese Parliament convened. Now the Congo is splitting up into a series of independent countries. There are already eight. Soon there will be twelve. Soon there will be thirty or forty. Each tribe will declare its own independence and claim its own state. They are already talking of this. The precedent has been created to divide the Congo into a series of unworkable fragments.

I asked about reports that the U.A.R. was sending arms to Gizenga (leftist Congolese). He replied:

That is nonsense. It is geographically impossible. I am a military officer and I can tell you one cannot send arms to Gizenga's part of the Congo through the Sudan. It is a trip of five thousand kilometers and mostly through swamps and deserts without roads. I have sent no arms to Gizenga, either overland or by air. There is no airlift to Gizenga, and it is impossible to send anything by truck. I have given Gizenga no help and I have sent him no technicians.

I asked if diplomatic relations would be restored with France should peace come in Algeria. He answered: "That would remove one of the main obstacles. But there is another very serious one which is the continuous French supply of arms to Israel. They are giving Israel planes and tanks and nuclear equipment. Algerian peace would eliminate only one main obstacle."

I asked about relations with Moscow and Peking. He said: "Relations with Russia are going on well and there are no disagreements. With Peking they are normal. We had some friction with China in 1959, when they attacked our position on the Communists in the U.A.R. But now relations are again being normalized."

I told Nasser that when I last saw him three years ago, I had asked his impression on religious freedom for Soviet Muslims and he had said, "Ask me after I come back from my own visit." I now wanted to know. He said:

I can only tell you what I saw. I saw freedom. I worshipped at mosques in Moscow, Leningrad, and Tashkent. And there were many people in the mosques. Last year, the Soviet radio broadcast Ramadan services just as we do here. That is what I saw, religious freedom. But I will admit that I noticed the mosques were mainly filled with older people. I don't think the younger people are very interested in religion.

I asked Nasser if the Yemen were still a member of the U.A.S. (United Arab States), and how that was developing. To my astonishment, Nasser didn't even know what the U.A.S. was—even though he founded it—until Heikal reminded him. Then he said: "Yes, it continues as a confederation, but we remain as two independent countries."

I reminded him that both in 1955 and in 1958, he spoke to me of his worry about an Israeli invasion and said that he feared war "as long as Israel exists." Did he still feel that way? He answered:

Of course. It could happen any day or any night. That is our experience with Israel. Seven days before the 1956 invasion, Ben Gurion said publicly he wanted peace. I read in the Israeli newspapers that Israel is preparing again for war. Just a few days ago the Israeli chief of staff issued an order that his soldiers should be prepared. We fear the threat of a war madness beside us. And the French are arming the Israelis with the latest Vautour fighter-bombers and Mirages to replace their Mystères.

Furthermore, we are suspicious that the Israeli nuclear plant is not for peaceful purposes because they built it secretly and first called it a textile factory. We told the UN about our own nuclear laboratories. France and Israel are cooperating in the atomic fields.

I asked Nasser if he would tell me what the famous Lavon incident really was. He said:

An Israeli colonel came to Cairo under a foreign passport to organize sabotage and terror. The group burned various cinemas and American libraries with time bombs. We were trying to protect American property, but they were trying to destroy it, to poison U.S. relations with us, pretending we had done it. One bomb went off prematurely and injured the man who left it. We caught him and interrogated him and forced him to confess all the details of the plot. We arrested all the conspirators in 1954, and tried them early in 1955. The colonel committed suicide.

I then asked what he thought of the Eichmann trial. He said:

I hear that Eichmann is being moved continually from place to place and drugged. It is not Israel's right to try Eichmann. He should be tried in a German court. Israel didn't even exist during the period of the crimes he is charged with. The Israelis say Eichmann killed six million Jews. How many Jews were there in Germany or the entire world before the war and after the war? It is easy to check the figures and see that these claims are not true. Maybe one or two million were killed.

I looked at Nasser and saw him suddenly glance across at Heikal, who must have made some sign because Nasser then said: "But, of course, killing is killing, anyway. We merely think the figure is exaggerated for propaganda reasons."

I asked how many Communists were now in prison in the U.A.R. He thought a moment and then said:

There are eighty in jail in Syria and about two hundred in Egypt. They conspired against the state as Communists. Many were arrested originally, but we released about two hundred in Egypt and about one hundred and forty in Syria, and they are all now behaving themselves. There is no Communist underground opposing us.

We think that to rebuild our country we must have national unity, so we decided to liquidate all parties and rebuild the country on a new basis.

The former parties were all dominated by the same class. We want to bring the different classes to the same level, and this will change the social structure of the country. Before the revolution, there were four parties, but they all represented the feudalist minority in their leadership. Twenty-five years from now there will be farm cooperatives, small ownership (with ten acres for each family), no landlords, industrial cooperatives, government-owned factories, privately owned factories, and factories half-privately owned and half-state owned. There will be small capitalists holding small numbers of securities. This will be a different society and one cannot foresee its political shape.

If we were to admit free political parties today there would be three: one prowestern bloc, one proeastern bloc, and one independent and national. Their arguments would destroy unity and bring us the Cold War.

I asked Nasser to tell me a bit about his personal life. He answered:

I am an easy man, always relaxed; and that helps me with my work. Sometimes I work for twenty-four hours without interruption and without feeling tired. I have no fixed routine. I don't need rest because I feel happy. I have no problems with my family. I don't worry. After you leave this evening I may go to my bedroom and read some papers or some books, or I may look at television or a movie with my children, or I may go back to my office. Sometimes I take two- or three-day holidays so I don't get tired.

Did he still play tennis? He smiled and said: "Unfortunately, we are now sitting in the tennis court. I haven't played for eight months, but I hope to start again soon. Now I play ping-pong with the children."

I asked what books he was reading. He said:

I read as many as ten books at the same time. I read on planning, on history, on Israel, novels. Now I am reading Lenin again. I read him in 1958. I am also reading India's third Five Year Plan. I am reading an Arab history of Israel. Also an Arabic book on the Middle East, a novel by Somerset Maugham, G. D. H. Cole's work on socialism, and an American book on China called *Impatient Giant*. I read at night. It is my only free moment. I also read *The New York Times*, the *Herald Tribune*, and British and Arabic newspapers.

He told me he goes to sleep at 2 A.M. and generally rises at 8 or 9 A.M.

At this point I was ready to go, but I had to ask why *The New York Times* stringer had been arrested. I did not wish to be impertinent but I felt it necessary to ask about anything that had to do with *The New York Times*; Fahmy worked for us as well as others. Nasser looked grim. He said it had nothing to do with *The New York Times*, but that Fahmy had been "sending many lies about me." He would be punished for this. He mentioned Lord Beaverbrook so I know that at least one of the reasons for his arrest was the *Daily Express* story claiming Nasser had diabetic comas. I said I would like to be able to tell this to Fahmy's wife because she didn't know why her husband was being held incommunicado. "She knows," said Nasser. I don't envy Maurice.

We then got up, shook hands in a friendly fashion, and I departed. Whether Nasser looked at a movie, a ping-pong table, or Lenin, I do not know.

PARIS, *April 6, 1961*

AT a hen luncheon party where Isabelle Norstad was present, Mrs. Burgess, wife of the outgoing NATO ambassador, said, "That fool Sulzberger doesn't know anything about NATO. Just because he sees General Norstad and plays golf with him doesn't mean he is well informed. Everybody knows that Norstad doesn't know anything about NATO." Isabelle said nothing.

PARIS, *April 7, 1961*

YESTERDAY evening, Gavin gave a reception for Vice President Johnson, which I attended with Marina. When Johnson spotted me he rushed over and grabbed me by the arm and took me into a corner for a talk. It became quite embarrassing. The reception was in his honor and people were being brought up to be introduced all the time. I kept trying to get out of the way, but he held me by the arm. When Winthrop Aldrich tottered up I slipped away. But Randy Kidder came up afterward and said, "The Vice President has given me orders to clear everybody out of the way because he wants you to come back and talk to him some more." I did.

He reached into his pocket and hauled out a letter from the President to him sent from Palm Beach just before he left America and addressed "Dear Lyndon." The President said he wanted to use Johnson's trip to Senegal as a symbol of American interest in Africa, and in order "to help Ed Murrow" (USIA boss) on the propaganda side. He also wanted Johnson to see Ambassador Art Dean in Geneva to get a lead on the present situation of the nuclear-test talks with Russia in order to muster Congressional support for our position. Then he wanted him to go to Paris to confer with Gavin and Norstad.

Johnson asked me what I thought of his speech at NATO this afternoon. I said I thought it gave the impression of American leadership, but really didn't commit us to anything and threw the ball back across the Atlantic on the nuclear arming of NATO.

He then reached into his pocket and hauled out another document. This was a carbon copy of a cable from Finletter to the Secretary of State marked "Secret—Eyes only—for Secretary of State to be passed on to President." The cable reported that Johnson's speech had made a profound and favorable impression on our allies and had already considerably changed the atmosphere.

Tom Finletter was at the reception and later observed that other NATO ambassadors were most impressed by Johnson's speech. "Yes," I said, "I saw your cable." "What cable?" he asked. "The one you just sent to the Secretary of State." "Good God!" he said. "I just sent it. It was in the highest possible classification. How did you ever see it?"

Johnson told me:

> You must have been puzzled by my reaction in our last conversation. But now I have something to say. Things are moving. There is real leadership. There were a lot of doubting Thomases who thought we had forgotten NATO. But we haven't. This trip was an ideal way to show that we are in favor of self-determination in Africa and elsewhere, but at the same time we are not weakening in our alliance.

At the door, when leaving, his right-hand man, Horace Busby, Johnson's aide, buttonholed me. He said:

> Just before we flew up to Washington after seeing the President, Johnson said there was one man he wanted to see in Paris and that was Sulzberger. He told the President that the most valuable talk he had had over here had been with you [much to my astonishment]. He likes frank talk. The only trouble was that you weren't frank enough. He wants you to tell him "This is what you fellows ought to do because this is the situation."

Interesting luncheon conversation with André de Staercke. He says Finletter is the first man the U.S. has ever had in the NATO council who speaks French. The Kennedy administration gives the impression of being more dynamic. But there has been no significant change in strategy. The Allied Defense Plan for 1970, MC-70, was developed on the idea that nuclear power would have to be built up to compensate for the lack of conventional forces. It appears Kennedy wants to place more stress on conventional forces. He doesn't yet seem to realize, however, that it is impossible to have a limited war in the NATO area.

PARIS, *April 8, 1961*

LUNCHED with Philippe Baudet. Relations between France and the United States are extremely bad. De Gaulle was so furious when Ambassador Walmsley in Tunis conferred with two FLN leaders, that he was on the verge of canceling President Kennedy's visit to Paris. He is still boiling with anger and considers this question something the U.S. has no right to concern itself with.

It is absolutely positive that de Gaulle will quit if he cannot settle the

Algerian question. One should make no mistake about this. And the outlook is exceedingly bad. The French army remains "in discipline," but it is watching and hoping for a breakdown.

The most important question between France and the U.S. is the question of nuclear arms. It is most delicate and difficult to broach, but everything else, including NATO and Big Three relationships, is linked to that, and Kennedy is the man to bring it up; de Gaulle won't.

GENEVA, *April 9, 1961*

I DROVE to Geneva today and had a long talk and drinks with my old friend Arthur Dean, now head of the American delegation to the nuclear-test talks which have resumed here.

When Dean was called in by President Kennedy to take this assignment, after studying the problem, he insisted we should take a draft treaty banning nuclear tests on the earth and in space. With Kennedy's authority he got an agreed program out of the State Department, the Atomic Energy Commission, and the Pentagon to lay out a way for policing these tests. The Pentagon and the Atomic Energy Commission had previously been particularly opposed to banning tests in outer space.

The Russians began these negotiations by demanding a ban on all kinds of tests. They claimed that all tests, even underground, could be monitored. However, in 1958, the Rand Corporation and the Livermore Laboratory of the University of California staged, on behalf of the government, a series of underground explosions called "Hardtack." These were exploded in a kind of soft rock called tuff. They demonstrated that if such explosions were arranged in a salt-packed, underground cave it was feasible by a process called "decoupling" to stage a detonation at least three hundred times greater than what would be registered as suspicious on a seismograph. This threw all U.S. calculations out of kilter. It gave such people as Professor Teller, the scientist, and Tom Murray, of the AEC (both of whom had strongly opposed continuing the moratorium on nuclear tests), a complete new argument against any ban.

In the meantime, diplomatic pressures have continued to build up. There are now nine series of resolutions at the UN calling for various nuclear curbs, such as the destruction of all existing atomic stocks or a ban on the manufacture and an end to the testing of such devices. Despite such world pressures, there are many Americans who feel that we risk our national safety in envisioning any treaty we cannot enforce 100 percent.

There is a further problem. Many scientists contend it is ridiculous to forgo the use of nuclear explosives for peacetime purposes; that, for example, we could put a new canal across Panama or develop a huge harbor in Alaska by peaceful nuclear detonations. But the Russians have opposed this also.

The question of tests in outer space is particularly interesting. It is possible to have remarkably valuable nuclear tests as far as one million kilometers from the earth's gravitational pull. Our world would be a mere pinpoint in the distance of space. If a device were exploded at that distance, the chances of any radiation effect on the surface of the earth would be infinitely small. And yet scientists could learn as much from such an explosion far from the earth's gravitational pull as they could learn from exploding a bomb in their own back yard.

We therefore propose that six solar satellites with seismic, electronic, photographic, and transmitting equipment should be launched to control against such space explosions. But even there it is possible to cheat. Tests could be held in outer space by devices equipped to release a balloon with a lead shield between the earth and the explosion. This would so decrease the heat of the explosion that it would not register on earth.

The odd thing, Art says, is that while there are limits to what scientists can learn in underground research, there are *no* limits to what they can learn from outer-space explosions.

Dean's strategy is to invite everybody to sign a treaty. But then, if all the nuclear powers did not sign—if only one refused to sign—anybody could denounce the treaty. The Russians have hinted more than once in a curious way—always informally and never in regular sessions—that if the British and the Americans can get the French to cease testing, "We will take care of China." There have been recent rumors that China has served notice on Moscow that it won't take any such Russian orders.

The big thing our military scientists want to do is to stage new tests in order to reduce the weight and increase the yield of our weapons. This is not like an agricultural problem such as increasing the yield by getting more wheat per acre. It is increasing the yield by getting more dead per dollar.

De Gaulle does not *want* to join the talks because that would mean ending French tests. In fact, at the recent SEATO meeting in Bangkok, Dean Rusk urged Couve de Murville to postpone the next French test scheduled in May because of the bad effect this would have on proposed Algerian peace negotiations. Couve said he thoroughly agreed and had urged this himself, but de Gaulle paid no attention.

We talked a lot about Foster Dulles, who was Art's law partner and one of his best friends. Art hopes to write a decent biography of him one of these days and I sincerely hope he will.

Art said that both Dulles and Eden were seriously ill at the worst moment of the Suez crisis in 1956. Tuesday was election day. But Friday night, Dulles fell desperately ill, was taken to the hospital, and operated on. Eisenhower asked Dean to stand by and work with Allen Dulles during that critical period as the Israelis, British, and French moved on Suez.

On Monday afternoon, the day before election day, a message came in from Menzies, the Australian Prime Minister. Menzies said the British had violated the ANZAM accord by not confiding to Australia and New Zealand that they were going into Suez. Menzies said Australia intended to quit the Commonwealth if Britain did not halt the Suez invasion. That same afternoon, a message came from Nehru saying that India would quit the Commonwealth if Britain did not halt the invasion. And the Russians announced that they might rocket France if the invasion did not halt.

Yet Dulles, whose mistakes (Dean admits) might have helped Britain and France into the invasion, took no decisions at all during this critical period. He was in a coma. He did not even know what was going on until the Friday after election day.

As for Eden, for some six weeks (unknown to him and unknown to his doctors) he had been suffering from uremic poisoning. He had previously had an operation attaching new plastic urethras to his kidneys, and these had become displaced, as later surgery proved. And it is clinically known that uremic poisoning affects the brain.

This was a strange paradox. The two men most associated with Suez in the popular mind were both ill at the height of the crisis.

Dean recalled my argument that lawyers made bad secretaries of state. He said that Dulles was more influenced by his religious antecedents (a long line of ministers) than by his legal training. (Incidentally, apropos of that legal training, he had no law degree. He had gone with his grandfather as a young secretary to represent the Chinese Republic at the Hague Conference, while he was at Princeton, and then he went to George Washington Law School which, says Dean, "was then no good at all and nothing but a diploma factory." (Dulles did not finish the full three years but just did two years.)

Dean said Dulles had a very Jesuitical approach in diplomacy, stemming from his religious conviction that we were always right and therefore could use *any* means to achieve our ends.

He talked of Dulles's hatred for Eden. Dean said: "This was really just a repetition of the old dislike of the Roundhead for the Cavalier. He detested Eden's aristocratic persiflage, he hated his long hair and a way he had of dangling his long, aristocratic hands from a loose wrist in front of his face. 'Why doesn't that man get a haircut?' Foster would ask. 'What does he mean by always dangling his hands in front of his face? Does he think he's impressing me by his aristocratic bearing?' "

MUNICH, *April 13, 1961*

SPENT yesterday at Bad Tölz, thirty-five miles south of here, a little spa now being used by the U.S. army as a training center for the 10th Special Services Group, airborne. This is the only U.S. guerrilla warfare unit in Europe.

The commandant is a tough, small colonel of forty-five who has the DSO, two Silver Stars, and numerous other decorations. He is a West Point graduate and has made eighty-two parachute jumps. His parents were born in Hungary. He is decent, honest, tough, but distinctly dumb.

The 10th has four special services companies training in unconventional warfare. This means guerrilla war, counterguerrilla war, liaison with resistance units, evasion, and escape. All actions are designed to take place behind an enemy's lines and to support indigenous personnel. Small detachments of military advisors would go behind enemy lines in uniform and observe the conventions of war, including the Geneva Convention, always representing the U.S. government openly. They would not "command" native guerrillas, but would aid their responsible leader with logistic support and advice, trying to coordinate his actions to help our strategy.

This particular unit is delighted that President Kennedy has asked for new funds for this type of work and they have begun to call themselves "The President's Own," like some of the royal British regiments.

MUNICH, *April 14, 1961*

DINED with Franz-Josef Strauss, dynamic young minister of defense and political boss of Bavaria. We met in a restaurant called the "Schwarzwälder Weinstube," where we enjoyed a good meal and enormous quantities of Palatinate white wine. Later, Frau Strauss, who had been to the theater, joined us: A most attractive, tall brunette who, although she is eight and a half months pregnant, doesn't show it. We thrashed over everything, from my column on the German-Spanish bases deal, which caused a furor, to Strauss's personal history and ambitions. Strauss, a heavy man, drank copious amounts of wine and sweated profusely.

He interprets Kennedy's new defense policy as a return to the theories of Generals Max Taylor and Gavin, who resigned from the army when their ideas were turned down. Kennedy is now giving them what they originally asked for—a considerable buildup of conventional forces. At present, the "nuclear threshold" is really zero. We have no plan to fight a conventional war beyond the divisional level.

This means there can be no pause in fighting for the purpose of negotiating a settlement if war breaks out in Europe, because Europe is defended primarily by tactical nuclear weapons. The best we can hope for immediately is to bring the nuclear threshold up to somewhere between brigade and divisional levels. The goal should be to bring it to the corps level. If a Soviet invasion can be blocked at the corps level without recourse to nuclear weapons, there could be a sufficient pause allowing settlement by negotiation.

Strauss said Bonn assumed that for the life of the North Atlantic Treaty, SACEUR (Supreme Allied Commander in Europe) would be an American. Germany would not accept a commander from any other nation. This formula is opposed by France and the British are uncertain.

Adenauer complained recently to Acheson that German divisions now have their Honest John battalions, but they don't know if their nuclear warheads are with them or not. These are kept locked up under American custody and brought in (camouflaged)—and removed—at night. So the divisional commander is never positive whether he has the right thing or not; and this is a serious psychological hazard. Everybody knows where the stockpiles are because of the peculiar type of security measures necessitated. But the commander never knows whether the real thing is in the stockpile or not.

I asked Strauss about France. He replied:

The U.S.A. thinks on a broad scale, but we think on a European scale. History tells us that Europe depends on Franco-German relations. As long as Franco-German relations are bad, Europe is filled with fear and unrest. Today's Communist menace is the heritage of a tragic past in bad Franco-German relations. Germany needs closer relations with France than any other European country—both practically and psychologically.

Strategically speaking, the distance from east to west in West Germany varies only from 115 to 320 miles. In our rear there is only France. And technical developments have overhauled us. Even if Germany were to be reunified, it would be too small now to be a strategic power by itself. But France and Germany are a single strategic unit. If Germany goes Communist, so does France. Germany cannot be defended without France. We must go it with France. We don't admit that there is a choice between France and NATO; it must be with France inside NATO.

I am not interested in becoming Chancellor. I have never had much in my life. I finished university in 1939, although I came from a very poor family. I was at war for six years and have been in politics ever since. I am physically strong, but there are limits. My political ambitions have been fully exhausted.

I am a convinced enemy of any German hegemony in Europe. The time for a European balance of power has gone. Europe is no longer the center of the world. German policy is a function of European policy, which in turn is a component of Atlantic policy. I see our future in these terms. It is intellectual nonsense to think of a disengaged, neutral Germany. A German today must be for a strong western Europe with Germany as a component; or he will seem to manoeuver between East and West and succumb to the East.

I asked Strauss who had influenced him most. He said he had studied two men very carefully: Thucydides and St. Augustine (*De Civitate Dei* and the *Confessions*). No living man had exercised much influence on him except Adenauer. "And yet," he continued, "nobody has fought so many battles with Adenauer as I. I am a Bavarian autonomist. But I admire Adenauer's instinct for liquidating a tragic past and seeking a new road for German historic orientation."

Strauss draws a comparison between Adenauer and de Gaulle and says there is "a soul community between them." De Gaulle has weakened Parliament, but he has maintained the characteristics of a legal state. He thinks that no parliament, provincial or national, can decide more than he personally is able to oversee. He maintains and safeguards the elements of a legal democratic state and all civil rights—except one. He wants to preserve for himself alone the right to take essential decisions.

De Gaulle is not a dictator. He would not mind paying a police fine of 500 francs for a traffic violation whereas a dictator would. But he allows no one else to take basic political decisions.

The same is true for Adenauer. Everything goes on as in a democracy —justice, administration, etc.—but there is *no* parliament or cabinet or anyone else to take vital decisions. Adenauer has achieved this eminence by political push, age, experience, and historical legend. This makes for the peculiar heart relationship between de Gaulle and Adenauer.

He told me, very off-the-record, that there are special military relations between Israel and Germany. Germany is now sending more arms to Israel than France is, but this is top secret and would cause a furor in the Arab states if it became known.

We talked about the whole Spanish deal. Strauss said he had learned a lesson from this. He said,

I marked my proposal to be classified as Cosmic and it was only later reduced in classification to NATO SECRET. Yet somebody leaked it. I know whom you play golf with, and I don't mean any generals. [Clearly he was thinking of Frank Roberts.] Golf is a good game and maybe I will take it up someday. But I have learned one thing from this experience. I will not confide any future major secrets to NATO.

I bet Strauss twelve bottles of French champagne that by January 1, 1970, he would either be Chancellor or would have been Chancellor of Germany.

PARIS, *April 19, 1961*

LUNCHED today with Kim (Kermit) Roosevelt. He is now vice president of Gulf Oil Company in charge of government relations, but he is still linked with the CIA. He is gloomy about the Cuban situation. History teaches this is not the moment for this kind of an operation. Yet we have to win, even if we have to send troops in. If we are going to be blamed for an American "Hungary," we might as well at least get results.

Kim was in charge of the operation in Iran when we got rid of Mossadegh in 1953. That one was relatively easy as we were able to calculate that if we could produce an open fight between Mossadegh and the Shah, the Shah would gain popular support. He did. The British had tried to get us to take the line of intervention many months earlier, but we waited until the local situation was right—unlike Cuba.

Kim was on a secret mission in the Middle East early in 1955 with Bob Anderson, later Eisenhower's Secretary of the Treasury. The mission, sent out by Eisenhower himself, sought to try and make peace between Egypt and Israel. Anderson and Kim talked to Nasser hour after hour. There was a corollary mission to Ben Gurion.

Chet Bowles offered Kim these ambassadorial posts: Teheran, Cairo, and Rabat. Kim pointed out that he could not go to Iran because the Russians had evidence of what his activities had been in overthrowing Mossadegh in 1953. Likewise, Kim told Bowles it would be useless to send him to Cairo. At the time of the Iraqi revolution, Nasser sent a team into Baghdad which grabbed all the Baghdad Pact intelligence files—well filled with Kim's name. Were Kim to be our ambassador, Nasser would be in a position to blackmail him and us by releasing such documents whenever convenient. He and Nasser (they know each other by their first names and have talked for "hundreds of hours") joke about Nasser's possession of those files. Rabat was uninteresting.

PARIS, *April 21, 1961*

DINED last night at Norstad's. He was terribly gloomy about Cuba (Bay of Pigs) and said: "I think this is the worst defeat the U.S. has suffered since the war of 1812."

PARIS, *April 22, 1961*

AT dinner, Philippe Baudet admitted there had been secret negotiations between France and Spain. "After all, you know General de Gaulle." He said, "The General feels strongly that there are three essentials to European strategy. The front line is Germany. The fallback position is France; and the emergency redoubt [*redoute*] is Spain." He told me the negotiations had been headed by General Jean-Jacques Noiret and General Agustin Muñoz Grandes for Spain.

PARIS, *April 23, 1961*

EARLY this morning the news came of a new *coup d'état* in Algeria and things look bad. Norstad called at 8 P.M. to tell me it was very serious. He simply couldn't understand how General Challe was crazy enough to get into this.

This morning, I had a chat with X. All Algeria has now gone over to the mutineers except for two enclaves around Tlemcen and Mers el-Kebir (as I am dictating this Mers el-Kebir has also gone over). The government has almost lost contact with Algeria. The French army is inert and won't oppose the rebels. Draftees accept the orders of their officers.

Some secret pamphlets have been seized indicating the plot was timed to explode Monday, April 24. But the government got suspicious Friday night, and Colonel Yves Godard triggered it early. General Vanuxem, deputy commander in Germany, has been placed under house arrest. General Faure, who has been commanding around Bordeaux, is also under arrest. No important politician has as yet been implicated. The government is worried lest the French forces in Germany declare for the rebels.

Debré is terribly torn by de Gaulle's statements. His heart is really with the rebels. The government will try to quarantine Algeria and starve it out without taking military action. The odds are against the insurrection, which can be blockaded and cut off from food and money. In order to win they will have to come and get de Gaulle. Challe knows that de Gaulle will give no quarter to the leaders. However there is a big difficulty: Nobody can be expected to fire on the paratroopers.

The new OAS (Secret Army Organization) is linked with the army. Three months ago, a group of paratroop and Foreign Legion leaders were organizing a conspiracy. The Legion seems to be the main force of the plot. They approached several young generals in Algeria to take over leadership. These generals refused—but failed to report the treasonable officers to Paris. General Salan has disappeared from Madrid and can be expected to show up in Algeria. The *plastiqueurs* (plastic bombers in France) are increasingly active and seem to be directly linked to the conspiracy.

PARIS, *April 24, 1961*

AROUND 3 A.M. I drove around town. Noted considerable troop concentrations including armor around the Elysée. Crowds were pushing into the ministry of the interior and given arms in the courtyard. I saw a platoon of tanks and the Garde Mobile crossing the Pont de la Concorde from the Left bank, followed by truckloads of tommy gunners.

De Gaulle has ten thousand men—mainly CRS, gendarmes, Gardes Républicaines, and marine commandos—for the defense of Paris. He intends to stay at the Elysée, which will be guarded permanently by marine commandos. Villacoublay military airfield has been covered with trucks to block aircraft landings. A parachute assault may come in the night of the 24–25.

If they can take over, the rebels do not plan to shoot de Gaulle but to put him on public trial for violating the Constitution. They want a civilian government rather than a military dictatorship and seem to have some tame politicians of all complexions, including Socialists, ready to join them.

Paris is very worried about the position of the army in Germany. There are reports that the third armored division was moving from Germany toward Paris.

Personally, I have a feeling that de Gaulle is carrying on a clever war of nerves and is putting out a lot of phony rumors, including one of an imminent paratroop assault, in order to slow up the momentum of the rebels and establish full order in France once and for all before the conspiracy can capitalize upon its surprise. I think that was the meaning of Debré's speech at 11:30 P.M. last night warning of the possibility of a paratroop assault within a half-hour.

This afternoon, I went to see Baudet in his office at general headquarters. Baudet said Debré had been convinced since noon on Saturday that Challe would move on Paris. He realized Challe had a good mind and would recognize the strategic necessity of asserting himself beyond Algeria. Debré had an evaluation made on the planes and troops available to the rebels and decided the situation was very dangerous and that an airborne invasion was a real possibility.

Many generals disagreed. Nevertheless, they calculated a speech such as Debré's made by radio, warning against assault and asking popular aid, would be of great psychological warfare use, so they encouraged him to make it. The consensus is that although tonight is again likely to be tense, the chances of a parachute descent have diminished. I said that if I were General Challe, I would not attempt to obtain a lodgment in Paris but would move tonight on Pau and Toulouse. He smiled: "We have been taking very serious precautions there."

I asked about the situation of the army in Germany. He said General Vanuxem, second in command, has been locked up. "Several other generals have been arrested in France." I asked about General Lecomte at SHAPE headquarters. Baudet said: "I would be surprised if he showed up at his office today." I asked if General Valluy was under arrest. "Not yet," he said. "But he is being watched."

The same was true of Marshal Juin.

Challe's (rebel commander's) position doesn't seem as strong as yesterday. Reports received by Paris from Algeria show that a considerable number of units remain loyal. The big decision for the government now is whether or not to blockade Algeria.

The navy is loyal, but the air force is bad. It has gone over to the rebels in Algeria and it is wobbly in France. No single plane was allowed to take off in France last night for fear of treason. This, I now realize, is one of the reasons they were so scared of a parachute assault. They didn't dare to meet it in the air by fighters.

Baudet says the government is furious with Spain. The Spaniards quite clearly let Salan and the other extremists go; it was not a question of their escape.

PARIS, *April 25, 1961*

DINED last night at Philippe de Rothschild's. What an odd civilization producing that kind of meal in the middle of a roaring crisis. Among other things in the ten-course banquet, we had sole with a caviar sauce and six varieties of wine, the glasses set up in bowling-pin formation.

Michelet, the garde des Sceaux (equivalent of U.S. attorney general), a nice simple man, was happily eating away with his knife.

Incidentally, here is a copy of the menu:

Consommé à la Bohémienne
Soles Dnieper
Gigot de Pré-Salé Rôti
Purée de Haricots Blancs
Pointes d'Asperges au Beurre
Poulet Froid à la Crème
Salade de Riz à l'Orientale
Fromages
Glaces aux Fraises
Fruits

And the wines:

Ruinart Reserve
Batard Montrachet 1955
Mouton Rothschild 1945
Lafite Rothschild 1926
Mouton Rothschild 1899
Yquem 1944

AN ADVISORY ROLE

NORSTAD CALLED AND WE HAD A SOMEWHAT INDISCREET TELE-phone conversation. I say "indiscreet" because, although there is a civil war going on here, he had kind words to say about General Challe, the insurrectionist leader, and he surely must know telephones are tapped. Larry said things seem to be going better now for de Gaulle, but he "still cannot exclude an invasion of France."

He was deeply puzzled by the leadership of this rebellion and regretted that emotions took charge of such excellent men. He admired both Challe and General Zeller as "honest and competent officers." He continued: "Challe is a talented leader, which is a pretty rare thing in the present crop of French generals. He is a man of warmth and liveliness, a good man, clean as a whistle and greatly respected. He won't run off to South America with a suitcase full of gold when this thing finishes."

One thing was obvious: The rebels cannot afford to stand still. The rebellion must either grow or shrink; it cannot be static. He thought (this was at 12:30 P.M.) that it was still consolidating its position. Challe had shown his power Sunday night when he "caused real panic here." Norstad was referring to Debré's speech warning against a paratroop invasion. "From his own viewpoint, this panic served Challe's aims," said Norstad.

The rebels had "lots of supplies" in Algeria. If the army handles its resources with care and some rationing it has two months' worth of stores. The only thing we could do now was not to talk about any help and to avoid embarrassment. Norstad said Challe was extremely pro-American and pro-NATO.

While we were talking, Tom Finletter came in to see me. He brought with him a draft (marked secret) of his briefing for Kennedy for the latter's visit to de Gaulle. Tom said this represented the combined effort of himself and Gavin. (It looked to me like a slightly formalized version of the precise ideas I had given Finletter in an informal "briefing" Saturday.) Tom, who was accompanied by Arthur Schlesinger, asked if I would read the draft and make suggestions. I did. I suggested first of all there should be a separate corollary paper analyzing de Gaulle's personality and the best way of approaching it. Tom asked me if I would draft this myself.

I told Tom I thought recommendations should include some discussion of de Gaulle's negative attitude in UN, so the President would be prepared on this; to stress our common interests in keeping Germany tied to western Europe so it won't break loose after Adenauer's death; to have the President brief himself on de Gaulle's relations and irritations with the U.S.A., going right back to Franklin Roosevelt; and to prepare the President on how to respond if, when he offers nuclear help to de Gaulle, de Gaulle says he doesn't want it. I also told him that because of the present rebellion, the President should be especially careful to try and help de Gaulle's prestige vis-à-vis the army, which is going to be shattered.

Tom's paper proposes that discussions concerning Big Three cooperation outside the NATO area should be formalized by having the two men exchange their minutes and initialing this section. It suggests formalized cooperation by the Big Three outside the NATO area. It wants to tell de Gaulle we intend to treat France on exactly the same basis as England in all matters including nuclear matters and that we want to revise the McMahon Act to make this possible.

Afterward, I lunched with Schlesinger, who wanted a long briefing and took notes. He is going to report to Kennedy on his return. I asked him to give me a summary of his notes to help in preparing my corollary paper for the President. Schlesinger said the President especially wants this because I knew de Gaulle better than any other American. (I pointed out that this might be relatively true, but I was far from being his blood brother; it was merely a sad commentary on our relations with France.)

Schlesinger remarked: "Are you clairvoyant?" I asked "What the hell do you mean?" He said last Friday he was talking with Chip Bohlen about who could possibly replace Allen Dulles as head of the CIA and they both decided that Max Taylor was the best man. A moment later Mac Bundy, the President's foreign-policy assistant, joined them and had the same idea. The next day, as Arthur was taking off for Europe, he read my column saying Taylor would soon be appointed. It was evident that Allen Dulles had to go and that the President wanted to put somebody he could totally trust in charge of the CIA, and there were only two possibilities— Taylor and Bobby Kennedy, the President's brother. I said the latter choice would be disastrous; we had already had one brother act—Foster and Allen Dulles.

Schlesinger asked me who I thought would be the best American ambassador to France to succeed Gavin. I said I didn't know. He asked how about Finletter. I said Tom was doing an excellent job in NATO, but I really didn't think he was quite prestigious enough to get on with de Gaulle. Bohlen was really the only man. Bohlen told Schlesinger that he is tremendously happy with his job now and is in the White House more than at any time since the days of Franklin Roosevelt. He is very close to the President, says Schlesinger. I recommended to both him and Finletter that Tom should enlist Bohlen's aid in briefing the President for de Gaulle because he would find Bohlen essentially pro-French, although not necessarily pro-de Gaulle.

Schlesinger said he was now very friendly with Acheson, who was treating him with great cordiality after the coolness of recent years, but, "Dean hasn't really learned anything since 1952. For him the world hasn't changed. He regards me as one of the Harriman soft team."

PARIS, *April 27, 1961*

THIS morning, I had a long talk with Norstad. He respects Challe for giving himself up the way he did. Suicide would have been the easy way out. Challe realizes he failed but clearly thinks he was right to try to upset the present policy, and is doing a decent thing by facing trial. Norstad asked his intelligence people if the three missing generals (Salan, Zeller, and Jouhaud) had been located yet. The answer was no.

Larry was furious at the case of General Edwin Walker, who has been transferred because he was beginning to indoctrinate troops with the philosophy of the John Birch Society. He complained about "trial by the press." General Walker was perhaps the best combat commander we had in Europe. He likened the Walker case to the Patton soldier-slapping incident.

Norstad read me exchanges of telegrams he had had with Washington during the French crisis. His recommendation was that we should offer to be of assistance but be very careful not to "force" any aid on an "already sensitive and overburdened government."

What we did do—and advised the French thereof—was to issue special orders to U.S. units. We told air units that if there was any attempt to seize installations they should be blocked with obstacles but not with recourse to shooting. This meant that if an airfield radar system picked up indications that unexpected planes were coming, the field should be covered with trucks.

The big result of the insurrection, unhappily, is that "the French army has been destroyed. There must be an extensive cleanup and this will take time. De Gaulle must restore the confidence of the French people in their army. The army has a special position in French culture and in the French approach to life. It really may take a generation to accomplish this job."

PARIS, *April 28, 1961*

I AM disturbed by anti-American rumors to the effect that the U.S.A. was behind the recent anti-Gaullist coup and wanted to oust de Gaulle because of his opposition to NATO. This morning, I went around to see the local

CIA representative who assured me no CIA or State Department official saw any rebel of the insurrection in Algeria or elsewhere.

There is a legend that the pro-NATO U.S.A. would like to see a pro-NATO successor to de Gaulle, and since Cuba, it is à la mode to criticize the CIA. *Izvestia* had an article along these lines on April 25, and the Polish attaché has been peddling it here in Paris.

PARIS, *April 30, 1961*

LUNCHED in the country with Billotte. He said it was appalling to see how cowardly some of the ministers had been. Pierre said he received several telephone calls threatening to kill him. He claims only Michelet and Malraux showed guts.

Billotte says it is imperative that the generals and colonels who led this last conspiracy be shot. There is no other way of lancing the abcess. Unlike Norstad, Billotte (whose career has also been military, who was a general, and whose father was a general) says Challe and the other leading conspirators should have committed suicide. It was the last patriotic gesture they could have made for France.

The objectives of the plot were to seize all Algeria, to take southwest France from the Toulouse-Pau air and airborne bases, to start a move toward Paris from southwest France and from French Germany, and to ask the Rambouillet heavy tanks to coordinate with this plus an airborne landing from Algeria.

PARIS, *May 2, 1961*

THE recent spy case (Colonel Rudolf Abel) was broken by the CIA in Paris. A man came around to the CIA here and sounded like a lunatic. Nevertheless, everything he said smelled logical and the CIA passed on its information to the FBI, which in the end broke the case.

Just before the Summit meeting two big shots from the CIA came over and had a secret briefing session with de Gaulle. They told him precisely what the U-2 had been assigned to find out from Russia, what it had found out, and they showed him photographs of U-2 missions. De Gaulle was deeply impressed and very grateful.

PARIS, *May 5, 1961*

BEUVE-MÉRY, editor of *Le Monde,* says de Gaulle remains a prisoner of the wartime secret intelligence methods he had to adopt as head of an emigré plus internal-resistance movement.

Beuve-Méry saw de Gaulle several times between 1958 and 1960. But each meeting was increasingly bitter and finally de Gaulle said: "Alors, I understand your ideas." That was the last meeting.

Beuve is convinced that the United States made its initial error in European policy during World War II. The only reason we didn't accept Churchill's plan to move into Vienna, Prague, and Berlin was because we were concentrating on Japan (before the first atomic explosion was a success) and we wanted Russian help. Therefore we were prepared to pay a price in Europe.

He said: "The only *coup d'état* in Prague was that in the spring of 1945—made by the U.S.A.—and not that made by Russia in 1948." Patton's troops waited ten days, as close to Prague as if they had been in Rambouillet outside of Paris, for the Russians to take over. Naturally, when the Russians decided to assume full powers in 1948, they reckoned there would be no American interference because the Americans, in fact, had given them Prague. Beuve-Méry says he is convinced one reason the Americans detest him is that they assume he is "pro-Communist" because he was in Prague before the war and after the war supported Beneš, who in turn made a deal (by *force majeure*) with Moscow.

PARIS, *May 6, 1961*

LUNCHED with Areilza (Count of Motrico), now ambassador in Paris and formerly Spanish envoy in Washington. He is delightful and extremely funny. It is a lovely embassy, well decorated with Goya paintings and magnificent Goya tapestries of the same series that hang in the Pardo Palace.

Motrico said he had been tipped in advance that the recent insurrection against de Gaulle planned as its very first move to assassinate the President Friday night while he was attending an official performance at the theater. He passed this information to Geoffroy de Courcel at the Elysée.

Motrico told a fascinating story of a dinner party he attended two months prior to the insurrection. His hostess was a well-known, very elderly salonnière with a reputation for intellectual company and bad food. Several right-wing personages were there. After dinner, his hostess raised her glass and proposed a toast to the health of "the President of the Sixth Republic, le Maréchal Juin." Motrico was astounded.

GENEVA, *May 14, 1961*

LONG talk with Dean Rusk, our first meeting since he became Secretary of State. The Laotian conference is about to start and he had to confer with Lord Home, Couve, Krishna Menon, and others.

Rusk is an agreeable man of imposing presence, over six feet, erect, heavyset, but fit looking. He has a mild manner, obstinate face, and friendly aspect. However, I must say he did not impress me as being brilliant or profound.

I asked if we weren't meeting de Gaulle's demands for consultations on non-NATO area problems by our proposal that NATO should consult on all kinds of matters outside the North Atlantic area. Would that not permit a kind of invisible inner three *directoire* to form? Rusk said:

> The problem wasn't discussed on that basis. The consultation system will be open-ended and any governments interested enough in any particular subject can take part. We want to develop the habit of intensive consultation. The way to consult is by consulting. In the past, it has been rare that anyone has taken the initiative to express views on a problem in advance, before a formal consultation became necessary. We think that things must be talked out ahead of time on an ad hoc basis.

I then turned to Laos and Southeast Asia. Were we preparing to negotiate anything except Laos with Communist China here in Geneva? He said flatly no. I then asked how we could save South Vietnam and stop the rot in Thailand. Should we send in troops or was a new SEATO protocol required? He replied: "In both countries we need a broad effort by ourselves, by the whole free world, and by the local governments. There would be expanded economic help and educational and public-health programs. There must be increased military aid, but so far we have not reached any decision on whether to put in troops."

I thought the partition of Laos at the 17th parallel was preferable to a coalition government and the only way we could save South Vietnam was by partitioning Laos. What was his feeling? He answered:

> Partition won't solve the problem in South Vietnam. The Communists have been infiltrating South Vietnam through Laos already. Of course, if Laos becomes fully Communist, the infiltration problem would be greatly magnified.
> What are the alternatives? Maybe the Laotian leaders could make their own kind of an arrangement without any interference or outside help. Then partition would not be raised at all. Otherwise, there might come about a de facto partition. We don't see formal partition as an answer; nor has it been proposed by anyone. Frankly we prefer a neutral Laos to a partitioned Laos.

I then asked him if we should be prepared to see all of Southeast Asia neutralist providing that we could get India into the action as a sponsoring power. He said this was too impractical a question because it just couldn't work out. India had not been very active in Southeast Asia. He did admit the U.S.A. was trying to encourage Indian interest in the area.

I asked what minimal terms for a Laotian settlement the U.S.A. could sign. He said:

> It's not a question of minimal terms. It's a question of integrity. We won't sign something that is clearly only designed to gloss over a phony. If there is an agreement that makes Laos genuinely neutral, we will take it. But it is hard to make a precise definition. This is a very complicated problem. And, of course, we must be concerned with the reactions in the

other Southeastern Asian lands. Finally, much will depend in the end on the Laotian people themselves.

Rusk said Kennedy's message to de Gaulle during the recent mutiny had been made public by de Gaulle and not by the Americans. De Gaulle was very grateful for the message and it helped him a lot. But later on, his pride took charge and underground rumors circulated saying that the Americans were trying to grab credit.

He saw no signs of a clash between old-fashioned Russian and Chinese imperialism. It was odd to see them working in each other's backyards. Russia was pushing along in Southeast Asia, but the Chinese were extremely active in Latin America and Africa.

I asked how we could possibly sign any Laotian agreement that did not see to it that all foreign forces got out of the country; it would be extremely difficult for observers to tell the difference between a Laotian and a North Vietnamese. He merely replied: "We just won't sign anything unless *all* foreigners get out."

Long lunch with Averell Harriman, here as Rusk's right-hand man. When Rusk goes home, the baby will be left in Averell's lap, precisely the way Dulles left the Vietnam baby in Bedell Smith's lap in 1954. Averell is pretty gloomy and seems more inclined to a solution by partition than his boss. He confided:

I am not yet in the inner circle of this administration. I see all the telegrams—except I wasn't in on Cuba. But I am not really an intimate. I have known the President for some time but only slightly, and he always calls me "Governor," not "Averell." But I am confident that before things end up I will be in the inner circle. I started as a private with Roosevelt and worked to the top. And then I had to start as a private all over again with Truman and work to the top. That is what I intend to do again.

Averell thinks it was a great mistake to select Mac Bundy as the President's White House advisor on foreign policy. He is a Republican and simply won't feel free enough to criticize all errors of the past administration.

I asked what he thought of Rusk. He said: "He certainly impressed me as a forceful man when he was Assistant Secretary. But I don't know how he is going to be now when he bears the responsibility for action and not just for making recommendations."

Averell said Norodom Sihanouk, Prime Minister (and former king) of Cambodia, is either the vainest or the most self-assured man he had ever met. But he definitely doesn't want communism in his country. And he is a realist. He recognizes that the real forces in the world are the U.S.A., China, and Russia. He is not in the least impressed with India.

Harriman had been deeply disappointed in Nehru. He didn't think of Nehru as an important factor in Asia, not even in India itself, where the contest for succession had already begun. There isn't even a real Nehru policy.

Averell would not accept any neutral Laotian government in which there was a Communist as minister of foreign affairs, defense, interior, or justice. The Communists could only have minor posts. And even these were dangerous. He had been told that a Communist minister of religious affairs had succeeded in infiltrating the Buddhist Bonzes.

At one point during lunch Averell said he guessed his role here was as the "fall guy—the Bedell Smith." He thought the U.S.A. might have to put troops in Southeast Asia. If this happens we would like to get in Pakistani, Philippine, and Thai troops. The American contingent would neither be the largest nor the smallest in size.

He had told Kennedy orally—but not in writing—that in his talk with de Gaulle he should under no circumstances bring up either NATO or UN because he would not get anywhere on them. He should just tell de Gaulle that he would like to discuss these subjects after an Algerian settlement has been arranged.

Averell said Diem, in South Vietnam, is gradually retreating from his previously austere and monkish life. But he is still a very tough fellow. Diem insists the Laotian gap should be blocked—by partition if necessary. It is all important to get partition at the 17th parallel, if there is no other viable solution.

At one point, Averell said that instead of complaining about Russia we should be thankful for the existence of a dynamic U.S.S.R., because it stimulated competition and prevented us from getting smug and lazy. We must give help to underdeveloped areas and help the poorer parts of the world for reasons of moral decency and quite regardless of what the Russians do or do not do. It was a great error for Kennedy to express doubt as to whether our system or communism would triumph in the end. This might sound perfectly reasonable at home, but the echoes abroad were unfortunate.

PARIS, *May 17, 1961*

ALLEN Dulles sent a message congratulating me on my Saturday column on an "open society" versus a "naked society," saying this was "in the greatest tradition of American journalism."

Katie Macmillan has been staying with us. She assumed her brother, David Ormsby-Gore, will be named ambassador to Washington in July or August. He is forty-three—Kennedy's age—and an old personal friend of the entire Kennedy family. Furthermore, his wife and children are, like the Kennedys, Roman Catholic. From the English point of view, they could have nothing better on tap—above all because his sister is married to Prime Minister Macmillan's son and his cousin, the late Marquess of Hartington, was married to Kennedy's eldest sister, now also dead.

Lunched with Gajewski. He is disappointed in de Gaulle. The General is a great man, theatrically splendid, but the recent mutiny had exposed that there was no government and no army. When de Gaulle goes, there will be chaos and bloodshed. All political elements in France, including the Communists and the Socialists are rotten.

Gajewski thought Khrushchev would not move on Berlin this summer. He has already let five times the length of his original ultimatum go by without acting. If the U.S. Marines had taken Cuba, Khrushchev would have liquidated the western position in Berlin; and it probably would have been a good thing. There would have been no war.

Gajewski says we must not emphasize the strength of Khrushchev's present position. The economic situation in the Communist bloc is very bad and the agricultural situation is terrible in Russia, disastrous in China. There is still considerable opposition to Khrushchev in the Russian political world.

Furthermore, the Sino-Soviet problem is a very serious one and we should make no mistake about it. Finally, Khrushchev is absolutely and definitely opposed to any thought of war. Thus, despite the tide which has unquestionably been going with him during the last four or five weeks, Khrushchev continues to have his own internal problems and most assuredly wants to keep the peace.

PARIS, *May 20, 1961*

BREAKFAST with George Ball, under secretary of state for economic affairs. Last March, he met Ted Heath, the British Cabinet member in charge of European affairs, and for the first time they asked how our government would feel if the United Kingdom joined the Common Market. Ball told them that if Britain joined and took the full commitments of the Rome Treaty, the U.S. would think this a great contribution to western cohesion. It would help to build Europe. Therefore we would be prepared to accept additional commercial discrimination against American products. American interest was basically political. We supported the Little Six of the Common Market in order to institutionalize Franco-German understanding and to tie Germany more closely to the West.

When Macmillan visited Washington, the question was raised again. President Kennedy asked Ball to explain our point of view to Macmillan, which he did. The British are being driven inevitably toward the Common Market. They've had three successive bad years and are facing difficulties. They are concerned about trade discrimination against them in the Common Market and also that this will increase as the market grows. Finally, the British simply can't afford to stay outside of the Common Market because of its dynamism. The growth rate of the Common Market is far greater than that of Britain.

Ball observed: "I think Macmillan has made his decision now. He is merely trying to waffle the solution—as he always does."

George said the project of a meeting with Khrushchev was first talked about by Kennedy in February, whereas the idea of a meeting with de Gaulle was only mentioned in March. Thus, the Khrushchev meeting was not linked to the de Gaulle meeting. He thought it unfortunate that Kennedy was now going to see Khrushchev right after de Gaulle and right after the series of defeats we have suffered in space, in Cuba, in Laos, possibly in Korea, and in the disruption of the French army.

PARIS, *May 23, 1961*

LAST night at dinner, General Grossin, head of French intelligence, said that recently a domestic servant in a house near Algiers called the police and reported General Salan was hiding in that house. This information was passed up from administrative echelon to administrative echelon. By the time troops arrived, five hours later, Salan had skipped. He had been forewarned by at least four different phone calls from government officials.

Prince Paul of Jugoslavia was there and we reminisced about the Balkans. He said that if he had it to do over again, he would still sign the pact with Hitler he signed twenty years ago. General Nedić had reported at a Cabinet meeting that if the Germans occupied Bulgaria it would be impossible for Jugoslavia to hold out in case of war and the best they could expect would be to have a few Serbian units escape southward into Greece. As a result Maček and the Slovenian boss said that if Paul did not sign the pact with the Axis—which indicated nothing but neutrality, friendship, and no military-transit rights—Croatia and Slovenia would secede. "I was faced with the impossible choice of a partitioned country or defeat and occupation unless I signed."

He told me that on January 1, 1939, he had told Sir Ronald Campbell, the British minister, that his most secret codes were known to the Germans and the Italians. Ciano had given copies of two top-secret British messages to Paul's Prime Minister, Stojadinović, to show him. Campbell took a train back to London the next day to advise the Foreign Office so the codes could be changed. Six months later Paul was visiting the King of England. Chamberlain called upon him. Chamberlain knew nothing about the leakage. Lord Halifax, foreign minister, hadn't told him.

Paul also told me about another leakage which caused great trouble. President Roosevelt sent our minister Arthur Lane to tell Paul we had heard Hungary was trying to make a new arrangement loosening its ties with Germany and drawing closer to Jugoslavia. Count Csaky, the Hungarian foreign minister who had been negotiating secretly with Paul, was horrified. Apparently the Hungarians learned that this American information had leaked to the Germans.

Lunched today at Motrico's. François de Rose feared it had been a mistake of the State Department to chuck in Khrushchev on top of Kennedy's meeting with de Gaulle. Pompidou, who was there, said: "My impression is that the President's itinerary must have been arranged not by the State Department but by American Express."

PARIS, *May 30, 1961*

AT dinner, George Ball told me that when Kennedy went to see General MacArthur, the General said to him: "All the chickens are coming home to roost and you are living in the coop."

PARIS, *June 1, 1961*

BUSY first day of President Kennedy's visit to France. Drinks with Chip Bohlen. I was struck by his enthusiasm for the new administration.

He had heard from Mac Bundy of my paper for Kennedy, in which I recommended that he, Bohlen, should be the interpreter. He would not have minded doing it but is really out of practice. (Later on at de Gaulle's reception I saw my old classmate Charles Sedgwick fulfilling the role for Kennedy.) It isn't a question of the language, but one forgets the technique of taking notes and remembering exactly what was said, whether in English or in French. The last time he had tried this was for Dulles and he found he couldn't remember what Dulles was saying. "Perhaps this was Freudian," said Chip with a wry grin.

He says Kennedy is most impressive. Chip is right in the inner circle and has been called in on everything. Fortunately for him, he only saw the tail end of the Cuban mess.

Kennedy reads everything I write, Chip said, and was absolutely furious at the column I published May 24, in which I criticized the adding of Vienna and Khrushchev to the Paris-de Gaulle schedule. Bundy was particularly angry and both he and Chip thought this was a mischievous piece designed to harm the President.

The idea had been put up in February, because Khrushchev had been hinting that he wanted such an encounter. Then came Cuba, Laos, etc., and we thought the matter was dead. We were surprised when the Russians suggested in May a meeting could be arranged in Vienna or Geneva since Mr. Kennedy was going to be in Europe. Kennedy wrote de Gaulle and asked him what his opinion was, and de Gaulle sent back a particularly warm and cordial letter, signed "Bien cordialement," in which he approved of the idea.

Kennedy is extremely well briefed. He reads a great deal, including all important papers, and he sorts things out effectively. Furthermore, Bundy is absolutely first class. He is the most important man influencing Kennedy on foreign affairs.

Chip was struck by the excellent atmosphere at lunch at the Elysée yesterday. There is a tremendous value to Mrs. Kennedy's fluent French and charming youthfulness, and de Gaulle was visibly in a very good mood.

Once when Kennedy asked him to describe Khrushchev's personality, Chip went ahead and summed up his impression by saying the best word for him was French; namely, *méchanceté* (a sort of wicked maliciousness). He added: "I can't really translate this for you; you had better ask your wife to elaborate."

Chip thought it would be a great mistake if Kennedy were to bring up the subject of nuclear sharing with de Gaulle because there was obviously nothing we could do about it and Congress would never qualify France for nuclear aid. I told him I disagreed and that it would be much better to bring the matter up and have a frank talk rather than to continue to let it fester as Eisenhower had done.

Chip recommended to Kennedy—but did not yet know whether his idea had been accepted—that the so-called *directoire* problem should be settled accordingly: The old Churchill-Roosevelt system of exchanging ideas directly at the top should be revised on a three-way basis with de Gaulle. The chiefs of government would consult on everything except subjects having to do with nations tied by treaty to the U.S.A., in this instance; that is to say, formal treaties ratified by the Senate. I said to Chip that this was exactly what I had been proposing; namely, that we extend to France the same parity we give to England. I thought his idea specifying treaties ratified by the Senate was a good one because it would erase from de Gaulle's mind the fear that there was a secret treaty with England. Chip said there was no worry about Kennedy's not being pro-French. He was almost too pro-French and it was a question of restraining him.

He said Kennedy had an excellent sense of humor. At a recent gridiron dinner he told this story on himself. When Al Smith was running for the Presidency in 1928, the tale had it that after Hoover won the election, Smith sent the Pope a telegram saying "Unpack." Kennedy said that after the school bill fracas started in Congress this year, he had received a telegram from the Pope saying "Pack." At lunch today, he said French and

English were the languages spoken by the new nations, not Russian and Chinese. De Gaulle smiled with pleasure.

Lunched with André de Staercke. This afternoon, Kennedy is coming to NATO and André, as the council dean, will make a speech making plain that NATO doesn't approve the apparent American dropping of the Norstad plan for a NATO nuclear stockpile.

De Staercke is worried that there is more activity than diplomacy in the Kennedy administration and says: "I fear that the New Frontier is the last border." Perhaps Europe underestimated Eisenhower a posteriori and overestimated Kennedy a priori.

The whole Cuban thing was a terrible blow and its effects are graver and more far-reaching than Washington realizes. In a sense it was worse than Suez because the paramount power of the West was damaged. Kennedy is taking a middle-of-the-road course which gets hit from both sides. He supported the Cuban rebels without backing them and he backed them without supporting them.

PARIS, *June 2, 1961*

THIS afternoon, I had a forty-minute talk with President Kennedy in his apartment at the Quai d'Orsay; the first since he entered the White House. He was extremely friendly and informal. I was looking out of the window of his secretary's office when a cortege arrived from the Elysée, where he had paid his farewell call on de Gaulle. The Gardes Républicaines, lined up in their white breeches and dark blue coats, gave a roll of the drums as his limousine showed up behind a V of motorcyclists.

Moments later Kennedy strolled by an open door, saw me, turned around, and came in with his hand outstretched, saying, "Hi, Cy. How are you? Glad to see you." He took me into a large room where we sat down. Nobody else was present.

Right at the start he said: "I guess we had better settle on what basis this is. Is this for the record or background or what?" I said it would be a great break for me if he would let me put it on the record. He said: "Gee, Cy, I had better not. You know I have got all these fellows traveling around with me and this would just get me into a lot of trouble." Later on he added: "Please protect me on this. Don't indicate in any way that you have seen me and don't tell anybody. Don't let Reston or any of those other fellows know you have seen me. I haven't seen anybody. So please protect me."

Then we started a conversation which lasted longer than I had expected. I began by asking if he had initiated the discussion of allied, Big Three, and nuclear matters. He replied that he had and said—much more modestly than it sounds—"I moved the conversation on from subject to subject."

He said the paper I had sent on to him was "invaluable" and "very useful." I had suggested that the best strategy—to prepare a favorable atmosphere for the tough questions—would be to discuss first things last. I asked Kennedy if this was what he had done and he smiled and said yes. They began with Berlin and then moved on to Asia, Africa, Latin America, etc., before hitting the more direct problems. He said that Berlin was easy because we knew in advance we agreed with each other.

I asked if he would be prepared to ask Congress to qualify France for atomic aid under the McMahon Act if France ceases nuclear tests and joins the Geneva talks. He said he had better not answer this one—but actually he went into the subject on and off as our conversation evolved.

I asked if we would give the French missile aid anyway, since this did not require amendment to the McMahon Act. He said this was being reviewed. We were considering making France eligible for such technical devices as guidance systems. But we would first have to see where we were going on the test-ban negotiations at Geneva. Although the question of missiles was not subject to the McMahon Act and not directly involved in Geneva, it was indirectly involved. It is all important right now that we should not seem to take the initiative in proliferating nuclear military power. Furthermore, if we give the French such help, there will be great German pressure to join in. Nevertheless, we are certainly going to look into the problem and help France on these matters.

Were we now prepared to treat France, in terms of consultation both inside and outside the NATO area, on a basis of complete parity with the way we treat England? Without any hesitation he replied: "There is no doubt of this." He then said: "We will improve the consultation procedure in every respect." He then elaborated on the atomic question and said Congress was very worried. The recent Blake espionage case in England had alarmed many Congressmen because apparently there had been a leakage on our atomic-propulsion system.

There was absolutely "no deadline" for the moratorium on atomic testing. I asked if August 1 would not be a deadline because of the multinational disarmament talks there. He repeated: "There isn't any deadline at all."

I asked if we were prepared to discuss with Khrushchev any plan to neutralize areas such as central Europe, south Asia, or east Asia. He said it was hard to talk about this in advance, but he didn't really think we could envision doing this because "there will be no withdrawals—no withdrawals anywhere."

Would we be prepared under any circumstances to enter into any kind of agreement with Khrushchev whereby both sides would promise to refrain from propaganda and subversion activities in each other's areas?

He didn't think it would be in Khrushchev's interest to make such a proposal. "I am sure Khrushchev won't propose that," he said. He thought it was impossible from the Russian point of view and when we had tried it in 1933, by the Roosevelt-Litvinov agreement, of course, it had not worked out.

I said that Khrushchev claimed to be opposed to war except for "wars of national liberation," which he favored. Couldn't this reservation entitle us also to say we favored wars of national liberation from our viewpoint? Kennedy said that this problem of local wars raised the question of "escalation." There was a danger of any such local war and external commitments growing into a major war. We were very concerned about this. The Laos crisis is an example of what can evolve from this kind of war.

By that time, I had finished my questions and I tucked them in my pocket, but Kennedy kept chatting so I took advantage of his mood. He said the talks with de Gaulle had been "very useful" and had been vastly helpful to himself (Kennedy). De Gaulle had explained in detail his views on France and his responsibilities and hopes. The talks also served to help give de Gaulle a real impression of American policy.

This process of consultations was particularly valuable because we and the French are involved in a great many places together. Kennedy admitted the French had a deep suspicion that we had a secret consultation treaty with England, but he said he had helped to alleviate this a bit. He added: "We consult in such an intimate way with England because the English are easy to consult with. We have a kind of community point of view. But now we are going to try to improve our own procedures of consultation with France which is involved in so many regions with us and where we are interested, such as Africa and Laos. After all, the French are in Laos under the Geneva agreement—we are not."

Kennedy said that despite de Gaulle's austere public manner he had been very "warm during our conversations." Furthermore, he added:

These talks were very satisfactorily arranged from my point of view. Most of the time, there were only the two of us plus interpreters and we could talk very frankly. This enabled me to get a precise idea of local political theories. De Gaulle has a much more removed relationship from his government than we have. I think that is the main problem. A President who must finally accept responsibility and determine policy is far better off if his own contacts are accurate and broad. This is a difficulty for de Gaulle. But from my point of view it showed the advantage of a trip like this.

As a matter of fact, when I was leaving de Gaulle he said: "I have more confidence in your country now."

Kennedy again returned to the nuclear matter and said we would have to reserve our position until we see where we are going. He also returned to de Gaulle's suspicions of the U.S.A. and said: "You were quite right [in the paper I had sent him]. His anti-American feeling and suspicions go way back and are very deep-rooted."

It was only out of respect for French wishes that so little had been given out here in the form of background information "because you know how de Gaulle feels about the press. We had to go along. But I don't need to tell you this. You know de Gaulle very well."

He asked me if I was going to Vienna. I said I had a hotel room and a plane seat, but I hadn't made up my mind. "What's your advice as a former newspaperman?" I asked him. "Why don't you go? You might as well spend two days in Vienna as here and there news won't be banned. Chip Bohlen can give you some pretty good background stuff. I think you ought to go."

Just before I departed the President said:

> I think it is tremendously important for a man with my responsibility to know something about the people I have to deal with. That helps me make up my mind when the moment for decision comes. Thus, for example, if you ask Dean Acheson or Walter Lippmann a question on any issue you will always get 100 percent contradictory answers. You have to know the men themselves in order to be able to evaluate their words.

PARIS, *June 5, 1961*

TOMMY Thompson and Chip Bohlen have returned from Vienna with Rusk to brief NATO on the Kennedy-Khrushchev talks. Chip is going with Rusk to the Elysée this afternoon to brief de Gaulle. Tommy told me I had been wise not to go to Vienna; it was a rat race. The only appearance of yield by Khrushchev, and therefore the only appearance of potential agreement, was on Laos.

Khrushchev made it clear that he intends to move on the question of an East German treaty and Berlin, but he did not fix a timetable. Kennedy warned Khrushchev we will not yield on Berlin because this symbolizes our entire position in Europe. We pointed out the danger to Khrushchev of signing a separate treaty with East Germany. This would give the East Germans, in effect, control over war and peace because of their possible actions against western supply lines.

Tommy believes the Chinese have told the Russians they won't play ball even if the Russians sign a test ban. The Russians will be quite "sweet" this summer and may not even sign a German treaty in a hurry because Khrushchev doesn't want to push us too much.

Chip said nothing in Vienna represented a major departure from the previous views of either side. On Berlin, both had simply laid out their point of view firmly. Kennedy never used the word "escalation" in discussing the danger of limited war, but he did point out the great threat of a direct confrontation of the two power blocs on the Berlin issue.

Khrushchev again showed that his conception of the Troika system is now a fundamental of Soviet policy. He showed no disposition to cede, and Chip says his formula is still "peace at no price."

Thompson is convinced Khrushchev got into the Laos affair in order to keep the Chinese out. Neither he nor the North Vietnamese wanted China in. For this reason Khrushchev may seriously want a *temporary* deal on Laos.

Khrushchev was less crisp than usual. He was quiet, firm, and courteous and only became animated for one brief flash during the discussion on Berlin. He hammered us for supporting repressive regimes which did not represent the popular wish in many countries. We of course favor self-determination, but the way he interprets this means self-determination only so long as it moves toward communism.

Khrushchev was impressed by Kennedy much more than by Eisenhower. He found him a modern man not cluttered up by old formulas. Kennedy had done his homework well and never once had to turn to an advisor for information.

PARIS, *June 6, 1961*

TOM Finletter came for coffee and said the most important aspect of the Vienna meeting was that the U.S.A. and Russia exchanged aide-mémoires on the German situation. The Russian paper was serious, but close reading reveals there is no deadline or ultimatum.

Khrushchev warned Kennedy, when the President talked about the dangers of war by mistake: "We don't make mistakes. We will not make war by mistake." Tom hopes this is true because, although it has menacing implications, this would also reduce the chances of war by accident, which is the great danger.

PARIS, *June 7, 1961*

LAST night, I dined alone at Herbert Blankenhorn's (German ambassador) with Franz-Josef Strauss (German defense minister). Only yesterday, Tom Finletter had been remarking that Blankenhorn at public dinner parties would talk about Nazi Germany with contempt and almost as if it was another country inhabited by another people—although everybody knew Blankenhorn had been a member of the Nazi party.

Since 1945, Blankenhorn has become an intimate advisor of Adenauer and is the Chancellor's most trusted envoy. And yet last night he could not say nasty enough things about Adenauer. Clearly Blankenhorn wants Strauss to treat him as his own stooge if he eventually becomes Chancellor. Strauss looked rather pleased, like a plump little boy.

Strauss said secret but formal orders have been passed down to all ranks in the French army instructing soldiers and officers to report on any disloyalty of their superiors. This horrified him and "could never" happen in Germany. De Gaulle made the mistake of never confiding his real political plans—on NATO and Algeria—to his top commanders. Therefore, they were shocked when they found out his real program and this was what encouraged the recent mutiny. Strauss thought Challe had been correct to revolt against de Gaulle and he had talked to many French generals, such as Valluy, who agree.

At Finletter's previous urging, I told Blankenhorn and Strauss I thought Germany, for the sake of NATO, should have a better representative on the council than von Walther. Strauss said Walther was terrible. But it wasn't really the poor fellow's fault because the system of policy making in Germany was so bad that Walther could never get firm instructions. Nevertheless, Walther would have to be replaced.

Strauss complained the French were treating Germany as a kind of "Maginot line" to protect France with the thought of establishing French guerrilla units behind it. The French army—even if it is back in Europe—won't be a modern army with properly modern equipment until 1965 or 1966.

Khrushchev wants to neutralize Germany, reducing its army to the size of a police force. However, although he would be willing to sacrifice communism in East Germany to achieve this goal in a unified, neutral, non-NATO Germany, he dares not risk decommunizing East Germany and possible repercussions in other satellites because of Chinese rigidity and pressure.

Strauss seemed to display unconscious contempt for de Gaulle as well as for Adenauer. I felt he would continue stubbornly to build Germany's military power and, therefore, its political specific gravity, not only in the West but also in the entire world. This could lead to dangerous consequences.

Lunched with Motrico, the Spanish ambassador. He is very disturbed by Franco's policy, which is tying Spain to Portugal's doomed Salazar government in a world that is changing swiftly.

Motrico proclaims himself an out-and-out supporter of Don Juan. He is trying to arrange a meeting between Don Juan and Kennedy. It is necessary for Don Juan's prestige to have the U.S. behind him and Washington must get ready for the eventual Spanish succession.

Portugal, he says, is practicing an idiotic policy of force to hold on to its colonies—when it has no force. It doesn't have the troops, navy, or air transport to do the job. He is afraid Portugal may try to induce Franco, under the terms of the Iberian alliance, to give physical support to its

African policy. That would be a disaster. The immediate objective is to insure that when Portugal blows Spain can remain solid and will not erupt in a simultaneous revolution. The second objective is to arrange for the transition to Don Juan sometime afterward.

LONDON, *June 12, 1961*

LUNCHED with David Bruce, the Philippe de Rothschilds, and Colonel Dick Ellis, whom David brought home (we're staying at the embassy). Ellis is most interesting: small, pink cheeked, white haired, about seventy; an Australian who speaks perfect Russian and several other languages. He was with Dunsterforce in the Caucasus after 1917, where he gained a reputation as tough, ruthless, and brilliant. In World War II he was a big shot in intelligence.

He said the Russians all assume they can work out an accommodation with the West but are more worried about China. Khrushchev is desperately trying to fill Central Asia and the Chinese border with Slavs, above all Ukrainians. He is also shaking up the administration in Turkestan.

David said de Gaulle is foolish to think of the Ruhr barons or Krupp as being real powers in Germany and that "Krupp is no more dangerous than this glass of marc [de Bourgogne]." Not even Adenauer would publicly demand a war for the sake of Berlin. The West could accept the East Germans as "agents" of Russia, but Russia has refused this formula.

He thought it had been folly for the U.S. to "create" a Berlin question at the start by trading off Thuringia, Saxony, etc., for occupation rights without even a corridor. He regretted that we didn't know how to negotiate in a phony way like the Russians—posing impossible demands knowing they were impossible.

If the West recognizes East Germany, no West German government could last forty-eight hours. There would be chaos in Berlin and the Russians would begin preparations for eventual takeover of West Germany with an indigenous Communist party.

LONDON, *June 13, 1961*

DINED last night with Bill Deakin, warden of St. Antony's, Oxford. He is about to write a short book on Richard Sorge, the famous Soviet spy in Tokyo who gave Moscow advance information that Hitler would attack and Tokyo wouldn't move (allowing Russia to shift Siberian divisions westward). He also gave an advance tip on Pearl Harbor (which Moscow didn't pass on to Washington).

Told a fascinating story of Fosco Maraini, now at St. Antony's. Maraini was put in a concentration camp by the Japs when he declared for Badoglio. One day, he walked up to a sentry, grabbed his bayonet, hacked off his middle finger, threw it and the bayonet at the sentry's feet, and turned his back to show his contempt. After that, the Italian prisoners were given better food and treatment.

Lunched with David Bruce. He says the British can never again have the relationship they had with us under Eisenhower, when they had Ike pretty well in their pocket—and they know it.

There will be a grave Berlin crisis this year and we must make it clear we are ready for war if necessary. Ike did understand—and indicate to the Russians—that in this nuclear-missile age, the President can make war without Congress. Kennedy realizes this and tried to make it plain to Khrushchev.

David sought years ago (for Acheson) to arrange a restoration of the monarchy in Spain (he was then ambassador in Paris), with Franco being named a duke, head of the state council, and given a huge estate. But the matter got into the hands of the Spanish desk of the State Department and strangled in red tape.

PARIS, *July 4, 1961*

AVERELL Harriman was reminiscing last night at dinner about George Kennan, who was his number-two when Averell was ambassador in Moscow. He says Kennan writes beautifully but his judgment has major flaws. He argued with Harriman in 1945, that we had nothing to gain by being adamant on Poland where Stalin would not yield, and all we would do would be to irritate. Averell says this was immoral—and unwise in terms of American politics where there is such a heavy Polish vote.

Harriman said the Bohlen record of the Yalta talks should never have been made public. It was a perfectly correct record, but it did not explain that often Roosevelt was trying out trial balloons on Stalin to see how he would react and did not really mean what he appeared to mean—on Poland, for example.

Averell said the British had been much weaker at the Geneva talks on Laos than the French, and it was the British who had insisted (from the West) on the Pathet Lao sitting down at the conference table. Harriman is furious at the Republicans for trying to set up a right-wing government under General Phoumi just five weeks before the Democrats took over. This is what upset the apple cart.

PARIS, *July 6, 1961*

LUNCHED with Jean Laloy. He is working on the Berlin planning committee. Dean Acheson, who is in charge, has drawn up a contingency paper which is now being submitted to the National Security Council. His idea is that first of all the West must take visible military measures to impress Khrushchev with our seriousness on Berlin. We should not indicate a willingness to negotiate until October or November, and until the effect of these measures has had a chance to sink in.

Laloy thinks Khrushchev is rattling rockets in order to impress us with the seriousness of his own intentions. The Russians are doing to us just what we plan to do to them, and each side is insisting it really means business, while neither side seems to believe the other.

Despite Macmillan's recent tough statements on German reunification, the British would still like to make a deal by recognizing East Germany. But this would be disastrous and might cost us West German membership in NATO.

PARIS, *July 8, 1961*

YESTERDAY evening, Bob (Sir Pierson) Dixon, who is now British ambassador here, said Khrushchev is trying to settle everything once and for all on the western frontier of his ideological empire. His ultimate, long-range worry will be in terms of China. So he wants all quiet on the western front before he turns his attention eastward.

THE SHAH FLIRTS

WITH RUSSIA

TEHERAN, *July 17, 1961*

THIS MORNING I HAD A TWO-HOUR TALK WITH THE SHAH: FRIENDLY, agreeable, and informal. He confided he had been having diarrhea for the last three days—like everybody else around here. He received me in his large office in the Saadabad Palace on the hillside outside Teheran. During our chat, we had several cups of tea and American cigarettes. I recall that the first time I met him almost twenty years ago he bummed almost all my American cigarettes. This time I got back at him. Our conversation rambled all over the place. I have an infected arm so my notes weren't very good.

He said he was by disposition extremely pro-French. He had had a French governess as a kid and grew to love France as a student in Le Rosey school on the lake of Geneva. But in recent years, he had become increasingly disappointed with the French and thought they had lost their vitality. Maybe de Gaulle is bringing back to France a sense of mission and grandeur. He considers him a big man and admires him greatly.

I told him that in late 1952, before the Eisenhower administration took over, I had tried to persuade Byroade that the U.S. should try and develop the Saadabad Pact instead of inventing a new Middle East defense organization; that Russia had accepted the existence of the Saadabad Pact—which had never been denounced—so it could be gradually given teeth without fear of a new crisis. Likewise, by including Afghanistan instead of Pakistan it would really create a "northern-tier" to protect the Middle East and at the same time it would avoid the complication of a crisis with India. The Shah agreed that this might have been feasible, and said that actually, in juridical theory, the Saadabad Pact still existed. CENTO obviated the need to do anything about it now.

Everybody tells me the Shah is dictator of Iran today and has been the real boss ever since he returned when the CIA bounced Mossadegh. He is an agreeable fellow, but he certainly does not give the impression of being a strong, tough ruler.

The Shah said Russia's aim remained unchanging—to impose a Communist regime in Iran. Moscow hoped to do this either by subversion or by vote; one or another way to accomplish "a revolution by the masses." The Russians might try and offer some new kind of bribe to Iran to encourage neutralism.

Russian propaganda claims that Iran is ruining its economy by its arms program. But the Shah argues it would have to spend more on armaments if it were neutral. He insisted that if Iran remains allied to the West, its geographical and strategic position will enable Europe to protect the oil wealth of the Middle East. Iran and Turkey are the only countries between the Arab states and Russia. As long as they are strong, the Arabs have room for maneuvers and neutralism. It was the fact of a strong Iran and Turkey that prevented Iraq from going Communist after Kassim's *coup d'état.*

The entire economy of western Europe depends on Middle East oil. In 1975, the oil consumption of western Europe will be 340,000,000 tons a year. If Middle Eastern oil were not available, the U.S. and Venezuela could not make up the deficit. Should Iran fall to communism, a few days later Iraq would be gone. Before long Turkey would follow—probably within a year.

The Russians wouldn't be able to use the Middle Eastern oil themselves, but if they could deprive the West of access to it, they could take over Europe by economic war. The Russians know that oil is our greatest weakness. During the next thirty years—the life of one generation—oil will be the Achilles heel of western Europe and nuclear energy will be too expensive and impractical to replace it as a fuel.

The Shah said:

It is our job to point out the problems, and it is your job to appreciate the problems and to decide how to manage them. If you are convinced the arguments we put forth are correct, you are not taking adequate measures.

Now let me tell you something. Two-and-one-half years ago we became acutely fed up with the U.S. attitude in CENTO. For three or four years, CENTO had been meeting but the U.S. never took the full part expected of it. In effect, you rejected the programs elaborated by CENTO and you never told us why.

After the Iraqi revolution of 1958, the United States proposed a draft of a special bilateral treaty with us and also with Turkey and Pakistan. In its initial form, the draft proposed was meaningless. We were so fed up that we turned a listening ear to Russian proposals for a nonaggression pact. I can only say that as things turned out, it is fortunate Russian proposals came too late.

Finally, Moscow proposed that Iran could remain in CENTO but would still sign a fifty-year nonaggression pact with the Soviet Union instead of the bilateral pact you were then offering.

We told your government, and President Eisenhower wrote begging me not to accept the Russian proposal. The British, Turks, and Pakistanis echoed him. They claimed that if we accepted the Russian offer it would weaken the western camp and would constitute a psychological victory for Russia.

But the United States then sent us a more explicit draft. Eisenhower wrote me a personal letter recalling the fate of the Baltic states after they had signed nonaggression treaties with Russia. I succumbed to this argument, and sent the Russians off. Since then, they have been conducting a violent and continuous propaganda campaign against us. But also, since then, the United States has *not* increased its military, economic, or moral aid to Iran.

The Russians now want an assurance that no foreign military bases will be permitted in Iran. I say that such a pledge would be contrary to the sovereignty of our country. Furthermore, the Russians define "base" in a loose way to suit themselves. When I built a port in the Persian gulf, they called it a naval base. When I built an airport, they called it an airbase.

But your country, to save a few more dollars, is not strengthening us and I don't think this is honorable. You should increase, not decrease, your help. The United States says that Iran's job is to maintain itself in case of war for as long as possible while a nuclear-missile conflict is fought out. But we don't look at things that way.

Personally, I feel that the stronger the United States and Russia become in thermonuclear weapons, the less danger there is of a global war. But I also feel that this very fact consequently increases the danger of local war.

I don't question your good faith and your willingness to help us in case of a local aggression. But the United States simply would not have time to send troops here, nor would it be able to take an immediate quick decision to do so. It would have to consult all of its allies first, and this would take a few days. During those few days, our fate would be decided. The aggressor would grab as much as he could, benefiting from surprise, and who would be able to force him to withdraw?

If Iran were more ready to defend itself against an enemy, that enemy wouldn't start things. I don't mean that we could stand up against the Russians. But suppose they used a proxy like Afghanistan to serve their purpose. And by keeping Iran weak, you tempt our enemies.

Our neighbors, such as Iraq and Afghanistan, have modern Soviet weapons. We desperately need missiles and new planes. Our neighbors have greatly superior aircraft. We keep sending you shopping lists, but nothing happens.

I asked him to comment on Senator Humphrey's statement that the Iranian army was "only capable of coping with the civilian population," claiming the commander-in-chief of the Iranian army had told him this. He said: "I am the commander-in-chief and I didn't." He continued: "The United States stopped us from signing a pact with the Russians on the basis of your promises. But you are not living up to your pledge."

The Shah said the only territorial claim Iran had was for Bahrein and this was not active and did not damage relations with Britain, but he wished me to keep that statement off the record because it would embarrass him politically if people thought he were not pressing it.

He didn't think Iran could afford elections for five more years, no matter what the Constitution said. He added: "One mistake the United States made was trying to sell your kind of democracy to countries like Iran, Pakistan, and South Korea. You can't do it. There are no democratic regimes in the area around Iran. The experiment in Turkey failed. Democracy of the western type, when applied in underdeveloped countries, becomes only a weapon for subversion."

He regarded de Gaulle as France's benevolent dictator. The French had a high level of education, prosperity, and economy, and de Gaulle was able to use special methods there. "I am not sure if we could apply similar methods in Iran." He then continued sadly:

> This job of mine is a source of danger and of trial. But monarchy is the instrument that has saved Iran. And I wish to point out that I am not only a puppet and a figurehead. I control the army and that is why we have never had a military *coup d'état*. I can change governments by decree and without bloodshed or army takeover.
>
> My philosophy of government *was* that when the people are sufficiently educated and gathered into real political parties, they can form the basis of western democracy. But what is to happen before then? I had hoped we would reach that ultimate stage much earlier. But my hopes were destroyed.

The U.S. bilateral treaty only guaranteed the regime against a Communist overthrow but not against another kind of upset. He said land reform had been going on much too slowly here. There were not even any maps defining who owned which property. It was necessary to set up cooperatives, but there were inadequate experts to run them.

He had wanted to give away all his land immediately, but it had taken ten years to do what he has done so far. He had given up "well over 500,-000 acres," but he didn't know how much remained. He promised: "I am going to give up all the rest of my land within a year."

I asked if he thought Khrushchev were planning some kind of coup in Iran while all the world was looking at Berlin. He answered: "For heaven's sake, don't write this, but I can tell you that if I were in Khrushchev's place, that's what I would do."

I asked how he was educating his son to be a monarch in the nuclear age. With a sad smile he said:

I would prefer that he never became a monarch. But if that is his destiny, he should study sociology above all other things—the science of human relations. He should also study our history and find out what are the good things in it that should be retained. Everything, of course, will depend upon what stage society will have reached when he assumes power. My father took over when there was nothing and he made an almost socialistic system in which the state controlled virtually everything. I am convinced we have certain inherent advantages and that Iran is the only country in this area which has any chance of someday attaining a European level.

TEHERAN, *July 18, 1961*

THIS morning, I spent another hour and a half with the Shah. He doesn't think Khrushchev will make a new offer of a nonaggression pact. Next time, he is going to play the game whole hog. He will try and get the mob to install a national front government with a neutralist foreign policy. That wouldn't last two months and then Khrushchev would move in and take over the country.

When Mossadegh took power, according to records his police captured afterward, there were only 121 Iranian army officers who were secret members of the Tudeh (left-wing) party. By the time Mossadegh was kicked out there were close to seven hundred. Mossadegh had destroyed the financial stability of the country.

He has no use for Nasser, saying: "All he can boast is that he is up to the ears in debt." He was delighted when I told him of reports that Nasser discovered a Russian plot, right in his own Revolution Command Council, which aimed to murder him.

I told him Prince Naim (foreign minister) of Afghanistan had drawn a map for me running along the Hindu Kush and up to the northwest, claiming that everything south of that line could be held against the Russians if the U.S. gave adequate aid and built a proper base at Kandahar. "At least Naim knows that," said the Shah. "But does Prince Daud [Prime Minister]?"

JERUSALEM, *July 24, 1961*

THIS morning, I went to one of the last sessions of the Eichmann trial. I remembered the wartime trials in Jerusalem under the British mandate—when the Jews were the accused. It was remarkable to see a kind of justice so closely associated with British justice now being applied by the Jews to a German.

The courtroom is large and well equipped. The audience is provided with portable earphones for interpretation into English, French, and German. All the judges and the prosecutor speak German directly to Eichmann, but everything is meticulously translated into Hebrew for the record. Behind the three judges is a large seal of the menorah, the seven-branched candelabrum.

Eichmann is housed in a glass, bullet-proof cage to protect him against assassination. Right behind him sit two Israeli policemen. The men who were on duty today contrived in some odd way to look both alert and bored. They were considerably less Jewish looking than Eichmann himself, the great racist.

In fact, Eichmann makes a very curious impression, like a figure out of a Kafka book. He is thin, definitely Semitic, dark, with an intelligent face, pinched features, glasses. A strained tenseness shows in the canted angle at which he holds his neck: a politely obstinate and curiously unctuous manner. He seems to have almost filial respect for the president of the tribunal, Judge Landau, a calm and courteous man.

Incidentally, when I entered the compound where the trial is taking place I was searched for weapons.

Eichmann had odd things to say in today's testimony. For example: "An anti-Semite, I never was." He claimed he regarded the Nuremberg laws as laws that "would not be carried out." He said, with servile insistence: "I was not the one who sowed the seed of fear." At another point he added: "I was not a rude person, a driving and obnoxious man." When it was recalled to him that he had admitted grabbing a copy of the New Testament from his wife and tearing it up, he said with full earnestness: "I am not infallible, I must say." Later he made the extraordinary statement: "I tried as best I could to live according to Kant's categorical imperative."

I talked with various Israelis about the impact of the trial. Some say it killed off cynicism here. Some point out that it was a unifying force in a world where most of the current trends are against Israel—anticolonialism does not affect this country; regional groupings excluded it; communism passes it by. But the Eichmann trial has shown people that the state was a necessity and what the world does to Jews.

This afternoon, Ben Gurion received me in the Prime Ministry and I enjoyed the conversation but did not get much out of it. He is a remarkable physical specimen for seventy-five. His memory is excellent. He quoted from the Bible in both Hebrew and English. A compact but strong little man, he was wearing a white, open-collared shirt with short sleeves and light summer pants.

I reminded him that in October, 1955, he had told me if Nasser kept receiving arms from Russia, Israel would have to "smash him." One year later came the Sinai war. Nasser was again getting arms. What was Ben Gurion's view?

He replied: "The problem is different today. Then there were almost daily border attacks, but since Sinai there has been more or less general quiet, and there is no interference with our shipping through the Elath Straits [the Gulf of Aqaba]. Nasser still says he intends to smash Israel and we know of his intentions and of his improved armaments. But he has respect for our army. Maybe he will try again in the future, but, while there is quiet on our borders, we ourselves will keep quiet."

I then asked him what he thought of President Kennedy's present initiative with the Arabs aiming at the basis for a Palestine peace. He said that, unlike the Arab leaders, he had received no letter from Kennedy, nor had any special envoy been sent such as the secret Anderson mission under Eisenhower. He recognized that American policy seeks peace and that there was a great friendship for Israel in the United States, adding: "As human beings, all your presidents are nice men." On his recent trip to the United States, he had seen Kennedy and also Eisenhower and Truman. He lunched with Truman and told him he would be remembered not only in American history but in Jewish history. Truman was so moved that he wept.

But, Ben Gurion said, it was a delusion apparently still entertained by Washington to think that Israel can take back a large number of Arab refugees. The Arabs don't care about their refugees. During the Sinai war the Israelis lost only one prisoner to the Egyptians, a pilot. But they had captured six thousand. Nevertheless, it took a long, long time to arrange an exchange of one against six thousand.

For the Arabs the refugees were only a political weapon. Israel had taken in more than a million Jewish refugees, a larger number than the Arabs had driven from this country. Yet their Arab brothers did not integrate them into their own lands.

Ben Gurion predicted: "Nothing will change. The Arabs are out to destroy Israel. They only want to use the refugees to further that plan. And we are not insane; we won't commit suicide."

He said: "The Arab refugees would be used to destroy Israel. There are hundreds of millions of refugees elsewhere in the world; yet nobody worries about exchanging them—Germans, Poles, Indians, Pakistanis. We now have a population of 240,000 Arabs, including 30,000 admitted since our independence war. We accepted 500,000 Jewish refugees from Arab lands."

I asked about the prospects for Arab-Israeli peace. He said: "The time is not ripe. And you Americans cannot help now. This is the first year of your new administration and it is occupied with Laos, Cuba, Congo, and Berlin. There is no chance of a settlement today. It will depend on the development of East-West relationships."

I asked him about scientific advances. He said there has been some progress in solar energy. Israel is working on the problem of turning salt water into fresh water and hopes in about five years a cheap process can be found. "The biggest problem is water. It is an even bigger problem than Nasser. Without water people cannot live. We must settle the desert."

I then inquired whether Israel were working on guidance systems for its new rockets. He said: "We are trying to improve our rockets. We need a defense against airplanes. We have asked the United States for rockets, like the Hawk or the Nike, but Washington refused. Therefore we are now working on many things."

I asked him whether they were proceeding to build nuclear weapons from their Dimona pile. He said Israel's policy was to disarm and have mutual inspection for this country and its neighbors—even without world disarmament. The prophet Isaiah was the first prophet of world disarmament. He called my attention to the fourth verse of the second chapter which he read to me from an Old Testament on his desk (complaining all the time that one should read the Bible in Hebrew because it was impossible to translate good books).

When he had finished, he said: "I believe in that more than anything in the world." Isaiah was his favorite prophet of the Bible. "This book is the whole Bible." He then read me Isaiah's predictions that the Jews would come together again in this country from all nations and then war would be eliminated.

I asked if there were a written alliance with France. He said there was no written alliance and added:

Are alliances important? You can have written alliances that are broken and unwritten understandings that are kept.

We have no alliances in the technical sense of written alliances. But we have friends, and among these the first are the Americans. Your second President, John Adams, was the first to proclaim that the Jewish people would come back and built their own state here. In 1922, the American Congress supported the idea of an Israel. The U.S. government was the first to recognize our government. The first big loan came from the United States. But in terms of our defense, it is France. France saved Israel in 1956. Without French aid we would have been overrun by Nasser.

I asked him about the effect of the Eichmann trial. He replied:

The effect is about as I had expected. We have a new generation here, a new type of Jew. And then there are immigrants such as the Yemeni, who lived under foreign rule dependent on others for mercy. Many of our youths never really knew what happened in Germany. It was a useful shock for them. For the old ones, we were here in Israel even when we were not here. I was here in Israel when I was a child living in Russia. Our young generation is now for the first time—through the Eichmann trial—learning all about the horrors done to the Jews because they were Jews. Hitler killed Poles and others, but the only people he wished to destroy totally were the Jews. This knowledge is a useful shock for the young. The trial has brought home the whole tragedy and greatly strengthened the faith of our people in a Jewish destiny.

I asked him if he considered Israel a religious state or a racial state? He said adjectives were useless, but "my own adjective is Jewish. I now refuse to be called a Zionist. A Jew is a man who feels himself a Jew. No one knows why he is something—but he knows that he is. I have no quarrel with the American Jews, only the American Zionists. If they are real Zionists, they should come here."

I then asked him who had most influenced him. He replied, seizing the Old Testament in his hand: "This book. The Old Testament. This book has influenced me even more than Plato."

He then went off on one of his favorite subjects. The Jewish prophets had not been thinkers like the Greek philosophers. The Greeks had asked questions about the nature of things, but the Bible had given all the answers to the Jews; the Bible had said that God created everything, even the bad things; that God embodied everything. Therefore, the Jews did not create a science, like the Greeks, because they were not seeking for the answer.

He continued:

The first man was not a Jew, he was just a man, made by God, neither black nor white. Faith in this fact made the early Jews strong and they believed in redemption. I am not myself observant. I do believe there is a higher principle above all things, a principle of justice. This is a unique belief in ancient days and it was the teaching of our prophets. They taught that you should love your neighbor as yourself—but no more. They did not speak about turning the other cheek.

I asked if he still felt that the basic differences between the modern Israelis and the old Greeks was that the Israelis refused to accept the idea of fate or destiny. He replied:

Our people cannot understand destiny. They believe in the freedom of human choice. Human beings can make their own fate. All history proves this and most recently and specially the history of Israel. The history of Israel is a remarkable history above all because the Jews survived for two thousand years even without Israel. That was due to this book, this Bible. There is no abstract fate or destiny involved. We don't believe in fate.

I asked what the biggest need for Israel was today. He said: "More Jews —more good Jews." He thought these would come from America, Russia, and the Muslim countries. Many Jews in America and England were looking for a meaning in life which they could not find in the comfortable civilizations there. Israel needed pioneers, men of determination and vision, and would undoubtedly get some from America. This country could easily double its population today.

He added: "Our greatest asset is the people, with a great purpose in life. We know what we are doing and what we have to do. I think we have this feeling more than any people in the world."

JERUSALEM, *July 25, 1961*

SAW Mrs. Golda Meir, Israeli foreign minister, in the foreign ministry. We drank cold coffee, and I noticed that she smokes innumerable cigarettes. She is a homely but sympathetic-looking woman with a chignon of brown hair, heavy features, and a modest manner.

She said Israel would not take the initiative in seeking a French alliance because it did not wish to embarrass de Gaulle. A written alliance was unnecessary because France could do no more for Israel than she is already doing. If there were to be a change of policy after de Gaulle went, no agreement could affect the change.

Israel was now seeking essential security matériel from the United States. But the policy of Kennedy, like that of Eisenhower, is that America refuses to be the main armaments supplier to the Middle East. Even when Israel asks for things it cannot obtain in other countries, the U.S. answers no. It merely says it won't let Israel down. This is reassuring, but what does it mean?

The Sixth Fleet is in the neighborhood and were Kennedy to instruct the commander of the Sixth Fleet that he should steam toward this country any time Ben Gurion says there is trouble, that would really mean something. But obviously this cannot be done. She continued:

> The reality is that Nasser has bases in Egypt and Syria only a few minutes' flight from Tel Aviv, Haifa, and Israel's airfields. If he blew them up, he would have done his job even if fighting continued afterward.
>
> Even if it wished to act very swiftly, Washington would have to consult both the American government and the Security Council. The fastest possible action would take twelve hours, but the first three or four hours are the important ones to Israel. This is not Canada, but a tiny, vulnerable country.

Mrs. Meir says she is confident the United States would give Israel help if it were attacked, but everything might almost be over by then. If Tel Aviv and Haifa were bombed, it might be impossible to call up Israel's reserves, and if the airfields were bombed, planes could not take off.

Therefore, Israel has been requesting from the United States ground-to-air missiles in sufficient numbers to defend itself; but this request has been turned down. Mrs. Meir did not doubt American goodwill, but we cannot make the Russians cease helping Nasser.

It seemed to me the only war Israel could afford to fight was a war it started itself, because of the strategic weakness she had described. She said: "We will not start a war," but she admitted the sole deterrent to Nasser is the threat of another beating, and he must be made to know he is running a risk. "Nevertheless," she said, "peace is more important than any victory in war."

TEL AVIV, *July 27, 1961*

THIS morning, Teddy Kollek came for breakfast. I am laid up in bed with my arm in the cast and gout in both feet. Kollek told me that among the strange paradoxes of Israel is that "white" Jews (meaning Europeans and Sabras) are the officers of the paratroop brigade; but most of the enlisted paratroopers are "black" Jews from the Arab world.

Last night, I spent hours talking with ten young Israelis. One was an Arab who runs an Arab newspaper. One was an Iraqi Jew who also runs an Arab newspaper. The rest were Sabras. The Arab bitterly denounced the Jews and said: "You will never have peace until you Europeans cease looking down on us Arabs and also on Arab Jews." He suggested the atmosphere could be prepared for peace talks with Nasser if Israeli Arabs were treated as equals with full citizenship privileges and an end to military government; if Arabic became the official second language; if Israel proclaimed that it is prepared to discuss the question of refugees.

Several were quite prepared to disassociate Israel from world Jewry and integrate it into the Middle East. They all felt this country's only future lay in economic and political integration into the Middle East. But they were perplexed about how to bring it about. All insisted Israel should become a lay state. The tragedy was that although they prayed for peace, all were convinced there would be war again within the next decade.

They said Ben Gurion kept stressing this was a "Jewish" state but did not even know what a Jew was. They were remarkably free of complexes and clearly felt closer to each other and the Middle East than to American or Russian Jews.

TEL AVIV, *July 28, 1961*

THIS morning, because I am still laid up, General Moshe Dayan came to see me. He is a burly, sunburned, youthful-looking man with a bullet head, strong cheekbones, large white teeth, and a rather merry expression, despite the black patch that covers his left eye, lost in World War II. He is now minister of agriculture and is frequently mentioned as Ben Gurion's private choice to succeed him as boss of Mapai, the largest party, and Prime Minister of Israel. Dayan was wearing simple light khaki trousers and a half-sleeved white shirt open at the throat.

We started off with a discussion of ground-to-air missiles. He said Israel wanted whatever it could get and specifically mentioned the Nike and the

Hawk. If Israel had these, that mere fact might prevent war. One battalion of such first-class antiaircraft weapons located near Tel Aviv could protect the necessary airfields and population centers.

I observed that it was hard to expect Nikes when we do not have enough of them for the U.S.A., much less for our allies. He made the point that America hasn't sold Israel a single gun, aircraft, or tank, so that he, for one, never expected us to agree to sell the missiles.

He would not care if Nasser also had ground-to-air missiles. They were purely defensive weapons. Israel wants to be able to safeguard itself against surprise attack and would not mind if Nasser had similar safeguards. Likewise, he said when Israel asks for a U.S. guarantee it did not care if the U.S. guaranteed all the rest of the Middle East.

Dayan admitted the military situation was awkward but did not think Nasser was in a position to destroy this country by surprise attack. He said: "As the English say, nothing is ever as good or as bad as it seems. And that includes a surprise attack. We are a weak, small country. But even if Egypt attacked they could not prevent us from mobilizing. Unless they use atomic weapons they probably could not kill more than ten thousand people around Tel Aviv and in the morning the real war would start. And I don't think Russia is going to give Nasser atomic weapons now."

He thought the Arabs were not efficient enough to mount a fully successful surprise, even if instructed by the Russians. He did not believe Israel would be forced to start a war, although this might become necessary if there were a very massive buildup in the U.A.R. clearly directed toward Israel.

The most important thing in the Middle East today was to try and pull out of the Arabs' mind the thought that they could destroy Israel. The Arabs do not want to start a war and lose it. If Nasser doesn't think he can win a war, he won't talk about it so much. Dayan thought U.S. policy toward Israel was possibly even worse under Kennedy than under Eisenhower.

I asked if he thought Israel's future lay more with a Middle East confederation or with Europe and the West. Without hesitation, he replied:

In no way do we belong more to the Middle East than to Europe or America. I would like to see still stronger ties between Israel, the U.S.A., France, Scandinavia, and the Socialist countries of Africa.

What do we have in common with Syria and Egypt? Nothing as compared with the western world. And in any Middle Eastern confederation we would be a minority. We would always be outvoted and forced to go along. We are not part of this Middle Eastern world. Geography by itself is not important. Thus, for example, Greece is really more Levantine and Middle Eastern than European, but the Greeks call themselves European.

Dayan saw no chance of Middle East peace until there was world peace. The two power blocs provided arms here. If there were a real arms embargo, the chances of war would be erased.

He said that in 1956, during the Sinai campaign, which he commanded, *all* Egypt's units were bad. They simply did not have the proper morale and leadership. He did not think this situation could be changed for twenty-five years. Once an Egyptian became an officer he ceased trying to learn and educate himself.

He regarded Orde Wingate as a strategic genius. He had great influence on the entire Israeli army. Wingate had an enormous impact upon Dayan personally and he has tried to follow his ideas.

In concluding, Dayan said Israel would be delighted to accept a Middle Eastern arms freeze immediately and that the present balance was all right.

Incidentally, Dayan said it was not necessary for a good army officer to be intelligent. Many a fool was a leader and trusted by his men. But he could not be a coward and he had to be honest. Thus Montgomery was a great officer although he was a fool.

NICOSIA, CYPRUS, *July 31, 1961*

THIS morning, I visited Archbishop Makarios, President of the Republic of Cyprus. He was agreeable and friendly, but if he had a crew haircut and a shave he would be unimpressive. Nevertheless, there is no doubt he has immense prestige among Greek Cypriots.

I asked if he thought the formula for the new Cypriot state could be applied to settle the Algerian dispute. He said: "The evolution of the Cyprus question is not a good example. Something must be found to assure the protection of the Europeans in Algeria. The rights of the European minority *must* be protected. I do not think the two communities in Algeria could benefit from the example of Cyprus."

Makarios quite clearly does not think the Cyprus formula is too hot for Cyprus itself and still quite evidently favors union with Greece.

I asked if it were not a fact that Makarios and the Pope were the only religious leaders of states today (Vatican City). He stroked his graying beard and a slight smile came over his ivory face as he said: "That is right, the Pope and I. But the Pope is a permanent chief of state and I am not. I thought it my duty to offer my services, but I hope to retire in 1965, after my term as President ends."

Late this afternoon, I went to see Dr. Kutchuk, head of the Turkish community and Vice President of Cyprus. He is a pleasant little man with brown skin and worried face. He is living in the former house of the British Commissioner and is clearly pleased with it. The chief decoration on the table in his sitting room is a cigarette box with a brass plaque on the side which says, "With the compliments of the manufacturers of Players cigarettes."

Kutchuk said economic conditions were very bad, unemployment was increasing, and there had been four years of drought with the result that the peasants were suffering. There was a real need for funds to furnish long-term credits to the peasants and to help create jobs in the cities. If such a program was not forthcoming, communism would continue to gain. Communist agents had now moved into the villages, where they were making headway. If there were a secret ballot today, it would probably show that the Communists would win at least 40 percent. There is a very real danger that the next President of Cyprus will be a Communist.

Kutchuk has the oriental manner of address. He said to me: "You know, Your Excellency, my position has been based upon the support of the peasants and I had promised them aid, but their confidence in me is now going."

He admitted that there was no feeling of nationality in Cyprus. People still felt themselves Greeks or Turks.

NICOSIA, CYPRUS, *August 2, 1961*

CHET Bowles, Under Secretary of State, is here conducting a meeting with American diplomats from the Middle East and North Africa. During the last several weeks, he has been having a row in Washington.

Chet said he had learned from Washington experience that "You should never get too far away from a microphone." The reason he had been hurt in the press was that for six months he had been keeping his mouth shut and seeing hardly any newspaper reporters.

This evening, I had a long talk with Ed Murrow, head of the USIA, who has been consulting with his representatives in the Middle East and Africa. One big propaganda problem is books. The Russians alone published forty million books last year in the languages of non-Communist countries. The Chinese are printing books in Hong Kong and distributing them from there in order to avoid embargos on goods from Communist China. Last year's USIA budget was $110,000,000. Yet Russia spends $120,000,000 a year only to jam our transmissions. The USIA budget is less than the cost of one combat-loaded Polaris submarine.

Ed said: "We must ask ourselves whether our kind of system, without change, can successfully compete with the Communists or whether we will have to discipline ourselves by such moves as revising the antitrust acts."

CORFU, GREECE, *August 7, 1961*

KING Paul invited me to Mon Repos, his summer palace, and I flew up at breakfast time. Corfu is pleasant and beautiful but too soft, muggy, and

Italian. The mountains on the Albanian coast are just across the way and the straits are only four miles wide at their narrows. There were lots of boats in the harbor as European sailing races are taking place. Evzone guards in their white kilts and pompoms marched to and from the palace in town, although only policemen guard Mon Repos outside.

The King received me informally, wearing a blue T-shirt and light pants. We began talking about his profession and its future. He said that while the royal family was in exile, he had worked under an assumed name in 1925 in an aircraft factory in Coventry, England, and had also wandered around the United States in 1928. This brought him into contact with ordinary people from whom his education by private tutors had isolated him.

When Prince Constantine visited the U.S.A. in 1959, it had done him good. He had been under the direct tutelage of the Secretary of Defense and was able to participate in all kinds of military things, even becoming a frogman. At that time, Queen Frederika was touring atomic sites.

King Paul thought that twenty years hence—just as now—a king would not be able to be the real commander of his armed forces because he could not keep up with military complications. A king could not specialize too much. His father had been able to serve as a real commander, but now military science with its vast general staffs was too complicated and no king could know the problems of all services.

The next generation of kings would not need any more specialized knowledge of economics or foreign affairs. But kings might have to take more active decisions as the need for decision making will increase.

In Scandinavia, kings did not play an important role. These countries had kings "only because they have always had them. But here in Greece a king is necessary because otherwise there would be chaos."

The basic need for a king was common sense. A strong man was useful at the head of any democracy, although the ideal democracy was Switzerland, where nobody even knew the President's name.

The method of ruling was now more democratic, but the role of king was just as necessary as in earlier days. People needed a symbol which was also responsible. It was impossible to establish the same kind of affectionate relationship between the public and a president because presidents changed too fast. Also a king could serve as a repository of knowledge as he gained experience with time. A king was a nonpolitical figure who could even work with a Socialist government if necessary—although it would be impossible to work with Communists.

At this point, the Queen came in, looking fresh and pretty. She shook hands and said: "How white you have become. How do you like my gray hair?" She sat down on the sofa and joined the conversation, talking rapidly and flashing her numerous rings.

Frederika thinks there will be a war over Berlin unless some drastic solution is produced. Otherwise it will be impossible to stop an explosion in East Germany and West German intervention. King Paul said the people of Greece did not want to be either Red or dead but would fight if necessary.

Greece was having trouble with Rumania because of the way he treated his nephew, former King Michael. He said: "Once a king always a king, of course" (clearly the basic motto of the fraternal order of kings, all of whom recognize the danger they may be bounced). Michael always came to Greece at Christmas and Easter; the King received him officially with the Royal Guard. The Rumanians have begun to raise a rumpus about this.

He then referred to Cyprus, saying: "Remember, you and I started that one. The present system cannot last. But something had to be done and this was a good arrangement to get over the trouble. Eden behaved very stupidly so that Papagos lost his temper and sent Grivas in while I was out of the country. Twice before, Papagos had tried to send Grivas, but I refused to give him permission. He waited until I was away."

He could not understand why Russia had pulled out of Albania and left it to Chinese influence. He said he had once told Tito: "Why don't you leave southern Albania to me and you take the north?" But Tito replied: "I already have a million Albanians—and that is too much."

King Paul said his gamble in putting in Caramanlis had paid off. The Queen said: "My husband gets on well with Caramanlis, but I do not like him. I like his wife and I like Averoff. But I admit the Prime Minister and his wife export well. They are beautiful and a good advertisement for Greece."

Frederika said: "I would like to tell you my idea about how to solve the Berlin crisis, but you must not betray me. You must not tell anybody. You will see why." She then suggested that Khrushchev needed help desperately. He had to raise the standard of living in eastern Europe to prevent an explosion. There was no chance of unifying East and West Germany, "and I do not want to see it because I do not like the Prussians. Leave things as they are."

The U.S.A. had helped Stalin win the war by an enormous lend-lease program, although Stalin never told the Russian people and they did not realize there had been serious American aid. She then said: "You must help Khrushchev the same way so he can improve things in eastern Europe, but you must not tell people you are helping. Let him get the credit. I could have suggested this idea to Eisenhower who was a big man but I do not know the new people in your government." She indicated disapproval for Kennedy's administration and described Stevenson as "an egghead and pinkish."

The King disclosed deep mistrust for Turkey. He had warned Washington fourteen years ago that, "If there is a war the Turks will never fight.

You'll see, they will make some arrangement to remain neutral, just as they did last time." He did not know whether Jugoslavia would aid Greece if Bulgaria attacked this country, but a couple of times each year Athens and Belgrade exchanged "ideas on strategy."

At this point, the Queen said we had better go in to lunch and explained the house was filled with young royalty. There were about two dozen at table including: Paul, Frederika, Crown Prince Constantine, Princess Sophia, Princess Irene (very pretty and like her mother), Don Juan Carlos, son of the pretender to the Spanish throne, Princess Beatrix (heir to the Dutch throne) and her sister, Prince Michael of Kent, a Princess Radziwill (no relation to Stash), and lots of the Queen's Hessian relatives.

The youngsters were cheerful and talkative. I was particularly impressed by the Dutch Princess Beatrix, plain but exceedingly nice and independent minded. She announced to me that all Dutch are Calvinists and Puritans, even the Catholics, and they all dress up in black and go to church on Sunday. She was very indignant with Frederika when the Queen said she refused to go and hear Maria Callas because Callas had twice let the audience down by refusing to sing. Beatrix insisted: "But she gives everything to art. She is a great artist. Once you hear her you forget everything." English was the lingua franca—although Juan Carlos does not speak it too well and has a marked accent.

I found Constantine (everybody calls him Tino) a friendly, unpretentious kid. He was very nervous about the finals in the European sailing race in which he is competing against an Italian. He kept saying: "I know the Italian is better than I am." He has great admiration for Niarchos, who has put in a midget car track on his island.

When the Queen saw me struggling with my food because of my bad arm, she offered to feed me. It was a simple, chatty group and the Queen explained it was a great joy to have the youngsters, but she would not invite their parents because that would spoil things.

The King said that when he went to see the Pope nobody had been smart enough to brief him on the fact that this Pope had been Nuncio when Paul was married and had then paid his respects. The Pope told him he had chosen the name John because it had the largest numeral after it (XXIII). In his formal speech of welcome he read one paragraph in demotic Greek which was wholly incomprehensible. The Queen said: "You should have seen them at the formal review of the Swiss Guard. There was my husband walking along with long strides and this funny fat little priest trying to keep up with him."

The Queen got into a long discussion on religion. She said religion was one of the great troubles today. It concerned itself too much with form and not enough with spirituality. She did not care if there had ever been such a being as Christ. It was the idea and the legend and the teaching that mattered. But priests concern themselves almost entirely with archaic forms. She said: "All our priests are bad—except our favorite one in the palace." Priests should be like other people and go and mix with them and keep their difference only inside, spiritually, but instead they try to separate themselves from other people by ridiculous formalities. Three hundred years from now, people would be astonished when they looked back upon the behavior of our contemporary priests.

Nuclear science taught that everything was an extraordinary manifestation of atomic energy. We do not see the extraordinary manifestations of ourselves that others see. Religion should begin to ponder these facts, but her theories were too radical for any priest to accept.

She told me Tito was a violent atheist. "That man hates religion," she said. Tito told her that when he was a boy his mother used to stand him in a corner as a punishment if he did not pray.

King Paul said no emperor has ever lived the way Tito does. "Why, he has two or three palaces everywhere. He has his own heated, salt-water swimming pool where he swims a half-hour every evening. He certainly likes the good life. He could never go into the mountains again. He has gotten too fat and his health is bad—they say it is rheumatism." The King said once he was on a yacht with Tito and his principal advisers and told him: "You people are not Communist." Tito laughed, but the rest were quite angry.

At this point the Queen mentioned Major Titov, the second Russian spaceman. I had left Athens before the newspapers were out so I did not know anything about him. This delighted everybody, especially the kids, the fact that a newspaper man had to learn the news from a queen. King Paul still did not believe that there was a man up there in space; it was only a tape recording. He said: "I do not believe Gagarin went up and I won't believe in this fellow until I see him on television actually landing."

The Queen said the English and the French had been incredibly stupid in 1956—they should have let Israel handle Nasser alone. The Israelis would have captured Cairo. But because of Anglo-French stupidity, Eisenhower had been right to move in because he saved the world from war.

We talked about what might happen when Khrushchev goes to Rome if he sees the Pope. The Queen said the Pope should line up all his priests with incense and when Khrushchev comes they should blow it at him. "You mean like chasing the devil away?" asked the King. "Yes," said the Queen.

The Queen was convinced the Russians were primarily European and was surprised that de Gaulle shared this idea ("I did not know he was so profound"). She said she had told the Russian ambassador, "We must stand together against the Chinese." He was somewhat startled.

The King said there had been no troubles with the U.S.A. since the Cyprus issue. This prompted the Queen to say: "That Dulles. What mistakes he made. I told his nice brother Allen: 'Why does not your brother ever make a gaffe on our side, in our favor?'"

PARIS, *August 31, 1961*

SATURDAY night, August 26, I was in Spetsais, Greece, on holiday, when the village postman brought a cable saying: PLEASE FIND MR. CYRUS SULZBERGER AND ASK HIM TO PHONE ME MOSCOW 418580 STOP GEORGY ZHUKOV CHAIRMAN COMMITTEE FOR CULTURAL RELATIONS.

Sunday, I went to the little telephone office and tried to call Moscow. No luck. So I took the boat to Athens and tried all Sunday evening and again Monday morning. Sometimes I was told it was impossible to get Moscow. Sometimes I was told the line was down. Sometimes I was told the number didn't answer. Sometimes I was told the number answered, but they had never heard of Mr. Zhukov.

At one point I got somebody who spoke French and claimed to be the Moscow operator and said they had not heard of Mr. Zhukov at that number. I told her to call the Kremlin and get the number. "Quel numéro au Kremlin?" she asked. I told her that was for her to find out. "Ah, mon Dieu," she said hanging up.

Then I called my secretary in Paris and dictated a long urgent cable to Zhukov. He called the Soviet embassy in Athens and told them to be helpful.

I went to the embassy where the chargé d'affaires received me warmly. He said: "You seem like such a nice fellow, such a friendly man. Why do you write such hostile pieces about us?"

He telephoned Zhukov. Presto! Zhukov wanted to know if I were prepared to interrupt my holiday and come to Moscow. I said yes, if I could see Khrushchev. He recommended that I should come on September 3 or 4, and he said: "I can make no promises but I think it would be good to be here." I decided to go. He gave orders on the telephone to issue a visa pronto. I didn't even have to fill out a form or sign a paper. I had the visa in three minutes. I flew back to Paris and will leave for Moscow Sunday.

KHRUSHCHEV

ON PARADISE

D ROVE AROUND TOWN WITH A GUIDE WHO BOASTED THE NAME Irene Urine and who knew enough English to be embarrassed by it.

Dined last night with Tommy Thompson who thought the Berlin-German crisis would only come to a real head in February. In October, Khrushchev will have his party conference; in November, he will summon a meeting of all states to sign an East German peace treaty. The meeting will then be held, but the Russians are very legalistic and it will take until January to ratify the treaty and deposit ratifications.

Lunched with Frank Roberts (British ambassador), who thought Khrushchev had staked his prestige entirely on settling the Berlin question this year. He is now trying to scare the West and that is why he has resumed nuclear testing and keeps brandishing the 100-megaton bomb.

A month ago, Khrushchev said that if West Germans lost faith in the West "they will turn to us. They have no place else to go." As a result Frank said: "We must be very careful. Morale in Berlin is dissolving fast." Within the past three days, Khrushchev has warned Norway, Denmark, and Greece against actions he interprets as hostile. Khrushchev considers that he can control and guide the crisis. But the fact is that he *cannot* control other nations and their public opinion.

I am still struck by problems of daily life. I lost a button from my shirt and asked the maid to sew on a new one. With great embarrassment she explained this was impossible unless she could remove another button from my shirt as a substitute.

Moscow, *September 5, 1961*

THIS morning, Mikhail Kharlamov, head of the foreign ministry press section, asked if I could come over right away so he could give me details of my Khrushchev interview.

Kharlamov said: "We wanted you to see Khrushchev some weeks ago, but you were traveling. We follow your movements and Khrushchev reads all your columns. You will find him quite well informed about you. And now that he is really going to get to know you, he may send for you again."

Kharlamov told me Khrushchev was going to give me a formal, prepared statement and wanted me to promise *The New York Times* would publish this. I said I was confident *The Times* would. (As it turned out, he gave me no such statement.) In exchange, I extracted a promise that anything Khrushchev told me would not be printed in the Soviet press, announced on its radio, or distributed by Tass or to foreign correspondents until *The Times* had published it.

Kharlamov asked if I had prepared any questions in advance. I plunked down a list of over sixty. He was appalled and said: "That agenda will take three days. You know how he talks." He suggested that in my own interest I should cut the list of questions to ten. When I got back to my hotel room I did reduce it—to twenty-one. This was done entirely by myself and there was no effort by the Russians to strike out embarrassing questions.

At 1 P.M., I went to Zhukov's office; Kharlamov was there. They asked if they could have my questions in order to translate them and send them to Khrushchev. They sent them up at 3 P.M. and I saw him at 4 P.M., so I really doubt if he had much chance to read them before we talked.

While my questions were being translated, we had sandwiches and chatted. Zhukov had an interpreter read some dreary passages from a war book he had written which praised Khrushchev lavishly. Yuri is clearly *the* chief public relations man vis-à-vis the West.

Today, Khrushchev told me he is prepared to meet Kennedy again in another effort "to resolve pressing international problems." He hopes such a new encounter can be "fruitful" and that both sides "will display understanding." He would always be glad to meet the U.S. President to resolve urgent world problems such as those of peace and war. For this, he "would spare neither strength nor time. But the main thing is that such a meeting must be fruitful.

"In Vienna, we compared viewpoints. The task now is to find solutions for the major international issues causing concern. And if President Kennedy agrees to a meeting it will be important that both sides display understanding of the need to resolve such important matters as the signing of a German peace treaty and the solution on this basis of the question of West Berlin, as well as the problem of disarmament under strict international control."

I had the impression that Khrushchev is supremely confident he can win the present test of wills without recourse to war and that although he admits the crisis is now acute, he is sure the West will in the end come to accept his basis for a new Berlin formula.

He is not ready to forgo nuclear testing in the atmosphere, recently resumed by Russia. He wishes to link the problem of tests directly to disarmament and, anyway, he sees no point in another ban by the three big atomic powers so long as France continues to conduct explosions. He professes to believe that the French tests are being conducted on behalf of NATO.

Khrushchev said the Soviet Union had given no nuclear warheads or long-range missiles to Communist China or to Russia's Warsaw Pact allies. The only such weapons remain in the hands of the Soviet armed forces and none are stationed outside Soviet territory except "perhaps in East Germany."

He proposed that it might be useful, in easing tension, for both East and West to revoke recent steps toward greater military preparedness and then, possibly, to discuss such ideas as the creation of a nuclear-free zone in Europe. But this did not include revoking of his own new testing program.

On the contrary, Khrushchev spoke of arming his forces with "several" 100-megaton bombs despite his acknowledgment that their destructive power is devastating. He indicated these will be manufactured in order to warn any other power against starting a war. At the same time, he promised Russia will never be the first to fight.

His attitude was tough and relentless but he insisted that since 1958, he has been seeking agreement to his desire for separate peaces with each part of divided Germany and the creation of a free city of West Berlin under new statutes. Western dillydallying forced him to adopt a hard approach. He argued that the United States provided him with a precedent for unilateral action by its manner of signing a peace treaty with Japan.

He seems convinced logic is on his side, both the logic of history and the logic of power. In a strange Darwinian interpretation of the advance of nations, Khrushchev jokingly considers that the United States is still in the stage of "jumping" while the Soviet Union has learned how to "fly." This referred to the earth-orbiting successes of the Soviet space men, Gagarin and Titov.

Khrushchev believes absolutely that if it comes to a showdown, Britain, France, and Italy would refuse to join the United States in a war over Berlin for fear of their absolute destruction. Quite blandly, he asserts these countries are "figuratively speaking, hostages to us and a guarantee against war."

Khrushchev expressed optimism that an early agreement would be reached in the dispute in Laos. Such a settlement, he said, might improve the world atmosphere. He thought any German settlement, however, must take into account the prestige needs of both East and West. At one point, Khrushchev indicated guarded willingness to aid Cuba if that country was attacked, but he hoped U.S. and Soviet soldiers would always stand shoulder to shoulder, never face to face. The Soviet Union and the United States together could guarantee world peace. He suggested that they agree to ban the export of either revolution or counterrevolution.

At two widely separated points in our lengthy discussion he mentioned a possible invitation to Kennedy to visit Russia when relations were better. Once he spoke of a possible state visit. Another time, jocularly, he suggested the President join him on a bear hunt.

Our conversation, which continued without a moment's pause for almost four and a half hours, touched on the future of Francis Gary Powers, the U-2 pilot shot down last year, on how best to cook bear meat, and on the relative approach of religious people and atheists to the death threat of war. It dealt with duck shooting, the tastiest way to eat pike, and neutron warheads for antimissile missiles. It speculated on international armies under tripartite command, once disarmament had been achieved, and on the problems of sending a man to the moon and bringing him back alive.

Throughout, Khrushchev remained impeccably courteous and although he raised his voice occasionally in order to stress major points and interrupted his doodling or fiddling with an orange ball-point pen to make stabbing gestures with his right forefinger, his manner was calm, polite, earnest, and friendly. He refrained from any of the major histrionics of which he is so capable.

We talked from 4 P.M. until almost 8:30 P.M. I was conducted to the Premier's office by Zhukov, and we were joined by Kharlamov and Viktor M. Sukhodrev, Khrushchev's elegant young interpreter who takes shorthand notes in his own strange mixture of English and Russian. A battery of women stenographers quietly moved in and out of the room to keep a running account.

When Khrushchev's door opened, it exposed a long, rather narrow room with plain, wood walls and simple furniture, the main articles of which were a large desk with a small table and two armchairs before it and a conference table covered with green baize and girded with chairs. At his desk and by Khrushchev's side at the conference table were twin sets of green and yellow telephones. At one end was a large engraving of Lenin; at the other a large engraving of Marx. This was once Stalin's office.

Khrushchev, who was sitting alone at the head of the conference table looking somewhat small, arose and came forward with a broad smile to shake my hand warmly. He posed beside me while several photographers took pictures and then waved the others to join the group saying, "We are all in this together." He then signaled the interpreter to the head of the table, seating me on the right and himself on the interpreter's left. When he noticed the sun striking my face, he arose and drew a ruffled yellow curtain. On the table was a tray holding mineral water, lemon soft drinks, and some green ashtrays. Late in the talk, when I asked if I might smoke, Khrushchev told me by all means and apologized for being remiss "because I am a nonsmoker myself."

Khrushchev was extremely well dressed in a fawn-colored suit, white, silk shirt with cuff links, and a gray tie. His pink complexion was mildly tanned by the Black Sea sun, where he had been taking a holiday. He observed that he had ordered all Soviet officials to take at least a month's holiday each year, but added ruefully: "As so often happens, the man who makes the rules is the first to break them."

The atmosphere was so cordial, indeed cozy, that it seemed paradoxical: an odd experience to sit so amiably across from the chunky, powerful little man whose will and actions the western powers hold responsible for the terrible situation in which the world finds itself. At times, during our talk, Khrushchev was gravely severe and at times he was sad or regretful. On occasion he was even gay.

I opened the conversation with a remark about the masses of pencils placed before each seat. Khrushchev laughed and said all pencils in Russia had once been American made. An American millionaire named Hammer, he continued, had received a concession from Lenin to manufacture them. "We have had a long business acquaintance with American millionaires," Khrushchev said. "Some of them are very intelligent."

I then plunged in. "Mr. Khrushchev," I enquired, "do you still believe war is neither inevitable nor desirable?" He replied:

Yes, and very profoundly, too. In spite of the acute crisis which, as you say, has now taken shape, I believe in the common sense of statesmen who bear the responsibility for the destiny of their countries.

They cannot but understand that in our day wars must not be a means of settling any issue and I hope they come to the conclusion that it is necessary to resolve urgent international problems peacefully—first and foremost the German problem. This can and must be settled by conclusion of a peace treaty with the two German states now in existence.

Khrushchev's ideas for a German settlement are well known. He wants all World War II belligerents to sign treaties with both East and West Germany and then draw up a special status for West Berlin, guaranteeing it freedom to have its own form of government and free access on the basis of an agreement with East Germany.

He considers this the task of the victor nations, but he is not averse to
UN discussion of the question if the Big Four powers are unable to agree.

If there is outside initiative, the Soviet Union does not attach much
importance to whether it comes from East, West, UN, or the neutrals.
A reasonable initiative is always a commendable thing for those who
launch it. We have already taken such an initiative by preparing our
ideas for a peace treaty and a free West Berlin.

I have already met President Kennedy and when it serves a useful
purpose I am prepared to meet him again. The question of where to
meet is of no particular importance as far as I am concerned. If the need
for such a meeting arises it will be easy to agree on the place and time.
The main thing is to insure that such a meeting is fruitful.

I met the President in Vienna and had comprehensive talks. It was
our introduction, in which we, so to say, felt each other out. We parted
after the meeting, each sticking to his own opinion. That is natural for
a first contact. But if, at a second meeting, we were to limit ourselves
to an exposition of each other's position, which both of us know, the
situation will of course not improve but, on the contrary, might even
deteriorate.

It would be another thing if both sides were to come to the meeting
prepared to relieve tension and reach agreement on the conclusion of a
German peace treaty, on giving West Berlin the status of a free city,
and especially on the more important problem of disarmament. In that
case, we could achieve important positive solutions and that would be
a great happiness for our peoples. I consider we must spare neither our
strength nor time for achievement of this goal. But the impression one
gets at present is that the American side is not yet ready for this. The
warlike measures being taken by the American side show Washington
evidently has no desire to resolve urgent problems peacefully and prefers
to increase its armed forces, threaten us with war, and prevent us from
signing a German peace treaty. That is the main obstacle to settling
urgent problems.

At this point, I asked Khrushchev his reaction to the Kennedy-Macmillan
cable asking an end to atmospheric nuclear tests. He opposed this idea
vigorously. His essential argument was that such a ban would leave France
free to continue testing—with American aid—on NATO's behalf and that
there should be no new test moratorium anyway until there is an accord
on world disarmament. He also claimed the West had carried out many
more nuclear tests to date than Russia and therefore he felt he had a
moral right to equal conditions.

Khrushchev said the 100-megaton bomb planned by the Soviet Union
would indeed have immense destructive power but was needed "to make
would-be aggressors think twice." He wanted this terrible weapon to warn
"those who dare to attack that they will perish if they do so."

I then asked: "Does Russia have any guaranteed defense against western
weapons—such as an antimissile missile with a neutron warhead?" In

theory, such a device could explode incoming missiles long before they struck. He replied: "I would like to put a counterquestion. Do you believe your military specialists are sure the defensive warheads which they have prepared against our rockets are truly effective?"

I answered that I was rather ignorant of such matters. Khrushchev continued:

I may know more about these things than you because my position obliges me to handle such questions. You are intruding on the most secret ground of any country and there is not a leading statesman who would disclose to you everything that he has, all the more so in such tense times.

I tell you this frankly. So I will have to bear in mind your advice to be discreet with my replies, for you have said there are no indiscreet questions but there are indiscreet answers. I can only tell you that at the same time we told our scientists and engineers to develop intercontinental rockets we told another group to work out means to combat such rockets. We expressed our great satisfaction with the work of the experts who produced the ICBM [intercontinental ballistic missiles]. At the same time, we remain very satisfied with the work of those who produced the means for combating such rockets.

Would the Soviet Union agree never to be the first nation to use nuclear weapons in war? He replied obliquely by saying his country would never start a war but any conflict that might develop would perforce be thermonuclear. He did not believe his Berlin and nuclear-testing policies caused any risk that the Soviet Union might not be able to accomplish the long-range aims outlined in the party program he is presenting to the twenty-second Congress of the Soviet Communist party next month. He did not think his foreign policy jeopardized the party program and, in this connection, made his remark that France, Britain, and Italy were figurative "hostages" against war.

I asked if he favored some kind of East-West deal outlining and respecting spheres of influence. He scoffed at this formula as imperialistic and a cause of colonial wars, a policy that was outmoded. Instead, he proposed a nonaggression pact between NATO and the Warsaw Treaty bloc.

However, while opposing war but favoring "wars of liberation," did he not inferentially justify other powers' declaring that wars against Communist states were wars of liberation? He answered by saying that no war as such was permissible but that national uprisings, as in Algeria, were justified.

He suggested that, since Russia and America were now projecting satellites above each other's territory, it might be desirable to negotiate agreements defining the frontiers of space. But cooperative use of space would be impossible without a prior disarmament accord, since space satellites are launched by ICBMs.

Another question concerned a statement by Marshal Malinovsky, Soviet defense minister, that the base from which any military aircraft made an authorized flight over a "Socialist" country would be subjected to rocket fire. I asked whether this implied protection for any country calling itself "Socialist," whether allied to the Soviet Union or not. The governments of both Jugoslavia and Cuba called themselves "Socialist" but were not allies. Khrushchev replied that he opposed any such flights, but, in the case of a Socialist state like Jugoslavia, he would be in no position to know if such an intrusion into its airspace was with the consent of the Belgrade Government or not. However, if Jugoslavia were attacked by "an imperialist power" and requested aid, that aid would be provided.

He drew a sharp distinction here with Cuba. He said Castro was "not a member of the Communist party" but "a revolutionary and a patriot. If he does join the party, he would be a worthy addition, but that depends on him," Khrushchev declared. He made no blanket commitment, but did assert that "If Cuba were subjected to attack, it would have every right to expect assistance from other peace-loving countries. There is no treaty obligation, but we would certainly not ignore a request for assistance."

During their Vienna talks, Khrushchev recalled,

President Kennedy said to me: "Our forces are equal. We have the ability to destroy each other." I agree with this, although privately I contest his analysis, as I feel we are stronger. But certainly we should not start a war to find out who is right. That would be savagery. Let us simply recognize that we are equal and can destroy each other and draw from this the conclusion that together we can guarantee world peace. Let us compete not in an arms race but in the development of our economies and the material benefits of our peoples, and let history decide who is the victor—without a war.

Khrushchev said there was a provision in Soviet law for the early release of prisoners but that he was not sure whether this could technically apply to Powers, the U-2 pilot. Nevertheless, he hinted that Powers, who is serving a ten-year sentence, might be released if and when relations between Moscow and Washington improve.

Powers himself is not of such value to us that we would consider it necessary to make him serve his full sentence. His sentence could be appealed to the Supreme Soviet, but such a step would be misunderstood right now by both Americans and our own people. The time has not come for such a move. After all, when Mr. Kennedy was elected, we freed the two V-47 fliers [members of the crew of a reconnaissance plane shot down over the Barents Sea, July 1, 1960]. We had hoped that this display of goodwill would be correctly understood and relations would improve. That would have led to the release of Powers, too. But to our regret, our relations at present are in such a state that it prevents any possibility of releasing Powers.

It is difficult for me to indulge in speculation. Nevertheless, my impression after our Vienna meeting was that Mr. Kennedy understands the need to improve relations between our countries. But evidently he is meeting with many difficulties. If you want to know what these are, I suggest you ask him.

He said there was not yet any fixed schedule for the landing of a Soviet citizen on the moon. He gave this explanation:

It is not a question of mooning him but of demooning him. Our national emblem is already on the moon, but we don't want to place a coffin beside it. We are now studying the possibilities of such a flight, but I cannot yet say when it would be scheduled. We can fly a man to the moon, but the difficulty is getting him away from there.

We can now take off from the earth and land again. If we compare our development to yours, we believe it is a higher development. You remember Darwin's theories on the maturation of species—from those which crawled, like reptiles, to those which jumped and those which flew. Well, you are still in the jumping stage, while we have already learned how to fly, and to land again. But that is still insufficient. We still have to learn how to land on other planets and then to take off from them back to this earth.

At this point we had concluded that phase of our talk guided by twenty-one questions that had been typed out in advance and translated into Russian.

Khrushchev then took off his bifocal glasses, and said: "We want to be strong in politics, but to do that you must be frank. I do not remember who it was who said that a diplomat is given a tongue in order to conceal his thoughts. He who does that is no diplomat but a cheap politician. His policy is bound to end in failure. I do not belong to that sort."

After some reminiscing, Khrushchev expressed hope that the United States and the Soviet Union would never fight each other and said he had told this to Eisenhower.

We would consider it a great happiness if the soldiers of these two countries should never stand face to face but always shoulder to shoulder. We are the strongest countries in the world and if we united for peace there can be no war. Then if any madman wanted war, we would but have to shake our fingers to warn him off.

Now the United States is arming and we are too. We are spending money and energy in preparations to destroy people. We are making nuclear tests. But what the hell do we want with tests? You cannot put a bomb in soup or make an overcoat out of it. Nevertheless, we are compelled to test.

After a digression into the pleasures of field sport, Khrushchev expressed the hope that—after a German peace treaty has been signed—"I will invite President Kennedy to come and shoot bear with me." He then mused about different ways of decreasing international tension—the need to end military bases on foreign soil, the desirability of a nuclear-free zone in central Europe, and the reduction of garrisons stationed in foreign countries. He thought: "We should agree to revoke our orders we both [the Soviet Union and the United States] have given to strengthen our military forces."

I expressed the opinion that the United States was a strong nation and did not like to be bullied. I thought his methods of seeking a German settlement were of that nature, that my country felt he was threatening it. Khrushchev said:

That is true. I understand it and take it into account. But for my part, I would like to say we proposed the conclusion of a German peace treaty as far back as 1958. This was followed by the Geneva Foreign Ministers' meeting. I discussed the matter with Macmillan, Eisenhower, and de Gaulle. In other words we broke a lot of china discussing this. That is why one cannot say we are imposing a solution acceptable only to us. They want to treat us like schoolboys—sit still, put your hands on the desk, don't dare take a pen to sign a peace treaty. But we are men, too, and we are a strong nation to boot.

When you wanted a peace treaty with Japan you disregarded us and went ahead and signed it. Now that we are telling you a peace treaty must be signed with Germany we are told, "If you dare you will have your ears boxed." That is an insult to which we cannot reconcile ourselves. We must reciprocally spare each other's feelings. The West wants to threaten us with force and deny us the right to sign a peace treaty. But nothing will come of that. We will sign it just the same because we also have strength.

I ventured that the United States was disappointed by Soviet failure to appreciate its change of policy on the civil war in Laos. Khrushchev implied acceptance of this complaint. He said:

We reached agreement on this in Vienna, Kennedy and myself. We reached agreement speedily. But it is difficult for us to apply this agreement quickly. But we are both evidently facing difficulties. It is not us, Russia, which is negotiating in Laos. What can I do with those three Princes? Or Kennedy? We can only advise. But I feel the ice is beginning to melt on this question. I feel we are approaching a solution. We are seeking no goals of our own there. I told this to President Kennedy. We want nothing in Laos. Far from impeding matters, we are trying to help.

Khrushchev summed up his veiws in a give-and-take conversation. He said:

Nothing can be resolved by war. I hope this crisis will be settled by the signing of peace treaties with the two Germanys. The most reasonable way to liquidate this crisis, as you put it, would be for those countries to bear the responsibility of putting an end to the state of war with Germany, to recognize the need for doing so, and to sign a German peace treaty.

To do this neither UN nor the neutrals are needed, since it is an elementary thing that after a thunderstorm there always comes a lull, a cool period; and after a war there always comes peace. Sixteen years have passed since the end of the last war and that is quite a sufficient period.

If the statesmen of the nations concerned do not do this, if UN has to be asked, it would mean the intervention of the world population and all the states of the world for the purpose of compelling those who do not understand the necessity of the treaty to understand it. If the UN or the neutrals should need to intervene, we would not be adverse.

At one point, when we were discussing what was needed in the world, Khrushchev said: "The correct treatment for the militaristic spirit in the West is disarmament and disarmament alone. This alone would eliminate the danger of war and create conditions for peaceful coexistence."

My notes on his discussion of the 100-megaton bomb have him saying: "But if war is imposed on us and a threat is made to destroy our country and annihilate our people, we won't stop at anything to deal a retaliatory blow. Therefore it is useful to have *several* 100-megaton bombs to protect our country."

When he got talking about Germans, including Hitler, Adenauer, Brandt, and Strauss, he pounded the table lightly with his fist and stuttered a bit trying to put his point across. At a later point Khrushchev said: "We will never at any time start a war against any country." He added he was certain that, "if war breaks out it will be a thermonuclear war."

Khrushchev said he thought it would be "foolish" to launch a war over Berlin if Russia signs a peace treaty with East Germany and declares West Berlin a free city, allowing access to West Berlin on the basis not of the occupation status but on agreement with the GDR. He said:

The circumstances of the matter would remain as before but access would be on a new fundamental basis. It would be much better to have access juridically certified in a peace treaty, which would then be registered with UN. This would assure communications with West Berlin and the outer world. We are not in any way encroaching on the political setup of West Berlin. There would be no interference in its affairs by the Socialist countries.

My belief that there will be no war is based on my belief that western statesmen haven't lost their reason and understand that war would lead to destruction. If Adenauer and Brandt have frightened the West Berliners so now they are shouting louder than I, there will be negotiations and no war.

He was sure common sense would prevail and Russia would go ahead with its economic program and, "I bet there will be a time when your mouth will water at the tremendous development of the Soviet Union."

At one point Khrushchev told me: "Domination of the U.S. over UN is coming to an end and it would be best for Americans themselves to become more aware of this and act accordingly."

He thought that the U.S. would do well to display "British wisdom." He continued: "The most rabid colonialists were the British, but they have always been able to leave their colonies five minutes before they were kicked out. Some countries don't know when to get out until they are struck with a knee in a certain place."

In discussing peace vis-à-vis peaceful coexistence Khrushchev said that under truly peaceful coexistence the export of both revolution and counter-revolution should be banned; there should be recognition of each other's form of society and noninterference and renunciation of war.

I then asked Khrushchev a somewhat philosophical question: "Don't you think that Communists, who by their convictions are atheists and do not believe in divinity and afterlife, might not fear war more than religious people, who by virtue of their religion believe in an afterlife following their earthly existence?"

He replied:

A very interesting question! I will be glad to answer it. I have lived a lot and seen a lot. I've seen war and I've seen death, but I have never seen anybody, even clergymen who consider themselves closer to God and, consequently, know more of the afterlife, who would be in a hurry to enter that afterworld. Imperialists, monopolists, colonialists, who also say that they believe in God, although they are sooner the devil's allies, are not in a hurry to enter the afterworld and prefer to send their soldiers to war promising them paradise after death, while they want to live longer on earth next to their safes and strongboxes of gold and dollars. So I have never noticed a special desire in religious people to get to so-called paradise in a hurry.

Soviet people, who are mostly not religious, although we do have our religious people, love earthly life and have no desire to get to paradise in heaven. They want paradise on earth. They want to live and work and enjoy the fruits of their labor, and we are quite successful in that. In forty-four years since the revolution, we have achieved great successes and now our road into a real, a Communist paradise is paved by the draft of our party's new program and we shall spare no effort to have this program implemented and make it come true. With the implementation of this program, we shall have crossed the threshold and will build communism.

As to paradise and heaven, we have heard a lot about it from the priests. So we decided to find out for ourselves what it is like there, and we sent up our explorer Yuri Gagarin. He circled the globe and found it nothing like paradise. So we decided to send another explorer up. We sent German Titov and told him to fly for a whole day. After all, Gagarin was up there for only a hour and a half and he might have missed paradise, so you take a good look. Well, he took off, came back, and confirmed Gagarin's conclusion and reported that there was nothing there.

All this, of course, does not mean that our people will not fight once there is no afterlife. Hitler, who unleashed a war against us, counted on the Soviet people refusing to fight for the Soviet Socialist system. But what was the result? The whole world sees that we are alive and prospering and are adopting a new program of Communist construction, while Hitler is gone and decayed and his associates have either been hanged or committed suicide.

So we Communists do not believe in afterlife and want to live and progress in peace. But if we are attacked we shall fight like lions against imperialism, against aggression.

He asked me when I next saw Cyrus Eaton "to convey my best wishes. He is a good man and his wife is a wonderful woman. We have a very good relationship with them and I hold it very dear. See what strange things happen when a Communist makes friends with a capitalist. We have different views, but we are at one on keeping the peace."

We had a long discussion about shooting and fishing. He told me one of his favorite fish was stuffed pike "which has to be cooked by a Jewish cook; they are the only ones who know how." He had been duck shooting last weekend. But he said: "My character doesn't allow me to fish. I would have to be chained down. But with a gun you are active." We had a long discussion about the best cut of the bear to eat. I was for the steak; he was for the ham. He said you should cook it in its own fat and it was quite good with cranberry sauce.

We talked at length about development of the virgin soil of Siberia. At first there were not enough women in the eastern camps but Khrushchev had induced the Komsomol organizations to appeal to girls to move out and now there was quite a family life. Many youngsters were going out to the east, to the Taiga forest to build power stations, to the swamps to be eaten by mosquitoes with a heroic spirit like that of a soldier.

Khrushchev said: "We have overtaken the U.S., but we are still poorer than you are. Yet we use the means at our disposal better. This year we produced 71,000,000 tons of steel. But in 1965, it will be 98 to 100,000,-000 tons. We are now developing at a higher pace than was foreseen in our Seven Year Plan and we are overfulfilling the target."

Khrushchev gave me a long off-the-record analysis of the American political scene. He said:

I have said a lot about Eisenhower in my time. I consider him intelligent, chivalrous, and honorable. These are good qualities and were especially manifest during the war. I said this to McCloy. When our troops were advancing on Vienna the Germans wanted to surrender to the Americans. But when Stalin advised Eisenhower of this he told the Germans to surrender to the Russians. For a general to do this, to make that sacrifice, shows him to be a man of high principles. He was later severely criticized in the U.S. for just this action.

There was a similar incident with Rokossovsky. The Germans he routed fled toward the British and Stalin approached Churchill on this—but Montgomery took them all prisoner. There you see the two men, Eisenhower and Montgomery. Naturally I don't know who took the second decision, whether it was Churchill or Montgomery. But Eisenhower's decision reflected his chivalry.

When I talked with Eisenhower I felt he was sincere. He didn't want war. He would never start a war. But due to his age and character he was indecisive. Dulles had a great influence on him. Eisenhower relegated all his work to Dulles. But Dulles was a man of a different sort and character, and this was not to Eisenhower's advantage.

American policy under Eisenhower was therefore far from brilliant. I have already spoken of the U-2 incident. I am sure Eisenhower knew of the overall plan for such flights. But I am sure also that he had no knowledge of that individual flight of Powers. That was something Allen Dulles cooked up. I just can't conceive of Eisenhower sending over a plane on the eve of the Paris Conference.

That was something done to put me in a difficult spot in Paris. It was supposed to show that the Soviet Union was incapable of protecting its own territory. This kind of position would embarrass any state. It was supposed to put me on the spot, but we shot down the plane and Eisenhower was put on the spot.

I am quite sure that Eisenhower wanted to apologize to me in Paris. When I proposed that Eisenhower should publicly voice his regrets he leaned toward Herter. My interpreter heard Eisenhower murmur to Herter: "I don't see why something like that could not be done." But evidently Herter said no and nothing was done.

The advantages Eisenhower had over Kennedy were that he was an older man, a hero of World War II, a man who commanded great respect in the U.S., and therefore if he said the U.S.A. should not go to war no one would dare accuse him of being afraid. And Dulles had also benefited from this prestige.

President Kennedy is in a different position. Politically he has a much broader outlook. When I talked with him in Vienna I found him a worthy partner. He himself conducted the talks without depending on Rusk the way Eisenhower always depended on Dulles.

At Geneva, in 1955, Eisenhower always waited for Dulles to scribble something on a piece of paper telling him what to do before he said anything. He took everything from Dulles and read it out. We were amazed. Nothing like that could happen here.

Kennedy formulates his own ideas. That is his superiority to Eisenhower. I had a feeling he understood things better. I am sure if Kennedy himself were able to decide matters he would not enter into any argument over Berlin and Germany. Views like those cannot be defended in an argument. It is opposed to common sense. No lawyer would risk defending that case in court. If he did, he would assume he would not stand much of a chance of winning. You cannot win that argument and Kennedy understands this. But he cannot break out of the situation. He is not a lawyer; he is a President.

Franklin Roosevelt would have agreed to our solution in Kennedy's place. He would have said it is foolish to fight over this. Many people would have opposed Roosevelt, but the population would have supported him.

Kennedy is too young. He lacks the authority and prestige to settle this issue correctly. He is afraid to take up that position and that is why he has induced those mobilization measures. But he doesn't want to fight. Only an idiot wants war.

But we will sign our peace treaty and arrange that access to a free West Berlin must be within the GDR. Macmillan, Fanfani, de Gaulle, and Adenauer all understand this, but nobody wants to be the first to say so.

The U.S. is the leader in the West. If Roosevelt were in power he would by now have appealed to the people. If Kennedy appealed to the people—if he voiced his real inner thoughts and stated that there was no use fighting over Berlin, no use losing a drop of blood—the situation would be settled quickly. All this talk of our desire to seize West Berlin is an invention.

Why? If Kennedy does the logical thing, the opposition will raise its voice and accuse him of youth, cowardice, and a lack of statesmanship. He is afraid of that. Eisenhower could have said this and no one could have accused him of being young, inexperienced, or afraid. Even though not understanding questions of state, Kennedy is probably abler than Eisenhower.

It is difficult for me to say how he will find his way out of this. If he musters up enough courage and signs a treaty, that is what's necessary and his prestige will be enhanced and he will undoubtedly be elected to a second term. Otherwise, the opposition will force him into a stand that will buy him no glory.

Of course, there will not be a war. Only men lacking reason want war. Kennedy is reasonable. Kennedy is reasonable but he is taking a very wrong stand now.

Here came the punch. Zhukov had told Khrushchev I had arranged his meeting with Bohlen, where the basis for a Korean cease-fire was worked out.* Khrushchev now asked me if I would take a message from him to Kennedy.

If you are personally in a position to meet Kennedy, I would not be loath to establishing some sort of contacts with him to find a means, without damaging the prestige of the U.S., to reach a settlement. But on the basis of a peace treaty and a free Berlin. And through such informal contacts, the President might say what is on his mind in ways of solving

* See C. L. Sulzberger, *A Long Row of Candles*, Macmillan, 1969, pp. 668, 954.

the problem—if he agrees on the principle of a peace treaty and a free city of West Berlin. Otherwise there is no use in contacts.

If he does wish to make such contact he can express his own opinions on the various forms and stages of a settlement and how to prepare public opinion so as not to endanger Kennedy's prestige and that of the U.S.

I said to Khrushchev if he wanted such a message to go to Kennedy he should send it through Ambassador Thompson. He begged me to do it personally. He said: "Thompson is very able but he is an ambassador. He would have to send such a message to Secretary Rusk. Rusk would tell Kennedy what was wrong with it before he told him what the message was and Kennedy would end up wearing Rusk's corset. Kennedy could not get a fair initial reaction, and Rusk is just a tool of the Rockefellers."

My feeling was that Khrushchev really wants informal contact—not through diplomats—and he would like to circumvent his own foreign office and government and save his own prestige.

Zhukov then embellished again his tale of how he and Bohlen arranged the Korean peace in my house in Paris—and I had never written about it —a somewhat souped up version of what really happened. In some respects, Zhukov is a kind of Soviet Walter Mitty.

Khrushchev said: "Kennedy has spoken of the necessity of revising the position of your military bases and eliminating some of them. He is now actually taking some steps in that sense. Many military men see the logic of this—men like Montgomery and MacArthur. This is a good trend. Also, some day, I don't see why we shouldn't have a nonaggression treaty between NATO and the Warsaw Pact—or some version of the Rapacki Plan—and a gradual reduction of troops by both sides in areas outside their own countries."

I was struck by Khrushchev's continual use of the word "prestige." He spoke resentfully about how our signature of the Japanese peace treaty had harmed Soviet prestige. He said: "We must mutually take into account each other's prestige. You went ahead and signed the Japanese treaty and now you want to prevent us from signing a German treaty. We cannot tolerate that; we have rights of our own."

Khrushchev told me off-the-record: "I believe if we can settle the Laos question it will improve the atmosphere for Berlin and Germany. That appeals to Kennedy; it doesn't affect my position. I want to help Kennedy."

The sun had long since set and, after a period of gathering darkness in the room, Khrushchev signaled for the lights to be turned on. In the sudden blaze he rubbed his eyes and looked a bit fatigued. He said: "We hope that we shall be able to resolve reasonably all the questions at issue between our two countries. Thereby the possibility would present itself for me to invite President Kennedy to this country as our guest. We will give

him a warm reception and all the honors that are due to him as a President
and a guest."*

MOSCOW, *September 6, 1961*

THIS evening, the day after I saw Khrushchev, I went over to Ambassador
Thompson's. I asked him to come out to the garden because there was less
chance of the trees being bugged, although it is perfectly feasible to wire
trees. I told him that I was in the embarrassed position of having been
given a message for Kennedy by Khrushchev which he had specifically
asked me not to tell Tommy about. I intended to get the message off as
soon as I got to Paris and I would request the President to deal Tommy in
on it immediately. Tommy was very understanding and sympathetic about
my quandary.

MOSCOW, *September 8, 1961*

THIS afternoon, I rode with Zhukov and his wife to the Kremlin where
Khrushchev was giving a reception for Nehru. When Khrushchev saw me
he came rushing up and thanked me for the way I had handled my dis-

---

* Much later, October 24, 1966, I read the newly published *With Kennedy* by Pierre
Salinger, which contains the following inaccurate version of Khrushchev's message to
Kennedy:

The night of our arrival in Manhattan, I had a call from Georgi Bolshakov, a
one-man troika himself. The Russian interpreter, editor, and spy said it was most
important that I have dinner with Kharlamov. . . . I replied merely that I was tied
up for dinner but could see Kharlamov at seven-fifteen the next night—a Saturday—
in my room at the Carlyle. . . .
"The storm in Berlin is over," was Kharlamov's opening shot.
"Over?" I told him I thought the situation there couldn't be much worse.
"Just wait my friend," was his mysterious reply. He then came straight to the
point of his visit. Earlier that month in Moscow, Khrushchev had given an exclusive
interview to Cyrus L. Sulzberger, Paris correspondent [sic] of *The New York Times*.
But he had also given him a most urgent message for JFK. Had Sulzberger delivered
it yet? I said I didn't know. [The message had long since been sent through Bundy,
highly classified. Salinger simply wasn't told.]
"Then I will repeat the message to you," said Kharlamov, "and you will deliver
it to the President."
The message was urgent. Khrushchev saw the increase in our military forces in
Germany as an imminent danger to peace. He was now willing, for the first time,
to consider American proposals for a rapprochement on Berlin. He was eager for
an early summit but would leave the timing up to JFK because of the President's
"obvious political difficulties." . . .
"But not too much time," said Kharlamov. There was intense pressure on Khrushchev from within the Communist bloc to recognize East Germany. But apart from
that, the danger of a major military incident in Berlin was too great to delay a settlement very much longer. . . .
I had left a call for the President and he sent for me at 1 A.M. I found him sitting
up in bed, reading and chewing on an unlit cigar. He hadn't heard from Sulzberger
[not true]. This was his first knowledge of Khrushchev's message and he had me
repeat the key points a number of times.

patch. I said: "You know we must have had to cut down twenty thousand spruce trees in Canada to print all that crap." When this was translated he roared with laughter. Later, when he spotted me again, he grabbed me for another chat and introduced me to his wife, Gagarin, and Titov.

Gromyko came sidling up, looking pale, somber. He said: "Now I see *The New York Times* is sending in the heavy artillery." God alone knows what that was supposed to mean. The place was packed with the new class —old Voroshilov; Marshal Budenny, astonishingly tough and sturdy for a man of eighty, his enormous moustaches still quite brown; Marshals Malinovsky and Rokossovsky, looking as if they had been cut from blocks of granite; Majors Gagarin and Titov. Titov is a particularly impressive man, handsome and with an intelligent sensitive face. When Khrushchev introduced us I said: "You may be surprised to know that in October, 1959, I circled the earth eight times in an hour and a half." Khrushchev looked startled. Gagarin and Titov laughed when I added: "At the South Pole."

I was interested to see how they cordon off the superbrass in a kind of ghetto: members of the Presidium, ambassadors, and Nehru's party in one little section of the huge St. George's Hall, carefully protected from infiltration (by plainclothesmen). I was allowed in the ghetto where I had talks with various ambassadors and also Nehru. Nehru seemed gloomy. He complained about being tired because he had to stay up until three in the morning every night in Belgrade. He said Khrushchev had talked to him at length about my conversation with him. Nehru recounted an idiotic story about how his sister had been in Greece recently and sent him a cable because she didn't know how to buy postage stamps in Greek.

Arnold Smith, the Canadian ambassador, told me that Furtseva and Yuri Zhukov hate each other. But Yuri seems to be on the way up. Arnold said he had put Fanfani up to suggest to the Russians that there should be two Germanys, both of them in the UN, and two Chinas, both of them in UN. The Russians were quite angry about the two Chinas suggestion.

Incidentally, I could not help reflecting after watching Khrushchev at the Kremlin reception with guys like Zhukov and his own son-in-law Adzhubei sucking around all the time. Khrushchev is really not a very good judge of men when he allows fellows like those two to get so obviously close to him.

On Wednesday, when I showed Tommy the first draft of my on-the-record interview with Khrushchev before the two significant changes he made the next day, Tommy was very gloomy. He said: "This means war. All of us are going to be dead." Again we had a long talk out in the garden . . . to avoid being bugged.

Kharlamov, incidentally, told me Khrushchev is an excellent shot. He has seen Khrushchev successively knock down ten saucers pitched into the air. He watched Khrushchev trying to teach Gromyko how to shoot. No luck. Gromyko was an awful goof and hardly knew which end of the gun went off. I gather Gromyko is kind of a comic-relief character; they all seem to kid about him.

Something happened in the Kremlin Wednesday, September 6, that caused Khrushchev to make a drastic shift in his Cold War tactics. This can probably be linked to his talks with Nehru, which began that day.

Tuesday, Khrushchev told me: "We already have a 100-megaton bomb and we shall test it." This phrase appeared textually in the Russian transcript of our talk, taken down by a secretary, and in the official English translation.

Also, I originally wrote that Khrushchev saw "no use" in another meeting "at this time with President Kennedy unless the President is ready to agree at least to the essentials of a settlement along such lines"—meaning Soviet concepts for a German and West Berlin formula. I added: "I deduce from Khrushchev's remarks that he considered a meeting with the President at this juncture would be untimely."

I prepared a dispatch including those remarks and then, Wednesday, September 6, went over it painstakingly together with Zhukov, Kharlamov, and Sukhodrev, the interpreter.

There was meticulous comparison of all quotations with the stenographic record. I had no English stenographer with me, but I compiled sixty-two pages of notes in a large notebook, as against a 23,000-word Russian text of everything said on the record. Once the text of my dispatch had been agreed upon in terms of accuracy, it was sent to the Kremlin together with the stenographic account. Khrushchev apparently read these papers Wednesday night.

Thursday morning, Zhukov said two changes were desired by Khrushchev. One was in the official stenographic record. Here, referring to the 100-megaton bomb, he wished it phrased, "We already have such a bomb and shall test the exploding device for it." In other words, instead of announcing his intention to test the ghastly weapon itself, as he had first told me, he spoke only of testing its detonator, a vast difference. Also, he sent me a special statement dictated that morning and saying he "would always be glad to meet with the United States President to resolve pressing international problems."

These two changes are significant. As a result of the alterations, tension is less cruel than it might have become. I cannot pretend to know what caused the switch. Thursday's changes were in Khrushchev's attitude, not the text. I assume Nehru's argument induced Khrushchev to soften his stand.

In my presence, the rewritten first page of my account of the interview was read over the telephone to Khrushchev. He expressed satisfaction to me personally in the Kremlin today.

PARIS, *September 9, 1961*

As soon as I got back to Paris, I went to see Cecil Lyon, chargé d'affaires. I explained that I had a top-secret message for Kennedy from Khrushchev but I didn't want to go back to the States immediately; on the other hand, I couldn't be remiss in giving the message. I had therefore written it out in a sealed envelope for the President. Cecil put it in another sealed envelope with a letter to Mac Bundy and sent it off by swiftest courier.

I wrote Bundy in my own covering note that it might be wise to refer to the Khrushchev message in code henceforth so he could confirm receipt and ask questions through embassy cables without disclosing the subject. I proposed to call it "The Rockefeller Letter" since Mr. K claims Rusk and the State Department are Rockefeller tools. It became known as this during its brief history and among the handful of Americans in on the secret.

PARIS, *September 11, 1961*

WENT out to see Larry Norstad and spent an hour and a quarter with him. I was saddened to see how badly he looked: older, strained, overtired. He is carrying a heavy burden. I thought back to those chunky, Soviet marshals I saw in the Kremlin, who looked as if they didn't have a nerve— or a soul—in their bodies. It frightened me.

Larry had originally felt the crisis would build up gradually and come to a real head next spring. Now it was coming much quicker and might hit us this month or in October. We were going ahead with our preparations and were both stronger in an absolute sense and in a relative sense vis-à-vis the Russians than we both had been six months ago. He is firm that we must in no way yield, but he is obviously extremely worried—more than anything by the prospect of miscalculation.

PARIS, *September 18, 1961*

PLAYED golf and had drinks yesterday with Gavin. Gavin said Norstad could not understand de Gaulle. He had now complicated the argument over putting our bombers and warheads back in France to such a degree that Norstad probably wouldn't accept if de Gaulle suddenly agreed.

Gavin said that some day he hoped to go through Pentagon records and straighten out the story on the decision to leave Berlin to the Russians. He says Eisenhower claims that decision was made by the Allied Committee in London in September, 1944. Nevertheless, as late as March, 1945, he (Gavin) was in charge of a training operation for an American parachute capture of Berlin. If the decision had been made in September, 1944, what the hell was he doing in March, 1945, he asks.

DRINKS with Cecil Lyon. He told me George Kennan, ambassador in Belgrade, was now calculating that chances of war were fifty-fifty.

Cecil told me the most astonishing thing. "You know the reason Gavin was so sensitive about the column you wrote saying he didn't speak French was because somehow he got it into his mind or heard from someone that you were being considered for the job of ambassador to France and he thought you wanted it." I expressed bewilderment. That was not my trade. I wouldn't touch it with a ten-foot pole. Cecil then asked if Uncle Arthur was after it. I said no and, anyway, his health was much too bad. Lord knows where Gavin picked that one up.

PLEASANT chat with Dean Rusk. I had gone to see George Ball, who is now under secretary and number-two man, and had just lit a cigarette and started to talk when Rusk's secretary burst in and said, "Secretary Rusk wants to see Mr. Sulzberger immediately."

George sent me off and I was ushered right in. Rusk said we are distinctly disturbed at the Jugoslavs' non-neutral neutrality as expressed at Belgrade (the recent neutrals meeting), and are warning them not to take continued American aid for granted.

The West Germans are dealing with East Germany on a de facto basis already. The phrase "de facto recognition" really means very little. We shouldn't forget that Adenauer exchanged ambassadors with Moscow although the Russians had already granted diplomatic recognition to East Germany—despite the fact that Adenauer claims he will break relations with countries recognizing East Germany.

Rusk was very worried about France and thought the OAS threat increasingly grave. He was anxious that de Gaulle would be overthrown and also that there would be *no* solution in Algeria.

I asked him about the Palestine question. He said we could do nothing "in public" about working out peace between the Arabs and Israelis.

"For your private information," he added, "I assure you that the United States had nothing to do with the recent Syrian uprising." I smiled. We don't plan on recognizing Syrian independence for a few days yet because we aren't sure they will be able to maintain independence and there are indications a countercoup is being mustered.

Rusk said he had been trying to make two things clear to the Russians:
1. We aren't going to buy the same horse again. In other words, we had made the exchange of Thuringia-Saxony against West Berlin and we had inferentially honored their control of East Germany. We weren't going to give them the rest of what we had gained from our part in the war; and

2. We were not negotiating our presence in West Berlin. We do not consider Berlin a city on the border between two countries—like Jerusalem between Israel and Jordan—and we are there.

WASHINGTON, *October 4, 1961*

THIS afternoon I went up to the White House for a talk with President Kennedy. I was so tired and feeling so lousy that I am surprised he didn't throw me out after five minutes. Also I was a damn fool. I have a feeling that if I had asked him, he would have let me write an interview. But I was too fatigued and unalert to respond to his mood. He talked very freely.

Afterward, Kay Graham, with whom I am staying asked me what I was going to do with it. I said nothing. She suggested I call Pierre Salinger and ask what use I might make of what the President said. I said I thought this was a shoddy way of doing it. Salinger hadn't been there and I wasn't going to pass the buck.

At the east gate, Dave Powers was waiting for me. Powers is a Massachusetts Irishman who is assistant to Kenneth O'Donnell. He has been part of the Kennedy political machine since 1952. He escorted me to the living quarters of the White House.

I finally saw the President in his study on the second floor.

First, Powers gave me a guided tour and served me a couple of scotch and sodas. He showed me what is now called the Queen's bedroom because Queen Elizabeth slept there, boasting about the plumbing arrangements and pointing out the Queen's bathroom with a fine modern tub and a very comfortable armchair-type toilet covered with wickerwork.

As we had drinks, Powers told me a little about the President's life. Each morning a list is prepared of people who are allowed to get through to him by telephone at night. Normally this includes the head of the CIA, Secretary McNamara, Secretary Rusk, and his own family, especially Bobby and their father.

The President has the same breakfast every day—fresh orange juice, toast, coffee, and a four-minute egg. He reads a couple of papers before he bathes, shaves, and is met with the day's agenda. He likes to have an occasional quiet group of friends for dinner and to show a movie. He tries to get to bed by 11 P.M. and to get up at 7:30. He always sits in the same armchair with the telephone beside him.

There is quite a change from Eisenhower days. On the victrola was a long-playing record with excerpts from Italian songs. The shelves were filled with stimulating books including Poe, Baudelaire, Betjeman, a work on Crete and Cnossos, David Douglas Duncan's book on the Kremlin, Charlie Thayer's *Diplomat,* Malraux, *Dr. Zhivago,* several volumes of Arthur Schlesinger, a copiously illustrated study on Meissen pottery, a presentation book on Vienna's Spanish Riding School, numerous cook-books including that of Alice B. Toklas.

I noted two books in the President's oval study, which he obviously must be in the process of reading: one on the major governments of Asia, the other, Stendhal's *Roman Journal*. I also saw paintings by Berthe Morizot and one by Boudin. All in all, quite a change from the Zane Gray atmos-phere of Eisenhower.

I was delayed because the President was having an extremely important strategy talk. The first to emerge were the civilians, preceding the Defense Department people by about ten minutes: Dean Rusk, Foy Kohler, Paul Nitze; then General Lemnitzer, General Maxwell Taylor, Admiral Ander-son (now chief of naval operations), General Norstad, who told me he was leaving right away for Paris, Allen Dulles, Mac Bundy.

While I was waiting Ted Sorensen, the President's personal political assistant, came in with one of his aides.

I called Bob Amory, at whose house I was to meet Marina, to leave word that she should go back to the Graham's, where I would eventually see her much later. I was on the phone when the President came by and grabbed me by the arm.

By the time I had hung up, he was at work with Sorensen and his aide on the two messages concerning bills. He took great care, adding some phrases of his own to the previously prepared texts. As he was finishing up he pointed to the study and suggested I wait for him there.

I was browsing among the books when he came in and sat down in his old New England soft-seat rocking chair and waved me to the armchair just a foot away. He has a quick, abrupt, nervous way of rocking back and forth.

He seemed extremely well, suntanned and fit, but his face is a bit puffy. Also, he looks a lot older than he did in Los Angeles last summer. He was friendly and relaxed. He said: "I met your wife at lunch." The Grahams had taken her to a *Washington Post* book luncheon honoring Harvard's publication of a volume of the Adams papers, and I knew they were going to take her to meet the President at a cocktail party before.

He asked: "Is she French?" I said, "No, Greek." "But then how can she be an Adams?" I said: "What do you mean?" He had thought most of the people at drinks were Adamses. I got the drift, explained we were staying with the Grahams (who later called Marina "the Greek Adams").

Then we started talking about serious things. First of all, he brought up the message Khrushchev asked me to give him and which I had sent. It was pretty hard to figure out just what it meant. I said that to me the only way to interpret this was in terms of Aesopian language; that one must stress the point of *prestige*, but wherever the word "Kennedy" was used the word "Khrushchev" must be substituted and wherever the word "Rusk" was used the word "Gromyko" must be substituted.

The President said he had noted my analysis and had talked it over with his experts, but he still couldn't be sure. He was going to talk it over with Tommy Thompson when he came here Friday.

I told the President I wasn't sure of my interpretation by any means and particularly in reference to what Khrushchev said about Rockefeller, but to me the message made absolutely no sense unless one used such an interpretation. I said I had no pretentions of being an expert on these questions and people like Bohlen and Thompson knew infinitely more. I had been very embarrassed about sending the message directly, without having read it to Thompson, and I was pleased that both Bohlen and Rusk had now seen it and hoped that Thompson would. He told me that Rusk had passed it on to Thompson.

He said Kharlamov had asked Salinger if the Khrushchev message had been delivered. This interested me because Salinger at a cocktail party told me: "Your memo was very interesting; it is imperative that the President should see you." I knew Salinger hadn't seen the memo from what Bohlen had told me.

The President said the 1959 German peace plan we had proposed to the Russians at the Foreign Ministers' Conference in Geneva was obviously not serious and we knew it could never be accepted. We had suggested a plebiscite in both Germanys and later on a meeting between the two governments, chosen by guaranteed free elections. At least now we were serious.

Khrushchev had been "much softer" recently in his approach to the Berlin problem. He said he had noticed a distinct change, "since I saw him in Vienna" (in June). Later he modified this and said Khrushchev regarded his July 24 speech as "an ultimatum," as he had indicated to McCloy, but he had eased afterward. At Vienna, Khrushchev had been very polite but rigid and narrow in his approach to the situation. He had shown no realization of the fact that American prestige was involved. *Now* he does and his attitude is less rigid.

I asked the President if the Vienna Conference with Khrushchev had been useful. He said: "Yes it was useful for me in judging this man. One always has a tendency to think that reason will prevail in personal conversation, but now I have been able to judge him. Now I know that there is *no* further need for talking. The only reason to meet again would be to make the final arrangements in any previously prepared settlement."

Khrushchev was treating Berlin in terms of the sheer military advantage surrounding the city and it was hard to shake him loose from that concept. I argued that the Russians had always taken the ground approach to strategy and had never studied naval or air strategy.

Kennedy said the American people must understand that, "We can't give what we haven't got." In other words, we don't have East Germany and it is not something we can bargain over. Furthermore, the American people should recognize how much de facto recognition West Germany gives East Germany, despite their propaganda against us on this point. He had no doubt at all that the people of the United States were ready to go to the brink of war on this Berlin issue.

At this point, he again said it was necessary to bring the Germans into any settlement, but also to bring them more solidly into allied defense in case there was no settlement, saying: "The chances of settling this without war are not yet too good."

It was very hard to explain to the American public such things as the fact that de Gaulle had already recognized the Oder-Neisse line (he pronounced this "Neesser") as Germany's eastern border. More than once when we were talking about Berlin he said: "If we push the button—if I push the button. . . ."

To my surprise, he thought Gromyko was a nice man. He had first met him in 1945, when UN was in the process of being formed, and he found him polite, agreeable, and human. When he smiled it was with a real smile, "not like our Russian ambassador here" (Menshikov). I ventured the opinion that Gromyko was a grumpy guy who didn't amount to a row of beans in the power structure of the Kremlin. This interested the President a great deal and he said he was going to ask Tommy Thompson. He is seeing Gromyko Friday on Berlin.

Kennedy said there might be a western summit meeting before the end of the year, but the probability was that there would only be a meeting of foreign ministers. It was likely there would be no East-West summit meeting.

He asked me how I thought Dulles would be viewed by history. I said I feared not too well. He jumped on this and said certainly not, with all those weak alliances like SEATO and CENTO.

The President talked at length about the problem of negotiating with our allies as well as with the Russians. No solution could be arranged that the West Germans would refuse to accept and participate in. But the West Germans had to recognize their responsibility in terms of preparing for the alternative of war. It was much easier for foreign statesmen like de Gaulle to refuse to associate themselves with a projected settlement. If war comes, they can blame us. And if war doesn't come, they can argue we yielded too much in advance.

He asked about de Gaulle and France and agreed when I worried about his position. He said: "De Gaulle's problem is that he wants to be tough on Berlin because he has to yield in Algeria." He talked at length about his difficulty in trying to help de Gaulle. Congress was very leery. They were concerned about the French security problem—both now and after de Gaulle. There had been a lot of trouble in trying to give the French the atomic submarine information.

Rather sadly, the President said that one of his biggest difficulties was that most Americans don't realize that we no longer have any overwhelming military advantage. However, Russia was not yet in a position to totally destroy us with long-range missiles. It simply did not have the capability. This was the importance of Khrushchev's statement to me that Britain, France, and West Germany were his hostages because he can pulverize Europe but not yet us.

He was concerned about the arguments whether the United States would use nuclear weapons to defend its interests, as discussed in the speech of Senator Margaret Chase Smith. But Kennedy said: "I think we have convinced Khrushchev on that." (Senator Smith said, September 21, that the Kennedy administration apparently lacked the will to use nuclear weapons. She said this had weakened the country's capacity to deal with the Soviet Union. The consequence, she said, was an increasingly aggressive Soviet foreign policy.)

I asked Kennedy about project "Defender," and said I thought the next shift in power balances would be when one side or the other got possession of a total weapon or a total defense. He agreed but thought a satisfactory antimissile missile was still far away for both sides. "Any missile coming our way with a nuclear warhead would not be alone and several could be decoys sent with it." Such a breakthrough would have a tremendous effect on foreign policy.

The President thought the situation in Southeast Asia was getting rapidly worse, above all in South Vietnam. At least in Europe, over the Berlin crisis, it was perfectly plain how we would have to fight a war if war broke out, but it is far more difficult to face the problem of fighting a war in Southeast Asia.

I said Khrushchev had told me he thought the situation in Laos would soon improve. Kennedy believed this was the line Khrushchev was putting out, but he figured Khrushchev thought Laos might soon fall into his lap. At another time during our conversation, the President repeated it was more a clearcut problem to defend Berlin than to defend Southeast Asia.

At one point we talked about Syria. The President said that nationalism reasserted itself there and remained a potent force among the satellites and would continue to for many, many years.

We could argue that if we give atomic information to France we would have to give it to Germany. But Khrushchev has no such argument in refusing to give nuclear weapons to China—and this must be quite a source of embarrassment to him.

He discussed recent journalistic visits to Khrushchev and said that Lippmann was very confused these days. Khrushchev, in his personal contacts, had one great advantage. He was a rough, tough man, so he was even more impressive to people when he was polite, as he was to me. Senator McCarthy and Jimmy Hoffa had this same advantage and they maintained good contacts even with critical elements of the press.

He asked me what I was working on now and said he had been most impressed by my two pieces on Berlin versus Munich, which expressed his view precisely and he hoped I would go on with this subject.

Kennedy was surprised that the Russians let me write that "hostages" statement from Moscow. I pointed out to him that there had been no censorship. I am astonished that he didn't realize this.

All this time he was rocking back and forth rather jerkily. He suddenly looked at his watch, found that an hour and five minutes had gone by, jumped up, and said he really had to be going. We walked down the hall and he saw me out.

NEW YORK, *October 6, 1961*

I WAS walking down the street today when I heard someone holler: "Meester Sulzberger! Meester Sulzberger!"

I looked around. Running toward me was Kharlamov. He is here with Gromyko. He could not have been more friendly. He asked me how things were—rather unusual for a Russian. I told him I was going off fishing this evening. He looked envious. I asked what he thought of my handling of the Khrushchev interview and the columns thereon. "Very fair," he said, "you were very fair."

NEW YORK, *October 31, 1961*

WE dined last night with Adlai Stevenson in his UN ambassador's residence on the forty-second floor of the Waldorf Towers, a lovely apartment and extremely nicely furnished. Adlai has a few modern French paintings of his own and the collection is fleshed out with museum and government loans, including early American portraits, a fine Sargent, and one of the most famous Whistlers.

Adlai was very nice. He has gotten plump and roly-poly and has quite considerable vanity, although he is most agreeable. Among the people there were Turgut Menemençioglu and his wife. I hadn't seen Turgut in twenty years; then he was going off as an army recruit with his hair all shaved. He is now an exceedingly distinguished diplomat, Turkish delegate to the UN General Assembly and President of the Security Council. I was much impressed by the elegant lucidity of his thought.

Also present were Pepe Figueres and his wife. Figueres is the former President of Costa Rica and now ambassador to the UN. He is a favorite of the non-Communist left among American diplomats, but rather pessimistic. His wife is American.

Adlai said it is essential to remember, when considering Latin America, that North America was settled by colonists who came to live permanently in a spirit of revolt against Europe and a search for change. The Europeans who came to Latin America were conquerors who came to make their fortune and return home. They brought with them the accepted religious and social traditions of their homeland rather than a spirit of revolt.

Figueres complained that the U.S. has not succeeded in instilling among Latin Americans a feeling that it represents the wave of the future. Russia has. Latin Americans regard Castro as a kind a Robin Hood stealing from the big rich Yankee.

The Panama Canal zone should be given by the U.S. to the Organization of American States and called an Inter-American zone and the OAS offices should be moved there. The OAS should then give primary responsibility for the defense of the canal to America.

The 1948 civil war in Costa Rica was the first of three Communist efforts to establish a Latin foothold. It failed. Next was Guatemala, where the President was overthrown. The third was Cuba. Washington did not recognize the Costa Rican affair for what it was in Cold War terms. Figueres said he and his friends fought and bled against the Communists in 1948. He was not going to fight a second time.

Turgut says all underdeveloped countries, including Latin America, aspire to the American dream of comfortable cars, stoves, and iceboxes, but they think the shortcut to this dream is Russia's formula of dictatorship plus massive industrialization. The U.S. has not succeeded in selling any convincing formula of its own.

THIS HURTS ME MORE

THAN IT HURTS YOU

MEXICO CITY, *November 3, 1961*

AMBASSADOR (THOMAS) MANN, A SANDY-HAIRED, SLIM MAN WITH glasses, knowledgeable and shrewd, says Latin America including Mexico, secretly wanted the U.S. to win in Cuba. The leaders realize Castro is a bigger threat to them than we are. Formally they had to oppose the U.S. intervention, but now they see all of them face the threat of left-wing revolution.

There was shock and disbelief at our failure in Cuba and a fear of consequences here. This may come to a head in a struggle for control in two or three years. Latin America has always argued that there is no danger of communism because, firstly, this is a Catholic area and, secondly, the U.S.A. would prevent communism as it did in Guatemala. Cuba changed this self-confidence.

In the past, Latin America has always thought that it could sit on its hands and the U.S.A. would do everything in the end. It saw in Cuba that we could not save societies from revolution but only at best could intervene afterward when the top of such a society was already done for. Leading Mexicans now see that if Mexico doesn't act on its own, they will someday be in Los Angeles or San Antonio like Cubans in Miami. They cannot merely depend on us to halt subversion.

The common denominator of all problems, political, economic and social, is the birthrate. The population grows about 4 percent a year. And this is imposed on existing misery in the countryside where the campesinos are no better off than before, while, on the other hand, the industrial economy and the cities are growing. There is a widening gap between countryside and city.

The PRI (the Institutional Revolutionary Party) aims for the common man's benefit and shifts its dictator every six years. One problem is to erase the old Spanish idea of evading tax payments. There is lots of corruption and stealing which is more or less accepted if it is not exorbitant; nepotism is general. The President is quite left-of-center, anticlerical, a free mason, but not per se anti-American.

MEXICO CITY, *November 4, 1961*

THIS morning, I visited President Adolfo Lopez Mateos at his private house in the San Angel district. He entertains in the Presidential Palace.

His home is surrounded by a wall and guarded inside by presidential guards: brown, grim, small. His sitting room is filled with books and an extensive collection of arms. Through the open door, I could see a lovely garden and swimming pool.

Lopez Mateos is slender, well dressed, dark complected. He is a lawyer by profession, former minister of labor, and at fifty-one, a good orator and a compromiser rather than a leader.

He said Castroism was trying to gain support for its own revolution in Mexico but, "We will not permit any interference with our government. Some leftists here sympathize with Castroism; we will permit no foreign interference."

Russia's aim is to transform the regime here. Propaganda is quiet. Anyway, the Mexican people seek entertainment rather than propaganda on radio and television.

Said he: "I am a genuine product of the Mexican revolution. In a political sense I am a democrat. I believe in guaranteeing human liberties. Economically, I see the need of raising living standards, improving health and education."

The U.S. has always worried about Communist influence in Latin America, but it thought in terms of political defense, not economic action. Washington should concentrate on the Alliance for Progress. "If any Latin American country goes Communist it will be because of hunger, not doctrine."

MEXICO CITY, *November 6, 1961*

YESTERDAY, we took a tour of Mexico City, Xochimilco, and Cuernavaca. Most impressed by both new and old residential quarters of the capital. Where does the wealth come from? Hundreds of really luxurious houses and modern architecture in the new quarter near the university. How much of it is graft? The President comes of modest circumstances, and yet what a splendid home and swimming pool.

Fine roads and overpasses out of this handsome city. Then contrast of Sunday markets swarming with poor Indians in villages. Lovely trip across Sierra Madre to Cuernavaca where we lunched at one of the most attractive places I've ever seen! Excellent food and drinks outside on a lawn swarming with peacocks and parrots, multicolored with clipped wings, who climbed up on chairs to be fed.

GUATEMALA CITY, *November 8, 1961*

THIS evening, we went to a farewell dinner by President Ydigoras for Ambassador John Muccio and his wife, who are leaving. When we got to the palace (which they use for entertainment and call "our Blair House"), I was grabbed by Mariano Lopez-Herrarte, younger brother of my old friend "Turk." Lopez is minister of health, the only representative of the social aristocracy in the government, and close to the CIA.

He guided me around, showed me how the marimba was played (by a team of expressionless Indians drumming wooden gongs, chewing gum, dressed in regimental uniform). He carefully pointed where Castillo-Armas was shot, fingering each bullet hole, including one in a patio window.

We stood around drinking more than an hour. The popular offering was a green creamy cocktail which Miguelito, son of the President and reputedly in charge of his financial gains (married to a lovely Gibraltar girl), said was an experiment of the presidential chef. Those present were the President, Miguelito and wife, the Honduran ambassador, dean of the corps, the auxiliary bishop (a jolly, intelligent, malicious-looking Spaniard), and a seedy bunch of U.S. brass.

An instant after we met, Ydigoras startled me by saying, "As soon as the first atom bomb drops, anywhere on earth, we will invade Belize [British Honduras]. They are with us and the British respect force."

Ydigoras said Mexico was to Guatemala as the U.S.A. is to Mexico. Every time the U.S. had snatched a piece of Mexico in the north, Mexico had snatched a piece of Guatemala in the south.

Dinner was served at a long table beneath chandeliers in paneled room. Indian reporters and photographers standing in background were taking snaps and notes. Indian servants in silver and black dinner jackets served soup, Pacific lobster, quail, sweets, and we drank white, red, and champagne wines (surprisingly lousy coffee).

Lopez-Herrarte told me the armed forces totaled nine thousand, that the cream goes into regimental marimba bands who used to hire out for dough, but that's been stopped.

GUATEMALA CITY, *November 9, 1961*

THIS morning, I had a long talk with Lopez-Herrarte. He said the Arbenz regime was pro-Communist and was overthrown in 1954, with U.S. aid. The Communists were put down by Castillo, a paternalistic dictator. He was killed in 1957, and no one was prepared to take over. Ydigoras was elected on a wave of anti-Castillo sentiment.

"Democracy in Central America is like self-rule at a children's party; you must have a grown-up directing operations."

Only leftists attend student meetings, although U.S. friends are in the majority.

Latin America is female; the U.S. is male; here women obey the men. We admire strength and determination. If the U.S. had had the gumption to land troops in Cuba, Ecuador [where there has just been a coup] wouldn't have happened. The trouble with the average American is he would rather be called an sob than an imperialist. When he gets over this complex, the trouble will be over. Sometimes you should be imperialistic for our sake, saying, "This hurts me more than it hurts you."

The only thing respected in 1961, is fear and fear alone. If you're more afraid of Russia you're a leftist. If you're more afraid of the U.S. you're a rightist.

GUATEMALA CITY, *November 10, 1961*

Two hours with General Ydigoras Fuentes, President of Guatemala. Julio Vielman, our stringer, delivered me at the Presidential Palace and left hastily as the last time he saw Ydigoras the President took a swing at him, missed, and then aimed a kick at his most sensitive parts.

The offices were crowded with hordes of people, rich and poor, blind, hale and healthy, many of them waving telegrams. Finally an officer came up to me and said in Spanish (no one there spoke English), "Casa Crema?" That is the President's private home, the Cream House. I was shipped off in a jeep station wagon.

The Casa Crema is protected by two steel-sheeted doors with sentries in helmets and with rifles. Inside, the place swarmed with armed men. One officer with a pistol sticking out of his pocket was oddly wandering around with the handle of a toothbrush protruding from his mouth. After a while I was taken to the President. Outside the patio, was a hideous statue of a man in armor. The patio itself was entirely taken up by a vast net cage filled with tropical birds.

The President received me in a room heavy with the odor of roses from two huge vases. There was a large portrait of himself, pictures of his grandchildren, and, among other things, an Arab metal coffee table.

He looked tired and careworn. I gave Ydigoras a letter from Paul Kennedy, our Central American correspondent (who was bounced out on his last visit for writing about anti-Castro training camps). The President immediately said Paul was a Castro spy. He then added, for good luck, that Herbert Matthews of *The Times* had invented Castro and was a Russian stooge.

He insisted Guatemala is pro-U.S.A. and spurns the alternatives of neutralism or pro-Russia. He dismissed Castro as a Russian puppet. He claims economic pressure or blockade is not enough to oust Castro; force is needed.

He saw little difference between Eisenhower and Kennedy. Both were trying to seek a compromise with Castro where none was possible. Khrushchev was a world problem, but Castro was an American problem. Both Ike and Kennedy had the same policy of words, not action, too much delay.

I asked him about Ecuador. He sniffed: "It's finished. As Francis I said after the battle of Pavia, all is lost, even honor."

He said the right (as well as the left) was attacking the U.S.A., saying: "Don't believe the gringoes, they will only help the left. If you don't get rid of Castro in a year, you'll have more Castros in Central America. Already the U.S. is pushing Dominica toward a new Castro."

He said Guatemala would become a second Cuba if the U.S. didn't help more. "Things are getting uneasy. The Alliance for Progress is just words—like Shakespeare. In the beginning, the U.S. was strong. You were pioneers. You fought. You fought the Indians, the bison, the forests, but now you are weak as a widow with a lost husband. We want more action and less words."

GUATEMALA CITY, *November 11, 1961*

LOPEZ-HERRARTE took us on a drive to Antigua, the Spanish colonial capital, and then to his own coffee-sugar-and-beef *finca*. Lopez came from a very wealthy family (says their estates were about the size of one-eighth of Guatemala) that went broke in 1929. He is clearly rich again and bought this estate of many hundred acres five years ago.

Antigua is charming, a sleepy town of one-storied houses, painted in pastels. It is set beneath two large volcanos and ringed by hills, and contains the old Captain General's palace and a couple of fine Spanish churches utterly ruined by the 1763 earthquake that caused removal of the capital to Guatemala City.

The finca itself reminded me of the sleepy Uruguayan tales of W. H. Hudson—low, reddish, old-fashioned houses, macaws and parrots in the luxurious garden, huge trees, a tame deer, lots of horses, hundreds of chickens, acres of well-tended coffee and sugar, a rushing stream stocked with brown trout, tropical forest, and pastureland tenanted by a herd including six Charolais cows he says are worth $15,000 each and a priceless Charolais bull flown down as a gift from Mexico.

He said Kennedy's Latin American policy reminds him of this: Latin America is a young bride whose husband has been sitting at the bedside for six months telling her how good it's going to be.

Guatemala was taken from the Communists in 1954, by three planes (from Nicaragua) and two hundred men (from Honduras) plus a good conspiracy inside, aided by CIA. Central American operations, I note, are on a tiny scale. Only a few men are needed, as in the Conquistadores' days, to accomplish big things.

In 1957, the CIA sent down a man to settle the electoral dispute between

Ydigoras and Cruz, after Castillo-Armas's assassination. He was a tall, gray-haired man who said he was a lawyer and came in a U.S. air force plane. He met Lopez-Herrarte and refused to identify himself, saying: "Call me Joe." The CIA had been opposing Ydigoras. They prevailed on Cruz to withdraw by getting him a Cabinet post, and Lopez "assumes," offering him a bribe. He said they had suggested $200,000 "for electoral expenses," but Ydigoras refused to agree to this because "the presidency is not for sale."

The CIA set aside $20,000,000 to overthrow Arbenz and little of this was spent. He wonders what happened to the rest. (So do I.) Peurifoy, when he came here as ambassador, saw Lopez first and asked him if the U.S. ceased buying Guatemalan coffee, would this overthrow Arbenz? Lopez replied that the coffee would merely be smuggled out via Salvador and suggested cutting off gasoline and "the government will fall in a week." He says, "Peurifoy seemed much more CIA than State Department to me."

PANAMA CITY, *November 14, 1961*

CREDE Calhoun, for many years our stringer here, an old Panama hand (now about seventy-five, retired), says one minister runs the biggest whorehouse in Colon; another runs the biggest whorehouse in Panama City. President Chiari is honest but unimpressive.

He will probably be ousted in favor of Harmodio Arias, father of Tito Arias (husband of Margot Fonteyn) who staged the 1959 "landing." The other leading member of the numerous Arias dynasty, Ricardo Arias, is politically finished now. The CIA backed him in the last elections. Chiari licked him.

This morning, I saw President Roberto Chiari in the Presidencia, a seventeenth-century building, modest but well proportioned, redone after World War I. The courtyard is filled with glittering pillars, set with pieces of glass, and a small fountain around which stroll white flamingoes and a cat. There are lots of security police wearing pistols and batons with leather thongs like whips.

Chiari is a shortish man of middle age with glasses and an earnest appearance. He said for this generation at the very least there is no thought of asking for control of the Canal which Panama is not prepared to run. But "We should have better participation in its benefits."

LIMA, *November 21, 1961*

CALLED on President Manuel Prado in his palace on the Plaza de Armas, diagonally across from the old Spanish cathedral containing Pizarro's mummified body. The entrance is guarded by Indian soldiers in early nineteenth-century Hussar uniforms bearing submachine guns with bayonets, a curious mixture.

Prado, whom I had met in Paris, was most friendly. We spoke French. His office is large, comfortable with an Inca-patterned rug, heavy Spanish furniture, and a massive ebony desk-table. He is a dapper little man of more than seventy, with thin, Greco-like features.

The OAS is behaving in ridiculous fashion. It investigates the Dominican Republic but not Cuba. When Peru sought to do the latter, Brazil and Ecuador opposed and the U.S. was too weak. If we now give aid to Ecuador we will encourage the left in Bolivia and Brazil. Such a policy would be "grotesque."

"This is not a moment for vacillation. You must choose whether you support democracy or communism in Latin America. And how can you apply nonintervention in Cuba while Cuba applies intervention everywhere else?"

Lunched with Sir Berkeley Gage, British ambassador, who had some wise things to say as well as excellent Pisco sours.

The U.S.A. should invest here in joint ventures (fifty-fifty Peruvian money) instead of all U.S. And the non-Peruvian part should be shared with Britain, Germany, or other western lands to reduce the political impact. The U.S. should be tough in attaching strings to loans but very discreet in presenting this.

The barriadas (slums) are *not* explosive. We should try and help the people in the Andes, not improve the slums which are already better than their mountain homes.

In Peru the rich "live in the eighteenth century" and the *cholos* (half-breeds) are their slaves. "Not even in Colombia is there such racial prejudice."

I visited slums by the Rimac river which are ghastly: dreadful smell, heaps of garbage burning by spontaneous combustion, piles of scrap, herds of pigs rushing by, no water (except from the river), electricity, or sewage. Families continue rudimentary village organizations from their Andes villages.

SANTIAGO, CHILE, *November 23, 1961*

TEA in the presidential palace, called La Moneda, the Mint, with President Alessandri. Alessandri, who speaks Italianate French, is the son of a previous and famous president, a large, aggressive man with a surprising resemblance to Mussolini: thrust-out jaw, bald, high forehead, square face, and gleaming, slightly insane-looking blue eyes; really the face of a fanatic.

He talked contemptuously of almost everyone. (John Jova, embassy counsellor, said later he had been blocking Alessandri's desire to visit the U.S.A., adding, "Can you imagine him making a speech at the National Press Club?")

I asked what chance the Communists had of coming in by vote. He began a tirade:

We must change our very bad political methods. The democratic institutions of the West are not adapted to the needs of the modern world. They lead to bad and dangerous political practices.

We can't build an economic and social policy and act with enough speed and unity. We must introduce constitutional reform to adapt parliamentary methods to our times. If Parliament has the right to institute social measures it becomes impossible for the government to solve the critical problems.

Parliamentary powers must be limited. Deputies are too much subject to the electoral influence and interests of private groups. There must be more importance given to the real social needs of the community. Each deputy wants to be reelected, so he curries favor with his constituents.

Parliament is now forcing up the cost of living. We must amend the Constitution and curb Parliament. The reforms I suggest are not needed only in Chile. They are needed throughout the western world. There is an illness in the democratic system.

BUENOS AIRES, *December 1, 1961*

THIS morning, I had a long talk and drink with Juan Bramuglia, once foreign minister under Peron ánd now a Peronista leader seeking to recapture power. He is a lawyer and generally regarded as a moderate in the movement.

His last contact with Peron was two and a half months ago in Madrid. Bramuglia said: "I am more loyal to Peron's ideas than I am to him." He said Peronism was not capitalistic but it stopped communism; it was a version of Christian socialism.

"Castro for us is the antithesis of Peron. He is a tool of Khrushchev. We are pro-West, not neutral; but we are not strongly procapitalism. We must stand with the western bloc. But there are several different positions within that bloc."

I spent the afternoon with Alberto Gainza Paz, publisher of *La Prensa*. He called at the hotel and drove me up to his office where he proudly showed off his mementos including a "freedom" award while he was in exile under Peron. He said it was all he could do when he returned to his office from exile to keep back the tears. Gainza Paz strikes me as a very decent, honest, liberal-conservative.

He says there would be trouble if the Peronistas won an election but the armed forces could be counted upon to keep them out. In the last analysis, the army and the navy are the ultimate power; but they don't want to exercise it.

The armed forces are anti-Communist and anti-Peron. But they don't want to break the constitutional system. They saw what happened in 1943, when a junta took over and Colonel Peron grabbed power. Nevertheless, if pushed, the army would keep out both the Communists and the Peronistas. Peron's main strength lies in the labor unions, where his name remains a valuable slogan.

I remarked that Peron's position reminded me of that of the Cid after he had died and was carried into battle dead, strapped to his horse, by the army; or like Stalin between his death in 1953, and his denunciation in 1956, when everything was done in his name.

BUENOS AIRES, *December 3, 1961*

EXCELLENT talk at *La Prensa* with Gainza Paz. He showed me a report from President Frondizi's office marked "Secret" on the April, 1961, conference in Uruguayana, Brazil, between Frondizi and the then Brazilian president, Quadros, a screwball who is already out.

At the Uruguayana meeting Quadros and Frondizi agreed that a nebulous bloc should be established among Brazil, Argentina, Chile, Bolivia, Paraguay, Uruguay—thus strengthening their attitude and bargaining position vis-à-vis the U.S.A. Quadros said the U.S. had made serious mistakes in Cuba (the Bay of Pigs invasion was then under way) and compared these with French and British "mistakes" in Suez. He insisted Brazil's foreign policy had to be related to internal politics which were tending towards a neutralist mood.

Frondizi conceded neutralism might satisfy public opinion. But without economic development, a president pursuing a neutralist policy would prove to be merely a theoretician. The main point, said Frondizi, is to achieve economic development. And, in addition to a national effort, this requires foreign aid. That foreign aid must perforce come from the West, whose fundamental financial center was the U.S.A.

BUENOS AIRES, *December 4, 1961*

SUMMING-UP. The two big external events in Latin America—Napoleon's invasion of Iberia, and the 1929–1930 stock market crash and depression.

We must get Canada into the Alliance for Progress and the Organization of American States. The latter should be easier once Britain joins the European Common Market.

The price of food in Argentina increased 600 percent in five years—as against 200 percent in Europe.

There is no real threat from the left; the military would jump down its throat.

RIO DE JANEIRO, *December 6, 1961*

LAST night, dined with Linc Gordon, our new ambassador, exceptionally bright and able, a college classmate. He is a Harvard professor.

Gordon points out the curious cycle of Brazilian dependence on single crops (until the depression stimulated the beginnings of industrialization). As each crop declined, a residue of subsistence farmers was left in the area where it had been grown; Brazil wood (sixteenth century); then sugar (through seventeenth); gold and diamonds (eighteenth); coffee (nineteenth); rubber (late nineteenth and early twentieth), combination of coffee and industrialization.

When Kubitschek came in six years ago, the total length of paved roads was less than in the state of Vermont. Kubitschek messed up fiscal affairs, above all by building Brasilia, but did a lot for the national infrastructure.

The Juliao (leftist peasant) movement in the northeast is significant; both among subsistence farmers and cane cutters. Those people are so ignorant they don't even know who's President of Brazil and can't comprehend Castroism or communism.

During, and for a long time after the empire, the army's professional officers' corps was an elite force and it has always considered itself proconstitutional. When it takes power it is not for power's sake and it prefers to hand over eventually and step out. But the army is now beginning to reflect divisions in national life.

A phony legend says there is no color prejudice in Brazil. But no one who can't "pass" as white is ever seen at "society" gatherings. The British try always to have a colored attaché on their embassy staff; and often they run into difficulty getting him hotel rooms.

RIO DE JANEIRO, *December 9, 1961*

TALK with Francisco Santiago Dantas, minister of foreign affairs, in the Foreign Ministry (Itamaraty) office where his famous predecessor, Rio Branco, worked, lived (slept on a cot), and died. It is a charming room, large, square, with green walls and a view over a garden in the old city.

He said Brazil has no territorial claims at all and specifically none on the Guianas. He admitted there were rumors Quadros had intended to press for British Guiana, "but we could find no evidence of this in the files when we came in."

Brazil sought a position like Britain's. No one could say Britain was not a faithful ally. Yet Britain always considered questions in terms of her own interest and then made policy decisions accordingly. Brazil similarly wanted an "independent" position pursuing its own interests but with the West.

Brazil opposed the export of Castro's revolution but also opposed intervention against Castro, even while admitting his was not a democratic regime.

This afternoon, President "Jango" Goulart received me at his apartment in the Preludio Building on Copacabana beach. He spoke in Portuguese and there were two interpreters.

Jango, as everyone calls him, is forty-three, swarthy, and looks like a smooth version of an old-fashioned Capone gangster. His comfortable apartment was filled with hangers-on, tough-looking ginks in shirt sleeves. His little children often piled in and crawled all over papa to his delight. I looked carefully for the shoulder holster he is supposed always to wear, saw none.

I asked if Quadros were planning a comeback and what his chances were. He said:

Quadros is popular. He could easily be elected deputy or senator. Or perhaps governor of Sao Paulo. But it is difficult to know whether he has any chance for real power. His actions show he is unstable.

After the events of August—following seventy-two years in which Brazil had been under a presidential regime—we are now in a parliamentary system. It is natural that things should be uneasy. It is natural to have rumors of a coup. Our parliamentarianism is new and the situation is difficult.

I asked what he thought should be done about Castro. He said:

We have a line on this—neither for nor against Castro. We are not interested in his personality. We always defend the principle of freedom and self-determination. If the Cuban people decide tomorrow that Castro is making mistakes and harming the national interest, the Cubans will oust him. In that way many dictatorships have been ousted by their people. I think Trujillo would still be in power had he been supported by his people.

Latin American sentiment isn't pro-Fidel; it is pro-small country. But the Latin Americans are Christian and not Communist. His declaration that he is a Communist did not help Fidel. It hurt him and helped the U.S.A. in Latin America.

PARIS, *December 16, 1961*

LAST night, I had an exceptionally interesting talk with Dean Rusk at the embassy residence. When I arrived, he was talking with Larry Norstad, who said the situation had gotten much worse in France particularly vis-à-vis the army.

Rusk was more chatty than I have ever seen him and exceptionally friendly. He explained to me: "You have found me in a bad mood because I am so god-damned sore at de Gaulle." Then he took off.

He had spent three and a half unnecessary hours—the meeting of foreign ministers—hammering out the communiqué on the NATO meeting which ended yesterday. The argument was about one word—"negotiated" —with reference to efforts to achieve a Berlin settlement. Couve de Murville had agreed previously, with reservations, that the allies could go ahead and explore the possibility of negotiations with Moscow, but de Gaulle vetoed this. Couve was placed in the position of having to argue interminably against insertion of the word "negotiated."

Rusk growled: "De Gaulle doesn't worry about any political problems at home and therefore he can blandly oppose the issue of any reference to negotiation. He simply doesn't accept that other governments are responsible to public opinion."

There are deep divisions between the six European powers, inside UN, in SEATO, in relations with Britain and in NATO, and they all stemmed "from France, and de Gaulle's isolation."

He is deeply suspicious of France's real policy. He says:

If you really mean business about going to war on Berlin the first thing is to have contact with the enemy, because you and the enemy thus know that you do mean business. But does a refusal to have contact—such as de Gaulle's—indicate seriousness of intentions as de Gaulle pretends? We *are* serious and we must know what we have to do. I wonder if de Gaulle means what he says.

I asked what inherent reasons there were for the present NATO disarray, which seemed worse than ever before. He said: "The only reason for any sense of disarray is de Gaulle. The military strength of NATO and economic progress are much better now than ever. There is intensive consultation on all questions and everything is moving—except de Gaulle."

But what had happened between the Kennedy visit last spring and now to worsen relations with France? Rusk said: "Nothing has happened except the argument on negotiations with Russia, and there really isn't any disarray except for France. It is a question of fourteen nations against one."

I said it seemed the split between the U.S. and Europe was widening. Rusk insisted this was not true.

I asked if we weren't being put in a position of disagreeing more and more with the former colonial powers on colonial questions like Angola, the Congo, etc. He replied:

On these colonial issues people cannot get it through their heads that the people of the United States really believe that governments derive power from the consent of the governed. It is only on this basis that decent relations can be worked out between different nations. But some of our friends don't accept this formula. That is the case of Goa. The best defense of Portugal would be to ask the Goans what they want. Portugal knows perfectly well that Nehru would not accept this. But they won't do it.

I said perhaps the Portuguese were concerned about the precedent because if there were a plebiscite in Goa they might have to have one in Angola. He admitted this but said the Portuguese had to face the changes in the world. "After all," he said, "there is more British money invested in India today than under the empire." The British and French empires had dissolved before the popular will of the former colonial peoples. But the Belgians and Dutch had not gone along so willingly.

What were the preconditions for the U.S. acceptance of Khrushchev's idea of a nonaggression agreement between NATO and the Warsaw Pact, and, anyway, what was the value of such an agreement? Rusk replied that the West Germans and the western powers had said no attempt would be made to change existing boundaries by force. The Russians know we won't extend the nuclear club by giving weapons to other nations on an international basis (as distinct from NATO as a unit) and that we were not helping the French in any way on atomic matters; that we would not help the Germans.

Therefore the Russians already have all the assurances that could be put in a legitimate nonaggression pact. But *if* there were a stabilized agreement on the situation in central Europe, we could work out a formula for the agreement Khrushchev seems to want.

This would not be de facto recognition of existing frontiers in central Europe, but it would be a commitment not to change them by force. The Russians would have to give precise pledges against the use of force, but they have already made such pledges in the past and ignored them. Therefore, such an agreement would tend to hoodwink the free world.

I asked what the U.S. attitude was now on the Norstad plan. To my great interest, he said, "Do you mean the surprise attack plan?" I said no, I referred to the NATO nuclear stockpile. He said the council would now discuss this seriously. The U.S. feels it is solvable and we didn't oppose it but we want to know what the allies feel first. "We can't say 'This is it,' and try to lay down the law. This would break up the alliance. At the heart is a question of sovereign responsibility of governments. Under what circumstances would governments delegate huge responsibilities to another authority? We can't push on this issue."

Was de Gaulle's proposal for a *directoire* absolutely dead or were there any substitute ideas under consideration? He said there are frequent tripartite consultations, although the U.S. also consults other allies on other matters. There cannot be a tripartite *directoire* for the free world. There is some permanent consultation of the Big Three through the Standing Group, but we cannot go further in excluding the vital interests of other nations.

PARIS, *December 17, 1961*

DINED with Averoff, Greek foreign minister. The Greeks are trying to get the United States and France to move in to support Albania and prevent it from being gobbled up by Tito with Khrushchev's support.

If Tito invades Albania—with Soviet agreement (and he would not make such a move without Moscow's blessing)—it is perfectly clear any new Albanian government would not only be pro-Tito but also pro-Moscow. Tito clearly could not risk putting himself in the position of destroying a "Socialist" regime.

The only two countries in a good position to help are France and the United States. Hoxha, Albanian boss, studied French and the French still have an embassy in Tirana. The U.S. has reserved its opinions, arguing it was better to let the Albanians depend on China. China is now in very bad shape and even the little bit of aid required by Albania creates problems. Also, the more Peking helped Albania, the more the Soviet-Chinese argument would be increased.

PARIS, *December 18, 1961*

LUNCHED with Gavin. He told me his career had not been conventional. He studied at night to get through high school and then got into West Point, starting off at the bottom of his class and graduating around 100th in his class—in the first third.

He has an idea that because our alliances are in disarray we should form an alliance "holding company," the Alliance for Freedom, which would be above NATO, SEATO, CENTO, and the OAS. This sounds extraordinarily like Montgomery.

Berlin is absolutely lost but everybody is afraid to say so. Even he is afraid to say it in his cables to Washington. It was lost when we let Russia get away with building the wall on August 13. The Russians are now sure they have Berlin and they have moved the center of tension from central Europe to Scandinavia. Finland is in a bad way.

But we can now fight a conventional war on terms favorable to ourselves in Scandinavia, whereas we could not do this in Berlin. Gavin thinks we can beat the Russians in a conventional way. I told him I thought he was crazy. Both NATO and the Russians have said in public statements that any war in Europe would automatically be a nuclear war.

He fears Russia might move into West Germany with conventional arms merely saying it was seeking revanchists and Nazis and offer to negotiate a settlement after occupying Nuremberg. It might then propose all-German unification and commercial advantages to Bonn. We would be too weak to try to push the Soviets out by conventional means and couldn't very well blow up hundreds of thousands of Germans to destroy 50,000 Russians in order to "liberate" Nuremberg. I said it would not be done that way, that we would offer to blow up Kiev.

I thought de Gaulle was obdurate because he was in a weak position and that he was always at his most obdurate then; and he was perfectly happy to see Berlin go because that would insure carrying out Richelieu's old idea of dividing Germany and also forcing West Germany more closely into the Common Market.

Gavin told me when he saw Kennedy last autumn, the President instructed him to talk tough with de Gaulle, which he did. De Gaulle was polite but angry and showed it by the distant expression in his eyes.

He said that in his 1958 letter, de Gaulle had not only proposed a Big Three political controlling group, but had suggested the world be divided up into theaters of operation and as it were spheres of influence. This idea had an appeal to the Russians who respect the idea of consolidating their strength as in UN.

He added that he had read all of Galbraith's cables from India and they were beautifully written but obviously Nehru had deceived him because Galbraith had predicted the Indians would not use force in Goa.

When Rusk saw de Gaulle he raised the Southeast Asia problem. De Gaulle merely shrugged his shoulders and said, "We have had a great deal of experience in that area. I wish you well." He made no offer to help and showed no desire to cooperate.

PARIS, *December 21, 1961*

LUNCHEON with General Paul Stehlin, chief of staff of the French air force. He was an assistant air attaché in Berlin under François-Poncet and Coulondre during the years prior to the outbreak of war in 1939. Stehlin, who was born in Lorraine, is bilingual in French and German. He says François-Poncet's German is so excellent that he is probably one of the thousand best German speakers in the world. François-Poncet used to irritate Hitler by deliberately speaking such perfect German that he not only put Hitler to shame (with his Austrian patois) but forced Hitler to consult his experts on what François-Poncet was really saying.

At a dinner party, Stehlin, as a young unmarried captain, was seated next to Goering's sister. He made a great impression on her and the very next night was ordered by François-Poncet to cancel his engagements and dine with her at her invitation. Stehlin said that although Goering's sister (whose husband was not in Berlin) looked remarkably like Hermann, one's country demanded great sacrifices. Through her he came to know Goering very well. Goering was very much against World War II, foresaw disaster, and knew the weaknesses of the Luftwaffe. Goering also told him in April, 1939, that Germany was seriously considering signing a pact with Russia. Goering explained that, after all, there were no great differences between the two systems—Russian socialism and German socialism.

PARIS, *December 22, 1961*

THIS morning Antoine Pinay came in to see me in my office and spent an hour and twenty minutes explaining his ideas. Pinay, who used to be Prime Minister, served in de Gaulle's Cabinet a couple of years. Now he is a bitter enemy. He was bluntly fired.

He is a dapper little man who looks rather like Charlie Chaplin: nice, honest, courteous, and full of common sense. He is very pro-American. He told me he was going to be seventy years old in eight days. I was astonished. I would have said he was about fifty-eight. He said he was very "sober" and never drank even a glass of wine. We had an elevator failure today and he had walked up six flights unwinded. I asked how long de Gaulle would last. He said that "without an event"—meaning some great blowup—"he can last a long time."

Who did he think would succeed de Gaulle, or what type of government? This was difficult. It depended on the condition in which de Gaulle left the country and how he would leave office himself. He added: "He has divided the country, the army, the police, the courts. But everything that counts in France is now against him. When a doctor diagnoses a patient, he treats him. But then if the treatment doesn't work, he changes that treatment. All de Gaulle does is to double the dose."

He found people preoccupied and afraid. He added: "We live in a police state." I asked what his attitude to the OAS was. He said this had been "created" by de Gaulle's mistakes; "But, it is not French." It represented little in France, although it meant much more in Algeria.

Pinay said that he had always been in opposition to de Gaulle within the Cabinet—primarily on NATO. He also disagreed on European unity and economic policy. He said: "Because I defended myself strongly, de Gaulle kept accusing me of being pro-American—and finally fired me."

Pinay complained that his telephone was tapped and that he was followed all the time by police agents. But this didn't bother him. He had not in any way been persecuted but he felt that a dossier was being collected on him to be used in case they wanted to persecute him later on. De Gaulle was building up an increasingly powerful police apparatus of his own. Pinay continued, "This is a police state. But it is still better than communism. The United States should exert pressure to loosen the dictatorship, but not to change the regime."

Pinay said that in Cabinet meetings de Gaulle is completely dominant. "He fascinates the ministers. No one dares to speak." He believes "ruse" is the first element of power. Pinay concluded: "I think loyalty is the first element of power."

X tells me: "Don't leave Paris in January. That is the month." He says there is a new secret organization in the army—much more secret than the oas—which is trying to enlist American aid. But Washington has refused.

PARIS, *December 28, 1961*

LONG talk with Couve de Murville at the Quai d'Orsay. He sat back puffing his pipe while I fired questions. I started by remarking that I had been away seven months and had the impression U.S.-French relations were now the worst since World War II. He replied:

Certainly, there is a great amount of irritation on both sides. Everybody in Washington is very excited about our attitude on Berlin. And then, of course, there is the Congo argument.

As for Berlin, let us look at the facts. Everything depends on Russia. The NATO discussions this month were ridiculous. Everybody there seemed to believe NATO could make decisions on Berlin. That is folly. The problem is not between France and the rest of the NATO powers; it is between the West and Russia.

I am sure the U.S. is honest in its belief that it would fight to save Berlin if negotiations break down. But what is important is not the impression you make upon your own public opinion, but the impression you make upon your enemies. You may look good to your public opinion; but the Russians will interpret any negotiations as an act of weakness. The only way to embarrass Khrushchev is to wait and force him to act.

I don't really believe that the U.S. is defeatist. The U.S. and France, in fact, agree in substance more than the U.S. and Britain. But once you begin negotiations they are hard to break off. The British will be increasingly eager for an agreement. And the Germans would be more anxious for one than they are perhaps now.

We had an example of this in 1959, at the Geneva Foreign Ministers Conference. The U.S. became so anxious to avoid a breakdown that Eisenhower invited Khrushchev to visit the U.S. without telling any of the rest of us. Then the Conference went on without any of us knowing how meaningless it had become.

We cannot forget this. When the U.S. says you are ready to fight we don't disbelieve you. But we say that if you ask for negotiations it shows weakness.

I asked what he thought should be done to improve relations between the U.S. and France. He said: "I don't know. It is very unfortunate. The rift should be healed."

I asked if he thought it was any use reviving de Gaulle's so-called *directoire* suggestion of 1958. Couve answered: "But the *directoire* really exists. There is no point in reviving it. Consultations go on on a satisfactory basis." I asked if de Gaulle agreed with him on this and he said, "Certainly." This stunned me.

He continued: "On the German affair, de Gaulle takes his position because he feels that is the best position. That is all. When Kennedy was here, de Gaulle thought Kennedy held the same opinion as he did on Berlin, and he was disappointed afterward to find he had been wrong."

I then asked if anything could be done on atomic matters. He replied:

We accept the facts of the situation as they are. We know that the U.S. will always be strongly against other countries getting nuclear weapons. We would do the same in your position. I am sure you already regret the relatively unimportant aid you gave to the British. We have no illusions. And there was no change in this between us as a result of the de Gaulle-Kennedy talks. It is not really a problem.

He admitted there was a "problem" on Southeast Asia. Britain and France opposed the U.S. policy. He added: "We have had the same opinion for five years—that Laos cannot be a stronghold for the West and that the least-bad solution is to neutralize it. But there is a difference in U.S. policy. Politicians like Kennedy and Harriman share our opinion. But your army and others have another policy. There is a difference between your proclaimed policy and what you do in Laos. Tout le monde a ses ultras."

I asked what he thought of Nassar's flirtation with Russia. He replied:

Nasser is in great difficulty. He has lost his prestige with the Arab world. He lost his prestige on Syria and he is at odds with almost all the Arab countries. Therefore he is much weaker internationally. And the situation inside Egypt is very bad. It is a desperate economic condition.

Nasser's game has always been to play off East against West, courting both sides alternately and he plays up to Russia and the U.S.A. and they both pay him. Early this year, he was on bad terms with the Russians and Washington developed great hope. But now he has turned eastward again. He will shift back.

He has made many deals with Moscow. Almost all of Egypt's arms come from the Communist world and now new ships are being sent there by Russia. But I doubt if Russia would be silly enough to put a military base in Egypt. It could not rely on the Egyptians and any such base could be destroyed in five minutes by the Sixth Fleet if a war came. And if the Russians have put a base into Nasser's hands, it need not concern us because it isn't dangerous.

PARIS, *December 30, 1961*

YESTERDAY, I spent three hours with Norstad. It has now been agreed that General Wheeler will succeed General Palmer as American commander in

Europe around March 1. It is also virtually a certainty that Wheeler will succeed Norstad at SHAPE when Larry leaves.

Larry told me something about the Norstad Plan against surprise attack. It is based on the military aspect of control-inspection in the NATO and Warsaw Pact areas if there is ever a nuclear agreement. The plan concludes that control-inspection could be useful and would free us from a great part of the dangers of attack by surprise. The ideal area to be inspected would be between the Urals and the Bay of Biscay. A smaller, but useful area would begin at the Soviet-Polish border and include both Germanys plus two or three European powers, such as Denmark and Holland, for example, also Alaska and a great part of Siberia. Under such a system, both sides would exchange blueprints and form joint mobile-inspection teams.

The Common Market has increased Europe's relative political weight and thus U.S. leadership is less respected than in the past. This is an unfortunate truth. The U.S. is too often in the position of starting with shaking its fist and ending up shaking its finger.

We talked about Khrushchev's statement to me about the Europeans being "hostages." Norstad said Khrushchev has the MRBM forces to strike against Europe, but the Europeans have shown great strength of character in the face of this and have not weakened.

The U.S. must convince the allies not only of our capability but also of our determination to use nuclear weapons. The allies were worried until three or four months ago on the score of our determination. This is all important because the Europeans will believe us more than they will believe each other—in terms of going to war.

PARIS, *January 5, 1962*

I SPENT an unhappy hour this afternoon with Jim Gavin. I mentioned that the Spanish ambassador had said that Chip Bohlen, on the way down to Madrid after the NATO meeting, told him that he, Chip, was going to be appointed ambassador to France and he was worried as to whether he will have enough money. Gavin then took off. His conversation ranged all over the place and he showed me various documents. The basic point he sought to prove was that he was a first-class ambassador.

He said when Rusk first saw de Gaulle last August he was horrified and formed an impression of him as a devil with horns and a tail. Rusk reported on the conversation to the President and said de Gaulle treated Gavin with "calculated indifference." Gavin told Rusk he must try to understand de Gaulle's strange personality and that actually Gavin got on well with him. He got Rusk to delete the word "calculated."

On October 30, immediately after returning to France from Washington, Gavin requested an appointment with de Gaulle and saw him at 3:30 P.M. He showed me two telegrams he sent after the talk. The first said he had conveyed Kennedy's suggestion that the chiefs of government of Britain,

France, and the United States should meet together in Bermuda if there appeared to be any prospect of an agreement on how to approach Russia on Berlin. If no agreement appeared possible the United States would have to continue probing on its own. The U.S. was arming in order to parley, and had to explain the problem to American public opinion, explaining why national sacrifices were necessary over the Berlin crisis. The telegram said de Gaulle had merely nodded and said he had taken note of the message. The second cable told the President that Gavin had accurately reported to de Gaulle on a Kennedy-Macmillan phone conversation on the subject of a Bermuda meeting.

Last autumn, rumors began to appear in the American press that Gavin was going to be replaced as ambassador, and some even mentioned Chip as the successor. Gavin said that when he had been home he had personally taken the matter up with Bohlen, saying: "Obviously I am not going to be there forever. If you want the job I would be glad to put in a good recommendation." (I am horrified by this tale and can easily imagine Chip's reaction.)

When Rusk was here last month for the NATO meeting, Gavin thought he would raise the question, but Rusk didn't mention it; therefore Gavin didn't either. Rusk saw de Gaulle and de Gaulle spoke English (I doubt this!) and was very friendly. Rusk realized, after all, that de Gaulle did not have horns. I told Gavin he was wrong about Rusk's impression and recounted what Rusk had said to me in Gavin's own residence the night of December 15.

During the Christmas season, rumors of Gavin's imminent departure continued. Therefore, on December 28, Gavin sent a letter to Rusk together with a carbon copy and covering letter to the President. In these, Gavin took note of the continued rumor campaign and said it was harming him, his position as ambassador, and the United States. He asked that the State Department issue an official denial. If there were any thought of replacing him, he was willing to fly to Washington to talk it over.

On January 3, Rusk telephoned. He told him not to worry and there was no thought of replacing him. There would not be an official denial but this would be handled "in our own way."

Gavin is clearly worried. The poor man does not understand the political infighting that goes on in Washington. He is an easy target for harpoons.

He ended this part of the conversation by assuring me once again: "You know I am doing a damn good job. I know de Gaulle well—of course not as well as you do. He was very nice to me at the New Year's reception this week."

Gavin agreed that relations were very bad and were going to get worse very soon. De Gaulle hopes to have a nuclear deterrent force in 1963. At first, the warheads will be carried by the Mirage but there will be missiles fairly soon. The French have solved the problem of solid-fuel packing and the missile. They had a second test recently that went off very well.

The Germans are au courant on this and they have their own problem. When the NATO foreign ministers met, McNamara made it plain that the United States would not use any nuclear weapons in the defense of Germany until it had to—in other words until it became plain there was no other means of checking a Russian invasion. At the same time, Strauss made it clear that Germany expected nuclear rockets with a long enough range to drop missiles on Russian, not satellite, soil.

De Gaulle is very worried about the possibility of some limited Russian attack on Germany which would be made by conventional means (and then the Russians would halt and offer to negotiate German reunification in exchange for certain conditions). The Germans share this worry and that is why they want missiles that will reach Russia. Gavin suspects that the Germans are willing to pay the French half of the cost of a gaseous-diffusion atomic plant, which will cost about $1,200,000,000, in exchange for a share of French nuclear weapons.

PARIS, *January 6, 1962*

GAVIN called up and asked me to stop by. He is very concerned about two problems; himself and France.

Apparently, last night, he saw the Laotian prince Souvanna Phouma, who inquired whether he was going to be in Paris long and gave the impression of treating Gavin like a lame-duck ambassador.

The second problem arose because Gavin was called in the middle of the night to be informed that the long-awaited civil war was breaking out. French intelligence said the OAS was mounting an attack on Rocher Noir (headquarters outside Algiers) with naval artillery support. The French rushed a cruiser to the area, but the attack didn't come. A phony report. Nevertheless, we are getting near the edge.

I had heard Kennedy telephoned de Gaulle in the middle of the NATO meeting last month. He confirmed this. Kennedy called to urge de Gaulle's agreement on seeking negotiations on Berlin, speaking from the White House with Bill Tyler of the State Department beside him. Tyler, translating for Kennedy, spoke to de Gaulle in the Elysée. Nevertheless, on December 16, Couve de Murville was still taking the stand that if the word "negotiation" appeared in the communiqué there would be no communiqué because this had to be unanimously approved and France wouldn't sign.

Gavin showed me a long personal letter from Kennedy to de Gaulle dated December 31, and handed on by Gavin January 2. In substance, this said, in the most friendly way, that the United States simply had to explore the possibilities of a negotiated settlement on Berlin because American public opinion would not support going to war without first knowing everything had been done for peace. Kennedy said he was convinced that Khrushchev could not indefinitely put off signature of a separate peace treaty with East Germany—what de Gaulle had so aptly called "his treaty with himself." It was therefore better to arrange some kind of settlement before this treaty was signed.

Kennedy was sure that he and de Gaulle agreed on basic long-range objectives even though they disagreed on tactics. He then turned to the subject of nuclear arms. As politely as possible, he said that no country other than Russia and the U.S. could afford an independent nuclear deterrent by itself. For the present, Europe was well protected by the American deterrent, and Kennedy said U.S. policy on this was that we would use nuclear weapons to defend Europe and gave personal assurances that it was his own policy as well. However, someday it might be advisable to have some kind of group control over the nuclear weapons in Europe. The U.S. was opposed to the spread of nuclear powers. Had it not been for long-standing agreements with England dating back to World War II, Britain would be treated in exactly the same way as France, but of course the United States could not renege on an agreement. Nevertheless not even Britain was strong enough to arm itself with this kind of weapon.

If France persevered in its atomic capability, it was inevitable that Germany would seek to do the same thing, but this could not be permitted by the United States. There was still too great a memory and fear of Germany. He hoped de Gaulle would understand our view. Kennedy concluded by saying (after almost three thousand words) that he was sticking only to Berlin and nuclear arms because there was not space for anything else and these were the two most important matters.

He referred to his meeting with Macmillan and said preparations were now being made to resume testing in the atmosphere, but no decision had yet been taken as to whether or when these tests would be resumed. The President said he had not yet made up his mind.

After showing me these messages, Gavin gave me a rather long account about his military theories and his experience at the NATO Naples command after the war and how the southwest portion of Russia would be invaded and occupied during a war.

He thought Khrushchev was seeking a new marine naval base to replace Saseno (Albania) and hoped someday to have access to Bizerte and Mers el-Kebir. He cited Harold Nicolson as saying an ambassador must interest himself in negotiating, in appearing as a popular image and as an accurate reporter of conditions in the country to which he is sent. He assured me he had reported the plain, unvarnished truth about France, but the State Department disliked de Gaulle and did not believe him.

He was worried about my column saying U.S.-French relations were at a low ebb. He rebuked me for pulling the rug out from under his feet. The issue was dead; why bring it up again? I said I thought the situation was a live one and if anything the Kennedy letter proved it. The second problem, his personal one, was also alive and Souvanna's comment proved it.

Poor guy—I feel sorry for him.

PARIS, *January 8, 1962*

LUNCHED with Laloy. When Adenauer visited Kennedy last autumn, Kennedy tried to get his acceptance on two key points: 1. Both Russia and the U.S.A. promise they will not give atomic weapons to countries not producing them themselves (in other words, dealing out the two Germanies, among others); 2. Abandon Bonn's insistence that it represents West Berliners abroad automatically and force Bonn to negotiate a new statute for West Berlin covering this point. Adenauer was most embarrassed.

France is all too ready to sign a peace with the FLN; but the FLN won't sign. No one knows what's holding things up. When the peace is signed, of course, the OAS uprising will take place. It is hard to know how powerful it is. It is doubtful if the French army in Oran, for example, would fire on the OAS.

DE GAULLE: FRANCE COULD "TEAR OFF AN ARM" OF RUSSIA

I SAW GAVIN AGAIN. HE HAS HAD A VERY NICE LETTER FROM KEN-
nedy expressing his complete confidence in him as ambassador. He
told me François de Rose indicates that France would join in a NATO
nuclear-sharing agreement if France received enriched uranium from us
as well as help in fabricating weapons that could be used in NATO but
could also be employed nationally. Gavin claims McCone, Symington, and
others have told the French this is possible under our laws. I thought this
was unlikely and he was being overoptimistic.

Gavin showed me a letter from de Gaulle to Kennedy of January 11,
replying to President Kennedy's letter to him. It is about three thousand
words long and very cold although polite. De Gaulle says France cannot
participate in any negotiations on Berlin at present and will not do so
until there is reason to believe the Russians have changed their attitude.
This would show weakness and greatly risks neutralizing West Germany,
which is Russia's main ambition and, he adds, a neutralized Germany
means a neutralized Europe, which would be dangerous for the United
States as well.

De Gaulle sniffs at Kennedy's references to the dangers of giving
nuclear weapons to Germany and says that France understood much better
than the United States the dangers of a resurgent Germany. He wholly
ignores Kennedy's plea that France should participate in a supranational
NATO nuclear-sharing arrangement. He goes on to explain that France must
maintain control of its own striking force. He recognizes that France has

neither the money nor the space to develop a really powerful force of this sort. Nevertheless, it will continue in its present program. Russia might have ten times the killing power of France with such a weapon, but if France could demonstrate that it could "tear off an arm" of Russia this might have a deterring influence. Anyway, France's national contribution would add to overall western strength.

Then—rather to my astonishment—de Gaulle went right back to his September, 1958, directorate plan. He said the West should have regular, formal systems of meetings between the chiefs of government, the foreign ministers, and the defense ministers of the United States, Britain, and France.

Gavin admits de Gaulle is trying to speak for Germany. He also says de Gaulle can offer a blackmail—giving atomic weapons to West Germany in exchange for German help in financing the gaseous diffusion plant— even though this violates treaties. We can't kick Germany out of the alliance over this since it is essential it stay in.

Gavin is discouraged and has dropped all thought of trying to arrange a meeting between Kennedy and de Gaulle this year. He is going to see Couve this week but admits this is useless.

Gavin says our only policy is to stick with de Gaulle until he achieves an Algerian settlement and then to drop him like a hot potato.

PARIS, *January 16, 1962*

NURI Birgi (Turkey's NATO ambassador) told me with tears in his eyes that Zorlu, the foreign minister who was hanged, had been his best friend. He said, of course no one should have been hanged, but if there had to be executions for reasons of state, only Bayar and Menderes should have died. Had President Gursel really wanted, he could have stopped the executions.

PARIS, *January 18, 1962*

COURCEL, de Gaulle's directeur de cabinet, called up the Quai d'Orsay and raised hell with them yesterday about my column on the letters between de Gaulle and Kennedy.

PARIS, *January 19, 1962*

CHRIS Herter and his wife came to lunch. Chris told me when he was Secretary of State, Sekou Touré was invited to dinner at the White House. At the last minute, he refused to come unless a member of his entourage was also invited. She was officially his secretary. To avoid any complications at the State Department, where he was invited to lunch the next day, he named her a secretary of state.

Chris said he thought our policy in the Congo had been lousy but, fortunately it had worked because the Sudan had prevented Egypt, Russia's agent in the Congo, from overflying the Sudan to Eastern Province. The Sudan deserved great credit.

PARIS, *January 20, 1962*

THIS morning I saw de Gaulle for an hour and twenty minutes at the Elysée, one of the best conversations I have had.

In the past it has been my experience to find that although I prepared a large number of questions to ask him, at the end he always seemed to have time to spare and he would throw out his arms and say: "Tiens. Qu'est-ce que vous pensez de la situation?" Therefore I decided today not to risk running short on questions. I had thirty-eight to ask. He answered them all, patiently and amiably.

Incidentally, I cannot help but recollect that—despite my lamentable French—I have yet to hear de Gaulle (after nineteen years) ever say anything in English. Not one word. This surprises me, because he does know some.

I asked whether he could count on the French army's loyalty to him. He answered that the OAS had no important influence left in the army. The army had met its last test in April, 1961. The army's commanders in Algeria had tried to revolt but, apart from a few very special units, like some of the Foreign Legion, the army did not follow the insurrectionists. The idea represented by the OAS was finished in the army; of this he was confident.*

I then inquired if, now that he was confident of base rights in Mers el-Kebir, he thought it would be equally easy to obtain an accord from Tunisia for similar rights in Bizerte. He answered:

Alas that is not the same thing. We *are* in Mers el-Kebir. Our presence is there and we do not have to yield anything. But Bizerte is part of Tunisia. [I was most struck by this reply because I remember his saying in the past that Bizerte was a base of primordial importance to France.]

We have always [and he stressed the word always] recognized the Tunisian state. When France governed Tunisia, it was as a protectorate, just as in Morocco. The French resident proposed decrees to the Bey of Tunis. But Tunisia was an entity like Morocco. I don't know about the outcome of the negotiations but that is a small question for me. [I remarked the way he said "me" instead of "us."] It is a big question for Bourguiba.

* See de Gaulle's further comments, pp. 73–74, 74.

I asked whether he hoped to bring all French forces back from Algeria in the near future. He replied, "I have already brought back two divisions. I am bringing back two other divisions soon." Newspaper speculation suggests he might slow this process up. De Gaulle blandly says he will continue. "And I will continue. And if there is a cease-fire I will bring almost all our forces back from Algeria swiftly."

I persisted. Did the agreements in principle guarantee the continuation of French nuclear testing in the Sahara? He regarded me inquisitively for a second and then said, "Yes we must continue."*

I then asked if he attached much significance to the rumors of difficulties inside Russia. He wrinkled his nose, shrugged his shoulders, and said:

Certainly there are difficulties inside the Communist world. This is no secret. Khrushchev himself advertises it. He has his difficulties inside Russia and also it is evident that he has his difficulties with China and Albania. It is the same thing as yesterday with Czechoslovakia. [I was extremely puzzled by the last remark and said so, but he blandly went on and I suddenly realized that he meant Jugoslavia and was referring to Tito's fight with Stalin.]

There are big difficulties in the Soviet world, but these result from what are essentially national differences. The differences between Russia and China do not stem from conditions of ideology. They merely indicate the rivalry between two big neighbors.

Also, certainly there is a progressive change in the life and the state of mind inside the Communist world. There are more and more intellectuals, more students and professors, and as a result they develop a more critical spirit.

And, furthermore, the people want more liberty and a greater well-being. And today there is no war. There is no more war in the name of which the people can be repressed as in the days of Stalin. Khrushchev realizes these truths. He weds himself to the popular desire for more freedom and well-being because, after all, Khrushchev is a politician.†

I then said to de Gaulle, "Mon Général, once you told me you thought Russia, regardless of its present ideology, was essentially a white, European, and western nation. Do you think that someday we can look to a true accord with Moscow and, perhaps, even an agreement between NATO and the Warsaw Pact?" "There can never be an alliance of that sort," he said. "NATO was created against Russia and the Warsaw Pact was created against NATO."

Did he envisage the possibility of a unified North Africa, a unified Maghreb? Here, as usual, he waxed sarcastic and quite funny. Indeed, he has as great a gift for mimicry as Henri Tisot, who has made a fortune mimicking de Gaulle. The General said:

---

* See de Gaulle's further comments, pp. 42, 74.
† See de Gaulle's further comments, p. 87.

"When one speaks of the Arabs one can never know what one is talking about . . . And who can unify the western Arabs? No one, I venture to say. But the question is unimportant."*

If Germany paid a substantial part of the cost of the proposed new French atomic production plant, would France give Germany access to its atomic stockpile? To my surprise, he took this one in his stride. He said: "Germany is not investing in our nuclear plants."

I then asked him if there was any plan which envisaged such an investment. He said: "We see no reason to change. France is building atomic plants with its own money."

Admittedly, this did not wholly answer the question.†

What did he think the West should do if the present exploratory talks with Russia on Berlin should break down? He said:

Obviously, it will not be necessary to do anything. I have not, in any way, prevented the present exploratory conversations. But I am sure they will lead to nothing. Of course, I do not wish to see any *real* negotiations on this. There is no reason for a real negotiation. If the present exploratory conversations lead to any real negotiations, we will not participate. Only the U.S.A. and Britain will participate. France will *not*.

But why should we not be able to continue as before? After all, the present situation marks no change from Potsdam. Why should this not continue? There is no reason, on our side, for this change. Khrushchev can make peace if *he* wants. Then we can have real negotiations.

But you cannot negotiate in the middle of a cold war. If you start such a procedure, it leads only to abandonment of your position.‡

I asked if he thought the European community, should it create a political confederacy, could afterward build its own nuclear force. He answered: "That is very possible. Of course, it cannot happen right away. First it must create its political union, but afterward, it is indeed possible. In the meantime, we are beginning to create our own atomic force. And we are in Europe so, after all, that is the beginning of a European force."

Why didn't he think the present informal system of consultation between the United States, Britain, and France was sufficient, why was it necessary to formalize such an arrangement? He replied:

Unless there is an organized system, there is clearly no engagement for a common policy. Look at the situation. The West must have a common policy in the world. But there is no common policy in the Congo or in Berlin or in the Far East.

But a common policy is a primordial necessity. It is a primordial necessity that there should be a western world policy confronting a

* See de Gaulle's further comments, p. 65.
† See de Gaulle's further comments, p. 65.
‡ See de Gaulle's further comments, p. 46.

Soviet world policy. The whole world looks for a *real western* global policy. But because there is no such policy the whole world suffers.

We need a permanent cooperation of the three main western powers. That is indispensable. And these powers are the United States, Britain, and France. The others are less important. They would have to follow us.

And how about the Germans? He answered: "Even the Germans. What could Germany do except follow? Anyway Germany has no world interests, no world obligations, no political undertakings. For example in Africa, in Asia. Those areas do not in the end really interest Germany."*

I then said I wanted to ask some personal questions and started off on the following. I had often heard from various people that he wished to retire and write a final volume of his *Mémoires*. He smiled quite sadly and said: "Retire? Yes. Write another volume? No. Writing about the war; that was one thing. Now, that is another. Retire? Yes. But not another volume. Colombey? Yes. But not writing."

He went on to say that he thought he would like to stay on in power to supervise the necessary constitutional changes and get France launched on its new governing system. He was a little vague about how long this would take.†

At this point, one hour and twenty minutes had gone by and the old man looked like an old man. I folded up my last page of paper, listing questions, and put it in my coat pocket, tucking my notebook in with it. "Alors," said he with a smile and a raised eyebrow, looking at me in a most friendly way, "Je dois vous quitter."

We arose simultaneously and he came to the doorway with me as he always does in his impeccably courteous way. I wished him good luck in this trying moment and also good health. He opened the door for me and said, "Good luck and good health to you."

PARIS, *January 23, 1962*

THIS morning I had a talk with Gavin. He was worried about the security aspect of the embassy apropos of the column I wrote last Wednesday about the exchange of letters between de Gaulle and Kennedy. He had had hints from the French that they knew the source. He was worried that perhaps his own office is tapped. He knew his home was tapped and also his telephone—and he never took any classified documents home. He said he was very pleased I had written the piece to show what Kennedy was up against.

I had a chat with Cecil Lyon. Lyon told me both he and Gavin were told that de Gaulle was furious about the column. The Quai d'Orsay thought de Gaulle would be so angry that he wouldn't receive me. I told Cecil this

* See de Gaulle's further comments, pp. 37–38.
† See de Gaulle's further comments, p. 84.

confirmed the ignorance concerning the Elysée that existed in the Quai d'Orsay; that de Gaulle had actually embellished the subject matter of the letters.

PARIS, *January 26, 1962*

AT dinner François de Rose, Foreign Ministry atomic expert, claimed the French were angry with Kennedy on one point in his last letter to de Gaulle. Kennedy said England was in a different situation vis-à-vis the U.S. on nuclear matters because of special arrangements in effect since the first wartime collaboration. This is not true. From 1946, when the McMahon Act was passed, until 1948, when the British were considered specially qualified for nuclear aid, there was *no* U.S.-British cooperation.

GHARDAIA, ALGERIA, *February 11, 1962*

SPENT three days on a French government tour of the Sahara, run by Olivier Guichard, Saharan délégué général. It included Manlio Brosio, Italian ambassador; Cecil Lyon, U.S. minister; and a batch of others, among whom were Jacques Baumel, senator from the Seine; Jean Leveque, technical counsellor in de Gaulle's secretariat general; Alain Peyrefitte, deputy from the Seine-et-Marne.

On February 9, we arrived at Hassi-Messaoud, main petroleum exploitation center. But there was an OAS strike and we couldn't see much. It was the regular OAS system with which I became familiar in Algiers. An employee of a company is killed (sometimes by the FLN; sometimes by the OAS), then the OAS orders a strike for "more protection."

On to Ouargla, a little oasis town surrounded by date palms with an old mosque and chapel. We dined with prefects and officers, all of whom were somewhat disquieted by the fact that the previous day the first OAS plastic bomb had been exploded there.

On February 10, we went to Touggourt where we spent most of the time being shown the complicated trucking operations of a Monsieur Deviq, deputy from the Oases, a millionaire and the grandson of a man who went out from France in 1878, after phylloxera had ruined his vineyards, to start a camel-caravan operation.

Deviq invited us all to an enormous méchoui in his garden: roast lamb on a spit which you are allowed to eat only with your right hand (no knives or forks or plates). You grab a piece and start pulling the meat off, not letting go even though it may be terribly hot because it is impolite to leave a touched piece for someone else. The méchoui was accompanied (strictly non-Muslim) by great quantities of booze and preceded by makhtouma, chorba, a sugared couscous called mesfouf, and various forms of pastry; grebia, bradj, honeyed makrout; finally dates and mint tea.

Today, we flew off in our private plane to El-Goléa, an absolutely lovely oasis in the vast desert which was known to André Gide. It is filled with date palms and wells and dominated by a tenth-century ksar or château-fort. We had another enormous méchoui, squatting on cushions and attended by many officers in the strange, baggy bloomer pants the military (including the Méharistes and camel corps we visited near Ouargla) sport with their regular army jackets. Afterward, we were taken to the tomb of Père Foucauld (founder of the Pères Blancs and a former army officer and vicomte), who was murdered at Tamanrasset by marauding Senussi tribesmen.

Then we flew on to Ghardaia, principal town of seven Mozabite settlements in the Mzab dry level valley. The Mozabites are a heretical and fundamentalist Muslim sect who escaped from orthodox Arab persecution in the Middle Ages. Dined with a collection of prefects, officers, and Mozabite dignitaries. The latter did not seem very happy at the prospect of living in an independent Algeria.

ALGIERS, *February 16, 1962*

ALGIERS is a nervous, cruel city. It was cold and rainy and the constant strikes made this particularly disagreeable. The lights were off a large part of the time and I had to type by candles. Bill Porter, U.S. consul general with whom I stayed, has an extensive radio tapping outfit (he is a licensed ham operator) and we used to sit around in the evenings listening to secret signals of the security forces. "Albatross" is the code name by which they contact each other and "Alerte Chicago" is the sign of violence.

I telephoned my old friend André Jouyne at Maréchal Foch. General Salan is supposed to be hiding somewhere in that area and I was going to see Jouyne. By a particularly interesting coincidence, his house was once Massu's headquarters. However, Porter said rumors were already being spread about U.S. contacts with the OAS and indicated he would prefer I kept my skirts clean since I was staying with him (so I didn't see Jouyne).

I saw one OAS character, Dr. Morizot, a clean-cut young man who used to be an officer in the first REP (paratroop regiment of the Foreign Legion). A nice fellow, but without any idea of the world. He told me that Colonel Y, who had been down in Katanga with the "affreux" mercenaries, was now up here with the OAS, sleeping with the daughter of General A (one of Salan's associates) and apparently linked with the murder of commandoes of a former Belgian Rexist.

I was impressed by the size of the armored car park, in front of the Délégation Générale, which is now primarily a barracks occupied only by unimportant officers since the real French government moved into the new fortified offices at Rocher Noir, twenty-five miles away.

Paul Hofmann, our correspondant, told me of a recent murder he saw.

He had just finished lunch, heard a shot, saw a Muslim man lying on the ground with his blood and brains running out. There was a queue waiting to get into a movie theater. The body lay for an hour and nobody paid any attention to it. In Oran, where a Muslim was being beaten to death, a kindly Frenchman called the police. A cop arrived and finished the man off with a bullet in the neck.

Had a drink with John Wallis of the *Daily Telegraph*. The previous afternoon he had seen a man kicked to death. A Muslim threw a grenade out of a bar, but missed. A crowd of Europeans formed. There were two harkis (native soldiers) taking the man off under arrest when the crowd broke in and kicked him to pieces. An officer with a few troops lagged behind until the job had been done. Then the harkis dragged the corpse off by its heels.

I heard another eyewitness account from Oran. This time a European youngster of about sixteen had his throat suddenly cut by four Muslims, who vanished immediately afterward. The kid staggered down the street trying to call for help, the blood spurting in all directions and women fainting.

Nice atmosphere!

On January 1, Archbishop Léon-Etienne Duval issued a New Year's message saying the "evil" can be defeated only by "absolute fidelity to the requirements of justice." The only result of that message was that the OAS ordered its followers to boycott church the next Sunday.

Went to a reception given by the French admiral and attended by all principal officials, including Jean Morin, délégué général, General Ailleret, the Archbishop, the consular corps, and others. A Frenchman (from the Metropole) cornered me and extolled the virtues of the OAS for an hour. He turned out to be a government official.

I have been rereading Camus and noted the following: From "l'Hôte" in *l'Exile et le Royaume*: "In this vast country which he had loved so much he was alone." From *La Peste*: "Stupidity has a knack of getting its way. We had nothing left us but the past, and even if some were tempted to live in the future, they had speedily to abandon the idea." In one chapter, a Jesuit priest in Oran, Father Paneloux, gives a sermon saying, "Calamity has come to us, my brethren; and, my brethren, you deserve it. We walk in darkness, in the thick darkness of this plague."

On February 14, I rode out to Rocher Noir to see Morin. I hired a taxi driven by a character who turned out to be a second-generation Algérois of Spanish-Jewish antecedents and, I suspect, an agent for every known conspiratorial group. He was very pleasant, except for a habit of driving madly at 75 mph through a rainstorm with a half-inch coating of mud obscuring his broken windshield. He didn't like to halt along the road in that crazy countryside.

Rocher Noir is a large set of buildings along the seashore, surrounded by barbed wire, troops, and fortified positions, and protected by the CRS.

At the gate you have to give up your papers in exchange for a pass and are very thoroughly checked. When I finished with Morin, my chauffeur sped home because the police had told him they heard the OAS was going to machine-gun certain cars on that road that evening.

Morin is swarthy with ruddy complexion and almost bald. We sat in his office with a picture window beyond which armed sentries patrolled the beach. I asked what he thought would happen and when. He said:

I thought for a long time the OAS would start operations itself, seizing public buildings and beginning a revolt in Algiers and Oran. Now this seems less probable. Little by little, their chance of gaining army support is decreasing and army lassitude grows. The army is suffering a crise de conscience and has been very bothered by OAS murders of officers.

The OAS says the French army won't fire on Frenchmen, but they have learned this is not so. Since they began to murder French officers, they have seen the patrols fire when necessary on anybody who violates roadblocks—French or Muslim. The OAS can always kill a number of Muslims in order to start trouble and show that no racial community is possible. But the military deserters will not be able to grab power. The French *colons* want to maintain and hold on to the land under their own direction, not that of the deserters. What they would like perhaps is partition.

Now we are at a difficult point. I presume an accord will soon be announced giving guarantees to the Europeans and this will produce uncertainty in the OAS. Most of the Algerian French want to stay in Algeria, whereas the OAS wants to seek power in France.

He said France wanted to settle with the FLN quickly and was pulling out divisions from Algeria "as a sign of good faith." This was to demonstrate that France did not intend to apply any pressure during the provisional joint administration following an armistice. De Gaulle was thus alleviating FLN fears of being tricked.

The French army is being held back as a strategic reserve despite efforts to entice it into security actions. Some officers are still individually doubtful and nostalgic for the past, but they won't do anything. The majority sees that subversion would be a catastrophe, a dead-end street. The big mass remains in discipline and hopes the OAS won't be foolish, but it is prepared to crush it if it is. There are not many doubtful units now. The Foreign Legion has been sent to the frontiers and the paratroopers have been moved from strategic areas.

Morin said that until a few months ago there were some Israeli Irgun agents in the OAS, but they have all gone. The Jews are very disconsolate and fear the Muslims. Some of them are leaving despite the OAS ban on emigration. The OAS is a hodgepodge, including both fascists and anti-fascists.

I have made a collection of OAS tracts. One claims, "A contingent of ladies of doubtful reputation has been sent to Algeria with the order to use their charms to detect patriots. Be warned about easy pickups." Bill Porter, reporting this to the State Department, added that a French journalist had come up to him and complained, "I am a patriot. Where are they?"

One industrious lady functions in the Hotel Aletti, where most foreign journalists live. She goes from room to room, spends twenty minutes, and collects 5,000 francs. She is described as moderately pretty—which can mean anything in somber Algiers. French reporters blandly charge her services on expense accounts under an item listed as "on n'est pas fait de bois."

One "order of mobilization" was issued in Bône and signed by "Général d'Armée Raoul Salan." This said: "You should consider yourself mobilized *sur place* and keep yourself at the disposition of the OAS in your town, the only legitimate authority." It commanded that shelter should be given to any "patriot pursued by the Gaullist Gestapo." It said: "Total war is henceforth and already declared and engaged against the most shameful treason in our history."

Execution orders—meaning permits for murder—read as follows: "After trial and death sentence, the special sections of the OAS have proceeded to execute sentence on the following persons . . ." These warn: "The OAS strikes where it wants, when it wants, whom it wants." Some concluded: "From Dunkerque to Tamanrasset, we will stay. Raoul Salan."

They talk of "true dictatorship in France" maintained by "guerrillas, dicks [barbouzes], traitors, and political assassination." The OAS boasts that de Gaulle is no longer considered a "worthwhile interlocutor by the FLN," because he is "unable to impose his will on the French resistance." It adds, "Neither suitcase nor coffin. One gun, one country."

On January 4, 1962, "General Raoul Salan, superior commander of the OAS, decreed general mobilization." This supposedly applies to all the French population of Algeria and "any departure from Algeria will be considered desertion and treated as such." Brochures argue that "fighting the OAS today is to prepare genocide and pogroms for tomorrow."

The latest journal, called "Appel de la France," claims there will be no putsch but merely a progressive mobilization gradually taking over. It talks of "la guerre révolutionnaires" and how instructions will be issued step by step to those mobilized. Soldiers must remain ready *sur place* like the Swiss army, Israeli kibbutniks, and the workers of the Iberian anarchist federation during the battle of Madrid. It says patriots have understood that "il ne s'agit donc nullement d'un putsch, mais d'une levée en masse, progressive, méthodique de toute la population."

PARIS, *February 20, 1962*

CECIL Lyon called. He had just read my column on the OAS to the effect that their motto should be "Down with Intelligence, Up with Death." Quite seriously, he counseled that I should get a police guard at my house to insure against plastic bombs. The embassy would be glad to arrange this.

I thanked him for his concern but considered it was the duty of the city of Paris to protect its inhabitants. He commented that the city of Paris might be too preoccupied and might have skipped my column.

Marina, who is worried about the servants, is making them sleep upstairs in the children's rooms because, normally speaking, the bombs go off on the ground floor and could splinter them with glass fragments.

PARIS, *February 21, 1962*

BREAKFAST with Walt Rostow, head of the State Department Policy Planning division and author of a theory on the stages of development for underdeveloped countries. He has a nice, easygoing approach: an agreeable, smiling fellow of middle age, medium height, a tiny bit overweight, sallow complexion, getting bald, bespectacled. On the whole, he looks like an affable college professor, which he is.

Rostow is convinced the gradual accumulation of American power, the increased arms budget, and the evident resolution to keep open Berlin access routes has really impressed Khrushchev.

He said the question posed by the famous Berlin "wall" was whether we were ready to risk war to liberate East Germany or to prevent Khrushchev from consolidating order there. Kennedy decided in the negative. He recognized that any action to change the situation in East Germany ultimately meant opening up the entire Soviet empire in eastern Europe. He was prepared to go to war to keep open access routes to West Berlin— but not to liberate eastern Europe.

Rostow thinks Khrushchev is very worried about China and that, as is always the case with Russia, he wants to patch up relations in the West when he has troubles in the East. But he has not yet made up his mind as to how far he is prepared to go in accommodating the West.

The real danger area is the Far East. The crisis in South Vietnam is the one which presents the most possibility of escalating into nuclear war. Kennedy saved Laos last spring by ordering our Pacific fleet into maneuvers with aircraft carriers and ten thousand Marines aboard. It was this determination to save the Mekong Valley which impressed Khrushchev with our resolve. We are determined to hold the Mekong because of its importance to Thailand.

We definitely prefer a neutral Laos to partition. If we could hold Laos intact under a neutral government, the Pathet Lao, which is poorly organized, might eventually disintegrate. However, if such a neutral state proves to be impossible, we may be forced into a partition position, extending a protective finger which would isolate Thailand.

There are many ultimate solutions to the South Vietnam problem. Either we can clean up the guerrilla action in South Vietnam—and then diplomatically plug the Laos leak; or militarily we may have to punish North Vietnam (a dangerous operation which could escalate into trouble).

PARIS, *February 22, 1962*

GAVIN saw de Gaulle two days ago and came away convinced the General is going to be just as tough after Algeria as before. Jim flies back Monday to see Rusk and the President. He fears he is going to make himself quite unpopular by telling them the facts about de Gaulle, who already talks as if the Algerian crisis had ended and is concentrating on French policy toward Europe.

Gavin thinks France and Germany are increasingly close, that "they are already in bed together." He suspects the French and Germans are edging toward a secret agreement under which France would supply Germany with nuclear warheads which the U.S. refuses to give either country. I called Jim's attention to a September 28 accord between France and Germany signed "for the mutual safeguard of the secrecy of inventions and technical information of interest to defense."

Gavin says France and Germany have already agreed on the manufacture of a joint tank and a joint helicopter. He knows enough about these things to realize that they have to exchange all kinds of information on electronic equipment, radios, ammunition, etc. It is a very detailed kind of undertaking and would lead naturally and evidently to atomic exchanges.

The Germans have nuclear aspirations just as the French do. Both Germany and France figure they might be threatened with a limited aggression in which the Russians would grab a piece of real estate and then sit tight, finding the U.S. in the embarrassed position of not wishing to risk the nuclear rocketing of New York and Washington in order to achieve the liberation of such captured European territories. Furthermore, the Germans want the capacity to retaliate against any Soviet assault by rocketing Russian territory.

I suggested a formula that might be able to break the log jam in our relations with France. He would have to sell it first in Washington, then sit on it until the right moment here. My idea: We should propose to the French a NATO Security Council (the old Spaak plan) of three permanent members and two shifting members; and at the same time get France's acceptance of Kennedy's Ottawa plan for stationing Polaris submarines under NATO. De Gaulle takes the cynical view that it doesn't matter if such submarines are present under NATO because General Norstad is simply an American commander and it is our own business whether we shift submarines from one American admiral to another American general. The reasoning might be fallacious, but, nevertheless, we might be able to obtain the fact of his agreement if we at least went part way toward solving his 1958 *directoire* request.

Jim was extremely interested and will try and sell it to the President. He asked me not to write anything about it now because it would embarrass him to have something appear in print just as he was raising it in Washington.

PARIS, *February 23, 1962*

DINED last night at the Norstads', in honor of Harry Labouisse, now envoy to Greece. He is worried that the Greek monarchy is putting itself out on a limb that can easily be sawed off by such actions as buying a yacht, giving a huge dowry to Princess Sophia, and generally behaving in an old-fashioned way.

George Kennan, ambassador to Jugoslavia, was there. Kennan thinks we are playing a dangerous game in always assuming the Russians are bluffing and that if we get tough they will back down.

Lunched with Kennan. I am impressed by his earnestness, sincerity, and thoughtfulness.

He was head of the Policy Planning group at the time NATO first was formed and his outfit actively opposed the concept of NATO as it has worked out. But since they were working for Secretaries of State—Marshall and Acheson—who had their own policy ideas, they had to function according to those ideas. As a result, Kennan himself headed the drafting committee which prepared the first outline of the North Atlantic Treaty.

In those days, he envisioned the relationship between North America and western Europe in the shape of a dumbbell. One large end represented the U.S. and Canada and the other large end represented the five countries joined in the Brussels Treaty. What Kennan would have liked was to have the U.S.A. give a military guarantee to the Brussels Pact but not join it. Then, eventually, a real Atlantic community might have worked out, including true Atlantic countries, such as, for example, Spain and Portugal. He had specifically thought it was unwise to include the Scandinavian countries, Italy, and later Greece and Turkey in NATO.

He says the Jugoslavs have the ridiculous impression that they are almost "honorary Africans" and back Nasser's line 100 percent on the Black African movement. This alienates them from England. They have no relations with West Germany. The French have just pulled out their ambassador because the Jugoslavs recognized the FLN "government." Relations with Italy are bad; and the Jugoslavs are not making much headway with us.

It is a pity Tito never made an official visit to the U.S.A. and that he was shabbily treated by the Eisenhower administration when he was in New York for the UN. It is unlikely he could go now because things are getting worse rather than better. In fact, Tito is probably more hated in the U.S. than Khrushchev. This is almost entirely the result of organized McCarthyite Catholics.

George thinks that we can never be in a position to handle our foreign policy correctly and win the Cold War unless we can reduce the lobbying power of individual groups. He cites as an example the McCarthyist Catholics and organized emigré groups. He says two "nations" listed as "members" of the Assembly of Captive European Nations have never existed.

The great trouble with Tito is that he remains a devout Marxist-Leninist with no realization of how much Stalinism there was in Lenin. In essence, he is still convinced of the ultimate triumph of communism and the doom of the western world. He and Nasser tend to infect each other in this respect and unfortunately the U.S. has never taken sufficient trouble to deconvince them.

PARIS, *February 28, 1962*

YESTERDAY evening, I had drinks with Bobby Kennedy, who is here on a brief visit concluding his Asian tour. I know him for a very able, hard-boiled fellow, but he gives the impression of a modest, naive, youthful college boy: very thin, somewhat shorter than his brother, with a slightly innocent expression and a habit of continually playing with his curly forelocks. He ordered a beer and then sat talking slowly, saying nothing remarkable but always completely at ease and giving the appearance of being completely frank.

He thinks Indonesia and Holland are very near to a settlement now, but that we must help both sides because we are respected and nobody else is doing anything to achieve harmony. He stressed the importance of our informal good offices. He found no resentment against the U.S. in Holland —and was struck by how popular we were in Indonesia and how well Ambassador Howard Jones is doing there. At the meetings which Jones attends with Sukarno and other ambassadors, he always gets a much bigger hand from the crowd than any other ambassador. This is a proof of U.S. popularity and, by inference, of Jones's popularity. The source of all this information is Jones.

He had a feeling that it was necessary for Japan to come more actively into the problem of helping underdeveloped areas. Japan could be of great use in Indonesia and other Southeast Asian countries. I mildly remonstrated that Japan was scarcely popular in the Philippines, but he was very earnest and did not smile. He thought it would be a good idea for the

Japanese to organize their own form of Peace Corps. I cannot help but think this is a rather delicate operation because the last Japanese Peace Corps seeking to establish the "greater East Asian coprosperity sphere" from 1941–1945 used methods that could hardly be described as popular.

Yesterday morning, he saw de Gaulle for forty minutes. Gavin was along. I asked him who interpreted, and he said it was one of their people but he thought Gavin "understood some of what went on." He said it was very interesting to meet de Gaulle. But the conversation was on a "very high level—philosophy and that sort of thing."

I asked who had impressed him most of the people he had met on this trip. It was between de Gaulle and Adenauer. He was tremendously struck by their age. "My goodness," he said, "Adenauer is eighty-six." But he also said he had been impressed by all he had read about these men before, especially referring to de Gaulle. "Think of all he has done and all he has done for his country."

He couldn't help thinking that it was noteworthy the West could produce leaders like this and the Communists could not. This was a great advantage we had. At one point he turned to me and said, "I will bet you can't guess who is the man who most influenced Adenauer and whom he most admires in terms of all his years of public service." I said I believed the man who had most influenced him in terms of his whole life was a school teacher named Petit, but the one he most admired in public life was without any doubt Foster Dulles. Kennedy was astonished. "How did you guess that?" he asked. I said it was fairly well known and it was also fairly natural that a man should so admire another man who was in a position of power and whom he was able to influence so heavily.

PARIS, *March 1, 1962*

LUNCHED today with Olivier Guichard, delegate general for Saharan affairs, who was de Gaulle's directeur de cabinet during the spring of 1958, when he returned to power. Guichard, who is only forty-one, is the son of a naval officer (Admiral Darlan's chef de cabinet). He was one of the prime organizers of the Rassemblement du Peuple Français, de Gaulle's one experiment in forming a political party.

He says General Jouhaud (OAS) is a fool. He has always mistrusted Salan. He was not able to persuade de Gaulle on this mistrust. Among de Gaulle's faults is that he thinks he can regulate military affairs by handing out promotions and decorations. He is simply unaware of the fact that he, de Gaulle, never made the slightest imprint on the French army. The army was against him during World War II and the army was against him during the period of his exile in Colombey. In fact, there was really no conspiracy during the spring of 1958. There was only a handful of people like Guichard and Foccart in Paris and Delbecque and Lieutenant

Neuwirth (a businessman serving as a lieutenant in a strategic position), in Algeria.

Guichard said Debré is heartbroken about being put on the skids. He never understood that the May 13 "complot" was merely to bring back de Gaulle and settle Algeria in the best possible terms—and was not at any time an "Algérie Française" plot. Now he is shattered by a realization of the truth.

The next Prime Minister will be either Chaban-Delmas or Pompidou. Chaban is very ambitious but would not be too disappointed if he remained on as president of the Assembly. Pompidou is a cold, smooth, competent intellectual. He was not with de Gaulle during the war but was brought in in a very low position as part of the entourage afterward. He worked his way up and de Gaulle became fond of him.

Guichard said de Gaulle was a desperately lonely man and he thought that if he had a few years of retirement he would be driven by internal forces to write another volume of his *Mémoires*. He hopes so. But if not, in any case, André Malraux would surely write a brilliant biography.

I asked Guichard why de Gaulle was so antipress. He really didn't know: "The General was once a journalist himself. In the 1930s de Gaulle was military correspondent of *l'Echo de Paris*. I know, because my father wrote the naval reports for *l'Echo*."

PARIS, *March 2, 1962*

LUNCHED with Jean-Jacques Servan-Schreiber and his charming twenty-four-year-old wife, Sabine (daughter of a professional army officer). Jean-Jacques, who criticizes the OAS, lives in a regular fortress: the fifth floor of an old-fashioned Paris apartment house. At the door to the building was a uniformed policeman who did not let me enter until I gave my name. Inside the door, were two plainclothes characters who asked for identification. One took me to the elevator. At the fifth floor, a burly character again asked my name before he let me in. Standing in the corner was a .22 automatic rifle.

The offices of *l'Express* are protected by a volunteer corps under the command of one of the staff, a retired officer. The volunteers, mostly admiring readers, are all armed with .22 automatic carbines. I thought this rather ineffective; Why not tommy guns? Jean-Jacques said it was against the law to use anything except sporting weapons; even pistols were banned. No permit was required for the .22s.

Jean-Jacques is a brave, intellectual, dynamic young fellow. I enjoy reading his magazine, but I cannot say that his logic impresses me. He hammers away at de Gaulle and yet admits de Gaulle is the only man who can save France. He criticizes de Gaulle's methods for trying to arrange peace in Algeria and then says de Gaulle is the only man who can arrange peace. He is convinced France is not inclined toward fascism. If de Gaulle fails he thinks the people will preserve republican order.

He is afraid that by the time the FLN and the French government have signed an Algerian peace, it will have already been overtaken by events and the OAS will be in a position to prevent either the FLN or France from imposing a settlement. The position of the army is still very doubtful. Although on the whole it dislikes the OAS and detests its indiscriminate murders and its *plasticages*, it is anti-de Gaulle. The luckiest thing for France is that Salan heads the OAS because Salan is generally disliked by the military.

One of the greatest OAS trumps is the fact that the French government has failed to put through a statute—which could be done in half an hour— granting insurance against *plasticage* damage. Apparently, French insurance companies are not allowed, legally, to pay off claims resulting from "civil war." The OAS damages are considered "civil war."

The result is that many people pay blackmail to the OAS to avoid damage which could bankrupt them. Gaston Defferre's (Socialist politician) apartment was plasticated, damaging it as well as splitting the building, a cooperative. The other owners demanded that Defferre pay for the damages.

PARIS, *March 5, 1962*

RECENTLY I have noticed some strange ginks hanging around my house. I mentioned this to Al Ulmer at dinner. He confessed to me that Cecil Lyon, after being turned down by me on his kind suggestion that my house should be guarded, asked Al to make arrangements with the French security to do just that—and not tell me. That is who those guys are.

PARIS, *March 6, 1962*

LUNCHED with Jean Laloy. Laloy thinks the French decision not to attend the Geneva seventeen-nation Disarmament Conference is lunatic. After twenty years of hard work, they have gotten themselves back to the isolated position of Yalta. The decision was taken by de Gaulle himself without consulting anybody.

Laloy thinks the West is foolish not to stress in its propaganda the ludicrous fact that China and Russia, the two big Communist states advertising themselves as examples to the underdeveloped world, are respectively starving and undernourished. Neither one has solved its agricultural problem.

The origin of the Sino-Soviet dispute centers about three things: the Chinese were furious that Khrushchev should proceed with de-Stalinization without even having advised them in advance; the Chinese don't like his approach to non-Communist nationalist movements; the two disagree on Soviet approaches to the West. Perhaps one reason for de-Stalinization and ending the "cult of personality" was to destroy not only the dead Stalin but the living Tito and Mao.

Saw Jean Monnet at his apartment-office on the Avenue Foch. Sunburned after a holiday in Switzerland, he is astonishingly youthful and vigorous for a man well past seventy.

I have the feeling that he simplifies too much, that he is overconfident, but he is also an extremely shrewd, practical, and old-fashioned economist. He advocates common sense, yet has the gift for dreaming great dreams.

He thought it hard to forecast the effect of the Common Market on the U.S. economy.

Until now, the U.S. economy has been the strongest in the world and has far and away the most advanced productivity. But it is not good for any one country to be in a position of superiority and to meet no competition. This relaxes the necessary effort.

The separate European states are too small, as individuals, with limited means. But together—taking for granted that Britain will join them—they will produce more efficiently than in the past and will compete more directly with the U.S.A. This competition will stimulate a greater U.S. effort. And competition is the essence of your economy.

The effect on the U.S. economy will be to stimulate production and there will be a similar effect on Europe. What this produces will be stimulation on a competitive basis in a system where there is no protection and where gradually European living standards will move toward those existing in the U.S.A.

Why does the U.S. industrialist invest in Europe? It is not to get behind Common Market walls, which are in the process of going down as tariffs are reduced. He is investing in order to get nearer to his market, to his customers. There is a much larger margin of opportunity for the sale of consumer goods in the Common Market than in the U.S. because there is a smaller stock of these goods proportionately in Europe.

I think the Russians and especially the Chinese are politically bound, whether or not they have the means to help other lands, to do their level best to appear as if they will help other lands. What *they* have to offer is the example. *We* can give help but not an example. We cannot pay the underdeveloped countries to do what we have done. They are too far behind. They simply cannot do it.

When westerners go to these countries as technicians, they want to continue living a comfortable life, but when Russian experts go to underdeveloped areas they live just like the local people. This undoubtedly creates a vast and favorable impression.

The only western country that can provide an example to underdeveloped lands is Israel, an example we cannot duplicate because we are too advanced. But we should get Israel to work with us. They have been doing very effective work in Africa. They should head this kind of program. Their big asset is the ability to show poor countries what to do. We can help but we have no example.

I said to Monnet, "I note you always assume that England will without any doubt enter the Common Market." He said, "Why, of course, it will come in this year. The forces working for this are too strong. And the British are being reasonable. No one could take the responsibility of keeping them out."

PARIS, *March 7, 1962*

THIS afternoon I went to see Chaban-Delmas, president of the Assembly: well dressed, dapper. He had a splendid war resistance record and ended up a general while he was still in his twenties.
Chaban said:

I myself told de Gaulle it would not be good to use me as Prime Minister. I am president of the Assembly and in France the president of the Assembly should only become Prime Minister when there is no other choice, as the last possible solution.

Today, it is evident that the competition is between Pompidou, Joxe, and me. I am the only Gaullist he can consider absolutely sure but who is not an unconditional fetishist. And I am also considered a "European" and a "liberal." These facts are of particular importance in my position as president of the Assembly. Of course, from my own point of view, being kept in reserve makes me run the risk that I might never be appointed. But it is better from de Gaulle's point of view that I should have to take that risk.

I asked if he thought it would be necessary to have purge trials of OAS leaders after the insurrection is crushed. He answered: "The situation in Algeria itself will be very tough and there will be lots of chaos there—but no real repercussions. The position of the army is sure. The army is not happy, but it will do what it has to do, although certain units may commit minor follies. The heads of the OAS will either emigrate or they will be killed when they are captured."

We talked about Pompidou. He said: "Pompidou is very intelligent and has a knack for adapting himself. But he should not be named Prime Minister before the elections. The Communists would then say de Gaulle is the same thing as the Rothschild bank—which might easily give the Communists twenty or thirty extra seats because for the last fifty years there has been prejudice against the Rothschild bank similar to the prejudice against the Rockefellers that used to apply in your country."

PARIS, *March 8, 1962*

GAVIN thinks the Russians broke through in two respects during their last tests last summer and autumn. These were achievements of a neutron warhead for missile defense and the explosion of various types of nuclear warheads in missiles. We have not yet exploded warheads in missiles though we are confident such weapons systems are already operational.

As a result of their last tests, the Russians have gotten ahead in a high-yield, high-altitude antimissile as well as in missile delivery and warheads. The neutron warhead is all important because it can "melt" the business end of any nuclear or thermonuclear weapon probably at a distance of about 1,000 yards.

Gavin showed me a cable he had sent to the State Department February 21, the day after he had seen de Gaulle, analyzing the French situation accordingly: De Gaulle was intent on developing "Europe" into a strong and influential political, economic, and military community. He did not elaborate very much on the "military" aspects.

De Gaulle, the telegram continued, hoped eventually to accomplish de facto the objectives of his 1958 *directoire* letter by having France speak for "Europe" in world affairs. He was resolutely determined to achieve this, although backing and filling en route toward his goal just the way he did en route toward an Algerian settlement.

Jim recommends we should continue to deal as much as we can with NATO and to support all our other NATO allies as closely as we can in bilateral dealings. But we should never forget the essentials of French policy. Nor should we deceive ourselves that de Gaulle is going to be easier to deal with after an Algerian settlement; on the contrary, he will be tougher.

De Gaulle reckons on keeping Germany under his control. It is wise for us whenever possible to point out to the Germans the superior value of their alliance with the U.S. as compared with their alliance with France.

PARIS, *March 9, 1962*

THIS afternoon, I went to see Prime Minister Debré at the Matignon. I haven't liked him in the past, but I must say my heart went out to him: He looked tired and nervous as if worn to the marrow. He took off his thick spectacles and came around and sat on my side of the desk after absentmindedly shaking hands twice.

I asked whether he was optimistic about squashing the OAS. He said the only big problem was in Algiers and Oran. He couldn't foresee how long that would continue, but, "We will make the necessary effort for true peace after the cease-fire. We will act against terrorism no matter from which direction it comes and all terrorists will be severely punished."

I then inquired whether the real source of difficulties between France and the U.S.A. was all to be reduced to nuclear questions. He said:

I think that there are basic differences in conception between our countries. For France, European defense requires a continental military power which is France. But the U.S. does not want to see *any* other atomic power. Even Britain is an addition the U.S. can only accept because of its old and special ties with London. Above all the U.S.A. is opposed to France as a nuclear power. The U.S.A. thinks that its own atomic guarantee is enough for the defense of NATO.

Thus there is a fundamental difference of conception. But this does not prevent the continuation of our alliance of solidarity and friendship. However, the problem must be recognized as such because it is serious.

Our position is really very clear. We think that a nuclear striking force must be national. It is too serious a matter to be shared with other countries. Only France should control its own nuclear force.

France could provide nuclear weapons, as a national force, for the European Little Six. None of the other five countries were even vaguely interested in building their own nuclear force except for Germany, which was banned from having such by the Paris accords. It was untrue that Germany was contributing money to a new nuclear separation plant with the promise of warheads in exchange.

He admitted the division between France and the U.S.A. was grave and that no solution was in sight. "But we must live with this difference and we will stay friendly and allied. Our viewpoints are as far apart as black and white. This is not a problem you can just stick in the icebox and forget. But things evolve. One day France will have its own nuclear striking force and then competition will vanish."

PARIS, *March 10, 1962*

LUNCHED with Etienne Burin des Roziers, de Gaulle's right hand in the Elysée. Etienne admitted France was very distressed by our viewpoint and based its suspicions on Kissinger's book, which said that no country could afford to start a nuclear war except in defense of its own individual territory. That was why France had its program. France had just as much interest as the U.S.A. in preventing Germany from having its own nuclear weapons. Etienne said it was too bad Kennedy and de Gaulle had never had time in their one meeting to really discuss this at length.

He went on at length about French anger at American misunderstanding concerning France's nuclear program. This was the kind of thing that simply could not be talked about between ambassadors and de Gaulle. Furthermore, de Gaulle didn't talk well. In 1945, just before Yalta, Harry Hopkins came to see de Gaulle together with Ambassador Caffery. To begin with, de Gaulle is incapable of understanding the position of an anomalous official like Hopkins. He kept asking, "What is his position? What is his authority?"

Etienne said de Gaulle is again convinced that some day not only all eastern Europe but also Russia will move toward an appreciation of the role of the individual in society—which means the West. Two months ago, before Etienne left Warsaw (where he was French ambassador), the Communist ambassadors all spoke to him about the difficulties between Russia and China.

GENEVA, *March 11, 1962*

LUNCHED with Art Dean who flew in last night with Rusk. He said that three days ago Khrushchev told Thompson: "Berlin is the testicles of the West. Every time I give them a yank they holler." I added: "Macmillan is the first guy to say ouch."

Dean says the British are absolutely lying when they say they have made a breakthrough on recording underground tests, thus permitting smaller inspection setup. They have not, and they know nothing, despite the fact we lent them a test site at Laramie. Ormsby-Gore came to see him and Dean produced a U.S. scientist who laid this fact on the line. Ormsby-Gore was under instructions, couldn't argue; just pretended he had another appointment.

Dean knows Krishna Menon well, having dealt with him much during the Korea talks, and says, "If he isn't a Communist he's awfully close. But he's also highly intelligent and does his homework."

GENEVA, *March 13, 1962*

LAST night, I had a pleasant talk with Dean Rusk. I found him all alone in his modest hotel suite, just finishing dinner, wearing a shirt and sweater, no necktie. Very friendly, he asked me if I didn't want a bite, but I told him I had already dined. He is a decent, simple, man.

He said:

The Russians must think of West Berlin as if it were on the border in a normal sense and not as if it were an island inside their territory. We *are* there and we will stay there. If Khrushchev wishes to push us out there will be war.

They want us out. There is no question on this. Khrushchev is out on a limb with long and heavy commitments. His problem is how to get off that limb without a war. He is gambling on western disunity to help him. There is a theory that Khrushchev's proposal for a free city was an attempt to save his public position as well as the face of the West.

But he is failing in this also. The latest information I have received is that the population of Berlin is going up, not down. Quite a few young married people are settling there. Mayor Brandt reports a steady population rise; yet Khrushchev had hoped for a drop. And new offices are being set up there; trade is going up. Therefore Khrushchev's gamble on erosion is beginning to look like a bad gamble.

The only thing for us to do is to deal with the problems of access as they arise. It doesn't matter much if Soviet planes fly in the corridors if they are not in the way. The West does not claim exclusive use of the Berlin air corridors. But they are crowding in on us.

It is hard to analyze just why Khrushchev chose to start another Berlin crisis now. It is probably an effort to consolidate his East German position. East Germany has been a second-class province of the Soviet empire. And Khrushchev has treated his own Germans as second-class citizens. After all, he extracted enormous reparations.

The westward flight of East Germans was not encouraged by the West. It was simply that Khrushchev could not keep them in. In fact, we preferred our friends to stay on where they were. But Khrushchev had a demonstrated failure and could not even hold his own people. Now he is trying to pass this problem on to us. He is stuck with Ulbricht who is not a success. Where can he find a successor to Ulbricht or any success in the situation? The twenty Russian divisions in East Germany are not just there to face us. They know NATO won't attack. They are there because of the discontent in East Germany and, to a degree, to frighten the Poles and the Czechs. Khrushchev wants to stabilize his east Europe.

Rusk thought it unwise to assume any secret French design to make a deal with Germany giving them nuclear warheads. "De Gaulle would like to hold the Germans to their commitments and the French would like to remain the sole nuclear power in continental western Europe. But France finds the nuclear club is very expensive to join and might want to make a continental partnership if the U.S.A. won't help her."

I asked Rusk if he had read my recent columns on brush-fire peace and whether it might not be a good idea to start off negotiations like this looking for fundamental points of agreement, no matter how subsidiary, instead of always concentrating on disagreement. He smiled and said:

This is precisely our approach. We want to put bone and flesh on any theoretical points of agreement. Khrushchev said the foreign ministers could meet, "despite the polemics." We are prepared to meet seriously right here and not to start off with propaganda. We feel there has been very meager food for optimism.

We are looking for points of agreement and we are anxious to see if there cannot be an accord on such things as outer space. We are trying to arrange a Laos agreement. But on the questions of a major sort like Berlin, Russian words mean different things from Russian actions. Nevertheless, from the U.S. point of view, the philosophical basis of this conference is to seek an agreement and not to argue disarmament.

Rusk had not yet mentioned Laos in his talks with Gromyko. He added: "I fear there is little Washington or Moscow can do on this. I have the impression the Russians would like to see a settlement of that situation but the Chinese are messing things up. We are worried about Chinese influence in Hanoi being in the ascendency. We have no hard proof, but there are indications that the Chinese are gaining and this represents a reversal of the trend."

I asked if there were a prospect for a de Gaulle-Kennedy meeting this spring. He said probably there would be a meeting moderately soon and it was not a big problem where, but there was nothing yet in the wind. He wondered whether such a meeting would be an answer to our difficulties with de Gaulle. The big question remained whether the U.S.A. would help France to become a nuclear power.

The fact of the matter was that the U.S.A. was less, not more, sovereign as a result of its nuclear strength. We have explained to de Gaulle that a nation in fact loses by having a nuclear force. There is no such thing as a divisible use of nuclear-military forces by the free world. Everybody is of course affected. It is impossible for the U.S. to make a decision to use nuclear weapons in Europe without Europe's consent.

PARIS, *March 20, 1962*

GAVIN has just been to see General Puget, chief of staff of the French armed forces, together with General Max Taylor, Kennedy's special military advisor. François de Rose was there. Taylor asked de Rose point blank: "If we give you nuclear systems [similar to those given England by the U.S.], will you cooperate with a NATO nuclear force?" De Rose answered categorically "yes."

Norstad told Taylor yesterday that between 50 percent and 75 percent of the French officers corps was anti-de Gaulle. Gavin is surprised there has been no action in Algeria since the cease-fire. He hears rumors that de Gaulle is making a secret deal with Salan and might let him out to Argentina and put a deposit in a Swiss bank for him. This is why Billotte was not named high commissioner in Algeria because Billotte wanted to get right to work and rout out Salan and all the others. I told Gavin I didn't believe this; that de Gaulle would never deal with a dirty man like Salan.

PARIS, *March 21, 1962*

THIS morning, I had a good, efficient talk with General Max Taylor, who is in Europe on a quick "orientation trip." His role is a kind of souped-up version (for Kennedy) of that played by Admiral Leahy for President Roosevelt.

I asked if the U.S. is now planning only for a NATO seaborne nuclear force and if so, why isn't it possible to get France to accept this? He said there is a fundamental confusion in all this talk about a NATO nuclear force. Behind it is the purely military requirement for modernization. General Norstad's bombers are getting obsolescent just like our SAC bombers are getting obsolescent. Provision must be made to replace them with missiles. If, when meeting this need, we can get an international aspect to the solution, that will be all to the good. We must give the Germans a feeling that they have a share in such a force, but the basic requirement remains the modernization of NATO.

But why, I inquired, doesn't France legally qualify for U.S. nuclear aid on the same basis as Britain? Taylor replied that President Kennedy has not yet decided to qualify France for such aid. This is a presidential decision and there is no fixed definition on what such qualification must be. But clearly his decision would be closely crossexamined by Congress. People simply don't like to see the nuclear club expanded. I added that there is some false logic here because France obviously is *in* the nuclear club and even Russia recognizes the fact.

Did we still really need thirty NATO divisions between Switzerland and the Baltic, and if so, why can't we get them? He said it was perfectly obvious that a rich Europe could provide these units. There was no reason why we could not reach the goal. But it was not only the fault of Europe. The U.S. had for too long a time preached its total reliance on atomic weapons and there is a hangover of this doctrine in European minds which leads to a reluctance to produce expensive conventional units.

I asked what would be the role of a national French atomic force in western defense—when de Gaulle has his small nuclear striking force in 1965. Taylor said:

If a NATO nuclear force is worth the trouble of creating, we must improvise a plan very quickly. We could ship one or two Polaris submarines there earmarked as part of SAC. The same would be true of Britain's V-bombers. Then the French could come in later when they have their force.

The central and major problem is whether a NATO force is worthwhile. You get into all kinds of arguments on this. There is a good deal of discussion of a U.S. veto. What is this? There is a legal requirement that the President must take a decision to release atomic weapons for use by non-U.S. forces. He could, of course, delegate his control of such forces to another American. But authorization to use such forces is different from authority to release them. Who gives the order to fire? What happens if there is a split vote among the fifteen allied powers? If there are both a U.S. nuclear force and a NATO nuclear force and the President delegates power to release certain nuclear weapons to the NATO force, who gives NATO the right to use that force if the U.S. national force is used? Is it possible to establish an executive committee inside NATO of the U.S.A., France, Britain, and Germany instead of a fifteen-member executive committee to control the firing of nuclear weapons? And actually are we much better off with four fingers on the trigger than with fifteen fingers on the trigger? We are still all tied up on those questions and I don't really know whether a NATO force is really worthwhile.

PARIS, *March 22, 1962*

LUNCHED with Pierre Billotte, amusing and interesting. He is ambitious, conceited, full of courage and intelligence. I like him. He told me de Gaulle had asked him to the Elysée to name him as high commissioner in Algeria after the cease-fire and told him he had no right to refuse. Billotte accepted the appointment on his fifty-sixth birthday, March 8. The idea has been cancelled.

De Gaulle assured Pierre he could take his orders directly from him and would not have to pass through Debré for whom de Gaulle expressed contempt. The President and Prime Minister are an odd pair. Pierre claims that Debré's ambition is to keep the Algerian troubles going so that he will stay on as Prime Minister and eventually succeed de Gaulle; that his inner sympathies are with the OAS.

Debré apparently cautioned de Gaulle that Billotte was trying to become a little Napoleon in Algeria with the idea of political fame in France and eventually edging into power. De Gaulle was also irked by all the newspaper leaks put out by Debré's office. In the meantime, Billotte had received telephone warnings from the OAS that he was number one on the murder list after de Gaulle.

Pierre had access to all the Elysée documents. These show that Salan is planning a *pourrissement* of the situation in Algeria in the hopes of gradually starting a war between the Europeans and the Muslims and winning the army over piecemeal to the Europeans. Only then would a select set of assassinations take place in France.

His own original plan was to send General Catroux with Ben Bella to Morocco to win de Gaulle popularity among the Arabs; to start an immediate offensive against the OAS and to lock up several generals in France. But he said there was no use moving sharply against the OAS in Algeria as his work was going to be betrayed by Debré.

In the end, Debré succeeded in turning de Gaulle against Billotte and they are no longer on speaking terms. Pompidou twice personally warned Billotte that Debré was in the process of betraying him. He had already written an opening speech and the proclamation for his arrival in Algiers plus his plan of action.

The weekend before last, while Pierre was scheduled for the Algerian job, the police had sent a force of 125 gendarmes to his place in the country to protect him. Now practically all have been withdrawn. Carloads of OAS guerrillas have been around the neighborhood. When he goes out he rarely uses his car but prefers a taxi. Sometimes he carries a revolver but says it really isn't much use because the thugs have tommy guns.

PARIS, *March 26, 1962*

I LUNCHED at Camp des Loges (St. Germain) with General Earle G. Wheeler, newly appointed deputy U.S. commander in Europe and scheduled to succeed Norstad at SHAPE. He is tall, well built, with an intelligent, strong face. He seemed self-possessed and modest.

He promised to give me some material on new "antisubversion" literature being used to instruct American troops for "defensive" antiguerrilla and sabotage work as contrasted with the "offensive" type of thing at Bad Tölz. In May, some allied countries will be sending prospective candidates for the first time to Bad Tölz. He admitted that the West German troops were there working under a subterfuge (playing the part of "native antiguerrilla troops") because Germany is forbidden this type of operation under the WEU agreements.

PARIS, *March 29, 1962*

LUNCHED with François de Rose. He says that under the McMahon Act a country can qualify for U.S. nuclear aid on two bases: it must prove its technical eligibility in terms of its own atomic accomplishments; and it must be politically eligible.

Since France has shown it is fully qualified technically and has mastered the secrets of plutonium weapons (not thermonuclear weapons—but there were no such things in 1946 when the McMahon Act was passed), it is clearly scientifically eligible. Therefore, logic leads to the conclusion that we consider France politically ineligible. If the U.S. considers France politically ineligible, why should France cooperate with the U.S. in NATO and other political fields?

It is insulting for the U.S. to tell France it doesn't want to give Paris nuclear aid for fear of German complaints. Nobody wants to give Germany nuclear aid, but if we continue to refuse this privilege to France, some future French government may feel forced to help the Germans. But that would be politically disastrous because even one German atomic bomb would completely solidify relations between the east European satellites and Russia, which have a very genuine fear of Germany.

If the U.S. and France can arrange a deal giving the French nuclear systems the Russians will be put on the spot vis-à-vis China. They don't want to give China such aid and yet if they are smoked out in public this will embarrass their relations with Peking and ruin any pretenses of solidarity in the Communist bloc.

ADENAUER: RUSSIA
CONTRADICTS MARX

CADENABBIA, ITALY, *April 2, 1962*

DROVE FROM MILAN TO CADENABBIA ON COMO TODAY AND SPENT an hour and three-quarters with old Adenauer in his villa above the lake. He was particularly friendly. Poured out coffee (assuring me it was "not Italian") and got up to get me a second cup. He allowed me to smoke and apologized for being a nonsmoker himself. We chatted about all sorts of things.

I mentioned de Gaulle's observation that Khrushchev's historic role could not be judged until we knew whether he intended to make peace or war and had succeeded or failed. He said: "In my opinion, Khrushchev will not make war. There are two reasons for this opinion: He is a Russian nationalist and he is a Communist.

"As a Russian nationalist he wants to be seen as the creator of Russia's economy coming, as he does, after Stalin's enormous expansion of Russia and after Lenin's development of Marxism. That is why he has no use for war. War would wreck the Russian economy. The second reason why he doesn't want war is the menace of Red China."

He then sat forward in his chair, rumpling his black suit, staring at me earnestly from a slightly tanned face, as if he were about to confide some very wise words:

I was in Moscow in the autumn of 1955. At that time, at Khrushchev's invitation, I had intimate talks with him about China, where he frankly expressed his concern. He showed himself perfectly aware that in case of a war, whatever its outcome, Russia would be greatly weakened and China would therefore be much more dangerous.

I agree with de Gaulle that one cannot judge Khrushchev's historical position before you knew what his final policy has been and how it succeeded. However, I was with Khrushchev three times a day for a period of six days. During our talks, he sometimes had his emotional moments but I noticed that he was always fully self-controlled.

I asked what he thought were the chances of some progress toward disarmament in the current Geneva talks. He didn't think there was any:

> For this reason, simply; Khrushchev doesn't trust the United States.
> This brings me to President Kennedy and his policy. This differs from what it was in the days of Eisenhower and Dulles. Then it was based on a conviction of the abominable aspect of communism, a conviction that communism *must* not be permitted to expand anywhere, that the aim should be to liberate the satellites.
> Khrushchev doesn't yet really believe the United States now wants to coexist. This makes it difficult for Kennedy to apply his policy of talking with the Russians as much as possible in the hopes of reducing misunderstanding.
> Khrushchev is still influenced by his reaction to the former policy. This may diminish, of course, as mistrust is eliminated.
> But because of the philosophical basis of mistrust under which Khrushchev believed the previous administration could not take up an attitude of coexistence, he is not yet persuaded of a change. Clearly, Kennedy is trying to do away with this skepticism because he thinks that then a modus vivendi can be established.
> Don't get me wrong. I don't reproach the Eisenhower-Dulles team for their policy. At that time, Communist domination was not so strong as it is today nor was it so firmly stabilized and one could still believe in the possibility of liberation. But the years have passed and the Communist hold has increased.
> If they were in power today, Eisenhower and Dulles would have the same policy as Kennedy. It is necessary now to make pragmatic decisions the way Kennedy does. Kennedy is prepared to attempt a modus vivendi; but this must be honestly received and met by the Soviet side.

I told him Djilas recalls Stalin saying that an army installs its own political system where it goes. Adenauer commented:

> Do you think that the present Soviet system is real, genuine communism? I think it has moved away and towards another dictatorial form of government in which a group, not an individual, has all the power. Khrushchev doesn't hold all the power.
> Russia has continued to develop differently from what Stalin had imagined. This makes an absurdity of the Stalinist doctrine. Even today, the East German regime is much harder than that in Russia itself. The Russians venerate Marx as the founder of communism. Yet Marx imagined a classless, stateless society. The present Russian social system is one of the omnipotence of the state, the exact reverse of Marx. And Stalinism is no longer accepted by Khrushchev. His opinions have been discarded by him and I don't think he will accept even the kind of doctrine of Stalin you now mention.

I then asked Adenauer if he envisioned a "Europe" in the future as united on a federal or a confederal basis. He said:

In international law, the terms federal and confederal are much discussed. Europe's political union should be developed, however, in stages, like the Common Market. One must not be too confused by theoreticians.

After all, you have only to look at German history. In the first half of the nineteenth century there was the North German Customs Union. Then there came the All German Customs Union and this eventually developed into a political structure.

I said I had an impression that de Gaulle would subtly keep Britain from entering the Common Market. Adenauer commented:

I'm not yet sure they'll come in. Certainly we cannot accept the Commonwealth into the Market. That would end our political objective by making it no longer a European grouping.

When Kennedy recently spoke of U.S. interests in the Common Market, some people began to call for an Atlantic community. But that is not possible. Partnership, yes; but not a community. That would kill the European idea. And I think Kennedy sees this also, that he agrees with my point of view.

I asked Adenauer if he didn't fear that some neutral countries would be damaged by exclusion from the Common Market and that Jugoslavia, for example, might not be driven back toward Russia's arms. He said: "We must not give up our great objective of an economically and politically strong Europe because of any difficulties existing elsewhere. I think it quite possible that future historians will see that the friendship of France and Germany and the resulting creation of a strong Europe will prove to have been the most constructive factor of this epoch."

I wondered if West Germany hoped or expected to receive nuclear arms from either the United States or France. There were many rumors of some kind of deal between the French and the West Germans under which the West Germans would get nuclear help in exchange for investing in French production. He answered:

In the position of France today, I think de Gaulle had no choice but to appeal to the nationalistic spirit of his army and the fatherland by playing up the idea of nuclear weapons for France in order to counteract OAS appeals to nationalistic spirit.

But let me stress that we do not want such weapons for Germany and I don't think there will ever be an agreement to grant them to Germany. I also think that the relations between the United States and de Gaulle will improve after he has settled his Algerian problem.

Let me add, the United States has always considered Algeria as a colonial problem. France did not. This created tension. But once the problem is solved, and thank God it appears to be in the process of being solved, I think that things will be better.

May I remind you that when Western European Union was founded in London, I made a declaration that we Germans waived the rights to ABC weapons. And I tell you now today that I waive them again.

At the time I met with Stikker here at his villa on Lake Como, General Norstad presented a plan and I thought it was good. He passed this on to President Eisenhower's administration. But they did not study it closely because it was too near the election period. I hear that President Kennedy is now continuing to study the question of a NATO force. I certainly do not think that the matter has been shelved.

How were relations now between Bonn and Washington, I asked. "Perhaps for a while, it may have seemed rather difficult to me. I had very close relations, after all with President Eisenhower and Foster Dulles. But now my personal relations with Kennedy, Rusk, and McNamara are very good."

He said it was a pity we couldn't send David Bruce back as ambassador to Bonn. He would either like to have Bruce himself or somebody who was just like Bruce and preferably named Bruce. He asked me to pass this on.

ROME, *April 4, 1962*

THIS evening had a talk with Pietro Nenni, left-wing Socialist boss. Very nice and friendly. Welcomed me like an old buddy. Spoke quite fluent French without inhibition. With his sloppy, plump frame and thick glasses, he looked like a shrewd, aging owl.

He described the reforms being attempted by the government under the "opening to the left," with the Socialists as "at the most like those of the U.S. New Deal." But even there, he said, the right was making difficulties from the start.

He hoped the "opening" would "stabilize the democratic forces of Italy sufficiently to give full guarantees that our Constitution will be truly applied; this is not yet the case. If the experiment succeeds we would then have the problem of an organic collaboration with the Christian-Democrats and our open support of them. But this must await the 1963 elections to ascertain if there has been enough progress in reform."

Nenni said his minimum economic objective is to see a leveling-out of differences between north and south and country and city. "These are the weak points of our social, economic, and political structure. There is less of a contrast than in Spain or Latin America; but there are some of the same characteristics. This makes for social and political instability."

In foreign policy, Nenni said: "We don't pose the problem of being in or out of NATO. We accept the fact of membership. The question is what we should do both inside and outside the alliance. We would like to see

Italy active in the quest for peaceful solutions, for disarmament, an end to nuclear tests. It is a question of which role we play—that of a Dulles or that of a Macmillan."

The "objective" differences between Russia and China were more important than the "subjective" differences. China was in the Stalinist phase of the early 1930s and the first Plans. Russia was already a stable, advanced society with problems of production and consumption. Therefore, Russia wants international détente and progress on disarmament while China is more interested in the struggle against colonialism.

ROME, *April 5, 1962*

LUNCHED with Enrico Mattei, said to be the most powerful man in Italy and chief of the national fuel trust. En route to his private dining room in the Hotel Eden, Mattei was accompanied by his bodyguard. He has had permanent protection since he received threatening letters from the OAS, which dislikes his North African oil maneuvers.

Mattei said:

For me, Italy had to make this experiment of an opening to the left. This is only a start. The country must gain on the social plan and social justice. I have followed these principles in terms of what might be called friendship with the neutrals because I have been working to extend friendly relations in Africa and the Middle East for years. You must remember that Nenni's party supported Mollet in France on the Suez adventure. But now he seems to have changed. He is following me. I don't stay behind. I am ahead.

I am personally against NATO and for neutralism. We Italians have nothing to gain from NATO. I believe our country can advance its own prestige by its own work. Everyone abroad keeps saying that Italy doesn't have the qualities of hard work and production techniques. They think of us as a country of the *dolce far niente*. That isn't true. Everybody, starting with the British, always says that the Italians are only fit for music, song, and wine. For years we have only exported men as laborers; we have not exported goods.

I was astounded by Mattei's inferiority complex. It is both personal and national. He simply couldn't avoid showing it on and on and on. For example, he told me the following strange tale.

In 1958, he celebrated Christmas in Poland—with a group of Communists—Russians, Poles, Hungarians, Czechoslovakians, East Germans, and one Chinese. They all sang because of the holiday and then at the end they asked him to sing. He apologized and said he didn't know how. He claimed they were appalled and said: "But every Italian sings." His rueful comment was that even behind the Iron Curtain they considered Italy a song and dance country.

He then made the curious remark that both Fanfani and Gronchi shared his own ideas of neutralism but were forced to keep this secret. Officially they were opposed to him, but in private they were with him.

He made a long pitch for aid to China. He said:

There are no Russian technicians left in China now. They have all gone. And the Russians have begun to charge China in foreign currency for aid debts. There is a big vacuum and the West should move in and help China to develop. If the West doesn't, who will? Obviously it will be Japan. We must help China and maybe by doing this we will isolate Russia.

I asked him if it were true that he was really bitterly anti-American. He replied quite frankly: "Yes, I am anti-American. We need to work here. We need to export the product of our work. We need cheap oil. And yet you try to keep us out of markets abroad. Your policy is run by your oil companies. I agree with Khrushchev that the oil companies run American policy."

Mattei said the Mediterranean basin with all its petroleum and natural gas would come to be a future "Ruhr," providing the energy for a new wave of industrialization in Europe. Italy was in the center of this, and thanks to its geographical position and its ports, it would be the fulcrum. This he regarded as an economic law, a historical necessity. It was inevitable and inescapable.

Mattei said there were two real forces in Italy today: the church and communism. He admitted that he was "tougher" and more hostile to other western countries now because "everybody has been against me." He made an astonishing boast when we were talking about China. He referred to his fuel center at Metanopoli. He said: "The republic of Italy has not yet recognized China, but the republic of Metanopoli has." He had made a $200,-000,000 a year trade agreement with China—half for exports and half for imports.

I asked Mattei what he would like to be doing in ten years' time—when he is sixty-five. Without hesitation he replied "go fishing." Fishing is his only other passion in life besides oil. Apart from that I think he just occasionally amuses himself with high-priced whores.

This evening, I saw Prime Minister Fanfani. He is now installed in the former Foreign Office, the Palazzo Chigi. Fanfani received me warmly— despite the contretemps I had with him in late 1958, when I wrote a series of columns about his so-called Mau Mau. No mention was made of the past. He is a very short, little man, now running to weight, and his hair has turned gray.

I asked if he thought Britain would come into the Common Market, and told him Adenauer had seemed optimistic, but I was more skeptical. He replied: "I am convinced Britain will come in—and soon. I have thought so, indeed, for years. I used to be alone in my thinking, but now everybody else is coming around. De Gaulle told me that he wants Britain in. He only wonders if it will be possible in terms of Britain's Commonwealth obligations. De Gaulle has big dreams about the project, but I think the most practical thing is for us to start with what is possible right now."

I told Fanfani I was worried about the strength of neutralism in Italy. I referred to the fact that Nenni had told me of his own neutralist ideas, that these accorded with Mattei's, that Mattei had admitted to me that he was anti-NATO. Fanfani replied:

Mattei is not against the Alliance. [This certainly does not jibe with what Mattei told me.] But he doesn't like the war made against him by the members of the Alliance. [This refers to oil competition from American, British, French, and Dutch firms.] At any rate, we don't listen to Mattei on foreign policy. We only listen to him on petroleum.

As for the neutralism of Nenni—that is already a conversion from his position of a few years earlier. Then he was openly pro-Moscow. One must remember where he started. Where was Nenni two years ago on communism, on foreign policy, on economic policy? That is what must be remembered.

The Americans have been very stupid not to contact Mattei directly. He feels like a hurt woman. I told President Eisenhower twice that I thought it would be a wise thing for the United States to invite Mattei on a visit. Each time Eisenhower agreed—but nothing was done. Then last year I said the same thing to President Kennedy. He agreed. But no one did anything about it.

I asked Fanfani what were the minimum social goals of his present operation of the "opening to the left." He replied:

The political goals are to try and reform democracy in Italy and win the Socialists over from communism. It became obvious that it was necessary to divide the Socialists from the Communists.

We saw the experience of reforms in your country under Franklin Roosevelt and also the French experience and how these managed to reduce friction and dispersion by governmental directions. This is what we are after.

PARIS, *April 18, 1962*

DINNER with Henry Byroade, ambassador in Afghanistan until last January. He is now the top State Department man in Bill Foster's Disarmament Agency.

Byroade is hard working and intelligent, but says he still can't understand the language of disarmament. And yet he had to present our treaty draft to NATO. He complained the State Department should have been prepared last March with some kind of draft to table because it was well known the Russians were going to table their own version. Ever since the Russian plan was put forth at Geneva, we have been under enormous pressure from the neutrals there to produce a plan of our own. Byroade and his associates have been working at top speed ever since.

At my house, where we went for drinks after dinner, Byroade admitted he had made a mistake in suggesting the "northern-tier" or Baghdad Pact alliance to Dulles. The words "northern-tier" were his own phrase. He now agrees with me that it would have been wiser to revive the Saadabad Pact, linking Turkey, Iraq, Iran, and Afghanistan, instead of creating the Baghdad Pact (now CENTO). Nobody in the State Department really knew very much about the Middle East in those days.

It would have been sensible for Washington to give Nasser arms—instead of pushing him into the Soviet arms deal—because we would have kept control of the supply of spare parts. But the State Department ignored his recommendations as ambassador to Egypt.

PARIS, *April 20, 1962*

LUNCHED with Gavin. The last time he saw de Gaulle, the General said the Common Market could never admit "the Commonwealth." Gavin thinks he really meant England.

Gavin is haunted by a fear that Macmillan is going to offer de Gaulle nuclear aid in exchange for his OK on England joining the Market. This will leave the U.S.A. on a hook and getting no benefit from the orders for nuclear equipment.

He thinks the plan for a supranational NATO force is no good. We would have to change our laws to bring it about. As the law stands, we cannot give our allies the power to get us involved in a war. The present concept is that there could be nuclear submarines put at the disposal of the alliance but with American commanders in charge.

WEST BERLIN, *April 24, 1962*

LONG talk with General Lucius Clay in his office at American headquarters on Clayallee. I wanted to know what essential changes there had been in U.S. Berlin policy since 1960. He answered:

In our expressed policy we have made stronger commitments under this administration than in the past—starting with Vice President Johnson's visit to West Berlin after the wall was erected. We have specifically and openly pledged to insist on maintenance of access on the ground, unrestricted air access, and the protection of freedom. And we have precisely pledged ourselves to maintain Berlin's economic viability. We have said that we support maintenance of the existing ties between West Berlin and the Federal Republic—although we have not accepted these ties on the same basis. We are also committed to maintain U.S. forces here as long as this is desired by the people of West Berlin. Thus, this administration has publicly strengthened our commitments.

But, I wondered, would it ever be possible for us to work out an agreement which, by bringing in more nations and organizations, could forestall future attempts by the Russians to apply a Berlin squeeze? He thought it was a good idea to bring in more nations on new agreements covering either ground or air access. There would have to be concurrent agreements with both West and East Germany on such access rights in order to get a complete package. However, the real essential guarantee in West Berlin was to maintain the strength of NATO and our own relative nuclear advantage over Russia. This was the only way to insure agreements entered into would be self-enforcing.

What had made the present negotiations with Moscow on Berlin possible was the evidence of our intention to increase military strength. If all the NATO allies had behaved with similar resolve, there probably never would have been a 1961 Berlin crisis.

Incidentally, Clay spoke very bitterly about de Gaulle and said his attitude was nonsensical—the insistence on not even talking about Berlin. The point was we should always talk, but we should talk about what was currently important. If the Russians were buzzing airplanes we should talk about buzzing airplanes. "Nothing is ever gained by not talking. To talk doesn't mean to yield. If you are molested, you talk about being molested—and not about negotiations."

Clay insisted: "With the commitments we have made, Berlin is as secure from the point of view of investment as any city in Europe. The real problem is the difficulty of getting in and out. Workers, for example, cannot count on driving off for the weekend without being arrested."

I asked him if we should do something about knocking down the wall. He said the time was "not yet ripe." It would have to be done during a period of tension or when we had given up all hope of settlement by negotiation. This would not be a popular action to take under present conditions. Undoubtedly a lot of people would get killed in such an action, and the allies must be fully ready in advance to support it.

I asked Clay how we could be absolutely positive the Russians could realize we were ready to fight for West Berlin after we had done nothing for Budapest in 1956, or in Berlin last August 13. He said the answer was "Friedrichstrasse." That was where U.S. and Soviet tanks met head on on October 23, 1961, in the first direct American-Russian confrontation of the Cold War. "And the Russians didn't like it. They retreated and tried to paint off Soviet insignias from their tanks so they would look like East

Germans. The next morning they barricaded their tanks in the rear and tried to hide them."

PARIS, May 7, 1962

GAVIN has come back from Washington glum and disappointed. Apparently he didn't even fight for his views on this last trip. He saw it was useless and that all he would do would be to damage his cause and make personal enemies. He thinks the best thing to do now is to lie low and stay out of the public prints for some weeks and, above all, not let it be known that he came back with empty hands.

The President explained to him the whole question of nuclear aid to France had been shelved for the moment. It is in the icebox. So is the prospect of any de Gaulle-Kennedy meeting. The decision was not taken as a result of any National Security Council accord. Instead there was a private meeting in the White House attended only by the President, Rusk, Bundy and McNamara. Both Rusk and Bundy produced long arguments against giving any nuclear aid to France.

Gavin is very gloomy. He saw Professor Kissinger, who shares his views, and who told him he was positive the President would have to reverse himself within a year. But Gavin thinks this may be too late and at best we would not get any quid pro quo from France, not even any gratitude.

When Macmillan saw Kennedy he painted a black picture. He said it was absolutely imperative for England to get into the Common Market. If she did not succeed she might have to withdraw her troops from Europe and eventually even quit NATO. We expect the British were exaggerating but nevertheless it is clear they are in a position where they may feel forced to help the French.

The State Department is convinced de Gaulle will not be indefinitely at the helm in France and that things will change when he is done. Gavin says he has argued that de Gaulle will be around a long time and that he has left such an impress that even when he goes his policies will continue.

ROCQUENCOURT, FRANCE, May 8, 1962

INTERESTING talk with Norstad this morning. I was struck by his judgment, firmness of attitude, and moderation of language as shown in the Berlin crisis. He read me some of his top-secret telegrams during the worst period; they were admirable.

Larry said there really had been quite a stink after I published my column to the effect that General Wheeler would replace him next winter as supreme commander. Practically all the NATO ambassadors produced official protests from their governments to the effect that the United States had no right to take a decision like this, that NATO only had the right to accept resignations and nominate successors. However, everything is now going well.

Larry remarked with a sour smile that he saw I was criticizing our policy of not giving the French nuclear aid. He was glad that at last we had made up our mind instead of diddling the French, but he personally thought it was a wise decision. The American people were not prepared to support such aid and de Gaulle himself realized this.

There really was no military significance to the pledge of the United States to place five Polaris submarines under NATO control. The submarines were already based at Holy Loch. All the pledge means is that they will now stay in the North Atlantic area unless granted permission by the alliance to leave. "You cannot double the effect of the same number of missiles," he said.

We talked at great length about Berlin. It was clear Norstad thought Lucius Clay too excitable and changeable, although he had done a very good job on restoring morale during the crisis of last autumn and winter. Norstad had vetoed Clay's desire to have planes fly in above the altitude of 10,000 feet and also to send fighters as escorts. The essence of the problem was to maintain access to Berlin and we would fly in planes above 10,000 feet when it was technically needed. It is not yet needed.

On March 14, Norstad advised Washington that the U.S. should be prepared if necessary to go it alone in Berlin, but that it would be far more desirable to have the support of Britain and France, which also had garrisons there, because of the effect on NATO. Our prime objective, he said, was to assure safe air access to Berlin; and we were doing as much.

In a secret cable to Washington on March 10, when the Russians started flying planes in the corridors at altitudes between 7–10,000 feet—used by most of our aircraft—and dropping chaff, Norstad urged that we act "quietly, promptly, and firmly," but without the use of fighters, and merely flying through. The Soviets soon abandoned this unprecedented effort to interfere at our usual flight levels.

PARIS, *May 9, 1962*

DINED with Brosio, the Italian ambassador. He says de Gaulle sees clearly that Britain's membership in the Common Market will completely change the kind of Europe he wants. It would be dominated by Britain and Germany instead of by France with German support.

He is alarmed about U.S. negotiating techniques. Washington continues to give and gets nothing in return. Brosio adds that we help Russia by withholding nuclear aid from our allies.

Brosio expressed surprise at the degree of Rusk's personal vindictiveness toward de Gaulle. Last December, he accompanied Segni on a visit to Rusk during the NATO meeting. Rusk, in a rage, kept wondering aloud whether France was "worth it."

PARIS, *May 16, 1962*

TOM Finletter bought lunch today. I said there was curious inconsistency in our NATO policy. We had always supported the idea of a U.S.-U.K.-French Standing Group—even when France had no armed forces—and yet we had always opposed the idea of a similar political Standing Group. Likewise, we gave the British nuclear cooperation while refusing it to the French. Finletter agreed. He had attended a briefing on the Christmas Island atomic tests and only prayed that no Frenchman would find out the extent of our cooperation with the British.

I called up Gavin this afternoon to firm up our golf date for tomorrow. He speculated about tomorrow's weather. I said I did not think it would be any more disagreeable than the conversation he had had at lunch today. (Gavin lunched with de Gaulle.) He seemed startled and said: "What did you hear? Do you mean to say you have already heard about my luncheon?"

I said, "Certainly, I have all kinds of little canary birds that come in the windows all the time."

He said, "Well, it certainly was a frank talk, I will tell you about it tomorrow."

I said I thought that he and I were being squeezed into a corner together. He chuckled and replied: "Let's add Kissinger. He told me when I saw him at Harvard during my recent trip home that the White House had asked him to come down to discuss policy. Kissinger said the hell with it; he disagreed with our German policy, our French policy, and everything else and there wasn't any point. Let's include him in our corner," said Gavin.

PARIS, *May 17, 1962*

LUNCHED and golfed with Gavin. Jim said he had found de Gaulle friendly and optimistic. De Gaulle told Gavin that he thought he had been very kind to the U.S. in his press conference Tuesday. Gavin pointed out that American reaction had not been favorable and the press was hostile. "J'ai l'habitude," de Gaulle replied.

PARIS, *May 21, 1962*

LUNCHED with General Paul Stehlin at his air ministry private dining room. I was interested to note antiaircraft guns still mounted because of the OAS, although I didn't see any soldiers. Stehlin said they were probably asleep.

He said France has had five explosions of atomic equipment so far but does not yet possess a bomb. De Gaulle doesn't understand nuclear questions at all and has never seen an explosion. The General hates the words "integration" and "association" but he likes the word "cooperation." Thus he is willing to talk about possibly cooperating with other countries of Europe on nuclear matters, but not to "associate."

Jouhaud should not be executed. Paul knows him well. They overlapped at St. Cyr. He is nice but stupid and uncultivated and should never have been promoted above the rank of brigadier general. He comes from a poor *pied-noir* family and was speaking the truth when he said all he possessed was a few meters of cemetery space. Salan is different. He is more intelligent and governed by ambition. But Stehlin does not believe he should be executed; he opposes capital punishment.

Stehlin admitted that the French gaseous-diffusion plant under construction is costing a fortune—much more than was anticipated or is yet admitted. The concept of a French striking force based on atomic bombs in the Mirage IV is silly because it will be outmoded before it is even started. When he discusses such things with de Gaulle, the General takes the view that either there will be no war at all or it will be over at the start, "it" being the entire world.

De Gaulle has the curious and illogical argument that if, for example, Moscow sends an ultimatum and orders France to put in a government under Maurice Thorez and France refuses, Moscow might give point to its argument by destroying Lyon. De Gaulle then says he would reply by destroying Kiev. But this is pointless. The Russians would have no interest in destroying Lyon. All his approach assures is that Europe would be destroyed before America in any conceivable war.

Stehlin is acutely aware of the growth of anti-American sentiment in France. One of his officers recently prepared a report for him and there was an anti-American statement within the first few lines. Stehlin announced to his entire staff: "I agree with you that every single thing going wrong in France is the fault of the Americans. Everything. As a result I don't want to ever hear you accuse the Americans again either orally or on paper. I will not have any more of this."

PARIS, *May 23, 1962*

I WENT to the Salan trial this afternoon at the Palais de Justice. It is strange to see him in the dock between two gendarmes. The top of his hair is still dyed reddish-brown, which was part of his disguise at the time he was captured. However, the temples have grown back white. He looks pale but relaxed.

What a contrast to see him in new civilian clothes, faced by a court either in uniform or in scarlet and ermine medieval robes, the lawyers wearing black gowns with white cravats and ribbon decorations.

PARIS, *May 31, 1962*

LUNCHED with Jean-Marie Soutou, head of the European section of the Quai d'Orsay, a brilliant young man. Soutou lunched at the Elysée twenty days ago. De Gaulle was relaxed and absolutely brilliant: vibrant, active, and warm. Tuesday, Soutou was back for the ceremony at which the new Albanian minister presented his letters of credence. He was appalled at the change in de Gaulle—old, tired, feeble, haggard. De Gaulle assembled his staff prior to receiving the Albanian. There were four colonels and a general in the military group. De Gaulle said to them: "For that Communist only one officer is necessary." Four of them left. De Gaulle gave a brief talk to the Albanian, saying France had had relations with his country for a long time and it was unnecessary to say anything else.

If England does get into the Common Market, it will change completely. If England does not get in, the Common Market will disintegrate. If England is not admitted, the Conservative government will fall. Chauvel, in his last telegram to the Quai d'Orsay this spring before leaving as French ambassador in London, predicted that if Britain is kept out of the Common Market the Tories will fall and that they will *never* forget that France was responsible and will become anti-French for years to come.

French insistence on becoming a nuclear power predates and will postdate de Gaulle. Europe will never accept the possibility of depending wholly upon American atomic support. What would happen if at some future date the Russians grabbed Lübeck in a *coup d'état* with purely conventional forces and then said they were prepared to negotiate? The U.S. knows that by 1966, the initial casualties in a nuclear war would probably amount to 75,000,000 dead. Would we be willing automatically to pay this horrible figure because Lübeck had been captured? The French doubt it. After all, what would France or other European countries do to help the U.S.A. in Cuba? The answer is nothing.

It is inescapable and unavoidable that France should want nuclear weapons of its own, even if on a minor scale, because without them France could have no pretensions to being a power of any sort. De Gaulle may not understand all the military implications of nuclear arms, but he does understand the political implications.

The U.S. operates on a false equation. We think first of all that we can get the Europeans to produce conventionally armed defenses while we keep the nuclear key to ourselves. Europe is not psychologically or politically ready to provide conventional armed Janissaries for the West, all alone. If Europe has no nuclear arms of its own it is bound in the end to become neutral.

The U.S. is wrong in thinking that Britain will give up its own national nuclear strength. This would mean yielding an excuse for its presently favored position with the U.S. It would also mean yielding the only trump it has vis-à-vis Europe, in a diplomatic bargaining sense.

The U.S. was probably not aware of the fact that France had made enormous scientific advances in its nuclear explorations—even if it remained well behind in its military potential. In fact, the French had been able to give Israel secrets of potentially vast importance which were causing a great deal of alarm in the Arab world.

PARIS, *June 7, 1962*

LUNCHED today with Stikker (NATO secretary-general) at his apartment in the George V. He found it more convenient than the NATO house for the secretary-general on the Villa Said.

Stikker is convinced de Gaulle has now decided to accept Britain into the Common Market because Macmillan persuaded him he was genuinely "European" in last weekend's talks. Brosio saw de Gaulle earlier this week, after the talks, and this was the impression he received. As a result, Brosio has wired Rome that they should stop trying to search for a compromise formula—Italy's role in recent weeks—because the whole matter is settled.

Stikker is disturbed by the lack of an American approach to NATO for help on South America. When Walt Rostow talked to NATO on this subject, he made an exceedingly bad impression. All he did was try and offer platitudinous excuses for our failure in Cuba. He showed unwillingness to consult in any serious way on the real problems of Latin America. A U.S. "Monroe Doctrine complex" always interferes.

There are problems about NATO MRBM missiles. One idea being studied is putting missiles on a barge that can be towed around in shallow water— for example off the coast of Holland or Greece. These barges could continually be moved around. It is also feasible to put missiles on trailers or railway cars to be moved around continually. The bridge and tunnel structure of Europe would permit this. Finally there will be a certain number of permanent hard-sited missiles.

In September, 1960, when the Norstad plan for NATO nuclear missile force was endorsed at Como by Adenauer, Spaak, and Stikker, the meeting had been actually held for another purpose. The U.S., at that time, was concerned about Algeria and considering taking active steps in support of the Muslim rebels. Adenauer was persuaded to take the lead in blocking this and a telegram was drafted there which was then sent by Norstad to Washington begging that we should do nothing. Only after this was the nuclear business discussed.

PARIS, *June 8, 1962*

I SAW Couve de Murville and asked him what had provoked the present crisis between France and the United States. He said:

If anything, the accelerated pace of difficulties resulted from the growing crisis between Germany and the U.S.A. The deterioration in Franco-American relations had been developing each month since Kennedy visited Paris in early June, 1961. But more irritation was caused—and increasingly—by Washington's feeling that we had conspired with Germans to disagree with you on Berlin.

It was not a result of the nuclear differences, the nuclear fuss. That is really an American fuss. We don't publish statements on it; you do. We knew the Washington situation. Under the Eisenhower administration we got an agreement for help to France on nuclear submarines, including the provision of one atomic engine. But this had already been canceled under Eisenhower and we never asked for anything else since then.

When Kennedy came in, he put under review all the nuclear problem. He brought into the administration with him a lot of bright boys with big ideas. They discovered that atomic warfare was dangerous and they sought various means of preventing it. They thought that conventional wars were better than atomic wars and therefore they decided to develop conventional arms. They wanted to prevent other nations from having nuclear arms in order to prevent their spread and at the same time the U.S. put its stress on conventional weapons.

All this happened when you Americans discovered that nuclear warfare was as dangerous for you as it was for other nations—after the Russians launched their Sputnik and you realized the implications. But it takes a long time for such developments to penetrate public opinion.

Then, some time ago, there were discussions between the U.S.A. and France on the technical level about military expenditures. These were very high for the U.S., which is worried about its gold leakage. The U.S.A. said it would be helpful to compensate and ease the pressures by selling weapons to us for dollars. France agreed. The U.S.A. said that maybe it could sell the equipment for two divisions to France—the two divisions coming back from Algeria.

France said it intended to reequip these two divisions, but this could be done with French equipment and there was no need to purchase it abroad. But France said maybe it could purchase *other* arms from the U.S.A. As a result of these talks General Lavaud's mission to Washington developed. Lavaud gave you a list of possible purchases in which we might be interested. None of the items was prohibited under the McMahon Act but several were related to nuclear military equipment. Lavaud's list was not accepted.

We had not asked to produce this list. We had not taken this initiative. We had been requested by Washington to act. But naturally we will only buy from the U.S. what is of interest to us, not what is of interest to the U.S. That is where the situation is today.

Relations are undoubtedly bad, but I don't know what we can do. We do not blindly follow U.S. policy. That is the real crisis. And, of course, we are the only country in NATO that takes this viewpoint—of not blindly following U.S. policy.

All we can do is to live with our disagreement. You people have already recognized that the best thing they can do with Russia is to live with their disagreement. Surely it is easier between France and the U.S. than between Russia and the U.S. to live in such a way.

He said that at last weekend's de Gaulle-Macmillan talks: "The nuclear subject was not raised. Britain and France have the same views and the same policy on this question—for the same reasons. But the British were fortunate. They got their nuclear assistance from the U.S.A. under the Eisenhower administration. They could never have received it under the Kennedy administration. That is our bad luck."

He understood that the U.S.A. could not give its nuclear weapons to other powers and that France would have a similar attitude in the same position. But, this being the case, why should the U.S. object to its allies' making their own nuclear weapons?

I asked if France intended to send troops to Southeast Asia under SEATO, even a token force, like the British contribution. He replied: "We will not send any forces. We were never asked to. The decision to send western troops to Southeast Asia was not a SEATO decision. It was an American decision."

I asked if France would be prepared to see an American general named as successor to Norstad at SHAPE. With a shrug he replied: "Who else but an American general if SACEUR is not to be just a figurehead? If a French general, for example, was named, he would have to have at his right hand an American general to do the atomic job under the situation as it now prevails. The only honest solution would be to have an American general."

Couve said the new troubles between France and the U.S.A. had started in June, 1961, right after the Kennedy visit to de Gaulle when the U.S. President continued on to see Khrushchev in Vienna. Kennedy began to diverge from his Paris policy as soon as he got to Vienna.

There was no doubt that if France, Britain, and Germany got together they could produce a nuclear force eventually on the same scale as that of the U.S. and Russia. It was impossible for a nation to be considered a power unless it had its own nuclear force. After all, no nation in preatomic days could consider itself a power if it were minus an army or minus a navy. One had to think of things in this sense.

The U.S.A. was wholly unrealistic in its approach. The only logical thing would have been for Washington to settle this matter in 1945 or 1946. At that time Washington could simply have said to Moscow: "We will destroy you if you start to experiment with atomic weapons." But naturally it was impossible to ever conceive of such a policy. The fact remains that once Russia embarked in the nuclear field, it became too late to try and slam down the lid of the box. Now this was impossible. Many countries besides France could make atomic arms today.

Received June 13, 1962
From Annecy-Geneva

Capitaine Clémence
OAS
Réseau Fidélite-Serment
GAAC

Dear Mr. Sulzberger,

At last in hoping you read me I'm in France after some days in Algeria—1½ hour ago I still was in Geneva as a free man, and now on my land. I have to be prudent if I want to live on to fight the Cos [Communists]. . . .

I, as the chief of the Anti-Communist action group for France and Algeria, and in spite of my bad command of American language, I've to inform you still once that we OAS fight for the Free World against Communism. Yes we are to be defeated very soon. We do know that Algeria will become a "Free" (so to speak) land, and a Communist one too, we do know all that.

Don't you see that this man de Gaulle is a danger for the free world, and for that we are hoping to murder him. Yes we want to replace him with a Pro-American and Anti-Communist government.

Yes we are to kill de Gaulle (that naughty old devil-inspired man). Yes we are to kill him in spite of HIM and of the Communists who thanks to their Soviet-manned spy group do inform de Gaulle of all they know about OAS. . . .

I've seen 5 days ago—General———, Colonel———, ———. And the like, all did tell me to inform you that we are lost and the States too in Algeria. . . .

Be sure that very soon there will be a Saint Bartholomew (as we say in France). . . .

VIVE LA FRANCE et les U.S.A.

PARIS, *June 13, 1962*

LUNCHED today with Burin des Roziers. The Elysée worries that the OAS diehards are transferring their bitterness and their operations to metropolitan France and may continue to try to assassinate de Gaulle. I then told him of a letter I had received from an unknown OAS officer, Captain Clémence, who spoke of OAS determination to "murder" de Gaulle and replace him with a "pro-American" government.

He outlined the Elysée view of Kennedy's "grand design." Washington figures that no matter who starts a war, the U.S.A. must finish it. Therefore, it wishes to eliminate the possibility that any of its allies might be in a position to start a war. For this reason, the U.S. wants to keep control of all nuclear weapons in the West. However, this is a heavy responsibility and costs a great deal. The U.S. would like economic assistance from its allies in order to help support the burden of such responsibility.

From a logical point of view, this policy is comprehensible but it could never be accepted by Europe. The French simply could not place all their reliance upon the U.S. for an indefinite future period. This would put France and other European countries in the position of satellites and ultimately they would lose all interest in their defense. They would not even want to have armies or navies of their own if their only real protection was a U.S. umbrella.

The argument was miscast. Apart from the realities of the situation—which found several countries in a position to manufacture their own nuclear arsenal whether or not France did—France and Europe would be more valuable allies to the U.S.A. if they had some nuclear stockpile of their own. Furthermore, de Gaulle wished to interest the French army in its own atomic military future as part of the aftermath of the Algerian mess.

Etienne admitted quite frankly that France wished to keep Germany divided and not reunited. He said it was necessary to recognize a certain de facto status quo in Europe as it now is. Once bilateral discussions between Moscow and Washington finally break down, Europe, with French prodding, might wish to start itself on a series of discussions to achieve a de facto settlement of frontiers on the continent.

PARIS, *June 14, 1962*

TALKED with Gavin for an hour this morning. Gavin thinks the U.S. must either change its policy toward de Gaulle and cooperate with him or make the tough decision to isolate and ultimately overthrow him. I said I thought either decision was unnecessary; it was better to wait six months.

Gavin said Strauss (Bonn's defense minister) was now in the U.S. where he had already contracted to purchase about $120,000,000 worth of Pershing missiles. Technically, these were still listed as having short range (under 400 miles), but in fact they could easily be souped up to 800 or more miles and were in reality MRBMS. The Germans will thus not only have access to guidance systems and their operation—which we are still refusing to the French—but will also have the missiles themselves.

Lunched with Y. He told me that in September, 1961, at UN, Rusk and Gromyko reached a private understanding: both Russia and the U.S. would do their best to prevent proliferation of nuclear weapons. In reality, this meant the U.S. would keep them from Germany and France and Russia would keep them from China. On its part, Russia promised also not to try to cut off our access rights to Berlin. Had France been wise enough to keep active as one of the Big Three western powers it could have prevented this foolish deal—because obviously Russia doesn't want to give atomic arms to China.

Y is impressed by Pompidou's method of operating with de Gaulle. De Gaulle will say to Pompidou that it would be simply terrible to do such and such a thing—in terms of foreign policy. Pompidou will nod agreement and say, "You are indeed right, General, I will prepare my views and bring them back to you." A day or two later he will come back with a paper stating in effect: "The first alternative you have presented is certainly very disagreeable. But the only other two choices are as follows: the second choice is clearly out of the question and the third choice is impossible." De Gaulle will then nod grudgingly and say, "I agree with you, Pompidou. Obviously, the only solution is choice number one. Go ahead and do what you want on it."

French intelligence managed to get recordings of private conversations between Gajewski, the Polish envoy, and Vinogradov, the Soviet ambassador, in which Gajewski was talking about the Americans and the West in exactly the same way he speaks to Westerners about Russia.

PARIS, *June 18, 1962*

MOST agreeable luncheon with Pompidou in his private dining room in the Hotel Matignon. There were six of us: in addition to the Prime Minister and myself, Alain Peyrefitte (minister of information), Colonel Jean Deguil, Robert de Souza, and Christian Chavanon. Deguil, who used to be General Ely's directeur de cabinet, is now Pompidou's military aide. De Souza is Pompidou's military aide and liaison with the Quai d'Orsay. Chavanon is a *maître des requêtes au Conseil d'Etat* and director of the Agence Havas.

While we were having a glass of sherry, I asked Pompidou why the OAS wanted to assassinate de Gaulle. He said diehards wanted to kill de Gaulle for two reasons: to take personal vengeance on the man they blame for all their troubles and also to establish their own government.

In January, 1960, at the time of the "barricades" incident, the Algérie Française people had circulated a list of a future "French government" with Pinay as President and Bidault as foreign minister. Juin would have been minister of defense and Lacoste Lareymondie minister of finance. "Fortunately," Pompidou added, "I was in America so I did not figure on the list." There was ample indication that Bidault and Soustelle were sympathetic to the OAS.

Pompidou said that in a sense there were only two parties in France today—the government and the opposition. The opposition, apart from the Communists, was made up of the active Vichyists, including the Independents and part of the Radicals. He stressed: "When I say active Vichyists I mean *active*. After all, 90 percent of France was Vichyist at one time or another."

I asked Pompidou how he thought it would be possible to find a compromise between the U.S. and French policy. He looked at me somewhat quizzically and asked if I had read McNamara's speech. There was no chance of a compromise between McNamara's speech and the French viewpoint. He thought it was a lack on the part of the French that they had not produced their own objective propositions for a NATO program. Peyrefitte interrupted and said de Gaulle's September, 1958, letter still served as the basis. Pompidou added that this had never been answered.

He thought it essential that England join the Common Market and was confident that England had a view of "confederated" Europe similar to de Gaulle's. This new "Europe" would establish its own nuclear force based upon an initial British and French contribution. This force would then be tied into NATO by treaties within the alliance obligating its use in a way similar to the pledges of other forces under the allies, including the U.S. strategic bombing force.

At one point, we discussed the secret Rusk-Gromyko compact banning proliferation of nuclear assistance in exchange for a Russian guarantee on Berlin access. Pompidou talked happily about this. He said France did not want to be put in the position of paying the price of keeping West Berlin free.

He said that in Athens during the NATO meeting, Rusk had indicated a desire to come to France in July. This visit was clearly a result of Rusk's intention to visit Germany and the obvious implication that a visit just to Germany, without France, would be tactless. He then turned to me and said, puffing a cigar after luncheon:

> Let me tell you—not as Prime Minister but as a Frenchman. If the U.S.A. ever tries to turn against us—for example by trying to break our good relations with Germany—we will turn to Russia. This will be a third force. Such is the normal law of politics. If your friend turns against you, you turn toward your enemy. This is precisely what happened with the OAS vis-à-vis de Gaulle. The OAS decided that de Gaulle was an enemy so it turned toward its real enemy, the FLN.

I asked him how presidential candidates would be nominated, and he said there would not be any problem there. After all, France had always been able to choose its Prime Ministers from among many parties and could choose its President the same way. The net result would be that France would either have a strong President or a strong Prime Minister. De Gaulle was very much hipped on the idea of trying to give as much prestige as possible to his successor and he was increasingly concerned with the problem of succession. But Pompidou thought frankly that it was impossible for de Gaulle to pass on such prestige.

He said there was a lot of confused talk about a presidential system. I added I had received the impression from de Gaulle that he did not want a vice president, and it was not a question of this. Pompidou said with a somewhat sardonic smile, "It depends on the day. Some days, the General is very much in favor of a vice president and some days he is very much opposed."

Pompidou talked at length about the French nuclear program. This was not a de Gaulle policy but a French policy. Colonel Deguil then interrupted and said, "I know from my own experience—before de Gaulle took over —Mr. Sulzberger used to talk with General Ely when he explained the need for a French nuclear force." Pompidou took this up and added, "It is both pre-de Gaulle and post-de Gaulle. Americans make a great mistake if they don't understand this."

He then went back to his earlier observations that if the U.S.A. tried to wreck the rapprochement of France and Germany it would be a fatal mistake. He said France was going to make a major effort on Adenauer's visit next month in order to get the idea across to public opinion that France and Germany were friends and allies. "If we don't succeed in this with Adenauer," he added, "we will never succeed with any German."

He said the important aspect of the de Gaulle-Macmillan conversations had been Macmillan's insistence that joining Europe was a "political" not an "economic" thing. It was not just a question of adhering to the Rome Treaty of the Common Market, but a matter of changing the whole impetus of British policy. This clearly had its ultimate implications in terms of developing a European nuclear striking force.

The American attitude towards national nuclear forces was simply impossible. He said that, after all, China would be an atomic power within five years.

France and the U.S.A. could live with their present differences. After all, they had had very strong differences on Laos and they still got along. We were now for the neutralization of Laos. We even might be for the neutralization of South Vietnam in the near future. We had different views on Berlin conversations with the Russians, but we still remained friends.

Rather to my astonishment, Pompidou asked me where I got my sunburn and I told him trout fishing in Normandy. He asked me how I fished and I said dry fly. He remarked that was difficult and then said I would be most surprised to know how he fished trout. "A la main," he continued. (In English "trout tickling.")

PARIS, *June 19, 1962*

YESTERDAY afternoon, after finishing work, I went to see Gavin. I asked if he would mind taking a walk for ten or fifteen minutes, so he put his briefcase and mine in his car and told the driver to meet us near the Rond-Point. In the street, I told him it seemed perfectly logical to me that his embassy was being tapped since, after all, I had been told the Russian embassy was tapped and that they had got records of the ambassador's private talks and distributed them to the Quai d'Orsay. There was nothing superconfidential about what I wanted to pass on but, since I didn't work for the U.S. government, I didn't want to give the French the impression I did and that I rushed to tell him everything they told me. Nevertheless, considering the fact the Rusk was arriving the next day, I thought he should know what my host at luncheon had told me, above all the warnings not to try to break up the Franco-German entente and also the warnings that if we got nasty to the French they might turn eastward.

Gavin said he had previously suspected there were "bugs" in his office, and he had mentioned this once before. This worries him.

He told me the Malraux-Kennedy conversations were very tough— despite the cordial propaganda put out—and that after Malraux came back Gavin detected a change in the French attitude. De Gaulle had been very nice to him a few days before Malraux returned, but then, after he had talked with Malraux, the General was quite nasty at their next meeting.

Gavin reported this to Washington and Mac Bundy called up to ask what it was all about. Gavin cautioned Bundy on the telephone that their conversation was certainly being listened to but Bundy didn't seem to care.

Jim thinks Kennedy is too influenced by Francophobes. Nor does he see how seriously damaging McNamara's speech was at this moment. Some NATO members are angry that McNamara chose to make a public speech repeating the substance of a secret speech to the Athens Alliance meeting— without advising in advance that this would be declassified. He asked rhetorically: "Is Washington just trying to go out of its way to make my mission a failure? The way things are going we might as well break relations right now."

Today, lunched with Louis Joxe, now minister of Algerian affairs. He is concerned about the state of Franco-U.S. relations. The timing of Rusk's visit here is unfortunate and nothing can come out of it. It would be a serious mistake to try and arrange a de Gaulle-Kennedy meeting for a long time to come. It is just silly to send a Secretary of State on a trip that can produce nothing. There is a serious gap between France and the U.S. The Americans have not been careful enough to try and analyze the realities of the French viewpoint and, for that matter, the European viewpoint.

He says de Gaulle will undoubtedly finish his term in office. He will then be almost seventy-five and will surely want to quit. The trouble is to find any kind of system to follow. There is a curious direct relationship between de Gaulle and the country which has been made possible by television. The normal middleman role between the voting public and the government that used to be occupied by the parties and the politicians has been eliminated and Joxe is very puzzled about how it can be either re-created or substituted for. Whatever happens, he says, the old Fourth Republic system won't come back.

The government was genuinely worried last week about the possibility that de Gaulle might be assassinated. A police guard was placed around him plus UNR party barbouzes. Joxe himself has been getting plenty of threats. For a long time, the OAS didn't menace him and respected him for not having changed his opinion, the way Debré did, and for trying to do something for the European minority in Algeria. But that is over. Joxe never tells anybody where he is going because he thinks this is the best precaution you can take. "Also I am well guarded."

He thought I was wise not to identify Bidault with the OAS despite Salan's letter saying that Bidault was its chief, "because after all somebody could say he was the chief of the FLN and it would prove nothing." He likes Bidault and says they were in the same "promotion" entering the government service. He is just sorry for him. As for Soustelle, he says he wanders in a cloud of conspiracy and loves it. "What a pity," he adds, "he was such a good archeologist. He should have stayed in Mexico."

PARIS, *June 21, 1962*

CHIP Bohlen dropped in for a drink, here as part of Rusk's entourage. I asked about the Rusk-Gromyko deal of September—refusal to proliferate atomic arms on both sides plus Soviet guarantee to keep Berlin access open. He denies there was a "deal," only agreement to discuss—if Berlin worked out.

I said I didn't disbelieve him but he should convince the French. Even if the "deal" isn't a fact, it is a fact that they think it is and they feel the U.S.A. is, in effect, making France pay the price of keeping our access to Berlin. He was horrified and said he wished he had known this before Rusk saw Pompidou. "Why doesn't Gavin report this?" he asked.

PARIS, *June 22, 1962*

LAST night at dinner, General Stehlin told me France's nuclear arms policy was started by the government of Felix Gaillard in 1957–1958 and not by the government of Guy Mollet in 1956. After Suez, Mollet agreed on a blueprint for such a policy but was politically too wobbly to put it through.

It was Gaillard who took the actual decision. De Gaulle adopted it and pushed it further.

PARIS, *June 25, 1962*

DINED last night with Professor Henry Kissinger. I was surprised at how young he is—only about thirty-eight. He was a private in the last war and didn't finish college until 1946. He started out as a professor of government. Tom Finletter sent him a letter some years ago via Arthur Schlesinger and it was as a result of his reply to this that he was brought into the government as an adviser on nuclear strategy.

Kissinger told me he ceased being adviser to the administration because he simply could not bring himself to argue in favor of theories he didn't believe. Our nuclear policy is crazy and we don't take into account basic political and human facts. There is absolutely no escaping the existence of a French national atomic force.

PARIS, *June 26, 1962*

SPENT yesterday with Couve de Murville, golfing at Morfontaine, then having gin and tonics, finally a late lunch. Very agreeable. He plays poor golf but enjoys it and is perfectly good-natured about the disasters that occur.

He thinks the only way the U.S. can solve the problem of gold leakage is by revaluing the dollar, sometime probably in one to three years. After all, the last revaluation was in 1933—almost thirty years ago. Therefore this would not so much be a revaluation as an adjustment. He thought we were spending too much overseas and wasting money in some of our defense installations and these could be cut down. But a basic decision would have to be taken eventually. Raising the price of gold would benefit South Africa and Russia, but this would be merely an initial benefit and ultimately there would have to be a whole series of international currency adjustments.

Couve told me that no matter what crises arose, he sleeps well at night. One of the first things de Gaulle asks a statesman he has never met before is how he sleeps. De Gaulle feels this is very indicative of a man's inner repose and capability as a leader. The General always sleeps well.

Couve expressed serious concern about Strauss. He considered him able and energetic but without principles. He was convinced Strauss was working to have Erhard succeed Adenauer as Chancellor because Erhard was weak and was old and Strauss wanted to make a play to succeed him—after the failure of an Erhard government.

Couve said that when Rusk was here, "Dean asked me how we felt about preventing the proliferation of nuclear weapons. I told him the last chance to prevent this was in 1945, when you should have sent an ultimatum to Russia warning them not to make the atomic bomb." Of course, Couve said to me, it was impossible for America to do that, philosophically and politically. "I don't think America will send even us an ultimatum," he added with a grin.

Couve thought Adenauer was a very fine man and his influence on German youth had been considerable. Adenauer was so old that he had never been infected by the hysteria and complexes of World Wars I and II. He was sane and normal. But the future of Germany remained a vitally important and dangerous question.

Discussing the origins of French nuclear policy, he said in 1952, the Pinay government had made the first decision to build Marcoule (an atomic pile), which was clearly devoted only to military purposes since there was a decision to make plutonium. The original schedule called for exploding the first bomb in 1960. Mendès-France later endorsed this policy as did the Edgar Faure government in 1956. In 1956, Mollet was worried and postponed the scheduled explosion until 1961, because there was to be another election and he didn't want anything to harm his appeal to the voters. Afterward, the Gaillard government moved this back.

Couve wasn't worried about the possibility of Red Chinese aggression despite the current reports of troops concentrations. These were purely defensive. Australia and Canada were feeding the Chinese. If they didn't do this, China would be weakened by still more starvation, although there would be no serious internal troubles or uprisings.

Ultimately, he sees an inevitable Sino-Soviet split because of the conflict between neighboring great powers. But there is nothing the West can do to accelerate development of such a split. The big problem will ultimately be the question of Chinese immigration into the empty spaces of Siberia— the way they are now immigrating into Mongolia.

PARIS, *June 27, 1962*

THE Gavins gave a dance last night. Various Frenchmen collared me to complain about Kennedy's press conference statement saying again that the U.S. would give no nuclear aid to France. Both General Stehlin and Soutou of the Quai d'Orsay, each of whom is very pro-American, were horrified by the President's use of the word "inimical." Soutou said, "We rarely use that word even vis-à-vis Russia. The U.S. will pay many months for this unnecessary affront."

PARIS, *June 29, 1962*

THIS afternoon, I asked Gavin: "Is Washington trying to cut your throat or to stab you in the back?" I was referring to agency dispatches saying Gavin would soon be replaced by Chip Bohlen.

Jim told me he took this job on the understanding that he would be here no more than eighteen months. His company gave him a year's salary to help him out and indicated it would like to have him back at the end of his service.

He has always planned to leave before two years were up. He is unhappy about the position of his children here; it is not wise to bring up kids "on the streets of Paris." (An odd remark!) He is determined to send them to school in the U.S.A. next September and can't afford to pay for boarding schools and have them fly back here holidays. He would like to terminate his assignment here in September.

Nevertheless, he is clearly hurt by the rumors saying he is on his way out. The State Department has been continually cutting his throat; also Mac Bundy. He finds it increasingly difficult to reach the President. He showed me his correspondence with the President and Rusk. A letter sent by Kennedy on January 4, 1962, said how pleased Kennedy was with the job he had been doing in Paris and described him as "the best envoy we have had there since Franklin." A curious way to reassure a man while cutting his throat. The White House never published an official denial to the rumors circulating last winter about his replacement, despite Gavin's request they do so.

After Gavin talked with the President explaining his desire to leave later this year, Kennedy sent him a letter that was so private he didn't even put it in the top-secret pouch but had a Marine flown over to deliver it by hand. This asked Gavin to make recommendations as to who should succeed him.

On May 23, Gavin replied. He showed me the letter in which he discussed two names they had apparently mentioned in Washington, Barry Bingham and Bohlen. Gavin said in his letter he thought both of them were good men but that the President would be "better served" by Bingham. Gavin contended at length to me that Chip had aged, was no longer "hungry" or "receptive" to new ideas.

Last winter, Gavin had one of his staff inquire why the State Department did not deny rumors that he was going. Bohlen remarked: "But maybe he will be going." Gavin feels hurt.

He has drawn up a letter with the idea of making it public stating why he has to resign to go home in September, after considerably less than two years service. He added to me, after showing me the letter, "After all, lots of ambassadors have served less than two years. Look at the President's father in London." I replied that Joe Kennedy was a disaster in London. Gavin had placed a telephone call to the President in Mexico City, where Kennedy had just begun an official visit. He was going to ask for clearance to publish his letter in the press.

I strongly urged against this. After he had convinced me that he simply must leave in September for family and financial reasons, I urged him at least to ride out the present storm and, only after it had subsided, to make the news public in August when most people would be away on holiday. Thus much less political significance would be read into the change.

Regardless of the facts, the French would immediately interpret his departure as signifying a new and tough U.S. policy toward France, resulting from the nuclear argument. They would say Gavin had been fired because he was known to be sympathetic to the French viewpoint. He thought this was very sound advice and will withhold the letter until August. There the matter rests.

I recalled that many people had been skeptical about his qualifications as an ambassador when he was named and that this included both French and Americans. I reminded him I had been among the skeptics. But I thought he had done a good job and must be very careful not to leave at the wrong moment. He should recognize the significance of this shift.

I told him Chip was one of my closest friends and that naturally it would be a personal pleasure to see him here, but there was no doubt that there would be something behind the implication of a tougher policy.

PARIS, *July 2, 1962*

GOLFED and lunched with Couve de Murville yesterday. He thinks the big worry in West Germany after Adenauer is that there will be an equivalent of France's Fourth Republic—dictatorship by the Parliament and continual shifts in ministers.

There is some logic in the fact that the OAS proclaimed itself as pro-American. The OAS wanted the French army to stay in Algeria and protect France's colonial domain while leaving the protection of France itself to the U.S. and NATO. De Gaulle hopes to change the psychology of the army when it is fully back in France by training with its own nuclear equipment.

Couve told me a bit about his family. One of his ancestors emigrated to Mauritius and stayed there until the English captured it. Then he returned to Marseille and eventually Bordeaux. Couve and his immediate ancestors are from Paris. He still has relatives in Mauritius but has never been there.

The family became Protestant in an unusual way. It used to be Catholic, but after the revolution one of his ancestors and his brother married two Protestant girls and turned Protestant themselves. He has an odd background because it includes French Protestants and English Catholics.

He talked about the rumors that Gavin might be going. He is of the impression that the State Department is pro-French but the White House entourage of the President is anti-French. He bases this on his impressions of Rusk. I think he underestimates anti-French elements in the State Department.

Couve commented sadly on Kennedy's statement last Wednesday opposing French nuclear policy. He had learned that one should never write a letter that one was not prepared to see published and one should make as few speeches as possible and then be very cautious in them.

He spoke warmly of David Bruce and thought him very competent but said he had entirely misunderstood the French attitude toward EDC (European army). Bruce wrongly thought this project would be passed. There was never any chance. But the American government was badly informed and believed its courtiers among the French and those politicians "in its pay."

One grievous tendency of the U.S. now was to interfere in the internal affairs of other countries. The British had done this for years. It seems to be an "Anglo-Saxon habit." He especially blamed the CIA for meddling in French politics.

He much preferred to have U.S. career diplomats here because there was less danger that they would report the situation inaccurately. That is to say, if he had a conference with a career man, he was more confident this conversation would be correctly reported back to Washington. With non-career men, one was forced to depend too much on the second man in the embassy. But he spoke warmly of Gavin.

He was worried about the Algerian situation and said there was going to be a serious struggle for power between extremists and the moderates. In two or three days, the French government will declare Algeria's independence.

Couve said the only basis for NATO was the common interest in the alliance of all its members. Sometimes Americans tended to forget that hard-boiled national interest alone was the basis for alliances. We were not allied in an anti-Communist pact but in a pact to prevent Europe from being overrun by Russia—any kind of Russia.

Alliances often have strange ideological associations. He cited as two instances the U.S. alliance with Russia during World War II, and the alliance between King François I of France and the Sultan of Turkey. As long as France and the U.S. retained the same essential interests they would remain allied.

To my surprise, Couve said this time that Malraux really had no noteworthy conversations in Washington. Malraux didn't understand policy, knew nothing about France's viewpoint, and was not permitted to speak for France in his foreign missions.

PARIS, *July 5, 1962*

WENT over to say good-bye to Gavin and had a nice chat. When he was in the Joint Chiefs of Staff, he took part in all discussion of bombing targets —this was before the era of missiles. There was a big argument about "anti-urban" bombing. Admiral Radford had been opposed to urban bombing as immoral, but a lot of air force people, including General Spaatz, favored it.

There was also a big discussion of the need to "crater" Russian airfields of which we estimated about two hundred would have to be wrecked so their reprisal forces could not take off. This required the use of large nuclear weapons and surface, not air, bursts to insure that runways were put out of action for at least several days. But it was calculated such a heavy fallout would be caused by the number of bombs needed for these surface bursts that perhaps 400,000,000 people would be killed.

Some twenty-five days out of each month the wind patterns of Europe are such that they sweep right across Russia and, incidentally, Japan, which would be obliterated. The only exception is in the southeast where they go down across Greece and Turkey and hook back westward again. In brutal logic, you could start a bomb pattern near the western frontier of the satellites and its effect would sweep on into Russia.

McNamara's counterforce strategy simply doesn't work. Furthermore, seaborne missiles are not accurate enough to strike any but large, immobile military targets and cities. They would be of no use, for example, on 1,500 moving tanks.

He told me he never got through to the President in Mexico but called up Bundy two days ago. They have agreed to work out a release date in early August. He said I had given him very good advice and Washington had played ball accordingly, putting out denials and the matter was now forgotten. Today he lunched with Joxe and Lucet and they seemed to think he was going to be here "forever."

He told Bundy he would like very much to be sure the President carefully read his letter recommending replacements—unless he had already made his decision, in which case it wasn't worthwhile. Bundy said the decision had been made.

LONDON, *July 9, 1962*

DAVID Bruce says Kennedy's "Declaration of Independence" was admired as a speech here, but people are still waiting for a concrete idea. David is confident Macmillan would never make a deal with the French to give them nuclear aid as this would violate the spirit of our agreement with Britain. Anyway, de Gaulle is unbribable.

Dined with the Radziwills who invited me to Ravello with Jackie Kennedy. Stash says the world situation has considerably improved since JFK took over. Incidentally, JFK hates Virginia and Glen Ora, detests horses. Spent his first weekend at Camp David (he had been there one day before) and rather liked it, primarily because it's in Maryland and not Virginia. His back still bothers him and he can't play golf. Stash found him tense.

I WAS received this afternoon by President de Valera in his lovely presidential residence in Phoenix Park, once the home of the English Lord Lieutenants. De Valera was sitting alone at his desk when I was introduced by his aide de camp. He rose fairly briskly but the poor old man is so blind that he extended his hand off at an angle. I shook it and he courteously waved me to an armchair beside his desk.

He is massive, although he is almost eighty, still well over six feet and, except for his eyesight, seems remarkably preserved. He used to be very thin but has filled out. His face is pale and long-featured and he has a slight twitching of the cheeks when he talks. But despite this indication of nervousness he speaks calmly in a soft drawl. Once or twice he wrote reminders to himself on a white memorandum pad with a huge black crayon.

I began by observing that the postwar era had been a time for old statesmen—Churchill, de Gasperi, de Gaulle, and Adenauer, to say nothing of himself. What did he consider to be the advantages and disadvantages of age in a national leader?

He replied:

The disadvantages are obvious because as one gets old one loses one's strength and energy and if by some freak chance you still retain these, none of those around you would be convinced. The advantages are, however, that if your faculties are all right you have a lifetime of experience behind you upon which to rely. You have seen all the moods of life and your judgment should be sound. Another disadvantage, of course, is that an old man is perhaps not very venturesome. He is not as inclined to take risks readily.

The plus and minus can be fairly well balanced. The ideal thing is to have a good team of ministers. Most democratic governments have a leader with a group of members and an old man is well served if he can gather around him vigorous younger men. I would rather drive a team that I have to hold in than to have a team I have to whip on. Older men should be capable of giving their younger colleagues a general inspiration and pass on ideas for the younger men to execute. But it is necessary for the old leader both to have his faculties about him and to assemble a good team.

It is a mistake to think of a government only in terms of its chief. But there are exceptions in times of crisis. Take the case of de Gaulle. I do not know him but it seems to me that he depends more upon himself than would be true in ordinary democratic government. But that is a special case because of crisis. The ancients were wise enough to place power in the hands of one man during times of crisis and this was true of the Greeks, the Romans, and the Celts. Even in the United States, it is ultimately one man who must take the major decisions under a system of checks and balances. For, as they say, a council of war never fights. You must have leadership. You can have a body of vigorous young people who nevertheless find decisions difficult.

It seemed to me that nationalism was beginning to fade, in favor of broader movements like continentalism. He commented:

Just the other day I was speaking of this to some friends. I do not think nationalism as such is dying. We have all the qualities for success in our country if we only remain true to ourselves. The right approach I think is through *inter*nationalism and not through cosmopolitanism. We must keep our national boundaries and amities.

De Gaulle seems to have that idea in France and I think he is right. Under internationalism, a country can nevertheless remain true to itself. Each nation has individual contributions to make.

There will, I imagine, be a pull toward eliminating boundaries. This will be directed by the big nations, not the small ones, because the big nations figure they have nothing to lose. It is like the old movement for free trade which was originated by the big states in order to push their goods on the small states. This country is a typical case. When I was speaking in the United States, forty years ago, we were only four or five million people in Ireland and yet we purchased more goods from England than all of India. The English didn't want us to have protection.

Today, the pull of the big nations is not only for free trade, but also for the wiping out of nationalities for the little fellows. Even a country like England feels it can survive as England in the Common Market. England is being driven into the Common Market in order to build up a strong resisting power to oppose the power of communism. The big countries [and here it was clear he meant the United States] try to force the little countries to make sacrifices.

It is all right to combine with other nations providing you don't destroy your own personality. I think nationality will survive as a concept. I have never yet met a man, no matter how poor he was, who should wish to give up his individuality. Every man and every nation wants to hang on his own little ego.

I asked whether he thought a nation could be morally committed and still remain politically neutral. He answered: "As you know I am not in the government and I cannot speak for it in my present nonpolitical position as President. But I remember the feeling during the last war. If you had had a vote in Ireland, the majority of our people would have voted against Hitler because of his crimes and his aggressions. But it would have been madness for Ireland to engage in the war. We had no defenses."

I asked him my favorite question: Who had been the greatest influence on his life? He said:

There was no one in particular. I had the good fortune of living and working with great selfless men, men of first-class quality, but there was no single dominant influence. I took things as they came along.

My early education was in the country. For most of my first sixteen years I was brought up as a country boy. I wouldn't give up that experience for anything. I only regret that my own children and grand-children have not had a similar opportunity. After that, my education was based on the classics and mathematics. This gives you two feet to stand on and you can go on either into science or the humanities.

I learned languages. Language is very important. Most people don't know what the Irish language really is. It is a sister language to Latin and Greek. But unfortunately it had few great writers during its classical period because when its literature should have been flowering our people were not independent and they were prevented from producing a great literature. But Irish is as much a language as theirs and I am not talking nonsense. It is a great linguistic medium, a wonderful medium for expressing human thought. My grandmother spoke Irish but the British who sought to assimilate us considered the Irish language was a means of resistance and it is not widely spoken.

I was struck by the fact that this was an age of partitioned countries— Ireland, Korea, Germany, Vietnam. Did he think unity was an undying necessity for a nation? He paused and then said:

Of course, France was France without Alsace and Lorraine before the first war. Ireland is Ireland without the North. But the North of Ireland is a piece of our national territory which has been cut off without regard to the views of the inhabitants. The British wanted to provide a continuous majority in the area around Belfast which they worked out by gerrymandering. The town of Derry was overwhelmingly nationalist but majority expression was ignored. Don't forget that until 1920, this island was always regarded as one Ireland.

Of course partition will ultimately disappear.

Gazing up toward the lovely park which the poor man is unable to see, de Valera said:

Someone will sit right here one day who will speak for all the country. Partition is the easy way to solve things but it is not permanent. If in the North there are people who spiritually want to be English rather than Irish, they can go and we will see that they get the adequate, right compensation for their property. Materially, we can make compensation, although of course there are sentimental longings attached.

Partition is a facile political solution but it won't last. Partition will bring trouble wherever it is. It might even start the next war in Germany or Korea.

At the end he reflected sadly: "Remember what we talked about at first. About the advantages and disadvantages of age. The days of one's youth always look better. You think that they were the gilded times. One must watch oneself. One sees how other peoples' memories gild the past and one must avoid this in oneself."

DUBLIN, *July 12, 1962*

LAST night, the minister for external affairs, Frank Aiken, gave a most stimulating dinner for me. Among those present were Ambassador Boland, Irish representative at UN, Dr. Andrews, transportation boss, and Desmond Williams. Aiken is a tall, handsome, well-built man of military bearing. At the age of twenty-three he commanded an IRA division during the rebellion against England. He strikes me as sincere, thoughtful, honest.

At table (and incidentally the food and drink were excellent) we talked about Algeria. Andrews contended the argument between Ben Khedda and Ben Bella was very similar to the argument that developed in Ireland right after liberation in 1922, which broke out in civil war. This touched off considerable disagreement, but Andrews stuck to his guns.

After dinner we sat around for hours. The conversation rambled. Aiken is most excited about the prospects of joining the Common Market. He and the others admire de Gaulle but seem a little skeptical about President Kennedy's abilities.

During the afternoon, I had an excellent long talk with Sean Lemass, Prime Minister. He is short, wiry, hard-looking, in his early sixties. He spoke with logic and common sense. Although less than twenty years younger than de Valera, he is intellectually of a new generation.

Lemass explained that the President was nonpolitical whereas the Prime Minister was elected by vote of the Dail. The President was a symbol and de Valera was the last man who could complain of this because he himself had devised it.

Lemass thought the Constitution must have worked pretty well because the proof was it had never been amended. However, it might have to be amended if Ireland accedes to the Common Market, above all to adhere to the Court of Justice established under the Rome Treaty.

Ultimately, the whole problem of partition would fade away through the Common Market. The effect of membership would be profound upon both Britain and Ireland and the change would inevitably lead to a new political climate. Lemass said the government of Northern Ireland would deny this, but he found in his contacts with the Belfast community a wide body of opinion which thought the existing division of Ireland would one day become anomalous within the Common Market. Lemass made the point that in the Common Market only Ireland would press the viewpoint of the people in the six counties of the North because their interests were common; this would not be true of Britain.

In the North, a new generation was growing up "which is forgetting the old slogans and heroes. A new attitude is developing. Of course this is still impeded by a certain amount of religious bigotry. But one hopes even that is slowly fading away." Concerning Ireland itself, Lemass said:

> We are working away from neutrality as a word. We don't wish to appear neutral as between communism and the free world. Of course we have no formal military ties, but we certainly don't wish to appear neutral and you may rest assured that in any crisis we will help the democracies.
>
> In 1949, when the North Atlantic Treaty was originally drawn up, Ireland decided to interpret the Treaty as implying acceptance of the partition boundary. When we were asked to join we therefore declined, but we stressed that we agreed with the aims of the Treaty apart from this matter of partition.
>
> And we have accepted the principle of European integration. This is not solely because of economic necessity. We are also attracted by the idea of political confederation. This is not a reversal of policy for us as it is with Britain. In our history, we have a long association of attachment for Europe. No one here has opposed joining the Common Market because of political integration. The only arguments have been on the pace of the progress. We recognize that a military commitment will be an inevitable consequence of our joining the Common Market and ultimately we would be prepared to yield even the technical label of neutrality. We are prepared to go into this integrated Europe without any reservations as to how far this will take us in the field of foreign policy and defence.

LONDON, *July 16, 1962*

GOOD talk with Lord Home, the foreign secretary. I asked what were the odds on Britain entering the Common Market. He said:

> We have reduced the matters in question to narrow limits. Only now we are coming into details on questions which might be difficult. Politically, the question is whether the Common Market will be something federal or short of that. Gaitskell, when he was over in Brussels, said England can never join a federated Europe. I must admit this was not far off the mark. But I doubt if the issue will ever be joined. Here and there we may have to surrender a little sovereignty. But the basic issue is unlikely to come up.
>
> We have been careful not to bring it forward. There is no need. Once we are joined with the six, Norway, Denmark, and others will come into the Iron and Steel Community, EURATOM, etc. These steps may bring small surrenders of sovereignty, as required. The difficulties now are really on certain commodities—like New Zealand butter and mutton, Australian and Canadian wheat. But if there is a world agreement in wheat in five years, it will really leave only the butter and mutton questions. Surely the Common Market can work that one out.

I asked if he envisioned the possibility of a European nuclear striking force. He said:

This can be handled in NATO at the start. There are military problems, problems of MRBMs and independent nuclear force. First, the military must decide what it wants. Then it should decide how this should be organized and then finally it must consider whether a European deterrent should be created or not. Britain feels you can't have a purely European deterrent. This must be tied into arrangements with the United States.

I don't think de Gaulle has any precise idea of what he wants. How his military capacity should be tied to us is something on which he has been unclear. He has always been annoyed, of course, by certain existing situations. But he has no program on how to reorganize NATO, for example.

What would Britain do if it didn't manage to join the Market? He said:

This is terribly difficult to answer. We must, behind the scenes, contemplate this possibility. But we should not allow ourselves to think that it may come about. We must be flat out to get in. We cannot hedge and hesitate. This might jeopardize our chances. Of course, if we can't join, it would be terribly bad for us. Europe, without us, would become more introspective and protectionist. It is hard for Britain to remain a first-class industrial nation if we are isolated from the Common Market. We would have had it economically. The Commonwealth cannot provide us with an alternative market.

We discussed Southeast Asia. I thought the Laotian agreement a phony. Home smiled and said:

It should be possible to close the highway across Laos from North to South Vietnam. The Laotians will pledge themselves to remain unaligned and not to permit any foreign troops to operate in their country. Of course the North Vietnamese are foreigners.

But I must say, Couve de Murville told me that this north-south drive across Laos from North Vietnam to South Vietnam is one that has been going on for thirty years along that same geographical path and long antedated the present Communist situation.

MACMILLAN: "A SPIRIT
OF THE DYNASTS
TAKES CONTROL"

LONDON, *July 16, 1962*

THIS EVENING, I HAD A TALK AND DRINKS WITH PRIME MINISTER Macmillan. It was an interesting moment because today he effected the biggest political execution Britain has seen this century, bluntly discharging over a dozen ministers with absolutely no advance notice. When I went in to see him at 6:30 P.M., the final slaughter was being announced to the press.

Macmillan received me in Admiralty House (No. 10 Downing Street is being repaired) in the Cabinet room where he was seated at the long, green-baize council table with a whisky and soda before him. He promptly offered me one. He was wearing striped pants and a long coat because he had entertained the Nigerian Prime Minister at lunch. The rest of the day had been devoted to brief interviews with incoming and outgoing ministers. Macmillan looked well for his sixty-eight years, sunburned and ruddy. But he was clearly under the combined influence of nervous strain and drink and he talked unconsecutively.

I reminded him of the time he said Britain's role was not to be too large, something between the bee and the dinosaur, and asked him how this affected its special position in the Common Market—if Britain is admitted. He said:

We cannot get into the Common Market on terms that are dishonorable to the white Commonwealth, to the EFTA [Free Trade Area] and to our own agriculture. We must protect all these obligations. If you took a purely intellectual view at this moment it would look only as if there were a fifty-fifty chance of our joining. Yet I feel in my knees that great world movements are irresistible. And there is a movement in what is left of Europe—west of the Stettin-Trieste line—to develop into one sound unit. The negotiations may be very difficult. But when things finally begin to move it will be hard to resist the trend.

There is a confederating spirit, a spirit of the ages, the dynasts, that takes control. Sometimes that movement is for ill purposes and sometimes it is for good. Napoleon could not help himself when he was led on by the world spirit of revolution—to evil.

What are the European people? For 2,500 years, starting in the Mediterranean basin, they have been making what we call modern civilization. Some, like the English, spread overseas to what I call the Byzantium of New York. But what are the Americans but Europeans? I am half-American and I know.

There are two streams of thought and philosophy. One is from the Christian civilization based on a Judaic origin. One is from the great Roman tradition based on order. These have mingled to make the modern world.

Twice in my lifetime, by tragic series of events, the Europeans have turned on each other and destroyed themselves. It is because of this that they have lost their automatic predominance.

In the United Nations, the Europeans—and I include America—are no longer the predominant group. Even thirty years ago the Europeans governed more than half the world. But the whole background has changed. Since that time, there has risen the Russian colossus. It is a great power, even if that power is sometimes exaggerated, and half-Asiatic, half-European.

What do we do? What is left? All that is left of free Europe is a small appendix of some 200,000,000 people, very intelligent and energetic, who have been through all kinds of ups and downs after five hundreds years of dark ages.

When I think of the Common Market I see that the economic side is vital. But it is not as vital as the political side. If we all work together, we can play a great role in the next stage of world development.

There will be 2,000,000,000 Chinese by the end of the century, even if you people don't seem to bother much about them. Napoleon said China was a sleeping giant and we should not wake it. But now the giant has been woken.

Your country and ours, and we are brothers practically, can play a role in the beginning of an enormous new period of history. But we want to work with Europeans so that they see our viewpoint—not because we are a proud people or want to keep an empire—but because we have something special to contribute. New countries are coming into being like mushrooms, some of them too soon. We try to teach them how to govern themselves. I want to keep an influence on them through the Commonwealth.

This is a completely new period of history starting now. There is an enormous change in the balance of power and also in the importance of power. I told de Gaulle that I am sixty-eight and he is seventy-two and in our childhood we would never have thought of a Common Market. We would have thought of ourselves only as an Englishman and a Frenchman. But the world has changed.

But I do believe—and I was struck by President Kennedy's speech on this, and I may say he repeated things I had previously said in Boston and elsewhere—in the theory of interdependence. There must be a larger cooperation. People have been given a religion and a civilization and we must work to maintain and spread these. This is not a very complex concept, but it is difficult to achieve.

And the role of Britain? We must do what we can. We are a fairly stable and experienced people; a very kind people who are against cruelty, whether to animals or to children. We have a good tradition of moderation and good sense. I hope we can contribute a lot to Europe— and Europe to us. We are pragmatic and not very logical—the way they are across the Channel—and maybe that will illumine our fogbound minds.

When you join a show, any form of partnership, you try to bring what you have got into a common pool. Our special relations with the U.S., based on common traditions, language, and ways of doing business, are part of what we can contribute. Some of these are slightly different from European ways. You know, I sometimes think it would be interesting if we televised meetings of foreign statesmen. People would see that we don't always speak logically and that the representatives of all nations don't think or work exactly the same. But we English are a pragmatic people. We rather distrust principles and theories. The Europeans have clearer and more astringent minds. It might help us to be associated with that because we are a bit sloppy. There are advantages in both systems.

Until this point I really hadn't been able to get a word in edgewise to start the trend into a channel. However, I now asked whether Macmillan thought Britain's nuclear capabilities would be part of what it could contribute to the new Europe. He said:

It is not beyond our power to settle these nuclear things. We already know enough nuclear power is stored in the world to destroy us all. This is comforting from one point of view but distressing from another. We must arrange so that we don't destroy each other. Neither the Russians nor the West has the slightest intention of starting an atomic war.

On the other hand, the very size of the danger makes things less dangerous. Had we known when we were all mobilizing for World War I that this would produce such incredible destruction, we would not have gone ahead to mobilize. And there are certain advantages in terror.

I am not very much for conventional war, although I know some of you people are. I have lived through two wars and found them very disagreeable. I was wounded three times in the first. I don't want any kind of war, conventional or otherwise.

I think we can play a useful role as the member of a European community still connected with the Commonwealth and the U.S.A. with special lines to each. We bring tradition, history, knowledge, and will, if not power. This all adds to the total, doesn't detract. If you think jealously you may be against these things, but if you think magnanimously you are for them.

I commented that de Gaulle was opposed to admitting Britain as long as it had special relations with the Commonwealth and the U.S.A. Macmillan retorted: "De Gaulle is a very proud Frenchman. But he is in a sense an old-fashioned nationalist. In some ways he is rather advanced. And there you have a duality. Some are half-narrow and half-broad and there are two ways of looking at things. The whole thing should be to get out of our private ivory towers."

I asked how England could help to bridge the nuclear gap between France and the U.S.A. He said:

I don't know. We are all obsessed by the nuclear problem. When I was in Russia three or four years ago, I told Khrushchev that if there was a nuclear war we would all be destroyed. He said: "Not all, the only ones left would be the Asians and the Africans." Khrushchev felt like a European. He meant to imply: "I am a civilized man."

In the end we must get the Russians into Europe. This will come very gradually. But they are gradually being corrupted by bourgeois influences. After all, they are ordinary chaps who want ordinary things, very decent people. We must just be very patient and avoid war and in a generation or two things will change. The Russians are civilized, intelligent people, but for the moment we cannot do much with them politically. They talk a lot of nonsense now but this won't go on forever. Our policy must be: never give in and never provoke.

Their big problem is farming. Isn't that what Khrushchev and all of us, whether in Europe or America, are worried about? The agricultural problem, what to do with the farmers.

And in Berlin, Khrushchev makes la politique. Actually I doubt if he wants a summit right now. It is hard to know what he wants. But if the leading men of the world have a sense of purpose and a sense of honor, we will get through.

I was very pleased with my de Gaulle meeting. It was very useful. I have a very high regard for him, although I don't always agree with him. I knew him in the bad times. I knew him well during the war. But he is not immortal. France will go on and some ideas will change. De Gaulle has courage, however.

Macmillan said he hoped the Common Market problems would be decided by Christmas. I asked what would happen if Britain didn't get in. He looked at me with mild horror, like a handsome bloodhound and said:

I have always made it a rule in my life to avoid fall-back positions. When you have a fall-back position, you always fall back. You just have to go on. And if what you are seeking fails, you must look around, take a deep breath, chuck it, and try something else. There was no fall-back position in the Battle of Britain. Churchill had no fall-back position. After all, if we had used pure reason in 1940, we might have sought a compromise peace.

And the Common Market question is as important to history as the battle of Britain. We have put up reasonable proposals. But we won't betray our friends. We can't make an honorable thing out of a dishonorable thing. If the Europeans say to us that they can't help New Zealand with its butter and mutton, we are not going to betray, 3,500,000 New Zealanders. There are practical ways around these problems. If you want to find these ways you can. If you don't you won't. If the Europeans pretend that it is economically impossible to adjust to such a miniature problem it will mean that politically they really don't want us.

Macmillan then sent out for two "strictly-confidential" memoranda Churchill had given his Cabinet in 1940. The first, dated May 29 (before the fall of France), predicted that France would not collapse and that anyway if it did there would be no thought of a separate peace. The second, dated July 4, cautioned Churchill's lieutenants against any thought of compromise. Citing these two documents, Macmillan said he didn't intend even to consider an alternative to Common Market membership, but, "If they won't meet us on these technical points, it means they really don't want us."

If Britain does get into the Common Market, "the next step will be a larger confederation working along the lines of interdependence President Kennedy spoke of. The final, ultimate step would be world government, but we are far from ready for that yet. I sometimes wonder if we ever will be. This planet may be too small."

From there on Macmillan meandered about, wondering why people wanted to go to the moon and what they could possibly imagine finding there and how they could build a life there. He took a sip of his drink, looked at me sadly and said somewhat pathetically (for a man who had been chopping off his colleagues' political heads): "I have tried my best. I am doing what I think is right. I have seen two wars and three times I was wounded. All I can do I am doing."

PARIS, *July 19, 1962*

LUNCHED with Motrico, the Spanish ambassador. He says big changes are going on in Spain and the lunatics are being chucked out. Many of the military leaders and "fanatics" in Spain had been strongly pro-OAS. However, he had warned Franco that de Gaulle was going to win and persuaded the Generalissimo to send a personal letter of congratulations when peace was finally achieved. De Gaulle replied in a warm, four-page letter. Motrico said: "You may be appalled to hear this—and I don't blame you—but this was the first personal exchange of letters between chiefs of the French and Spanish states since 1930."

Gil Robles, attacked in Madrid for attending a European meeting in Munich, complained to him: "It is bad enough to be charged with communism because you attend a meeting with people like Maurice Faure, René Mayer, Paul Reynaud, and Jacqueline Patenôtre. But it is too much when you are charged with treason because you shake hands with a man like Madariaga, twenty-five years after the end of a civil war." To which Motrico added: "Sheer insanity. My God, only seventeen years after the Germans were sending thousands of Frenchmen to ovens, de Gaulle and Adenauer reviewed a joint march-past of their troops."

GENEVA, *July 24, 1962*

DINED last night with Harriman at Le Lion d'Or above the lake. He leaves today, having finished the Laos negotiations and signed the accords. He recalled we had lunched at the same place the day before the negotiations began last year. Although browned off with me for a very pessimistic column of mine on Laos, he couldn't have been friendlier.

Averell estimates it would cost about $700,000,000 per annum to raise the annual Chinese calory intake by an average of 100 calories; 16,000,000 tons of grain would provide the Chinese with about 1,500 to 1,900 calories. The shipping costs are immense. This means $1 per Chinaman per 100 calories.

He speculated about what might have happened had FDR lived and been well enough to stay on in office. He never would have allowed the Communists to grab China; it had been a mistake to force Chiang to collaborate with the Communists. Roosevelt "had his Dutch jaw stuck out on China," on which Churchill always disagreed with him. Averell says Stalin truly respected Roosevelt as "something new and different."

Roosevelt also would never have ceded to Joint Chiefs of Staff pressure to pull our troops out of Germany so fast to send them to the Pacific. He would have insisted on keeping them on the Elbe River line.

Averell says Harry Hopkins and General Marshall were considered by Churchill the Americans who helped him most. He himself liked his job as aid administrator, in London until 1943, best of all the numerous government jobs he's had because it was fascinating, he saw Churchill all the time, and he was "right in the war."

Averell thinks the U.S.A. must now retreat from "the front lines" in Southeast Asian policy and let others more visibly share the burden. He is furious at a State Department secret cable he showed me insisting the French must follow our policy even where it is wrong.

He says the CIA has gotten us into terrible messes and cites Burma,

Laos, and Indonesia as examples (Burma being the Chinese Nationalist troops hodgepodge). We should have recognized Mao in 1949. Now we must wait and see what happens.

Last week, Averell flew secretly to Vienna to see Burma's General Ne Win who was there on a medical trip. On the whole, impressed. Says Ne Win is a real nationalist and clearly not too pro-American—"but he has locked up all his Communists."

Pleasant gossip with Dean Rusk this evening in his room at the Hotel Richemont. He took off his jacket, proposed I do the same, then poured a couple of drinks.

Rusk said that if you leave out Iceland and Luxembourg, Washington had agreed more than any other NATO capital with Norstad's policy. But he kept making the point: "How could Norstad have a policy that was a NATO policy? What is a NATO policy? In the end, he has to speak as an American. There is only one American policy."

He also assured me the coming Gavin shift had nothing to do with policy. There had been some differences between Gavin and Washington but there always were between Washington and any ambassador. Rusk said: "These new appointments didn't turn on a policy examination of the attitudes of each man. Gavin had certain views not endorsed in Washington but this wasn't a shift done for policy reasons."

I asked if he had been able to deduce here from Gromyko what Khrushchev is up to on Berlin. Rusk apologized that "I am not a Kremlinologist," then went on:

No, I don't see any new Soviet ideas. There doesn't seem to be any change. Khrushchev is probably trying to build up public pressure and also a little private pressure to find out how far he can go.

He has a huge problem in East Germany. The regime there has failed to produce a sense of reasonable contentment for its people. East Germany is not even keeping up with the rest of the bloc. This is partly because the Russians hate the Germans and have always treated them as second-class members of their camp.

The situation in East Germany has produced enormous pressures on Khrushchev. He would like to transfer these pressures to us—to get us out of Berlin. Khrushchev has de-Stalinized in Russia far more than in East Germany. Things would be far less tense in East Germany with a Polish-type regime instead of Ulbricht.

He sees the situation as tantalizing—a West Berlin surrounded by East Germany. I am sure his army tells him that it would probably be a simple operation just to close the throat. But the situation is more tantalizing in appearance than reality because the U.S.A. is *in* Berlin. West Berlin is therefore no more vulnerable than any other place where the U.S.A. is committed with its forces. The gut of the problem is that if both sides come to the table convinced that neither will fight a nuclear war, that is a good way of starting one.

We must remind ourselves that the Russians really hate and fear the Germans. They are concerned about the revival of the Federal Republic and about its possible claim to nuclear weapons. If they maintain their pressure they will produce just what they don't want—nationalism, a nuclear West Germany, and real trouble in East Germany. They risk being their own worst enemies. While we look at a multilateral force as limiting the spread of national capabilities, they think of it as a phony cover for national capabilities.

I asked if there had been *any* progress on disarmament and a test ban. He said, "On general and complete disarmament—no progress. But on some aspects of stage one there is a possibility of moving forward. But the Russians still insist they will accept only national, not international inspections."

India's views on these matters, he said, had been governed by Krishna Menon, who is hostile to us. Arthur Lall, India's representative, is a Menon man. "Nehru is old and ill; he is also Prime Minister. He is *in* office but he doesn't *fill* it. Thus, each department becomes a kind of separate principality. Menon figures his own future depends on a proeastern policy. Friendship for the West has already been preempted by others."

I asked if he still considered SEATO and CENTO valid alliances. He answered:

They're rather different problems. CENTO is basically Iran, since all its other members are in other alliances also, and was designed as a means of assuring Iran. [This is wholly untrue!] The situation in Iran is now very complicated. But CENTO is a rather artificial device and has no sense of regional solidarity.

SEATO is more important to its area. But it should not stand in the way of solidarity among Southeast Asian states. We would like to draw Malaya and Burma and Cambodia into regional friendships. We hope SEATO will remain insurance against attacks on the countries in the area, whether they're in SEATO or not.

You may remember the Truman administration looked into both possibilities—alliances in those areas—and found the areas themselves were not united in support of the idea; so it was dropped.

There is a great deal of milling around on Katanga, a lot of dirty work going on and U Thant wasn't too wrong when he referred to Tshombé and his group as clowns. You can't write this but we have learned there were elements in the U.S.A. who advised Tshombé that if he could get UN troops to shoot some women—this was before the hundreds of women were organized to march—it was a sure thing the UN bond issue could be blocked in Congress. This is pretty dirty stuff.

I mentioned to Rusk the French tale that he and Gromyko, last September, had reached agreement not to give atomic arms to other nations, etc. Rusk bridled, said it was a canard. "All I told Gromyko was what we have been saying publicly since 1945—that we are opposed to the proliferation of nuclear weapons. The French have been resentful at being forced to yield territory and prestige steadily since 1945, and they don't seem to see the opportunities presented for another kind of prestige by a man like Jean Monnet."

GENEVA, *July 25, 1962*

DINED with Bill Sullivan, a bright young foreign service officer, number-two man on our delegation for the Laos negotiations. He says Russia has inhibitions about signing a German peace treaty because of the ultimate implications as a precedent for Two Chinas.

China seems to be weaker militarily than India in the frontier area they are disputing. Yet it insists on pressing the issue. The Indians are getting irked and feel the Chinese are so weak they can be pushed. But the Chinese response has been tough.

We are confident things are moving our way and not the Communist way in China. The Chinese can no longer set themselves up as an example in Asia of how to achieve success quickly. And they can't expand militarily while the U.S. Seventh Fleet is in the western Pacific and we are on Taiwan. Thus they can neither develop their "great leap forward" as a political and propaganda example nor successfully threaten their neighbors as a bully.

The litmus test indicating the Communists will think the jig is up will be when they institute a major birth-control program. This will imply realization they must live in their territory without Taiwan and on their own resources; that they can't afford a 15–20,000,000 population increase each year. As long as they stress the increase in population, they indicate an assumption that someday they will be the masters of all Asia.

BONN, WEST GERMANY, *July 26, 1962*

LONG talk with Franz-Josef Strauss, defense minister. I asked how he interpreted Norstad's resignation. He said:

Norstad undoubtedly is 100 percent loyal to his administration. He always was, is, and will be. On the other hand, his statement [on missiles] could have been interpreted as being not in full compliance with the new U.S. concepts. Norstad wanted an MRBM force. The Kennedy administration is not against MRBMs; but several times it has expressed the view that they are not absolutely necessary from a military viewpoint and their utility is politically doubtful; that Europeans should concentrate on conventional forces.

Norstad is of the opinion that no troop commander should be in a position to physically command warheads and resort to them in case he is hard pressed in war. But up to now the problem has not been actual. In terms of a "threshold," Norstad introduced the term of "pause." I think we should endeavor to make serious efforts to restore any military situation, after an attack, without resort to nuclear weapons —but we must leave open the question of when, where, and how they might or would be applied. The purpose of this is to leave an element of doubt in the minds of an aggressor so he cannot calculate our reaction.

The aim of NATO's military policy must be to maintain a credible deterrence in a form making it impossible for an aggressor to calculate the degree of his risk, and by so doing to eliminate the threat of any kind of military conflict. There should be *no* proving ground for a European war without the risk of atomic weapons. Were the possibility of such a proving ground to exist, it would destroy the internal coherence of the alliance.

I asked if he thought Taylor's new position (chairman of the Joint Chiefs) did not bode changes for Europe. He answered:

In his book, *Uncertain Trumpet*, Taylor was undoubtedly right to criticize the past and to demand that U.S. forces should be more flexible; to insist that a far greater guerrilla capacity is necessary for you with your worldwide commitments in Asia, Africa, and Latin America. All this is correct.

But the same theory cannot be applied to Europe. That would dissolve the structure and internal coherence of the alliance. We can never allow an aggressor to think he might try a military probing action without assuming an automatic risk of nuclear rebuttal. The Russians must be made to fear a nuclear risk of retaliation directly on the Soviet Union should they move in Germany.

Taylor in his book indicated that U.S. national survival was the only basic excuse for using atomic weapons. You can imagine how we feel about that.

I asked Strauss what he considered would be the role of Germany in any "European" nuclear force. He said: "From a military viewpoint and taking into consideration the known French attitude, we accept a European force as the least bad solution. But from a political viewpoint, we don't love the idea—the idea of a political directorate in NATO, which is what it would amount to [meaning the force would be comprised only of U.S., U.K., and French contributions]. Therefore, we can't push the idea. But we feel a better solution for Europe is a multilateral force."

BAD GODESBERG, WEST GERMANY, *July 29, 1962*

GASTONE Guidotti, Italian ambassador (with whom I am staying) says whenever you mention Naziism, concentration camps, Jews, or any other embarrassing thing to Germans, their eyes unconsciously drift away and they reveal an intimate, silent moment of embarrassment. In *Baedeker* (the new editions), Dachau is described without even speaking of the concentration camp there, Belsen isn't mentioned, and Amsterdam is cited for the "departure" of 70 percent of its Jews, who didn't come back —without saying who deported them or why they didn't return.

BRUSSELS, *July 30, 1962*

LUNCHED with Spaak. He thought Brussels was de facto becoming the capital of the new "Europe" and only regretted that his government had stupidly let the Coal and Steel Community go to Luxembourg. He insisted that Britain must come into Europe politically as well as economically. But he did not think it would be a complete disaster if Britain failed to get into the Market; things could still be salvaged by a good commercial accord.

PARIS, *August 2, 1962*

LUNCHED with André de Staercke who said at the start Europe was afraid we were too trigger-happy but now it is afraid we aren't trigger-happy enough. This is the real meaning behind demands for a European nuclear force.

ROCQUENCOURT, FRANCE, *August 3, 1962*

THIS morning, I had a long, long talk with Norstad, the first since his resignation was announced. He told me the story.

On July 12, he was in Bonn to tell the Germans he expected at the December NATO meeting to announce his resignation effective as of March. When he returned to Paris, there was a message from McNamara asking him to fly back to discuss personnel changes.

In Washington, McNamara told him Taylor was becoming chief of staff, referred to Norstad's previous statements that he was ready to retire late this year or early next, and said they'd like to announce it now in order to name Lemnitzer to SHAPE. Lemnitzer normally would have had a second two-year term as chairman of the joint chiefs. Norstad said OK if that's the way they wanted it; that Lemnitzer was an admirable man but of course he had been training Wheeler for the job.

He then went to see Kennedy. For fifty minutes they talked and the President never mentioned the forthcoming resignation. Norstad then brought it up and the President said: "Oh yes, I wanted to talk about that." He added nothing to McNamara's explanation.

I reminded Larry he had told me he might have something to "leak" to me in February and said I could guess what the subject was. Wasn't it a secret arrangement between France and Germany for German investment in the French atomic diffusion plant in exchange for warheads? He smiled and said, "Indirectly, that is the subject."

PARIS, *August 4, 1962*

DINED at Norstad's last night: Isabelle's fiftieth birthday. A rather sad little party—just eight of us. Larry is worried about U.S. policy. Both our military and our diplomatic policies are driving France and Germany closer together (against us) as we talk to each about the dangers of the other; and our attitude encourages more and more talk about "Europe" and less and less about NATO.

ROME, *August 9, 1962*

DINED at the Barzinis with Giovanni Malagodi, head of the Liberal party (of which Luigi is a deputy). Malagodi is a portly, young-looking fifty-eight, speaks impeccable English. He is a banker and represented Italy at Marshall Plan talks in Paris. From this he drifted into politics and was named head of the Liberal party in 1954.

He says more money is spent every year in Sicily than in Israel. In 1903, the first law was passed for the industrialization of Naples. The South used to be called "a cemetery for public works." The preconditions for a modern society are now developing in the south. Naples is a problem in itself; an ancient capital, like Vienna, with an enormous population and the habit of living on a court. Naples was the first meridional problem to be tackled—in 1903—and will be the last to be solved. There is an old saying: "There are inner Neapolitans, outer Neapolitans, points on the frontier of Naples, peasants in the field, Christians, and Turks; that is the world." You see the same faces on the waiters of Naples as in Vienna, who once served grand dukes. Naples is the only Middle Eastern (Levantine) city without a European quarter.

Malagodi considers corruption, as in Italy, a phenomenon of social and economic development rather than a geographical or racial habit. It existed in France until the end of the monarchy, in England through the eighteenth century, flourished in America in the nineteenth. It marks a stage of political development. Graft in Greece, Turkey, Italy, and Iberia is part of the grab for power.

RAVELLO, ITALY, *August 17, 1962*

SPENT a couple of days at the villa of Stash Radziwill where Stash and Lee were entertaining her sister Jackie Kennedy, for a fortnight, together with her daughter, Caroline. Apart from myself and the above, the other guests were Gianni Agnelli and Marella, his wife (Agnelli is the owner of Fiat and exceptionally nice), and Benno (Gilbert) Graziani and his wife, Nicole, a beautiful young blonde.

The Villa Episcopio is lovely, just below the town square and on a cliff high above Amalfi and the sea. It is a complicated arrangement. Several secret-service agents have been flown over from Washington to handle the Kennedys' security. One of them, named Hill, is always with Jackie and even traveled aboard Agnelli's yacht with us when we sailed to Paestum, keeping in touch with his colleagues in a police motor launch by miniature transistor walkie-talkie. An Italian-speaking T-man from the Treasury antinarcotics service was along on loan; also cordons of Italian security agents. The secret-service fellows were always just outside the house and were used as drivers of beach cars, children's nannies, etc.

The security operation was complex. For example, to go swimming required the following. We all climbed into Fiat beach cars and the security people walkie-talkied to those below to clear the entire road to Amalfi. We then drove down and loaded on motor boats. The police launches kept everyone away and we rode over to a beach across the bay where they had another little place called the Beach House, to change, etc. Swam in front of this. When we went to Paestum the police ordered cars to a beach away from the crowd, the Italian agents tried to keep all people away and no one else was allowed with our party or in the museum.

Jackie is a strange girl and also strange looking, but quite lovely despite the fact her eyes are set too far apart. She is a good athlete, swims, water skis, and dances well, has a fine figure. She has an odd habit of halting consistently as she talks, a kind of pause rather than a stutter, so sometimes you think she's through saying something when she isn't.

I didn't have the impression that she was particularly brilliant, despite her reputation for so being, or unusually cultivated. Speaks good French (spent a year living with a French family after Vassar—which she hated; wishes she'd gone to Radcliffe) and some Italian. A rather typical society girl but sweet, exceptionally fond of Caroline, and somehow on the whole unspoiled. Jack (the President) called up twice (at 3:00 A.M.) while I was there and it seems a most affectionate family.

She adores Lee and told me several times: "Aren't I lucky to have a sister who lives on this side of the ocean so I can come and see her."

We talked a good deal at various times and here are some odds and ends I remember. She has immense admiration, love (and I felt a little fear) for her father-in-law whom she refers to as "Mr. Kennedy." Says he can't speak at all since his stroke and it is tragic when he tries to tell Jack something; the President keeps asking, "Do you mean this, or that?" and can't get through. She thinks Old Joe had had several small strokes before and planned to go off suddenly; was sad he didn't die. He had been given decoagulents at that early stage and chucked them away.

Mrs. Kennedy, Sr., and Ethel are immensely religious. I was struck by the fact Jackie herself went to mass almost every day. But she said with evident disapproval that Ethel goes with her children to the 7:30 A.M. mass every day of the summer.

She said Bobby is immensely ambitious and will never feel that he has succeeded in life until he has been elected to something, even mayor of Hyannisport. Being appointed to office isn't enough.

She admires Malraux enormously. Thinks she made a hit with de Gaulle and is proud that at the Elysée dinner he leaned across the table and announced she knew more about French history than most French women.

Says de Gaulle told her (as they were in Paris en route to Vienna) to beware of Mme Khrushchev who was "plus maline que lui." She thinks Mrs. K is hard and tough. But she rather liked K and likes his daughter, Mrs. Adzhubei, very much. Can't stand Adzhubei (an opinion I heartily share) and said she had the impression Khrushchev didn't really like him either and wasn't particularly close to him.

Says the White House life isn't too bad because at least she has all the family together, unlike the campaigning period. And she can retreat to the privacy of Glen Ora.

She is fascinated by scuba diving but only did it once, after hours of lessons at the bottom of Charlie Wrightsman's swimming pool; and then, to her terror, she was approached by a shark and two small barracuda. But she followed the teacher's advice and stayed still, not rising to the surface, and they ignored her.

Jackie is vastly impressed by John Glenn, the astronaut. She says he is the most controlled person on earth. Even Jack, who is highly self-controlled and has the ability to relax easily and to sleep as and when he wishes, to shrug off the problems of the world, seems fidgety and loose compared to Glenn. Glenn is the most dominating man she ever met, I gather, save for old Joe Kennedy. Mrs. Glenn is very nice too. Jackie thinks Glenn could do anything: that, for example, he would be a fine ambassador in Moscow.

Jackie says it isn't true that the spacemen are specially quizzed on their marital relationships. The wives apparently all pray a great deal when a launching is about to take place. Says Jackie: "Even if you didn't believe in God, wouldn't you pray?"

NEW YORK, *August 28, 1962*

A FEW days in New York. One featured lunch with Adlai Stevenson. He talked very critically about Teddy Kennedy as a candidate in Massachusetts and thought the administration would be more hurt by Teddy's victory than by his defeat because of the image of the entire family which is thrust increasingly upon the public.

He blamed the administration for allowing the deadlock to build up over Berlin and thinks we should have always stressed unification of Berlin as being good instead of unification of Germany which no one wants. We lost by not reacting to the construction of the Berlin wall last year and now Russia would never consider a change of status for East Berlin, although demanding that West Berlin should be internationalized.

He saw Tito this summer on his Adriatic island hideout and was overwhelmed by the imperial splendor in which he lives. He was received on Tito's seventieth birthday and they drank copious quantities of wine, every bottle of which had been laid down in the year 1892, when the Jugoslav was born. They only rode around in a golf cart, ate, and drank. The wine was served in ceramic boots.

Adlai said Tito intends to be recognized before his death as a senior Communist leader of his time. He complained about the "damned Common Market" and said this had damaged Jugoslav trade heavily.

ATHENS, *October 1, 1962*

HARRY Labouisse, ambassador to Greece, complains that the new embassy building is most impractical. It was idiotic to build a glass-walled chancery in a country like Greece. The Russians are trying to buy a house across the way, and with modern techniques it is easy to photograph at long range and pick up sounds. We made a test from another house across the street and were able to photograph confidential documents at a distance of 100 yards. Therefore, blinds have to be drawn all the time. Also where you have a volatile population it is rather silly to have a glass wall; Greek mobs are adroit at throwing bricks.

Harry told us the sad tale of Lyndon Johnson's visit. Johnson was not invited by the Greek government although a communiqué said he was. He merely decided to come but, having announced—erroneously—that this was at the invitation of Greece, he declined to stay in either the government guest house or the American embassy. He made statements about our $20,000,000 aid cut which served only to revive a moribund issue. He declined a private lunch by the seashore Caramanlis had arranged for him. Driving with the Prime Minister in the official motorcade tour, he stopped the car and got out to shake hands with people and invited two old ladies to join him. He shoved them in back beside the startled Caramanlis and sat in front beside the chauffeur. It wasn't even his car.

ATHENS, *October 2, 1962*

GOOD talk with Prime Minister Caramanlis. He said Greek-American relations were neither better nor worse as a result of the Lyndon Johnsons' trip. The U.S. made a great mistake in trying to interpret Greek democracy in American terms. We always expected other countries to practice our precise form of government despite different circumstances and traditions.

There was really too much liberty in Greece today. In a way, the Papandreou opposition was verging on the insurrectional. They were trying to paralyze the state and refused to recognize either the King or the government because they claimed the October, 1961, elections were fraudulent. In fact, Caramanlis insisted, he had seen to it personally that the opposition should have a particularly generous allotment of seats in Parliament.

PARIS, *October 17, 1962*

CECIL Lyon, chargé d'affaires during the interim between Gavin and Bohlen, invited me for lunch with Walt Rostow, Assistant Secretary of State for Policy and Planning. To my astonishment, I found a distinguished group assembled, including Gaston Palewski, minister for atomic affairs; General Pierre Gallois, retired air force intellectual; Olivier Wormser, head of the economic division of the Quai d'Orsay; Jean Laloy; Claude Lebel, head of the North African section of the Quai; Paul Delouvrier, delegate general to the district of the region of Paris; Pierre Uri, an economist who works with Monnet.

Cecil asked Rostow if he would give an exposition of American policy. The outline was brilliantly clear but left me worried and dissatisfied.

He said there have been two major Soviet Cold War offensives. The first began southward in Greece and the U.S. moved to block it in 1947, through the Truman Doctrine. The Berlin airlift checked it as it shifted westward. It was finally brought to an end by our battlefield victories in Korea in 1951, where brilliant use of mobile artillery broke up an onslaught by one million Chinese. This offensive was featured by a Soviet shift from backing of popular-front movements around the world to outright support of subversion and guerrilla insurrections in places like the Philippines, Malaya, etc. It was ended by relative stabilization of the

European "front" and finally by freezing the existing status quo in the Far East.

The second or Khrushchev offensive began in approximately 1957, and is still under way. The Russians seem to feel their successes with Sputnik were of such an order that they could trade their advantage for more real estate. In this they have been proven wrong. They have not been able to get going in Southeast Asia or Indonesia and have lost where they hoped to advance in Africa. They have been squeezed out of the Congo and their efforts in Guinea were disastrous. They spent millions and incurred nothing but hostility.

We know by studying his record that Khrushchev is a gambler. He gambled on the Moscow subway and he gambled in the Ukraine. But we calculate he must be faced with toughness in order to make him back down. When President Kennedy took the hard decision to send Marines to Laos in the spring of 1961, Khrushchev recognized the dangers. He admitted this in Vienna to Kennedy.

We now consider that the second offensive is drawing to a close. In fact, Rostow prepared a paper that was secretly circulated and was entitled "Khrushchev at Bay." This is the moment for toughness.

If we could now frustrate the second and new Khrushchev offensive it would be possible to foresee a gradual dwindling of the Cold War and that maybe ten years hence it might be replaced by another situation.

Rostow said we are *not* concerned about Cuba and that it is not an ultimate danger. Despite Russia, Castro was being squeezed out and there was no dynamic threat. He was very confident about this! (The missile crisis was just mounting behind the scenes!)

The Sino-Soviet split is far deeper than people realize. This year, when China was desperately hard up and in need of food, the Russians insisted on payment of $200,000,000 in hard currency for their past aid debts. The Chinese are in desperate difficulties and don't even pretend to be menacing in such areas as Formosa. They seem to be using the Indian frontier crisis just to attract public opinion away from their own problems. Indeed China is in a very strange position. What keeps it from absolute collapse is western food and Soviet oil. If either one were to be cut off, the place might come apart.

The second part of Rostow's exposition dealt with nuclear matters. There had been three basic American policies. Originally, after the Baruch plan failed, our policy was one of an American weapons monopoly for the West. This was succeeded by the McMahon plan, which placed a premium on the independent nuclear development of other allies, promising aid once they had achieved a certain level. We have now quite consciously abandoned that. The primary reason is Germany.

We are convinced that once France is given nuclear aid by the U.S., it will not be long before West Germany demands such aid and that would present dangerous problems. He admitted Adenauer had forsworn German nuclear weapons. This attitude was conditional on no change in the existing nuclear club membership. Rostow claims the Germans made it quite plain to us that they will change their attitude if France gets aid.

Afterward I cautioned Rostow against making statements like this to groups of Frenchmen who would immediately misreport them to Bonn. I thought the German excuse we kept producing was unsatisfactory. He strongly disagreed.

But Walt did say we were modifying our nuclear policy. We are prepared to give atomic arms assistance to a group of our allies, through "Europe" or NATO. And we are prepared for their control without any American veto power. Rostow thought such a group arrangement could contain the German problem. It was up to the Europeans to work out a system of control.

(Afterward he told me that Norstad had not been relieved because of a disagreement over giving NATO an MRBM force, but it was a question of whether such missiles should be land-based or sea-based.)

What worries me is the picture of a bright professor, decent, liberal, and sincere, with almost arrogant confidence in the truth of his own analysis of Soviet policy, its raison d'être and the best means of checking it. I don't think he gives enough thought to the possibility that this analysis may at least in some respects be wrong; or to the human and political effects upon our allies. I like Rostow but am frightened.

PARIS, *October 19, 1962*

PLEASANT talk with Pompidou. He looked very well and sat back, sleek and well fed, puffing his cigar, while we chatted in his office at the Matignon.

He thought it probable that before the end of 1963, de Gaulle would have paid a visit to Washington: "Were I making a bet on this right now, I would bet in favor."

I said de Gaulle seemed to pose the referendum question in the terms: either me or the deluge. Pompidou said this wasn't really it. In France there were two concepts of power. The first has it coming from the President who names the government and orients national policy. The second has it emanating from Parliament with the President only a respected figurehead. These were the philosophical concepts posed.

De Gaulle happens to feel there are too many parties in France and that this means continuance of weak, divided governments if power stems from Parliament. If there were only two parties, the question would not present itself. De Gaulle is trying to push toward the ultimate solution by the system of deuxième scrutin (second balloting). This will force right and left to divide on the second round—the left referring to the non-Communist left. De Gaulle hopes to push toward what in effect would be a two-party division on the second ballot.

He said the OAS was still active but is now divided into two camps. The first is the "Belgian" group with headquarters in Belgium and directed by Colonel Argoud. The second is the "Spanish" group and includes General Gardy and some of the Algerian colonels like Gardes and Chateau-Jobert. The "Belgians" want to kill de Gaulle but would like an alliance with the politicians. The "Spanish" are less eager to kill de Gaulle but are also more reluctant to establish an entente with the political parties.

PARIS, *October 24, 1962*

I SAW Larry Norstad this afternoon. He thinks the odds are better than three to one against nuclear war over Cuba. Khrushchev must be muttering about these "mad Americans" and is somewhat nonplussed. He doubts if Khrushchev will try anything in Berlin because anything serious would mean war and he now realizes this.

Khrushchev might order all his ships not bearing offensive weapons to continue on to Cuba, to disregard warnings, and to get shot at. He could multiply the number of corpses if necessary; that is no trouble. Then he could demand a neutral UN investigation of the damaged ships, spread with corpses and carrying no hot cargo. But ships carrying hot weapons would either have to be ordered to turn back or be definitely sunk.

We cannot let missiles continue in Cuba. The quarantine does nothing about overthrowing Castro. We simply have to take Cuba now—either by starting trouble on the island or starting some kind of a fake demonstration off the coast of Florida to give an excuse for a police action. And this would have to be total and extremely swift.

We cannot risk failure and it would be a crime to stop. We have to follow through. But on the other hand, we should not push too far or too quickly and this is against the American nature, which likes noise and action. Norstad is a bit worried about the judgment and sangfroid of the team in control in Washington.

NATO has stood up remarkably well. Our actions against Cuba are not popular. But all NATO members are resolved not to be split by Khrushchev. De Gaulle has been particularly good.

PARIS, *October 25, 1962*

DINED last night at Tom Finletter's, a farewell party for von Walther. After dinner, Tom made a little speech, stressing what a great friend and valuable colleague Walther had been. I was appalled when I remembered how Tom had asked me to request Strauss to get him removed as a "menace." I told Tom I was extremely embarrassed, recalling all this, and that for the sake of my own conscience I wanted someday to tell the true story to von Walther and Strauss. Tom begged me not to. I said I had no intention of doing this until after he had left as ambassador to NATO.

Tom then asked me to establish close contact as soon as possible with Grewe, von Walther's successor, until recently German ambassador to Washington. Washington had given him all kinds of advance and unfavorable warnings about Grewe and he asked me "as a public service" to tell him (Tom) how I sized Grewe up. I said I would be damned if I would ever be so foolish as to get caught up in a maneuver like the last one. I pointed out that Grewe had started out well in Washington before the administration conceived a dislike for him. After all, he had thought von Walther was a crumb and then drastically changed his mind. He said wryly that he was "more interested in people who finish well than in people who start well."

On Cuba, von Walther, de Staercke, Boyesen (Norwegian ambassador to NATO), and Alessandrini were all convinced Khrushchev would not move simultaneously in Berlin, would initially pull back, and would force a negotiation on Kennedy which would ultimately prove embarrassing.

If Khrushchev played this cleverly he could win a smashing victory in the UN Assembly and gain a great deal of world opinion. He could then offer to meet Kennedy and Kennedy could not turn this down, because point 7 of his proclamation on Cuba said: "He [Khrushchev] has an opportunity . . . by participating in a search for peaceful and permanent solutions. This nation is prepared to present its case . . . or in any other meeting that could be useful. . . . We are prepared to discuss new proposals for the removal of tensions on both sides."

Point 4 of the U.S. draft resolution given by Stevenson in the Security Council said: "[The Security Council] urgently recommends that the United States of America and the Union of Soviet Socialist Republics confer promptly on measures to remove the existing threat to the security of the Western Hemisphere and the peace of the world."

De Staercke said that when there is a negotiation it means that both sides must concede something. The blockade cannot continue indefinitely. The only way to remove missile bases from Cuba is to take Cuba, which would cause immense damage to the U.S. position in the world; or by getting the Russians to withdraw them. But the Russians could legitimately say they would not withdraw them unless we did something equal—such as dismantling our missile bases in Turkey. De Staercke thought we should take the initiative in making such an offer. After all, the entire concept of NATO now favored a maritime MRBM force which rendered such bases obsolescent anyway. Finletter thought it impossible for us either to make such a suggestion or to agree to it at this time, for reasons of prestige and American public opinion.

Lunched with Cecil Lyon. Dean Acheson (and Cecil went along with him) handled himself beautifully with de Gaulle three days ago. Cecil, who shares my admiration for de Gaulle, remarked upon the fact that it is the squeaky wheel that always gets the grease—in this case from Uncle Sam.

He has heard a tale attributed to de Gaulle when he was advised that Chip was coming over as ambassador: "Well, if it has to be an American, he is the most suitable man."

Dined with Chip and Avis Bohlen tonight. They only arrived in Paris yesterday and Chip presents his letters of credence to de Gaulle the day after tomorrow. Chip told me a cable from the President (signed by Rusk) was waiting for him when he arrived, complaining about my column published yesterday and asking Chip to set me straight. He assured me the discovery of the Soviet missile bases in Cuba was a total surprise.

CAMBRIDGE, MASSACHUSETTS, *October 27, 1962*

ISAIAH Berlin came for coffee this morning. He had just been in Washington and dined with the President.

He talked a lot about Kennedy. He feels the President is still psychologically dominated by his father and his father's record as ambassador during the period of appeasement in England that preceded World War II. Jack Kennedy's early book, *While England Slept*, inferentially seemed to excuse his father's record by pointing out that a state must move early to confront an aggressor or otherwise it cannot really fight. England should have acted against the occupation of the Rhineland but should not have guaranteed Poland.

Berlin says the President is surrounded by a group of activists who are very stimulating but who are not long-range thinkers. Isaiah wonders if deep in the President's mind he may not have a presentiment that he may not live a long time because of his illness and that he must make his mark on history quickly.

NEW YORK, *October 31, 1962*

WE spent yesterday evening with Adlai Stevenson, first drinks at the Waldorf Towers, then dinner chez Mrs. Vincent Astor with Ham and Christa Armstrong.

Time and again Adlai's obvious dislike of Kennedy intruded by innuendo. He thought Khrushchev had gone into Cuba because he thought this would change the military balance and allow Russia to negotiate with us on missiles. For my money, that's too simple.

I asked Adlai if he would describe the difference between the Kennedy-Stevenson technique in UN as compared with the Eisenhower-Lodge technique. I here report what he said—but must add that he assured me that it was he and he alone who had made the decision on how to play things differently.

He said the world is changing rapidly and more and more inexperienced countries are joining UN. The Soviet bloc had been making great inroads among the Afro-Asian nations. Our first job, therefore, was to decide how to play the East-West Cold War among these new lands. There were various ways of doing this. Should we depend upon private contacts with individuals among the Afro-Asian delegations? Adlai said we tried hard and he had spent a great deal of time sitting on floors in Harlem or eating indigestible food in the homes of African delegates.

But we also had to identify ourselves with their aspirations and distinguish ourselves from the general category "the West." This produced difficulties in NATO. Above all, there was trouble because we were so linked to Portugal. Thoughtful delegates from western Europe realized they were under a cloud and that the United States could help them. We did our best to identify ourselves in UN votes with Afro-Asia and Stevenson said he thought the fact that he had traveled in those countries labeled as a "liberal Democrat" was helpful.

The second change in our technique showed itself in an effort to cool off the Cold War. Here again, we used personal contacts with various delegations. We sought to make them see we were positively interested in peace and not in a continuation of the Cold War. Adlai said he wanted to ease tension because he realized the neutrals were not interested either in the West or in the Cold War. Instead of trying to reeducate them, we began to try to redirect them.

The Cuba crisis had been "a gratuitous break" for the U.S. Our position on Soviet perfidy had helped. The Afro-Asian nations had been taking a line of "a plague on both your houses," but when Khrushchev was exposed in Cuba it tended to confirm what we had been saying.

Without UN, it is possible that no third body could have stopped the

Cuba crisis. We might have had to invade and, as a result, keep our Marines there for years. It is hard to imagine a substitute device.

When the Soviet missiles were discovered, thirty-two of them were targeted on U.S. areas. How long could we have waited under this menace with a restive American public opinion?

Lunched with Raymond Laporte. SDECE (French intelligence) reported almost a month ago that a serious crisis was about to develop in Cuba.

Raymond thinks Khrushchev backtracked so suddenly on Cuba because of fear that an American commando expedition might capture intact Soviet medium-range and intermediate-range ballistic missiles with their warheads, revealing to us Soviet secrets.

WASHINGTON, *November 6, 1962*

THIS morning I had a good talk with Dickie Bissel, former CIA number-two, father of the U-2, who now runs an outfit called the Institute for Defense Analysis (IDA). A brilliant fellow.

He said the Russians want to compete with us on all fronts. They even sent two race horses to Bowie. They don't have large capitalists with stables. This was a governmental decision and symbolic of this competitive spirit.

In 1955, they felt they had a considerable lead in rocket technology and wished to leapfrog our bomb advantage. This helped accelerate their interest in Sputnik and they also realized its enormously dramatic technical accomplishment would enhance their prestige. By the autumn of 1954, CIA became convinced that satellites would soon be orbited and the first one would have a huge propaganda impact comparable to the first nuclear detonation.

Bissel doesn't think space activities can become a major influence in the real balance of power except for reconnaissance. The Russians may feel that by stimulating us to get to the moon first, they might divert us from more useful activities. But they have to compete to insure against a U.S. breakthrough giving us a real advantage. And they wish to advertise themselves as the leading great power in technology and science.

We talked at length about the U-2. He said it was a near miss S.A.-2 that caused an engine flame-out in Powers' plane in 1960. It is not so important for Russia to have such reconnaissance as they can find out what they need from our open society where they can even get aerial photography services to work for them.

In June, 1956, Eisenhower made the decision that for ten days we would fly reconnaissance over Russia, weather permitting. The first U-2 flight over Russia took place then, above Moscow. The Russians protested secretly and for a while the program was halted.

Killian had a great deal to do with getting the U-2 developed from a paper proposal even before December, 1954, when Bissel was put in charge of the program. In about two years, satellites will be able to take pictures as good as those of the U-2, but they do not have the flexibility.

WASHINGTON, *November 7, 1962*

THIS morning, I had a talk with Ed Martin, Assistant Secretary of State for Latin America. He said:

> The Cuban crisis has strengthened the U.S. position and weakened communism. New support has been given to the leadership of the center and right groups. This explains the recent agitation in the press and parties of Mexico and Chile for a break in relations with Cuba. A previously dormant attitude has been revived.
>
> There is a great deal of evidence that the Communists have been confused by the situation. It is much harder for them now to defend Castro as a Latin American revolutionist. Since Castro declared himself a Communist—and since the October crisis—he is increasingly defined as a Soviet puppet.
>
> Castroism has been tarnished as a "wave of the future." The Soviet refusal to stand up and be counted has hurt Castroism's repute.

KENNEDY:

NIXON HAS "A SPLIT

PERSONALITY"

WASHINGTON, *November 9, 1962*

MARINA AND I DINED LAST NIGHT AT THE WHITE HOUSE. THE others present were (in addition to our host and hostess): Joe and Susan-Mary Alsop, Isaiah and Aline Berlin, Arthur and Marian Schlesinger, S. N. Behrman, the playwright, and a very pretty young blonde named Mrs. Meyer.

The atmosphere was extremely informal. The President looked well, calm and relaxed, and sat around chatting until 11 P.M. The rest of us stayed on another half-hour with Jackie, listening to phonograph records including a folk song that has just been put out—"PT 109." Jackie seems to know the words by heart and loves it. She seemed a little ill at ease and also looked as if she might be pregnant again.

When we entered, we were taken up in the elevator to the first floor where the President has his office and apartment. Little Caroline was wandering around the hall in her nightgown. We went into the private sitting room and sat over our drinks a long time. We were served excellent caviar and crabmeat on toothpicks. The dinner was fairly good, if pretentious—turtle soup, some sort of lobster soufflé, beef, and a kind of iced mousse. There were white and red wines, and champagne. After dinner the men sat over coffee and brandy in the dining room.

The President drank one highball but only toyed with his wine and took nothing afterward. Nothing was served after the brandy or when we rejoined the ladies.

The President was extremely friendly and clearly wanted to talk only about politics or foreign policy. He made only rudimentary efforts to converse with the ladies at dinner and none before and after. When he greeted me he said: "You have come over at an interesting time," grinning from ear to ear. When he went off to bed at 11, as he was shaking hands he asked: "Am I going to see you again?" I hoped so. Here are some of the things he said:

"Nixon is a nice fellow in private and a very able man. I worked with him on the Hill for a long time, but he seems to have a split personality and he is very bad in public. And nobody likes him."

All the Russian missiles will be out of Cuba by Monday (November 12). "I am astonished at how fast they've been able to get them out." But, when I inquired, Kennedy said he did not think the Russians had had an advance emergency plan for a speedy evacuation in case this proved necessary. They had merely been able to improvise brilliantly.

There should be some way that the press can be answered back and restrained from excesses. He could understand Nixon's complaints. "But we politicians can't do it. It is quite right that the press should take after us. Nevertheless, the uncontrolled attacks by the press should be stopped. There should be some means in the press itself to take care of this."

I said I thought he exaggerated the importance of the press and recalled that Franklin Roosevelt had been heavily opposed by almost all newspapers during his last three elections; and yet he won. Kennedy contended that FDR would have won much more handsomely if he had been better supported by the press. The press is extremely powerful and he pointed out various examples in different states. Two papers in Tennessee—the *National Banner* and the *Chattanooga Times*—had made it possible to keep Gore in the Senate. All the papers were Republican in Michigan and Ohio and this had had a big influence in the last election.

Kennedy said TV was very useful, but it did not make up for mass press opposition. I interjected that de Gaulle had managed to win his referendum with TV support (government controlled) against the press. Kennedy did not think this was the same sort of situation.

He told me he had had a very hard time "communicating" with André Malraux when he was over here. He didn't seem much impressed by Malraux—above all on political or diplomatic matters.

At one point, I said to the President I had heard he was angry about a column I wrote. "Which column was that?" he asked. "I thought your columns were pretty good recently. How did you get that idea?" I told him Chip Bohlen had received a cable giving him that impression. "Well, I didn't send that cable," Kennedy said. (It was signed "Rusk.")

Kennedy said he could not understand why Khrushchev went into Cuba. If he had thought America wasn't going to fight in the heart of an area of its own vital national interest, he surely must have assumed we weren't going to fight in Berlin. Therefore, "Why didn't he go straight for Berlin?" He said: "Tommy [Ambassador Thompson] has views on this," and asked me if I had talked to Tommy about them. I said I hadn't.

Several times Kennedy talked about his "terrible responsibility" in terms of making war or peace. "I know the figures," he said. "One-hundred million Europeans would be dead in a day—and eighty million here. A war can destroy humanity."

He complained that "Europe wants a free ride in its defense." What he meant was that the NATO allies weren't doing enough to build western defense and were counting too much on our protection. He said: "Our press is too kind to Europe. They're not kind to us." I replied: "That is a pretty unkind cut, Mr. President." He grinned and said: "Well, maybe I didn't mean you, Cy."

Europe had to build greater conventional forces and refused to do so. This was particularly true for France and Germany. The French had only one and one-half divisions in NATO. De Gaulle has no actual nuclear capability and cannot rely on atoms for defense. The Cuban crisis showed that large conventional forces are needed. We would have had to go into Cuba with conventional forces had we attacked. The Europeans want an atomic umbrella. They won't build up the necessary conventional forces.

Kennedy told me his father will never again be able to talk but still manages to communicate his ideas and his mind was all right. "But it is better to 'go' fast," he added. His father had been deeply interested in Teddy's campaign and was most excited about the results.

Two telephone calls came during the course of the evening. During one of them (I don't know to whom he was talking), he said: "I don't want to make an issue of that just now." He was quick, decisive, and un-hesitating. He allowed Arthur Schlesinger to take the second call and said as he did so: "You had better turn down that music. We don't want too much background." I had a feeling Arthur was more intellectual court jester than peer of the realm.

Kennedy said Khrushchev could not have thought of really getting us to dismantle the Turkey bases. He complained about Walter Lippmann's column suggesting this and said he simply could not understand it.

The President seemed to have an obsession about de Gaulle and made it clear that he thought him a very great man, although he has lots of trouble with him. He kept coming back to him time and time again during the evening.

He thought the Russians, once they saw how determined we were, were afraid that we might capture some of their missiles in Cuba. The real alternative to a naval quarantine would have been a conventional assault on Cuba, not an air attack. There was too much danger that in the chaos resulting from an air attack, someone might have gotten excited and started off a terrible war.

He wasn't ever sure that Khrushchev really believed we wouldn't fight as the Russians said to Robert Frost. After all: "You can't believe what Frost tells you. He is not very reliable as a reporter."

Kennedy warned that it was always easy for the United States to make a deal on Berlin and avoid war. The Europeans should realize this and do more about arming themselves instead of relying on us. We couldn't go on forever carrying the burden largely alone.

He also complained that Europe wasn't doing enough about foreign aid and again he singled out France and Germany. Throughout, he betrayed a considerable distaste for and suspicion of the Germans with particular reference to Adenauer and Strauss.

This morning, I had a good talk with Tommy Thompson. He said our Polaris success threw off Russian expectations to get ahead in missiles. In early 1960, the marshals apparently indicated they were not prepared to risk a showdown unless Khrushchev did more to meet their military requirements. They considered it too dangerous to have a summit meeting and Khrushchev broke it up. They tried to gain a weapons' breakthrough in the test series begun in 1961.

In Spring, 1962, the decision on the Cuban venture was made. Moscow knew a showdown, probably on Berlin, was looming and the army was again asking for more before risking confrontation. So Cuba was tried instead. Khrushchev announced he would not make trouble on Berlin until after our November 6 election—by which time he hoped to have installed his Cuban missiles, without our discovery. Then he planned to go to UN and trade off Cuba against Berlin or bases, also scaring Latin America.

Tommy last saw Khrushchev in July. Khrushchev said he wanted to get the Berlin problem settled and resume the road to coexistence. He really believes he *can* win by peaceful competition and wants to get on with it. He also wants good relations with us because of China. Khrushchev has a genuine fear that the military could seize control of the U.S. He was also afraid that we would really let go on Berlin. Tommy does not think Cuba was a mousetrap operation designed to entice invasion.

Khrushchev is still firmly in the Russian saddle but weaker in the bloc and among neutrals, who now fear they could be traded off. Tommy does not think Khrushchev's head will fall but possibly Malinovsky's or Suslov's.

The Soviet military tells the party: You make policy but we will say what is needed if there are risks. Khrushchev can overrule them as he did on demobilization and a cutback on plane production in exchange for more missiles.

Khrushchev needs a success. But he is unlikely to move against Berlin now. He will probably work for a better atmosphere by something like a testing agreement.

The question in Cuba now is: Where are the nuclear warheads? It is unlikely that the Russians would leave them with the unsteady Castro. Castro did not go to the November 7 Soviet reception; nor did his brother Raul.

Lunched with Walt Rostow. He said this administration is not bound together by a particular ideology. Its members are not just Republicans or Democrats or New Dealers, etc. Their common link is that they were junior officers in World War II, and that is the way they reacted on the Cuba affair—like members of a command post and not like members of a high-up general headquarters.

The Russians tried to get a quick fix on the nuclear balance by the Cuban experiment. Now they will have to spend much more money on something like ICBMs, submarines, or a weapon in space. Or they can decide to end the armaments race and accept inspection. They will probably delay a decision and lie low for a while.

Each nation has a central complex. Russia worries about invasion from the West. The United States worries about another Pearl Harbor. The Russians touched our deepest nerve by their Cuban deception and the way Gromyko knew nothing about it when he talked with Kennedy.

WASHINGTON, *November 11, 1962*

SPENT the day at Paul Nitze's farm in La Plata, Maryland. Nitze told us the story of Dean Acheson's visit to Paris via London, where he spent a few hours briefing David Bruce and showing him the pictures. He had with him Sherman Kent of the CIA to explain the latter, plus a security aide to guard Kent.

When Acheson got to Paris he was smuggled into de Gaulle's office by an underground tunnel from across the street. Acheson went in alone except for the Elysée interpreter. Not even Sherman Kent was allowed. De Gaulle greeted him, then said: "Je vous écoute." Acheson explained everything, and added he had brought along pictures to confirm what he was saying. De Gaulle said: "It is not necessary to show me the pictures because obviously a great government like yours would not risk war for nothing."

Acheson said de Gaulle never made any small talk but when he saw Adenauer the next day the old Chancellor started off by talking at length about bowling. He had recently been down in Italy where he bowled with a Cardinal and had done very well. "Did you win?" Acheson asked. The answer was: "No, I think his prayers went more directly to heaven."

Adenauer had been briefed on the Cuban crisis the day before by Ambassador Red Dowling, so he was all prepared. He told Acheson the United States should have gone ahead and attacked the Russian installations in Cuba without bothering to consult the allies. Acheson replied: "But wouldn't you have protested that you were not being consulted about something which might directly affect German interests?" Adenauer smiled and admitted he would have.

WASHINGTON, *November 20, 1962*

THIS evening, I had a long talk with the President. I waited in the office of his principal secretary, Mrs. Evelyn Lincoln, a very nice woman.

Mrs. Lincoln's walls are hung with presidential mementos. These include a mounted whale's tooth; she told me the President collects these unsightly objects. Also pictures of his late brother, Joe, Jr., in football uniform and as an officer; the President's Pulitzer Prize citation for *Profiles in Courage*; honorary degrees; and a galaxy of photographs, some in color and some in black and white of Kennedy, his family, and various distinguished visitors. The latter included Nkrumah, Adenauer, and Macmillan. Macmillan had sent a large photograph and an effusive inscription revising the well-known quotation to read as follows: "Ask not what your country can do for you but what we can do together for all mankind." There were also quite a few cartoons. One of these was of Nixon and Kennedy and inscribed by Nixon: "To Jack Kennedy, my neighbor, wishing him the best success in almost everything. Dick Nixon." They were neighbors in the Senate office building.

The door to the President's office was open when he came in through another entrance. He spotted me and rushed into Mrs. Lincoln's room, saying: "Hello Cy, I'm sorry I got tied up. Come on in."

I knew he had been at work since 8:30 that morning and our conversation did not end until late but he looked well and resilient. The only sign of nervousness was a fidgeting with an unlit cigarette. He was calm, collected, and moved easily from subject to subject across a broad spectrum. I am always impressed by his remarkable memory.

My fundamental impression was that despite his very considerable victory in Cuba (he had just announced that Russia was withdrawing its troops and bomber planes) and despite the Chinese-Indian cease-fire proclaimed today, he was by no means overoptimistic. I shall now give a detailed account of our conversation based on the notes I scribbled down. I had taken out my notebook from the word "go" and told him I did not want to waste his time because I knew he had had a cruel day and I did not intend to make it any crueller. He grinned and told me not to worry, to take it easy, he had plenty of time. He asked me what I intended to do with my notes on what he said. I told him I wasn't entirely sure but I thought I would drop out bits of material in various columns during the coming weeks.

I asked if we were trying to devise any new approach in advance of renewed test-ban negotiations, providing inspection safeguards. He said that his letters to and from Khrushchev and the McCloy-Kuznetzov conversations had been concerned only with Cuba and had not in any way touched on other things. Nor had we formulated another approach. We still insisted upon minimal means of direct inspection on-site. We would not accept the Russian suggestion of "black-boxes." The idea of a selective rationing series of zones eligible for inspection was only partially acceptable to us and anyway the Russians were adamantly opposed. The situation remained that we demanded inspection safeguards which they refused to grant.

I inquired whether there had been the slightest advance toward a formula for disarmament. He said the deadlock remained unchanged. Likewise, there had been no new approaches on the subject of disengagement and he repeated his emphasis that we were not engaged in any political talks with the Russians apart from Cuba.

Given this deadlock, I asked if it might not be advisable for the United States to revive Eisenhower's 1955 proposal for "open skies," which had been rejected by Moscow. He said: "There has been no consideration of this, I must admit. I will have to read that policy proposal and see what it consists of before I can even consider it. You must remember that the last political talks I have had with any Russians were when Gromyko came to see me [just before the Cuban crisis exploded last month], and this came to nothing."

Did he intend to press Congress to give its OK on making a nuclear submarine available to France? He answered with a categorical "yes." He intended to "implement the Gilpatric commitment." (In September, 1962, Deputy Defense Secretary Roswell L. Gilpatric arranged with French Defense Minister Pierre Messmer during meetings in Paris that we should renew our offer to sell the French an atomic-powered submarine in fulfillment of a promise made four years ago.)

In his recent letters to de Gaulle, had he ever answered the General's 1958 request for a *directoire*? Kennedy said he had not personally answered the *directoire* request but thought that it had been "bypassed by events." Anyway, the French request was "tied with Germany now." Furthermore, "De Gaulle has not brought it up lately. I guess that in a sense he has carved himself a de facto position already even if this is not formally acknowledged in just the way he would like. We'd better leave the matter alone."

I wondered what he thought about the possibility that France was demanding, as the price of admission to the Common Market, Britain's cooperation in a European nuclear force. The President replied: "We don't have any evidence that this is the price and we have an equity on that. It hasn't come up. But we would have to look at it very carefully if it should arise and consider whether we would release the British from their obligations to us."

I asked if, when Adenauer was here last week, the German Chancellor had given any backing to a new Berlin approach that might be considered after the Cuban mess has finally been settled. He answered in the negative. Adenauer did not think that the time would come soon, anyway, for another Berlin negotiation, but Kennedy thought it was likely that the Chancellor would eventually agree to consider new approaches. "But we have not yet considered this. We would only have to review the possibility in the light of the chances of an equitable approach [meaning a quid pro quo arrangement]. The last exchange on Berlin was in October [presumably during the Gromyko conversation]. We have to be ready for possible new solutions but there is no point working out this in detail in advance."

In exchange for concessions, might we ever consider de facto recognition of East Germany or of the Oder-Neisse frontier? He replied: "I couldn't tell you now on this. There simply aren't any indications that the Russians are interested in the Oder-Neisse line question. We must first know if the Russians are interested. There is no use in trying to work out an attitude on such an issue causing tension inside the alliance, if the Russians are not even interested in the matter."

Did we have any way today of checking as to whether the Russians had left any nuclear warheads in Cuba? He said quite flatly: "No, there is not any way, but I certainly assume they won't do so." I asked: "You mean they wouldn't leave such toys in the hands of such screwballs?" "That's right," he said.

Were there Chinese troops or weapons in Cuba? He said: "We don't have any evidence to that effect. It may be true but we certainly don't have any evidence."

I told him Arthur Lall had asked me if the United States would ever consider sending tactical nuclear weapons to help India against the Chinese. Kennedy was startled and said: "Arthur Lall? Why he is one of Krishna Menon's men." I said he was trying to wriggle off the hook. Kennedy then said there wasn't any policy about what to do on helping India until after Harriman got back from the mission there on which he leaves tomorrow.

I wondered if we were making any new effort to end the Kashmir argument. He said this was very hard for us to do but added: "Unless there is a Kashmir agreement, our help to India imperils our relations with Pakistan. A Kashmir agreement would certainly release Indian troops for use against China, but we have made no headway in efforts to mediate between India and Pakistan."

I asked if the Yemen revolt were to spread to Saudi Arabia, whether it would be in our national interest to support the Saudi Arabian monarchy. He said this had tricky aspects. "If U.A.R. or Yemeni troops were to invade Saudi Arabia I think we would assist Saudi Arabia, but we would not have any obligation to do this if it were just a local insurrection and there were no evidence of an invasion. The real problem is the withering away of the Saudi Arabian monarchy. There is the same problem in Jordan. The wheel certainly turns quickly. Just a short time ago Nasser was in the ash can. Now look what he is up to."

Had we any intention of offering new inducements to our NATO allies to provide more conventional divisions? He shrugged his shoulders and said: "What more can we do? Sooner or later they will have to produce more conventional forces or otherwise there will be no sense to NATO." Did he mean that we would have to go through an agonizing reappraisal? He said: "If ultimately they do not produce more conventional strength, perhaps we will have to rethink our approach. Of course Berlin is the key to all this. We would need less troops without Berlin."

Did he plan any new offer to the allies on a multilateral nuclear force? He answered: "No—our position is that we are awaiting their proposals in reply to our standing offer." During the recent Khrushchev correspondence there had been no mention of any eventual Kennedy visit to Russia. Nor had there been references to a summit meeting at a later date. "I can't see what use such a meeting would be right now."

I was interested in what he had said about the problem of national security and the press and inquired whether he had ever considered trying to produce a U.S. version of an official secrets act. He answered: "I doubt if either Congress or the press would ever accept that kind of an approach. I talked with the newspaper publishers a year ago on this and on self-policing by the press in terms of security. But they wouldn't take it. They always suspect that this is a form of managing the news. I think somebody, like Columbia, for example, should take a look at how the press uses news and not just how we seem to use the news. Columbia should study this and I think they would find this was a very provocative subject."

I turned to personal matters. I could see what a killing job it was to be President: Did he try in any way to go into training or follow certain physical regimes to keep himself fit? He did not precisely do this, but he did try to swim every day and also every evening he took twenty-five minutes of back exercises. He was going off to do these as soon as I left. He also kept Sundays free. He had realized after the first few months that he had to keep his schedule more simple and try to see fewer people and ration his ceremonial efforts.

The only chance he had to read for pleasure was on Sunday, and he really had little opportunity for reading. He did look at a lot of magazines. But the only two books he had seen recently were *Seven Days in May* (about a military coup in America) and *Fail-Safe*. Leland Hayward is thinking of making a play or movie on the latter and wanted to be sure it would not damage the national interest. Kennedy asked me if I had read it and I said: "Yes, and I thought it was a lot of crap, although the first part was interesting." Unfortunately, by that interjection I prevented him from expressing his opinion. He said of *Seven Days in May*: "That is about seizing the presidency and naturally it is a subject I am interested in."

He then sat back and surveyed the world situation. He said Khrushchev had backed down "a little bit" but the crisis wasn't over and "also look at China." The world was still filled with trouble and, "the human race remains in peril." Apropos of this, he thought that "Europe should realize the advantage of adequate conventional defense which would give us a chance in case of trouble to have time to pause and negotiate."

I told him I wanted to ask a question I had posed to many other leaders: Who was the person who had most influenced him? Without hesitation he said: "I suppose you would say my father and the atmosphere he created around all of us as we were growing up. But there is not any special public figure. We have seen a number of impressive ones, but I don't think I could talk in terms of influence. De Lattre certainly was an impressive man. I ran into him in Indochina. He was a very vivid and vital personality who loved to create an effect." I asked if there had been any particular philosopher or statesman who influenced him and he said, "No." He then continued:

As far as the presidency is concerned, nobody can really help there. Some people used to say that Nixon had certain advantages because he had learned a good deal and assumed responsibilities as Vice President. But being Vice President isn't enough. In this job there is nothing like experience. And that is also true in the Cabinet. It is unlike the British system, where you can have a Shadow Cabinet with different people working for many years and having knowledge about the government operations in particular departments. We suddenly bring men in and dump them into the situation. It is a very tough problem. And it would be hard to devise a Shadow Cabinet system here.

When you take over a job like this, you simply have to depend on the judgment of the men around you. And you don't know them at first. They may have good records and excellent reputations but their judgment may be lousy—generals and diplomats and others. And you can't tell at the start. Of course, after you have had a few months you gain a hell of an advantage.

I asked him if he had been scared by the immensity of the task and its responsibility at the start. He said with a grin:

No, not scared. At the beginning, you are protected by the value of your own ignorance. But I can do the job much better now and I could have done this much better earlier if I had had experience.

Let me show you what I mean. After Cuba—the Bay of Pigs—we began to talk about maybe going into Laos. But all the generals and other people disagreed about this and you don't know whom to believe and whom to disbelieve. It is a very hard thing at first.

Kennedy said more and more problems crept up all the time. Every day, there was something new. The Congo was getting worse again and there may be a new crisis in Laos. Brazil was rapidly heading toward bankruptcy. There was the Indian crisis, trouble was coming in Chile, Guatemala might very well elect a Communist President next year. There was nothing but trouble looming ahead.

PARIS, *November 30, 1962*

LAST night, our first since returning, we dined à quatre with the Bohlens. Chip said he has seen de Gaulle twice since presenting his letters of credence to explain the dénouement of the Cuban crisis. De Gaulle assured Kennedy at the height of the crisis that if it should end up in war, the U.S. could count entirely on French support.

As a result, France's stock is now very high again. Chip insists the effort to give France an atomic submarine does not affect our basic atomic policy, but he seems to show the beginnings of a marked admiration for de Gaulle and says he will soon prepare a report for the Department on the man as a character, stressing his shyness. Chip admits that he is one of the very few great men he has ever known.

PARIS, *December 5, 1962*

DINED last night at the Bohlens, a farewell for Norstad. Interesting postprandial conversation with Bohlen, Norstad, Pierre Messmer (minister of defense), and François de Rose.

It seemed to me everybody was arguing in favor of what he didn't want. Messmer was saying that if he were an American his nuclear policy would be the same as ours. Bohlen and Norstad were criticizing Walter Lippmann's speech explaining our nuclear policy. And de Rose was blandly proclaiming that France of course didn't wish to consider its own small nuclear force as a "trigger" of our own.

Norstad thinks our nuclear policy toward Europe has been silly. All this talk about a multilateral force is meaningless and confusing. The biggest mistake was that five years ago we should have pledged to the

NATO allies that we would not remove any of the nuclear installations we were bringing over here.

We should saturate Europe with nuclear devices and work out a control arrangement. We haven't taken sufficient initiative ourselves in trying to work out the controls and he can understand why Europeans worry about leaving everything in our hands. NATO, in fact, is probably the world's second nuclear power today—ahead of Russia. Europe could suck us into a NATO arrangement now and we will have to accept whatever they come up with.

Lunched with Burin des Roziers. He asked what I thought of Nehru and I said, "Not much." He had translated at two conversations—one between Nehru and de Gaulle and one between Nehru and Malraux. The Nehru-de Gaulle colloquy was very banal. As for that with Malraux, it simply didn't make any sense. He said: "Don't forget, it's impossible to translate Malraux into French, much less into English. I merely did my best to put what he said directly into English. I must say Nehru looked very puzzled. I don't blame him."

ROCQUENCOURT, FRANCE, *December 5, 1962*

MARATHON talk with Norstad. Since Kennedy started discussing increased conventional forces eighteen months ago, some progress has been made. But such progress had already been predictable. There is absolutely no sense in demanding new conventional units before we have met the need to beef up our existing European units and have met existing goals. It is plain nonsense to speak of more paper divisions as the administration is doing.

Of course, the U.S. would prefer to have all nuclear weapons and control in its own hands. But politically that won't work. We should say that we think a multilateral force is the second-best solution and we should discuss this on a NATO basis. After all, being blown up is just as important to a Belgian or a Frenchman as it is to an American, even if they aren't in the same nuclear league as we are.

The idea of a seaborne force politically panders to the worst instincts in an alliance. First of all, it is pretended this is cheaper whereas probably it is more expensive. Secondly, it implies to the various allies that because they won't have any missiles on their soil they won't become targets in a war; that they will have the benefits of an alliance without its responsibilities. This weakens the moral fiber.

PARIS, *December 6, 1962*

DINED at the Jean Dutourds' last night. The Pompidous were there. Highly cultivated, a Normalien and scholar on Racine, Pompidou gives the impression of being a good, steady, rather "Anglo-Saxon" type fellow with common sense.

The OAS is practically finished, he said. They are rapidly running out of money. They had a fat war chest which they took away from Algeria, but they have been living well and have virtually spent it all. During the next few weeks, there are still likely to be some assassination plots but the danger is rapidly diminishing and any thought of a putsch is gone.

He said Khrushchev was undoubtedly a better man than his successor would probably be, but we must not exaggerate and cater to him too much. Cuba had proved that the Russians definitely don't want war and are not overconfident about their military position.

He thinks Macmillan will soon run the risk of losing all chance of getting into the Common Market. The decision will be taken during the next ten days at the Macmillan-de Gaulle talks. The argument boils down to whether Commonwealth agriculture will make concessions to French agriculture or vice versa, and, naturally, the agriculture of France is in a stronger bargaining position.

The American embassy had been very surprised by de Gaulle's election victory because the embassy "dines out en ville and listens to the wrong people."

Pompidou said he no longer gets any chance to write. He had once started a novel about "Paris intellectuals," but he never got around to finishing it. He added, concerning the subject matter, "I suppose you would have had to call that a comic novel."

PARIS, *December 7, 1962*

THIS evening, Bill Porter came around for drinks. He is now ambassador to Algeria. The situation is an awful mess. Ben Bella is naive and inexperienced but he is learning and at present seems to be backed by Boumedienne and the army. They are all a bunch of wild-eyed innocents.

The U.S. has told Ben Bella it will undertake to feed four million Algerians through February. This is approximately 40 percent of the population. Ben Bella was touched that we should do this despite his expressed hostility in Havana. The Algerians now recognize this was a mistake and they are impressed by the way we made the Russians back down in Cuba.

PARIS, *December 10, 1962*

LUNCHED with Brosio at the Italian embassy. Khrushchev sent a message to Macmillan to this effect: Don't try to push us around on Berlin and make no mistake in thinking that the Cuban incident proves that we are soft. The Berlin situation is just the opposite of Cuba. In Cuba, the

U.S. proved that if you have a superiority in conventional forces on the spot you can win; or force the other fellow to be the first to use nuclear weapons. It is just the reverse in Berlin. The West should realize this.

PARIS, *December 12, 1962*

DINED last night at the Philippe de Rothschilds'. A very small dinner for Guy Mollet. I was quite interested to see the head of the Socialist party tuck into a good Rothschild meal.

Mollet said that just prior to the 1956 Suez crisis, Ben Gurion and the Israeli defense minister came secretly to confer with him in France. The British delayed for two months before agreeing to the Suez action and only on condition that they could run it militarily and politically.

He said the press was suffering under de Gaulle but the big thing was that television was entirely at the service of the regime. I recalled that the Fourth Republic, including his own government, had several times closed papers and magazines. He said this was only in the interest of national security. He went on: "You Americans would not let a Communist paper appear." I told him he was wrong.

PARIS, *December 16, 1962*

LAST night, I had a long talk with Dean Rusk over at Bohlen's residence. The NATO meeting finished yesterday and Rusk left this morning for Ireland and the U.S.A.

I must say he was extremely nice and forthright and I like him. He is very courteous and patient and was quite relaxed as we sat and drank and chatted. But there is within him an element of pique at the frustrations of his office. And I often detect only a thin wall between his anger at some of the countries that disagree with him and his calm exterior.

I asked what the U.S. would do in its own policy if Britain didn't come into the Common Market. He said, "The consequences would be so serious that we simply hate to contemplate failure. It would affect the entire U.S. attitude toward Atlantic unity and would be a cause of disillusionment throughout the alliance."

What would his attitude be if there was no compromise on the nuclear argument with France? He said:

> That is a phony issue. We have an existing policy in this field in NATO. It was not voted; it just developed that way. Some people in Europe think the present situation is not satisfactory. We say, OK, one alternative is a multilateral force. During the last two months, we have given the most detailed information to these people to try and help them arrive at a conclusion.
>
> And there are differences inside Europe on this. If we put forward a

U.S. plan and Europe disagrees, it could divide the alliance. Europe has not made any suggestion of its own. Not a single country in Europe has made such a suggestion. I think everybody is waiting until the British Common Market negotiations are completed.

The countries of Europe don't agree with each other. If you want to join this nuclear club you have to join it in a major-league way. The U.S. has over $100,000,000,000 invested in atomic energy. No country can pretend to be big league unless it is ready to shell out on such a scale. Some European countries would like us to play the role of a soft touch. But we Americans look at the question from our own point of view. The Europeans haven't really begun to look at the issue.

I then asked what the U.S. would do if NATO simply refuses to raise the needed conventional forces and whether we would consider some kind of "agonizing reappraisal" in our basic policy. Rusk said there had been some improvement in the conventional force levels as a result of our needling. This is important with respect to agreed force levels. It has nothing to do with revising NATO strategy. The agreed force levels are at a minimum and we must honor our pledges.

Otherwise, if Europe doesn't stick by its promises, someday there will be a movement in the U.S. against the idea of the U.S.A. as a world policeman. *We* draft our men and levy taxes and suffer casualties in distant places like South Vietnam. Europe hasn't begun to plumb its capabilities. It is a matter of will. The Europeans haven't begun to approach the level of national effort they achieved in 1939, when they were quarreling with each other.

We provide the cannon fodder as well as the nuclear produce and it is ridiculous for people to say that we should accept to serve as their cannon fodder. We have 400,000 men in NATO and are the only member that has met its agreed force goals. Why should we draft a Kansas farmer and send him to Britain where there is no conscription and where that same Kansas farmer sees Englishmen lolling about? This will become a political problem at home if something isn't done about it. Congress will —and should—ask what they intend to do.

I then repeated the question about an alternative U.S. policy if nothing is done. Rusk said:

All the Kennedy administration did was to say that NATO should produce the agreed force. This is not a revolutionary event. And these forces have been steadily increasing. We are not discouraged.

Our interest in NATO is identical with our own security. De Gaulle doesn't realize that and recognizes U.S. security as separate from that of western Europe. There is no question of an "agonizing reappraisal" but just of getting people off their cans.

If the Russian intelligence service could point to the gap between the actual forces of NATO—which they know—and NATO's announced goals—which are also known to them—Soviet agents would probably give advice to Moscow on western intentions which might lead the Kremlin to believe there is a weakness in the will to defend the West. We must head off such misconclusions.

We are more worried about what Moscow thinks on this matter than about what Washington thinks.

He said France's nuclear arms won't make a difference for many years to come. He continued on his familiar tack. "This is a big-league problem. The minor leagues can't play a significant role there. It is simply not a practical problem. We are ready to discuss with France until it runs out of their ears. But the French should realize that we consult with them not because they have a few nuclear weapons, but because they are France."

I asked if we were contemplating any action if Laos continues to deteriorate. He said that Gromyko had mentioned Laos in his speech yesterday (Saturday, the day I talked with Rusk). We know that much of the Viet Minh has left Laos but some of them are still there. We are watching carefully to see if the agreements are carried out. "But Laos is a spooky place, filled with confusion." Rusk then added that no westerner could really understand Laos and recalled how the civil war was interrupted when the King buried his father and all sides observed an armistice.

I then asked him if he thought Secretaries of State were now "condemned" to travel. I pointed out that Dulles had been criticized by the Democrats for traveling so much and now here was Rusk hopping about like a traveling salesman. Was there any way to put an end to this? He said:

As long as the Under Secretary can serve as acting Secretary when the Secretary himself is away, it is not as serious a problem as it might be. But it might be desirable to have someone with the prestige of a Cabinet member to do the traveling job.

Truman tried to work out a system like this when he had Phil Jessup as ambassador at large. As a matter of fact, Truman once suggested that we should appoint a Secretary of Foreign Affairs—which was Jefferson's first title—and let him do the traveling.

The Dutch actually had two foreign ministers for a while, right after the war. Now in England you have Lord Home in the House of Lords and Heath in the Commons and also handling the Common Market negotiations, so there is a kind of divided labor. But it is difficult to work things out that way for those who belong to several clubs—like NATO, SEATO, CENTO, ANZUS, and the OAS.

One of Dulles's troubles was that he often took leaders of the State Department traveling with him and tried to run the Department from his vest pocket as he moved around. My theory is to leave the Department in the hands of the acting Secretary. Like General Marshall, when

I travel I see myself as a kind of ambassador. Sometimes I even ask the State Department for instructions. I don't send instructions from abroad the way Dulles did. I just don't think you can run foreign policy from your vest pocket while you are traveling.

Lunched with Norstad. He said Washington's arrogance was turning all Europe against us. In a sad way, we were doing what Stalin had once done—uniting Europe.

Clark Clifford was there. He is working on a constitutional amendment to divide up the duties of the President by giving the ceremonial functions to the Vice President, much as they are divided between the Prime Minister and the Queen in England.

PARIS, *December 20, 1962*

LUNCHED today with Alain Peyrefitte, information minister. He didn't think de Gaulle would stay beyond January, 1966. The contenders for the succession are Pompidou, Debré, and Chaban-Delmas.

De Gaulle would never agree to Chaban who, apart from everything else, is a flibbertigibbet and a womanizer which de Gaulle won't take. Debré is too excitable. Obviously Pompidou is the man.

He told me, by the way, that he had had lunch at the Elysée with Eisenhower and de Gaulle in August, and that Eisenhower had told de Gaulle, "I am reading a book about you by Cy Sulzberger and I advise you to read it."

PARIS, *December 21, 1962*

LUNCHED with General Lemnitzer, Norstad's successor, in my old hangout, Lucas Carton. His aide fixed our rendezvous for 12:30 P.M., not the customary hour in Paris, and I thought he would want a quick snack. Not at all. I didn't get out until 2:40 P.M.—two hours and ten minutes of food, drink, and conversation. That is par for a Frenchman, but not for American military.

Lemnitzer showed up in full uniform with decorations stretching down to his navel. He is likeable and simple. He comes from Homesdale, Pennsylvania, and decided to go to West Point just as World War I was ending. His father was in the shoe business.

Lemnitzer asked me how the press was and whether he should trust foreign journalists to background briefings. I advised that he should have such briefings, and tried to explain what background meant, but I said he should never really say anything he didn't wish to say on-the-record.

He has had a lot to do with Europe. During World War II, he and

Terence Airey were the two principal negotiators with S.S. Lieutenant General Wolff, who arranged the German surrender in Italy in the spring of 1945. Lemnitzer was sent over to discuss the birth of NATO with the "military committee" of the five original WEU nations. And he has just held the highest post of our armed services—chairman of the Joint Chiefs of Staff.

Lemnitzer agreed that the French regarded nuclear weapons as a political and diplomatic trump versus the allies, whereas we only thought of nuclear weapons as arms versus enemies.

PARIS, *December 27, 1962*

LUNCHED chez Jean-Jacques Servan-Schreiber. There were no longer any guards outside the door. They had been removed right after the elections a month ago.

The most interesting part of our conversation was on French politics. I was struck by Servan-Schreiber's great ambition and also his naiveté. I really don't think he knows much about French politics and he certainly knows nothing about American politics. He questioned me eagerly about how Kennedy had organized his machine to gain control of the Democratic party.

Jean-Jacques begged me during our conversation always to "play him down" as "unimportant" if anybody mentioned his name. What he wants is simply this. He thinks all the old parties in France are destroyed. Big business, which is not reactionary and which favors expansion but which considers only its own interests, is behind de Gaulle. Therefore, the left must organize a brand new party: the old ones are finished; the Socialists, what was left of the Radicals, the PSU, etc. And the old leaders are discredited, even including so able a man as Pierre Mendès-France.

What de Gaulle has achieved is the end of the Third Republic. The Fourth Republic was a temporary phenomenon that never counted for much. The Third was based on a series of brilliant personalities with several parties acting as their individual cliques. That era is gone. It is only possible to deal with mass national parties now and de Gaulle's UNR will continue that way even after his disappearance, despite the fact that it has hardly any important leaders.

The people of France have experienced a revolution and are no longer interested in small parties run by individual personalities. Accepting this situation, Jean-Jacques hopes to build a new left party, putting together the fragments of the old. The only hope will be to get together a party that is stronger than the Communists. It is impossible to deal with the Communists. But if you have a party that gets more votes than the Communists, they will support you without trying to make a deal first. He wants to get a group of tough young men with political experience and form a kind of "Kennedy clique" to work on a behind-the-scenes basis and eventually take over.

He is disgusted with the old leaders like Mollet. It is ridiculous to complain that de Gaulle used television in a "fascist" way to win the last elections. He found to his own chagrin while campaigning in Normandy (unsuccessfully) that the trouble with television was that the opposition leaders were allowed to appear. When France saw people like Mollet, Monnerville, Reynaud, and Maurice Faure, it promptly voted for de Gaulle. Furthermore, the press is certainly not oppressed under de Gaulle more than under the Fourth Republic; probably less so. It is influenced in two ways. First of all, it is losing circulation, so it tries to cater to what it imagines public interest to be and avoids provocative subjects. Secondly, it is under pressure from big-business interests that favor the regime.

PARIS, *December 28, 1962*

MARINA and I took the Norstads to Chez Anna for lunch. In his six years in Paris, this was the first time that Larry had been in a bistro. He becomes a civilian on Wednesday (five days from now) for the first time since he was nineteen.

Incidentally, Madame Anna knew who my guest was, not only because I had told her in advance in order to secure the best banquette in her tiny restaurant, but also because two French flatfeet came in to inspect the place this morning and two more arrived with Norstad. She whispered into my ear as we were leaving, "Are you going to replace the general?" I am afraid my answer disappointed her.

PARIS, *January 2, 1963*

WENT out to SHAPE for the formal ceremonies at which Lemnitzer took over from Norstad. It was extremely moving and many people had tears in their eyes when they saw the march-past of dress-uniformed troops from each nation, from skirted Greek evzones to Dutch grenadiers in bearskins. Larry will be missed.

PARIS, *January 3, 1963*

THIS morning's *Figaro* says General de Gaulle confided at a small reception of regular Elysée correspondents the list of his Christmas holiday reading. This included: *Ce que Je Crois* by François Mauriac, speeches to the French Academy by René Clair and Cardinal Tisserand, a book on Asia by d'Harcourt, and my book on de Gaulle.

De Gaulle commented, when asked what he was reading, "Oh, also a book by Sulzberger." According to the official account, a journalist asked in a low voice, "*En Observant de Gaulle?*" The General then said, "Yes, that is it." A moment passed before he added haughtily, "It is interesting."

PARIS, *January 4, 1963*

LUNCHED with Bohlen. At 3:30 he sees de Gaulle to start complex negotiations for settling the nuclear dispute between the U.S.A. and France. He asked if I had any advice. I said only that I thought we should hew to the concept of a small pilot-project multilateral-force with the U.S.A., Britain, and France each contributing a percentage of their stockpile, thus getting the thing started on a test-tube basis.

Chip was at the Nassau talks between Kennedy and Macmillan. He talked at length with Kennedy there and at Palm Beach. Kennedy's fear was that de Gaulle might refuse the Nassau offer out of hand, thus preventing any subsequent negotiations. But de Gaulle transmitted a message to Washington in which he left the door open.

Chip claims de Gaulle's nuclear policy is contradictory because, by insisting on a national deterrent which would have an influence in keeping France's ascendancy vis-à-vis Germany, it also encourages the Germans to claim a similar national deterrent.

All he wants to do is make broad statements to the General from which de Gaulle cannot possibly dissent. Thus he intends to point out that so long as Russia is governed by a Communist regime similar to that now in power, NATO is essential to the West. If there should be a radical change in Russia as a result of some internal convolution, all countries might have to revise their policy, but that is a long time off.

PARIS, *January 7, 1963*

GOLFED and lunched with Bohlen yesterday. De Gaulle expressed the opinion that it was always difficult for a nation to recapture control of its own national force when it had been committed to a supranational undertaking. Chip, thinking of the Strasbourg incident in World War II (when de Gaulle occupied the city in violation of Eisenhower's orders), remonstrated. De Gaulle caught the innuendo and said Strasbourg was only "un petit incident."

Bohlen claims that when someone asked de Gaulle about the recent Rambouillet meeting with Macmillan the General replied: "It reminds me of Edith Piaf's song 'Ne Pleurez Pas Milord.' "

PARIS, *January 8, 1963*

LUNCH with Stikker, who looks remarkably well considering that he has had two heart attacks and a serious cancer operation.

We will never, he said, be able to make a deal with the Russians getting something in exchange for the withdrawal of land-based missiles in Turkey and Italy. The Russians would only ask us with what we were replacing them and one Polaris submarine is more powerful. We should only do what is needed by NATO.

The basic need of NATO is to reaffirm its determination to pursue a forward strategy. This is above all necessary to reassure the Germans. Once a forward strategy has been reaffirmed, it can be decided how much money is available and whether this can be best expended on conventional or on nuclear forces. That will get things back into proportion. They have been wholly twisted out of proportion by McNamara's thoughtless statements and silly American demands, such as the one for a flat 20 percent increase in NATO contributions by each ally—utterly impossible to meet.

De Gaulle has a "backward strategy." His only forward strategy is to defend France in Germany to the last German.

I was most interested when Stikker at one point said, "I know you play golf with Couve often and he tells you interesting things. I saw that telegram Lyon [U.S. chargé] sent after your golf game last weekend. I know everything that goes on and I would just like to be helpful. I know you miss Norstad as much as I do. So please feel free to call me up any time you want advice and I will try to help you."

PARIS, *January 9, 1963*

DINED last night at the Alain de Rothschilds in honor of the Bohlens. The Pompidous were there. After dinner, I sat in on an interesting dialogue between Pompidou and Bohlen. Pompidou recounted all the old arguments in favor of a French national "force de frappe" but then went on and said perhaps a "European deterrent" might be useful. Bohlen immediately urged him to go ahead with this concept, saying the U.S. had been eagerly requesting its allies to produce their own ideas.

Pompidou talked at length about the contrasts between Britain and the Continent. There was no escaping the fact that the British not only felt but thought differently. They were not truly Europeans and could not become such. I thought that this significantly hinted France would never let the British into the Common Market.

Bohlen saw a contradiction in French policy. By proceeding to build a national "force de frappe," France would inevitably encourage the Germans to emulate them by their own national nuclear deterrent. To my surprise Pompidou agreed.

Chip said the French argument was wrong—that the U.S. might change its policy and cease protection of Europe. After all, nations must base their policy on probabilities; it was impossible to always reckon on certainties. Obviously Russia would not change in any significant way for ten years at the very least; therefore the risk of Communist expansion would remain with us for a time. Naturally, if ever there was a significant change in Russia, all of us—each NATO ally—might have to reconsider policy.

In the meantime, Europe should reckon with the "probabilities" of American policy just as the U.S. has reckoned on certain "probabilities" in postulating its attitude toward Europe. For example, 20 percent of all Frenchmen vote for the Communists, so there has always been a discernible chance that France might have a Communist government. But Washington always reckons on the "probability" this would not occur.

Pompidou said there were great differences between Britain and France with respect to the Nassau proposals of December. It would be years before submarines and Polaris missiles were ready for delivery under the terms of the offer made to France. In the meantime, France required a small warhead which the British already had. Bohlen said all the U.S. wants to do at this stage is to keep the door open, to keep discussing things.

Pompidou argued that each of the allies had a different degree of interest in different problems. For example, West Germany was vitally interested in Berlin. France was a little less vitally interested, Britain still less so, and the U.S. even more removed.

Bohlen said he didn't think this was a fair analysis. We had more troops in Berlin than either France or England. We had six divisions in Europe and France must therefore assume that quite obviously we were vitally interested in the defense of Europe. Pompidou, puffing a cigar, smiled and said: "Yes, that is why we were able to withdraw our two divisions to Algeria."

Nevertheless, he said it was impossible to assume that the U.S. would respond immediately with a nuclear attack or risk the destruction of the U.S. for every localized incident in Europe. We must remember the old cry before World War II, "Is it worth dying for Danzig?" It was terribly hard to calculate what would be considered a real casus belli by the U.S. Cuba, of course, was an admirable one, making it much easier for the U.S. to face up to the Russians. But what would be a proper casus belli (from the American point of view) involving Europe?

Pompidou made the interesting statement that India's fate is a much more important question than the French atomic "force de frappe." If India comes under Chinese domination, thus forming a bloc of one billion people, "We shall all be eaten in the long run."

PARIS, *January 11, 1963*

LUNCH with Soutou, responsible for Africa and the Near East at the Quai. Bohlen is an expert and de Gaulle respects him. Soutou told me, to my interest, that in considering the human relations of de Gaulle I should not forget de Gaulle's liking for me. I expressed doubt about this but Jean-Marie said that on the airplane back from Turin last spring the General expressed particular regard for me.

He said the moment it renounced the idea of war—as Khrushchev has —communism was finished. In this respect, China is correct. It is like Islam after its big period of conquest. Russia is being slowly engulfed by new concepts. And it *is* really western. Like the rest of Europe, its philosophical origins are in Jerusalem, Athens, and Rome. If one looks back over history one can say that when Russia embraced Marxism in 1917, it was embracing western philosophy. Nor should we forget that the Russians are inherently racists. They are both racially and historically against the Chinese.

PARIS, *January 18, 1963*

LUNCHED with Pierre Billotte. He claims Philippe de Gaulle, the son, and Alain de Boissieu, son-in-law, have some influence on de Gaulle and have the guts to speak up. They both call him "père" instead of "papa" and *vouvoyer* him. The two boys aided in a reconciliation between Billotte and de Gaulle. Boissieu was with him in Moscow in 1941, because he had escaped from prison camp shortly after Billotte. Likewise, he says, in September, 1944, "I saved young de Gaulle's life." At Chaumont, near Colombey-les-deux-Eglises, young de Gaulle (then a naval lieutenant) took a handful of tanks out as a flank guard on Billotte's right. They were surrounded by Germans and, since Billotte heard the gunfire, he sent a large force through to save them because "after all I didn't want de Gaulle's son killed or taken prisoner."

PARIS, *January 21, 1963*

DINED with the Bohlens and Maurice and Katie Macmillan. They are very gloomy about the European crisis. Maurice thinks England will have to take immediate emergency steps beginning with an embargo on the removal of capital and control of imports and exports.

He says the French argument that his father knew about the Nassau deal when he was at Rambouillet is untrue. It was Harold Macmillan's idea that an emergency provision be written into the Nassau agreement allowing Britain to use Polaris submarines for national purposes at moments of great national interest. Macmillan pointed out to Kennedy that unless there were such a safety valve, there would never be an alternative for an ally but the extremes of remaining 100 percent loyal or negotiating with an enemy.

Maurice said his parents' visit to the de Gaulles had been unexpectedly livened up. The General had ordered that a movie be shown one evening and a young cultural attaché at the Quai d'Orsay had selected and sent as "suitable" a travelogue about Polynesia. But he had obviously neglected to see the film through himself. The entire last reel was taken up with tribal preparations for battle during which the warriors carefully, explicitly, and painstakingly decorate their private parts. Mme de Gaulle was appalled—as the four watched in bleak silence.

PARIS, *January 22, 1963*

IN the morning mail arrived a plain envelope addressed in hand, which I thought was a bill. I ripped it open and found a two-page letter from General de Gaulle written in pen and ink on his personal stationery, a plain piece of paper headed in the upper left corner "Le Général de Gaulle."

It was dated January 20, and mailed yesterday, January 21 at 5:45 P.M. from rue Cler in the 7th arrondissement. I note the time because on January 20, Adenauer arrived in Paris to sign a Franco-German treaty with de Gaulle which Washington is calling the "Bonn-Paris Axis." The letter said, in part:

I read your book, *The Test*, with much interest. I will refrain from judging your opinions since you are passing judgment on me. But I must say that the facts you recount are, to my knowledge, exact on the whole and that your work is very vivid and very clear. Moreover, how could I fail to appreciate the sympathy toward me I felt in it.

C. de Gaulle

I was pleased that the facts I recounted are confirmed as exact.

Somehow it seems strange—in this age of teleprompters, ghost writers, electric typewriters, etc.—to think of a seventy-two-year-old chief of state writing a letter all by himself (despite his bad eyes), then addressing and licking the envelope. And also, the envelope is completely unmarked and of somewhat inferior quality. Had it not been mailed over at rue Cler in the 7th arrondissement, I could easily imagine that the old man, after writing it, had jammed on his hat and coat and gone out to put it in the postbox.

BARBIZON, FRANCE, *January 23, 1963*

MOST interesting lunch with General Speidel at the Bas Bréau. Speidel was in Greece in October and lunched with the royal family. He claims Crown Prince Constantine dangerously passed his car on the road to Tatoi and he reprimanded the young man in front of his parents—who agreed. Speidel finds him spoiled and lazy. He speaks no French and very little German. (Today it was announced that Constantine will marry a Danish princess.)

Speidel thinks the Franco-German alliance signed yesterday is a pleasant

symbol but means nothing. All the German generals think the idea pointless.

He agrees that France has a backward strategy while Germany has a forward strategy and no meeting of minds is possible on this, General Ailleret doesn't know anything about troops but is only interested in his
nuclear projects. The last French maneuvers were a disaster and entirely
contrary to the meaning of NATO. But de Gaulle is still intent on defending France alone in case of war and reckons on a Russian breakthrough. It is hard to imagine where the thirty divisions on the central
front will come from if de Gaulle doesn't play ball. It is an anomaly to
find Germany "specially" allied to the one western power which formally
favors the Oder-Neisse frontier and the division of Germany.

PARIS, *January 24, 1963*

LUNCHED with General Pierre Gallois, now a liaison man for the Marcel
Dassault aircraft corporation. Among the officers present was Colonel
René Chesnais of the French air force who used to be Al Gruenther's
aide-de-camp at SHAPE. He is now a member of General de Gaulle's
Elysée staff. Gallois says:

The United States bases strategy today on a choice of options. It wants
to be able to choose between concession and nuclear war. It openly
seeks a rational and flexible policy. But the crux of the difficulty is that
France does not want a choice of options. France does not want to offer
the Russians a chance of anything between concession and nuclear holocaust. France has been invaded three times during the last century. It
doesn't think it possible to have conventional war in Europe and its
policy does not contemplate an alternative between any form of invasion
and holocaust.

The U.S.A. complains that France only has a very small number of divisions and should increase its conventional forces. Gallois points out
that Britain has 400,000 men under arms but only four divisions. The
U.S.A. has 2,500,000 men under arms but only sixteen divisions. The
Russians are doing much better about producing divisions from their
population.

I foresaw a serious problem at the end of this year when the French
"force de frappe" was finally in being as a small group of Mirages,
armed with atomic bombs. At that point, the issue would arise in NATO
as to whether France, with its countercity strategy, would agree to coordinate its choice of targets with NATO's counterforce strategy.

Gallois thought the best France could do would be exactly what the
British had done prior to Nassau. The British had promised NATO their
V-bomber force would take on five missions on D-day, five missions on
D-day plus one, etc. The missions were not specified but presumably

could be coordinated with NATO plans. France might be able to work out a similar small percentage basis on the number of missions committed; that was all.

De Gaulle was adjusting to the 1960s his original idea of the 1930s for an "armée de metier." In the 1930s, he wanted a small professional force of six armored divisions with air support. That would reduce the huge number of men mobilized in a conventional force and release them to industry—also cutting costs. This was approximately the idea today, adjusted to the nuclear age.

Gallois recalled that in 1954, when he was a high SHAPE official, NATO based its plans on the idea of a "crust" force of less than twenty divisions stationed within 50 kilometers of the Iron Curtain and protected by low-yield nuclear weapons. Strategy was not based on defense requirements but on the estimates of what the allies were ready to produce rather than what they needed. He himself had participated in planning with Andy Goodpaster.

The original basis for what we now call the "thirty divisional requirement" on the central front was a demand for twenty-eight NATO divisions on that front when we talked of 150 Soviet divisions. Why, asked Gallois, have we now moved that figure on our side from twenty-eight to thirty divisions while, at the same time, we say the Russian force has been reduced to 150 divisions? The answer again is only in terms of what the allies can produce, not what they need.

France does *not* believe in a conventional strategy. The U.S.A. tells Europe it has two hundred million men and only eighteen divisions— and that isn't enough. France answers that the U.S.A. has 185 million inhabitants and only sixteen divisions. There is a standoff. Both sides of the Atlantic have high living standards to protect and don't want massive mobilization.

The Kennedy administration has been obsessed by a new emphasis on fear. It fears two things; nuclear war by miscalculation and by escalation. But Europe is less scared by the idea of escalation, which is what most frightens the U.S.A. now that it realizes that it is directly under the ICBM barrel.

As a result of American fears, Washington now wants to withdraw tactical nuclear weapons from Europe. But until this policy started, tactical nuclear weapons had in fact been a safety valve. They filled the gap between armed "incidents" and holocaust. McNamara's present policy is what widens the gap between conventional war and holocaust, instead of vice versa.

Furthermore, Polaris submarines, envisioned in a multilateral force, are only countercity weapons and not counterforce weapons. It requires at least two aimed Polaris missiles to insure destruction of any target. It would require some 1,600 Polaris missiles to do the job, on a counterforce basis, or perhaps four hundred land-based missiles. And anyway, paradoxically enough, Polaris submarines are only designed for countercity purposes while we talk of a counterforce strategy.

British military policy has not changed one iota despite the Nassau agreement. In fact, British policy is much closer to that of France than to that of the U.S.A. The British have hardly any conventional troops and a very small commitment in Germany. And they are planning to keep a strong national independent nuclear deterrent, no matter what the Americans say about the Nassau agreement.

The heart of the problem is that what is *less* than general war for the U.S.A. *is* general war for France. What is a minor incident for the U.S.A. is a major incident for Europe. General Taylor in his *Uncertain Trumpet* suggests that war should be redefined. For Taylor, war is a nuclear exchange between the U.S.A. and the U.S.S.R. Anything else is "localized conflict." France uses the same logic. France agrees with Taylor. It is for this reason that Paris and Washington are today so far apart.

Gallois carries his argument to a disagreeable extreme. He says: "Can you reconcile the existence of atomic weapons to any system of military alliance such as NATO?" The answer is a flat no. In the end, the only answer for atomic "have" powers is "chacun pour soi." The only alliances possible today are among nations which do not have nuclear weapons.

In 1950, Britain and France urged the U.S.A. not to use nuclear weapons during the Korean war, when the U.S. had immense superiority over Russia. As a result, the Americans fought a stupid, costly war in which they lost 100,000 men and spent so much money that they lost the first lap of the space race. This American experience in itself is one reason why France does not rely on conventional weapons.

In 1954, the French lost out in Indochina, despite last-minute American support, because the British opposed the use of nuclear weapons. In 1956, Washington opposed France and Britain and they lost Suez because they had no nuclear support. In 1958, Britain and the U.S. reacted to events in Iraq and Lebanon and, although their effort was clearly sabotaged by France, they won because of the implied nuclear strength of the U.S.A. In 1961–1962, all three powers disagreed on Laos and the result was a fiasco.

In the atomic age, alliances are inherently weak and there is no escape from this. They must respond to their lowest common denominator. In an alliance today, you don't add the strength of contributing nations, you divide it. You don't add to the combined wills of the nations; you divide.

NATO is preparing for a war which in fact cannot take place. It is planning for many months of a war which would only last for a few minutes.

NATO should be turned upside down. It should produce machine tools and distribute weapons; and then it should tell its members that, in a time of crisis, they are free to die if they wish to do so. That is all the alliance can hope to achieve.

Gallois argues that so long as NATO bases its philosophy on the Dulles concept it is—and was—valid. Dulles understood that the U.S.A. had to brandish its nuclear weapons with some irrationality—as we showed in Quemoy and Matsu. With a man like Dulles, the Russians never knew just what an adventure would lead to.

We are at a disadvantage if we talk to Khrushchev only in rational terms. He frightened the wits out of Averell Harriman when he told him that if one single Russian soldier was killed around Berlin he had already given orders to his marshals to unleash their rockets against the U.S.A. This was irrational but it worked.

In 1958, Dulles succeeded in bluffing out a victory at Quemoy, 6,000 miles away from the U.S. coastline. In 1962, Kennedy succeeded in bluffing the Russians out of Cuba less than 100 miles from the U.S. coastline. The U.S.A. has lost more than 5,000 miles in four years.

PARIS, *January 29, 1963*

LUNCHED today with John Mowinckel. He says Galbraith has such a high and mighty way of presenting his views to Washington that Rusk cabled him last Christmas: "Happy Birthday."

Baldwin, ambassador in Malaya, cabled the Peace Corps over his signature saying one of the Peace Corps doctors wanted a rectal thermometer for the buffaloes. He stipulated: "Require a seven-inch instrument. Five inches not enough." Shriver sent a deadpan memo to Kennedy, his brother-in-law, saying, "I think you should know what your envoy to Malaya requires."

PARIS, *January 30, 1963*

TODAY I saw Chris Herter who said: "For God's sake, please continue to write your columns explaining what de Gaulle really thinks; nobody else does."

Herter thought it possible there would be a trade war in the western world as a result of the Common Market crisis. This would be very costly and the Russians could exploit it, above all by unloading cheap oil.

He is now Kennedy's principal trade negotiator but doesn't know whether under our laws the U.S.A. could deal with individual members of the Common Market or only with the Market as a bloc.

It is apparent, now that the concept of a conventional shield for NATO is finished, we will have to get back to the strategy of immediate nuclear defense against any attack in Europe. The U.S.A. simply isn't going to get the divisions it wants.

Received a letter from Eisenhower, who is in Palm Springs, saying in part:

I do not mind saying that, while I believe that at the very beginning, NATO was conceived largely as strictly a defensive mechanism, my administration tried, starting soon after my inauguration, to give a broader base of interest for the organization—hoping for collective consideration of questions entirely outside of the military. Moreover, while I have not in recent months read the NATO agreement, it is my impression that there was clearly implied the purpose of keeping the free world unified in their approach to common problems; even though the language emphasized, almost exclusively, military aspects.

DE GAULLE:

"EUROPE COULD NOT

DEFEND ITSELF ALONE"

PARIS, *January 31, 1963*

I SAW GENERAL DE GAULLE THIS AFTERNOON. HE SAID IIE NOTICED *The New York Times* had been hostile to him. I said I just wrote my own opinions. "I know that," he said. "And I want to tell you once again how much I appreciate your book." I then hauled out a massive list of questions, spreading them out in front of me on his desk and took out my notebook.*

"Allons-y," he said. I started off by asking if he intended to retire upon completion of his term as President in January, 1966. Without any hesitation he replied: "Yes, I hope to retire."†

I asked if, as things now stood, there were any particular three or four men he thought might be qualified to succeed him in the post of President. He said: "Really I would not like to answer that. I cannot say. Surely there are men who are qualified but it would be incorrect for me to express an opinion on this subject."‡

Did he plan to write a fourth volume of his *Mémoires*? He replied:

No, definitely not. Not at all. You must remember that the other three volumes were *mémoires de guerre*. For the period since then, the period after that which I covered in those three volumes, history can speak for itself in facts and documents, even if not through the press, which has been most distorted. But there were no such facts and docu-

---

* See de Gaulle's further comments, p. 82.
† See de Gaulle's further comments, p. 38.
‡ See de Gaulle's further comments, p. 38.

ments really available for the period of the war and therefore I could not leave that tale untold. But I can assure you I will not write a fourth volume.*

I wondered if he thought France retained a prejudice against the U.S. and Britain, as a result of wartime disagreements between 1940 and 1945. He said: "It is very evident that during the war both the U.S. and Britain tried to control France and the affairs of France according to their own desires. And it is true that I opposed the U.S. and Britain in such efforts. I opposed them for the very reason I have just cited and I can assure you I did well."†

I then moved the conversation to the subject of foreign affairs and began by asking if he thought a meeting between himself and Kennedy would be useful at any time in the near future.

Rather to my surprise he said: "I prefer to reserve my answer." I waited for him to add something, staring back at him, but he said nothing. I then asked: "But in principle, might such a meeting be useful?"

He said: "I have always had the impression that such meetings are only of value for agreements (pour s'accorder)."

I then asked if he thought it would be useful to prepare the ground first, but I could not nudge anything further out of him on this subject.

I inquired whether he thought there could or should be such a thing as interdependence between Europe and North America. He said:

Alas, first there must be a Europe. Right now it is very convenient for the U.S. There is a France and a Germany and an Italy and a Great Britain. And the U.S. plays each one against the other.

But if there were a real Europe, that would be different. There would have to be a real Europe with its own economy, its own policy, and its own defense. Once there is such a Europe, it should have an organized accord with the U.S., but what, after all, is interdependence? I don't know what is meant by this, and there must be "rapports" between Europe and America. That is interdependence, I suppose.

But certainly, in terms of defense, if there is a Soviet threat, Europe could not defend itself alone. Nor really could the U.S.A. The U.S.A. could defend itself with missiles but not in a moral sense and vis-à-vis the free world.‡

I said Messmer had announced the "force de frappe" would be in existence by the end of this year and asked if France, as part of its coordination, would work out and select targets in accord with NATO. He said: "Of course we are ready to cooperate technically and also strategically.

* See de Gaulle's further comments, pp. 37, 38, 55, 85–86.
† See de Gaulle's further comments, p. 55.
‡ See de Gaulle's further comments, pp. 65–66.

'There should be no problem." (I fear there will be a big problem when it comes to choosing between "counterforce" and "countercity" targets.)*

I said I understood that in June, 1940, de Gaulle himself had received Monnet's and Lord Vansittart's proposal to unite France and Britain and that de Gaulle had personally submitted this to Churchill. He said my information was correct. I then said: "If you considered Britain a European country then why isn't it European today?"

He said: "Ah, but of course, Britain can be in Europe. It was European then. But it doesn't want to be European today. It was obliged by the circumstance of war to be European at that moment. Now it must come back to things in a European way."

I then asked him if he thought German signature of the Treaty of Reconciliation implied formal acceptance of de Gaulle's own view that the Oder-Neisse line was the permanent border between Germany and Poland.

He answered: "I didn't discuss this with Adenauer. This is not a current question for the Germans. Berlin is. Berlin is the only real point. I don't think there were any new commitments on the Oder-Neisse line."

I asked if France were working for a unified Germany and would be willing to see it neutralized and demilitarized in exchange for unification.

"This is not a question now," he said. "Our treaty supports Germany in terms of the status quo, the status quo in Berlin. This is its only significance in those terms."

Would he be prepared to see a demilitarized Germany in exchange for reunification? He said: "If Germany were neutralized, France would be quickly neutralized also. We are for a Germany allied to the West and militarily effective. Our view has not changed."

I asked if France intended an alliance with Spain and whether he expected to visit Spain. He did not intend any treaty like that with Germany. Nevertheless, Spain required much help and was a militarily important country. The Spanish should be brought into western defense. This must be arranged because there were certain essentials that had to be faced. But he was planning neither a treaty nor a visit.

I remarked there had been rumors in some newspapers to the effect that he would like to make a deal with Russia of a private sort. The General said this was absurd; the Communist menace remained and France remained attached to its ideals and obligations.

We got up together and he escorted me to the door. Absentmindedly he wished me a happy New Year, hastily adding:

"Of course, it is already January 31, yet most of this year is before you and I do hope you have a good year."

* See de Gaulle's further comments, pp. 42, 46, 55–56, 56.

PARIS, *February 1, 1963*

FIRST-CLASS talk with Pompidou. He came in puffing a cigar, looking very sleek and content. He is solid but not big, giving a curious air of comfortable confidence. We moved to his inner office, sitting at a table by the window, looking over the lovely garden. I regretted there was so much to talk about today because relations between our countries were not what we would like them. He smiled sadly and said yes, he agreed.

Many people, I began, were speculating about a "deal" between Paris and Moscow; was there any substance to such reports? He said on the contrary, there wasn't the slightest truth in them. Ambassador Vinogradov had gone to see de Gaulle a couple of days ago, but only to complain about the Franco-German treaty. All he did was to worry about the treaty with Adenauer.

How did he envision the role of the United States and Britain vis-à-vis the kind of "Europe" France was looking forward to? He said:

The role of Britain is evident. In the end Britain must be in. It is inevitable. The normal role for Britain is to be part of Europe because it is so closely linked by history and geography.

But this will mean, undoubtedly, a great historical change for Britain. After all, the British are used to their links with the Commonwealth and the United States. Also it has been British doctrine for so long to prevent any European unity. This was the traditional British policy until 1940. But there has been a profound change in everything and it is perfectly clear that ultimately Britain will be part of Europe.

As for the United States, the day will come when the U.S.A. and Europe must work together on an equal basis. Once this essential fact is recognized, we can plan and work together and end our current difficulties.

I then asked if he thought NATO was outmoded, or if France, in any case, was planning to withdraw from NATO. He said:

I will give you my idea. This is only my idea, but I would like to tell you what I think. NATO is not outmoded at the present moment. But for us, NATO is still the United States. It is dominated and run by the United States.

NATO will be in this sense outmoded when the United States no longer dominates it. But the forces exist to create another balance in the West.

In the future, once a Europe has been organized, NATO will reflect a separate change, a repartition of strength, a more precise balance of forces. At that time, Europe will be able to defend itself in a better and more effective way—but allied to the United States. It would become an alliance of two powers instead of fifteen nations. But this is for the future. We must go along with the concept of NATO as it is for the present, despite disagreements. It is ridiculous that France wants to quit NATO.

What did he think Europe's ultimate role would be? He observed:

Certainly, it is excluded that Europe would be a "third force." Naturally, we all hope, all of us, that Russia will become more civilized and will turn westward, cut off from China and establishing its own freedoms. I think Russia will turn toward us and eventually aspire to join with European nations just the way Poland and Spain are now turning toward us. Europe is certainly closer to Russia than the United States is, for example. But there would never be any effort to set up a balance, from the European viewpoint, playing between Washington and Moscow. Such a concept couldn't come for years.

Did he consider Russia a more "European" country than Britain? He replied categorically, "Certainly not. Britain is certainly more European than Russia. It is more European than Russia ever could be. But on the other hand, Russia is probably more European than the United States."

I asked if Britain would now be in the Common Market if she had joined the Gaullist idea of a "European" nuclear force. He said:

I think you exaggerate the point. Certainly we would have been obliged to make Britain see the need for an economic solution, whether or not there had been such an agreement. Had Britain decided to come into a European nuclear force, it would have proved Britain's desire to become truly European. Then, in that context, other problems would have been more easily solved—such problems as wheat, mutton— and we could have even made transitional agreements to help the British out. And we would have been ready for compromise. It is hard to envision a European atomic force without British participation.

Pompidou said France remained sternly against the idea of Germany receiving atomic weapons. He repeated de Gaulle's arguments, saying that Germany was forbidden by its own commitments to have atomic weapons. The new treaty with Germany was in a sense aimed against this. "France believes that the Germans themselves have interdicted themselves from having such weapons. We cannot consider changing the situation."

On Spain he said:

Spain is a neighbor and we are on bad terms. We have been on bad terms since the days of Napoleon. And then of course, during more recent days, there was the argument that always persisted over Morocco. Our relations with Spain were poisoned over Morocco just the way our relations with Britain were poisoned over the Middle East—Syria, and the Lebanon and Palestine, even Egypt. But the Spanish regime has changed. It is becoming more liberal. It has opened a new window to the West. Spain is lowering the barrier of the Pyrenees. And we must recognize these changes.

I talked of new American senatorial desires to withdraw U.S. troops from Europe. Was France taking sufficient care to understand our public opinion? He replied: "Quite frankly, France certainly wants the United States to continue stationing its six divisions in Europe. Surely that is so. We need them. We need the United States and France and the United States must work together. It is a disservice to both countries to exaggerate present difficulties."

Was he astounded by the vigor of reaction to de Gaulle's veto of Britain in the Common Market and spurning of Kennedy's Nassau offer on Polaris? He said: "No, I am not astounded. I expected that the reaction would be sharp and strong. One of de Gaulle's principal characteristics is to say exactly what he thinks. And after all, this is a turning point. One cannot escape that fact. It is normal to have a sharp reaction. Nevertheless, I must confess that I am somewhat startled by its violence."

I told him that I had talked with de Gaulle about the degree of anti-Americanism in the French press and de Gaulle was astonished because he had exactly the contrary feeling. What did he think? Pompidou said: "I think you are both right. Both observations are true. There is certainly an anti-American element in the French press today and there is also an anti-de Gaulle element in the French press. As far as I am concerned, I deplore both. They can do no good."

Pompidou said the "basis" of French policy is that Europe must have its *own* nuclear force. It must be able to defend itself to some degree. Otherwise, Europe would not be in a position to prevent a possible deal, someday, between the U.S. and Russia, when both are looking for a détente. It is the reverse of what the Americans say France is after. The obvious thing that would have to be dealt with, if Washington and Moscow ever got together, would be some sort of arrangement to neutralize Germany. And that would be fatal for France. France must keep the Germans tied to them, tied to the West. This was absolutely essential and the whole point of the Adenauer-de Gaulle treaty of "reconciliation" was to make it impossible to have a neutralized Germany.

I then returned, at the risk of redundancy, to the idea of nuclear weapons for Germany. He said: "After all, I must admit, it is hard to prevent the Germans from wanting nuclear weapons. It is very hard to stop them. But we are certainly going to try to stop them for just as long as we can. De Gaulle, of course, could not announce this at his press conference. This was not the kind of thing he could talk about in public. But really, one of the essential reasons for the recent treaty between Germany and France is simply to prevent the Germans from having nuclear weapons."

I then remarked rather acidly that it seemed to me Paris and Washington had an identical policy toward Germany in this respect and it was strange that they were in such an argument about it. He said: "Yes, we do have the same policy there. But we can't let all this go through Washington. We have to have a control ourselves. We ourselves cannot risk that someday Washington might decide to neutralize Germany, without even asking us."

He seemed in a mood to chat. A curious thing was that in the next British elections de Gaulle would be a major factor. But: "I can promise you de Gaulle will be very happy if he is a major factor and this helps Macmillan win. Macmillan is the best man to govern Britain from our point of view. We hope he gets back and we won't mind in the least if he campaigns to victory on an anti-de Gaulle platform."

I mentioned, as I was saying farewell, that de Gaulle told me he thought it was no longer possible to revive the *directoire* idea, but that at the same time he regretted the fact that the Big Three western powers were not consolidating their views enough in advance. Pompidou agreed the *directoire* idea was dead. He said that, after all, Germany had been reestablished as a major power and could not now be excluded. So there never could be a "Big Three" in the West, the way it had been possible in 1958.

On the way out, I dropped in on Simonne Servais, his press aide. She told me that, at the time of the last putsch, when de Gaulle was in danger, he sent a private letter to his physician André Lichtwitz, perhaps his only confidant. This was a private political testament, enclosed in an envelope marked: "To be opened if anything happens to me." And that envelope was in another addressed personally to the doctor, containing a request to return it to de Gaulle if nothing did happen. Lichtwitz returned it after the crisis. De Gaulle gave him the outer envelope, saying: "Keep this: it is historical. I shall dispose of the rest."

PARIS, *February 2, 1963*

DINED last night with Chris Herter and then went to the embassy where Bohlen, who has just been ill, was pacing up and down, eager to discuss de Gaulle. The General told him when he last saw him January 4, that he considered it "inevitable" West Germany would someday have atomic weapons.

Chip is bitter because he feels he was personally double-crossed. He had been telling Washington the door was open for further nuclear negotiations. De Gaulle apparently had indicated as much in the letter he sent Kennedy on January 3, the day before he saw Chip. Then on January 14, without any subsequent letter, de Gaulle spurned the Nassau-Polaris offer and announced in a public press conference a series of blatantly contrary views. Chip complained: "How can you say de Gaulle is courteous when he does a discourteous thing like making such a public announcement without even advising the President first?"

Chip wonders if the implication of de Gaulle's present policy is preparing an ultimate deal with Russia.

PARIS, *February 14, 1963*

INTERESTING tête-à-tête luncheon with Blankenhorn (German ambassador). "I am going to speak very frankly," he said, and then proceeded to unload.

He has deep-seated mistrust for de Gaulle. He says: "I know what I am talking about because I have been through this once before in terms of Hitler." (He was co-opted into the Nazi party himself in 1936, as were all State officials.) He claims de Gaulle is determined to exclude the Americans and British from Europe and to replace them with a French-dominated coalition strong enough to make its own deal with Russia after the embourgeoisement of that country is far enough advanced to permit an adjustment.

There is much more to the Spanish negotiations than the French admit. The French are trying to work out a military alliance with Spain that will not only include bases in the Canary Islands, but will also cover such things as joint maneuvers and the supplying of French arms to Spain.

France has violated its German treaty several times already. It did not consult the Germans prior to de Gaulle's decision to exclude the British from the Common Market or refuse the U.S. Polaris offer. It did not consult the Germans prior to starting the Spanish negotiations.

PARIS, *February 15, 1963*

LAST night at dinner, Mme Jean-Claude Servan-Schreiber, who dislikes her cousin-in-law Jean-Jacques, told me that Jean-Jacques was trying to build up a small press empire in order to launch himself politically so he can run for President a few years hence. Just a few days ago, he tried to buy up *France Observateur*, but at the last minute this flopped. Jean-Jacques had hoped to turn *L'Express* into a daily and use *France Observateur* as the equivalent of the present *L'Express*. He is trying to gain control of *Les Echos*, run by Jean-Claude.

Lunched with Alessandrini. He insists de Gaulle is beginning to follow in the footsteps of Mussolini and Hitler (another ex-fascist telling me this; rather gloomily impressive). We cannot afford to let him blackmail us.

The Russians will never make a deal with de Gaulle because he doesn't matter to them and what they are thinking about is the reality of American strength. Alex is convinced Moscow and Washington made a deal on removing missiles almost simultaneously from Cuba and Italy and Turkey.

PARIS, *February 18, 1963*

JEAN Laloy thinks it a terrible mistake ever to permit two statesmen to be entirely alone because they never completely understand each other and dictate contradictory accounts of their meeting. Both Macmillan and de Gaulle will probably write their own versions of what they said to each other during the recent Rambouillet talks—simply because they didn't understand each other.

For a long time, de Gaulle hoped that Russia would slowly be changed by "embourgeoisement" under the leadership of the good old muzhik, Khrushchev. But Khrushchev's second visit to France completely removed this illusion.

At one point, I said de Gaulle rather liked children but didn't know how to behave with them. Laloy commented: "It is the way Swift liked babies. Somebody once asked him, 'Do you like babies?' Swift replied, 'Yes, boiled.' "

The other day at the Quai d'Orsay, Jean was talking to Couve and explaining that he should never forget there was an element of idealism in American policy. Couve replied: "Surely, I know better than any of you how Puritans can manage to suit their ideals to their political interests." (Couve is a Protestant, Laloy a Catholic.)

PARIS, *February 22, 1963*

DINED at Blankenhorn's. Among those present were Tony Rumbold (British minister) and Soldati (the Swiss ambassador). Tony insists Macmillan and de Gaulle were never alone for one minute. They were always accompanied by Zulueta (Macmillan's right-hand man), Burin des Roziers, and Andronikov (the official French interpreter).

Tony saw the official French version of the conversations. The only substantial difference between the French and British versions was this. De Gaulle said to Macmillan: "And what if we two join in the manufacture of missiles?" He did not mention nuclear warheads, although this seems to be implicit. Macmillan didn't answer. De Gaulle, when he went over the compte-rendu, struck out this sentence, presumably so that he would not appear on the record as a supplicant.

Soldati says that one year ago he predicted that Britain would never be in the Common Market. He could not understand how a great power like the United States could base its entire foreign policy on the single assumption that Jean Monnet was right in saying that Britain would join.

I wish there would be a strike of the electrical workers in Washington, D.C., in order to stop the computers and allow the State Department a chance to think.

PARIS, *February 25, 1963*

LUNCHED with Senator Jacques Baumel, secretary-general and boss of the UNR-UDT (the Gaullist party). He is forty-five, agreeable. I find him pro-American; nobody else does.

He is convinced de Gaulle will stand for reelection in 1966, but sure he will resign before his second term is over. He wants to get the European question fixed—vis-à-vis England—and that cannot happen for four or five more years. But the General has a fear of decaying in office while chief of state—not physically but mentally. De Gaulle believes "la vieillesse est un naufrage" (old age is a shipwreck), and he has a horror of it.

PARIS, *February 26, 1963*

LUNCHED today with General Stehlin. De Gaulle has explained his strategic concepts to him. Either there will never be another war on a major scale because it is too dangerous, or the entire world will be destroyed in such a war. Either way, you cannot plan for the results so there is no need to worry about logical defense. But France must make an effort to join the nuclear club. One member of the French Automobile Club may have a Rolls-Royce and the other a 2 CV (Mini), but one can't join the Automobile Club if one doesn't have the 2 CV. Furthermore, de Gaulle wants his force as a diplomatic weapon.

Stehlin said the insoluble confrontation between the U.S.A. and France would come late this year when there is an actual small Mirage force and French and NATO planners discuss targeting. There cannot really be any compromise between counterforce and countercity strategies. But de Gaulle doesn't understand this. From an American viewpoint, all we have to do is tell the French: "We already have such and such a target covered by six missiles. If you want to join in we can cover it with seven, thanks to your help. That is up to you." But if France wants to aim at Kiev and we don't, trouble starts.

PARIS, *February 27, 1963*

LUNCH with Tom Finletter. He is a strong opponent of McNamara and thinks it shocking that a man with so little experience in international affairs should have such a big impact on American foreign policy. He also thinks it ridiculous that the Secretary of State was not even present at the Nassau meeting. He sneers at George Ball as too much under the influence of Jean Monnet, quoting Senator Aiken's remark that Ball should have been registered as a foreign lobbyist when he worked for Monnet.

PARIS, *March 4, 1963*

GOLFED with Couve de Murville. He complained that the whole world is badgered by the farm problem. Farmers always have powerful political lobbies and are coddled by governments, which give them artificial subsidies and then charge the consumers and taxpayers the costs.

PARIS, *March 6, 1963*

COUVE, Pompidou, and de Gaulle himself have told me the General's 1958 *directoire* letter was never answered by Eisenhower. And Kennedy plus two American ambassadors "confirmed" this. The Americans, at any rate, hadn't taken the trouble to look into the facts.

At last I got the story from Chip Bohlen. Chip, who had been doing some homework, took me back to the embassy to show me the actual texts. He is going to wire Rusk asking permission for me to write the truth.

On September 17, 1958, de Gaulle wrote Eisenhower a letter a bit more than a page long—to which was appended a memorandum which was being sent in duplicate to Macmillan. The General said France understood the worries of the U.S.A. on Formosa (then a crisis) and suggested that an "organization"—the word *directoire* was not used—be composed of the Big Three western powers to make basic decisions in all the world, including the use of nuclear weapons.

On October 21, 1958, Eisenhower sent back a letter by himself and marked as a NIACT (meaning urgent, night-action telegram) for Cecil Lyon (then chargé d'affaires) and Randy Burgess (then U.S. ambassador to NATO) explaining the American viewpoint. It stressed the necessity of considering the viewpoints of other NATO allies in any political decisions. The letter was in the embassy files.

Chip had been startled to discover this answer only a week ago. Before then, he also had believed the U.S.A. had never answered de Gaulle. There had obviously been a ridiculous lapse in American governmental methods.

PARIS, *March 15, 1963*

LAST night we went to a very small dinner Couve de Murville gave at the Quai d'Orsay. One of the troubles with American policy, he says, is the curious system we have inherited from our earliest origins. It is the habit in the U.S.A. to elect a man President who has had no governmental experience. When he campaigns he is surrounded by "experts" on different subjects and he brings them along to the White House after his election. This tends to create a kind of second Cabinet where a man like Mac Bundy can have more importance than the Secretary of State.

France, on the other hand, has a long tradition of centralized authority, dating back to the monarchy. It has the habit of a small executive aided by a formal Cabinet of what the French call the "governement," and underneath the professional civil-service functions. The Cabinet carries out policy on orders from the executive and in the case of de Gaulle the executive is an unusually strong man. But there are three or four principal ministers in the Cabinet among whom Couve—with no false modesty—includes himself, adding: "I have much more to do with policy than Dean Rusk has in the U.S.A."

He considered it most unlikely that the Russians and the Chinese would be able to reach a settlement. In any case, it was silly for the western countries to gamble on probabilities. It was ridiculous to argue that we must not do such and such a thing because it would weaken Khrushchev's position and bring about something worse.

Khrushchev's problem vis-à-vis China was very comparable to that of the U.S.A. vis-à-vis France. The Chinese wanted independent nuclear strength, but the Russians could not afford to give that to the Chinese because they would lose some of their power if they did so.

Couve said that Britain had made the classical error of gambling on French internal politics. It only really got started on serious Common Market negotiations last October. Then it tried to delay while betting de Gaulle would be defeated in the elections. They guessed wrong.

Macmillan had no sensible policy but tried to ride two horses at once. He wanted the economic conveniences of the Common Market while at the same time retaining special relations with the U.S.

The British had hoped to drag out negotiations and gradually isolate France while winning the support of the other five continental powers. France thus decided it was necessary to act brutally in order to prevent Britain from carrying out this plan and that was the reason for the sudden, dramatic dénouement.

Couve admitted that if Britain had joined France in a nuclear missile force it undoubtedly could have gotten into the Common Market because it would have proven it was genuinely European. But it chose Nassau instead.

Couve thinks the multilateral-navy concept (MLF) Washington now pushes is a mistake. Both France and the U.S. agree on the basic aim of delaying the creation of a German national nuclear force. However, the multilateral idea will do nothing but whet the German appetite. The Germans are expected to pay 40 percent of the cost and therefore they will be in a strong position to request acceleration of their own atomic demands.

LONDON, *March 16, 1963*

DAVID Bruce, with whom we are staying in London, told me he thought it was a great mistake for Kennedy to go to the Nassau Conference without his Secretary of State. The President had told him he and Rusk had decided it was not advisable for the two to be out of the country at the same time. But this agreement has never been put into practice. Furthermore the two men are going to Costa Rica for the OAS Conference.

LONDON, *March 18, 1963*

I ASKED Bruce what effect a Labour victory in the next elections would have on British relations with the U.S.A. and NATO. He said: "My guess is Britain won't repudiate the Nassau agreement, but might cease building ships for the Polaris force." The Labour party would certainly give up an independent nuclear deterrent and increase conventional forces. The Tories are also pledged to increase conventional forces and it would probably not be easy for Labour to rely exclusively on the U.S.A. for atomic protection.

Labour is probably more anticolonial than the Conservatives. The Tories would also want to give independence to former colonies *if* they can. But only when these dependencies are prepared to govern themselves. Labour would try to speed up the process. This doesn't bother us. Economically, nationalization and capital levies will be pushed if Labour comes in, but the U.S.A. doesn't need to worry about this unless it causes an economic crisis.

All this, of course, subject to the reservation that Labour will make one of its basic objectives a desire to get along with the U.S.A. David simply cannot imagine an anti-American government in Britain as we are too essential to Britain's material interest.

Bruce said Acheson was right when he said de Gaulle was a great man and we must not think he was petty or entirely "bad" just because his policy runs against ours. There was no point in having a violent argument with him. The basic underlying issue on the NATO force was to give the Germans an equal status. Nevertheless, Bruce says it is very hard for the U.S. to expand political control over the West's nuclear forces. You can't be in the position of having 97 percent of the West's nuclear strength and deal with your allies on its use.

LONDON, *March 19, 1963*

LUNCHED with Patrick Gordon Walker, shadow foreign secretary in the Labour leadership and probably foreign minister in any Harold Wilson Cabinet.

Gordon Walker has an intellectual, sad, long face, and his head is growing bald. He talked willingly and in a most friendly fashion, seeming rather disappointed when I told him I didn't intend to quote him. He said:

> Broadly speaking, a Labour government would be nearer to the philosophy of Kennedy in Washington than the present government. Our big problem is to try not to look as if we are trailing along behind the U.S. Defense policy would certainly change. We would be closer to the McNamara viewpoint. It doesn't pay to go on with an illusory, independent nuclear deterrent. That is a waste of money. It would pay to spend the same money on better conventional forces. The extra influence obtained through them would increase the influence of our views in the U.S.
>
> We think the Common Market is a good thing for Europe and we are not anti-French. But we don't want to join the Common Market. We want to improve relations between the Common Market and EFTA [Free Trade Area].

LONDON, *March 20, 1963*

THIS afternoon, I saw Harold Wilson, new leader of the Labour party, in his office in the House of Commons. He is a small, pipe-smoking man, with an unctuous manner, a very middle-class accent, and bright blue eyes: the face of a halibut, with shark's eyes. He was friendly and briskly answered all questions.

I started by asking if a Labour government would give up an independent deterrent. He answered in the affirmative and added:

> We cannot afford to experiment on missiles ourselves. Our policy is wholly against an independent deterrent. An independent British deterrent does not add to western strength. The western deterrent *must* be American. We are now using up, in a useless nuclear effort, resources which could be put into conventional forces where we are falling down on our obligations. Not enough is left over for brush-fire forces Britain needs. Britain insists on developing its own nuclear weapons and by doing this helps to frustrate the hopes that such weapons would not be proliferated. This is a contradictory policy and it has been Britain's official policy for three years.

He said that the general principle of the Labour party was to get Britain out of the entire nuclear business. A Labour government would not want to repudiate the Nassau agreement. Nassau was merely a sop thrown to Britain by the dominant American partner in order to help Macmillan out. A Labour government would look at the defense situation and try to repair the shambles. But Nassau envisages (in Article 6) an independent deterrent. Therefore a Labour government would want to denegotiate the Nassau agreement.

Wilson continued:

We are against a European deterrent without the U.S.A. We don't want a further division of resources in the alliance and a German finger on the trigger. Nor do we want a NATO multilateral force. At least not until we know more what it means. We think the U.S.A. is and should remain the custodian of the western deterrent. We don't like the thought that in a multilateral force there would be more fingers on the trigger. All we want is more fingers on the safety catch.

After all, if the Russians were to drop a bomb and the West is allowed only three minutes to reply, there is not time for consultation. But if there is a crisis that lasts a week, there is time for consultation. Methods must be worked out facing these different eventualities. My own impression is that the U.S. doesn't want a multilateral NATO force but made the offer just to call Europe's bluff.

Wilson would like to see Britain phase out its existing stockpiles of atomic arms, putting the entire responsibility for western nuclear defense on the U.S.A., but improving consultation methods and increasing Europe's contribution of conventional forces. If nuclear weapons are phased out it will improve the possibilities of consultation.

A Labour government would be ready to reduce Britain to Germany's level rather than to try to bring Germany up by giving it qualified access to nuclear weapons. He suspects that Macmillan, as "a part of a bribe" to France to obtain membership in the Common Market, promised to send de Gaulle plutonium. He suspects that such plutonium is actually being sent now, but I doubt this.

He thought a Labour victory would have a good effect on U.S.-U.K. relations. The so-called "special" Anglo-American relations meant very little. Eisenhower and Macmillan had an "old-boy" relationship, but the Kennedy administration was entirely too modern for that sort of thing.

LONDON, *March 21, 1963*

LUNCHED with Stash Radziwill. He told me Kennedy was so positive that de Gaulle would visit him in the U.S.A. after the Nassau Conference that he got Charlie Wrightsman to actually evacuate his house in Palm Beach so it could be prepared to lodge de Gaulle. All I could say was, "What lunacy!"

LONDON, *March 22, 1963*

TODAY, I drove to Alton in Hampshire to see Field Marshal Lord Montgomery at Isington Mill, his little country home. It was an interesting and in some ways moving experience.

His place is *really* modest and simple. When I returned to London, I happened to pass Aspley House, the enormous mansion (almost a palace) on Piccadilly given by the grateful British people to the Duke of Wellington after the Napoleonic wars. I fear that Montgomery did not do so well. Whatever one may think of him, he is undoubtedly the most famous British general since Wellington.

The Mill is about a mile off the main road to Winchester and beside a little stream in which Monty says there are trout. But that doesn't interest him. There is a more luxurious house next door, so I first rang the bell there and a maid told me I was in the wrong place. I then walked to his little place where there was a young male servant in a sweater working in the garage. The doorbell didn't work but the servant finally let me in and Monty greeted me.

Monty was wearing a dark blue knitted sweater and over it an open, leather windbreaker. He led me through the dining room upstairs to his study. The dining room was the most impressive in the small house and had some very nice silver which had undoubtedly been presented to the Field Marshal. The room was decorated with a lot of bad oil paintings, at least four of which were full length portraits of Monty.

His study proved to be plain, tasteless, spotlessly neat, with hideous but not uncomfortable furniture and an enormous mass of knickknacks. Everything was in apple-pie order, including the desk. He doesn't seem to have any secretary and I suppose when he writes a book a publisher must arrange to lend him one.

The room was filled with the most extraordinary hodgepodge of souvenirs, all meticulously hung at mathematically equidistant points or placed along the window ledges and mantel. In a peculiarly ugly cage was the only other living thing in the house, a somnolent blue parakeet with a celluloid fake companion. There were at most twenty books on a shelf by his desk and I imagine this comprises his entire library. Prominent among the books were *Burke's Peerage* and the 1963 *Who's Who*. I could just imagine the old codger reading himself to sleep with those after his usual dinner of mutton.

Among the decorations in this study were several signed snapshots of King George VI together with Montgomery. There were also signed photographs from Tito, Churchill, Mountbatten, Queen Elizabeth, Nehru, Truman, Eisenhower, Smuts, Princess Margaret (with her baby), etc. Churchill had inscribed his picture: "To Monty. Hard times; stern conflict; victorious commander! Winston S. Churchill 1946." Among the bad oil paintings were one by Churchill and one by Field Marshal Alexander.

The knickknacks were extraordinary. They included a few postcard reproductions of religious paintings placed on the bare wooden mantel above a stove with burning coal briquets; also a complicated, spotless silver replica of a tank; an ugly Bavarian bottle top; a silly little brass tag naming Monty an honorary member of a West Canadian press club.

Monty sat on a sofa opposite the stove. He seemed cocky, tough, positive, intolerant, ignorant, and unbelievably vain. He has a stubborn, grumpy face, but looks extremely fit for a man of his age. There is not an ounce of fat on him and there is a healthy gleam in his cold, blue eyes. I dislike him and think that his supreme military gift is confirmed by the fact that his own army didn't shoot him in the back. He thinks he has the answers to everything—military, political, psychological, etc.— and all in curt, simple Saxon words.

I began by asking him what he thought of the idea of a multilateral force for NATO. He said:

Nonsense. Absolute nonsense. Just assume you have a ship with a crew of one-third Belgian, one-third Portuguese, and one-third Danish. It won't work. Won't work. You might get over the language barrier. Politically maybe the idea seems good, but militarily it's poppycock.

People fight differently. I know. I have commanded all sorts of people. The European army broke down on that issue. You must keep people together in national units under national control. Maybe you can weld these units together into a fighting machine. That depends. The politicians don't understand these things. The politicians never fought or commanded troops in battle. They never commanded.

Why, you couldn't even put the British and the Americans together on the same ship. They are different. Anyone is a fool to think the British and the Americans are the same. Our sailors owe allegiance to the Queen; yours owe allegiance to the President. We have a different kind of discipline. It is all right to have British ships with British sailors, but don't let the biscuits on the same ship. You could not have a people more different than the British and the Americans. I have commanded both. I know. You should not try to mix them up in the same box of tricks.

I asked if he thought Britain should keep an independent nuclear deterrent. He answered curtly: "Yes, naturally; the French are going to. You can't have England without one. You can't let the French be the only European country with their own deterrent. Is Britain to be completely dependent on the U.S.A. for their deterrent? That would be ridiculous: Politics change; men change; people change. But we can't risk it. I am against being completely dependent on the U.S."

Should there be a European deterrent? He said:

That is all right if it is based on national contingents. I am for a strong western Europe on its own. But I mean the Continent and without Britain and the Common Market. I am for a strong Commonwealth and I am also for a strong Anglo-American alliance. I think de Gaulle is completely right. I know something about this. I started Western Defense in 1948, through Western Union. This was later absorbed into NATO.

There will be no peace, no lasting peace, until you get the armed forces of different countries back behind their borders and get the Russians back into Russia. Keep the Germans in Germany. Get the Americans back to America, the Canadians back to Canada, and the British back to Britain. Then you can do something. I don't believe the people who say that once the Americans go home they will never come back to Europe in a war. I have never known the Americans to break their word. They have signed a treaty. They will stick to it.

And there is another thing. You can't give the Germans any kind of nuclear weapons. The moment you do this you will find that the Russians are likely to go to war.

If the Russians march west, that is war. At once. But you don't have to have the Americans and the British in front line. There are fifty million Germans and if you want to know what fifty million Germans are like when they are fighting, I can tell you. They will hold the NATO front. And there are fifty million Frenchmen. Why do they want us over here?

I asked Montgomery if he favored disengagement. He said:

Disengagement is the wrong word. You have got the Germans and the French in the front line and there is no need for the Americans and the British to be there: This isn't NATO disengagement.

Of course, twice the Americans came into the war too late and people suspect them. But you must chuck this silly name calling. Maybe it would be a good idea to have just a few Americans and British in the front line to get killed right away if the Russians attack, just to bring everybody in immediately. I used to say when I was at NATO that I would shoot an American myself if a war started, just to make sure. We should have one armored-car regiment of Americans and one armored-car regiment of British up front to be killed on D-day.

But the moment Russian troops are engaged, NATO troops being attacked on a common frontier, that is war. And nuclear weapons should be used at once. But this war won't happen. I have explained this to Khrushchev. He is a clever fellow. He understands me.

The key to peace is China. Khrushchev is scared silly of China. Soon there will be a billion Chinese armed with nuclear weapons. That is a huge country at his back. I have had it out with him. He is too clever.

We should detach China from Russia and vice versa and get them looking our way. But you people are too emotionally involved. Your politicians are silly.

I asked him if he thought NATO were outmoded. He replied: "No, it needs a spring clean, an overhauling. It has succeeded in its original purpose, stopping Soviet aggression, but now it needs streamlining. The whole thing needs looking at. It should have a fundamental redesign."

Did he think it was essential to get thirty divisions on the central front. He sniffed. He said:

At Lisbon our goal was ninety divisions all around. But there was never any hope of getting this. So they arrived at the figure of thirty for central Europe. This figure wasn't arrived at by reasoning; it was only what they thought they might get. I was there. I know. And they don't have it. They don't have thirty divisions.

Why, in 1939, the French mobilized one hundred divisions. Now I'd say they have three. In 1939, the Belgians mobilized twenty-five divisions. Now they have two. This is all nonsense. They want us to do the fighting. The only way to get them to build up defenses is for us to go home and at the same time make it clear that we will use nuclear weapons if a war is on.

I asked him who, living or dead, had most influenced his life. "No general," he answered (although in a moment he contradicted himself). "The best soldier ever produced during my time was Alanbrooke. He had a great influence on me. I met him in the 1920s. The greatest leader I have met is Churchill. Stalin was a great leader, ruthless, brutal. But without Stalin I think the Russians would have quit the war."

He told me: "Eisenhower doesn't speak to me anymore." This had occurred since Monty had published his memoirs.

I said some nice things about Ike. But I put on record our entire correspondence on the Normandy campaign. I told Ike if he didn't pull back Patton on the right and hit the Germans a smashing blow in 1944, the war would last until spring. But Ike didn't follow my advice. He lost a lot of lives. Eighty thousand American boys in the Ardennes alone. Damned fool Ike.

I don't know why Ike was angry. He wrote the first book after the war, *Crusade in Europe*. And he said some bad things about Alanbrooke and me. But I did nothing. I didn't mind.

Monty told me:

I know de Gaulle very well. He is quite right to avoid the domination of an Anglo-Saxon bloc. If Britain got into Europe through the Common Market, we would be pushed around by the U.S. That would prevent any chance of an agreement with Russia. And de Gaulle wants some kind of agreement. He is quite right. And he has given France back her soul.

He chucked out the useless politicians. Now he has a proper setup in France.

Now you can see what's what. You may not agree with me. But you know what I think. And I am right.

This evening, David Bruce told me Finletter had wanted to see Prime Minister Macmillan personally and suggest he name a better British ambassador to NATO. What a conspirator!

PARIS, *March 29, 1963*

LUNCHED with Chip Bohlen. He told me Bruce sent a telegram to the State Department saying my analysis of the Labour party's attitude on nuclear weapons is completely accurate.

Bob Murphy, in town last week, told Chip that Couve de Murville had worked for some time for the Vichy government and handled certain financial negotiations with the Germans. This was in no sense against Couve, who had eventually escaped to Spain, joining the Committee of National Liberation in Algiers.

But during the winter of 1943–1944, Henry Morgenthau had exerted enormous successful pressure and forced his dismissal from the committee. I told Chip I had never detected any hangover of anti-American resentment.

PARIS, *April 4, 1963*

LONG and agreeable talk with Couve de Murville. He saw no point in thinking of a revision of SEATO; it might just as well stay as it is. It can never be a dynamic alliance because it is composed of such extremely different parts. But it has been a useful, stabilizing factor. The sole reality is that of U.S. military force. The only thing France had in Southeast Asia was a small training mission in Laos and France had no intention of sending any further units. "Where would they go?" he asked with a quizzical smile.

South Vietnam is the real trouble in the SEATO area today. On the basis of its own sad experiences and the facts reported to it from both North and South, France feels it is impossible to produce any military solution in South Vietnam. The only solution can be political. And this is very difficult to imagine. It is not a question of reunifying all Vietnam, but of just finding a political solution in South Vietnam. However, nobody is going to win the war there, neither the Americans nor the Communists.

Couve saw no reason for the West to take any initiative now toward new East-West negotiations.

The Russians are simply not in a position to negotiate. They have various internal problems, to say nothing of the repercussions of China and Cuba. It is hard to say just what Khrushchev's position is at this time because we get little accurate information. But it is evident that for a long time, Khrushchev's policy has been a complete failure. It was a failure in Berlin. He is at odds with China. He looked ridiculous in Cuba. He has failed in his efforts to subvert the underdeveloped areas. In Africa, he failed in the Congo, Guinea, and Mali. In the Middle East, all the Arab countries are chasing out the Communists. All this, of course, weakens Khrushchev's situation at home. And the arms race presents him with a continually heavier burden. This is also heavier for the U.S., but the U.S. is a richer country. And finally Khrushchev has not been able to solve the agricultural difficulties.

I asked if he thought there was any use in trying, one or another way, to resume talks with Britain about the Common Market. He said there was no point in this and everyone agreed it would be unrealistic although things might be different in some years. Some solution other than British membership would have to be evolved.

I asked if France thought there would be any point in new talks about creating a European nuclear force by pooling the atomic arms of France and Britain and obtaining aid from Germany. He answered:

First you must know which British government you are dealing with. Macmillan's chances don't look very good. In the past, we always thought the start for a modern Europe would be a European nuclear defense based on Anglo-French cooperation. And kind of European union joined on an equal basis with the U.S. must have its own atomic force. But this idea was ignored. You have chosen the solution of the multilateral force. But I can assure you that the multilateral force is already dead.

The difficulty in our previous talks with Britain was in its relationship with the U.S.A. If we talked to the British about these things, they reported to Washington that France was asking them to betray America. This is precisely what happened when Macmillan came to Rambouillet.

PARIS, *April 5, 1963*

LUNCHED with Cecil Lyon and Tony Rumbold. The interesting aspect was nonpolitical. Monsieur Alex invited us down to his cave. Tony had a date and Cecil had to escort Stevenson (who is back here) to see Joxe. But I told them they could not let me down and had to follow through, so they obliged.

We had an excellent 1913 Marc de Bourgogne and a complete tour, including the area Alex had sealed off from the Germans during the occupation. (He worked with two trusted employees every night until 5 A.M. cementing the passage and then put in a false case of empty bottles to camouflage the entrance to the place where his most valuable drinks were.) Incidentally, he told me he thought the best wine in the world was a 1904 Château Latour served in the magnum.

In 1932, he bought the house which is now the Hotel La Pérouse for 3,000,000 francs and it is worth 1,300,000,000 today. He says he makes money out of his hotel while he sleeps and out of the restaurant during daytime.

PARIS, *April 8, 1963*

LUNCHED today with Stikker. I like him no matter how unpopular he is with his colleagues. I also feel very sorry for him. He confided to me that he must have another operation in June; it must be cancer again.

Stikker comments wryly on the fact that de Gaulle gave a reception for the SEATO ministers and Pompidou is going to the NATO building for a SEATO conference, although this was never done for NATO.

Stikker says you can't kill nationalism and it is silly of the U.S.A. to keep talking about it.

At Athens in 1962, he tried to persuade McNamara not to make his statement opposing any national nuclear forces, saying this would offend France and might offend Britain. McNamara refused—with Rusk present. Stikker thinks Rusk is a weak man and although he likes McNamara, considers him dangerously naive.

PARIS, *April 22, 1963*

GOLFED and lunched with Bohlen. Chip spent Tuesday in Palm Beach with the President sitting by the swimming pool discussing France. Kennedy asked why Peyrefitte was so anti-American. Chip said he really wasn't anti-American but like all Frenchmen he had a certain tendency toward *méchanceté* and doesn't like many foreigners or most other Frenchmen. We would just have to recognize the facts of the French character.

He found absolutely no disposition by the President or those around him to arrange a Kennedy-de Gaulle meeting as part of Kennedy's European tour. Furthermore, Chip doesn't think de Gaulle would like a tête-à-tête. He would be embarrassed by direct questions on France's plans, above all on the nuclear business. He just doesn't know enough about the problem and would not be able to hold up his end well enough so he would prefer to avoid a conversation at this time.

Lunched with Jean-Jacques Servan-Schreiber. He told me he had no ambition personally to try and run in the contest to succeed de Gaulle. Gaston Defferre was much more qualified and he wanted to back him.

This contrasts greatly with my last luncheon conversation when Jean-Jacques confided his own ambitions. By next autumn, he hopes to have a pretty solid political machine of his own, including representatives of the *syndicats* and the *patronats* and other groups prepared to unite in the struggle for succession against de Gaulle.

I told him I thought he and France should thank de Gaulle for having destroyed the older political generation in France so that the struggle for succession would take place among young men instead of old politicos.

"THREE THINGS
THE AMERICANS
CAN'T STAND"

D INED AT BOHLEN'S LAST NIGHT WITH AVERELL HARRIMAN, HERE for the day in search of a solution to the Laos question. He saw Couve this afternoon and will see Lord Home tomorrow. Says the French are very helpful and reasonable on Southeast Asia.

The only other people present (Marina was going to the theater) were Chip and Avis, Bill Sullivan, a Far Eastern expert in the State Department, and Mike Forrestal. I don't know exactly what Mike's job is at present. I believe he is on Mac Bundy's staff in the White House.

Avis gave us Russian vodka and caviar, Château Haut Brion, with a splendid entrée and a soufflé with white wine, followed by a remarkable champagne and framboise. Averell, who was sprightly, gay and in a delightful mood (he is seventy-one), got Avis furious by saying: "This is exactly the same meal we had on the airplane last night."

When he was home last week Kennedy said to Bohlen: "I don't see any reason for me ever to see Khrushchev again. There is nothing to be gained from it. But I am glad I saw him once. It was valuable in terms of the effect on me."

Chip said the first thing that happened at Yalta—which has never been written—was that one day as Roosevelt was looking out of his window, he spotted a very pretty lemon tree and happened to express admiration for its beauty to one of the Russians. Next thing he knew the damn thing was dug up and four Russians came in and told him Stalin had presented it to him. It was sent home but nobody knows what became of it. Chip said:

"The Republicans could have really made something of Russia handing out not just a lemon but a whole tree of lemons to Roosevelt."

Averell said he was present when General Marshall, then chief of staff, came to Roosevelt and told him that Bill Bullitt had leaked the information about the impending "Torch" operation to de Gaulle. ("Torch" was the code name for the invasion of North Africa.) Marshall said intelligence had made a very careful check and found out not only that de Gaulle had been tipped off but that it was Bullitt and this was one reason why he turned so anti-Roosevelt and anti-Democratic party.

Averell admitted that the U.S. government now endorses partition as a solution for Laos but doesn't dare say so, Diem has been for this for some time and he thinks the Russians have been playing ball lately during this latest Laos crisis and their ambassador in Vientiane has been relatively helpful. De facto partition has already been established. No decision has been taken on whether we should send troops there or once again send an expeditionary force to Thailand.

It really didn't matter that the SEATO umbrella had been withdrawn from Laos because if the Laotian government asked UN for help, we could immediately move in troops just the same as we did in Korea. In other words, we would use UN instead of SEATO.

The very important thing was to insure that the Communists didn't have access to the Mekong River, which is the real highway into South Vietnam. The so-called "Ho Chi Minh trail" is barely a footpath and they can't send much in the way of supplies over it to fight Diem.

Things are going much better in South Vietnam now. Ambassador Nolting has done a good job although he is tired and would like to be replaced. Diem has put through practically all the reforms we have demanded of him. But he very foolishly insists on continuing to govern with a family or clan apparatus. All the intellectuals in Saigon are against him. If he brought five or six of these intellectuals into his team they would shut up.

Harriman offered the theory that the present Laos crisis was obviously not prompted by Russia but was also not pushed by China; that it was purely done by North Vietnam. I can't imagine North Vietnam doing it without at least tacit Chinese support.

Mike said—with the hearty approval of Harriman—that the real trouble started in Laos just before Christmas of 1959, when the CIA was permitted to take over U.S. policy and sought to impose a right-wing government by forcible means.

Bohlen told an amusing story about Hector McNeil, late British Minister of State, and Guy Burgess, the British defector, who used to work for Hector as personal assistant. Before Burgess went to the U.S. for the first time Hector said to him, "Guy, there are three things the Americans can't stand: communism, homosexuality, and the race question." Burgess replied, "I see what you mean, Hector, I mustn't make a pass at Paul Robeson."

PARIS, *April 30, 1963*

GOLFED with Bohlen and John McCone, head of the CIA. McCone is an amiable, white-haired man with glasses. He told me he thought by far the most important aspect of intelligence was the analysis of information acquired and judgment based thereon.

McCone believed it impossible to partition Laos because the Communists had already extended too far south along the Ho Chi Minh trail. I argued the only kind of partition that could be considered would be similar to that in Vietnam; but there had been large Communist forces south of the partition line in Vietnam at that time.

I mentioned the French opinion that there could probably never be a military solution to the South Vietnam war. He thought that this was probably a correct observation.

He assured me that Castro is an exceptionally able and intelligent man and we should not underrate him. Donovan, who arranged the prisoner exchange, is very impressed with him and likes him. Castro has incredible energy and can stay up all night, wandering around town and then going to work the next day.

The idea of a "hot line" between Washington and Moscow was first discussed at the Camp David meeting between Eisenhower and Khrushchev. It is much easier to arrange such a thing via teletype than telephone because it is very complicated to put an unscrambler on a line involving two languages. Teletype is swifter than telephone because of translation.

PARIS, *May 10, 1963*

DINED last night at de Staercke's. Present were the Finletters, the Speidels, Sir Evelyn Shuckburgh, now British ambassador to NATO, and Lady Shuckburgh.

Speidel said the only sensible strategy for the West to handle limited Soviet thrusts would be to prepare immediate conventional counterthrusts. Thus, if the Russians tried a "police" action to seize a city like Lübeck, we should have a conventional striking force or armor ready immediately to seize a town like Leipzig or Dresden. But it is impossible to prepare for such a strategy until the thirty-divisions goal is reached on the central front. We need at least four or five more divisions.

PARIS, *May 13, 1963*

YESTERDAY, we went to the Windsors for a small lunch at which Dixon, the British ambassador, and his wife were the principal guests.

The Duke thinks Montgomery is a vain, petty, obnoxious man but a good general. He first met Monty shortly before the phony war ended in 1940, and Monty was commanding a division. He sat next to him at lunch and asked: "General, what do you think of the phony war?" Monty replied: "The only way to win the war is to kill Germans."

The Duchess told me he takes Spanish lessons twice a week and she takes French. His French is execrable, but he is quite good at Spanish and was brought up speaking German. (He has always had German sympathies.)

She has purchased an amusing bell shaped like a turtle which rings when you push the tail. This is placed on the table and when the Duke and his cronies are reminiscing and simply can't remember things, if somebody comes through and remembers correctly she rings it.

OTTAWA, *May 19, 1963*

TODAY being Sunday, I walked out to Ambassador Walt Butterworth's and had lunch with him and Virginia, à trois. Butterworth says the most important fact of Pearson's electoral victory is that the U.S. and Canada have resumed willingness and ability to communicate frankly and unemotionally.

The problem of Quebec nationalism is very serious.

U.S. philosophy is to create a melting pot but Canada's is to recognize the existence of two cultures and languages with equality in certain areas. In Ottawa and Quebec, the languages have equal value but not in Manitoba, Saskatchewan, etc. And in rural Quebec areas the French don't try and teach their children English. The English speakers, though not the first settlers and only 10 percent of Quebec, "own" the province through disproportionate control of finance, power, etc.

The U.S.A. would have an immense problem if secession came. The west of a fragmented Canada would ask to join us, dumping the Quebec problem in our lap. It's better to have poor East-West (English-French) relations in Canada than bad North-South continental relations.

OTTAWA, *May 22, 1963*

I TOOK a walk today with Gerard Smith in order to discuss our nuclear policy. Smith was first brought into the State Department by Dulles, after having worked with the Atomic Energy Commission, and at one time heading the Policy and Planning division. Together with Bob Bowie, he is a father of our current international nuclear-sharing program: a nice, quiet, intelligent man who is firmly convinced that the project for a multilateral force (MLF) is the only solution. The basic problem remains that there is a legitimate demand in Europe for long-range missiles to match the Soviet batteries. The U.S. dilemma is whether to sell such weapons to individual allied nations or to produce a joint force.

OTTAWA, *May 23, 1963*

THIS morning, I visited Lester (Mike) Pearson, now Prime Minister. He looks exceedingly well and visibly pleased by his electoral success.

Pearson speculated that it might in the end be better if the four Canadian air squadrons now in Europe were eventually brought back to North America. It was very expensive for Canada to support these overseas units and they might be more economically deployed on this continent. Was it sensible to have U.S. squadrons based in Canada and Canadian squadrons based in Europe?

Neutralism was not an important factor in Canada, although it was more widespread than ten years ago. It tended to rise and fall in direct relationship to fear of Russia. When the U.S.A. makes mistakes—such as the Bay of Pigs—it rises. Neutralism could also be related to the trouble in Quebec. The Quebec separatists are also neutralists.

This evening, at two parties, I saw Rusk, McNamara, Couve de Murville, and Spaak; all here for the NATO meeting. McNamara was most friendly, direct, forthright. He thought Bohlen, Bruce, and Dowling were the best trio of ambassadors the U.S. has ever had. He is sincere but appallingly naive. He thinks the British are double-crossers but brilliant, that they will stick by the MLF in the end. He has no use for nor understanding of de Gaulle.

Rusk, by the way, told me he plays golf with George Ball, "the only man I can beat," for fifty-cent bets. Says he'd rather hit a ball 230 yards in any direction than get satisfaction out of a straight shot.

Spaak said he had been most profoundly influenced in his life by Churchill. He hates de Gaulle, considers him a "great personality" but not a "great man."

NEW YORK, *May 30, 1963*

I RAN into Steve Dedijer, who has been lecturing, first at Harvard, then at Yale, and is flying back to Sweden in two days to see his wife and their six-day-old boy. Steve, once a Jugoslav Communist and head of its Atomic Energy Commission, expects to become a Swedish citizen soon.

Steve is fed up with ideology and feels a free man, attacking both communism and capitalism. In 1949, just after the split with Stalin, the Jugoslav government decided it wanted to manufacture an atomic bomb. Steve advised the bosses they were nuts, it couldn't be done.

The atmosphere was so dictatorial that he told Ranković (minister of the interior) he intended to go around with a card marked "Steve Dedijer, International Spy," and to pass these around if the regime persisted in suspecting everybody who disagreed with them.

He says Marxism is crazy and capitalism is booming in a way Marxism refuses to admit. Communism is still governed by what wits call "Meyer's Law." This says: "If the facts don't fit the theory, discard the facts."

The Jugoslav social system is undermined by bureaucratic lassitude. A general he knows confides: "Everything is coming to pieces. But if I tell the truth I will lose my job, my car, and my villa. So what the hell."

WASHINGTON, *June 5, 1963*

LUNCHED with General Heusinger, former chief of the German general staff and now chairman of the Permanent Military Committee of NATO.

He said that General Lemnitzer, NATO commander, must be given the weapons to make several alternative plans, which cannot be done unless he receives MRBMs. Heusinger pointed this out to McNamara, recalling an incident from German history in 1914. The Kaiser suggested to Moltke that he put more divisions in the east against Russia. Moltke replied: "Your Majesty, I have only one plan and it is in the west." Lemnitzer should be given the opportunity of having more than one plan.

If we had an adequate conventional force in Europe, it would place the Russians in a very difficult position. If they wished to plan a war, they would have to import more troops into eastern Europe. This requires time and we could spot their movement. This would give the West a period in which to make diplomatic inquiries as well as military preparations. Or, if the Russians wished a war, they would have to start an all-out atomic holocaust at the beginning and this would mean Moscow would face an excruciatingly difficult choice.

Heusinger is convinced there will never be a multilateral nuclear force (MLF) and that NATO will never get its thirty divisions on the central front. Yet, despite these obvious shortcomings, Washington continues obstinately to oppose all thought of land-based MRBMs and gets angry with Lemnitzer when he requests them—as he must do to fulfill his responsibilities.

I asked Heusinger if it would be hypothetically possible for some small and well-disciplined group of German staff officers to secretly conduct arms research in both Israel (nuclear) and Egypt (missiles). After all, Special Group R worked for Seeckt in Russia in 1921, prior to the Rapallo Treaty and without the knowledge of any civilian officials. Heusinger gulped, then said he was sure this was not being done—but hypothetically it could be.

Later, I had a very amicable chat with John McCone in the new CIA building which is quite a place—almost on a Pentagon scale in size and filled with all kinds of security labyrinths and elevators that only operate with special keys.

He says the Israeli atomic plant at Dimona was started in the winter of 1956–1957 with French aid and the U.S.A. didn't learn a thing about it until late 1960. We have seen the French design for the reactor. It does not include a plutonium separation plant for potential military purposes. But the Israelis are very sophisticated and surely can produce plutonium for weapons even if that phase is not yet operational.

As for Egypt, McCone says the Soviets sent in a test reactor in 1958. This was similar to Russian help for such lands as Jugoslavia and Czechoslovakia. It makes only a small quantity of weapons fuel but could make chemical-type devices for radiation purposes. McCone does not think this chemical-type weapon is alarming. Cheaper and more effective bacteriological and chemical weapons already exist.

The Germans in Egypt could be testing and developing missile devices, something they cannot do in Germany. But they could probably work more efficiently and with more security at home in Germany on bacteriological and chemical weapons. The Germans have reactors and laboratories, a large chemical industry, many engineers and scientists.

Referring to the old German-Russian accord of the 1920s, McCone said they never risked dangerous results in case of discovery because both partners were isolated and without allies. Furthermore, there was a minimal chance of discovery in the huge Soviet land mass.

After leaving McCone, I saw Dick Helms, who succeeded Frank Wisner as CIA deputy in charge of operations. We talked about the Penkovsky case. He said that in 1959, Colonel Popov, who was in a comparable position, was arrested and condemned for the same sort of thing. We now believe he has been shot, although the Russians hint he is still alive.

The Penkovsky trial showed there has been some kind of change in Russia. Many people were involved. And Marshal Vorontsov, head of the rocket force, has been demoted together with other officers. Almost three hundred Soviet intelligence officers have been called back to Russia since Penkovsky's arrest. There is an intensive reexamination of Red army intelligence and the KGB, both of which operated abroad as separate and competitive apparatuses. There seems to be a scrutiny of Soviet intelligence personnel and of Penkovsky's relationships with Soviet political leaders. Kosygin's son-in-law was Penkovsky's boss.

WASHINGTON, *June 6, 1963*

MAC Bundy invited me for lunch at the Metropolitan Club. I was having a drink with Kim Roosevelt when he came and joined us. Rather coldly, he asked Kim: "Are you still spreading the same poison around?" Kim, of course, disagrees very strongly with the administration on Nasser.

I asked Mac what was the story of the present correspondence between Khrushchev and Kennedy? Bundy said that since 1961, they had been in communication in a variety of ways. The present topic is the test ban. We have had no answer to our suggestions and probably won't until after the Russians have met with the Chinese.

Kennedy would like to see de Gaulle again. He invited him last autumn and suggested meeting in Florida in order to avoid all the fuss of Washington. De Gaulle said he respected Kennedy but did not wish to create false expectations that agreement would be forthcoming when such agreement was unlikely.

Bundy admitted that European suspicions of direct, bilateral U.S.-Soviet negotiations represented a real problem and had been revived by the hot-line agreement. He added: "If we thought we could get a major settlement, we would not be deterred from bilateral discussions with Russia. We would not make allied representation a precondition to such talks. But this is not an immediate problem, only theoretical. There is no such thing going on now." This is a *most* important statement.

Long and excellent talk with McNamara in the Pentagon. He has a huge office, one of the biggest I have ever seen. I was fascinated to note de Gaulle's three volumes of *Mémoires* (in English) right behind his desk. The man must be a masochist.

I asked him first of all why the British were double-crossing us on MLF. He thought this was primarily for political reasons. The financial excuses adduced were not of major importance. Macmillan feels Britain cannot be in the MLF and also justify an independent nuclear deterrent.

I asked what were the prospects of either a U.S. or Soviet breakthrough toward creating an effective defensive umbrella. He said we had two programs: Nike Zeus and Nike X—which is an advance phase of Zeus and was our first program. The Kwajalein tests had proven these weapons capable of intercepting, but there were still severe limitations to their capability. Then there was the Defender study and other various research programs. Neither we nor the Russians had come anywhere near finding a true antimissile umbrella.

McNamara thought a lodgment on the moon had no serious military importance in terms of foreseeable technology. There was some conceivable advantage of space in terms of nuclear testing, but space tests were very costly and difficult and extremely hard to carry out undetected.

He said there was no doubt that in terms of a holocaust the U.S.A. could absorb a Soviet surprise attack, survive, and obliterate the Soviet Union. But we needed NATO in another sense.

There was a great spectrum running from the Cold War and the Berlin wall to Cuba, to localized incidents, and on to all-out nuclear holocaust. If one starts with the Berlin wall on the left, Cuba near the center, and holocaust on the extreme right, the line of deterrence moves to the right. NATO helps to prevent Soviet aggression in all fields less than an all-out nuclear surprise attack. It helps to deter in a political and economic sense as well as in a conventional military sense.

McNamara admitted there was a paradox. We can handle the extreme of holocaust alone. But we cannot handle anything less than that extreme alone. Without NATO, the Soviet Union could gradually destroy us by salami tactics.

I observed that the Pentagon perhaps intruded too much into United States foreign policy. He replied: "I don't think the State Department believes this. The consequences of Skybolt or U.S.-Canada atomic relationships did not stem from any Pentagon usurpation of foreign-policy prerogatives. The State Department is responsible for foreign policy and has primacy in such matters. When the Pentagon prepares a defense program which has foreign-policy implications, we first must discuss this with the State Department. Defense is the servant, not the master of foreign policy."

I asked McNamara how he thought it would be possible to target the French nuclear force, which is explicitly countercity, together with NATO targeting, which is counterforce. He said: "From a military viewpoint, it isn't even worth discussing targets with the French. From a political viewpoint, the matter will be settled. Of course, de Gaulle uses his atomic force to divide the United States from Europe."

Frank Wisner told a most amusing and true story, later confirmed by Alphand. A high-ranking French official was instructed by Paris to call on Bob Lovett, Under Secretary of State, and protest on some long-forgotten problem. He argued the French case in his heavily accented English. Lovett sat back stonily. When the official had finished, he looked at Lovett and asked for his reaction.

"I have just three things to say. First of all, this is a ridiculous and picayune complaint. Secondly, I have rarely seen a case so miserably presented. And thirdly, your fly is open."

The poor man, flustered and embarrassed, looked down and found his zipper fly indeed open. He leaned forward to zip it up and in the process his necktie got caught in the zipper, which, as these things do, jammed. He couldn't zip it up or down and he couldn't get his necktie out so he was bent over like a horseshoe. His diplomatic aplomb vanished; he had to shake hands and say good-bye to Lovett and hobble out of the office stooped over like a cripple.

WASHINGTON, *June 7, 1963*

LONG talk with Attorney General Robert Kennedy. He is, of course, on the side of the angels now, and I am glad to have his energies as well as his family influence working in a just cause. But I cannot forget, when talking with him, that it was not very difficult for him at another time to think that Joe McCarthy was hot stuff.

He was quiet, unexcitable, friendly, energetic, tough as wire. Even more than his brother, he gives the impression of being a quick reactor rather than a thoughtful planner with vision that carries into the future, and he seems more concerned with winning than with what he is winning. I say this despite the fact that he could not have been more friendly and agreeable. He received me in the approved New Frontier style: shirt sleeves rolled up.

During our conversation the President called up from California. He is going to Honolulu this evening. When the desk phone rang, he picked it up. They started chatting informally about all kinds of things. At one point Bobby said: "Oh, he's a great guy. You'll like him. He's a real good Democrat."

I told Bobby I was very concerned by the tarnish to our reputation abroad caused by grim events such as Alabama; what were we trying to do to try and offset this. He said Thurgood Marshall was going on a trip to three or four African countries to talk, meet intellectuals, political leaders, and student groups. When African leaders come here they are invited to the Department of Justice where we tell them what we are doing on this difficult issue.

"The State Department does less about this. The Justice Department keeps both USIA and State briefed on what is being done. We try to show how difficult the problem is for a democratic society, where things can't be settled too swiftly without dictatorship." He made the point that in South Africa the government is on the wrong side, unlike the U.S.A.

Bobby said Washington was determined that more would be done to employ American Negroes in government positions abroad. He welcomed my suggestion that we should ask businesses to make a point of sending able Negro citizens to positions overseas.

WASHINGTON, *June 8, 1963*

GEORGE Ball says farmers have an extraordinary and malign influence on policy on both sides of the Iron Curtain. Their problems are universal and transcend ideology. The new agricultural technology multiplies productivity. More and more western countries are becoming agriculturally self-sufficient or acquiring agricultural surpluses for export.

In the East, population increases outrun the increase in farm productivity. In the West, great problems are posed as the impact of new agricultural technology is felt. This is particularly true in the United States, which is relatively ten years ahead of Europe. We have more efficient fertilizers and equipment and Europe is handicapped by smaller land holdings.

As living standards improve, there is a general shift in the more advanced lands from cereal to protein consumption. Fortunately for the West, the cow is an inefficient machine. It requires eight to ten pounds of cereal to produce one pound of beef. But there has been a revolution in chicken production. The chicken has become a remarkable protein factory. It leads a serene and uneventful life. The ratio of cereal to meat in chickens is approaching two pounds of cereal to one pound of meat, whereas it used to be four to one. This makes chicken meat increasingly cheap and this fact has political repercussions.

The United States depends quite heavily on its agricultural exports to Europe in order to maintain a surplus in our trade balance. And this in turn helps to pay for Europe's defense. United States agricultural imports from the Common Market area during recent years remained relatively steady at around $200,000,000 per annum. But during the same period our agricultural exports rose from $900,000,000 to $1,200,000,000. The resulting $1,000,000,000 gap between our agricultural imports from and exports to Europe pays a large share of European defense and aid to underdeveloped lands because the export-import gap between us and Europe on nonagricultural goods is very small.

Until 1958, we exported about $3,000,000 worth of chickens to the Common Market area. But by last year, this had risen to $50,000,000. We want Europe's agriculture to develop normally and without too high an artificial price level. The increased protein consumption in Europe will offset greater technological productivity. The key to price levels is the price of grain—which is used to feed chickens. In fact, the key is the wheat price, which sets relations of other cereal prices.

In the Communist world, the big agricultural problem is the failure of the farmers to produce enough. This is the Achilles' heel of communism. Russia has not yet recovered from the liquidation of the kulaks. In the West, too few farmers are producing too much food. In the East, too many farmers are not producing enough food.

I spent an hour with Dean Rusk. He likes to think things are or should be as he would desire in a "good" world and, it seems to me, he frequently does not face disagreeable facts if they do not coincide with his high moral and patriotic opinions.

I recalled our early discussions, when he first took office, on my idea of a "brush-fire peace," meaning an effort to draw together with the Russians on points where we agree instead of always stressing points where we disagree. He said we were still pursuing this approach wherever possible.

We still consider it important to try and keep contact with the Russians on points where there *can* be an eventual solution. But now there is evidently a period of pause in the Soviet Union. The Russian-Chinese talks are coming up and there is no sign of motion in Moscow.

Did he think maybe a time had come to redefine the phrase "Cold War" and call it instead "Cold Armistice"? He said:

There's not enough to support this conclusion. There have indeed been pauses for weeks or for months, but things do continue to happen. And we cannot rely on the continuation of a pause.

Yet things are not going badly from our point of view. The Soviets have sent almost $1,000,000,000 to Indonesia, yet the Indonesian Communist party is going toward China and Indonesia is more clearly nonaligned and less pro-Communist than in the past. The Russians have spent several hundred-million dollars in Iraq and the Iraqi government shoots and jails Communists, so you can see the Russians have their own problems.

On some points, there is certainly an objective underlying common interest between Russia and the United States. Two of these are the needs to halt the arms race and prevent the proliferation of nuclear weapons. Each side has stated that its policy is against the proliferation of nuclear weapons. The trouble is that the Russians did help China in the past—until 1959—and now the Chinese are getting to the point where they may soon explode a device.

What was the present status on a test ban and disarmament? Rusk said we were still hung up on two points. The Russians argue that national means of nuclear detection are sufficient and international inspection is tantamount to espionage. We think this can be dealt with pragmatically. Russians, looking at the United States, can conclude that national means of detection are sufficient because we have an open society given to leaks and favoring espionage. But when we look at them it is different because they have a closed society and can hide many things within their huge land mass. We simply do not have the national means to ensure detection, and we tell them that if they have any devices unknown to us, we would like proof that national means are sufficient.

I asked if it might now be time to consider partitioning Laos. He said we strongly opposed "formal partition." But he added there had been a kind of de facto partition for a long time. The Soviets must find a way of making good on their commitment in Laos. We went a long way to find agreement. Khrushchev is committed on this. So there is no point in trying to do to tiny Laos what was done to Vietnam.

Didn't he think the Pentagon was interfering too much in United States foreign policy? He got very indignant and said:

> This is phony. There has never been a time when the Pentagon was more responsive to foreign policy problems than during the last two years. The Pentagon works on many matters of foreign policy—status of forces, nuclear problems, burden sharing in the alliances, the gold flow. But they work along with us. Some of the things that create irritation abroad and which are laid to the Pentagon are simply part of U.S. foreign policy. But the Pentagon is merely part of the basket of alibis thrown at the U.S.A. and excuses for doing things.

> The refusal of the alliance to contribute sufficient conventional forces and the excuses used are just balls. Force goals were established on a fair and even basis and set according to the minimum needed in the event of a nuclear war. Therefore, any arguments about the fact that they don't have to be brought up to the fixed limits in order to ensure a pause are beside the point. The goals fixed must be met in terms of a nuclear war and are therefore the minimum for any kind of strategy. Kennedy insists that we all agree on this and that all the allies must live up to their promises. The U.S.A. has done so. So should the others. Arguments about this view of strategy are simply a phony alibi by some of the allies for not getting off their rumps.

Later, I lunched with Hervé Alphand. He seems bitter and emotionally anti-British, rather antiadministration.

He says there are two great Frenchmen nowadays, de Gaulle and Jean Monnet. But the United States overestimates the importance of Monnet. American diplomats are continually deceived into thinking the anti-de Gaulle feeling one encounters in Paris at dinner parties actually represents French opinion.

He says British propaganda is brilliantly effective and produces visible results in the administration. Mac Bundy talks so much like Ormsby-Gore that he even uses the same phrases.

THIS afternoon, I went over to see U Thant, Secretary-General of UN, in his office on the 38th floor. U Thant is about five foot eight, but he looks sturdier than his photographs indicate. Although his round Asian features give him a slightly soft and weak appearance in photographs, a good deal of inner strength emerges when you see him. We spent an hour —very relaxed—chatting while I smoked cigarettes and he puffed a little cheroot. Behind his glasses his eyes frequently twinkled. I liked him.

I inquired whether he thought anyone but a neutral could be an effective Secretary-General. He said: "To begin with, anyone who came from a country other than those that are nonaligned couldn't be elected."

Anybody who took the job of Secretary-General would more or less have to forgo any future career so that he could not be suspected of using the world post to advance himself later in a national sense.

I asked if he thought the Secretary-General should be "morally neutral" or if, despite his political neutrality, he had to take forthright stands on issues where he felt there was a distinction between right and wrong? Without hesitation, he answered:

> I can't be neutral on moral issues. One cannot escape decisions on such matters. And take, for example, the case of my country. Burma has been neutral, or nonaligned, in the sense of not belonging to a military bloc. But Burma is neutral only in this and no other sense; only militarily. We have taken stands as a country on moral issues. In 1956, we denounced Russia on Hungary. Nevertheless, we never joined SEATO because we did not think that was in our interest and we were geographically exposed with our long frontier with China. No Secretary-General worthy of the name can ever afford to be morally neutral.

I wondered whether tiny lands such as San Marino, Andorra, Monaco, and Liechtenstein technically were eligible for membership. He said technically they were. Cyprus has only 450,000 citizens. Kuwait, the last member, came in with 350,000 inhabitants. If a country applies for membership such an application is examined by the Security Council, and if the Council recommends membership, it is placed before the Assembly to vote on. In this respect, U Thant said that theoretically the Vatican State could apply for membership.

Was there any acceptable formula to allow the admission of partitioned countries bracketed together—like both halves of Germany, Korea, or Vietnam? He said the Russians wanted this; it was a matter of outright East-West argument. But the question has never been raised in the General Assembly.

I asked what a country lost by not being a UN member. He said this was tantamount to the situation of a province in a nation which was not represented in its own Parliament and therefore could not speak on its own legislative needs. He admitted that in the case of Switzerland, the Swiss actually gained by not being UN members because it did not hurt their basic interests, they paid no dues, and they made money out of the UN through its Geneva office. He also conceded that the Chinese probably gained at present because they were not inhibited by UN rules and obligations.

PARIS, *June 28, 1963*

LUNCHED with Laloy. He was astonished when I asked him about his conversation yesterday with Mac Bundy. This had been kept a deep secret and Laloy had not even told Couve de Murville.

Jean said that at their Rambouillet meeting de Gaulle told Macmillan he did not want Britain in the Common Market because he did not think Britain was ready but suggested to Macmillan that Britain should join with France in missile manufacture—and obviously implied she should also join in nuclear projects. But Britain could not dream of joining in a nuclear-missile project while being spurned by the Common Market.

This helped explain Macmillan's mood when he left immediately for Nassau. De Gaulle insisted on modifying the official text of the conversations and struck from it (as Tony Rumbold had previously told me) references to his missile offer to Macmillan. Laloy says de Gaulle always modifies history and the best proof of this is his own *Mémoires*.

Mac Bundy told him yesterday that Kennedy was not trying to provoke any new debate with de Gaulle and France was not really a major problem for the U.S., which was more concerned with such things as relations with Russia. Bundy said de Gaulle tended to mask or obscure real problems.

Laloy said Russia hoped to get another agreement out of China—at the forthcoming Moscow talks—that would avoid an open break.

What the Russians obviously want this time is a three-way agreement on spheres of ideological interest. Chinese dogmatism would be acknowledged in the Orient because of such special situations as Formosa, Korea, and Vietnam. Polycentrism and revisionism would be acknowledged in Europe to suit Togliatti and others who desire a popular front. And Russia would remain in between as a kind of arbiter.

Laloy says the U.S. clearly wants to encourage Khrushchev against China. He was recently at a SHAPE exercise where George Kennan spoke. To Laloy's horror, Kennan endorsed outright the Titoist theory that Khrushchev is a good man who does everything possible for peace and therefore must be helped and backed by the U.S.A. Laloy made the sour observation that Khrushchev had not shown any such kindly instincts in Cuba last October.

He made some acid comments on Kennedy's remarks in Berlin that the proudest boast today was to say, "I am a citizen of Berlin." I said all Americans seemed to go nuts in Berlin and remembered that it was there, in 1954, that Dulles had likened Bidault to Abraham Lincoln. Laloy thought Kennedy's Berlin statement was cheap and that Sorensen was a cheap intellectual who kept studding speeches for his boss with Goethe quotations taken out of a dictionary.

Jean thinks there will be a post-de Gaulle examination of truth in recent years, exhuming the General's role in plots and counterplots— much like the de-Stalinization program in Russia. General Dulac, in his testimony at the OAS generals' treason trials, made it clear that de Gaulle had first sponsored and then double-crossed the May, 1958, uprising by the army.

PARIS, *July 3, 1963*

JEAN Monnet, as usual, was exceedingly nice when I saw him this afternoon, but also, neither fascinating nor thought provoking. He is widely acknowledged as an inspiring man, but to me he seems intent on talking in platitudes. He has much common sense and little originality.

Yet he is admirable. A truly remarkable physical specimen, at seventy-five he looks fifty-five, and has the sturdy, stocky build of a French peasant. He tries to walk a mile almost every day and loves any time he can spend in the country. The room in his office-apartment where we sat and I drank whisky had several paintings on the walls by his wife.

Monnet said it was necessary to build a "European-controlled" nuclear force in partnership with the U.S.A. At present the security of the West was assured by American strength. A European-controlled force remained, however, in the distance because it was so costly and technically difficult to construct.

But one must always keep in mind the *objective* of such a force, which would work in conjunction with that of the U.S.A. A European-controlled force—a term he used time and again—could only be formed subsequent to what is being sought today; namely, a multilateral nuclear force in which European membership would join with the U.S.A.

What was now needed was a common partnership of the U.S.A. and the European partners in this venture with a certain equality. When the MLF comes into being and begins to grow, it will help the growth of partnership and understanding between the U.S.A. and Europe.

It would be a fundamental error to think of the U.S.A. and Europe as separate. They must act together as equal partners. Ultimately, the MLF must evolve in time into an organism combining a European-controlled force together with a U.S. force under NATO. These cannot be separate forces. But before there is a European-controlled force there must be the gradual creation of some kind of European institution to *control* the European force.

We must keep the objectives in sight—the U.S. nuclear force and the European-controlled force together in NATO. But at present, the situation between Europe and the U.S.A. is distorted by the intellectual gap. Europe is behind in knowledge and feels unequal. The Europeans don't feel they are really participating.

There might have been a foundation for a European force if Britain and France had come together to create it. But this dream was indefinitely delayed by the events of last December and January. De Gaulle might be able to go ahead with his national force regardless of expense, even though Monnet thinks the idea is folly. In time of war money didn't count and in time of peace—now—France might spend what is necessary on such a force, although this would cut into social progress. The French were going through the same experiences that the British had acquired earlier and would find in the end that it cost too much to produce too little in terms of a national nuclear force.

Lunched with Pierre Billotte. He says de Gaulle told him he reckons the Labour party will win the next British elections and will make such a mess of things in England that about two years later the Conservatives will come back and plead to join the Common Market on any terms whatsoever.

PARIS, *July 11, 1963*

PLEASANT tête-à-tête lunch today with André de Staercke, just back from Moscow and Kiev where he and Spaak saw Khrushchev. The Belgian party was flown from Moscow to Kiev and taken twenty miles away to Khrushchev's dacha above the river. It was a hot summer day and their host was wearing a long peasant shirt and straw hat.

Mrs. Adzhubei, Khrushchev's daughter, and several of his grandchildren were there. Peasants were harvesting the crops. It was an agreeable, Chekovian atmosphere. Khrushchev seemed full of beans, although he admitted that just a few days previously the doctor had looked at him for hypertension.

Khrushchev was prepared to reconsider the 1957 Disarmament Commission's plan for insurance against surprise attack. This envisioned a line drawn through central Europe and a zone of 800 kilometers on each side which would be inspected both by air and on the ground by each side to insure against the movement of troops or supplies necessary as a preliminary to surprise assault.

He mocked the West for not having accepted his original Berlin "ultimatum" terms for a separate peace treaty with East Germany. That would have been an "incomplete" treaty and he might now have been embarrassed vis-à-vis Ulbricht. But he still had his grip around Berlin and he intended to use it to our embarrassment. He recalled the Chekov story about the peasant who stole bolts from railway ties to use as weights on his fishing lines. The judge berated him and said it might cause a terrible accident. The peasant said he knew this wouldn't be the case because the villagers had been stealing them for years. And they never stole too many bolts from any set of tracks; they left enough not to upset the balance. That is the way he planned to continue taking bolts from Berlin. Spaak said: "Not a single bolt; we won't let you take another." Khrushchev smiled and said he would take them—but never too many at a time.

There wouldn't be a war; probably not for generations. He didn't wish disaster; nor did the West. It was now up to the West, however, whether Russia adopted a hard or soft policy. The implication was not that he might turn toward China, but that he might make another play at Berlin or a threat elsewhere.

Khrushchev talked sneeringly of France, England, and all the western powers but the U.S.A. He said the Germans would be disappointed with de Gaulle. Then, ultimately, they would look to Russia for another Rapallo Pact. He didn't think this would happen soon. It might be done by Erhard's successor, or the latter's successor, or even his successor. But inevitably Germany would seek it. De Gaulle, at great expense, was producing a tiny nuclear force that could convince no great power.

As for Wilson, Khrushchev had not been impressed by him and thought England was without influence. He told Spaak "not to worry" about Wilson because he would have just the same policy as Macmillan; seemed to think he was a poor type. He showed open contempt for both France and England as factors in the world. He compared de Gaulle with the king who wore no clothes as described in the Hans Christian Andersen fairy tale.

He was firmly opposed to any on-site inspection in a test-ban accord. He said Russia would no more allow inspectors in the U.S.S.R. to travel about than any men, apart from eunuchs, were once allowed in oriental harems.

LONDON, *July 16, 1963*

EXCELLENT lunch with David Bruce on a little table in his office—first-class food, drink, and conversation. What a fine man and public servant.

David doesn't think there has been any decay in the moral fiber of Britain, as implied by the Profumo case. Perhaps only the vices of the upper class have merely spread a bit; there has been a significant rise in illegitimate births around the country. The habit of demonstration, as exemplified in the Greek visit, is deeply rooted—as, for example, the pro-Boer demonstrations three generations ago. The important thing here is that, by and large, the public supports the police and is not "agin" them.

Harold Wilson is very clever and won't make mistakes; but not at all a warm type, although a most skilled parliamentary debater. On a personal level, a Wilson government would have less cozy relations with the U.S.A.—no comfortable weekends with wives. Nor will British policy coincide too easily with ours—except on yielding the national nuclear deterrent.

LONDON, *July 17, 1963*

DINED last night with R. H. S. Crossman, Labour MP and a close friend of Harold Wilson. Crossman is minister of science in the Shadow Cabinet. He is a member of the establishment, his father was a judge and he went to Winchester where he was head of the school. He is one of the intellectuals who moved left. On the English scale, he is quite prosperous.

When he finished Oxford, during the pre-Hitler period, he went to Germany and came to know well Willy Münzenberg, the brilliant, personable head of the Comintern apparatus for the West.

He calls Harold Wilson a tough, cynical, practical, puritanical politician. He is not so puritanical that he doesn't have some personal weaknesses. Nevertheless, he has always been rather isolated and now, since he succeeded Hugh Gaitskell, he has more than ever chosen deliberately to isolate himself from his friends.

The Labour party cannot really hope to benefit much from the Profumo case and other scandals. The simple British farmer and workingman consider that all politicians are lax and live the fat life in London—regardless of party. Therefore the fallout from these scandals, if Labour tried to exploit it too much, would hit the Labour party as well as the Conservative leaders.

The biggest shock in terms of the Macmillan government has been its laxness on security. It tended to think of all its officials on an old boy basis and therefore never fired irresponsible civil servants, figuring it was impossible for the members of the "club" to be disloyal. This attitude goes back to the Burgess and Maclean period.

Pleasant talk at the Foreign Office this morning with Ted Heath, Lord Privy Seal. Heath handled all the Common Market negotiations and was applauded for the grace with which he accepted failure.

He is a rather heavy man with florid face, gray hair, and a calm, pleasant manner. Were he not a bachelor, he might very well be the leading candidate to succeed Macmillan as Tory chief. He is said to be Macmillan's own choice. Unfortunately, in scandal-ridden Britain, a happily married life is now essential in politics.

I asked whether Heath thought the new formula to restore contacts between Britain and the Common Market Six through WEU was a useful one. He didn't think it was really practical or sensible and certainly not what Britain had wished. Nevertheless, regular WEU meetings are a good thing and Britain will accept the formula on the assumption that it can lead to better relations with the European community.

We then turned to the Middle East. Heath said: "The U.S. and Britain are, in fact, closer than ever before on Middle East policy. The U.S. has made it clear to Nasser that it regards Aden and the Persian Gulf as important to U.S. interests. The oil coming from this region is useful to both the U.S. and Britain. We have told Nasser that these are vital western interests."

I said I had been surprised by Heath's statement yesterday in the House of Commons that there were nuclear weapons already in the Middle East; and then the Foreign Office had put out a communiqué explaining he only meant means of delivery, presumably referring to Egyptian rockets. I had the impression that, in fact, he really meant what he said and, by innuendo, was referring to imminent Israeli warheads. Heath, with an agreeable smile, said, "Perhaps that was in the back of my mind."

BONN, WEST GERMANY, *July 20, 1963*

THIS morning, I saw Gerhard Schröder, foreign minister. Forthright, fit, sunburned, brisk. It was a Saturday morning on a fine weekend but there he was working away in his flower-filled office above the Rhine.

I asked what he thought of the text of the proposed Soviet draft for a nonaggression pact between NATO and the Warsaw allies. He said: "We have always been convinced that the Soviet intention is, either via a separate peace or by some other accord, to gain an influence beyond the Soviet occupied zone and inside the Federal Republic itself."

The Germans thought any new declaration in the field of nonaggression could not be given free of charge. There must be some quid pro quo. The only use it might have would be if in turn there were a specific improvement of the present situation. Germany opposed any freezing of the status quo or giving influence to Khrushchev in the West.

The West should seek improvements in either Berlin or on the whole German question and these must be a specific objective. Such an improvement would at least be discussed as a precondition to a nonaggression pact. We should do nothing for nothing; there must be a return, a counterpart.

I asked what he thought was the real value of the Franco-German treaty. He said de Gaulle *never* should have been "in error" about us.

> We have always been clear on our position. I told de Gaulle our position. There are certain fundamental interests of German policy which seems to us very clear. It is vital for us to have a close relationship with the United States and the existence of such a relationship is a fact. But this does not exclude good relations with France. In fact, it makes these more necessary. We are all together in a great alliance. France and Germany are the two most important continental neighbors of western Europe in NATO. They serve as a kind of nucleus of Europe. If de Gaulle had any thought that a special relationship between Germany and France could counterbalance the special relationship between England and the United States, this was not based on reality. That would be a false parallel and a wrong assessment of the real interests involved. France is not militarily a great power. Things could have been different had France been a great power.

ADENAUER:

"I THINK OF DEATH

WITH EQUANIMITY"

BONN, WEST GERMANY, *July 22, 1963*

THIS AFTERNOON, I SPENT AN HOUR AND TWENTY MINUTES WITH Chancellor Adenauer at the Schaumburg Palace, in what is very likely to be my last visit to him—certainly as Chancellor. It was an exceptionally interesting and agreeable talk.

He said:

If de Gaulle put all his forces under NATO, this would end him in France because of military resentment. It is vital to remember this in assessing French policy. And if de Gaulle were not there in France all Europe would be Communist.

I see it this way. What would the world look like if my partners' desires were fulfilled? And I would like to tell you something that may interest you. As we have often discussed together before, I was in Moscow in 1955. At that time, when I talked to Khrushchev, Bulganin was present but he didn't say anything. Khrushchev said he could not master the Red Chinese. He was so serious about this that I often remembered that event afterward and I felt that one day its result would be the lessening of Soviet pressures on us.

And now that these events are coming about, I wonder if the U.S. will go the right way. There are many curious developments. The U.S., Britain, and Russia are all supporting India. Why? Pakistan says that if India attacks Pakistan, China will help Pakistan. The Kashmir problem is very hot. I only raise the question. I don't have an opinion on it. But of course this quarrel between India and Pakistan and China's support of Pakistan lessens Chinese pressure on Russia and therefore has its effect on Europe.

We should always look at what the Russians are doing in eastern Siberia. Eastern Siberia has been under Russian control since 1858. Previously it was Chinese. Eastern Siberia is a territory of 7,000,000 square kilometers. The U.S. has 9,300,000 square kilometers and China has 9,500,000 square kilometers. You can see how important it is. And the Russians have declared eastern Siberia a restricted military area and won't let anyone travel there. They have built large power stations there and the area has many mineral resources.

The Russians are building cities and are forcing population to settle in the area. Once the Russians develop eastern Siberia, a large new center of power will be established there. Then the Red Chinese will have against them a strong Russia plus an India strengthened by U.S. and Soviet aid. And the Chinese will be supported by Pakistan. I don't know how far U.S. policy will permit Russia to build up its strength against China.

At this point I intruded. I told him this was probably the last time I would see him as Chancellor and I wanted to ask some questions relating to his accomplishments in history. I started off by asking: "What do you consider your greatest achievement?" He thought for a moment and then he said:

Perhaps there are two. One is this: After the first Bundestag election in 1949, the CDU-CSU (Christian-Socialist bloc) had the possibility of joining with the Socialists and with the FDP and Deutschepartei. It was a temptation to join the Socialists. I was able to prevail upon a meeting of twenty of our party leaders at my Rhöndorf house and persuade them that we should not join with the Socialists because the attitude of Dr. Schumacher and of other leaders toward Russia was unsatisfactory. This, in the end, determined our policy for all subsequent years including our membership in NATO.

The second outstanding achievement, I think, is our treaty with France. Together with France, Germany can exercise a great influence in foreign relationships. Alone, without such a treaty, we cannot.

I wondered what he considered his greatest failure? A smile broke out on his wooden face and he said:

I never asked myself this question. This sounds rather immodest, but it is a fact. Those two things I mentioned as achievements are most important for Germany. They served as the basis for our union with the West and prevented anything happening against us. Nothing else really counts.

I feel that Germany is a vibrant democracy. The failures of the Nazis were so striking, apart from their crimes, that they virtually persuaded the German people that dictatorship is wholly wrong. This reactivated the democratic idea which had been here before the Nazis and which became vigorous and strong. It is of course necessary to see the democratic idea properly explained. It is not possible to teach democracy academically like a catechism. People must only be allowed to become aware of its principles and how to use them naturally.

I then asked how he planned to use his retirement—writing, lecturing, traveling, or what? He said: "I want to write my memoirs. Secondly, I want to use the authority I have to insure the preservation of the policies I wish, acting as a kind of elder statesman. The most important thing in German policy is to insure its consistency and to stabilize it."

I asked Adenauer who was the greatest man he had met and dealt with as Chancellor. To my surprise he did not mention de Gaulle. He said: "I hesitate between Truman and Dulles. I know Dulles better and therefore I would say that he was the man."

I then told the Chancellor I wanted to pose the most indiscreet question that had ever been put to him. Although I was much younger than he, I was much interested in death and had written a book on it. I wondered if it would be possible for him to tell me precisely what he thought death was. He smiled sadly but then began to talk. He said:

> No human knows that answer. If I could tell you that—but no one can. It is perhaps a gift of God that I myself have little if any fear. I think of death with equanimity.
>
> I cannot imagine that the soul, which is our life, could fade to nothing when death comes. Somehow it must continue to exist. Man is not permitted to know how—but it must. Because the origins of life, life itself, is as much of a mystery as death and we are unable to explain either phenomenon. The highest commandment has always been that which others hand on to us—to do one's duty.

These are not very profound expressions, but there was something most moving about his earnest, simple sincerity.

I asked if as a young man he had had any special ambitions, such as writing a play or traveling to a certain country, which he had never been able to achieve. He said: "You may think this funny; you may not believe it. But my dream was to live as a notary in the country with my family with just enough money to get along and not too much work. We cannot control our wishes."

At this point the Chancellor looked at me with a very strange and somewhat amused glance, saying: "Now, I want to ask you a question. Why is Kennedy so irritated with you?" I said I would certainly answer his question but I wanted first to ask another question which was, why did he have that impression? He said: "I have seen him irked when your name was mentioned." I then said I expected the President might feel I was too sympathetic in what I wrote about General de Gaulle and that I was not sufficiently optimistic about the possibilities of a multilateral nuclear force (MLF). In each case, Adenauer nodded and said he thought I was probably right.

BRUSSELS, *July 23, 1963*

THIS afternoon, I had a talk with Spaak in his office on the top floor of the new Foreign Ministry. He said:

Big countries must from time to time use the representatives of small countries to make contacts and soundings the way I was able to do when I saw Khrushchev in Kiev this month. When a representative of the U.S. makes a similar endeavor, he is automatically inhibited because he represents a great power and the implications are that he speaks with more responsibility. Khrushchev disquieted me by speaking too much about Germany. I warned him that he should not try to make any German agreement a precondition for a test-ban accord. I said to him: "You will lose all in an impasse if you adopt this."

Coming from a representative of a small country, this is rather easier because I don't have to be held responsible, and at worst people might merely say that I had been imprudent. This is an advantage we in the West have. A man like Gomulka, for example, could not see Kennedy on a similar basis. He could not speak freely the way I did with Khrushchev. And I assure you that when I talk to Khrushchev I do not in any sense feel I have to say "yes" on everything.

He then read me a three-page letter in which he advised Khrushchev not to push the German matter too fast because he would have no chance of succeeding. He suggested that Khrushchev first arrange an agreement on nuclear tests, then an accord on inspection and controls against ground surprise attacks, then an accord on on-site inspections against underground nuclear tests; then a nonaggression pact between NATO and the Warsaw alliance. Only at that point should he bring up either NATO or Germany.

PARIS, *July 29, 1963*

LUNCHED at the Bohlens' with former Vice President Nixon, his wife, and two daughters. Nixon could not have been nicer or more agreeable. He rushed across the room when he spotted me and said that when he had been in Greece the Queen assured him that, although she was somewhat worried about her projected trip to London, she and the King would at least get a fair break in "anything Cy Sulzberger wrote." I told Nixon I feared that they must have been deceived because I wrote a piece saying it was a damn fool trip.

He also told me he had taken with him on his trip a column I wrote saying one result of the Sino-Soviet fight was to make communism look more respectable and to heighten the danger of popular-front movements in Europe. He had successively tried this idea out on the leaders of

Morocco, Egypt, Greece, Italy, and Germany and found they all agreed. Considering that in late October, 1960, I wrote a column saying that if anybody voted for Nixon they had nothing to lose but their brains, I thought this was rather decent of the guy.

He agreed with Adenauer that it would be a mistake for the West to get too mixed up in the Sino-Soviet row; we should be in a position to play both sides rather subtly and to see if we could not develop some kind of indirect contacts with the Chinese—not recognition but at least a means of keeping touch. They were both against us and we should not put all our eggs in Khrushchev's basket.

Essentially there were really no major differences between the foreign-policy attitudes of the Democrats and the Republicans and it wasn't any use talking about Cuba (meaning the Bay of Pigs), because that was an affair of the past. The big issue in the 1964 elections would be foreign policy and not race. The race issue was simply too big. Both parties were devoured by it. It would be impossible for the Republicans either to run on a platform such as that Javits wanted—of promising more than Kennedy—or a kind of lily-white, retrograde and outright racist platform.

Nixon said he was, technically speaking, titular head of the Republican party today as the last defeated candidate, and he proposed to use his influence when he gets home to achieve three things: 1. To insure that there will be an internationalist and nonisolationist foreign-policy plank; 2. To insure that there is no retrograde racist plank; and 3. To insure that there is a sound economic plank, "because after all I am a free enterpriser myself."

From his conversation it seemed he was definitely anti-Goldwater. He likes Goldwater but thinks he is too poorly informed. A time comes when any politician has to cut the umbilical cord that ties him to a party group and Goldwater will face that problem—probably between now and January, but certainly before the New Hampshire primaries—vis-à-vis the Birchers and the right-wing lunatic fringe. They have a lot of money. "I know that because they used it against me." But he is going to have to make a choice.

It is ridiculous and impossible for a party to attempt to tie itself to a temporary emotional issue like desegregation versus segregation and the Republicans would lick themselves if they opposed progress just because they thought they could gain votes in the South. Goldwater has quite a lot of support among the rich élite in some cities like Los Angeles, Chicago, and Detroit. But the big powers in New York, Philadelphia, and the northeast haven't made up their minds.

Nixon said he had developed political interests fairly young. He had not gone into the law deliberately in order to get into politics, but it had been in his mind and, although he was elected to the California state assembly somewhat accidentally, he was delighted. He talked a good deal about the technique of public speaking and said it was always necessary to prepare a speech in advance, even for a small audience. In fact, it was easier to speak to a large audience because you did not feel the personal connections. Television was a special new gimmick and would play a very important role in 1964. The best thing is to use the press-conference technique such as "Meet the Press" programs and always to look right into the eye of the camera so the audience felt you were talking directly to it.

This is all I can remember from an agreeable lunch. Obviously my stock with Nixon has gone up. I judge this from the fact that I was sitting next to his little fifteen-year-old daughter Julie. She was saying how excited she was to be going to England and her father leaned across the table and said, "You must talk to Mr. Sulzberger about this because he knows all the royal family intimately." I didn't bother to disillusion him.

PARIS, *July 30, 1963*

GOLFED and had an excellent chat over drinks today with Nixon, Bohlen, and Cecil Lyon. Dick (we have now gotten to a first-name basis) and I beat the two diplomats by steady, undistinguished play. "We fived them to death," said Nixon happily. His form is more determined than stylish or powerful.

He was very cheerful and not at all depressed by what the uncertain world of politics had done to him. He said that one had to go on living no matter what happened. Furthermore, he said, anent the Republican party, that it had to count on the solid center block of American opinion and not just on "the extremists" who favored Goldwater. Despite his own defeats, he expected to have a good deal of influence at the 1964 Republican Convention.

I must say, he is doggedly persistent in his political intentions and good-humored about adversity.

PARIS, *August 3, 1963*

GOOD talk with Pompidou. I asked if Kennedy's latest offer of nuclear aid had in any way indicated it could satisfy France's requirements. He said: "There have not been any offers; that is to say, real offers. There was only a vague or tentative hint in the President's letter. The last real offer we had was the Polaris offer after the Nassau meeting and of course we turned that down for reasons you know well."

Pompidou went on to say that U.S. nuclear secrets and nuclear devices could only be satisfactory if they were given to France as such and not to France as part of any large organization. He said:

We must have our independent force—of course within the alliance—just as the U.S. has its own independent force within the alliance. After all, if Kennedy had wanted to bomb Cuba last autumn, he could have done so. We intend to be in a position where, if we wish to bomb Corsica, for example, we can do so.

We insist on a completely free position and the Nassau accord offered to us did not include such freedom. We don't have our own atomic force yet like the British. We must first have our H-bomb and in order to get this we have to test.

He didn't think it was conceivable that the U.S.A. would offer France sufficient secrets and weapons to obviate the need of tests. The Kennedy letter contained no proposition but only vague allusions. De Gaulle doesn't believe the U.S. will ever make France such an offer. He told Nixon and Bohlen at the Elysée luncheon that he was certain the U.S. would not give France such equipment because it was not in U.S. interest and he added that he would not do so either if he were in America's place.

He said:

I doubt very much if we can negotiate. Basically there are two differences:

1. U.S. interest is to keep the possession of nuclear weapons limited to the U.S.A. and Russia. France's interest is to have such weapons and to have them under France's own independent control.

2. We differ on our conception of détente. For us détente means the Russians must cease provoking tension and pressure because they are the only authors of the tensions. They must give more guarantees on Berlin and ease the situation in the satellites. We think the Russians know they need a détente because Cuba showed they could not fight the U.S.A. and satellite demands for improvement are mounting. Furthermore, the Russians are being pressed at their back by China which is even eyeing Siberia. And as certain Soviet diplomats say, the Chinese are "racists."

We think it is rather annoying that the U.S.A. contemplates giving Khrushchev the satisfaction of announcing a détente and an end to aggression—which the West has never threatened. The U.S.A. contemplates giving its own seal to an agreement that by implication accepts the Berlin situation, Germany's partition, and the satellites, just as events were beginning to move to repair those situations.

France didn't really need American atomic secrets now because its theoreticians are pretty well up to date, but they can only measure their technical advances by testing. One reason France opposed the Polaris offer was that French industry was not yet ready to make the equivalent of the latest U.S. missiles and miniaturized warheads.

If the U.S. offered France weapons to keep it from testing, how could the French be absolutely positive these weapons would work if they had not tried them. Pompidou said the U.S.A. gave secrets to Britain—but only in exchange for British guarantees that France would not be ready to give herself. The British were getting a little fed up with their own nuclear program anyway.

I asked Pompidou if Bonn accepted the wording of an ultimate non-aggression pact with Russia, would Paris then also accept? He said yes, France did not wish to be more royalist than the king.

Pompidou then summed things up by saying that a French-U.S. negotiation would not be difficult if the U.S. accepted the idea that France will make its own nuclear force by its own means. Once this has been agreed, the two countries can get along with things and there will not be any more major problems.

"But the U.S. plainly doesn't quite understand things yet. When Kennedy says that the U.S.A. gave atomic bombs to French planes in Germany, this proves he doesn't want to see our problem accurately. These planes are put at U.S. disposal for the overall sake of the alliance. They work for the alliance under U.S. command and therefore it is up to the U.S. how they are armed. If they are recalled to France they would have to leave their bombs behind. That is not enough."

ROME, *August 5, 1963*

THIS morning, I was received by Giovanni Leone, Prime Minister of the makeshift, stopgap Italian government that is trying to arrange terms for a formal alliance with the Nenni Socialists.

He is most odd looking, with an elfin face and shape; about five feet five inches tall, round and built like a turnip, dressed in a black suit this steaming day, squat, with pointed ears, very long nose, glasses, a great graying shock of hair, little moustache, bright but somewhat surprised expression. He might have been invented by Walt Disney.

I asked if he thought Italy had solved the problem of effective, democratic self-government. He said, from a constitutional viewpoint, yes; but from a political viewpoint, no stable majority existed in Parliament.

Would the opening of the left work in the long run? He said: "I have the greatest confidence in this provided there is a clear understanding between our party and the Socialists. That would lead to a large majority in Parliament and to the isolation of the Communists. It must be understood that in no case would the Communists be permitted to join in contributing to that majority."

NICOSIA, CYPRUS, *August 17, 1963*

I PAID an agreeable visit to Archbishop Makarios in his air-conditioned presidential palace. Makarios was charming and his English is much improved. Nevertheless, he is vain (flattery takes on him), overconfident, naive. He likes the prerogatives of being chief of state.

Makarios is tall by Cypriot standards, especially when he has his priest's hat off. He greeted me bareheaded—he is almost bald—and without his outer black robe, only a dark blue inner one. He spoke easily in a soft voice and was quite willing to discuss anything but his answers were scarcely illuminating.

I began by inquiring whether, as an ecclesiastical head, he found any conflict, in his dual role, between that which is God's and that which is Caesar's. He said:

No, there is no conflict of interest. I am not really a party leader trying to create a political career for myself. I was asked to offer myself to the people during their first steps in this new life of independence and I thought it my duty to serve. I accept the office of President not to satisfy any ambition of my own, but only in order to aid our state in its difficult first steps.

Perhaps, there are some advantages to having an ecclesiastic as a ruler. There might also be some disadvantages; for example, it takes time away from normal religious duties; but I find it doesn't really interfere. And, after all, even in politics there is no different standard of right and wrong from that in religious life. What is right in the latter is also right in the former. Something cannot be both just and unjust.

I asked if he thought religion were a good training for politics. He said, "Yes, religion teaches morality and morality should always lie at the base of political life, as it should in all other aspects of life."

ATHENS, *August 22, 1963*

THIS morning, I went to see Panayotis Pipinellis, now Prime Minister. He is a career diplomat and, although very conservative, a level-headed man who is highly intelligent and, unlike most Greeks, not governed by emotion. He is a tiny fellow who used to be quite plump but has been seriously ill.

It seemed to me that under the constitutional system the Crown was under obligation to follow the advice of the government. If this were so, had not the Crown lost position by violating such constitutional obligations when the King and Queen went to London against the advice of Prime Minister Caramanlis?

He commented:

Our historical and psychological connections with Byzantium are much more powerful than they are with classical times. This helps explain the overwhelming importance of the church. Likewise, the Crown has a particular importance despite any legal limitations. It has immense moral and psychological prestige. The King has no authority to refuse assent to government decisions. He has a right to be consulted, to advise, and to warn. It is under this last interpretation that the King *can* disagree with the Prime Minister and warn against unwise decisions. This was the real political issue of the London trip. The King was on firm constitutional grounds even though perhaps he acted unwisely.

He said the Communists have gained. They are taking advantage of the disintegration of the Center. The Center, by making excessive demands, has succeeded in divorcing itself from those people who crave nothing but tranquility and stability. The Communists have also been helped by the fact that they have assumed a more respectable international position thanks to the Vatican's attitude and Khrushchev's better relations with the West.

ATHENS, *October 1, 1963*

THIS morning, I took a taxi out to the Kastri, some miles outside Athens, to visit George Papandreou, leader of the Center Union opposition. He is seventy-four but incredibly youthful, lean, tanned, and full of energy. He received me in the book-lined study of his comfortable, suburban house out in this pinewood area. Tall, gray haired, with a tiny dot of a moustache, he seemed amazingly vigorous.

Papandreou was very optimistic about his chances in the November elections. As a result of pressures and strong statements, he has forced the King to dissolve Parliament and install a nonpolitical caretaker government.

Papandreou said the major issue was realization of political democracy. In all western countries, political democracy exists and the struggle has turned into a struggle for social democracy. But in Greece, political democracy has ceased to exist. The 1961 elections were not free.

Caramanlis established a quasi-totalitarian regime. This monopolized the radio for political purposes and the gendarmes hampered the circulation of opposition papers outside the principal cities. Finally the secret service, KYP, is used to discourage free speech and opposition in general. As a result the peasants are politically terrorized despite the fact that there is a free Parliament and freedom in the press of the cities.

Everything is done in the name of anticommunism. The formula that is presented is that EDA equals communism, the Center equals fellow-traveling, and ERE (Caramanlis's party) equals nationalism. Papandreou said: "We must reconquer democracy which has been lost to us in the name of anticommunism."

ATHENS, *October 2, 1963*

LUNCH with Harry Labouisse. I asked what was the importance to the United States in terms of the election results. He said Caramanlis and

Averoff had proved they could run the country. Greece has moved forward under their administration. The opposition, on the other hand, has seemed irresponsible. Papandreou and the other opposition leaders are pro-West and pro-U.S.A. But the statements they are making are irresponsible and there is no doubt we would prefer to continue dealing with those we have dealt with in the past. It was a good five to one bet that Caramanlis would come back. (On the whole, it is clear that Harry is strongly wedded to the Caramanlis party. I wonder if he may not be a little overboard on the subject.)

We chatted about the forthcoming holiday visit of Jackie Kennedy. Harry feels that it is bad taste for her to stay in the house of Nomikos (where she also stayed in 1961). At least one of the Nomikos ships has been trading with Cuba. Likewise, Harry thinks it's bad for her to go cruising on Onassis's yacht, the *Christina*. There is nothing actually wrong in terms of violating the proprieties, but it leaves a poor impression.

ATHENS, *October 3, 1963*

THIS morning I called on Caramanlis, former Prime Minister and head of the ERE (right-wing) party. His apartment is comfortable, old-fashioned, and rather luxurious. The *objets* and furniture are polished to a gleaming finish: everything bright and brilliant. The walls were lined with books. Outside the gates stood some surly policemen.

Caramanlis looked pale and tired. He started off by saying: "It is a terrible situation, terrible. There has been abuse of freedom here. There has been a steady blackmail by the opposition. The press and the Communists and the opposition abuse democracy and hamper its working."

Caramanlis predicted that EDA (the extreme left) would get 20 percent or more of the vote in next month's balloting. It had been helped by Papandreou's "clamor about a police state and fascism." The Greek Communist party is one of the most active in the world, despite its relatively small size. It has already staged three rounds of a revolt. Although it has been outlawed, it operates with full freedom and is protected by Papandreou under the guise of "democracy."

Caramanlis surprised me by saying that after the elections "I must take legal measures against the opposition." Obviously, he intends to clamp down on them and this smells bad in terms of his rather authoritarian inclinations.

This afternoon, I drove out to Tatoi to see King Paul at his country palace. He received me informally, dressed in white-summer admiral's uniform. I asked why he had so suddenly seemed to change his mind, dismissing Parliament and replacing Pipinellis with a new caretaker Cabinet. He said:

There really had been genuine pressure from all quarters, including the Conservatives. Papandreou was strongly opposed to Pipinellis. Frankly, I don't quite know why because I think Pipinellis is an honest, intelligent man, in fact a gentleman. And there aren't so many gentlemen among our politicians.

But Papandreou evolved a blackmail method. He kept threatening all kinds of things and I thought it better to yield on this issue. But I put a navy man I trust in as under secretary of the interior in order to keep strict order. Papandreou protested against this but I wouldn't give in.

The King said that four or five days ago, "I realized the whole tendency was in favor of changing the government. It went against the grain with me. I like standing up for people. But I felt that in this case I had to do it."

He claimed Caramanlis is not dictatorial but "is teased to extremes by Papandreou." When Caramanlis resigned last spring, he recommended the majority system should be used in the elections. But this would have facilitated a popular front.

The Constitution obliges people to vote, so it would have been difficult if Papandreou had tried to blackball elections. Papandreou had told him he was considering ordering his supporters to vote for Caramanlis rather than throwing in blank ballots. That would have eliminated the opposition by producing just two parties—the Communist-led EDA and Caramanlis. This would have been idiotic. It would have benefitted only EDA. But it was an oriental tactic and by these blackmail methods Papandreou succeeded.

"Everything is personal here. Parties don't exist, only leaders. In the old days, before the Greek kingdom, every bandit chief had his followers, his own ideas, and his own policies."

The King told me Venizelos had no followers and even wanted to quit politics. It was funny the way Venizelos and Papandreou played together. They kept forming alliances and splitting. Some time ago, the King said to Papandreou, when he had just gotten together again with Venizelos: "Is this a marriage under the Greek Orthodox church or is it a marriage under the Roman church—where you can't divorce?" A little bit later they split up again and the King sent word to Papandreou: "Have you got the Pope's permission?"

The King claims Caramanlis chose a "phony issue" to resign because otherwise he faced a good deal of trouble over the Salonika affair (the murder of Lambrakis) and the trouble that Makarios was starting in Cyprus. He would have landed in trouble, but now he is better off because he was away all summer.

The King talked at length about de Gaulle's visit. De Gaulle was a splendid man. He was rather interested to see how de Gaulle's naval aide looked after him. He always stood just a bit behind the General at his left and, as it were, seemed to guide him without touching him when the

General had trouble with his eyes. De Gaulle was very impatient with the Greek police and broke through to mix with people. There was a great problem for the police when he disappeared into the crowd. The King was astonished at what beautiful French de Gaulle spoke [sic].

He said one strange thing. At the time de Gaulle went to Salonika, King Paul had an emergency appendicitis operation so he sent his son, the Crown Prince, along. Constantine said to him afterward that one of the French generals in the party was most impressed by the parade in Salonika. He turned to him and said: "This is the best parade I have seen since the Germans entered Paris." "Astonishing!" said the King. I agreed.

Eisenhower had told him he wanted to offer Khrushchev a joint U.S.-Soviet trip to the moon back in 1960. This is the offer that Kennedy recently made at the UN. However, the U-2 affair and the breakup of the Paris Summit followed and Eisenhower was never able to make his speech.

He told me also that he had recently been informed that in 1956, at the time of Suez, the President sent a signal to the Sixth Fleet, saying: "Are you prepared to meet the enemy?" The reply sent back to Washington was: "Which enemy?"

Farewell drink with Harry and Eve Labouisse. Harry is all upset. Jackie Kennedy arrived this morning on a strictly "incognito" holiday trip. She was invited to lunch at the Palace and refused to go because she dislikes the Queen. Harry persuaded her to agree to go to tea, but she wants to bring along her sister and Stash Radziwill. And the Queen hates Stash and doesn't want to have him.

PARIS, *October 11, 1963*

THIS evening, I spent an hour and a quarter with Couve de Murville, who has just come back from conversations in Washington with Kennedy. He seemed sad and had a bad cold in the head, gray, with dripping nose; even if things had gone well—which they had not—he was scarcely the man to advertise cheerfulness.

He was afraid his talks only clarified the existence of an anti-de Gaulle clique in Washington, very similar to that which existed in 1944, and "even including some of the same people." I expressed surprise that he could say some of the same people were there almost twenty years later. But he is convinced that the higher echelons of the State Department are personally hostile to de Gaulle and that the same is true of the White House. It was clear he particularly meant Bundy.

Couve believes Washington is absolutely convinced that anything emanating from France originates personally with de Gaulle and is therefore automatically bad. He feels the U.S. government has decided

as a matter of policy that it cannot do any business with France until
de Gaulle is out of power. This is not a U.S. governmental position, he
said, nor even a Kennedy position. But it is the position of so many
influential people in the government that it has a preponderant influence
on the U.S. attitude.

His conversation with Kennedy was very relaxed and friendly. Kennedy had wanted to have things explained to him and he "listened well."
Toward the end, he asked: "Just why are we so far apart then?"

It had always been agreed that de Gaulle would repay the visit Kennedy
had paid him here. It is assumed this will take place some time in 1964.
If one looks at Kennedy's political calendar, it is evident this means
fairly early in the year; and it would be a working visit rather than a
state visit. "But," said Couve, "frankly I doubt if it would be good for
de Gaulle to go to Washington in the present atmosphere. No one really
wants to discuss things and I would not be surprised if in the end the visit
did not come off."

I said France is always talking of the need for reforming NATO. Had
there been any working paper prepared outlining France's views of desirable reforms? He answered:

I explained to your people that NATO should be revised giving both
more burdens and more responsibilities to the European countries and
thus leaving less of both to you. Europe should pay a larger share of
defense, but it also should have more responsibilities.

Frankly, I don't find any of our partners share this opinion. Most of
them are satisfied to do nothing. I told your people that most of the NATO
allies don't want to do anything for defense—but want to do it inside
NATO, while Uncle Sam pays the bill. Of course, this is not true of the
Germans.

We are the only ones in NATO who accept the concept of Europe
taking more into its own hands. So it is hard to see how we can discuss
reform inside NATO seeking a better balance, because most European
countries are satisfied with the present system.

That being so, we have made our own military decisions to put more
of our defense in our own hands—with certain implications to NATO. As
you know, we have limited our forces in Germany to two divisions. We
have changed the command of our Mediterranean and Atlantic fleets
and we have initiated our own atomic program.

And we will continue all this until there is a real NATO reform—
which is not for today. We think that for the time being things can
remain there and there is no use in always harping on French sins.

I asked whether France proposed to recognize Communist China and if
any soundings would be made during the forthcoming trip of Edgar Faure
to Peking. Couve said: "Clearly it is quite normal in the situation in which
we find ourselves after the Moscow treaty to have a rapprochement. The
Chinese want relations with us but nothing has been done—*for the present.*"

While he was in Washington he stressed the "battle" of the U.S.A. versus France in Germany and the efforts of Washington to block Franco-German cooperation. He said:

I tried to explain that such a policy was disadvantageous to all three of us—the U.S.A., France, and Germany—and helped only the Russians. I said it was normal for Germany to have close relations with both France and the U.S.A. But these relations could not be exactly the same. There were differences in the size of power of the countries involved and also in geography.

We are not going to exchange military units with the German army inside the U.S.A. but in France. We are increasing exchanges of German and French youth inside our countries but this is not in the U.S.A. We give the Germans military facilities because we are neighbors. This cannot be done in the U.S.A. We are working out many economic problems in common inside the Common Market, but we have no Common Market with the U.S.A. I explained all this and I can't really judge what your reaction was. The only trouble is that the Franco-German treaty was signed by two men who are hated in the U.S.A.— Adenauer and de Gaulle.

There is a sort of Russo-American effort against France through the Moscow treaty. They reproach us for not signing the treaty and claim that it helps the Chinese. China and France are the only two countries for which the signing of the Moscow treaty had any significance. All the others have either finished their testing or had no intention of making any tests. So it is not a surprise that the position of France and China on this coincides. It would be a logical thing for France and China to draw closer together now.

Couve said he was frankly bewildered by the fact that the U.S. now thought it was a "vital" U.S. interest to have Britain in the Common Market. This undoubtedly stimulated a French suspicion that Kennedy's grand design was determined to end the Common Market. After all, only a few years ago, the U.S. preferred to have Britain out of the Common Market.

He then recalled that in 1956, during the Suez crisis, there had been a very difficult situation and Dulles at that time had said that things could "never" be the same again between France and the U.S. But this made for no enduring difficulties between Britain and the U.S. There were even Americans who strongly preferred Mollet to de Gaulle, although Mollet was the man who arranged the expedition behind Washington's back.

PARIS, *October 12, 1963*

YESTERDAY evening, I went over and had a drink with Bohlen, who has just come back from Washington, where he took part in the conversations between Kennedy, Rusk, and Couve de Murville. I warned him Paris seemed getting ready to recognize Peking. He was skeptical.

CAIRO, *October 19, 1963*

LUNCHED with Sir Harold Beeley (British ambassador) and his wife. He says there is no doubt that despite the suffering of the upper class (who see the foreigners most) and minorities, Egypt is better off after eleven years of the revolutionary regime.

He told me a fine story about the Ethiopian ambassador here. A group of Eritrean students organized in Cairo and started a demonstration against the Ethiopian embassy, hauling a tank of gasoline behind them, all set for a bonfire. The ambassador called up the Foreign Office to protest and demand protection; the only result was that the one guard stationed before his embassy opened the gate to the demonstrators. So the ambassador hauled out a revolver, shot two of the students and the guard. Everyone fled. Some time later, another protest was organized. The ambassador called the Foreign Office, demanded protection, and said: "If it is not forthcoming, this time I shall use a machine gun." Immediately twenty soldiers arrived and broke up the demonstration.

CAIRO, *October 20, 1963*

THIS morning I visited the elderly Rector of the Al Azhar, outstanding figure in the world of Islam. The seventy-year-old Rector, called "Your Eminence" by his colleagues, received me in his exceedingly modest flat in Heliopolis. His full title is Sheikh Mahmoud Shaltout, Sheikh el Islam, Rector of Al Azhar University. He was sitting in one of two small reception rooms in his ground-floor apartment. There were several chairs around the walls, a table in the middle. The chairs were imitation French and gilded; the floor was covered with a modern, machine-made oriental rug. On the wall was a painting of the Sheikh in a garden.

He is stooped with kind, strong face, a bad right eye (trachoma), and a fringe of gray beard. His lower lip was thrust forward and he seemed to be toothless. He appeared somewhat feeble but spoke in a strong voice and smiled often. The room was a bit smelly and there were quite a few flies. We were served glasses of excellent mango juice and small cups of bitter Egyptian (Turkish) coffee.

The Sheikh said: "There is no authority in Islam save for the *Koran* itself. There are some leaders such as the Rectors of Al Azhar and other universities, but they have no authority in a clerical sense. In fact, the Caliph never had any religious authority. This belongs to God alone as revealed in the *Koran*. There is no single man or group above others in Islam; each man thinks for himself."

How did he explain that Islam was spreading more rapidly in Sub-Saharan Africa than any other faith? He said: "The answer can be both simple and complex. First of all, there is the simplicity of belief in Islam itself. Islam says the religion of God is one expressed by different prophets in different ages. The various revealed religions are all expressions of a single one. But what I might call the more complicated factor is that people in that part of Africa never had bad experiences with Islamic conquerors. And Muslims, when they go there, live with them as brothers; they stress brotherhood."

He said:

Islam has no formal directing organization or clergy. Every individual is God's vice-gerent on earth. [I thought to myself, how strange; Islam has God but no clergy; Buddhism has a clergy but no God.]

I then asked what was the Rector's feeling toward the Black Muslim movement in America. He appeared to know little about it. He said:

It is extremely difficult to pass judgment on a group without thoroughly understanding its beliefs. But we have a criterion in Islam, a criterion of Islamic life and ideas. There is one God who is not choosy and belongs to no single group. The nature of mankind does not differ. Islam knows no color—white, black, red, or yellow—for man. It knows only the man, goodness, and justice. Muhammad was the prophet of Islam and these beliefs were revealed through him and are fundamental. If anyone believes in God, in all his prophets including Moses, Jesus, and Muhammad, and in the idea of resurrection and the mission of Muhammad, then he is a Muslim.

CAIRO, *October 21, 1963*

THIS morning, I went to Al Ahram for a long talk and coffee with Mohammed Hassanein Heikal, the editor, and Nasser's close friend. A small, energetic man with mobile features and much charm, he greeted me warmly and we had a good talk.

He said Castro has endangered the theory of nonalignment by choosing a camp. The U.A.R. never allowed a Soviet base to be built here at the time of the Suez danger. The Cuban crisis of 1962 convinced the world of the rightness of the U.S. view. At the start, Cairo suspected that the talk of Soviet missiles was a phony excuse for use of force. Everyone was astonished and shocked by Russian admission of their missiles— and their withdrawal.

CAIRO, *October 22, 1963*

THIS morning, I had a long talk with Ambassador John Badeau, a former missionary-teacher, ex-Near East Foundation Arabist. He is a tall man with lined, pleasant face, and an easy manner, who seems pleased with the fact of being a diplomat. He said the major U.S. interest involved in this region is Saudi Arabian oil. It is of paramount importance to keep it available to the West. What can protect this access?

Reasonable stability in Saudi Arabia is needed. Otherwise, it would fall apart into its three main provinces of Hassa (oil), Nejd, and Hejaz. And were it imperiled internally, it might suck in other forces from abroad.

A year ago, when the trouble in Yemen became critical, conditions in Saudi Arabia were bad. King Saud was ineffective and there was some dissidence. The forces for destruction are greater in Saudi Arabia than the forces for construction.

U.S. policy wanted to prevent Yemen from sucking Saudi Arabia into a vortex of destruction and war with the U.A.R. Such a war would have posed the problem: Would the U.S.A. have defended Saudi Arabia in a shooting war?

The U.S. told Faisal that the real problem of Saudi Arabia is modernization and change; Kennedy said this to Faisal in person. It is our belief that at present the royal family is the only alternative to chaos; but Faisal hasn't moved fast enough.

The Bunker mission for Yemen peace negotiated with both sides in April, 1963. The start of Yemen disengagement was held up two months by UN because U Thant wished to avoid another Congo morass and was unsure of what the Russians would do; also there was the problem of finances.

And General von Horn, the Swede, was most depressed, having had enough difficulty in Palestine. He was horrified on reaching Yemen and, among other things, he sardonically included two hundred coffins among the list of essentials he needed.

NASSER:

"ONE LEARNS TO

BE MORE PATIENT"

CAIRO, *October 23, 1963*

THIS EVENING, I HAD A LONG TALK WITH NASSER IN HIS HELIOPOLIS house; Heikal came along. The conversation lasted two full hours. Nasser speaks very fluent English and, after taking twenty-one pages of notes, I was dead beat.

I asked if he detected any difference in the foreign policy of the Eisenhower and Kennedy administrations. He said:

I think the main characteristic of this administration is its attempt to be frank in discussing all problems. Frankness is a great help. It overcomes suspicion and a lack of trust.

During the last two and a half years, relations between ourselves and Washington have been progressing. Also, I may add, before—at the end of the Eisenhower administration—things were already getting better. There is now a better understanding, an attempt to comprehend the problems of the Middle East.

I said I had the impression that there were no longer any bilateral problems, only problems affecting third countries such as Israel or Saudi Arabia. Nasser replied: "That is correct. There are only problems of third countries. We no longer feel your interference or pressure as we did during the early days of the revolution. Of course we always believe that the U.S. is not fair on the question of Israel and the Arabs and takes the side of Israel."

I asked whether the thaw in world relations was not perplexing to the nonaligned countries. He said:

The philosophy of nonalignment means I must adopt a wholly independent policy, independent of the two camps, and not be influenced in my point of view. And I think this attitude on the part of nonaligned nations has done much to ease international tension. We are always for peace, for coexistence, for negotiations, and for improving contacts between the two camps. But we do not have pretensions.

The two blocs remain, NATO and the Communist camp remain. Should there be a war, all the members on one side or on the other side would stick to their blocs. We don't want to get involved. Nonalignment doesn't have the mission of mediation. We express our views whether these please others or not. But anything that is against peace we oppose. In this kind of a situation we try to help mediate. [This is a rather odd statement from a man who is sponsoring a military operation in Yemen and is backing one side in another military operation on the Algerian-Moroccan border.]

Nasser then said that during the Cuban crisis a year ago, the U.A.R. had infuriated all parties. At the UN it suggested that Cuba should be nonaligned and quit its Soviet ties—which angered Castro. It suggested that all bases—Russian missiles and U.S. installations at Guantanamo—should be withdrawn. This infuriated both Washington and Moscow. Nasser smiled happily and said this proved his nonalignment.

He continued:

We feel that U.S. Middle Eastern policy is based on good relations with all countries, all *governments*, despite the contradictions which are deep. On the other hand, Soviet policy seeks the confidence and trust of the *peoples* of the Middle East, despite prevailing contradictions.

We feel that the U.S., despite complications, wants good relations with all governments, even though their ideologies may be contradictory—as in the case of Israel, Jordan, Saudi Arabia, Yemen, Iraq, and Syria. This is a clever policy.

I was struck by the distinction he made as between governments and peoples. He answered:

Yes, there is a deliberate distinction between governments and peoples. Look at the difference between the broadcasts in Arabic on the VOA and Radio Moscow. The VOA stresses governments, without raising problems. Because, after all, you have interests in the Middle East. I mean interests like petroleum and pipelines in the Gulf, Iraq, and Syria. Russia doesn't have such interests and the Russian radio just appeals to peoples.

I asked what "color" Egypt felt itself to be and whether it objected to China's recent efforts to introduce racism into the Communist quarrel. He said: "People here don't read all those long statements. And racism doesn't occur here. We are a variety of shades. And anyway, there is no racial discrimination in our religion, which forbids all thought of race."

I asked what he thought of the future of Arab unity. He said:

The peoples are united and have the same feelings and reactions. But there is the second term of constitutional unity. To reach this is not easy; any faction may create a civil war. After all, it wasn't easy for the U.S. to federate, and afterward you had a civil war.

There are the ambitions of politicians, the differences between classes, and these encourage contradictions which make constitutional Arab unity more difficult. The exploiters or the beneficiaries of certain politicians oppose unity because this would deprive them of their advantages. That is why there is unrest and instability.

I asked Nasser what he thought was the ultimate future of Saudi Arabia. He grinned and said:

I don't know, but the people have radios and this is a small world. They even hang transistors around the necks of camels. They listen to all the different broadcasts. You can't isolate people anymore. And another factor is education. There is now a new class of intellectuals. The son of the Bedouin is now becoming an intellectual. Regardless of class, the people are being educated and they realize that oil revenues are not being used enough for their development. People oppose what is going on—even inside the royal families. They recognize the need for economic development and equality. They feel they are human beings and not slaves.

I said I was a bit puzzled by the argument between Nasser and Syria's Baath, because they both seemed to profess progressive ideas. What was the difference? He said:

The main difference is that they have slogans without any definitions. We have asked them, "What do you mean by freedom? What is democracy? Do you want political parties?" But there is no clear answer. One of them said: "We support western democracy when we are out of power, but when we are in power we favor a single party."

They have no definition of Arab unity. Their policy is based on promises, maneuvers, and lies. It is a policy of bad character.

Nasser said that he was deliberately investing beyond the national capacity. He thought it was better to have a hard-currency crisis and to invest money rather than to build up hard-currency reserves. This policy gave work to everybody. And now, for the first time, there was labor shortage in two provinces and he had to give more attention to mechanization.

It seemed paradoxical to me to see Cairo with all its traffic and consumers goods built on a country with a pitifully low average wage when even Moscow couldn't support such luxury. He said: "We adopted something contrary to the Soviet and Communist line. Our plan started by concentrating on consumers goods and food. Then we started with some heavy, strategic industries such as steel. We are now turning to heavy industry. But we know our people and they need everything and want everything at low prices."

I asked Nasser: "What have you personally learned as a result of the revolution and being in power yourself for more than a decade?" He looked puzzled for a moment and then he smiled in a rather disarming way. He said: "Well, I was always very patient. But one learns to be more patient. I always thought I was very good in dealing with people. But there, too, one learns more. One learns more tolerance and one learns better how to deal with people. I have also learned not to go to bed later than 2 o'clock."

I said to him that his enemies call his government a dictatorship and a police state. What did he think?

"Our object is to free the individual. This makes a free society. Such a free society is impossible if it's dominated by landlords and capitalists, whether or not there is a parliament. We have our own pragmatic system. We don't follow any ideology."

He said the Communist party was still illegal. In 1959, Communists had been arrested. "Some of them were still in jail and those who have been released are quiet." His government opposed all organizations that were against his regime; the Muslim Brotherhood no longer functioned.

I then asked him if he had been at all influenced by de Gaulle or his ideas. He said:

I started to admire de Gaulle during World War II. I remember his pictures. [It was rather moving to think of this young Egyptian captain admiring the lonely Frenchman at a distance.] I remember the pictures showing him when he returned to Paris and marched in a parade to the Arch of Triumph. I admired him during the war as an officer who insisted on carrying on the fight despite all odds.

De Gaulle was courageous also on Algeria, where he faced the situation bluntly. Now he tries to be independent by all means. It is a question of dignity. I think he is a man of principle. It is different to deal with him than to deal with the politicians, even if there are difficulties. It is a great advantage to deal with a man of principle.

BEIRUT, *October 27, 1963*

LAST night, Charles Malik, former foreign minister and president of the UN Assembly, told me he was one of the seconders for the nomination of Martin Buber for the Nobel Literary Prize—and hopes he gets it next year. He had to do this secretly because, although living now in Switzerland, eighty-five-year-old Buber is an Israeli. He wrote a long letter (also secretly) to Buber telling him what an immense influence he had had on

Malik's life and Buber wrote a touching reply. Malik, by the way, is urging Paul Hoffman for the Nobel Peace Prize (also a bit dashing for an Arab because Hoffman's wife is Jewish).

AMMAN, JORDAN, *October 28, 1963*

THIS afternoon, immediately after flying in from Beirut, I taxied to the Palace to keep a rendezvous with King Hussein. At the gate of the palace, my taxi was checked carefully for bombs; then a soldier with red head-dress and khaki uniform, carrying a tommy gun, got in the front seat and rode up with me to the entrance. Inside, the door to Hussein's office was guarded by two well-built Circassians in black cossack dress with kara-kul hats, cartridge bandoliers across their breasts, and silver daggers.

The King was standing at the door and a court photographer took several pictures of us. He is a very short man, although slim, powerfully built (as I was to discover later when I went down to Aqaba and swam with him). He is a first-class athlete—fencing, rifle and shotgun, riding, sports car and go-cart racing. He learned recently to water ski very well (he can now turn around and go backwards on skis).

Hussein is said to go armed constantly (shoulder holster). He is very brave and good in crises; but not at all intellectual, never reads, and mixes with a rather inferior group of young English men and women with whom he has go-cart races.

I started off by remarking on his reputation for courage and asking him to define that quality. He said: "All I have done has been out of fear that I might otherwise do something contrary to my convictions. One must do what accords with one's conscience and one must stick to one's principles; that is all."

I asked if he thought a central, dominant figure—whether king or dictator—were necessary in Arab nations today. He said:

A central, dominant figure is a sign of weakness in a nation, I believe. My greatest ambition is to create a system of government that has the solid support of the people so that Jordan will not be dependent upon me. It is a weakness when a nation feels it must put all its hopes on the life span or the ability of one leader. In principle I am against this.

As for kings—naturally there are good and bad kings; and maybe the same is true of dictators also. Perhaps one might criticize Nasser and his regime for this, just as Nasser criticizes me. But I am not, as such, contrary to any particular form of regime. I believe in the freedom of each people to choose the kind of system they consider beneficial, but I like to see this done in an orderly manner.

In the Arab world, the monarchies and the other governmental systems should cooperate for the betterment of the Arab world as a whole. There are both advantages and disadvantages to the monarchic system.

Certainly monarchy offers continuity and thus should insure a certain amount of stability. It is surely not the only governing solution; but, at the same time, it is surely not so bad that it must go.

Talking about himself he mused:

Many men have influenced me. Here in Jordan there was my grandfather [Emir Abdullah], whom I respected a great deal and whom I loved. And then there are the people of Jordan themselves. It is not easy to be a Jordanian. But we are slowly coming together to form what we call the Jordanian family.

I wondered what he thought of the Fertile Crescent idea, remarking that I had discussed this with his grandfather years ago. He said: "This is a sound regional idea. If you quote me on my views, I know I'll get into trouble; but go ahead and quote me anyway. I think that Iraq-Syria-Lebanon-Jordan, as a bloc, should cooperate in all fields. How should this Crescent be started? I think the political aspect should come last. We should first learn to live with each other now and tighten our cooperation in the future."

In the later afternoon, drinks with Bill McComber, our ambassador to Jordan. He reasons:

Jordan is the heartland of the east Arab-Israeli world. A coup here could not be limited. If the Jordan plateau crumbles, an area conflagration is almost certain. And any successor regime here would be less satisfactory to Israel. Nasserism or Baathism in Jordan would have Israel by the throat. Therefore Israel would move if there were a Jordan coup. It simply cannot afford to have an aggressively hostile state on its longest frontier.

And if Israel moves into the West bank, all the Arabs would join to fight against Israel. This would suck in the great powers and there is at least an outside chance that chaos would spread beyond the area immediately involved.

McComber says Hussein worries more about Nasser than Israel. Although enemies, Jordan and Israel have much in common. They recognize they have a certain community of interest. They both worry about Nasser. They have a tacit understanding not to mess each other up and to try and control fanatical elements who provoke incidents on their border. In the U.S. Congress, Israeli pressures support Jordanian appropriations. Despite public demonstrations, their joint frontier is quiet. Nevertheless, there are terrible passions and hatreds among the Palestinians and the fact the two are "successor states" of Palestine is just the reverse of a common bond.

McComber says Hussein is very brave but no intellectual. He is a true aristocrat, conscious of his direct descent from the Prophet. Princess Muna, his wife, told McComber the hardest thing for her to get used to in this new life was seeing her husband, when he got dressed, strap on a shoulder holster. Hussein is convinced he will not die a natural death and that when he is killed it will be by a man in uniform standing behind him.

Jordan is really two countries—two-thirds Palestinian and one-third tribesmen. Jerusalem has been described as a golden bowl, filled with vipers.

AQABA, JORDAN, *October 30, 1963*

SPENT the night here after a most interesting trip by automobile yesterday to the ancient Nabatean capital of Petra. Drove down from Amman in the early morning, first stopping at a Bedouin brigade post where Jordanian soldiers in red Arab headdress checked our car. At El Giza, sheep and camels were being watered by their Bedouin owners in a long reservoir made out of an old Roman cistern. Bedouin girls in black robes with long braids and tattooed faces (unveiled) walked by firmly and gracefully with cans of water on their heads. Flocks of goats and donkeys grazed on the sparse shrubs of the desert.

Petra was on the caravan route from Saudi Arabia and Yemen to Damascus. The former city of the Edomites and Nabateans is approached through a narrow passage with towering rock walls called the Siq. Shortly before you get to Petra there is a rich village called Wadi Musa (Moses), where Moses stopped on the way from Egypt. Wadi Musa boasts numerous springs. Petra, with its pink and red structures carved out of the walls of sandstone canyons, is a remarkable and dramatic ruin to which we rode on horseback after the road became impassable.

From Petra we motored through the desert past Bedouin camps of dark brown goats' wool tents to Ras al Nageb, where the railway from Damascus ends. Lawrence of Arabia blew it up not far from Maan in 1917, and the stretch from Maan to Medina has never been rebuilt.

We reached Aqaba at 5:15, after driving through the most extraordinary desert filled with vast, abrupt, jagged peaks. We first spotted the Gulf in an extraordinary purple-brown landscape; sea and sky, mountains rumbling toward the Gulf from all directions. Aqaba is only swimming distance from Elath, the Israeli port. A good swimmer could, within a day, traverse Egyptian, Israeli, Jordanian, and Saudi waters: They all meet here.

Hussein was down in his simple villa water skiing and took us out in his new glass-bottomed boat to look at the fish.

DAMASCUS, SYRIA, *November 1, 1963*

THIS afternoon I called on Michel Aflak, founder and secretary-general of the Baath party. He is supposed to be a great intellectual, but he struck me as a pretty third-rate character. The Baath is an underground organization and perhaps he was just camouflaging his intellect. If so, he was most successful.

Aflak received me in his unattractive, second-floor flat, in a middle-class, tawdry neighborhood. The building would not be noticeable except for an armed sentry stationed at the entrance. One sees a lot of military signs in Damascus these days and there are plenty of tanks and armed troops stationed at key centers around the town.

After going through a smelly hallway, up a dismal flight of stairs, I rang the bell and was admitted by a young girl who seemed startled. I made my way past a little hall filled with women and screaming children. I was conducted into a very small parlor by a charming young gentleman who is the brother of Madame Aflak and who explained to me in English that the Baath leader was in bed. Apparently he sits up all night gassing with his colleagues.

The parlor was very cold and had a stone floor. The furniture comprised eight chairs and a little sofa, all covered with hideous orange slipcovers. There was a bare wooden table in the center and on the walls some cheap Chinese prints. In a little stand in one corner were some Japanese dolls and in another corner was the ugliest lamp I have ever seen in the center of which stood a flower pot.

After he got dressed, Aflak came in. Aflak is a Christian, very rare among Arab leaders, and a graduate of the Sorbonne. He was once a high-school teacher. We talked French, which he doesn't speak as well as a Sorbonne graduate should. He has a soft voice and the most infuriating manner of talking slowly. There is a pause of several seconds between every phrase and between many words, even the simplest. This halting mannerism, almost an intellectual stutter, is most upsetting. It seems to take him about a minute even to say a simple sentence like, "It is not raining anymore."

Nevertheless, I was interested to quiz him on the organization and ideology of the Baath, which now is beginning to rival Nasserism for influence among the Arabs and which, incidentally, enrages Nasser when it is mentioned. I persevered through our tedious conversation for a couple of hours during which Aflak, a very polite man, passed around cigarettes, we were served cups of Turkish coffee, he fiddled with a small rosary, groups of his retainers came in quietly and sat down to listen, and children screamed with immensely loud voices in the hall outside.

I began by inquiring when and how the Baath was organized.

It was started in 1940, in Damascus by me and my comrade, Bitar. [Bitar is now Syrian Prime Minister.] We began with ten students. We were teachers at the time. The party remained very small until 1943, with only about thirty members. But we evolved our basic ideas then and these principles have not changed.

Since our student days, Bitar and I have always been interested in politics and nationalism. Before World War II, there was a current toward progressivism among many young intellectuals. But there was no contact with national sources. Many intellectuals were pro-Communist or extreme leftists and antinational. At the same time, there was a traditional nationalist current which neglected these intellectual forces and contented itself only with working for independence and an end of the French mandate.

There was a divorce, accordingly, between national and social forces. This was the first point on which our party sought a rebirth. [Baath means renaissance.] We determined to ally nationalism and socialism. Prior to this, progressives were suspect among nationalists and vice versa.

When we started in 1940, we had already read many critiques of Marxism and communism. I personally had contradictory and somewhat paradoxical affinities. I was interested in Nietzsche, Marx, and German philosophers such as Kant. And we also profited greatly from prewar political thinking of the period from 1933–1939, which sought to bring together unrelated thinkers such as Marx and Nietzsche.

I read much on Nazism in that period, but we had little in common with it. We sought more the basic current of realism in German thought and its dislike of the abstract. In this sense, Marx is too abstract and we sought this through the Germans. But we were never influenced by Nazism. Above all there was a contradiction between our own national cause and Nazism which saw all Semitic peoples as inferior.

This is silly. The Nazis courted the Arabs despite their Semitic antecedents.

I asked why it had taken so long (twenty-three years) for the Baath to attain power in Syria during a time of revolt and independence throughout the world. He replied: "We foresaw that because we realize that the Arabs are living through a period where they lack almost everything. It isn't like in other countries. There is an interruption between the present and the past. To be an authentic revolutionary movement, you can't be a small intellectual minority or merely copy others such as the Communists. To be an authentic organization, a party must have the truths and values learned only by struggle. You must have time and learn such political experience and organization slowly."

I wondered how the Baath stood on East-West alignment. He said:

Our party was one of the first in the world to proclaim neutralism. Even before the war, before the birth of our party, we were tending toward a neutralist line. We have always rejected both the Communist and the traditional nationalist solutions. What we have done is to keep the positive elements of both nationalism and Marxism and to bring them together in a synthesis.

Communism as a doctrine and a world movement is something that we as neutralists do not regard as an enemy. But communism in the Arab world is something else. Communism here took a detour and is anti-Arab. We have suppressed it for this reason because it opposes Arab unity. Communism is in principle against Arab unity and thus became opposed to the will of the masses. It became a rootless minority party.

I asked Aflak why Nasser's concept of Arab socialism and that of the Baath were at war with each other when they appear to have similar aspirations. Aflak smiled ruefully and said:

The Baath spread its ideas well ahead of the Egyptian revolution. Nasser really took his line only after the crisis of 1956 and that of 1958. In fact, it was only in 1961, after the rupture of the Egyptian-Syrian union, that Nasser in his pact of social union took the Baath slogan of "Unity, Liberty, Socialism." Indeed, the first time Nasser ever spoke of socialism in Egypt was in 1957. Nasser has no philosophical basis; he is more opportunistic or, perhaps, empirical.

Even today, there is a difference in reality. We have a past. Nasser has only slogans, mere words. [This is precisely what Nasser said about the Baath.] There is an essential difference. For the Baath there is a concept: an Arab nation which exists, although it is now fragmented, underdeveloped, and largely under reactionary regimes. It needs a revolution both spiritual and social. And such a revolution needs a party with a popular base as the instrument for its unification.

Egypt is the largest Arab nation including a population that is one-third of the Arab world. It is richer and more advanced than most Arab countries and geographically holds a key position. Egypt, through Nasser, seeks a hegemony. Nasser wants a theoretical justification for this and for such a theoretical justification he takes the Baath's ideas. But this is not sincere.

SDE BOKER, ISRAEL, *November 10, 1963*

MOST interesting talk with Ben Gurion, who is now living on a kibbutz here in a particularly unattractive and barren part of the Negev Desert. His house is a bit better than the others: terrible, little, dirty, green wooden boxes, plunked down amid the dust. Ben Gurion's is somewhat larger and is outfitted with television, plumbing, good army telephone communications, and a sentry outside the door. But it is still pretty simple stuff for a man who might be living the relatively fat life of Tel Aviv.

I only saw two rooms: a comfortable, plain, book-lined study and a slightly larger sitting room filled with equally comfortable but ugly furniture and a few photographs and remembrances from the past. Mrs.

Ben Gurion came in while I was talking to her husband and brought us coffee in a motherly way. The old man himself looked remarkably fit, nearly bald with white thatches of hair, but very vigorous with extremely young hands, dressed in simple khaki shirt and trousers.

I asked if he thought basic French policy had been changed under de Gaulle. No he didn't, although France obviously wanted friends in the Middle East now. It was understandable that de Gaulle wished to restore French influence in this area, but he was convinced it was not at the expense of Israel; Israel can still count on France as a source of military equipment.

Was there any chance of Israel's establishing diplomatic relations with West Germany? Speaking as if he were still Prime Minister, Ben Gurion said: "We will not propose establishment of relations. This must come from Bonn. If Bonn proposes the idea we are ready to discuss it. Adenauer I think always wanted to exchange ambassadors. Probably he refrained because of the effect on East Germany and an Arab reaction."

Did he think the Arabs would react in a military way when Israel starts to pump water from Jordan into the Negev and when would this begin? Ben Gurion said:

> You can never tell if the Arabs will react. Syria is one of the most unstable states in the Middle East. The Syrians feel they have to do something about the Jordan situation, but they talk too much about it. Iraq might help them if they start trouble, but we are not afraid of them. And I don't think Egypt will come in on this. During our war of independence, after the second truce, Egypt did not comply with the terms. I [and I note the way he used this word "I"] attacked, but none of the others moved to help Egypt. The same was true during the Sinai campaign, when neither Syria nor Jordan helped Egypt. And there was a Syria-Jordan-Egypt treaty putting all their troops under Nasser's command. What will happen in the Jordan situation depends a great deal on Iraq, which is a more stable country than Syria. Sometime next year this is going to come to a head, but we can deal with Syria and Iraq.

I observed that there was speculation as to whether the Israelis were experimenting with atomic weapons manufacture at their Negev reactor in Dimona. Ben Gurion commented:

> There are contradictory imperatives and we must choose. We must have atomic power in a peaceful sense because we will always have a shortage of water. Experts disagree, but, nevertheless, we think that in six or eight years, atomic power here will be relatively cheaper because we have no coal or oil and we will need power for the desalinization of water. Without water you cannot live. With atomic power, desalinization will be cheaper.
>
> In eight or ten years, atomic power will provide cheaper electricity for us than conventional power and we have to prepare and acquire the

know-how. This was the purpose of the Dimona reactor. Nevertheless, Nasser is getting atomic help in his experiments from India. I know he is working for this goal of military nuclear capability. He has not given up on his dream of being the dictator of the Arab world. He has lost a good deal of prestige, but if he defeats Israel he can recapture that prestige and therefore he won't give up on this ambition.

Nasser won't risk war with us until he is sure he will win because otherwise he would lose everything.

He then went on to say he thought Nasser was working on nuclear weapons. When I asked again if Israel were doing likewise, he hinted as much by indirect innuendo, but added: "Nasser has a large desert in which to test, but we cannot test here."

I recalled that in May, 1963, he had proposed a Soviet-U.S. guarantee of the Middle East and in lieu of this a defense pact with the U.S.A. I asked him how he felt about these ideas now. He said it was impractical to think of a Russo-American guarantee today and he doubted Russia could come any nearer to the West so long as its Chinese problem continued. There had been some parallelism in Washington and Moscow policy in 1948 and 1956. But even in 1956, Bulganin's letters to him had been very different in tone from that Eisenhower wrote him. Bulganin had been hostile and threatening destruction whereas Eisenhower had been polite. At this point he observed: "Eisenhower, in a human way, was a lovely, nice, honest man."

Then he returned to his theory that only Russia and the U.S. together could impose a real détente in the Middle East and that Russia's view depended on China. He thought it was a great mistake that the U.S.A. did not recognize China.

I asked him about Russia's attitude toward the Jews and he said:

The Jews see no future in Russia. If Khrushchev now allowed the Jews out, I am sure one million would leave. And Khrushchev cannot admit that he runs a country whose population would like to leave. But Russia is gradually changing. Education is spreading and the standard of living is improving. This must inevitably lead to more freedom and the time will come when Russia cannot remain a dictatorship. No country with an educated population and good living standards can remain a dictatorship [a statement denied by history]. But anti-Semitism will remain among the Russian people and the Jews will continue wishing to leave.

He then began a strange, meandering conversation. He contended that Periclean Athens was great but that half its population was made up of slaves. The old Jews also had slaves but he claimed they were not badly treated. He continued: "We had prophets and prophets did not exist elsewhere. These were men who objected with passion against any quality of discrimination."

He admitted that Plato had not been a democrat, although he said it was unfair to call him a fascist. Plato deserved greatness for opposing wars among the Greek peoples, although he regarded all non-Greeks as barbarians. But he insisted (without historical justification) that 3,800 years ago the Jewish prophets had spoken out passionately against all forms of discrimination and any distinction between Jews and pagans. They had always emphasized "justice and leniency" as primary qualities, although this is not the general interpretation of the law of Moses. "Our prophets taught that Jews and pagans were equal as human beings, whereas the Greeks considered themselves superior to barbarians and favored a caste system.

"Nevertheless, what we should do is base our civilization on Greek society, which includes science, plus the Jewish teachings of the prophets, which taught that all the people of the world should live in peace and justice, goodness and grace."

JERUSALEM, *November 11, 1963*

PLEASANT chat this afternoon with Abba Eban, deputy (now acting) foreign minister, a large, intelligent, witty man. Last May, when Ben Gurion wrote Kennedy, he pointed out that Egypt, Syria, and Iraq had proclaimed a new unity and unified army under Cairo's command; that Hussein was tottering and it looked as if Jordan would go; therefore Israel wanted a U.S. pact or a combined U.S.-Soviet guarantee. By the time Kennedy answered, Hussein was reestablished and the union had dissolved. So Kennedy merely said the circumstances, as Ben Gurion must agree, seemed changed; and he should count on our support against aggression. Israel says the big question is: Do the Arabs believe all this? How can we convince them of the reality of a U.S. supporting deterrent?

I had an agreeable talk with Prime Minister Levi Eshkol, an extremely decent man whom I had never met before. He has a strong, quiet face and manner, is bald, wears glasses, and speaks English with a heavy accent but fluently.

I asked if he weren't afraid that when Israel starts piping water from the Jordan into the Negev, the Arabs might react with a military attack. He would like to hope that nothing would happen despite threats.

Eric Johnston was sent here by Eisenhower to negotiate water-sharing and we were all about to sign an agreement. But at the last moment, the Arabs did not sign, although it was understood on both sides that we would continue a water program based on the provisions of the plan. We did not want to aggravate the situation of our friend Hussein, but I think he will stay quiet and take his share of water. I would say that Nasser won't interfere.

What were the prospects of some kind of settlement of the Arab refugee problem based on Joe Johnson's report? He said:

I see no new doors. Our approach is that the only solution is to settle the refugees in the Arab states. They have plenty of room. This is partly being done in Jordan, where there are tens of thousands being incorporated into the economy. We would be prepared to sit down and discuss how we could help in paying compensation. But we have taken in tens of thousands of Arabs already.

I asked him how dependent Israel was on U.S. aid, both governmental and from private Jewish sources. He answered:

If Israel were to decide to take no more Jews from poor countries, maybe we could manage without any aid at all. But if we take in 70,000 penniless immigrants this year—at least 15,000 families—we must invest in houses, synagogues, schools, hospitals, jobs. This costs about $10,000–12,000 per family or about $180,000,000 per annum. Israel gets $50,000,000 a year from American Jewish charities [the UJA] plus bonds [now being repaid] or about $50–60,000,000 a year. Then there is U.S. government aid amounting to about $70,000,000. But if you add this together it amounts to $180,000,000 and all goes to the new immigrants. And in this situation you have Israel spending almost as great a percentage (11 percent) of the GNP on defense as the U.S.A. does.

He thought the French were improving their relations with the Arab states. "There is no danger of de Gaulle trying to barter us away to the Arabs. We feel a special sympathy exists for us among the French people themselves and there has been no change in France's arms supply to us."

Eshkol is most concerned about the cost of defense and said:

I cry with one eye when I look at our defense budget, as a former finance minister, but I smile with the other eye because I know I am giving security to our people. Our enemies want our blood. They have three or four times the number of tanks and planes we have, as well as rockets and missile ships. The Hawks [ground-to-air missiles] we bought from you cost $25,000,000. We need a low-interest loan from the U.S.A. Of course, we would prefer aid without a loan such as Nasser gets from Khrushchev but a long-range low-interest loan would help a lot.

You have no idea how much these things cost. We started with the Primus stove in 1948, and have climbed up to the jet—but it costs millions to buy planes and train pilots.

Eshkol talked a bit about Israel's African program and admitted it stemmed from a desire to outflank Nasser and gain votes in the UN Assembly. The only nearby countries friendly to Israel were Turkey, Iran, and Ethiopia. But Israel has now sent some two thousand technicians and experts to Africa. "This is costing us many millions of dollars, but it is worth a lot."

JERUSALEM, *November 12, 1963*

DINED tonight with Eliahu Elath and his wife. Eliahu is now president of Hebrew University. He first met Ben Gurion in 1922, when he, Elath, was eighteen and went to a secret Zionist meeting in Moscow. He considers Ben Gurion a phony, in an intellectual sense, who doesn't know much classical Greek and is not really a serious scholar of anything— just a man of action.

Eliahu was ambassador to Washington, then London. He made such a good impression that Truman gave him access to photostats of U.S. state papers which Elath is using in the preparation of his memoirs, although the State Department won't release the papers for years to come.

Eden was Prime Minister at the time Britain was Israel's ally during the Suez campaign. Eliahu says Eden was weak and is convinced he did not really intend to quit the British Cabinet in 1938 over the Munich crisis, but hoped he would precipitate the government's downfall and then be able to take over as Prime Minister. Eden was in such bad shape when the Suez campaign commenced seven years ago that Elath cabled his government there was no serious hope of British support.

Despite Bevin's reputation as anti-Semitic, Elath liked and trusted him far more than Eden. One knew where he stood with Bevin. He was desperately worried once when he had invited him to his own residence for an official dinner. Bevin's doctors warned that he should not give him much to eat or drink because the Foreign Secretary's health was bad. Elath worked out a menu which was at the absolute minimum and Bevin ate everything but the plate. Eliahu was terrified that if his guest had a seizure he would be blamed for poisoning this "enemy" of Israel.

TEL AVIV, *November 13, 1963*

THIS evening, I got to the root of the basic question in Israeli security. Ben Gurion had intimated that Israel suspected Nasser was receiving help in military atomics from India. Tonight I dined chez Spencer Barnes. Professor Bergman, head of the Israeli Atomic Energy Commission, was there.

He thinks that India—and if it goes ahead and aids Nasser, also Egypt—will be able to produce a kind of poison warhead from isotopes or nuclear "garbage" within about two years. This would not have great explosive power, but if one such warhead were to land on Tel Aviv, for example, the entire area would have to be evacuated and perhaps could not be lived in again for thirty years. Nasser is behind on guidance systems, but were he to aim ten missiles at Tel Aviv, it is a dead certainty that at least one would land in the necessary area. There would not necessarily be any heavy casualties when the missile landed and there would be time for people to move out because the warhead could be detected through Geiger counters.

Ambassador Wally Barbour was present during the conversation. He told me later this was the missing link in all his dealings. The Israelis know that no matter how many ground-to-air missiles they have, they can't prevent such an attack. That is why they are demanding ground-to-ground missiles from us. It is possible they are working on a small kind of warhead, for their own deterrent. They have not yet had to take a formal decision on whether to make nuclear weapons or just have an atoms-for-peace program because the Dimona reactor is not yet in production. But it could clearly make military products as well as peacetime power.

The big problem for Israel is the deterrent. They believe our promises that if Egypt attacks we will defend Israel. However, they don't have the time or space to trade. They could be blown up and pushed into the sea before we had decided to surface a Polaris submarine and menace Egypt. They need an immediate deterrent and we don't like to give it to them.

I asked Barbour what he thought we would do if the following happened: One day Nasser claims the Israelis have killed seventy Egyptians in a frontier raid so he fires a missile at Tel Aviv in retaliation. He says the missile has a conventional warhead as is proven by a small explosion. But the Israelis say it has a poison warhead and they have to evacuate Tel Aviv. Do we immediately blow up Cairo? Barbour didn't have the answer.

There was a charming old lady at dinner named Shapiro. She is a veteran Zionist who had been living in the U.S.A.—although she was born in Russia—and came to Palestine in 1919. She worked for years for the Jewish Agency. She was secretary to Sharett (then named Shertok).

In May, 1948, when the state of Israel was created, she and Sharett and a chauffeur were the only members of the Israeli Foreign Office. The very first job was to announce the existence of Israel officially to the approximately seventy governments in the world. She and Sharett sat up until 2 A.M. drafting telegrams to each government and then they got into a car together with the chauffeur and drove to the cable and wireless office to send the telegrams. Sharett wanted to take them in but she said, "No, you are now foreign minister and you have to stay in the car." She took them up to the counter and the boy spent hours counting each word and then said, "All right, that will cost so many hundred dollars."

She told him to charge it to the government; but he said he had had no such instructions and only the Jewish Agency had a charge account. So she had to go down and get Sharett out of the car and the two of them persuaded the man at the counter that they would personally act as guarantors for twenty-four hours until collect arrangements could be made.

Jewish Agency representatives in the different countries were prepared to assume the functions of ambassadors and ministers as soon as recognition was granted, but they had no diplomatic codes and in looking for embassy buildings they had no idea how much they would be paid and how much the government would be willing to spend for buildings, so they had to use their own judgment.

When Mrs. Meir was sent that year as the first ambassador to Moscow, Miss Shapiro went along. Mrs. Meir didn't know what kind of clothes to take. She never wore hats so Miss Shapiro had to buy her some. The Russians had never had a female diplomat accredited so their protocol had nothing in it for the costume that should be worn. It was finally agreed that Mrs. Meir should wear a long-sleeved dinner dress when she presented her letters of credence (this has since become regulation Soviet protocol) and Miss Shapiro lent Mrs. Meir her own very modest string of pearls. (There had been one woman ambassador before, an Indian, but she wore a sari.)

The Israelis had no diplomatic bag and when Miss Shapiro left Moscow for Stockholm to buy furniture for the new embassy in Moscow she put all the official letters in her suitcase and tied it up in a string. She had the first diplomatic pouch designed in a Stockholm department store.

Wally Barbour and I had a nightcap. He added some disagreeable details to the Lyndon Johnson legend. Shortly after the 1960 elections in the U.S.A., Vice President-elect Johnson came to London with Lady Bird, Senator Fulbright, and others. Barbour was chargé d'affaires because Jock Whitney had already resigned. Lord Home made a special effort to give a cocktail party in Johnson's honor on a Saturday afternoon, canceling a shoot in the country to do so. And Macmillan also canceled his weekend to give Johnson a dinner.

When Johnson arrived at the embassy in Regent's Park he decided not to go to the cocktail party. Barbour could not dissuade him and finally Fulbright went along to try and reduce some of the irritation. Johnson then arrived thirty-five minutes late at the Prime Minister's house while Barbour chewed his lips. Promptly at 10 P.M. *he* got up, said he was tired, and left. As soon as he got into the car, driven by the staid and elderly U.S. ambassador's chauffeur, he said to the latter, "What nightclub do we go to here?" The chauffeur knew nothing about nightclubs. But they finally did find one and Johnson and his wife were there until 3 A.M. They were too stupid to realize that one carload of American security agents and one carload of British security agents were following them and had to sit around outside the nightclub until almost dawn. British security told Macmillan and the British press got hold of the story, but Macmillan issued instructions to have it played down.

PARIS, *November 22, 1963*

PRESIDENT Kennedy was murdered this evening!

Bill and Pussy Deakin are staying with us and we were dining early before the theater when the appalling news came. I had to rush to the office and send another column; Bill came along.

It is too soon to even imagine what it all means or who may have been behind it. Television adds a new instantaneous reality to terror in this age; and everyone is terrified of the implications. How much of a change does this mean in the U.S.A.? I think of the weeping, belly-scratching, beagle-loving, nightclubbing Texan who takes power.

Poor Kennedy, he didn't really have a chance to get things moving as he hoped. And poor Jackie. This was the most attractive couple we have had in the White House—ever. Now, so soon, before anything really happened, the dream is over.

PARIS, *November 25, 1963*

CHIP said that at one of the discussions after the Bay of Pigs in April, 1961, Johnson complained of the bad counsel of one of the leading officials and Kennedy turned sharply to him saying: "None of that, Lyndon. This is a joint responsibility and we are all in it together. I won't have any more talk like that."

During the one and a half hours between Kennedy's death and Johnson's swearing-in, a special alert was wired to our armed forces because there was no one legally commanding them and in a position to push the emergency button.

PARIS, *November 29, 1963*

MOTRICO told me very secret negotiations had been going on between him and Vinogradov, the Soviet ambassador, hinting at the establishment of diplomatic relations between Franco's Spain and Soviet Russia. The original contacts had been arranged by Brosio, the Italian ambassador who served in Moscow for some years.

Last week M talked to Vinogradov on possible ways of improving trade relations between Spain and Russia; and Vinogradov said he thought it was far more important to discuss diplomatic relations than to discuss commerce. Motrico indicated at once that he had been given a free hand by Madrid to explore the possibilities for such a relationship.

Motrico asked what I thought of Johnson's view of de Gaulle. I didn't think this mattered until after his reelection—if it comes—a year hence. But in such an event, Johnson seemed inclined to listen more to the generals and admirals than to the professors and computer experts; and the generals and admirals were less anti-French.

PARIS, *December 1, 1963*

GOLFED and lunched with Couve de Murville and Chip Bohlen. Chip asked if Couve thought de Gaulle would run again. Couve said nobody knows, but after all de Gaulle might not live that long and, anyway, the General was certainly worried about decrepitude in office. Chip replied: "That's your answer, I think. He won't run."

Chip told me that two weeks after I saw Couve on the subject in October, Couve told the Japanese foreign minister that France might recognize China. Nevertheless Couve and de Gaulle have been denying this to Bohlen. At least, they say, such a move would not take place for quite a while.

Couve insists that the day of parliaments is over, even in the U.S.A. Democracy must discover a way of expressing itself in a newer and more efficient form.

I observed that de Gaulle had told me he thinks this the era of a stronger executive and economic *dirigisme*. Couve agreed with the General on the first part but not on *dirigisme*. He said de Gaulle does not understand economics although, now that he realizes how important the subject is, "he tries hard."

LONDON, *December 3, 1963*

THIS morning I had a long talk with Harold Wilson in his office in the House of Commons. Wilson, pink and efficient, dressed in a neat black suit, seemed to have grown more at ease with himself, his position, and the world.

I asked what he thought might be the effect on British elections and the world of the extraordinary historical concatenation of recent events— Macmillan's illness and resignation, Adenauer's resignation, and Kennedy's assassination.

He said Douglas-Home was the candidate Labour most wanted as the Tory to oppose. He said: "After all, we want to win the election."

"As for Erhard's replacement of Adenauer in command at Bonn—it is now possible that there can be somewhat more joint Anglo-American approach to Germany on world problems. There is a better chance of getting across the candid approach on allied access to Berlin."

Of the change caused by the assassination, Wilson said:

I expect the first effect would be to help the Conservatives for the short term. When there is a storm in the world you tend to cling more tightly to the hand of nurse.

As for the long-term effect, the Conservatives now claim that Home will become the leader of the western alliance. I think this is silly and it underrates Johnson. After all, Johnson almost became the presidential nominee himself. All we know of him suggests he will be a strong President.

I asked Wilson if his views on the MLF had changed. He replied:

No. The position is unchanged. Washington assumes the Germans wish to be a nuclear power. I do not believe this. The U.S. government thinks the MLF could sublimate German nuclear ambitions. I think this is a dangerous assumption. There are many signs that this could only whet the German appetite, if there is one. If you have a boy and wish to sublimate his sex appetite, it may not be wise to take him to a striptease show.

I had an impression that in England voters tended to vote for an image, not for a policy; if so, what kind of image was Wilson trying to create for Labour? He said my analysis was sound and that he had been trying, as he showed in the party's Scarborough Conference, to get across a positive image emphasizing youth, change, and the mobilization of science.

Happily, from a Labour viewpoint, Home was helping in this respect. Had I seen yesterday's newspapers showing Home with a sticking plaster on his jaw, accompanying a group of cronies on a shoot. "We could not find the money to pay for better election propaganda." Wilson said. "The Tories insist on continuing an image completely remote from the ordinary people and the youth of Britain."

Wilson said that even before he became party leader—and above all afterward—he had decided not to associate himself with any Labour clique or faction. The leader must be accessible to all members of the party and not just to particular groups.

But I refuse to go in for social life with party members. This is partly because of my own situation; I have no time. And I need time to read and write.

But there is more to it than that. Some of our party members live in nice London homes and have things like large wine cellars. Others come from outside London and live here in modest digs. Why should I spend more time with the prosperous party members in London? If I have any time in the evening I like to sit in the House of Commons' members dining room with any of our MPs who happen to be there. My wife and I don't enjoy entertaining. When I can come home we like to have a quiet evening during which I catch up on my reading.

It was the Socialists, not Conservatives, who would have the task of stopping Russian penetration in Europe. Wilson added, with a certain amount of smug pride, "I have been to Moscow eleven times. Home has only been there once."

But he has little use for the French Socialists and thinks nothing of Guy Mollet who was "A man of Suez." He says, "We worried about Mollet's visit to Moscow. After all, he went as Khrushchev's guest. I never went on a Khrushchev basis but a parliamentary basis. And the communiqué issued after Mollet's visit was in very Marxist language. It looked to us as if Mollet were trying to work out a deal for some kind of popular-front voting arrangement in France."

LONDON, *December 5, 1963*

LONG talk with Foreign Secretary Rab Butler, a tall, slightly misshapen, heavy man with blotchy and ravaged features. He has a deformity of the right hand with which apparently he even has difficulty in writing. But he is self-confident, highly intelligent, well educated. He sat down in one arm chair, waving me across to another, and pulled up a straight chair on which to rest his feet while we talked.

The idea of a special relationship with America was an orthodox British view, shared by the opposition. The alliance was all-important to Europe's future.

This is where we differ from de Gaulle. We think that NATO is the right way to solve the problems both of Europe and America. An autarchic Europe would not work out. It could not be a substitute. We do not see ourselves as a third force. But de Gaulle does. He appears to be on the edge of making a great nuisance of himself.

The special relationship goes back to the 1939–1940 period and it is an absolute lifeline. After all, you are the most powerful nation and we are proud to have you as friends. I think this was very well demonstrated during the service in St. Paul's for Kennedy.

What did he think were the effects of Britain's exclusion from the Common Market? He said:

The big effect of de Gaulle's action was that Macmillan suffered politically. A good deal of Macmillan's decline in Conservative fortunes dates from that time. People felt Macmillan had put his whole mind to the Common Market and he went into a political slump afterward.

But I must admit our farmers are pleased. About eighty Tory seats come from farming districts and these are much easier to fight now.

There was a political slump at the beginning after the first Common Market shock, but there has been both economic and political recovery since then.

I asked what Butler thought was Britain's special international role.

We regard ourselves as a power. We have our own nuclear deterrent and fifty million inhabitants. We have interests in every part of the world. We are involved in Hong Kong, Singapore, Australia, and New Zealand, and through the length and breadth of Africa. We are as much a world power as the U.S.A., although we recognize that we are not nearly as powerful in terms of population, resources, and gross national product.

That is why the U.S. relationship is so important to us. But you also depend to a heavy degree on us and on our presence in places, in Aden or the oil areas. We cannot carry out our role without the special relationship, but I think the same applies to you. And I think you people see this.

Butler is very much one of the "old-boy club": polished, intelligent, smug, insular. Of a recent ministerial dinner in the Hague he said: "I sat next to Mr. Pickioney [Piccioni]. He did not say a word—thank God."

LONDON, *December 10, 1963*

LATE this afternoon, I saw Sir Alec Douglas-Home at No. 10 Downing Street. It is the first time I have seen him since he became Prime Minister and, incidentally, since he became Sir Alec instead of the Earl of Home.

He received me in the Cabinet room and we sat side by side, the long table covered with pads and pencils where the ministers gather. He was inconspicuously but extremely well dressed, very elegant and at ease; tall, thin, and looking quite healthy, no doubt as a result of his steady weekend routine of shooting parties.

I wondered if Douglas-Home, by dropping his title didn't feel like a man who has lost his shadow. He grinned and said: "Well, I must admit that I still have to be careful when I sign my name because I don't always remember. But you know I have done this before. First I was Douglas-Home and then for thirty years I was Lord Douglas. Then I became Home. We have unusual customs over here."

I asked if it would be possible for Britain to commit itself in a governmental sense on the MLF before the general elections. He said: "On the present going, this is out of the question. I don't see how the matter can be far enough advanced before the elections. I doubt if it will be up for a decision by this government."

Was the Common Market now dead as an issue now in England? He replied: "It is inconceivable that we could open the issue again before the elections. If the opportunity should come along after the elections, the decision would ultimately have to be made by Parliament. A great deal must happen before it comes to that point."

I recalled that Macmillan had told me last year that Britain's basic European policy was to join the Common Market and that it was impossible to even contemplate a fall-back position in case of failure. But the policy had failed. What alternative European policy did the present government have?

Douglas-Home said:

There is nothing comparable to the Common Market. Had there been we would have been less eager to join. Of course, we have EFTA [European Free Trade Area] and special economic and trade ties with the Commonwealth. But the Common Market has 250,000,000 people and is of much greater potential importance.

I had been very much struck by the intense reaction here to President Kennedy's murder and while I knew he had been much admired and widely liked in England, I was astonished at the degree and depth of the emotional reaction. The Prime Minister commented: "I think we always realized that he was an exceptional man. He had a direct appeal, above all to the younger generation. We always knew he had a huge popularity. He represented the absolute essence of a free society, and a free life, and at the same time, although he was clearly determined to defend this freedom, it was perfectly clear that he would do everything possible to avoid war. People felt these ideas and also his determination to maintain peace, and I think this added up together."

I asked if he thought Kennedy's death would have any effect on Anglo-American ties. He said: "Certainly not from our angle. We are as keen as ever to continue the closest possible link. I had a very short talk with President Johnson when I was over there for the funeral and he said that this would be his policy too."

Could he define our so-called special relationship? He answered:

I suppose it is very hard to define and maybe that is one of the things that helps it. It is certainly founded on a common language. And there is also the fact that we have a great respect for your achievements. The U.S. is an outstanding example of the operation of a free society. We have all that in common. And we fought together in two wars and have developed the habit of working together. And I suppose we have an affection for you as a former colony [he added this with a mischievous grin]. It is a rather intangible thing.

The United States is a young country which has made a marvelous job of it. A man in your country has a fine and equal opportunity to get ahead and this is very refreshing to see. Of course, you have many faults and so do we. But we value each other's virtues.

He didn't think de Gaulle intended, at least at this next NATO meeting, to put the alliance "against the wall." But he was struck by the fact that the General had completely changed his ideas on strategy. He said:

I know for a fact that eighteen months ago his view was that you don't have to put all your divisions right up in front, but that it was just necessary to back up the Germans.

Now he has developed this concept of an immediate trip-wire. You people think that it might be possible to continue a conventional war in Europe for weeks. We don't entirely share your view and think it could only last for a much shorter time. But de Gaulle now seems to think it is a matter of hours at most. He wants an immediate nuclear retaliation in case of any kind of attack in Europe. No matter what type of aggression de Gaulle would like to let go with everything.

I asked Douglas-Home how he liked the job of Prime Minister. He answered:

I like it. Naturally, at first there were some strange aspects and I had to do things I was unused to, such as appointing bishops. And I had to get the feel of the House of Commons again. After all, I had not been in the House for many, many years. But I do feel that I can handle it and that it isn't too much of a strain. You have to organize yourself and your time. I find I can manage this.

PARIS, *December 12, 1963*

THIS afternoon, I saw de Gaulle at the Elysée. I was rather puzzled when I entered the gate and was escorted to the waiting room outside his office, because the courtyard was filled with the large navy blue buses that are generally used to transport policemen. I wondered if some sort of putsch was expected. I found out, however, from Bonneval that today was the traditional affair given by the President of the Republic for school children; the kids had been transported in the buses.*

I began by saying it seemed to me very difficult even to contemplate any agreement between ourselves and France on the issue of nuclear forces, since we preferred to strike back only at an enemy's military installations whereas France, as I understood it, would strike at an enemy's cities. "Yes," he said, "it is very hard to compromise I admit. We certainly would attack cities."

I mentioned that Norstad had recently made a speech in which he suggested there should be a nuclear directorate of the four leading allies: the U.S.A., Britain, France, and West Germany. I wondered whether

* See de Gaulle's further comments, pp. 43, 66.

de Gaulle favored this and whether he thought the so-called *directoire* concept, about which he wrote to President Eisenhower in 1958, was worth reviving.

He answered:

Every day this becomes more difficult. And anyway, why should there be four members of such a directorate? The Germans do not have any nuclear weapons, and, furthermore, it is better they should not have any. Why give them nuclear weapons? And why should they be allowed to participate in such a *directoire*?

Certainly, it would be very hard now to form such a directorate. The U.S. now has an American strategy, not a European strategy. Therefore it isn't practical to conceive of a directorate. Naturally, it is necessary that the allied governments should exchange political and strategic ideas and they must remain allies. They must reciprocally explain their own situations and conceptions. But the U.S. has chosen to take back its own freedom of action. And France has also chosen to take back its own freedom of action.

Therefore, it seems to me it would be very hard to create a directorate now. Of course, if a war came there would be a directorate, as always. This is the way wars have been fought by allies in the past. But I don't see how there can be a directorate before a war. We must have contacts and explain ideas and exchange information. But this is all we can do because it is apparent we have different strategies.

I asked the General if, apart from the issue of strategy, he had any ideas on how the structure of NATO as it now stands should be reformed.

He answered this rather obliquely and certainly negatively. He said: "The states in NATO are allies and they all understand that they must make war in common if war comes. We believe in this."*

I then asked if now that the "force de dissuasion" was beginning, although not yet wholly born, France would be prepared to participate in nuclear disarmament talks with Russia, the U.S., and Britain. He replied:

If there were real measures discussed for real disarmament France would participate. Naturally we are in favor of nuclear disarmament. We don't wish to keep atomic weapons if the U.S. and Russia are ready to give them up. If they wish to negotiate a suppression of such arms we are ready to join in talks. But the present Geneva talks are meaningless. They can lead to nothing. They have no purpose except to amuse diplomats and please the journalists. They have no reality. They only represent lost time, and I see no reason to waste time.†

I asked if Edgar Faure, who has recently been in China and who had seen the General both before and after his trip, had brought back with him

---

* See de Gaulle's further comments, pp. 57–58, 67.
† See de Gaulle's further comments, pp. 51–52, 57, 77.

any invitation from the Chinese for de Gaulle to visit that country. He said: "No, nothing. Faure had been there before and he knows China somewhat. He came back and reported to me on general indications but he brought no invitation with him."*

I asked him if he thought Algeria were living up to its commitments in the Evian agreement. He said: "Yes, until now they have respected the agreements. And our relations are not bad with them. There is no hostility on either side."

I said that twice in the past he had told me he hoped to retire to Colombey when he had finished his first term; what was his intention now. He said: "I don't know my plan. That is to say, I know what I will do but I won't say. I won't tell anyone."

Did he think it would be useful to have a vice president in France? He was categorically against it. He said: "This would not be very useful here. I am not speaking only of the situation as it affects me. But if any President of the Republic dies or is unable to continue in office he must be replaced by elections within two or three weeks. And an interim regime is perfectly capable of governing until then."

I asked what he thought were the basic tasks remaining to him. He said: "There are always tasks ahead, although they are less dramatic now than they were five years ago. Above all, there is the matter of organizing the country, especially in terms of social and economic organization. The political reorganization of France has been accomplished and it works. It works for France even if the opposition doesn't like it."

I inquired if he still favored the old idea of labor-capital "associations." He said: "The 'association' idea is now making progress. We are still working on it. But you can see that the old-fashioned class war is now much less ardent in France. Naturally there are 'interests' that work for discord. But there is far less class warfare."

Did he think it necessary to make any further basic reforms in the Constitution? He said: "The essential has been done. The Constitution has been made. Of course Constitutions are subject to amendment. Your Constitution has often been amended. We have several small changes, perhaps, to make; but they are only small. The proof of the value of our Constitution is that it works and that it is good for France even if it is not good for the opposition."

I then recalled that once when I had talked to him about Khrushchev and inquired whether he thought he was an important man, he had said you could not assess a man in a historical sense until the end of his life and he had quoted Sophocles to say that the day could best be judged only in the evening. In those terms, how did he now assess President Kennedy?

* See de Gaulle's further comments, pp. 46, 67, 77–78.

He answered:

I cannot really say. He was very likable and he certainly had great value. He wanted to solve problems, but, unfortunately, he lacked the necessary time. He wanted to solve enormous problems: the race problem in your country, the problem of the dollar, the underdeveloped lands, Latin America, Europe, disarmament. Those were and are enormous problems and they require a great amount of time. History will probably say of Kennedy that he was a man of great ability who lacked the time to prove himself.

With this icy and exact logic, penetrating the emotional storms of that tragic moment, I conclude this volume.

INDEX